Philips'

CONCISE ATLAS

OF THE WORLD

GEORGE PHILIP

Edited by:
Bill Willett, B.A., Cartographic Editor, George Philip and Son Ltd
Consultant Cartographer Harold Fullard, M.Sc.
Maps prepared by George Philip Cartographic Services Ltd
under the direction of Alan Poynter, M.A., Director of Cartography

Fourth Edition 1986
Reprinted 1988

British Library Cataloguing in Publication Data

Philips' concise atlas of the world — 4th ed.
  1. Atlases, British
  912   G1021
  ISBN 0 540 05518 2

Printed in Hong Kong

Preface

The **Concise Atlas** has been devised as a useful reference book that will meet most people's needs. The map coverage of the world is comprehensive and at scales suitable to the area concerned. Each continental section is introduced with two maps, one to show the political divisions and one to show the relief of land. Within each continental section maps of the important political, cultural or geographical regions, such as Italy and the Balkans, precede those at larger scales of the individual countries and more densely populated regions.

The majority of the maps are coloured to the relief of the land, shown by layer colours with relief shading in grey. On this physical background are shown the patterns of settlement and communications.

Spellings of names are in the form given in the latest official lists and generally agree with the rules of the Permanent Committee on Geographical Names and the United States Board on Geographic Names. This means that for many well-known places the local spelling is used, with the English conventional form given in parentheses, for example, Roma (Rome) or Warszawa (Warsaw). The index refers the reader from the conventional form to the local form.

The index contains over 45,000 names and shows the map page number and the geographical coordinates for each entry.

B.M. Willett

Contents

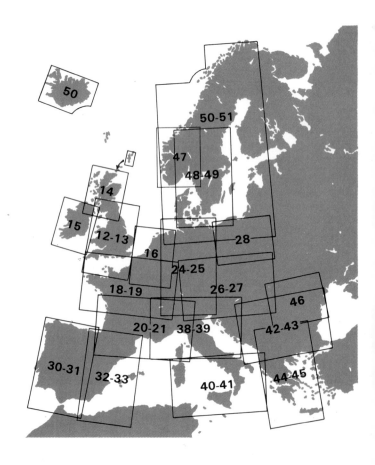

Contents

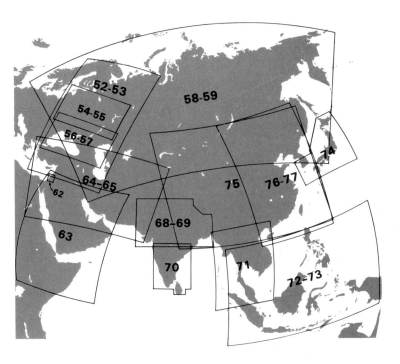

Asia

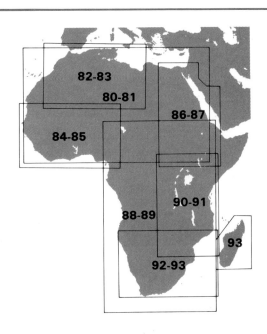

Africa

Contents

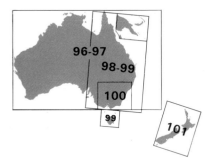

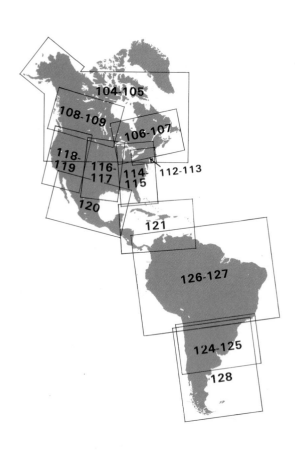

Index

Principal Countries of the World

Country	Area in thousands of square km.	Population in thousands	Density of population per sq. km.	Capital Population in thousands
Afghanistan	647	17 222	27	Kabul (1 036)
Albania	29	2 841	98	Tiranë (202)
Algeria	2 382	20 500	9	Algiers (1 740)
Angola	1 247	8 339	7	Luanda (700)
Argentina	2 767	29 627	11	Buenos Aires (9 927)
Australia	7 687	15 369	2	Canberra (251)
Austria	84	7 549	90	Vienna (1 516)
Bangladesh	144	94 651	657	Dhaka (3 459)
Belgium	31	9 856	318	Brussels (989)
Belize	23	156	5	Belmopan (3)
Benin	113	3 720	33	Porto-Novo (132)
Bhutan	47	1 360	29	Thimphu (60)
Bolivia	1 099	6 082	5	Sucre (63) La Paz (881)
Botswana	600	1 007	2	Gaborone (60)
Brazil	8 512	129 662	15	Brasilia (1 306)
Brunei	6	209	35	Bandar Seri Begawan (58)
Bulgaria	111	8 946	81	Sofia (1 064)
Burkina Faso	274	6 607	24	Ouagadougou (286)
Burma	677	36 750	54	Rangoon (2 276)
Burundi	28	4 540	162	Bujumbura (157)
Cambodia (Kampuchea)	181	6 981	39	Phnom Penh (400)
Cameroon	475	9 165	19	Yaoundé (485)
Canada	9 976	24 907	2	Ottawa (738)
Central African Rep.	623	2 450	4	Bangui (302)
Chad	1 284	4 789	4	Ndjamena (303)
Chile	757	11 682	15	Santiago (4 132)
China	9 597	1 039 677	108	Peking (9 231)
Colombia	1 139	27 190	24	Bogota (4 056)
Congo	342	1 651	5	Brazzaville (422)
Costa Rica	51	2 379	47	San José (272)
Cuba	115	9 884	86	Havana (1 951)
Cyprus	9	655	73	Nicosia (161)
Czechoslovakia	128	15 415	120	Prague (1 186)
Denmark	43	5 118	119	Copenhagen (1 382)
Djibouti	22	332	15	Djibouti (150)
Dominican Republic	49	5 962	121	Santo Domingo (1 313)
Ecuador	284	9 251	32	Quito (881)
Egypt	1 001	45 915	46	Cairo (5 074)
El Salvador	21	5 232	249	San Salvador (429)
Equatorial Guinea	28	381	14	Rey Malabo (37)
Ethiopia	1 222	33680	28	Addis Abeba (1 478)
Fiji	18	670	37	Suva (68)
Finland	337	4 863	14	Helsinki (922)
France	547	54 652	99	Paris (8 510)
French Guiana	91	78	1	Cavenne (39)
Gabon	268	1 127	4	Libréville (252)
Gambia	11	696	63	Banjul (109)
Germany, East	108	16 864	156	East Berlin (1 173)
Germany, West	249	61 638	248	Bonn (294)
Ghana	239	12 700	53	Accra (738)
Greece	132	9 848	75	Athens (3 027)
Greenland	2 176	52	0.02	Godthåb (10)
Guatemala	109	7 699	71	Guatemala (793)
Guinea	246	5 704	23	Conakry (763)
Guinea-Bissau	36	836	23	Bissau (109)
Guyana	215	922	4	Georgetown (188)
Haiti	28	5 201	186	Port-au-Prince (888)
Honduras	112	4 092	37	Tegucigalpa (485)
Hong Kong	1	5 313	5 313	Hong Kong (1 184)
Hungary	93	10 702	115	Budapest (2 067)
Iceland	103	236	2	Reykjavik (84)
India	3 288	732 256	223	Delhi (5 729)
Indonesia	2 027	156 442	77	Jakarta (6 503)
Iran	1 648	42 070	26	Tehran (4 496)
Iraq	435	14 654	34	Baghdad (2 969)
Irish Republic	70	3 508	50	Dublin (525)
Israel	21	4 097	195	Jerusalem (424)
Italy	301	56 836	189	Rome (2 831)
Ivory Coast	322	9 300	29	Abidjan (850)
Jamaica	11	2 260	205	Kingston (671)
Japan	372	119 259	320	Tokyo (8 139)
Jordan	98	3 489	36	Ammān (681)
Kenya	583	18 784	32	Nairobi (1 048)
Korea, North	121	19 185	158	Pyŏngyang (1 500)
Korea, South	98	39 951	408	Seoul (8 367)
Kuwait	18	1 672	93	Kuwait (775)
Laos	237	4 209	18	Vientiane (90)
Lebanon	10	2 739	274	Beirut (702)
Lesotho	30	1 444	48	Maseru (45)
Liberia	111	2 113	19	Monrovia (306)
Libya	1 760	3 356	2	Tripoli (980)
Luxembourg	3	365	121	Luxembourg (79)
Madagascar	587	9 400	16	Antananarivo (400)
Malawi	118	6 429	54	Lilongwe (103)
Malaysia	330	14 860	45	Kuala Lumpur (938)
Mali	1 240	7 528	6	Bamako (419)
Malta	0.3	377	1 256	Valletta (14)
Mauritania	1 031	1 779	2	Nouakchott (135)
Mauritius	2	993	496	Port Louis (149)
Mexico	1 973	75 103	38	Mexico (14 750)
Mongolia	1 565	1 803	1	Ulan Bator (419)
Morocco	447	22 110	49	Rabat (842)
Mozambique	783	13 311	17	Maputo (384)
Namibia	824	1 040	1	Windhoek (61)
Nepal	141	15 738	112	Katmandu (210)
Netherlands	41	14 362	350	Amsterdam (936)
New Zealand	269	3 203	12	Wellington (343)
Nicaragua	130	3 058	23	Managua (820)
Niger	1 267	6 040	5	Niamey (225)
Nigeria	924	89 022	96	Lagos (1 477)
Norway	324	4 129	13	Oslo (624)
Oman	212	1 131	5	Muscat (25)
Pakistan	804	89 729	112	Islamabad (201)
Panama	76	2 089	27	Panama (655)
Papua New Guinea	462	3 190	7	Port Moresby (123)
Paraguay	407	3 472	8	Asunción (602)
Peru	1 285	18 790	15	Lima (4 601)
Philippines	300	52 055	173	Manila (1 630)
Poland	313	36 571	117	Warsaw (1 641)
Portugal	92	10 056	109	Lisbon (818)
Puerto Rico	9	3 350	372	San Juan (1 086)
Romania	238	22 638	95	Bucharest (1 979)
Rwanda	26	5 700	219	Kigali (116)
Saudi Arabia	2 150	10 421	5	Riyadh (667)
Senegal	196	6 316	32	Dakar (799)
Sierra Leone	72	3 672	51	Freetown (214)
Singapore	0.6	2 502	4 170	Singapore (2 517)
Somali Republic	638	5 269	8	Mogadishu (400)
South Africa	1 221	31 008	25	Pretoria (739) Cape Town (2 517)
Spain	505	38 228	76	Madrid (3 159)
Sri Lanka	66	15 416	234	Colombo (1 412)
Sudan	2 506	20 362	8	Khartoum (561)
Surinam	163	407	2	Paramaribo (151)
Swaziland	17	605	36	Mbabane (23)
Sweden	450	8 331	19	Stockholm (1 409)
Switzerland	41	6 482	158	Bern (289)
Syria	185	9 660	52	Damascus (1 251)
Taiwan	36	18 700	519	Taipei (2 271)
Tanzania	945	20 378	22	Dar-es-Salaam (757)
Thailand	514	49 459	96	Bangkok (5 468)
Togo	56	2 756	49	Lomé (247)
Trinidad and Tobago	5	1 202	240	Port of Spain (66)
Tunisia	164	6 886	42	Tunis (597)
Turkey	781	47 279	61	Ankara (2 239)
Uganda	236	14 625	62	Kampala (332)
United Arab Emirates	84	1 206	14	Abu Dhabi (449)
U.S.S.R.	22 402	272 500	12	Moscow (8 396)
United Kingdom	245	56 377	230	London (6 755)
United States	9 363	234 496	25	Washington (3 061)
Uruguay	178	2 968	17	Montevideo (1 173)
Venezuela	912	16 394	18	Caracas (2 944)
Vietnam	330	57 181	173	Hanoi (2 571)
Western Samoa	3	159	53	Apia (36)
Yemen, North	195	6 232	32	Sana' (448)
Yemen, South	288	2 158	7	Aden (285)
Yugoslavia	256	22 800	89	Belgrade (1 407)
Zaïre	2 345	31 151	13	Kinshasa (2 242)
Zambia	753	6 242	8	Lusaka (641)
Zimbabwe	391	7 740	20	Harare (656)

Principal Cities of the World

The population figures used are from censuses or more recent estimates and are given in thousands for towns and cities over 500,000 (over 750,000 in China, India, the U.S.S.R. and the U.S.A.) Where possible the population of the metropolitan area is given e.g. Greater London, Greater New York, etc.

AFRICA

ALGERIA (1977)
Alger 1 740
Oran 543

ANGOLA (1982)
Luanda 700

CAMEROON (1983)
Douala 708

EGYPT (1976)
El Qâhira 5 074
El Iskandarîya 2 318
El Giza 1 230

ETHIOPIA (1983)
Addis Abeba 1 478

GHANA (1970)
Accra 738

GUINEA (1980)
Conakry 763

IVORY COAST (1976)
Abidjan 850

KENYA (1983)
Nairobi 1 048

MOROCCO (1981)
Casablanca 2 409
Rabat-Salé 842
Fès 562
Marrakech 549

NIGERIA (1975)
Lagos 1 477
Ibadan 847

SENEGAL (1976)
Dakar 779

SOUTH AFRICA (1980)
Johannesburg 1 726
Cape Town 1 491
Durban 961
Pretoria 739
Port Elizabeth 585

SUDAN (1980)
El Khartûm, 561

TANZANIA (1978)
Dar-es-Salaam 757

TUNISIA (1984)
Tunis 597

ZAIRE (1975)
Kinshasa 2 242

ZAMBIA (1980)
Lusaka 641

ZIMBABWE (1983)
Harare 681

ASIA

AFGHANISTAN (1979)
Kābul 1 036

BANGLADESH (1982)
Dhaka 3 459
Chittagong 1 388
Khulna 623

BURMA (1977)
Rangoon 2 276

CHINA (1970)
Shanghai 11 860
Beijing 9 231
Tianjin 7 764
Shenyang 2 800
Wuhan 2 560
Guangzhou 2 500
Chongqing 2 400
Nanjing 1 750
Harbin 1 670
Dalian 1 650
Xi'an 1 600
Lanzhou 1 450
Taiyuan 1 350
Qingdao 1 300
Chengdu 1 250
Changchun 1 200
Kunming 1 100
Jinan 1 100
Fushun 1 080
Anshan 1 050
Zhengzhou 1 050
Hangzhou 960
Tangshan 950
Baotou 920
Zibo 850
Changsha 825
Shijiazhuang 800
Qiqihar 760

HONG KONG (1981)
Kowloon 2 450
Hong Kong 1 184
Tsuen Wan 599

INDIA (1981)
Calcutta 9 194
Bombay 8 243
Delhi 5 729
Madras 4 289
Bangalore 2 922
Ahmedabad 2 548
Hyderabad 2 546
Pune 1 686
Kanpur 1 639
Nagpur 1 302
Jaipur 1 015
Lucknow 1 008
Coimbatore 920
Patna 919
Surat 914
Madurai 908
Indore 829
Varanasi 797
Jabalpur 757

INDONESIA (1980)
Jakarta 6 503
Surabaya 2 028
Bandung 1 462
Medan 1 379
Semarang 1 026
Palembang 787
Ujung Pandang 709
Malang 512

IRAN (1976)
Tehrān 4 496
Esfahān 672
Mashhad 670
Tabrīz 599

IRAQ (1970)
Baghdād 2 969

JAPAN (1982)
Tōkyō 11 676
Yokohama 2 848
Ōsaka 2 623
Nagoya 2 093
Kyōto 1 480
Sapporo 1 465
Kobe 1 383
Fukuoka 1 121
Kitakyūshū 1 065
Kawasaki 1 055
Hiroshima 898
Sakai 809
Chiba 756
Sendai 662
Okayama 551
Kumamoto 522
Kagoshima 514
Amagasaki 510
Higashiōsaka 501

JORDAN (1981)
'Ammān 681

KOREA, NORTH (1972)
Pyŏngyang 1 500

KOREA, SOUTH (1980)
Sŏul 8 367
Pusan 3 160
Taegu 1 607
Inchŏn 1 085
Kwangju 728
Taejon 652

KUWAIT (1975)
Al-Kuwayt 775

LEBANON (1980)
Bayrūt 702

MALAYSIA (1980)
Kuala Lumpur 938

PAKISTAN (1981)
Karachi 5 103
Lahore 2 922
Faisalabad 1 092
Rawalpindi 806
Hyderabad 795
Multan 730
Gujranwala 597
Peshawar 555

PHILIPPINES (1981)
Manila 1 630
Quezon City 1 166
Davao 610

SAUDI ARABIA (1974)
Ar Riyād 667
Jiddah 561

SINGAPORE (1983)
Singapore 2 517

SRI LANKA (1981)
Colombo 1 412

SYRIA (1982)
Dimashq 1 112
Halab 985

TAIWAN (1981)
Taipei 2 271
Kaohsiung 1 227
Taichung 607
Tainan 595

THAILAND (1982)
Bangkok 5 468

TURKEY (1982)
İstanbul 2 949
Ankara 2 276
İzmir 1 083
Adana 864
Konya 691
Bursa 658
Gaziantep 526

VIETNAM (1973-79)
Phanh Bho Ho Chi Minh 3 420
Hanoi 2 571
Haiphong 1 279

AUSTRALIA AND NEW ZEALAND

AUSTRALIA (1982)
Sydney 3 310
Melbourne 2 837
Brisbane 1 124
Adelaide 960
Perth 948

NEW ZEALAND (1982)
Auckland 839

EUROPE

AUSTRIA (1981)
Wien 1 516

BELGIUM (1983)
Brussel 989

BULGARIA (1982)
Sofiya 1 064

CZECHOSLOVAKIA (1983)
Praha 1 186

DENMARK (1981)
København 1 382

FINLAND (1982)
Helsinki 922

FRANCE (1982)
Paris 8 510
Lyon 1 170
Marseille 1 080
Lille 935
Bordeaux 628
Toulouse 523

GERMANY, EAST (1982)
East Berlin 1 173
Leipzig 557
Dresden 521

GERMANY, WEST (1980)
West Berlin 1 896
Hamburg 1 645
München 1 299
Köln 977
Essen 648
Frankfurt am Main 629
Dortmund 608
Düsseldorf 590
Stuttgart 581
Duisburg 558
Bremen 555
Hannover 535

GREECE (1981)
Athínai 3 027
Thessaloníki 706

HUNGARY (1983)
Budapest 2 067

IRISH REPUBLIC (1981)
Dublin 525

ITALY (1981)
Roma 2 831
Milano 1 635
Napoli 1 211
Torino 1 104
Genova 760
Palermo 700

NETHERLANDS (1983)
Rotterdam 1 025
Amsterdam 936
's-Gravenhage 674

NORWAY (1980)
Oslo 624

POLAND (1983)
Warszawa 1 641
Łódź 848
Kraków 735
Wrocław 631
Poznań 571

PORTUGAL (1981)
Lisboa 818

ROMANIA (1982)
Bucureşti 1 979

SPAIN (1981)
Madrid 3 159
Barcelona 1 753
Valencia 745
Sevilla 646
Zaragoza 572
Málaga 502

SWEDEN (1983)
Stockholm 1 409

SWITZERLAND (1982)
Zürich 705

U.S.S.R. (1983)
Moskva 8 396
Leningrad 4 779
Kiyev 2 355
Tashkent 1 944
Baku 1 638
Kharkov 1 519
Minsk 1 405
Gorkiy 1 382
Novosibirsk 1 370
Sverdlovsk 1 269
Kuybyshev 1 242
Dnepropetrovsk 1 128
Tbilisi 1 125
Odessa 1 097
Yerevan 1 095
Omsk 1 080
Chelyabinsk 1 077
Donetsk 1 055
Perm 1 037
Ufa 1 034
Kazan 1 031
Alma-Ata 1 023
Rostov 977
Volgograd 962
Saratov 887
Riga 867
Krasnoyarsk 845
Zaporozhye 835
Voronezh 831

UNITED KINGDOM (1983)
London 6 754
Birmingham 1 013
Glasgow 751
Leeds 714
Sheffield 543
Liverpool 502

YUGOSLAVIA (1981)
Beograd 1 407
Zagreb 1 175
Skopje 507

SOUTH AMERICA

ARGENTINA (1980)
Buenos Aires 9 927
Córdoba 982
Rosario 955
Mendoza 597
La Plata 560

BOLIVIA (1982)
La Paz 881

BRAZIL (1980)
São Paulo 8 732
Rio de Janeiro 5 539
Belo Horizonte 1 937
Salvador 1 502
Recife 1 433
Fortaleza 1 307
Brasília 1 306
Pôrto Alegre 1 221
Nova Iguaçu 1 184
Curitiba 943
Belém 934
Goiánia 680
Duque de Caxias 666
São Gonçalo 660
Santo André 634
Campinas 587

CHILE (1983)
Santiago 4 132

COLOMBIA (1978)
Bogotá 4 056
Medellín 1 507
Cali 1 316
Barranquilla 855

ECUADOR (1982)
Guayaquil 1 279
Quito 881

PARAGUAY (1978)
Asunción 602

PERU (1981)
Lima 4 601

URUGUAY (1981)
Montevideo 1 173

VENEZUELA (1980)
Caracas 2 944
Maracaibo 901
Valencia 506

NORTH AMERICA

CANADA (1983)
Toronto 3 067
Montréal 2 862
Vancouver 1 311
Ottawa 738
Edmonton 699
Calgary 634
Winnipeg 601
Québec 580
Hamilton 548

CUBA (1981)
La Habana 1 925

DOMINICAN REP. (1981)
Santo Domingo 1 313

GUATEMALA (1979)
Guatemala 793

HAITI (1982)
Port-au-Prince 888

JAMAICA (1980)
Kingston 671

MEXICO (1979)
Mexico 14 750
Guadalajara 2 468
Netzahualcóyotl 2 331
Monterrey 2 019
Puebla de Zaragoza 711
Ciudad Juárez 625
León de los Aldamas 625
Tijuana 566

NICARAGUA (1981)
Managua 820

PANAMA (1981)
Panama 655

PUERTO RICO (1980)
San Juan 1 086

UNITED STATES (1980)
New York 16 121
Los Angeles 11 498
Chicago 7 870
Philadelphia 5 548
San Francisco 5 180
Detroit 4 618
Boston 3 448
Houston 3 101
Washington 3 061
Dallas 2 975
Cleveland 2 834
Miami 2 644
St. Louis 2 356
Pittsburgh 2 264
Baltimore 2 174
Minneapolis-St. Paul 2 114
Seattle 2 093
Atlanta 2 030
San Diego 1 817
Cincinnati 1 660
Denver 1 621
Milwaukee 1 570
Tampa 1 569
Phoenix 1 509
Kansas City 1 327
Indianapolis 1 306
Portland 1 243
Buffalo 1 243
New Orleans 1 187
Providence 1 096
Columbus 1 093
San Antonio 1 072
Sacramento 1 014
Dayton 1 014
Rochester 971
Salt Lake City 936
Memphis 913
Louisville 906
Nashville 851
Birmingham 847
Oklahoma 834
Greensboro 827
Norfolk 807
Albany 795
Toledo 792
Honolulu 763

GENERAL REFERENCE

Abbreviations of measures used — ft Feet; mm { Millimetres / Millimeters } cm { Centimetres / Centimeters } m { Metres / Meters } Km { Kilometres / Kilometers } mb Milibars

City and Town symbols in order of size

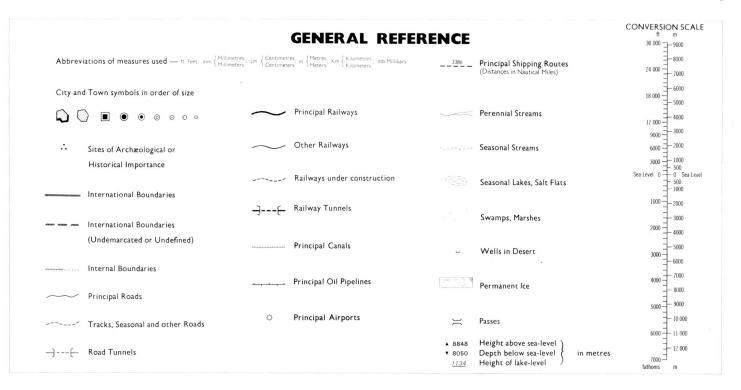

∴ Sites of Archæological or Historical Importance

International Boundaries

International Boundaries (Undemarcated or Undefined)

Internal Boundaries

Principal Roads

Tracks, Seasonal and other Roads

Road Tunnels

Principal Railways

Other Railways

Railways under construction

Railway Tunnels

Principal Canals

Principal Oil Pipelines

☼ Principal Airports

3386 — Principal Shipping Routes (Distances in Nautical Miles)

Perennial Streams

Seasonal Streams

Seasonal Lakes, Salt Flats

Swamps, Marshes

⌄ Wells in Desert

Permanent Ice

⌣ Passes

▲ 8848 Height above sea-level
▼ 8050 Depth below sea-level } in metres
1134 Height of lake-level

CONVERSION SCALE

```
ft        m
30 000 — 9000
       — 8000
24 000 — 7000
       — 6000
18 000 — 5000
       — 4000
12 000 — 3000
9000
6000   — 2000
3000   — 1000
         500
Sea Level 0 — 0 Sea Level
         500
         1000
1000   — 2000
       — 3000
2000   — 4000
       — 5000
3000   — 6000
       — 7000
4000   — 8000
       — 9000
5000   — 10 000
       — 11 000
6000   — 12 000
7000
fathoms  m
```

THE WORLD
Physical
1:150 000 000

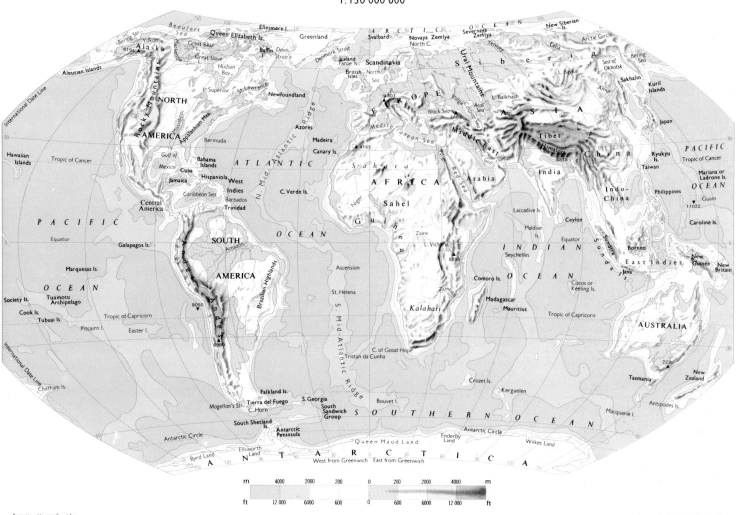

```
m    4000   2000   200   0   200   2000   4000   m
ft   12 000  6000   600   0   600   6000   12 000  ft
```

Projection: Hammer Equal Area

Projection: *Hammer Equal Area*

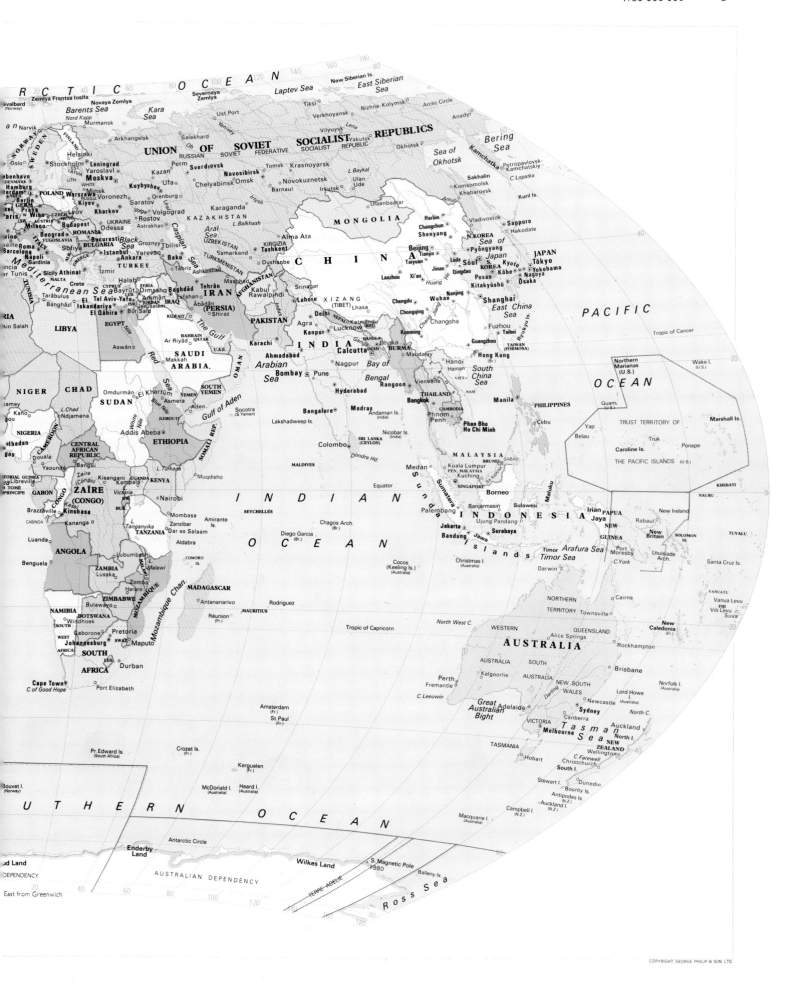

A R C T I C   O C E A N

Svalbard (Norway)
Zemlya Frantsa Iosifa
Novaya Zemlya
Severnaya Zemlya
Laptev Sea
New Siberian Is.
East Siberian Sea
Barents Sea
Kara Sea
Ust Port
Tiksi
Verkhoyansk
Nizhne-Kolymsk
Arctic Circle
Anadyr
a n Narvik
Nord Kapp
Murmansk
Yenisey
Vilyuysk
Lena
Yakutsk
Bering Sea
Arkhangelsk
Salekhard
Okhotsk
Sea of Okhotsk
Kamchatka
Petropavlovsk-Kamchatskiy
C. Lopatka
NORWAY SWEDEN FINLAND
Helsinki
UNION   OF   SOVIET
RUSSIAN
SOCIALIST   REPUBLICS
SOVIET FEDERATIVE
SOCIALIST REPUBLIC
Ulan Ude
Sea of Okhotsk
Sakhalin
Khabarovsk
Kuril Is.
Sapporo
Hakodate
Oslo Stockholm Leningrad
Perm
Sverdlovsk
Tomsk Krasnoyarsk
L. Baykal
kbenhavn DENMARK
Kazan
Yaroslavl
Novosibirsk
Irkutsk
Ulaanbaatar
Vladivostok
N.KOREA
Sea of Japan
LITH. Moskva
Kuybyshev
Ufa
Chelyabinsk Omsk
Novokuznetsk
MONGOLIA
Harbin
Changchun
Shenyang
Pyŏngyang
JAPAN
POLAND Warszawa Minsk
Kiyev Voronezh
Saratov
Orenburg
Karaganda
Beijing
KOREA
Sŏul
Kyoto Tōkyō
Berlin
Kharkov
Volga
Volgograd
KAZAKHSTAN
L. Balkhash
Tianjin
Taiyuan
Jinan
Pusan Kōbe Nagoya Yokohama
Praha CZECH. Lvov UKRAINE
Rostov
Aral Sea
Alma Ata
KIRGIZIA
Lanzhou
Xi'an
Qingdao
Ōsaka
 Wien AUSTRIA Budapest
Odessa
Astrakhan
UZBEKISTAN
Tashkent
C H I N A
Huang He
Kitakyūshū
Milano ROMANIA Bucuresti
Black Sea
Groznyy Tbilisi
TURKMENISTAN
Dushanbe
Srinagar
Chengdu
Wuhan
Nanjing
Shanghai
Beograd YUGOSLAVIA BULGARIA
Sofiye Istanbul
Yerevan
Baku
Ashkhabad
AFGHANISTAN
Kabul
Rawalpindi
XIZANG (TIBET)
Lhasa
Chongqing
Chang Jiang
East China Sea
Roma ITALY
Sicily Athinai GREECE
TURKEY
Izmir
Tabriz
Mashhad
Lahore
Delhi
NEPAL Katmandu
BHUTAN
Changsha
Fuzhou
Taibei
TAIWAN (FORMOSA)
Sardinia
Crete CYPRUS SYRIA
Halab
Tehrān
Eşfahān
Agra
Kanpur
Lucknow
BANGLA. Dhaka
Kunming
Guangzhou
Tunis MALTA
Mediterranean Sea
Bayrūt Dimashq Baghdād
IRAN (PERSIA)
Ābādān
Shirāz
Karachi
I N D I A
Nagpur
Calcutta
DESH
BURMA
Mandalay
Hong Kong
Tel Aviv-Yafo
ISR. JORDAN
IRAQ
Jerusalem
Bür Sa'īd
KUWAIT
PAKISTAN
Ahmadabad
Hyderabad
Hanoi
Hainan
Iskandarīya El Qâhira
Bahrain QATAR
The Gulf
U.A.E.
Arabian Sea
Bombay Pune
Bay of Bengal
Rangoon
South China Sea
LIBYA
EGYPT
Nile
Aswân
SAUDI ARABIA
OMAN
Hyderabad
Madras
Andaman Is. (India)
THAILAND
Bangkok
Manila
PHILIPPINES
Ain Salah
Red Sea
Makkah
Bangalore
Lakshadweep Is.
Nicobar Is. (India)
CAMBODIA
Phnom Penh
Cebu
NIGER **CHAD**
Omdurmân El Khartum
YEMEN
Gulf of Aden
SRI LANKA (CEYLON)
Phan Bho Ho Chi Minh
iamey
L.Chad Ndjamena
SUDAN
Blue Nile
Asmera
SOUTH YEMEN
Aden
Colombo
MALDIVES
MALAYSIA
BRUNEI SABAH
Yap
Guam (U.S.)
TRUST TERRITORY OF
NIGERIA
White Nile
Addis Abeba
DJIBOUTI
Socotra (S. Yemen)
Dondra Hd.
Medan
Kuala Lumpur
PEN. MALAYSIA
Belau
Marshall Is.
Yaoundé
CENTRAL AFRICAN REPUBLIC
ETHIOPIA
L. Turkana
SOMALI REP.
Muqdisho
Equator
Kuching
SINGAPORE
Caroline Is.
Truk
Ponape
THE PACIFIC ISLANDS (U.S.)
Douala
Bangui
Zaire (Congo)
Kisangani UGANDA KENYA
Kampala
MALDIVES
Borneo
Banjarmasin
Sulawesi
Maluku
NAURU
KIRIBATI
ZAÏRE (CONGO)
Victoria
Nairobi
SEYCHELLES
I N D I A N
Palembang
I N D O N E S I A
Irian Jaya
PAPUA NEW GUINEA
New Ireland
Brazzaville Kinshasa
CABINDA
Mombasa
Zanzibar
Amirante Is.
Chagos Arch. (Br.)
Jakarta
Sumatera
Ujung Pandang
Rabaul
Luanda
Kananga
TANZANIA
Dar es Salaam
Aldabra
Diego Garcia (Br.)
O C E A N
Bandung
Jawa
Surabaya
GUINEA
New Britain
SOLOMON Is.
TUVALU
ANGOLA
Lubumbashi
COMORO Is.
Christmas I. (Australia)
Timor
Arafura Sea
Port Moresby
Louisiade Arch.
Santa Cruz Is.
Benguela
ZAMBIA
Lusaka
L. Malawi
Cocos (Keeling Is.) (Australia)
Timor Sea
C. York
VANUATU
Vanua Levu
FIJI Viti Levu Suva
NAMIBIA
Bulawayo
ZIMBABWE
Zomba
Harare
MADAGASCAR
Antananarivo
Rodriguez
MAURITIUS
Réunion (Fr.)
Darwin
NORTHERN
Cairns
New Caledonia
Windhoek
BOTSWANA
Gaborone
MOZAMBIQUE
Mozambique Chan.
TERRITORY
Townsville
Norfolk I. (Australia)
Johannesburg SWAZ. Maputo
Pretoria
Tropic of Capricorn
North West C.
WESTERN
Alice Springs
QUEENSLAND
Rockhampton
SOUTH AFRICA
LES. Durban
Amsterdam (Fr.)
St.Paul (Fr.)
AUSTRALIA
SOUTH
Brisbane
Cape Town C. of Good Hope
Port Elizabeth
AUSTRALIA
Perth
Fremantle
Kalgoorlie
AUSTRALIA
NEW SOUTH WALES
Lord Howe I. (Australia)
Pr.Edward Is. (South Africa)
Crozet Is. (Fr.)
C.Leeuwin
Great Australian Bight
Adelaide
Darling
Newcastle
North C.
Sydney
Canberra
Auckland
Kerguelen (Fr.)
VICTORIA
Melbourne
Tasman Sea
NEW ZEALAND
Wellington
Bouvet I. (Norway)
McDonald I. (Australia)
Heard I. (Australia)
TASMANIA
Hobart
Stewart I.
Bounty Is. (N.Z.)
C.Farewell
South I.
Christchurch
Dunedin
Antipodes Is. (N.Z.)
Auckland Is. (N.Z.)
S O U T H E R N   O C E A N
Macquarie I. (Australia)
Campbell I. (N.Z.)
ud Land
DEPENDENCY
Antarctic Circle
Enderby Land
Wilkes Land
S. Magnetic Pole 1980
Balleny Is.
AUSTRALIAN DEPENDENCY
TERRE ADÉLIE
Ross Sea
East from Greenwich

PACIFIC OCEAN

Tropic of Cancer
Northern Marianas (U.S.)
Wake I. (U.S.)

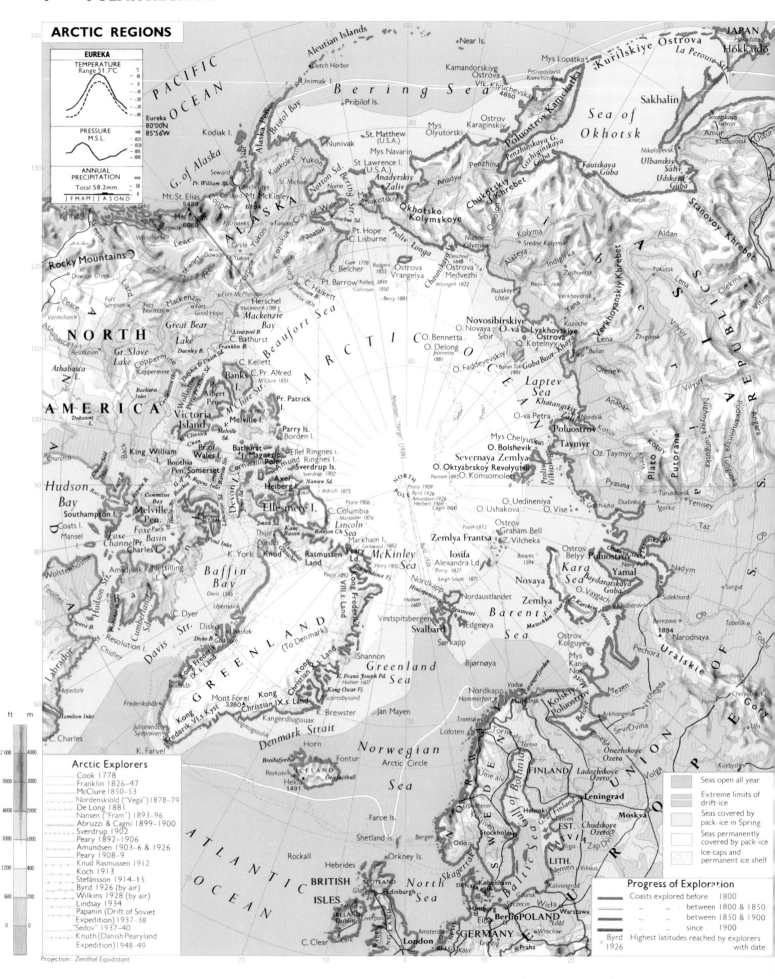

ARCTIC REGIONS

EUREKA
TEMPERATURE
Range 51.7°C

Eureka
80°00'N
85°56'W

PRESSURE
M.S.L.

ANNUAL
PRECIPITATION
Total 58.2mm.

J F M A M J J A S O N D

Arctic Explorers

Cook 1778
Franklin 1826–47
McClure 1850–53
Nordenskiold ("Vega") 1878–79
De Long 1881
Nansen ("Fram") 1893–96
Abruzzi & Cagni 1899–1900
Sverdrup 1902
Peary 1892–1906
Amundsen 1903–6 & 1926
Peary 1908–9
Knud Rasmussen 1912
Koch 1913
Stefánsson 1914–15
Byrd 1926 (by air)
Wilkins 1928 (by air)
Lindsay 1934
Papanin (Drift of Soviet
  Expedition) 1937–38
"Sedov" 1937–40
Knuth (Danish Pearyland
  Expedition) 1948–49

Projection: Zenithal Equidistant

Progress of Exploration

Coasts explored before 1800
"   "   between 1800 & 1850
"   "   between 1850 & 1900
"   "   since 1900
Highest latitudes reached by explorers
  with date

Seas open all year
Extreme limits of drift-ice
Seas covered by pack-ice in Spring
Seas permanently covered by pack-ice
Ice-caps and permanent ice shelf

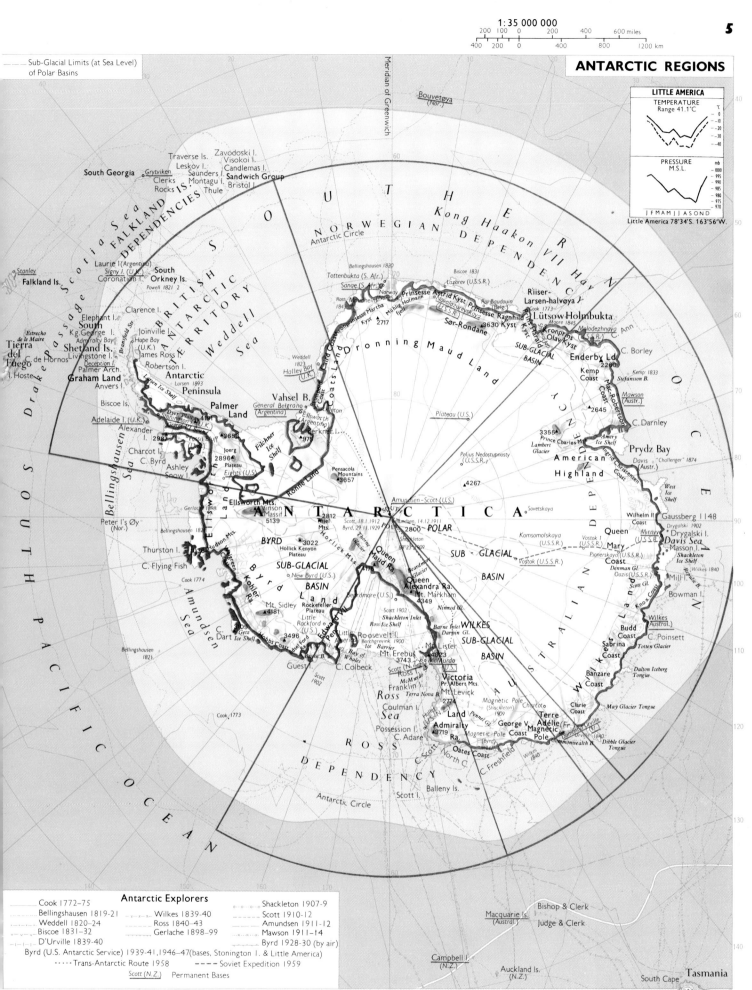

ANTARCTIC REGIONS

1:35 000 000

LITTLE AMERICA
TEMPERATURE
Range 41.1°C

PRESSURE
M.S.L.

Little America 78°34'S. 163°56'W.

Sub-Glacial Limits (at Sea Level)
of Polar Basins

Antarctic Explorers

Cook 1772–75
Bellingshausen 1819-21
Weddell 1820–24
Biscoe 1831–32
D'Urville 1839–40
Wilkes 1839–40
Ross 1840–43
Gerlache 1898–99
Shackleton 1907-9
Scott 1910-12
Amundsen 1911–12
Mawson 1911–14
Byrd 1928-30 (by air)
Byrd (U.S. Antarctic Service) 1939-41,1946–47(bases, Stonington I. & Little America)
Trans-Antarctic Route 1958
Soviet Expedition 1959
Scott (N.Z.)   Permanent Bases

COPYRIGHT. GEORGE PHILIP & SON. LTD.

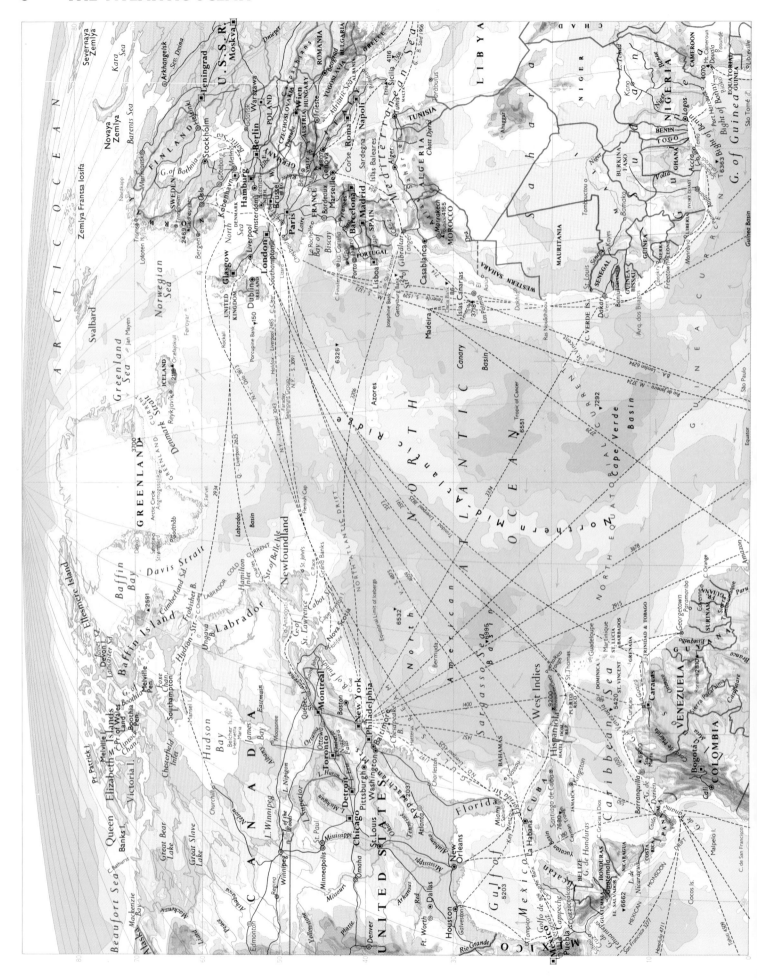

→ Direction of Currents

COPYRIGHT GEORGE PHILIP & SON, LTD.

Principal Shipping Routes
(Distances in Nautical Miles)

3778

Projection: Mollweide

PACIFIC OCEAN

SOUTH ATLANTIC OCEAN

SOUTHERN OCEAN

BRAZIL

ARGENTINA

CHILE

BOLIVIA

PERU

PARAGUAY

URUGUAY

ECUADOR

Andes

Amazonas

Mato Grosso

Gran Chaco

Pampas

Patagonia

Galápagos

Lima

Santiago

Córdoba

Buenos Aires

Montevideo

Asunción

La Paz

Rosario

São Paulo

Rio de Janeiro

Belo Horizonte

Salvador

Recife

Fortaleza

Belém

Pôrto Alegre

Valparaíso

Concepción

Tierra del Fuego

Cape Horn

Drake Passage

Falkland Is.

FALKLAND IS.
DEPENDENCIES

South Georgia

Scotia Sea

Weddell Sea

BRITISH ANTARCTIC TERRITORY

Antarctic Peninsula

Graham Land

Palmer Land

Ellsworth Land

Byrd Land

Ross Sea

Dronning Maud Land

Enderby Land

Coats Land

South Sandwich Is.

Tristan da Cunha

Gough I.

Bouvetøya

Ascension

St. Helena

Fernando de Noronha

Trindade

Martin Vaz

SOUTH AFRICA

Cape Town

ANGOLA

NAMIBIA

CONGO

Brazzaville

Luanda

BENGUELA COLD CURRENT

PERUVIAN COLD CURRENT

SOUTH EQUATORIAL CURRENT

Tropic of Capricorn

Mid-Atlantic Ridge

Brazil Basin

Angola Basin

Cape Basin

Agulhas Basin

Argentine Basin

Atlantic Indian Ridge

Walvis Ridge

Chile Rise

Antarctic (Southern Pacific) Basin

South East Pacific Basin

WEST WIND DRIFT

Equatorial Limit of Iceberg

Southern Ocean

Antarctic Circle

m ft
18 000 6000
12 000 4000
9000 3000
6000 2000
4500 1500
3000 1000
1200 400
600 200
0 0
0
200 600
2000 6000
4000 12 000
5000 15 000
6000 18 000
8000 24 000
m ft

1:17 500 000

100   0   100   200   300   400   500 miles
100   0   200   400   600   800 km

Nordkapp   Nordkinn

Lofoten

Kebnekaise
2123

L. Inari   *Lappland*

Kanin
Peninsula

Kola
Peninsula

White
Sea

Mezen

Tundra   d Pechora

Telpos Iz.
1617

Narodnaya
1894

West Siberian Plain

Ob

Irtysh

Scandinavia

Torne älv

Ume älv

Indalsälven

Gulf of Bothnia

Finland

Lake
Ladoga

Svir

L.
Onega

Onega

N. Dvina

Kama

Tobol

Piggen
2469

Osio

Stockholm

Åland Is.

Helsinki

Gulf of Finland

L.
Chudskoye

Neva   Leningrad

Rybinsk
Res.

Gorkiy

Volga

Ural Mountains

Vänern

Mälaren

Valdai
Hills

Volga

Moskva o

Oka

Obshchi Syrt

Skaw

Vättern

Gotland

Central Russian Uplands

P l a i n

Dvina

Ural

Volga Heights

Katte
gat

København

BALTIC SEA

North   *European*   Neman

Pripet

Ukraine

Dnieper

Don

Tsimlyansk
Res.

Volga

Kirgiz Steppe

Berlin

Oder

Vistula

Warszawa

Pripet
Marshes

Kiyevo

Dnieper

Bug

Ural

Ust Urt Plateau

Ore Mts.
Prahao

Sudetes

Bohemian Forest

Moravia
Hts.

Tatra
2655

Carpathians

Dniester

Odessa

Dnieper

Sea of
Azov

Kuban

Terek

Caucasus

Elbrus

Karagiye Depression
-132

Kara
Bogaz

Caspian Sea

Inn

Danube

Wien

Budapest

Bakony Forest

Plain of
Hungary

Drava

Sava

Tisza

Mureş

Prut

Transylvanian Alps

Bucureşti

Crimea

Strait of Kerch

Black Sea

2211

5633

Transcaucasia

Kura

Baku o

Araks

Dinaric Alps

Dalmatia

Beograd

Morava

Danube

Wallachia

Balkans

Balkan Peninsula

Sofiya

Rhodope

Istanbul   Bosporus

Pontine Mts.

Ararat
5165

L. Van

L. Urmia

Kurdistan

Elburz Mts.

Tehran

Adriatic Sea

Apennines

Gran
Sasso
2914

Pindus

Dardanelles

Sea of
Marmara

Ankara o

Kizil

Anatolia

Mts

Transcaucasia

Calabria

Strait of Messina

Etna 3263

Ionian Sea

Ionian Is.

Morea

Athinai

Ankara o

L. Tuz

Erciyas
3710

Taurus Mts.

Halab

Euphrates

Mesopotamia

Tigris

Baghdad

Sicily

C. Spartivento

5121

C. Matapan

Rhodes

Cyprus

Bayrut o

Syrian

Desert

Persian
Gulf

Ileria

Malta

Crete

Tel Aviv-
Yafo o

Nile Delta

Dead
Sea
-395

Levant

Tripoli

AN   *SEA*

Gulf of Sidra

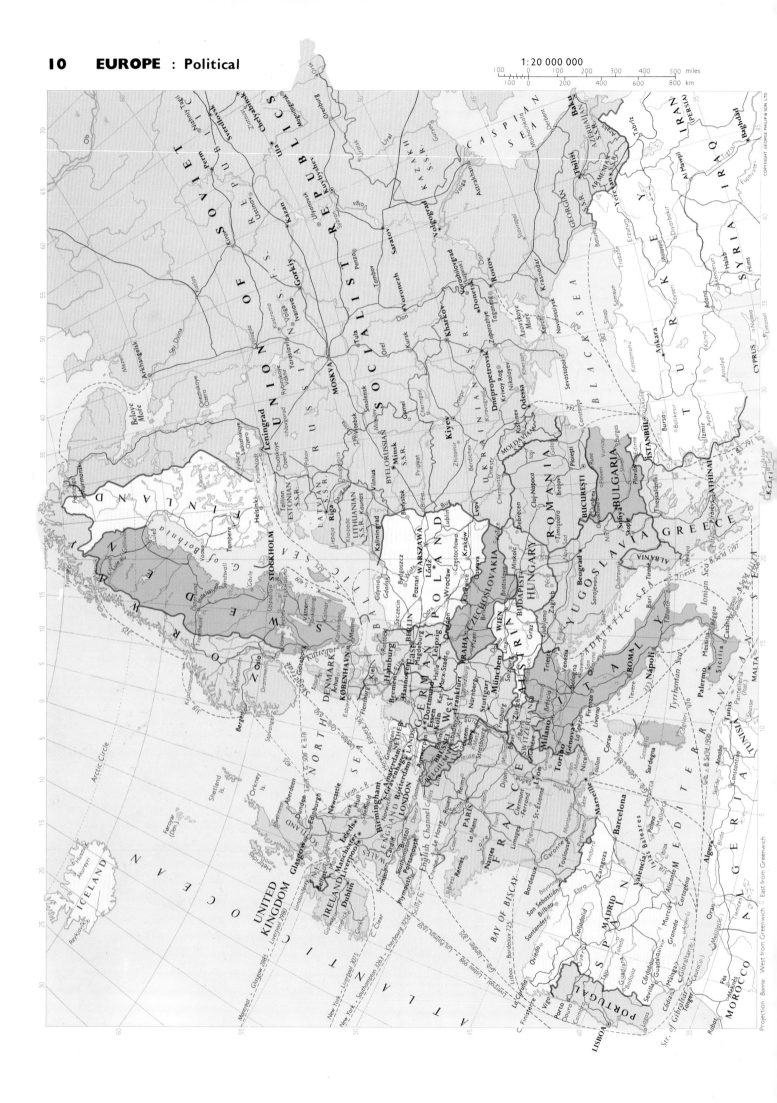

1 : 4 000 000

The DISTRICTS of Northern Ireland have been numbered and can be identified by reference to this table.

1	Londonderry	14	Craigavon
2	Limavady	15	Armagh
3	Coleraine	16	Newry & Mourne
4	Ballymoney	17	Banbridge
5	Moyle	18	Down
6	Larne	19	Lisburn
7	Ballymena	20	Antrim
8	Magherafelt	21	Newtownabbey
9	Cookstown	22	Carrickfergus
10	Strabane	23	North Down
11	Omagh	24	Ards
12	Fermanagh	25	Castlereagh
13	Dungannon	26	Belfast

1 Merseyside
2 Greater Manchester
3 West Yorkshire
4 South Yorkshire
5 West Glamorgan
6 Mid Glamorgan
7 South Glamorgan

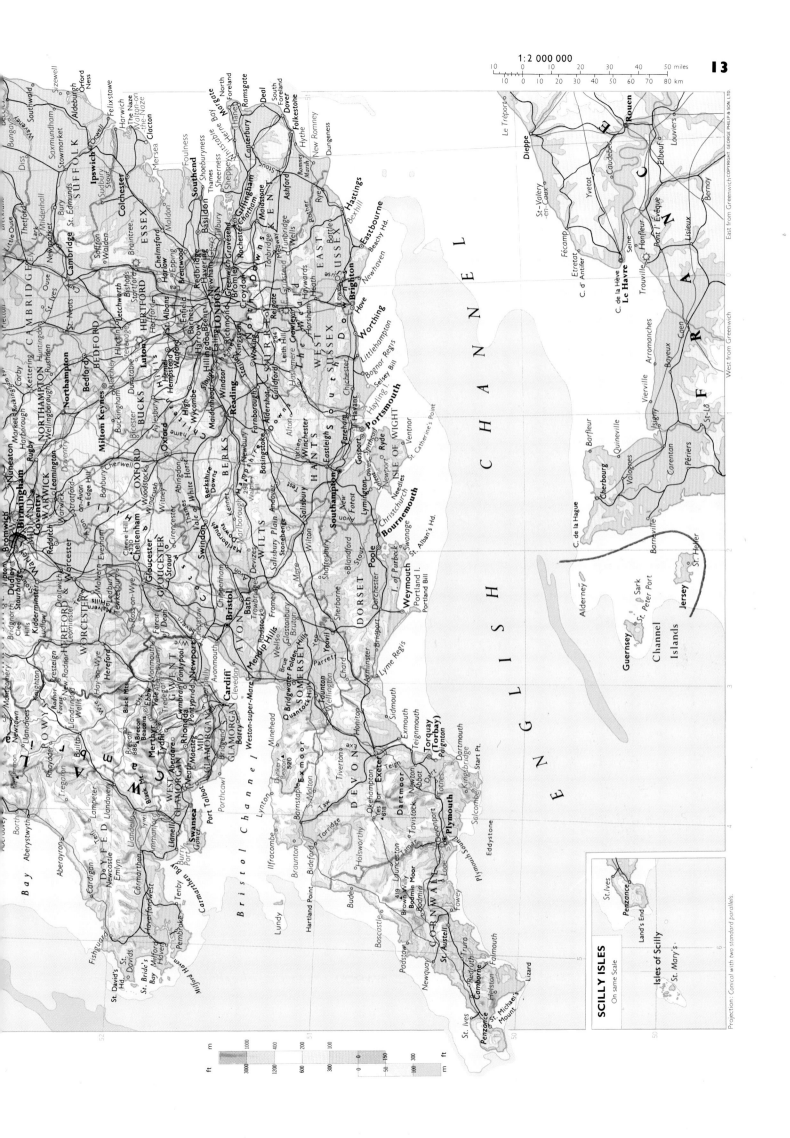

1 : 2 000 000

SCILLY ISLES
On same Scale

Isles of Scilly

1:2 000 000

10 0 10 20 30 40 50 miles
10 0 10 20 30 40 50 60 70 80 km

ORKNEY IS.
On same scale

Scapa Flow · Hoy · South Ronaldsay · Westray · North Ronaldsay · Rousay · Eday · Sanday · Stronsay · Stromness · Mainland · Shapinsay · ORKNEY · Kirkwall · Scapa Flow · Hoy · South Ronaldsay · Pentland Firth · Dunnet Hd. · John o'Groats

Orkney Is. · Pentland Firth · Dunnet Hd. · John O'Groats · Hoy · Scapa Flow · South Ronaldsay · Noss Hd. · C. Wrath · Strathy Pt. · Thurso · Wick · Durness · L. Eriboll · Tongue · Dounreay · Halladale · Lybster · Eddrachillis Bay · Ben Hope 927 · Reay Forest · Ord of Caithness · L. Laxford · Naver · Helmsdale · Lochinver · Enard Bay · L. Assynt · B. More Assynt · Loch Shin · Lairg · Brora · Golspie · Ullapool · L. Broom · Oykell · Dornoch · L. Fannich · Strathpeffer · Dingwall · Cromarty · Lossiemouth · Cullen · Portsoy · Banff · Macduff · Kinnaird's Head · Fraserburgh · B. Dearg 1081 · Ben Wyvis 1045 · Conon · Beauly · Fortrose · Nairn · Forres · Elgin · Rothes · Keith · Deveron · Turriff · Buckie · Rattray Head · Peterhead · Buchan Ness · Elton · Ythan · Huntly · Dufftown · Tomintoul · BUCHAN · GRAMPIAN · Inverurie · Alford · Don · Aberdeen · Girdle Ness

WESTERN ISLES · Flannan Is. · Butt of Lewis · L. Roag · Broad Bay · Stornoway · Eye Pen. · Lewis · Tarbert · Harris · L. Seaforth · Sound of Harris · North Uist · Lochmaddy · Monach Is. · Benbecula · South Uist · Lochboisdale · Sound of Barra · Barra · Barra Hd.

OUTER HEBRIDES · North Minch · Little Minch · INNER HEBRIDES · Rubha Hunish · L. Gairloch · Trotternish · L. Maree · SKYE · Rubha Reidh · Portree · Raasay · Rona · Scalpay · Sound of Raasay · Kyle of Lochalsh · Cuillin Hills · L. Bracadale · Cuillin Sound · Canna · Rhum · Eigg · Muck · Coll · Tiree · Staffa · Iona · Mull · Ben More 966 · Colonsay · Gometra

WEST HIGHLANDS · HIGHLAND · NORTH WEST HIGHLANDS · Glen More · Loch Ness · Inverness · Culloden Moor · Grantown-on-Spey · Aviemore · Strath Spey · Cairn Gorm 1245 · CAIRNGORM MTS · Ben Macdhui 1311 · Ballater · Aboyne · Dee · Banchory · Stonehaven · Inverbervie · Braemar · Lochnagar 1154 · Balmoral · Braes of Angus · Laurencekirk · Brechin · Montrose · Strathmore · Forfar · Arbroath · Broughty Ferry · Carnoustie · Firth of Tay · St. Andrews · Fife Ness · Anstruther

Stromeferry · Dornie · Glen Affric · Glen Moriston · Fort Augustus · Glen Garry · L. Oich · Kingussie · Newtonmore · Cairn Toul 1292 · Badenoch · GRAMPIAN HIGHLANDS · Forest of Atholl · Blair Atholl · Pass of Killiecrankie · Pitlochry · Kirriemuir · Alyth · Blairgowrie · Sidlaw Hills · TAYSIDE · Scone · Dundee · Tayport · Cupar · FIFE · Leven · Glenrothes · Buckhaven · Kirkcaldy · Cowdenbeath · Kinross · Loch Leven

Mallaig · L. Morar · Arisaig · Glen Spean · LOCHABER · Fort William · Ben Nevis 1343 · Ardgour · Glen Coe · Ballachulish · Rannoch Moor · L. Rannoch · L. Tummel · Aberfeldy · Tay · Dunkeld · Killin · Ben Lawers 1214 · Breadalbane · Crieff · Perth · L. Earn · Ben Vorlich 983 · Comrie · Callander · Trossachs · L. Katrine · Ben Lomond 974 · Dunblane · Stirling · Bannockburn · Dunfermline · Rosyth · Leith · North Berwick · Dunbar

Morvern · Sound of Mull · Tobermory · Loch Sunart · L. Shiel · L. Eil · L. Linnhe · Glen Etive · Ben Cruachan 1124 · Oban · Loch Awe · Inveraray · B. Vorlich 943 · Ben More 1174 · CENTRAL · Alloa · Grangemouth · Falkirk · Linlithgow · Bathgate · Livingston · Musselburgh · Haddington · Lammermuir Hills · St. Abb's Head · Eyemouth

ATLANTIC OCEAN · Firth of Lorn · Sound of Jura · Crinan · Lochgilphead · Helensburgh · Dunoon · Dumbarton · Clydebank · Greenock · Port Glasgow · Paisley · Johnstone · Renfrew · Glasgow · Airdrie · Coatbridge · Motherwell · Wishaw · Edinburgh · LOTHIAN · Dalkeith · Penicuik · Berwick-upon-Tweed · Holy I.

Jura · Sound of Islay · Gigha · Tarbert · KINTYRE · Bute · Rothesay · Largs · Rutherglen · E. Kilbride · Hamilton · Lanark · Carstairs · Peebles · Moorfoot Hills · Galashiels · Coldstream · Tweed · Duns · Kelso

Islay · Bowmore · Port Ellen · Rubh' a' Mhail · Campbeltown · Mull of Kintyre · Ardrossan · Saltcoats · Arran · Goat Fell 874 · Brodick · Troon · Prestwick · Ayr · Irvine · Kilmarnock · Ayr · Cumnock · Biggar · Broad Law 840 · SOUTHERN UPLANDS · Selkirk · Melrose · Hawick · Jedburgh · CHEVIOT HILLS · The Cheviot 816 · Coquet

SHETLAND IS. · On same scale · Unst · Fetlar · Yell · Yell Sound · Whalsay · SHETLAND · Mainland · Bressay · Foula · Scalloway · Lerwick · Sumburgh Hd.

Rathlin · Fair Hd. · Ballycastle · Trostan 554 · NORTHERN IRELAND · Ballymena · Larne · Belfast · Belfast Lough · Bangor · Newtownards · North Channel · Ailsa Craig · Girvan · Dalmellington · Doon · Sanquhar · Nith · Leadhills · Moffat · Merrick 843 · Ken · DUMFRIES AND GALLOWAY · Dumfries · Lockerbie · Langholm · Esk · N. Tyne · ENGLAND · Hexham · Stranraer · Portpatrick · GALLOWAY · Newton Stewart · Castle Douglas · Dalbeattie · Gatehouse of Fleet · Kirkcudbright · Wigtown Bay · Annan · Gretna Green · Carlisle · HADRIAN'S WALL · S. Tyne · Alston · Wear · Luce Bay · Whithorn · Mull of Galloway · Solway Firth · Workington · Derwent · Penrith · Skiddaw 931 · Cross Fell 893 · Ullswater · Tees · Barnard Castle · CUMBRIAN MTS.

NORTH SEA · Bass Rock · Firth of Forth · Musselburgh · Preston pans

ft m · 3000 1000 · 1200 400 · 600 200 · 300 100 · 0 0 · 50 150 · 100 300 · m ft

Projection: Conical with two standard parallels.

West from Greenwich

COPYRIGHT. GEORGE PHILIP & SON. LTD.

1:2 000 000

10   0   10   20   30   40   50 miles
10   0   10   20   30   40   50   60   70   80 km

ATLANTIC OCEAN

NORTH CHANNEL

IRISH SEA

St. George's Channel

Kintyre   Arran
Campbeltown
Mull of Kintyre   Ailsa Craig
Stranraer
Portpatrick

Malin Hd.
Tory I.   Horn Hd.   Sheep Haven   Lough Swilly
Bloody Foreland   Carndonagh   Portrush   Giant's Causeway   Rathlin I.   Fair Hd.
Gweedore   Inishowen Pen.   Moville   Ballycastle
Aran I.   Errigal 752   Derryveagh Mts.   Buncrana   Coleraine   Ballymoney   554 Trostan
Letterkenny   Limavady
Gweebarra B.   **Londonderry**   Sperrin Mts.   Ballymena   Larne   I. Magee
DONEGAL   Lifford   Strabane   Sawel 683   Magherafelt   Antrim   Carrickfergus   Belfast L.
Glenties   Bluestack 676   Derg   Cookstown   Antrim   Donaghadee
Loughros More B.   Finn   Mourne   **Belfast**   **Bangor**   Newtownards
Rossan Pt.   Killybegs   Ballyshannon   Omagh   U L S T E R   NORTHERN IRELAND   **Lisburn**   Strangford L.
Rathlin O Birne I.   **Donegal**   Bundoran   L. Erne   Dungannon   Lurgan (Craigavon)   Ards Pen.
Downpatrick Hd.   Killala B.   Donegal Bay   Erne   Enniskillen   Invinestown   Blackwater   Portadown   Banbridge   Downpatrick
Broad Haven   Erris Hd.   Sligo B.   Sligo   Upper   Clones   Monaghan   **Armagh**   Slieve Donard 852   Newcastle
Belmullet   Killala   LEITRIM   L. Erne   Finn   Annalee   MONAGHAN   Newry   Sl. Gullion 577   Mourne Mts.   Dundrum Bay
Mullet Peninsula   Ballina   SLIGO   Colooney   L. Allen   Belturbet   Cootehill   Castleblayney   Carlingford L.   Greenore
Achill Hd.   Moy   Ox Mts.   Arrow   Leitrim   CAVAN   Carrickmacross   Louth   **Dundalk**   Dundalk Bay
Achill   Nephin 806   L. Conn   Boyle   Carrick-on-Shannon   Cavan   Kingscourt   LOUTH
Achill I.   Clare I.   Clew Bay   Castlebar   ROSCOMMON   L. Gowna   L. Sheelin   Ceannannas Mór (Kells)   Ardee
Croagh Patrick 765   Westport   Castlereagh   Granard   Oldcastle   Blackwater   An Uaimh (Navan)   Drogheda
Inishbofin   Mweelrea 819   L. Mask   Robe   Longford   L. Ree   Athboy   Trim   MEATH   Balbriggan
Killary Harbour   CONNACHT   Ballinrobe   LONGFORD   Inny   Mullingar   Boyne   Swords   Lambay I.
Clifden   Twelve Pins   Tuam   L. Corrib   Suck   WESTMEATH   Maynooth   **DUBLIN**   Ireland's Eye
Slyne Hd.   CONNEMARA   GALWAY   I R E L A N D   **Athlone**   Clara   Edenderry   **Dublin** (Baile Átha Cliath)   Howth Head
GALWAY   Ballinasloe   Brosna   Tullamore   Liffey   Celbridge   Dublin Bay
Galway   Clare   Athenry   Loughrea   OFFALY   Bog   Daingean   Droichead Nua   Naas   **Dun Laoghaire**
Galway Bay   Kilkieran B.   Slieve Aughty   Portumna   Shannon   Birr   Portarlington   Mountmellick   Kildare   KILDARE   Kippure 754   Bray
Inishmore   Aran Is.   Gort   Sl. Bloom   Port Laoise   Poulaphouca Res.   Wicklow
Hags Hd.   Ennistymon   L. Derg   LAOIS   LEINSTER   Athy   Barrow   WICKLOW   Wicklow Hd.
Liscannor Bay   CLARE   Roscrea   Lugnaquilla 923   Rathdrum   Mizen Hd.
Mal Bay   Miltown Malbay   Ennis   Nenagh   Templemore   Nore   Carlow   Tullow   Shillelagh   Avoca   Arklow
Kilkee   Killaloe   Ballina   Keeper 694   Thurles   CARLOW   Muine Bheag   Mt. Leinster 796   Gorey
Loop Hd.   Rineanna   Ardnacrusha   TIPPERARY   **Kilkenny**   Enniscorthy
R. Shannon   **Limerick**   Cashel   KILKENNY   Callan   WEXFORD   Cahore Pt.
Foynes   Golden Vale   Tipperary   Slievenamon   New Ross
Rathkeale   LIMERICK   Galtymore 920   Caher   722 Carrick-on-Suir   **Wexford**   Wexford Harbour   Rosslare
Listowel   Newcastle   Galty Mts.   Clonmel   Greenore Pt.
Kerry Hd.   Tralee Bay   Feale   Rath Luirc (Charleville)   Knockmealdown Mts.   Comeragh Mts.   **Waterford**   Tuscar Rock   Carnsore Pt.
Brandon Bay   **Tralee**   MUNSTER   Mitchelstown   Blackwater   WATERFORD   Tramore   Hook Hd.   Saltee Is.
Brandon Mt. 953   St. Mish   Maine   Newmarket   Fermoy   Lismore   Dungarvan   Waterford Harbour
Dingle   Killarney   Kanturk   Blackwater   Dungarvan Bay   St. David's Hd.
Valentia Harbour   Macgillycuddy's Reeks   Lakes of Killarney   Mallow   Boggeragh Mts.   Youghal   Youghal Harbour
Carrauntuohill 1040   **Cork**   Blarney   Midleton
Valentia I.   Cahirciveen   Kenmare   Macroom   Lee   CORK   Cobh   Crosshaven
Skellig Rocks   Caha Mts.   Glengarriff   Passage West   Cork Harbour   Old Head of Kinsale
Ballinskelligs B.   Kenmare River   Bandon   Bandon   Kinsale
Castletown Bearhaven   Bantry   Clonakilty
Bear I.   Bantry Bay   Skibbereen   Clonakilty Bay
Crow Hd.   Dunmanus Bay   Skull   Baltimore
Mizen Hd.   Fastnet Rock   Clear I.   C. Clear

Projection: Conical with two standard parallels.   West from Greenwich   COPYRIGHT. GEORGE PHILIP & SON. LTD.

ft   m
3000   1000
1200   400
600   200
300   100   300
0
100   300
200   600
m   ft

Towns underlined in Northern Ireland give their names to the Districts in which they stand
The remaining Districts are:—
1	Fermanagh	5	Castlereagh
2	Moyle	6	Ards
3	Newtownabbey	7	Down
4	North Down	8	Newry & Mourne

1:2 500 000

10   0   10   20   30   40   50 miles
10   0   10   20   30   40   50   60   70   80 km

NORTH SEA

ENGLAND

Great Yarmouth
Lowestoft
North Walsham
Caister
Beccles
Southwold
Aldeburgh
Orford Ness

Dover
Calais
Cap Gris Nez
Boulogne-sur-Mer
Le Touquet-Paris-Plage
Berck
Étaples
Montreuil
St-Pol-sur-Ternoise
Dunkerque (Dunkirk)
Gravelines
St-Omer
Hazebrouck
Lille
Roubaix
Tourcoing
Tournai
Valenciennes
Douai
Arras
Béthune
Lens
Cambrai
Amiens
St-Quentin
Abbeville
Beauvais
Compiègne
Soissons
Laon
Reims
Épernay
Châlons-sur-Marne
St-Dizier
Chaumont
Paris
Versailles
St-Germain
St-Denis
Meaux
Charleville-Mézières
Sedan
Verdun
Metz
Nancy
Lunéville
Strasbourg
Saverne
Haguenau
Saarbrücken
Saarlouis
Trier
Luxembourg
Thionville
Longwy
Arlon
Bastogne

NETHERLANDS
Groningen
Leeuwarden
Assen
Emmen
Zwolle
Amsterdam
Haarlem
Leiden
's-GRAVENHAGE (The Hague)
ROTTERDAM
Dordrecht
Utrecht
Apeldoorn
Deventer
Enschede
Arnhem
Nijmegen
'S-Hertogenbosch
Eindhoven
Tilburg
Breda
Middelburg
Vlissingen
Den Helder
Texel
Zaandam
Hilversum
Amersfoort
Venlo
Roermond
Maastricht
Heerlen

BELGIUM
Antwerpen
Gent (Gand)
Brussel (Bruxelles)
Brugge
Oostende (Ostend)
Kortrijk
Mechelen
Leuven
Namur
Liège
Charleroi
Mons
Hasselt
Genk
Verviers

LUXEMBOURG

GERMANY
Bremerhaven
Oldenburg
Emden
Wilhelmshaven
Osnabrück
Münster
Dortmund
ESSEN
DUISBURG
DÜSSELDORF
KÖLN (Cologne)
Bonn
Aachen
Mönchengladbach
Krefeld
Wuppertal
Bochum
Gelsenkirchen
Wiesbaden
Mainz
Koblenz
Kaiserslautern

OSTFRIESISCHE INSELN
Norderney
Langeoog
Borkum
Juist
Ijsselmeer
Noordoostpolder
WADDENEILANDEN
Terschelling
Ameland
Schiermonnikoog
Vlieland

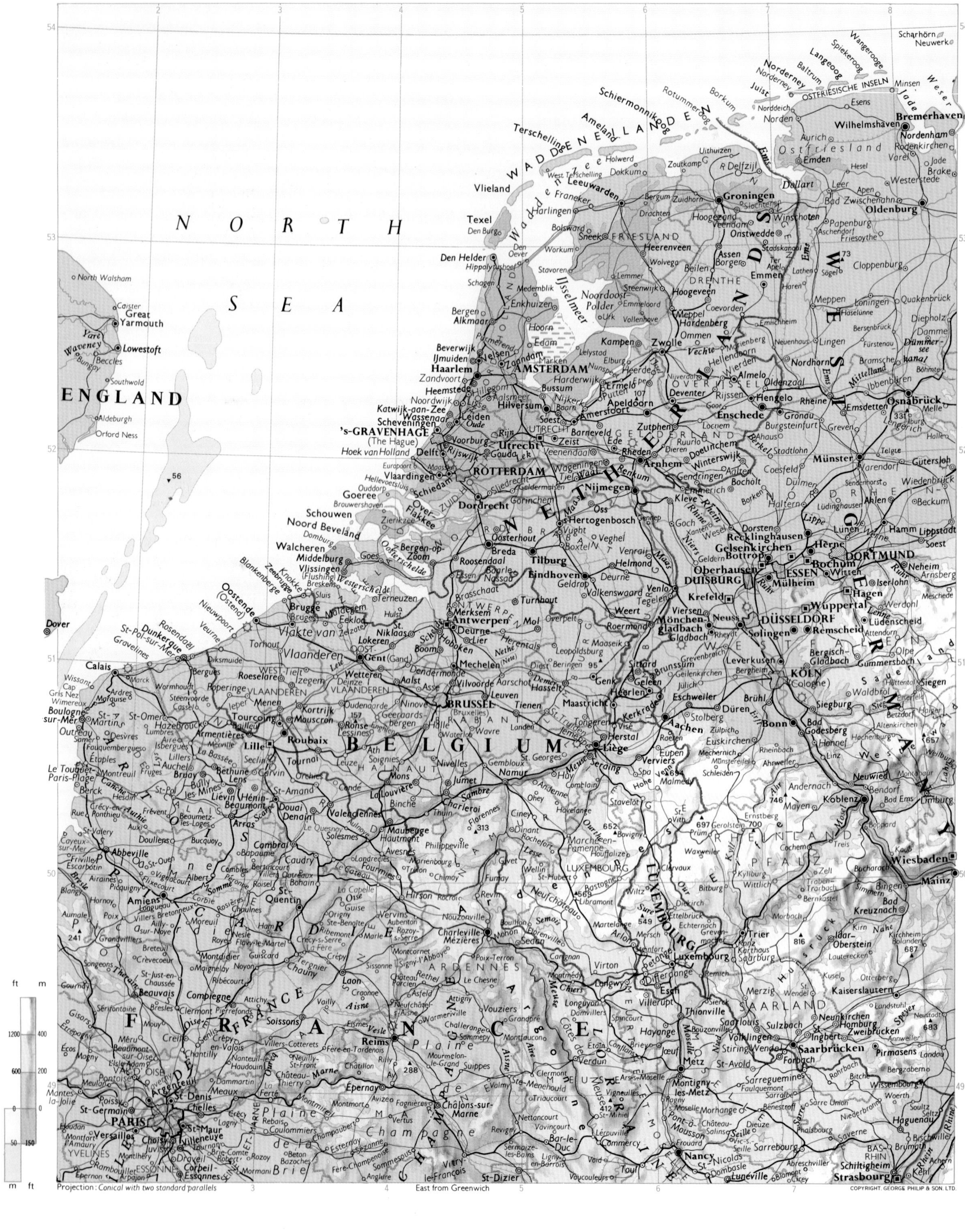

Projection: Conical with two standard parallels
East from Greenwich
COPYRIGHT GEORGE PHILIP & SON, LTD.

1:5 000 000

20 10 0 20 40 60 80 100 miles
40 20 0 40 80 120 160 km

CORSICA
On same scale

Corse

Haute-Corse
Corse du Sud

MEDITERRANEAN SEA

ENGLISH CHANNEL

BAY OF BISCAY

GERMANY

BELGIUM

SWITZERLAND

ALPS

PROVENCE

DAUPHINÉ

MASSIF Central

PYRÉNÉES

East from Greenwich
West from Greenwich

Projection: Conical with two standard parallels

DÉPARTEMENTS IN THE PARIS AREA

1 Ville de Paris   3 Val-de-Marne
2 Seine-St.-Denis 4 Hauts-de-Seine

Projection: Conical with two standard parallels

West from Greenwich   East from Greenwich

BELGIUM

GERMANY

LUXEMBOURG

SAARLAND

FRANCE

SWITZERLAND

ITALY

PARIS

BRUSSEL
Bruxelles

KÖLN

FRANKFURT

Wiesbaden
Mainz

Worms

Ludwigshafen
Mannheim

Karlsruhe

Strasbourg

Freiburg

Mulhouse

Basel

Bern

Lausanne

Genève

Lyon
Lyons

Dijon

Reims

Metz

Nancy

Épinal

Besançon

Neuchâtel

Bourges

Nevers

Troyes

Auxerre

Amiens

Lille

Clermont-Ferrand

Vichy

Moulins

Montluçon

Chaumont

Bar-le-Duc

Verdun

Luxembourg

Thionville

Saarbrücken

Koblenz

Bonn

Aachen

Liège

Namur

Charleroi

Maubeuge

Laon

Soissons

Compiègne

Beauvais

St-Quentin

Charleville-Mézières

Versailles

Melun

Fontainebleau

Sens

Chalon-sur-Saône

Mâcon

Bourg-en-Bresse

Annecy

Chambéry

Aosta

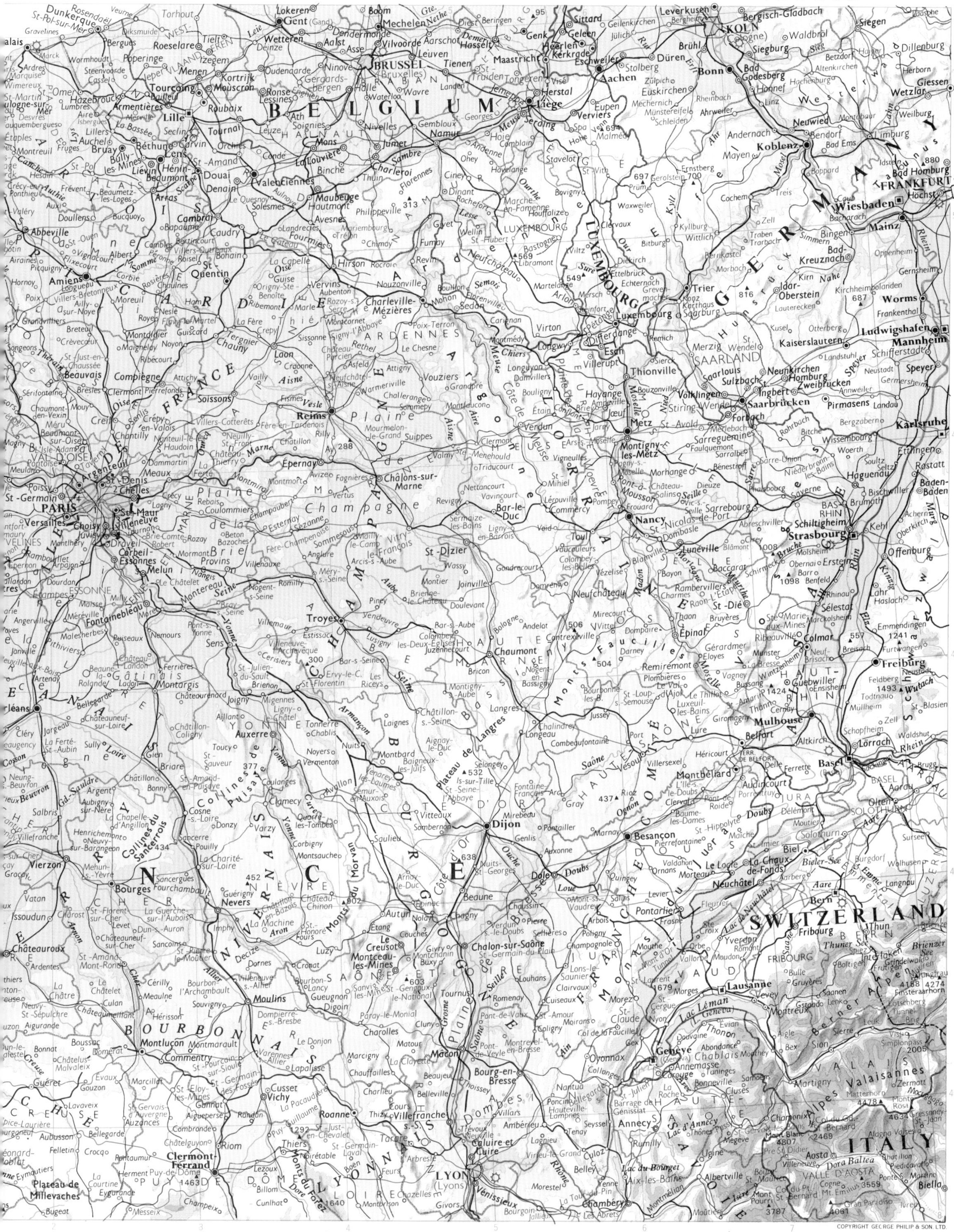

COPYRIGHT GEORGE PHILIP & SON LTD.

1:2 500 000

10 0 10 20 30 40 50 miles
10 0 10 20 30 40 50 60 70 80 km

SWITZERLAND

FRANCHE COMTE

BERN

VAUD

VALAIS

GRISONS

CENTRAL

ITALY

MILANO
(Milan)

TORINO

GENOVA

Golfo di Génova

LIGURIAN SEA

ALPES-DE-
HAUTE-PROVENCE

ALPES
MARITIMES

PROVENCE

VAUCLUSE

BOUCHES
DU RHONE

MARSEILLE

Toulon

Côte d'Azur

ILES D'HYÈRES

u Lion

MEDITERRANEAN SEA

CORSICA

HAUTE-CORSE

CORSE-
DU-SUD

Ajaccio

Iles Cerbicale

COPYRIGHT. GEORGE PHILIP & SON. LTD.

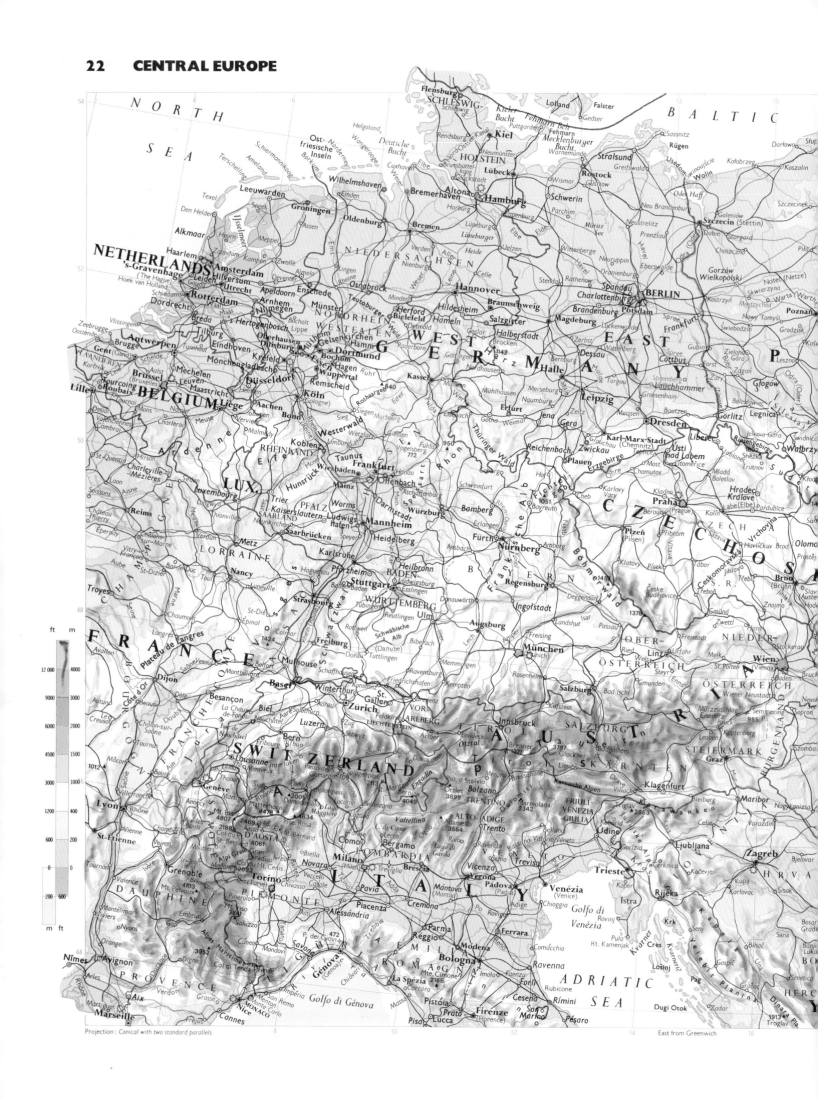

1:5 000 000

50   0   50   100 miles
50   0   50   100   150 km

**CENTRAL
EUROPE
POLITICAL**
1:25 000 000

DENMARK
København
's-Gravenhage
NETH.
BELGIUM
Brussel
LUX.
FRANCE
Berlin
WEST
GERMANY
EAST
Bonn
Praha
CZECHOSLOVAKIA
POLAND
Warszawa
U.S.S.R.
SWITZ.
Bern
LIECHT.
AUSTRIA
Wien
HUNGARY
Budapest
ROMANIA
ITALY
MONACO
SAN MARINO
Roma
YUGOSLAVIA
Beograd
București
BULGARIA
Sofiya

POLAND

Zatoka Gdańska
Zelenogradsk
Kaliningrad (Königsberg)
Pregolya
Chernyakhovsk
LITHUANIAN S.S.R.
Vilnius
Gdynia
Sopot
Gdańsk (Danzig)
Elbląg
R.S.F.S.R.
Gusev
Braniewo
Lyna
Chernyakhovsk
Varena
Starogard
Malbork
Kwidzyń
Ostróda
Olsztyn
Pojezierze Mazurski
Gizycko
Ketrzyn
309
Suwałki
Augustów
Alitus
Lida
Grudziądz
Chełmno
Wąbrzeźno
Iława
Mława
Ostrołęka
Sokółka
238
Grodno
Mosty
Neman
Novogrudok
BYELORUSSIAN
Toruń
Rypin
Lipno
Ciechanów
Ostrów Mazowiecka
Brańsk
Hajnówka
Volkovysk
Slonim
S.S.R.
Łomza
Białystok
Bereza
Włocławek
Płock
Pułtusk
Bug
Czeremcha
Zhabinka
Gniezno
Września
Wisła (Vistula)
Warszawa (Warsaw)
Mińsk Mazowiecki
Siedlce
Biała Podlaska
Brest
Kutno
Łowicz
Pruszków
Żyrardów
Skierniewice
Grójec
Otwock
Łuków
Międzyrzec Podlaska
Pripyat
Konin
Koło
Łęczyca
Łódź
Pilica
Radom
Puławy
Kozienice
Włodawa
Kalisz
Zduńska Wola
Tomaszów Mazowiecki
Piotrków Trybunalski
Końskie
Radomsko
Lublin
Chełm
Zamość
Dubrovitsa
Polésy
Sarny
Ostrów Wielkopolski
Wieluń
Warta
Kielce
Ostrowiec Świetokrzyski
Krasnik
Włodawa
Vladimir Volynskiy
Lutsk
Kovel
Styr
Goryn
Korosten
Radomyshl
Opole
Częstochowa
Sandomierz
Tarnobrzeg
390
San
Przeworsk
Sokal
Dubno
Ostrog
Shepetovka
Zhitomir
Kiyev
Borispol
Zabrze
Bytom
Gliwice
Chorzów
Sosnowiec
Katowice
Kraków
Wieliczka
Tarnów
Jarosław
Przemyśl
Gorodok
Lvov
Zolochev
Brody
Radekhov
Kremenets
Starokonstantinov
Berdichev
Kazatin
Belaya Tserkov
Raciborz
Ostrava
Bielsko-Biała
Nowy Sącz
Jasło
Krosno
Sanok
Sambor
Dnestr
Ternopol
Khmelnitskiy
Vinnitsa
384
UKRAINIAN S.S.R.
U.S.S.R.
Frýdek Místek
Cieszyn
Český Těšín
1725
Tatry
2655
Dukelský Pr.
602
Drogobych
Borislav
Stryi
471
Buchach
Chortkov
Zaleshchiki
Kamenets-Podolskiy
Dnestr
Zhmerinka
Uman
Západné Beskydy
Vychodné Beskydy
4730
CARPATHIANS
Turka
Ivano-Frankovsk
Kolomyya
Snyatyn
Khotin
Magilev-Podolskiy
Bug
Pervomaisk
Gottwaldov
Žilina
SLOVAK S.S.R.
Ružomberok
Prešov
1881
Nadvornaya
Yablonitse
Yedintsy
Soroki
Kotovsk
Nizké Tatry
Košice
Uzhgorod
Mukachevo
931
Chernovtsy
Storozhinets
MOLDAVIAN
Kremnica
Banská Bystrica
Zvolen
Slovenské Rudohorie
Sátoraljaújhely
Beregovo
Khust
2061
Storozhinets
Dorohoi
Beltsy
S.S.R.
Nitra
Banská Štiavnica
Lučenec
Sajó
Tokaj
Rădăuți
Botoșani
429
Kishinev
Nové Zámky
Hron
N.
Miskolc
Nyíregyháza
Satu Mare
Sighetu
Pietrosul
2305
Baia Mare
Vatra-Dornei
Suceava
Iași
Benderų
Tiraspol
Komárno
Vác
Eger
Mezőkövesd
Hajdúböszörmény
Carei
Someş
Bistrita
2102
Pietrosu
Roman
Odessa
Győr
Tatabánya
Esztergom
Jászberény
Debrecen
Dej
Bistrita
Piatra Neamt
Vaslui
Belgorod Dnestrovskiy
BUDAPEST
Újpest
Karcag
Oradea
Salonta
Cluj-Napoca
Turda
Tîrgu Mureş
Praid
Bacău
Veszprém
Székesfehérvár
Cegléd
Szolnok
Nagykőrös
Mezőtúr
Negru
Aiud
Odorheiul Secuiesc
Miercurea Ciuc
Bîrlad
Kecskemét
Kiskunfélegyháza
Békéscsaba
Mții Bihor
1848
Abrud
Sighișoara
Medias
Bretcu
Tecuci
Kagul
Kalocsa
Kiskőrös
Kiskunhalas
Szentes
Hódmezővásárhely
Gyula
Brad
Alba-Iulia
Mureş
Sfîntu Gheorghe
Focșani
Reni
Baja
Szeged
Makó
Arad
Deva
Simeria
Sibiu
Fagaras
Brașov
Rîmnicu Sărat
Galați
Batászék
Szekszárd
Subotica
Senta
Kikinda
Timișoara
Lugoj
Hunedoara
Carpatii Meridionali
2535
Vf. Negoiu
Vf. Omul
2507
Cîmpina
Buzău
Brăila
467
Tulcea
Sulina
Pécs
Mohács
Sombor
Bečej
Zrenjanin (Petrovgrad)
Caransebeş
ROMANIA
Banat
2518
350
Peleaga
Paringul Mare
Tîrgu Jiu
Cîmpulung
Tîrgoviște
Ploiești
Ialomita
Cernavodă
BLACK
Osijek
Novi Sad
Vršac
Porta Orientalis
2509
Vîlcea
Pitești
Arges
București (Bucharest)
Constanța
Drava
Sremska Mitrovica
Bela Crkva
Mehadia
Portile de Fier
Turnu-Severin
Orșova
Valahia
Dîmbovita
Călărași
SEA
Odžak
Brčko
Bijeljina
Zemun
Pančevo
Smederevo
Požarevac
Slatina
Oltenita
Silistra
Mangalia
Bosna
Tuzla
Beograd (Belgrade)
Sava
Morava
Negotin
Craiova
Caracal
Vedea
Olt
Giurgiu
Ruse (Ruschuk)
Tolbukhin
YUGOSLAVIA
1346
Kragujevac
Čačak
Timok
Vidin
Lom
Dunărea (Danube)
Corabia
Turnu Măgurele
BULGARIA
Sarajevo
Titovo Užice
Zaječar
Sofiya

COPYRIGHT. GEORGE PHILIP & SON. LTD.

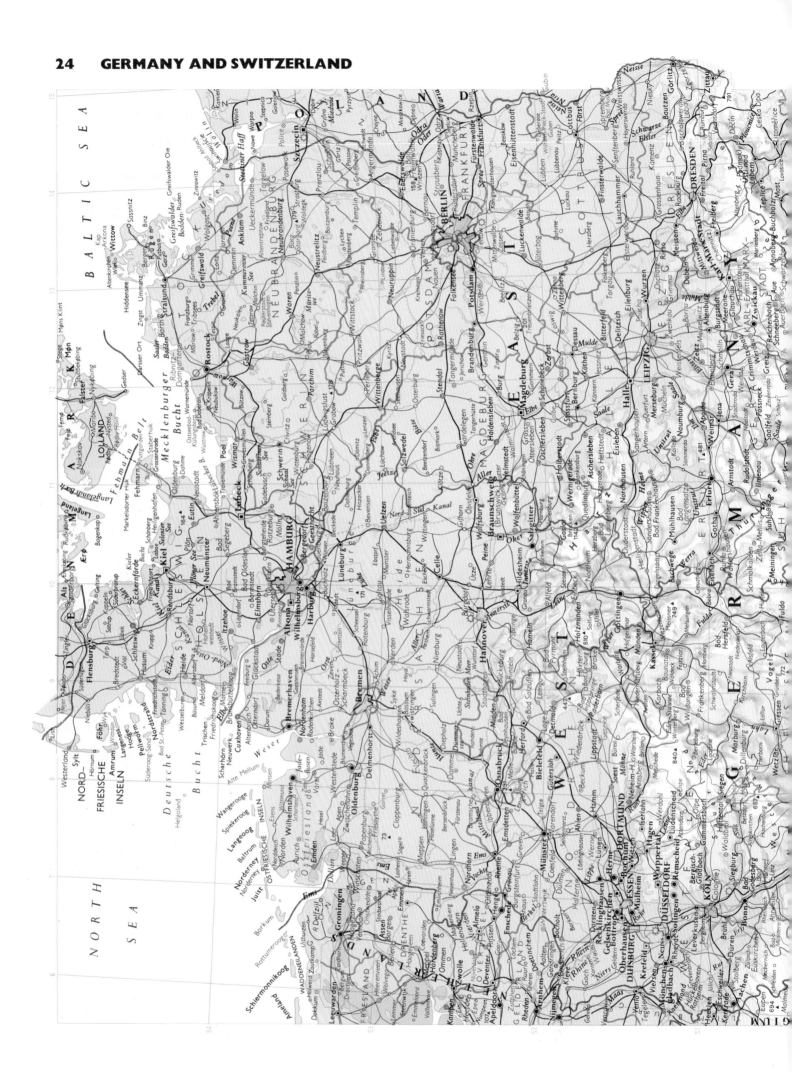

1 : 2 500 000

COPYRIGHT GEORGE PHILIP & SON, LTD.

East from Greenwich

Conical with two standard parallels

1:2 500 000

East from Greenwich

COPYRIGHT. GEORGE PHILIP & SON. LTD.

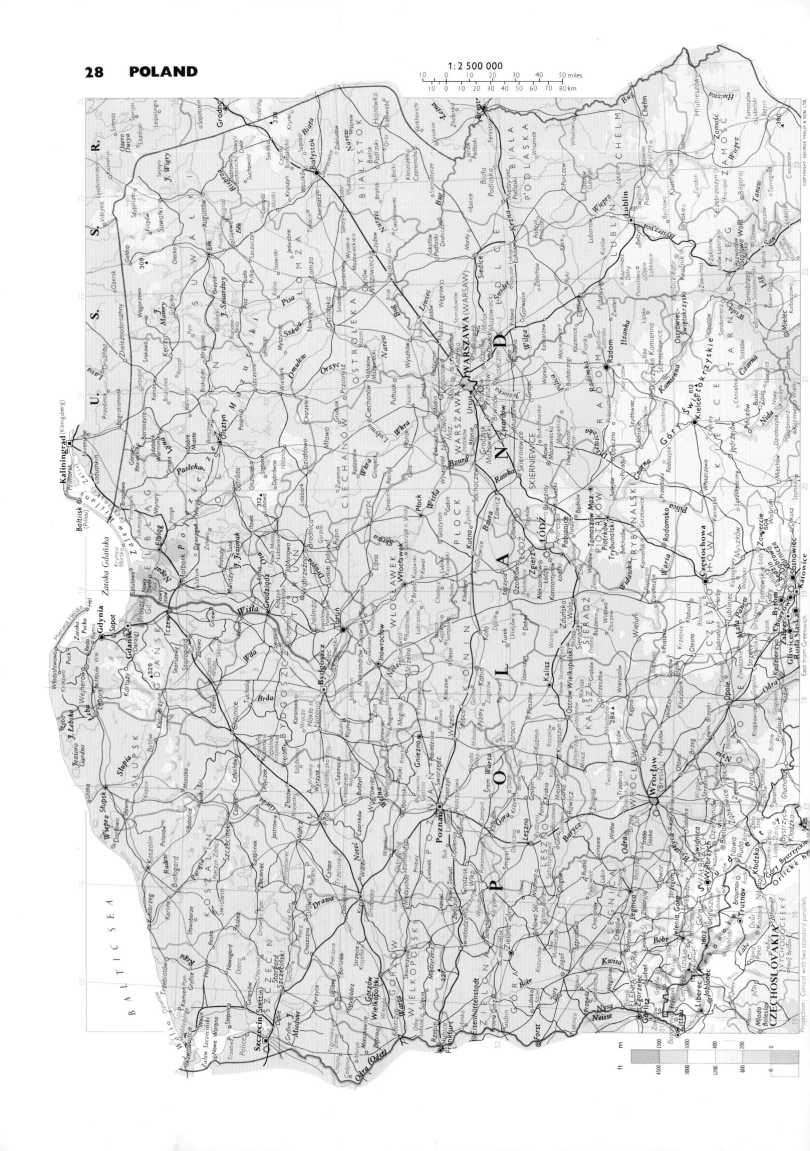

1 : 2 500 000

1:5 000 000

50   0   50   100 miles

50   0   50   100   150 km

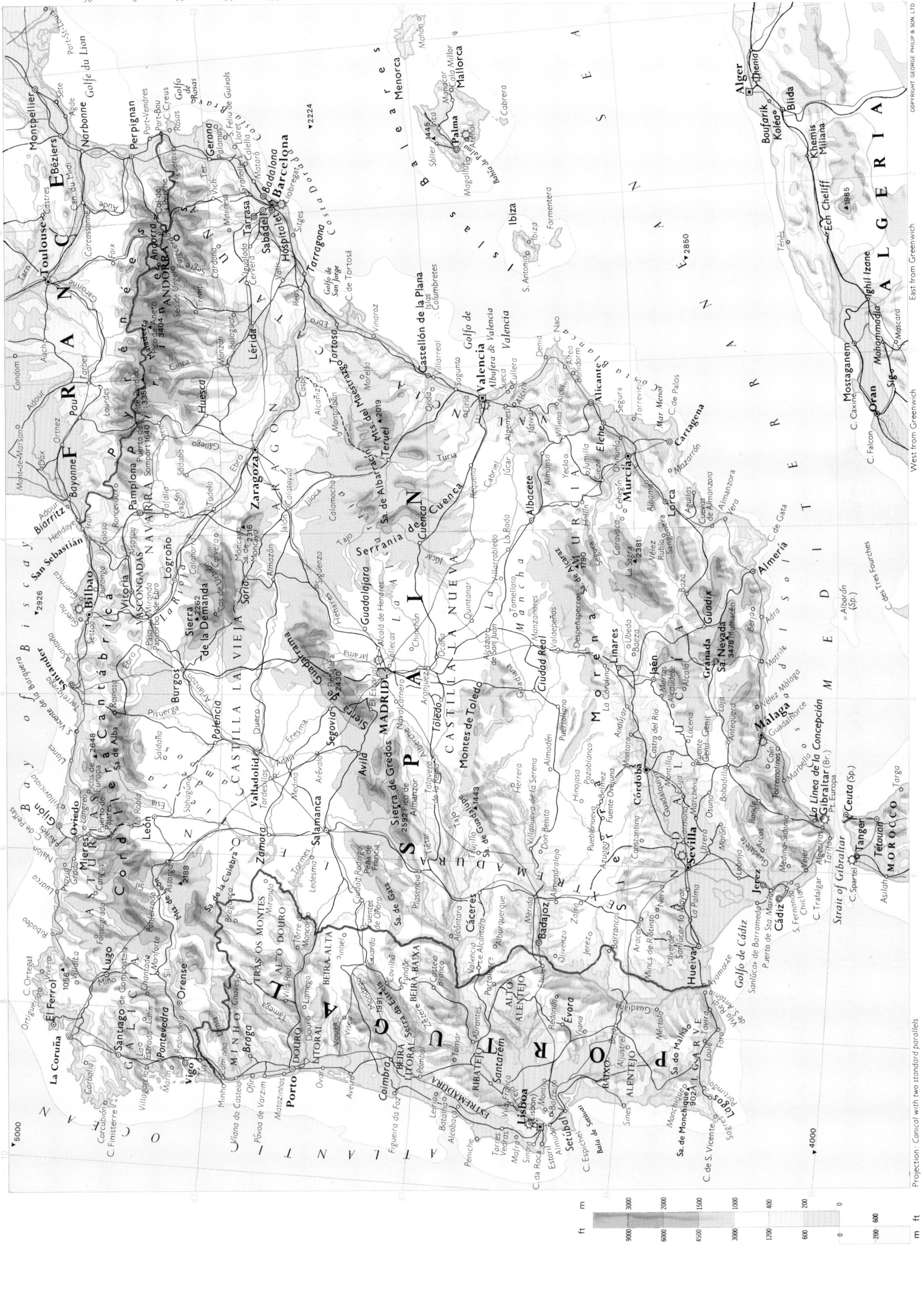

COPYRIGHT GEORGE PHILIP & SON LTD.

East from Greenwich

West from Greenwich

Projection : Conical with two standard parallels

FRANCE

PORTUGAL

ALGERIA

MOROCCO

ATLANTIC OCEAN

MEDITERRANEAN SEA

Bay of Biscay

Balearic Is.

Golfo de Cádiz

Strait of Gibraltar

Golfe du Lion

Mallorca   Menorca   Ibiza   Formentera   Cabrera

Palma

MADRID

Barcelona   Badalona   Sabadell   Tarrasa   Hospitalet

Zaragoza   Huesca   Lérida   Tortosa

Valencia   Castellón de la Plana   Alicante   Elche   Murcia   Cartagena

Granada   Málaga   Almería   Guadix   Jaén   Linares   Córdoba

Sevilla   Cádiz   Jerez   Huelva   Badajoz   Cáceres   Mérida

Ciudad Real   Albacete   Cuenca   Guadalajara   Toledo

Valladolid   Salamanca   Ávila   Segovia   Zamora   León   Palencia   Burgos   Soria   Logroño

Bilbao   San Sebastián   Santander   Gijón   Oviedo   Mieres   Vitoria   Pamplona

La Coruña   Santiago de Compostela   Pontevedra   Vigo   Orense   Lugo   El Ferrol

Lisboa   Porto   Coimbra   Setúbal   Évora   Braga   Santarém

Andorra   ANDORRA

Alger   Blida   Boufarik   Koléa   Oran   Mostaganem   Tetouán   Tanger   Ceuta   Gibraltar

Perpignan   Narbonne   Béziers   Montpellier   Toulouse   Bayonne   Biarritz   Pau   Tarbes

GALICIA   ASTURIAS   CASTILLA LA VIEJA   CASTILLA LA NUEVA   ARAGON   NAVARRA   VASCONGADAS   CATALUÑA   VALENCIA   MURCIA   ANDALUCIA   EXTREMADURA   LEON

Pirineos   Pyrénées   Cordillera Cantábrica   Sierra de Guadarrama   Sierra Morena   Sierra Nevada   Montes de Toledo   Serranía de Cuenca   Sierra de Gredos

m   3000   2000   1500   1000   400   200   0

ft   9000   6000   4500   3000   1200   600   0

5000   4000

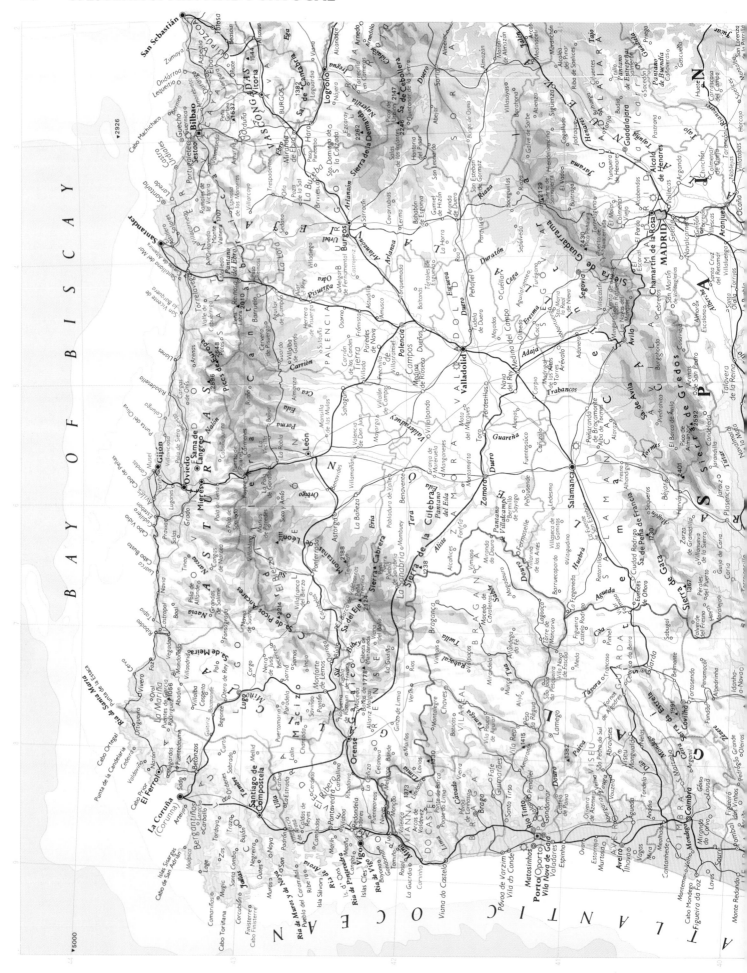

1 : 2 500 000

MEDITERRANEAN SEA

MOROCCO

Golfo de Cádiz

PORTUGAL

ALGARVE

LISBOA (LISBON)

Sevilla

Córdoba

Granada

Málaga

Gibraltar (Br.)

Ceuta (Sp.)

Melilla (Sp.)

Tangér (Tanger)

Tétouan

Badajoz

Ciudad Real

Projection: Conical with two standard parallels

COPYRIGHT GEORGE PHILIP & SON LTD.

West from Greenwich

1:2 500 000

10 0 10 20 30 40 50 miles
10 0 10 20 30 40 50 60 70 80 km

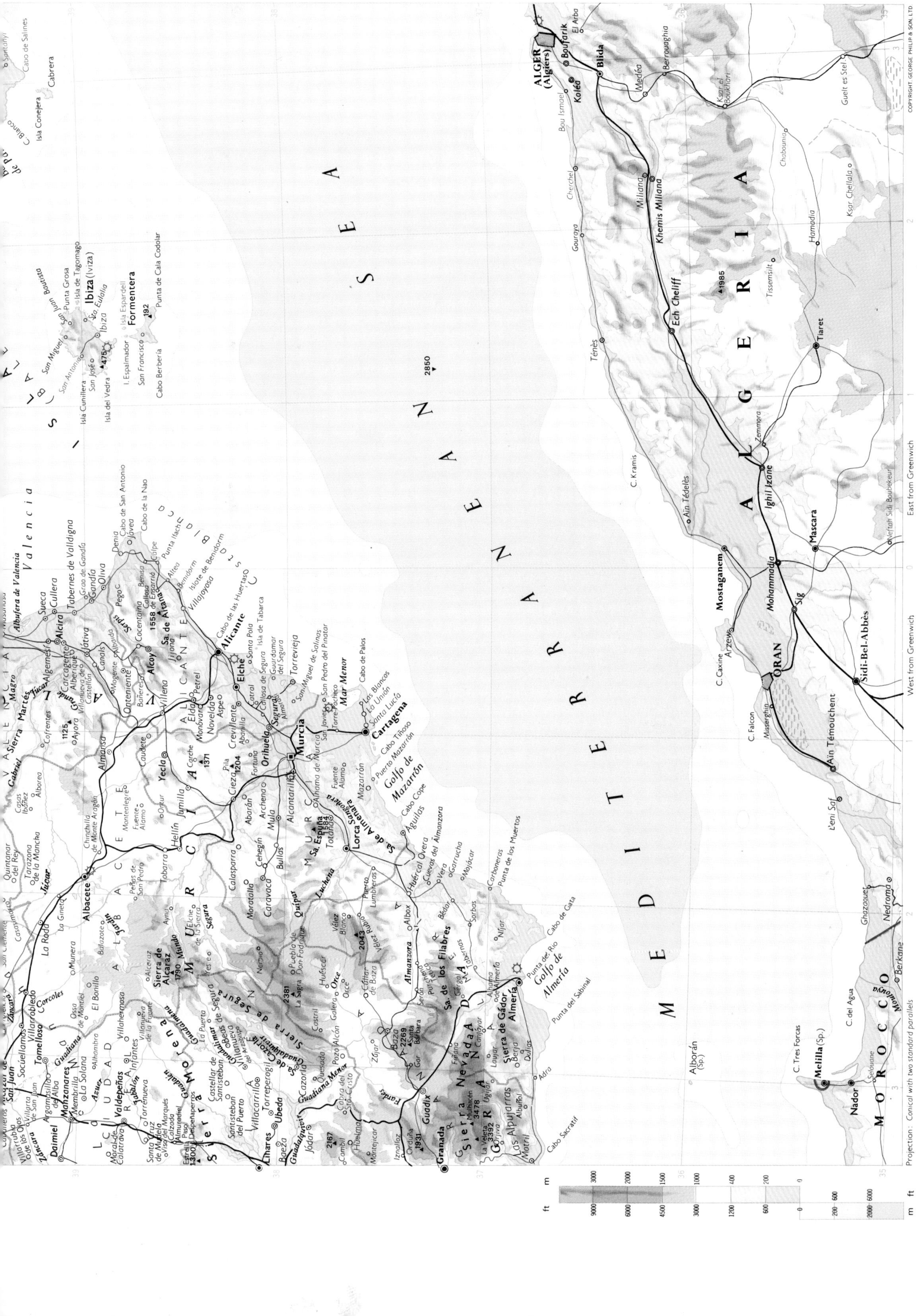

M E D I T E R R A N E A N   S E A

B A L E A R I C   I S L E S

Ibiza (Iviza)
Formentera

ALGER
(Algiers)
Boufarik
El Arba
Blida
Koléa
Medéa
Berrouaghia

A L G E R I A

Khemis Miliana
Miliana
Ech Cheliff
Ténès
Tiaret
Ighil Izane
Mascara
Mostaganem
Arzew
Mohammadia
Sig
ORAN
Sidi-Bel-Abbès
Aïn Témouchent
L'eni Saf

M O R O C C O
Melilla (Sp.)
Nador
Berkane
Nedroma
Ghazaouet

Valencia
Albufera de Valencia
Sueca
Cullera
Gandía
Denia
Cabo de San Antonio
Cabo de la Nao

Alicante
Elche
Alcoy
Játiva
Albacete
Murcia
Orihuela
Cartagena
Mar Menor
Cabo de Palos
Golfo de Mazarrón
Lorca
Granada
Sierra Nevada
Mulhacén 3478
Almería
Golfo de Almería
Guadix
Baza
Úbeda

M U R C I A

Sierra de Cazorla
Sierra de Segura
Sierra de Alcaraz

Projection: Conical with two standard parallels

East from Greenwich
West from Greenwich

COPYRIGHT GEORGE PHILIP & SON LTD

m ft
9000
6000
4500
3000
1200
600
0
200
2000
6000

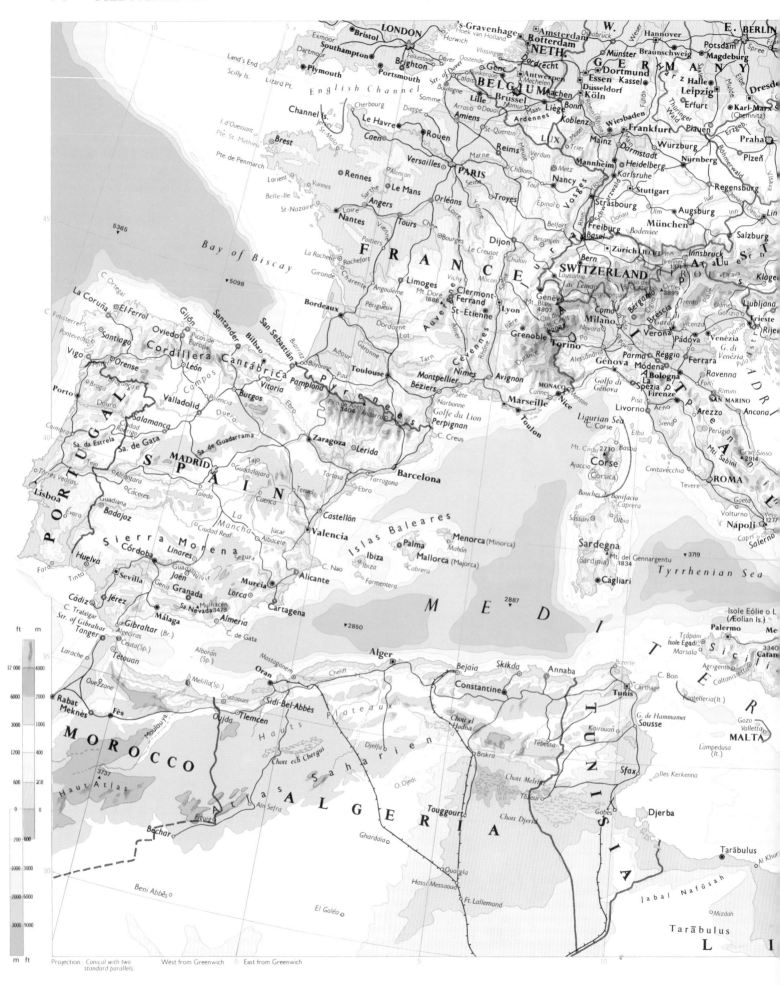

HOULGATE

NR. MORLAIX

LUCCA - ITALY
P38.

10.4 W
43. 8 N

1:10 000 000

50   0   50   100   150   200 miles

50   0   100   200   300   km

POLAND
Poznań
Łódź
Warszawa
Płock
Wisła (Vistula)
Brest
Radom
Lublin
Kielce
Chorzów
Kraków
Tarnów
Przemyśl
Lvov
Ostrava
Jablunkovský Pr.
550
Tatry
2655
CHOSLOVAKIA
egnica
Wrocław
Sudety
Slavkov
Vah
Banská Stiavnica
Košice
Bratislava
Miskolc
HUNGARY
Budapest
Kecskemét
Debrecen
Oradea
Cluj-Napoca
Szeged
Hódmezővásárhely
Arad
Körös
ROMANIA
Pécs
Subotica
Timişoara
Mureş
Carpaţii Meridionali
Negoiu 2535
Braşov (Orasul Stalin)
Zagreb
Novi Sad
Petrovaradin
Sibiu
Sombor
Beograd
Smederevo
Kragujevac
Craiova
Pitesti
Ploieşti
Bucureşti
Silistra
Ruse
Tolbukhin
Varna
Sofiya
Plovdiv
BULGARIA
Rhodopi Planina
Edirne
Burgas

BLACK SEA

Istanbul
Üsküdar
Marmara Denizi
Bursa
Eskişehir
Ankara
TURKEY
Afyon Karahisar
Konya
Izmir
Antalya
Adana
Gaziantep

SYRIA
Halab
Ḥamāh
Ḥimṣ
Dimashq
(Damascus)
Bayrūt (Beirut)
LEBANON
JORDAN
Tel Aviv-Yafo
Jerusalem
ISRAEL
ʿAmmān
Dead Sea

EGYPT
El Qâhira
Suweis
Canal
Sinai
El Faiyûm
Beni Suef
Nile

MEDITERRANEAN SEA

AFRICA
LI BY A
Banghāzī
Barqa
Khalīj Surt

------ Division between Greeks
and Turks in Cyprus;
Turks to the north.

ITALY AND THE BALKAN STATES

Brenner 1371

SWITZERLAND

Passo del S. Gottardo 2108

P Merano

Bressanone

Alpi Carniche

Drave

Villach

Klagenfurt Bleiburg

Maribor

Nagykani

2757 Pso. d. Stelvio

Bolzano

Marmolada 3342

TRENTINO ALTO-ADIGE

Triglav 2863 Kobarid (Caporetto)

Karawanken

FRIULI VENEZIA GIULIA

Udine

Gorizia

Celje

Varaždin

Bernina 4049

Chiavenna

Adamello 3554

Trento

Belluno

Vittorio Veneto

Ljubljana

Kočevje

Cerknica

Zagreb

Bjelovar

Geneve Martigny Rhône Domodóssola

Lago

Lugano

L. di Como

Lecco

Rovereto

Rivaro

Schio

Bassano

Vicenza

Treviso

Padova

Venezia (Venice)

Koper

Postojna

Rijeka (Fiume)

Karlovac

Kupa

HRVAT

Lyon Rhône

Anneey Thones

Mt. Blanc 4807

Matterhorn Mte. Rosa 4478 4634

V. D'AOSTA

Gran Paradiso 4061 Ivrea

Como Bergamo

LOMBARDIA

Lago di Garda

Verona

Pádova (Padua)

Venézia

Golfo di Venézia

Rovinj

Pula (Pola)

Rt. Kamenjak

Krk

Cres

Senj

Sisak

Unac

BOSN

Busto Arsizio Biella

Novara Milano (Milan)

Brescia

Mántova (Mantua)

Adige

Chióggia

Losinj

Pag

Velebit Planina

Gospić Bihać

Banja

Grac

Vercelli

Pavia

Ticino

Cremona

Rovigo

Comácchio

Krk

Kvarner

Kvarnerić

Kremen 1591

HERC

Torino (Turin)

PIEMONTE

Chivasso

Casale

Piacenza

Parma

Ferrara

Ravenna

Dugi Otok

Zadar

Troglav 1913

Split

Y

Grenoble

Mt. Pelvoux 4103 Briançon

Susa Pinerolo Émi Viso

Asti Alba

Alessándria

Tánaro

Réggio Módena

Bologna

Imola Faenza

Forli

Cesena

Rímini

Rubicone

San Benedetto

Šibenik

Brač

Hvar

DAUPHINÉ

Montélimar

Embrun

Saluzzo Cúneo Mondoví

P. dei Giovi 472

Génova (Genoa)

Chiávari

EMILI ROMAG

Mte. Cimone 2165

Pistóia

Pso. di Porretta

San Marino

Pésaro

Fano

Urbino

Ancona

Loreto

Vis

Lastovo

Korčul

Orange Nyons

Tende

Riv. di Ponente

Riv. di Levante

La Spézia

Carrara

Lucca Prato

Firenze (Florence)

Civitanova

Fabriano

Macerata

Palagruža (Yugoslavia)

Avignon

PROVENCE

Digne

Alpi Marittimes 3052

MONACO

Monte Carlo

Imperia

San Remo

Golfo di Génova

Arno

Pisa

Pontedera

TOSCANA Siena

Arezzo

Cortona

Perúgia

Assisi Foligno

UMBRIA

Ascoli Piceno

Téramo

Gran Sasso 2914

Pescara

Chieti

ADRIATIC

Aix Marseille Toulon

Dragnignan Grasse Cannes Nice Menton

Côte d'Azur

Golfo di Génova

Volterra

L. Trasimeno

Ombrone

Chiusi

Amiata 1738

L. di Bolsena

Orvieto

Spoleto 2478

Terni

Rieti

L'Aquila

ABRU

Mt. Amaro 2795 Vasto

Ortona

Lanciano

Térmoli

SE

Iles d'Hyères

LIGURIAN SEA

C. Corse

Capraia

Piombino

Portoferráio

Elba

Grosseto

Mte. Argentário

Fiora

Viterbo

Bracciano

Civitavécchia

Campagna

Tívoli

ROMA (Rome)

Frasinone

MOLISE

S. Severo

Campobasso

Monte S. Ángelo 1056

Monte Gargano

Sannicandro

TYRRHENIAN

Calvi

Bastia

Mt. Cinto 2710

CORSE (CORSICA) (Fr.) Ajaccio

Aléria

Sartene

Pto. Vecchio

Bonifácio

Orbetello

Velletri

Óstia

Ánzio

Latina

Sabáudia

Terracina

Fondi

Gaeta

Ísole Ponziane

Garigliano

Volturno

Benevento

Caserta

Averso

Vesúvio 1277

Fóggia

G. di Manfredónia

Cerignola Barletta

Andria Corato

Trani

Molfetta

Bari

Putignano

Asinara

C. Falcone

2855

Golfo dell' Asinara

Porto Tórres

Maddalena

Caprera

Capri

Ólbia (Terranova)

Golfo Aranci

Bouches de Bonifácio

3719

Ísole

Nápoli (Naples)

Torre Annunziata

Sorrento

Castellammare

Salerno

Sele

Avellino

Nocera

Éboli

Potenza

Spinazzola

Matera

BASILICATA

Taranto

Sássari

Alghero

Bosa

Núoro

Orosei

SARDEGNA (SARDINIA)

C. Mte. Santo

Agri

Pisciotta

Golfo di Táran

2271

Iglésias

Oristano

Terralba

Sorgono

Tirso

Mt. Gennargentu 1834

Arbatax

Ierzu

MALTA
1:1 000 000

C. S. Dimitri

Gozo (Ghawdex)

Comino (Kemmuna)

Victoria (Rabat)

Mdina

Rabat

St. Pauls Bay

Mosta

Hamrun

Luqa

Sliema

Valletta

Marsaxlokk

Zurrieq

Birzebbuga

Cágliari

Golfo di Cágliari

C. Spartivento

C. Carbonara

Iglésias Portoscuso Carbonia

G. di Pálmas

Cosenza

CALABR 1929

Crotone

Nicastro

Sambiase

Catanzar

Pizzo

Corigliano

Ústica (It.)

Isole Eólie o Lípari

Strómboli

Salina

Lípari

Vulcano

C. Peloro

Milazzo

Palmi

Taurianova

Scilla

Réggio

C. Spartivento

Palermo

Castellammare

Términi

Cefalù

Patti

Messina

Str. di Messina

Trápani

Érice

Isole Égadi

Favignana

Marsala

Alcamo Segesta

Monti Nébrodi

Mistretta

Enna

Adrano

Etna 3340

Giarre

Catánia

Lentini

Augusta

Castelvetrano

Selinunte

Menfi Sciacca

Caltanissetta

Piazza

Caltagirone

Ferla

Siracusa (Syracuse)

C. Bon

AFRICA

Platani

Pto. Empédocle Agrigento

Licata

Salso

Gela

Vittória

Módica

Ragusa

Noto

Ispica

C. Passero

Pantelleria (Ital.)

1730

MEDIT

Gozo

Comino

Valletta

Mdina MALTA

Lampedusa (Ital.)

S.E. EUROPE
POLITICAL
1:25 000 000

Bern SWITZ. LIECHT

AUSTRIA

Wien

Budapest

HUNGARY

U.S.S.R.

FRANCE

Venezia Trieste

SAN MARINO

YUGOSLAVIA

Beograd

ROMANIA

Bucureşti

Corse (Fr.)

ITALY

Roma

ADRIATIC SEA

ALBANIA

Tirana

Sofija

BULGARIA

Thessaloniki

GREECE

AEGEAN SEA

TURKEY

Napoli

Sicilia

MALTA

Athínai

Kríti

MEDITERRANEAN SEA

Projection: Conical with two standard parallels

1:5 000 000

50   0   50   100 miles

50   0   50   100   150   km

East from Greenwich

COPYRIGHT. GEORGE PHILIP & SON. LTD.

Projection: Conical with two standard parallels

East from Greenwich

1 : 2 500 000

10   10   20   30   40   50 miles

10   0   10   20   30   40   50   60   70   80 km

AUSTRIA

Innsbruck   Salzach   Niedere Tauern   Fohnsdorf   Knittelfeld   Peggau   Weiz   Neudau

Graz   Gleisdorf   Fürstenfeld   Güssing   Körmend   Vasvár

Hohe Tauern   Hofgastein   Judenburg   1989   Voitsberg   Stainz

HUNGARY

Nagykanizsa   SOMOGY

Klagenfurt   Wörther See   Maribor   Sveti Lenart   Donya Lendava

Villach   Karawanken   Drava   Ptuj   Varaždin

Bolzano (Bozen)   Marmolada   3342

VENEZIA GIULIA   FRIULI

Udine   Gorizia   **Ljubljana**

Trieste   Monfalcone

YUGOSLAVIA

Zagreb   Karlovac

Treviso   **Venézia** (Venice)   Laguna Veneta

Pádova (Padua)   Mestre

Golfo di Venézia

Vicenza   Rovigo   Ádria   Chióggia

Rijeka (Fiume)   Opatija   Istra

Ferrara   Porto Tolle   Foci del Po

Pola   Medulin   Cres   Kvarner

Argenta   Ravenna   Comácchio

Krk   Senj   Rab   Pag

Imola   Faenza   Forlì   Cérvia

BOSNA   Banja Luka

Bihać   HERCEGOVINA

Cesena   **Rímini**   Riccione

SAN MARINO   Pésaro   Fano

Zadar   Biograd

DALMACIJA

Ancona   Senigállia

Šibenik   Trogir   **Split**

Dinara Planina   2006

Arezzo   MARCHE   Osimo

Brač   Hvar   Makarska

Perúgia   Assisi   Macerata   Fermo

Korčula   Pelješac

UMBRIA   Foligno   Áscoli Piceno

Vis   Lastovo   Mljet

Todi   Spoleto   Téramo

Lastovski Kanal

Terni   Narni   Rieti   L'Aquila   **Pescara**   Chieti

ABRUZZI   Gran Sasso d'Italia   2914

Viterbo   L. di Bolsena   L. di Bracciano

MOLISE   Vasto   Térmoli

ROMA (ROME)   Tívoli   Tévere

Civitavécchia   LAZIO

ADRIATIC SEA

Tremiti   Vieste   Gargano   Monte Sant'Ángelo

Iles Sanguinaires
G. d'Ajaccio
C. di Muro
G. de Valinco
Táravo
Petreto
Propriano
Sartène
Bonifacio
CORSE
CORSE-DU-SUD
Bouches de Bonifacio
2136 Zonza
Levie
Porto-Vecchio
Iles Cerbicales
I. de Cavallo
Solenzara
Favone
CORSICA

Santa Teresa Gallura
Maddalena
La Maddalena
Caprera
Asinara
Punta dello Scorno
Golfo dell'
Asinara
Coghinas
Aggius
Tempio Pausania
1362
M. Limbara
Pto. Cervo
Arzachena
Costa
Smeralda
Golfo Aranci
Olbia
Tavolara
G. di Ólbia

Porto Tórres
C. dell'Argentiera
Sássari
Osilo
Sorso
Sennori
Oschiri
L. di Coghinas
Posada
Tanaunella

Fertília
Alghero
Ittiri
Ozieri
Pattada
Buddusó
Siniscola
C. Comino

Villanova
Monteleone
1259
Bororva
1170
Bitti
Orune
C. Comino

Bosa
Macomer
Oliena
Dorgali
Golfo di
Orosei

Temo
SARDEGNA
Nuoro
L. del Tirso
Fonni
Sorgono
Monti del
Gennargentu
1834
Baunei
Arbatax
C. di Monte Santu

C. Mannu
Oristano
Cabras
SARDEGNA
M. Arci
812
Láconi
Lanusei
Ílbono

Golfo di
Oristano
Arborea
Terralba
Mandas
Nurri
Senorbì

Gúspini
Morreale
Sanluri
Villacidro
Serramanna
S. Vito
Villaputzu
Muravera

C. Pécora
1236
M. Línas
Gonnosfanádiga
Doliánova
Serpentara

Fluminimaggiore
Iglésias
Cixerri
Assémini
Sestu
Selárgius
Quartu Sant'Elena
C. Ferrato

Portoscuso
Gonnesa
Siliqua
Sínnai
1069
Pta. Serpeddì

Carloforte
Carbónia
1116
Cágliari

San Pietro
Sant'Antíoco
Santadi
Golfo di
Cágliari

Sant'
Antíoco
Porto Botte
Pula
Teulada
Serpentara
C. Carbonara

G. di Pálmas
C. Spartivento

SARDINIA

TYRRHENIAN
▽
3719

SEA
3589
▽

Ustica

Vatican City
ROMA
(Rome)
Tívoli
Conca
del Fúcino

Fregene
Tévere (Tiber)
Palestrina
Sóbiaco
Trevico

Lido di Óstia
(Lido di Roma)
Anzio
Velletri
Angen
Alatri
Veroli
Sora

Prática
di Mare
Albano
Lazio
Cisterna di Latina
Ferentino
Frosinone
Monte S. Gio

Aprília
Cisterna
Sezze
Priverno
Isola del L

Anzio
Nettuno
Latina
Pontínia
Sonnino
Fondi
1533
Fórmia

Sabáudia
Monte Circeo
541
Terracina
Gaeta
Mintumo
Mondragon

Zannone
Golfo di
Gaeta

Palmarola
Ponza
Ísole
Ponziane
283
Ventotene
Voltur
Cas

 Íschia
788

G. di
Castellammare del Golfo
C. Gallo
PALERMO
Bagheria

C. San Vito
G. di Castellammare
Carini
Móreale
Mísilmeri
Términi I

Levanzo
Trápani
Érice
1110
Partinico
S. Giuseppe
Iato
Ísole Égadi
Maréttimo
Alcamo
Camporeale
Corleone
1613
Marineo

Favignana
Paceco
Calatafimi
Salemi
Gibellina
Lercara
Alia

Marsala
Partanna
Bisacquino
Pálizzi
M
SICI

Castelvetrano
Santa Margherita
Sambuca
di Sicilia
Burgio
San Cata
Calt

Mazara
del Vallo
Menfi
Mussomeli
Castelter

Campobello di Mazara
Belice
Sciacca
Caltabellotta
Ríbera
Bivona
Platani
Racalmuto
San Cata

Cattólica Eraclea
Siculiano
Agrigento
Naro
Can

Porto Empédocle
Raffadali
Favara
Palma di Montechiaro
Campobello di
Lic

Sciacca
Sicilian Channel

Iles de la
Galite

C. Blanc
Cani
Bizerte
(Binzert)
C. Serrat
Menzel-Bourguiba
Plane
Zembra
C. Bon

El Kala
Tabarka
Mateur
Golfe de Tunis
C. Bon

ALGERIA
Teboursouk
Tébourba
TUNIS
Halq el Oued
Kelibia

Bou Salem
Béja
Medjerda
Menzel-
Temime

Mellegue
Soliman
Pantelleria
Pantelleria
836
(It.)

TUNISIA
Nabeul
Zaghouan
Hammamet

MEDITE
1319
▽

ft m
9000 3000
6000 2000
4500 1500
3000 1000
1200 400
600 200
0 0
200 600
2000 6000
4000 12 000
m ft

1 : 2 500 000

10   0   10   20   30   40   50 miles

10   0   10   20   30   40   50   60   70   80 km

A D R I A T I C

S E A

Strait of Otranto

I O N I A N

S E A

Golfo di Táranto

Golfo di Sant'Eufémia

Golfo di Squillace

Isole Eólie o Lípari (Æolian Is.)

G. di Salerno

G. di Manfredónia

BASILICATA

CALABRIA

G. di Policastro

ALBANIA

Kérkira (Corfu)

East from Greenwich

1:2 500 000

10 0 10 20 30 40 50 miles

10 0 10 20 30 40 50 60 70 80 km

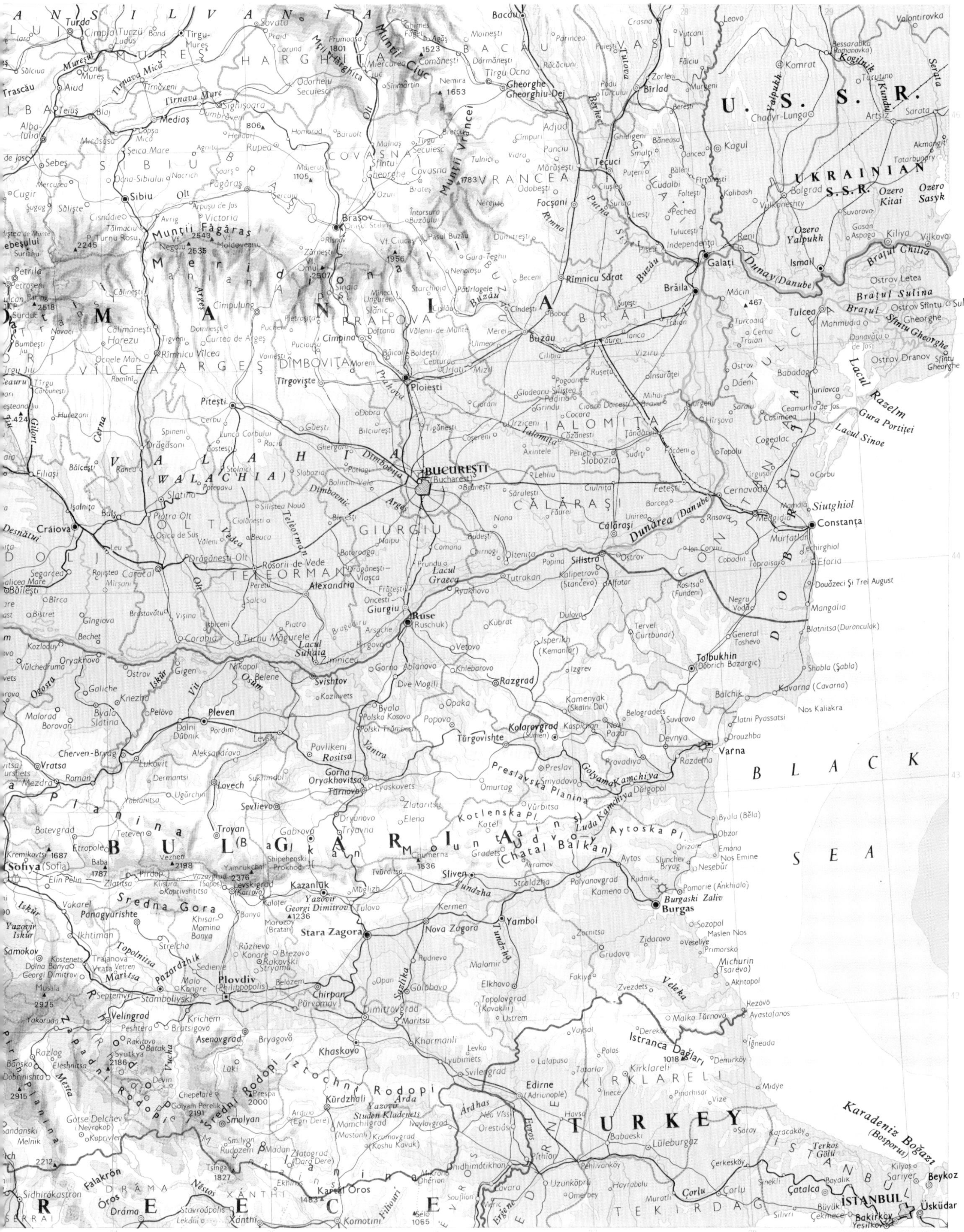

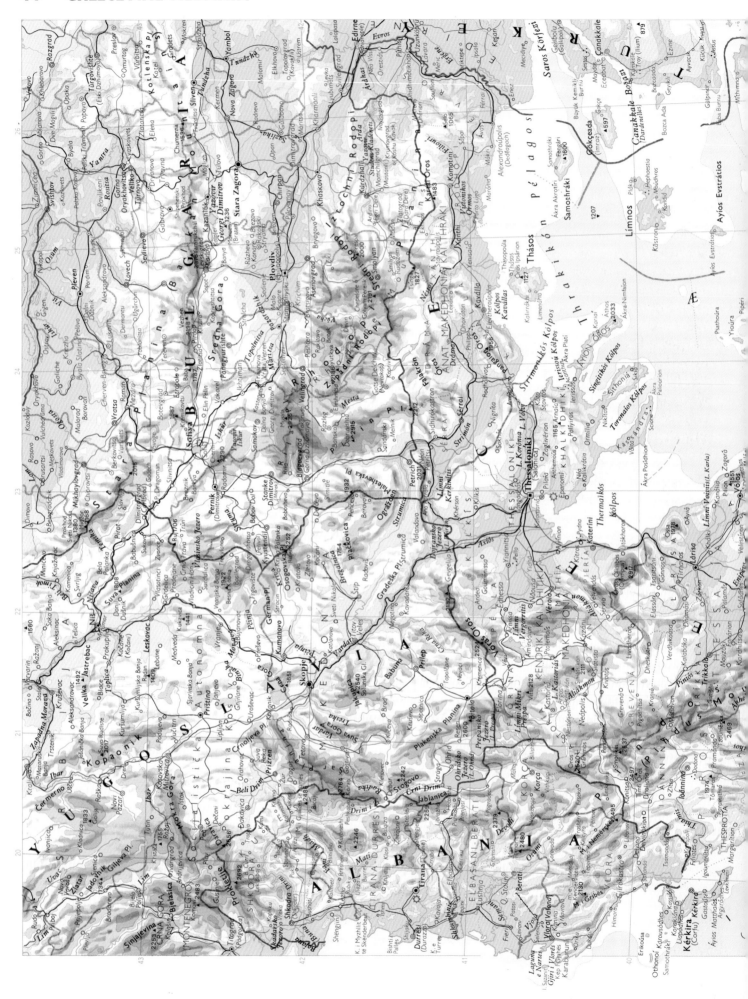

1 : 2 500 000

miles
10 0 10 20 30 40 50 miles
10 0 10 20 30 40 50 60 70 80 km

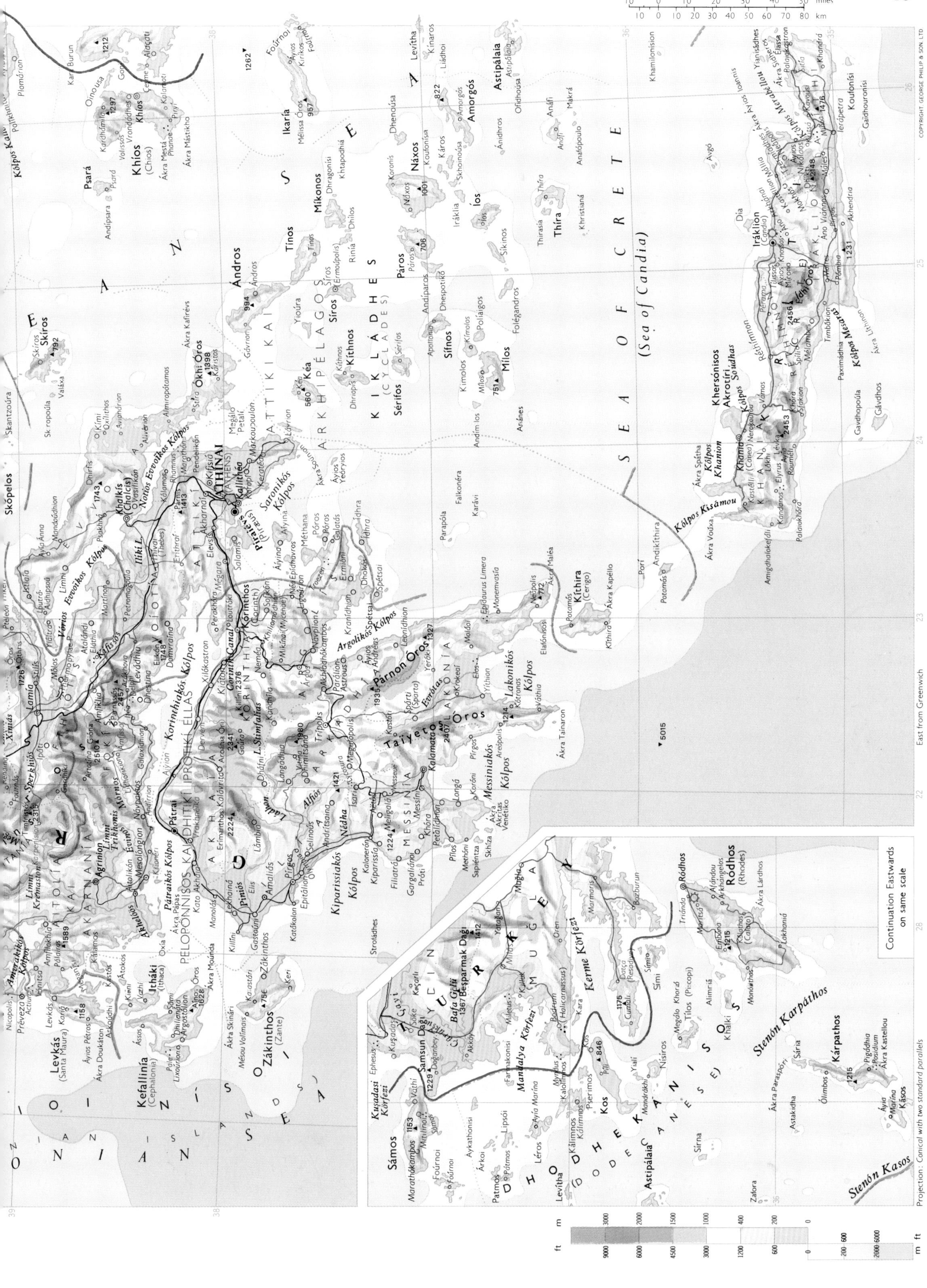

East from Greenwich

Continuation Eastwards
on same scale

Projection: Conical with two standard parallels

Major labels

Kólpos Kallonís
Plomárion
Kará Burun 1212
Oinoúsa
Kardhámila 1297
Vrondádos
Khíos (Chios)
Akra Mastikho
Psará
Andípsara Psará
Ikaría 1262
Mélissa Óros 957
Foúrnoi
Áyios Kírikos
Kínaros
Lévitha
Astipálaia
Oúdhioúsa
Anáfi
Makrá
Khamilonísion
Koufonísi
Ierápetra
Khondrá

Mikonos
Tinos
Ándros
Ándros
Náxos
Koufonísi
Káros
Íos
Sikinos
Thíra
Thirasía
Iráklia
Dhragonísi

ARKHIPÉLAGOS
KIKLÁDHES (CYCLADES)
Páros
Andíparos
Síros
Ermoúpolis
Kéa
Kíthnos
Sérifos
Sífnos
Mílos
Kímolos
Folégandros
Dhespotikó
Poliaígos

ÓKhi Óros 1398
Kárislos
Stíra
Megálo Petalí

SEA OF CRETE
(Sea of Candia)

Khersónisos Akrotíri
Soúdhas
Khaniá (Canea)
RÉTHI MNON
Réthimnon
KHANIÁ
Iráklion (Candia)
Neápolis
LASÍTHI
Áyios Nikólaos
Ierápetra
Kólpos Mesarás
Akra Lithínon
Gávdhos
Gavdhopoúla

SKÓPELOS
Skíathos
Skíros 792
Skíros
Akra Kafirévs

ATTIKI KAI VOIOTIA
ATHÍNAI (ATHENS)
Kallithéa
Piraiévs (Piraeus)
Saronikós Kólpos
Salamís
Elevsís
Mégara
Aíyina
Méthana
Póros
Galatás
Ídhra
Spétsai
Ermióni

Khalkís (Chalcis)
Thívai (Thebes)
Levádhia
Korinthos (Corinth)
Korinthós Kólpos
Korinthiakós Kólpos
Korinth Canal

Lamía
Xiniás
Stereá
Sperkhiós
Ímittos
Parnassós
Giona
Vardúsia
Tríkkala

PELOPÓNNISOS
ÉLLAS
DHITIKI ÍLLAS
PROTHKI ÉLLAS
AKHAÏA
ARKADHIA
MESSINÍA
LAKONÍA
Pátrai
Korinthos
Árgos
Náfplion
Mikínai (Mycenae)
Trípolis
Spárti (Sparta)
Taïyetos Óros 2407
Parnon Óros 1935
Kalámata
Messiniakós Kólpos
Kiparissiakós Kólpos
Nísos
Pírgos
Piniós
Amaliás
Eléa
Filiatrá
Pílos
Methóni
Koróni
Areópolis
Akra Taínaron
Ákra Akrítas

Kíthira (Cerigo) 772
Akra Kapéllo
Andikíthira
Elafónisos
Monemvasía
Neápolis
Epídavros Limerá

IONIAN SEA
Levkás (Santa Maura)
Kefallinía (Cephalonia)
Itháki (Ithaca)
Zákinthos (Zante)
Préveza
Amvrakikós Kólpos
Aktion
AITOLIA KAI AKARNANIA
Agrínion
Trikhonís
Mesolóngion
Pátraïkós Kólpos
Strofádhes

Inset (lower right)

Kuşadasi Körfezi
Sámos
Vathí
Mitilíni
Marathókambos
Foúrnoi
Pátmos
Lipsoí
Léros
Kálimnos
Kos
Astipálaia
Nísiros
Tílos
Sími
Khálki
Ródhos (Rhodes)
Ródhos
Líndos
Akra Líndos
Kárpathos
Sténón Karpáthos
Kásos
Sténón Kasos

DHODEKÁNISOS (DODECANESE)
MUĞLA
AYDIN
Ephesus
Kuşadasi
Bafa Gölü
Milas
Bodrum
Marmaris
Fethiye
Samsun Dağı
Beşparmak Dağı 1367
Menderes
Kerme Körfezi

Elevation scale

m	ft
3000	9000
2000	6000
1500	4500
1000	3000
400	1200
200	600
0	0

1:2 500 000

EXTENSION WESTWARDS
At the same scale as main map

COPYRIGHT GEORGE PHILIP & SON LTD.

Projection: Conical with two standard parallels

East from Greenwich

1:2 500 000

10 0 10 20 30 40 50 miles
10 0 10 20 30 40 50 60 70 80 km

Projection: Conical with two standard parallels

East from Greenwich

COPYRIGHT GEORGE PHILIP & SON, LTD.

ft m

6000 — 2000
4500 — 1500
3000 — 1000
1200 — 400
600 — 200
0 — 0
200 — 600

m ft

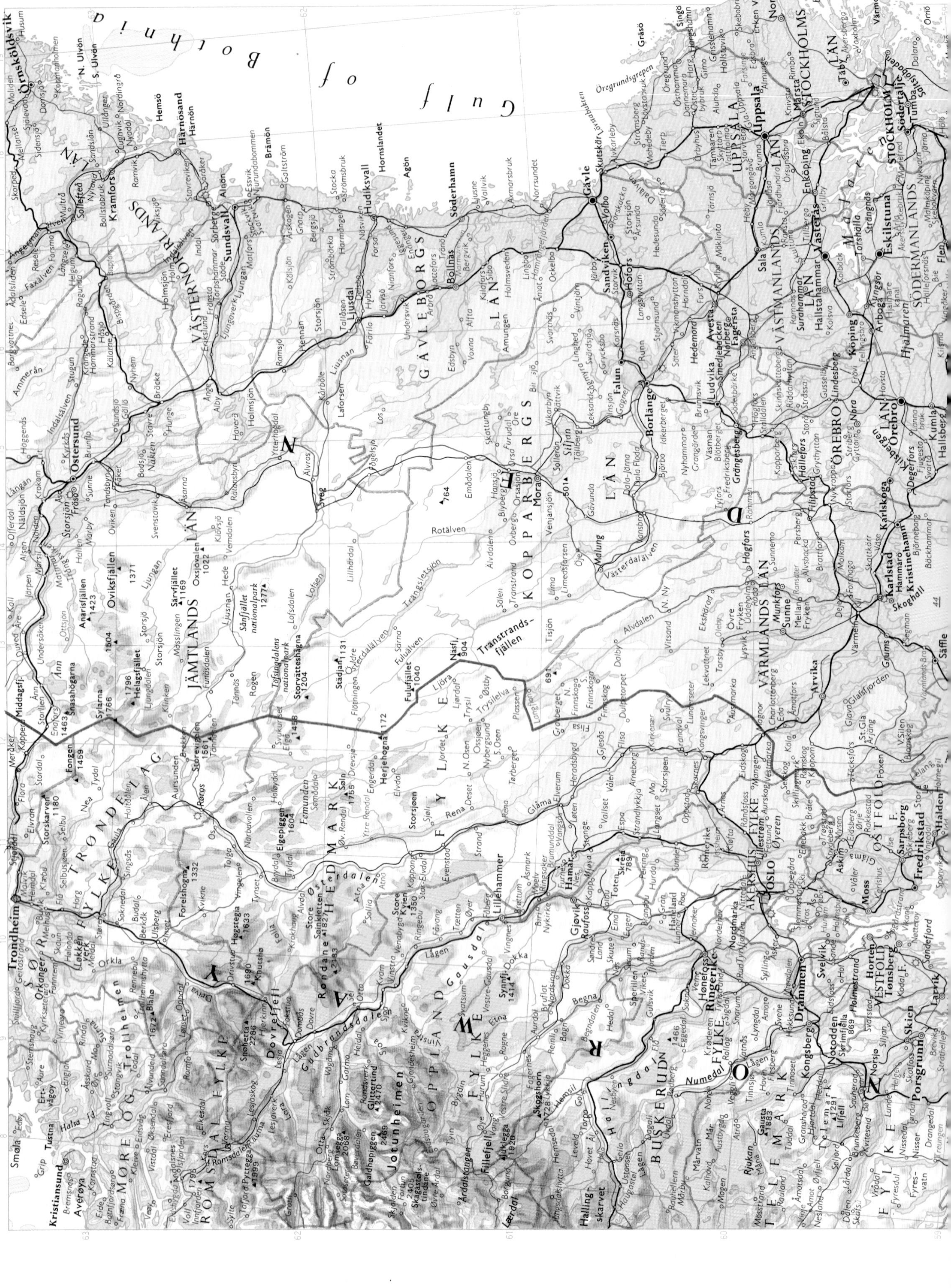

Gulf of Bothnia

VÄSTERNORRLANDS LÄN

GÄVLEBORGS LÄN

JÄMTLANDS LÄN

KOPPARBERGS LÄN

VÄRMLANDS LÄN

VÄSTMANLANDS LÄN

UPPSALA LÄN

STOCKHOLMS LÄN

SÖDERMANLANDS LÄN

ÖREBRO LÄN

TRÖNDELAG

SØR-TRØNDELAG FYLKE

MØRE OG ROMSDAL FYLKE

HEDMARK FYLKE

OPPLAND FYLKE

AKERSHUS FYLKE

BUSKERUD FYLKE

VESTFOLD FYLKE

TELEMARK FYLKE

ØSTFOLD

Örnsköldsvik · Härnösand · Sundsvall · Hudiksvall · Söderhamn · Gävle · Bollnäs · Ljusdal · Östersund · Falun · Borlänge · Mora · Uppsala · STOCKHOLM · Södertälje · Eskilstuna · Västerås · Köping · Örebro · Karlstad · Karlskoga · Trondheim · Røros · Lillehammer · Hamar · Gjøvik · Oslo · Drammen · Kongsberg · Skien · Porsgrunn · Sarpsborg · Fredrikstad · Moss · Kristiansund

1 : 2 500 000

miles
km

459

809

Projection : Conical with two standard parallels

East from Greenwich

COPYRIGHT GEORGE PHILIP & SON, LTD.

POLAND

Słupsk

BALTIC SEA

Gotland
Visby
Lummelunda
Västergarn
Klintehamn
Stora Karlsö
Hoburgen

ÖLAND
Kalmar
Öland s. udde

Bornholm
Rønne
Nexö
Svaneke
Allinge

Nyköping
Oxelösund
Norrköping
Linköping
Motala
Mjölby
ÖSTERGÖTLANDS
Tranås
Skövde
Falköping
Jönköping
Huskvarna
Nässjö
Vetlanda
Eksjö
KALMAR LÄN
Oskarshamn
Västervik
Vimmerby
JÖNKÖPINGS LÄN
Värnamo
Ljungby
Växjö
KRONOBERGS LÄN
Alvesta
BLEKINGE LÄN
Karlskrona
Karlshamn
Ronneby
Lidköping
Mariestad
Vänersborg
Alingsås
Borås
Trollhättan
Uddevalla
Kungälv
Göteborg
Mölndal
HALLANDS LÄN
Varberg
Falkenberg
Halmstad
Laholm
Ängelholm
Helsingborg
Landskrona
MALMÖHUS
Lund
Malmö
Trelleborg
Ystad
KRISTIANSTADS LÄN
Kristianstad
Hässleholm
Eslöv

GERMANY
Hiddensee
Rügen
Arkona
Kiel
Flensburg
Schleswig
Husum
Rendsburg

DENMARK
Skagen
Frederikshavn
Hjørring
NORDJYLLANDS
Ålborg
Nørresundby
Hobro
Randers
Viborg
VIBORG AMT.
Skive
Mors
Nykøbing
Thisted
RINGKØBING AMT.
Holstebro
Herning
Ringkøbing
Esbjerg
RIBE AMT.
JYLLAND
Silkeborg
ÅRHUS
Århus
Djursland
Grenå
Skanderborg
Horsens
Vejle
VEJLE AMT.
Fredericia
Kolding
SØNDERJYLLANDS AMT.
Haderslev
Åbenrå
Tønder

FYN
Odense
Middelfart
Svendborg
Faborg
Nyborg
Assens

SJÆLLAND
København (COPENHAGEN)
Roskilde
Helsingør
Hillerød
Frederikssund
Frederiksværk
Holbæk
Kalundborg
Slagelse
Sorø
Ringsted
Næstved
Korsør
Vordingborg

LOLLAND
FALSTER
Nykøbing
Nakskov
Maribo
Gedser

STORSTRØM

Møn

Fehmarn

Kattegat
Ålborg Bugt
Anholt
Læsø
Samsø

Skagerrak

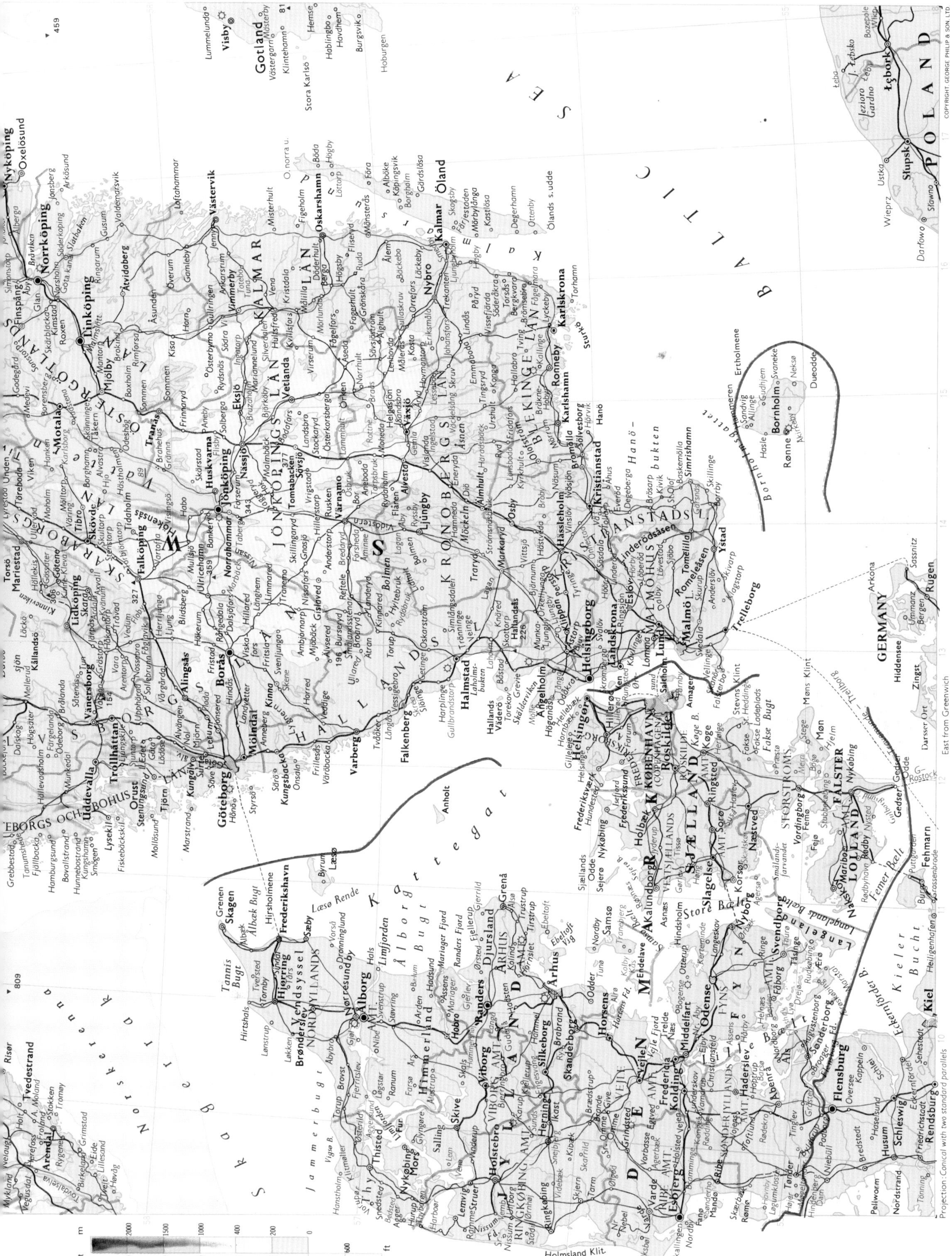

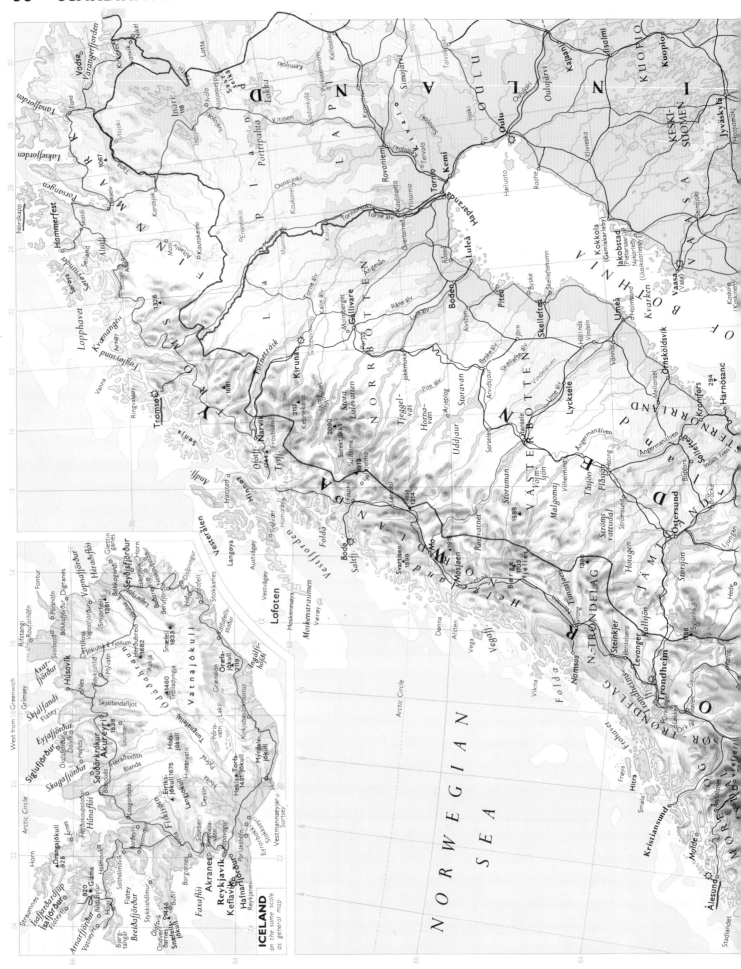

ICELAND
on the same scale
as general map

1:5 000 000

20 10 0 20 40 60 80 100 miles
40 20 0 40 80 120 160 km

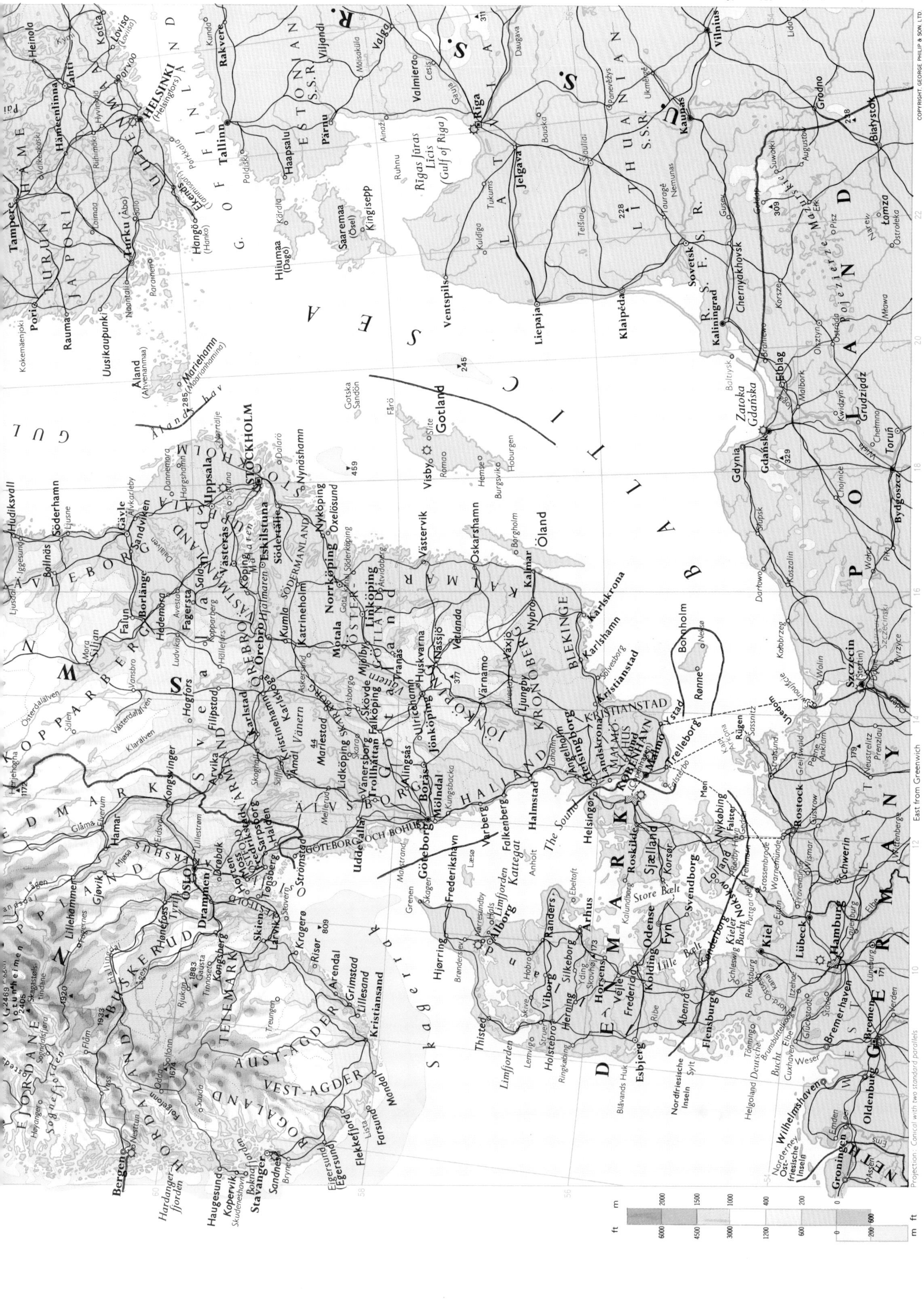

FINLAND

Heinola
Kotka
Lovisa (Loviisa)
Lahti
Kouvola
Hämeenlinna
Porvoo
HELSINKI (Helsingfors)
Tampere
HÄME
TURUN JA PORI
Turku (Åbo)
Hangö (Hanko)
Pori
Rauma
Uusikaupunki
Naantali
Parainen

ESTONIAN S.S.R.
Tallinn
Haapsalu
Pärnu
Viljandi
Rakvere
Valga
Hiiumaa (Dagö)
Saaremaa (Ösel)
Kingisepp
Kärdla

LATVIAN S.S.R.
Riga
Valmiero
Cēsis
Daugava
Jelgava
Tukums
Bauska
Ventspils
Kuldiga
Liepaja
Telšiai
Rigas Jūras Līcis (Gulf of Riga)
Ruhnu

LITHUANIAN S.S.R.
Klaipeda
Šiauliai
Tauragė
Nemunas
Kaunas
Vilnius
Kaišiadorys
Sovetsk
Chernyakhovsk

R.S.F.S.R.
Kaliningrad

POLAND
Gdynia
Zatoka Gdańska
Gdańsk
Elbląg
Malbork
Grudziądz
Toruń
Bydgoszcz
Grodno
Białystok
Łomża
Ostrołęka
Suwałki
Augustów
Olsztyn
Szczecin (Stettin)
Koszalin
Słupsk
Kołobrzeg

BALTIC SEA

Gotland
Visby
Slite
Fårö
Gotska Sandön
Öland
Borgholm
Bornholm
Rønne

SWEDEN
STOCKHOLM
Uppsala
Gävle
Söderhamn
Hudiksvall
Bollnäs
Ljusdal
Sandviken
Falun
Borlänge
Mora
Siljan
Hedemora
Avesta
Fagersta
Sala
Västerås
Köping
Eskilstuna
Södertälje
Nyköping
Oxelösund
Nynäshamn
Katrineholm
Norrköping
Linköping
Motala
Örebro
Kumla
Karlskoga
Filipstad
Karlstad
Arvika
Kristinehamn
Lidköping
Skövde
Skara
Mariestad
Trollhättan
Vänersborg
Uddevalla
GÖTEBORG
Borås
Alingsås
Mölndal
Jönköping
Nässjö
Huskvarna
Tranås
Vetlanda
Västervik
Oskarshamn
Kalmar
Nybro
Växjö
Värnamo
Ljungby
Karlskrona
Karlshamn
Kristianstad
Halmstad
Falkenberg
Varberg
Ängelholm
Landskrona
MALMÖ
Helsingborg
Lund
Ystad
Trelleborg

VÄRMLAND
DALARNA
KOPPARBERG
ÖREBRO
VÄSTMANLAND
SÖDERMANLAND
ÖSTERGÖTLAND
SMÅLAND
KRONOBERG
BLEKINGE
HALLAND
KALMAR
GÖTEBORG OCH BOHUS
ÄLVSBORG
SKARABORG
JÖNKÖPING

NORWAY
OSLO
Bergen
Stavanger
Sandnes
Haugesund
Kopervik
Egersund (Eigersund)
Flekkefjord
Farsund
Mandal
Kristiansand
Lillesand
Grimstad
Arendal
Risør
Kragerø
Larvik
Skien
Porsgrunn
Tønsberg
Horten
Drammen
Kongsberg
Notodden
Hønefoss
Gjøvik
Lillehammer
Hamar
Kongsvinger
Moss
Fredrikstad
Sarpsborg
Halden

HORDALAND
ROGALAND
VEST-AGDER
AUST-AGDER
TELEMARK
BUSKERUD
OPPLAND
HEDMARK
ØSTFOLD
AKERSHUS
Sognefjorden
Hardangerfjorden
Jotunheimen
Galdhøpiggen 2469

DENMARK
KØBENHAVN
Sjælland
Roskilde
Korsør
Slagelse
Næstved
Nykøbing
Svendborg
Odense
Fyn
Nyborg
Kolding
Fredericia
Vejle
Horsens
Århus
Randers
Viborg
Silkeborg
Herning
Holstebro
Thisted
Hjørring
Ålborg
Frederikshavn
Skagen
Esbjerg
Ribe
Åbenrå
Sønderborg
Haderslev
Flensburg
Falster
Lolland
Bornholm
Limfjorden
Kattegat
Skagerrak
The Sound
Store Bælt
Lille Bælt

GERMANY
Hamburg
Lübeck
Kiel
Flensburg
Rostock
Schwerin
Wismar
Stralsund
Greifswald
Rügen
Bremen
Bremerhaven
Wilhelmshaven
Oldenburg
Emden
Cuxhaven
Lüneburg
Schleswig
Rendsburg
Neumünster
Itzehoe
Neustrelitz
Neubrandenburg
Prenzlau
Güstrow
Weser
Elbe

NETHERLANDS
Groningen

GULF OF BOTHNIA

m   ft
6000
4500
3000
1200
600
200
0

53

1:10 000 000

Projection: Conical with two standard parallels

------- Division between Greeks and Turks in Cyprus; Turks to the North.

East from Greenwich

COPYRIGHT. GEORGE PHILIP & SON, LTD.

Projection: Conical with two standard parallels

East from Greenwich

1:5 000 000

50   0   50   100 miles
50   0   50   100   150 km

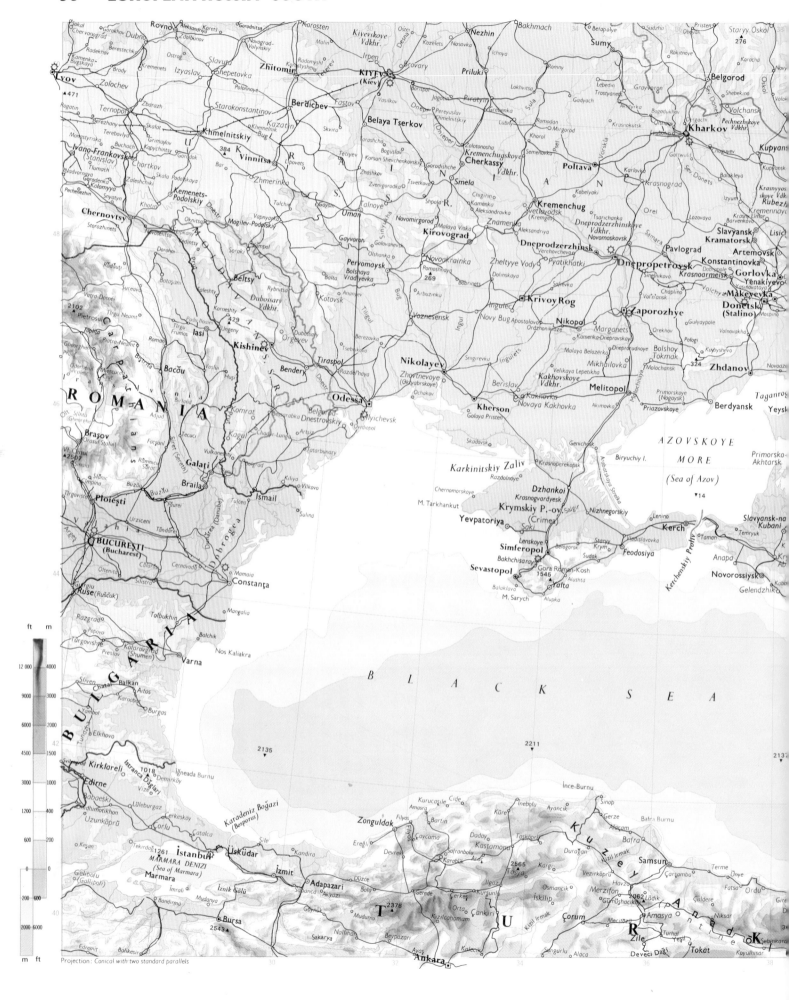

Projection: Conical with two standard parallels

1:5 000 000

50   0   50   100 miles
50   0   50   100   150 km

Yelan-Kolenovskiy
Georgiu-Dezh
Ostrogozhsk
Kamenka
Bobrov
Talovaya
Buturlinovka
239
Povorino
Peski
Uryupinsk
Khrenovoye
Novokhopersk
Buzuluk
Yelan
Samoylovka
Krasnoarmeysk
Zhirnovsk
Krasnyy Kut
Orlov Gay
Oz.Chalkar
Chalkar
Dzhambeyty
Pavlovsk
Boguchar
Kantemirovka
Kalach
Novoannenskiy
Panfilovo
Medveditsa
Danilovka
Ilovlya
V'dkhr.
Rovnoye
Piterka
Novouzensk
Mergenevskiy
Karsha
Millerovo
Meshkovo
Kazanskaya
Serafimovich
Kletskiy (Kletskaya)
Ilovlya (Iloulyskaya)
Dubovka
Kamyshin
Nikolayevsk
Bykovo
Iovatka
Aleksandrov Gay
Kaztalovka
Furmanovo
Antonovo
Indernorskiy
Starobelsk
Melovoye
Cherktovo
Veshenskaya
Don
Frolovo
Olkhovka
Volgogradskoye
Urda
Kushum
Inderborskiy
Voroshilovgrad (Lugansk)
Glubokiy
Belaya Kalitva
Morozovsk
Lenin
Surovikino
Kalach na Donu
Volgograd (Stalingrad)
Krasnoslobodsk
Volzhskiy
Leninsk
Kapustin Yar
Vladimirovka
Shungay
Makhambet (Yamankhalinka)
Zelënyy
Kommunarsk
Krasnodon
Krasnyy Luch
Sverdlovsk
Gukovo
Kamensk-Shakhtinskiy
Tsimlyanskoye Vdkhr.
Chernyshkovskiy
Krasnoarmeysk
Akhtubinsk (Petropavlovskoye)
Verkhniy Baskunchak
Novobogatinskoye
Guryev
Rovenki
Snezhnoye
Shakhty
Krasnyy Sulin
Artëmovsk
Tsimlyansk
Volgodonsk
Dubovskoye
Kotelnikovo
Obilnoye
Kopanovka
Yenotayevka
Novoshakhtinsk
Kamenolomni
Matveyev Kurgan
Tuzlov
Novocherkassk
Don
Bolshaya Martynovka
Zimovniki
Remontnoye
KALMYK A.S.S.R.
Krasnyy Yar
Kumyzyak
Taganrog
Rostov
Bataysk
Azov
Veselovskoye Vdkhr.
Mechetinskaya
Oz. Manych-Gudilo
Elista (Stepnoi)
Krasnoye
Astrakhan
Kirovskiy
Liman
CASPIAN SEA
Zernograd
Yeya
Proletarskaya
Yegorlykskaya
Gigant
Leninsk
Priyutnoye
Kaspiyskiy
Beloye Ozero
Starokorsunskaya
minskaya
Salsk
Peschanokopskoye
Pavlovskaya
Belaya Glina
Krasnogvardeyskoye
Divnoye
Kalaus
Arzgir
Kuma
Staryy Biryuzyak
O. Kulaly
Mangyshlakskiy Zaliv
M. Tyub Karagan
Fort Shevchenko
Tikhoretsk
Timashevsk
Korenovsk
Novoaleksandrovskaya
Ipatovo
Svetlograd (Petrovskoye)
Blagodarnoye
Budennovsk
Vladimirovka
Tyuleniy
Bryanskoye
P-ov. Mangyshlak
Krasnodar
Ust-Labinsk
Armavir
831 Kurganinsk (Kurgannaya)
Kuban
Stavropol
Nevinnomyssk
Zelenokumsk
Vorontsovo-Aleksandrovskoye
Kursavka
Shevchenko
Maykop
Labinsk
Urup
Mineralnyye Vody
Cherkessk
Georgievsk
Mozdok
Kizlyar
O. Chechen
Aleksandriyskaya
Lopatin
Khadyzhensk
Apsheronsk
Dakhovskaya
Yessentuki
Pyatigorsk
Prokhladnyy
CHECHENO-
Terek
Bolshoi
Sochi
Krasnaya Polyana
Kislovodsk
Karachayevsk
Nalchik
Nartkala
Malgobek
INGUSH
Gudermes
Sulak
Kizil Yurt
Makhachkala
Adler
Gagra
ABKHAZ A.S.S.R.
Teberda
KABARDINO-BALKAR A.S.S.R.
Elbrus 5633
5203
Grozny
Beslan
Khasavyurt
Kumtorkala
Kaspiysk
Gudauta
Novyy Afon
Tkvarcheli
Kodori
Ordzhonikidze
Balta
Buynaksk
Izberbash
Novokayakent
Sukhumi
Kazbek 5047
Tebulos 4492
Khunzakh
Kakhib
Akusha
Dogestanskiye Ogni
Ochamchire
Gali
Dzhvari
Tsageri
Rioni
Agvali
Tlyarata
Madzhalis
Derbent
800
Anaklia
Tskhaltubo
GEORGIA
Tskhinvali (Staliniri)
Kvareli
Kuli
Kasumkent
Kutaisi
Chiatura
S.S.R.
Dusheti
Telavi
Samus
Kutaisi
Sachkhere
Zestafoni
Khashuri
Gori
Mtskheta
Gurdzhaani
Zakataly
Akhty
Khachmas
Poti
Samtredia
Kobuleti
Makharadze
Borzhomi
Tbilisi
Kaspi
Signakhi
Citeli-Tskaro
Sheki (Nukha)
Kutkashen
Kuba
Mikhaylovka
Divichi
Batumi
ADZHAR A.S.S.R.
Akhaltsikhe
Vale
Khrami
Rustavi
Mtkvari
Mirzaani
Iori
Alazan
Mingechaurskoye Vdkhr.
Bazar Dyuzi 4466
Baba dag 3629
Siazan
Görele
Akçaabat
Hopa
Borçka
Pazar
Khulo
Akhalkalaki
Shaumyani
Akstafa
Kura
AZERBAIJAN
Agdash
Geokchay
Mashtaga
Sumgait
Surakhany
Trabzon
Rize
Kaçkar 3937
Artvin
Ardahan
Çildir
3192 K'siri
Alaverdi
Tauz
Shamkhor
Mingechaur
Yevlakh
Barda
S.S.R.
Kürdamir
BAKU
Tirebolu
Sürmene
İspir
Oltu
Ardanuç
Leninakan
Kirovakan
Kirovabad
Chanlar
Mir-Bashir
Agdzhabedi
Sabirabad
Kazi Magomed
Alyaty
Gümüşhane
Çakırgöl 3063
Narman
Sarikamiş
Selim
Kars
Araks 4090
Dilizhan
Sevan
Dashkesan
Terter
Agdam
Imishly
M. Byandovan
Bayburt
Tortum
Kağızman
Digor
Echmiadzin
Yerevan
ARMENIAN S.S.R.
Ozero Sevan
Kamo
Martuni
Sabirabad
Ali-Bayramly

Ergeni Vozyshennost
Privolzhskaya V'zyshennost
Prikaspiyskaya Nizmennost
KAZAKH S.S.R.
Bolshoi Kavkaz
Maliy Kavkaz Mountains
DAGESTAN A.S.S.R.
Armyanskoye Nagorye

East from Greenwich   COPYRIGHT GEORGE PHILIP & SON LTD

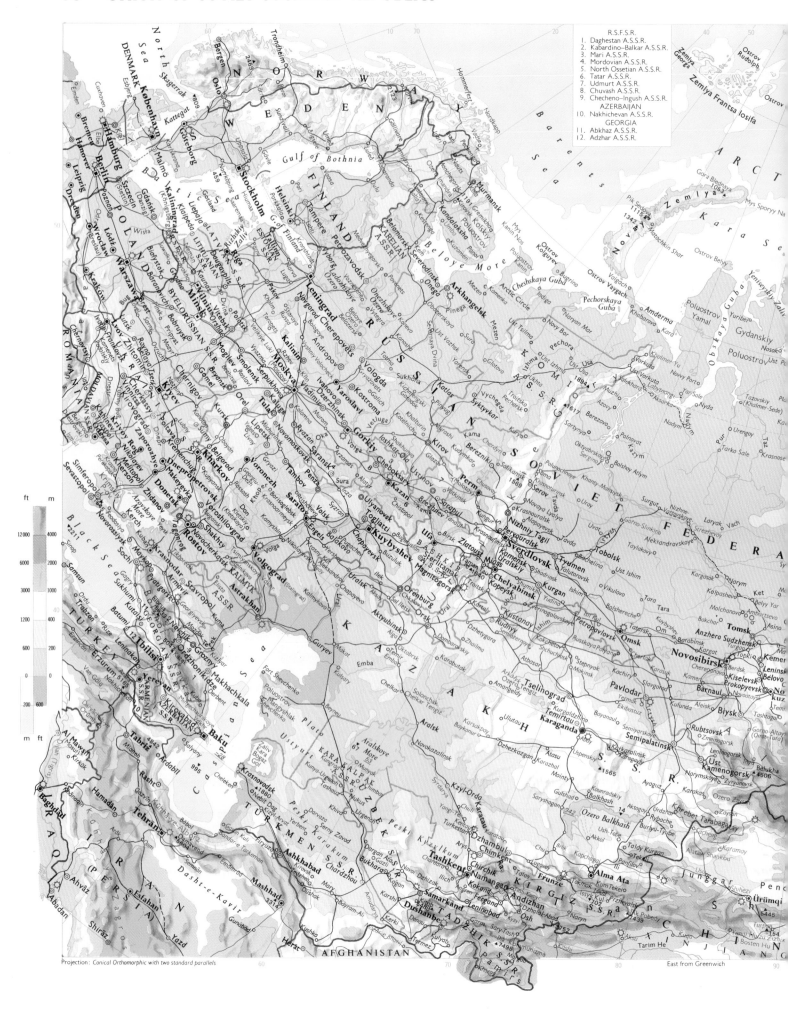

R.S.F.S.R.
1. Daghestan A.S.S.R.
2. Kabardino–Balkar A.S.S.R.
3. Mari A.S.S.R.
4. Mordovian A.S.S.R.
5. North Ossetian A.S.S.R.
6. Tatar A.S.S.R.
7. Udmurt A.S.S.R.
8. Chuvash A.S.S.R.
9. Checheno–Ingush A.S.S.R.
AZERBAIJAN
10. Nakhichevan A.S.S.R.
GEORGIA
11. Abkhaz A.S.S.R.
12. Adzhar A.S.S.R.

Projection: Conical Orthomorphic with two standard parallels

East from Greenwich

1:50 000 000

250   0   250   500   750   1000 miles
250   0   500   1000   1500 km

PACIFIC OCEAN

ARCTIC OCEAN

INDIAN OCEAN

Aleutian Is.
Bering Str.
C. Dezhnyov
Wrangel I.
New Siberian Is.
Severnaya Zemlya
Taimyr Peninsula
Chelyuskin
Laptev Sea
Kara Sea
Novaya Zemlya
Barents Sea
Svalbard
Greenland
Iceland
British Isles
North Sea
Baltic Sea
Scandinavia
Finland
Kola Pen.
White Sea
North Cape
Arctic Circle

Kamchatka Peninsula
Klyuchevsk Vol. 4780
Sredinny Ra.
Sea of Okhotsk
Sakhalin
Kolyma
Gydan Ra. (Kolyma)
Indigirka
Verkhoyansk Range
Stanovoy Ra.
Aldan
Lena
Central Siberian Plateau
Lower Tunguska
Olenek
Yenisei
Kotuy

West Siberian Plain
Ob
Irtysh
Tobol
Yablonovy Ra.
Angara
Selenga
Sayan Mts.
Altai
Belukha 4506
Tien Shan
Turfan Basin
Tarim Basin
Takla Makan
Lop Nor
Koko Nor
Plateau of Mongolia
Gobi
Sungari
Manchurian Plain
Great Khingan Mts.
Amur
Sikhote Alin Ra.
Korea
Yellow Sea
Hwang
Great Plain of China
Si-kiang
Hainan
G. of Tonkin
Mekong
Salween
Irrawaddy
Si China
China
East China Sea
Formosa
Ryukyu Is.
Korea Str.
Japan
Sea of Japan
Hokkaido
Kurile Is.
Honshu
Shikoku
Kyushu
Tropic of Cancer
Bonin Is.
10 522
Caroline Is.
Guam
Cape Johnson Deep 10 497
Philippine Is.
Luzon
Mindanao
Halmahera
Moluccas
Celebes
Celebes Sea
Sulu Sea
Palawan
Borneo
Kinabalu 4101
Macasar Strait
Ceram
Banda Sea
Flores
Timor
Java
Arafura Sea
New Guinea
Australia
Java Sea
East Sunda Is.
Bali
Sumatra
Sunda Str.
Malay Peninsula
Str. of Malacca
G. of Thailand
Chao Phraya
Andaman Is.
Nicobar Is.
Bay of Bengal
Ceylon
Polk Strait
Eastern Ghats
Western Ghats
Deccan
Godavari
Krishna
C. Comorin
Laccadive Is.
Maldive Is.
Chagos Arch.
Seychelles
Amirantes
Equator

Plateau of Tibet
Kunlun Shan
Himalaya
Karakoram
Everest 8848
Pamirs
Hindu Kush
Tsangpo
Brahmaputra
Ganges
India
Narmada
Thar Desert
Sulaiman Ra.
Indus
Ural Mountains 1640
Ural
Volga
Don
Steppe
Kirghiz
Syr Darya
Amu Darya
Aral Sea
Turanian Plain
Caspian Sea
Elburz Mts.
Plateau of Iran
Helmand
Zagros
Tigris
Euphrates
Mesopotamia
Ararat 5165
Caucasus
Elbruz 5633
Black Sea
Bosporus
Anatolia
Taurus Mts.
Cyprus
Mediterranean Sea
Adriatic Sea
Rhine
Danube
Carpathians
Vistula
Oder
Elbe
Dnepr
Dnepr
Central Russian Uplands
North European Plain
N. Dvina
Kolguyev I.

Syrian Desert
Dead Sea
Sinai Pen.
Suez Canal
Red Sea
Nile
Libyan Desert
Arabia
Mt. Rub'al Khali
Asir
Ras Asir (C. Guardafui)
Socotra
G. of Aden
G. of Oman
The Gulf
Arabian Sea
Somali Peninsula
Lake Victoria

m   6000   4000   2000   1000   400   200   0
ft   18 000   12 000   6000   3000   1200   600   0   200-600   2000   6000   4000 12 000   6000 18 000   8000 24 000   ft

Projection: Bonne
East from Greenwich

1:50 000 000
250 0 250 500 750 1000 miles
250 0 500 1000 1500 km

1:1 000 000

1949–1974 Armistice lines between
Israel and the Arab States.

MEDITERRANEAN SEA

LEBANON

SYRIA

JORDAN

EGYPT

Projection: Conical with two standard parallels

East from Greenwich

Continuation
Southwards
1:2 500 000

COPYRIGHT. GEORGE PHILIP & SON. LTD.

BIRKET RAM

Qiryat Shemona

Naharíyya
'Akko (Acre)
Qiryat Yam
HEFA (Haifa)
Qiryat Ata
Tirat Karmel
'ATLIT
Nazerat (Nazareth)
MEGIDDO
CAESAREA
Or 'Aqiva
Hadera
Netanya
Tülkarm
Et Taiyiba
SAMARIA
Nabulus
SHECHEM
JACOB'S WELL
TEL ARSHAF
Herzliyya
Ramat HaSharon
TEL AVIV
YAFO (Jaffa)
Bene Beraq
Ramat Gan
Petah Tiqwa
Or Yehuda
Bat Yam
Holon
Rishon le Ziyyon
Nes Ziyyona
Ramla
Rehovot
Lod (Lydda)
TEL GEZER
Ashdod
SHILO
Ashqelon
Qiryat Gat
BET GUVRIN
TEL LAKHISH
Al Khalil (Hebron)
Gaza
Gaza Strip
Khan Yunis
Be'er Sheva
MESADA
JERUSALEM (Yerushalayim, Al Quds)
Bayt Lahm (Bethlehem)
BIRAK SULAYMAN (SOLOMON'S POOLS)
QUMRAN
Ariha (Jericho)
'AMMAN
Az Zarqa'
As Salt
Irbid
Dar'a
Al Mafraq
Jarash
DEAD SEA (BAHR EL MIYET)

Hagalil (Galilee)
Shomron (Samaria)
Yam Kinneret (Sea of Galilee)
KEFAR NAHUM (CAPERNAUM)
Terverya
Emeq Yizre'el
Harei Shomron
Midbar Yehuda
Ha Negev
PETRA
Elat
'Aqaba

ISRAEL
EGYPT
JORDAN
Gaza Strip
Ghazzah
Khan Yunis
Be'er Sheva
Dimona
HORVOT SHIVTA
Mizpe Ramon
Har Ramon
Al Khalil (Hebron)
'Arad

Under Israeli Occupation

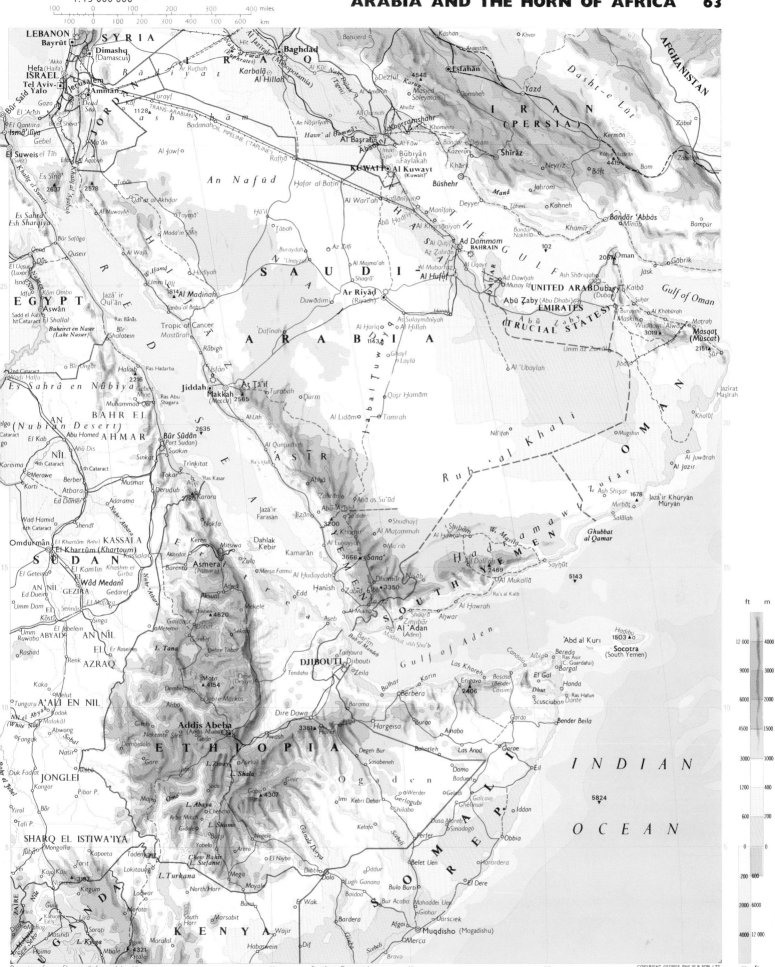

1:15 000 000

Projection: Sanson-Flamsteed's Sinusoidal   East from Greenwich   COPYRIGHT GEORGE PHILIP & SON LTD.

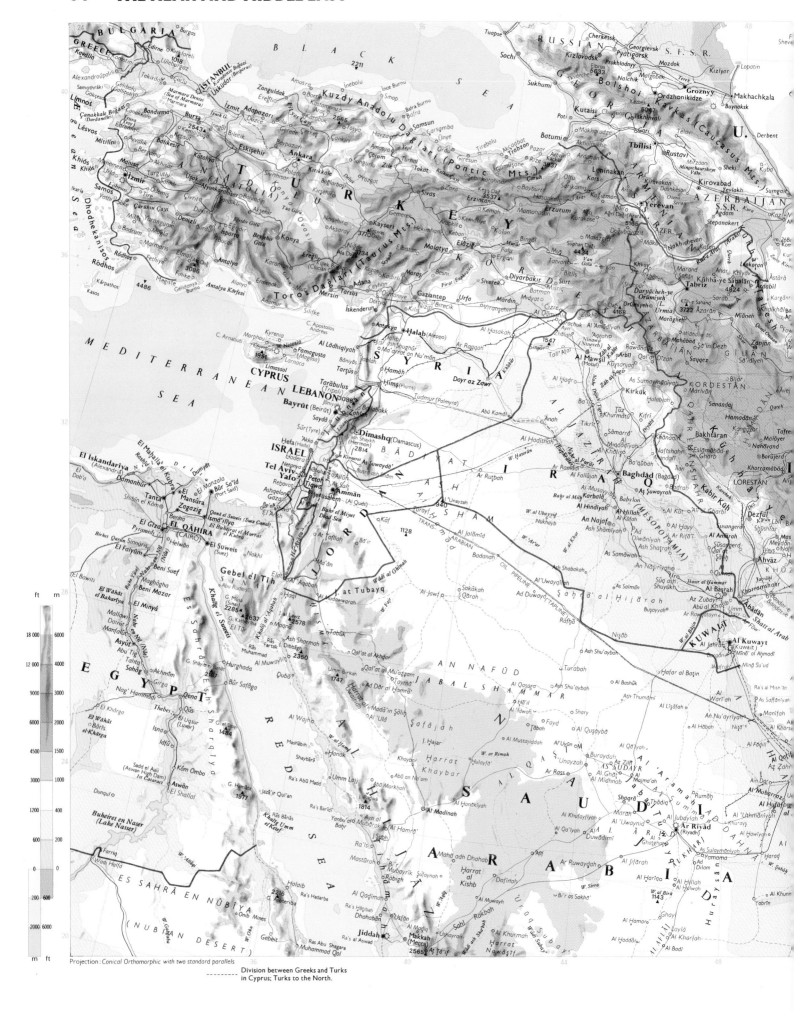

Projection: Conical Orthomorphic with two standard parallels

- - - - - - - - Division between Greeks and Turks
in Cyprus; Turks to the North.

Continuation Southwards
on same scale

Projection: Conical with two standard parallels

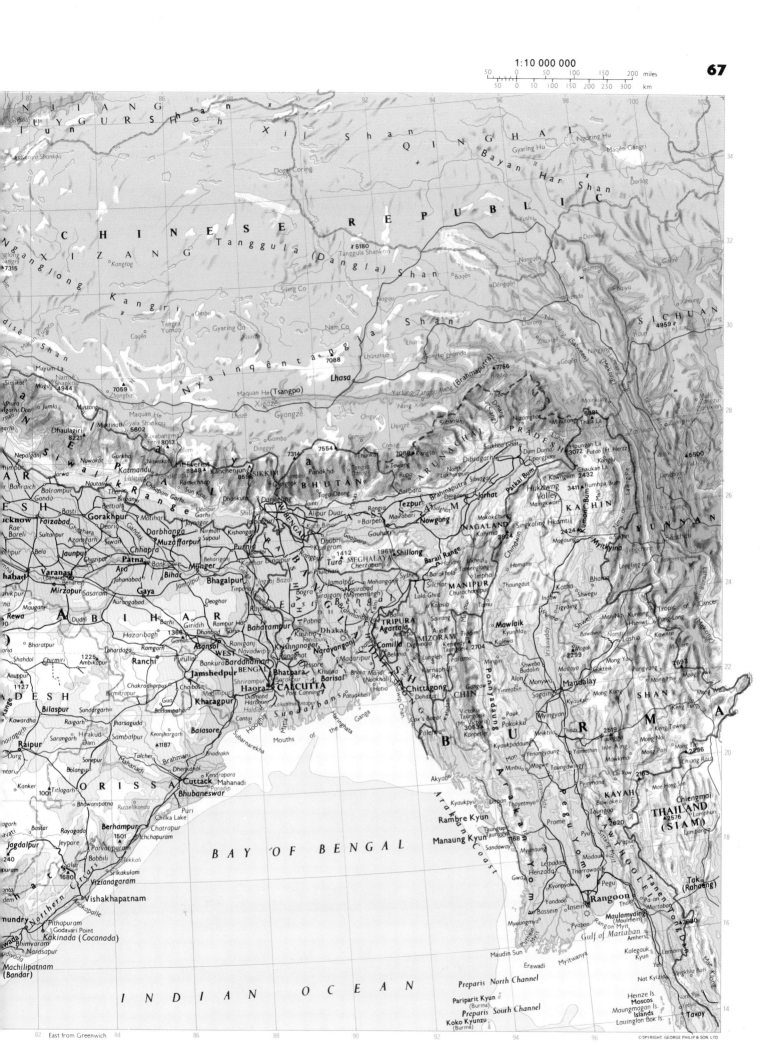

1:10 000 000

50   0   50   100   150   200 miles
50   0 50 100 150 200 250 300 km

N J I A N G
U Y G U R S
Hoh   Xil   Shan
QINGHAI
Ngoring Hu
Gyaring Hu
Dong   Coring
Bayan   Har   Shan
Dartag
CHINESE   REPUBLIC
XIZANG
Tanggula   ▲5180
Tanggula Shankou
(Dangla)   Shan
SICHUAN
Nang Xian
Yarlung Zangbo Jiang (Brahmaputra)
Lhasa

East   from   Greenwich

BAY OF BENGAL

I N D I A N   O C E A N

Preparis North Channel
Paripari Kyun
(Burma)
Preparis South Channel
Koko Kyunzu
(Burma)

COPYRIGHT. GEORGE PHILIP & SON LTD

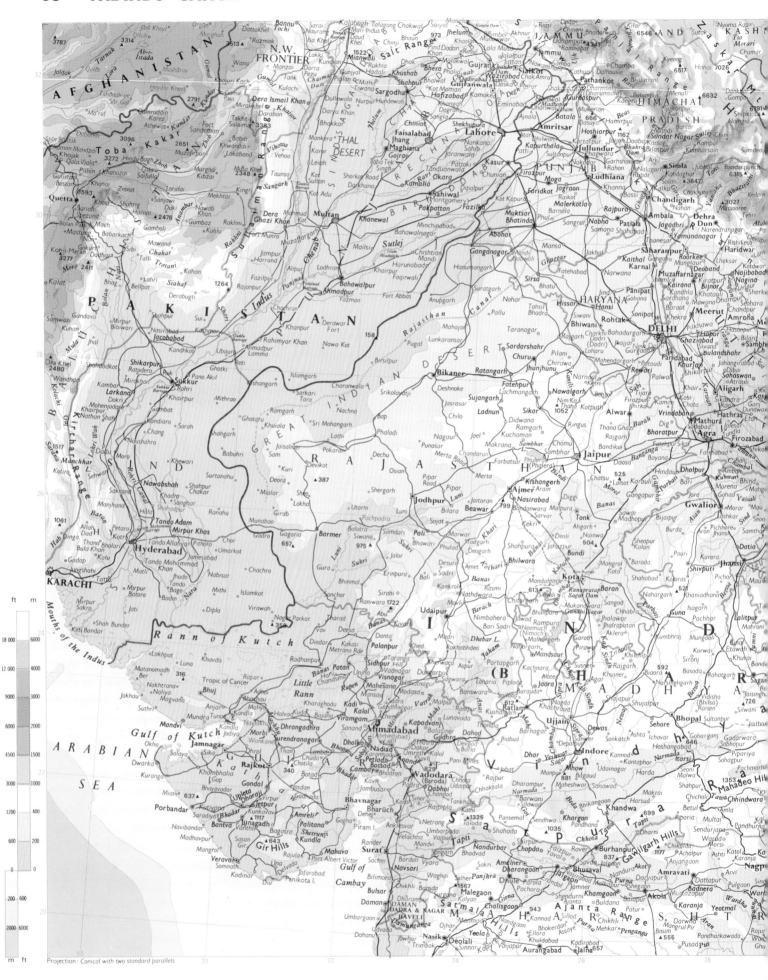

Projection: Conical with two standard parallels

1:6 000 000

50 0 50 100 150 miles
50 0 50 100 150 200 250 km

S. ASIA: IRRIGATION
1:40 000 000

Irrigated Areas

CHINESE REPUBLIC

TIBET

AFGHANISTAN KASHMIR

PAKISTAN

NEPAL BANGLA DESH

INDIA BURMA

Tropic of Cancer

SRI LANKA

CHINESE REPUBLIC

GXIZANG / Xizang KANGDISE SHAN

La'nga Co Mapam Yumco

Ngangla Kangri

Maquan He (Brahmaputra) Yarlung Zangbo Jiang (Brahmaputra)

NEPAL

Mt. Everest 8848

Kanchenjunga

SIKKIM Gangtok BHUTAN

Darjeeling

Katmandu Lalitpur Bhaktapur

MAHABHARAT Range

UTTAR PRADESH

Lucknow Faizabad Gorakhpur

Allahabad Varanasi (Banaras) (Benares)

Patna BIHAR

Gaya

MADHYA PRADESH

Jabalpur Bilaspur Raipur Bhilai

ORISSA

Cuttack Bhubaneswar Puri

Chilka Lake

BANGLADESH DHAKA (Dacca)

MEGHALAYA

TRIPURA

CALCUTTA Howrah

Jamshedpur Durgapur Asansol

Kharagpur

Sunderbans

Mouths of the Ganga

The Sandheads

BAY OF BENGAL

East from Greenwich

COPYRIGHT GEORGE PHILIP & SON LTD

1:6 000 000

MAHARASHTRA

MADHYA PRADESH

KARNATAKA

TAMIL NADU

ARABIAN SEA

BAY OF BENGAL

Coromandel Coast

BOMBAY
Pune (Poona)
Sholapur
HYDERABAD
Secunderabad
Warangal
Gulbarga
Bijapur
Kolhapur
Belgaum
GOA
Panaji (Panjim)
Marmagoa
Margao
Dharwad
Hospet
Bellary
Kurnool
Nellore
Vijayawada
Guntur
Tenali
Machilipatnam (Bandar)
Rajahmundry
Vishakhapatnam
Mangalore
BANGALORE
Mysore
MADRAS
Vellore
Pondicherry
Salem
Coimbatore
Calicut (Kozhikode)
Tiruchchirappalli (Trichinopoly)
Thanjavur (Tanjore)
Madurai
Cochin
Ernakulam
Alleppey
Quilon
Trivandrum
Nagercoil
C. Comorin

Gulf of Mannar

Palk Strait

Palk Bay

Pearl Banks

Projection: Conical with two standard parallels

East from Greenwich

SRI LANKA
On same scale

SRI LANKA (CEYLON)

Jaffna
Jaffna Lagoon
Elephant Pass
Mannar I.
Adam's Bridge
Trincomalee
Koddiyar Bay
Batticaloa
Anuradhapura
Kandy
Negombo
Colombo
Dehiwala
Moratuwa
Ratnapura
Galle
Matara

Great Basses
Little Basses

Palk Strait

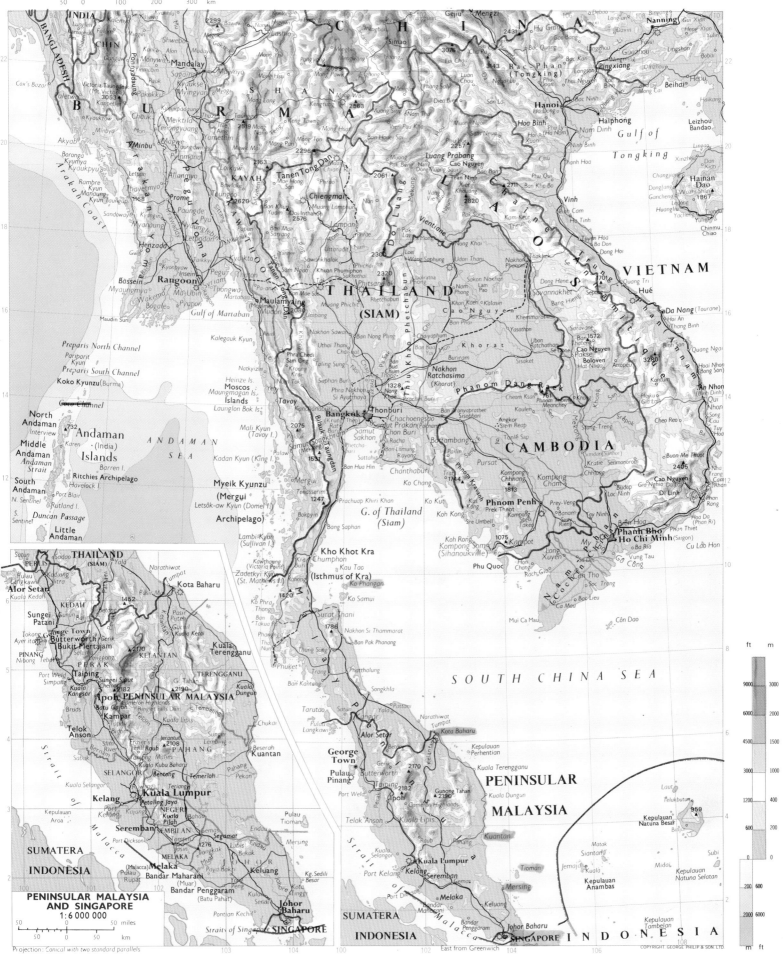

1:10 000 000

50 0 50 100 150 200 miles

50 0 100 200 300 km

CHINA

BURMA

INDIA

BANGLADESH

THAILAND (SIAM)

LAOS

VIETNAM

CAMBODIA

ANDAMAN SEA

Andaman Islands (India)

Gulf of Martaban

G. of Thailand (Siam)

SOUTH CHINA SEA

Gulf of Tongking

Hainan Dao

Rangoon

Mandalay

Bangkok

Thonburi

Hanoi

Haiphong

Vientiane

Phnom Penh

Ho Chi Minh (Saigon)

Phanh Bho Ho Chi Minh

PENINSULAR MALAYSIA

SUMATERA INDONESIA

Kuala Lumpur

Singapore

PENINSULAR MALAYSIA AND SINGAPORE

1:6 000 000

50 0 50 miles

50 0 50 km

Projection: Conical with two standard parallels

East from Greenwich

COPYRIGHT GEORGE PHILIP & SON LTD

ft	m
9000	3000
6000	2000
4500	1500
3000	1000
1200	400
600	200
0	0
200	600
2000	6000

m ft

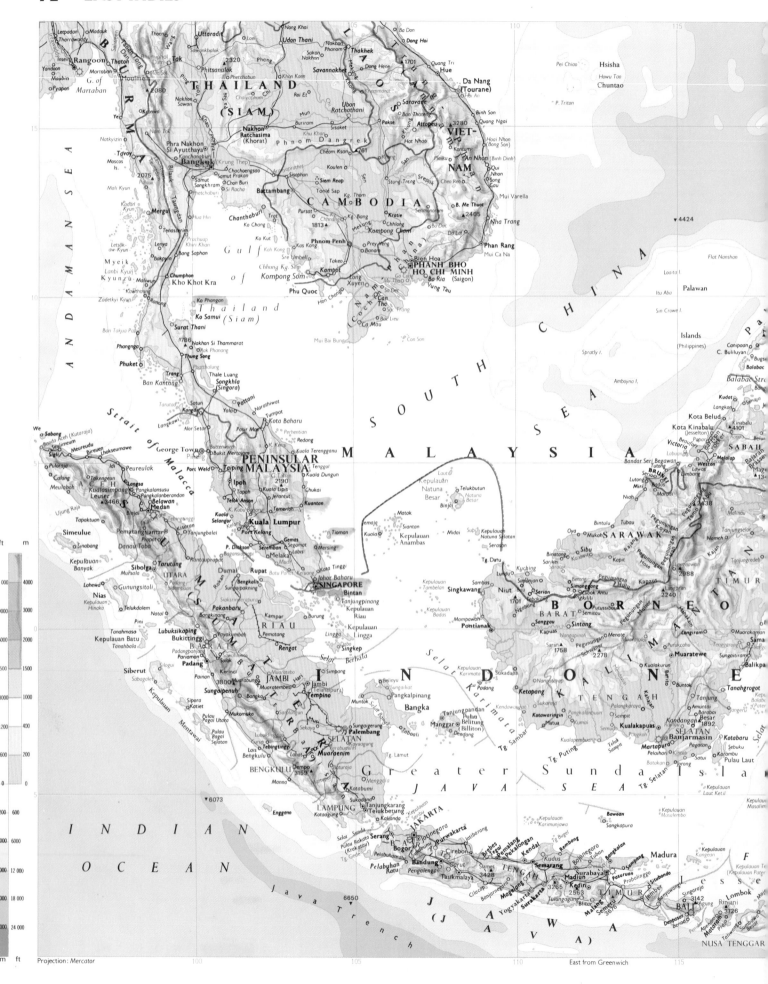

Projection: Mercator   East from Greenwich

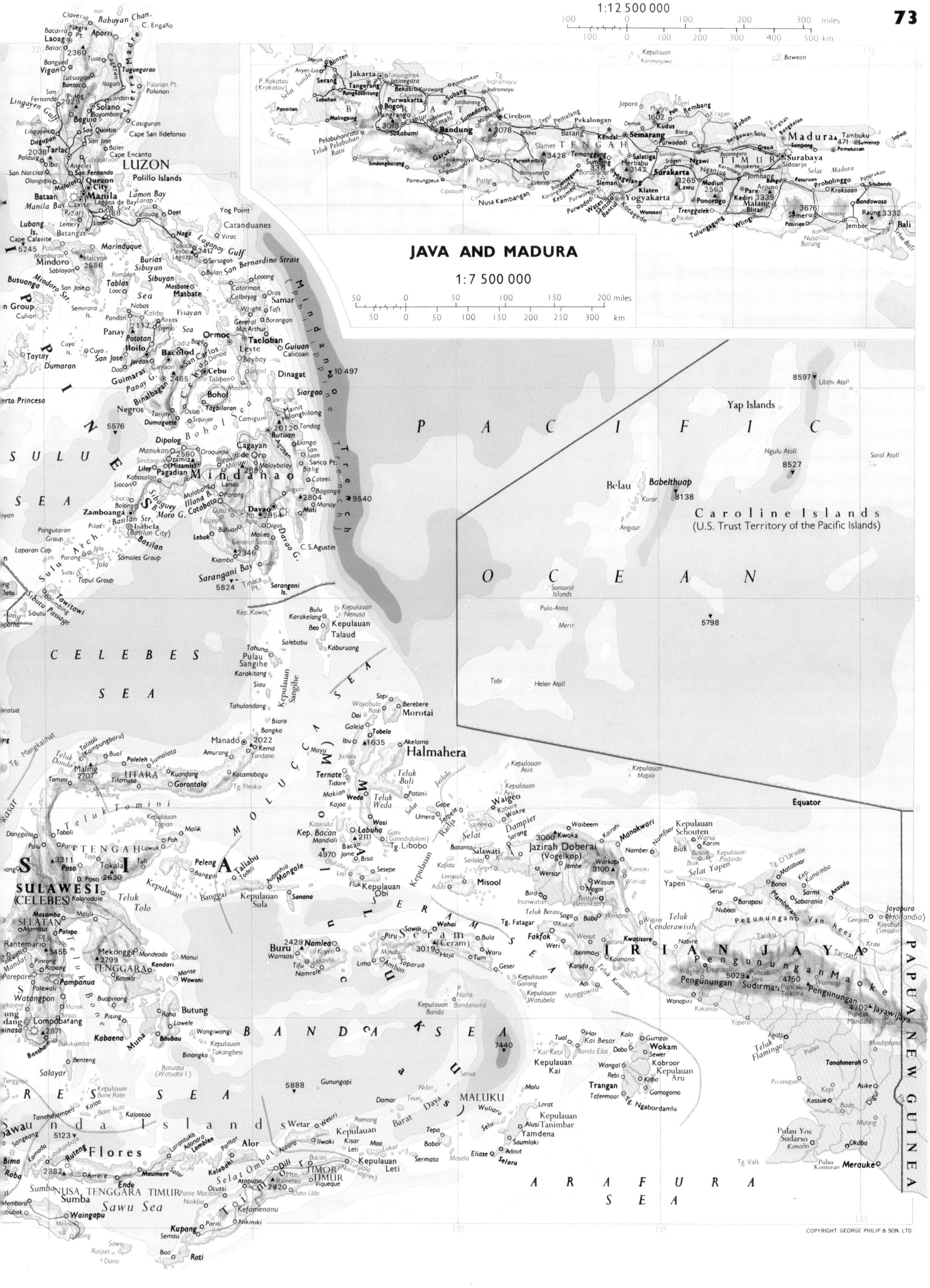

1:12 500 000

JAVA AND MADURA

1:7 500 000

LUZON

PACIFIC OCEAN

Caroline Islands
(U.S. Trust Territory of the Pacific Islands)

Yap Islands

Belau Babelthuap

CELEBES SEA

SULU SEA

Mindanao

MOLUCCA SEA

Halmahera

SULAWESI (CELEBES)

CERAM SEA

Buru Ceram (Seram)

IRIAN JAYA

BANDA SEA

MALUKU

ARAFURA SEA

Flores

NUSA TENGGARA TIMUR

TIMUR TIMUR

Sawu Sea

PAPUA NEW GUINEA

COPYRIGHT. GEORGE PHILIP & SON. LTD.

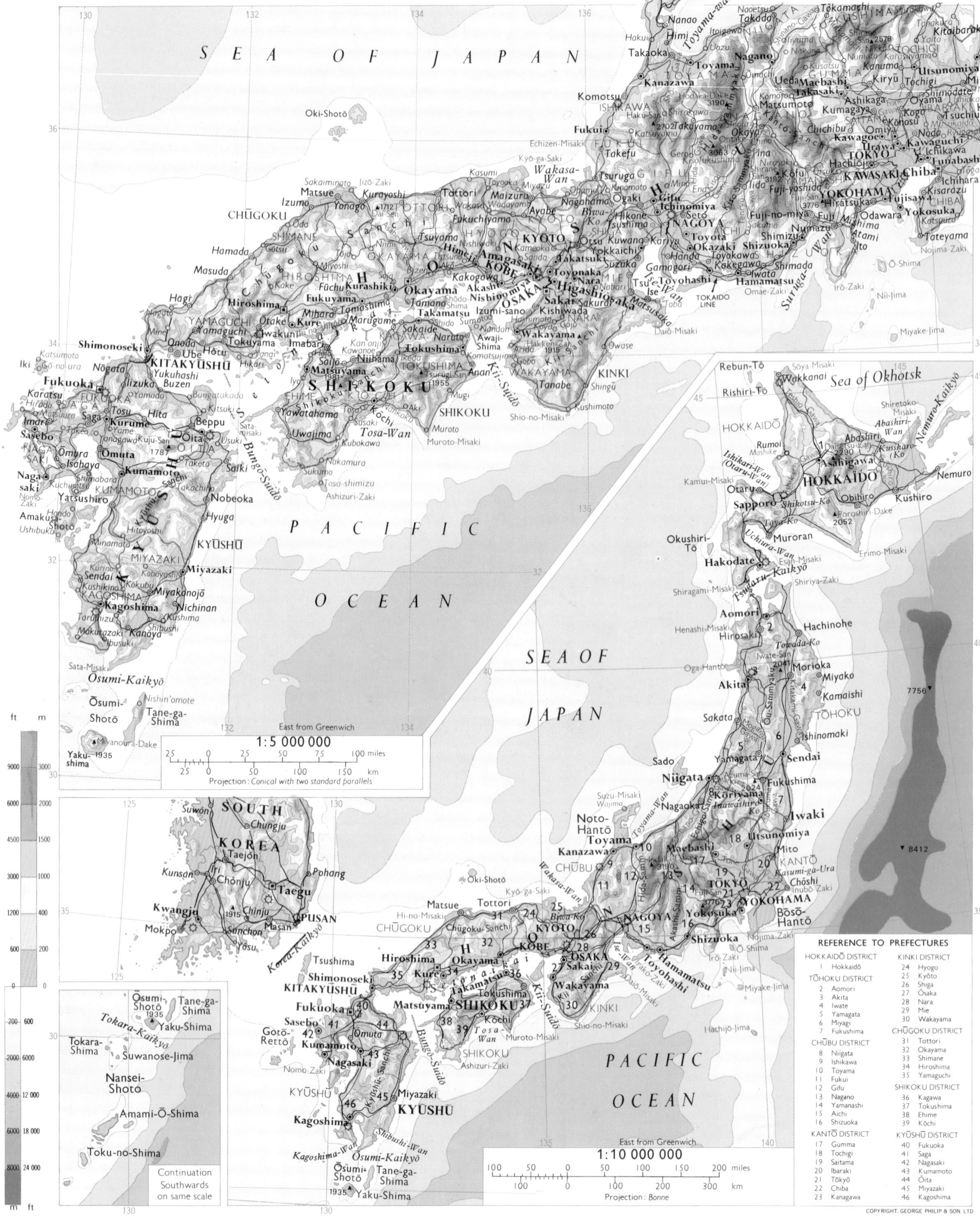

SEA OF JAPAN

Suzu-misaki
Wajima Suzu
Naoetsu Takada Tōkamachi
Nanao Toyama-wan Itoigawa
Himi TOYAMA Nagano
Takaoka Toyama Matsumoto
Kanazawa Ueda Takasaki
Komotsu ISHIKAWA Haku-San 3190 Maebashi Kiryū Tochigi
Fukui Takayama 2702 Chichibu Kawagoe TOKYO
Takefu 4063 Ina Kōfu Hachiōji KAWASAKI Chiba
Tsuruga GIFU Fuji-yoshida YOKOHAMA Kisarazu
Ichinomiya Gifu 3776 Hiratsuka Yokosuka
NAGOYA Toyota Numazu Odawara Tateyama
Kuwana Okazaki Shizuoka Atami
Toyohashi Hamamatsu TOKAIDO LINE
Handa Iwata

CHŪGOKU
Matsue Izumo Yonago Kurayoshi 1712 Tottori TOTTORI
SHIMANE Oda Wakasa-Wan
Hamada Gotsu Miyoshi OKAYAMA KYOTO Ōtsu
Masuda HIROSHIMA Fukuchiyama Ayabe Maizuru
Hagi YAMAGUCHI Okayama Himeji KOBE Amagasaki
Hiroshima Fukuyama OSAKA Higashiōsaka
Onoda Ube Kure Kurashiki Takatsuki Nara
KITAKYŪSHŪ Mihara Takamatsu Izumi-sano Kishiwada WAKAYAMA
Fukuoka Iwakuni Tokuyama Wakayama
FUKUOKA SAGA Matsuyama Marugame KINKI
Karatsu Tosu Hita EHIME SHIKOKU Tokushima
Sasebo Saga Kurume Beppu KŌCHI Tanabe
Imari Ōita Uwajima Tosa-Wan
Nagasaki KUMAMOTO Ōita Kōchi Shingu
Ōmuta Kumamoto Nobeoka Muroto-Misaki
KUMAMOTO Hyuga Shio-no-Misaki
KYŪSHŪ MIYAZAKI Miyazaki
Sendai Miyakonojō
KAGOSHIMA Nichinan
Kagoshima

PACIFIC OCEAN

Ōsumi-Kaikyō
Tane-ga-Shima
Yaku-Shima

SEA OF OKHOTSK
Rebun-Tō Sōya-Misaki Wakkanai
Rishiri-Tō Nemuro-Kaikyō
HOKKAIDŌ Abashiri-Wan
Rumoi Abashiri
Asahigawa Kushiro-Ko
Otaru Sapporo Obihiro Kushiro
Muroran Nemuro
Okushiri-Tō Uchiura-Wan
Hakodate Tsugaru-Kaikyō
Aomori Hachinohe
Hirosaki Towada-Ko
Iwate-San 2041 Morioka Miyako
Akita Kamaishi
TOHOKU
Sakata Ishinomaki
Sado Yamagata Sendai
Niigata Fukushima
Nagaoka Kōriyama
Noto-Hantō Iwaki
Toyama Utsunomiya
Kanazawa Maebashi KANTŌ
CHŪBU Mito
TOKYO
NAGOYA YOKOHAMA
Shizuoka Bōsō-Hantō

7756
8412

REFERENCE TO PREFECTURES

HOKKAIDŌ DISTRICT
1 Hokkaidō

TŌHOKU DISTRICT
2 Aomori
3 Akita
4 Iwate
5 Yamagata
6 Miyagi
7 Fukushima

CHŪBU DISTRICT
8 Niigata
9 Ishikawa
10 Toyama
11 Fukui
12 Gifu
13 Nagano
14 Yamanashi
15 Aichi
16 Shizuoka

KANTŌ DISTRICT
17 Gumma
18 Tochigi
19 Saitama
20 Ibaraki
21 Tōkyō
22 Chiba
23 Kanagawa

KINKI DISTRICT
24 Hyogo
25 Kyōto
26 Shiga
27 Ōsaka
28 Nara
29 Mie
30 Wakayama

CHŪGOKU DISTRICT
31 Tottori
32 Okayama
33 Shimane
34 Hiroshima
35 Yamaguchi

SHIKOKU DISTRICT
36 Kagawa
37 Tokushima
38 Ehime
39 Kōchi

KYŪSHŪ DISTRICT
40 Fukuoka
41 Saga
42 Nagasaki
43 Kumamoto
44 Ōita
45 Miyazaki
46 Kagoshima

SOUTH KOREA
Suwon Chungju
Taejon
Kunsan Chonju
Kwangju Chinju Taegu
Mokpo Sunchon PUSAN
Yosu Masan

Tsushima
Korea-Kaikyo

CHŪGOKU
Matsue Tottori
Chūgoku-Sanchi
Hiroshima Okayama KYOTO
Kure KOBE OSAKA Sakai
Shimonoseki Takamatsu Wakayama
KITAKYŪSHŪ SHIKOKU KINKI
Fukuoka Matsuyama Kōchi
Sasebo Ōmuta Kumamoto
Gotō-Rettō Nagasaki
Miyazaki
KYŪSHŪ
Kagoshima
Kagoshima-Wan
Ōsumi-Kaikyō
Tane-ga-Shima
Yaku-Shima

Ōsumi-Shotō Tane-ga-Shima
Tokara-Kaikyo Yaku-Shima
Tokara-Shima Suwanose-Jima
Nansei-Shoto
Amami-Ō-Shima
Toku-no-Shima

Continuation Southwards on same scale

1:5 000 000
East from Greenwich
Projection: Conical with two standard parallels

1:10 000 000
East from Greenwich
Projection: Bonne

PACIFIC OCEAN

SEA OF JAPAN

COPYRIGHT GEORGE PHILIP & SON LTD.

1:20 000 000

1:10 000 000

50   0   50   100   150   200   250 miles
50   0   50   100   150   200   250   300   350   400 km

COPYRIGHT GEORGE PHILIP & SON LTD

PACIFIC OCEAN

EAST CHINA SEA

KITAKYŪSHŪ
Fukuoka
Omuta
Sasebo
Nagasaki
Kagoshima
Makurazaki
Minamata
Sendai
JAPAN
Koshiki-jima
Uji-guntō
Kusagaki-jima
Gotō-rettō
Tsushima
Amakusa

Cheju
Cheju Do
(Quelpart)

Tokara-guntō
Amami-ō-shima
Amami guntō
Tokuno-shima
Okino-erabu-jima

Nansei-shotō

7507

Okinawa
Nago
Kozo
Naha
Okinawa-wa
Okinawa guntō
Oku
Kume

2370

Tropic of Cancer

Sekibi-shō
Ryūkyū-rettō
Senkaku guntō
Yaeyama-rettō
Iriomote
Ishigaki
Sakishima-guntō
Miyako
Miyako-rettō

6585

TAIWAN
(FORMOSA)

Jilong
TAIBEI
Taoyuan
Xinzhu
Miaoli
Taizhong
Nantou
Jiayi
Yunlin
Zhanghua
Tainan
Gaoxiong
Pingdong

3950
Yu Shan

Batan Is.
Batan
Sabtang
Babuyan
Camiguin
Babuyan Is.
Calayan
Dalupiri
Fuga

C. Engaño
Aparri
Laoag
LUZON
2360 Cagua

PHILIPPINES

SOUTH CHINA SEA

Shanghai
Nantong
Changshu
Wuxi
Suzhou
Zhenjiang
NANJING
Hefei
ANHUI
JIANGSU
Xuzhou
Bengbu
Huainan

ZHEJIANG
Hangzhou
Shaoxing
Ningbo
Wenzhou

FUJIAN
Fuzhou
Nanping
Quanzhou
Xiamen
Zhangzhou
Shantou

JIANGXI
Nanchang
Jingdezhen

HUBEI
WUHAN
Hankou
Hanyang

HENAN
Kaifeng
Zhengzhou
Luoyang

HUNAN
Changsha
Hengyang
Shaoyang

GUANGDONG
GUANGZHOU (Canton)
Kowloon
HONGKONG (Br.)
Macau (Port.)
Foshan
Zhanjiang

GUANGXI-ZHUANGZU
ZIZHIQU
Nanning
Guilin
Liuzhou
Wuzhou

GUIZHOU
Guiyang
Zunyi

SICHUAN
CHONGQING
Zigong
Luzhou
Neijiang

SHAANXI
XI'AN
Xianyang

Hainan
Haikou

VIETNAM
HANOI
Haiphong

m
4000
3000
2000
1500
1000
400
200
0

ft
12 000
9000
6000
4500
3000
1200
600
0

ft
2000
4000
6000

m
600
1200
1800

Projection: Lambert's Equivalent Azimuthal   East from Greenwich

1 : 40 000 000

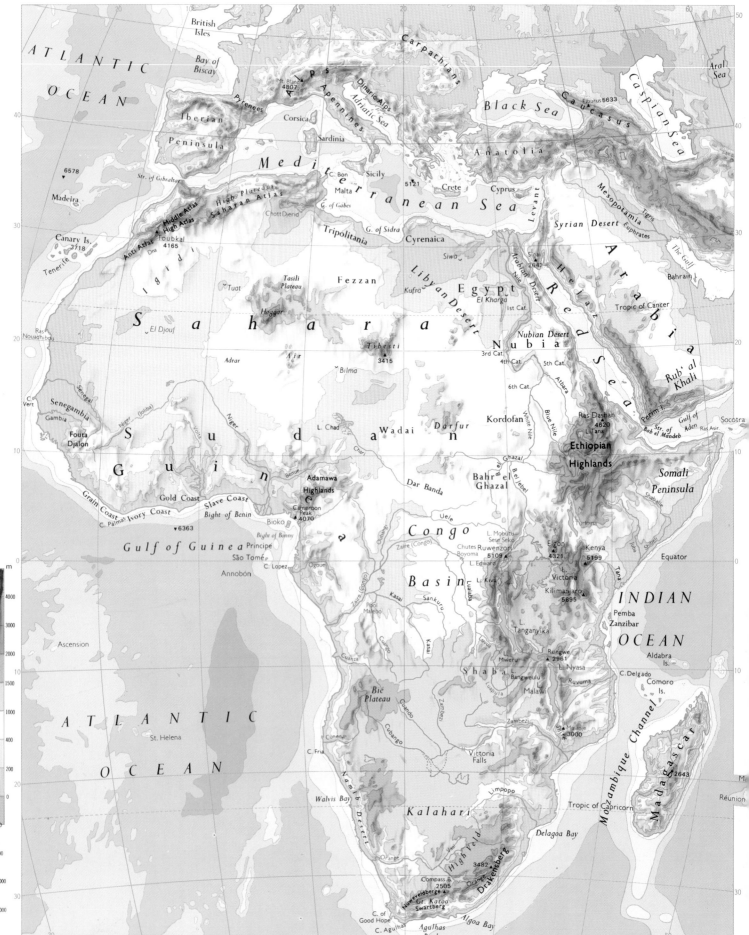

ATLANTIC OCEAN

British Isles

Bay of Biscay

Iberian Peninsula

Corsica

Sardinia

Madeira

6578

Str. of Gibraltar

Canary Is. 3718

Tenerife

Middle Atlas

High Atlas

Anti Atlas

Toubkal 4165

Igidi

El Djouf

Adrar

Ras Nouadhibou

C. Vert

Senegambia

Senegal

Gambia

Fouta Djalon

Grain Coast

C. Palmas Ivory Coast

Gold Coast

Slave Coast

Bight of Benin

Bioko

Mt. Blanc 4807

Alps

Apennines

Pyrenees

Dinaric Alps

Adriatic Sea

Carpathians

Black Sea

Caucasus

Elbrus 5633

Caspian Sea

Aral Sea

Anatolia

Mediterranean Sea

Sicily

Malta

Crete

Cyprus

C. Bon

5121

G. of Gabes

Chott Djerid

High Plateaux

Saharan Atlas

Tripolitania

G. of Sidra

Cyrenaica

Tasili Plateau

Fezzan

Tuat

Hoggar

Sahara

Air

Bilma

Tibesti 3415

Libyan Desert

Siwa

Egypt

Kufra

El Kharga

Mesopotamia

Euphrates

Tigris

Levant

Syrian Desert

Arabian Desert

Nile

1st Cat.

Sinai 2642

Red Sea

Hejaz

Arabia

The Gulf

Bahrain

Tropic of Cancer

Rub' al Khali

Nubian Desert

Nubia

3rd Cat.

4th Cat.

5th Cat.

6th Cat.

Atbara

Ras Dashan 4620

L. Tana

Ethiopian Highlands

Socotra

Ras Asir

Gulf of Aden

Str. of Bab el Mandeb

Perim I.

Somali Peninsula

Sudan

Wadai

Darfur

Kordofan

White Nile

Blue Nile

Bahr el Ghazal

Dar Banda

Bahr el Ghazal

Uele

Shabelle

Sudan

Guinea

Adamawa Highlands

Cameroon Peak 4070

6363

Gulf of Guinea

Principe

São Tomé

Annobón

Bight of Bonny

C. Lopez

Ogooué

Zaïre (Congo)

Ubangi

Congo

Basin

L. Mobutu Sese Seko

Chutes Boyoma

Ruwenzori 5109

L. Edward

L. Kivu

Lualaba

Turkana

Elgon 4321

Kenya 5199

Victoria

Kilimanjaro 5895

L. Tanganyika

Pemba

Zanzibar

INDIAN

OCEAN

Equator

Juba

Tana

Aldabra Is.

C. Delgado

Comoro Is.

Rungwe 2961

Mweru

L. Bangweulu

L. Nyasa

Ruvuma

Shaba

Malawi

Luapula

Bié Plateau

Cuango

Cuanza

Kwango

Kasai

Sankuru

Kasai

Lulua

Pool Malebo

Zaïre (Congo)

Kwilu

Shaba

Mulanje 3000

Zambezi

Cubango

Coando

Cunene

Ascension

St. Helena

ATLANTIC

OCEAN

Bié Plateau

Namib Desert

Walvis Bay

C. Fria

Kalahari

Orange

Victoria Falls

Zambezi

Limpopo

Tropic of Capricorn

Delagoa Bay

Mozambique Channel

Madagascar 2643

Réunion

High Veld

3482

Drakensberg

Compass B. 2505

Orange

Swartberg

Nieuweveldberge

Gt. Karoo

C. of Good Hope

C. Agulhas

Agulhas Bank

Algoa Bay

Projection: Zenithal Equidistant.

West from Greenwich

East from Greenwich

COPYRIGHT. GEORGE PHILIP & SON LTD.

1:40 000 000

200   0   200   400   600   800   1000 miles
200   0   200 400 600 800 1000 1200 1400 1600 km

ATLANTIC

OCEAN

UNITED
KINGDOM   **London**   NETH.   GERMANY   POLAND   **Warszawa**
BELG.   **Praha**   CZECHOSLOVAKIA   **Kiyev**
Paris   **Wien**   AUSTRIA   HUNGARY   **Volgograd**
FRANCE   SWITZ.   YUGOSLAVIA   ROMANIA   **Odessa**   U.   S.   S.   R.
Bay of
Biscay   ITALY   BULGARIA   *Black Sea*   Aral
Sea
Madrid   Corse   Sardegna   **Roma**   Adriatic Sea   GREECE   **Istanbul**   Ankara   **Baku**   Caspian Sea
SPAIN   **Athínai**   TURKEY
Lisboa   PORTUGAL   Sicilia   Kriti   **Al Mawşil**   **Tehrān**
Mediterranean   CYPRUS   Halab   SYRIA   **Dimashq**   **Baghdād**   Eşfahān
Tanger   **Alger**   **Tunis**   MALTA   Tel Aviv-Yafo   IRAN
Tétouan   Constantine   TUNISIA   Bür Said   **El Iskandarîya**   Jerusalem   ISRAEL   JORDAN   Al Başrah
Casablanca   **Rabat** Fès   Oran   Sfax   **El QAHIRA**   El Suweis   KUWAIT   The Gulf
MOROCCO   **Marrakech**   Banghāzi   El Faiyûm   SAUDI-   BAHRAIN   QATAR
Islas   ALGERIA   LIBYA   Sahrâ' Libiya   EGYPT   Asyût   **Al Madînah**   Tropic of Cancer
Canarias   Aswân   ARABIA   **Makkah**
WESTERN   In Salah   Ghudāmis   *Sahara*   Wadi Halfa   Es Sahrâ   Bür Südân   YEMEN   SOUTH YEMEN
SAHARA   Marzûq   en Nūbiya   Socotra
Fdérik   Ghat   Al Jawf   Dongola   G. of Aden   (South Yemen)
MAURITANIA   Atbara   Omdurmân   Kassala   Mitsiwa   Al 'Adan   Ras Asir
Nouakchott   Agadez   El Khartûm   **Asmera**   DJIBOUTI   Berbera
MALI   NIGER   CHAD   SUDAN   L. Tana   Djibouti   Hargeisa
SENEGAL   Tombouctou   Gao   El Fasher   El Obeid   ETHIOPIA   Harer
Dakar   Kayes   Niamey   Sokoto   Kano   Ndjamena   Abéché   **Addis Abeba**   SOMALI REP
GAMBIA   Bamako   BURKINA   Maiduguri   (Ft.-Lamy)   Sarh   Mongalla
GUINEA   FASO   Kaduna   Bauchi   CENTRAL AFRICAN   L. Turkana
BISSAU   GUINEA   Ouagadougou   NIGERIA   Bangui   REPUBLIC   UGANDA   KENYA   Equator
Conakry   Kankan   IVORY   GHANA   TOGO   Ibadan   Benue   CAMEROON   Yaoundé   L. Mobutu   Kampala   Nairobi   INDIAN
Freetown   SIERRA   COAST   Kumasi   BENIN   Lagos   Port Harcourt   Douala   Sese Seko   Kisangani   L.   Kisumu
LEONE   Bouaké   Accra   Porto Novo   Malabo   EQUATORIAL   ZAÏRE   Victoria
LIBERIA   Abidjan   Bioko   GUINEA   GABON   Mbandaka   RWANDA   Mombasa   OCEAN
Monrovia   Bight of Benin   SÃO TOMÉ   Libreville   CONGO   Kigali   BURUNDI   Pemba   Zanzibar
& PRINCIPE   Brazzaville   Kinshasa   Mwanza   TANZANIA   Dar-es-Salaam
Gulf of Guinea   Annobón   Pointe-Noire   Kananga   Mbuji-Mayi   Tabora   Dodoma
Cabinda   Boma   Shaba   Kalemie   L. Tanganyika   Aldabra Is.
Ascension   Luanda   Bukama   L. Mweru   COMOROS   Antsiranana
St. Helena   Benguela   Lobito   ANGOLA   Likasi   Lubumbashi   Kitwe   L. Malawi   Mahajanga
Huambo   Namibe   ZAMBIA   Lusaka   Lilongwe   MOZAMBIQUE   Moçambique
Lüderitz   NAMIBIA   Livingstone   Harare   Blantyre   Quelimane   MADAGASCAR   Antananarivo
(SOUTH   Windhoek   BOTSWANA   ZIMBABWE   Bulawayo   Beira   MAURITIUS
WEST   Swakopmund   Kalahari   Gaborone   Limpopo   Réunion   Fianarantsoa   Toliara
AFRICA)   Walvis-   TRANSVAAL   Tropic of Capricorn
bai   Pretoria   Maputo   Mozambique Channel
SOUTH AFRICA   Johannesburg   SWAZ.   Toamasina
Kimberley   Bloemf.   NATAL   Durban
CAPE PROVINCE   LES.
Cape Town   East London
Kaap die Goeie Hoop   Port Elizabeth
(Cape of Good Hope)

LES.   Lesotho
O. V.   Oranje-Vrystaat
SWAZ.   Swaziland

Projection: Zenithal Equidistant.   West from Greenwich   East from Greenwich   COPYRIGHT. GEORGE PHILIP & SON. LTD.

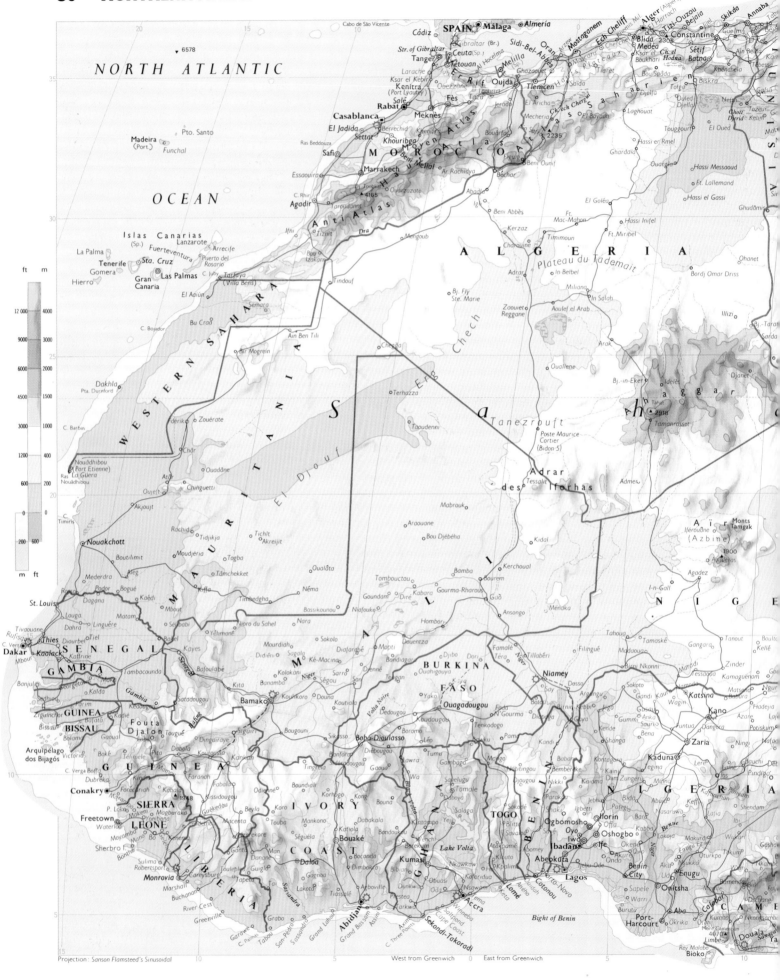

NORTH ATLANTIC

OCEAN

SPAIN

MOROCCO

WESTERN SAHARA

ALGERIA

MAURITANIA

MALI

NIGER

SENEGAL

GAMBIA

GUINEA BISSAU

GUINEA

SIERRA LEONE

LIBERIA

IVORY COAST

BURKINA FASO

GHANA

TOGO

BENIN

NIGERIA

CAMEROON

Projection: Sanson Flamsteed's Sinusoidal   West from Greenwich   East from Greenwich

100   0   100   200   300   400 miles
100   0   100   200   300   400   500   600 km

MEDITERRANEAN SEA

TURKEY

Pantelleria (It.)
Ragusa Sicily
C. Passero
Antalya
Antalya Körfezi
Halab
Al Mawşil (Mosul)
SYRIA
Nahr Dijlah (Tigris)
Lampedusa (It.)
MALTA
Krítí
Iráklion
Karpathos
Ródhos
Iskenderun Körfezi
Antakya
Al Ladhiqiya
Hamāh
Mesopotamia
 Les Kerkenna
Ras Kasr
CYPRUS
Nicosia
Limassol
Tarabulus
Hims
Nahr al Furāt
Tarābulus (Tripoli)
Al Khums
Zlītan
Misrātah
Banghāzi (Benghazi)
Banī Walīd
878
Tūkrah
Al Bayḍā' (Cyrene)
Darnah
Tubruq (Tobruk)
Khalīj Bunbah
Bardia
Ras Milh
Sīdī Barrānī
Marsá Matrūḥ
El 'Arîsh
Gaza
Beer Sheva
Dead Sea
LEBANON
Bayrūt
Dimashq (Damascus)
Ar Rutbah
IRAQ
Bādiyat
Al Qaḍārif
Gharyān
968
Banī Walīd
Surt
Khalīj Surt
Zueitina
Ajdābiyah
Al 'Uqaylah
Marsa Brega
Salūm
ISRAEL
Tel Aviv-Yafo
Haifa
Jerusalem (Al Quds)
Amman
JORDAN
'Akaba
ash Shām
Jādū
Mizdah
Hūn
Marādah
Awjilah
Al 'Irq
El Iskandarîya (Alexandria)
El 'Alamein
Damanhûr
Tanta
El Mahalla el Kubra
Dumyât
El Mansûra
Port Said
El Qantara
Ismâ'îlîya
El Suweis (Suez)
Buheirat el-Murrat el-Kubra
Gebel
Beer Sheba
Sînâ'
Elat
Al 'Aqabah
Ma'ān
Al Jawf
Taymā'
SAUDI
Zuwārah
Al Qaḍārif
Tarābulus
Ra's Al-Unuf
El Qâhira (Cairo)
El Gîza
Helwân
Khalîg el Suweis
Sinmûru
El Faiyum
Beni Suef
Beni Mazâr
El Minya
Mallawi
Es Sahrâ'
Esh Sharqîya
An Nafûd
Tabūk
ARABIA
Qâra
Siwa
Munkhafed el Qattâra (Qattâra Depression)
El Bawiti
El Wâhât el-Dakhla
Mût
El Qasr
Qasr Farâfra
Asyût
Manfalût
Abu Tig
Akhmîm
Girga
Sohâg
Tahta
Qena
Bûr Safâga
Qâseir
Madā'in Sālih
Al Wajh
Yanbu' al Bahr
Umm Lajj
Al Madînah
Cyrenaica
Sahrâ'
LIBYA
Sabhah
1200
Tasâwah
Marzûq
Tmassah
Zillah
Fezzan
Wâw al Kabîr
Al Qaṭrūn
Al Jaghbûb
El Wâhât el-Khârga
El Khârga
El Uqsur (Luxor)
Qûs
Bârîs
Isnâ
Edfu
1st Cataract
Aswân
Aswân High Dam
El Shallâl
Ras Bânâs
Bîr Shalatein
Bîr Ungat
Halaib
Ras Hadarba
Rabigh
Qasr
At Tā'if
Makkah (Mecca)
Jiddah
Idehan
Marzûq
Ma'tan as Sarra
Al Jazîrah
Adri
Sabhâ
Tasâwah
L î b î y e
E G Y P T
Tropic of Cancer
Toummo
r
a
Aozou
3150
Tarso Emissi
Woûr
Bardaï
Emi Koussi
3415
Tibesti
Zouar
Gouri
Ounianga-Kébir
Ounianga Sérir
Depression du Mourdi
Borkou
Ain Galakka
Faya-Largeau
Fada
Ennedi
Djourab
CHAD
Bahr el Ghazal (Soro)
Rebiana
Al Jawf
Al Kufrah
Uweinat
1893
Ayn al 'Uwaynat
El Wâhât el Selîma
2nd Cataract
Wadi Halfa
Es Sahrâ en Nûbîya
Muhammad Qol
2635
Bûr Sûdân (Port Sudan)
Suakin
Sinkat
Tokar
Trinkitat
Aqiq
Ras Kasar
Karora
(Nubian Desert)
Abu Hamed
BAHR EL AHMAR
3rd Cataract
Dongola
Argo
Delgo
Kosha
Abri
Nukheila
Abū Dis
4th Cataract
Kareima
Merowe
5th Cataract
Berber
Haiya Junction
Musmar
Derudeb
Nakfa
Kerea
Eritrea
Asmera
Akordat
Barentu
Mitsiwa
Zula
ESH SHAMALÎYA
El Khandaq
Ed Debba
Korti
Atbara
Ed Dāmer
Adarama
Kassala
Keren
Ad Ugri
Adwa
Aksum
Mekele
4620
Gondar
Mota
Debre Markos
Nukheila
Bir 'Atrun
Laqiya Arba'în
Gebel Abyad
SHAMÂL DÂRFÛR
6th Cataract
Shendi
Geili
El Khartûm Bahrî (Khartoum)
Omdurmân
El Khartûm
Wad Hamid
Khashm el Girba
Gedaref
Gallâbât
Metema
Lac Tchad
L. Tana
Debre Tabor
Zigey
Mao
Moussoro
Arada
Biltine
Tiné
Iriba
Malha
Hamrato esh Sheykh
Sodiri
SUDAN
Omdurmân
El Kamlin
Rufa'a
Khashm el Girba
KASSALA
Barentu
Ras Dashen
4620
Lalibela
Sekota
Ndjamena (Ft. Lamy)
Kousseri
Massakory
Ati
Oum Hadjer
Am Dam
Abéché
El Junaynah
Kabkabiya
El Fasher
Umm Keddada
En Nahud
Umm Bel
Bara
Ed Dueim
SHAMÂL KORDOFAN
GEZIRA
Wâd Medani
Sennâr
Kâsto
Kagmar
El Obeid
Dikwa
Bitkine
Mongo
Goz Beïda
Nyâlâ
Marrah
3088
Dârfûr
Zalingei
Geneina
Kutum
JANUB DÂRFÛR
Idd el Ghanam
Abū Zabad
Er Rahad
Rashad
El Odaiya
Dilling
El Laqâwa
Heiban
Kadûgli
Talodi
JANUB KORDOFAN
Kaka
Melut
Renk
AZRAQ
Ar Roseires
Kurmuk
Asosa
Gimbi
Nekemte
Dembidolo
Addis Abeba (Addis Ababa)
Addis Alem
ETHIOPIA
Gore
Gambela
Gimbi
Maroua
Kaélé
Garoua
Rei-Bouba
Tcholliré
Mondou
Moissala
Sarh
Kyabé
Birao
Songo
Ouanda Djallé
Kafia Kingi
Nyâmlêll
Râga
Deim Zubeir
BAHR EL GHAZAL
Wâw
Tonj
Meshra er Req
Gogrial
EL BUHEIRAT
Rumbek
Jur
S û d d
Bentiu
Nil el Abyad (White Nile)
Malakâl
Fangak
Abwong
Sobat
Nasir
Akōbō
A'ALI EN NIL
Kodok
Fashoda
Tûngaru
Abwong
Nekemte
Dembidolo
CENTRAL AFRICAN REPUBLIC
Bria
Yalinga
Bakouma
Djema
Bambari
Bakala
Ippy
Fort Sibut
Bossembélé
Bangui
Mobaye
Kouango
Bangassou
Ouango
Bomu
ZAÏRE (CONGO)
Yakoma
Bondo
Uere
GHARB EL ISTIWA'IYA
Marîdî
Tambura
Amadi
Yambio
Juba
Mongalla
Tombe
SHARQ EL ISTIWA'IYA
Kapoeta
JONGLEI
Bôr
Pibor P.
Kongor
Duk Faiwil
L. Turkana
Omo
L. Abaya
4200
L. Shamo
Chew Bahir (L. Stefanie)
Lokitaung
Todenyang
KENYA
Dungu
Faradje
Niangara

COPYRIGHT. GEORGE PHILIP & SON LTD.

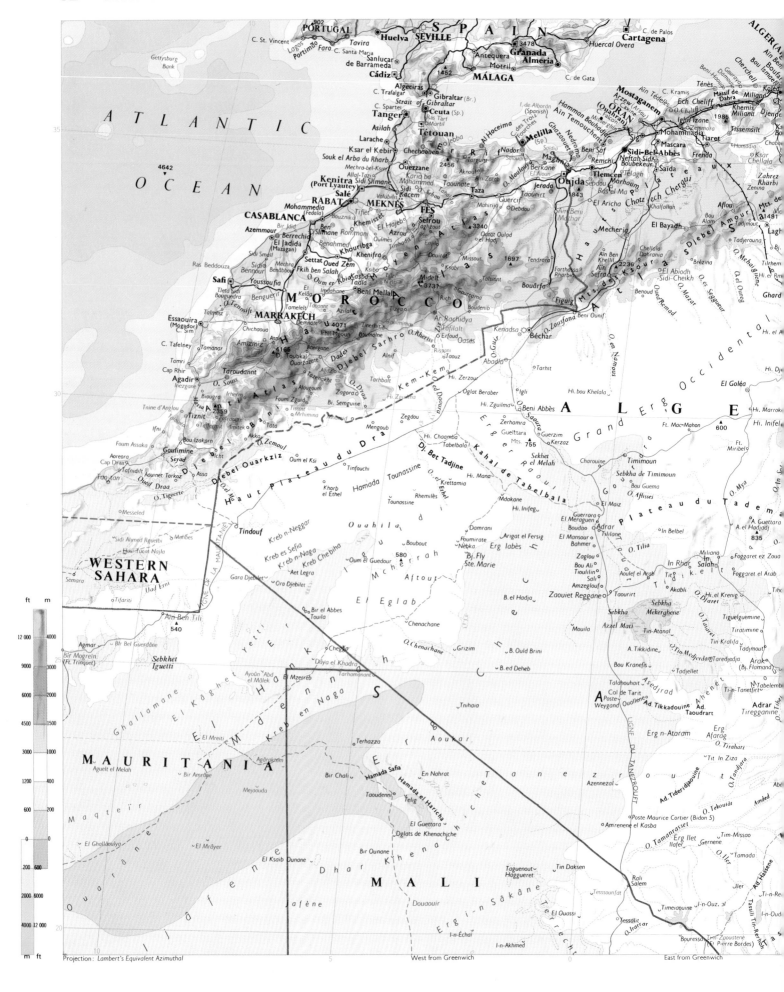

ft   m

12 000 4000

9000   3000

6000   2000

4500   1500

3000   1000

1200   400

600   200

0   0

200   600

2000   6000

4000   12 000

m   ft

Projection: Lambert's Equivalent Azimuthal

1:8 000 000

50 0 50 100 150 200 miles
50 0 50 100 150 200 250 300 km

SICILY Etna 3340
Marsala
Agrigento **Caltanissetta** **CATANIA**
Ragusa **Siracusa**
C. Spartivento
C. Passero

Gozo
Valletta
MALTA

Linosa I.
Lampione I.
Lampedusa

M E D I T E R R A N E A N   S E A

Menzel Bourguiba **Bizerte** (Binzert)
Galite Is.
Mateur C. Blanc
Tabarka C. Serrat
C. Rosa Djana I.
Skikda **Annaba** La Calle Golfe de Tunis
Collo Azzaba Béja C. Bon Zembra I.
Belaïa Jijel El Milia Medjez Kelibia
Jerissa R. Mostefa
CONSTANTINE Guelma Souk Ahras **TUNIS** Menzel-Temime
Bordj bou Arrerridj 2004 El Eulma Sedrata El Kef Soliman Nabeul Pantelleria (Italian)
Sétif Aïn M'lila El Kroubs Ouenza Thala Maktar Hammamet G. de Hammamet
Rass el Oued Oum-el-Bouaghi Aïn Beïda Kairouan Enfida
Batna Khenchela **Sousse**
Monastir
Moknine
Msaken
Djem Rass Kaboudia
Biskra Aurès 2328
1338 Menzel Chaker El Mahdia
Tolga Fériana Sbeitla **Sfax** Iles Kerkenna
Metlaoui Graïba
Négrine Maharès Kneiss Is.
1165 Cekhira
Gafsa Djebiniana
Nefta Chott el Fedjadj El Hamma **G. de Gabès**
Tozeur Chott Djerid Kebili **Gabès** Djerba I.
Matmata Adjim El Kantara
Douz Zarzis

Chott Melrhir
Ouled Djellal
El Meghaier
Djamâa
Guemar El Oued
Megarine
Touggourt Blidet Amor

Ouargla
Hassi Rhénami
Hassi Messaoud
Ft. Lallemand

Bahiret el Bibane
Médenine
Tataouine
Ben Gardane Zaltan **Tarâbulus** (Tripoli) Tâjûrâ Al Khums
Ben Aoune Zuwârah Sabrâtah Az Zâwiyah Zanzûr Al Qasabah Leptis Magna (Labdgh)
Nâlût Tiji Gharyân Tarhûnah Zlîtan
Jabal Nafûsah Misrâtah
Jâdû 968 Wâdî Bani Walîd Bi'r Dhu'jûn
716 Mizdah Tâwurghâ'
GHARYÂN Sabkhat Tâwurghâ'
Wâdi Sawfajjîn Al Qaddâhîyah
Shumaykh Bu'ayrât **Khalij Surt** (Gulf of Sidra)
KHUMS W. Zamzam Surt
Qasr As Sultân W. Thâmu
Al Qaryah ash Sharqîyah Bu Hâdi An Nawfalîyah Es Sider Ra's Al-Unuf
Ghudâmis Daraj W. Qizrah W. Ruais Quwayrât al Milh

Banghâzî (Benghazi)
Al Abyâr Banînah
Tûkrah
Suluq
Kurkûrah
Zueitina
Ajdâbiyah
Marsa Brega

MISRÂTAH

Al Hammâdah al Hamrâ'
Plateau du Tinrhert
Hasy Tissan Jabal Waddân Waddân Hûn Zillah
Jabal as Sawdâ' 840 Al Jufrah
Zarzaïtine Adrî Barqin Brach Wâdi ash Shâti' Sumnû
SABHAH
Bir al Qbî Al Haruj al Aswad
1200 Qaltat Bû As Su'ud
W. Bû Hijân
Awbârî **Sabhah** (Sebha) Ghadir Oâhirah Ar Rom
Godduà Umm al Arânib Tmassah
Tasâwuh Trâghân Tarbû
Marzûq Ma'fan Majdûl Marqa Wâw al Kabîr
L I B Y A
945
Idehan Marzûq
1428 Al Qatrûn
Al Barkât Madrusah Tajarbî B. Zâmûs 583 Wâw an Nâmûs

Tropic of Cancer

Sarîr Tibasti
J. Nuqayy Erissi
Ghelini

Toummo Passe de Kourizo
Toummo Dhoba Yedri Aozou Massif de Kemet Pic Bette 2286
Massif d'Afafi
Madama Tarso Ourâri Tuzugu
Fezzan Omchi Tarso Emissi 3150 Yebbi-Souma
Plateau du Djado Pic Touside 3265 Bardai Tiêbora
Orida Djado Tarso Tieroko 2910
Chirfa Zouar Tarso Ahon
Sara Sherda Emi Koussi 3415
Gouro

N I G E R **C H A D**

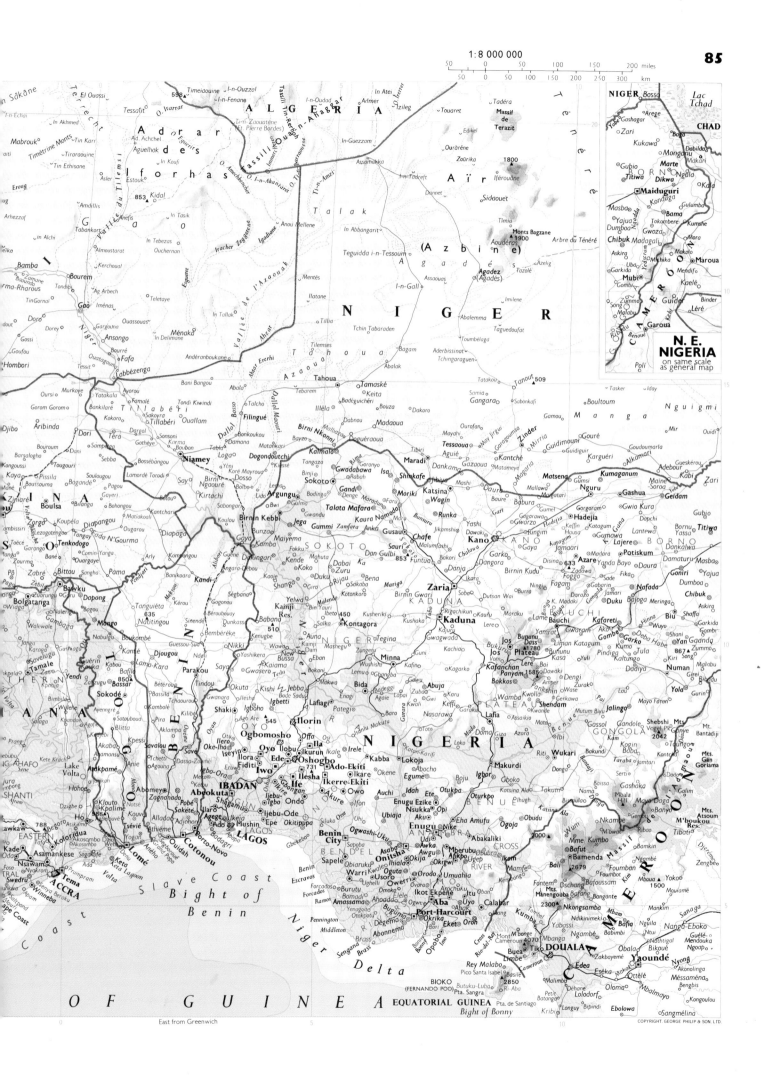

1:8 000 000

ALGERIA

Adrar de Iforhas

NIGER

Aïr

(Azbine)

Agadez
(Agadès)

NIGER

Tahoua

NIGER Bosso
Lac
Tchad
CHAD
N. E.
NIGERIA
on same scale
as general map

CAMEROON

Maiduguri

Maroua

Garoua

Niamey

Maradi

Zinder

Kano

Sokoto

Gusau

Katsina

Nguru

Gashua

Geidam

BORNO

Potiskum

Hadejia

Azare

Bauchi

Gombe

Zaria

KADUNA

Kaduna

Jos

PLATEAU

Minna

Bida

Abuja

Makurdi

BENUE

Ilorin

OYO

Ogbomosho

Oshogbo

Ado-Ekiti

IBADAN

Abeokuta

Ife

OGUN

LAGOS

Porto-Novo

Cotonou

Lomé

ACCRA

Tema

Benin
City

BENDEL

Warri

Enugu

ANAMBRA

Onitsha

Owerri

Aba

Port-Harcourt

Calabar

CAMEROON

DOUALA

Yaoundé

BIOKO
(FERNANDO POO)

EQUATORIAL GUINEA

Bight of
Benin

Niger

Delta

Slave Coast

Bight of Bonny

OF GUINEA

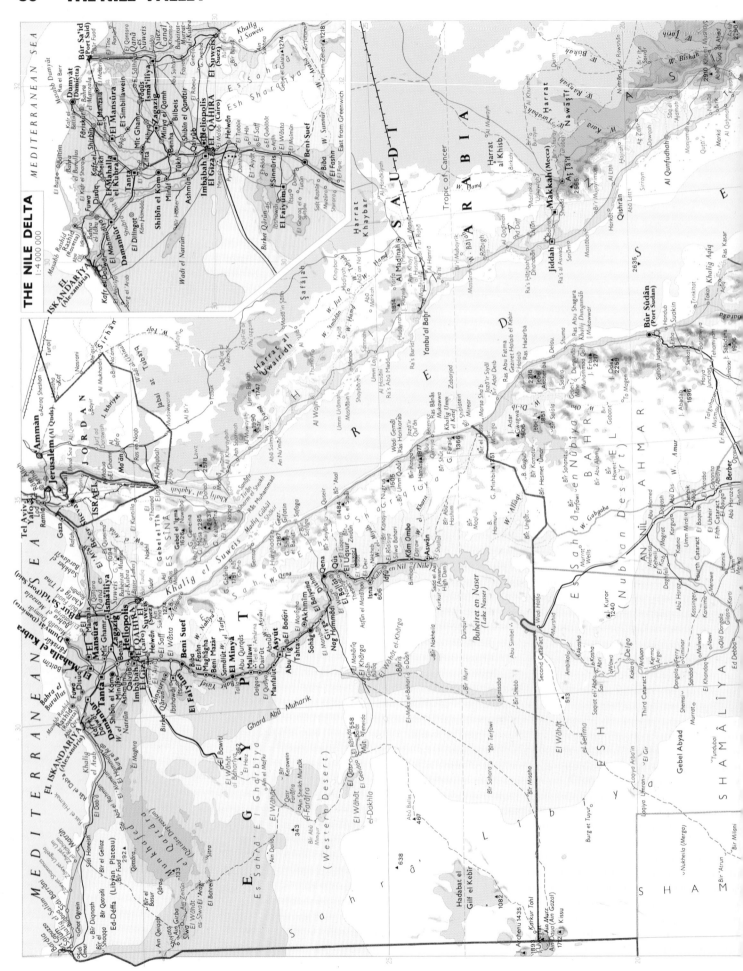

THE NILE DELTA
1:4 000 000

1:8 000 000

50   0   50   100   150   200 miles
50 0 50 100 150 200 250 300 km

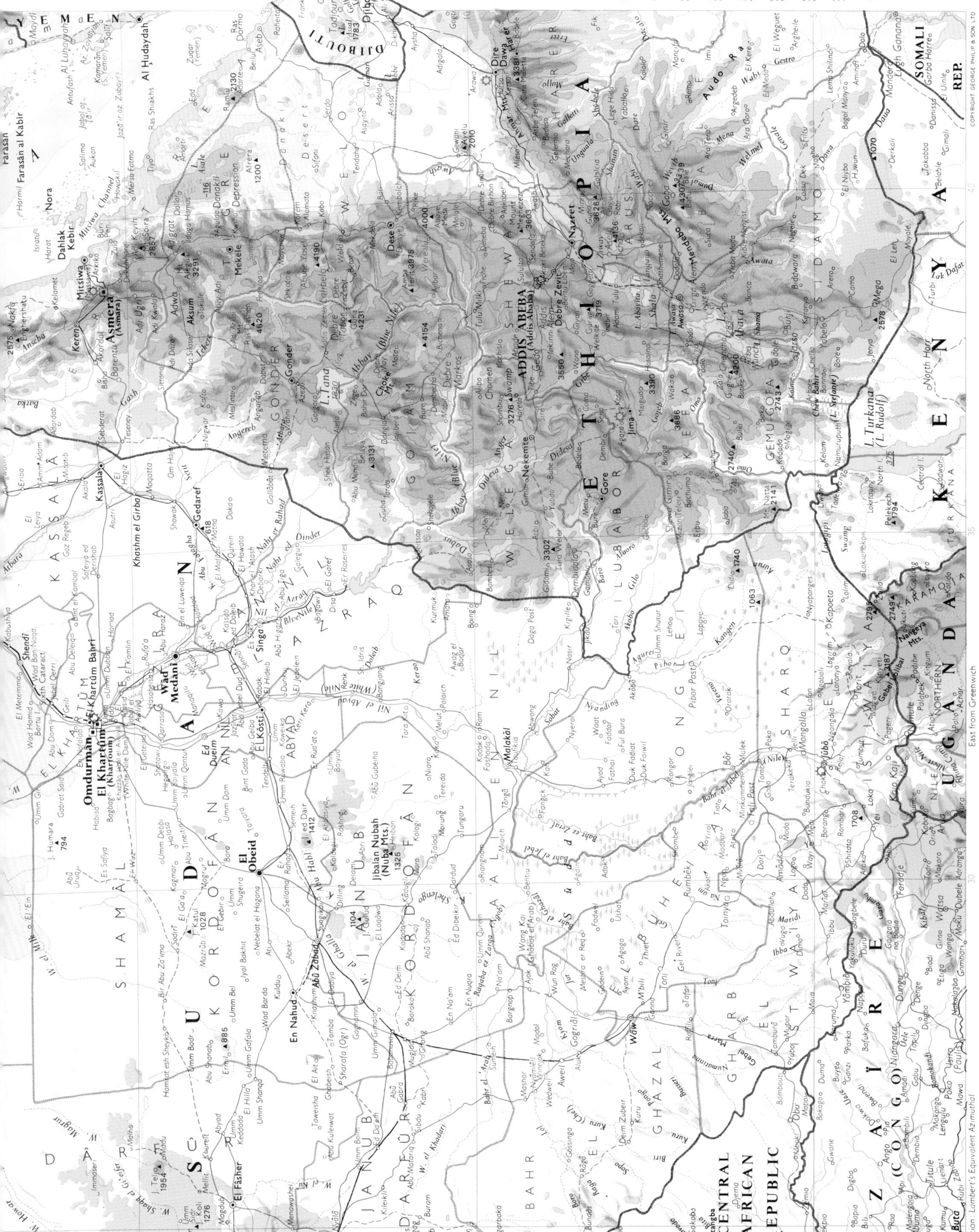

SOMALI REP.

COPYRIGHT GEORGE PHILIP & SON LTD

Y E M E N

Faràsàn
Faràsàn al Kabir

Nora

Dahlak
Kebir

Mitsiwa
Asmera
(Asmara)

Keren

Kassala

K A S S A L A

Gedaref

Khashm el Girba

Omdurmân
El Khartûm
(Khartoum)

**Wad
Medani**

Ed
Dueim

El Kôsti

Shendi

A N   N I L

S H A M Â L

K O R D O F Â N

El Obeid

Jibalan Nubah
(Nuba Mts.)
1325

D A R F U R

En Nahud

Abû Zabad

El Fâsher

S U D A N

J A N U B   D A R F U R

J A N U B   K O R D O F Â N

B A H R   E L   G H A Z A L

Wâw

C E N T R A L
A F R I C A N
R E P U B L I C

Z A Ï R E
(C O N G O)

DJIBOUTI
Djibouti

Dire
Dawa

Mekele

Aksum

Gonder

L.Tana

Dese

Debre Markos

ADDIS ABEBA
(ADDIS ABABA)

Nazret

E T H I O P I A

S H E W A

G O J A M

G O N D E R

W E L E G A

Nekemte

Gore

I L U B A B O R

Jima

K E F A

G E M U
G O F A

L.Turkana
(L.Rudolf)

K E N Y A

S I D A M O

A R U S S I

B A L E

H A R A R

W E L L O

E R I T R E A

T I G R A Y

A W S A

Malakâl

J O N G L E I

B A H R   E L   J E B E L

A L   I S T I W Â' I Y A

E L   B U H E Y R A T

W A Ï L Y A   G H A R B

Bôr

Jûbâ

U G A N D A

East from Greenwich

Projection: Lambert's Equivalent Azimuthal

m   ft
4000 12,000
3000 9000
2000 6000
1500 4500
1000 3000
400   1200
200   600
0   0
m ft

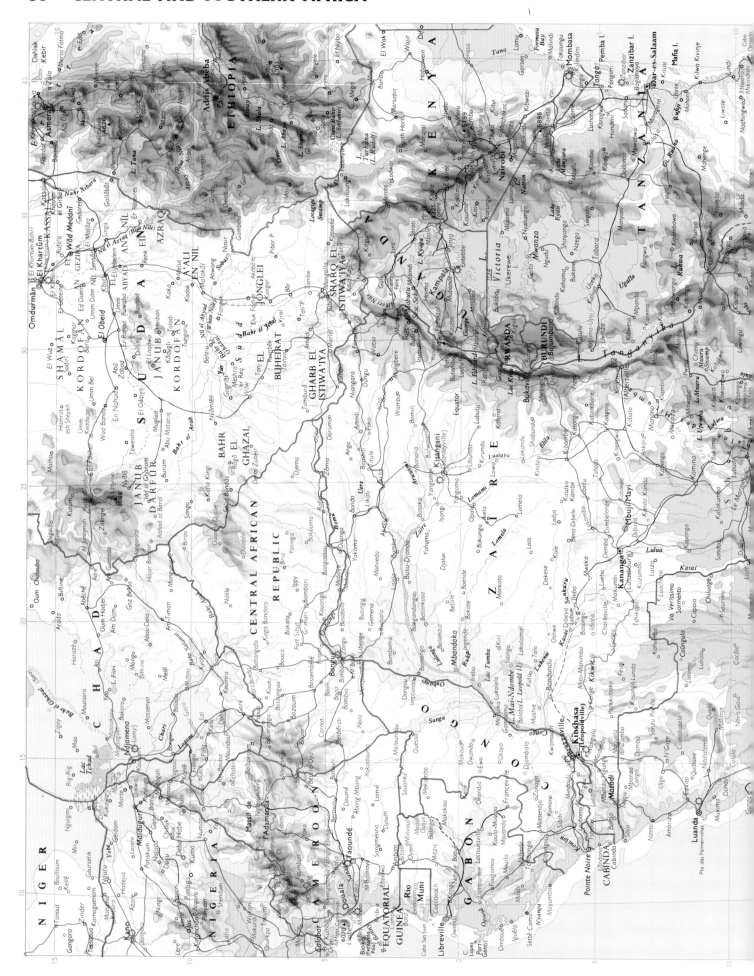

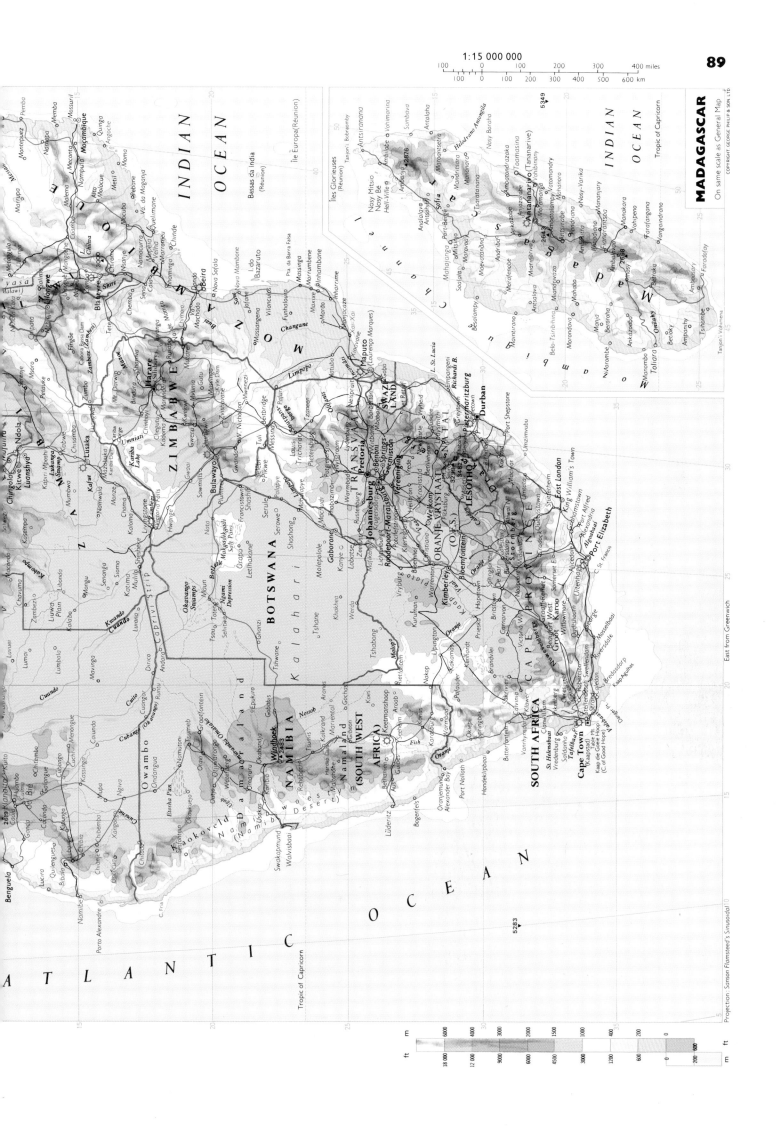

1:15 000 000

100   0   100   200   300   400 miles

100   0   100   200   300   400   500   600 km

MADAGASCAR
On same scale as General Map
COPYRIGHT GEORGE PHILIP & SON LTD

INDIAN

OCEAN

Tropic of Capricorn

Îles Glorieuses
(Réunion)

Nosy Mitsio
Nosy Be
Hell-Ville

Antsiranana

Île Europa (Réunion)

Bassas da India
(Réunion)

INDIAN   OCEAN

Antananarivo (Tananarive)

ATLANTIC   OCEAN

Projection: Samson Flamsteed's Sinusoidal

East from Greenwich

ZIMBABWE

ZAMBIA

BOTSWANA

Kalahari

NAMIBIA
(SOUTH WEST
AFRICA)

SOUTH AFRICA

Cape Town

CAPE PROVINCE

TRANSVAAL

Pretoria
Johannesburg

ORANGE
VRYSTAAT
(O.F.S.)

Bloemfontein

LESOTHO

SWAZI
LAND

NATAL

Durban

Port Elizabeth

MOZAMBIQUE

Maputo

Beira

Harare

Bulawayo

Gaborone

Windhoek

Tropic of Capricorn

m   6000   4000   3000   2000   1500   1000   400   200   0   ft
ft 18 000 12 000 9000 6000 4500 3000 1200 600 0   m

SOMALI REP.

ETHIOPIA

SUDAN

KENYA

UGANDA

TANZANIA

RWANDA

BURUNDI

ZAIRE

CENTRAL AFRICAN REPUBLIC

NAIROBI

MOMBASA

DAR ES SALAAM

Kampala

Kisangani

L. Turkana (L. Rudolf)

Lake Victoria

L. Kyoga

L. Albert

L. Tanganyika

L. Kivu

Pemba I.

Zanzibar

Equator

1:8 000 000

50   0   50   100   150   200 miles
50   0   100   200   300 km

INDIAN

OCEAN

Projection: Lambert's Equivalent Azimuthal

East from Greenwich

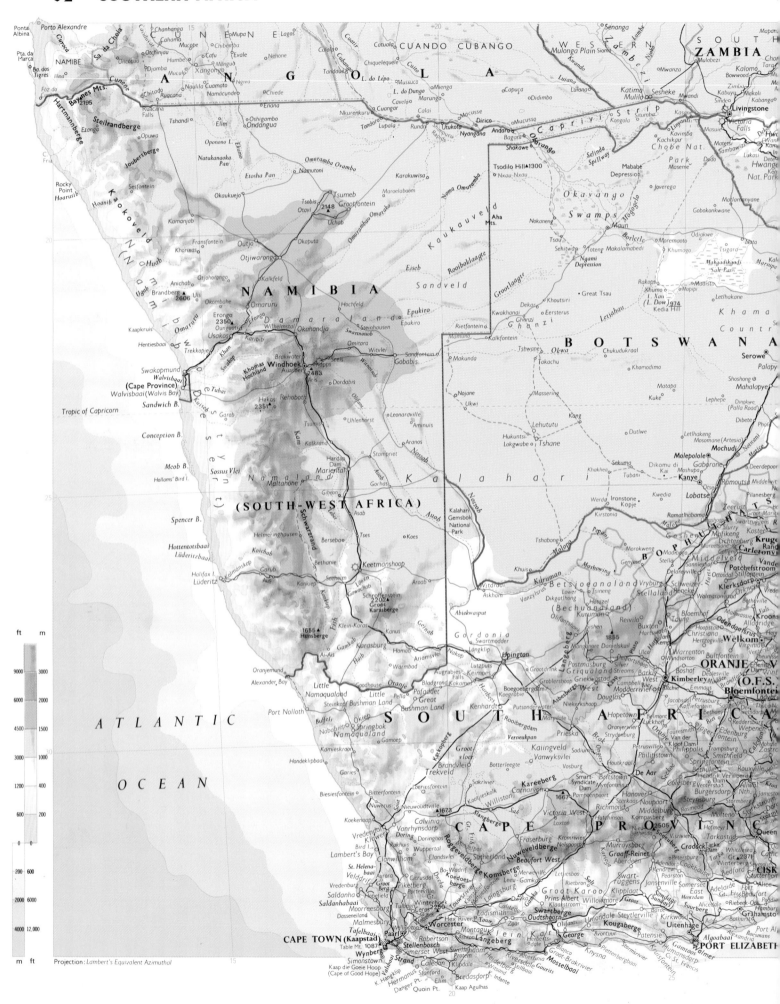

ATLANTIC

OCEAN

NAMIBIA

(SOUTH-WEST AFRICA)

BOTSWANA

SOUTH AFRICA

CAPE PROVINCE

ANGOLA

ZAMBIA

CUANDO CUBANGO

Kalahari

Tropic of Capricorn

Projection: Lambert's Equivalent Azimuthal

CAPE TOWN (Kaapstad)

PORT ELIZABETH

ORANJE (O.F.S.)

Bloemfontein

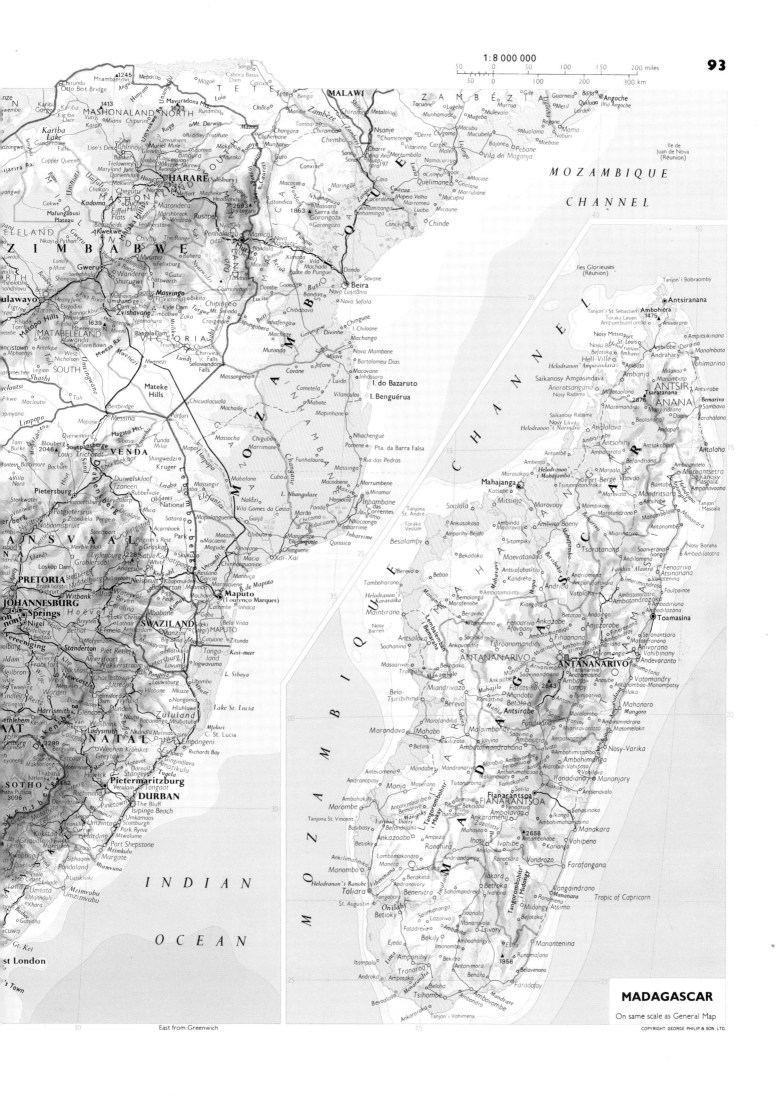

1:8 000 000

50   0   50   100   150   200 miles
100   0   100   200   300 km

MADAGASCAR

On same scale as General Map

COPYRIGHT. GEORGE PHILIP & SON. LTD.

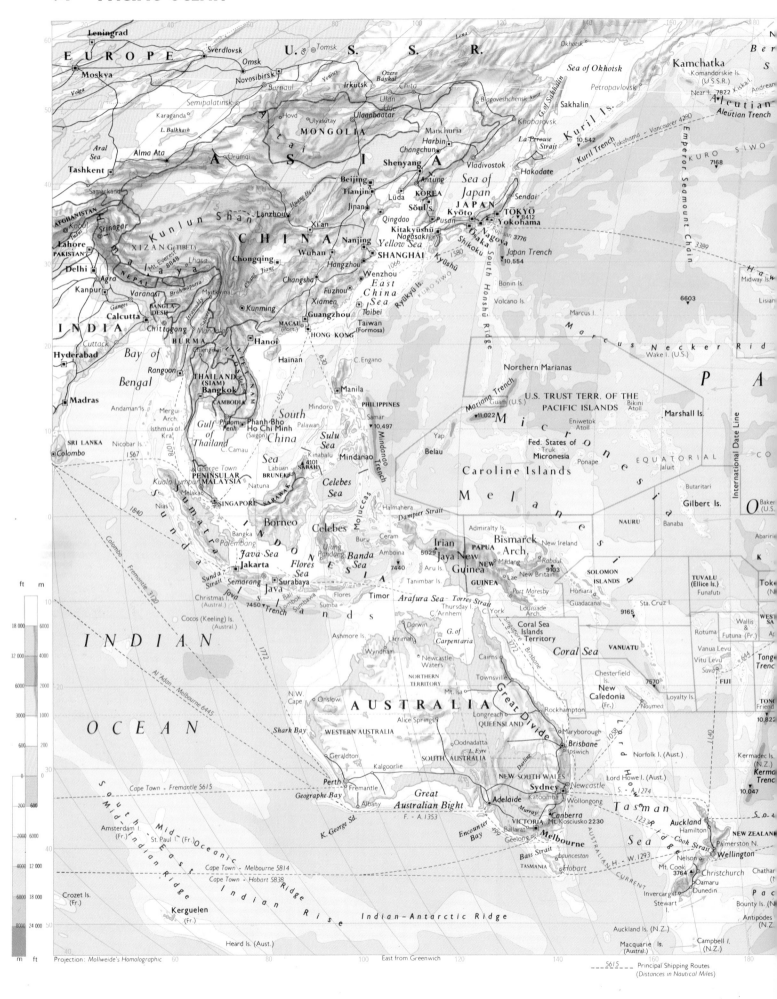

Leningrad

EUROPE U. S. S. R.

Moskva
Sverdlovsk
Omsk
Tomsk
Volga
Semipalatinsk
Novosibirsk
Barnaul
Irkutsk
Chita
Ulan Ude
Ozero Baykal
Hovd
Ulyasutay
Ulaanbaatar
Manchuria
Khabarovsk
Blagoveshchensk
Amur
Kamchatka
Komandorskie Is. (U.S.S.R.)
Petropavlovsk
Sea of Okhotsk
G. of Sakhalin
Sakhalin
La Perouse Strait
Near I. 7822
Kiska I.
Andreanof
Aleutian Trench

Aral Sea
Alma Ata
L. Balkhash
Urumqi
MONGOLIA
Changchun
Harbin
Shenyang
Antung
Vladivostok
Hakodate
Kuril Is.
Kuril Trench
Yokohama - Vancouver 4280
Emperor Seamount Chain
KURO SIWO
7168

Tashkent
Karaganda
Samarkand
A   S   I   A
Beijing
Tianjin
KOREA
Lüda
Sŏul's
Pusan
Sendai
Sea of Japan
JAPAN
TOKYO
Yokohama
8412
Fuji I. 3776
Nagoya
3389

AFGHANISTAN
Kabul
Srinagar
Kunlun Shan
XIZANG (TIBET)
Lanzhou
Xi'an
CHINA
Jinan
Yellow Sea
Nagasaki
Kitakyūshū
Kyōto
Osaka
Shikoku
Kyūshū
Japan Trench
10.554

Lahore
PAKISTAN
Delhi
Agra
Kanpur
Varanasi
Mt. Everest 8848
Lhasa
Nepal
Brahmaputra
Chongqing
Chang Jiang
Wuhan
Hangzhou
Nanjing
SHANGHAI
Bonin Is.
6603
Midway Is.
Lisian

INDIA
Calcutta
BANGLA DESH
Chittagong
Mandalay
Myitkyina
Kunming
Changsha
Fuzhou
Xiamen
Wenzhou
East China Sea
Ryūkyū Is.
Taibei
Marcus I.
Wake I. (U.S.)
Marcus   Necker   Rid
Midway Is.

Hyderabad
Cuttack
Bay of Bengal
BURMA
Chiengmai
Irrawaddy
Rangoon
THAILAND (SIAM)
Bangkok
Hanoi
Hainan
MACAU (Port.)
Guangzhou
HONG KONG
Taiwan (Formosa)
C. Engano
Northern Marianas
PA

Madras
Andaman Is.
Mergui Arch.
Isthmus of Kra
CAMBODIA
LAOS
VIETNAM
Phnom Penh
Ho Chi Minh (Saigon)
Manila
Mindoro
PHILIPPINES
Samar
Mariano Trench
Guam (U.S.)
11.022
U.S. TRUST TERR. OF THE PACIFIC ISLANDS
Bikini Atoll
Marshall Is.

SRI LANKA
Colombo
Nicobar Is.
1567
C. Camau
Gulf of Thailand
South China Sea
Palawan
Sulu Sea
Mindanao
Mindanao Trench
Yap
Belau
Eniwetok Atoll
Fed. States of Micronesia
Truk
Jaluit
EQUATORIAL
Baker I. (U.S.)

Kuala Lumpur
PENINSULAR MALAYSIA
Melaka
Nias
George Town
Kinabalu
Labuan
SABAH
BRUNEI
SARAWAK
Celebes Sea
Caroline Islands
Ponape
Butaritari
Gilbert Is.

SINGAPORE
Natuna
Borneo
Celebes
Moluccas
Halmahera
Dampier Strait
Admiralty Is.
New Ireland
NAURU
Banaba
Abaririri
K

Bangka
Palembang
Sumatra
Java Sea
Ceram
Buru
Amboina
Irian Jaya
5029
Bismarck Arch.
Rabaul
New Britain
SOLOMON ISLANDS
TUVALU (Ellice Is.)
Funafuti
Tok

Jakarta
Semarang
Surabaya
Bali
Flores Sea
Banda Sea
7440
Tanimbar Is.
Aru Is.
PAPUA NEW GUINEA
NEW GUINEA
Madang
Lae
9103
Honiara
Guadalcanal
Sta. Cruz I.
9165
WES SA

INDONESIA
Java
Java Trench
7450
Sumba
Sumbawa
Flores
Timor
Arafura Sea
Torres Strait
Thursday I.
C. York
Port Moresby
Louisiade Arch.
Rotuma
Wallis & Futuna (Fr.)

Christmas I. (Austral.)
Cocos (Keeling) Is. (Austral.)
Sunda Strait
1772
Darwin
Ashmore Is.
L. McKinlay
Arnhem
G. of Carpentaria
Coral Sea Islands Territory
Vanua Levu
Vitu Levu
Suva
FIJI

INDIAN
Fremantle 3720
N.W. Cape
Onslow
Wyndham
Newcastle Waters
Cairns
Townsville
Coral Sea
VANUATU
Chesterfield Is.
7570
New Caledonia (Fr.)
Nouméa
Loyalty Is.
Tong Trenc

OCEAN
Al Adan - Melbourne 6445
Shark Bay
NORTHERN TERRITORY
AUSTRALIA
Mt. Isa
Alice Springs
Longreach
QUEENSLAND
Rockhampton
Great Divide
Norfolk I. (Aust.)
TON Friend
10.822

WESTERN AUSTRALIA
Geraldton
Oodnadatta
L. Eyre
SOUTH AUSTRALIA
Maryborough
Brisbane
Ipswich
NEW SOUTH WALES
Lord Howe I. (Aust.)
Kermadec Is. (N.Z.)
Kerma Trenc
10.047

Cape Town - Fremantle 5615
Perth
Fremantle
Geographe Bay
Kalgoorlie
Albany
K. George Sd.
Great Australian Bight
F. - A. 1353
Adelaide
Katoomba
Sydney
Newcastle
Wollongong
Lord Howe I. (Aust.)
1274
Tasman Sea
Auckland
Hamilton
NEW ZEALAND
Cook Strait

South Mid Indian Ridge
Amsterdam (Fr.)
St. Paul I. (Fr.)
Mid Oceanic Ridge
East Indian Rise
Geelong
Ballarat
VICTORIA
Mt. Kosciusko 2230
Melbourne
Encounter Bay
Murray
Bass Strait
Launceston
TASMANIA
Hobart
H. W. 1293
Nelson
Mt. Cook 3764
Christchurch
Oamaru
Dunedin
Chatha

Crozet Is. (Fr.)
Kerguelen (Fr.)
Indian - Antarctic Ridge
Invercargill
Stewart
Bounty Is. (N.Z.)
Antipodes (N.Z.)
Pac

Heard Is. (Aust.)
Auckland Is. (N.Z.)
Macquarie Is. (Austral.)
Campbell I. (N.Z.)

Projection: Mollweide's Homolographic
East from Greenwich
5615   Principal Shipping Routes (Distances in Nautical Miles)

ALASKA
6050
Bristol Bay
Gulf of Alaska
Juneau
Sitka
Prince of Wales I.
Prince Rupert
Kitimat
Queen Charlotte Is.
GREENLAND
C. Farewell
Churchill
Hudson Bay
Belcher Is.
Dawson Creek
C A N A D A
Edmonton
Prince Albert
Lynn Lake
Scheffervile
Hamilton Inlet
Labrador
Strait of Belle Isle
N O R T H
NORTH AMERICA
Vancouver
Vancouver I.
Victoria
Seattle
Tacoma
Portland
Rocky Mountains
Calgary
Medicine Hat
Spokane
Helena
Butte
Boise
Regina
Winnipeg
L. Winnipeg
Saskatoon
Bismarck
Missouri
James Bay
Duluth
L. Superior
St. Paul
Minneapolis
Milwaukee
CHICAGO
Sault Ste. Marie
Montréal
Ottawa
Toronto
Québec
L. Huron
L. Ontario
L. Erie
Anticosti
G. of St. Lawrence
Fredericton
Saint John
Pr. Edward I.
C. Breton I.
C. Race
Newfoundland
Sable I.
Southampton 3091
NORTH
C. Blanco
Mendocino Seascarp
C. Mendocino
Sacramento
Oakland
San Francisco
4418
Salt Lake City
Denver
Cheyenne
Des Moines
Kansas
St. Louis
UNITED STATES
Santa Fé
Oklahoma
Detroit
Cincinnati
Indianapolis
Buffalo
Pittsburgh
Appalachian Mts.
Boston
C. Sable
NEW YORK
Philadelphia
Baltimore
Washington
Richmond
Norfolk
Little Rock
Memphis
Mississippi
Atlanta
C. Hatteras
ATLANTIC
New York - Liverpool
Bermuda (U.K.)
2419
Los Angeles
San Diego
2091
Murray Seascarp
CALIFORNIAN CURRENT
El Paso
Ciudad Juárez
Dallas
Austin
San Antonio
Houston
New Orleans
Galveston
Mobile
Savannah
Jacksonville
New York - Recife 3678
6741
Hawaiian Is.
(U.S.A.)
Ridge
Oahu
Honolulu
Hawaii
Tropic of Cancer
Guadalupe
6225
Pto. Eugenia
Gulf of California
Sierra Madre
MEXICO
C. S. Lucas
3277
Guadalajara
Aguascalientes
México
Revilla Gigedo Is.
(Mexico)
Tampico
San Luis Potosí
Torreón
Monterrey
Gulf of Mexico
Tampa
Miami
Florida Strait
BAHAMAS
OCEAN
N.Y. - C. 1972
Panamá 4530
Clarion Fracture Zone
Veracruz
Puebla 5700
Acapulco
La Habana
CUBA
Yucatan Channel
Mérida
West Indies
Hispaniola 9200
DOM. REP.
HAITI
7680
JAMAICA
Kingston
Santo Domingo
St. Thomas (U.S.)
Virgin Is.
PUERTO RICO
Guadeloupe (Fr.)
Leeward Is.
IFIC
4711
Clipperton Fracture Zone
Clipperton I. (Fr.)
S.E. MONSOON DRIFT
GUATEMALA
Guatemala
EL SALVADOR
BELIZE
HONDURAS
Tegucigalpa
Salvador
NICARAGUA
Managua
CENTRAL AMERICA
San José
COSTA RICA
Colón
PANAMA
Panamá Canal
Caribbean Sea
Barranquilla
Maracaibo
Curaçao (Ne.)
Martinique (Fr.)
Windward Is.
BARBADOS
TRINIDAD & TOBAGO
Caracas
Orinoco
VENEZUELA
CURRENT
Palmyra Is. (U.S.)
Teraina
Tabuaeran
Kiritimati
3666
Cocos I.
835
Medellín
Bogotá
Cali
COLOMBIA
rmas Island Ridge
EAN
Jarvis I. (U.S.)
Equator
Galápagos
(Ecuador)
C. S.Francisco
Quito
ECUADOR
Chimborazo 6267
Cuenca
Guayaquil
Iquitos
Amazon
Manaus
I
B A T I
Malden I.
Starbuck I.
Tahiti - Panamá 4570
C. Pariñas
Lobos I.
700
Chiclayo
Trujillo
BRAZIL
SOUTH
Tongareva
Penrhyn Is.
Manihiki
Suwarrow Is.
Vostok
Caroline I.
Flint I.
Marquesas Is.
Leeward Is.
6369
PERU
Lima
Callao
AMERICA
Cook Islands
(N.Z.)
1303
Society Is.
Windward Is.
Tahiti
FRENCH POLYNESIA
Tuamotu Archipelago
East Pacific Ridge
Auckland - Panamá 6510
Southeast
Pacific Basin
PERUVIAN CURRENT
Cuzco
L. Titicaca
Illampu & Ancohuma 6550
La Paz
6866
Arequipa
BOLIVIA
Manuae
Austral
Rarotonga
Seamount Chain
Tuamotu Ridge
Tropic of Capricorn
Sala-y-Gómez
(Chile)
San Félix (Chile)
San Ambrosio (Chile)
Iquique
Peru-
Chile
PARAGUAY
8050
Antofagasta
Trench
Tubuai Is.
(Austral Is.)
Pitcairn I. (U.K.)
Ducie I.
Rapa Iti
Easter Is.
(Chile)
792
Salta
Tucumán
Asunción
Corrientes
Pto. Alegre
Arch. de Juan Fernández
(Chile)
Alejandro Selkirk
Robinson Crusoe
Aconcagua 6960
Valparaíso
Santiago
Concepción
Córdoba
Rosario
Santa Fé
Paysandú
URUGUAY
Buenos Aires
La Plata
ARGENTINA
Río de la Plata
Montevideo
Mar del Plata
Pacific-Antarctic Ridge
WEST WIND DRIFT
Pacific-Antarctic Basin
Chile Rise
Chonos Arch.
G. of Penas
Wellington
CAPE HORN CURRENT
Neuquén
Patagonia
P.A. - Valparaíso
1414
1355
1295
Buenos Aires
Montevideo
SOUTH
P.A.
Sta. Cruz Arena
Punta Arenas
Str. of Magellan
Tierra del Fuego
C. Horn
P. Deseado
Stanley
Falkland Is. (U.K.)
South Georgia
Argentine Basin
6212
ATLANTIC
OCEAN
160
140
120
100
West from Greenwich
80
60
40
COPYRIGHT. GEORGE PHILIP & SON. LTD.

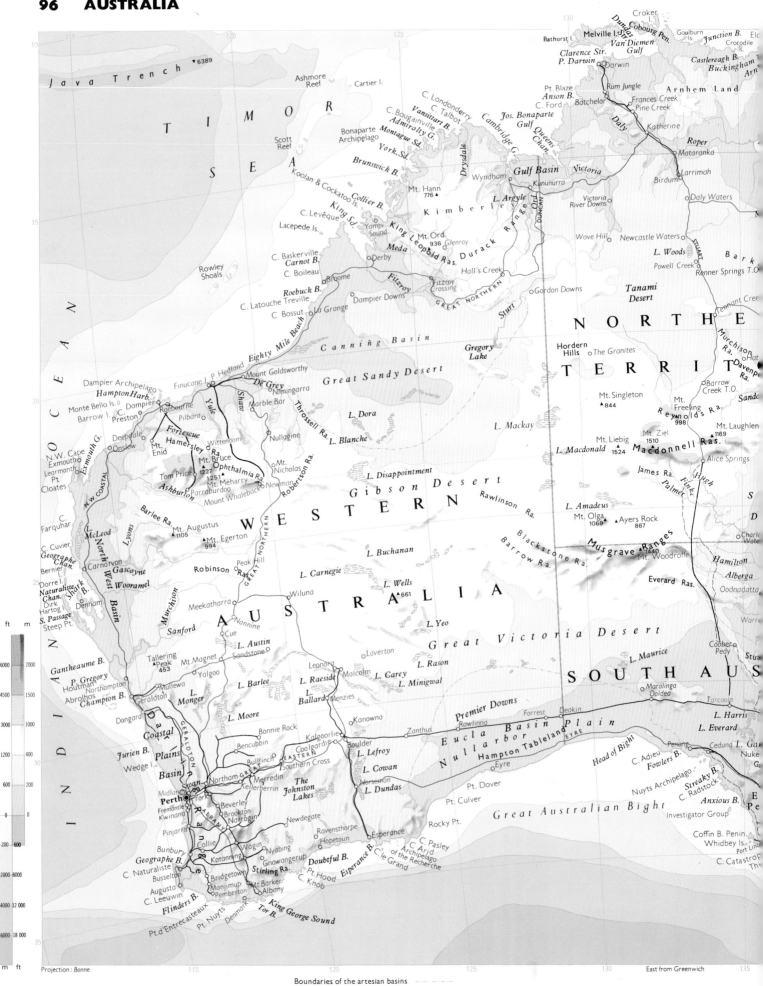

Boundaries of the artesian basins

Projection: Bonne   East from Greenwich

1:12 000 000

100   0   100   200   miles

100   0   100   200   300   400 km

AUSTRALASIA
POLITICAL
1:80 000 000

200   0   200   400   600   800   miles

400   0   400   800   1200   1600 km

INDONESIA

**PAPUA
NEW
GUINEA**

**NORTHERN
TERRITORY**

**WESTERN
AUSTRALIA**

QUEENSLAND

**SOUTH
AUSTRALIA**

**NEW
SOUTH
WALES**

VICTORIA

TASMANIA

**PACIFIC
OCEAN**

**NEW
ZEALAND**

INDIAN
OCEAN

SOUTHERN
OCEAN

Gulf
of

Carpentaria

Cape
York
Peninsula

Coral
Sea
Basin

Great
Barrier
Reef

QUEENSLAND

Great
Dividing
Range

Selwyn Range

Grey
Range

P A C I F I C

O C E A N

CORAL SEA ISLANDS
TERRITORY

Trinity Bay

Townsville

Tropic of Capricorn

Brisbane

NEW SOUTH WALES

Murray River

VICTORIA

Great
Dividing
Range

Australian Alps

SYDNEY
Wollongong

Canberra
CAP.
TERR.

Adelaide

MELBOURNE

Ballarat
Geelong

Tasman
Sea

TASMANIA

MELBOURNE
Ballarat
Geelong

King I.

Bass Strait

Flinders I.
Furneaux
Group

Hobart

on same scale

COPYRIGHT. GEORGE PHILIP & SON. LTD

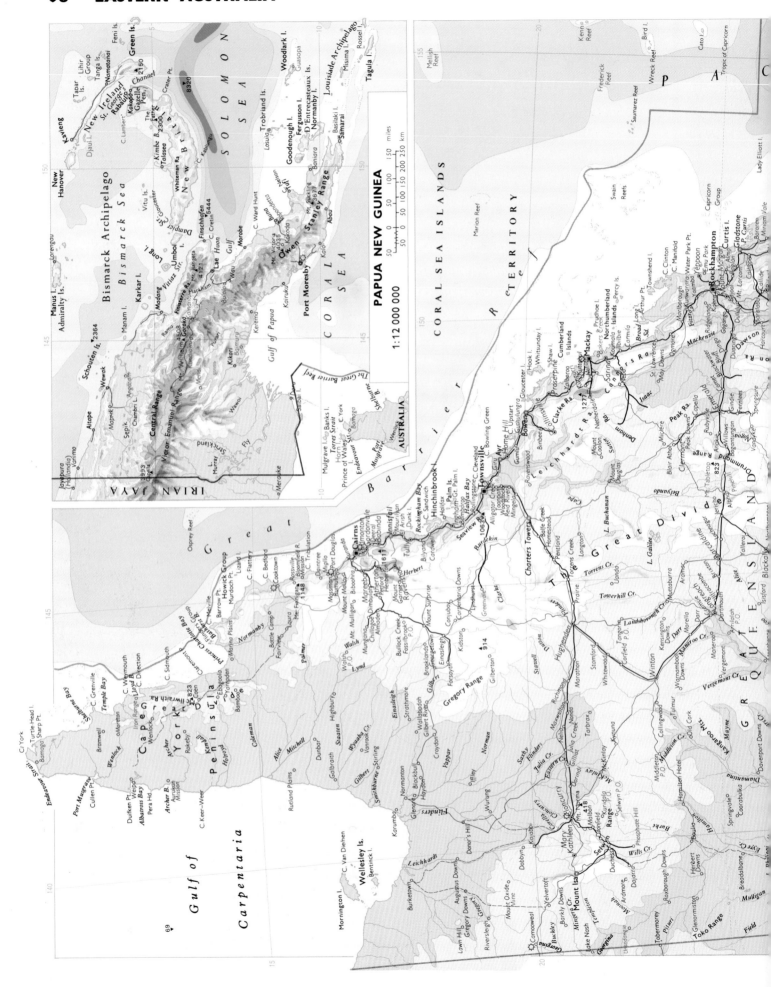

PAPUA NEW GUINEA

1:12 000 000

50	0	50	100	150		miles
50	0	50	100	150	200 250	km

AUSTRALIA

1:7 500 000

50 0 50 100 150 200 miles
50 0 50 100 150 200 250 300 km

F I C   O C E A N

T a s m a n   S e a

Continuation Southwards

TASMANIA

Bass Strait

Kent Group
Curtis Group
Flinders Island
Furneaux Group
King Island
Cape Barren I.
Launceston
Devonport
Burnie
Zeehan
Queenstown
Strahan
New Norfolk
Hobart
Glenorchy
S.E. Cape

NEW SOUTH WALES

SOUTH AUSTRALIA

Great Dividing Range

Darling Downs

Darling R.

Murray R.

BRISBANE
Redcliffe
Ipswich
Toowoomba
Warwick
Dalby
Gympie
Maryborough
Southport
Gold Coast
Byron Bay
Lismore
Grafton
Coffs Harbour
Armidale
Tamworth
Inverell
Moree
Newcastle
Maitland
Cessnock
SYDNEY
Wollongong
Parramatta
Liverpool
Katoomba
Bathurst
Orange
Dubbo
Wellington
Parkes
Forbes
Broken Hill
Bourke
CANBERRA
Goulburn
Cooma
Wagga Wagga
Albury
Griffith
Narrandera
Deniliquin
Echuca
Bendigo
Ballarat
MELBOURNE
Williamstown
Geelong
Warrnambool
Mount Gambier
Wentworth
Mildura
Wilsons Promontory

ADELAIDE
Gawler
Port Pirie
Port Augusta
Whyalla
Murray Bridge
Kangaroo I.
Lake Torrens
Lake Eyre (North)
Lake Eyre South
Lake Frome
Lake Blanche
Lake Gregory
Cooper Creek

Flinders Ranges
Barrier Ra.

Projection: Bonne

East from Greenwich

COPYRIGHT. GEORGE PHILIP & SON, LTD.

1 : 4 500 000

20   0   20   40   60   80   100 miles
20   0   40   80   120   160 km

TASMAN SEA

NEW SOUTH WALES

Taree
Newcastle
Stockton
Belmont
Swansea
The Entrance
Maitland
Cessnock
Woy Woy
Gosford
Manly
SYDNEY
Hornsby
Parramatta
Fairfield
Liverpool
Penrith
Lithgow
Katoomba
Cronulla
Campbelltown
Wollongong
Kiama
Picton
Bathurst
Orange
Mudgee
Wellington
Dubbo
Forbes
Parkes
Cowra
Young
Goulburn
Nowra
Canberra
AUSTRALIAN CAPITAL TERRITORY
Queanbeyan
Cootamundra
Junee
Wagga Wagga
Temora
Narrandera
Leeton
Griffith
Hillston
Hay
Albury
Broken Hill
Silver City
Wentworth
Mildura

VICTORIA

Echuca
Bendigo
Castlemaine
Ballarat
Maryborough
Ararat
Horsham
The Grampians
Hamilton
Portland
Mount Gambier
Geelong
MELBOURNE
Dandenong
Frankston
Sunshine
Williamstown
Warrnambool
Traralgon
Morwell
Sale
Bairnsdale
Lakes Entrance

SOUTH AUSTRALIA

ft   m
6000 2000
4500 1500
3000 1000
1200   400
 600   200
   0   0
2000 6000
4000 12 000

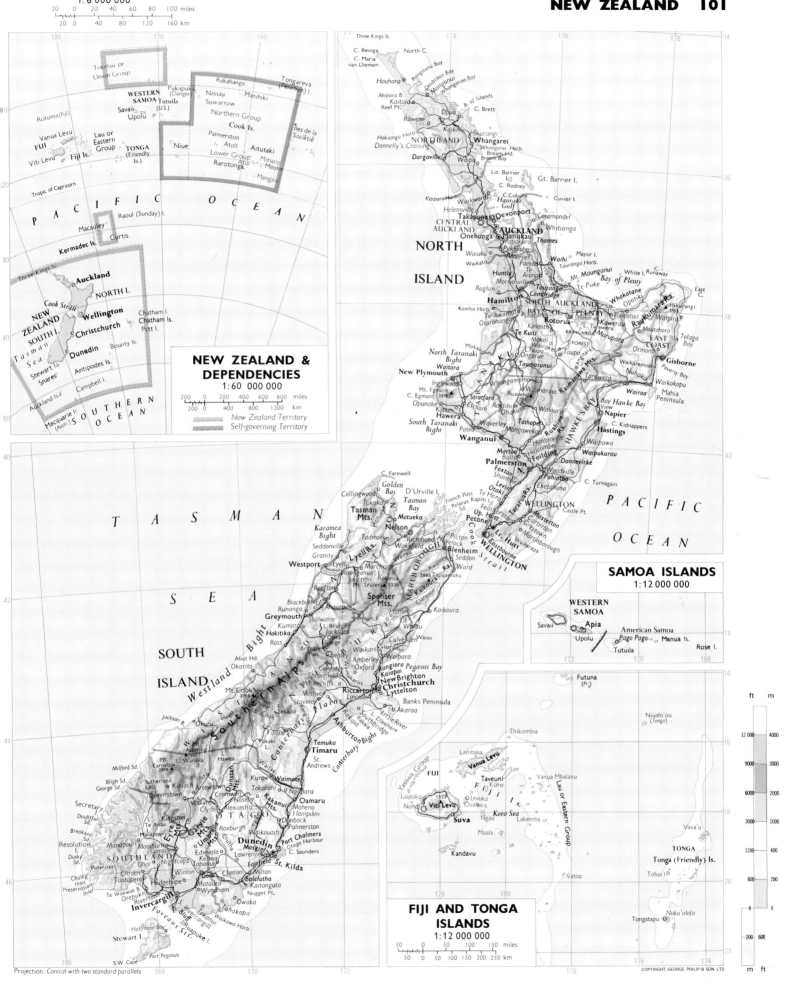

1:6 000 000

NEW ZEALAND &
DEPENDENCIES
1:60 000 000

New Zealand Territory
Self-governing Territory

SAMOA ISLANDS
1:12 000 000

FIJI AND TONGA
ISLANDS
1:12 000 000

Projection: Conical with two standard parallels

COPYRIGHT. GEORGE PHILIP & SON, LTD.

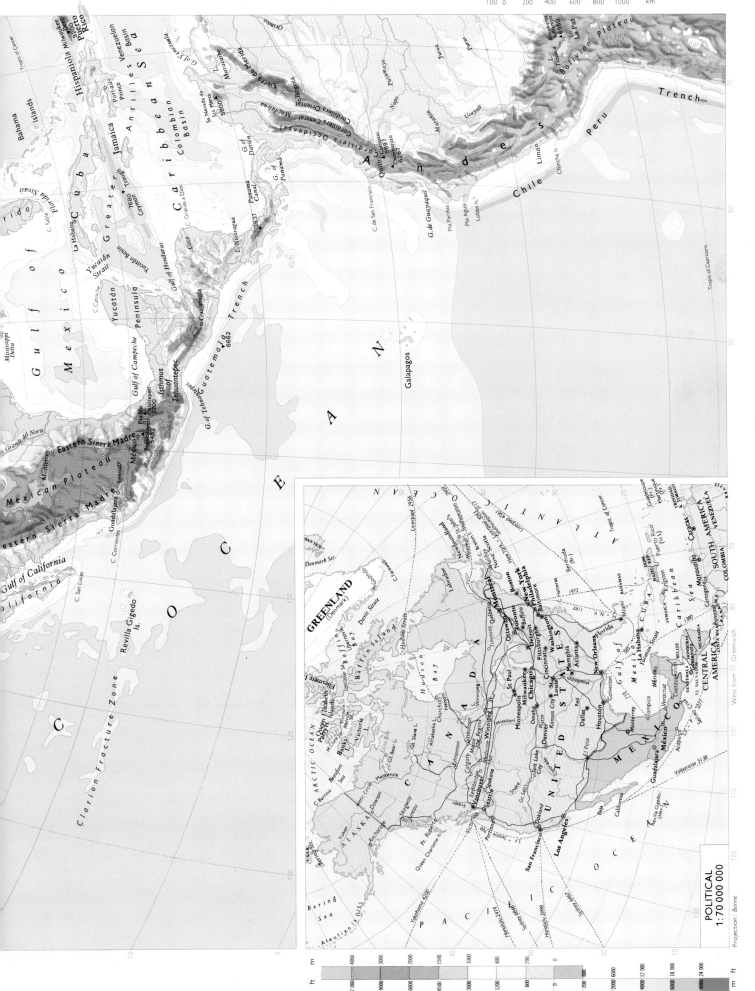

Projection: Bonne

ft   m

9000 3000

6000 2000

4500 1500

3000 1000

1200   400

600   200

0   0

200   600

2000   6000

m   ft

ALASKA
1 : 30 000 000

100 0   100 200 300 miles

100 0   100 200   400 km

West from Greenwich

GREENLAND

ATLANTIC

OCEAN

Baffin Bay

Davis Strait

BAFFIN ISLAND

Cumberland Peninsula

Cumberland Sd.

Hudson Strait

Frobisher Bay

Resolution I.

Foxe Basin

Foxe Channel

Southampton I.

Hudson Bay

Ungava Peninsula

Ungava Bay

PENINSULA

James Bay

COAST OF LABRADOR

NEWFOUNDLAND

QUEBEC

Gulf of St. Lawrence

St. John's

NEWFOUNDLAND

I. d'Anticosti

Cabot Str.

Cape Breton I.

ST-PIERRE et MIQUELON (Fr.)

Sydney

PR. EDWARD I.

Charlottetown

NEW BRUNSWICK

NOVA SCOTIA

Halifax

Dartmouth

MONTRÉAL

Québec

Ottawa

Saint John

Fredericton

MAINE

TORONTO

Lake Ontario

Lake Erie

Lake Huron

NEW YORK

Buffalo

BOSTON

MASS.

VERMONT

NEW HAMPSHIRE

Portland

DETROIT

Cleveland

Toledo

CHICAGO

NEW YORK

NEW JERSEY

PENNSYLVANIA

OHIO

INDIANA

N. W T E R R I T O R I E S

MANITOBA

H U D S O N   B A Y

North Belcher Is.
Baker's Dozen Is.
Kugong I.
Belcher Islands
Flaherty I.
Tukarak I.
Innetalling I.
Merry I.
Poste-de-la-Baleine

L. Minto
Nastapoka Is.
Nastapoka
L. Guillaume-Delisle
Petite Baleine
L. à l'Eau Claire
L. D'Iberville
Lac Bienville
Grand Baleine

Stupart
Knee L.
Edmund
Gods
Black Duck
Niskibi
Fort Severn
North Caribou
Braverstone
Beakin
Echoing
Severn
Winisk
Wabuk Pt.
C. Lookout
C. Henrietta Maria
Long I.
Pte. Louis-XIV
Burton
Roggan
Roggan River
Roggan L.
Kanaaupscow
Julian L.
Craven L.
L. Bérézuik
La Grande
Castor
Duncan
Sakami
Yasinski
Opinaca
Low L.
Eastmain
L. de la Corvette
Boyd
Frégate
L. de la Corvette
Lac Rossignol
Eastmain

Gods L.
Sharpe L.
Red Sucker L.
Sandy Lake
Stull L.
Sachigo L.
Favourable Lake
Ponask L.
Sachigo
Bearskin Lake
Finger L.
Sandy L.
Severn
Big Trout L.
Winisk
Attawapiskat
Shamattawa
Ekwan
Lakitusaki
Lake River
Ekwan Pt.
North Twin I.
South Twin I.
Akimiski I.
J A M E S B A Y
Weston I.
Fort Albany
Charlton
Trodely I.
Charlton I.
Eastmain
Fort Rupert (Rupert House)
Rupert B.
Nemiscau
Rupert
Mesgouez
Nottaway
L. Evans
L. Mistassini

MacDowell L. 396
North Caribou L.
Pipestone
Cat L.
Otoskwin
Central Patricia
Pickle Lake
Lansdowne House
Wunnummin
Mameigwess L.
Attawapiskat
Wapikopa L.
Winisk
Missisa
Kapiskau
Kinoje
North Twin I.
Weston I.
Hannah B.
Broadback
Nemiscau
Dana
L. Olga
Chibougamau
Waconichi
Opémisca 556

Committ Lake
Birch L.
Trout L.
Bowman
St. Joseph L.
Fort Hope
Eabamet
Atthameg
Albany
Ogoki
Fort Albany
Moose River
Moose Factory
Moosonee
Rupert B.
Nemiscau
Nottaway
Soscumica Matagami
Poncheville
L. au Goëland
L. Waswanipi
Chibougamau

O N T A R I O

Lac Seul
Savant Res.
Ghost River
Lookout
Sioux Lookout
Sturgeon
Collins
Armstrong
Ferland
Little Current
Kwataboahegan
Moose River
Hannah B.
Fort Albany
Q U E B E C
L. Olga
Waswanipi
Opémisca

Hudson
Minnitaki L.
Allanwater
Caribou L.
Auden
Kenogami
Nakina
Pagwa River
Calstock
Hearst
Mattice
Moonbeam
Fraserdale
Island Falls
Island Falls
Matagami
L. au Goëland
556

Ignace
White Otter
English River
Graham
Nipigon
Jellicoe
Long L.
Geraldton
Longlac
Niagaron
Hornepayne
Opasatika
Kapuskasing
Smooth Rock Falls
Cochrane
Norembega
Kesagami L.
Otter Rapids
Kenogami
L. Parent
Rés. Gouin
St-Fe

Marmion
Kawene
Koshabowic
Lac des Mille Lacs
Cameron Falls
Beardmore
Long L.
Hillsport
Oba
Kapuskasing
Smoky Falls
Groundhog
South Porcupine
Iroquois Falls
La Reine
La Sarre
Macamic
Amos
Barraute
L. Parent
Senneterre
Paradis
Rés. Cabonga

Atikokan
Lac la Croix
Quetico
Pickerel L.
Kakabeka Falls
Dog L.
Red Rock
Thunder Bay
St. Ignace
Slate Is.
Heron Bay
Marathon
Schreiber
Terrace Bay
Nipigon
Rossport
Esnagi
Franz
Missanabie
Foleyet
Fire River
Elsas
Peterbell
Kapuskasing
Matagami
Timmins
Schumacher
Abitibi
Kirkland Lake
Noranda
Rouyn
Cadillac
Val-d'Or
Mégiscane
Kempt
Vermilion

Northern Light
Birch L.
Grand Marais
Isle Royale
Copper Harbor
Manitou I.
LAKE SUPERIOR
Michipicoten
Michipicoten I.
Lake Superior Prov. Park
White River
Hawk Jct.
Wawa
Dalton
Chapleau
Horwood L.
Foleyet
Gogama
Ramsey
Sultan
Matachewan
Elk Lake
New Liskeard
Cobalt
Haileybury
Latchford
Temiscaming
Mattawa
Deux Rivières
L'Annonciation
Trois-Rivières

Duluth
Superior
Apostle Is.
Bayfield
Washburn
Ashland
Mellen
Ironwood
Hurley
Wakefield
Watersmeet
L'Anse
Baraga
Keweenaw B.
Houghton
Hancock
Laurium
Ontonagon
Ishpeming
Negaunee
Marquette
183
604
Caribou I. (Ontario)
648
Michipicoten
Batchawana
Montreal River
Thessalon
Blind River
Sproget
Elliot Lake
Sudbury
Copper Cliff
Espanola
Sturgeon Falls
North Bay
Nipissing
Callander
Mattawa
Klock
Kiosk
Brent
Pembroke
Petawawa
L. Kipawa
Fort Coulonge
Pontiac

Ashland
Republic
Iron River
Crystal Falls
Iron Mountain
Norway
Cooks
Manistique
Thompson
Gladstone
Escanaba
Rapid River
Nadeau
Stephenson
Gulliver
Naubinway
Epoufette
Brevort
Mackinaw City
St. Ignace
Cedarville
De Tour
Drummond I.
Cockburn I.
Meldrum
Thessalon
North Channel
Gore Bay
Manitoulin I.
Espanola
Little Current
Killarney
Byng Inlet
Britt
Key Harbour
Ottawa River
Rapides des Joachims
Chalk River
Rolphton
Pembroke
Renfrew
Arnprior
Carp
Ottawa
Hull

W I S C O N S I N
Wausau
Merrill
Antigo
Marinette
Menominee
Green Bay
Marshfield
Stevens Point
Wisconsin Rapids
Waupaca
Clintonville
Shawano
Oconto
Sturgeon Bay
Algoma
Kewaunee
Two Rivers
Manitowoc
Frankfort
Charlevoix
Petoskey
Boyne City
Gaylord
Mancelona
Traverse City
Alpena
Rogers City
Cheboygan
Mackinaw City
Tobermory
Wiarton
Owen Sound
Southampton
Port Elgin
Kincardine
Walkerton
Hanover
Durham
Collingwood
Meaford
Barrie
Orillia
Midland
Penetanguishene
Parry Sound
Georgian Bay
Huntsville
Bracebridge
Bancroft
Haliburton
Minden
Coe Hill
Bobcaygeon
Lindsay
Peterborough
Havelock
Kaladar
Tweed
Napanee
Kingston
Smiths Falls
Perth
556

Neenah
Menasha
Oshkosh
Appleton
Fond du Lac
Sheboygan
Manitowoc
Ludington
Manistee
Scottville
Baldwin
Reed City
Big Rapids
Clare
Harrisville
Au Sable Pt.
Tawas City
East Tawas
Standish
Bay City
Saginaw
Midland
Au Gres
Sable
Port Austin
Pte. aux Barques
Harbor Beach
Port Elgin
Goderich
Clinton
Wingham
Listowel
Harriston
Stratford
Kitchener
Guelph
Galt
Brampton
Cobourg
Port Hope
Trenton
Belleville
Wellington
Picton
Watertown
Carthage

Baraboo
Portage
Columbus
Beaver Dam
West Bend
Watertown
Milwaukee
Waukesha
Madison
Monroe
Beloit
Janesville
Oconomowoc
Whitewater
MILWAUKEE
Racine
Kenosha
Holland
Muskegon
Grand Haven
Grand Rapids
Ionia
Flint
Lansing
Owosso
Saginaw
Sanilac
Sandusky
Lapeer
Pontiac
Mount Clemens
Detroit
Dearborn
Windsor
Sarnia
London
Woodstock
Ingersoll
Brantford
Hamilton
TORONTO
Lake Ontario
St. Catharines
Niagara Falls
Welland
Buffalo
Lockport
Rochester
Fulton
Oswego
Rome
Utica
Syracuse
Auburn
Geneva
Penn Yan
Ithaca
Cortland
Binghamton
Elmira
Corning
Oneonta
Albany
Troy
Schenectady
Amsterdam
Gloversville
Saratoga Springs
Glens Falls
Rutland
Adirondack Mountains
Ticonderoga
Tupper Lake
Saranac Lake
Lake Placid
Plattsburg
Malone
Massena
Cornwall
Brockville
Ogdensburg
Potsdam
Canton
Gananoque
Napanee
Morrisburg
Prescott
MONTREAL
Valleyfield
Salaberry-de-Valleyfield
Lachine
Joliette
L'Assomption
Trois-Rivières
960

Madison
Rockford
Freeport
Dixon
Rochelle
Elgin
Aurora
Joliet
CHICAGO
Cicero
Evanston
Waukegan
Gary
East Chicago
Hammond
Michigan City
South Bend
Elkhart
Niles
Benton Harbor
St. Joseph
Kalamazoo
Battle Creek
Marshall
Albion
Jackson
Ann Arbor
Ypsilanti
Monroe
Toledo
Adrian
Hillsdale
Coldwater
Three Rivers
Sturgis
Mishawaka
Kendallville
Defiance
Napoleon
Bryan
Fremont
Sandusky
Lorain
Euclid
CLEVELAND
Lakewood
Ashtabula
Painesville
Conneaut
Erie
Dunkirk
Fredonia
Jamestown
Warren
Bradford
Olean
Salamanca
Wellsville
Hornell
Bath
Dansville
Geneseo
Batavia
Lake Erie
Leamington
Point Pelee
174

I N D I A N A   O H I O   P E N N S Y L V A N I A

I L L I N O I S

ft m
4500 1500
3000 1000
1200 400
600 200
0 0
200 600
2000 6000
4000 12 000
m ft

Lambert's Equivalent Azimuthal

COAST OF

NEW FOUNDLAND

LABRADOR

QUEBEC

Smallwood Reservoir

Churchill Falls

Labrador City

Schefferville

Goose Bay   Happy Valley

North-West River   Goose

Mealy Mts.   1128

L. Melville

Str. of Belle Isle   Belle I.

St. Anthony

Long Range Mts.

NEWFOUNDLAND

Gander

Corner Brook

Grand Falls

Deer Lake

Bay of Islands

St. John's

Avalon Peninsula

Cabot Strait

GULF OF ST. LAWRENCE

Î. d'Anticosti

Jupiter

Sept-Îles

Port-Cartier

Baie-Comeau

Gaspé

Pén. de Gaspé

Mts. Chic-Chocs

Matane

Rimouski

Rivière-du-Loup

St. Lawrence

Chicoutimi

Saguenay

NEW BRUNSWICK

Fredericton

Moncton

Saint John

Edmundston

Campbellton

Bathurst

PRINCE EDWARD ISLAND

Charlottetown

Summerside

NOVA SCOTIA

Halifax

Dartmouth

Truro

New Glasgow

Sydney

Glace Bay

Cape Breton Island

Louisbourg

Yarmouth

Lunenburg

Bridgewater

Liverpool

Shelburne

Digby

MAINE

Bangor

Augusta

Waterville

Portland

Lewiston

Auburn

BOSTON

Manchester

Nashua

Lowell

Brockton

Portsmouth

Dover

Sable I. (Nova Scotia)

SAINT-PIERRE ET MIQUELON (Fr.)

Miquelon

St. Pierre

Langlade

ATLANTIC

OCEAN

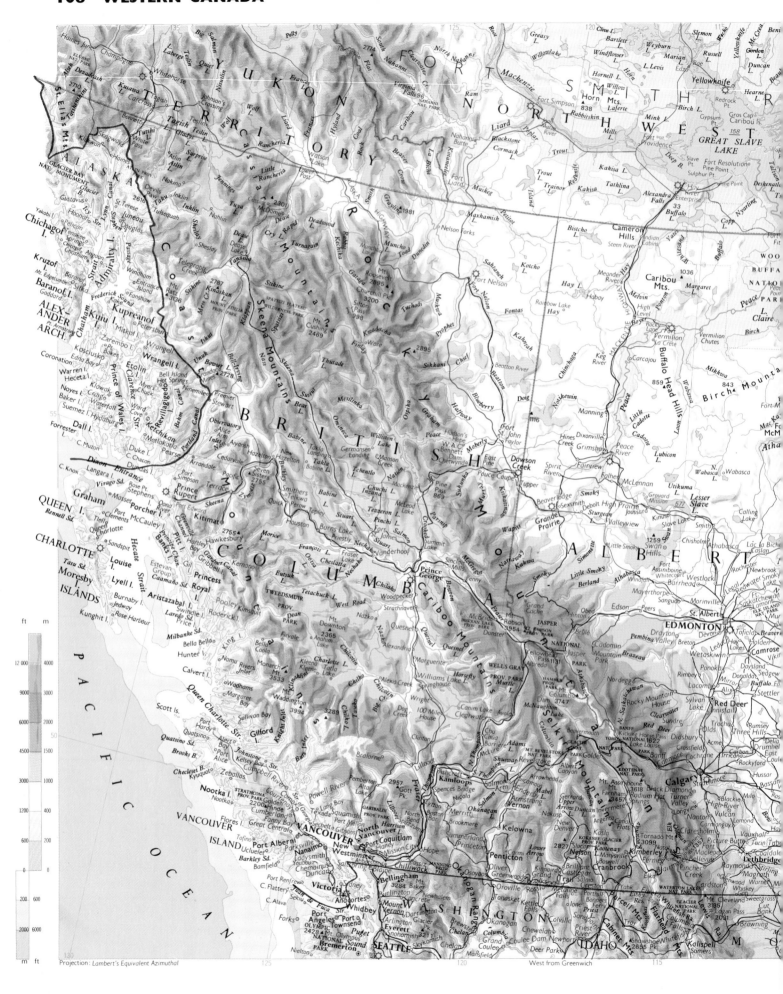

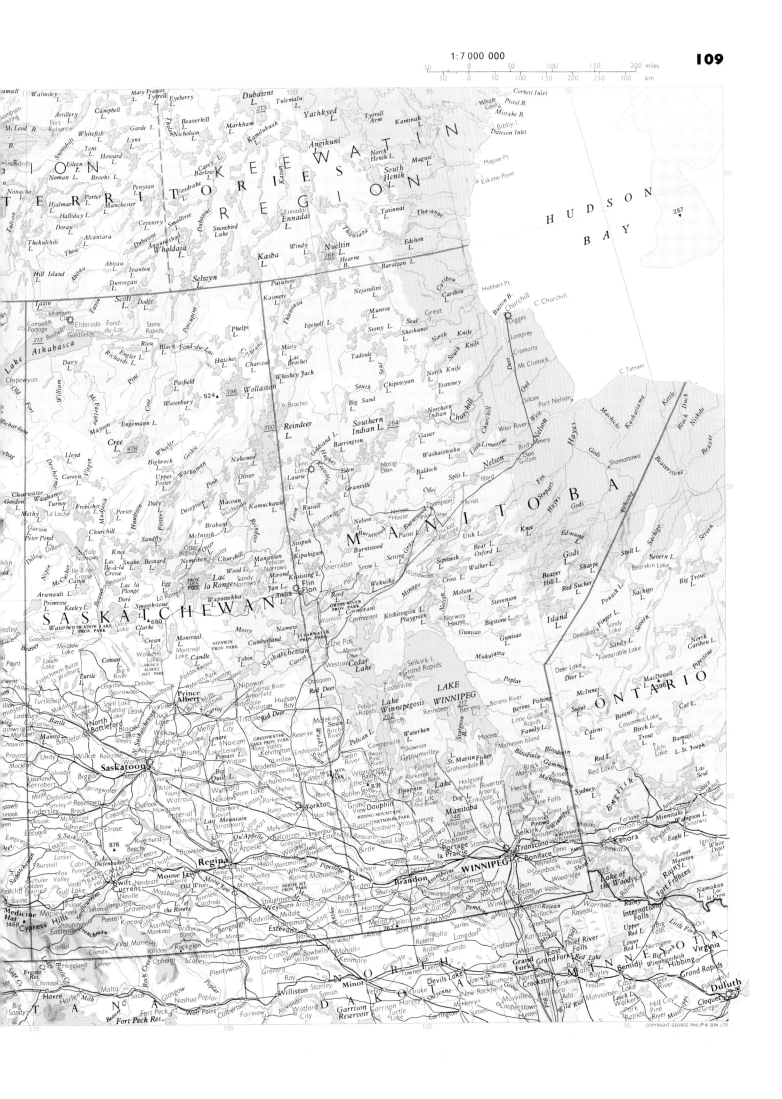

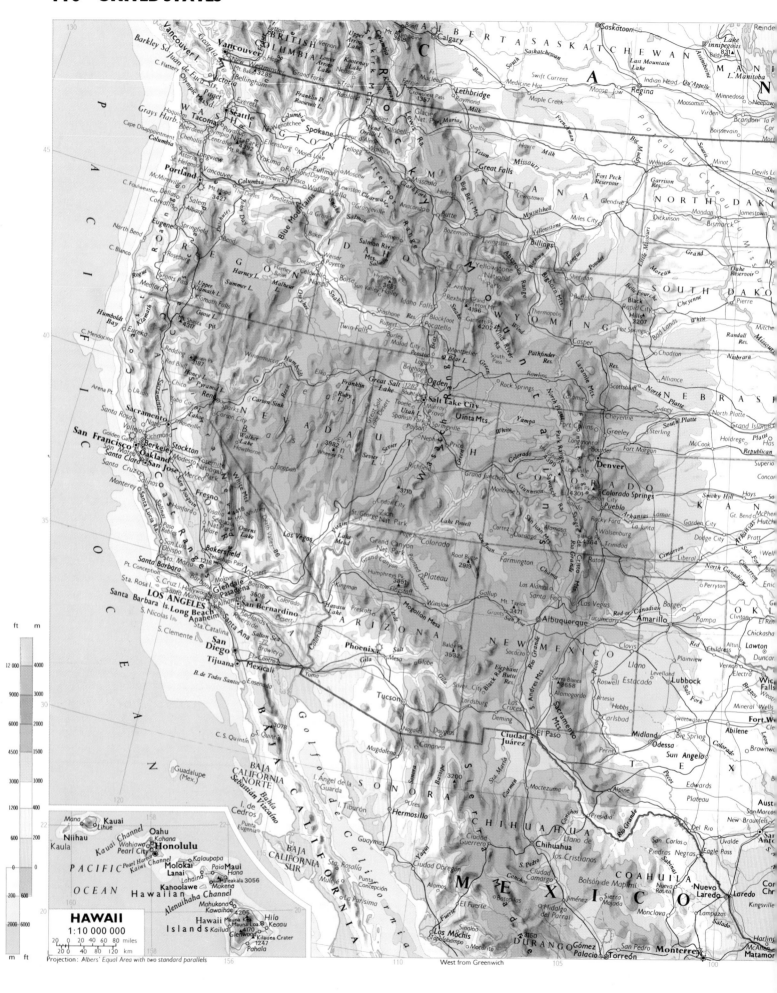

HAWAII
1:10 000 000

Projection: Albers' Equal Area with two standard parallels

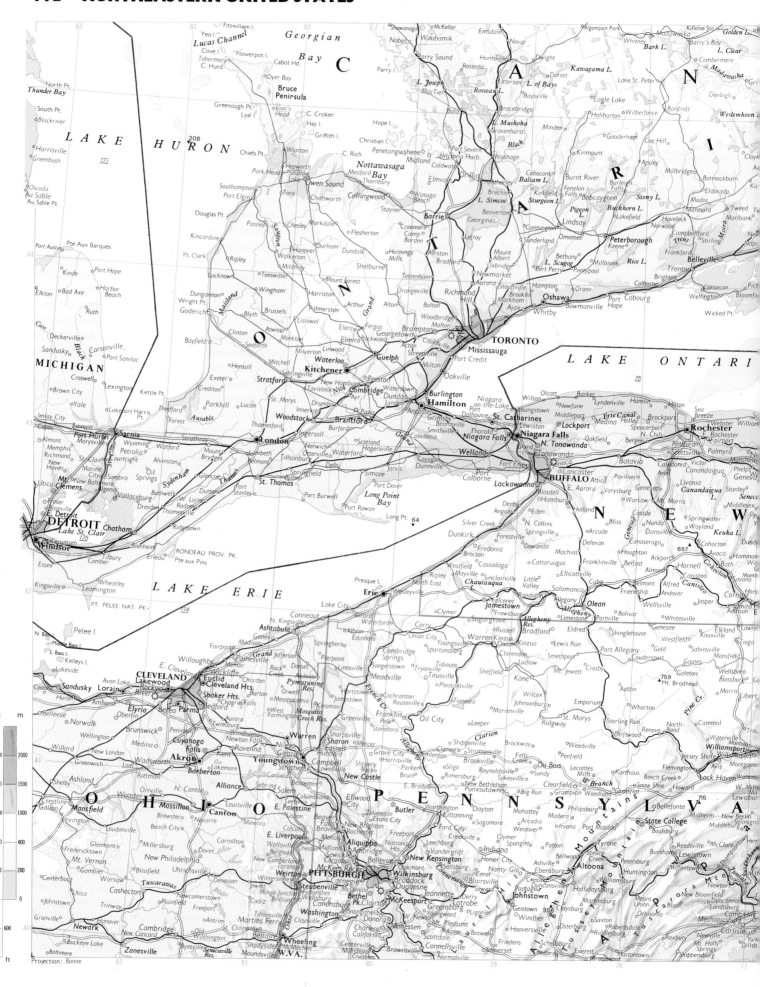

1:2 500 000

ATLANTIC OCEAN

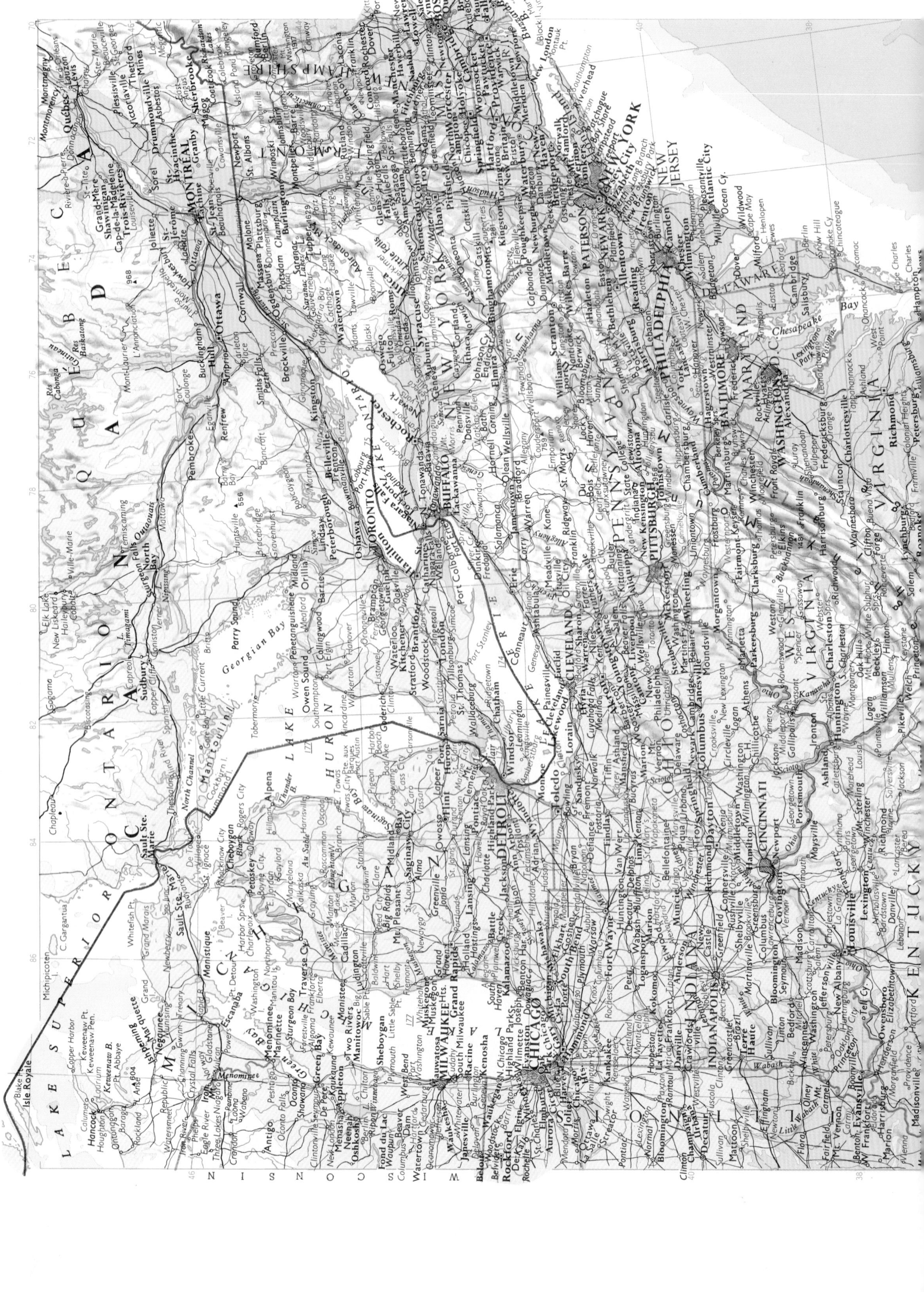
Q U É B E C
O N T A R I O
M I C H I G A N
W I S C O N S I N
O H I O
I N D I A N A
P E N N S Y L V A N I A
N E W Y O R K
W E S T V I R G I N I A
V I R G I N I A
K E N T U C K Y
M A R Y L A N D
D E L A W A R E
NEW JERSEY
L A K E S U P E R I O R
L A K E H U R O N
L A K E E R I E
L A K E O N T A R I O
Georgian Bay
Québec
MONTREAL
Ottawa
TORONTO
Hamilton
BUFFALO
Rochester
Syracuse
Albany
BOSTON
NEW YORK
PHILADELPHIA
BALTIMORE
WASHINGTON
PITTSBURGH
CLEVELAND
DETROIT
Toledo
Columbus
Dayton
CINCINNATI
Louisville
INDIANAPOLIS
CHICAGO
MILWAUKEE
Sault Ste. Marie
Lansing
Grand Rapids
Richmond
Charleston

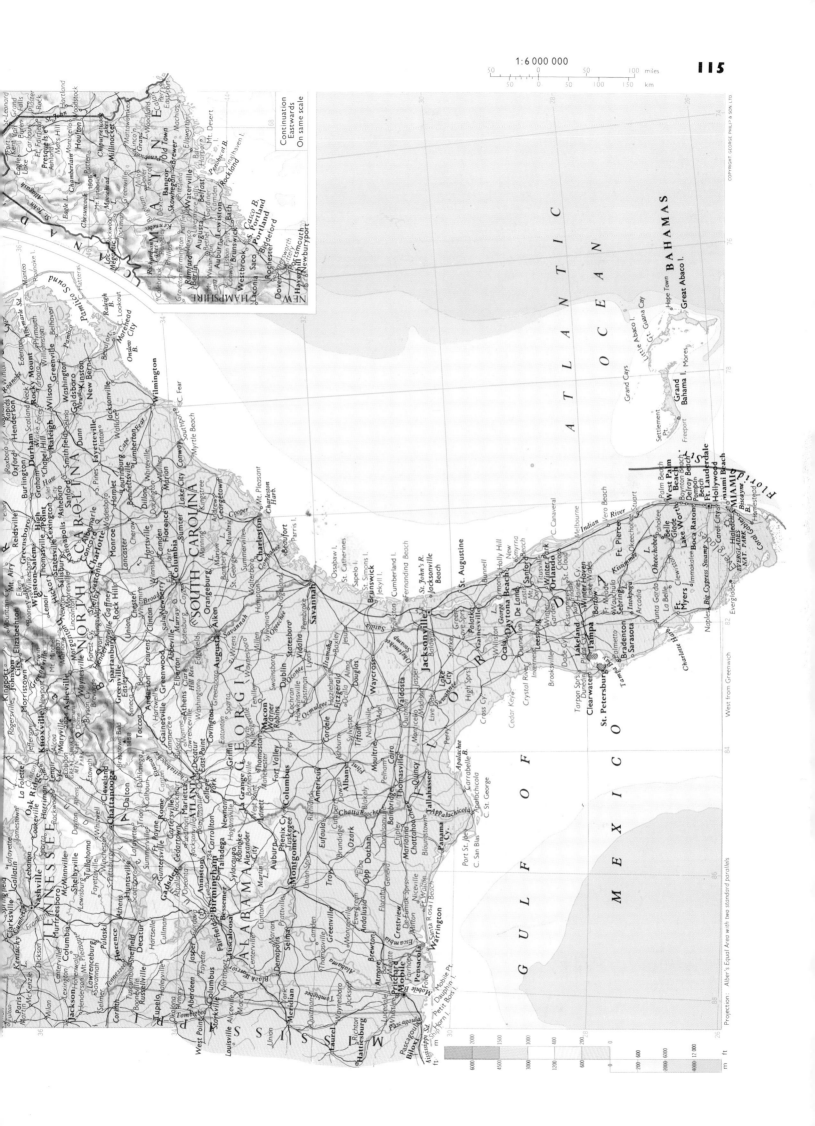

1:6 000 000

50   0   50   100 miles

50   0   50   100   150   km

Continuation
Eastwards
On same scale

COPYRIGHT GEORGE PHILIP & SON, LTD

MAINE

NEW HAMPSHIRE

Bangor
Skowhegan Old Town
Waterville Brewer
Augusta Belfast
Lewiston Camden
Auburn Gardiner
Brunswick Rockland
Bath
Portland
Biddeford

Berlin
Rumford Farmington
Groveton
Lisbon Falls
Concord Laconia Dover
Rochester Portsmouth
Haverhill Newburyport

ATLANTIC

OCEAN

BAHAMAS

Hope Town
Great Abaco I.

Little Abaco I.
Gt. Guana Cay

Grand Cays

Settlement Pt.
Grand
Bahama I. Mores.
Freeport

NORTH CAROLINA

Wilmington
Raleigh
Durham
Greensboro
Winston-Salem
High Point
Charlotte
Greenville
Goldsboro
New Bern
Kinston

SOUTH CAROLINA

Columbia
Charleston
Florence
Sumter
Orangeburg
Georgetown

GEORGIA

Savannah
Augusta
Macon
Columbus
Atlanta
Albany
Valdosta
Brunswick

ALABAMA

Montgomery
Birmingham
Mobile
Tuscaloosa
Selma
Dothan

TENNESSEE

Nashville
Chattanooga
Knoxville

FLORIDA

Jacksonville
St. Augustine
Daytona Beach
Orlando
Tampa
St. Petersburg
Clearwater
Sarasota
Ft. Myers
Miami
Ft. Lauderdale
Hollywood
West Palm Beach
Palm Beach
Boca Raton
Coral Gables
Homestead
Tallahassee
Pensacola
Panama Cy.

GULF OF MEXICO

West from Greenwich

Projection: Alber's Equal Area with two standard parallels

ft   m
6000 2000
4500 1500
3000 1000
1200   400
600   200
0   0
200
2000 600
6000 2000
12 000 4000

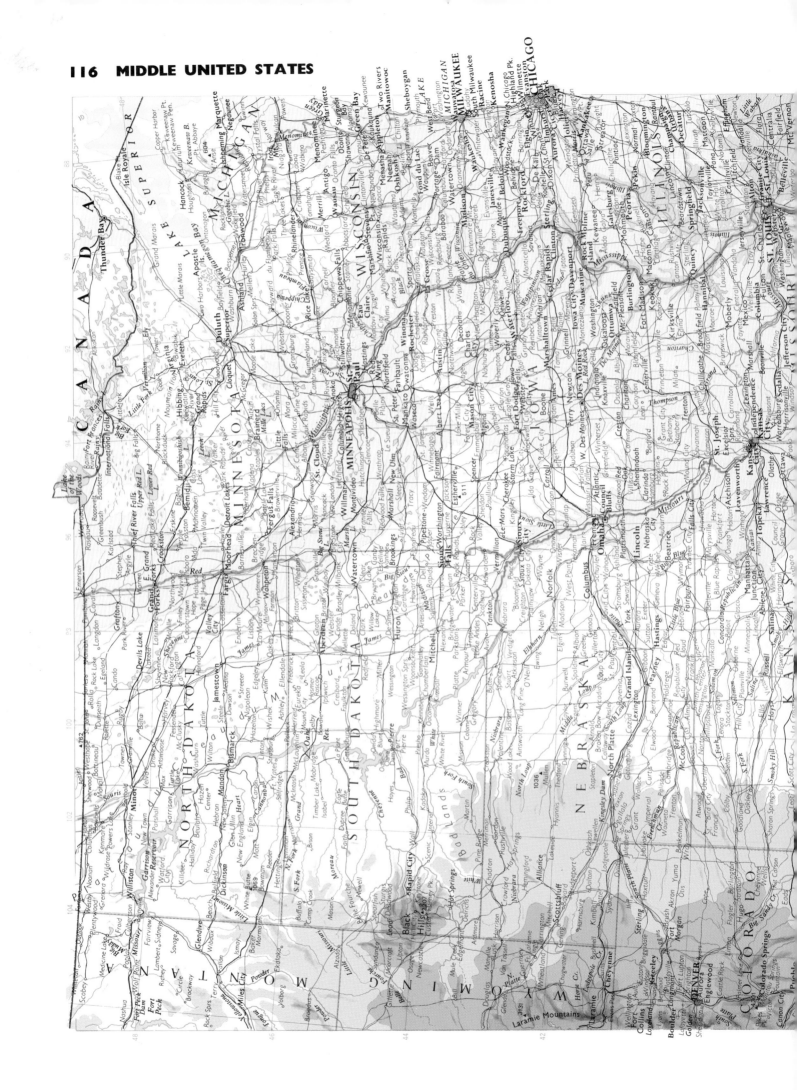

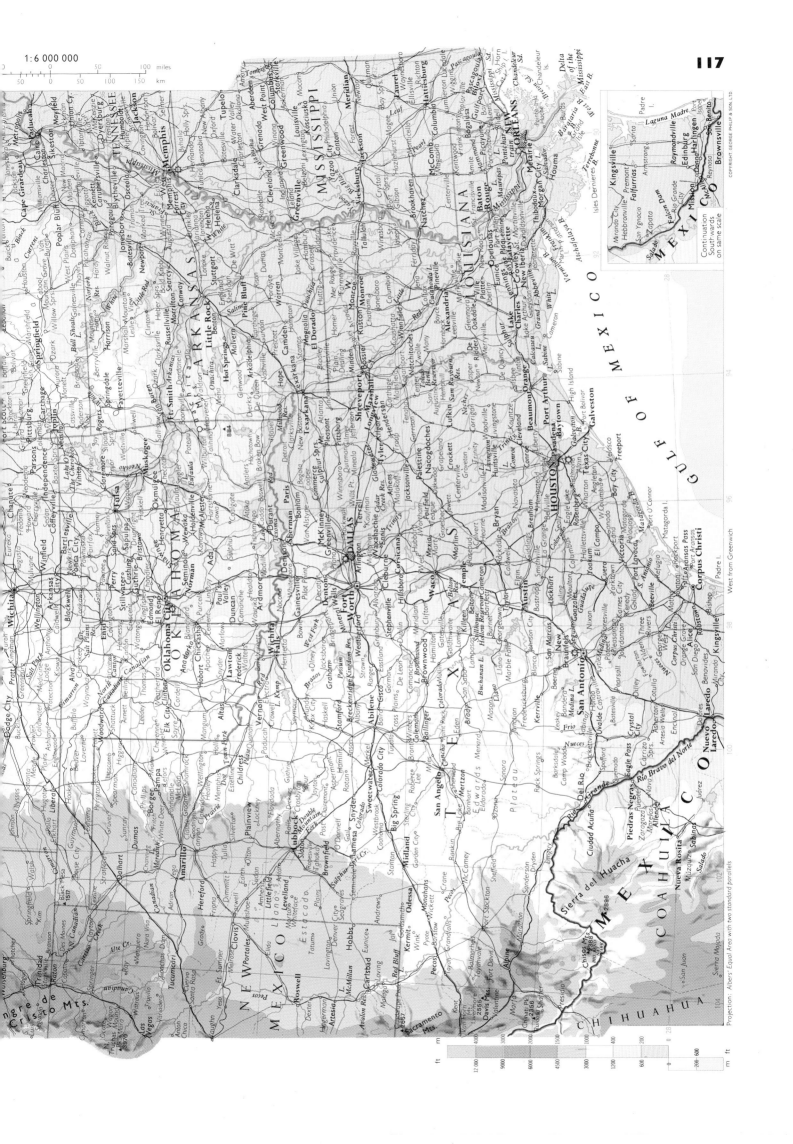

1:6 000 000

50   0   50   100 miles

50   0   50   100   150 km

COPYRIGHT GEORGE PHILIP & SON, LTD.

Continuation
South-wards
on same scale

Projection: Albers' Equal Area with two standard parallels

West from Greenwich

1:6 000 000

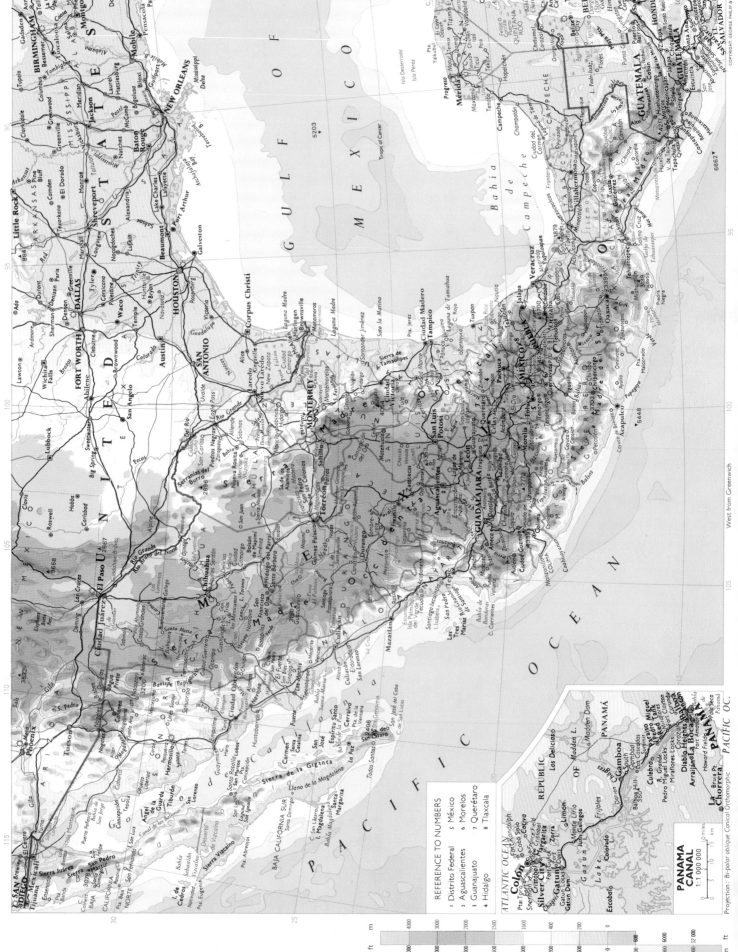

1:12 000 000

REFERENCE TO NUMBERS

1 Distrito Federal   5 México
2 Aguascalientes   6 Morelos
3 Guanajuato   7 Querétaro
4 Hidalgo   8 Tlaxcala

PANAMA CANAL
1:1 000 000

Projection: Bi-polar oblique Conical Orthomorphic
COPYRIGHT GEORGE PHILIP & SON, Ltd.

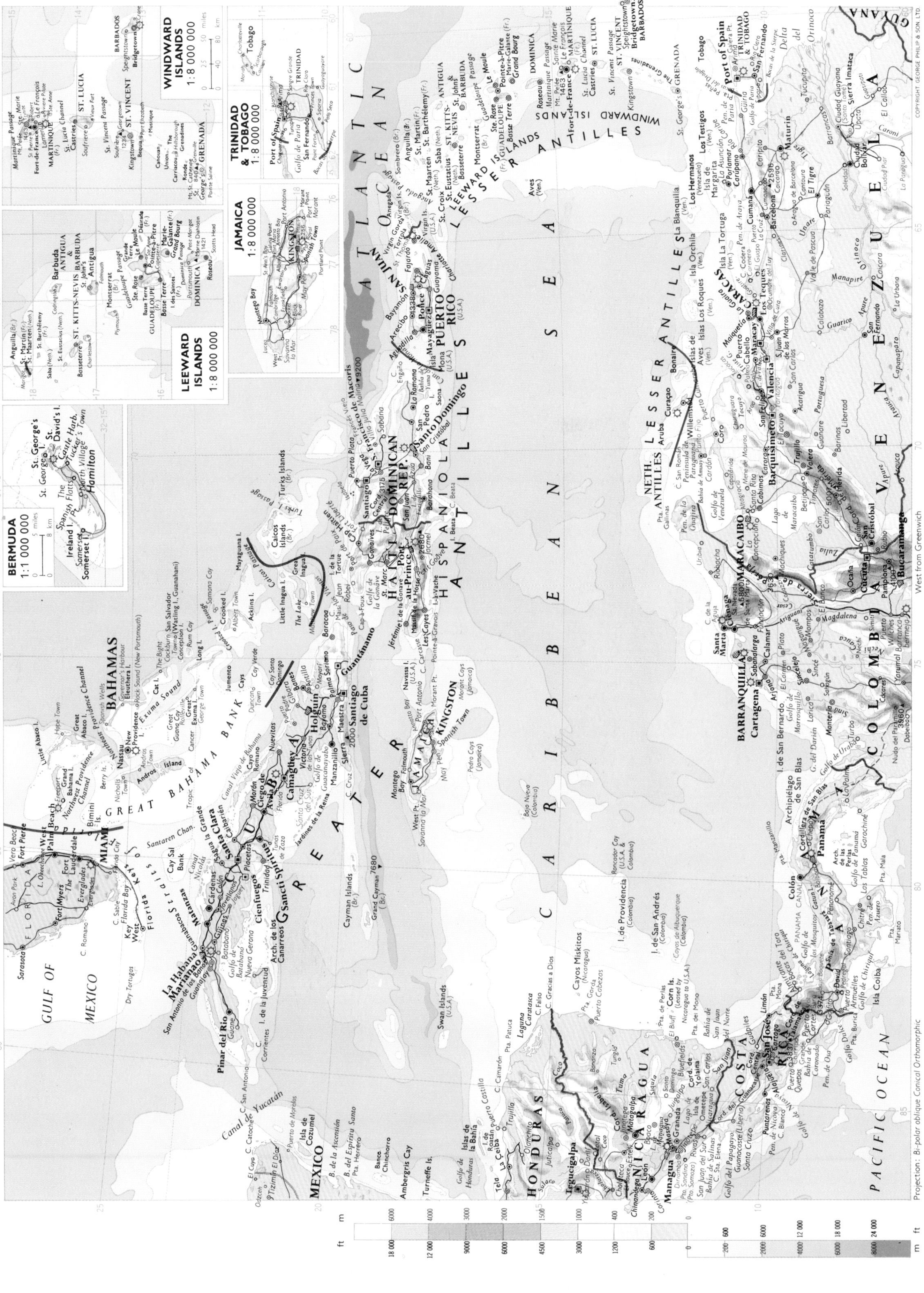

1:12 000 000

100   0   100   200 miles
100   0   100   200   300 km

WINDWARD ISLANDS
1:8 000 000

TRINIDAD & TOBAGO
1:8 000 000

JAMAICA
1:8 000 000

LEEWARD ISLANDS
1:8 000 000

BERMUDA
1:1 000 000

ATLANTIC OCEAN

CARIBBEAN SEA

GULF OF MEXICO

PACIFIC OCEAN

GREATER ANTILLES

LESSER ANTILLES

WINDWARD ISLANDS

LEEWARD ISLANDS

NETH. ANTILLES

HISPANIOLA

GREAT BAHAMA BANK

BAHAMAS

CUBA

JAMAICA

HAITI

DOMINICAN REP.

PUERTO RICO (U.S.A.)

FLORIDA

MEXICO

HONDURAS

NICARAGUA

COSTA RICA

PANAMA

COLOMBIA

VENEZUELA

GUIANA

West from Greenwich

Projection: Bi-polar oblique Conical Orthomorphic

COPYRIGHT GEORGE PHILIP & SON LTD.

m / ft
6000 4000 3000 2000 1500 1000 400 200 0
18000 12000 9000 6000 4500 3000 1200 600 0

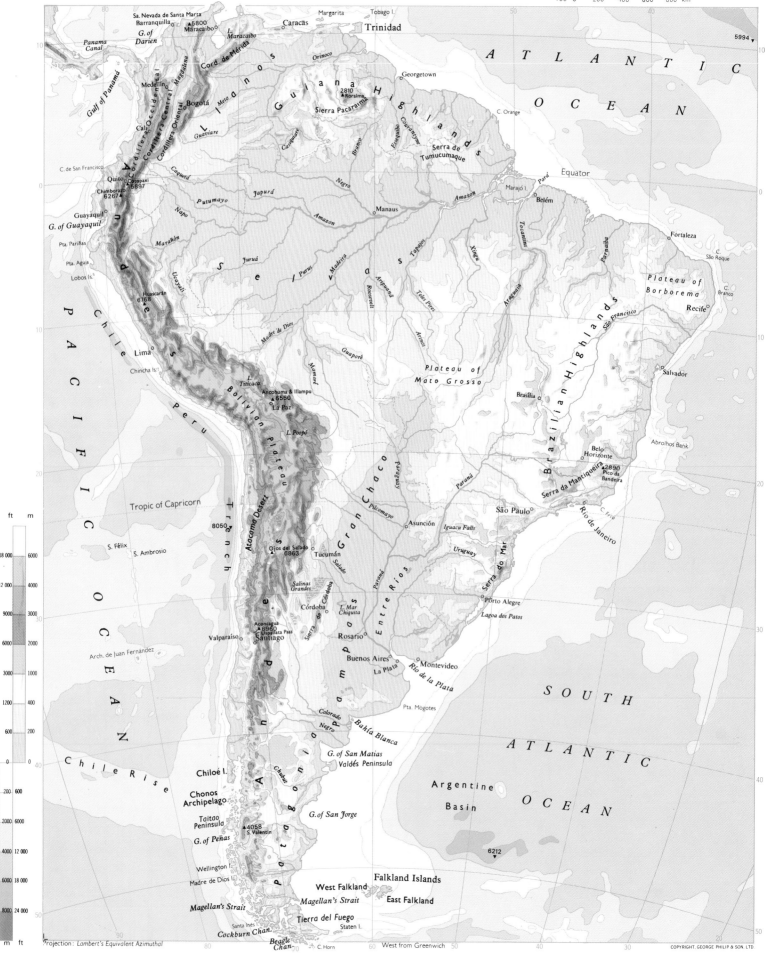

1:30 000 000

100 0 100 200 300 400 500 miles
100 0 200 400 600 800 km

5994 ▾

Panama Canal

Sa. Nevada de Santa Marta
Barranquilla
▲5800
Maracaibo
G. of Darien
L. Maracaibo
Margarita
Tobago I.
Caracas
Trinidad

A T L A N T I C

Orinoco
Georgetown

O C E A N

Cord. de Mérida
Medellín
Bogotá
Cali

Guiana Highlands

2810
▲Roraima

C. Orange

Sierra Pacaraima

Serra de Tumucumaque

Guaviare

C. de San Francisco

Equator

Quito Cotopaxi
Chimborazo ▲5897
6267

Caquetá
Putumayo
Japurá
Negro

Amazon

Manaus

Marajó I.
Pará
Belém

Fortaleza

C. de San Roque

G. of Guayaquil
Guayaquil

Napo
Marañón

S
Juruá
Purus

Amazon
Madeira
Tapajós
Xingu
Tocantins

Parnaíba

Plateau of Borborema

Pta. Pariñas
Pta. Aguja
Lobos Is.

Ucayali

e
l
v
a
s

Roosevelt
Aripuanã
Teles Pires
Arinos

Recife

Branco

Huascarán
6768▲

Madre de Dios
Guaporé
Mamoré

Plateau of Mato Grosso

São Francisco

Salvador

Lima

A
n
d
e
s

Chincha Is.

L. Titicaca
Ancohuma & Illampu
▲6550
La Paz

Bolivian Plateau

L. Poopó

Brasília

Brazilian Highlands

Abrolhos Bank

P
A
C
I
F
I
C

Chile

Peru

Tropic of Capricorn

8050

Ojos del Salado
6863

Gran Chaco

Paraná
Pilcomayo

Belo Horizonte
▲2890
Pico da Bandeira
Serra da Mantiqueira

S. Félix
S. Ambrosio

Atacama Desert

Tucumán
Salado

Asunción
Iguaçu Falls

São Paulo

C. Frio

Rio de Janeiro

O
C
E
A
N

Trench

Salinas Grandes
Sierra de Córdoba

Córdoba
L. Mar Chiquita

Uruguay

Serra do Mar

Pôrto Alegre
Lagoa dos Patos

Arch. de Juan Fernández

Aconcagua
▲6960
Uspallata Pass
Santiago

Rosario

Entre Ríos

Valparaíso

P
a
m
p
a
s

Buenos Aires
La Plata

Montevideo
Río de la Plata

S O U T H

ft m

18 000   6000
12 000   4000
9000   3000
6000   2000
3000   1000
1200   400
600   200
0   0
200   600
2000   6000
4000   12 000
6000   18 000
8000   24 000

m ft

Colorado
Negro

Bahía Blanca

Pta. Mógotes

A T L A N T I C

Chiloé I.

G. of San Matias
Valdés Peninsula

Chonos Archipelago

Chubut

A
n
d
e
s

P
a
t
a
g
o
n
i
a

Argentine Basin

O C E A N

Taitao Peninsula
▲4058
S. Valentin

G. of San Jorge

6212
▾

Wellington I.
Madre de Dios I.

Chile Rise

West Falkland

Falkland Islands

East Falkland

Magellan's Strait

Magellan's Strait

Santa Inés I.

Tierra del Fuego

Staten I.

Cockburn Chan.

Projection: *Lambert's Equivalent Azimuthal*

Beagle Chan.

C. Horn

West from Greenwich

COPYRIGHT. GEORGE PHILIP & SON. LTD.

1:30 000 000

Projection: Lambert's Equivalent Azimuthal

West from Greenwich

COPYRIGHT. GEORGE PHILIP & SON. LTD.

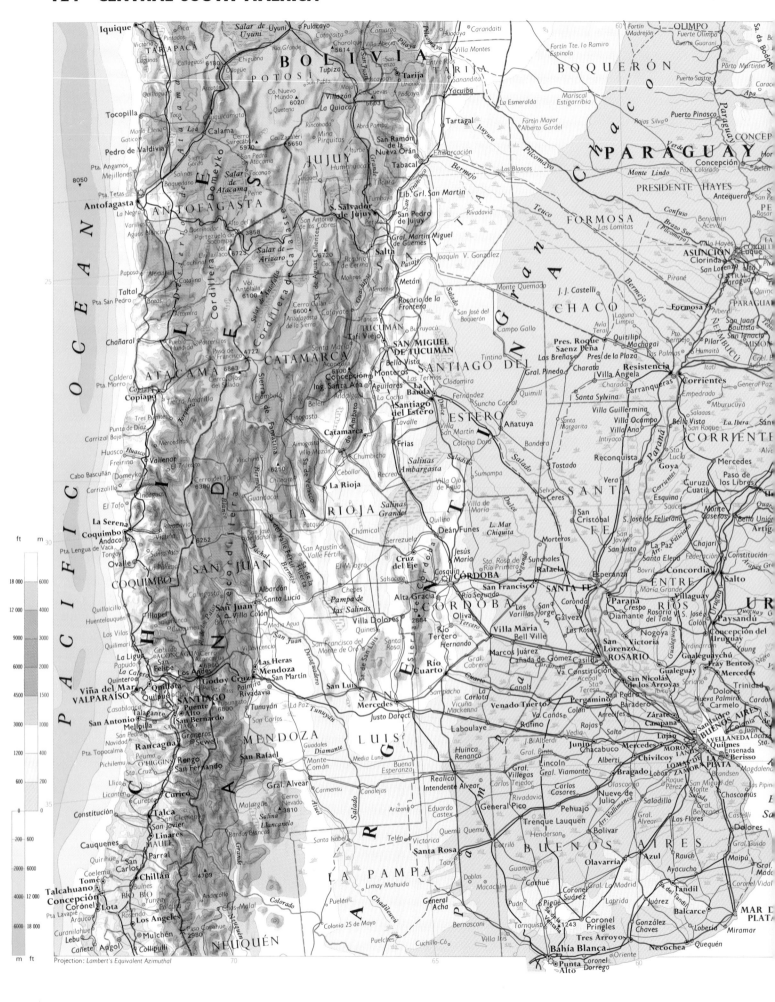

Projection: Lambert's Equivalent Azimuthal

ATLANTIC

OCEAN

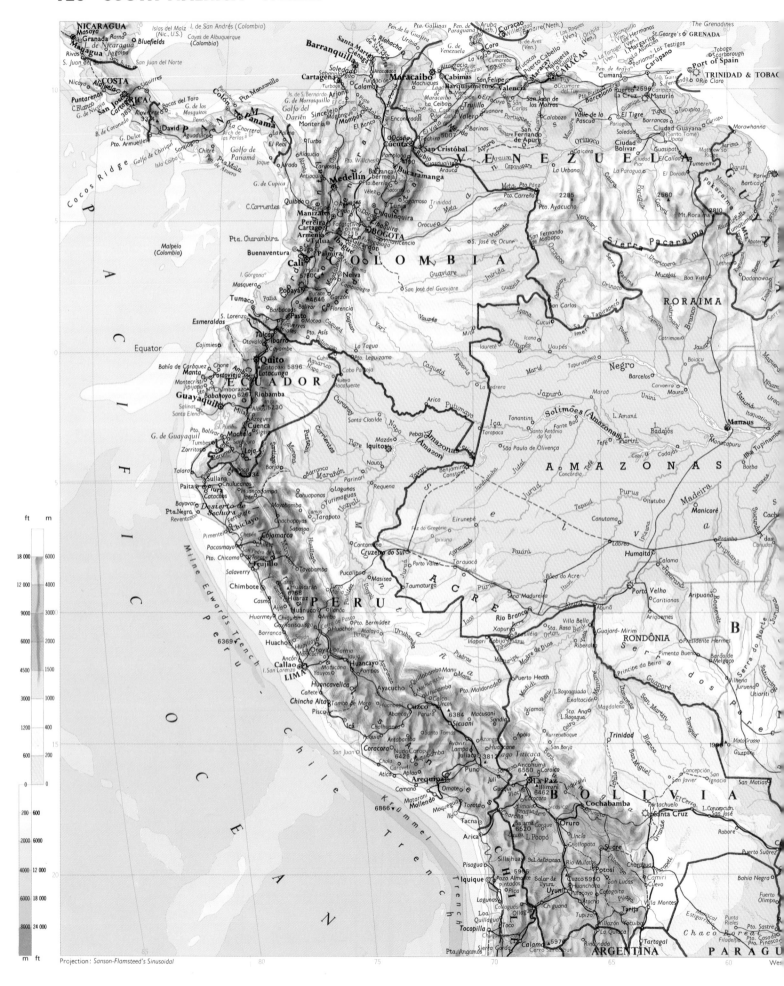

Projection: Sanson-Flamsteed's Sinusoidal

1:16 000 000

100   0   100   200   300   400   500 miles
100 0   100 200 300 400 500 600 700 800 km

A T L A N T I C

Paramaribo
Nieuw Amsterdam
Moengo Mana
Albina Irocoubo
St. Laurent Sinnomary
Kaw Cayenne
Approuague
C. Orange
FR.
St. Georges
GUIANA Oiapoque
NAM
Camopi
Oiapoque

Serra Tumucumaque
Amapá
Araguari
Meriruma C. do Norte

AMAPÁ

Estuario do
Rio Amazonas
Ilha Caviana
Macapá
Ilha Mexiana

Equator

A T L A N T I C   O C E A N

Óbidos
Santarém Amazonas (Amazon)
Belterra
Brasília Legal Prainha Almeirim
Altamira

Ilha de Maracá
Ilha de Marajó

B. de São Marcos
São Luís (Maranhão)
Barreirinhas
Luís Correia
Parnaíba Comocim
Granja
Fortaleza (Ceará)
Rocas
Fernando de Noronha
(Braz.)

PARÁ
MARANHÃO
CEARÁ
RIO GRANDE
DO NORTE Natal
C. de São Roque

PIAUÍ
PERNAMBUCO
RECIFE
(Pernambuco)

B R A Z I L

GOIÁS
BAHIA
Feira de
Santana
Salvador (Bahia)

GROSSO
Planalto do

Mato Grosso

DIST.
FED. Brasília
Anápolis

Goiânia

MINAS GERAIS

Belo Horizonte

Vitória

SÃO
PAULO

RIO DE JANEIRO

COPYRIGHT. GEORGE PHILIP & SON, LTD

1:16 000 000

100 50 0 100 200 300 miles
100 0 100 200 300 400 km

Projection: Sanson-Flamsteed's Sinusoidal

INDEX *

The number printed in bold type against each entry indicates the map page where the feature can be found. This is followed by its geographical coordinates. The first coordinate indicates latitude, i.e. distance north or south of the Equator. The second coordinate indicates longitude, i.e. distance east or west of the meridian of Greenwich in England (shown as 0° longitude). Both latitude and longitude are measured in degrees and minutes (with 60 minutes in a degree), and appear on the map as horizontal and vertical gridlines respectively. Thus the entry for Paris in France reads.

Paris, France   **19**   48 50 N   2 20 E

This entry indicates that Paris is on page 19, at latitude 48 degrees 50 minutes north (approximately five-sixths of the distance between horizontal gridlines 48 and 49, marked on either side of the page) and at longitude 2 degrees 20 minutes east (approximately one-third of the distance between vertical gridlines 2 and 3, marked at top and bottom of the page). Paris can be found where lines extended from these two points cross on the page. The geographical coordinates are sometimes only approximate but are close enough for the place to be located. Rivers have been indexed to their mouth or confluence.

An open square □ signifies that the name refers to an administrative subdivision of a country while a solid square ■ follows the name of a country. An arrow ↷ follows the name of a river.

The alphabetical order of names composed of two or more words is governed primarily by the first word and then by the second. This rule applies even if the second word is a description or its abbreviation, R.,L.,I. for example. Names composed of a proper name (Gibraltar) and a description (Strait of) are positioned alphabetically by the proper name. If the same place name occurs twice or more times in the index and all are in the same country, each is followed by the name of the administrative subdivision in which it is located. The names are placed in the alphabetical order of the subdivisions. If the same place name occurs twice or more in the index and the places are in different countries they will be followed by their country names, the latter governing the alphabetical order. In a mixture of these situations the primary order is fixed by the alphabetical sequence of the countries and the secondary order by that of the country subdivisions.

* *Please refer to the table at the end of the index for the recent place name changes in India, Iran, Mozambique and Zimbabwe.*

Abbreviations used in the index:

A. R.–Autonomous Region
A. S. S. R.–Autonomous Soviet Socialist Republic
Afghan.–Afghanistan
Afr.–Africa
Ala.–Alabama
Alas.–Alaska
Alg.–Algeria
Alta.–Alberta
Amer.–America
And. P.–Andhra Pradesh
Arch.–Archipelago
Argent.–Argentina
Ariz.–Arizona
Ark.–Arkansas
Atl. Oc. – Atlantic Ocean
Austral. – Australia
B. – Baie, Bahía, Bay, Bucht, Bugt
B.A. – Buenos Aires
B.C. – British Columbia
Bangla. – Bangladesh
Barr. – Barrage
Bay. – Bayern
Belg. – Belgium
Berks. – Berkshire
Bol. – Bolshoi
Boliv. – Bolivia
Bots. – Botswana
Br. – British
Bri. – Bridge
Bt. – Bight
Bucks. – Buckinghamshire
Bulg. – Bulgaria
C. – Cabo, Cap, Cape, Coast
C. Prov. – Cape Province
Calif. – California
Camb. – Cambodia
Cambs. – Cambridgeshire
Can. – Canada
Cent. – Central
Chan. – Channel
Co. – Country
Colomb. – Colombia
Colo. – Colorado
Conn. – Connecticut
Cord. – Cordillera
Cr. – Creek
Cumb. – Cumbria
Czech. – Czechoslovakia
D.C. – District of Columbia
Del. – Delaware
Dep. – Dependency
Derby. – Derbyshire
Des. – Desert
Dist. – District
Dj. – Djebel
Dumf. & Gall. – Dumfries and Galloway
E. – East
Eng. – England
Fed. – Federal, Federation
Fla. – Florida
For. – Forest
Fr. – France, French
Fs. – Falls
Ft. – Fort

G. – Golfe, Golfo, Gulf, Guba
Ga. – Georgia
Ger. – Germany
Glam. – Glamorgan
Glos. – Gloucestershire
Gr. – Grande, Great, Greater, Group
H.K. – Hong Kong
H.P. – Himachal Pradesh
Hants. – Hampshire
Harb. – Harbor, Harbour
Hd. – Head
Here. & Worcs. – Hereford and Worcester
Herts. – Hertfordshire
Hts. – Heights
Hung. – Hungary
I.o.M. – Isle of Man
I.(s). – Île, Ilha, Insel, Isla, Island, Isle
Id. – Idaho
Ill. – Illinois
Ind. – Indiana
Ind. Oc. – Indian Ocean
Indon. – Indonesia
J. – Jabal, Jabel, Jazira
Junc. – Junction
K. – Kap, Kapp
K. – Kuala
Kal. – Kalmyk A.S.S.R.
Kans. – Kansas
Kep. – Kepulauan
Ky. – Kentucky
L. – Lac, Lacul, Lago, Lagoa, Lake, Limni, Loch, Lough
La. – Lousiana
Lancs. – Lancashire
Leb. – Lebanon
Leics. – Leicestershire
Lim. – Limerick
Lincs. – Lincolnshire
Lit. – Little
Lr. – Lower
Mad. P. – Madhya Pradesh
Madag. – Madagascar
Malay. – Malaysia
Man. – Manitoba
Manch. – Manchester
Maran. – Maranhão
Mass. – Massachusetts
Md. – Maryland
Me. – Maine
Mend. – Mendoza
Mér. – Méridionale
Mich. – Michigan
Mid. – Middle
Minn. – Minnesota
Miss. – Mississippi
Mo. – Missouri
Mong. – Mongolia
Mont. – Montana
Moroc. – Morocco
Mozam. – Mozambique
Mt.(e). – Mont, Monte, Monti, Montaña, Mountain
Mys. – Mysore
N. – Nord, Norte, North, Northern, Nouveau

N.B. – New Brunswick
N.C. – North Carolina
N.D. – North Dakota
N.H. – New Hampshire
N.I. – North Island
N.J. – New Jersey
N. Mex. – New Mexico
N.S. – Nova Scotia
N.S.W. – New South Wales
N.T. – Northern Territory
N.W.T. – North West Territory
N.Y. – New York
N.Z. – New Zealand
Nat. – National
Nat.Park. – National Park
Nebr. – Nebraska
Neth. – Netherlands
Nev. – Nevada
Newf. – Newfoundland
Nic. – Nicaragua
Northants. – Northamptonshire
Northumb. – Northumberland
Notts. – Nottinghamshire
O. – Oued, ouadi
Occ. – Occidentale
O.F.S. – Orange Free State
Okla. – Oklahoma
Ont. – Ontario
Or. – Orientale
Oreg. – Oregon
Os. – Ostrov
Oxon. – Oxfordshire
Oz. – Ozero
P. – Pass, Passo, Pasul, Pulau
P.E.I. – Prince Edward Island
P.N.G. – Papua New Guinea
P.O. – Post Office
P. Rico.–Puerto Rico
Pa. – Pennsylvania
Pac. Oc. – Pacific Ocean
Pak. – Pakistan
Parag. – Paraguay
Pass. – Passage
Pen. – Peninsula, Peninsule
Phil. – Philippines
Pk. – Peak
Plat. – Plateau
P-ov. – Poluostrov
Port. – Portugal, Portuguese
Prom. – Promontory
Prov. – Province, Provincial
Pt. – Point
Pta. – Ponta, Punta
Pte. – Pointe
Qué. – Québec
Queens. – Queensland
R. – Rio, River
R.I. – Rhode Island
R.S.F.S.R. – Russian Soviet Federative Socialist Republic
Ra.(s). – Range(s)
Raj. – Rajasthan
Reg. – Region
Rep. – Republic
Res. – Reserve, Reservoir
Rhld. – Pfz. – Rheinland–Pfalz

S. – San, South
S. Afr. – South Africa
S. Austral. – South Australia
S.C. – South Carolina
S.D. – South Dakota
S.-Holst. – Schleswig-Holstein
S.I. – South Island
S. Leone–Sierra Leone
S.S.R. – Soviet Socialist Republic
Sa. – Serra, Sierra
Sard. – Sardinia
Sask. – Saskatchewan
Scot. – Scotland
Sd. – Sound
Sept. – Septentrionale
Sev. – Severnaja
Sib. – Siberia
Som. – Somerset
Span. – Spanish
Sprs. – Springs
St. – Saint
Sta. – Santa, Station
Staffs. – Staffordshire
Ste. – Sainte
Sto. – Santo
Str. – Strait, Stretto
Switz. – Switzerland
T.O. – Telegraph Office
Tas. – Tasmania
Tenn. – Tennessee
Terr. – Territory
Tex. – Texas
Tg. – Tanjung
Thai. – Thailand
Tipp. – Tipperary
Trans. – Transvaal
U.K. – United Kingdom
U.S.A. – United States of America
U.S.S.R. – Union of Soviet Socialist Republics
Ukr. – Ukraine
Ut.P. – Uttar Pradesh
Utd. – United
V. – Vorota
Va. – Virginia
Vdkhr. – Vodokhranilishche
Venez. – Venezuela
Vic. – Victoria
Viet. – Vietnam
Vol. – Volcano
Vt. – Vermont
W. – Wadi, West
W.A. – Western Australia
W. Isles–Western Isles
W. Va. – West Virginia
Wash. – Washington
Wilts. – Wiltshire
Wis. – Wisconsin
Wlkp. – Wielkopolski
Wyo. – Wyoming
Yorks. – Yorkshire
Yug. – Yugoslavia
Zap. – Zapadnaja
Zimb. – Zimbabwe

Aachen Ain el Mafki

A

Aachen 24 50 47N 6 4 E
Aâlâ en Nîl □ 87 8 50N 29 55 E
Aalen 25 48 49N 10 6 E
Aalsmeer 16 52 17N 4 43 E
Aalst 16 50 56N 4 2 E
Aalten 16 51 56N 6 35 E
Aarau 25 47 23N 8 4 E
Aarberg 25 47 2N 7 16 E
Aare → 25 47 33N 8 14 E
Aargau □ 25 47 26N 8 10 E
Aarschot 16 50 59N 4 49 E
Aba, Nigeria 85 5 10N 7 19 E
Aba, Zaïre 90 3 58N 30 17 E
Âbâ, Jazîrat 87 13 30N 32 31 E
Ābādān 64 30 22N 48 20 E
Abade, Ethiopia 87 9 22N 38 3 E
Abade, Iran 65 31 8N 52 40 E
Abadin 30 43 21N 7 29W
Abadla 82 31 2N 2 45W
Abaetetuba 127 1 40 S 48 50W
Abagnar Qi 76 43 52N 116 2 E
Abai 125 25 58 S 55 54W
Abak 85 4 58N 7 50 E
Abakaliki 85 6 22N 8 2 E
Abakan 59 53 40N 91 10 E
Abal Nam 86 25 20N 38 37 E
Abalemma 85 16 12N 7 50 E
Abanilla 33 38 12N 1 3W
Abano Terme 39 45 22N 11 46 E
Abarán 33 38 12N 1 23W
Abarqū 65 31 10N 53 20 E
'Abasān 62 31 19N 34 21 E
Abashiri 74 44 0N 144 15 E
Abashiri-Wan 74 44 0N 144 30 E
Abau 98 10 11 S 148 46 E
Abaújszántó 27 48 16N 21 12 E
Abay 58 49 38N 72 53 E
Abaya L. 87 6 30N 37 50 E
Abaza 58 52 39N 90 6 E
Abbadia San Salvatore 39 42 53N 11 40 E
Abbay (Nîl el Azraq) → 87 15 38N 32 31 E
Abbaye, Pt. 114 46 58N 88 4W
Abbé, L. 87 11 8N 41 47 E
Abbeville, France 19 50 6N 1 49 E
Abbeville, La., U.S.A. 117 30 0N 92 7W
Abbeville, S.C., U.S.A. 115 34 12N 82 21W
Abbiategrasso 38 45 23N 8 55 E
Abbieglassie 99 27 15 S 147 28 E
Abbotsford, B.C., Can. 108 49 5N 122 20W
Abbotsford, Qué., Can. 113 45 25N 72 53W
Abbotsford, U.S.A. 116 44 55N 90 20W
Abbottabad 66 34 10N 73 15 E
Abd al Kūrī 63 12 5N 52 20 E
Abéché 81 13 50N 20 35 E
Abejar 32 41 48N 2 47W
Abekr 87 12 45N 28 50 E
Abêlessa 82 22 58N 4 47 E
Abengourou 84 6 42N 3 27W
Åbenrå 49 55 3N 9 25 E
Abensberg 25 48 49N 11 51 E
Abeokuta 85 7 3N 3 19 E
Aber 90 2 12N 32 25 E
Aberaeron 13 52 15N 4 16W
Aberayron = Aberaeron 13 52 15N 4 16W
Abercorn 99 25 12 S 151 5 E
Abercorn = Mbala 91 8 46 S 31 17 E
Abercrombie → 100 33 54 S 149 8 E
Aberdare 13 51 43N 3 27W
Aberdare Ra. 90 0 15 S 36 50 E
Aberdeen, Austral. 99 32 9 S 150 56 E
Aberdeen, Can. 109 52 20N 106 8W
Aberdeen, S. Afr. 92 32 28 S 24 2 E
Aberdeen, U.K. 14 57 9N 2 6W
Aberdeen, Ala., U.S.A. 115 33 49N 88 33W
Aberdeen, Idaho, U.S.A. 118 42 57N 112 50W
Aberdeen, S.D., U.S.A. 116 45 30N 98 30W
Aberdeen, Wash., U.S.A. 118 47 0N 123 50W
Aberdovey 13 52 33N 4 3W
Aberfeldy 14 56 37N 3 50W
Abergaria-a-Velha 30 40 41N 8 32W
Abergavenny 13 51 49N 3 1W
Abernathy 117 33 49N 101 49W
Abert L. 118 42 40N 120 8W
Aberystwyth 13 52 25N 4 6W
Abha 86 18 0N 42 34 E
Abhayapuri 69 26 24N 90 38 E
Abidiya 86 18 18N 34 3 E
Abidjan 84 5 26N 3 58W
Abilene, Kans., U.S.A. 116 39 0N 97 16W
Abilene, Texas, U.S.A. 117 32 22N 99 40W
Abingdon, U.K. 13 51 40N 1 17W
Abingdon, Ill., U.S.A. 116 40 53N 90 23W
Abingdon, Va., U.S.A. 115 36 46N 81 56W
Abitau → 109 59 53N 109 3W
Abitau L. 109 60 27N 107 15W
Abitibi L. 106 48 40N 79 40W
Abiy Adi 87 13 39N 39 3 E
Abkhaz A.S.S.R. □ 57 43 0N 41 0 E
Abkit 59 64 10N 157 10 E
Abnûb 86 27 18N 31 4 E
Åbo 51 60 28N 22 15 E
Abo, Massif d' 83 21 41N 16 8 E
Abocho 85 7 35N 6 56 E
Abohar 68 30 10N 74 10 E
Aboisso 84 5 30N 3 5W
Abomey 85 7 10N 2 5 E
Abondance 21 46 18N 6 42 E
Abong-Mbang 88 4 0N 13 8 E
Abonnema 85 4 41N 6 49 E
Abony 27 47 12N 20 3 E
Aboso 84 5 23N 1 57W
Abou-Deïa 81 11 20N 19 20 E
Aboyne 14 57 4N 2 48W
Abra Pampa 124 22 43 S 65 42W
Abrantes 31 39 24N 8 7W
Abraveses 30 40 41N 7 55W
Abreojos, Pta. 120 26 50N 113 40W
Abreschviller 19 48 39N 7 6 E
Abrets, Les 21 45 32N 5 35 E
Abri, Esh Shimâliya, Sudan 86 20 50N 30 27 E
Abri, Janub Kordofân, Sudan 87 11 40N 30 21 E
Abrud 46 46 19N 23 5 E
Abruzzi □ 39 42 15N 14 0 E
Absaroka Ra. 118 44 40N 110 0W
Abū al Khaṣīb 64 30 25N 48 0 E
Abū 'Alī 64 27 20N 49 27 E
Abu 'Arīsh 63 16 53N 42 48 E
Abû Ballas 86 24 26N 27 36 E
Abu Deleiq 87 15 57N 33 48 E
Abū Dhabī 65 24 28N 54 36 E
Abū Dīs 62 31 47N 35 16 E
Abû Dis 86 19 12N 33 38 E
Abû Dom 87 16 18N 32 25 E
Abû Gabra 87 11 2N 26 50 E
Abū Ghaush 62 31 48N 35 6 E
Abû Gubeiha 87 11 30N 31 15 E
Abu Habl, Khawr → 87 12 37N 31 0 E
Abu Hamed 86 19 32N 33 13 E
Abu Haraz 87 14 35N 33 30 E
Abû Haraz 86 19 8N 32 18 E
Abû Higar 87 12 50N 33 59 E
Abū Kamāl 64 34 30N 41 0 E
Abū Madd, Ra's 64 24 50N 37 7 E
Abū Markhah 64 25 4N 38 22 E
Abu Qir 86 31 18N 30 0 E
Abu Qireiya 86 24 5N 35 28 E
Abu Qurqâs 86 28 1N 30 44 E
Abû Rudies 86 29 0N 33 15 E
Abu Salama 86 27 10N 35 51 E
Abû Simbel 86 22 18N 31 40 E
Abu Tig 86 27 4N 31 15 E
Abu Tiga 87 12 47N 34 12 E
Abû Zabad 87 12 25N 29 10 E
Abū Zābī 65 24 28N 54 22 E
Abuja 85 9 16N 7 2 E
Abukuma-Gawa → 74 38 06N 140 52 E
Abunã 126 9 40 S 65 20W
Abunã → 126 9 41 S 65 20W
Aburo, Mt. 90 2 4N 30 53 E
Abut Hd. 101 43 7 S 170 15 E
Abwong 87 9 2N 32 14 E
Åby 49 58 40N 16 10 E
Aby, Lagune 84 5 15N 3 14W
Acámbaro 120 20 0N 100 40W
Acanthus 44 40 27N 23 47 E
Acaponeta 120 22 30N 105 20W
Acapulco 120 16 51N 99 56W
Acatlán 120 18 10N 98 3W
Acayucan 120 17 59N 94 58W
Accéglio 38 44 28N 6 59 E
Accomac 114 37 43N 75 40W
Accra 85 5 35N 0 6W
Accrington 12 53 46N 2 22W
Acebal 124 33 20 S 60 50W
Aceh □ 72 4 15N 97 30 E
Acerenza 41 40 50N 15 58 E
Acerra 41 40 57N 14 22 E
Aceuchal 31 38 39N 6 30W
Achalpur 68 21 22N 77 32 E
Achenkirch 26 47 32N 11 45 E
Achensee 26 47 26N 11 45 E
Acher 68 23 10N 72 32 E
Achern 25 48 37N 8 5 E
Achill 15 53 56N 9 55W
Achill Hd. 15 53 59N 10 15W
Achill I. 15 53 58N 10 5W
Achill Sound 15 53 53N 9 55W
Achim 24 53 1N 9 2 E
Achinsk 59 56 20N 90 20 E
Achol 87 6 35N 31 32 E
Acireale 41 37 37N 15 9 E
Ackerman 117 33 20N 89 8W
Acklins I. 121 22 30N 74 0W
Acland, Mt. 97 24 50 S 148 20 E
Acme 108 51 33N 113 30W
Aconcagua □, Argent. 124 32 50 S 70 0W
Aconcagua □, Chile 124 32 15 S 70 30W
Aconcagua, Cerro 124 32 39 S 70 0W
Aconquija, Mt. 124 27 0 S 66 0W
Açores, Is. dos = Azores 6 38 44N 29 0W
Acquapendente 39 42 45N 11 50 E
Acquasanta 39 42 46N 13 24 E
Acquaviva delle Fonti 41 40 53N 16 50 E
Acqui 38 44 40N 8 28 E
Acre = 'Akko 62 32 55N 35 4 E
Acre □ 126 9 1 S 71 0W
Acre → 126 8 45 S 67 22W
Acri 41 39 29N 16 23 E
Acs 27 47 42N 18 0 E
Actium 44 38 57N 20 45 E
Acton 112 43 38N 80 3W
Ad Dahnā 64 24 30N 48 10 E
Ad Dammām 64 26 20N 50 5 E
Ad Dār al Ḥamrā' 64 27 20N 37 45 E
Ad Dawhah 65 25 15N 51 35 E
Ad Dilam 64 23 55N 47 10 E
Ada, Ghana 85 5 44N 0 40 E
Ada, Minn., U.S.A. 116 47 20N 96 30W
Ada, Okla., U.S.A. 117 34 50N 96 45W
Ada, Yugo. 42 45 49N 20 9 E
Adaja → 30 41 32N 4 52W
Ådalslinden 48 63 27N 16 55 E
Adam 65 22 15N 57 28 E
Adamaoua, Massif de l' 85 7 20N 12 20 E
Adamawa Highlands = Adamaoua, Massif de l' 85 7 20N 12 20 E
Adamello, Mt 38 46 10N 10 34 E
Adami Tulu 87 7 53N 38 41 E
Adaminaby 99 36 0 S 148 45 E
Adams, Mass., U.S.A. 113 42 38N 73 8W
Adams, N.Y., U.S.A. 114 43 50N 76 3W
Adams, Wis., U.S.A. 116 43 59N 89 50W
Adam's Bridge 70 9 15N 79 40 E
Adams Center 113 43 51N 76 1W
Adams L. 108 51 10N 119 40W
Adams, Mt. 118 46 10N 121 28W
Adam's Peak 70 6 48N 80 30 E
Adamuz 31 38 2N 4 32W
Adana 64 37 0N 35 16 E
Adanero 30 40 56N 4 36W
Adapazarı 64 40 48N 30 25 E
Adarama 87 17 10N 34 52 E
Adare, C. 5 71 0 S 171 0 E
Adaut 73 8 8 S 131 7 E
Adavale 97 25 52 S 144 32 E
Adda → 38 45 8N 9 53 E
Addis Ababa = Addis Abeba 87 9 2N 38 42 E
Addis Abeba 87 9 2N 38 42 E
Addis Alem 87 9 0N 38 17 E
Addison 112 42 9N 77 15W
Adebour 85 13 17N 11 50 E
Adel 115 31 10N 83 28W
Adelaide, Austral. 97 34 52 S 138 30 E
Adelaide, Madag. 93 32 42 S 26 20 E
Adelaide I. 5 67 15 S 68 30W
Adelaide Pen. 104 68 15N 97 30W
Adélie, Terre 5 68 0 S 140 0 E
Ademuz 32 40 5N 1 13W
Aden = Al 'Adan 63 12 45N 45 12 E
Aden, G. of 63 13 0N 50 0 E
Adendorp 92 32 25 S 24 30 E
Adgz 82 30 47N 6 30W
Adhoi 68 23 26N 70 32 E
Adi 73 4 15 S 133 30 E
Adi Daro 87 14 20N 38 14 E
Adi Keyih 87 14 51N 39 22 E
Adi Kwala 87 14 38N 38 48 E
Adi Ugri 87 14 58N 38 48 E
Adieu, C. 96 32 0 S 132 10 E
Adigala 87 10 24N 42 15 E
Adige → 39 45 9N 12 20 E
Adigrat 87 14 20N 39 26 E
Adilabad 70 19 33N 78 20 E
Adin 118 41 10N 121 0W
Adin Khel 65 32 45N 68 5 E
Adirampattinam 70 10 28N 79 20 E
Adirondack Mts. 114 44 0N 74 15W
Adjim 83 33 47N 10 50 E
Adjohon 85 6 41N 2 32 E
Adjud 46 46 7N 27 10 E
Adjumani 90 3 20N 31 50 E
Adlavik Is. 107 55 2N 57 45W
Adler 57 43 28N 39 52 E
Admer 83 20 21N 5 27 E
Admer, Erg d' 83 24 0N 9 5 E
Admiralty B. 5 62 0 S 59 0W
Admiralty G. 96 14 20 S 125 55 E
Admiralty I. 104 57 40N 134 35W
Admiralty Inlet 118 48 0N 122 40W
Admiralty Is. 94 2 0 S 147 0 E
Admiralty Ra. 5 72 0 S 164 0 E
Ado 85 6 36N 2 56 E
Ado Ekiti 85 7 38N 5 12 E
Adok 87 8 10N 30 20 E
Adola 87 11 14N 41 44 E
Adonara 73 8 15 S 123 5 E
Adoni 70 15 33N 77 18W
Adony 27 47 6N 18 52 E
Adour → 20 43 32N 1 32W
Adra, India 69 23 30N 86 42 E
Adra, Spain 33 36 43N 3 3W
Adrano 41 37 40N 14 49 E
Adrar 82 27 51N 0 11W
Adré 81 13 40N 22 20 E
Adrī 83 27 32N 13 2 E
Ádria 39 45 4N 12 3 E
Adrian, Mich., U.S.A. 114 41 55N 84 0W
Adrian, Tex., U.S.A. 117 35 19N 102 37W
Adriatic Sea 34 43 0N 16 0 E
Adua 73 1 45 S 129 50 E
Adur 70 9 8N 76 40 E
Adwa 87 14 15N 38 52 E
Adzhar A.S.S.R. □ 57 42 0N 42 0 E
Adzopé 84 6 7N 3 49W
Ægean Sea 35 37 0N 25 0 E
Æolian Is. = Eólie 41 38 30N 14 50 E
Aerht'ai Shan 75 46 40N 92 45 E
Ærø 49 54 52N 10 25 E
Ærøskøbing 49 54 53N 10 24 E
Aëtós 45 37 15N 21 50 E
Afafi, Massif d' 83 22 11N 15 10 E
Afándou 45 36 18N 28 12 E
Afarag, Erg 82 23 50N 2 47 E
Affreville = Khemis Miliania 82 36 11N 2 14 E
Afghanistan ■ 65 33 0N 65 0 E
Afgoi 63 2 7N 44 59 E
'Afīf 64 23 53N 42 56 E
Afikpo 85 5 53N 7 54 E
Aflisses, O. → 82 28 40N 0 50 E
Aflou 82 34 7N 2 3 E
Afognak I. 104 58 10N 152 50W
Afragola 41 40 54N 14 15 E
Afrera 87 13 16N 41 5 E
Africa 78 10 0N 20 0 E
Afton 113 42 14N 75 31W
Aftout 82 26 50N 3 45W
Afuá 127 0 15 S 50 20W
Afula 62 32 37N 35 17 E
Afyonkarahisar 64 38 45N 30 33 E
Aga 86 30 55N 31 10 E
Agadès = Agadez 85 16 58N 7 59 E
Agadez 85 16 58N 7 59 E
Agadir 82 30 28N 9 35W
Agano → 74 37 57N 139 8 E
Agapa 59 71 27N 89 15 E
Agar 68 23 40N 76 2 E
Agaro 87 7 50N 36 38 E
Agartala 67 23 50N 91 23 E
Agaş 46 46 28N 26 15 E
Agassiz 108 49 14N 121 46W
Agats 73 5 33 S 138 0 E
Agattu I. 104 52 25N 172 30 E
Agbélouvé 85 6 35N 1 14 E
Agboville 84 5 55N 4 15W
Agdam 57 40 0N 46 58 E
Agdash 57 40 44N 47 22 E
Agde 20 43 19N 3 28 E
Agde, C. d' 20 43 16N 3 28 E
Agdzhabedi 57 40 5N 47 27 E
Agen 20 44 12N 0 38 E
Ager Tay 83 20 0N 17 41 E
Agersø 49 55 13N 11 12 E
Ageyevo 55 54 10N 36 27 E
Agger 49 56 47N 8 13 E
Ággius 40 40 56N 9 4 E
Aghil Mts. 69 36 0N 77 0 E
Aginskoye 59 51 6N 114 32 E
Agira 41 37 40N 14 30 E
Agly → 20 42 46N 3 3 E
Agnibilékrou 84 7 10N 3 11W
Agnita 46 45 59N 24 40 E
Agnone 41 41 49N 14 20 E
Agofie 85 8 27N 0 15 E
Agogna → 38 45 4N 8 52 E
Agogo 87 7 50N 28 45 E
Agon 18 49 2N 1 34W
Agön 48 61 34N 17 23 E
Ágordo 39 46 18N 12 2 E
Agout → 20 43 47N 1 41 E
Agra 68 27 17N 77 58 E
Agramunt 32 41 48N 1 6 E
Agreda 32 41 51N 1 55W
Agri → 41 40 13N 16 44 E
Ağri Daği 64 39 50N 44 15 E
Ağri Karakose 64 39 44N 43 3 E
Agrigento 40 37 19N 13 33 E
Agrinion 45 38 37N 21 27 E
Agrópoli 41 40 23N 14 59 E
Água Clara 127 20 25 S 52 45W
Agua Prieta 120 31 20N 109 32W
Aguadas 126 5 40N 75 38W
Aguadilla 121 18 27N 67 10W
Aguanish 107 50 14N 62 2W
Aguanus → 107 50 13N 62 5W
Aguapey → 124 29 7 S 56 36W
Aguaray Guazú → 124 24 47 S 57 19W
Aguarico → 126 0 59 S 75 11W
Aguas → 32 41 20N 0 30W
Aguas Blancas 124 24 15 S 69 55W
Aguas Calientes, Sierra de 124 25 26 S 66 40W
Aguascalientes 120 21 53N 102 12W
Aguascalientes □ 120 22 0N 102 20W
Agudo 31 38 59N 4 52W
Águeda 30 40 34N 8 27W
Águeda → 30 41 2N 6 56W
Aguié 85 13 31N 7 46 E
Aguilafuente 30 41 13N 4 7W
Aguilar 31 37 31N 4 40W
Aguilar de Campóo 30 42 47N 4 15W
Aguilares 124 27 26 S 65 35W
Aguilas 33 37 23N 1 35W
Agulaa 87 13 40N 39 40 E
Agulhas, Kaap 92 34 52 S 20 0 E
Agung 72 8 20 S 115 28 E
'Agur 62 31 42N 34 55 E
Agur 90 2 28N 32 55 E
Agusan → 73 9 0N 125 30 E
Agvali 57 42 36N 46 8 E
Aha Mts. 92 19 45 S 21 0 E
Ahaggar 83 23 0N 6 30 E
Ahamansu 85 7 38N 0 35 E
Ahar 64 38 35N 47 0 E
Ahaus 24 52 4N 7 1 E
Ahelledjem 83 26 37N 6 58 E
Ahipara B. 101 35 5 S 173 5 E
Ahiri 70 19 30N 80 0 E
Ahlen 24 51 45N 7 52 E
Ahmadabad (Ahmedabad) 68 23 0N 72 40 E
Ahmadnagar (Ahmednagar) 70 19 7N 74 46 E
Ahmadpur 68 29 12N 71 10 E
Ahmar Mts. 87 9 20N 41 15 E
Ahoada 85 5 8N 6 36 E
Ahr → 24 50 33N 7 17 E
Ahrensbök 24 54 0N 10 34 E
Ahrweiler 24 50 31N 7 3 E
Aḥsā', Wāḥat al 64 25 50N 49 0 E
Ahuachapán 120 13 54N 89 52W
Åhus 49 55 56N 14 18 E
Ahvāz 64 31 20N 48 40 E
Ahvenanmaa = Åland 51 60 15N 20 0 E
Ahwar 63 13 30N 46 40 E
Ahzar 85 15 30N 3 20 E
Aichach 25 48 28N 11 9 E
Aichi □ 74 35 0N 137 15 E
Aidone 41 37 26N 14 26 E
Aiello Cálabro 41 39 6N 16 12 E
Aigle 25 46 18N 6 58 E
Aigle, L' 18 48 46N 0 38 E
Aignay-le-Duc 19 47 40N 4 43 E
Aigre 20 45 54N 0 1 E
Aigua 125 34 13 S 54 46W
Aigueperse 20 46 3N 3 13 E
Aigues-Mortes 21 43 35N 4 12 E
Aigues-Mortes, G. d' 21 43 31N 4 3 E
Aiguilles 21 44 47N 6 51 E
Aiguillon 20 44 18N 0 21 E
Aiguillon, L' 20 46 20N 1 16W
Aigurande 20 46 27N 1 49 E
Aihui 75 50 10N 127 30 E
Aija 126 9 50 S 77 45W
Aijal 67 23 40N 92 44 E
Aiken 115 33 34N 81 50W
Aillant-sur-Tholon 19 47 52N 3 20 E
Aillik 107 55 11N 59 18W
Ailly-sur-Noye 19 49 45N 2 20 E
Ailsa Craig 14 55 15N 5 7W
'Ailūn 62 32 18N 35 47 E
Aim 59 59 0N 133 55 E
Aimere 73 8 45 S 121 3 E
Aimogasta 124 28 33 S 66 50W
Aimorés 127 19 30 S 41 4W
Ain □ 21 46 5N 5 20 E
Ain → 21 45 45N 5 11 E
Ain Banaiyan 65 23 0N 51 0 E
Aïn Beïda 83 35 50N 7 29 E
Aïn ben Khellil 82 33 15N 0 49W
Aïn Ben Tili 82 25 59N 9 27W
Aïn Beni Mathar 82 34 1N 2 0W
Aïn Benian 82 36 48N 2 55 E
Aïn Dalla 86 27 20N 27 23 E
Ain Dar 64 25 55N 49 10 E
Ain el Mafki 86 27 30N 28 15 E

Aïn Galakka Alexandria

Aïn Galakka **81** 18 10N 18 30 E
Ain Girba **86** 29 20N 25 14 E
Aïn M'lila **83** 36 2N 6 35 E
Ain Qeiqab **86** 29 42N 24 55 E
Aïn-Sefra **82** 32 47N 0 37W
Ain Sheikh Murzûk **86** 26 47N 27 45 E
Ain Sukhna **86** 29 32N 32 20 E
Aïn Tédelès **82** 36 0N 0 21 E
Aïn-Témouchent **82** 35 16N 1 8W
Aïn Touta **83** 35 26N 5 54 E
Ain Zeitûn **86** 29 10N 25 48 E
Aïn Zorah **82** 34 37N 3 32W
Ainabo **63** 9 0N 46 25 E
Ainaži **54** 57 50N 24 24 E
Aínos Óros **45** 38 10N 20 35 E
Ainsworth **116** 42 33N 99 52W
Aïr **85** 18 30N 8 0 E
Airaines **19** 49 58N 1 55 E
Airdrie **14** 55 53N 3 57W
Aire **19** 50 37N 2 22 E
Aire ~→, France **19** 49 18N 4 55 E
Aire ~→, U.K. **12** 53 42N 0 55W
Aire, I. del **32** 39 48N 4 16 E
Aire-sur-l'Adour **20** 43 42N 0 15W
Airvault **18** 46 50N 0 8W
Aisch ~→ **25** 49 46N 11 1 E
Aisne □ **19** 49 42N 3 40 E
Aisne ~→ **19** 49 26N 2 50 E
Aitana, Sierra de **33** 38 35N 0 24W
Aitape **98** 3 11 S 142 22 E
Aitkin **116** 46 32N 93 43W
Aitolía Kai Akarnanía □ **45** 38 45N 21 18 E
Aitolikón **45** 38 26N 21 21 E
Aiud **46** 46 19N 23 44 E
Aix-en-Provence **21** 43 32N 5 27 E
Aix-la-Chapelle = Aachen **24** 50 47N 6 4 E
Aix-les-Bains **21** 45 41N 5 53 E
Aix-sur-Vienne **20** 45 48N 1 8 E
Aiyansh **108** 55 17N 129 2W
Aíyina **45** 37 45N 23 26 E
Aiyínion **44** 40 28N 22 28 E
Aiyion **45** 38 15N 22 5 E
Aizenay **18** 46 44N 1 38W
Aizpute **54** 56 43N 21 40 E
Ajaccio **21** 41 55N 8 40 E
Ajaccio, G. d' **21** 41 52N 8 40 E
Ajanta Ra. **70** 20 28N 75 50 E
Ajax **112** 43 50N 79 1W
Ajdâbiyah **83** 30 54N 20 4 E
Ajdovščina **39** 45 54N 13 54 E
Ajibar **87** 10 35N 38 36 E
Ajka **27** 47 4N 17 31 E
'Ajmân **65** 25 25N 55 30 E
Ajmer **68** 26 28N 74 37 E
Ajo **119** 32 18N 112 54W
Ajok **87** 9 15N 28 28 E
Ak Dağ **64** 36 30N 30 0 E
Akaba **85** 8 10N 1 2 E
Akabli **82** 26 49N 1 31 E
Akaki Beseka **87** 8 55N 38 45 E
Akala **87** 15 39N 36 13 E
Akaroa **101** 43 49 S 172 59 E
Akasha **86** 21 10N 30 32 E
Akashi **74** 34 45N 135 0 E
Akbou **83** 36 31N 4 31 E
Akelamo **73** 1 35N 129 40 E
Åkernes **47** 58 45N 7 30 E
Akershus fylke □ **47** 60 0N 11 10 E
Akeru ~→ **70** 17 25N 80 0 E
Aketi **88** 2 38N 23 47 E
Akhaïa □ **45** 38 5N 21 45 E
Akhalkalaki **57** 41 27N 43 25 E
Akhaltsikhe **57** 41 40N 43 0 E
Akharnaí **45** 38 5N 23 44 E
Akhelóös ~→ **45** 38 36N 21 14 E
Akhendria **45** 34 58N 25 16 E
Akhéron ~→ **44** 39 20N 20 29 E
Akhisar **64** 38 56N 27 48 E
Akhladhókambos **45** 37 31N 22 35 E
Akhmîm **86** 26 31N 31 47 E
Akhtopol **43** 42 6N 27 56 E
Akhtubinsk (Petropavlovskiy) **57** 48 13N 46 7 E
Akhty **57** 41 30N 47 45 E
Akhtyrka **54** 50 25N 35 0 E
Akimiski I. **106** 52 50N 81 30W
Akimovka **56** 46 44N 35 0 E
Åkirkeby **49** 55 4N 14 55 E
Akita **74** 39 45N 140 7 E
Akita □ **74** 39 40N 140 30 E
Akjoujt **84** 19 45N 14 15W
Akka **82** 29 22N 8 9W
'Akko **62** 32 55N 35 4 E
Akkol **58** 45 0N 75 39 E
Akköy **45** 37 30N 27 18 E
Aklampa **85** 8 15N 2 10 E
Aklavik **104** 68 12N 135 0W
Akmonte **31** 37 13N 6 38W
Aknoul **82** 34 40N 3 55W
Ako **85** 10 19N 10 48 E
Akobo ~→ **87** 7 48N 33 3 E
Akola **68** 20 42N 77 2 E
Akonolinga **85** 3 50N 12 18 E
Akordat **87** 15 30N 37 40 E
Akosombo Dam **85** 6 20N 0 5 E
Akot, India **68** 21 10N 77 10 E
Akot, Sudan **87** 6 31N 30 9 E
Akpatok I. **105** 60 25N 68 8W
Akranes **50** 64 19N 21 58W
Åkrehamn **47** 59 15N 5 10 E
Akreïjit **84** 18 19N 9 11W
Akritas Venétiko, Ákra **45** 36 43N 21 54 E
Akron, Colo., U.S.A. **116** 40 13N 103 15W
Akron, Ohio, U.S.A. **114** 41 7N 81 31W
Akrotiri, Ákra **44** 40 26N 25 27 E
Aksai Chih **69** 35 15N 79 55 E
Aksaray **64** 38 25N 34 2 E
Aksarka **58** 66 31N 67 50 E
Aksay **52** 51 11N 53 0 E
Akşehir **64** 38 18N 31 30 E
Aksenovo Zilovskoye **59** 53 20N 117 40 E
Akstafa **57** 41 7N 45 27 E
Aksu **75** 41 5N 80 10 E
Aksum **87** 14 5N 38 40 E
Aktogay **58** 46 57N 79 40 E
Aktyubinsk **53** 50 17N 57 10 E
Aku **85** 6 40N 7 18 E
Akure **85** 7 15N 5 5 E
Akureyri **50** 65 40N 18 6W
Akusha **57** 42 18N 47 30 E
Al Abyār **83** 32 9N 20 29 E
Al 'Adan **63** 12 45N 45 0 E
Al Amāda03yah **64** 37 5N 43 30 E
Al Amārah **64** 31 55N 47 15 E
Al 'Aqabah **62** 29 31N 35 0 E
Al 'Aramah **64** 25 30N 46 0 E
Al Ashkhara **65** 21 50N 59 30 E
Al 'Ayzarīyah (Bethany) **62** 31 47N 35 15 E
Al 'Azīzīyah **83** 32 30N 13 1 E
Al Badī' **64** 22 0N 46 35 E
Al Barkāt **83** 24 56N 10 14 E
Al Başrah **64** 30 30N 47 50 E
Al Bāzūrīyah **62** 33 15N 35 16 E
Al Bīrah **62** 31 55N 35 12 E
Al Bu'ayrāt **83** 31 24N 15 44 E
Al Buqay'ah **62** 32 15N 35 30 E
Al Dīwaniyah **64** 32 0N 45 0 E
Al Fallūjah **64** 33 20N 43 55 E
Al Fāw **64** 30 0N 48 30 E
Al Fujayrah **65** 25 7N 56 18 E
Al Ghaţghaţ **64** 24 40N 46 15 E
Al Hābah **64** 27 10N 47 0 E
Al Haddār **64** 21 58N 45 57 E
Al Ḩadīthah **64** 34 0N 41 13 E
Al Hāmad **64** 31 30N 39 30 E
Al Ḩamar **64** 22 23N 46 6 E
Al Hamādah al Ḩamrā' **83** 29 30N 12 0 E
Al Hamrā **64** 24 2N 38 55 E
Al Ḩarīq **64** 23 29N 46 27 E
Al Harīr, W. ~→ **62** 32 44N 35 59 E
Al Harūj al Aswad **83** 27 0N 17 10 E
Al Ḩasakah **64** 36 35N 40 45 E
Al Ḩawīyah **64** 24 40N 49 15 E
Al Ḩawrah **63** 13 50N 47 35 E
Al Ḩawţah **63** 16 5N 48 20 E
Al Ḩayy **64** 32 5N 46 5 E
Al Ḩillah, Iraq **64** 32 30N 44 25 E
Al Ḩillah, Si. Arab. **64** 23 35N 46 50 E
Al Hindīyah **64** 32 30N 44 10 E
Al Ḩişnn **62** 32 29N 35 52 E
Al Hoceïma **82** 35 8N 3 58W
Al Ḩudaydah **63** 14 50N 43 0 E
Al Ḩufrah, Awbārī, Libya **83** 25 32N 14 1 E
Al Ḩufrah, Misrātah, Libya **83** 29 5N 18 3 E
Al Hūfuf **64** 25 25N 49 45 E
Al Ḩulwah **64** 23 24N 46 48 E
Al Husayyāt **83** 30 24N 20 37 E
Al 'Idwah **64** 27 15N 42 35 E
Al Irq **81** 29 5N 21 35 E
Al Ittihad = Madīnat ash Sha'b **63** 12 50N 45 0 E
Al Jāfūrah **64** 25 0N 50 15 E
Al Jaghbūb **81** 29 42N 24 38 E
Al Jahrah **64** 29 25N 47 40 E
Al Jalāmīd **64** 31 20N 39 45 E
Al Jawf, Libya **81** 24 10N 23 24 E
Al Jawf, Si. Arab. **64** 29 55N 39 40 E
Al Jazır **63** 18 30N 56 31 E
Al Jazirah, Libya **81** 26 10N 21 20 E
Al Jazirah, Si. Arab. **64** 33 30N 44 0 E
Al Jubayl **64** 27 0N 49 50 E
Al Jubaylah **64** 24 55N 46 25 E
Al Junaynah **81** 13 27N 22 45 E
Al Juwārah **63** 19 0N 57 13 E
Al Khābūrah **65** 23 57N 57 5 E
Al Khalīl = Hebron **62** 31 32N 35 6 E
Al Khalūf **63** 20 30N 58 13 E
Al Kharfah **64** 22 0N 46 35 E
Al Kharj **64** 24 0N 47 0 E
Al Khufayfīyah **64** 24 50N 44 35 E
Al Khums **83** 32 40N 14 17 E
Al Khums □ **83** 31 20N 14 10 E
Al Khurmah **64** 21 58N 42 3 E
Al Kufrah **81** 24 17N 23 15 E
Al Kūt **64** 32 30N 46 0 E
Al Kuwayt **64** 29 30N 47 30 E
Al Lādhiqīyah **64** 35 30N 35 45 E
Al Lidām **63** 20 33N 44 45 E
Al Līth **86** 20 9N 40 15 E
Al Lubban **62** 32 9N 35 14 E
Al Luḩayyah **63** 15 45N 42 40 E
Al Madīnah **64** 24 35N 39 52 E
Al-Mafraq **62** 32 17N 36 14 E
Al Majma'ah **64** 25 57N 45 22 E
Al Manāmāh **65** 26 10N 50 30 E
Al Marj **81** 32 25N 20 30 E
Al Maşīrah **63** 20 25N 58 50 E
Al Matamma **63** 16 10N 44 30 E
Al Mawşil **64** 36 15N 43 5 E
Al Mazra **62** 31 16N 35 31 E
Al Midhnab **64** 25 50N 44 18 E
Al Miqdādīyah **64** 34 0N 45 0 E
Al Mish'āb **64** 28 12N 48 36 E
Al Mubarraz **64** 25 30N 49 40 E
Al Muḩarraq **65** 26 15N 50 40 E
Al Mukallā **63** 14 33N 49 2 E
Al Mukhā **63** 13 18N 43 15 E
Al Musayyib **64** 32 40N 44 25 E
Al Mustajiddah **64** 26 30N 41 50 E
Al Muwayliḩ **64** 27 40N 35 30 E
Al Qaddāhīyah **83** 31 15N 15 9 E
Al Qadīmah **64** 22 20N 39 13 E
Al Qāmishli **64** 37 10N 41 10 E
Al Qaryah ash Sharqīyah **83** 30 28N 13 40 E
Al Qaşabāt **83** 32 39N 14 1 E
Al Qaţīf **64** 26 35N 50 0 E
Al Qaţrūn **83** 24 56N 15 3 E
Al Quaisūmah **64** 28 10N 46 20 E
Al Quds **62** 31 47N 35 10 E
Al Qunfidha **86** 19 3N 41 4 E
Al Quraiyat **65** 23 17N 58 53 E
Al Qurnah **64** 31 1N 47 25 E
Al 'Ulá **64** 26 35N 38 0 E
Al Uqaylah ash Sharqīgah **83** 30 12N 19 10 E
Al Uqayr **64** 25 40N 50 15 E
Al 'Uthmānīyahyah **64** 25 5N 49 22 E
Al 'Uwaynid **64** 24 50N 46 0 E
Al' 'Uwayqīlah ash Sharqīgah **64** 30 30N 42 10 E
Al 'Uyūn **64** 26 30N 43 50 E
Al Wajh **86** 26 10N 36 30 E
Al Wakrah **65** 25 10N 51 40 E
Al Wari'āh **64** 27 51N 47 25 E
Al Wātīyah **83** 32 28N 11 57 E
Al Yāmūn **62** 32 29N 35 14 E
Ala **38** 45 46N 11 0 E
Alabama □ **115** 33 0N 87 0W
Alabama ~→ **115** 31 8N 87 57W
Alaçati **45** 38 16N 26 23 E
Alaejos **30** 41 18N 5 13W
Alagna Valsésia **38** 45 51N 7 56 E
Alagoa Grande **127** 7 3 S 35 35W
Alagoas □ **127** 9 0 S 36 0W
Alagoinhas **127** 12 7 S 38 20W
Alagón **32** 41 46N 1 12W
Alagón ~→ **31** 39 44N 6 53W
Alajuela **121** 10 2N 84 8W
Alakamisy **93** 21 19 S 47 14 E
Alakurtti **52** 67 0N 30 30 E
Alameda, Spain **31** 37 12N 4 39W
Alameda, Idaho, U.S.A. **118** 43 2N 112 30W
Alameda, N. Mex., U.S.A. **119** 35 10N 106 43W
Alamitos, Sierra de los **120** 37 21N 115 10W
Alamo **119** 36 21N 115 10W
Alamogordo **119** 32 59N 106 0W
Alamos **120** 27 0N 109 0W
Alamosa **119** 37 30N 106 0W
Åland **51** 60 15N 20 0 E
Aland **70** 17 36N 76 35 E
Alandroal **31** 38 41N 7 24W
Alandur **70** 13 0N 80 15 E
Alange, Presa de **31** 38 45N 6 18W
Alanis **31** 38 3N 5 43W
Alanya **64** 36 38N 32 0 E
Alaotra, Farihin' **93** 17 30 S 48 30 E
Alapayevsk **58** 57 52N 61 42 E
Alar del Rey **30** 42 38N 4 20W
Alaraz **30** 40 45N 5 17W
Alaşehir **53** 38 23N 28 30 E
Alaska □ **104** 65 0N 150 0W
Alaska, G. of **104** 58 0N 145 0W
Alaska Highway **108** 60 0N 130 0W
Alaska Pen. **104** 56 0N 160 0W
Alaska Range **104** 62 50N 151 0W
Alássio **38** 44 1N 8 10 E
Alataw Shankou **75** 45 5N 81 57 E
Alatri **40** 41 44N 13 21 E
Alatyr **55** 54 45N 46 35 E
Alatyr ~→ **55** 54 52N 46 36 E
Alausi **126** 2 0 S 78 50W
Álava □ **32** 42 48N 2 28W
Alava, C. **118** 48 10N 124 40W
Alaverdi **57** 41 15N 44 37 E
Alawoona **99** 34 45 S 140 30 E
Alayor **32** 39 57N 4 8 E
Alazan ~→ **57** 41 5N 46 40 E
Alba **38** 44 41N 8 1 E
Alba □ **46** 46 10N 23 30 E
Alba de Tormes **30** 40 50N 5 30W
Alba Iulia **46** 46 8N 23 39 E
Albac **46** 46 28N 23 1 E
Albacete **33** 39 0N 1 50W
Albacete □ **33** 38 50N 2 0W
Albacutya, L. **99** 35 45 S 141 58 E
Ålbæk **49** 57 36N 10 25 E
Ålbæk Bucht **49** 57 35N 10 40 E
Albaida **33** 38 51N 0 31W
Albalate de las Nogueras **32** 40 22N 2 18W
Albalate del Arzobispo **32** 41 6N 0 31W
Albania ■ **44** 41 0N 20 0 E
Albano Laziale **40** 41 44N 12 40 E
Albany, Austral. **96** 35 1 S 117 58 E
Albany, Ga., U.S.A. **115** 31 40N 84 10W
Albany, Minn., U.S.A. **116** 45 37N 94 38W
Albany, N.Y., U.S.A. **114** 42 35N 73 47W
Albany, Oreg., U.S.A. **118** 44 41N 123 0W
Albany, Tex., U.S.A. **117** 32 45N 99 20W
Albany ~→ **106** 52 17N 81 31W
Albardón **124** 31 20 S 68 30W
Albarracín **32** 40 25N 1 26W
Albarracín, Sierra de **32** 40 30N 1 30W
Albatross B. **97** 12 45 S 141 30 E
Albegna ~→ **39** 42 30N 11 11 E
Albemarle **115** 35 27N 80 15W
Albemarle Sd. **115** 36 0N 76 30W
Albenga **38** 44 3N 8 12 E
Alberche ~→ **30** 39 58N 4 46W
Alberdi **124** 26 14 S 58 20W
Alberes, Mts. **32** 42 28N 2 56 E
Alberique **33** 39 7N 0 31W
Albersdorf **24** 54 8N 9 19 E
Albert **19** 50 0N 2 38 E
Albert Canyon **108** 51 8N 117 41W
Albert L. **99** 35 30 S 139 10 E
Albert, L. = Mobutu Sese Seko, L. **90** 1 30N 31 0 E
Albert Lea **116** 43 32N 93 20W
Albert Nile ~→ **90** 3 36N 32 2 E
Alberta □ **108** 54 40N 115 0W
Alberti **124** 35 1 S 60 16W
Albertinia **92** 34 11 S 21 34 E
Albertirsa **27** 47 14N 19 37 E
Alberton **107** 46 50N 64 0W
Albertville **21** 45 40N 6 22 E
Albertville = Kalemie **90** 5 55 S 29 9 E
Alberz, Reshteh-Ye Kūhhā-Ye **65** 36 0N 52 0 E
Albi **20** 43 56N 2 9 E
Albia **116** 41 0N 92 50W
Albina **127** 5 37N 54 15W
Albina, Ponta **92** 15 52 S 11 44 E
Albino **38** 45 47N 9 48 E
Albion, Idaho, U.S.A. **118** 42 21N 113 37W
Albion, Mich., U.S.A. **114** 42 15N 84 45W
Albion, Nebr., U.S.A. **116** 41 47N 98 0W
Albion, Pa., U.S.A. **112** 41 53N 80 21W
Albocácer **32** 40 21N 0 1 E
Albōke **49** 56 57N 16 47 E
Alborán **31** 35 57N 3 0W
Alborea **33** 39 17N 1 24W
Ålborg **49** 57 2N 9 54 E
Ålborg B. **49** 56 50N 10 35 E
Albox **33** 37 23N 2 8W
Albreda **108** 52 35N 119 10W
Albuera, La **31** 38 45N 6 49W
Albufeira **31** 37 5N 8 15W
Albula ~→ **25** 46 38N 9 30 E
Albuñol **33** 36 48N 3 11W
Albuquerque **119** 35 5N 106 47W
Albuquerque, Cayos de **121** 12 10N 81 50W
Alburg **113** 44 58N 73 19W
Alburno, Mte. **41** 40 32N 15 15 E
Alburquerque **31** 39 15N 6 59W
Albury **97** 36 3 S 146 56 E
Alby **48** 62 30N 15 28 E
Alcácer do Sal **31** 38 22N 8 33W
Alcaçovas **31** 38 23N 8 9W
Alcalá de Chisvert **32** 40 19N 0 13 E
Alcalá de Guadaira **31** 37 20N 5 50W
Alcalá de Henares **32** 40 28N 3 22W
Alcalá de los Gazules **31** 36 29N 5 43W
Alcalá la Real **31** 37 27N 3 57W
Alcamo **40** 37 59N 12 55 E
Alcanadre **32** 42 24N 2 7W
Alcanadre ~→ **32** 41 43N 0 12W
Alcanar **32** 40 33N 0 28 E
Alcanede **31** 39 25N 8 49W
Alcanena **31** 39 27N 8 40W
Alcañices **30** 41 41N 6 21W
Alcaníz **32** 41 2N 0 8W
Alcântara **127** 2 20 S 44 30W
Alcántara **31** 39 41N 6 57W
Alcantara L. **109** 60 57N 108 9W
Alcantarilla **33** 37 59N 1 12W
Alcaracejos **31** 38 24N 4 58W
Alcaraz **33** 38 40N 2 29W
Alcaraz, Sierra de **33** 38 40N 2 20W
Alcarria, La **32** 40 31N 2 45W
Alcaudete **31** 37 35N 4 5W
Alcázar de San Juan **33** 39 24N 3 12W
Alcira **33** 39 9N 0 30W
Alcoa **115** 35 50N 84 0W
Alcobaça **31** 39 32N 9 0W
Alcobendas **32** 40 32N 3 38W
Alcolea del Pinar **32** 41 2N 2 28W
Alcora **32** 40 5N 0 14W
Alcoutim **31** 37 25N 7 28W
Alcova **118** 42 37N 106 52W
Alcoy **33** 38 43N 0 30W
Alcubierre, Sierra de **32** 41 45N 0 22W
Alcublas **32** 39 48N 0 43W
Alcudia **32** 39 51N 3 7 E
Alcudia, B. de **32** 39 47N 3 15 E
Alcudia, Sierra de la **31** 38 34N 4 30W
Aldabra Is. **3** 9 22 S 46 28 E
Aldan **59** 58 40N 125 30 E
Aldan ~→ **59** 63 28N 129 35 E
Aldeburgh **13** 52 9N 1 35 E
Aldeia Nova **31** 37 55N 7 24W
Alder **118** 45 27N 112 3W
Alderney **18** 49 42N 2 12W
Aldershot **13** 51 15N 0 43W
Aldersyde **108** 50 40N 113 53W
Aledo **116** 41 10N 90 50W
Alefa **87** 11 55N 36 55 E
Aleg **84** 17 3N 13 55W
Alegre **125** 20 50 S 41 30W
Alegrete **125** 29 40 S 56 0W
Aleisk **58** 52 40N 83 0 E
Alejandro Selkirk, I. **95** 33 50 S 80 15W
Aleksandriya, Ukraine S.S.R., U.S.S.R. **54** 50 37N 26 19 E
Aleksandriya, Ukraine S.S.R., U.S.S.R. **56** 48 42N 33 3 E
Aleksandriyskaya **57** 43 59N 47 0 E
Aleksandrov **55** 56 23N 38 44 E
Aleksandrovac, Srbija, Yugo. **42** 44 28N 21 13 E
Aleksandrovac, Srbija, Yugo. **42** 43 28N 21 3 E
Aleksandrovka **56** 48 55N 32 20 E
Aleksandrovo **43** 43 14N 24 51 E
Aleksandrovsk-Sakhaliniskiy **59** 50 50N 142 20 E
Aleksandrovskiy Zavod **59** 50 40N 117 50 E
Aleksandrovskoye **58** 60 35N 77 50 E
Aleksandrów Kujawski **28** 52 53N 18 43 E
Aleksandrów Łódżki **28** 51 49N 19 17 E
Alekseyevka **55** 50 43N 38 40 E
Aleksin **55** 54 31N 37 9 E
Aleksinac **42** 43 31N 21 42 E
Além Paraíba **125** 21 52 S 42 41W
Alemania, Argent. **124** 25 40 S 65 30W
Alemania, Chile **124** 25 10 S 69 55W
Ålen **47** 62 51N 11 17 E
Alençon **18** 48 27N 0 4 E
Alenuihaha Chan. **110** 20 25N 156 0W
Aleppo = Ḩalab **64** 36 10N 37 15 E
Aléria **21** 42 5N 9 26 E
Alert Bay **108** 50 30N 126 55W
Alès **21** 44 9N 4 5 E
Aleşd **46** 47 3N 22 22 E
Alessándria **38** 44 54N 8 37 E
Ålestrup **49** 56 42N 9 29 E
Ålesund **47** 62 28N 6 12 E
Alet-les-Bains **20** 43 0N 2 14 E
Aleutian Is. **104** 52 0N 175 0W
Aleutian Trench **94** 48 0N 180 0
Alexander **116** 47 51N 103 40W
Alexander Arch. **104** 57 0N 135 0W
Alexander B. **92** 28 36 S 16 33 E
Alexander City **115** 32 58N 85 57W
Alexander I. **5** 69 0 S 70 0W
Alexandra, Austral. **99** 37 8 S 145 40 E
Alexandra, N.Z. **101** 45 14 S 169 25 E
Alexandra Falls **108** 60 29N 116 18W
Alexandria, B.C., Can. **108** 52 35N 122 27W
Alexandria, Ont., Can. **106** 45 19N 74 38W
Alexandria, Romania **46** 43 57N 25 24 E
Alexandria, S. Afr. **92** 33 38 S 26 28 E
Alexandria, Ind., U.S.A. **114** 40 18N 85 40W
Alexandria, La., U.S.A. **117** 31 20N 92 30W
Alexandria, Minn., U.S.A. **116** 45 50N 95 20W
Alexandria, S.D., U.S.A. **116** 43 40N 97 45W
Alexandria, Va., U.S.A. **114** 38 47N 77 1W

Alexandria Amursk

Alexandria = El Iskandarîya **86** 31 0N 30 0 E
Alexandria Bay **114** 44 20N 75 52W
Alexandrina, L. **97** 35 25 S 139 10 E
Alexandroúpolis **44** 40 50N 25 54 E
Alexis → **107** 52 33N 56 8W
Alexis Creek **108** 52 10N 123 20W
Alfambra **32** 40 33N 1 5W
Alfândega da Fé **30** 41 20N 6 59W
Alfaro **32** 42 10N 1 50W
Alfatar **43** 43 59N 27 13 E
Alfeld **24** 52 0N 9 49 E
Alfenas **125** 21 20 S 46 10W
Alfiós → **45** 37 40N 21 33 E
Alfonsine **39** 44 30N 12 1 E
Alford **14** 57 13N 2 42W
Alfred, Me., U.S.A. **113** 43 28N 70 40W
Alfred, N.Y., U.S.A. **112** 42 15N 77 45W
Alfreton **12** 53 6N 1 22W
Alfta **48** 61 21N 16 4 E
Alga **58** 49 53N 57 20 E
Algaba, La **31** 37 27N 6 1W
Algar **31** 36 40N 5 39W
Ålgård **47** 58 46N 5 53 E
Algarinejo **31** 37 19N 4 9W
Algarve **31** 36 58N 8 20W
Algeciras **31** 36 9N 5 28W
Algemesí **33** 39 11N 0 27W
Alger **82** 36 42N 3 8 E
Algeria ■ **82** 35 10N 3 11 E
Alghero **40** 40 34N 8 20 E
Algiers = Alger **82** 36 42N 3 8 E
Algoabaai **92** 33 50 S 25 45 E
Algodonales **31** 36 54N 5 24W
Algodor → **30** 39 55N 3 53W
Algoma, Oreg., U.S.A. **118** 42 25N 121 54W
Algoma, Wis., U.S.A. **114** 44 35N 87 27W
Algona **116** 43 4N 94 14W
Algonac **112** 42 37N 82 32W
Alhama de Almería **33** 36 57N 2 34W
Alhama de Aragón **32** 41 18N 1 54W
Alhama de Granada **31** 37 0N 3 59W
Alhama de Murcia **33** 37 51N 1 25W
Alhambra, Spain **33** 38 54N 3 4W
Alhambra, U.S.A. **119** 34 2N 118 10W
Alhaurín el Grande **31** 36 39N 4 41W
Alhucemas = Al-Hoceïma **82** 35 8N 3 58W
'Alī al Gharbī **64** 32 30N 46 45 E
Ali Bayramly **57** 39 59N 48 52 E
Ali Sabieh **87** 11 10N 42 44 E
Ália **40** 37 47N 13 42 E
'Alīābād **65** 28 10N 57 35 E
Aliaga **32** 40 40N 0 42W
Aliákmon → **44** 40 30N 22 36 E
Alibag **70** 18 38N 72 56 E
Alibo **87** 9 52N 37 5 E
Alibunar **42** 45 5N 20 57 E
Alicante **33** 38 23N 0 30W
Alicante □ **33** 38 30N 0 37W
Alice, S. Afr. **92** 32 48 S 26 55 E
Alice, U.S.A. **117** 27 47N 98 1W
Alice →, Queens., Austral. **98** 24 2 S 144 50 E
Alice →, Queens., Austral. **98** 15 35 S 142 20 E
Alice Arm **108** 55 29N 129 31W
Alice, Punta dell' **41** 39 23N 17 10 E
Alice Springs **96** 23 40 S 133 50 E
Alicedale **92** 33 15 S 26 4 E
Aliceville **115** 33 9N 88 10W
Alick Cr. → **98** 20 55 S 142 20 E
Alicudi, I. **41** 38 33N 14 20 E
Alida **109** 49 25N 101 55W
Aligarh, Raj., India **68** 25 55N 76 15 E
Aligarh, Ut. P., India **68** 27 55N 78 10 E
Alīgūdarz **64** 33 25N 49 45 E
Alijó **30** 41 16N 7 27W
Alimena **41** 37 42N 14 4 E
Alimnia **45** 36 16N 27 43 E
Alingsås **49** 57 56N 12 31 E
Alipur **68** 29 25N 70 55 E
Alipur Duar **69** 26 30N 89 35 E
Aliquippa **114** 40 38N 80 18W
Aliste → **30** 41 34N 5 58W
Alitus **54** 54 24N 24 3 E
Alivérion **45** 38 24N 24 2 E
Aliwal North **92** 30 45 S 26 45 E
Alix **108** 52 24N 113 11W
Aljezur **31** 37 18N 8 49W
Aljustrel **31** 37 55N 8 10W
Alkamari **85** 13 27N 11 10 E
Alkmaar **16** 52 37N 4 45 E
All American Canal **119** 32 45N 115 0W
Allada **85** 6 41N 2 9 E
Allah Dad **68** 25 38N 67 34 E
Allahabad **69** 25 25N 81 58 E
Allakh-Yun **59** 60 50N 137 5 E
Allal Tazi **82** 34 30N 6 20W
Allan **109** 51 53N 106 4W
Allanche **20** 45 14N 2 57 E
Allanmyo **67** 19 30N 95 17 E
Allanridge **92** 27 45 S 26 40 E
Allanwater **106** 50 14N 90 10W
Allaqi, Wadi → **86** 23 7N 32 47 E
Allariz **30** 42 11N 7 50W
Allassac **20** 45 15N 1 29 E
Allegan **114** 42 32N 85 52W
Allegany **112** 42 6N 78 30W
Allegheny → **114** 40 27N 80 0W
Allegheny Mts. **114** 38 0N 80 0W
Allegheny Res. **112** 42 0N 78 55W
Allègre **20** 45 12N 3 41 E
Allen, Bog of **15** 53 15N 7 0W
Allen, L. **15** 54 12N 8 5W
Allenby (Hussein) Bridge **62** 31 53N 35 33 E
Allende **120** 28 20N 100 50W
Allentown **114** 40 36N 75 30W
Allentsteig **26** 48 41N 15 20 E
Alleppey **70** 9 30N 76 28 E
Aller → **24** 52 57N 9 10 E
Allevard **21** 45 24N 6 5 E
Alliance, Nebr., U.S.A. **116** 42 10N 102 50W
Alliance, Ohio, U.S.A. **114** 40 53N 81 7W
Allier □ **20** 46 25N 3 0 E
Allier → **19** 46 57N 3 4 E
Allingåbro **49** 56 28N 10 20 E
Allinge **49** 55 17N 14 50 E
Alliston **106** 44 9N 79 52W
Alloa **14** 56 7N 3 49W
Allos **21** 44 15N 6 38 E
Alma, Can. **107** 48 35N 71 40W
Alma, Ga., U.S.A. **115** 31 33N 82 28W
Alma, Kans., U.S.A. **116** 39 1N 96 22W
Alma, Mich., U.S.A. **114** 43 25N 84 40W
Alma, Nebr., U.S.A. **116** 40 10N 99 25W
Alma, Wis., U.S.A. **116** 44 19N 91 54W
'Almā ash Sha'b **62** 33 7N 35 9 E
Alma Ata **58** 43 15N 76 57 E
Almada **31** 38 40N 9 9W
Almaden **98** 17 22 S 144 40 E
Almadén **31** 38 49N 4 52W
Almagro **31** 38 50N 3 45W
Almanor, L. **118** 40 15N 121 11W
Almansa **33** 38 51N 1 5W
Almanza **30** 42 39N 5 3W
Almanzor, Pico de **30** 40 15N 5 18W
Almanzora → **33** 37 14N 1 46W
Almarcha, La **32** 39 41N 2 24W
Almaş, Mţii. **46** 44 49N 22 12 E
Almazán **32** 41 30N 2 30W
Almazora **32** 39 57N 0 3W
Almeirim, Brazil **127** 1 30 S 52 34W
Almeirim, Port. **31** 39 12N 8 37W
Almelo **16** 52 22N 6 42 E
Almenar **32** 41 43N 2 12W
Almenara **32** 39 46N 0 14W
Almenara, Sierra de **33** 37 34N 1 32W
Almendralejo **31** 38 41N 6 26W
Almería **33** 36 52N 2 27W
Almería □ **33** 37 20N 2 20W
Almería, G. de **33** 36 41N 2 28W
Almirante **14** 9 10N 82 30W
Almiropótamos **45** 38 16N 24 11 E
Almirós **45** 39 11N 22 45 E
Almodôvar **31** 37 31N 8 2W
Almodóvar del Campo **31** 38 43N 4 10W
Almogia **31** 36 50N 4 32W
Almonaster la Real **31** 37 52N 6 48W
Almont **112** 42 53N 83 2W
Almonte **113** 45 14N 76 12W
Almonte → **31** 39 41N 6 28W
Almora **69** 29 38N 79 40 E
Almoradi **33** 38 7N 0 46W
Almorox **30** 40 14N 4 24W
Almoustarat **85** 17 35N 0 8 E
Älmult **49** 56 33N 14 8 E
Almuñécar **31** 36 43N 3 41W
Almunia de Doña Godina, La **32** 41 29N 1 23W
Alnif **82** 31 10N 5 8W
Alnwick **12** 55 25N 1 42W
Aloi **90** 2 16N 33 10 E
Alonsa **109** 50 50N 99 0W
Alor **73** 8 15 S 124 30 E
Alor Setar **71** 6 7N 100 22 E
Alora **31** 36 49N 4 46W
Alosno **31** 37 33N 7 7W
Alougoum **82** 30 17N 6 56W
Alpedrinha **30** 40 6N 7 27W
Alpena **114** 45 6N 83 24W
Alpes-de-Haute-Provence □ **21** 44 8N 6 10 E
Alpes-Maritimes □ **21** 43 55N 7 10 E
Alpha **97** 23 39 S 146 37 E
Alpi Apuane **38** 44 7N 10 14 E
Alpi Lepontine **25** 46 22N 8 27 E
Alpi Orobie **38** 46 7N 10 0 E
Alpi Retiche **25** 46 30N 10 0 E
Alpiarça **31** 39 15N 8 35W
Alpine, Ariz., U.S.A. **119** 33 57N 109 4W
Alpine, Tex., U.S.A. **117** 30 25N 103 35W
Alps **22** 47 0N 8 0 E
Alpujarras, Las **33** 36 55N 3 20W
Alrø **49** 55 52N 10 5 E
Alsace **19** 48 15N 7 25 E
Alsask **109** 51 21N 109 59W
Alsásua **32** 42 54N 2 10W
Alsen **48** 63 23N 13 56 E
Alsfeld **24** 50 44N 9 19 E
Alsónémedi **27** 47 20N 19 15 E
Alsten **50** 65 58N 12 40 E
Alta **50** 69 57N 23 10 E
Alta Gracia **124** 31 40 S 64 30W
Alta Lake **108** 50 10N 123 0W
Alta, Sierra **32** 40 31N 1 30W
Altaelva → **50** 69 46N 23 45 E
Altafjorden **50** 70 5N 23 5 E
Altagracia **126** 10 45N 71 30W
Altai = Aerhatai Shan **75** 46 40N 92 45 E
Altamaha → **115** 31 19N 81 17W
Altamira, Brazil **127** 3 12 S 52 10W
Altamira, Chile **124** 25 47 S 69 51W
Altamira, Cuevas de **30** 43 20N 4 5W
Altamont **113** 42 43N 74 3W
Altamura **41** 40 50N 16 33 E
Altanbulag **75** 50 16N 106 30 E
Altar **120** 30 40N 111 50W
Altata **120** 24 30N 108 0W
Altavista **114** 37 9N 79 22W
Altay **75** 47 48N 88 10 E
Altdorf **25** 46 52N 8 36 E
Alte Mellum **24** 53 45N 8 6 E
Altea **33** 38 38N 0 2W
Altenberg **24** 50 46N 13 47 E
Altenbruch **24** 53 48N 8 44 E
Altenburg **24** 50 59N 12 28 E
Altenkirchen, Germ., E. **24** 54 38N 13 20 E
Altenkirchen, Germ., W. **24** 50 41N 7 38 E
Altenmarkt **26** 47 43N 14 39 E
Altenteptow **24** 53 42N 13 15 E
Alter do Chão **31** 39 12N 7 40W
Altkirch **19** 47 37N 7 15 E
Altmühl → **25** 48 54N 11 54 E
Alto Adige = Trentino-Alto Adige **38** 46 30N 11 0 E
Alto Araguaia **127** 17 15 S 53 20W
Alto Chindio **91** 16 19 S 35 25 E
Alto Cuchumatanes = Cuchumatanes, Sa. de los **120** 15 30N 91 10W
Alto del Inca **124** 24 10 S 68 10W
Alto Ligonha **91** 15 30 S 38 11 E
Alto Molocue **91** 15 50 S 37 35 E
Alto Paraná □ **125** 25 0 S 54 50W
Alton, Can. **112** 43 54N 80 5W
Alton, U.S.A. **116** 38 55N 90 5W
Alton Downs **99** 26 7 S 138 57 E
Altona, Austral. **100** 37 51 S 144 50 E
Altona, Ger. **24** 53 32N 9 56 E
Altoona **114** 40 32N 78 24W
Altopáscio **38** 43 50N 10 40 E
Altötting **25** 48 14N 12 41 E
Altstätten **25** 47 22N 9 33 E
Altun Shan **75** 38 30N 88 0 E
Alturas **118** 41 36N 120 37W
Altus **117** 34 30N 99 25W
Alucra **57** 40 22N 38 47 E
Aluksne **54** 57 24N 27 3 E
Alùla **63** 11 50N 50 45 E
Alupka **56** 44 23N 34 2 E
Alushta **56** 44 40N 34 25 E
Alusi **73** 7 35 S 131 40 E
Alustante **32** 40 36N 1 40W
Alva **117** 36 50N 98 50W
Alvaiázere **30** 39 49N 8 23W
Älvängen **49** 57 58N 12 8 E
Alvarado, Mexico **120** 18 40N 95 50W
Alvarado, U.S.A. **117** 32 25N 97 15W
Alvaro Obregón, Presa **120** 27 55N 109 52W
Alvdal **47** 62 6N 10 37 E
Alvear **124** 29 5 S 56 30W
Alverca **31** 38 56N 9 1W
Alvesta **49** 56 54N 14 35 E
Alvie **99** 38 14 S 143 30 E
Alvin **117** 29 23N 95 12W
Alvinston **113** 42 49N 81 52W
Alvito **31** 38 15N 8 0W
Älvros **48** 62 3N 14 38 E
Älvsborgs län □ **49** 58 30N 12 30 E
Älvsbyn **50** 65 40N 21 0 E
Älvsered **49** 57 14N 12 51 E
Alwar **68** 27 38N 76 34 E
Alwaye **70** 10 8N 76 24 E
Alxa Zuoqi **76** 38 50N 105 40 E
Alyangula **97** 13 55 S 136 30 E
Alyaskitovyy **59** 64 45N 141 30 E
Alyata **57** 39 58N 49 25 E
Alyth **14** 56 38N 3 15W
Alzada **116** 45 3N 104 22W
Alzano Lombardo **38** 45 44N 9 43 E
Alzey **25** 49 48N 8 4 E
Am Dam **81** 12 40N 20 35 E
Am Géréda **81** 12 53N 21 14 E
Am-Timan **81** 11 0N 20 10 E
Amadeus, L. **96** 24 54 S 131 0 E
Amâdi **87** 5 29N 30 25 E
Amadi **90** 3 40N 26 40 E
Amadjuak **105** 64 0N 72 39W
Amadjuak L. **105** 65 0N 71 8W
Amadora **31** 38 45N 9 13W
Amagasaki **74** 34 42N 135 20 E
Amager **49** 55 37N 12 35 E
Amakusa-Shotō **74** 32 15N 130 10 E
Åmål **48** 59 3N 12 42 E
Amalapuram **70** 16 35N 81 55 E
Amalfi **41** 40 39N 14 34 E
Amaliás **45** 37 47N 21 22 E
Amalner **68** 21 5N 75 5 E
Amambaí **125** 23 5 S 55 13W
Amambaí → **125** 23 22 S 53 56W
Amambay □ **125** 23 0 S 56 0W
Amambay, Cordillera de **125** 23 0 S 55 45W
Amándola **39** 42 59N 13 21 E
Amangeldy **58** 50 10N 65 10 E
Amantea **41** 39 8N 16 3 E
Amapá **127** 2 5N 50 50W
Amapá □ **127** 1 40N 52 0W
Amara **87** 10 25N 34 10 E
Amarante, Brazil **127** 6 14 S 42 50W
Amarante, Port. **30** 41 16N 8 5W
Amaranth **109** 50 36N 98 43W
Amaravati → **70** 11 0N 78 15 E
Amareleja **31** 38 12N 7 13W
Amargosa **127** 13 2 S 39 36W
Amarillo **117** 35 14N 101 46W
Amaro, Mt. **39** 42 5N 14 6 E
Amarpur **69** 25 5N 87 0 E
Amasra **64** 41 45N 32 30 E
Amassama **85** 5 1N 6 2 E
Amasya **64** 40 40N 35 50 E
Amatikulu **93** 29 3 S 31 33 E
Amatitlán **120** 14 29N 90 38W
Amatrice **39** 42 38N 13 16 E
Amazon = Amazonas → **127** 0 5 S 50 0W
Amazonas □ **126** 4 0 S 62 0W
Amazonas → **127** 0 5 S 50 0W
Ambad **70** 19 38N 75 50 E
Ambahakily **93** 21 36 S 43 41 E
Ambala **68** 30 23N 76 56 E
Ambalangoda **70** 6 15N 80 5 E
Ambalapuzha **70** 9 25N 76 25 E
Ambalavao **93** 21 50 S 46 56 E
Ambam **88** 2 20N 11 15 E
Ambanja **93** 13 40 S 48 27 E
Ambarchik **59** 69 40N 162 20 E
Ambarijeby **93** 14 56 S 47 41 E
Ambarnath **70** 19 12N 73 22 E
Ambaro, Helodranon' **93** 13 23 S 48 38 E
Ambartsevo **58** 57 30N 83 52 E
Ambasamudram **70** 8 43N 77 25 E
Ambato **126** 1 5 S 78 42W
Ambato Boeny **93** 16 28 S 46 43 E
Ambato, Sierra de **124** 28 25 S 66 10W
Ambatofinandrahana **93** 20 33 S 46 48 E
Ambatolampy **93** 19 20 S 47 35 E
Ambatondrazaka **93** 17 55 S 48 28 E
Ambatosoratra **93** 17 37 S 48 31 E
Ambenja **93** 15 17 S 46 58 E
Amberg **25** 49 25N 11 52 E
Ambergris Cay **120** 18 0N 88 0W
Ambérieu-en-Bugey **21** 45 57N 5 20 E
Amberley **101** 43 9 S 172 44 E
Ambert **20** 45 33N 3 44 E
Ambidédi **84** 14 35N 11 47W
Ambikapur **69** 23 15N 83 15 E
Ambikol **86** 21 20N 30 50 E
Ambinanindrano **93** 20 5 S 48 23 E
Ambjörnarp **49** 57 25N 13 17 E
Ambleside **12** 54 26N 2 58W
Ambo, Ethiopia **87** 12 20N 37 30 E
Ambo, Peru **126** 10 5 S 76 10W
Ambodifototra **93** 16 59 S 49 52 E
Ambodilazana **93** 18 6 S 49 10 E
Ambohimahasoa **93** 21 7 S 47 13 E
Ambohimanga **93** 20 52 S 47 36 E
Ambon **73** 3 35 S 128 20 E
Amboseli L. **90** 2 40 S 37 10 E
Ambositra **93** 20 31 S 47 25 E
Ambovombé **93** 25 11 S 46 5 E
Amboy **119** 34 33N 115 51W
Amboyna I. **72** 7 50N 112 50 E
Ambridge **112** 40 36N 80 15W
Ambriz **88** 7 48 S 13 8 E
Ambur **70** 12 48N 78 43 E
Amby **99** 26 30 S 148 11 E
Amchitka I. **104** 51 30N 179 0W
Amderma **58** 69 45N 61 30 E
Ameca **120** 20 30N 104 0W
Ameca → **120** 20 40N 105 15W
Amecameca **120** 19 7N 98 46W
Ameland **16** 53 27N 5 45 E
Amélia **39** 42 34N 12 25 E
Amélie-les-Bains-Palalda **20** 42 29N 2 41 E
Amen **59** 68 45N 180 0 E
Amendolaro **41** 39 58N 16 34 E
American Falls **118** 42 46N 112 56W
American Falls Res. **118** 43 0N 112 50W
American Highland **5** 73 0 S 75 0 E
American Samoa **101** 14 20 S 170 40W
Americana **125** 22 45 S 47 20W
Americus **115** 32 0N 84 10W
Amersfoort, Neth. **16** 52 9N 5 23 E
Amersfoort, S. Afr. **93** 26 59 S 29 53 E
Amery **109** 56 34N 94 3W
Amery Ice Shelf **5** 69 30 S 72 0 E
Ames **116** 42 0N 93 40W
Amesbury **113** 42 50N 70 52W
Amesdale **109** 50 2N 92 55W
Amfiklia **45** 38 38N 22 35 E
Amfilokhía **45** 38 52N 21 9 E
Amfípolis **44** 40 48N 23 52 E
Ámfissa **45** 38 32N 22 22 E
Amga **59** 60 50N 132 0 E
Amga → **59** 62 38N 134 32 E
Amgu **59** 45 45N 137 15 E
Amgun → **59** 52 56N 139 38 E
Amherst, Burma **67** 16 2N 97 20 E
Amherst, Can. **107** 45 48N 64 8W
Amherst, Mass., U.S.A. **113** 42 21N 72 30W
Amherst, Ohio, U.S.A. **112** 41 23N 82 15W
Amherst, Tex., U.S.A. **117** 34 0N 102 24W
Amherst I. **113** 44 8N 76 43W
Amherstburg **106** 42 6N 83 6W
Amiata, Mte. **39** 42 54N 11 40 E
Amiens **19** 49 54N 2 16 E
Amigdhalokefáli **45** 35 23N 23 30 E
Amindaion **44** 40 42N 21 42 E
Amirante Is. **3** 6 0 S 53 0 E
Amisk L. **109** 54 35N 102 15W
Amite **117** 30 47N 90 31W
Amizmiz **82** 31 12N 8 15W
Åmli **47** 58 45N 8 32 E
Amlwch **12** 53 24N 4 21W
Amm Adam **87** 16 20N 36 1 E
'Ammān **62** 31 57N 35 52 E
Ammanford **13** 51 48N 4 0W
Ammerån **48** 63 9N 16 13 E
Ammerån → **48** 63 9N 16 13 E
Ammersee **25** 48 0N 11 7 E
Ammi'ad **62** 32 55N 35 32 E
Amnéville **19** 49 16N 6 9 E
Amorebieta **32** 43 13N 2 44W
Amorgós **45** 36 50N 25 57 E
Amory **115** 33 59N 88 29W
Amos **106** 48 35N 78 5W
Åmot, Buskerud, Norway **47** 59 54N 9 54 E
Åmot, Telemark, Norway **47** 59 34N 8 0 E
Åmotsdal **47** 59 37N 8 26 E
Amour, Djebel **82** 33 42N 1 37 E
Amoy = Xiamen **76** 24 25N 118 4 E
Ampanihy **93** 24 40 S 44 45 E
Ampasindava, Helodranon' **93** 13 40 S 48 15 E
Ampasindava, Saikanosy **93** 13 42 S 47 55W
Amper **85** 9 25N 9 40 E
Amper → **25** 48 30N 11 57 E
Ampère **83** 35 44N 5 27 E
Ampezzo **39** 46 25N 12 48 E
Amposta **32** 40 43N 0 34 E
Ampotaka **93** 25 3 S 44 41 E
Ampoza **93** 22 20 S 44 44 E
Amqa **62** 32 59N 35 10 E
Amqui **107** 48 28N 67 27W
Amraoti **68** 20 55N 77 45 E
Amreli **68** 21 35N 71 17 E
Amrenene el Kasba **82** 22 10N 0 30 E
Amritsar **68** 31 35N 74 57 E
Amroha **68** 28 53N 78 30 E
Amrum **24** 54 37N 8 21 E
Amsel **83** 22 47N 5 29 E
Amsterdam, Neth. **16** 52 23N 4 54 E
Amsterdam, U.S.A. **114** 42 58N 74 10W
Amsterdam, I. **3** 37 30 S 77 30 E
Amstetten **26** 48 7N 14 51 E
Amudarya → **58** 43 40N 59 0 E
Amund Ringnes I. **4** 78 20N 96 25W
Amundsen Gulf **104** 71 0N 124 0W
Amundsen Sea **5** 72 0 S 115 0W
Amungen **48** 61 10N 15 40 E
Amuntai **72** 2 28 S 115 25 E
Amur → **59** 52 56N 141 10 E
Amurang **73** 1 5N 124 40 E
Amuri Pass **101** 42 31 S 172 11 E
Amurrio **32** 43 3N 3 0W
Amursk **59** 50 14N 136 54 E

Amurzet Arapkir

Amurzet 59 47 50N 131 5 E
Amusco 30 42 10N 4 28W
Amvrakikós Kólpos 45 39 0N 20 55 E
Amvrosiyevka 57 47 43N 38 30 E
Amzeglouf 82 26 50N 0 1 E
An Nafūd 64 28 15N 41 0 E
An Najaf 64 32 3N 44 15 E
An Nāqūrah 62 33 7N 35 8 E
An Nāṣirīyah 64 31 0N 46 15 E
An Nawfaliyah 83 30 54N 17 58 E
An Nhon (Binh Dinh) 71 13 55N 109 7 E
An Nîl □ 86 19 30N 33 0 E
An Nîl el Abyad □ 87 14 0N 32 15 E
An Nîl el Azraq □ 87 12 30N 34 30 E
An Nu'ayrīyah 64 27 30N 48 30 E
An Uaimh 15 53 39N 6 40W
Āna-Sira 47 58 17N 6 25 E
Anabar → 59 73 8N 113 36 E
'Anabtā 62 32 19N 35 7 E
Anaconda 118 46 7N 113 0W
Anacortes 118 48 30N 122 40W
Anadarko 117 35 4N 98 15W
Anadia 30 40 26N 8 27W
Anadolu 64 38 0N 30 0 E
Anadyr 59 64 35N 177 20 E
Anadyr → 59 64 55N 176 5 E
Anadyrskiy Zaliv 59 64 0N 180 0 E
Anáfi 45 36 22N 25 48 E
Anafópoulo 45 36 17N 25 50 E
Anagni 40 41 44N 13 8 E
'Ānah 64 34 25N 42 0 E
Anahim Lake 108 52 28N 125 18W
Anáhuac 120 27 14N 100 9W
Anai Mudi, Mt. 70 10 12N 77 4 E
Anaimalai Hills 70 10 20N 76 40 E
Anakapalle 70 17 42N 83 06 E
Anakie 98 23 32 S 147 45 E
Anaklia 57 42 22N 41 35 E
Analalava 93 14 35 S 48 0 E
Anambar → 68 30 15N 68 50 E
Anambas, Kepulauan 72 3 20N 106 30 E
Anamoose 116 47 55N 100 20W
Anamosa 116 42 7N 91 30W
Anamur 64 36 8N 32 58 E
Anan 74 33 54N 134 40 E
Anand 68 22 32N 72 59 E
Anandpur 69 21 16N 86 13 E
Anánes 45 36 33N 24 9 E
Anantapur 70 14 39N 77 42 E
Anantnag 69 33 45N 75 10 E
Ananyev 56 47 44N 29 47 E
Anapa 56 44 55N 37 25 E
Anápolis 127 16 15 S 48 50W
Anār 65 30 55N 55 13 E
Anārak 65 33 25N 53 40 E
Anatolia = Anadolu 64 38 0N 30 0 E
Anatone 118 46 9N 117 4W
Añatuya 124 28 20 S 62 50W
Anaunethad L. 109 60 55N 104 25W
Anaye 81 19 15N 12 50 E
Ancenis 18 47 21N 1 10W
Anchorage 104 61 10N 149 50W
Anciāo 30 39 56N 8 27W
Ancohuma, Nevada 126 16 0 S 68 50W
Ancón 126 11 50 S 77 10W
Ancona 39 43 37N 13 30 E
Ancud 128 42 0 S 73 50W
Ancud, G. de 128 42 0 S 73 0W
Anda 76 46 24N 125 19 E
Andacollo, Argent. 124 37 10 S 70 42W
Andacollo, Chile 124 30 5 S 71 10W
Andalgalá 124 27 40 S 66 30W
Åndalsnes 47 62 35N 7 43 E
Andalucia 31 37 35N 5 0W
Andalusia 115 31 19N 86 30W
Andalusia = Andalucia 31 37 35N 5 0W
Andaman Is. 71 12 30N 92 30 E
Andaman Sea 72 13 0N 96 0 E
Andaman Str. 71 12 15N 92 20 E
Andara 92 18 2 S 21 9 E
Andelot 19 48 15N 5 18 E
Andelys, Les 18 49 15N 1 25 E
Andenne 16 50 30N 5 5 E
Andéranboukane 85 15 26N 3 2 E
Andermatt 25 46 38N 8 35 E
Andernach 24 50 24N 7 25 E
Andernos-les-Bains 20 44 44N 1 6W
Anderslöv 49 55 26N 13 19 E
Anderson, Calif., U.S.A. 118 40 30N 122 19W
Anderson, Ind., U.S.A. 114 40 5N 85 40W
Anderson, Mo., U.S.A. 117 36 43N 94 29W
Anderson, S.C., U.S.A. 115 34 32N 82 40W
Anderson → 104 69 42N 129 0W
Anderson, Mt. 93 25 5 S 30 42 E
Anderstorp 49 57 19N 13 39 E
Andes 126 5 40N 75 53W
Andes, Cord de los 126 20 0 S 68 0W
Andfjorden 50 69 10N 16 20 E
Andhra, L. 70 18 54N 73 32 E
Andhra Pradesh □ 70 16 0N 79 0 E
Andikíthira 45 35 52N 23 15 E
Andimilos 45 36 47N 24 12 E
Andiparos 45 37 0N 25 3 E
Andipaxoi 45 39 9N 20 13 E
Andipsara 45 38 30N 25 29 E
Andirrion 45 38 24N 21 46 E
Andizhan 58 41 10N 72 0 E
Andkhvoy 65 36 52N 65 8 E
Andol 70 17 51N 78 4 E
Andong 76 36 40N 128 43 E
Andorra ■ 32 42 30N 1 30 E
Andorra La Vella 32 42 31N 1 32 E
Andover, U.K. 13 51 13N 1 29W
Andover, N.Y., U.S.A. 112 42 11N 77 48W
Andover, Ohio, U.S.A. 112 41 35N 80 35W
Andrahary, Mt. 93 13 37 S 49 17 E
Andraitx 32 39 39N 2 25 E
Andramasina 93 19 11 S 47 35 E
Andranopasy 93 21 17 S 43 44 E
Andreanof Is. 104 52 0N 178 0W
Andreapol 54 56 40N 32 17 E
Andrespol 28 51 45N 19 34 E
Andrews, S.C., U.S.A. 115 33 29N 79 30W
Andrews, Tex., U.S.A. 117 32 18N 102 33W
Ándria 41 41 13N 16 17 E
Andriba 93 17 30 S 46 58 E
Andrijevica 42 42 45N 19 48 E
Andrítsaina 45 37 29N 21 52 E
Androka 93 24 58 S 44 2 E
Ándros 45 37 50N 24 57 E
Andros I. 121 24 30N 78 0W
Andros Town 121 24 43N 77 47W
Andrychów 27 49 51N 19 18 E
Andújar 31 38 3N 4 5W
Aneby 49 57 48N 14 49 E
Anegada I. 121 18 45N 64 20W
Anegada Passage 121 18 15N 63 45W
Anécho 85 6 12N 1 34 E
Anergane 82 31 4N 7 14W
Aneto, Pico de 32 42 37N 0 40 E
Ang Thong 71 14 35N 100 31 E
Angamos, Punta 124 23 1 S 70 32W
Ang'angxi 75 47 10N 123 48 E
Angara → 59 58 30N 97 0 E
Angarab 87 13 11N 37 7 E
Angarsk 59 52 30N 104 0 E
Angaston 99 34 30 S 139 8 E
Ånge 48 62 31N 15 35 E
Angel de la Guarda 120 29 30N 113 30W
Angeles 73 15 9N 120 33 E
Ängelholm 49 56 15N 12 58 E
Angellala 99 26 24 S 146 54 E
Angels Camp 119 38 8N 120 30W
Ängelsberg 48 59 58N 16 0 E
Anger → 87 9 37N 36 6 E
Angereb → 87 13 45N 36 40 E
Ångermanälven → 48 62 40N 18 0 E
Angermünde 24 53 1N 14 0 E
Angers, Can. 113 45 31N 75 29W
Angers, France 18 47 30N 0 35W
Angerville 19 48 19N 2 0 E
Ångesån → 50 66 50N 22 15 E
Anghiari 39 43 32N 12 3 E
Angikuni L. 109 62 0N 100 0W
Angkor 71 13 22N 103 50 E
Anglés 32 41 57N 2 38 E
Anglesey 12 53 17N 4 20W
Anglet 20 43 29N 1 31W
Angleton 117 29 12N 95 23W
Anglin → 20 46 42N 0 52 E
Anglure 19 48 35N 3 50 E
Angmagssalik 4 65 40N 37 20W
Ango 90 4 10N 26 5 E
Angoche 91 16 8 S 40 0 E
Angoche, I. 91 16 20 S 39 50 E
Angol 124 37 56 S 72 45W
Angola, Ind., U.S.A. 114 41 40N 85 0W
Angola, N.Y., U.S.A. 112 42 38N 79 2W
Angola ■ 89 12 0 S 18 0 E
Angoon 108 57 40N 134 40W
Angoram 98 4 4 S 144 4 E
Angoulême 20 45 39N 0 10 E
Angoumois 20 45 50N 0 25 E
Angra dos Reis 125 23 0 S 44 10W
Angren 58 41 1N 70 12 E
Angu 90 3 25N 24 28 E
Anguilla 121 18 14N 63 5W
Angus, Braes of 14 56 51N 3 10W
Anhanduí → 125 21 46 S 52 9W
Anholt 49 56 42N 11 33 E
Anhua 77 28 23N 111 12 E
Anhui □ 75 32 0N 117 0 E
Anhwei □ = Anhui □ 75 32 0N 117 0 E
Anidhros 45 36 38N 25 43 E
Anie 85 7 42N 1 8 E
Animas 119 31 58N 108 58W
Ånimskog 49 58 53N 12 35 E
Anin 71 15 36N 97 50 E
Anina 42 45 6N 21 51 E
Anivorano 93 18 44 S 48 58 E
Anjangaon 68 21 10N 77 20 E
Anjar 68 23 6N 70 10 E
Anjidiv I. 70 14 40N 74 10 E
Anjou 18 47 20N 0 15W
Anjozorobe 93 18 22 S 47 52 E
Anju 76 39 36N 125 40 E
Anka 85 12 13N 5 58 E
Ankang 75 32 40N 109 1 E
Ankara 64 40 0N 32 54 E
Ankaramena 93 21 57 S 46 39 E
Ankazoabo 93 22 18 S 44 31 E
Ankazobe 93 18 20 S 47 10 E
Ankisabe 93 19 17 S 46 29 E
Anklam 24 53 48N 13 40 E
Anklesvar 68 21 38N 73 3 E
Ankober 87 9 35N 39 40 E
Ankoro 90 6 45 S 26 55 E
Anlu 77 31 15N 113 45 E
Ånn 48 63 19N 12 34 E
Ann Arbor 114 42 17N 83 45W
Ann C., Antarct. 5 66 30 S 50 30 E
Ann C., U.S.A. 114 42 39N 70 37W
Anna, U.S.A. 117 37 28N 89 10W
Anna, U.S.S.R. 55 51 28N 40 23 E
Annaba 83 36 50N 7 46 E
Annaberg-Buchholz 24 50 34N 12 58 E
Annalee → 15 54 3N 7 15W
Annam = Trung-Phan 71 16 30N 107 30 E
Annamitique, Chaîne 71 17 0N 106 0 E
Annan 14 55 0N 3 17W
Annan → 14 54 58N 3 18W
Annapolis 114 38 95N 76 30W
Annapolis Royal 107 44 44N 65 32W
Annapurna 69 28 34N 83 50 E
Anneberg 49 57 32N 12 6 E
Annecy 21 45 55N 6 8 E
Annecy, L. d' 21 45 52N 6 10 E
Annemasse 21 46 12N 6 16 E
Anning 75 24 55N 102 26 E
Anniston 115 33 45N 85 50W
Annobón 79 1 25 S 5 35 E
Annonay 21 45 15N 4 40 E
Annonciation, L' 106 46 25N 74 55W
Annot 21 43 58N 6 38 E
Annotto Bay 121 18 17N 77 3W
Annuello 99 34 53 S 142 55 E
Annville 113 40 18N 76 32W
Annweiler 25 49 12N 7 58 E
Áno Arkhánai 45 35 16N 25 11 E
Áno Porróia 44 41 17N 23 2 E
Áno Viánnos 45 35 2N 25 21 E
Anoka 116 45 10N 93 26W
Anorotsangana 93 13 56 S 47 55 E
Anqing 75 30 30N 117 3 E
Anren 77 26 43N 113 18 E
Ansāb 64 29 11N 44 43 E
Ansai 76 36 50N 109 20 E
Ansbach 25 49 17N 10 34 E
Anse au Loup, L' 107 51 32N 56 50W
Anse, L' 106 46 47N 88 28W
Anseba → 87 16 0N 38 30 E
Anshan 76 41 5N 122 58 E
Anshun 75 26 18N 105 57 E
Ansirabe 93 19 55 S 47 2 E
Ansley 116 41 19N 99 24W
Ansó 32 42 51N 0 48W
Anson 117 32 46N 99 54W
Anson B. 96 13 20 S 130 6 E
Ansongo 85 15 25N 0 35 E
Ansonia 113 41 21N 73 6W
Anstruther 14 56 14N 2 40W
Ansudu 73 2 11 S 139 22 E
Antabamba 126 14 40 S 73 0W
Antakya 64 36 14N 36 10 E
Antalaha 93 14 57 S 50 20 E
Antalya 64 36 52N 30 45 E
Antalya Körfezi 64 36 15N 31 30 E
Antananarivo 93 18 55 S 47 31 E
Antananarivo □ 93 19 0 S 47 0 E
Antanimbaribe 93 21 30 S 44 48 E
Antarctic Pen. 5 67 0 S 60 0W
Antarctica 5 90 0 S 0 0
Antelope 91 21 2 S 28 31 E
Antequera, Parag. 124 24 8 S 57 7W
Antequera, Spain 31 37 5N 4 33W
Antero Mt. 119 38 45N 106 15W
Anthemoús 44 40 31N 23 15 E
Anthony, Kans., U.S.A. 117 37 8N 98 2W
Anthony, N. Mex., U.S.A. 119 32 1N 106 37W
Anti Atlas, Mts. 82 30 0N 8 30W
Antibes 21 43 34N 7 6 E
Antibes, C. d' 21 43 31N 7 7 E
Anticosti, Î. d' 107 49 30N 63 0W
Antifer, C. d' 18 49 41N 0 10 E
Antigo 116 45 8N 89 5W
Antigonish 107 45 38N 61 58W
Antigua 120 14 34N 90 41W
Antigua & Barbuda ■ 121 17 0N 61 50W
Antilla 121 20 40N 75 50W
Antimony 119 38 7N 112 0W
Antioch 118 38 7N 121 45W
Antioche, Pertuis d' 20 46 6N 1 20W
Antioquia 126 6 40N 75 55W
Antipodes Is. 94 49 45 S 178 40 E
Antler 116 48 58N 101 18W
Antler → 109 49 8N 101 0W
Antlers 117 34 15N 95 35W
Antofagasta 124 23 50 S 70 30W
Antofagasta □ 124 24 0 S 69 0W
Antofagasta de la Sierra 124 26 5 S 67 20W
Antofalla 124 25 30 S 68 5W
Antofalla, Salar de 124 25 40 S 67 45W
Anton 117 33 49N 102 5W
Anton Chico 119 35 12N 105 5W
Antongila, Helodrano 93 15 30 S 49 50 E
Antonibé 93 15 7 S 47 24 E
Antonibé, Presqu'île d' 93 14 55 S 47 20 E
Antonina 125 25 26 S 48 42W
Antonito 119 37 4N 106 1W
Antonovo 57 49 25N 51 42 E
Antrain 18 48 28N 1 30W
Antrim 15 54 43N 6 13W
Antrim □ 15 54 55N 6 20W
Antrim, Mts. of 15 54 57N 6 8W
Antrodoco 39 42 25N 13 4 E
Antropovo 55 58 26N 42 51 E
Antsalova 93 18 40 S 44 37 E
Antsiranana 93 12 25 S 49 20 E
Antsohihy 93 14 50 S 47 59 E
Antwerp 113 44 12N 75 36W
Antwerp = Antwerpen 16 51 13N 4 25 E
Antwerpen 16 51 13N 4 25 E
Antwerpen □ 16 51 15N 4 40 E
Anupgarh 68 29 10N 73 10 E
Anuradhapura 70 8 22N 80 28 E
Anvers = Antwerpen 16 51 13N 4 25 E
Anvers I. 5 64 30 S 63 40W
Anvik 104 62 37N 160 20W
Anxi, Fujian, China 77 25 2N 118 12 E
Anxi, Gansu, China 75 40 30N 95 43 E
Anxious B. 96 33 24 S 134 45 E
Anyama 84 5 30N 4 3W
Anyang 76 36 5N 114 21 E
Anyer-Lor 73 6 6 S 105 56 E
Anyi, Jiangxi, China 77 28 49N 115 25 E
Anyi, Shanxi, China 77 35 2N 111 2 E
Anyuan 77 25 9N 115 21 E
'Anzah 62 32 22N 35 12 E
Anzhero-Sudzhensk 58 56 10N 86 0 E
Ánzio 40 41 28N 12 37 E
Aoiz 32 42 46N 1 22W
Aomori 74 40 45N 140 45 E
Aomori □ 74 40 45N 140 40 E
Aonla 68 28 16N 79 11 E
Aoreora 82 28 51N 10 53W
Aosta 38 45 43N 7 20 E
Aoudéras 85 17 45N 8 20 E
Aouinet Torkoz 82 28 31N 9 46W
Aoukar 82 23 50N 2 45W
Aouker 84 17 40N 10 0W
Aoulef el Arab 82 26 55N 1 2 E
Apa → 124 22 6 S 58 2W
Apache, Ariz., U.S.A. 119 31 46N 109 6W
Apache, Okla., U.S.A. 117 34 53N 98 22W
Apalachee B. 115 30 0N 84 0W
Apalachicola 115 29 40N 85 0W
Apapa 85 6 25N 3 25 E
Apaporis → 126 1 23 S 69 25W
Aparri 73 18 22N 121 38 E
Apateu 46 46 36N 21 47 E
Apatin 42 45 40N 19 0 E
Apàtity 52 67 34N 33 22 E
Apatzingán 120 19 0N 102 20W
Apeldoorn 16 52 13N 5 57 E
Apen 24 53 12N 7 47 E
Apenam 72 8 35 S 116 13 E
Apennines 9 44 20N 10 20 E
Apia 101 13 50 S 171 50W
Apiacás, Serra dos 126 9 50 S 57 0W
Apizaco 120 19 26N 98 9W
Aplao 126 16 0 S 72 40W
Apo, Mt. 73 6 53N 125 14 E
Apolda 24 51 1N 11 30 E
Apollo Bay 100 38 45 S 143 40 E
Apollonia 45 36 58N 24 43 E
Apollonia = Marsá Susah 81 32 52N 21 59 E
Apolo 126 14 30 S 68 30W
Apostle Is. 116 47 0N 90 30W
Apóstoles 125 28 0 S 56 0W
Apostolovo 56 47 39N 33 39 E
Apoteri 126 4 2N 58 32W
Appalachian Mts. 114 38 0N 80 0W
Appalachicola → 115 29 40N 85 0W
Appennini 41 41 0N 15 0 E
Appennino Ligure 38 44 30N 9 0 E
Appenzell-Ausser Rhoden □ 25 47 23N 9 23 E
Appenzell-Inner Rhoden □ 25 47 20N 9 25 E
Appiano 39 46 27N 11 17 E
Apple Hill 113 45 13N 74 46W
Appleby 12 54 35N 2 29W
Appleton 114 44 17N 88 25W
Approuague 127 4 20N 52 0W
Aprelevka, U.S.S.R. 55 55 33N 37 4 E
Aprelevka, U.S.S.R. 55 55 34N 37 4 E
Apricena 41 41 47N 15 25 E
Aprigliano 41 39 17N 16 19 E
Aprilia 40 41 38N 12 38 E
Apsheronsk 57 44 28N 39 42 E
Apt 21 43 53N 5 24 E
Apucarana 125 23 55 S 51 33W
Apulia = Púglia 41 41 0N 16 30 E
Apure → 126 7 37N 66 25W
Apurimac → 126 12 17 S 73 56W
Apuseni, Munții 46 46 30N 22 45 E
Aqabah = Al 'Aqabah 86 29 13N 35 0 E
'Aqabah, Khalīj al 64 28 15N 33 20 E
Āqcheh 65 37 0N 66 5 E
Aqīq 86 18 14N 38 12 E
Aqīq, Khalīg 86 18 20N 38 10 E
Aqrabā 62 32 9N 35 20 E
Aqrah 64 36 46N 43 45 E
Aquidauana 127 20 30 S 55 50W
Áquila, L' 39 42 21N 13 24 E
Aquiles Serdán 120 28 37N 105 54W
Ar Rachidiya 82 31 58N 4 20W
Ar Rafīd 62 32 57N 35 52 E
Ar Ramādī 64 33 25N 43 20 E
Ar Raml 83 26 45N 19 40 E
Ar Ramthā 62 32 34N 36 0 E
Ar Raqqah 64 36 0N 38 55 E
Ar Rass 64 25 50N 43 40 E
Ar Rifā'ī 64 31 50N 46 10 E
Ar Riyāḍ 64 24 41N 46 42 E
Ar Rummān 62 32 9N 35 48 E
Ar Ruṭbah 64 33 0N 40 15 E
Ar Ruwayḍah 64 23 40N 44 40 E
Arab, Bahr el → 87 9 50N 29 0 E
Arab, Khalîg el 86 30 55N 29 0 E
Arab, Shatt al 64 30 0N 48 31 E
Arabatskaya Strelka 56 45 40N 35 0 E
Arabba 39 46 30N 11 51 E
Arabia 60 25 0N 45 0 E
Arabian Sea 60 16 0N 65 0 E
Arac 64 41 15N 33 21 E
Aracaju 127 10 55 S 37 4W
Aracataca 126 10 38N 74 9W
Aracati 127 4 30 S 37 44W
Araçatuba 125 21 10 S 50 30W
Aracena 31 37 53N 6 38W
Aracena, Sierra de 31 37 50N 6 50W
Araçuai 127 16 52 S 42 4W
'Arad 62 31 15N 35 12 E
Arad 42 46 10N 21 20 E
Arad □ 42 46 20N 22 0 E
Arada 81 15 0N 20 20 E
Aradu Nou 42 46 8N 21 20 E
Arafura Sea 73 9 0 S 135 0 E
Aragats 57 40 30N 44 15 E
Aragón 32 41 25N 1 0W
Aragón → 32 42 13N 1 44W
Aragona 40 37 24N 13 36 E
Araguacema 127 8 50 S 49 20W
Araguaia → 127 5 21 S 48 41W
Araguari 127 18 38 S 48 11W
Araguari → 127 1 15N 49 55W
Arak 82 25 20N 3 45 E
Arāk 64 34 0N 49 40 E
Arakan Coast 67 19 0N 94 0 E
Arakan Yoma 67 20 0N 94 40 E
Arákhova 45 38 28N 22 35 E
Araks = Aras, Rūd-e → 64 39 10N 47 10 E
Aral Sea = Aralskoye More 58 44 30N 60 0 E
Aralsk 58 46 50N 61 20 E
Aralskoye More 58 44 30N 60 0 E
Aramā, Mții. de 46 47 10N 22 30 E
Aramac 97 22 58 S 145 14 E
Arambagh 69 22 53N 87 48 E
Aran I. 15 55 0N 8 30W
Aran Is. 15 53 5N 9 42W
Aranda de Duero 32 41 39N 3 42W
Aranđelovac 42 44 18N 20 27 E
Aranjuez 30 40 1N 3 40W
Aranos 92 24 9 S 19 7 E
Aransas Pass 117 27 55N 97 9W
Araouane 84 18 55N 3 30W
Arapahoe 116 40 22N 99 53W
Arapey Grande → 124 30 55 S 57 49W
Arapkir 64 39 5N 38 30 E

Arapongas Aska

Arapongas	125	23 29 S	51 28W
Araranguá	125	29 0 S	49 30W
Araraquara	127	21 50 S	48 0W
Ararás, Serra das	125	25 0 S	53 10W
Ararat	97	37 16 S	143 0 E
Ararat, Mt. = Ağri Daği	64	39 50N	44 15 E
Araria	69	26 9N	87 33 E
Araripe, Chapada do	127	7 20 S	40 0W
Araruama, Lagoa de	125	22 53 S	42 12W
Aras, Rūd-e →	64	39 10N	47 10 E
Arauca	126	7 0N	70 40W
Arauca →	126	7 24N	66 35W
Arauco	124	37 16 S	73 25W
Arauco □	124	37 40 S	73 25W
Arawa	87	9 57N	41 58 E
Araxá	127	19 35 S	46 55W
Araya, Pen. de	126	10 40N	64 0W
Arba Minch	87	6 0N	37 30 E
Arbatax	40	39 57N	9 42 E
Arbaza	59	52 40N	92 30 E
Arbīl	64	36 15N	44 5 E
Arboga	48	59 24N	15 52 E
Arbois	19	46 55N	5 46 E
Arbore	87	5 3N	36 50 E
Arborea	40	39 46N	8 34 E
Arborfield	109	53 6N	103 39W
Arborg	109	50 54N	97 13W
Arbrå	48	61 28N	16 22 E
Arbresie, L'	21	45 50N	4 26 E
Arbroath	14	56 34N	2 35W
Arbuckle	118	39 3N	122 2W
Arbus	40	39 30N	8 33 E
Arbuzinka	56	47 0N	31 59 E
Arc	19	47 28N	5 34 E
Arc →	21	45 34N	6 12 E
Arcachon	20	44 40N	1 10W
Arcachon, Bassin d'	20	44 42N	1 10W
Arcade	112	42 34N	78 25W
Arcadia, Fla., U.S.A.	115	27 20N	81 50W
Arcadia, La., U.S.A.	117	32 34N	92 53W
Arcadia, Nebr., U.S.A.	116	41 29N	99 4W
Arcadia, Pa., U.S.A.	112	40 46N	78 54W
Arcadia, Wis., U.S.A.	116	44 13N	91 29W
Arcata	118	40 55N	124 4W
Arcévia	39	43 29N	12 58 E
Archangel = Arkhangelsk	52	64 40N	41 0 E
Archar	42	43 50N	22 54 E
Archbald	113	41 30N	75 31W
Archena	33	38 9N	1 16W
Archer →	97	13 28 S	141 41 E
Archer B.	98	13 20 S	141 30 E
Archers Post	90	0 35N	37 35 E
Archidona	31	37 6N	4 22W
Arci, Monte	40	39 47N	8 44 E
Arcidosso	39	42 51N	11 30 E
Arcila = Asilah	82	35 29N	6 0W
Arcis-sur-Aube	19	48 32N	4 10 E
Arco, Italy	38	45 55N	10 54 E
Arco, U.S.A.	118	43 45N	113 16W
Arcola	109	49 40N	102 30W
Arcos	32	41 12N	2 16W
Arcos de los Frontera	31	36 45N	5 49W
Arcos de Valdevez	30	41 55N	8 22W
Arcot	70	12 53N	79 20 E
Arcoverde	127	8 25 S	37 4W
Arcs, Les	21	43 27N	6 29 E
Arctic Bay	105	73 1N	85 7W
Arctic Ocean	4	78 0N	160 0W
Arctic Red River	104	67 15N	134 0W
Arda →, Bulg.	43	41 40N	26 29 E
Arda →, Italy	38	44 53N	9 52 E
Ardabīl	64	38 15N	48 18 E
Ardahan	64	41 7N	42 41 E
Ardakān	65	30 20N	52 5 E
Årdal, Aust-Agder, Norway	47	58 42N	7 48 E
Årdal, Rogaland, Norway	47	59 9N	6 13 E
Ardales	31	36 53N	4 51W
Årdalstangen	47	61 14N	7 43 E
Ardatov	55	54 51N	46 15 E
Ardea	44	40 58N	22 3 E
Ardèche □	21	44 42N	4 16 E
Ardèche →	21	44 16N	4 39 E
Ardee	15	53 51N	6 32W
Arden	112	44 43N	76 56W
Arden Stby.	49	56 46N	9 52 E
Ardennes	16	50 0N	5 10 E
Ardennes □	19	49 35N	4 40 E
Ardentes	19	46 45N	1 50 E
Ardestān	65	33 20N	52 25 E
Ardgour	14	56 45N	5 25W
Árdhas →	44	41 36N	26 25 E
Ardila →	31	38 12N	7 28W
Ardino	43	41 34N	25 9 E
Ardjuno	73	7 49 S	112 34 E
Ardlethan	99	34 22 S	146 53 E
Ardmore, Austral.	98	21 39 S	139 11 E
Ardmore, Okla., U.S.A.	117	34 10N	97 5W
Ardmore, Pa., U.S.A.	113	39 58N	75 18W
Ardmore, S.D., U.S.A.	116	43 0N	103 40W
Ardnacrusha	15	52 43N	8 38W
Ardnamurchan, Pt. of	14	56 44N	6 14W
Ardore Marina	41	38 11N	16 10 E
Ardres	19	50 50N	2 0 E
Ardrossan, Austral.	99	34 26 S	137 53 E
Ardrossan, U.K.	14	55 39N	4 50W
Ards □	15	54 35N	5 30W
Ards Pen.	15	54 30N	5 25W
Ardud	46	47 37N	22 52 E
Ardunac	57	41 8N	42 5 E
Åre	48	63 22N	13 15 E
Arecibo	121	18 29N	66 42W
Areia Branca	127	5 0 S	37 0W
Aremark	47	59 15N	11 42 E
Arenas	30	43 17N	4 50W
Arenas de San Pedro	30	40 12N	5 5W
Arendal	47	58 28N	8 46 E
Arendsee	24	52 52N	11 27 E
Arenys de Mar	32	41 35N	2 33 E
Arenzano	38	44 24N	8 40 E
Areópolis	45	36 40N	22 22 E
Arequipa	126	16 20 S	71 30W
Arero	87	4 41N	38 50 E
Arès	20	44 47N	1 8W
Arévalo	30	41 3N	4 43W
Arezzo	39	43 28N	11 50 E
Arga →	32	42 18N	1 47W
Argalastí	44	39 13N	23 13 E
Argamasilla de Alba	33	39 8N	3 5W
Arganda	32	40 19N	3 26W
Arganil	30	40 13N	8 3W
Argelès-Gazost	20	43 0N	0 6W
Argelès-sur-Mer	20	42 34N	3 1 E
Argens →	21	43 24N	6 44 E
Argent-sur-Sauldre	19	47 33N	2 25 E
Argenta, Can.	108	50 20N	116 55W
Argenta, Italy	39	44 37N	11 50 E
Argentan	18	48 45N	0 1W
Argentário, Mte.	39	42 23N	11 11 E
Argentat	20	45 6N	1 56 E
Argentera	38	44 23N	6 58 E
Argentera, Monte del	38	44 12N	7 5 E
Argenteuil	19	48 57N	2 14 E
Argentia	107	47 18N	53 58W
Argentiera, C. dell'	40	40 44N	8 8 E
Argentière, L'	21	44 47N	6 33 E
Argentina ■	128	35 0 S	66 0W
Argentino, L.	128	50 10 S	73 0W
Argenton-Château	18	46 59N	0 27W
Argenton-sur-Creuse	20	46 36N	1 30 E
Argeş □	46	45 0N	24 45 E
Argeş →	46	44 30N	25 50 E
Arghandab →	66	31 30N	64 15 E
Argo	86	19 28N	30 30 E
Argolikós Kólpos	45	37 20N	22 52 E
Argolís □	45	37 38N	22 50 E
Argonne	19	49 0N	5 20 E
Árgos	45	37 40N	22 43 E
Árgos Orestikón	44	40 27N	21 26 E
Argostólion	45	38 12N	20 33 E
Arguedas	32	42 11N	1 36W
Arguello, Pt.	119	34 34N	120 40W
Argun →	59	53 20N	121 28 E
Argungu	85	12 40N	4 31 E
Argyle	116	48 23N	96 49W
Argyrádhes	44	39 27N	19 58 E
Århus	49	56 8N	10 11 E
Århus Amtskommune □	49	56 15N	10 15 E
Ariamsvlei	92	28 9 S	19 51 E
Ariana	83	36 52N	10 12 E
Ariano Irpino	41	41 10N	15 4 E
Ariano nel Polèsine	39	44 56N	12 5 E
Aribinda	85	14 17N	0 52W
Arica, Chile	126	18 32 S	70 20W
Arica, Colomb.	126	2 0 S	71 50W
Arid, C.	96	34 1 S	123 10 E
Aridh	64	25 0N	46 0 E
Ariège □	20	42 56N	1 30 E
Ariège →	20	43 30N	1 25 E
Arieş →	46	46 24N	23 20 E
Arilje	42	43 44N	20 7 E
Arima	121	10 38N	61 17W
Arinos →	126	10 25 S	58 20W
Ario de Rosales	120	19 12N	102 0W
Aripuanã	126	9 25 S	60 30W
Aripuanã →	126	5 7 S	60 25W
Ariquemes	126	9 55 S	63 6W
Arisaig	14	56 55N	5 50W
Arîsh, W. el →	86	31 9N	33 49 E
Arissa	87	11 10N	41 35 E
Aristazabal I.	108	52 40N	129 10W
Arivaca	119	31 37N	111 25W
Arivonimamo	93	19 1 S	47 11 E
Ariyalur	70	11 8N	79 8 E
Ariza	74	41 19N	2 3W
Arizaro, Salar de	124	24 40 S	67 50W
Arizona	124	35 45 S	65 25W
Arizona □	119	34 20N	111 30W
Arizpe	120	30 20N	110 11W
Årjäng	48	59 24N	12 8 E
Arjeplog	50	66 3N	18 2 E
Arjona, Colomb.	126	10 14N	75 22W
Arjona, Spain	31	37 56N	4 4W
Arka	59	60 15N	142 0 E
Arkadak	55	51 58N	43 19 E
Arkadelphia	117	34 5N	93 0W
Arkadhía □	45	37 30N	22 20 E
Arkaig, L.	14	56 58N	5 10W
Arkalyk	58	50 13N	66 50 E
Arkansas □	117	35 0N	92 30W
Arkansas →	117	33 48N	91 4W
Arkansas City	117	37 4N	97 3W
Árkathos →	44	39 20N	21 4 E
Arkhángelos	45	36 13N	28 7 E
Arkhangelsk	52	64 40N	41 0 E
Arkhangelskoye	55	51 32N	40 58 E
Arkiko	87	15 33N	39 30 E
Arklow	15	52 48N	6 10W
Árkoi	45	37 24N	26 44 E
Arkona, Kap	24	54 41N	13 26 E
Arkonam	70	13 7N	79 43 E
Arkösund	49	58 29N	16 56 E
Arkoúdhi	45	38 33N	20 43 E
Arkticheskiy, Mys	59	81 10N	95 0 E
Arkul	55	57 17N	50 3 E
Arlanc	20	45 25N	3 42 E
Arlanza →	30	42 6N	4 9W
Arlanzón →	30	42 3N	4 17W
Arlberg Pass	25	47 9N	10 12 E
Arlee	118	47 10N	114 4W
Arles	21	43 41N	4 40 E
Arlington, S. Afr.	93	28 1 S	27 53 E
Arlington, Oreg., U.S.A.	118	45 48N	120 6W
Arlington, S.D., U.S.A.	116	44 25N	97 4W
Arlington, Va., U.S.A.	114	38 52N	77 3W
Arlington, Wash., U.S.A.	118	48 11N	122 4W
Arlon	16	49 42N	5 49 E
Arlöv	49	55 38N	13 5 E
Arly	85	11 35N	1 28 E
Armagh	15	54 22N	6 40W
Armagh □	15	54 18N	6 37W
Armagnac	20	43 44N	0 10 E
Armançon →	19	47 59N	3 30 E
Armavir	57	45 2N	41 7 E
Armenia	126	4 35N	75 45W
Armenian S.S.R. □	57	40 0N	44 0 E
Armeniş	46	45 13N	22 17 E
Armentières	19	50 40N	2 50 E
Armidale	97	30 30 S	151 40 E
Armour	116	43 20N	98 25W
Armstrong, B.C., Can.	108	50 25N	119 10W
Armstrong, Ont., Can.	106	50 18N	89 4W
Armstrong, U.S.A.	117	26 59N	97 48W
Armur	70	18 48N	78 16 E
Arnaía	44	40 30N	23 40 E
Arnaouti, C.	64	35 0N	32 20 E
Arnarfjörður	50	65 48N	23 40W
Arnaud →	105	60 0N	70 0W
Arnay-le-Duc	19	47 10N	4 27 E
Arnedillo	32	42 13N	2 14W
Arnedo	32	42 12N	2 5W
Árnes	50	66 1N	21 31W
Årnes	47	60 7N	11 28 E
Arnett	117	36 9N	99 44W
Arnhem	16	51 58N	5 55 E
Arnhem B.	96	12 20 S	136 10 E
Arnhem, C.	97	12 20 S	137 30 E
Arnhem Land	96	13 10 S	134 30 E
Arni	70	12 43N	79 19 E
Árnissa	44	40 47N	21 49 E
Arno →	38	43 41N	10 17 E
Arnold, Nebr., U.S.A.	116	41 29N	100 10W
Arnold, Pa., U.S.A.	112	40 36N	79 44W
Arnoldstein	26	46 33N	13 43 E
Arnon →	19	47 13N	2 1 E
Arnot	109	55 56N	96 41W
Arnøy	50	70 9N	20 40 E
Arnprior	106	45 26N	76 21W
Arnsberg	24	51 25N	8 2 E
Arnstadt	24	50 50N	10 56 E
Aroab	92	26 41 S	19 39 E
Aroánia Óri	45	37 56N	22 12 E
Aroche	31	37 56N	6 57W
Arolsen	24	51 23N	9 1 E
Aron →	19	46 50N	3 27 E
Arona	38	45 45N	8 32 E
Arosa, Ria de →	30	42 28N	8 57W
Arpajon, Cantal, France	20	44 54N	2 28 E
Arpajon, Essonne, France	19	48 37N	2 12 E
Arpino	40	41 40N	13 35 E
Arrabury	99	26 45 S	141 0 E
Arrah	69	25 35N	84 32 E
Arraiján	120	8 56N	79 36W
Arraiolos	31	38 44N	7 59W
Arran	14	55 34N	5 12W
Arrandale	108	54 57N	130 0W
Arras	19	50 17N	2 46 E
Arrats →	20	44 6N	0 52 E
Arreau	20	42 54N	0 22 E
Arrecife	80	28 57N	13 37W
Arrecifes	124	34 06 S	60 9W
Arrée, Mts. d'	18	48 26N	3 55W
Arriaga	120	21 55N	101 23W
Arrilalah P.O.	98	23 43 S	143 54 E
Arromanches-les-Bains	18	49 20N	0 38W
Arronches	31	39 8N	7 16W
Arros, R	20	43 40N	0 2W
Arrou	18	48 6N	1 8 E
Arrow, L.	15	54 3N	8 20W
Arrow Rock Res.	118	43 45N	115 50W
Arrowhead	108	50 40N	117 55W
Arrowtown	101	44 57 S	168 50 E
Arroyo de la Luz	31	39 30N	6 38W
Arroyo Grande	119	35 9N	120 32W
Års	49	56 48N	9 30 E
Ars	20	46 13N	1 30W
Ars-sur-Moselle	19	49 5N	6 4 E
Arsenault L.	109	55 6N	108 32W
Arsiero	39	45 49N	11 22 E
Arsikere	70	13 15N	76 15 E
Arsk	55	56 10N	49 50 E
Árta	45	39 8N	21 2 E
Artá	32	39 41N	3 21 E
Árta □	44	39 15N	21 5 E
Arteaga	120	18 50N	102 20W
Arteijo	30	43 19N	8 29W
Artem, Ostrov	57	40 28N	50 20 E
Artemovsk, R.S.F.S.R., U.S.S.R.	59	54 45N	93 35 E
Artemovsk, Ukraine S.S.R., U.S.S.R.	56	48 35N	38 0 E
Artemovski	57	47 45N	40 16 E
Artenay	19	48 5N	1 50 E
Artern	24	51 22N	11 18 E
Artesa de Segre	32	41 54N	1 3 E
Artesia	117	32 55N	104 25W
Artesia Wells	117	28 17N	99 18W
Artesian	116	44 2N	97 54W
Arthez-de-Béarn	20	43 29N	0 38W
Arthington	84	6 35N	10 45W
Arthur →	99	41 2 S	144 40 E
Arthur Pt.	98	22 7 S	150 3 E
Arthur's Pass	101	42 54 S	171 35 E
Artigas	124	30 20 S	56 30W
Artik	57	40 38N	43 58 E
Artillery L.	109	63 9N	107 52W
Artois	19	50 20N	2 30 E
Artotína	45	38 42N	22 2 E
Artsiz	56	46 4N	29 26 E
Artvin	64	41 14N	41 44 E
Aru, Kepulauan	73	6 0 S	134 30 E
Aru Meru □	90	3 20 S	36 50 E
Arua	90	3 1N	30 58 E
Aruanã	127	14 54 S	51 10W
Aruba	121	12 30N	70 0W
Arudy	20	43 7N	0 28W
Arun →	69	26 55N	87 10 E
Arunachal Pradesh □	67	28 0N	95 0 E
Aruppukottai	70	9 31N	78 8 E
Arusha	90	3 20 S	36 40 E
Arusha □	90	4 0 S	36 30 E
Arusha Chini	90	3 32 S	37 20 E
Arusi □	87	7 45N	39 00 E
Aruvi →	70	8 48N	79 53 E
Aruwimi →	90	1 13N	23 36 E
Arvada	118	44 43N	106 6W
Arvakalu	70	8 20N	79 58 E
Arvayheer	75	46 15N	102 48 E
Arve →	21	46 11N	6 8 E
Arvi	68	20 59N	78 16 E
Arvida	107	48 25N	71 14W
Arvidsjaur	50	65 35N	19 10 E
Arvika	48	59 40N	12 36 E
Arxan	75	47 11N	119 57 E
Arys	58	42 26N	68 48 E
Arzachena	40	41 5N	9 27 E
Arzamas	55	55 27N	43 55 E
Arzew	82	35 50N	0 23W
Arzgir	57	45 18N	44 23 E
Arzignano	39	45 30N	11 20 E
Aš	26	50 13N	12 12 E
'As Saffānīyah	64	28 5N	48 50 E
Aş Şāfī	62	31 2N	35 28 E
As Salt	62	32 2N	35 43 E
As Samāwah	64	31 15N	45 15 E
As Samū'	62	31 24N	35 4 E
As Sanamayn	62	33 3N	36 10 E
As Sulaymānīyah	64	24 9N	47 18 E
As Sulţan	83	31 4N	17 8 E
As Sumaymānīyah	64	35 35N	45 29 E
As Summān	64	25 0N	47 0 E
As Suwaih	65	22 10N	59 33 E
As Suwaydā'	64	32 40N	36 30 E
Aş Şuwayrah	64	32 55N	45 0 E
Asab	92	25 30 S	18 0 E
Asaba	85	6 12N	6 38 E
Asafo	84	6 20N	2 40W
Asahigawa	74	43 46N	142 22 E
Asale, L.	87	14 0N	40 20 E
Asamankese	85	5 50N	0 40W
Asansol	69	23 40N	87 1 E
Åsarna	48	62 39N	14 22 E
Asbe Teferi	87	9 4N	40 49 E
Asbesberge	92	29 0 S	23 0 E
Asbestos	107	45 47N	71 58W
Asbury Park	114	40 15N	74 1W
Ascensión, B. de la	120	19 50N	87 20W
Ascension I.	7	8 0 S	14 15W
Aschach	26	48 22N	14 2 E
Aschaffenburg	25	49 58N	9 8 E
Aschendorf	24	53 2N	7 22 E
Aschersleben	24	51 45N	11 28 E
Asciano	39	43 14N	11 32 E
Áscoli Piceno	39	42 51N	13 34 E
Áscoli Satriano	41	41 11N	15 32 E
Ascope	126	7 46 S	79 8W
Ascotán	124	21 45 S	68 17W
Aseb	87	13 0N	42 40 E
Åseda	49	57 10N	15 20 E
Asedjrad	82	24 51N	1 29 E
Asela	87	8 0N	39 0 E
Asenovgrad	43	42 1N	24 51 E
Aseral	47	58 37N	7 25 E
Asfeld	19	49 27N	4 5 E
Asfûn el Matâ'na	86	25 26N	32 30 E
Åsgårdstrand	47	59 22N	10 27 E
Ash Fork	119	35 14N	112 32W
Ash Grove	117	37 21N	93 36W
Ash Shām, Bādiyat	64	32 0N	40 0 E
Ash Shāmiyah	64	31 55N	44 35 E
Ash Shāriqah	65	25 23N	55 26 E
Ash Shaţrah	64	31 30N	46 10 E
Ash Shu'aybah	64	27 53N	42 43 E
Ash Shu'bah	64	28 54N	44 44 E
Ash Shūnah ash Shamālīyah	62	32 37N	35 34 E
Asha	52	55 0N	57 16 E
Ashaira	86	21 40N	40 40 E
Ashanti □	85	7 30N	1 30W
Ashburn	115	31 42N	83 40W
Ashburton	101	43 53 S	171 48 E
Ashburton →	96	21 40 S	114 56 E
Ashby-de-la-Zouch	12	52 45N	1 29W
Ashcroft	108	50 40N	121 20W
Ashdod	62	31 49N	34 35 E
Ashdot Yaaqov	62	32 39N	35 35 E
Asheboro	115	35 43N	79 46W
Asherton	117	28 25N	99 43W
Asheville	115	35 39N	82 30W
Asheweig →	106	54 17N	87 12W
Ashford, Austral.	99	29 15 S	151 3 E
Ashford, U.K.	13	51 8N	0 53 E
Ashford, U.S.A.	118	46 45N	122 2W
Ashikaga	74	36 28N	139 29 E
Ashizuri-Zaki	74	32 44N	133 0 E
Ashkhabad	58	38 0N	57 50 E
Ashland, Kans., U.S.A.	117	37 13N	99 43W
Ashland, Ky., U.S.A.	114	38 25N	82 40W
Ashland, Me., U.S.A.	107	46 34N	68 26W
Ashland, Mont., U.S.A.	118	45 41N	106 12W
Ashland, Nebr., U.S.A.	116	41 5N	96 27W
Ashland, Ohio, U.S.A.	114	40 52N	82 20W
Ashland, Oreg., U.S.A.	118	42 10N	122 38W
Ashland, Pa., U.S.A.	113	40 45N	76 22W
Ashland, Va., U.S.A.	114	37 46N	77 30W
Ashland, Wis., U.S.A.	116	46 40N	90 52W
Ashley, N.D., U.S.A.	116	46 3N	99 23W
Ashley, Pa., U.S.A.	113	41 12N	75 55W
Ashley Snow I.	5	73 35 S	77 6W
Ashmont	108	54 7N	111 35W
Ashmore Reef	96	12 14 S	123 5 E
Ashmûn	86	30 18N	30 55 E
Ashq'elon	62	31 42N	34 35 E
Ashtabula	114	41 52N	80 50W
Ashti	70	18 50N	75 15 E
Ashton, S. Afr.	92	33 50 S	20 5 E
Ashton, U.S.A.	118	44 6N	111 30W
Ashton-under-Lyne	12	53 30N	2 8W
Ashuanipi, L.	107	52 45N	66 15W
Asia	60	45 0N	75 0 E
Asia, Kepulauan	73	1 0N	131 13 E
Asiago	39	45 52N	11 30 E
Asifabad	70	19 20N	79 24 E
Asike	73	6 39 S	140 24 E
Asilah	82	35 29N	6 0W
Asinara, G. dell'	40	41 0N	8 30 E
Asinara I.	40	41 5N	8 15 E
Asino	58	57 0N	86 0 E
'Asīr □	63	18 40N	42 30 E
Asir, Ras	63	11 55N	51 10 E
Aska	70	19 2N	84 42 E

Asker Babana

Asker 47 59 50N 10 26 E
Askersund 49 58 53N 14 55 E
Askim 47 59 35N 11 10 E
Askja 50 65 3N 16 48W
Asl 86 29 33N 32 44 E
Asmār 65 35 10N 71 27 E
Asmera (Asmara) 87 15 19N 38 55 E
Asnæs 49 55 40N 11 0 E
Asni 82 31 17N 7 58W
Aso 74 33 0N 131 5 E
Asola 38 45 12N 10 25 E
Asoteriba, Jebel 86 21 51N 36 30 E
Asotin 118 46 20N 117 3W
Aspe 33 38 20N 0 40W
Aspen 119 39 12N 106 56W
Aspermont 117 33 11N 100 15W
Aspiring, Mt. 101 44 23 S 168 46 E
Aspres 21 44 32N 5 44 E
Aspromonte 41 38 10N 16 0 E
Aspur 68 23 58N 74 7 E
Asquith 109 52 8N 107 13W
Assa 82 28 35N 9 6W
Assâba 84 16 10N 11 45W
Assam □ 67 26 0N 93 0 E
Assamakka 85 19 21N 5 38 E
Asse 16 50 24N 4 10 E
Assekrem 83 23 16N 5 49 E
Assémini 40 39 18N 9 0 E
Assen 16 53 0N 6 35 E
Assens, Fyn, Denmark 49 56 41N 10 3 E
Assens, Fyn, Denmark 49 55 16N 9 55 E
Assini 84 5 9N 3 17W
Assiniboia 109 49 40N 105 59W
Assiniboine → 109 49 53N 97 8W
Assis 125 22 40 S 50 20W
Assisi 39 43 4N 12 36 E
Assos 45 38 22N 20 33 E
Assus 44 39 32N 26 22 E
Assynt, L. 14 58 25N 5 15W
Astaffort 20 44 4N 0 40 E
Astakidha 45 35 53N 26 50 E
Astara 53 38 30N 48 50 E
Asti 38 44 54N 8 11 E
Astipálaia 45 36 32N 26 22 E
Astorga 30 42 29N 6 8W
Astoria 118 46 16N 123 50W
Åstorp 49 56 6N 12 55 E
Astrakhan 57 46 25N 48 5 E
Astrakhan-Bazàr 53 39 14N 48 30 E
Astudillo 30 42 12N 4 22W
Asturias 30 43 15N 6 0W
Asunción 124 25 10 S 57 30W
Asunción, La 126 11 2N 63 53W
Asutri 87 15 25N 35 45 E
Aswa → 90 3 43N 31 55 E
Aswad, Ras al 86 21 20N 39 0 E
Aswân 86 24 4N 32 57 E
Aswân High Dam = Sadd el Aali 86 24 5N 32 54 E
Asyût 86 27 11N 31 4 E
Asyûti, Wadi → 86 27 11N 31 16 E
Aszód 27 47 39N 19 28 E
At Ţafīlah 64 30 45N 35 30 E
At Ta'if 86 21 5N 40 27 E
Aţ Ţur 62 31 47N 35 14 E
Aţ Ţurrah 62 32 39N 35 59 E
Atacama □ 124 27 30 S 70 0W
Atacama, Desierto de 124 24 0 S 69 20W
Atacama, Salar de 124 23 30N 68 20W
Atakor 83 23 27N 5 31 E
Atakpamé 85 7 31N 1 13 E
Atalándi 45 38 39N 22 58 E
Atalaya 126 10 45 S 73 50W
Atami 74 35 5N 139 4 E
Atapupu 73 9 0 S 124 51 E
Atâr 80 20 30N 13 5W
Atara 59 63 10N 129 10 E
Ataram, Erg n- 82 23 57N 2 0 E
Atarfe 31 37 13N 3 40W
Atascadero 119 35 32N 120 44W
Atasu 58 48 30N 71 0 E
Atauro 73 8 10 S 125 30 E
Atbara 86 17 42N 33 59 E
'Atbara → 86 17 40N 33 56 E
Atbasar 58 51 48N 68 20 E
Atchafalaya B. 117 29 30N 91 20W
Atchison 116 39 40N 95 10W
Atebubu 85 7 47N 1 0W
Ateca 32 41 20N 1 49W
Aterno → 39 42 11N 13 51 E
Atesine, Alpi 38 46 55N 11 30 E
Atessa 39 42 5N 14 27 E
Ath 16 50 38N 3 47 E
Ath Thāmāmi 64 27 45N 44 45 E
Athabasca 108 54 45N 113 20W
Athabasca → 109 58 40N 110 50W
Athabasca, L. 109 59 15N 109 15W
Athboy 15 53 37N 6 55W
Athenry 15 53 18N 8 45W
Athens, Can. 113 44 38N 75 57W
Athens, Ala., U.S.A. 115 34 49N 86 58W
Athens, Ga., U.S.A. 115 33 56N 83 24W
Athens, N.Y., U.S.A. 113 42 15N 73 48W
Athens, Ohio, U.S.A. 114 39 25N 82 6W
Athens, Pa., U.S.A. 113 41 57N 76 36W
Athens, Tenn., U.S.A. 115 35 45N 84 38W
Athens, Tex., U.S.A. 117 32 11N 95 48W
Athens = Athinai 45 37 58N 23 46 E
Atherley 112 44 37N 79 20W
Atherton 97 17 17 S 145 30 E
Athiéme 85 6 37N 1 40 E
Athinai 45 37 58N 23 46 E
Athlone 15 53 26N 7 57W
Athni 70 16 44N 75 6 E
Atholl, Forest of 14 56 51N 3 50W
Atholville 107 47 59N 66 43W
Áthos, Mt. 44 40 9N 24 22 E
Athy 15 53 0N 7 0W
Ati, Chad 81 13 13N 18 20 E
Ati, Sudan 87 13 5N 29 2 E
Atiak 90 3 12N 32 2 E
Atico 126 16 14 S 73 40W
Atienza 32 41 12N 2 52W
Atikokan 106 48 45N 91 37W
Atikonak L. 107 52 40N 64 32W
Atka 59 60 50N 151 48 E
Atkarsk 55 51 55N 45 2 E
Atkinson 116 42 35N 98 59W
Atlanta, Ga., U.S.A. 115 33 50N 84 24W
Atlanta, Tex., U.S.A. 117 33 7N 94 8W
Atlantic 116 41 25N 95 0W
Atlantic City 114 39 25N 74 25W
Atlantic Ocean 6 0 0 20 0W
Atlin 104 59 31N 133 41W
Atlin, L. 108 59 26N 133 45W
'Atlit 62 32 42N 34 56 E
Atløy 47 61 21N 4 58 E
Atmakur 70 14 37N 79 40 E
Atmore 115 31 2N 87 30W
Atna → 47 61 44N 10 49 E
Atoka 117 34 22N 96 10W
Átokos 45 38 28N 20 49 E
Atouguia 31 39 20N 9 20W
Atoyac → 120 16 30N 97 31W
Atrak → 65 37 50N 57 0 E
Ätran 49 57 7N 12 57 E
Atrauli 68 28 2N 78 20 E
Atri 39 42 35N 14 0 E
Atsbi 87 13 52N 39 50 E
Atsoum, Mts. 85 6 41N 12 57 E
Attalla 115 34 2N 86 5W
Attawapiskat 106 52 56N 82 24W
Attawapiskat → 106 52 57N 82 18W
Attawapiskat, L. 106 52 18N 87 54W
Attendorn 24 51 8N 7 54 E
Attersee 26 47 55N 13 32 E
Attica 114 40 20N 87 15W
Attichy 19 49 25N 3 3 E
Attigny 19 49 28N 4 35 E
Attikamagen L. 107 55 0N 66 30W
Attiki □ 45 38 10N 23 40 E
'Attīl 62 32 23N 35 4 E
Attleboro 114 41 56N 71 18W
Attock 66 33 52N 72 20 E
Attopeu 71 14 48N 106 50 E
Attur 70 11 35N 78 30 E
Atuel → 124 36 17 S 66 50W
Åtvidaberg 49 58 12N 16 0 E
Atwater 119 37 21N 120 37W
Atwood, Can. 112 43 40N 81 1W
Atwood, U.S.A. 116 39 52N 101 3W
Au Sable → 114 44 25N 83 20W
Au Sable Pt. 106 46 40N 86 10W
Aubagne 21 43 17N 5 37 E
Aube □ 19 48 15N 4 0 E
Aube → 19 48 34N 3 43 E
Aubenas 21 44 37N 4 24 E
Aubenton 19 49 50N 4 12 E
Aubigny-sur-Nère 19 47 30N 2 24 E
Aubin 20 44 33N 2 15 E
Aubrac, Mts. d' 20 44 38N 2 58 E
Auburn, Ala., U.S.A. 115 32 37N 85 30W
Auburn, Calif., U.S.A. 118 38 53N 121 4W
Auburn, Ind., U.S.A. 114 41 20N 85 0W
Auburn, N.Y., U.S.A. 114 42 57N 76 39W
Auburn, Nebr., U.S.A. 116 40 25N 95 50W
Auburn Range 99 25 15 S 150 30 E
Auburndale 115 28 5N 81 45W
Aubusson 20 45 57N 2 11 E
Auch 20 43 39N 0 36 E
Auchel 19 50 30N 2 29 E
Auchi 85 7 6N 6 13 E
Auckland 101 36 52 S 174 46 E
Auckland Is. 94 50 40 S 166 5 E
Aude □ 20 43 8N 2 28 E
Aude → 20 43 13N 3 14 E
Auden 106 50 14N 87 53W
Auderville 18 49 43N 1 57W
Audierne 18 48 1N 4 34W
Audincourt 19 47 30N 6 50 E
Audo Ra. 87 6 20N 41 50 E
Audubon 116 41 43N 94 56W
Aue 24 50 34N 12 43 E
Auerbach 24 50 30N 12 25 E
Auffay 18 49 43N 1 07 E
Augathella 97 25 48 S 146 35 E
Augrabies Falls 92 28 35 S 20 20 E
Augsburg 25 48 22N 10 54 E
Augusta, Italy 41 37 14N 15 12 E
Augusta, Ark., U.S.A. 117 35 17N 91 25W
Augusta, Ga., U.S.A. 115 33 29N 81 59W
Augusta, Kans., U.S.A. 117 37 40N 97 0W
Augusta, Me., U.S.A. 107 44 20N 69 46W
Augusta, Mont., U.S.A. 118 47 30N 112 29W
Augusta, Wis., U.S.A. 116 44 41N 91 8W
Augustenborg 49 54 57N 9 53 E
Augusto Cardosa 91 12 40 S 34 50 E
Augustów 28 53 51N 23 00 E
Augustus Downs 98 18 35 S 139 55 E
Augustus, Mt. 96 24 20 S 116 50 E
Aukan 87 15 29N 40 50 E
Aulla 38 44 12N 10 0 E
Aulnay 20 46 2N 0 22W
Aulne → 18 48 17N 4 16W
Aulnoye 19 50 12N 3 50 E
Ault 116 40 40N 104 42W
Ault-Onival 18 50 5N 1 29 E
Aulus-les-Bains 20 42 49N 1 19 E
Aumale 19 49 46N 1 46 E
Aumont-Aubrac 20 44 43N 3 17 E
Auna 85 10 9N 4 42 E
Aundh 70 17 33N 74 23 E
Aunis 20 46 5N 0 50W
Auponhia 73 1 58 S 125 27 E
Aups 21 43 37N 6 15 E
Auraiya 69 26 28N 79 33 E
Aurangabad, Bihar, India 69 24 45N 84 18 E
Aurangabad, Maharashtra, India 70 19 50N 75 23 E
Auray 18 47 40N 3 0W
Aurès 83 35 8N 6 30 E
Aurich 24 53 28N 7 30 E
Aurillac 20 44 55N 2 26 E
Aurlandsvangen 47 60 55N 7 12 E
Auronza 39 46 33N 12 27 E
Aurora, Can. 112 44 0N 79 28W
Aurora, S. Afr. 92 32 40 S 18 29 E
Aurora, Colo., U.S.A. 116 39 44N 104 55W
Aurora, Ill., U.S.A. 114 41 42N 88 12W
Aurora, Mo., U.S.A. 117 36 58N 93 42W
Aurora, Nebr., U.S.A. 116 40 55N 98 0W
Aurora, Ohio, U.S.A. 112 41 21N 81 20W
Aurskog 47 59 55N 11 26 E
Aurukun Mission 98 13 20 S 141 45 E
Aus 92 26 35 S 16 12 E
Aust-Agder fylke □ 47 58 55N 7 40 E
Austad 47 58 58N 7 37 E
Austerlitz = Slavkov 27 49 10N 16 52 E
Austevoll 47 60 5N 5 13 E
Austin, Minn., U.S.A. 116 43 37N 92 59W
Austin, Nev., U.S.A. 118 39 30N 117 1W
Austin, Pa., U.S.A. 112 41 40N 78 7W
Austin, Tex., U.S.A. 117 30 20N 97 45W
Austin, L. 96 27 40 S 118 0 E
Austral Downs 97 20 30 S 137 45 E
Austral Is. = Tubuai Is. 95 23 0 S 150 0W
Austral Seamount Chain 95 24 0 S 150 0W
Australia ■ 94 23 0 S 135 0 E
Australian Alps 97 36 30 S 148 30 E
Australian Cap. Terr. □ 97 35 30 S 149 0 E
Australian Dependency □ 5 73 0 S 90 0 E
Austria ■ 26 47 0N 14 0 E
Austvågøy 50 68 20N 14 40 E
Auterive 20 43 21N 1 29 E
Authie → 19 50 22N 1 38 E
Authon 18 48 12N 0 55 E
Autlán 120 19 40N 104 30W
Autun 19 46 58N 4 17 E
Auvergne 20 45 20N 3 15 E
Auvézère → 20 45 12N 0 50 E
Auxerre 19 47 48N 3 32 E
Auxi-le-Château 19 50 15N 2 8 E
Auxonne 19 47 10N 5 20 E
Auzances 20 46 2N 2 30 E
Auzat 20 45 27N 3 19 E
Avallon 19 47 30N 3 53 E
Avalon Pen. 107 47 30N 53 20W
Avalon Res. 117 32 30N 104 30W
Avanigadda 70 16 0N 80 56 E
Avaré 125 23 4 S 48 58W
Ávas 44 40 57N 25 56 E
Aveiro, Brazil 127 3 10 S 55 5W
Aveiro, Port. 30 40 37N 8 38W
Aveiro □ 30 40 40N 8 35W
Āvej 64 35 40N 49 15 E
Avellaneda 124 34 50 S 58 10W
Avellino 41 40 54N 14 46 E
Averøya 47 63 0N 7 35 E
Aversa 41 40 58N 14 11 E
Avery 118 47 22N 115 56W
Aves, I. de 121 15 45N 63 55W
Aves, Is. de 121 12 0N 67 30W
Avesnes-sur-Helpe 19 50 8N 3 55 E
Avesta 48 60 9N 16 10 E
Aveyron □ 20 44 22N 2 45 E
Aveyron → 20 44 7N 1 5 E
Avezzano 39 42 2N 13 24 E
Avgó 45 35 33N 25 37 E
Aviá Terai 124 26 45 S 60 50W
Aviano 39 46 3N 12 35 E
Avigliana 38 45 7N 7 13 E
Avigliano 41 40 44N 15 41 E
Avignon 21 43 57N 4 50 E
Ávila 30 40 39N 4 43W
Ávila □ 30 40 30N 5 0W
Ávila, Sierra de 30 40 40N 5 0W
Avilés 30 43 35N 5 57W
Avionárion 45 38 31N 24 8 E
Avisio → 39 46 7N 11 5 E
Aviz 31 39 4N 7 53W
Avize 19 48 59N 4 0 E
Avoca, Austral. 100 37 5 S 143 26 E
Avoca, Ireland 15 52 52N 6 13W
Avoca, U.S.A. 112 42 24N 77 25W
Avoca → 100 35 40 S 143 43 E
Avola, Can. 108 51 45N 119 19W
Avola, Italy 41 36 56N 15 7 E
Avon, N.Y., U.S.A. 112 43 0N 77 42W
Avon, S.D., U.S.A. 116 43 0N 98 3W
Avon □ 13 51 30N 2 40W
Avon →, Avon, U.K. 13 51 30N 2 43W
Avon →, Hants., U.K. 13 50 44N 1 45W
Avon →, Warwick, U.K. 13 52 0N 2 9W
Avon Downs 97 19 58 S 137 25 E
Avon, Îles 97 19 37 S 158 17 E
Avon Lake 112 41 28N 82 3W
Avondale 91 17 43 S 30 58 E
Avonlea 109 50 0N 105 0W
Avonmore 113 45 10N 74 58W
Avonmouth 13 51 30N 2 42W
Avramov 43 42 45N 26 38 E
Avranches 18 48 40N 1 20W
Avre → 18 48 47N 1 22 E
Avrig 46 45 43N 24 21 E
Avrillé 20 46 28N 1 28W
Avtovac 42 43 9N 18 35 E
Awag el Baqar 87 10 10N 33 10 E
'Awālī 65 26 0N 50 30 E
Awarja → 70 17 5N 76 15 E
'Awartā 62 32 10N 35 17 E
Awasa, L. 87 7 0N 38 30 E
Awash 87 9 1N 40 10 E
Awash → 87 11 45N 41 5 E
Awaso 84 6 15N 2 22W
Awatere → 101 41 37 S 174 10 E
Awbārī 83 26 46N 12 57 E
Awbārī □ 83 26 35N 12 46 E
Awe, L. 14 56 15N 5 15W
Aweil 87 8 42N 27 20 E
Awgu 85 6 4N 7 24 E
Awjilah 81 29 8N 21 7 E
Ax-les-Thermes 20 42 44N 1 50 E
Axarfjörður 50 66 15N 16 45W
Axel Heiberg I. 4 80 0N 90 0W
Axim 84 4 51N 2 15W
Axintele 46 44 37N 26 47 E
Axiós → 44 40 57N 22 35 E
Axmarsbruk 48 61 3N 17 10 E
Axminster 13 50 47N 3 1W
Axstedt 24 53 26N 8 43 E
Axvall 49 58 23N 13 34 E
Ay 19 49 3N 4 0 E
Ayabaca 126 4 40 S 79 53W
Ayabe 74 35 20N 135 20 E
Ayacucho, Argent. 124 37 5 S 58 20W
Ayacucho, Peru 126 13 0 S 74 0W
Ayaguz 58 48 10N 80 0 E
Ayakudi 70 10 28N 77 56 E
Ayamonte 31 37 12N 7 24W
Ayan 59 56 30N 138 16 E
Ayancık 56 41 57N 34 18 E
Ayas 56 40 10N 32 14 E
Ayaviri 126 14 50 S 70 35W
Āybaq 65 36 15N 68 5 E
Ayenngré 85 8 40N 1 1 E
Ayeritam 71 5 24N 100 15 E
Ayer's Cliff 113 45 10N 72 3W
Ayers Rock 96 25 23 S 131 5 E
Aygues → 21 44 7N 4 43 E
Ayiá 44 39 43N 22 45 E
Ayia Anna 45 38 52N 23 24 E
Ayia Marina 45 35 27N 26 53 E
Ayia Marina 45 37 11N 26 48 E
Ayia Paraskevi 44 39 14N 26 16 E
Ayia Rouméli 45 35 14N 23 58 E
Ayiássos 45 39 5N 26 23 E
Áyion Óros 44 40 25N 24 6 E
Áyios Andréas 45 37 21N 22 45 E
Áyios Evstrátios 44 39 34N 24 58 E
Áyios Evstrátios 44 39 30N 25 0 E
Áyios Ioannis, Ákra 45 35 20N 25 40 E
Áyios Kiríkos 45 37 34N 26 17 E
Áyios Matthaios 44 39 30N 19 47 E
Áyios Mírono 45 35 15N 25 1 E
Áyios Nikólaos 45 35 11N 25 41 E
Áyios Pétros 45 38 38N 20 33 E
Áyios Yeóryios 45 37 28N 23 57 E
Aykathonisi 45 37 28N 27 0 E
Aykin 52 62 15N 49 56 E
Aylesbury 13 51 48N 0 49W
Aylmer 112 42 46N 80 59W
Aylmer L. 104 64 0N 110 8W
'Ayn al Mubārak 64 24 10N 38 10 E
'Ayn 'Arīk 62 31 54N 35 8 E
'Ayn Zaqqūt 83 29 0N 19 30 E
Ayn Zhālah 64 36 45N 42 35 E
Ayna 33 38 34N 2 3W
Ayolas 124 27 10 S 56 59W
Ayom 87 7 49N 28 23 E
Ayon, Ostrov 59 69 50N 169 0 E
Ayora 33 39 3N 1 3W
Ayr, Austral. 97 19 35 S 147 25 E
Ayr, U.K. 14 55 28N 4 37W
Ayr → 14 55 29N 4 40W
Ayre, Pt. of 12 54 27N 4 21W
Aysha 87 10 50N 42 23 E
Aytos 43 42 42N 27 16 E
Aytoska Planina 43 42 45N 27 30 E
Ayu, Kepulauan 73 0 35N 131 5 E
Ayutla 120 16 58N 99 17W
Ayvalık 64 39 20N 26 46 E
Aẓ Ẓāhirīyah 62 31 25N 34 58 E
Aẓ Ẓahrān 64 26 10N 50 7 E
Az Zarqā 62 32 5N 36 4 E
Az Zāwiyah 83 32 52N 12 56 E
Az-Zilfī 64 26 12N 44 52 E
Az Zubayr 64 30 20N 47 50 E
Azambuja 31 39 4N 8 51W
Azamgarh 69 26 5N 83 13 E
Azaouak, Vallée de l' 85 15 50N 3 20 E
Āzārbāījān □ 64 37 0N 44 30 E
Azare 85 11 55N 10 10 E
Azay-le-Rideau 18 47 16N 0 30 E
Azazga 83 36 48N 4 22 E
Azbine = Aïr 85 18 0N 8 0 E
Azeffoun 83 36 51N 4 26 E
Azemmour 82 33 20N 9 20W
Azerbaijan S.S.R. □ 57 40 20N 48 0 E
Azezo 87 12 28N 37 15 E
Azilal, Beni Mallal 82 32 0N 6 30W
Azimganj 69 24 14N 88 16 E
Aznalcóllar 31 37 32N 6 17W
Azogues 126 2 35 S 78 0W
Azor 62 32 2N 34 48 E
Azores 6 38 44N 29 0W
Azov 57 47 3N 39 25 E
Azov Sea = Azovskoye More 56 46 0N 36 30 E
Azovskoye More 56 46 0N 36 30 E
Azovy 58 64 55N 64 35 E
Azpeitia 32 43 12N 2 19W
Azrou 82 33 28N 5 19W
Aztec 119 36 54N 108 0W
Azúa de Compostela 121 18 25N 70 44W
Azuaga 31 38 16N 5 39W
Azuara 32 41 15N 0 53W
Azuer → 31 39 8N 3 36W
Azuero, Pen. de 121 7 30N 80 30W
Azul 124 36 42 S 59 43W
Azzaba 83 36 48N 7 6 E
Azzano Décimo 39 45 53N 12 46 E

B

Ba Don 71 17 45N 106 26 E
Ba Ngoi = Cam Lam 71 11 50N 109 10 E
Ba Xian 76 39 8N 116 22 E
Baa 73 10 50 S 123 0 E
Baamonde 30 43 7N 7 44W
Baarle Nassau 16 51 27N 4 56 E
Baarn 16 52 12N 5 17 E
Bāb el Māndeb 63 12 35N 43 25 E
Baba 43 42 44N 23 59 E
Baba Burnu 44 39 29N 26 2 E
Baba dag 57 41 0N 48 19W
Babadag 46 44 53N 28 44 E
Babaeski 43 41 26N 27 6 E
Babahoyo 126 1 40 S 79 30W
Babana 85 10 31N 3 46 E

Babar Bandula

Place	Page	Latitude	Longitude
Babar, Alg.	**83**	35 10N	7 6 E
Babar, Indon.	**73**	8 0 S	129 30 E
Babar, Pak.	**68**	31 7N	69 32 E
Babarkach	**68**	29 45N	68 0 E
Babayevo	**55**	59 24N	35 55 E
Babb	**118**	48 56N	113 27W
Babenhausen	**25**	49 57N	8 56 E
Babia Gora	**27**	49 38N	19 38 E
Babile	**87**	9 16N	42 11 E
Babinda	**98**	17 20 S	145 56 E
Babine	**108**	55 22N	126 37W
Babine →	**108**	55 45N	127 44W
Babine L.	**108**	54 48N	126 0W
Babo	**73**	2 30 S	133 30 E
Babócsa	**27**	46 2N	17 21 E
Bābol	**65**	36 40N	52 50 E
Bābol Sar	**65**	36 45N	52 45 E
Baborówo Kietrz	**27**	50 7N	18 1 E
Baboua	**88**	5 49N	14 58 E
Babuna	**42**	41 30N	21 40 E
Babura	**85**	12 51N	8 59 E
Babušnica	**42**	43 7N	22 27 E
Babuyan Chan.	**73**	19 10N	122 0 E
Babylon, Iraq	**64**	32 40N	44 30 E
Babylon, U.S.A.	**113**	40 42N	73 20W
Bač	**42**	45 29N	19 17 E
Bac Kan	**71**	22 5N	105 50 E
Bac Ninh	**71**	21 13N	106 4 E
Bac Phan	**71**	22 0N	105 0 E
Bac Quang	**71**	22 30N	104 48 E
Bacabal	**127**	4 15 S	44 45W
Bacan, Kepulauan	**73**	0 35 S	127 30 E
Bacan, Pulau	**73**	0 50 S	127 30 E
Bacarès, Le	**20**	42 47N	3 3 E
Bacarra	**73**	18 15N	120 37 E
Bacau	**73**	8 27 S	126 27 E
Bacău	**46**	46 35N	26 55 E
Bacău □	**46**	46 30N	26 45 E
Baccarat	**19**	48 28N	6 42 E
Bacchus Marsh	**100**	37 43 S	144 27 E
Bacerac	**120**	30 18N	108 50W
Băceşti	**46**	46 50N	27 11 E
Bacharach	**25**	50 3N	7 46 E
Bachelina	**58**	57 45N	67 20 E
Bachuma	**87**	6 48N	35 53 E
Bačina	**42**	43 42N	21 23 E
Back →	**104**	65 10N	104 0W
Bačka Palanka	**42**	45 17N	19 27 E
Bačka Topola	**42**	45 49N	19 39 E
Bäckefors	**49**	58 48N	12 9 E
Bački Petrovac	**42**	45 29N	19 32 E
Backnang	**25**	48 57N	9 26 E
Backstairs Passage	**97**	35 40 S	138 5 E
Bacolod	**73**	10 40N	122 57 E
Bacqueville	**18**	49 47N	1 0 E
Bacs-Kiskun □	**27**	46 43N	19 30 E
Bácsalmás	**27**	46 8N	19 17 E
Bad →	**116**	44 22N	100 22W
Bad Aussee	**26**	47 43N	13 45 E
Bad Axe	**106**	43 48N	82 59W
Bad Bergzabern	**25**	49 6N	8 0 E
Bad Bramstedt	**24**	53 56N	9 53 E
Bad Doberan	**24**	54 6N	11 55 E
Bad Driburg	**24**	51 44N	9 0 E
Bad Ems	**25**	50 22N	7 44 E
Bad Frankenhausen	**24**	51 21N	11 3 E
Bad Freienwalde	**24**	52 47N	14 3 E
Bad Godesberg	**24**	50 41N	7 4 E
Bad Hersfeld	**24**	50 52N	9 42 E
Bad Hofgastein	**26**	47 17N	13 6 E
Bad Homburg	**25**	50 17N	8 33 E
Bad Honnef	**24**	50 39N	7 13 E
Bad Ischl	**26**	47 44N	13 38 E
Bad Kissingen	**25**	50 11N	10 5 E
Bad Kreuznach	**25**	49 47N	7 47 E
Bad Lands	**116**	43 40N	102 10W
Bad Langensalza	**24**	51 6N	10 40 E
Bad Lauterberg	**24**	51 38N	10 29 E
Bad Leonfelden	**26**	48 31N	14 18 E
Bad Lippspringe	**24**	51 47N	8 46 E
Bad Mergentheim	**25**	49 29N	9 47 E
Bad Münstereifel	**24**	50 33N	6 46 E
Bad Muskau	**24**	51 33N	14 43 E
Bad Nauheim	**25**	50 24N	8 45 E
Bad Oeynhausen	**24**	52 16N	8 45 E
Bad Oldesloe	**24**	53 48N	10 22 E
Bad Orb	**25**	50 16N	9 21 E
Bad Pyrmont	**24**	51 59N	9 15 E
Bad Reichenhall	**25**	47 44N	12 53 E
Bad St.-Peter	**24**	54 23N	8 32 E
Bad Salzuflen	**24**	52 8N	8 44 E
Bad Segeberg	**24**	53 58N	10 16 E
Bad Tölz	**25**	47 43N	11 34 E
Bad Waldsee	**25**	47 56N	9 46 E
Bad Wildungen	**24**	51 7N	9 10 E
Bad Wimpfen	**25**	49 12N	9 10 E
Bad Windsheim	**25**	49 29N	10 25 E
Badagara	**70**	11 35N	75 40 E
Badagri	**85**	6 25N	2 55 E
Badajoz	**31**	38 50N	6 59W
Badajoz □	**31**	38 40N	6 30W
Badakhshan □	**65**	36 30N	71 0 E
Badalona	**32**	41 26N	2 15 E
Badalzai	**66**	29 50N	65 35 E
Badampahar	**69**	22 10N	86 10 E
Badanah	**64**	30 58N	41 30 E
Badas	**72**	4 33N	114 25 E
Badas, Kepulauan	**72**	0 45N	107 5 E
Baddo →	**66**	28 0N	64 20 E
Bade	**73**	7 10 S	139 35 E
Baden, Austria	**27**	48 1N	16 13 E
Baden, Can.	**112**	43 14N	80 40W
Baden, Switz.	**25**	47 28N	8 18 E
Baden-Baden	**25**	48 45N	8 15 E
Baden-Württemberg □	**25**	48 40N	9 0 E
Badgastein	**26**	47 7N	13 9 E
Badger	**107**	49 0N	56 4W
Bādghīsāt □	**65**	35 0N	63 0 E
Badia Polèsine	**39**	45 6N	11 30 E
Badin	**68**	24 38N	68 54 E
Badnera	**68**	20 48N	77 44 E
Badogo	**84**	11 2N	8 13W
Badong	**77**	31 1N	110 23 E
Badrinath	**69**	30 45N	79 30 E
Baduen	**63**	7 15N	47 40 E
Badulla	**70**	7 1N	81 7 E
Baena	**31**	37 37N	4 20W
Baeza	**33**	37 57N	3 25W
Bafa Gölü	**45**	37 30N	27 29 E
Bafang	**85**	5 9N	10 11 E
Bafatá	**84**	12 8N	14 40W
Baffin B.	**4**	72 0N	64 0W
Baffin I.	**105**	68 0N	75 0W
Bafia	**88**	4 40N	11 10 E
Bafilo	**85**	9 22N	1 22 E
Bafing →	**84**	13 49N	10 50W
Bafoulabé	**84**	13 50N	10 55W
Bafoussam	**85**	5 28N	10 25 E
Bafra	**56**	41 34N	35 54 E
Bafra, C.	**56**	41 44N	35 58 E
Bāft, Esfahān, Iran	**65**	31 40N	55 25 E
Bāft, Kermān, Iran	**65**	29 15N	56 38 E
Bafut	**85**	6 6N	10 2 E
Bafwasende	**90**	1 3N	27 5 E
Bagalkot	**70**	16 10N	75 40 E
Bagamoyo	**90**	6 28 S	38 55 E
Bagamoyo □	**90**	6 20 S	38 30 E
Baganga	**73**	7 34N	126 33 E
Bagansiapiapi	**72**	2 12N	100 50 E
Bagasıa	**68**	21 30N	71 0 E
Bagawi	**87**	12 20N	34 18 E
Bagdarin	**59**	54 26N	113 36 E
Bagé	**125**	31 20 S	54 15W
Bagenalstown = Muine Bheag	**15**	52 42N	6 57W
Baggs	**118**	41 8N	107 46W
Baghdād	**64**	33 20N	44 30 E
Bagheıhat	**69**	22 40N	89 47 E
Bagheria	**40**	38 5N	13 30 E
Bāghīn	**65**	30 12N	56 45 E
Baghlān	**65**	36 12N	69 0 E
Baghlān □	**65**	36 0N	68 30 E
Bagley	**116**	47 30N	95 22W
Bagnacavallo	**39**	44 25N	11 58 E
Bagnara Cálabra	**41**	38 16N	15 49 E
Bagnères-de-Bigorre	**20**	43 5N	0 9 E
Bagnères-de-Luchon	**20**	42 47N	0 38 E
Bagni di Lucca	**38**	44 1N	10 37 E
Bagno di Romagna	**39**	43 50N	11 59 E
Bagnoles-de-l'Orne	**18**	48 32N	0 25W
Bagnoli di Sopra	**39**	45 13N	11 55 E
Bagnolo Mella	**38**	45 27N	10 14 E
Bagnols-les-Bains	**20**	44 30N	3 40 E
Bagnols-sur-Cèze	**21**	44 10N	4 36 E
Bagnoıégio	**39**	42 38N	12 7 E
Bagolino	**38**	45 49N	10 28 E
Bagotville	**107**	48 22N	70 54W
Bagrdan	**42**	44 5N	21 11 E
Baguio	**73**	16 26N	120 34 E
Bahabón de Esgueva	**32**	41 52N	3 43W
Bahadurgarh	**68**	28 40N	76 57 E
Bahama, Canal Viejo de	**121**	22 10N	77 30W
Bahamas ■	**121**	24 0N	75 0W
Baharîya, El Wâhât al	**86**	28 0N	28 50 E
Bahau	**71**	2 48N	102 26 E
Bahawalnagar	**68**	30 0N	73 15 E
Bahawalpur	**68**	29 24N	71 40 E
† Bahawalpur □	**68**	29 5N	71 3 E
Baheri	**69**	28 45N	79 34 E
Bahi	**90**	5 58 S	35 21 E
Bahi Swamp	**90**	6 10 S	35 0 E
Bahia = Salvador	**127**	13 0 S	38 30W
Bahia □	**127**	12 0 S	42 0W
Bahía Blanca	**124**	38 35 S	62 13W
Bahía de Caráquez	**126**	0 40 S	80 27W
Bahía, Islas de la	**121**	16 45N	86 15W
Bahía Laura	**128**	48 10 S	66 30W
Bahía Negra	**126**	20 5 S	58 5W
Bahir Dar	**87**	11 37N	37 10 E
Bahmer	**82**	27 32N	0 10W
Bahönye	**27**	46 25N	17 28 E
Bahr Aouk →	**88**	8 40N	19 0 E
Bahr el Ahmar □	**86**	20 0N	35 0 E
Bahr el Ghazâl □	**87**	7 0N	28 0 E
Bahr el Jebel →	**87**	7 30N	30 30 E
Bahr Salamat →	**81**	9 20N	18 0 E
Bahr Yûsef →	**86**	28 25N	30 35 E
Bahra el Burullus	**86**	31 28N	30 48 E
Bahraich	**69**	27 38N	81 37 E
Bahrain ■	**65**	26 0N	50 35 E
Bai	**84**	13 35N	3 28W
Baia Mare	**46**	47 40N	23 35 E
Baia-Sprie	**46**	47 41N	23 43 E
Baïbokoum	**81**	7 46N	15 43 E
Baicheng	**76**	45 38N	122 42 E
Băicoi	**46**	45 3N	25 52 E
Baidoa	**63**	3 8N	43 30 E
Baie Comeau	**107**	49 12N	68 10W
Baie-St-Paul	**107**	47 28N	70 32W
Baie Trinité	**107**	49 25N	67 20W
Baie Verte	**107**	49 55N	56 12W
Baignes	**20**	45 23N	0 25W
Baigneux-les-Juifs	**19**	47 31N	4 39 E
Ba'ījī	**64**	35 0N	43 30 E
Baikal, L. = Baykal, Oz.	**59**	53 0N	108 0 E
Bailadila, Mt.	**70**	18 43N	81 15 E
Baile Atha Cliath = Dublin	**15**	53 20N	6 18W
Bailei	**87**	6 44N	40 18 E
Bailén	**31**	38 8N	3 48W
Băileşti	**46**	44 01N	23 20 E
Bailhongal	**70**	15 55N	74 53 E
Bailleul	**19**	50 44N	2 41 E
Bailundo	**89**	12 10 S	15 50 E
Baimuru	**98**	7 35 S	144 51 E
Bain-de-Bretagne	**18**	47 50N	1 40W
Bainbridge, Ga., U.S.A.	**115**	30 53N	84 34W
Bainbridge, N.Y., U.S.A.	**113**	42 17N	75 29W
Baing	**73**	10 14 S	120 34 E
Bainville	**116**	48 8N	104 10W
Bā'ir	**64**	30 45N	36 55 E
Baird	**117**	32 25N	99 25W
Baird Mts.	**104**	67 10N	160 15W
Bairin Youqi	**76**	43 30N	118 35 E
Bairin Zuoqi	**76**	43 58N	119 15 E
Bairnsdale	**97**	37 48 S	147 36 E
Baise →	**20**	44 17N	0 18 E
Baissa	**85**	7 14N	10 38 E
Baitadi	**69**	29 35N	80 25 E
Baiyin	**76**	36 45N	104 14 E
Baiyu Shan	**76**	37 15N	107 30 E
Baiyuda	**86**	17 35N	32 07 E
Baja	**27**	46 12N	18 59 E
Baja California	**120**	31 10N	115 12W
Baja, Pta.	**120**	29 50N	116 0W
Bajah, Wadi →	**86**	23 14N	39 20 E
Bajana	**68**	23 7N	71 49 E
Bajimba, Mt.	**99**	29 17 S	152 6 E
Bajina Bašta	**42**	43 58N	19 35 E
Bajmok	**42**	45 57N	19 24 E
Bajo Nuevo	**121**	15 40N	78 50W
Bajoga	**85**	10 57N	11 20 E
Bajool	**98**	23 40 S	150 35 E
Bak	**27**	46 43N	16 51 E
Bakala	**88**	6 15N	20 20 E
Bakar	**39**	45 18N	14 32 E
Bakchav	**58**	57 1N	82 5 E
Bakel	**84**	14 56N	12 20W
Baker, Calif., U.S.A.	**119**	35 16N	116 8W
Baker, Mont., U.S.A.	**116**	46 22N	104 12W
Baker, Nev., U.S.A.	**118**	38 59N	114 7W
Baker, Oreg., U.S.A.	**118**	44 50N	117 55W
Baker I.	**94**	0 10N	176 35W
Baker, L.	**104**	64 0N	96 0W
Baker Lake	**104**	64 20N	96 3W
Baker Mt.	**118**	48 50N	121 49W
Baker's Dozen Is.	**106**	56 45N	78 45W
Bakersfield, Calif., U.S.A.	**119**	35 25N	119 0W
Bakersfield, Vt., U.S.A.	**113**	44 46N	72 48W
Bakhchisaray	**56**	44 40N	33 45 E
Bakhmach	**54**	51 10N	32 45 E
Bakhtīārī □	**64**	32 0N	49 0 E
Bakinskikh Komissarov, im 26	**64**	39 20N	49 15 E
Bakırköy	**43**	40 59N	28 53 E
Bakkafjörður	**50**	66 2N	14 48W
Bakkagerði	**50**	65 31N	13 49W
Bakony →	**27**	47 35N	17 54 E
Bakony Forest = Bakony Hegység	**27**	47 10N	17 30 E
Bakony Hegység	**27**	47 10N	17 30 E
Bakori	**85**	11 34N	7 25 E
Bakouma	**88**	5 40N	22 56 E
Bakov	**26**	50 27N	14 55 E
Baku	**57**	40 25N	49 45 E
Bala	**112**	45 1N	79 37W
Bal'ā	**62**	32 20N	35 6 E
Bala, L. = Tegid, L.	**12**	52 53N	3 38W
Balabac I.	**72**	8 0N	117 0 E
Balabac, Str.	**72**	7 53N	117 5 E
Balabakk	**64**	34 0N	36 10 E
Balabalangan, Kepulauan	**72**	2 20 S	117 30 E
Bălăciţa	**46**	44 23N	23 8 E
Balaghat	**69**	21 49N	80 12 E
Balaghat Ra.	**70**	18 50N	76 30 E
Balaguer	**32**	41 50N	0 50 E
Balakhna	**55**	56 25N	43 32 E
Balaklava, Austral.	**99**	34 7 S	138 22 E
Balaklava, U.S.S.R.	**56**	44 30N	33 30 E
Balakleya	**56**	49 28N	36 55 E
Balakovo	**55**	52 4N	47 55 E
Balanda	**55**	51 30N	44 40 E
Balangir	**69**	20 43N	83 35 E
Balapur	**68**	20 40N	76 45 E
Balashikha	**55**	55 49N	37 59 E
Balashov	**55**	51 30N	43 10 E
Balasinor	**68**	22 57N	73 23 E
Balasore	**69**	21 35N	87 3 E
Balassagyarmat	**27**	48 4N	19 15 E
Balât	**86**	25 36N	29 19 E
Balaton	**27**	46 50N	17 40 E
Balatonfüred	**27**	46 58N	17 54 E
Balatonszentgyörgy	**27**	46 41N	17 19 E
Balazote	**33**	38 54N	2 09W
Balboa	**120**	9 0N	79 30W
Balboa Hill	**120**	9 6N	79 44W
Balbriggan	**15**	53 35N	6 10W
Balcarce	**124**	38 0 S	58 10W
Balcarres	**109**	50 50N	103 35W
Balchik	**43**	43 28N	28 11 E
Balclutha	**101**	46 15 S	169 45 E
Bald Knob	**117**	35 20N	91 35W
Baldock L.	**109**	56 33N	97 57W
Baldwin, Fla., U.S.A.	**115**	30 15N	82 10W
Baldwin, Mich., U.S.A.	**114**	43 54N	85 53W
Baldwinsville	**114**	43 10N	76 19W
Bale	**39**	45 4N	13 46 E
Bale □	**87**	6 20N	41 30 E
Baleares □	**32**	39 30N	3 0 E
Baleares, Islas	**32**	39 30N	3 0 E
Balearic Is. = Baleares, Islas	**32**	39 30N	3 0 E
Băleni	**46**	45 48N	27 51 E
Baler	**73**	15 46N	121 34 E
Balfe's Creek	**98**	20 12 S	145 55 E
Balfour	**93**	26 38 S	28 35 E
Balfouriyya	**62**	32 38N	35 18 E
Bali, Camer.	**85**	5 54N	10 0 E
Bali, Indon.	**72**	8 20 S	115 0 E
Bali □	**72**	8 20 S	115 0 E
Bali, Selat	**73**	8 30 S	114 35 E
Baligród	**27**	49 20N	22 17 E
Balikesir	**64**	39 35N	27 58 E
Balikpapan	**72**	1 10 S	116 55 E
Balimbing	**73**	5 10N	120 3 E
Baling	**71**	5 41N	100 55 E
Balipara	**67**	26 50N	92 45 E
Baliza	**127**	16 0 S	52 20W
Balkan Mts. = Stara Planina	**43**	43 15N	23 0 E
Balkan Pen.	**9**	42 0N	22 0 E
Balkh	**65**	36 44N	66 47 E
Balkh □	**65**	36 30N	67 0 E
Balkhash	**58**	46 50N	74 50 E
Balkhash, Ozero	**58**	46 0N	74 50 E
Ballachulish	**14**	56 40N	5 10W
Balladoran	**100**	31 52 S	148 39 E
Ballarat	**97**	37 33 S	143 50 E
Ballard, L.	**96**	29 20 S	120 10 E
Ballarpur	**70**	19 50N	79 23 E
Ballater	**14**	57 2N	3 2W
Ballenas, Canal de las	**120**	29 10N	113 45W
Balleny Is.	**5**	66 30 S	163 0 E
Ballia	**69**	25 46N	84 12 E
Ballina, Austral.	**97**	28 50 S	153 31 E
Ballina, Mayo, Ireland	**15**	54 7N	9 10W
Ballina, Tipp., Ireland	**15**	52 49N	8 27W
Ballinasloe	**15**	53 20N	8 12W
Ballinger	**117**	31 45N	99 58W
Ballinrobe	**15**	53 36N	9 13W
Ballinskelligs B.	**15**	51 46N	10 11W
Ballon	**18**	48 10N	0 14 E
Ballycastle	**15**	55 12N	6 15W
Ballymena	**15**	54 53N	6 18W
Ballymena □	**15**	54 53N	6 18W
Ballymoney	**15**	55 5N	6 30W
Ballymoney □	**15**	55 5N	6 23W
Ballyshannon	**15**	54 30N	8 10W
Balmaceda	**128**	46 0 S	71 50W
Balmazújváros	**27**	47 37N	21 21 E
Balmoral, Austral.	**99**	37 15 S	141 48 E
Balmoral, U.K.	**14**	57 3N	3 13W
Balmorhea	**117**	31 2N	103 41W
Balonne →	**97**	28 47 S	147 56 E
Balrampur	**69**	27 30N	82 20 E
Balranald	**97**	34 38 S	143 33 E
Balş	**46**	44 22N	24 5 E
Balsas →	**120**	17 55N	102 10W
Bålsta	**48**	59 35N	17 30 E
Balston Spa	**113**	43 0N	73 52W
Balta, Romania	**46**	44 54N	22 38 E
Balta, U.S.A.	**116**	48 12N	100 7W
Balta, R.S.F.S.R., U.S.S.R.	**57**	42 58N	44 32 E
Balta, Ukraine S.S.R., U.S.S.R.	**56**	48 2N	29 45 E
Baltanás	**30**	41 56N	4 15W
Baltic Sea	**51**	56 0N	20 0 E
Baltîm	**86**	31 35N	31 10 E
Baltimore, Ireland	**15**	51 29N	9 22W
Baltimore, U.S.A.	**114**	39 18N	76 37W
Baltrum	**24**	53 43N	7 25 E
Baluchistan □	**65**	27 30N	65 0 E
Balurghat	**69**	25 15N	88 44 E
Balygychan	**59**	63 56N	154 12 E
Bam	**65**	29 7N	58 14 E
Bama	**85**	11 33N	13 41 E
Bamako	**84**	12 34N	7 55W
Bamba	**85**	17 5N	1 24W
Bambari	**88**	5 40N	20 35 E
Bamberg, Ger.	**25**	49 54N	10 53 E
Bamberg, U.S.A.	**115**	33 19N	81 1W
Bambesi	**87**	9 45N	34 40 E
Bambey	**84**	14 42N	16 28W
Bambili	**90**	3 40N	26 0 E
Bamboo	**98**	14 34 S	143 20 E
Bamenda	**85**	5 57N	10 11 E
Bamfield	**108**	48 45N	125 10W
Bāmīān □	**65**	35 0N	67 0 E
Bamiancheng	**76**	43 15N	124 2 E
Bamkin	**85**	6 3N	11 27 E
Bampūr	**65**	27 15N	60 21 E
Ban Aranyaprathet	**71**	13 41N	102 30 E
Ban Ban	**71**	19 31N	103 30 E
Ban Bua Chum	**71**	15 11N	101 12 E
Ban Houei Sai	**71**	20 22N	100 32 E
Ban Khe Bo	**71**	19 10N	104 39 E
Ban Khun Yuam	**71**	18 49N	97 57 E
* Ban Me Thuot	**71**	12 40N	108 3 E
Ban Phai	**71**	16 4N	102 44 E
Ban Thateng	**71**	15 25N	106 27 E
Baña, Punta de la	**32**	40 33N	0 40 E
Banaba	**94**	0 45 S	169 50 E
Banadar Daryay Oman □	**65**	27 30N	56 0 E
Banalia	**90**	1 32N	25 5 E
Banam	**71**	11 20N	105 17 E
Banamba	**84**	13 29N	7 22W
Banana	**98**	24 28 S	150 8 E
Bananal, I. do	**127**	11 30 S	50 30W
Banaras = Varanasi	**69**	25 22N	83 8 E
Banas →, Gujarat, India	**68**	23 45N	71 25 E
Banas →, Madhya Pradesh, India	**69**	24 15N	81 30 E
Bânâs, Ras.	**86**	23 57N	35 50 E
Banbridge	**15**	54 21N	6 17W
Banbridge □	**15**	54 21N	6 16W
Banbury	**13**	52 4N	1 21W
Banchory	**14**	57 3N	2 30W
Bancroft	**106**	45 3N	77 51W
Band	**43**	46 30N	24 25 E
Band-e Torkestān	**65**	35 30N	64 0 E
Banda	**68**	25 30N	80 26 E
Banda Aceh	**72**	5 35N	95 20 E
Banda Banda, Mt.	**99**	31 10 S	152 28 E
Banda Elat	**73**	5 40 S	133 5 E
Banda, Kepulauan	**73**	4 37 S	129 50 E
Banda, La	**124**	27 45 S	64 10W
Banda Sea	**73**	6 0 S	130 0 E
Bandama →	**84**	6 32N	5 30W
Bandanaira	**73**	4 32 S	129 54 E
Bandanwara	**68**	26 9N	74 38 E
Bandar = Machilipatnam	**70**	16 12N	81 12 E
Bandār 'Abbās	**65**	27 15N	56 15 E
Bandar-e Būshehr	**65**	28 55N	50 55 E
Bandar-e Chārak	**65**	26 45N	54 20 E
Bandar-e Deylam	**64**	30 5N	50 10 E
Bandar-e Lengeh	**65**	26 35N	54 58 E
Bandar-e Ma'shur	**64**	30 35N	49 10 E
Bandar-e Nakhīlū	**65**	26 58N	53 30 E
Bandar-e Rīg	**65**	29 30N	50 45 E
Bandar-e Shāh	**65**	37 0N	54 10 E
Bandar-e Shāhpūr	**64**	30 30N	49 5 E
Bandar-i-Pahlavī	**64**	37 30N	49 30 E
Bandar Seri Begawan	**72**	4 52N	115 0 E
Bandawe	**91**	11 58 S	34 5 E
Bande	**30**	42 3N	7 58W
Bandeira, Pico da	**125**	20 26 S	41 47W
Bandera, Argent.	**124**	28 55 S	62 20W
Bandera, U.S.A.	**117**	29 45N	99 3W
Banderas, Bahía de	**120**	20 40N	105 30W
Bandia →	**70**	19 2N	80 28 E
Bandiagara	**84**	14 12N	3 29W
Bandırma	**64**	40 20N	28 0 E
Bandon	**15**	51 44N	8 45W
Bandon →	**15**	51 40N	8 41W
Bandula	**91**	19 0 S	33 7 E

† *Now part of Punjab* □

* *Renamed Buon Me Thuot*

Bandundu

Baume-les-Dames

Bandundu **88** 3 15 S 17 22 E
Bandung **73** 6 54 S 107 36 E
Băneasa **46** 45 56N 27 55 E
Bañeres **33** 38 44N 0 38W
Banes **121** 21 0N 75 42W
Bañeza, La **30** 42 17N 5 54W
Banff, Can. **108** 51 10N 115 34W
Banff, U.K. **14** 57 40N 2 32W
Banff Nat. Park **108** 51 30N 116 15W
Banfora **84** 10 40N 4 40W
Bang Hieng → **71** 16 10N 105 10 E
Bang Lamung **71** 13 3N 100 56 E
Bang Saphan **71** 11 14N 99 28 E
Bangala Dam **91** 21 7 S 31 25 E
Bangalore **70** 12 59N 77 40 E
Bangante **85** 5 8N 10 32 E
Bangaon **69** 23 0N 88 47 E
Bangassou **88** 4 55N 23 7 E
Bangeta, Mt. **98** 6 21 S 147 3 E
Banggai **73** 1 40 S 123 30 E
Banggi, P. **72** 7 17N 117 12 E
Banghāzī **83** 32 11N 20 3 E
Banghāzī □ **83** 32 7N 20 4 E
Bangil **73** 7 36 S 112 50 E
Bangjang **87** 11 23N 32 41 E
Bangka, Pulau, Sulawesi, Indon. **73** 1 50N 125 5 E
Bangka, Pulau, Sumatera, Indon. **72** 2 0 S 105 50 E
Bangka, Selat **72** 2 30 S 105 30 E
Bangkalan **73** 7 2 S 112 46 E
Bangkinang **72** 0 18N 101 5 E
Bangko **72** 2 5 S 102 9 E
Bangkok = Krung Thep **71** 13 45N 100 35 E
Bangladesh ■ **67** 24 0N 90 0 E
Bangolo **84** 7 1N 7 29W
Bangor, N. Ireland, U.K. **15** 54 40N 5 40W
Bangor, Wales, U.K. **12** 53 13N 4 9W
Bangor, Me., U.S.A. **107** 44 48N 68 42W
Bangor, Pa., U.S.A. **113** 40 51N 75 13W
Bangued **73** 17 40N 120 37 E
Bangui **88** 4 23N 18 35 E
Banguru **90** 0 30N 27 10 E
Bangweulu, L. **91** 11 0 S 30 0 E
Bangweulu Swamp **91** 11 20 S 30 15 E
Bani **121** 18 16N 70 22W
Bani → **84** 14 30N 4 12W
Bani Bangou **85** 15 3N 2 42 E
Bani, Djebel **82** 29 16N 8 0W
Banī Na'īm **62** 31 31N 35 10 E
Banī Suhaylah **62** 31 21N 34 19 E
Bania **84** 9 4N 3 6W
Baniara **98** 9 44 S 149 54 E
Banīnah **83** 32 0N 20 12 E
Bāniyās **64** 35 10N 36 0 E
Banja Luka **42** 44 49N 17 11 E
Banjar **73** 7 24 S 108 30 E
Banjarmasin **72** 3 20 S 114 35 E
Banjarnegara **73** 7 24 S 109 42 E
Banjul **84** 13 28N 16 40W
Bankeryd **49** 57 53N 14 6 E
Banket **91** 17 27 S 30 19 E
Bankilaré **85** 14 35N 0 44 E
Bankipore **69** 25 35N 85 10 E
Banks I., B.C., Can. **108** 53 20N 130 0W
Banks I., N.W.T., Can. **4** 73 15N 121 30W
Banks I., P.N.G. **97** 10 10 S 142 15 E
Banks Pen. **101** 43 45 S 173 15 E
Banks Str. **99** 40 40 S 148 10 E
Bankura **69** 23 11N 87 18 E
Bankya **42** 42 43N 23 8 E
Bann →, Down, U.K. **15** 54 30N 6 31W
Bann →, Londonderry, U.K. **15** 55 10N 6 34W
Bannalec **18** 47 57N 3 42W
Banning **119** 33 58N 116 52W
Banningville = Bandundu **88** 3 15 S 17 22 E
Bannockburn, Can. **112** 44 39N 77 33W
Bannockburn, U.K. **14** 56 5N 3 55W
Bannockburn, Zimb. **91** 20 17 S 29 48 E
Bañolas **32** 42 16N 2 44 E
Banon **21** 44 2N 5 38 E
Baños de la Encina **31** 38 10N 3 46W
Baños de Molgas **30** 42 15N 7 40W
Bánovce **27** 48 44N 18 16 E
Banská Bystrica **27** 48 46N 19 14 E
Banská Štiavnica **27** 48 25N 18 55 E
Bansko **43** 41 52N 23 28 E
Banswara **68** 23 32N 74 24 E
Banten **73** 6 5 S 106 8 E
Bantry **15** 51 40N 9 28W
Bantry, B. **15** 51 35N 9 50W
Bantul **73** 7 55 S 110 19 E
Bantva **68** 21 29N 70 12 E
Bantval **70** 12 55N 75 0 E
Banya **43** 42 33N 24 50 E
Banyak, Kepulauan **72** 2 10N 97 10 E
Banyo **85** 6 52N 11 45 E
Banyuls **20** 42 29N 3 8 E
Banyumas **73** 7 32 S 109 18 E
Banyuwangi **73** 8 13 S 114 21 E
Banzare Coast **5** 68 0 S 125 0 E
Banzyville = Mobayi **88** 4 15N 21 8 E
Baocheng **77** 33 12N 106 56 E
Baode **76** 39 1N 111 5 E
Baoding **76** 38 50N 115 28 E
Baoji **77** 34 20N 107 5 E
Baojing **77** 28 45N 109 41 E
Baokang **77** 31 54N 111 12 E
Baoshan **75** 25 10N 99 5 E
Baotou **76** 40 32N 110 2 E
Baoying **77** 33 17N 119 20 E
Bap **68** 27 23N 72 18 E
Bapatla **70** 15 55N 80 30 E
Bapaume **19** 50 7N 2 50 E
Bāqa el Gharbīyya **62** 32 25N 35 2 E
Ba'qūbah **64** 33 45N 44 50 E
Baquedano **124** 23 20 S 69 52W
Bar, U.S.S.R. **56** 49 4N 27 40 E
Bar, Yugo. **42** 42 8N 19 8 E
Bar Harbor **107** 44 15N 68 20W
Bar-le-Duc **19** 48 47N 5 10 E
Bar-sur-Aube **19** 48 14N 4 40 E
Bar-sur-Seine **19** 48 7N 4 20 E
Barabai **72** 2 32 S 115 34 E
Barabinsk **58** 55 20N 78 20 E
Baraboo **116** 43 28N 89 46W
Baracoa **121** 20 20N 74 30W
Baradero **124** 33 52 S 59 29W
Baraga **116** 46 49N 88 29W
Barahona, Dom. Rep. **121** 18 13N 71 7W
Barahona, Spain **32** 41 17N 2 39W
Barail Range **67** 25 15N 93 20 E
Baraka → **86** 18 13N 37 35 E
Barakhola **67** 25 0N 92 45 E
Barakot **69** 21 33N 84 59 E
Barakula **99** 26 30 S 150 33 E
Baralaba **98** 24 13 S 149 50 E
Baralzon L. **109** 60 0N 98 3W
Baramati **70** 18 11N 74 33 E
Baramba **69** 20 25N 85 23 E
Barameiya **86** 18 32N 36 38 E
Baramula **69** 34 15N 74 20 E
Baran **68** 25 9N 76 40 E
Baranof I. **104** 57 0N 135 10W
Baranovichi **54** 53 10N 26 0 E
Baranów Sandomierski **28** 50 29N 21 30 E
Baranya □ **27** 46 0N 18 15 E
Barão de Melgaço **126** 11 50 S 60 45W
Baraolt **46** 46 5N 25 34 E
Barapasi **73** 2 15 S 137 5 E
Barasat **69** 22 46N 88 31 E
Barat Daya, Kepulauan **73** 7 30 S 128 0 E
Barataria B. **117** 29 15N 89 45W
Baraut **68** 29 13N 77 7 E
Barbacena **125** 21 15 S 43 56W
Barbacoas **126** 1 45N 78 0W
Barbados ■ **121** 13 0N 59 30W
Barban **39** 45 5N 14 4 E
Barbastro **32** 42 2N 0 5 E
Barbate **31** 36 13N 5 56W
Barberino di Mugello **39** 44 1N 11 15 E
Barberton, S. Afr. **93** 25 42 S 31 2 E
Barberton, U.S.A. **114** 41 0N 81 40W
Barbezieux **20** 45 28N 0 9W
Barbigha **69** 25 21N 85 47 E
Barbourville **115** 36 57N 83 52W
Barbuda I. **121** 17 30N 61 40W
Barca, La **120** 20 20N 102 40W
Barcaldine **97** 23 43 S 145 6 E
Barcarrota **31** 38 31N 6 51W
Barcellona Pozzo di Gotto **41** 38 8N 15 15 E
Barcelona, Spain **32** 41 21N 2 10 E
Barcelona, Venez. **126** 10 10N 64 40W
Barcelona □ **32** 41 30N 2 0 E
Barcelonette **21** 44 23N 6 40 E
Barcelos **126** 1 0 S 63 0W
Barcin **28** 52 52N 17 55 E
Barcoo → **97** 25 30 S 142 50 E
Barcs **27** 45 58N 17 28 E
Barczewo **28** 53 50N 20 42 E
Barda **57** 40 25N 47 10 E
Bardai **83** 21 25N 17 0 E
Bardas Blancas **124** 35 49 S 69 45W
Bardejov **27** 49 18N 21 15 E
Bardera **63** 2 20N 42 27 E
Bardi **38** 44 38N 9 43 E
Bardi, Ra's **64** 24 17N 37 31 E
Bardia **81** 31 45N 25 0 E
Bardo **28** 50 31N 16 42 E
Bardoli **68** 21 12N 73 5 E
Bardolino **38** 45 33N 10 43 E
Bardsey I. **12** 52 46N 4 47W
Bardstown **114** 37 50N 85 29W
Bareilly **69** 28 22N 79 27 E
Barentin **18** 49 33N 0 58 E
Barenton **18** 48 38N 0 50W
Barents Sea **4** 73 0N 39 0 E
Barentu **87** 15 2N 37 35 E
Barfleur **18** 49 40N 1 17W
Barga, China **75** 30 40N 81 20 E
Barga, Italy **38** 44 5N 10 30 E
Bargal **63** 11 25N 51 0 E
Bargara **98** 24 50 S 152 25 E
Barge **38** 44 43N 7 19 E
Barge, La **118** 42 12N 110 4W
Bargnop **87** 9 32N 28 25 E
Bargteheide **24** 53 42N 10 13 E
Barguzin **59** 53 37N 109 37 E
Barh **69** 25 29N 85 46 E
Barhaj **69** 26 18N 83 44 E
Barham **100** 35 36 S 144 8 E
Barhi **69** 24 15N 85 25 E
Bari, India **68** 26 39N 77 39 E
Bari, Italy **41** 41 6N 16 52 E
Bari Doab **68** 30 20N 73 0 E
Bariadi □ **90** 2 45 S 34 40 E
Barīm **63** 12 39N 43 25 E
Barinas **126** 8 36N 70 15W
Baring C. **104** 70 0N 117 30W
Baringo **90** 0 47N 36 16 E
Baringo □ **90** 0 55N 36 0 E
Baringo, L. **90** 0 47N 36 16 E
Baripada **69** 21 57N 86 45 E
Bârîs **86** 24 42N 30 31 E
Barisal **69** 22 45N 90 20 E
Barisan, Bukit **72** 3 30 S 102 15 E
Barito → **72** 4 0 S 114 50 E
Barjac **21** 44 20N 4 22 E
Barjols **21** 43 34N 6 2 E
Barjūj, Wadi → **83** 25 26N 12 12 E
Bark L. **112** 45 27N 77 51W
Barka = Baraka → **87** 18 13N 37 35 E
Barkah **65** 23 40N 58 0 E
Barker **112** 43 20N 78 35W
Barkley Sound **108** 48 50N 125 10W
Barkly Downs **98** 20 30 S 138 30 E
Barkly East **92** 30 58 S 27 33 E
Barkly Tableland **97** 17 50 S 136 40 E
Barkly West **92** 28 5 S 24 31 E
Barkol, Wadi → **86** 17 40N 32 0 E
Barksdale **117** 29 47N 100 2W
Barlee, L. **96** 29 15 S 119 30 E
Barlee Ra. **96** 23 30 S 116 0 E
Barletta **41** 41 20N 16 17 E
Barleur, Pointe de **18** 49 42N 1 16W
Barlinek **28** 53 0N 15 15 E
Barlow L. **109** 62 00N 103 0W
Barmedman **99** 34 9 S 147 21 E
Barmer **68** 25 45N 71 20 E
Barmera **99** 34 15 S 140 28 E
Barmouth **12** 52 44N 4 3W
Barmstedt **24** 53 47N 9 46 E
Barnagar **68** 23 7N 75 19 E
Barnard Castle **12** 54 33N 1 55W
Barnato **99** 31 38 S 145 0 E
Barnaul **58** 53 20N 83 40 E
Barne Inlet **5** 80 15 S 160 0 E
Barnes **99** 36 2 S 144 47 E
Barnesville **115** 33 6N 84 9W
Barnet **13** 51 37N 0 15W
Barneveld, Neth. **16** 52 7N 5 36 E
Barneveld, U.S.A. **113** 43 16N 75 14W
Barneville **18** 49 23N 1 46W
Barney, Mt. **97** 28 17 S 152 44 E
Barngo **99** 25 3 S 147 20 E
Barnhart **117** 31 10N 101 8W
Barnsley **12** 53 33N 1 29W
Barnstaple **13** 51 5N 4 3W
Barnsville **116** 46 43N 96 28W
Baro **85** 8 35N 6 18 E
Baro → **87** 8 26N 33 13 E
Baroda **68** 25 29N 76 35 E
Baroda = Vadodara **68** 22 20N 73 10 E
Barpali **69** 21 11N 83 35 E
Barqin **83** 27 33N 13 34 E
Barques, Pte. aux **114** 44 5N 82 55W
Barquinha **31** 39 28N 8 25W
Barquisimeto **126** 10 4N 69 19W
Barr **19** 48 25N 7 28 E
Barra, Brazil **127** 11 5 S 43 10W
Barra, U.K. **14** 57 0N 7 30W
Barra do Corda **127** 5 30 S 45 10W
Barra do Piraí **125** 22 30 S 43 50W
Barra Falsa, Pta. da **93** 22 58 S 35 37 E
Barra Hd. **14** 56 47N 7 40W
Barra Mansa **125** 22 35 S 44 12W
Barra, Sd. of **14** 57 4N 7 25W
Barraba **99** 30 21 S 150 35 E
Barrackpur **69** 22 44N 88 30 E
Barrafranca **41** 37 22N 14 10 E
Barranca, Lima, Peru **126** 10 45 S 77 50W
Barranca, Loreto, Peru **126** 4 50 S 76 50W
Barrancabermeja **126** 7 0N 73 50W
Barrancas **126** 8 55N 62 5W
Barrancos **31** 38 10N 6 58W
Barranqueras **124** 27 30 S 59 0W
Barranquilla **126** 11 0N 74 50W
Barras **127** 4 15 S 42 18W
Barraute **106** 48 26N 77 38W
Barre **114** 44 15N 72 30W
Barreal **124** 31 33 S 69 28W
Barreiras **127** 12 8 S 45 0W
Barreirinhas **127** 2 30 S 42 50W
Barreiro **31** 38 40N 9 6W
Barreiros **127** 8 49 S 35 12W
Barrême **21** 43 57N 6 23 E
Barren I. **71** 12 17N 93 50 E
Barren, Nosy **93** 18 25 S 43 40 E
Barretos **127** 20 30 S 48 35W
Barrhead **108** 54 10N 114 24W
Barrie **106** 44 24N 79 40W
Barrier Ra. **97** 31 0 S 141 30 E
Barrière **108** 51 12N 120 7W
Barrington, Ill., U.S.A. **114** 42 8N 88 5W
Barrington, R.I., U.S.A. **113** 41 43N 71 20W
Barrington L. **109** 56 55N 100 15W
Barrington Tops **97** 32 6 S 151 28 E
Barrow **104** 71 16N 156 50W
Barrow → **15** 52 10N 6 57W
Barrow Creek T.O. **96** 21 30 S 133 55 E
Barrow I. **96** 20 45 S 115 20 E
Barrow-in-Furness **12** 54 8N 3 15W
Barrow Pt. **98** 14 20 S 144 40 E
Barrow Ra. **96** 26 0 S 127 40 E
Barrow Str. **4** 74 20N 95 0W
Barruecopardo **30** 41 4N 6 40W
Barruelo **30** 42 54N 4 17W
Barry **13** 51 23N 3 19W
Barry's Bay **106** 45 29N 77 41W
Barsalogho **85** 13 25N 1 3W
Barsi **70** 18 10N 75 50 E
Barsø **49** 55 7N 9 33 E
Barstow, Calif., U.S.A. **119** 34 58N 117 2W
Barstow, Tex., U.S.A. **117** 31 28N 103 24W
Barth **24** 54 20N 12 36 E
Bartica **126** 6 25N 58 40W
Bartin **64** 41 38N 32 21 E
Bartle Frere, Mt. **97** 17 27 S 145 50 E
Bartlesville **117** 36 50N 95 58W
Bartlett **117** 30 46N 97 30W
Bartlett, L. **108** 63 5N 118 20W
Bartolomeu Dias **91** 21 10 S 35 8 E
Barton-upon-Humber **12** 53 41N 0 27W
Bartoszyce **28** 54 15N 20 55 E
Bartow **115** 27 53N 81 49W
Barumba **90** 1 3N 23 37 E
Baruth **24** 52 3N 13 31 E
Barvenkovo **56** 48 57N 37 0 E
Barwani **68** 22 2N 74 57 E
Barycz → **28** 51 42N 16 15 E
Barysh **55** 53 39N 47 8 E
Bas-Rhin □ **19** 48 40N 7 30 E
Bašaid **42** 45 38N 20 25 E
Bāsa'idū **65** 26 35N 55 20 E
Basankusa **88** 1 5N 19 50 E
Bascuñán, C. **124** 28 52 S 71 35W
Basel (Basle) **25** 47 35N 7 35 E
Basel-Stadt □ **25** 47 35N 7 35 E
Baselland □ **25** 47 26N 7 45 E
Basento → **41** 40 21N 16 50 E
Bashkir A.S.S.R. □ **52** 54 0N 57 0 E
Basilaki I. **98** 10 35 S 151 0 E
Basilan **73** 6 35N 122 0 E
Basilan Str. **73** 6 50N 122 0 E
Basildon **13** 51 34N 0 29 E
Basilicata □ **41** 40 30N 16 0 E
Basim **70** 20 3N 77 0 E
Basin **118** 44 22N 108 2W
Basingstoke **13** 51 15N 1 5W
Basirhat **69** 22 40N 88 54 E
Baška **39** 44 58N 14 45 E
Baskatong, Rés. **106** 46 46N 75 50W
Baskerville C. **96** 17 10 S 122 15 E
Basle = Basel **25** 47 35N 7 35 E
Basmat **70** 19 15N 77 12 E
Basoda **68** 23 52N 77 54 E
Basoka **90** 1 16N 23 40 E
Basongo **88** 4 15 S 20 20 E
Basque Provinces = Vascongadas **32** 42 50N 2 45W
Basra = Al Başrah **64** 30 30N 47 50 E
Bass Rock **14** 56 5N 2 40W
Bass Str. **97** 39 15 S 146 30 E
Bassano **108** 50 48N 112 20W
Bassano del Grappa **39** 45 45N 11 45 E
Bassar **85** 9 19N 0 57 E
Basse Santa-Su **84** 13 13N 14 15W
Basse-Terre **121** 16 0N 61 40W
Bassée, La **19** 50 31N 2 49 E
Bassein **70** 19 26N 72 48 E
Basseterre **121** 17 17N 62 43W
Bassett, Nebr., U.S.A. **116** 42 37N 99 30W
Bassett, Va., U.S.A. **115** 36 48N 79 59W
Bassi **68** 30 44N 76 21 E
Bassigny **19** 48 0N 5 10 E
Bassikounou **84** 15 55N 6 1W
Bassum **24** 52 50N 8 42 E
Båstad **49** 56 25N 12 51 E
Bastak **65** 27 15N 54 25 E
Bastar **70** 19 15N 81 40 E
Basti **69** 26 52N 82 55 E
Bastia **21** 42 40N 9 30 E
Bastia Umbra **39** 43 4N 12 34 E
Bastide-Puylaurent, La **20** 44 35N 3 55 E
Bastogne **16** 50 1N 5 43 E
Bastrop **117** 30 5N 97 22W
Basuto **92** 19 50 S 26 25 E
Bat Yam **62** 32 2N 34 44 E
Bata, Eq. Guin. **88** 1 57N 9 50 E
Bata, Romania **46** 46 1N 22 4 E
Bataan **73** 14 40N 120 25 E
Batabanó **121** 22 40N 82 20W
Batabanó, G. de **121** 22 30N 82 30W
Batac **73** 18 3N 120 34 E
Batagoy **59** 67 38N 134 38 E
Batak **43** 41 57N 24 12 E
Batakan **72** 4 5 S 114 38 E
Batalha **31** 39 40N 8 50W
Batama **90** 0 58N 26 33 E
Batamay **59** 63 30N 129 15 E
Batang, China **75** 30 1N 99 0 E
Batang, Indon. **73** 6 55 S 109 40 E
Batangafo **88** 7 25N 18 20 E
Batangas **73** 13 35N 121 10 E
Batanta **73** 0 55 S 130 40 E
Batatais **125** 20 54 S 47 37W
Batavia **114** 43 0N 78 10W
Bataysk **57** 47 3N 39 45 E
Batchelor **96** 13 4 S 131 1 E
Bateman's B. **97** 35 40 S 150 12 E
Batemans Bay **99** 35 44 S 150 11 E
Batesburg **115** 33 54N 81 32W
Batesville, Ark., U.S.A. **117** 35 48N 91 40W
Batesville, Miss., U.S.A. **117** 34 17N 89 58W
Batesville, Tex., U.S.A. **117** 28 59N 99 38W
Bath, U.K. **13** 51 22N 2 22W
Bath, Maine, U.S.A. **107** 43 50N 69 49W
Bath, N.Y., U.S.A. **114** 42 20N 77 17W
Bathgate **14** 55 54N 3 38W
Bathurst, Austral. **97** 33 25 S 149 31 E
Bathurst, Can. **107** 47 37N 65 43W
Bathurst = Banjul **84** 13 28N 16 40W
Bathurst B. **97** 14 16 S 144 25 E
Bathurst, C. **104** 70 34N 128 0W
Bathurst Harb. **99** 43 15 S 146 10 E
Bathurst I., Austral. **96** 11 30 S 130 10 E
Bathurst I., Can. **4** 76 0N 100 30W
Bathurst In. **104** 68 10N 108 50W
Bathurst Inlet **104** 66 50N 108 1W
Batie **84** 9 53N 2 53W
Batinah **65** 24 0N 56 0 E
Batlow **99** 35 31 S 148 9 E
Batman **64** 37 55N 41 5 E
Batna **83** 35 34N 6 15 E
Batočina **42** 44 7N 21 5 E
Batoka **91** 16 45 S 27 15 E
Baton Rouge **117** 30 30N 91 5W
Batopilas **120** 27 0N 107 45W
Batouri **88** 4 30N 14 25 E
Battambang **71** 13 7N 103 12 E
Batticaloa **70** 7 43N 81 45 E
Battipáglia **41** 40 38N 15 0 E
Battīr **62** 31 44N 35 8 E
Battle, Can. **109** 52 58N 110 52W
Battle, U.K. **13** 50 55N 0 30 E
Battle → **109** 52 43N 108 15W
Battle Camp **98** 15 20 S 144 40 E
Battle Creek **114** 42 20N 85 6W
Battle Harbour **107** 52 16N 55 35W
Battle Lake **116** 46 20N 95 43W
Battle Mountain **118** 40 45N 117 0W
Battlefields **91** 18 37 S 29 47 E
Battleford **109** 52 45N 108 15W
Battonya **27** 46 16N 21 3 E
Batu **87** 6 55N 39 45 E
Batu Gajah **71** 4 28N 101 3 E
Batu, Kepulauan **72** 0 30 S 98 25 E
Batu Pahat **71** 1 50N 102 56 E
Batuata **73** 6 12 S 122 42 E
Batumi **57** 41 30N 41 30 E
Baturaja **72** 4 11 S 104 15 E
Baturité **127** 4 28 S 38 45W
Bau **72** 1 25N 110 9 E
Baubau **73** 5 25 S 122 38 E
Bauchi **85** 10 22N 9 48 E
Bauchi □ **85** 10 30N 10 0 E
Baud **18** 47 52N 3 1W
Baudette **116** 48 46N 94 35W
Baugé **18** 47 31N 0 8W
Baule-Escoublac, La **18** 47 18N 2 23W
Baume-les-Dames **19** 47 22N 6 22 E

Baunatal Benavente

Baunatal	**24**	51 13N	9 25 E
Baunei	**40**	40 2N	9 41 E
Bauru	**125**	22 10 S	49 0W
Baús	**127**	18 22 S	52 47W
Bauska	**54**	56 24N	25 15 E
Bautzen	**24**	51 11N	14 25 E
Baux, Les	**21**	43 45N	4 51 E
Bavanište	**42**	44 49N	20 53 E
Bavaria = Bayern ☐	**25**	49 7N	11 30 E
Båven	**48**	59 0N	16 56 E
Bavi Sadri	**68**	24 28N	74 30 E
Bavispe →	**120**	29 30N	109 11W
Baw Baw, Mt.	**100**	37 49 S	146 19 E
Bawdwin	**67**	23 5N	97 20 E
Bawean	**72**	5 46 S	112 35 E
Bawku	**85**	11 3N	0 19W
Bawlake	**67**	19 11N	97 21 E
Baxley	**115**	31 43N	82 23W
Baxter Springs	**117**	37 3N	94 45W
Bay Bulls	**107**	47 19N	52 50W
Bay City, Mich., U.S.A.	**114**	43 35N	83 51W
Bay City, Oreg., U.S.A.	**118**	45 45N	123 58W
Bay City, Tex., U.S.A.	**117**	28 59N	95 55W
Bay de Verde	**107**	48 5N	52 54W
Bay, Laguna de	**73**	14 20N	121 11 E
Bay Minette	**115**	30 54N	87 43W
Bay St. Louis	**117**	30 18N	89 22W
Bay Shore	**114**	40 44N	73 15W
Bay Springs	**117**	31 58N	89 18W
Bay View	**101**	39 25 S	176 50 E
Baya	**91**	11 53 S	27 25 E
Bayamo	**121**	20 20N	76 40W
Bayamón	**121**	18 24N	66 10W
Bayan	**76**	46 5N	127 24 E
Bayan Har Shan	**75**	34 0N	98 0 E
Bayan Hot = Alxa Zuoqi	**76**	38 50N	105 40 E
Bayan Obo	**76**	41 52N	109 59 E
Bayana	**68**	26 55N	77 18 E
Bayanaul	**58**	50 45N	75 45 E
Bayanhongor	**75**	46 8N	102 43 E
Bayard	**116**	41 48N	103 17W
Bayázeh	**65**	33 30N	54 40 E
Baybay	**73**	10 40N	124 55 E
Bayburt	**64**	40 15N	40 20 E
Bayerischer Wald	**25**	49 0N	13 0 E
Bayern ☐	**25**	49 7N	11 30 E
Bayeux	**18**	49 17N	0 42W
Bayfield, Can.	**112**	43 34N	81 42W
Bayfield, U.S.A.	**116**	46 50N	90 48W
Baykal, Oz.	**59**	53 0N	108 0 E
Baykit	**59**	61 50N	95 50 E
Baykonur	**58**	47 48N	65 50 E
Baymak	**52**	52 36N	58 19 E
Baynes Mts.	**92**	17 15 S	13 0 E
Bayombong	**73**	16 30N	121 10 E
Bayon	**19**	48 30N	6 20 E
Bayona	**30**	42 6N	8 52W
Bayonne, France	**20**	43 30N	1 28W
Bayonne, U.S.A.	**113**	40 41N	74 7W
Bayovar	**126**	5 50 S	81 0W
Baypore →	**70**	11 10N	75 47 E
Bayram-Ali	**58**	37 37N	62 10 E
Bayreuth	**25**	49 56N	11 35 E
Bayrischzell	**25**	47 39N	12 1 E
Bayrūt	**64**	33 53N	35 31 E
Bayt Awlá	**62**	31 37N	35 2 E
Bayt Fajjār	**62**	31 38N	35 9 E
Bayt Fūrīk	**62**	32 11N	35 20 E
Bayt Ḩānūn	**62**	31 32N	34 32 E
Bayt Jālā	**62**	31 43N	35 11 E
Bayt Lahm	**62**	31 43N	35 12 E
Bayt Rīma	**62**	32 2N	35 6 E
Bayt Sāḩūr	**62**	31 42N	35 13 E
Bayt Ummar	**62**	31 38N	35 7 E
Bayt 'ūr al Taḩtā	**62**	31 54N	35 5 E
Baytīn	**62**	31 56N	35 14 E
Baytown	**117**	29 42N	94 57W
Baytūniyā	**62**	31 54N	35 10 E
Bayzo	**85**	13 52N	4 35 E
Baza	**33**	37 30N	2 47W
Bazar Dyuzi	**57**	41 12N	47 50 E
Bazarny Karabulak	**55**	52 15N	46 20 E
Bazarnyy Syzgan	**55**	53 45N	46 40 E
Bazartobe	**57**	49 26N	51 45 E
Bazaruto, I. do	**93**	21 40 S	35 28 E
Bazas	**20**	44 27N	0 13W
Bazhong	**77**	31 52N	106 46 E
Beach	**116**	46 57N	103 58W
Beach City	**112**	40 38N	81 35W
Beachport	**99**	37 29 S	140 0 E
Beachy Head	**13**	50 44N	0 16 E
Beacon	**114**	41 32N	73 58W
Beaconia	**109**	50 25N	96 31W
Beaconsfield	**97**	41 11 S	146 48 E
Beagle, Canal	**128**	55 0 S	68 30W
Bealanana	**93**	14 33N	48 44 E
Beamsville	**112**	43 12N	79 28W
Béar, C.	**20**	42 31N	3 8 E
Bear I.	**15**	51 38N	9 50W
Bear L., B.C., Can.	**108**	56 10N	126 52W
Bear L., Man., Can.	**109**	55 8N	96 0W
Bear L., U.S.A.	**118**	42 0N	111 20W
Bearcreek	**118**	45 11N	109 6W
Beardmore	**106**	49 36N	87 57W
Beardmore Glacier	**5**	84 30 S	170 0 E
Beardstown	**116**	40 0N	90 25W
Béarn	**20**	43 8N	0 36W
Bearpaw Mt.	**118**	48 15N	109 30W
Bearskin Lake	**106**	53 58N	91 2W
Beas de Segura	**33**	38 15N	2 53W
Beasain	**32**	43 3N	2 11W
Beata, C.	**121**	17 40N	71 30W
Beatrice, U.S.A.	**116**	40 20N	96 40W
Beatrice, Zimb.	**91**	18 15 S	30 55 E
Beatrice, C.	**97**	14 20 S	136 55 E
Beatton →	**108**	56 15N	120 45W
Beatton River	**108**	57 26N	121 20W
Beatty	**119**	36 58N	116 46W
Beaucaire	**21**	43 48N	4 39 E
Beauce, Plaine de la	**19**	48 10N	1 45 E
Beauceville	**107**	46 13N	70 46W
Beaudesert	**99**	27 59 S	153 0 E
Beaufort, Austral.	**100**	37 25 S	143 25 E
Beaufort, Malay.	**72**	5 30N	115 40 E
Beaufort, N.C., U.S.A.	**115**	34 45N	76 40W
Beaufort, S.C., U.S.A.	**115**	32 25N	80 40W
Beaufort Sea	**4**	72 0N	140 0W
Beaufort West	**92**	32 18 S	22 36 E
Beaugency	**19**	47 47N	1 38 E
Beauharnois	**106**	45 20N	73 52W
Beaujeu	**21**	46 10N	4 35 E
Beaulieu	**20**	44 59N	1 50 E
Beaulieu →	**108**	62 3N	113 11W
Beauly	**14**	57 29N	4 27W
Beauly →	**14**	57 26N	4 28W
Beaumaris	**12**	53 16N	4 7W
Beaumetz-les-Loges	**19**	50 15N	2 40 E
Beaumont, Dordogne, France	**20**	44 45N	0 46 E
Beaumont, Sarthe, France	**18**	48 13N	0 8 E
Beaumont, U.S.A.	**117**	30 5N	94 8W
Beaumont-de-Lomagne	**20**	43 53N	0 59 E
Beaumont-le-Roger	**18**	49 4N	0 47 E
Beaumont-sur-Oise	**19**	49 9N	2 17 E
Beaune	**19**	47 2N	4 50 E
Beaune-la-Rolande	**19**	48 4N	2 25 E
Beaupréau	**18**	47 12N	1 00W
Beauséjour	**109**	50 5N	96 35W
Beausset, Le	**21**	43 10N	5 46 E
Beauvais	**19**	49 25N	2 8 E
Beauval	**109**	55 9N	107 37W
Beauvoir	**18**	46 55N	2 1W
Beauvoir-sur-Niort	**20**	46 12N	0 30W
Beaver, Alaska, U.S.A.	**104**	66 20N	147 30W
Beaver, Okla., U.S.A.	**117**	36 52N	100 31W
Beaver, Pa., U.S.A.	**112**	40 40N	80 18W
Beaver, Utah, U.S.A.	**119**	38 20N	112 45W
Beaver →, B.C., Can.	**108**	59 52N	124 20W
Beaver →, Sask., Can.	**109**	55 26N	107 45W
Beaver City	**116**	40 13N	99 50W
Beaver Dam	**116**	43 28N	88 50W
Beaver Falls	**114**	40 44N	80 20W
Beaver I.	**106**	45 40N	85 31W
Beaver, R	**106**	55 55N	87 48W
Beaverhill L., Alta., Can.	**108**	53 27N	112 32W
Beaverhill L., Man., Can.	**109**	54 5N	94 50W
Beaverhill L., N.W.T., Can.	**109**	63 2N	104 22W
Beaverlodge	**108**	55 11N	119 29W
Beavermouth	**108**	51 32N	117 23W
Beaverstone →	**106**	54 59N	89 25W
Beaverton	**112**	44 26N	79 9W
Beawar	**68**	26 3N	74 18 E
Bebedouro	**125**	21 0 S	48 25W
Beboa	**93**	17 22 S	44 33 E
Bebra	**24**	50 59N	9 48 E
Beccles	**13**	52 27N	1 33 E
Bečej	**42**	45 36N	20 3 E
Beceni	**46**	45 23N	26 48 E
Becerreá	**30**	42 51N	7 10W
Béchar	**82**	31 38N	2 18W
Bechyně	**26**	49 17N	14 29 E
Beckley	**114**	37 50N	81 8W
Beckum	**24**	51 46N	8 3 E
Bécon	**18**	47 30N	0 50W
Bečva →	**27**	49 31N	17 40 E
Bédar	**33**	37 11N	1 59W
Bédarieux	**20**	43 37N	3 10 E
Bédarrides	**21**	44 2N	4 54 E
Beddouza, Ras	**82**	32 33N	9 9W
Bedele	**87**	8 31N	36 23 E
Bederkesa	**24**	53 37N	8 50 E
Bedeso	**87**	9 58N	40 52 E
Bedford, Can.	**106**	45 7N	72 59W
Bedford, S. Afr.	**92**	32 40 S	26 10 E
Bedford, U.K.	**13**	52 8N	0 29W
Bedford, Ind., U.S.A.	**114**	38 50N	86 30W
Bedford, Iowa, U.S.A.	**116**	40 40N	94 41W
Bedford, Ohio, U.S.A.	**114**	41 23N	81 32W
Bedford, Pa., U.S.A.	**112**	40 1N	78 30W
Bedford, Va., U.S.A.	**114**	37 25N	79 30W
Bedford ☐	**13**	52 4N	0 28W
Bedford, C.	**97**	15 14 S	145 21 E
Będków	**28**	51 36N	19 44 E
Bednja →	**39**	46 12N	16 25 E
Bednodemyanovsk	**55**	53 55N	43 15 E
Bedónia	**38**	44 28N	9 36 E
Bedourie	**97**	24 30 S	139 30 E
Bedous	**20**	43 0N	0 36W
Będzin	**28**	50 19N	19 7 E
Beech Grove	**114**	39 40N	86 2W
Beechworth	**99**	36 22 S	146 43 E
Beechy	**109**	50 53N	107 24W
Beelitz	**24**	52 14N	12 58 E
Beenleigh	**99**	27 43 S	153 10 E
Be'er Sheva'	**62**	31 15N	34 48 E
Be'er Sheva' →	**62**	31 12N	34 40 E
Be'er Toviyya	**62**	31 44N	34 42 E
Be'eri	**62**	31 25N	34 30 E
Be'erotayim	**62**	32 19N	34 59 E
Beersheba = Be'er Sheva'	**62**	31 15N	34 48 E
Beeskow	**24**	52 9N	14 14 E
Beeston	**12**	52 55N	1 11W
Beetzendorf	**24**	52 42N	11 6 E
Beeville	**117**	28 27N	97 44W
Befale	**88**	0 25N	20 45 E
Befotaka	**93**	23 49 S	47 0 E
Bega	**97**	36 41 S	149 51 E
Bega, Canalul	**42**	45 37N	20 46 E
Bégard	**18**	48 38N	3 18W
* Begemdir & Simen ☐	**87**	12 55N	37 30 E
Bègles	**20**	44 45N	0 35W
Begna →	**47**	60 41N	10 0 E
Begonte	**30**	43 10N	7 40W
Begu-Sarai	**69**	25 24N	86 9 E
Behbehān	**64**	30 30N	50 15 E
Behror	**68**	27 51N	76 20 E
Behshahr	**65**	36 45N	53 35 E
Bei Jiang →	**75**	23 2N	112 58 E
Bei'an	**75**	48 10N	126 20 E
Beibei	**75**	29 47N	106 22 E
Beihai	**75**	21 28N	109 6 E
Beijing	**76**	39 55N	116 20 E
Beijing ☐	**76**	39 55N	116 20 E
Beilen	**16**	52 52N	6 27 E
Beilngries	**25**	49 1N	11 27 E
Beilpajah	**99**	32 54 S	143 52 E
Beilul	**87**	13 2N	42 20 E
Beira	**91**	19 50 S	34 52 E
Beirut = Bayrūt	**64**	33 53N	35 31 E
Beit Lāhiyah	**62**	31 32N	34 30 E
Beitaolaizhao	**76**	44 58N	125 58 E
Beitbridge	**91**	22 12 S	30 0 E
Beiuş	**46**	46 40N	22 21 E
Beizhen	**76**	37 20N	118 2 E
Beja	**31**	38 2N	7 53W
Béja	**83**	36 43N	9 12 E
Beja ☐	**31**	37 55N	7 55W
Bejaia	**83**	36 42N	5 2 E
Béjar	**30**	40 23N	5 46W
Bejestān	**65**	34 30N	58 5 E
Bekasi	**73**	6 20 S	107 0 E
Békés	**27**	46 47N	21 9 E
Békés ☐	**27**	46 45N	21 0 E
Békéscsaba	**27**	46 40N	21 5 E
Bekily	**93**	24 13 S	45 19 E
Bekoji	**87**	7 40N	39 17 E
Bekok	**71**	2 20N	103 7 E
Bekwai	**85**	6 30N	1 34W
Bela, India	**69**	25 50N	82 0 E
Bela, Pak.	**66**	26 12N	66 20 E
Bela Crkva	**42**	44 55N	21 27 E
Bela Palanka	**42**	43 13N	22 17 E
Bela Vista, Brazil	**124**	22 12 S	56 20W
Bela Vista, Mozam.	**93**	26 10 S	32 44 E
Bélâbre	**20**	46 34N	1 8 E
Belalcázar	**31**	38 35N	5 10W
Belanovica	**42**	44 15N	20 23 E
Belavenona	**93**	24 50 S	47 4 E
Belawan	**72**	3 33N	98 32 E
Belaya →	**52**	56 0N	54 32 E
Belaya Glina	**57**	46 5N	40 48 E
Belaya Kalitva	**57**	48 13N	40 50 E
Belaya Kholunitsa	**55**	58 41N	50 13 E
Belaya, Mt.	**87**	11 25N	36 8 E
Belaya Tserkov	**54**	49 45N	30 10 E
Belceşti	**46**	47 19N	27 7 E
Bełchatów	**28**	51 21N	19 22 E
Belcher, C.	**4**	71 0N	161 0W
Belcher Is.	**106**	56 15N	78 45W
Belchite	**32**	41 18N	0 43W
Belebey	**52**	54 7N	54 7 E
Belém (Pará)	**127**	1 20 S	48 30W
Belén, Argent.	**124**	27 40 S	67 5W
Belén, Parag.	**124**	23 30 S	57 6W
Belen	**119**	34 40N	106 50W
Belene	**43**	43 39N	25 10 E
Bélesta	**20**	42 55N	1 56 E
Belet Uen	**63**	4 30N	45 5 E
Belev	**55**	53 50N	36 5 E
Belfast, S. Afr.	**93**	25 42 S	30 2 E
Belfast, U.K.	**15**	54 35N	5 56W
Belfast, Maine, U.S.A.	**107**	44 30N	69 0W
Belfast, N.Y., U.S.A.	**112**	42 21N	78 9W
Belfast ☐	**15**	54 35N	5 56W
Belfast, L.	**15**	54 40N	5 50W
Belfield	**116**	46 54N	103 11W
Belfort	**19**	47 38N	6 50 E
Belfort ☐	**19**	47 38N	6 52 E
Belfry	**118**	45 10N	109 2W
Belgaum	**70**	15 55N	74 35 E
Belgioioso	**38**	45 9N	9 21 E
Belgium ■	**16**	50 30N	5 0 E
Belgorod	**56**	50 35N	36 35 E
Belgorod-Dnestrovskiy	**56**	46 11N	30 23 E
Belgrade	**118**	45 50N	111 10W
Belgrade = Beograd	**42**	44 50N	20 37 E
Belhaven	**115**	35 34N	76 35W
Beli Drim →	**42**	42 6N	20 25 E
Beli Manastir	**42**	45 45N	18 36 E
Beli Timok →	**42**	43 53N	22 14 E
Belice →	**40**	37 35N	12 55 E
Belin	**20**	44 30N	0 47W
Belinga	**88**	1 10N	13 2 E
Belingwe	**91**	20 29 S	29 57 E
Belingwe, N.	**91**	20 37 S	29 55 E
Belinskiy (Chembar)	**55**	53 0N	43 25 E
Belinţ	**42**	45 48N	21 54 E
Belinyu	**72**	1 35 S	105 50 E
Belitung, P.	**72**	3 10 S	107 50 E
Beliu	**46**	46 30N	22 0 E
Belize ■	**120**	17 0N	88 30W
Belize City	**120**	17 25N	88 0W
Beljanica	**42**	44 08N	21 43 E
Belkovskiy, Ostrov	**59**	75 32N	135 44 E
Bell →	**106**	49 48N	77 38W
Bell Bay	**99**	41 6 S	146 53 E
Bell I.	**107**	50 46N	55 35W
Bell-Irving →	**108**	56 12N	129 5W
Bell Peninsula	**105**	63 50N	82 0W
Bell Ville	**124**	32 40 S	62 40W
Bella Bella	**108**	52 10N	128 10W
Bella Coola	**108**	52 25N	126 40W
Bella Unión	**124**	30 15 S	57 40W
Bella Vista, Corrientes, Argent.	**124**	28 33 S	59 0W
Bella Vista, Tucuman, Argent.	**124**	27 10 S	65 25W
Bellac	**20**	46 7N	1 3 E
Bellágio	**38**	45 59N	9 15 E
Bellaire	**114**	40 1N	80 46W
Bellary	**70**	15 10N	76 56 E
Bellata	**99**	29 53 S	149 46 E
Belle Fourche	**116**	44 43N	103 52W
Belle Fourche →	**116**	44 25N	102 19W
Belle Glade	**115**	26 43N	80 38W
Belle-Île	**18**	47 20N	3 10W
Belle Isle	**107**	51 57N	55 25W
Belle-Isle-en-Terre	**18**	48 33N	3 23W
Belle Isle, Str. of	**107**	51 30N	56 30W
Belle, La	**115**	26 45N	81 22W
Belle Plaine, Iowa, U.S.A.	**116**	41 51N	92 18W
Belle Plaine, Minn., U.S.A.	**116**	44 35N	93 48W
Belle Yella	**84**	7 24N	10 0W
Belledonne	**21**	45 30N	6 10 E
Belledune	**107**	47 55N	65 50W
Bellefontaine	**114**	40 20N	83 45W
Bellefonte	**114**	40 56N	77 45W
Bellegarde, Ain, France	**21**	46 4N	5 49 E
Bellegarde, Creuse, France	**20**	45 59N	2 18 E
Bellegarde, Loiret, France	**19**	48 0N	2 26 E
Bellême	**18**	48 22N	0 34 E
Belleoram	**107**	47 31N	55 25W
Belleville, Can.	**106**	44 10N	77 23W
Belleville, Rhône, France	**21**	46 7N	4 45 E
Belleville, Vendée, France	**18**	46 48N	1 28W
Belleville, Ill., U.S.A.	**116**	38 30N	90 0W
Belleville, Kans., U.S.A.	**116**	39 51N	97 38W
Belleville, N.Y., U.S.A.	**113**	43 46N	76 10W
Bellevue, Can.	**108**	49 35N	114 22W
Bellevue, Idaho, U.S.A.	**118**	43 25N	114 23W
Bellevue, Ohio, U.S.A.	**112**	41 20N	82 48W
Bellevue, Pa., U.S.A.	**112**	40 29N	80 3W
Belley	**21**	45 46N	5 41 E
Bellin (Payne Bay)	**105**	60 0N	70 0W
Bellingen	**99**	30 25 S	152 50 E
Bellingham	**118**	48 45N	122 27W
Bellingshausen Sea	**5**	66 0 S	80 0W
Bellinzona	**25**	46 11N	9 1 E
Bellona Reefs	**97**	21 26 S	159 0 E
Bellows Falls	**114**	43 10N	72 30W
Bellpat	**68**	29 0N	68 5 E
Bellpuig	**32**	41 37N	1 1 E
Belluno	**39**	46 8N	12 13 E
Bellville	**117**	29 58N	96 18W
Bellwood	**112**	40 36N	78 21W
Belmar	**113**	40 10N	74 2W
Bélmez	**31**	38 17N	5 17W
Belmont, Austral.	**99**	33 4 S	151 42 E
Belmont, Can.	**112**	42 53N	81 5W
Belmont, U.S.A.	**112**	42 14N	78 3W
Belmonte, Brazil	**127**	16 0 S	39 0W
Belmonte, Port.	**30**	40 21N	7 20W
Belmonte, Spain	**32**	39 34N	2 43W
Belmopan	**120**	17 18N	88 30W
Belmullet	**15**	54 13N	9 58W
Belo Horizonte	**127**	19 55 S	43 56W
Belo-sur-Mer	**93**	20 42 S	44 0 E
Belo-Tsiribihina	**93**	19 40 S	44 30 E
Belogorsk, R.S.F.S.R., U.S.S.R.	**59**	51 0N	128 20 E
Belogorsk, Ukraine S.S.R., U.S.S.R.	**56**	45 3N	34 35 E
Belogradchik	**42**	43 53N	22 15 E
Belogradets	**43**	43 22N	27 18 E
Beloha	**93**	25 10 S	45 3 E
Beloit, Kans., U.S.A.	**116**	39 32N	98 9W
Beloit, Wis., U.S.A.	**116**	42 35N	89 0W
Belokorovichi	**54**	51 7N	28 2 E
Belomorsk	**52**	64 35N	34 30 E
Belonia	**67**	23 15N	91 30 E
Belopolye	**54**	51 14N	34 20 E
Beloretsk	**52**	53 58N	58 24 E
Belovo	**58**	54 30N	86 0 E
Beloye More	**52**	66 30N	38 0 E
Beloye, Oz.	**52**	60 10N	37 35 E
Beloye Ozero	**57**	45 15N	46 50 E
Belozem	**43**	42 12N	25 2 E
Belozersk	**55**	60 0N	37 30 E
Belpasso	**41**	37 37N	15 0 E
Belsito	**40**	37 50N	13 47 E
Beltana	**99**	30 48 S	138 25 E
Belterra	**127**	2 45 S	55 0W
Beltinci	**39**	46 37N	16 20 E
Belton, S.C., U.S.A.	**115**	34 31N	82 39W
Belton, Tex., U.S.A.	**117**	31 4N	97 30W
Belton Res.	**117**	31 8N	97 32W
Beltsy	**56**	47 48N	28 0 E
Belturbet	**15**	54 6N	7 28W
Belukha	**58**	49 50N	86 50 E
Beluran	**72**	5 48N	117 35 E
Beluša	**27**	49 5N	18 27 E
Belušić	**42**	43 50N	21 10 E
Belvedere Maríttimo	**41**	39 37N	15 52 E
Belvès	**20**	44 46N	1 0 E
Belvidere, Ill., U.S.A.	**116**	42 15N	88 55W
Belvidere, N.J., U.S.A.	**113**	40 48N	75 5W
Belvis de la Jara	**31**	39 45N	4 57W
Belyando →	**97**	21 38 S	146 50 E
Belyy	**54**	55 48N	32 51 E
Belyy, Ostrov	**58**	73 30N	71 0 E
Belyy Yar	**58**	58 26N	84 39 E
Belzig	**24**	52 8N	12 36 E
Belzoni	**117**	33 12N	90 30W
Bełżyce	**28**	51 11N	22 17 E
Bemaraha, Lembalemban' i	**93**	18 40 S	44 45 E
Bemarivo	**93**	21 45 S	44 45 E
Bemarivo →	**93**	15 27 S	47 40 E
Bemavo	**93**	21 33 S	45 25 E
Bembéréke	**85**	10 11N	2 43 E
Bembesi	**91**	20 0 S	28 58 E
Bembesi →	**91**	18 57 S	27 47 E
Bembézar →	**31**	37 45N	5 13W
Bemidji	**116**	47 30N	94 50W
Ben 'Ammi	**62**	33 0N	35 7 E
Ben Cruachan	**14**	56 26N	5 8W
Ben Dearg	**14**	57 47N	4 58W
Ben Gardane	**83**	33 11N	11 11 E
Ben Hope	**14**	58 24N	4 36W
Ben Lawers	**14**	56 33N	4 13W
Ben Lomond, Austral.	**97**	41 38 S	147 42 E
Ben Lomond, U.K.	**14**	56 12N	4 39W
Ben Macdhui	**14**	57 4N	3 40W
Ben Mhor	**14**	57 16N	7 21W
Ben More, Central, U.K.	**14**	56 23N	4 31W
Ben More, Strathclyde, U.K.	**14**	56 26N	6 2W
Ben More Assynt	**14**	58 7N	4 51W
Ben Nevis	**14**	56 48N	5 0W
Ben Slimane	**82**	33 38N	7 7W
Ben Vorlich	**14**	56 22N	4 15W
Ben Wyvis	**14**	57 40N	4 35W
Bena	**85**	11 20N	5 50 E
Bena Dibele	**88**	4 4 S	22 50 E
Benagalbón	**31**	36 45N	4 15W
Benagerie	**99**	31 25 S	140 22 E
Benahmed	**82**	33 4N	7 9W
Benalla	**97**	36 30 S	146 0 E
Benambra, Mt.	**100**	36 31 S	147 34 E
Benamejí	**31**	37 16N	4 33W
Benanee	**99**	34 31 S	142 52 E
Benares = Varanasi	**69**	25 22N	83 8 E
Bénat, C.	**21**	43 5N	6 22 E
Benavente, Port.	**31**	38 59N	8 49W

* *Renamed Gonder ☐*

Benavente Bilaspur

Benavente, Spain 30 42 2N 5 43W
Benavides, Spain 30 42 30N 5 54W
Benavides, U.S.A. 117 27 35N 98 28W
Benbecula 14 57 26N 7 21W
Bencubbin 96 30 48 S 117 52 E
Bend 118 44 2N 121 15W
Bendel □ 85 6 0N 6 0 E
Bender Beila 63 9 30N 50 48 E
Bendery 56 46 50N 29 30 E
Bendigo 97 36 40 S 144 15 E
Bendorf 24 50 26N 7 34 E
Benē Beraq, Israel 62 32 6N 34 51 E
Benē Beraq, Israel 62 32 6N 34 51 E
Bénéna 84 13 9N 4 17W
Benenitra 93 23 27 S 45 5 E
Benešŏv 26 49 46N 14 41 E
Bénestroff 19 48 54N 6 45 E
Benet 20 46 22N 0 35W
Benevento 41 41 7N 14 45 E
Benfeld 19 48 22N 7 34 E
Benga 91 16 11 S 33 40 E
Bengal, Bay of 60 15 0N 90 0 E
Bengawan Solo → 73 7 5 S 112 35 E
Bengbu 75 32 58N 117 20 E
Benghazi = Banghāzī 83 32 11N 20 3 E
Bengkalis 72 1 30N 102 10 E
Bengkulu 72 3 50 S 102 12 E
Bengkulu □ 72 3 48 S 102 16 E
Bengough 109 49 25N 105 10W
Benguela 89 12 37 S 13 25 E
Benguerir 82 32 16N 7 56W
Benguérua, I. 93 21 58 S 35 28 E
Benha 86 30 26N 31 8 E
Beni 90 0 30N 29 27 E
Beni → 126 10 23 S 65 24W
Beni Abbès 82 30 5N 2 5W
Beni-Haoua 82 36 30N 1 30 E
Beni Mazâr 86 28 32N 30 44 E
Beni Mellal 82 32 21N 6 21W
Beni Ounif 82 32 0N 1 10W
Beni Saf 82 35 17N 1 15W
Beni Suef 86 29 5N 31 6 E
Beniah L. 108 63 23N 112 17W
Benicarló 32 40 23N 0 23 E
Benidorm 33 38 33N 0 9W
Benidorm, Islote de 33 38 31N 0 9W
Benin ■ 85 10 0N 2 0 E
Benin, Bight of 85 5 0N 3 0 E
Benin City 85 6 20N 5 31 E
Benisa 33 38 43N 0 03 E
Benjamin Aceval 124 24 58 S 57 34W
Benjamin Constant 126 4 40 S 70 15W
Benkelman 116 40 7N 101 32W
Benkovac 39 44 2N 15 37 E
Benlidi 98 24 35 S 144 50 E
Bennett 108 59 56N 134 53W
Bennett, Ostrov 59 76 21N 148 56 E
Bennettsville 115 34 38N 79 39W
Bennington 114 42 52N 73 12W
Benoa 72 8 50 S 115 20 E
Bénodet 18 47 53N 4 7W
Benoni 93 26 11 S 28 18 E
Benoud 82 32 20N 0 16 E
Bensheim 25 49 40N 8 38 E
Benson 119 31 59N 110 19W
Bent 65 26 20N 59 31 E
Benteng 73 6 10 S 120 30 E
Bentinck I. 97 17 3 S 139 35 E
Bentiu 87 9 10N 29 55 E
Bento Gonçalves 125 29 10 S 51 31W
Benton, Ark., U.S.A. 117 34 30N 92 35W
Benton, Ill., U.S.A. 116 38 0N 88 55W
Benton Harbor 114 42 10N 86 28W
Bentong 71 3 31N 101 55 E
Bentu Liben 87 8 32N 38 21 E
Benue □ 85 7 30N 7 30 E
Benue → 85 7 48N 6 46 E
Benxi 76 41 20N 123 48 E
Beo 73 4 25N 126 50 E
Beograd 42 44 50N 20 37 E
Beowawe 118 40 35N 116 30W
Beppu 74 33 15N 131 30 E
Berati 44 40 43N 19 59 E
Berau, Teluk 73 2 30 S 132 30 E
Berber 86 18 0N 34 0 E
Berbera 63 10 30N 45 2 E
Berbérati 88 4 15N 15 40 E
Berberia, C. del 33 38 39N 1 24 E
Berbice → 126 6 20N 57 32W
Berceto 38 44 30N 10 0 E
Berchtesgaden 25 47 37N 12 58 E
Berck-sur-Mer 19 50 25N 1 36 E
Berdichev 56 49 57N 28 30 E
Berdsk 58 54 47N 83 2 E
Berdyansk 56 46 45N 36 50 E
Berea, Ky., U.S.A. 114 37 35N 84 18W
Berea, Ohio, U.S.A. 112 41 21N 81 50W
Berebere 73 2 25N 128 45 E
Bereda 63 11 45N 51 0 E
Berekum 84 7 29N 2 34W
Berenice 86 24 2N 35 25 E
Berens → 109 52 25N 97 2W
Berens I. 109 52 18N 97 18W
Berens River 109 52 25N 97 0W
Berestechko 54 50 22N 25 5 E
Bereşti 46 46 6N 27 50 E
Beretău → 46 46 59N 21 7 E
Berettyo → 27 46 59N 21 7 E
Berettyóújfalu 27 47 13N 21 33 E
Berevo, Majunga, Madag. 93 17 14 S 44 17 E
Berevo, Tuléar, Madag. 93 19 44 S 44 58 E
Bereza 54 52 31N 24 51 E
Berezhany 54 49 26N 24 58 E
Berezina → 54 52 33N 30 14 E
Berezna 55 51 35N 31 46 E
Berezniki 58 59 24N 56 46 E
Berezovka 56 47 14N 30 55 E
Berezovo 58 64 0N 65 0 E
Berg 47 59 10N 11 18 E
Berga, Spain 32 42 6N 1 48 E
Berga, Sweden 49 57 14N 16 3 E
Bergama 64 39 8N 27 15 E
Bérgamo 38 45 42N 9 40 E
Bergantiños 30 43 20N 8 40W
Bergedorf 24 53 28N 10 12 E
Bergen, Ger. 24 54 24N 13 26 E
Bergen, Neth. 16 52 40N 4 43 E
Bergen, Norway 47 60 23N 5 20 E
Bergen, U.S.A. 112 43 5N 77 56W
Bergen-op-Zoom 16 51 30N 4 18 E
Bergerac 20 44 51N 0 30 E
Bergheim 24 50 57N 6 38 E
Bergisch-Gladbach 24 50 59N 7 9 E
Bergkvara 49 56 23N 16 5 E
Bergsjö 48 61 59N 17 3 E
Bergues 19 50 58N 2 24 E
Bergum 16 53 13N 5 59 E
Bergvik 48 61 16N 16 50 E
Berhala, Selat 72 1 0 S 104 15 E
Berhampore 69 24 2N 88 27 E
Berhampur 70 19 15N 84 54 E
Berheci → 46 46 7N 27 19 E
Bering Sea 94 58 0N 167 0 E
Bering Str. 104 66 0N 170 0W
Beringen 16 51 3N 5 14 E
Beringovskiy 59 63 3N 179 19 E
Berislav 56 46 50N 33 30 E
Berisso 124 34 56 S 57 50W
Berja 33 36 50N 2 56W
Berkane 82 34 52N 2 20W
Berkeley 13 51 41N 2 28W
Berkeley Springs 114 39 38N 78 12W
Berkner I. 5 79 30 S 50 0W
Berkovitsa 43 43 16N 23 8 E
Berkshire □ 13 51 30N 1 20W
Berland → 108 54 0N 116 50W
Berlanga 31 38 17N 5 50W
Berleburg 24 51 3N 8 22 E
Berlenga, Ilhas 31 39 25N 9 30W
Berlin, Ger. 24 52 32N 13 24 E
Berlin, Md., U.S.A. 114 38 19N 75 12W
Berlin, N.H., U.S.A. 114 44 29N 71 10W
Berlin, Wis., U.S.A. 114 43 58N 88 55W
Berlin, E. □ 24 52 30N 13 30 E
Berlin, W. □ 24 52 30N 13 20 E
Bermeja, Sierra 31 36 30N 5 11W
Bermejo →, Formosa, Argent. 124 26 51 S 58 23W
Bermejo →, San Juan, Argent. 124 32 30 S 67 30W
Bermeo 32 43 25N 2 47W
Bermillo de Sayago 30 41 22N 6 8W
Bermuda ■ 121 32 45N 65 0W
Bern (Berne) 25 46 57N 7 28 E
Bern (Berne) □ 25 46 45N 7 40 E
Bernado 119 34 30N 106 53W
Bernalda 41 40 24N 16 44 E
Bernalillo 119 35 17N 106 37W
Bernam → 71 3 45N 101 5 E
Bernardo de Irigoyen 125 26 15 S 53 40W
Bernasconi 124 37 55 S 63 44W
Bernau, Germ., E. 24 52 40N 13 35 E
Bernau, Germ., W. 25 47 45N 12 20 E
Bernay 18 49 5N 0 35 E
Bernburg 24 51 40N 11 42 E
Berndorf 26 47 59N 16 1 E
Berne = Bern 25 46 57N 7 28 E
Berneck 25 51 3N 11 40 E
Berner Alpen 25 46 27N 7 35 E
Bernese Oberland = Oberland 25 46 27N 7 35 E
Bernier I. 96 24 50 S 113 12 E
Bernina, Piz 25 46 20N 9 54 E
Bernkastel-Kues 25 49 55N 7 04 E
Beror Hayil 62 31 34N 34 38 E
Béroubouay 85 10 34N 2 46 E
Beroun 26 49 57N 14 5 E
Berounka → 26 50 0N 13 47 E
Berovo 42 41 38N 22 51 E
Berrahal 83 36 54N 7 33 E
Berre, Étang de 21 43 27N 5 5 E
Berrechid 82 33 18N 7 36W
Berri 99 34 14 S 140 35 E
Berriane 82 32 50N 3 46 E
Berrigan 100 35 38 S 145 49 E
Berrouaghia 82 36 10N 2 53 E
Berry, Austral. 99 34 46 S 150 43 E
Berry, France 19 47 0N 2 0 E
Berry Is. 121 25 40N 77 50W
Berryville 117 36 23N 93 35W
Bersenbrück 24 52 33N 7 56 E
Berthold 116 48 19N 101 45W
Berthoud 116 40 21N 105 5W
Bertincourt 19 50 5N 2 58 E
Bertoua 88 4 30N 13 45 E
Bertrand 116 40 35N 99 38W
Berufjörður 50 64 48N 14 29W
Berwick 114 41 4N 76 17W
Berwick-upon-Tweed 12 55 47N 2 0W
Berwyn Mts. 12 52 54N 3 26W
Berzasca 42 44 39N 21 58 E
Berzence 27 46 12N 17 11 E
Besalampy 93 16 43 S 44 29 E
Besançon 19 47 15N 6 0 E
Besar 72 2 40 S 116 0 E
Beserah 71 3 50N 103 21 E
Beshenkovichi 54 55 2N 29 29 E
Beška 42 45 8N 20 6 E
Beskydy 27 49 35N 18 40 E
Beslan 57 43 15N 44 28 E
Besna Kobila 42 42 31N 22 10 E
Besnard L. 109 55 25N 106 0W
Besni 64 37 41N 37 52 E
Besor, N. → 62 31 28N 34 22 E
Beşparmak Dağı 45 37 32N 27 30 E
Bessarabiya 46 47 0N 28 10 E
Bessarabka 56 46 21N 28 58 E
Bessèges 21 44 18N 4 8 E
Bessemer, Ala., U.S.A. 115 33 25N 86 57W
Bessemer, Mich., U.S.A. 116 46 27N 90 0W
Bessin 18 49 21N 1 0W
Bessines-sur-Gartempe 20 46 6N 1 22 E
Bet Alfa 62 32 31N 35 25 E
Bet Dagan 62 32 1N 34 49 E
Bet Guvrin 62 31 37N 34 54 E
Bet Ha'Emeq 62 32 58N 35 8 E
Bet Hashitta 62 32 31N 35 27 E
Bet Qeshet 62 32 41N 35 21 E
Bet She'an 62 32 30N 35 30 E
Bet Shemesh 62 31 44N 35 0 E
Bet Tadjine, Djebel 82 29 0N 3 30W
Bet Yosef 62 32 34N 35 33 E
Betafo 93 19 50 S 46 51 E
Betanzos 30 43 15N 8 12W
Bétaré Oya 88 5 40N 14 5 E
Bétera 32 39 35N 0 28W
Bethal 93 26 27 S 29 28 E
Bethanien 92 26 31 S 17 8 E
Bethany, S. Afr. 92 29 34 S 25 59 E
Bethany, U.S.A. 116 40 18N 94 0W
Bethany = Al Ayzarīyah 62 31 47N 35 15 E
Bethel, Alaska, U.S.A. 104 60 50N 161 50W
Bethel, Pa., U.S.A. 112 40 20N 80 2W
Bethel, Vt., U.S.A. 113 43 50N 72 37W
Bethlehem, S. Afr. 93 28 14 S 28 18 E
Bethlehem, U.S.A. 114 40 39N 75 24W
Bethlehem = Bayt Lahm 62 31 43N 35 12 E
Bethulie 92 30 30 S 25 59 E
Béthune 19 50 30N 2 38 E
Béthune → 18 49 53N 1 9 E
Betioky 93 23 48 S 44 20 E
Beton Bazoches 19 48 42N 3 15 E
Betong, Malay. 72 1 24N 111 31 E
Betong, Thai. 71 5 45N 101 5 E
Betoota 99 25 45 S 140 42 E
Betroka 93 23 16 S 46 0 E
Betsiamites 107 48 56N 68 40W
Betsiamites → 107 48 56N 68 38W
Betsiboka → 93 16 3 S 46 36 E
Betsjoeanaland 92 26 30 S 22 30 E
Bettiah 69 26 48N 84 33 E
Bèttola 38 44 42N 9 32 E
Betul 68 21 58N 77 59 E
Betzdorf 24 50 47N 7 53 E
Beuca 46 44 14N 24 56 E
Beuil 21 44 6N 6 59 E
Beulah 116 47 18N 101 47W
Bevensen 24 53 5N 10 34 E
Beverley, Austral. 96 32 9 S 116 56 E
Beverley, U.K. 12 53 52N 0 26W
Beverly, Mass., U.S.A. 113 42 32N 70 50W
Beverly, Wash., U.S.A. 118 46 55N 119 59W
Beverly Hills 119 34 4N 118 29W
Beverwijk 16 52 28N 4 38 E
Bex 25 46 15N 7 0 E
Beyin 84 5 1N 2 41W
Beykoz 43 41 8N 29 7 E
Beyla 84 8 30N 8 38W
Beynat 20 45 8N 1 44 E
Beyneu 58 45 10N 55 3 E
Beypazarı 64 40 10N 31 56 E
Beyşehir Gölü 64 37 40N 31 45 E
Bezdan 42 45 50N 18 57 E
Bezet 62 33 4N 35 8 E
Bezhetsk 55 57 47N 36 39 E
Bezhitsa 54 53 19N 34 17 E
Béziers 20 43 20N 3 12 E
Bezwada = Vijayawada 70 16 31N 80 39 E
Bhadra → 70 14 0N 75 20 E
Bhadrakh 69 21 10N 86 30 E
Bhadravati 70 13 49N 75 40 E
Bhagalpur 69 25 10N 87 0 E
Bhaisa 70 19 10N 77 58 E
Bhakkar 68 31 40N 71 5 E
Bhakra Dam 68 31 30N 76 45 E
Bhamo 67 24 15N 97 15 E
Bhamragarh 70 19 30N 80 40 E
Bhandara 69 21 5N 79 42 E
Bhanrer Ra. 68 23 40N 79 45 E
Bharatpur 68 27 15N 77 30 E
Bharuch 68 21 47N 73 0 E
Bhatghar L. 70 18 10N 73 48 E
Bhatiapara Ghat 69 23 13N 89 42 E
Bhatinda 68 30 15N 74 57 E
Bhatkal 70 13 58N 74 35 E
Bhatpara 69 22 50N 88 25 E
Bhattiprolu 70 16 7N 80 45 E
Bhaun 68 32 55N 72 40 E
Bhaunagar = Bhavnagar 68 21 45N 72 10 E
Bhavani 70 11 27N 77 43 E
Bhavani → 70 11 0N 78 15 E
Bhavnagar 68 21 45N 72 10 E
Bhawanipatna 70 19 55N 80 10 E
Bhera 68 32 29N 72 57 E
Bhilsa = Vidisha 68 23 28N 77 53 E
Bhilwara 68 25 25N 74 38 E
Bhima → 70 16 25N 77 17 E
Bhimavaram 70 16 30N 81 30 E
Bhind 68 26 30N 78 46 E
Bhir 70 19 4N 75 46 E
Bhiwandi 70 19 20N 73 0 E
Bhiwani 68 28 50N 76 9 E
Bhola 69 22 45N 90 35 E
Bhongir 70 17 30N 78 56 E
Bhopal 68 23 20N 77 30 E
Bhor 70 18 12N 73 53 E
Bhubaneswar 69 20 15N 85 50 E
Bhuj 68 23 15N 69 49 E
Bhumibol Dam 72 17 15N 98 58 E
Bhusaval 68 21 3N 75 46 E
Bhutan ■ 69 27 25N 90 30 E
Biafra, B. of = Bonny, Bight of 85 3 30N 9 20 E
Biak 73 1 10 S 136 6 E
Biała 28 50 24N 17 40 E
Biała →, Białystok, Poland 28 53 11N 23 4 E
Biała →, Tarnów, Poland 27 50 3N 20 55 E
Biała Piska 28 53 37N 22 5 E
Biała Podlaska 28 52 4N 23 6 E
Biała Podlaska □ 28 52 0N 23 0 E
Biała Rawska 28 51 48N 20 29 E
Białobrzegi 28 52 27N 21 3 E
Białogard 28 54 2N 15 58 E
Białowieża 28 52 41N 23 49 E
Biały Bór 28 53 53N 16 51 E
Białystok 28 53 10N 23 10 E
Białystok □ 28 53 9N 23 10 E
Biancavilla 41 37 39N 14 50 E
Biaro 73 2 5N 125 26 E
Biarritz 20 43 29N 1 33W
Biasca 25 46 22N 8 58 E
Biba 86 28 55N 31 0 E
Bibala 89 14 44 S 13 24 E
Bibane, Bahiret el 83 33 16N 11 13 E
Bibbiena 39 43 43N 11 50 E
Bibby I. 109 61 55N 93 0W
Biberach 25 48 5N 9 49 E
Bibey → 30 42 24N 7 13W
Bibiani 84 6 30N 2 8W
Bibile 70 7 10N 81 25 E
Biboohra 98 16 56 S 145 25 E
Bibungwa 90 2 40 S 28 15 E
Bic 107 48 20N 68 41W
Bicaj 44 42 0N 20 25 E
Bicaz 46 46 53N 26 5 E
Biccari 41 41 23N 15 12 E
Biche, La → 108 59 57N 123 50W
Bichena 87 10 28N 38 10 E
Bicknell, Ind., U.S.A. 114 38 50N 87 20W
Bicknell, Utah, U.S.A. 119 38 16N 111 35W
Bida 85 9 3N 5 58 E
Bidar 70 17 55N 77 35 E
Biddeford 107 43 30N 70 28W
Biddiyā 62 32 7N 35 4 E
Biddū 62 31 50N 35 8 E
Biddwara 87 5 11N 38 34 E
Bideford 13 51 1N 4 13W
Bidor 71 4 6N 101 15 E
Bié, Planalto de 89 12 0 S 16 0 E
Bieber 118 41 4N 121 6W
Biebrza → 28 53 13N 22 25 E
Biecz 27 49 44N 21 15 E
Biel (Bienne) 25 47 8N 7 14 E
Bielawa 28 50 43N 16 37 E
Bielé Karpaty 27 49 5N 18 0 E
Bielefeld 24 52 2N 8 31 E
Bielersee 25 47 6N 7 5 E
Biella 38 45 33N 8 3 E
Bielsk Podlaski 28 52 47N 23 12 E
Bielsko-Biała 27 49 50N 19 2 E
Bielsko-Biała □ 27 49 45N 19 15 E
Bien Hoa 71 10 57N 106 49 E
Bienfait 109 49 10N 102 50W
Bienne = Biel 25 47 8N 7 14 E
Bienvenida 31 38 18N 6 12W
Bienville, L. 106 55 5N 72 40W
Biescas 32 42 37N 0 20W
Biese → 24 52 53N 11 46 E
Biesiesfontein 92 30 57 S 17 58 E
Bietigheim 25 48 57N 9 8 E
Biferno → 41 41 59N 15 2 E
Big → 107 54 50N 58 55W
Big B. 107 55 43N 60 35W
Big Beaver 109 49 10N 105 10W
Big Belt Mts. 118 46 50N 111 30W
Big Bend 93 26 50 S 32 2 E
Big Bend Nat. Park 117 29 15N 103 15W
Big Black → 117 32 0N 91 5W
Big Blue → 116 39 11N 96 40W
Big Cr. → 108 51 42N 122 41W
Big Cypress Swamp 115 26 12N 81 10W
Big Falls 116 48 11N 93 48W
Big Fork → 116 48 31N 93 43W
Big Horn 118 46 11N 107 25W
Big Horn Mts. = Bighorn Mts. 118 44 30N 107 30W
Big Lake 117 31 12N 101 25W
Big Moose 113 43 49N 74 58W
Big Muddy → 116 48 8N 104 36W
Big Pine 119 37 12N 118 17W
Big Piney 118 42 32N 110 3W
Big Quill L. 109 51 55N 104 50W
Big Rapids 114 43 42N 85 27W
Big River 109 53 50N 107 0W
Big Run 112 40 57N 78 55W
Big Sable Pt. 114 44 5N 86 30W
Big Sand L. 109 57 45N 99 45W
Big Sandy 118 48 12N 110 9W
Big Sandy Cr. → 116 38 6N 102 29W
Big Sioux → 116 42 30N 96 25W
Big Spring 117 32 10N 101 25W
Big Springs 116 41 4N 102 3W
Big Stone City 116 45 20N 96 30W
Big Stone Gap 115 36 52N 82 45W
Big Stone L. 116 45 30N 96 35W
Big Trout L. 106 53 40N 90 0W
Biganos 20 44 39N 0 59W
Bigfork 118 48 3N 114 2W
Biggar, Can. 109 52 4N 108 0W
Biggar, U.K. 14 55 38N 3 31W
Biggenden 99 25 31 S 152 4 E
Bighorn → 118 46 9N 107 28W
Bighorn Mts. 118 44 30N 107 30W
Bignona 84 12 52N 16 14W
Bigorre 20 43 6N 0 5 E
Bigstone L. 109 53 42N 95 44W
Bigtimber 118 45 53N 110 0W
Bigwa 90 7 10 S 39 10 E
Bihać 39 44 49N 15 57 E
Bihar 69 25 5N 85 40 E
Bihar □ 69 25 0N 86 0 E
Biharamulo 90 2 25 S 31 25 E
Biharamulo □ 90 2 30 S 31 20 E
Biharkeresztes 27 47 8N 21 44 E
Bihor □ 46 47 0N 22 10 E
Bihor, Munţii 46 46 29N 22 47 E
Bijagós, Arquipélago dos 84 11 15N 16 10W
Bijaipur 68 26 2N 77 20 E
Bijapur, Mad. P., India 70 18 50N 80 50 E
Bijapur, Mysore, India 70 16 50N 75 55 E
Bījār 64 35 52N 47 35 E
Bijeljina 42 44 46N 19 17 E
Bijelo Polje 42 43 1N 19 45 E
Bijie 77 27 20N 105 16 E
Bijnor 68 29 27N 78 11 E
Bikaner 68 28 2N 73 18 E
Bikapur 69 26 30N 82 7 E
Bikin 59 46 50N 134 20 E
Bikini Atoll 94 12 0N 167 30 E
Bikoué 85 3 55N 11 50 E
Bilād Banī Bū 'Ali 65 22 0N 59 20 E
Bilara 68 26 14N 73 53 E
Bilaspur, Mad. P., India 69 22 2N 82 15 E

Bilaspur **Bogalusa**

Bilaspur, Punjab, India	**68**	31 19N	76 50 E
Bilauk Taung dan	**71**	13 0N	99 0 E
Bilbao	**32**	43 16N	2 56W
Bilbeis	**86**	30 25N	31 34 E
Bilbor	**46**	47 6N	25 30 E
Bíldudalur	**50**	65 41N	23 36W
Bileća	**42**	42 53N	18 27 E
Bilecik	**64**	40 5N	30 5 E
Biłgoraj	**28**	50 33N	22 42 E
Bilibino	**59**	68 3N	166 20 E
Bilibiza	**91**	12 30 S	40 20 E
Bilir	**59**	65 40N	131 20 E
Bilishti	**44**	40 37N	21 2 E
Bill	**116**	43 18N	105 18W
Billabong Creek	**100**	35 5 S	144 2 E
Billingham	**12**	54 36N	1 18W
Billings	**118**	45 43N	108 29W
Billingsfors	**48**	58 59N	12 15 E
Billiton Is = Belitung	**72**	3 10 S	107 50 E
Billom	**20**	45 43N	3 20 E
Bilma	**81**	18 50N	13 30 E
Bilo Gora	**42**	45 53N	17 15 E
Biloela	**97**	24 24 S	150 31 E
Biloxi	**117**	30 24N	88 53W
Bilpa Morea Claypan	**99**	25 0 S	140 0 E
Biltine	**81**	14 40N	20 50 E
Bilyana	**98**	18 5 S	145 50 E
Bilyarsk	**55**	54 58N	50 22 E
Bima	**73**	8 22 S	118 49 E
Bimban	**86**	24 24N	32 54 E
Bimberi Peak	**100**	35 44 S	148 51 E
Bimbila	**85**	8 54N	0 5 E
Bimbo	**88**	4 15N	18 33 E
Bimini Is.	**121**	25 42N	79 25W
Bin Xian	**77**	35 2N	108 4 E
Bina-Etawah	**68**	24 13N	78 14 E
Binalbagan	**73**	10 12N	122 50 E
Binalong	**100**	34 40 S	148 39 E
Binalud, Kuh-e	**65**	36 30N	58 30 E
Binatang	**72**	2 10N	111 40 E
Binche	**16**	50 26N	4 10 E
Binda	**99**	27 52 S	147 21 E
Bindle	**99**	27 40 S	148 45 E
Bindura	**91**	17 18 S	31 18 E
Bingara, N.S.W., Austral.	**99**	29 52 S	150 36 E
Bingara, Queens., Austral.	**99**	28 10 S	144 37 E
Bingen	**25**	49 57N	7 53 E
Bingerville	**84**	5 18N	3 49W
Bingham	**107**	45 5N	69 50W
Bingham Canyon	**118**	40 31N	112 10W
Binghamton	**114**	42 9N	75 54W
Bingöl	**64**	38 53N	40 29 E
Binh Dinh = An Nhon	**71**	13 55N	109 7 E
Binh Son	**71**	15 20N	108 40 E
Binjai	**72**	3 20N	98 30 E
Binnaway	**99**	31 28 S	149 24 E
Binongko	**73**	5 55 S	123 55 E
Binscarth	**109**	50 37N	101 17W
Bint Jubayl	**62**	33 8N	35 25 E
Bintan	**72**	1 0N	104 0 E
Bintulu	**72**	3 10N	113 0 E
Bintuni (Steenkool)	**73**	2 7 S	133 32 E
Binyamina	**62**	32 32N	34 56 E
Binyang	**77**	23 12N	108 47 E
Binz	**24**	54 23N	13 37 E
Binzert = Bizerte	**83**	37 15N	9 50 E
Bío Bío □	**124**	37 35 S	72 0W
Biograd	**39**	43 56N	15 29 E
Biokovo	**42**	43 23N	17 0 E
Biougra	**82**	30 15N	9 14W
Biq'at Bet Netofa	**62**	32 49N	35 22 E
Bîr Abu Hashim	**86**	23 42N	34 6 E
Bîr Abu M'nqar	**86**	26 33N	27 33 E
Bîr Adal Deib	**86**	22 35N	36 10 E
Bi'r al Malfa	**83**	31 58N	15 18 E
Bir Aouine	**83**	32 25N	9 18 E
Bîr 'Asal	**86**	25 55N	34 20 E
Bir Autrun	**81**	18 15N	26 40 E
Bi'r Dhu'fān	**83**	31 59N	14 32 E
Bîr Diqnash	**86**	31 3N	25 23 E
Bir el Abbes	**82**	26 7N	6 9W
Bir el Ater	**83**	34 46N	8 3 E
Bîr el Basur	**86**	29 51N	25 49 E
Bîr el Gellaz	**86**	30 50N	26 40 E
Bîr el Shaqqa	**86**	30 54N	25 1 E
Bîr Fuad	**86**	30 35N	26 28 E
Bîr Haimur	**86**	22 45N	33 40 E
Bir Jdid	**82**	33 26N	8 0W
Bîr Kanayis	**86**	24 59N	33 15 E
Bîr Kerawein	**86**	27 10N	28 25 E
Bir Lahrache	**83**	32 1N	8 12 E
Bîr Maql	**86**	23 7N	33 40 E
Bîr Misaha	**86**	22 13N	27 59 E
Bir Mogrein	**82**	25 10N	11 25W
Bi'r Mubayrīk	**64**	23 22N	39 8 E
Bîr Murr	**86**	23 28N	30 10 E
Bi'r Nabālā	**62**	31 52N	35 12 E
Bîr Nakheila	**86**	24 1N	30 50 E
Bîr Qatrani	**86**	30 55N	26 10 E
Bîr Ranga	**86**	24 25N	35 15 E
Bir, Ras	**87**	12 0N	43 20 E
Bîr Sahara	**86**	22 54N	28 40 E
Bîr Seiyâla	**86**	26 10N	33 50 E
Bir Semguine	**82**	30 1N	5 39W
Bîr Shalatein	**86**	23 5N	35 25 E
Bîr Shebb	**86**	22 25N	29 40 E
Bîr Shût	**86**	23 50N	35 15 E
Bîr Terfawi	**86**	22 57N	28 55 E
Bîr Umm Qubûr	**86**	24 35N	34 2 E
Bîr Ungât	**86**	22 8N	33 48 E
Bîr Za'farâna	**86**	29 10N	32 40 E
Bîr Zāmūs	**83**	24 16N	15 6 E
Bi'r Zayt	**62**	31 59N	35 11 E
Bîr Zeidûn	**86**	25 45N	33 40 E
Bira	**73**	2 3 S	132 2 E
Bîra	**46**	47 2N	27 3 E
Birak Sulaymān	**62**	31 42N	35 7 E
Biramféro	**84**	11 40N	9 10W
Birao	**81**	10 20N	22 47 E
Birawa	**90**	2 20 S	28 48 E
Bîrca	**46**	43 59N	23 36 E
Birch Hills	**109**	52 59N	105 25W
Birch I.	**109**	52 26N	99 54W
Birch L., N.W.T., Can.	**108**	62 4N	116 33W
Birch L., Ont., Can.	**106**	51 23N	92 18W
Birch L., U.S.A.	**106**	47 48N	91 43W
Birch Mts.	**108**	57 30N	113 10W
Birch River	**109**	52 24N	101 6W
Birchip	**99**	35 56 S	142 55 E
Birchiş	**46**	45 58N	22 9 E
Bird	**109**	56 30N	94 13W
Bird City	**116**	39 48N	101 33W
Bird I., Austral.	**97**	22 10 S	155 28 E
Bird I., S. Afr.	**92**	32 3 S	18 17 E
Bird I. = Aves, I. de	**121**	12 0N	67 30W
Birdlip	**13**	51 50N	2 7W
Birdsville	**97**	25 51 S	139 20 E
Birdum	**96**	15 39 S	133 13 E
Birecik	**64**	37 0N	38 0 E
Bireuen	**72**	5 14N	96 39 E
Birifo	**84**	13 30N	14 0W
Birigui	**125**	21 18 S	50 16W
Birk	**86**	18 8N	41 30 E
Birka	**86**	22 11N	40 38 E
Birkenfeld	**25**	49 39N	7 11 E
Birkenhead	**12**	53 24N	3 1W
Birket Qârûn	**86**	29 30N	30 40 E
Birkfeld	**26**	47 21N	15 45 E
Birkhadem	**82**	36 43N	3 3 E
Bîrlad	**46**	46 15N	27 38 E
Birmingham, U.K.	**13**	52 30N	1 55W
Birmingham, U.S.A.	**115**	33 31N	86 50W
Birmitrapur	**69**	22 24N	84 46 E
Birni Ngaouré	**85**	13 5N	2 51 E
Birni Nkonni	**85**	13 55N	5 15 E
Birnin Gwari	**85**	11 0N	6 45 E
Birnin Kebbi	**85**	12 32N	4 12 E
Birnin Kudu	**85**	11 30N	9 29 E
Birobidzhan	**59**	48 50N	132 50 E
Birqīn	**62**	32 27N	35 15 E
Birr	**15**	53 7N	7 55W
Birrie ⤳	**99**	29 43 S	146 37 E
Birsilpur	**68**	28 11N	72 15 E
Birsk	**52**	55 25N	55 30 E
Birtin	**46**	46 59N	22 31 E
Birtle	**109**	50 30N	101 5W
Biryuchiy	**56**	46 10N	35 0 E
Birzai	**54**	56 11N	24 45 E
Bîrzava	**46**	46 7N	21 59 E
Bisa	**73**	1 15 S	127 28 E
Bisáccia	**41**	41 0N	15 20 E
Bisacquino	**40**	37 42N	13 13 E
Bisalpur	**69**	28 14N	79 48 E
Bisbal, La	**32**	41 58N	3 2 E
Bisbee	**119**	31 30N	110 0W
Biscarrosse, Étang de	**20**	44 21N	1 10W
Biscay, B. of	**6**	45 0N	2 0W
Biscayne B.	**115**	25 40N	80 12W
Biscéglie	**41**	41 14N	16 30 E
Bischofshofen	**26**	47 26N	13 14 E
Bischofswerda	**24**	51 8N	14 11 E
Bischwiller	**19**	48 41N	7 50 E
Biscoe Bay	**5**	77 0 S	152 0W
Biscoe I.	**5**	66 0 S	67 0W
Biscostasing	**106**	47 18N	82 9W
Biševo	**39**	42 57N	16 3 E
Bisha	**87**	15 30N	37 31 E
Bisha, Wadi ⤳	**86**	21 24N	43 26 E
Bishop, Calif., U.S.A.	**119**	37 20N	118 26W
Bishop, Tex., U.S.A.	**117**	27 35N	97 49W
Bishop Auckland	**12**	54 40N	1 40W
Bishop's Falls	**107**	49 2N	55 30W
Bishop's Stortford	**13**	51 52N	0 11 E
Bisignano	**41**	39 30N	16 17 E
Bisina, L.	**90**	1 38N	33 56 E
Biskra	**83**	34 50N	5 44 E
Biskupiec	**28**	53 53N	20 58 E
Bislig	**73**	8 15N	126 27 E
Bismarck	**116**	46 49N	100 49W
Bismarck Arch.	**94**	2 30 S	150 0 E
Bismarck Sea	**98**	4 10 S	146 50 E
Bismark	**24**	52 39N	11 31 E
Biso	**90**	1 44N	31 26 E
Bison	**116**	45 34N	102 28W
Bispfors	**50**	63 1N	16 37 E
Bispgården	**48**	63 2N	16 40 E
Bissagos = Bijagós, Arquipélago dos	**84**	11 15N	16 10W
Bissau	**84**	11 45N	15 45W
Bissett	**109**	51 2N	95 41W
Bissikrima	**84**	10 50N	10 58W
Bistcho L.	**108**	59 45N	118 50W
Bistreţu	**46**	43 54N	23 23 E
Bistrica = Ilirska-Bistrica	**39**	45 34N	14 14 E
Bistriţa	**46**	47 9N	24 35 E
Bistriţa ⤳	**46**	46 30N	26 57 E
Bistriţa Năsăud □	**46**	47 15N	24 30 E
Bistriţei, Munţii	**46**	47 15N	25 40 E
Biswan	**69**	27 29N	81 2 E
Bisztynek	**28**	54 8N	20 53 E
Bitam	**88**	2 5N	11 25 E
Bitburg	**25**	49 58N	6 32 E
Bitche	**19**	49 2N	7 25 E
Bitkine	**81**	11 59N	18 13 E
Bitlis	**64**	38 20N	42 3 E
Bitola (Bitolj)	**42**	41 5N	21 10 E
Bitonto	**41**	41 7N	16 40 E
Bitter Creek	**118**	41 39N	108 36W
Bitter L. = Buheirat-Murrat-el-Kubra	**86**	30 15N	32 40 E
Bitterfeld	**24**	51 36N	12 20 E
Bitterfontein	**92**	31 0 S	18 32 E
Bitterroot ⤳	**118**	46 52N	114 6W
Bitterroot Range	**118**	46 0N	114 20W
Bitti	**40**	40 29N	9 20 E
Bittou	**85**	11 17N	0 18W
Biu	**85**	10 40N	12 3 E
Bivolari	**46**	47 31N	27 27 E
Bivolu	**46**	47 16N	25 58 E
Biwa-Ko	**74**	35 15N	136 10 E
Biwabik	**116**	47 33N	92 19W
Bixad	**46**	47 56N	23 28 E
Biyang	**77**	32 38N	113 21 E
Biysk	**58**	52 40N	85 0 E
Bizana	**93**	30 50 S	29 52 E
Bizerte (Binzert)	**83**	37 15N	9 50 E
Bjargtangar	**50**	65 30N	24 30W
Bjelasica	**42**	42 50N	19 40 E
Bjelašnica	**42**	43 43N	18 9 E
Bjelovar	**42**	45 56N	16 49 E
Bjerringbro	**49**	56 23N	9 39 E
Björbo	**48**	60 27N	14 44 E
Björneborg	**48**	59 14N	14 16 E
Bjørnøya	**4**	74 30N	19 0 E
Bjuv	**49**	56 5N	12 55 E
Blace	**42**	43 18N	21 17 E
Blachownia	**28**	50 49N	18 56 E
Black ⤳, Can.	**112**	44 42N	79 19W
Black ⤳, Ark., U.S.A.	**117**	35 38N	91 19W
Black ⤳, N.Y., U.S.A.	**113**	43 59N	76 4W
Black ⤳, Wis., U.S.A.	**116**	43 52N	91 22W
Black Diamond	**108**	50 45N	114 14W
Black Forest = Schwarzwald	**25**	48 0N	8 0 E
Black Hills	**116**	44 0N	103 50W
Black I.	**109**	51 12N	96 30W
Black L., Can.	**109**	59 12N	105 15W
Black L., U.S.A.	**114**	45 28N	84 15W
Black Mesa, Mt.	**117**	36 57N	102 55W
Black Mt. = Mynydd Du	**13**	51 45N	3 45W
Black Mts.	**13**	51 52N	3 5W
Black Range	**119**	33 30N	107 55W
Black River	**121**	18 0N	77 50W
Black River Falls	**116**	44 23N	90 52W
Black Sea	**9**	43 30N	35 0 E
Black Sugarloaf, Mt.	**100**	31 18 S	151 35 E
Black Volta ⤳	**84**	8 41N	1 33W
Black Warrior ⤳	**115**	32 32N	87 51W
Blackall	**97**	24 25 S	145 45 E
Blackball	**101**	42 22 S	171 26 E
Blackbull	**98**	17 55 S	141 45 E
Blackburn	**12**	53 44N	2 30W
Blackduck	**116**	47 43N	94 32W
Blackfoot	**118**	43 13N	112 12W
Blackfoot ⤳	**118**	46 52N	113 53W
Blackfoot River Res.	**118**	43 0N	111 35W
Blackie	**108**	50 36N	113 37W
Blackpool	**12**	53 48N	3 3W
Blackriver	**112**	44 46N	83 17W
Blacks Harbour	**107**	45 3N	66 49W
Blacksburg	**114**	37 17N	80 23W
Blacksod B.	**15**	54 6N	10 0W
Blackstone	**114**	37 6N	78 0W
Blackstone ⤳	**108**	61 5N	122 55W
Blackstone Ra.	**96**	26 00 S	129 00 E
Blackville	**107**	46 44N	65 50W
Blackwater	**98**	23 35 S	148 53 E
Blackwater ⤳, Ireland	**15**	51 55N	7 50W
Blackwater ⤳, U.K.	**15**	54 31N	6 35W
Blackwater Cr. ⤳	**99**	25 56 S	144 30 E
Blackwell	**117**	36 55N	97 20W
Blaenau Ffestiniog	**12**	53 0N	3 57W
Blagaj	**42**	43 16N	17 55 E
Blagodarnoye	**57**	45 7N	43 37 E
Blagoevgrad (Gorna Dzhumayo)	**42**	42 2N	23 5 E
Blagoveshchensk	**59**	50 20N	127 30 E
Blain	**18**	47 29N	1 45W
Blaine	**118**	48 59N	122 43W
Blaine Lake	**109**	52 51N	106 52W
Blainville	**19**	48 33N	6 23 E
Blair	**116**	41 38N	96 10W
Blair Athol	**97**	22 42 S	147 31 E
Blair Atholl	**14**	56 46N	3 50W
Blairgowrie	**14**	56 36N	3 20W
Blairmore	**108**	49 40N	114 25W
Blairsville	**112**	40 27N	79 15W
Blaj	**46**	46 10N	23 57 E
Blake Pt.	**116**	48 12N	88 27W
Blakely	**115**	31 22N	85 0W
Blâmont	**19**	48 35N	6 50 E
Blanc, C.	**83**	37 15N	9 56 E
Blanc, Le	**20**	46 37N	1 3 E
Blanc, Mont	**21**	45 48N	6 50 E
Blanca, Bahía	**128**	39 10 S	61 30W
Blanca Peak	**119**	37 35N	105 29W
Blanchard	**117**	35 8N	97 40W
Blanche L., S. Austral., Austral.	**97**	29 15 S	139 40 E
Blanche L., W. Austral., Austral.	**96**	22 25 S	123 17 E
Blanco, S. Afr.	**92**	33 55 S	22 23 E
Blanco, U.S.A.	**117**	30 7N	98 30W
Blanco ⤳	**124**	30 20 S	68 42W
Blanco, C., C. Rica	**121**	9 34N	85 8W
Blanco, C., Spain	**33**	39 21N	2 51 E
Blanco, C., U.S.A.	**118**	42 50N	124 40W
Blanda ⤳	**50**	65 20N	19 40W
Blandford Forum	**13**	50 52N	2 10W
Blanding	**119**	37 35N	109 30W
Blanes	**32**	41 40N	2 48 E
Blanice ⤳	**26**	49 10N	14 5 E
Blankenberge	**16**	51 20N	3 9 E
Blankenburg	**24**	51 46N	10 56 E
Blanquefort	**20**	44 55N	0 38W
Blanquillo	**125**	32 53 S	55 37W
Blansko	**27**	49 22N	16 40 E
Blantyre	**91**	15 45 S	35 0 E
Blarney	**15**	51 57N	8 35W
Błaski	**28**	51 38N	18 30 E
Blatná	**26**	49 25N	13 52 E
Blatnitsa	**43**	43 41N	28 32 E
Blato	**39**	42 56N	16 48 E
Blaubeuren	**25**	48 24N	9 47 E
Blaydon	**12**	54 56N	1 47W
Blaye	**20**	45 8N	0 40W
Blaye-les-Mines	**20**	44 1N	2 8 E
Blayney	**99**	33 32 S	149 14 E
Blaze, Pt.	**96**	12 56 S	130 11 E
Błazowa	**27**	49 53N	22 7 E
Bleckede	**24**	53 18N	10 43 E
Bled	**39**	46 27N	14 7 E
Blednaya, Gora	**58**	76 20N	65 0 E
Bleiburg	**26**	46 35N	14 49 E
Blejeşti	**46**	44 19N	25 27 E
Blekinge län □	**49**	56 20N	15 20 E
Blenheim, Can.	**112**	42 20N	82 0W
Blenheim, N.Z.	**101**	41 38 S	173 57 E
Bléone ⤳	**21**	44 5N	6 0 E
Bletchley	**13**	51 59N	0 44W
Bleymard, Le	**20**	44 30N	3 42 E
Blida	**82**	36 30N	2 49 E
Blidet Amor	**83**	32 59N	5 58 E
Blidö	**48**	59 37N	18 53 E
Blidsberg	**49**	57 56N	13 30 E
Bligh Sound	**101**	44 47 S	167 32 E
Blind River	**106**	46 10N	82 58W
Blinishti	**44**	41 52N	19 58 E
Blitar	**73**	8 5 S	112 11 E
Blitta	**85**	8 23N	1 6 E
Block I.	**114**	41 11N	71 35W
Block Island Sd.	**113**	41 17N	71 35W
Bloemfontein	**92**	29 6 S	26 14 E
Bloemhof	**92**	27 38 S	25 32 E
Blois	**18**	47 35N	1 20 E
Blomskog	**48**	59 16N	12 2 E
Blönduós	**50**	65 40N	20 12W
Błonie	**28**	52 12N	20 37 E
Bloodvein ⤳	**109**	51 47N	96 43W
Bloody Foreland	**15**	55 10N	8 18W
Bloomer	**116**	45 8N	91 30W
Bloomfield, Can.	**112**	43 59N	77 14W
Bloomfield, Iowa, U.S.A.	**116**	40 44N	92 26W
Bloomfield, N. Mexico, U.S.A.	**119**	36 46N	107 59W
Bloomfield, Nebr., U.S.A.	**116**	42 38N	97 40W
Bloomfield River Mission	**98**	15 56 S	145 22 E
Bloomington, Ill., U.S.A.	**116**	40 27N	89 0W
Bloomington, Ind., U.S.A.	**114**	39 10N	86 30W
Bloomsburg	**114**	41 0N	76 30W
Blora	**73**	6 57 S	111 25 E
Blossburg	**112**	41 40N	77 4W
Blouberg	**93**	23 8 S	29 0 E
Blountstown	**115**	30 28N	85 5W
Bludenz	**26**	47 10N	9 50 E
Blue Island	**114**	41 40N	87 40W
Blue Lake	**118**	40 53N	124 0W
Blue Mesa Res.	**119**	38 30N	107 15W
Blue Mts., Austral.	**97**	33 40 S	150 0 E
Blue Mts., Ore., U.S.A.	**118**	45 15N	119 0W
Blue Mts., Pa., U.S.A.	**114**	40 30N	76 30W
Blue Mud B.	**97**	13 30 S	136 0 E
Blue Nile = An Nîl el Azraq □	**87**	12 30N	34 30 E
Blue Nile = Nîl el Azraq ⤳	**87**	15 38N	32 31 E
Blue Rapids	**116**	39 41N	96 39W
Blue Ridge Mts.	**115**	36 30N	80 15W
Blue Stack Mts.	**15**	54 46N	8 5W
Blueberry ⤳	**108**	56 45N	120 49W
Bluefield	**114**	37 18N	81 14W
Bluefields	**121**	12 20N	83 50W
Bluff, Austral.	**98**	23 35 S	149 4 E
Bluff, N.Z.	**101**	46 37 S	168 20 E
Bluff, U.S.A.	**119**	37 17N	109 33W
Bluffton	**114**	40 43N	85 9W
Blumenau	**125**	27 0 S	49 0W
Blumenthal	**24**	53 5N	8 20 E
Blunt	**116**	44 32N	100 0W
Bly	**118**	42 23N	121 0W
Blyberg	**48**	61 9N	14 11 E
Blyth, Can.	**112**	43 44N	81 26W
Blyth, U.K.	**12**	55 8N	1 32W
Blythe	**119**	33 40N	114 33W
Blytheswood	**112**	42 8N	82 37W
Bø	**47**	59 25N	9 3 E
Bo	**84**	7 55N	11 50W
Bo Duc	**71**	11 58N	106 50 E
Bo Hai	**76**	39 0N	120 0 E
Bo Xian	**77**	33 50N	115 45 E
Boa Vista	**126**	2 48N	60 30W
Boaco	**121**	12 29N	85 35W
Boal	**30**	43 25N	6 49W
Boatman	**99**	27 16 S	146 55 E
Bobai	**77**	22 17N	109 59 E
Bobbili	**70**	18 35N	83 30 E
Bóbbio	**38**	44 47N	9 22 E
Bobcaygeon	**106**	44 33N	78 33W
Böblingen	**25**	48 41N	9 1 E
Bobo-Dioulasso	**84**	11 8N	4 13W
Boboc	**43**	45 13N	26 59 E
Bobolice	**28**	53 58N	16 37 E
Boboshevo	**42**	42 9N	23 0 E
Bobov Dol	**42**	42 20N	23 0 E
Bóbr ⤳	**28**	52 4N	15 4 E
Bobraomby, Tanjon' i	**93**	12 40 S	49 10 E
Bobrinets	**56**	48 4N	32 5 E
Bobrov	**55**	51 5N	40 2 E
Bobruysk	**54**	53 10N	29 15 E
Bôca do Acre	**126**	8 50 S	67 27W
Boca, La	**120**	8 56N	79 30W
Boca Raton	**115**	26 21N	80 5W
Bocaiúva	**127**	17 7 S	43 49W
Bocanda	**84**	7 5N	4 31W
Bocaranga	**88**	7 0N	15 35 E
Bocas del Toro	**121**	9 15N	82 20W
Boceguillas	**32**	41 20N	3 39W
Bochnia	**27**	49 58N	20 27 E
Bocholt	**24**	51 50N	6 35 E
Bochov	**26**	50 9N	13 3 E
Bochum	**24**	51 28N	7 12 E
Bockenem	**24**	52 1N	10 8 E
Boćki	**28**	52 39N	23 3 E
Bocşa Montană	**42**	45 21N	21 47 E
Boda	**88**	4 19N	17 26 E
Böda	**49**	57 15N	17 3 E
Bodafors	**49**	57 48N	14 23 E
Bodaybo	**59**	57 50N	114 0 E
Boden	**50**	65 50N	21 42 E
Bodensee	**25**	47 35N	9 25 E
Bodenteich	**24**	52 49N	10 41 E
Bodhan	**70**	18 40N	77 44 E
Bodinayakkanur	**70**	10 2N	77 10 E
Bodinga	**85**	12 58N	5 10 E
Bodmin	**13**	50 28N	4 44W
Bodmin Moor	**13**	50 33N	4 36W
Bodrog ⤳	**27**	48 15N	21 35 E
Bodrum	**64**	37 5N	27 30 E
Bódva ⤳	**27**	48 19N	20 45 E
Boegoebergdam	**92**	29 7 S	22 9 E
Boën	**21**	45 44N	4 0 E
Boende	**88**	0 24 S	21 12 E
Boerne	**117**	29 48N	98 41W
Boffa	**84**	10 16N	14 3W
Bogalusa	**117**	30 50N	89 55W

Bogan Brabant L.

Bogan → **97** 29 59S 146 17 E
Bogan Gate **99** 33 7S 147 49 E
Bogantungan **98** 23 41S 147 17 E
Bogata **117** 33 26N 95 10W
Bogatić **42** 44 51N 19 30 E
Bogenfels **92** 27 25S 15 25 E
Bogense **49** 55 34N 10 5 E
Boggabilla **99** 28 36S 150 24 E
Boggabri **99** 30 45S 150 0 E
Boggeragh Mts. **15** 52 2N 8 55W
Bognor Regis **13** 50 47N 0 40W
Bogø **49** 54 55N 12 2 E
Bogo **73** 11 3N 124 0 E
Bogodukhov **54** 50 9N 35 33 E
Bogong, Mt. **97** 36 47S 147 17 E
Bogor **73** 6 36S 106 48 E
Bogoroditsk **55** 53 47N 38 8 E
Bogorodsk **55** 56 4N 43 30 E
Bogorodskoye **59** 52 22N 140 30 E
Bogoso **84** 5 38N 2 3W
Bogota **126** 4 34N 74 0W
Bogotol **58** 56 15N 89 50 E
Bogra **69** 24 51N 89 22 E
Boguchany **59** 58 40N 97 30 E
Boguchar **57** 49 55N 40 32 E
Bogué **84** 16 45N 14 10W
Boguslav **56** 49 47N 30 53 E
Boguszów **28** 50 45N 16 12 E
Bohain **19** 49 59N 3 28 E
Bohemia **26** 50 0N 14 0 E
Bohemian Forest = Böhmerwald **25** 49 30N 12 40 E
Bohena Cr. → **99** 30 17S 149 42 E
Bohinjska Bistrica **39** 46 17N 14 1 E
Böhmerwald **25** 49 30N 12 40 E
Bohmte **24** 52 24N 8 20 E
Bohol **73** 9 50N 124 10 E
Bohotleh **63** 8 20N 46 25 E
Boi **85** 9 35N 9 27 E
Boi, Pta. de **125** 23 55S 45 15W
Boiano **41** 41 28N 14 29 E
Boileau, C. **96** 17 40S 122 7 E
Boinitsa **42** 43 58N 22 32 E
Boise **118** 43 43N 116 9W
Boise City **117** 36 45N 102 30W
Boissevain **109** 49 15N 100 5W
Boite → **39** 46 5N 12 5 E
Boitzenburg **24** 53 16N 13 36 E
Boizenburg **24** 53 22N 10 42 E
Bojador C. **80** 26 0N 14 30W
Bojana → **42** 41 52N 19 22 E
Bojanowo **28** 51 43N 16 42 E
Bojnūrd **65** 37 30N 57 20 E
Bojonegoro **73** 7 11S 111 54 E
Boju **85** 7 22N 7 55 E
Boka **42** 45 22N 20 52 E
Boka Kotorska **42** 42 23N 18 32 E
Bokala **84** 8 31N 4 33W
Boké **84** 10 56N 14 17W
Bokhara → **99** 29 55S 146 42 E
Bokkos **85** 9 17N 9 1 E
Boknafjorden **47** 59 14N 5 40 E
Bokoro **81** 12 25N 17 14 E
Bokote **88** 0 12S 21 8 E
Bokpyin **71** 11 18N 98 42 E
Boksitogorsk **54** 59 32N 33 56 E
Bokungu **88** 0 35S 22 50 E
Bol, Chad **81** 13 30N 15 0 E
Bol, Yugo. **39** 43 18N 16 38 E
Bolama **84** 11 30N 15 30W
Bolan Pass **66** 29 50N 67 20 E
Bolaños → **120** 21 14N 104 8W
Bolbec **18** 49 30N 0 30 E
Boldeşti **46** 45 3N 26 2 E
Bole, China **75** 45 11N 81 37 E
Bole, Ethiopia **87** 6 36N 37 20 E
Bolekhov **54** 49 0N 24 0 E
Bolesławiec **28** 51 17N 15 37 E
Bolgatanga **85** 10 44N 0 53W
Bolgrad **56** 45 40N 28 32 E
Boli, China **76** 45 46N 130 31 E
Boli, Sudan **87** 6 2N 28 48 E
Bolinao C. **73** 16 23N 119 55 E
Bolívar, Argent. **124** 36 15S 60 53W
Bolívar, Colomb. **126** 2 0N 77 0W
Bolivar, Mo., U.S.A. **117** 37 38N 93 22W
Bolivar, Tenn., U.S.A. **117** 35 14N 89 0W
Bolivia ■ **126** 17 6S 64 0W
Boljevac **42** 43 51N 21 58 E
Bolkhov **55** 53 25N 36 0 E
Bollène **21** 44 18N 4 45 E
Bollnäs **48** 61 21N 16 24 E
Bollon **99** 28 2S 147 29 E
Bollstabruk **48** 63 1N 17 40 E
Bollullos **31** 37 19N 6 32W
Bolmen **49** 56 55N 13 40 E
Bolobo **88** 2 6S 16 20 E
Bologna **39** 44 30N 11 20 E
Bologne **19** 48 10N 5 8 E
Bologoye **54** 57 55N 34 0 E
Bolomba **88** 0 35N 19 0 E
Bolong **73** 7 6N 122 16 E
Boloven, Cao Nguyen **71** 15 10N 106 30 E
Bolpur **69** 23 40N 87 45 E
Bolsena **39** 42 40N 11 58 E
Bolsena, L. di **39** 42 35N 11 55 E
Bolshaya Glushitsa **55** 52 24N 50 29 E
Bolshaya Martynovka **57** 47 12N 41 46 E
Bolshaya Vradiyevka **56** 47 50N 30 40 E
Bolshereche **58** 56 4N 74 45 E
Bolshevik, Ostrov **59** 78 30N 102 0 E
Bolshezemelskaya Tundra **52** 67 0N 56 0 E
Bolshoi Kavkas **57** 42 50N 44 0 E
Bolshoy Anyuy → **59** 68 30N 160 49 E
Bolshoy Atlym **58** 62 25N 66 50 E
Bolshoy Begichev, Ostrov **59** 74 20N 112 30 E
Bolshoy Lyakhovskiy, Ostrov **59** 73 35N 142 0 E
Bolshoy Tokmak **56** 47 16N 35 42 E
Bol'shoy Tyuters, Ostrov **54** 59 51N 27 13 E
Bolsward **16** 53 3N 5 32 E
Boltaña **32** 42 28N 0 4 E
Boltigen **25** 46 38N 7 24 E
Bolton, Can. **112** 43 54N 79 45W
Bolton, U.K. **12** 53 35N 2 26W
Bolu **64** 40 45N 31 35 E
Bolvadin **64** 38 45N 31 4 E
Bolzano (Bozen) **39** 46 30N 11 20 E
Bom Despacho **127** 19 43S 45 15W
Bom Jesus da Lapa **127** 13 15S 43 25W
Boma **88** 5 50S 13 4 E
Bomaderry **99** 34 52S 150 37 E
Bombala **97** 36 56S 149 15 E
Bombarral **31** 39 15N 9 9W
Bombay **70** 18 55N 72 50 E
Bomboma **88** 2 25N 18 55 E
Bombombwa **90** 1 40N 25 40 E
Bomi Hills **84** 7 1N 10 38W
Bomili **90** 1 45N 27 5 E
Bomokandi → **90** 3 39N 26 8 E
Bomongo **88** 1 27N 18 21 E
Bomu → **88** 4 40N 23 30 E
Bon C. **83** 37 1N 11 2 E
Bonaire **121** 12 10N 68 15W
Bonang **99** 37 11S 148 41 E
Bonanza **121** 13 54N 84 35W
Bonaparte Archipelago **96** 14 0S 124 30 E
Boñar **30** 42 52N 5 19W
Bonaventure **107** 48 5N 65 32W
Bonavista **107** 48 40N 53 5W
Bonavista, C. **107** 48 42N 53 5W
Bondeno **39** 44 53N 11 22 E
Bondo **88** 3 55N 23 53 E
Bondoukou **84** 8 2N 2 47W
Bondowoso **73** 7 56S 113 49 E
Bone Rate **73** 7 25S 121 5 E
Bone Rate, Kepulauan **73** 6 30S 121 10 E
Bone, Teluk **73** 4 10S 120 50 E
Bonefro **41** 41 42N 14 55 E
Bo'ness **14** 56 0N 3 38W
Bong Son = Hoai Nhon **71** 14 28N 109 1 E
Bongandanga **88** 1 24N 21 3 E
Bongor **81** 10 35N 15 20 E
Bongouanou **84** 6 42N 4 15W
Bonham **117** 33 30N 96 10W
Bonifacio **21** 41 24N 9 10 E
Bonifacio, Bouches de **40** 41 12N 9 15 E
Bonin Is. **94** 27 0N 142 0 E
Bonke **87** 6 5N 37 16 E
Bonn **24** 50 43N 7 6 E
Bonnat **20** 46 20N 1 54 E
Bonne Terre **117** 37 57N 90 33W
Bonners Ferry **118** 48 38N 116 21W
Bonnétable **18** 48 11N 0 25 E
Bonneuil-Matours **18** 46 41N 0 34 E
Bonneval **18** 48 11N 1 24 E
Bonneville **21** 46 5N 6 24 E
Bonney, L. **99** 37 50S 140 20 E
Bonnie Rock **96** 30 29S 118 22 E
Bonny, France **19** 47 34N 2 50 E
Bonny, Nigeria **85** 4 25N 7 13 E
Bonny → **85** 4 20N 7 10 E
Bonny, Bight of **88** 3 30N 9 20 E
Bonnyville **109** 54 20N 110 45W
Bonoi **73** 1 45S 137 41 E
Bonorva **40** 40 25N 8 47 E
Bontang **72** 0 10N 117 30 E
Bonthain **73** 5 34S 119 56 E
Bonthe **84** 7 30N 12 33W
Bontoc **73** 17 7N 120 58 E
Bonyeri **84** 5 1N 2 46W
Bonyhád **27** 46 18N 18 32 E
Booker **117** 36 29N 100 30W
Boolaboolka, L. **99** 32 38S 143 10 E
Booligal **99** 33 58S 144 53 E
Boom **16** 51 6N 4 20 E
Boonah **99** 27 58S 152 41 E
Boone, Iowa, U.S.A. **116** 42 5N 93 53W
Boone, N.C., U.S.A. **115** 36 14N 81 43W
Booneville, Ark., U.S.A. **117** 35 10N 93 54W
Booneville, Miss., U.S.A. **115** 34 39N 88 34W
Boonville, Ind., U.S.A. **114** 38 3N 87 13W
Boonville, Mo., U.S.A. **116** 38 57N 92 45W
Boonville, N.Y., U.S.A. **114** 43 31N 75 20W
Boorindal **99** 30 22S 146 11 E
Boorowa **99** 34 28S 148 44 E
Boothia, Gulf of **105** 71 0N 90 0W
Boothia Pen. **104** 71 0N 94 0W
Bootle, Cumb., U.K. **12** 54 17N 3 24W
Bootle, Merseyside, U.K. **12** 53 28N 3 1W
Booué **88** 0 5S 11 55 E
Bopeechee **99** 29 36S 137 22 E
Bophuthatswana □ **92** 26 0S 26 0 E
Boppard **25** 50 13N 7 36 E
Boquete **121** 8 49N 82 27W
Bor **26** 49 41N 12 45 E
Bôr **87** 6 10N 31 40 E
Bor, Sweden **49** 57 9N 14 10 E
Bor, Yugo. **42** 44 8N 22 7 E
Borah, Mt. **118** 44 19N 113 46W
Borama **63** 9 55N 43 7 E
Borang **87** 4 50N 30 59 E
Borås **49** 57 43N 12 56 E
Borāzjān **65** 29 22N 51 10 E
Borba, Brazil **126** 4 12S 59 34W
Borba, Port. **31** 38 50N 7 26W
Borçka **57** 41 25N 41 41 E
Bordeaux **20** 44 50N 0 36W
Borden **107** 46 18N 63 47W
Borden I. **4** 78 30N 111 30W
Borders □ **14** 55 35N 2 50W
Bordertown **97** 36 19S 140 45 E
Borðeyri **50** 65 12N 21 6W
Bordighera **38** 43 47N 7 40 E
Bordj bou Arreridj **83** 36 4N 4 45 E
Bordj Bourguiba **83** 32 12N 10 2 E
Bordj el Hobra **83** 32 9N 4 51 E
Bordj Fly Ste. Marie **82** 27 19N 2 32W
Bordj-in-Eker **83** 24 9N 5 3 E
Bordj Menaiel **83** 36 46N 3 43 E
Bordj Messouda **83** 30 12N 9 25 E
Bordj Nili **82** 33 28N 3 2 E
Bordj Omar Driss **83** 28 10N 6 40 E
Bordj Zelfana **83** 32 27N 4 15 E
Borek Wielkopolski **28** 51 54N 17 11 E
Borensberg **49** 58 34N 15 17 E
Borgarnes **50** 64 32N 21 55W
Børgefjellet **50** 65 20N 13 45 E
Borger, Neth. **16** 52 54N 6 44 E
Borger, U.S.A. **117** 35 40N 101 20W
Borghamn **49** 58 23N 14 41 E
Borgholm **49** 56 52N 16 39 E
Bòrgia **41** 38 50N 16 30 E
Borgo San Dalmazzo **38** 44 19N 7 29 E
Borgo San Lorenzo **39** 43 57N 11 21 E
Borgo Valsugano **39** 46 3N 11 27 E
Borgomanero **38** 45 41N 8 28 E
Borgonovo Val Tidone **38** 45 1N 9 28 E
Borgorose **39** 42 12N 13 14 E
Borgosésia **38** 45 43N 8 17 E
Borgvattnet **48** 63 26N 15 48 E
Borislav **54** 49 18N 23 28 E
Borisoglebsk **55** 51 27N 42 5 E
Borisoglebskiy **55** 56 28N 43 59 E
Borisov **54** 54 17N 28 28 E
Borispol **54** 50 21N 30 59 E
Borja, Peru **126** 4 20S 77 40W
Borja, Spain **32** 41 48N 1 34W
Borjas Blancas **32** 41 31N 0 52 E
Borken **24** 51 51N 6 52 E
Borkou **81** 18 15N 18 50 E
Borkum **24** 53 36N 6 42 E
Borlänge **48** 60 29N 15 26 E
Borley, C. **5** 66 15S 52 30 E
Bormida → **38** 44 23N 8 13 E
Bórmio **38** 46 28N 10 22 E
Borna **24** 51 8N 12 31 E
Borneo **72** 1 0N 115 0 E
Bornholm **49** 55 10N 15 0 E
Bornholmsgattet **49** 55 15N 14 20 E
Borno □ **85** 12 30N 12 30 E
Bornos **31** 36 48N 5 42W
Bornu Yassa **85** 12 14N 12 25 E
Borobudur **73** 7 36S 110 13 E
Borodino **54** 55 31N 35 40 E
Borogontsy **59** 62 42N 131 8 E
Boromo **84** 11 45N 2 58W
Borongan **73** 11 37N 125 26 E
Bororen **98** 24 13S 151 33 E
Borotangba Mts. **87** 6 30N 25 0 E
Borovan **43** 43 27N 23 45 E
Borovichi **54** 58 25N 33 55 E
Borovsk **55** 55 12N 36 24 E
Borrby **49** 55 27N 14 10 E
Borriol **32** 40 4N 0 4W
Borroloola **97** 16 4S 136 17 E
Borşa **46** 47 41N 24 50 E
Borsod-Abaúj-Zemplén □ **27** 48 20N 21 0 E
Bort-les-Orgues **20** 45 24N 2 29 E
Borth **13** 52 29N 4 3W
Borujerd **64** 33 55N 48 50 E
Borzhomi **57** 41 48N 43 28 E
Borzna **54** 51 18N 32 26 E
Borzya **59** 50 24N 116 31 E
Bosa **40** 40 17N 8 32 E
Bosanska Brod **42** 45 10N 18 0 E
Bosanska Dubica **39** 45 10N 16 50 E
Bosanska Gradiška **42** 45 10N 17 15 E
Bosanska Kostajnica **39** 45 11N 16 33 E
Bosanska Krupa **39** 44 53N 16 10 E
Bosanski Novi **39** 45 2N 16 22 E
Bosanski Samac **42** 45 3N 18 29 E
Bosansko Grahovo **39** 44 12N 16 26 E
Bosansko Petrovac **39** 44 35N 16 21 E
Bosaso **63** 11 12N 49 18 E
Boscastle **13** 50 42N 4 42W
Boscotrecase **41** 40 46N 14 28 E
Bose **77** 23 53N 106 35 E
Boshan **76** 36 28N 117 49 E
Boshoek **92** 25 30S 27 9 E
Boshof **92** 28 31S 25 13 E
Boshrüyeh **65** 33 50N 57 30 E
Bosilegrad **42** 42 30N 22 27 E
Boskovice **27** 49 29N 16 40 E
Bosna → **42** 45 4N 18 29 E
Bosna i Hercegovina □ **42** 44 0N 18 0 E
Bosnia = Bosna □ **42** 44 0N 18 0 E
Bosnik **73** 1 5S 136 10 E
Bōsō-Hantō **74** 35 20N 140 20 E
Bosobolo **88** 4 15N 19 50 E
Bosporus = Karadeniz Boğazı **64** 41 10N 29 10 E
Bossangoa **88** 6 35N 17 30 E
Bossekop **50** 69 57N 23 15 E
Bossembélé **81** 5 25N 17 40 E
Bossier City **117** 32 28N 93 48W
Bosso **85** 13 43N 13 19 E
Bossut C. **96** 18 42S 121 35 E
Bosten Hu **75** 41 55N 87 40 E
Boston, U.K. **12** 52 59N 0 2W
Boston, U.S.A. **114** 42 20N 71 0W
Boston Bar **108** 49 52N 121 30W
Bosut → **42** 45 20N 19 0 E
Boswell, Can. **108** 49 28N 116 45W
Boswell, Okla., U.S.A. **117** 34 1N 95 50W
Boswell, Pa., U.S.A. **112** 40 9N 79 2W
Botad **68** 22 15N 71 40 E
Botevgrad **43** 42 55N 23 47 E
Bothaville **92** 27 23S 26 34 E
Bothnia, G. of **50** 63 0N 20 0 E
Bothwell, Austral. **99** 42 20S 147 1 E
Bothwell, Can. **112** 42 38N 81 52W
Boticas **30** 41 41N 7 40W
Botletle → **92** 20 10S 23 15 E
Botoroaga **46** 44 8N 25 32 E
Botoşani **46** 47 42N 26 41 E
Botoşani □ **46** 47 50N 26 50 E
Botro **84** 7 51N 5 19W
Botswana ■ **92** 22 0S 24 0 E
Bottineau **116** 48 49N 100 25W
Bottrop **24** 51 34N 6 59 E
Botucatu **125** 22 55S 48 30W
Botwood **107** 49 6N 55 23W
Bou Alam **82** 33 50N 1 26 E
Bou Ali **82** 27 11N 0 4W
Bou Djébéha **84** 18 25N 2 45W
Bou Guema **82** 28 49N 0 19 E
Bou Ismael **82** 36 38N 2 42 E
Bou Izakarn **82** 29 12N 9 46W
Bou Saâda **83** 35 11N 4 9 E
Bou Salem **83** 36 45N 9 2 E
Bouaké **84** 7 40N 5 2W
Bouar **88** 6 0N 15 40 E
Bouârfa **82** 32 32N 1 58 E
Bouca **88** 6 45N 18 25 E
Boucau **20** 43 32N 1 29W
Bouches-du-Rhône □ **21** 43 37N 5 2 E
Bouda **82** 27 50N 0 27W
Boudenib **82** 31 59N 3 31W
Boufarik **82** 36 34N 2 58 E
Bougainville C. **96** 13 57S 126 4 E
Bougaroun, C. **83** 37 6N 6 30 E
Bougie = Bejaia **83** 36 42N 5 2 E
Bougouni **84** 11 30N 7 20W
Bouillon **16** 49 44N 5 3 E
Bouïra **83** 36 20N 3 59 E
Boulder, Austral. **96** 30 46S 121 30 E
Boulder, Colo., U.S.A. **116** 40 3N 105 10W
Boulder, Mont., U.S.A. **118** 46 14N 112 4W
Boulder City **119** 36 0N 114 50W
Boulder Dam = Hoover Dam **119** 36 0N 114 45W
Bouli **84** 15 17N 12 18W
Boulia **97** 22 52S 139 51 E
Bouligny **19** 49 17N 5 45 E
Boulogne → **18** 47 12N 1 47W
Boulogne-sur-Gesse **20** 43 18N 0 38 E
Boulogne-sur-Mer **19** 50 42N 1 36 E
Bouloire **18** 47 58N 0 33 E
Boulsa **85** 12 39N 0 34W
Boultoum **85** 14 45N 10 25 E
Boumalne **82** 31 25N 6 0W
Bouna **84** 9 10N 3 0W
Boundiali **84** 9 30N 6 20W
Bountiful **118** 40 57N 111 58W
Bounty I. **94** 48 0S 178 30 E
Bourbon-Lancy **20** 46 37N 3 45 E
Bourbon-l'Archambault **20** 46 36N 3 4 E
Bourbonnais **20** 46 28N 3 0 E
Bourbonne-les-Bains **19** 47 59N 5 45 E
Bourem **85** 17 0N 0 24W
Bourg **20** 45 3N 0 34W
Bourg-Argental **21** 45 18N 4 32 E
Bourg-de-Péage **21** 45 2N 5 3 E
Bourg-en-Bresse **21** 46 13N 5 12 E
Bourg-St.-Andéol **21** 44 23N 4 39 E
Bourg-St.-Maurice **21** 45 35N 6 46 E
Bourganeuf **20** 45 57N 1 45 E
Bourges **19** 47 9N 2 25 E
Bourget **113** 45 26N 75 9W
Bourget, L. du **21** 45 44N 5 52 E
Bourgneuf, B. de **18** 47 3N 2 10W
Bourgneuf-en-Retz **18** 47 2N 1 58W
Bourgneuf-la-Fôret, Le **18** 48 10N 0 59W
Bourgogne **19** 47 0N 4 30 E
Bourgoin-Jallieu **21** 45 36N 5 17 E
Bourgueil **18** 47 17N 0 10 E
Bourke **97** 30 8S 145 55 E
Bournemouth **13** 50 43N 1 53W
Bourriot-Bergonce **20** 44 7N 0 14W
Bouscat, Le **20** 44 53N 0 32W
Boussac **20** 46 22N 2 13 E
Boussens **20** 43 12N 0 58 E
Busso **81** 10 34N 16 52 E
Boutilimit **84** 17 45N 14 40W
Boutonne → **20** 45 55N 0 43 E
Bouvet I. = Bouvetøya **7** 54 26S 3 24 E
Bouvetøya **7** 54 26S 3 24 E
Bouznika **82** 33 46N 7 6W
Bouzonville **19** 49 17N 6 32 E
Bova Marina **41** 37 59N 15 56 E
Bovalino Marina **41** 38 9N 16 10 E
Bovec **39** 46 20N 13 33 E
Bovigny **16** 50 12N 5 55 E
Bovill **118** 46 58N 116 27W
Bovino **41** 41 15N 15 20 E
Bow Island **108** 49 50N 111 23W
Bowbells **116** 48 47N 102 19W
Bowdle **116** 45 30N 99 40W
Bowen **97** 20 0S 148 16 E
Bowen → **98** 20 24S 147 20 E
Bowen Mts. **99** 37 0S 148 0 E
Bowie, Ariz., U.S.A. **119** 32 15N 109 30W
Bowie, Tex., U.S.A. **117** 33 33N 97 50W
Bowland, Forest of **12** 54 0N 2 30W
Bowling Green, Ky., U.S.A. **114** 37 0N 86 25W
Bowling Green, Ohio, U.S.A. **114** 41 22N 83 40W
Bowling Green, C. **97** 19 19S 147 25 E
Bowman **116** 46 12N 103 21W
Bowman I. **5** 65 0S 104 0 E
Bowmans **99** 34 10S 138 17 E
Bowmanville **106** 43 55N 78 41W
Bowmore **14** 55 45N 6 18W
Bowral **97** 34 26S 150 27 E
Bowraville **99** 30 37S 152 52 E
Bowron → **108** 54 3N 121 50W
Bowser L. **108** 56 30N 129 30W
Bowsman **109** 52 14N 101 12W
Bowwood **91** 17 5S 26 20 E
Boxelder Cr. → **118** 47 20N 108 30W
Boxholm **49** 58 12N 15 3 E
Boxtel **16** 51 36N 5 20 E
Boyabat **56** 41 28N 34 42 E
Boyce **117** 31 25N 92 39W
Boyer → **108** 58 27N 115 57W
Boyle **15** 53 58N 8 19W
Boyne → **15** 53 43N 6 15W
Boyne City **114** 45 13N 85 1W
Boyni Qara **65** 36 20N 67 0 E
Boynton Beach **115** 26 31N 80 3W
Bozburun **45** 36 43N 28 8 E
Bozcaada **44** 39 49N 26 3 E
Bozeman **118** 45 40N 111 0W
Bozen = Bolzano **39** 46 30N 11 20 E
Božepole Wielkopolski **28** 54 33N 17 56 E
Boževac **42** 44 32N 21 24 E
Bozouls **20** 44 28N 2 43 E
Bozoum **88** 6 25N 16 35 E
Bozovici **46** 44 56N 22 1 E
Bra **38** 44 41N 7 50 E
Brabant □ **16** 50 46N 4 30 E
Brabant L. **109** 55 58N 103 43W

Brabrand Bucharest

Brabrand 49 56 9N 10 7 E
Brač 39 43 20N 16 40 E
Bracadale, L. 14 57 20N 6 30W
Bracciano 39 42 6N 12 10 E
Bracciano, L. di 39 42 8N 12 11 E
Bracebridge 106 45 2N 79 19W
Brach 83 27 31N 14 20 E
Bracieux 19 47 30N 1 30 E
Bräcke 48 62 45N 15 26 E
Brackettville 117 29 21N 100 20W
Brački Kanal 39 43 24N 16 40 E
Brad 46 46 10N 22 50 E
Brádano → 41 40 23N 16 51 E
Braddock 112 40 24N 79 51W
Bradenton 115 27 25N 82 35W
Bradford, Can. 112 44 7N 79 34W
Bradford, U.K. 12 53 47N 1 45W
Bradford, Pa., U.S.A. 114 41 58N 78 41W
Bradford, Vt., U.S.A. 113 43 59N 72 9W
Brădiceni 46 45 3N 23 4 E
Bradley, Ark., U.S.A. 117 33 7N 93 39W
Bradley, S.D., U.S.A. 116 45 10N 97 40W
Bradley Institute 91 17 7S 31 25 E
Bradore Bay 107 51 27N 57 18W
Bradshaw 97 15 21S 130 16 E
Brady 117 31 8N 99 25W
Brædstrup 49 55 58N 9 37 E
Braeside 113 45 28N 76 24W
Braga 30 41 35N 8 25W
Braga □ 30 41 30N 8 30W
Bragado 124 35 2S 60 27W
Bragança, Brazil 127 1 0S 47 2W
Bragança, Port. 30 41 48N 6 50W
Bragança □ 30 41 30N 6 45W
Bragança Paulista 125 22 55S 46 32W
Brahmanbaria 69 23 58N 91 15 E
Brahmani → 69 20 39N 86 46 E
Brahmaputra → 67 24 2N 90 59 E
Braich-y-pwll 12 52 47N 4 46W
Braidwood 99 35 27S 149 49 E
Brăila 46 45 19N 27 59 E
Brăila □ 46 45 5N 27 30 E
Brainerd 116 46 20N 94 10W
Braintree, U.K. 13 51 53N 0 34 E
Braintree, U.S.A. 113 42 11N 71 0W
Brak → 92 29 35S 22 55 E
Brake, Niedersachsen, Ger. 24 53 19N 8 30 E
Brake, Nordrhein, Ger. 24 51 43N 9 12 E
Bräkne-Hoby 49 56 14N 15 6 E
Brakwater 92 22 28S 17 3 E
Brålanda 49 58 34N 12 21 E
Bralorne 108 50 50N 123 45W
Bramberg 25 50 6N 10 40 E
Bramminge 49 55 28N 8 42 E
Brämön 48 62 14N 17 40 E
Brampton 106 43 45N 79 45W
Bramsche 24 52 25N 7 58 E
Bramwell 98 12 8S 142 37 E
Branco → 126 1 20S 61 50W
Brande 49 55 57N 9 8 E
Brandenburg 24 52 24N 12 33 E
Brandfort 92 28 40S 26 30 E
Brandon, Can. 109 49 50N 99 57W
Brandon, U.S.A. 113 43 48N 73 4W
Brandon B. 15 52 17N 10 8W
Brandon, Mt. 15 52 15N 10 15W
Brandsen 124 35 10S 58 15W
Brandval 47 60 19N 12 1 E
Brandvlei 92 30 25S 20 30 E
Brandýs 26 50 10N 14 40 E
Branford 113 41 15N 72 48W
Braniewo 28 54 25N 19 50 E
Bransfield Str. 5 63 0S 59 0W
Brańsk 28 52 44N 22 51 E
Branson, Colo., U.S.A. 117 37 4N 103 53W
Branson, Mo., U.S.A. 117 36 40N 93 18W
Brantford 106 43 10N 80 15W
Brantôme 20 45 22N 0 39 E
Branxholme 99 37 52S 141 49 E
Branzi 38 46 0N 9 46 E
Bras d'or, L. 107 45 50N 60 50W
Brasiléia 126 11 0S 68 45W
Brasília 127 15 47S 47 55 E
Braslav 54 55 38N 27 0 E
Braslovce 39 46 21N 15 3 E
Braşov 46 45 38N 25 35 E
Braşov □ 46 45 45N 25 15 E
Brass 85 4 35N 6 14 E
Brass → 85 4 15N 6 13 E
Brassac-les-Mines 20 45 24N 3 20 E
Brasschaat 16 51 19N 4 27 E
Brassey, Banjaran 72 5 0N 117 15 E
Brasstown Bald, Mt. 115 34 54N 83 45W
Bratislava 27 48 10N 17 7 E
Bratsigovo 43 42 1N 24 22 E
Bratsk 59 56 10N 101 30 E
Brattleboro 114 42 53N 72 37W
Braţul Chilia → 46 45 25N 29 20 E
Bratul Sfîntu Gheorghe → 46 45 0N 29 20 E
Braţul Sulina → 46 45 10N 29 20 E
Bratunac 42 44 13N 19 21 E
Braunau 26 48 15N 13 3 E
Braunschweig 24 52 17N 10 28 E
Braunton 13 51 6N 4 9W
Brava 63 1 20N 44 8 E
Bråviken 48 58 38N 16 32 E
Bravo del Norte → 120 25 57N 97 9W
Brawley 119 32 58N 115 30W
Bray 15 53 12N 6 6W
Bray, Pays de 19 49 46N 1 26 E
Bray-sur-Seine 19 48 25N 3 14 E
Brazeau → 108 52 55N 115 14W
Brazil 114 39 32N 87 8W
Brazil ■ 127 10 0S 50 0W
Brazilian Highlands = Brasil, Planalto 122 18 0S 46 30W
Brazo Sur → 124 25 21S 57 42W
Brazos → 117 28 53N 95 23W
Brazzaville 88 4 9S 15 12 E
Brčko 42 44 54N 18 46 E
Brda → 28 53 8N 18 8 E
Breadalbane, Austral. 98 23 50S 139 35 E
Breadalbane, U.K. 14 56 30N 4 15W
Breaksea Sd. 101 45 35S 166 35 E
Bream Bay 101 35 56S 174 28 E
Bream Head 101 35 51S 174 36 E
Breas 124 25 29S 70 24W
Brebes 73 6 52S 109 3 E
Brechin, Can. 112 44 32N 79 10W
Brechin, U.K. 14 56 44N 2 40W
Breckenridge, Colo., U.S.A. 118 39 30N 106 2W
Breckenridge, Minn., U.S.A. 116 46 20N 96 36W
Breckenridge, Tex., U.S.A. 117 32 48N 98 55W
Břeclav 27 48 46N 16 53 E
Brecon 13 51 57N 3 23W
Brecon Beacons 13 51 53N 3 27W
Breda 16 51 35N 4 45 E
Bredaryd 49 57 10N 13 45 E
Bredasdorp 92 34 33S 20 2 E
Bredbo 99 35 58S 149 10 E
Bredstedt 24 54 37N 8 59 E
Bregalnica → 42 41 43N 22 9 E
Bregenz 26 47 30N 9 45 E
Bregovo 42 44 9N 22 39 E
Bréhal 18 48 53N 1 30W
Bréhat, I. de 18 48 51N 3 0W
Breiðafjörður 50 65 15N 23 15W
Breil 21 43 56N 7 31 E
Breisach 25 48 2N 7 37 E
Brejo 127 3 41S 42 47W
Brekke 47 61 1N 5 26 E
Breloux-la-Crèche 20 46 23N 0 19W
Bremangerlandet 47 61 51N 5 0 E
Bremen 24 53 4N 8 47 E
Bremen □ 24 53 6N 8 46 E
Bremerhaven 24 53 34N 8 35 E
Bremerton 118 47 30N 122 38W
Bremervörde 24 53 28N 9 10 E
Bremnes 47 59 47N 5 8 E
Bremsnes 47 63 6N 7 40 E
Brenes 31 37 32N 5 54W
Brenham 117 30 5N 96 27W
Brenner Pass 26 47 0N 11 30 E
Breno 38 45 57N 10 20 E
Brent, Can. 106 46 2N 78 29W
Brent, U.K. 13 51 33N 0 18W
Brenta → 39 45 11N 12 18 E
Brentwood 13 51 37N 0 19 E
Bréscia 38 45 33N 10 13 E
Breskens 16 51 23N 3 33 E
Breslau = Wrocław 28 51 5N 17 5 E
Bresle → 18 50 4N 1 22 E
Bresles 19 49 25N 2 13 E
Bressanone 39 46 43N 11 40 E
Bressay I. 14 60 10N 1 5W
Bresse, La 19 48 0N 6 53 E
Bresse, Plaine de 19 46 50N 5 10 E
Bressuire 18 46 51N 0 30W
Brest, France 18 48 24N 4 31W
Brest, U.S.S.R. 54 52 10N 23 40 E
Bretagne 18 48 0N 3 0W
Bretçu 46 46 7N 26 18 E
Breteuil, Eur, France 18 48 50N 0 53 E
Breteuil, Oise, France 19 49 38N 2 18 E
Breton 108 53 7N 114 28W
Breton, Pertuis 20 46 17N 1 25W
Breton Sd. 117 29 40N 89 12W
Brett, C. 101 35 10S 174 20 E
Bretten 25 49 2N 8 43 E
Brevard 115 35 19N 82 42W
Brevik 47 59 4N 9 42 E
Brewarrina 99 30 0S 146 51 E
Brewer 107 44 43N 68 50W
Brewster, N.Y., U.S.A. 113 41 23N 73 37W
Brewster, Wash., U.S.A. 118 48 10N 119 51W
Brewster, Kap 4 70 7N 22 0W
Brewton 115 31 9N 87 2W
Breyten 93 26 16S 30 0 E
Breytovo 55 58 18N 37 50 E
Brežice 39 45 54N 15 35 E
Brézina 82 33 4N 1 14 E
Březnice 26 49 32N 13 57 E
Breznik 42 42 44N 22 50 E
Brezno 27 48 50N 19 40 E
Brezovo 43 42 21N 25 5 E
Bria 88 6 30N 21 58 E
Briançon 21 44 54N 6 39 E
Briare 19 47 38N 2 45 E
Bribie I. 97 27 0S 152 58 E
Bricon 19 48 5N 5 0 E
Bricquebec 18 49 28N 1 38W
Bridgehampton 113 40 56N 72 19W
Bridgend 13 51 30N 3 35W
Bridgeport, Calif., U.S.A. 119 38 14N 119 15W
Bridgeport, Conn., U.S.A. 114 41 12N 73 12W
Bridgeport, Nebr., U.S.A. 116 41 42N 103 10W
Bridgeport, Tex., U.S.A. 117 33 15N 97 45W
Bridger 118 45 20N 108 58W
Bridgeton 114 39 29N 75 10W
Bridgetown, Austral. 96 33 58S 116 7 E
Bridgetown, Barbados 121 13 0N 59 30W
Bridgetown, Can. 107 44 55N 65 18W
Bridgewater, Can. 107 44 25N 64 31W
Bridgewater, Mass., U.S.A. 113 41 59N 70 56W
Bridgewater, S.D., U.S.A. 116 43 34N 97 29W
Bridgewater, C. 97 38 23S 141 23 E
Bridgnorth 13 52 33N 2 25W
Bridgton 113 44 5N 70 41W
Bridgwater 13 51 7N 3 0W
Bridlington 12 54 6N 0 11W
Bridport, Austral. 99 40 59S 147 23 E
Bridport, U.K. 13 50 43N 2 45W
Brie-Comte-Robert 19 48 40N 2 35 E
Brie, Plaine de la 19 48 35N 3 10 E
Briec 18 48 6N 4 0W
Brienne-le-Château 19 48 24N 4 30 E
Brienon 19 48 0N 3 35 E
Brienz 25 46 46N 8 2 E
Brienzersee 25 46 44N 7 53 E
Briey 19 49 14N 5 57 E
Brig 25 46 18N 7 59 E
Brigg 12 53 33N 0 30W
Briggsdale 116 40 40N 104 20W
Brigham City 118 41 30N 112 1W
Bright 99 36 42S 146 56 E
Brighton, Austral. 99 35 5S 138 30 E
Brighton, Can. 106 44 2N 77 44W
Brighton, U.K. 13 50 50N 0 9W
Brighton, U.S.A. 116 39 59N 104 50W
Brignogan-Plage 18 48 40N 4 20W
Brignoles 21 43 25N 6 5 E
Brihuega 32 40 45N 2 52W
Brikama 84 13 15N 16 45W
Brilliant, Can. 108 49 19N 117 38W
Brilliant, U.S.A. 112 40 15N 80 39W
Brilon 24 51 23N 8 32 E
Bríndisi 41 40 39N 17 55 E
Brinje 39 45 0N 15 9 E
Brinkley 117 34 55N 91 15W
Brinkworth 99 33 42S 138 26 E
Brion, Î. 107 47 46N 61 26W
Brionne 18 49 11N 0 43 E
Brionski 39 44 55N 13 45 E
Brioude 20 45 18N 3 24 E
Briouze 18 48 42N 0 23W
Brisbane 97 27 25S 153 2 E
Brisbane → 99 27 24S 153 9 E
Brisighella 39 44 14N 11 46 E
Bristol, U.K. 13 51 26N 2 35W
Bristol, Conn., U.S.A. 114 41 44N 72 57W
Bristol, Pa., U.S.A. 113 40 6N 74 52W
Bristol, R.I., U.S.A. 113 41 40N 71 15W
Bristol, S.D., U.S.A. 116 45 25N 97 43W
Bristol, Tenn., U.S.A. 115 36 36N 82 11W
Bristol B. 104 58 0N 160 0W
Bristol Channel 13 51 18N 4 30W
Bristol I. 5 58 45S 28 0W
Bristol L. 119 34 23N 116 50W
Bristow 117 35 55N 96 28W
British Antarctic Territory □ 5 66 0S 45 0W
British Columbia □ 108 55 0N 125 15W
British Guiana = Guyana ■ 126 5 0N 59 0W
British Honduras = Belize ■ 120 17 0N 88 30W
British Isles 8 55 0N 4 0W
Brits 93 25 37S 27 48 E
Britstown 92 30 37S 23 30 E
Britt 106 45 46N 80 34W
Brittany = Bretagne 18 48 0N 3 0W
Britton 116 45 50N 97 47W
Brive-la-Gaillarde 20 45 10N 1 32 E
Briviesca 32 42 32N 3 19W
Brixton 98 23 32S 144 57 E
Brlik 58 44 0N 74 5 E
Brno 27 49 10N 16 35 E
Bro 48 59 31N 17 38 E
Broach = Bharuch 68 21 47N 73 0 E
Broad → 115 33 59N 82 39W
Broad B. 14 58 14N 6 16W
Broad Haven 15 54 20N 9 55W
Broad Law 14 55 30N 3 22W
Broad Sd. 97 22 0S 149 45 E
Broadford 100 37 14S 145 4 E
Broads, The 12 52 45N 1 30 E
Broadsound Ra. 97 22 50S 149 30 E
Broadus 116 45 28N 105 27W
Broadview 109 50 22N 102 35W
Broager 49 54 53N 9 40 E
Broaryd 49 57 7N 13 15 E
Brochet 109 57 53N 101 40W
Brochet, L. 109 58 36N 101 35W
Brock 109 51 26N 108 43W
Brocken 24 51 48N 10 40 E
Brockport 114 43 12N 77 56W
Brockton 113 42 8N 71 2W
Brockville 106 44 35N 75 41W
Brockway, Mont., U.S.A. 116 47 18N 105 46W
Brockway, Pa., U.S.A. 112 41 14N 78 48W
Brocton 112 42 25N 79 26W
Brod 42 41 35N 21 17 E
Brodarevo 42 43 14N 19 44 E
Brodeur Pen. 105 72 30N 88 10W
Brodick 14 55 34N 5 9W
Brodnica 28 53 15N 19 25 E
Brody 54 50 5N 25 10 E
Brogan 118 44 14N 117 32W
Broglie 18 49 0N 0 30 E
Brok 28 52 43N 21 52 E
Broken → 100 36 24S 145 24 E
Broken Bay 100 33 30S 151 15 E
Broken Bow, Nebr., U.S.A. 116 41 25N 99 35W
Broken Bow, Okla., U.S.A. 117 34 2N 94 43W
Broken Hill 97 31 58S 141 29 E
Broken Hill = Kabwe 91 14 27S 28 28 E
Brokind 49 58 13N 15 42 E
Bromfield 13 52 25N 2 45W
Bromley 13 51 20N 0 5 E
Bromölla 49 56 5N 14 28 E
Brønderslev 49 57 16N 9 57 E
Brong-Ahafo 84 7 50N 2 0W
Bronkhorstspruit 93 25 46S 28 45 E
Bronnitsy 55 55 27N 38 10 E
Bronte, Italy 41 37 48N 14 49 E
Bronte, U.S.A. 117 31 54N 100 18W
Bronte Park 99 42 8S 146 30 E
Brookfield 116 39 50N 93 4W
Brookhaven 117 31 40N 90 25W
Brookings, Oreg., U.S.A. 118 42 4N 124 10W
Brookings, S.D., U.S.A. 116 44 20N 96 45W
Brooklands 98 18 10S 144 0 E
Brooklin 112 43 55N 78 55W
Brookmere 108 49 52N 120 53W
Brooks 108 50 35N 111 55W
Brooks B. 108 50 15N 127 55W
Brooks L. 109 61 55N 106 35W
Brooks Ra. 104 68 40N 147 0W
Brooksville 115 28 32N 82 21W
Brookton 96 32 22S 117 1 E
Brookville 114 39 25N 85 0W
Brooloo 99 26 30S 152 43 E
Broom, L. 14 57 55N 5 15W
Broome 96 18 0S 122 15 E
Broons 18 48 20N 2 16W
Brora 14 58 0N 3 50W
Brora → 14 58 4N 3 52W
Brösarp 49 55 43N 14 6 E
Brosna → 15 53 8N 8 0W
Broşteni 46 47 14N 25 43 E
Brothers 118 43 56N 120 39W
Brøttum 47 61 2N 10 34 E
Brou 18 48 13N 1 11 E
Brouage 20 45 52N 1 4W
Broughton Island 105 67 33N 63 0W
Broughty Ferry 14 56 29N 2 50W
Broumov 27 50 35N 16 20 E
Brouwershaven 16 51 45N 3 55 E
Brovary 54 50 34N 30 48 E
Brovst 49 57 6N 9 31 E
Browerville 116 46 3N 94 50W
Brown Willy 13 50 35N 4 34W
Brownfield 117 33 10N 102 15W
Browning 118 48 35N 113 0W
Brownlee 109 50 43N 106 1W
Brownsville, Oreg., U.S.A. 118 44 29N 123 0W
Brownsville, Tenn., U.S.A. 117 35 35N 89 15W
Brownsville, Tex., U.S.A. 117 25 56N 97 25W
Brownwood 117 31 45N 99 0W
Brownwood, L. 117 31 51N 98 35W
Brozas 31 39 37N 6 47W
Bru 47 61 32N 5 11 E
Bruas 71 4 31N 100 46 E
Bruay-en-Artois 19 50 29N 2 33 E
Bruce, Mt. 96 22 37S 118 8 E
Bruce Pen. 112 45 0N 81 30W
Bruche → 19 48 34N 7 43 E
Bruchsal 25 49 9N 8 39 E
Bruck an der Leitha 27 48 1N 16 47 E
Bruck an der Mur 26 47 24N 15 16 E
Brückenau 25 50 17N 9 48 E
Brue → 13 51 10N 2 59W
Bruges = Brugge 16 51 13N 3 13 E
Brugg 25 47 29N 8 11 E
Brugge 16 51 13N 3 13 E
Brühl 24 50 49N 6 51 E
Brûlé 108 53 15N 117 58W
Brûlon 18 47 58N 0 15W
Brumado 127 14 14S 41 40W
Brumath 19 48 43N 7 40 E
Brumunddal 47 60 53N 10 56 E
Brundidge 115 31 43N 85 45W
Bruneau 118 42 57N 115 55W
Bruneau → 118 42 57N 115 58W
Brunei = Bandar Seri Begawan 72 4 52N 115 0 E
Brunei ■ 72 4 50N 115 0 E
Brunflo 48 63 5N 14 50 E
Brunico 39 46 50N 11 55 E
Brunkeberg 47 59 26N 8 28 E
Brunna 48 59 52N 17 25 E
Brunnen 25 46 59N 8 37 E
Brunner 101 42 27S 171 20 E
Brunner, L. 101 42 37S 171 27 E
Brunnsvik 48 60 12N 15 8 E
Bruno 109 52 20N 105 30W
Brunsbüttelkoog 24 53 52N 9 13 E
Brunswick, Ga., U.S.A. 115 31 10N 81 30W
Brunswick, Md., U.S.A. 114 39 20N 77 38W
Brunswick, Me., U.S.A. 107 43 53N 69 50W
Brunswick, Mo., U.S.A. 116 39 26N 93 10W
Brunswick, Ohio, U.S.A. 112 41 15N 81 50W
Brunswick = Braunschweig 24 52 17N 10 28 E
Brunswick B. 96 15 15S 124 50 E
Brunswick, Pen. de 128 53 30S 71 30W
Bruntál 27 50 0N 17 27 E
Bruny I. 97 43 20S 147 15 E
Brusartsi 42 43 40N 23 5 E
Brush 116 40 17N 103 33W
Brushton 113 44 50N 74 62W
Brusio 25 46 14N 10 8 E
Brusque 125 27 5S 49 0W
Brussel 16 50 51N 4 21 E
Brussels, Can. 112 43 45N 81 25W
Brussels, Ont., Can. 112 43 44N 81 15W
Brussels = Bruxelles 16 50 51N 4 21 E
Bruthen 99 37 42S 147 50 E
Bruxelles 16 50 51N 4 21 E
Bruyères 19 48 10N 6 40 E
Brwinów 28 52 9N 20 40 E
Bryagovo 43 41 58N 25 8 E
Bryan, Ohio, U.S.A. 114 41 30N 84 30W
Bryan, Texas, U.S.A. 117 30 40N 96 27W
Bryan, Mt. 99 33 30S 139 0 E
Bryanka 57 48 32N 38 45 E
Bryansk 54 53 13N 34 25 E
Bryanskoye 57 44 20N 47 10 E
Bryant 116 44 35N 97 28W
Bryne 47 58 44N 5 38 E
Bryson City 115 35 28N 83 25W
Brza Palanka 42 44 28N 22 27 E
Brzava → 42 45 21N 20 45 E
Brzeg 28 50 52N 17 30 E
Brzeg Din 28 51 16N 16 41 E
Brześć Kujawski 28 52 36N 18 55 E
Brzesko 27 49 59N 20 34 E
Brzeszcze 27 49 59N 19 10 E
Brzeziny 28 51 49N 19 42 E
Brzozów 27 49 41N 22 3 E
Bū Athlah 83 30 9N 15 39 E
Bu Craa 80 26 45N 12 50W
Bua Yai 71 15 33N 102 26 E
Buabuq 86 31 29N 25 29 E
Buapinang 73 4 40S 121 30 E
Buayan 73 6 3N 125 6 E
Buba 84 11 40N 14 59W
Bubanza 90 3 6S 29 23 E
Bucak 64 37 28N 30 36 E
Bucaramanga 126 7 0N 73 0W
Bucchiánico 39 42 20N 14 10 E
Bucecea 46 47 47N 26 28 E
Buchach 54 49 5N 25 25 E
Buchan 14 57 32N 2 8W
Buchan Ness 14 57 29N 1 48W
Buchanan, Can. 109 51 40N 102 45W
Buchanan, Liberia 84 5 57N 10 2W
Buchanan, L., Queens., Austral. 98 21 35S 145 52 E
Buchanan, L., W. Australia, Austral. 96 25 33S 123 2 E
Buchanan, L., U.S.A. 117 30 50N 98 25W
Buchans 107 48 50N 56 52W
Bucharest = Bucureşti 46 44 27N 26 10 E

Buchholz
Caeté

Name	Page	Lat.	Long.
Buchholz	24	53 19N	9 51 E
Buchloe	25	48 3N	10 45 E
Bückeburg	24	52 16N	9 2 E
Buckeye	119	33 28N	112 40W
Buckhannon	114	39 2N	80 10W
Buckhaven	14	56 10N	3 2W
Buckie	14	57 40N	2 58W
Buckingham, Can.	106	45 37N	75 24W
Buckingham, U.K.	13	52 0N	0 59W
Buckingham □	13	51 50N	0 55W
Buckingham B.	97	12 10 S	135 40 E
Buckingham Can.	70	14 0N	80 5 E
Buckinguy	99	31 3 S	147 30 E
Buckland Newton	13	50 45N	2 25W
Buckley	118	47 10N	122 2W
Bucklin	117	37 37N	99 40W
Bucquoy	19	50 9N	2 43 E
Buctouche	107	46 30N	64 45W
Bucureşti	46	44 27N	26 10 E
Bucyrus	114	40 48N	83 0W
Budafok	27	47 26N	19 2 E
Budalin	67	22 20N	95 10 E
Budapest	27	47 29N	19 5 E
Budaun	68	28 5N	79 10 E
Budd Coast	5	68 0 S	112 0 E
Buddusò	40	40 35N	9 18 E
Bude	13	50 49N	4 33W
Budeşti	46	44 13N	26 30 E
Budge Budge	69	22 30N	88 5 E
Búðareyri	50	65 2N	14 13W
Búðir	50	64 49N	23 23W
Budia	32	40 38N	2 46W
Budjala	88	2 50N	19 40 E
Búdrio	39	44 31N	11 31 E
Budva	42	42 17N	18 50 E
Budzyń	28	52 54N	16 59 E
Buea	85	4 10N	9 9 E
Buena Vista, Colo., U.S.A.	119	38 56N	106 6W
Buena Vista, Va., U.S.A.	114	37 47N	79 23W
Buena Vista L.	119	35 15N	119 21W
Buenaventura, Colomb.	126	3 53N	77 4W
Buenaventura, Mexico	120	29 50N	107 30W
Buendía, Pantano de	32	40 25N	2 43W
Buenos Aires	124	34 30 S	58 20W
Buenos Aires □	124	36 30 S	60 0W
Buenos Aires, Lago	128	46 35 S	72 30W
Buffalo, Mo., U.S.A.	117	37 40N	93 5W
Buffalo, N.Y., U.S.A.	114	42 55N	78 50W
Buffalo, Okla., U.S.A.	117	36 55N	99 42W
Buffalo, S.D., U.S.A.	116	45 39N	103 31W
Buffalo, Wyo., U.S.A.	118	44 25N	106 50W
Buffalo →	108	60 5N	115 5W
Buffalo Head Hills	108	57 25N	115 55W
Buffalo L.	108	52 27N	112 54W
Buffalo Narrows	109	55 51N	108 29W
Buffels →	92	29 36 S	17 15 E
Buford	115	34 5N	84 0W
Bug →, Poland	28	52 31N	21 5 E
Bug →, U.S.S.R.	56	46 59N	31 58 E
Buga	126	4 0N	76 15W
Buganda □	90	0 0N	31 30 E
Buganga	90	0 3 S	32 0 E
Bugeat	20	45 36N	1 55 E
Bugel, Tanjung	72	6 26 S	111 3 E
Bugojno	42	44 2N	17 25 E
Bugsuk	72	8 15N	117 15 E
Bugt	76	48 47N	121 56 E
Bugue, Le	20	44 55N	0 56 E
Bugulma	52	54 33N	52 48 E
Buguma	85	4 42N	6 55 E
Buguruslan	52	53 39N	52 26 E
Buhăeşti	46	46 47N	27 32 E
Buheirat-Murrat-el-Kubra	86	30 15N	32 40 E
Buhl, Idaho, U.S.A.	118	42 35N	114 54W
Buhl, Minn., U.S.A.	116	47 30N	92 46W
Buhuşi	46	46 41N	26 45 E
Buick	117	37 38N	91 2W
Builth Wells	13	52 10N	3 26W
Buinsk	55	55 0N	48 18 E
Buir Nur	75	47 50N	117 42 E
Buis-les-Baronnies	21	44 17N	5 16 E
Buitrago	30	41 0N	3 38W
Bujalance	31	37 54N	4 23W
Buján	30	42 59N	8 36W
Bujanovac	42	42 28N	21 44 E
Bujaraloz	32	41 29N	0 10W
Buje	39	45 24N	13 39 E
Bujumbura (Usumbura)	90	3 16 S	29 18 E
Bük	27	47 22N	16 45 E
Buk	28	52 21N	16 30 E
Bukachacha	59	52 55N	116 50 E
Bukama	91	9 10 S	25 50 E
Bukavu	90	2 20 S	28 52 E
Bukene	90	4 15 S	32 48 E
Bukhara	58	39 48N	64 25 E
Bukima	90	1 50 S	33 25 E
Bukittinggi	72	0 20 S	100 20 E
Bukkapatnam	70	14 14N	77 46 E
Bukoba	90	1 20 S	31 49 E
Bukoba □	90	1 30 S	32 0 E
Bukowno	27	50 17N	19 35 E
Bukuru	85	9 42N	8 48 E
Bukuya	90	0 40N	31 52 E
Bula, Guin.-Biss.	84	12 7N	15 43W
Bula, Indon.	73	3 6 S	130 30 E
Bulan	73	12 40N	123 52 E
Bulandshahr	68	28 28N	77 51 E
Bûlâq	86	25 10N	30 38 E
Bulawayo	91	20 7 S	28 32 E
Buldana	68	20 30N	76 18 E
Bulgan	75	48 45N	103 34 E
Bulgaria ■	43	42 35N	25 30 E
Bulgroo	99	25 47 S	143 58 E
Bulhar	63	10 25N	44 30 E
Buli, Teluk	73	1 5N	128 25 E
Buliluyan, C.	72	8 20N	117 15 E
Bulki	87	6 11N	36 31 E
Bulkley →	108	55 15N	127 40W
Bull Shoals L.	117	36 40N	93 5W
Bullaque →	31	38 59N	4 17W
Bullas	33	38 2N	1 40W
Bulle	25	46 37N	7 3 E
Buller, Mt.	100	37 10 S	146 28 E
Bullfinch	96	30 58 S	119 3 E
Bulli	99	34 15 S	150 57 E
Bullock Creek	98	17 43 S	144 31 E
Bulloo →	97	28 43 S	142 30 E
Bulloo Downs	99	28 31 S	142 57 E
Bulloo L.	99	28 43 S	142 25 E
Bulls	101	40 10 S	175 24 E
Bully-les-Mines	19	50 27N	2 44 E
Bulnes	124	36 42 S	72 19W
Bulo Burti	63	3 50N	45 33 E
Bulolo	98	7 10 S	146 40 E
Bulqiza	44	41 30N	20 21 E
Bulsar	68	20 40N	72 58 E
Bultfontein	92	28 18 S	26 10 E
Bulu Karakelong	73	4 35N	126 50 E
Bulukumba	73	5 33 S	120 11 E
Bulun	59	70 37N	127 30 E
Bumba	88	2 13N	22 30 E
Bumbiri I.	90	1 40 S	31 55 E
Bumble Bee	119	34 8N	112 18W
Bumhpa Bum	67	26 51N	97 14 E
Bumi →	91	17 0 S	28 20 E
Buna, Kenya	90	2 58N	39 30 E
Buna, P.N.G.	98	8 42 S	148 27 E
Bunazi	90	1 3 S	31 23 E
Bunbah, Khalīj	81	32 20N	23 15 E
Bunbury	96	33 20 S	115 35 E
Buncrana	15	55 8N	7 28W
Bundaberg	97	24 54 S	152 22 E
Bünde	24	52 11N	8 33 E
Bundi	68	25 30N	75 35 E
Bundoran	15	54 24N	8 17W
Bundukia	87	5 14N	30 55 E
Bundure	100	35 10 S	146 1 E
Bungendore	100	35 14 S	149 30 E
Bungo-Suidō	74	33 0N	132 15 E
Bungoma	90	0 34N	34 34 E
Bungu	90	7 35 S	39 0 E
Bungun Shara	75	49 0N	104 0 E
Bunia	90	1 35N	30 20 E
Bunji	69	35 45N	74 40 E
Bunju	72	3 35N	117 50 E
Bunkerville	119	36 47N	114 6W
Bunkie	117	31 1N	92 12W
Bunnell	115	29 28N	81 12W
Buñol	33	39 25N	0 47W
Buntok	72	1 40 S	114 58 E
Bununu	85	9 51N	9 32 E
Bununu Dass	85	10 0N	9 31 E
Bunza	85	12 8N	4 0 E
Buol	73	1 15N	121 32 E
Buorkhaya, Mys	59	71 50N	132 40 E
Buqayq	64	26 0N	49 45 E
Buqei'a	62	32 58N	35 20 E
Bur Acaba	63	3 12N	44 20 E
Bûr Fuad	86	31 15N	32 20 E
Bûr Safâga	86	26 43N	33 57 E
Bûr Sa'îd	86	31 16N	32 18 E
Bûr Sûdân	86	19 32N	37 9 E
Bûr Taufiq	86	29 54N	32 32 E
Bura	90	1 4 S	39 58 E
Buraimī, Al Wāhāt al	65	24 10N	55 43 E
Burao	63	9 32N	45 32 E
Buras	117	29 20N	89 33W
Buraydah	64	26 20N	44 8 E
Burbank	119	34 9N	118 23W
Burcher	99	33 30 S	147 16 E
Burdekin →	98	19 38 S	147 25 E
Burdett	108	49 50N	111 32W
Burdur	64	37 45N	30 22 E
Burdwan	69	23 14N	87 39 E
Bure	87	10 40N	37 4 E
Bure →	12	52 38N	1 45 E
Bureba, La	32	42 36N	3 24W
Büren	24	51 33N	8 34 E
Bureya →	59	49 27N	129 30 E
Burford	112	43 7N	80 27W
Burg, Magdeburg, Ger.	24	52 16N	11 50 E
Burg, Schleswig-Holstein, Ger.	24	54 25N	11 10 E
Burg el Arab	86	30 54N	29 32 E
Burg et Tuyur	86	20 55N	27 56 E
Burgas	43	42 33N	27 29 E
Burgaski Zaliv	43	42 30N	27 39 E
Burgdorf, Ger.	24	52 27N	10 0 E
Burgdorf, Switz.	25	47 3N	7 37 E
Burgenland □	27	47 20N	16 20 E
Burgeo	107	47 37N	57 38W
Burgersdorp	92	31 0 S	26 20 E
Burghausen	25	48 10N	12 50 E
Búrgio	40	37 35N	13 18 E
Burglengenfeld	25	49 11N	12 2 E
Burgo de Osma	32	41 35N	3 4W
Burgohondo	30	40 26N	4 47W
Burgos	32	42 21N	3 41W
Burgos □	32	42 21N	3 42W
Burgstädt	24	50 55N	12 49 E
Burgsteinfurt	24	52 9N	7 23 E
Burgsvik	49	57 3N	18 19 E
Burguillos del Cerro	31	38 23N	6 35W
Burgundy = Bourgogne	19	47 0N	4 30 E
Burhanpur	68	21 18N	76 14 E
Burhou	18	49 45N	2 15W
Buri Pen.	87	15 25N	39 55 E
Burias	73	12 55N	123 5 E
Burica, Pta.	121	8 3N	82 51W
Burigi, L.	90	2 2 S	31 22 E
Burin	107	47 1N	55 14W
Būrīn	62	32 11N	35 15 E
Buriram	71	15 0N	103 0 E
Burji	87	5 29N	37 51 E
Burkburnett	117	34 7N	98 35W
Burke	118	47 31N	115 56W
Burke →	98	23 12 S	139 33 E
Burketown	97	17 45 S	139 33 E
Burk's Falls	106	45 37N	79 24W
Burley	118	42 37N	113 55W
Burlington, Can.	112	43 18N	79 45W
Burlington, Colo., U.S.A.	116	39 21N	102 18W
Burlington, Iowa, U.S.A.	116	40 50N	91 5W
Burlington, Kans., U.S.A.	116	38 15N	95 47W
Burlington, N.C., U.S.A.	115	36 7N	79 27W
Burlington, N.J., U.S.A.	114	40 5N	74 50W
Burlington, Vt., U.S.A.	114	44 27N	73 14W
Burlington, Wash., U.S.A.	118	48 29N	122 19W
Burlington, Wis., U.S.A.	114	42 41N	88 18W
Burlyu-Tyube	58	46 30N	79 10 E
Burma ■	67	21 0N	96 30 E
Burnaby I.	108	52 25N	131 19W
Burnet	117	30 45N	98 11W
Burnett →	97	24 45 S	152 23 E
Burney	118	40 56N	121 41W
Burnham	112	40 37N	77 34W
Burnie	97	41 4 S	145 56 E
Burnley	12	53 47N	2 15W
Burns, Oreg., U.S.A.	118	43 40N	119 4W
Burns, Wyo., U.S.A.	116	41 13N	104 18W
Burns Lake	108	54 20N	125 45W
Burnside →	104	66 51N	108 4W
Burnt River	112	44 41N	78 42W
Burntwood →	109	56 8N	96 34W
Burntwood L.	109	55 22N	100 26W
Burqā	62	32 18N	35 11 E
Burqān	64	29 0N	47 57 E
Burqin	75	47 43N	87 0 E
Burra	97	33 40 S	138 55 E
Burragorang, L.	100	33 52 S	150 37 E
Burreli	44	41 36N	20 1 E
Burrendong, L.	100	32 45 S	149 10 E
Burrewarra Pt.	100	35 50 S	150 15 E
Burriana	32	39 50N	0 4W
Burrinjuck Dam	100	35 0 S	148 34 E
Burrinjuck Res.	99	35 0 S	148 36 E
Burro, Serranías del	120	29 0N	102 0W
Burruyacú	124	26 30 S	64 40W
Burry Port	13	51 41N	4 17W
Bursa	64	40 15N	29 5 E
Burseryd	49	57 12N	13 17 E
Burstall	109	50 39N	109 54W
Burton L.	106	54 45N	78 20W
Burton-upon-Trent	12	52 48N	1 39W
Burtundy	99	33 45 S	142 15 E
Buru	73	3 30 S	126 30 E
Burullus, Bahra el	86	31 25N	31 0 E
Burundi ■	90	3 15 S	30 0 E
Burung	72	0 24N	103 33 E
Bururi	90	3 57 S	29 37 E
Burutu	85	5 20N	5 29 E
Burwell	116	41 49N	99 8W
Bury	12	53 36N	2 19W
Bury St. Edmunds	13	52 15N	0 42 E
Buryat A.S.S.R. □	59	53 0N	110 0 E
Buryn	54	51 13N	33 50 E
Burzenin	28	51 28N	18 47 E
Busalla	38	44 34N	8 58 E
Busango Swamp	91	14 15 S	25 45 E
Buşayyah	64	30 0N	46 10 E
Busca	38	44 31N	7 29 E
Bushati	44	41 58N	19 34 E
Bushell	109	59 31N	108 45W
Bushenyi	90	0 35 S	30 10 E
Bushnell, Ill., U.S.A.	116	40 32N	90 30W
Bushnell, Nebr., U.S.A.	116	41 18N	103 50W
Busia □	90	0 25N	34 6 E
Busie	84	10 29N	2 22W
Businga	88	3 16N	20 59 E
Buskerud fylke □	47	60 13N	9 0 E
Busko Zdrój	28	50 28N	20 42 E
Busoga □	90	0 5N	33 30 E
Busovača	42	44 6N	17 53 E
Busra ash Shām	64	32 30N	36 25 E
Bussang	19	47 50N	6 50 E
Busselton	96	33 42 S	115 15 E
Busseto	38	44 59N	10 2 E
Bussum	16	52 16N	5 10 E
Bustard Hd.	97	24 0 S	151 48 E
Busto Arsizio	38	45 40N	8 50 E
Busto, C.	30	43 34N	6 28W
Busu-Djanoa	88	1 43N	21 23 E
Busuanga	73	12 10N	120 0 E
Büsum	24	54 7N	8 50 E
Buta	90	2 50N	24 53 E
Butare	90	2 31 S	29 52 E
Bute	14	55 48N	5 2W
Bute Inlet	108	50 40N	124 53W
Butemba	90	1 9N	31 37 E
Butembo	90	0 9N	29 18 E
Butera	41	37 10N	14 10 E
Butha Qi	75	48 0N	122 32 E
Butiaba	90	1 50N	31 20 E
Butler, Mo., U.S.A.	116	38 17N	94 18W
Butler, Pa., U.S.A.	114	40 52N	79 52W
Butom Odrzánski	28	51 44N	15 48 E
Butte, Mont., U.S.A.	118	46 0N	112 31W
Butte, Nebr., U.S.A.	116	42 56N	98 54W
Butterworth	71	5 24N	100 23 E
Button B.	109	58 45N	94 23W
Butuan	73	8 57N	125 33 E
Butuku-Luba	85	3 29N	8 33 E
Butung	73	5 0 S	122 45 E
Buturlinovka	55	50 50N	40 35 E
Butzbach	24	50 24N	8 40 E
Bützow	24	53 51N	11 59 E
Buxar	69	25 34N	83 58 E
Buxton, S. Afr.	92	27 38 S	24 42 E
Buxton, U.K.	12	53 16N	1 54W
Buxy	19	46 44N	4 40 E
Buy	55	58 28N	41 28 E
Buyaga	59	59 50N	127 0 E
Buynaksk	57	42 48N	47 7 E
Büyük Çekmece	43	41 2N	28 35 E
Büyük Kemikli Burun	44	40 20N	26 15 E
Buzançais	18	46 54N	1 25 E
Buzău	46	45 10N	26 50 E
Buzău □	46	45 20N	26 30 E
Buzău →	46	45 10N	27 20 E
Buzău, Pasul	46	45 35N	26 12 E
Buzaymah	81	24 50N	22 2 E
Buzen	74	33 35N	131 5 E
Buzet	39	45 24N	13 58 E
Buzi →	91	19 50 S	34 43 E
Buziaş	42	45 38N	21 36 E
Buzuluk	52	52 48N	52 12 E
Buzuluk →	55	50 15N	42 7 E
Buzzards Bay	114	41 45N	70 38W
Bwana Mkubwe	91	13 8 S	28 38 E
Byala, Ruse, Bulg.	43	43 28N	25 44 E
Byala, Varna, Bulg.	43	42 53N	27 55 E
Byala Slatina	43	43 26N	23 55 E
Byandovan, Mys	57	39 45N	49 28 E
Bychawa	28	51 1N	22 36 E
Byczyna	28	51 7N	18 12 E
Bydgoszcz	28	53 10N	18 0 E
Bydgoszcz □	28	53 16N	17 33 E
Byelorussian S.S.R. □	54	53 30N	27 0 E
Byers	116	39 46N	104 13W
Byesville	112	39 56N	81 32W
Bygland	47	58 50N	7 48 E
Byglandsfjord	47	58 40N	7 50 E
Byglandsfjorden	47	58 44N	7 50 E
Byhalia	117	34 53N	89 41W
Bykhov	54	53 31N	30 14 E
Bykle	47	59 20N	7 22 E
Bykovo	57	49 50N	45 25 E
Bylas	119	33 11N	110 9W
Bylderup	49	54 57N	9 6 E
Bylot I.	105	73 13N	78 34W
Byrd, C.	5	69 38 S	76 7W
Byrd Land	5	79 30 S	125 0W
Byrd Sub-Glacial Basin	5	82 0 S	120 0W
Byrock	99	30 40 S	146 27 E
Byron, C.	97	28 38 S	153 40 E
Byrranga, Gory	59	75 0N	100 0 E
Byrum	49	57 16N	11 0 E
Byske	50	64 57N	21 11 E
Byske älv →	50	64 57N	21 13 E
Bystrzyca →, Lublin, Poland	28	51 21N	22 46 E
Bystrzyca →, Wrocław, Poland	28	51 12N	16 55 E
Bystrzyca Kłodzka	28	50 19N	16 39 E
Byten	54	52 50N	25 27 E
Bytom	28	50 25N	18 54 E
Bytów	28	54 10N	17 30 E
Byumba	90	1 35 S	30 4 E
Bzenec	27	48 58N	17 18 E
Bzura →	28	52 25N	20 15 E

C

Name	Page	Lat.	Long.
Ca Mau	71	9 7N	105 8 E
Ca Mau, Mui = Bai Bung	71	8 35N	104 42 E
Caacupé	124	25 23 S	57 5W
Caála	89	12 46 S	15 30 E
Caamano Sd.	108	52 55N	129 25W
Caazapá	124	26 8 S	56 19W
Caazapá □	125	26 10 S	56 0W
Caballeria, C. de	32	40 5N	4 5 E
Cabañaquinta	30	43 10N	5 38W
Cabanatuan	73	15 30N	120 58 E
Cabanes	32	40 9N	0 2 E
Cabano	107	47 40N	68 56W
Čabar	39	45 36N	14 39 E
Cabedelo	127	7 0 S	34 50W
Cabeza del Buey	31	38 44N	5 13W
Cabildo	124	32 30 S	71 5W
Cabimas	126	10 23N	71 25W
Cabinda	88	5 33 S	12 11 E
Cabinda □	88	5 0 S	12 30 E
Cabinet Mts.	118	48 0N	115 30W
Cabo Blanco	128	47 15 S	65 47W
Cabo Frio	125	22 51 S	42 3W
Cabo Pantoja	126	1 0 S	75 10W
Cabonga, Réservoir	106	47 20N	76 40W
Cabool	117	37 10N	92 8W
Caboolture	99	27 5 S	152 58 E
Cabora Bassa Dam	91	15 20 S	32 50 E
Caborca (Heroica)	120	30 40N	112 10W
Cabot, Mt.	113	44 30N	71 25W
Cabot Strait	107	47 15N	59 40W
Cabra	31	37 30N	4 28W
Cabra del Santo Cristo	33	37 42N	3 16W
Cábras	40	39 57N	8 30 E
Cabrera, I.	33	39 8N	2 57 E
Cabrera, Sierra	30	42 12N	6 40W
Cabri	109	50 35N	108 25W
Cabriel →	33	39 14N	1 3W
Cacabelos	30	42 36N	6 44W
Čačak	42	43 54N	20 20 E
Cáceres, Brazil	126	16 5 S	57 40W
Cáceres, Spain	31	39 26N	6 23W
Cáceres □	31	39 45N	6 0W
Cache Bay	106	46 22N	80 0W
Cachepo	31	37 20N	7 49W
Cachéu	84	12 14N	16 8W
Cachi	124	25 5 S	66 10W
Cachimbo, Serra do	127	9 30 S	55 0W
Cachoeira	127	12 30 S	39 0W
Cachoeira de Itapemirim	125	20 51 S	41 7W
Cachoeira do Sul	125	30 3 S	52 53W
Cachopo	31	37 20N	7 49W
Cacólo	88	10 9 S	19 21 E
Caconda	89	13 48 S	15 8 E
Cadarache, Barrage de	21	43 42N	5 47 E
Čadca	27	49 26N	18 45 E
Caddo	117	34 8N	96 18W
Cader Idris	12	52 43N	3 56W
Cadí, Sierra del	32	42 17N	1 42 E
Cadillac, Can.	106	48 14N	78 23W
Cadillac, France	20	44 38N	0 20W
Cadillac, U.S.A.	114	44 16N	85 25W
Cadiz	73	10 57N	123 15 E
Cádiz	31	36 30N	6 20W
Cadiz	112	40 13N	81 0W
Cádiz □	31	36 36N	5 45W
Cádiz, G. de	31	36 40N	7 0W
Cadomin	108	53 2N	117 20W
Cadotte →	108	56 43N	117 10W
Cadours	20	43 44N	1 2 E
Caen	18	49 10N	0 22W
Caernarfon	12	53 8N	4 17W
Caernarfon B.	12	53 4N	4 40W
Caernarvon = Caernarfon	12	53 8N	4 17W
Caerphilly	13	51 34N	3 13W
Caesarea	62	32 30N	34 53 E
Caeté	127	19 55 S	43 40W

Caetité | Carbon

Caetité	**127**	13 50S	42 32W
Cafayate	**124**	26 2S	66 0W
Cafu	**92**	16 30S	15 8E
Cagayan	**73**	9 39N	121 16E
Cagayan →	**73**	18 25N	121 42E
Cagayan de Oro	**73**	8 30N	124 40E
Cagli	**39**	43 32N	12 38E
Cágliari	**40**	39 15N	9 6E
Cágliari, G. di	**40**	39 8N	9 10E
Cagnano Varano	**41**	41 49N	15 47E
Cagnes-sur-Mer	**21**	43 40N	7 9E
Caguas	**121**	18 14N	66 4W
Caha Mts.	**15**	51 45N	9 40W
Cahama	**92**	16 17S	14 19E
Caher	**15**	52 23N	7 56W
Cahersiveen	**15**	51 57N	10 13W
Cahore Pt.	**15**	52 34N	6 11W
Cahors	**20**	44 27N	1 27E
Cahuapanas	**126**	5 15S	77 0W
Caianda	**91**	11 2S	23 31E
Caibarién	**121**	22 30N	79 30W
Caicara	**126**	7 38N	66 10W
Caicó	**127**	6 20S	37 0W
Caicos Is.	**121**	21 40N	71 40W
Caicos Passage	**121**	22 45N	72 45W
Cainsville	**112**	43 9N	80 15W
Caird Coast	**5**	75 0S	25 0W
Cairn Gorm	**14**	57 7N	3 40W
Cairn Toul	**14**	57 3N	3 44W
Cairngorm Mts.	**14**	57 6N	3 42W
Cairns	**97**	16 57S	145 45E
Cairo, Ga., U.S.A.	**115**	30 52N	84 12W
Cairo, Illinois, U.S.A.	**117**	37 0N	89 10W
Cairo = El Qâhira	**86**	30 1N	31 14E
Cairo Montenotte	**38**	44 23N	8 16E
Caithness, Ord of	**14**	58 9N	3 37W
Caiundo	**89**	15 50S	17 28E
Caiza	**126**	20 2S	65 40W
Cajamarca	**126**	7 5S	78 28W
Cajarc	**20**	44 29N	1 50E
Cajàzeiras	**127**	6 52S	38 30W
Čajetina	**42**	43 47N	19 42E
Čajniče	**42**	43 34N	19 5E
Çakirgol	**57**	40 33N	39 40E
Čakovec	**39**	46 23N	16 26E
Cala	**31**	37 59N	6 21W
Cala →	**31**	37 38N	6 5W
Cala Cadolar, Punta de	**33**	38 38N	1 35E
Calabar	**85**	4 57N	8 20E
Calábria □	**41**	39 24N	16 30E
Calaburras, Pta. de	**31**	36 30N	4 38W
Calaceite	**32**	41 1N	0 11E
Calafat	**46**	43 58N	22 59E
Calafate	**128**	50 19S	72 15W
Calahorra	**32**	42 18N	1 59W
Calais, France	**19**	50 57N	1 56E
Calais, U.S.A.	**107**	45 11N	67 20W
Calais, Pas de	**19**	50 57N	1 20E
Calalaste, Cord. de	**124**	25 0S	67 0W
Calama, Brazil	**126**	8 0S	62 50W
Calama, Chile	**124**	22 30S	68 55W
Calamar, Bolívar, Colomb.	**126**	10 15N	74 55W
Calamar, Vaupés, Colomb.	**126**	1 58N	72 32W
Calamian Group	**73**	11 50N	119 55E
Calamocha	**32**	40 50N	1 17W
Calañas	**31**	37 40N	6 53W
Calanda	**32**	40 56N	0 15W
Calang	**72**	4 37N	95 37E
Calangiánus	**40**	40 56N	9 12E
Calapan	**73**	13 25N	121 7E
Călăraşi	**46**	44 12N	27 20E
Calasparra	**33**	38 14N	1 41W
Calatafimi	**40**	37 56N	12 50E
Calatayud	**32**	41 20N	1 40W
Calauag	**73**	13 55N	122 15E
Calavà, C.	**41**	38 11N	14 55E
Calavite, Cape	**73**	13 26N	120 20E
Calbayog	**73**	12 4N	124 38E
Calbe	**24**	51 57N	11 47E
Calca	**126**	13 22S	72 0W
Calcasieu L.	**117**	30 0N	93 17W
Calci	**38**	43 44N	10 31E
Calcutta	**69**	22 36N	88 24E
Caldaro	**39**	46 23N	11 15E
Caldas da Rainha	**31**	39 24N	9 8W
Caldas de Reyes	**30**	42 36N	8 39W
Calder →	**12**	53 44N	1 21W
Caldera	**124**	27 5S	70 55W
Caldwell, Idaho, U.S.A.	**118**	43 45N	116 42W
Caldwell, Kans., U.S.A.	**117**	37 5N	97 37W
Caldwell, Texas, U.S.A.	**117**	30 30N	96 42W
Caledon	**92**	34 14S	19 26E
Caledon →	**92**	30 31S	26 5E
Caledon B.	**97**	12 45S	137 0E
Caledonia, Can.	**112**	43 7N	79 58W
Caledonia, U.S.A.	**112**	42 57N	77 54W
Calella	**32**	41 37N	2 40E
Calemba	**92**	16 0S	15 44E
Calera, La	**124**	32 50S	71 10W
Calexico	**119**	32 40N	115 33W
Calf of Man	**12**	54 4N	4 48W
Calgary	**108**	51 0N	114 10W
Calhoun	**115**	34 30N	84 55W
Cali	**126**	3 25N	76 35W
Calicoan	**73**	10 59N	125 50E
Calicut (Kozhikode)	**70**	11 15N	75 43E
Caliente	**119**	37 36N	114 34W
California, Mo., U.S.A.	**116**	38 37N	92 30W
California, Pa., U.S.A.	**112**	40 5N	79 55W
California □	**119**	37 25N	120 0W
California, Baja, T.N. □	**120**	30 0N	115 0W
California, Baja, T.S. □	**120**	25 50N	111 50W
California, Golfo de	**120**	27 0N	111 0W
California, Lr. = California, Baja	**120**	25 50N	111 50W
Călimăneşti	**46**	45 14N	24 20E
Călimani, Munţii	**46**	47 12N	25 0E
Călineşti	**46**	45 21N	24 18E
Calingasta	**124**	31 15S	69 30W
Calipatria	**119**	33 8N	115 30W
Calistoga	**118**	38 36N	122 32W
Calitri	**41**	40 54N	15 25E
Callabonna, L.	**97**	29 40S	140 5E
Callac	**18**	48 25N	3 27W
Callan	**15**	52 33N	7 25W
Callander	**14**	56 15N	4 14W
Callao	**126**	12 0S	77 0W
Callaway	**116**	41 20N	99 56W
Callide	**98**	24 18S	150 28E
Calling Lake	**108**	55 15N	113 12W
Callosa de Ensarriá.	**33**	38 40N	0 8W
Callosa de Segura	**33**	38 7N	0 53W
Calne	**12**	51 26N	2 0W
Calola	**92**	16 25S	17 48E
Calore →	**41**	41 11N	14 28E
Caloundra	**99**	26 45S	153 10E
Calpe	**33**	38 39N	0 3E
Calstock	**106**	49 47N	84 9W
Caltabellotta	**40**	37 36N	13 11E
Caltagirone	**41**	37 13N	14 30E
Caltanissetta	**41**	37 30N	14 3E
Caluire-et-Cuire	**21**	45 49N	4 51E
Calulo	**88**	10 1S	14 56E
Calumet	**114**	47 14N	88 27W
Calunda	**89**	12 7S	23 36E
Caluso	**38**	45 18N	7 52E
Calvados □	**18**	49 5N	0 15W
Calvert	**117**	30 59N	96 40W
Calvert I.	**108**	51 30N	128 0W
Calvinia	**92**	31 28S	19 45E
Calw	**25**	48 43N	8 44E
Calzada Almuradiel	**33**	38 32N	3 28W
Calzada de Calatrava	**31**	38 42N	3 46W
Cam →	**13**	52 21N	0 16E
Cam Lam	**71**	11 54N	109 10E
Cam Ranh	**71**	11 54N	109 12E
Camabatela	**88**	8 20S	15 26E
Camacupa	**89**	11 58S	17 22E
Camagüey	**121**	21 20N	78 0W
Camaiore	**38**	43 57N	10 18E
Camaná	**126**	16 30S	72 50W
Camaquã →	**125**	31 17S	51 47W
Camarat, C.	**21**	43 12N	6 41E
Camaret	**18**	48 16N	4 37W
Camargo	**126**	20 38S	65 15E
Camargue	**21**	43 34N	4 34E
Camariñas	**30**	43 8N	9 12W
Camarón, C.	**121**	16 0N	85 0W
Camarones	**128**	44 50S	65 40W
Camas	**118**	45 35N	122 24W
Camas Valley	**118**	43 0N	123 46W
Cambados	**30**	42 31N	8 49W
Cambará	**125**	23 2S	50 5W
Cambay	**68**	22 23N	72 33E
Cambay, G. of	**68**	20 45N	72 30E
Cambil	**33**	37 40N	3 33W
Cambo-les-Bains	**20**	43 22N	1 23W
Cambodia ■	**71**	12 15N	105 0E
Camborne	**13**	50 13N	5 18W
Cambrai	**19**	50 11N	3 14E
Cambria	**119**	35 39N	121 6W
Cambrian Mts.	**13**	52 25N	3 52W
Cambridge, Can.	**106**	43 23N	80 15W
Cambridge, N.Z.	**101**	37 54S	175 29E
Cambridge, U.K.	**13**	52 13N	0 8E
Cambridge, Idaho, U.S.A.	**118**	44 36N	116 40W
Cambridge, Mass., U.S.A.	**114**	42 20N	71 8W
Cambridge, Md., U.S.A.	**114**	38 33N	76 2W
Cambridge, Minn., U.S.A.	**116**	45 34N	93 15W
Cambridge, N.Y., U.S.A.	**113**	43 2N	73 22W
Cambridge, Nebr., U.S.A.	**116**	40 20N	100 12W
Cambridge, Ohio, U.S.A.	**114**	40 1N	81 35W
Cambridge Bay	**104**	69 10N	105 0W
Cambridge Gulf	**96**	14 55S	128 15E
Cambridge Springs	**112**	41 47N	80 4W
Cambridgeshire □	**13**	52 12N	0 7E
Cambrils	**32**	41 8N	1 3E
Cambuci	**125**	21 35S	41 55W
Camden, Ala., U.S.A.	**115**	31 59N	87 15W
Camden, Ark., U.S.A.	**117**	33 40N	92 50W
Camden, Me., U.S.A.	**107**	44 14N	69 6W
Camden, N.J., U.S.A.	**114**	39 57N	75 7W
Camden, S.C., U.S.A.	**115**	34 17N	80 34W
Camdenton	**117**	38 0N	92 45W
Camembert	**18**	48 53N	0 10E
Cámeri	**38**	45 30N	8 40E
Camerino	**39**	43 10N	13 4E
Cameron, Ariz., U.S.A.	**119**	35 55N	111 31W
Cameron, La., U.S.A.	**117**	29 50N	93 18W
Cameron, Mo., U.S.A.	**116**	39 42N	94 14W
Cameron, Tex., U.S.A.	**117**	30 53N	97 0W
Cameron Falls	**106**	49 8N	88 19W
Cameron Highlands	**71**	4 27N	101 22E
Cameron Hills	**108**	59 48N	118 0W
Cameroon ■	**88**	6 0N	12 30E
Camerota	**41**	40 2N	15 21E
Cameroun →	**85**	4 0N	9 35E
Cameroun, Mt.	**88**	4 13N	9 10E
Cametá	**127**	2 12S	49 30W
Camiguin	**73**	8 55N	123 55E
Caminha	**30**	41 50N	8 50W
Camino	**118**	38 47N	120 40W
Camira Creek	**99**	29 15S	152 58E
Cammal	**112**	41 24N	77 28W
Camocim	**127**	2 55S	40 50W
Camogli	**38**	44 21N	9 9E
Camooweal	**97**	19 56S	138 7E
Camopi →	**127**	3 10N	52 20W
Camp Crook	**116**	45 36N	103 59W
Camp Wood	**117**	29 41N	100 0W
Campagna	**41**	40 40N	15 5E
Campana	**124**	34 10S	58 55W
Campana, I.	**128**	48 20S	75 20W
Campanario	**31**	38 52N	5 36W
Campania □	**41**	40 50N	14 45E
Campbell	**112**	41 5N	80 36W
Campbell I.	**94**	52 30S	169 0E
Campbell L.	**109**	63 14N	106 55W
Campbell River	**108**	50 5N	125 20W
Campbell Town	**99**	41 52S	147 30E
Campbellford	**112**	44 18N	77 48W
Campbellsville	**114**	37 23N	85 21W
Campbellton	**107**	47 57N	66 43W
Campbelltown	**99**	34 4S	150 49E
Campbeltown	**14**	55 25N	5 36W
Campeche	**120**	19 50N	90 32W
Campeche □	**120**	19 50N	90 32W
Campeche, Bahía de	**120**	19 30N	93 0W
Camperdown	**99**	38 14S	143 9E
Camperville	**109**	51 59N	100 9W
Campi Salentina	**41**	40 22N	18 2E
Campidano	**40**	39 30N	8 40E
Campillo de Altobuey	**32**	39 36N	1 49W
Campillo de Llerena	**31**	38 30N	5 50W
Campillos	**31**	37 4N	4 51W
Campina Grande	**127**	7 20S	35 47W
Campiña, La	**31**	37 45N	4 45W
Campinas	**125**	22 50S	47 0W
Campli	**39**	42 44N	13 40E
Campo, Camer.	**88**	2 22N	9 50E
Campo, Spain	**32**	42 25N	0 24E
Campo Belo	**127**	20 52S	45 16W
Campo de Criptana	**33**	39 24N	3 7W
Campo de Gibraltar	**31**	36 15N	5 25W
Campo Formoso	**127**	10 30S	40 20W
Campo Grande	**127**	20 25S	54 40W
Campo Maíor	**127**	4 50S	42 12W
Campo Maior	**31**	38 59N	7 7W
Campo Túres	**39**	46 53N	11 55E
Campoalegre	**126**	2 41N	75 20W
Campobasso	**41**	41 34N	14 40E
Campobello di Licata	**40**	37 16N	13 55E
Campobello di Mazara	**40**	37 38N	12 45E
Campofelice	**40**	37 54N	13 53E
Camporeale	**40**	37 53N	13 3E
Campos	**125**	21 50S	41 20W
Campos Belos	**127**	13 10S	47 3W
Campos del Puerto	**33**	39 26N	3 1E
Campos Novos	**125**	27 21S	51 50W
Camprodón	**32**	42 19N	2 23E
Campuya →	**126**	1 40S	73 30W
Camrose	**108**	53 0N	112 50W
Camsell Portage	**109**	59 37N	109 15W
Can Tho	**71**	10 2N	105 46E
Canaan	**113**	42 1N	73 20W
Canada ■	**104**	60 0N	100 0W
Cañada de Gómez	**124**	32 40S	61 30W
Canadian	**117**	35 56N	100 25W
Canadian →	**117**	35 27N	95 3W
Canakkale	**44**	40 8N	26 30E
Canakkale Boğazi	**44**	40 0N	26 0E
Canal Flats	**108**	50 10N	115 48W
Canal latéral à la Garonne	**20**	44 25N	0 15E
Canalejas	**124**	35 15S	66 34W
Canals, Argent.	**124**	33 35S	62 53W
Canals, Spain	**33**	38 58N	0 35W
Canandaigua	**114**	42 55N	77 18W
Cananea	**120**	31 0N	110 20W
Canarias, Islas	**80**	28 30N	16 0W
Canarreos, Arch. de los	**121**	21 35N	81 40W
Canary Is. = Canarias, Islas	**80**	29 30N	17 0W
Canaveral, C.	**115**	28 28N	80 31W
Cañaveras	**32**	40 27N	2 24W
Canavieiras	**127**	15 39S	39 0W
Canbelego	**99**	31 32S	146 18E
Canberra	**97**	35 15S	149 8E
Canby, Calif., U.S.A.	**118**	41 26N	120 58W
Canby, Minn., U.S.A.	**116**	44 44N	96 15W
Canby, Ore., U.S.A.	**118**	45 16N	122 42W
Cancale	**18**	48 40N	1 50W
Canche →	**19**	50 31N	1 39E
Candala	**63**	11 30N	49 58E
Candas	**30**	43 35N	5 45W
Candé	**18**	47 34N	1 0W
Candela	**41**	41 8N	15 31E
Candelaria	**125**	27 29S	55 44W
Candelaria, Pta. de la	**30**	43 45N	8 0W
Candeleda	**30**	40 10N	5 14W
Candelo	**99**	36 47S	149 43E
Candia = Iráklion	**45**	35 20N	25 12E
Candia, Sea of = Crete, Sea of	**45**	36 0N	25 0E
Candle L.	**109**	53 50N	105 18W
Candlemas I.	**5**	57 3S	26 40W
Cando	**116**	48 30N	99 14W
Canea = Khaniá	**45**	35 30N	24 4E
Canelli	**38**	44 44N	8 18E
Canelones	**125**	34 32S	56 17W
Canet-Plage	**20**	42 41N	3 2E
Cañete, Chile	**124**	37 50S	73 30W
Cañete, Peru	**126**	13 8S	76 30W
Cañete, Spain	**32**	40 3N	1 54W
Cañete de las Torres	**31**	37 53N	4 19W
Canfranc	**32**	42 42N	0 31W
Cangas	**30**	42 16N	8 47W
Cangas de Narcea	**30**	43 10N	6 32W
Cangas de Onís	**30**	43 21N	5 8W
Canguaretama	**127**	6 20S	35 5W
Canguçu	**125**	31 22S	52 43W
Cangxi	**77**	31 47N	105 59E
Cangzhou	**76**	38 19N	116 52E
Cani, I.	**83**	36 21N	10 5E
Canicattì	**40**	37 21N	13 50E
Canicattini	**41**	37 1N	15 3E
Canim Lake	**108**	51 47N	120 54W
Canipaan	**72**	8 33N	117 15E
Canisteo	**112**	42 17N	77 37W
Canisteo →	**112**	42 15N	77 30W
Cañiza, La	**30**	42 13N	8 16W
Cañizal	**30**	41 12N	5 22W
Canjáyar	**33**	37 1N	2 44W
Cankırı	**64**	40 40N	33 37E
Cankuzo	**90**	3 10S	30 31E
Canmore	**108**	51 7N	115 18W
Cann River	**99**	37 35S	149 7E
Canna	**14**	57 3N	6 33W
Cannanore	**70**	11 53N	75 27E
Cannes	**21**	43 32N	7 0E
Canning Basin	**96**	19 50S	124 0E
Canning Town	**69**	22 23N	88 40E
Cannington	**112**	44 20N	79 2W
Cannock	**12**	52 42N	2 2W
Cannon Ball →	**116**	46 20N	100 38W
Canoe L.	**109**	55 10N	108 15W
Canon City	**116**	38 27N	105 14W
Canora	**109**	51 40N	102 30W
Canosa di Púglia	**41**	41 13N	16 4E
Canourgue, Le	**20**	44 26N	3 13E
Canowindra	**99**	33 35S	148 38E
Canso	**107**	45 20N	61 0W
Cantabria, Sierra de	**32**	42 40N	2 30W
Cantabrian Mts. = Cantábrica, Cordillera	**30**	43 0N	5 10W
Cantábrica, Cordillera	**30**	43 0N	5 10W
Cantal □	**20**	45 4N	2 45E
Cantanhede	**30**	40 20N	8 36W
Cantavieja	**32**	40 31N	0 25W
Čantavir	**42**	45 55N	19 46E
Canterbury, Austral.	**99**	25 23S	141 53E
Canterbury, U.K.	**13**	51 17N	1 5E
Canterbury □	**101**	43 45S	171 19E
Canterbury Bight	**101**	44 16S	171 55E
Canterbury Plains	**101**	43 55S	171 22E
Cantillana	**31**	37 36N	5 50W
Canton, Ga., U.S.A.	**115**	34 13N	84 29W
Canton, Ill., U.S.A.	**116**	40 32N	90 0W
Canton, Mass., U.S.A.	**113**	42 8N	71 8W
Canton, Miss., U.S.A.	**117**	32 40N	90 1W
Canton, Mo., U.S.A.	**116**	40 10N	91 33W
Canton, N.Y., U.S.A.	**114**	44 32N	75 3W
Canton, Ohio, U.S.A.	**114**	40 47N	81 22W
Canton, Okla., U.S.A.	**117**	36 5N	98 36W
Canton, S.D., U.S.A.	**116**	43 20N	96 35W
Canton = Guangzhou	**75**	23 5N	113 10E
• Canton I.	**94**	2 50S	171 40W
Canton L.	**117**	36 12N	98 40W
Cantù	**38**	45 44N	9 8E
Canudos	**126**	7 13S	58 5W
Canutama	**126**	6 30S	64 20W
Canutillo	**119**	31 58N	106 36W
Canyon, Texas, U.S.A.	**117**	35 0N	101 57W
Canyon, Wyo., U.S.A.	**118**	44 43N	110 36W
Canyonlands Nat. Park	**119**	38 25N	109 30W
Canyonville	**118**	42 55N	123 14W
Canzo	**38**	45 54N	9 18E
Cao Xian	**77**	34 50N	115 35E
Cáorle	**39**	45 36N	12 51E
Cap-aux-Meules	**107**	47 23N	61 52W
Cap-Chat	**107**	49 6N	66 40W
Cap-de-la-Madeleine	**106**	46 22N	72 31W
Cap-Haïtien	**121**	19 40N	72 20W
Capa Stilo	**41**	38 25N	16 35E
Capáccio	**41**	40 26N	15 4E
Capaia	**88**	8 27S	20 13E
Capanaparo →	**126**	7 1N	67 7W
Capbreton	**20**	43 39N	1 26W
Capdenac	**20**	44 34N	2 5E
Cape →	**98**	20 49S	146 51E
Cape Barren I.	**97**	40 25S	148 15E
Cape Breton Highlands Nat. Park	**107**	46 50N	60 40W
Cape Breton I.	**107**	46 0N	60 30W
Cape Charles	**114**	37 15N	75 59W
Cape Coast	**85**	5 5N	1 15W
Cape Dorset	**105**	64 14N	76 32W
Cape Dyer	**105**	66 30N	61 22W
Cape Fear →	**115**	34 30N	78 25W
Cape Girardeau	**117**	37 20N	89 30W
Cape May	**114**	39 1N	74 53W
Cape Montague	**107**	46 5N	62 25W
Cape Palmas	**84**	4 25N	7 49W
Cape Province □	**92**	32 0S	23 0E
Cape Tormentine	**107**	46 8N	63 47W
Cape Town (Kaapstad)	**92**	33 55S	18 22E
Cape Verde Is. ■	**6**	17 10N	25 20W
Cape Vincent	**113**	44 9N	76 21W
Cape York Peninsula	**97**	12 0S	142 30E
Capela	**127**	10 30S	37 0W
Capella	**98**	23 2S	148 1E
Capella, Mt.	**98**	5 4S	141 8E
Capelle, La	**19**	49 59N	3 50E
Capendu	**20**	43 11N	2 31E
Capernaum = Kefar Naḥum	**62**	32 54N	35 32E
Capestang	**20**	43 20N	3 2E
Capim →	**127**	1 40S	47 47W
Capitan	**119**	33 33N	105 41W
Capizzi	**41**	37 50N	14 26E
Čapljina	**42**	43 10N	17 43E
Capoche →	**91**	15 35S	33 0E
Capraia	**38**	43 2N	9 50E
Caprarola	**39**	42 21N	12 11E
Capreol	**106**	46 43N	80 56W
Caprera	**40**	41 12N	9 28E
Capri	**41**	40 34N	14 15E
Capricorn, C.	**97**	23 30S	151 13E
Capricorn Group	**98**	23 30S	151 55E
Caprino Veronese	**38**	45 37N	10 47E
Caprivi Strip	**92**	18 0S	23 0E
Captainganj	**69**	26 55N	83 45E
Captain's Flat	**99**	35 35S	149 27E
Captieux	**20**	44 18N	0 16W
Cápua	**41**	41 7N	14 15E
Capulin	**117**	36 48N	103 59W
Caquetá →	**126**	1 15S	69 15W
Caracal	**46**	44 8N	24 22E
Caracas	**126**	10 30N	66 55W
Caracol	**127**	9 15S	43 22W
Caradoc	**99**	30 35S	143 5E
Caráglio	**38**	44 25N	7 25E
Carajás, Serra dos	**127**	6 0S	51 30W
Carangola	**125**	20 44S	42 5W
Caransebeş	**46**	45 28N	22 18E
Carantec	**18**	48 40N	3 55W
Carapelle →	**41**	41 3N	15 55E
Caraş Severin □	**42**	45 10N	22 10E
Caraşova	**42**	45 11N	21 51E
Caratasca, Laguna	**121**	15 20N	83 40W
Caratinga	**127**	19 50S	42 10W
Caraúbas	**127**	5 43S	37 33W
Caravaca	**33**	38 8N	1 52W
Caravággio	**38**	45 30N	9 39E
Caravelas	**127**	17 45S	39 15W
Caraveli	**126**	15 45S	73 25W
Caràzinho	**125**	28 16S	52 46W
Carballino	**30**	42 26N	8 5W
Carballo	**30**	43 13N	8 41W
Carberry	**109**	49 50N	99 25W
Carbia	**30**	42 48N	8 14W
Carbó	**120**	29 42N	110 58W
Carbon	**108**	51 30N	113 9W

• *Renamed Abariringa*

Carbonara, C.	**40**	39 8N	9 30 E
Carbondale, Colo, U.S.A.	**118**	39 30N	107 10W
Carbondale, Ill., U.S.A.	**117**	37 45N	89 10W
Carbondale, Pa., U.S.A.	**114**	41 37N	75 30W
Carbonear	**107**	47 42N	53 13W
Carboneras	**33**	37 0N	1 53W
Carboneras de Guadazaón	**32**	39 54N	1 50W
Carbonia	**40**	39 10N	8 30 E
Carcabuey	**31**	37 27N	4 17W
Carcagente	**33**	39 8N	0 28W
Carcajou	**108**	57 47N	117 6W
Carcans, Étang d'	**20**	45 6N	1 7W
Carcasse, C.	**121**	18 30N	74 28W
Carcassonne	**20**	43 13N	2 20 E
Carche	**33**	38 26N	1 9W
Carcross	**104**	60 13N	134 45W
Cardamom Hills	**70**	9 30N	77 15 E
Cárdenas, Cuba	**121**	23 0N	81 30W
Cárdenas, San Luis Potosí, Mexico	**120**	22 0N	99 41W
Cárdenas, Tabasco, Mexico	**120**	17 59N	93 21W
Cardenete	**32**	39 46N	1 41W
Cardiff	**13**	51 28N	3 11W
Cardigan	**13**	52 6N	4 41W
Cardigan B.	**13**	52 30N	4 30W
Cardinal	**113**	44 47N	75 23W
Cardona, Spain	**32**	41 56N	1 40 E
Cardona, Uruguay	**124**	33 53 S	57 18W
Cardoner →	**32**	41 41N	1 51 E
Cardross	**109**	49 50N	105 40W
Cardston	**108**	49 15N	113 20W
Cardwell	**98**	18 14 S	146 2 E
Careen L.	**109**	57 0N	108 11W
Carei	**46**	47 40N	22 29 E
Careme	**73**	6 55 S	108 27 E
Carentan	**18**	49 19N	1 15W
Carey, Idaho, U.S.A.	**118**	43 19N	113 58W
Carey, Ohio, U.S.A.	**114**	40 58N	83 22W
Carey, L.	**96**	29 0 S	122 15 E
Carey L.	**109**	62 12N	102 55W
Careysburg	**84**	6 34N	10 30W
Cargados Garajos	**3**	17 0 S	59 0 E
Cargèse	**21**	42 7N	8 35 E
Carhaix-Plouguer	**18**	48 18N	3 36W
Carhué	**124**	37 10 S	62 50W
Caribbean Sea	**121**	15 0N	75 0W
Cariboo Mts.	**108**	53 0N	121 0W
Caribou	**107**	46 55N	68 0W
Caribou →, Man., Can.	**109**	59 20N	94 44W
Caribou →, N.W.T., Can.	**108**	61 27N	125 45W
Caribou I.	**106**	47 22N	85 49W
Caribou Is.	**108**	61 55N	113 15W
Caribou L., Man., Can.	**109**	59 21N	96 10W
Caribou L., Ont., Can.	**106**	50 25N	89 5W
Caribou Mts.	**108**	59 12N	115 40W
Carignan	**19**	49 38N	5 10 E
Carignano	**38**	44 55N	7 40 E
Carinda	**99**	30 28 S	147 41 E
Cariñena	**32**	41 20N	1 13W
Carinhanha	**127**	14 15 S	44 46W
Carini	**40**	38 9N	13 10 E
Carinola	**40**	41 11N	13 58 E
Carinthia □ = Kärnten	**26**	46 52N	13 30 E
Caripito	**126**	10 8N	63 6W
Caritianas	**126**	9 20 S	63 6W
Carlbrod = Dimitrovgrad	**42**	43 0N	22 48 E
Carlentini	**41**	37 15N	15 2 E
Carleton Place	**106**	45 8N	76 9W
Carletonville	**92**	26 23 S	27 22 E
Carlin	**118**	40 44N	116 5W
Carlingford, L.	**15**	54 0N	6 5W
Carlinville	**116**	39 20N	89 55W
Carlisle, U.K.	**12**	54 54N	2 55W
Carlisle, U.S.A.	**114**	40 12N	77 10W
Carlitte, Pic	**20**	42 35N	1 55 E
Carloforte	**40**	39 10N	8 18 E
Carlos Casares	**124**	35 32 S	61 20W
Carlos Tejedor	**124**	35 25 S	62 25W
Carlota, La	**124**	33 30 S	63 20W
Carlow	**15**	52 50N	6 58W
Carlow □	**15**	52 43N	6 50W
Carlsbad, Calif., U.S.A.	**119**	33 11N	117 25W
Carlsbad, N. Mex., U.S.A.	**117**	32 20N	104 14W
Carlyle, Can.	**109**	49 40N	102 20W
Carlyle, U.S.A.	**116**	38 38N	89 23W
Carmacks	**104**	62 5N	136 16W
Carmagnola	**38**	44 50N	7 42 E
Carman	**109**	49 30N	98 0W
Carmangay	**108**	50 10N	113 10W
Carmanville	**107**	49 23N	54 19W
Carmarthen	**13**	51 52N	4 20W
Carmarthen B.	**13**	51 40N	4 30W
Carmaux	**20**	44 3N	2 10 E
Carmel	**113**	41 25N	73 38W
Carmel-by-the-Sea	**119**	36 38N	121 55W
Carmel Mt.	**62**	32 45N	35 3 E
Carmelo	**124**	34 0 S	58 20W
Carmen, Colomb.	**126**	9 43N	75 8W
Carmen, Parag.	**125**	27 13 S	56 12W
Carmen de Patagones	**128**	40 50 S	63 0W
Carmen, I.	**120**	26 0N	111 20W
Cármenes	**30**	42 58N	5 34W
Carmensa	**124**	35 15 S	67 40W
Carmi	**114**	38 6N	88 10W
Carmila	**98**	21 55 S	149 24 E
* Carmona	**31**	37 28N	5 42W
Carnarvon, Queens., Austral.	**98**	24 48 S	147 45 E
Carnarvon, W. Austral., Austral.	**96**	24 51 S	113 42 E
Carnarvon, S. Afr.	**92**	30 56 S	22 8 E
Carnarvon Ra.	**99**	25 15 S	148 30 E
Carnaxide	**31**	38 43N	9 14W
Carndonagh	**15**	55 15N	7 16W
Carnduff	**109**	49 10N	101 50W
Carnegie	**112**	40 24N	80 4W
Carnegie, L.	**96**	26 5 S	122 30 E
Carnic Alps = Karnische Alpen	**26**	46 36N	13 0 E
Carnot	**88**	4 59N	15 56 E
Carnot B.	**96**	17 20 S	121 30 E
Carnsore Pt.	**15**	52 10N	6 20W
Caro	**114**	43 29N	83 27W
Carol City	**115**	25 5N	80 16W
Carolina, Brazil	**127**	7 10 S	47 30W

* Renamed N'gage

Carolina, S. Afr.	**93**	26 5 S	30 6 E
Carolina, La	**31**	38 17N	3 38W
Caroline I.	**95**	9 15 S	150 3W
Caroline Is.	**94**	8 0N	150 0 E
Caron	**109**	50 30N	105 50W
Caroni →	**126**	8 21N	62 43W
Carovigno	**41**	40 42N	17 40 E
Carpathians	**46**	49 50N	21 0 E
Carpaţii Meridionali	**46**	45 30N	25 0 E
Carpenédolo	**38**	45 22N	10 25 E
Carpentaria Downs	**98**	18 44 S	144 20 E
Carpentaria, G. of	**97**	14 0 S	139 0 E
Carpentras	**21**	44 3N	5 2 E
Carpi	**38**	44 47N	10 52 E
Carpino	**41**	41 50N	15 51 E
Carpinteria	**119**	34 25N	119 31W
Carpio	**30**	41 13N	5 7W
Carrabelle	**115**	29 52N	84 40W
Carrara	**38**	44 5N	10 7 E
Carrascosa del Campo	**32**	40 2N	2 45W
Carrauntohill, Mt.	**15**	52 0N	9 49W
Carrick-on-Shannon	**15**	53 57N	8 7W
Carrick-on-Suir	**15**	52 22N	7 30W
Carrickfergus	**15**	54 43N	5 50W
Carrickfergus □	**15**	54 43N	5 49W
Carrickmacross	**15**	54 0N	6 43W
Carrieton	**99**	32 25 S	138 31 E
Carrington	**116**	47 30N	99 7W
Carrión →	**30**	41 53N	4 32W
Carrión de los Condes	**30**	42 20N	4 37W
Carrizal Bajo	**124**	28 5 S	71 20W
Carrizalillo	**124**	29 5 S	71 30W
Carrizo Cr.	**117**	36 30N	103 40W
Carrizo Springs	**117**	28 28N	99 50W
Carrizozo	**119**	33 40N	105 57W
Carroll	**116**	42 2N	94 55W
Carrollton, Ga., U.S.A.	**115**	33 36N	85 5W
Carrollton, Ill., U.S.A.	**116**	39 20N	90 25W
Carrollton, Ky., U.S.A.	**114**	38 40N	85 10W
Carrollton, Mo., U.S.A.	**116**	39 19N	93 24W
Carrollton, Ohio, U.S.A.	**112**	40 31N	81 9W
Carron →	**14**	57 30N	5 30W
Carron, L.	**14**	57 22N	5 35W
Carrot →	**109**	53 50N	101 17W
Carrot River	**109**	53 17N	103 35W
Carrouges	**18**	48 34N	0 10W
Carruthers	**109**	52 52N	109 16W
Çarşamba	**64**	41 15N	36 45 E
Carse of Gowrie	**14**	56 30N	3 10W
Carsoli	**39**	42 7N	13 3 E
Carson	**116**	46 27N	101 29W
Carson City	**118**	39 12N	119 46W
Carson Sink	**118**	39 50N	118 40W
Carsonville	**114**	43 25N	82 39W
Carstairs	**14**	55 42N	3 41W
Cartagena, Colomb.	**126**	10 25N	75 33W
Cartagena, Spain	**33**	37 38N	0 59W
Cartago, Colomb.	**126**	4 45N	75 55W
Cartago, C. Rica	**121**	9 50N	85 52W
Cartaxo	**31**	39 10N	8 47W
Cartaya	**31**	37 16N	7 9W
Carteret	**18**	49 23N	1 47W
Cartersville	**115**	34 11N	84 48W
Carterton	**101**	41 2 S	175 31 E
Carthage, Ark., U.S.A.	**117**	34 4N	92 32W
Carthage, Ill., U.S.A.	**116**	40 25N	91 10W
Carthage, Mo., U.S.A.	**117**	37 10N	94 20W
Carthage, N.Y., U.S.A.	**114**	43 59N	75 37W
Carthage, S.D., U.S.A.	**116**	44 14N	97 38W
Carthage, Texas, U.S.A.	**117**	32 8N	94 20W
Cartier I.	**96**	12 31 S	123 29 E
Cartwright	**107**	53 41N	56 58W
Caruaru	**127**	8 15 S	35 55W
Carúpano	**126**	10 39N	63 15W
Caruthersville	**117**	36 10N	89 40W
Carvin	**19**	50 30N	2 57 E
Carvoeiro	**126**	1 30 S	61 59W
Carvoeiro, Cabo	**31**	39 21N	9 24W
Casa Branca	**31**	38 29N	8 12W
Casa Grande	**119**	32 53N	111 51W
Casa Nova	**127**	9 25 S	41 5W
Casablanca, Chile	**124**	33 20 S	71 25W
Casablanca, Moroc.	**82**	33 36N	7 36W
Casacalenda	**41**	41 45N	14 50 E
Casal di Principe	**41**	41 0N	14 8 E
Casalbordino	**39**	42 10N	14 34 E
Casale Monferrato	**38**	45 8N	8 28 E
Casalmaggiore	**38**	44 59N	10 25 E
Casalpusterlengo	**38**	45 10N	9 40 E
Casamance →	**84**	12 33N	16 46W
Casamássima	**41**	40 58N	16 55 E
Casarano	**41**	40 0N	18 10 E
Casares	**31**	36 27N	5 16W
Casas Grandes	**120**	30 22N	108 0W
Casas Ibañez	**33**	39 17N	1 30W
Casasimarro	**33**	39 22N	2 3W
Casatejada	**30**	39 54N	5 40W
Casavieja	**30**	40 17N	4 46W
Cascade, Idaho, U.S.A.	**118**	44 30N	116 2W
Cascade, Mont., U.S.A.	**118**	47 16N	111 46W
Cascade Locks	**118**	45 44N	121 54W
Cascade Ra.	**102**	47 0N	121 30W
Cascais	**31**	38 41N	9 25W
Cáscina	**38**	43 40N	10 32 E
Caselle Torinese	**38**	45 12N	7 39 E
Caserta	**41**	41 5N	14 20 E
Cashel	**15**	52 31N	7 53W
Cashmere	**118**	47 31N	120 30W
Casiguran	**73**	16 22N	122 7 E
Casilda	**124**	33 10 S	61 10W
Casimcea	**46**	44 45N	28 23 E
Casino	**97**	28 52 S	153 3 E
Casiquiare →	**126**	2 1N	67 7W
Caslan	**108**	54 38N	112 31W
Čáslav	**26**	49 54N	15 22 E
Casma	**126**	9 30 S	78 20W
Casola Valsenio	**39**	44 12N	11 40 E
Cásoli	**39**	42 7N	14 18 E
Caspe	**32**	41 14N	0 1W
Casper	**118**	42 52N	106 20W
Caspian Sea	**53**	43 0N	50 0 E
Casquets	**18**	49 46N	2 15W

Cass City	**114**	43 34N	83 24W
Cass Lake	**116**	47 23N	94 38W
Cassá de la Selva	**32**	41 53N	2 52 E
Cassano Iónio	**41**	39 47N	16 20 E
Cassel	**19**	50 48N	2 30 E
Casselman	**113**	45 19N	75 5W
Casselton	**116**	47 0N	97 15W
Cassiar	**108**	59 16N	129 40W
Cassiar Mts.	**108**	59 30N	130 30W
Cassino	**40**	41 30N	13 50 E
Cassis	**21**	43 14N	5 32 E
Cassville	**117**	36 45N	93 52W
Cástagneto Carducci	**38**	43 9N	10 36 E
Castéggio	**38**	45 1N	9 8 E
Castejón de Monegros	**32**	41 37N	0 15W
Castel di Sangro	**39**	41 47N	14 6 E
Castel San Giovanni	**38**	45 4N	9 25 E
Castel San Pietro	**39**	44 23N	11 30 E
Castelbuono	**41**	37 56N	14 4 E
Casteldelfino	**38**	44 35N	7 4 E
Castelfiorentino	**38**	43 36N	10 58 E
Castelfranco Emília	**38**	44 37N	11 2 E
Castelfranco Véneto	**39**	45 40N	11 56 E
Casteljaloux	**20**	44 19N	0 6 E
Castellabate	**41**	40 18N	14 55 E
Castellammare del Golfo	**40**	38 2N	12 53 E
Castellammare di Stábia	**41**	40 47N	14 29 E
Castellammare, G. di	**40**	38 5N	12 55 E
Castellamonte	**38**	45 23N	7 42 E
Castellana Grotte	**41**	40 53N	17 10 E
Castellane	**21**	43 50N	6 31 E
Castellaneta	**41**	40 40N	16 57 E
Castellar de Santisteban	**33**	38 16N	3 8W
Castelleone	**38**	45 19N	9 47 E
Castelli	**124**	36 7 S	57 47W
Castelló de Ampurias	**32**	42 15N	3 4 E
Castellón □	**32**	40 15N	0 5W
Castellón de la Plana	**32**	39 58N	0 3W
Castellote	**32**	40 48N	0 15W
Castelltersol	**32**	41 45N	2 8 E
Castelmáuro	**41**	41 50N	14 40 E
Castelnau-de-Médoc	**20**	45 2N	0 48W
Castelnaudary	**20**	43 20N	1 58 E
Castelnovo ne' Monti	**38**	44 27N	10 26 E
Castelnuovo di Val di Cécina	**38**	43 12N	10 54 E
Castelo	**125**	20 33 S	41 14 E
Castelo Branco	**30**	39 50N	7 31W
Castelo Branco □	**30**	39 52N	7 45W
Castelo de Paiva	**30**	41 2N	8 16W
Castelo de Vide	**31**	39 25N	7 27W
Castelsarrasin	**20**	44 2N	1 7 E
Casteltérmini	**40**	37 32N	13 38 E
Castelvetrano	**40**	37 40N	12 46 E
Casterton	**99**	37 30 S	141 30 E
Castets	**20**	43 52N	1 6W
Castiglione del Lago	**39**	43 7N	12 3 E
Castiglione della Pescáia	**38**	42 46N	10 53 E
Castiglione delle Stiviere	**38**	45 23N	10 30 E
Castiglione Fiorentino	**39**	43 20N	11 55 E
Castilblanco	**31**	39 17N	5 5W
Castilla La Nueva	**31**	39 45N	3 20W
Castilla La Vieja	**30**	41 55N	4 0W
Castilla, Playa de	**31**	37 0N	6 33W
Castille = Castilla	**30**	40 0N	3 30W
Castillon, Barrage de	**21**	43 53N	6 33 E
Castillon-en-Couserans	**20**	42 56N	1 1 E
Castillon-la-Bataille	**20**	44 51N	0 2W
Castillonès	**20**	44 39N	0 37 E
Castillos	**125**	34 12 S	53 52W
Castle Dale	**118**	39 11N	111 1W
Castle Douglas	**14**	54 57N	3 57W
Castle Harbour	**121**	32 17N	64 44W
Castle Point	**101**	40 54 S	176 15 E
Castle Rock, Colo., U.S.A.	**116**	39 26N	104 50W
Castle Rock, Wash., U.S.A.	**118**	46 20N	122 58W
Castlebar	**15**	53 52N	9 17W
Castleblaney	**15**	54 7N	6 44W
Castlegar	**108**	49 20N	117 40W
Castlegate	**118**	39 45N	110 57W
Castlemaine	**97**	37 2 S	144 12 E
Castlereagh	**15**	53 47N	8 30W
Castlereagh □	**15**	54 33N	5 53W
Castlereagh →	**97**	30 12 S	147 32 E
Castlereagh B.	**96**	12 10 S	135 10 E
Castletown	**12**	54 4N	4 40W
Castletown Bearhaven	**15**	51 40N	9 54W
Castlevale	**98**	24 30 S	146 48 E
Castor	**108**	52 15N	111 50W
Castres	**20**	43 37N	2 13 E
Castries	**121**	14 0N	60 50W
Castril	**33**	37 48N	2 46W
Castro, Brazil	**125**	24 45 S	50 0W
Castro, Chile	**128**	42 30 S	73 50W
Castro Alves	**127**	12 46 S	39 33W
Castro del Río	**31**	37 41N	4 29W
Castro Marim	**31**	37 13N	7 26W
Castro Urdiales	**32**	43 23N	3 11W
Castro Verde	**31**	37 41N	8 4W
Castrojeriz	**30**	42 17N	4 9W
Castropol	**30**	43 32N	7 0W
Castroreale	**41**	38 5N	15 15 E
Castrovillari	**41**	39 49N	16 11 E
Castroville	**117**	29 20N	98 53W
Castuera	**31**	38 43N	5 37W
Casummit Lake	**106**	51 29N	92 22W
Cat I., Bahamas	**121**	24 30N	75 30W
Cat I., U.S.A.	**117**	30 15N	89 7W
Cat L.	**106**	51 40N	91 50W
Čata	**27**	47 58N	18 38 E
Catacáos	**126**	5 20 S	80 45W
Cataguases	**125**	21 23 S	42 39W
Catahoula L.	**117**	31 30N	92 5W
Catalão	**127**	18 10 S	47 57W
Catalina	**107**	48 31N	53 4W
Catalonia = Cataluña	**32**	41 40N	1 15 E
Cataluña	**32**	41 40N	1 15 E
Catamarca	**124**	28 30 S	65 50W
Catamarca □	**124**	27 0 S	65 50W
Catanduanes	**73**	13 50N	124 20 E
Catanduva	**125**	21 5 S	48 58W
Catánia	**41**	37 31N	15 4 E
Catánia, G. di	**41**	37 25N	15 8 E

Catanzaro	**41**	38 54N	16 38 E
Catarman	**73**	12 28N	124 35 E
Catastrophe C.	**96**	34 59 S	136 0 E
Cateau, Le	**19**	50 6N	3 30 E
Cateel	**73**	7 47N	126 24 E
Cathcart	**92**	32 18 S	27 10 E
Cathlamet	**118**	46 12N	123 23W
Catio	**84**	11 17N	15 15W
Cativa	**120**	9 21N	79 49W
Catlettsburg	**114**	38 23N	82 38W
Cato I.	**97**	23 15 S	155 32 E
Catoche, C.	**120**	21 40N	87 8W
Catral	**33**	38 10N	0 47W
Catria, Mt.	**39**	43 28N	12 42 E
Catrimani	**126**	0 27N	61 41W
Catskill	**114**	42 14N	73 52W
Catskill Mts.	**114**	42 15N	74 15W
Cattaraugus	**112**	42 22N	78 52W
Cattólica	**39**	43 58N	12 43 E
Cattólica Eraclea	**40**	37 27N	13 24 E
Catuala	**92**	16 25 S	19 2 E
Catur	**91**	13 45 S	35 30 E
Cauca →	**126**	8 54N	74 28W
Caucaia	**127**	3 40 S	38 35W
Caucasus Mts. = Bolshoi Kavkas	**57**	42 50N	44 0 E
Caudebec-en-Caux	**18**	49 30N	0 42 E
Caudete	**33**	38 42N	1 2W
Caudry	**19**	50 7N	3 22 E
Caulnes	**18**	48 18N	2 10W
Caulónia	**41**	38 23N	16 25 E
Caúngula	**88**	8 26 S	18 38 E
Cauquenes	**124**	36 0 S	72 22W
Caura →	**126**	7 38N	64 53W
Cauresi →	**91**	17 8 S	33 0 E
Causapscal	**107**	48 19N	67 12W
Caussade	**20**	44 10N	1 33 E
Cauterets	**20**	42 52N	0 8W
Caux, Pays de	**18**	49 38N	0 35 E
Cava dei Tirreni	**41**	40 42N	14 42 E
Cávado →	**30**	41 32N	8 48W
Cavaillon	**21**	43 50N	5 2 E
Cavalaire-sur-Mer	**21**	43 10N	6 33 E
Cavalerie, La	**20**	44 0N	3 10 E
Cavalese	**39**	46 17N	11 29 E
Cavalier	**116**	48 50N	97 39W
Cavallo, Île de	**21**	41 22N	9 16 E
Cavally →	**84**	4 22N	7 32W
Cavan	**15**	54 0N	7 22W
Cavan □	**15**	53 58N	7 10W
Cavárzere	**39**	45 8N	12 6 E
Cave City	**114**	37 13N	85 57W
Cavendish	**99**	37 31 S	142 2 E
Caviana, I.	**127**	0 10N	50 10W
Cavite	**73**	14 29N	120 55 E
Cavour	**38**	44 47N	7 22 E
Cavtat	**42**	42 35N	18 13 E
Cawndilla, L.	**99**	32 30 S	142 15 E
Cawnpore = Kanpur	**69**	26 28N	80 20 E
Caxias	**127**	4 55 S	43 20W
Caxias do Sul	**125**	29 10 S	51 10W
Caxine, C.	**82**	35 56N	0 27W
Caxito	**88**	8 30 S	13 30 E
Cay Sal Bank	**121**	23 45N	80 0W
Cayambe	**126**	0 3N	78 8W
Cayce	**115**	33 59N	81 10W
Cayenne	**127**	5 0N	52 18W
Cayes, Les	**121**	18 15N	73 46W
Cayeux-sur-Mer	**19**	50 10N	1 30 E
Caylus	**20**	44 15N	1 47 E
Cayman Is.	**121**	19 40N	80 30W
* Cayo	**120**	17 10N	89 0W
Cayo Romano	**121**	22 0N	78 0W
Cayuga, Can.	**112**	42 59N	79 50W
Cayuga, U.S.A.	**113**	42 54N	76 44W
Cayuga L.	**114**	42 45N	76 45W
Cazalla de la Sierra	**31**	37 56N	5 45W
Căzănești	**46**	44 36N	27 3 E
Cazaux et de Sanguinet, Étang de	**20**	44 29N	1 10W
Cazères	**20**	43 13N	1 5 E
Cazin	**39**	44 57N	15 57 E
Čazma	**39**	45 45N	16 39 E
Čazma →	**39**	45 35N	16 29 E
Cazombo	**89**	11 54 S	22 56 E
Cazorla	**33**	37 55N	3 2W
Cazorla, Sierra de	**33**	38 5N	2 55W
Cea →	**30**	42 0N	5 36W
Ceamurlia de Jos	**43**	44 43N	28 47 E
Ceanannus Mor	**15**	53 42N	6 53W
Ceará = Fortaleza	**127**	3 43 S	38 35W
Ceará □	**127**	5 0 S	40 0W
Ceará Mirim	**127**	5 38 S	35 25W
Ceauru, L.	**46**	44 58N	23 11 E
Cebollar	**124**	29 10 S	66 35W
Cebollera, Sierra de	**32**	42 0N	2 30W
Cebreros	**30**	40 27N	4 28W
Cebu	**73**	10 18N	123 54 E
Ceccano	**40**	41 34N	13 18 E
Cece	**27**	46 46N	18 39 E
Cechi	**84**	6 15N	4 25W
Cecil Plains	**99**	27 30 S	151 11 E
Cécina	**38**	43 19N	10 33 E
Cécina →	**38**	43 19N	10 29 E
Ceclavin	**30**	39 50N	6 45W
Cedar →	**116**	41 17N	91 21W
Cedar City	**119**	37 41N	113 3W
Cedar Creek Res.	**117**	32 4N	96 5W
Cedar Falls	**116**	42 39N	92 29W
Cedar Key	**115**	29 9N	83 5W
Cedar L.	**109**	53 10N	100 0W
Cedar Rapids	**116**	42 0N	91 38W
Cedarburg	**114**	43 18N	87 55W
Cedartown	**115**	34 1N	85 15W
Cedarvale	**108**	55 1N	128 22W
Cedarville	**118**	41 37N	120 13W
Cedeira	**30**	43 39N	8 2W
Cedral	**120**	23 50N	100 42W
Cedrino →	**40**	40 23N	9 44 E
Cedro	**127**	6 34 S	39 3W
Cedros, I. de	**120**	28 10N	115 20W
Ceduna	**96**	32 7 S	133 46 E
Cedynia	**28**	52 53N	14 12 E
Cefalù	**41**	38 3N	14 1 E

* Renamed San Ignacio

Cega Chelmsford

Cega →	**30**	41 33N	4 46W
Cegléd	**27**	47 11N	19 47 E
Céglie Messápico	**41**	40 39N	17 31 E
Cehegín	**33**	38 6N	1 48W
Cehu-Silvaniei	**46**	47 24N	23 9 E
Ceiba, La	**121**	15 40N	86 50W
Ceica	**46**	46 53N	22 10 E
Ceira →	**30**	40 13N	8 16W
Cekhira	**83**	34 20N	10 5 E
Celano	**39**	42 6N	13 30 E
Celanova	**30**	42 9N	7 58W
Celaya	**120**	20 31N	100 37W
Celbridge	**15**	53 20N	6 33W
Celebes = Sulawesi	**73**	2 0 S	120 0 E
Celebes Sea	**73**	3 0N	123 0 E
Čelić	**42**	44 43N	18 47 E
Celina	**114**	40 32N	84 31W
Celje	**39**	46 16N	15 18 E
Celldömölk	**27**	47 16N	17 10 E
Celle	**24**	52 37N	10 4 E
Celorico da Beira	**30**	40 38N	7 24W
Cement	**117**	34 56N	98 8W
Cengong	**77**	27 13N	108 44 E
Cenis, Col du Mt.	**21**	45 15N	6 55 E
Ceno →	**38**	44 4N	10 5 E
Cenon	**20**	44 50N	0 33W
Centallo	**38**	44 30N	7 35 E
Center, N.D., U.S.A.	**116**	47 9N	101 17W
Center, Texas, U.S.A.	**117**	31 50N	94 10W
Centerfield	**119**	39 9N	111 56W
Centerville, Ala., U.S.A.	**115**	32 55N	87 7W
Centerville, Iowa, U.S.A.	**116**	40 45N	92 57W
Centerville, Miss., U.S.A.	**117**	31 10N	91 3W
Centerville, Pa., U.S.A.	**112**	40 3N	79 59W
Centerville, S.D., U.S.A.	**116**	43 10N	96 58W
Centerville, Tenn., U.S.A.	**115**	35 46N	87 29W
Centerville, Tex., U.S.A.	**117**	31 15N	95 56W
Cento	**39**	44 43N	11 16 E
Central	**119**	32 46N	108 9W
Central □, Kenya	**90**	0 30 S	37 30 E
Central □, Malawi	**91**	13 30 S	33 30 E
Central □, U.K.	**14**	56 10N	4 30W
Central □, Zambia	**91**	14 25 S	28 50 E
Central African Republic ■	**88**	7 0N	20 0 E
Central City, Ky., U.S.A.	**114**	37 20N	87 7W
Central City, Nebr., U.S.A.	**116**	41 8N	98 0W
Central, Cordillera, Colomb.	**126**	5 0N	75 0W
Central, Cordillera, C. Rica	**121**	10 10N	84 5W
Central I.	**90**	3 30N	36 0 E
Central Islip	**113**	40 49N	73 13W
Central Makran Range	**65**	26 30N	64 15 E
Central Patricia	**106**	51 30N	90 9W
Central Ra.	**98**	5 0 S	143 0 E
Central Russian Uplands	**9**	54 0N	36 0 E
Central Siberian Plateau	**59**	65 0N	105 0 E
Centralia, Ill., U.S.A.	**116**	38 32N	89 5W
Centralia, Mo., U.S.A.	**116**	39 12N	92 6W
Centralia, Wash., U.S.A.	**118**	46 46N	122 59W
Centúripe	**41**	37 37N	14 41 E
Cephalonia = Kefallinía	**45**	38 15N	20 30 E
Cepin	**42**	45 32N	18 34 E
Ceprano	**40**	41 33N	13 30 E
Ceptura	**46**	45 1N	26 21 E
Cepu	**73**	7 12 S	111 31 E
Ceram = Seram	**73**	3 10 S	129 0 E
Ceram Sea = Seram Sea	**73**	2 30 S	128 30 E
Cerbère	**20**	42 26N	3 10 E
Cerbicales, Îles	**21**	41 33N	9 22 E
Cerbu	**46**	44 46N	24 46 E
Cercal	**31**	37 48N	8 40W
Cercemaggiore	**41**	41 27N	14 43 E
Cerdaña	**32**	42 22N	1 35 E
Cerdedo	**30**	42 33N	8 23W
Cère →	**20**	44 55N	1 49 E
Cerea	**39**	45 12N	11 13 E
Ceres, Argent.	**124**	29 55 S	61 55W
Ceres, Italy	**38**	45 19N	7 22 E
Ceres, S. Afr.	**92**	33 21 S	19 18 E
Céret	**20**	42 30N	2 42 E
Cerignola	**41**	41 17N	15 53 E
Cerigo = Kíthira	**45**	36 15N	23 0 E
Cérilly	**20**	46 37N	2 50 E
Cerisiers	**19**	48 8N	3 30 E
Cerizay	**18**	46 50N	0 40W
Çerkeş	**64**	40 49N	32 52 E
Cerknica	**39**	45 48N	14 21 E
Cermerno	**42**	43 35N	20 25 E
Cerna	**46**	45 4N	28 17 E
Cerna →	**46**	44 45N	24 0 E
Cernavodă	**46**	44 22N	28 3 E
Cernay	**19**	47 44N	7 10 E
Cernik	**42**	45 17N	17 22 E
Cerralvo	**120**	24 20N	109 45 E
Cerreto Sannita	**41**	41 17N	14 34 E
Cerritos	**120**	22 27N	100 20W
Cerro	**119**	36 47N	105 36W
Certaldo	**38**	43 32N	11 2 E
Cervaro →	**41**	41 30N	15 52 E
Cervera	**32**	41 40N	1 16 E
Cervera de Pisuerga	**30**	42 51N	4 30W
Cervera del Río Alhama	**32**	42 2N	1 58W
Cérvia	**39**	44 15N	12 20 E
Cervignano del Friuli	**39**	45 49N	13 20 E
Cervinara	**41**	41 2N	14 36 E
Cervione	**21**	42 20N	9 29 E
Cervo	**30**	43 40N	7 24W
Cesaro	**41**	37 50N	14 38 E
Cesena	**39**	44 9N	12 14 E
Cesenático	**39**	44 12N	12 22 E
Çësis	**54**	57 17N	25 28 E
Česká Lípa	**26**	50 45N	14 30 E
Česka Socialistická Republika □	**26**	49 30N	14 40 E
Česká Třebová	**27**	49 54N	16 27 E
České Budějovice	**26**	48 55N	14 25 E
České Velenice	**26**	48 45N	15 1 E
Ceskomoravská Vrchovina	**26**	49 30N	15 40 E
Český Brod	**26**	50 4N	14 52 E
Český Krumlov	**26**	48 43N	14 21 E
Český Těšin	**27**	49 45N	18 39 E
Ceşme	**45**	38 20N	26 23 E
Cessnock	**97**	32 50 S	151 21 E
Cestas	**20**	44 44N	0 41W
Cestos →	**84**	5 40N	9 10W
Cetate	**46**	44 7N	23 2 E
Cétin Grad	**39**	45 9N	15 45 E
Cetina →	**39**	43 26N	16 42 E
Cetinje	**42**	42 23N	18 59 E
Cetraro	**41**	39 30N	15 56 E
Ceuta	**82**	35 52N	5 18W
Ceva	**38**	44 23N	8 3 E
Cévennes	**20**	44 10N	3 50 E
Ceyhan	**64**	37 4N	35 47 E
Ceylon = Sri Lanka ■	**70**	7 30N	80 50 E
Cèze →	**21**	44 13N	4 43 E
Cha Pa	**71**	22 20N	103 47 E
Chabeuil	**21**	44 54N	5 1 E
Chablais	**21**	46 20N	6 36 E
Chablis	**19**	47 47N	3 48 E
Chabounia	**82**	35 30N	2 38 E
Chacabuco	**124**	34 40 S	60 27W
Chachapoyas	**126**	6 15 S	77 50W
Chachro	**68**	25 5N	70 15 E
Chaco □	**124**	26 30 S	61 0W
Chad ■	**81**	15 0N	17 15 E
Chad, L. = Tchad, L.	**81**	13 30N	14 30 E
Chadan	**59**	51 17N	91 35 E
Chadileuvú →	**124**	37 46 S	66 0W
Chadiza	**91**	14 45 S	32 27 E
Chadron	**116**	42 50N	103 0W
Chadyr-Lunga	**56**	46 3N	28 51 E
Chagda	**59**	58 45N	130 38 E
Chagny	**19**	46 57N	4 45 E
Chagoda	**54**	59 10N	35 15 E
Chagos Arch.	**60**	6 0 S	72 0 E
Chágres →	**120**	9 10N	79 40W
Chāh Bahār	**65**	25 20N	60 40 E
Chāh Gay Hills	**65**	29 30N	64 0 E
Chaillé-les-Marais	**20**	46 25N	1 2W
Chaise-Dieu, La	**20**	45 20N	3 40 E
Chaize-le-Vicomte, La	**18**	46 40N	1 18W
Chaj Doab	**68**	32 15N	73 0 E
Chajari	**124**	30 42 S	58 0W
Chake Chake	**90**	5 15 S	39 45 E
Chakhansur	**65**	31 10N	62 0 E
Chakhansur □	**65**	30 0N	62 0 E
Chakonipau, L.	**107**	56 18N	68 30W
Chakradharpur	**69**	22 45N	85 40 E
Chakwal	**68**	32 56N	72 53 E
Chala	**126**	15 48 S	74 20W
Chalais	**20**	45 16N	0 3 E
Chalakudi	**70**	10 18N	76 20 E
Chalcis = Khalkís	**45**	38 27N	23 42 E
Chaleur B.	**107**	47 55N	65 30W
Chalhuanca	**126**	14 15 S	73 15W
Chalindrey	**19**	47 48N	5 26 E
Chaling	**77**	26 58N	113 30 E
Chalisgaon	**70**	20 30N	75 10 E
Chalkar	**57**	50 35N	51 52 E
Chalkar Oz.	**57**	50 33N	51 45 E
Chalky Inlet	**101**	46 3 S	166 31 E
Challans	**18**	46 50N	1 52W
Challapata	**126**	18 53 S	66 50W
Challerange	**19**	49 18N	4 46 E
Challis	**118**	44 32N	114 25W
Chalna	**69**	22 36N	89 35 E
Chalon-sur-Saône	**19**	46 48N	4 50 E
Chalonnes	**18**	47 20N	0 45W
Châlons-sur-Marne	**19**	48 58N	4 20 E
Châlus	**20**	45 39N	0 58 E
Cham	**25**	49 12N	12 40 E
Chama	**119**	36 54N	106 35W
Chaman	**66**	30 58N	66 25 E
Chamarajnagar-Ramasamudram	**70**	11 52N	76 52 E
Chamartín de la Rosa	**32**	40 28N	3 40W
Chamba	**68**	32 35N	76 10 E
Chambal →	**69**	26 29N	79 15 E
Chamberlain	**116**	43 50N	99 21W
Chambers	**119**	35 13N	109 30W
Chambersburg	**114**	39 53N	77 41W
Chambéry	**21**	45 34N	5 55 E
Chambly	**113**	45 27N	73 17W
Chambois	**18**	48 48N	0 6 E
Chambon-Feugerolles, Le	**21**	45 24N	4 18 E
Chambord	**107**	48 25N	72 6W
Chambri L.	**98**	4 15 S	143 10 E
Chamical	**124**	30 22 S	66 27W
Chamonix	**21**	45 55N	6 51 E
Champa	**69**	22 2N	82 43 E
Champagne, Can.	**108**	60 49N	136 30W
Champagne, France	**19**	49 0N	4 40 E
Champagne, Plaine de	**19**	49 0N	4 30 E
Champagnole	**19**	46 45N	5 55 E
Champaign	**114**	40 8N	88 14W
Champaubert	**19**	48 50N	3 45 E
Champdeniers	**20**	46 29N	0 25W
Champeix	**20**	45 37N	3 8 E
Champion B.	**96**	28 44 S	114 36 E
Champlain, Can.	**106**	46 27N	72 24W
Champlain, U.S.A.	**114**	44 59N	73 27W
Champlain, L.	**114**	44 30N	73 20W
Champotón	**120**	19 20N	90 50W
Chamusca	**31**	39 21N	8 29W
Chañaral	**124**	26 23 S	70 40W
Chanasma	**68**	23 44N	72 5 E
Chandalar	**104**	67 30N	148 35W
Chandannagar	**69**	22 52N	88 24 E
Chandausi	**68**	28 27N	78 49 E
Chandeleur Is.	**117**	29 48N	88 51W
Chandeleur Sd.	**117**	29 58N	88 40W
Chandigarh	**68**	30 43N	76 47 E
Chandler, Can.	**107**	48 18N	64 46W
Chandler, Ariz., U.S.A.	**119**	33 20N	111 56W
Chandler, Okla., U.S.A.	**117**	35 43N	96 53W
Chandmani	**75**	45 22N	98 2 E
Chandpur, Bangla.	**69**	23 8N	90 45 E
Chandpur, India	**68**	29 8N	78 19 E
Chandrapur	**70**	19 57N	79 25 E
Chang	**68**	26 59N	68 30 E
Chang Jiang →, Jiangsu, China	**75**	31 48N	121 10 E
Chang Jiang →, Shanghai, China	**75**	31 35N	121 15 E
Changanacheri	**70**	9 25N	76 31 E
Changbai	**76**	41 25N	128 5 E
Changbai Shan	**76**	42 20N	129 0 E
Changchiak'ou = Zhangjiakou	**76**	40 48N	114 55 E
Ch'angchou = Changzhou	**75**	31 47N	119 58 E
Changchun	**76**	43 57N	125 17 E
Changde	**75**	29 4N	111 35 E
Changfeng	**77**	32 28N	117 10 E
Changhai = Shanghai	**75**	31 15N	121 26 E
Changjiang	**75**	19 20N	108 55 E
Changjin-chŏsuji	**76**	40 30N	127 15 E
Changle	**77**	25 59N	119 27 E
Changli	**76**	39 40N	119 13 E
Changning	**77**	26 28N	112 22 E
Changping	**76**	40 14N	116 12 E
Changsha	**75**	28 12N	113 0 E
Changshou	**77**	29 51N	107 8 E
Changshu	**77**	31 38N	120 43 E
Changshun	**77**	26 3N	106 25 E
Changtai	**77**	24 35N	117 42 E
Changting	**75**	25 50N	116 22 E
Changyang	**77**	30 30N	111 10 E
Changzhi	**76**	36 10N	113 6 E
Changzhou	**75**	31 47N	119 58 E
Chanhanga	**92**	16 0 S	14 8 E
Chanlar	**57**	40 25N	46 10 E
Channapatna	**70**	12 40N	77 15 E
Channel Is., U.K.	**18**	49 30N	2 40W
Channel Is., U.S.A.	**119**	33 55N	119 26W
Channel-Port aux Basques	**107**	47 30N	59 9W
Channing, Mich., U.S.A.	**114**	46 9N	88 1W
Channing, Tex., U.S.A.	**117**	35 45N	102 20W
Chantada	**30**	42 36N	7 46W
Chanthaburi	**71**	12 38N	102 12 E
Chantilly	**19**	49 12N	2 29 E
Chantonnay	**18**	46 40N	1 3W
Chantrey Inlet	**104**	67 48N	96 20W
Chanute	**117**	37 45N	95 25W
Chanza →	**31**	37 32N	7 30W
Chao Hu	**77**	31 30N	117 30 E
Chao Phraya →	**71**	13 32N	100 36 E
Chao'an	**75**	23 42N	116 32 E
Chaoyang, Guangdong, China	**75**	23 17N	116 30 E
Chaoyang, Liaoning, China	**76**	41 35N	120 22 E
Chapala	**91**	15 50 S	37 35 E
Chapala, Lago de	**120**	20 10N	103 20W
Chapayevo	**57**	50 25N	51 10 E
Chapayevsk	**55**	53 0N	49 40 E
Chapecó	**125**	27 14 S	52 41W
Chapel Hill	**115**	35 53N	79 3W
Chapelle-d'Angillon, La	**19**	47 21N	2 25 E
Chapelle-Glain, La	**18**	47 38N	1 11W
Chapleau	**106**	47 50N	83 24W
Chaplin	**109**	50 28N	106 40W
Chaplino	**56**	48 8N	36 15 E
Chaplygin	**55**	53 15N	40 0 E
Chapra	**69**	25 48N	84 44 E
Châr	**80**	21 32N	12 45 E
Chara	**59**	56 54N	118 20 E
Charadai	**124**	27 35 S	60 0W
Charagua	**126**	19 45 S	63 10W
Charaña	**126**	17 30 S	69 25W
Charata	**124**	27 13 S	61 14W
Charcas	**120**	23 10N	101 20W
Charcoal L.	**109**	58 49N	102 22W
Charcot I.	**5**	70 0 S	75 0W
Chard	**13**	50 52N	2 59W
Chardara	**58**	41 16N	67 59 E
Chardon	**112**	41 34N	81 17W
Chardzhou	**58**	39 6N	63 34 E
Charente	**20**	45 40N	0 5 E
Charente □	**20**	45 50N	0 16 E
Charente →	**20**	45 57N	1 5W
Charente-Maritime □	**20**	45 30N	0 35W
Charentsavan	**57**	40 35N	44 41 E
Chārīkār	**65**	35 0N	69 10 E
Charité, La	**19**	47 10N	3 0 E
Chariton →	**116**	39 19N	92 58W
Charkhari	**69**	25 24N	79 45 E
Charkhi Dadri	**68**	28 37N	76 17 E
Charleroi	**16**	50 24N	4 27 E
Charlerol	**112**	40 8N	79 54W
Charles, C.	**114**	37 10N	75 59W
Charles City	**116**	43 2N	92 41W
Charles L.	**109**	59 50N	110 33W
Charles Town	**114**	39 20N	77 50W
Charleston, Ill., U.S.A.	**114**	39 30N	88 10W
Charleston, Miss., U.S.A.	**117**	34 2N	90 3W
Charleston, Mo., U.S.A.	**117**	36 52N	89 20W
Charleston, S.C., U.S.A.	**115**	32 47N	79 56W
Charleston, W. Va., U.S.A.	**114**	38 24N	81 36W
Charleston Harb.	**115**	32 46N	79 55W
Charlestown, S. Afr.	**93**	27 26 S	29 53 E
Charlestown, U.S.A.	**114**	38 29N	85 40W
Charlesville	**88**	5 27 S	20 59 E
Charleville	**97**	26 24 S	146 15 E
Charleville = Rath Luirc	**15**	52 21N	8 40W
Charleville-Mézières	**19**	49 44N	4 40 E
Charlevoix	**114**	45 19N	85 14W
Charlieu	**21**	46 10N	4 10 E
Charlotte, Mich., U.S.A.	**114**	42 36N	84 48W
Charlotte, N.C., U.S.A.	**115**	35 16N	80 46W
Charlotte Amalie	**121**	18 22N	64 56W
Charlotte Harbor	**115**	26 58N	82 4W
Charlotte Waters	**96**	25 56 S	134 54 E
Charlottenberg	**48**	59 54N	12 17 E
Charlottesville	**114**	38 1N	78 30W
Charlottetown	**107**	46 14N	63 8W
Charlton, Austral.	**99**	36 16 S	143 24 E
Charlton, U.S.A.	**116**	40 59N	93 20W
Charlton I.	**106**	52 0N	79 20W
Charmes	**19**	48 22N	6 17 E
Charny	**107**	46 43N	71 15W
Charolles	**21**	46 27N	4 16 E
Charost	**19**	47 0N	2 7 E
Charouine	**82**	29 0N	0 15W
Charre	**91**	17 13 S	35 10 E
Charroux	**20**	46 9N	0 25 E
Charters Towers	**97**	20 5 S	146 13 E
Chartre, La	**18**	47 42N	0 34 E
Chartres	**18**	48 29N	1 30 E
Chascomús	**124**	35 30 S	58 0W
Chasefu	**91**	11 55 S	33 8 E
Chasovnya-Uchurskaya	**59**	57 15N	132 50 E
Chasseneuil-sur-Bonnieure	**20**	45 52N	0 29 E
Chata	**68**	27 42N	77 30 E
Châtaigneraie, La	**18**	46 38N	0 45W
Chatal Balkan = Udvoy Balkan	**43**	42 50N	26 50 E.
Château-Chinon	**19**	47 4N	3 56 E
Château-du-Loir	**18**	47 40N	0 25 E
Château-Gontier	**18**	47 50N	0 48W
Château-la-Vallière	**18**	47 30N	0 20 E
Château-Landon	**19**	48 8N	2 40 E
Château, Le	**20**	45 52N	1 12W
Château-Porcien	**19**	49 31N	4 13 E
Château-Renault	**18**	47 36N	0 56 E
Château-Salins	**19**	48 50N	6 30 E
Château-Thierry	**19**	49 3N	3 20 E
Châteaubourg	**18**	48 7N	1 25W
Châteaubriant	**18**	47 43N	1 23W
Châteaudun	**18**	48 3N	1 20 E
Châteaugiron	**18**	48 3N	1 30W
Châteauguay	**113**	45 23N	73 45W
Châteaulin	**18**	48 11N	4 8W
Châteaumeillant	**20**	46 35N	2 12 E
Châteauneuf	**18**	48 35N	1 15 E
Châteauneuf-du-Faou	**18**	48 11N	3 50W
Châteauneuf-sur-Charente	**20**	45 36N	0 3W
Châteauneuf-sur-Cher	**19**	46 52N	2 18 E
Châteauneuf-sur-Loire	**19**	47 52N	2 13 E
Châteaurenard	**21**	43 53N	4 51 E
Châteauroux	**19**	46 50N	1 40 E
Châteaux-Arnoux	**21**	44 6N	6 0 E
Châtelaillon-Plage	**20**	46 5N	1 5W
Châtelaudren	**18**	48 33N	2 59W
Châtelet, Le, Cher, France	**20**	46 40N	2 20 E
Châtelet, Le, Seine-et-Marne, France	**19**	48 30N	2 47 E
Châtelguyon	**20**	45 55N	3 4 E
Châtellerault	**18**	46 50N	0 30 E
Châtelus-Malvaleix	**20**	46 18N	2 1 E
Chatfield	**116**	43 15N	91 58W
Chatham, N.B., Can.	**107**	47 2N	65 28W
Chatham, Ont., Can.	**106**	42 24N	82 11W
Chatham, U.K.	**13**	51 22N	0 32 E
Chatham, La., U.S.A.	**117**	32 22N	92 26W
Chatham, N.Y., U.S.A.	**113**	42 21N	73 32W
Chatham Is.	**94**	44 0 S	176 40W
Chatham Str.	**108**	57 0N	134 40W
Châtillon, Loiret, France	**19**	47 36N	2 44 E
Châtillon, Marne, France	**19**	49 5N	3 43 E
Chatillon	**38**	45 45N	7 40 E
Châtillon-Coligny	**19**	47 50N	2 51 E
Châtillon-en-Bazois	**19**	47 3N	3 39 E
Châtillon-en-Diois	**21**	44 41N	5 29 E
Châtillon-sur-Indre	**18**	46 59N	1 10 E
Châtillon-sur-Seine	**19**	47 50N	4 33 E
Châtillon-sur-Sèvre	**18**	46 56N	0 45W
Chatmohar	**69**	24 15N	89 15 E
Chatra	**69**	24 12N	84 56 E
Chatrapur	**69**	19 22N	85 2 E
Châtre, La	**20**	46 35N	1 59 E
Chats, L. des	**113**	45 30N	76 20W
Chatsworth, Can.	**112**	44 27N	80 54W
Chatsworth, Zimb.	**91**	19 38 S	31 13 E
Chattahoochee	**115**	30 43N	84 51W
Chattanooga	**115**	35 2N	85 17W
Chaudanne, Barrage de	**21**	43 51N	6 32 E
Chaudes-Aigues	**20**	44 51N	3 1 E
Chauffailles	**21**	46 13N	4 20 E
Chauk	**67**	20 53N	94 49 E
Chaukan La	**67**	27 0N	97 15 E
Chaulnes	**19**	49 48N	2 47 E
Chaumont, France	**19**	48 7N	5 8 E
Chaumont, U.S.A.	**113**	44 4N	76 9W
Chaumont-en-Vexin	**19**	49 16N	1 53 E
Chaumont-sur-Loire	**18**	47 29N	1 11 E
Chaunay	**20**	46 13N	0 9 E
Chauny	**19**	49 37N	3 12 E
Chausey, Îs.	**18**	48 52N	1 49W
Chaussin	**19**	46 59N	5 22 E
Chautauqua	**112**	42 17N	79 30W
Chauvigny	**18**	46 34N	0 39 E
Chauvin	**109**	52 45N	110 10W
Chaux-de-Fonds, La	**25**	47 7N	6 50 E
Chaves, Brazil	**127**	0 15 S	49 55W
Chaves, Port.	**30**	41 45N	7 32W
Chavuma	**89**	13 4 S	22 40 E
Chaykovskiy	**52**	56 47N	54 9 E
Chazelles-sur-Lyon	**21**	45 39N	4 22 E
Chazy	**113**	44 52N	73 28W
Cheb (Eger)	**26**	50 9N	12 28 E
Cheboksary	**55**	56 8N	47 12 E
Cheboygan	**114**	45 38N	84 29W
Chebsara	**55**	59 10N	38 59 E
Chech, Erg	**82**	25 0N	2 15W
Chechaouen	**82**	35 9N	5 15W
Chechen, Os.	**57**	43 59N	47 40 E
Checheno-Ingush A.S.S.R. □	**57**	43 30N	45 29 E
Chęciny	**28**	50 46N	20 28 E
Checleset B.	**108**	50 5N	127 35W
Checotah	**117**	35 31N	95 30W
Chedabucto B.	**107**	45 25N	61 8W
Cheduba I.	**67**	18 45N	93 40 E
Cheepie	**99**	26 33 S	145 1 E
Chef-Boutonne	**20**	46 7N	0 4W
Chegdomyn	**59**	51 7N	133 1 E
Chegga	**82**	25 27N	5 40W
Chehalis	**118**	46 44N	122 59W
Cheiron	**21**	43 49N	6 58 E
Cheju Do	**77**	33 29N	126 34 E
Chekalin	**55**	54 10N	36 10 E
Chekiang = Zhejiang □	**75**	29 0N	120 0 E
Chela, Sa. da	**92**	16 20 S	13 20 E
Chelan	**118**	47 49N	120 0W
Chelan, L.	**108**	48 5N	120 30W
Cheleken	**53**	39 26N	53 7 E
Chelforó	**128**	39 0 S	66 33W
Chéliff, O. →	**82**	36 0N	0 8 E
Chelkar	**58**	47 48N	59 39 E
Chelkar Tengiz, Solonchak	**58**	48 0N	62 30 E
Chellala Dahrania	**82**	33 2N	0 1 E
Chelles	**19**	48 52N	2 33 E
Chełm	**28**	51 8N	23 30 E
Chełm □	**28**	51 15N	23 30 E
Chełmek	**27**	50 6N	19 16 E
Chełmno	**28**	53 20N	18 30 E
Chelmsford	**13**	51 44N	0 29 E

Chelmsford Dam Cilician Gates P.

Chelmsford Dam 93 27 55 S 29 59 E
Chelmża 28 53 10N 18 39 E
Chelsea, Austral. 100 38 5 S 145 8 E
Chelsea, Can. 113 45 30N 75 47W
Chelsea, Okla., U.S.A. 117 36 35N 95 35W
Chelsea, Vt., U.S.A. 113 43 59N 72 27W
Cheltenham 13 51 55N 2 5W
Chelva 32 39 45N 1 0W
Chelyabinsk 58 55 10N 61 24 E
Chemainus 108 48 55N 123 42W
Chemillé 18 47 14N 0 45W
Chemnitz = Karl-Marx-Stadt 24 50 50N 12 55 E
Chemult 118 43 14N 121 47W
Chen, Gora 59 65 16N 141 50 E
Chen Xian 75 25 47N 113 1 E
Chenab → 68 30 23N 71 2 E
Chenachane, O. → 82 25 20N 3 20W
Chenango Forks 113 42 15N 75 51W
Chencha 87 6 15N 37 32 E
Chenchiang = Zhenjiang 75 32 12N 119 24 E
Cheney 118 47 29N 117 34W
Chengbu 77 26 18N 110 16 E
Chengcheng 77 35 8N 109 56 E
Chengde 76 40 59N 117 58 E
Chengdu 75 30 38N 104 2 E
Chenggu 77 33 10N 107 21 E
Chengjiang 75 24 39N 103 0 E
Ch'engtu = Chengdu 75 30 38N 104 2 E
Chengyang 76 36 18N 120 21 E
Chenxi 77 28 2N 110 12 E
Cheo Reo 71 13 25N 108 28 E
Cheom Ksan 71 14 13N 104 56 E
Chepelare 43 41 44N 24 40 E
Chepén 126 7 15 S 79 23W
Chepes 124 31 20 S 65 35W
Chepo 121 9 10N 79 6W
Cheptsa → 55 58 36N 50 4 E
Cheptulil, Mt. 90 1 25N 35 35 E
Chequamegon B. 116 46 40N 90 30W
Cher □ 19 47 10N 2 30 E
Cher → 18 47 21N 0 29 E
Cheran 69 25 45N 90 44 E
Cherasco 38 44 39N 7 50 E
Cheraw 115 34 42N 79 54W
Cherbourg 18 49 39N 1 40W
Cherchell 82 36 35N 2 12 E
Cherdakly 55 54 25N 48 50 E
Cherdyn 52 60 24N 56 29 E
Cheremkhovo 59 53 8N 103 1 E
Cherepanovo 58 54 15N 83 30 E
Cherepovets 55 59 5N 37 55 E
Chergui, Chott ech 82 34 21N 0 25 E
Cherikov 54 53 32N 31 20 E
Cherkassy 56 49 27N 32 4 E
Cherkessk 57 44 15N 42 5 E
Cherlak 58 54 15N 74 55 E
Chernaya Kholunitsa 55 58 51N 51 52 E
Cherni 43 42 35N 23 18 E
Chernigov 54 51 28N 31 20 E
Chernikovsk 52 54 48N 56 8 E
Chernobyl 54 51 13N 30 15 E
Chernogorsk 59 53 49N 91 18 E
Chernomorskoye 56 45 31N 32 40 E
Chernovskoye 55 58 48N 47 20 E
Chernovtsy 56 48 15N 25 52 E
Chernoye 59 70 30N 89 10 E
Chernyakhovsk 54 54 36N 21 48 E
Chernyshkovskiy 57 48 30N 42 13 E
Chernyshovskiy 59 63 0N 112 30 E
Cherokee, Iowa, U.S.A. 116 42 40N 95 30W
Cherokee, Okla., U.S.A. 117 36 45N 98 25W
Cherokees, L. O'The 117 36 50N 95 12W
Cherquenco 128 38 35 S 72 0W
Cherrapunji 67 25 17N 91 47 E
Cherry Creek 118 39 50N 114 58W
Cherryvale 117 37 20N 95 33W
Cherskiy 59 68 45N 161 18 E
Cherskogo Khrebet 59 65 0N 143 0 E
Chertkovo 57 49 25N 40 19 E
Cherven 54 53 45N 28 28 E
Cherven-Bryag 43 43 17N 24 7 E
Chervonograd 54 50 25N 24 10 E
Cherwell → 13 51 46N 1 18W
Chesapeake 114 36 43N 76 15W
Chesapeake Bay 114 38 0N 76 12W
Cheshire □ 12 53 14N 2 30W
Cheshskaya Guba 52 67 20N 47 0 E
Cheslatta L. 108 53 49N 125 20W
Chesley 112 44 17N 81 5W
Chesne, Le 19 49 30N 4 45 E
Cheste 33 39 30N 0 41W
Chester, U.K. 12 53 12N 2 53W
Chester, Calif., U.S.A. 118 40 22N 121 14W
Chester, Ill., U.S.A. 117 37 58N 89 50W
Chester, Mont., U.S.A. 118 48 31N 111 0W
Chester, N.Y., U.S.A. 113 41 22N 74 16W
Chester, Pa., U.S.A. 114 39 54N 75 20W
Chester, S.C., U.S.A. 115 34 44N 81 13W
Chesterfield 12 53 14N 1 26W
Chesterfield, Îles 94 19 52 S 158 15 E
Chesterfield In. 104 63 25N 90 45W
Chesterfield Inlet 104 63 30N 90 45W
Chesterton Range 99 25 30 S 147 27 E
Chesterville 113 45 6N 75 14W
Chesuncook L. 107 46 0N 69 10W
Chetaibi 83 37 1N 7 20 E
Chéticamp 107 46 37N 60 59W
Chetumal 120 18 30N 88 20W
Chetumal, Bahía de 120 18 40N 88 10W
Chetwynd 108 55 45N 121 36W
Chevanceaux 20 45 18N 0 14W
Cheviot Hills 12 55 20N 2 30W
Cheviot Ra. 99 25 20 S 143 45 E
Cheviot, The 12 55 29N 2 8W
Chew Bahir 87 4 40N 36 50 E
Chewelah 118 48 17N 117 43W
Cheyenne, Okla., U.S.A. 117 35 35N 99 40W
Cheyenne, Wyo., U.S.A. 116 41 9N 104 49W
Cheyenne → 116 44 40N 101 15W
Cheyenne Wells 116 38 51N 102 10W
Cheylard, Le 21 44 55N 4 25 E
Chhabra 68 24 40N 76 54 E
Chhatarpur 69 24 55N 79 35 E
Chhindwara 68 22 2N 78 59 E
Chhlong 71 12 15N 105 58 E
Chi → 71 15 11N 104 43 E
Chiamis 73 7 20 S 108 21 E
Chiamussu = Jiamusi 75 46 40N 130 26 E
Chiang Mai 71 18 47N 98 59 E
Chiange 89 15 35 S 13 40 E
Chiapa → 120 16 42N 93 0W
Chiapas □ 120 17 0N 92 45W
Chiaramonte Gulfi 41 37 1N 14 41 E
Chiaravalle 39 43 38N 13 17 E
Chiaravalle Centrale 41 38 41N 16 25 E
Chiari 38 45 31N 9 55 E
Chiatura 57 42 15N 43 17 E
Chiávari 38 44 20N 9 20 E
Chiavenna 38 46 18N 9 23 E
Chiba 74 35 30N 140 7 E
Chiba □ 74 35 30N 140 20 E
Chibabava 93 20 17 S 33 35 E
Chibatu 73 7 6 S 107 59 E
Chibemba, Angola 89 15 48 S 14 8 E
Chibemba, Angola 92 16 20 S 15 20 E
Chibia 89 15 10 S 13 42 E
Chibougamau 106 49 56N 74 24W
Chibougamau L. 106 49 50N 74 20W
Chibuk 85 10 52N 12 50 E
Chic-Chocs, Mts. 107 48 55N 66 0W
Chicacole = Srikakulam 70 18 14N 84 4 E
Chicago 114 41 53N 87 40W
Chicago Heights 114 41 29N 87 37W
Chichagof I. 108 58 0N 136 0W
Chichaoua 82 31 32N 8 44W
Chichén Itzá 120 20 40N 88 32W
Chichester 13 50 50N 0 47W
Chichibu 74 36 5N 139 10 E
Ch'ich'ihaerh = Qiqihar 75 47 26N 124 0 E
Chickasha 117 35 0N 98 0W
Chiclana de la Frontera 31 36 26N 6 9W
Chiclayo 126 6 42 S 79 50W
Chico 118 39 45N 121 54W
Chico →, Chubut, Argent. 118 44 0 S 67 0W
Chico →, Santa Cruz, Argent. 128 50 0 S 68 30W
Chicomo 93 24 31 S 34 6 E
Chicopee 114 42 6N 72 37W
Chicoutimi 107 48 28N 71 5W
Chidambaram 70 11 20N 79 45 E
Chidenguele 93 24 55 S 34 11 E
Chidley C. 105 60 23N 64 26W
Chiede 92 17 15 S 16 22 E
Chiefs Pt. 112 44 41N 81 18W
Chiemsee 25 47 53N 12 27 E
Chiengi 91 8 45 S 29 10 E
Chienti → 39 43 18N 13 45 E
Chieri 38 45 0N 7 50 E
Chiers → 19 49 39N 5 0 E
Chiese → 38 45 8N 10 25 E
Chieti 39 42 22N 14 10 E
Chifeng 76 42 18N 118 58 E
Chigirin 56 49 4N 32 38 E
Chignecto B. 107 45 30N 64 40W
Chiguana 124 21 0 S 67 58W
Chihli, G. of = Bo Hai 76 39 0N 120 0 E
Chihuahua 120 28 40N 106 3W
Chihuahua □ 120 28 40N 106 3W
Chiili 58 44 20N 66 15 E
Chik Bollapur 70 13 25N 77 45 E
Chikhli 68 20 20N 76 18 E
Chikmagalur 70 13 15N 75 45 E
Chikodi 70 16 26N 74 38 E
Chikwawa 91 16 2 S 34 50 E
Chilako → 108 53 53N 122 57W
Chilanga 91 15 33 S 28 16 E
Chilapa 120 17 40N 99 11W
Chilas 69 35 25N 74 5 E
Chilcotin → 108 51 44N 122 23W
Childers 97 25 15 S 152 17 E
Childress 117 34 30N 100 15W
Chile ■ 128 35 0 S 72 0W
Chile Rise 95 38 0 S 92 0W
Chilecito 124 29 10 S 67 30W
Chilete 126 7 10 S 78 50W
Chililabombwe 91 12 18 S 27 43 E
Chilin = Jilin 76 43 55N 126 30 E
Chilka L. 69 19 40N 85 25 E
Chilko → 108 52 0N 123 40W
Chilko, L. 108 51 20N 124 10W
Chillagoe 97 17 7 S 144 33 E
Chillán 124 36 40 S 72 10W
Chillicothe, Ill., U.S.A. 116 40 55N 89 32W
Chillicothe, Mo., U.S.A. 116 39 45N 93 30W
Chillicothe, Ohio, U.S.A. 114 39 20N 82 58W
Chilliwack 108 49 10N 121 54W
Chilo 68 27 25N 73 32 E
Chiloane, I. 93 20 40 S 34 55 E
Chiloé, I. de 128 42 30 S 73 50W
Chilpancingo 120 17 30N 99 30W
Chiltern Hills 13 51 44N 0 42W
Chilton 114 44 1N 88 12W
Chiluage 88 9 30 S 21 50 E
Chilubula 91 10 14 S 30 51 E
Chilumba 91 10 28 S 34 12 E
Chilwa, L. 91 15 15 S 35 40 E
Chimacum 118 48 1N 122 46W
Chimay 16 50 3N 4 20 E
Chimbay 58 42 57N 59 47 E
Chimborazo 126 1 29 S 78 55W
Chimbote 126 9 0 S 78 35W
Chimishliya 46 46 34N 28 44 E
Chimkent 58 42 18N 69 36 E
Chimoio 91 19 4 S 33 30 E
Chimpembe 91 9 31 S 29 33 E
Chin □ 67 22 0N 93 0 E
Chin Ling Shan = Qinling Shandi 77 33 50N 108 10 E
China 120 25 40N 99 20W
China ■ 75 30 0N 110 0 E
Chinan = Jinan 76 36 38N 117 1 E
Chinandega 121 12 35N 87 12W
Chinati Pk. 117 30 0N 104 25W
Chincha Alta 126 13 25 S 76 7W
Chinchilla 99 26 45 S 150 38 E
Chinchilla de Monte Aragón 33 38 53N 1 40W
Chinchón 32 40 9N 3 26W
Chinchorro, Banco 120 18 35N 87 20W
Chinchou = Jinzhou 76 41 5N 121 3 E
Chincoteague 114 37 58N 75 21W
Chinde 91 18 35 S 36 30 E
Chindwin → 67 21 26N 95 15 E
Chinga 91 15 13 S 38 35 E
Chingleput 70 12 42N 79 58 E
Chingola 91 12 31 S 27 53 E
Chingole 91 13 4 S 34 17 E
Ch'ingtao = Qingdao 76 36 5N 120 20 E
Chinguetti 80 20 25N 12 24W
Chingune 93 20 33 S 35 0 E
Chinhae 76 35 9N 128 47 E
Chinhanguanine 93 25 21 S 32 30 E
Chiniot 68 31 45N 73 0 E
Chinju 76 35 12N 128 2 E
Chinle 119 36 14N 109 38W
Chinnamanur 70 9 50N 77 24 E
Chinnampo 76 38 52N 125 10 E
Chinnur 70 18 57N 79 49 E
Chino Valley 119 34 54N 112 28W
Chinon 18 47 10N 0 15 E
Chinook, Can. 109 51 28N 110 59W
Chinook, U.S.A. 118 48 35N 109 19W
Chinsali 91 10 30 S 32 2 E
Chintamani 70 13 26N 78 3 E
Chióggia 39 45 13N 12 15 E
Chios = Khios 45 38 27N 26 9 E
* Chipai L. 106 52 56N 87 53W
Chipata 91 13 38 S 32 28 E
Chipatujah 73 7 45 S 108 0 E
Chipewyan L. 109 58 0N 98 27W
Chipinga 91 20 13 S 32 28 E
Chipiona 31 36 44N 6 26W
Chipley 115 30 45N 85 32W
Chiplun 70 17 31N 73 34 E
Chipman 107 46 6N 65 53W
Chipoka 91 13 57 S 34 28 E
Chippawa 112 43 5N 79 2W
Chippenham 13 51 27N 2 7W
Chippewa → 116 44 25N 92 10W
Chippewa Falls 116 44 55N 91 22W
Chiprovtsi 42 43 24N 22 52 E
Chiquián 126 10 10 S 77 0W
Chiquimula 120 14 51N 89 37W
Chiquinquira 126 5 37N 73 50W
Chir → 57 48 30N 43 0 E
Chirala 70 15 50N 80 26 E
Chiramba 91 16 55 S 34 39 E
Chirawa 68 28 14N 75 42 E
Chirayinkil 70 8 41N 76 49 E
Chirchik 58 41 29N 69 35 E
Chirfa 83 20 55N 12 22 E
Chiricahua Pk. 119 31 53N 109 14W
Chirikof I. 104 55 50N 155 40W
Chiriquí, Golfo de 121 8 0N 82 10W
Chiriquí, Lago de 121 9 10N 82 0W
† Chiriquí, Vol. de 121 8 55N 82 35W
Chirivira Falls 91 21 10 S 32 12 E
Chirnogi 46 44 7N 26 32 E
Chirpan 43 42 10N 25 19 E
Chirripó Grande, Cerro 121 9 29N 83 29W
Chisamba 91 14 55 S 28 20 E
Chisholm 108 54 55N 114 10W
Chishtian Mandi 68 29 50N 72 55 E
Chisimaio 79 0 22 S 42 32 E
Chisimba Falls 91 10 12 S 30 56 E
Chisineu Criş 42 46 32N 21 37 E
Chisone → 38 44 49N 7 25 E
Chisos Mts. 117 29 20N 103 15W
Chistopol 55 55 25N 50 38 E
Chita 59 52 0N 113 35 E
Chitapur 70 17 10N 77 5 E
Chitembo 89 13 30 S 16 50 E
Chitipa 91 9 41 S 33 19 E
Chitokoloki 89 13 50 S 23 13 E
Chitorgarh 68 24 52N 74 38 E
Chitrakot 70 19 10N 81 40 E
Chitral 66 35 50N 71 56 E
Chitravati → 70 14 45N 78 15 E
Chitré 121 7 59N 80 27W
Chittagong 67 22 19N 91 48 E
Chittagong □ 67 24 5N 91 0 E
Chittoor 70 13 15N 79 5 E
Chittur 70 10 40N 76 45 E
Chiusa 39 46 38N 11 34 E
Chiusi 39 43 1N 11 58 E
Chiva 33 39 27N 0 41W
Chivasso 38 45 10N 7 52 E
Chivilcoy 124 34 55 S 60 0W
Chiwanda 91 11 23 S 34 55 E
Chizela 91 13 10 S 25 0 E
Chkalov = Orenburg 52 52 0N 55 5 E
Chkolovsk 55 56 50N 43 10 E
Chlumec 26 50 9N 15 29 E
Chmielnik 28 50 37N 20 43 E
Choba 90 2 30N 38 5 E
Chobe National Park 92 18 0 S 25 0 E
Chocianów 28 51 27N 15 55 E
Chociwel 28 53 29N 15 21 E
Chodaków 28 52 16N 20 18 E
Chodavaram 70 17 50N 82 57 E
Chodecz 28 52 24N 19 2 E
Chodziez 28 52 58N 16 58 E
Choele Choel 128 39 11 S 65 40W
Choisy-le-Roi 19 48 45N 2 24 E
Choix 120 26 40N 108 23W
Chojna 28 52 58N 14 25 E
Chojnice 28 53 42N 17 32 E
Chojnów 28 51 18N 15 58 E
Choke Mts. 87 11 18N 37 15 E
Chokurdakh 59 70 38N 147 55 E
Cholet 18 47 4N 0 52W
Choluteca 121 13 20N 87 14W
Choma 91 16 48 S 26 59 E
Chomen Swamp 87 9 20N 37 10 E
Chomu 68 27 15N 75 40 E
Chomutov 26 50 28N 13 23 E
Chon Buri 71 13 21N 101 1 E
Chonan 76 36 48N 127 9 E
Chone 126 0 40 S 80 0W
Chong'an 77 27 45N 118 0 E
Chongde 77 30 32N 120 26 E
Chongjin 76 41 47N 129 50 E
Chŏngju 76 39 40N 125 5 E
Chŏngju 76 36 39N 127 27 E
Chongli 76 40 58N 115 15 E
Chongqing 75 29 35N 106 25 E
Chongzuo 77 22 23N 107 20 E
Chŏnju 76 35 50N 127 4 E
Chonming Dao 77 31 40N 121 30 E
Chonos, Arch. de los 128 45 0 S 75 0W
Chopda 68 21 20N 75 15 E
Chopim → 125 25 35 S 53 5W
Chorley 12 53 39N 2 39W
Chorolque, Cerro 124 20 59 S 66 5W
Choroszcz 28 53 10N 22 59 E
Chorrera, La 120 8 50N 79 50W
Chortkov, U.S.S.R. 54 49 2N 25 46 E
Chortkov, U.S.S.R. 56 49 1N 25 42 E
Chŏrwŏn 76 38 15N 127 10 E
Chorzele 28 53 15N 20 55 E
Chorzów 28 50 18N 18 57 E
Chos-Malal 124 37 20 S 70 15W
Chosan 76 40 50N 125 47 E
Chōshi 74 35 45N 140 51 E
Choszczno 28 53 7N 15 25 E
Choteau 118 47 50N 112 10W
Chotila 68 22 23N 71 15 E
Chowchilla 119 37 11N 120 12W
Choybalsan 75 48 4N 114 30 E
Christchurch, N.Z. 101 43 33 S 172 47 E
Christchurch, U.K. 13 50 44N 1 33W
Christian I. 112 44 50N 80 12W
Christiana 92 27 52 S 25 8 E
Christiansfeld 49 55 21N 9 29 E
Christie B. 109 62 32N 111 10W
Christina → 109 56 40N 111 3W
Christmas I., Ind. Oc. 94 10 30 S 105 40 E
* Christmas I., Pac. Oc. 95 1 58N 157 27W
Chrudim 26 49 58N 15 43 E
Chrzanów 27 50 10N 19 21 E
Chtimba 91 10 35 S 34 13 E
Chu 58 43 36N 73 42 E
Chu → 71 19 53N 105 45 E
Chu Chua 108 51 22N 120 10W
Ch'uanchou = Quanzhou 75 24 55N 118 34 E
Chūbu □ 74 36 45N 137 30 E
Chubut → 128 43 20 S 65 5W
Chuchi L. 108 55 12N 124 30W
Chudovo 54 59 10N 31 41 E
Chudskoye, Oz. 54 58 13N 27 30 E
Chūgoku □ 74 35 0N 133 0 E
Chūgoku-Sanchi 74 35 0N 133 0 E
Chuguyev 56 49 55N 36 45 E
Chugwater 116 41 48N 104 47W
Chukai 71 4 13N 103 25 E
Chukhloma 55 58 45N 42 40 E
Chukotskiy Khrebet 59 68 0N 175 0 E
Chukotskoye More 59 68 0N 175 0W
Chula Vista 119 32 39N 117 8W
Chulman 59 56 52N 124 52 E
Chulucanas 126 5 8 S 80 10W
Chulym → 58 57 43N 83 51 E
Chumbicha 124 29 0 S 66 10W
Chumerna 43 42 45N 25 55 E
Chumikan 59 54 40N 135 10 E
Chumphon 71 10 35N 99 14 E
Chumuare 91 14 31 S 31 50 E
Chuna → 59 57 47N 94 37 E
Chun'an 77 29 35N 119 3 E
Chunchŏn 76 37 58N 127 44 E
Chunga 91 15 0 S 26 2 E
Chungking = Chongqing 75 29 35N 106 25 E
Chunian 68 30 57N 74 0 E
Chunya 91 8 30 S 33 27 E
Chunya □ 90 7 48 S 33 0 E
Chuquibamba 126 15 47 S 72 44W
Chuquicamata 124 22 15 S 69 0W
Chuquisaca □ 126 23 30 S 63 30W
Chur 25 46 52N 9 32 E
Churachandpur 67 24 20N 93 40 E
Churchill 109 58 47N 94 11W
Churchill →, Man., Can. 109 58 47N 94 12W
Churchill →, Newf., Can. 107 53 19N 60 10W
Churchill, C. 109 58 46N 93 12W
Churchill Falls 107 53 36N 64 19W
Churchill L. 109 55 55N 108 20W
Churchill Pk. 108 58 10N 125 10W
Churu 68 28 20N 74 50 E
Chushal 69 33 40N 78 40 E
Chusovoy 52 58 15N 57 40 E
Chuvash A.S.S.R.□ 55 55 30N 47 0 E
Ci Xian 76 36 20N 114 25 E
Ciacova 42 45 35N 21 10 E
Cianjur 73 6 51 S 107 7 E
Cibadok 73 6 53 S 106 47 E
Cibatu 73 7 8 S 107 59 E
Cicero 114 41 48N 87 48W
Cidacos → 32 42 21N 1 38W
Cide 56 41 53N 33 1 E
Ciechanów 28 52 52N 20 38 E
Ciechanów □ 28 53 0N 20 30 E
Ciechanowiec 28 52 40N 22 31 E
Ciechocinek 28 52 53N 18 45 E
Ciego de Avila 121 21 50N 78 50W
Ciénaga 126 11 1N 74 15W
Cienfuegos 121 22 10N 80 30W
Cieplice Śląskie Zdrój 28 50 50N 15 40 E
Cierp 20 42 55N 0 40 E
Cies, Islas 30 42 12N 8 55W
Cieszanów 28 50 14N 23 8 E
Cieszyn 27 49 45N 18 35 E
Cieza 33 38 17N 1 23W
Cifuentes 32 40 47N 2 37W
Cijara, Pantano de 31 39 18N 4 52W
Cijulang 73 7 42 S 108 27 E
Cikajang 73 7 25 S 107 48 E
Cikampek 73 6 23 S 107 28 E
Cilacap 73 7 43 S 109 0 E
Çıldır 57 41 10N 43 20 E
Cilician Gates P. 64 37 20N 34 52 E

* Renamed Wapikopa, L.

† Renamed Barú, Vol.

* Renamed Kiritimati

Cîlnicu Columbus

Cîlnicu **46** 44 54N 23 4 E
Cimahi **73** 6 53 S 107 33 E
Cimarron, Kans., U.S.A. **117** 37 50N 100 20W
Cimarron, N. Mex., U.S.A. **117** 36 30N 104 52W
Cimarron → **117** 36 10N 96 17W
Cimone, Mte. **38** 44 10N 10 40 E
Cîmpic Turzii **46** 46 34N 23 53 E
Cîmpina **46** 45 10N 25 45 E
Cîmpulung, Argeş, Romania **46** 45 17N 25 3 E
Cîmpulung, Moldovenesc, Romania **46** 47 32N 25 30 E
Cîmpuri **43** 46 0N 26 50 E
Cinca → **32** 41 26N 0 21 E
Cincer **42** 43 55N 17 5 E
Cincinnati **114** 39 10N 84 26W
Cîndeşti **46** 45 15N 26 42 E
Ciney **16** 50 18N 5 5 E
Cingoli **39** 43 23N 13 10 E
Cinigiano **39** 42 53N 11 23 E
Cinto, Mt. **21** 42 24N 8 54 E
Ciorani **46** 44 45N 26 25 E
Ciotat, La **21** 43 12N 5 36 E
Čiovo **39** 43 30N 16 17 E
Circeo, Monte **40** 41 14N 13 3 E
Circle, Alaska, U.S.A. **104** 65 50N 144 10W
Circle, Montana, U.S.A. **116** 47 26N 105 35W
Circleville, Ohio, U.S.A. **114** 39 35N 82 57W
Circleville, Utah, U.S.A. **119** 38 12N 112 24W
Cirebon **73** 6 45 S 108 32 E
Cirencester **13** 51 43N 1 59W
Cireşu **46** 44 47N 22 31 E
Cirey-sur-Vezouze **19** 48 35N 6 57 E
Ciriè **38** 45 14N 7 35 E
Cirò **41** 39 23N 17 3 E
Cisco **117** 32 25N 99 0W
Cislău **46** 45 14N 26 20 E
Cisna **27** 49 12N 22 20 E
Cisnădie **46** 45 42N 24 9 E
Cisterna di Latina **40** 41 35N 12 50 E
Cisternino **41** 40 45N 17 26 E
Citeli-Ckaro **57** 41 33N 46 0 E
Citlaltépetl **120** 19 0N 97 20W
Citrusdal **92** 32 35 S 19 0 E
Città della Pieve **39** 42 57N 12 0 E
Città di Castello **39** 43 27N 12 14 E
Città Sant' Angelo **39** 42 32N 14 5 E
Cittadella **39** 45 39N 11 48 E
Cittaducale **39** 42 24N 12 58 E
Cittanova **41** 38 22N 16 5 E
Ciuc, Munţii **46** 46 25N 26 5 E
Ciucaş **46** 45 31N 25 56 E
Ciudad Acuña **120** 29 20N 100 58W
Ciudad Altamirano **120** 18 20N 100 40W
Ciudad Bolívar **126** 8 5N 63 36W
Ciudad Camargo **120** 27 41N 105 10W
Ciudad de Valles **120** 22 0N 99 0W
Ciudad del Carmen **120** 18 38N 91 50W
Ciudad Delicias = Delicias **120** 28 10N 105 30W
Ciudad Guayana **126** 8 0N 62 30W
Ciudad Guerrero **120** 28 33N 107 28W
Ciudad Guzmán **120** 19 40N 103 30W
Ciudad Juárez **120** 31 40N 106 28W
Ciudad Madero **120** 22 19N 97 50W
Ciudad Mante **120** 22 50N 99 0W
Ciudad Obregón **120** 27 28N 109 59W
Ciudad Real **31** 38 59N 3 55W
Ciudad Real □ **31** 38 50N 4 0W
Ciudad Rodrigo **30** 40 35N 6 32W
Ciudad Trujillo = Sto. Domingo **121** 18 30N 70 0W
Ciudad Victoria **120** 23 41N 99 9W
Ciudadela **32** 40 0N 3 50 E
Ciulniţa **46** 44 26N 27 22 E
Cividale del Friuli **39** 46 6N 13 25 E
Civita Castellana **39** 42 18N 12 24 E
Civitanova Marche **39** 43 18N 13 41 E
Civitavécchia **39** 42 6N 11 46 E
Civitella del Tronto **39** 42 48N 13 40 E
Civray **20** 46 10N 0 17 E
Çivril **64** 38 20N 29 43 E
Cixerri → **40** 39 20N 8 40 E
Cizre **64** 37 19N 42 10 E
Clacton-on-Sea **13** 51 47N 1 10 E
Clain → **18** 46 47N 0 33 E
Claire, L. **108** 58 35N 112 5W
Clairemont **117** 33 9N 100 44W
Clairton **112** 40 18N 79 54W
Clairvaux-les-Lacs **21** 46 35N 5 45 E
Claise → **18** 46 56N 0 42 E
Clamecy **19** 47 28N 3 30 E
Clanton **115** 32 48N 86 36W
Clanwilliam **92** 32 11 S 18 52 E
Clara **15** 53 20N 7 38W
Clare, Austral. **99** 33 50 S 138 37 E
Clare, U.S.A. **114** 43 47N 84 45W
Clare □ **15** 52 20N 9 0W
Clare → **15** 53 22N 9 5W
Clare I. **15** 53 48N 10 0W
Claremont **114** 43 23N 72 20W
Claremont Pt. **98** 14 1 S 143 41 E
Claremore **117** 36 40N 95 37W
Claremorris **15** 53 45N 9 0W
Clarence →, Austral. **97** 29 25 S 153 22 E
Clarence →, N.Z. **101** 42 10 S 173 56 E
Clarence I. **5** 61 10 S 54 0W
Clarence, I. **128** 54 0 S 72 0W
Clarence Str., Austral. **96** 12 0 S 131 0 E
Clarence Str., U.S.A. **108** 55 40N 132 10W
Clarendon, Ark., U.S.A. **117** 34 41N 91 20W
Clarendon, Tex., U.S.A. **117** 34 58N 100 54W
Clarenville **107** 48 10N 54 1W
Claresholm **108** 50 0N 113 33W
Clarie Coast **5** 68 0 S 135 0 E
Clarinda **116** 40 45N 95 0W
Clarion, Iowa, U.S.A. **116** 42 41N 93 46W
Clarion, Pa., U.S.A. **112** 41 12N 79 22W
Clarion → **112** 41 9N 79 41W
Clarion Fracture Zone **95** 20 0N 120 0W
Clark **116** 44 55N 97 45W
Clark Fork **118** 48 9N 116 9W
Clark Fork → **118** 48 9N 116 15W
Clark Hill Res. **115** 33 45N 82 20W
Clark, Pt. **112** 44 4N 81 45W
Clarkdale **119** 34 53N 112 3W
Clarke City **107** 50 12N 66 38W
Clarke, I. **97** 40 32 S 148 10 E
Clarke L. **109** 54 24N 106 54W
Clarke Ra. **98** 20 45 S 148 20 E
Clark's Fork → **118** 45 39N 108 43W
Clark's Harbour **107** 43 25N 65 38W
Clarks Summit **113** 41 31N 75 44W
Clarksburg **114** 39 18N 80 21W
Clarksdale **117** 34 12N 90 33W
Clarkston **118** 46 28N 117 2W
Clarksville, Ark., U.S.A. **117** 35 29N 93 27W
Clarksville, Tenn., U.S.A. **115** 36 32N 87 20W
Clarksville, Tex., U.S.A. **117** 33 37N 94 59W
Clatskanie **118** 46 9N 123 12W
Claude **117** 35 8N 101 22W
Claveria **73** 18 37N 121 4 E
Clay Center **116** 39 27N 97 9W
Clayette, La **21** 46 17N 4 19 E
Claypool **119** 33 27N 110 55W
Claysville **112** 40 5N 80 25W
Clayton, Idaho, U.S.A. **118** 44 12N 114 31W
Clayton, N. Mex., U.S.A. **117** 36 30N 103 10W
Cle Elum **118** 47 15N 120 57W
Clear L. **118** 39 5N 122 47W
Clear, C. **15** 51 26N 9 30W
Clear I. **15** 51 26N 9 30W
Clear Lake, S.D., U.S.A. **116** 44 48N 96 41W
Clear Lake, Wash., U.S.A. **118** 48 27N 122 15W
Clear Lake Res. **118** 41 55N 121 10W
Clearfield, Pa., U.S.A. **114** 41 0N 78 27W
Clearfield, Utah, U.S.A. **118** 41 10N 112 0W
Clearmont **118** 44 43N 106 29W
Clearwater, Can. **108** 51 38N 120 2W
Clearwater, U.S.A. **115** 27 58N 82 45W
Clearwater →, Alta., Can. **108** 52 22N 114 57W
Clearwater →, Alta., Can. **109** 56 44N 111 23W
Clearwater Cr. **108** 61 36N 125 30W
Clearwater, Mts. **118** 46 20N 115 30W
Clearwater Prov. Park **109** 54 0N 101 0W
Cleburne **117** 32 18N 97 25W
Clécy **18** 48 55N 0 29W
Cleethorpes **12** 53 33N 0 2W
Cleeve Cloud **13** 51 56N 2 0W
Clelles **21** 44 50N 5 38 E
Clerks Rocks **5** 56 0 S 34 30W
Clermont, Austral. **97** 22 49 S 147 39 E
Clermont, France **19** 49 23N 2 24 E
Clermont-en-Argonne **19** 49 5N 5 4 E
Clermont-Ferrand **20** 45 46N 3 4 E
Clermont-l'Hérault **20** 43 38N 3 26 E
Clerval **19** 47 25N 6 30 E
Clervaux **16** 50 4N 6 2 E
Cléry-Saint-André **19** 47 50N 1 46 E
Cles **38** 46 21N 11 4 E
Cleveland, Austral. **99** 27 30 S 153 15 E
Cleveland, Miss., U.S.A. **117** 33 43N 90 43W
Cleveland, Ohio, U.S.A. **114** 41 28N 81 43W
Cleveland, Okla., U.S.A. **117** 36 21N 96 33W
Cleveland, Tenn., U.S.A. **115** 35 9N 84 52W
Cleveland, Tex., U.S.A. **117** 30 18N 95 0W
Cleveland □ **12** 54 35N 1 8 E
Cleveland, C. **97** 19 11 S 147 1 E
Cleveland Heights **112** 41 32N 81 30W
Clevelândia **125** 26 24 S 52 23W
Clew B. **15** 53 54N 9 50W
Clewiston **115** 26 44N 80 50W
Clifden, Ireland **15** 53 30N 10 2W
Clifden, N.Z. **101** 46 1 S 167 42 E
Cliff **119** 33 0N 108 36W
Clifton, Austral. **99** 27 59 S 151 53 E
Clifton, Ariz., U.S.A. **119** 33 8N 109 23W
Clifton, Tex., U.S.A. **117** 31 46N 97 35W
Clifton Forge **114** 37 49N 79 51W
Climax **109** 49 10N 108 20W
Clinch → **115** 36 0N 84 29W
Clingmans Dome **115** 35 35N 83 30W
Clint **119** 31 37N 106 11W
Clinton, B.C., Can. **108** 51 6N 121 35W
Clinton, Ont., Can. **106** 43 37N 81 32W
Clinton, N.Z. **101** 46 12 S 169 23 E
Clinton, Ark., U.S.A. **117** 35 37N 92 30W
Clinton, Ill., U.S.A. **116** 40 8N 89 0W
Clinton, Ind., U.S.A. **114** 39 40N 87 22W
Clinton, Iowa, U.S.A. **116** 41 50N 90 12W
Clinton, Mass., U.S.A. **114** 42 26N 71 40W
Clinton, Mo., U.S.A. **116** 38 20N 93 46W
Clinton, N.C., U.S.A. **115** 35 5N 78 15W
Clinton, Okla., U.S.A. **117** 35 30N 99 0W
Clinton, S.C., U.S.A. **115** 34 30N 81 54W
Clinton, Tenn., U.S.A. **115** 36 6N 84 10W
Clinton C. **98** 22 30 S 150 45 E
Clinton Colden L. **104** 63 58N 107 27W
Clintonville **116** 44 35N 88 46W
Clipperton Fracture Zone **95** 19 0N 122 0W
Clipperton, I. **95** 10 18N 109 13W
Clisson **18** 47 5N 1 16W
Clive L. **108** 63 13N 118 54W
Cloates, Pt. **96** 22 43 S 113 40 E
Clocolan **93** 28 55 S 27 34 E
Clodomira **124** 27 35 S 64 14W
Clonakilty **15** 51 37N 8 53W
Clonakilty B. **15** 51 33N 8 50W
Cloncurry **97** 20 40 S 140 28 E
Cloncurry → **98** 18 37 S 140 40 E
Clones **15** 54 10N 7 13W
Clonmel **15** 52 22N 7 42W
Cloppenburg **24** 52 50N 8 3 E
Cloquet **116** 46 40N 92 30W
Clorinda **124** 25 16 S 57 45W
Cloud Peak **118** 44 23N 107 10W
Cloudcroft **119** 33 0N 105 48W
Cloverdale **118** 38 49N 123 0W
Clovis, Calif., U.S.A. **119** 36 47N 119 45W
Clovis, N. Mex., U.S.A. **117** 34 20N 103 10W
Cloyes **18** 48 0N 1 14 E
Cluj-Napoca **46** 46 47N 23 38 E
Cluj □ **46** 46 45N 23 30 E
Clunes **99** 37 20 S 143 45 E
Cluny **21** 46 26N 4 38 E
Cluses **21** 46 5N 6 35 E
Clusone **38** 45 54N 9 58 E
Clutha → **101** 46 20 S 169 49 E
Clwyd □ **12** 53 5N 3 20W
Clwyd → **12** 53 20N 3 30W
Clyde, Can. **105** 70 30N 68 30W
Clyde, N.Z. **101** 45 12 S 169 20 E
Clyde, U.S.A. **112** 43 8N 76 52W
Clyde → **14** 55 56N 4 29W
Clyde, Firth of **14** 55 20N 5 0W
Clydebank **14** 55 54N 4 25W
Clymer **112** 42 3N 79 39W
Côa → **30** 41 5N 7 6W
Coachella **119** 33 44N 116 13W
Coahoma **117** 32 17N 101 20W
Coahuayana → **120** 18 41N 103 45W
Coahuila de Zaragoza □ **120** 27 0N 103 0W
Coal → **108** 59 39N 126 57W
Coalane **91** 17 48 S 37 2 E
Coalcomán **120** 18 40N 103 10W
Coaldale **108** 49 45N 112 35W
Coalgate **117** 34 35N 96 13W
Coalinga **119** 36 10N 120 21W
Coalville, U.K. **12** 52 43N 1 21W
Coalville, U.S.A. **118** 40 58N 111 24W
Coari **126** 4 8 S 63 7W
Coast □ **90** 2 40 S 39 45 E
Coast Mts. **108** 55 0N 129 0W
Coast Ranges **102** 41 0N 123 0W
Coastal Plains Basin **96** 30 10 S 115 30 E
Coatbridge **14** 55 52N 4 2W
Coatepeque **120** 14 46N 91 55W
Coatesville **114** 39 59N 75 55W
Coaticook **107** 45 10N 71 46W
Coats I. **105** 62 30N 83 0W
Coats Land **5** 77 0 S 25 0W
Coatzacoalcos **120** 18 7N 94 25W
Cobadin **46** 44 5N 28 13 E
Cobalt **106** 47 25N 79 42W
Cobán **120** 15 30N 90 21W
Cobar **97** 31 27 S 145 48 E
Cóbh **15** 51 50N 8 18W
Cobija **126** 11 0 S 68 50W
Cobleskill **114** 42 40N 74 30W
Coboconk **112** 44 39N 78 48W
Cobourg **106** 43 58N 78 10W
Cobourg Pen. **96** 11 20 S 132 15 E
Cobram **99** 35 54 S 145 40 E
Cobre **118** 41 6N 114 25W
Coburg **25** 50 15N 10 58 E
Coca **30** 41 13N 4 32W
Cocanada = Kakinada **70** 16 50N 82 11 E
Cocentaina **33** 38 45N 0 27W
Cocha, La **124** 27 50 S 65 40W
Cochabamba **126** 17 26 S 66 10W
Cochem **25** 50 8N 7 7 E
Cochemane **91** 17 0 S 32 54 E
Cochin **70** 9 59N 76 22 E
Cochin China = Nam-Phan **71** 10 30N 106 0 E
Cochise **119** 32 6N 109 58W
Cochran **115** 32 25N 83 23W
Cochrane, Alta., Can. **108** 51 11N 114 30W
Cochrane, Ont., Can. **106** 49 0N 81 0W
Cochrane → **109** 59 0N 103 40W
Cochrane, L. **128** 47 10 S 72 0W
Cockatoo I. **96** 16 6 S 123 37 E
Cockburn **99** 32 5 S 141 0 E
Cockburn, Canal **128** 54 30 S 72 0W
Cockburn I. **106** 45 55N 83 22W
Coco → **121** 15 0N 83 8W
Coco Chan. **71** 13 50N 93 25 E
Coco Solo **120** 9 22N 79 53W
Cocoa **115** 28 22N 80 40W
Cocobeach **88** 0 59N 9 34 E
Cocora **46** 44 45N 27 3 E
Cocos I. **95** 5 25N 87 55W
Cocos Is. **94** 12 10 S 96 55 E
Cod, C. **111** 42 8N 70 10W
Codajás **126** 3 55 S 62 0W
Coderre **109** 50 11N 106 31W
Codigoro **39** 44 50N 12 5 E
Codó **127** 4 30 S 43 55W
Codogno **38** 45 10N 9 42 E
Codróipo **39** 45 57N 13 0 E
Codru, Munţii **46** 46 30N 22 15 E
Cody **118** 44 35N 109 0W
Coe Hill **106** 44 52N 77 50W
Coelemu **124** 36 30 S 72 48W
Coen **97** 13 52 S 143 12 E
Coesfeld **24** 51 56N 7 10 E
Coeur d'Alene **118** 47 45N 116 51W
Cœur d'Alene L. **118** 47 32N 116 48W
Coevorden **16** 52 40N 6 44 E
Coffeyville **117** 37 0N 95 40W
Coffs Harbour **97** 30 16 S 153 5 E
Cofrentes **33** 39 13N 1 5W
Cogealac **46** 44 36N 28 36 E
Coghinas → **40** 40 55N 8 48 E
Coghinas, L. di **40** 40 46N 9 3 E
Cognac **20** 45 41N 0 20W
Cogne **38** 45 37N 7 21 E
Cogolludo **32** 40 59N 3 10W
Cohagen **118** 47 2N 106 36W
Cohoes **114** 42 47N 73 42W
Cohuna **99** 35 45 S 144 15 E
Coiba, I. **121** 7 30N 81 40W
Coig → **128** 51 0 S 69 10W
Coihaique **128** 45 30 S 71 45W
Coimbatore **70** 11 2N 76 59 E
Coimbra, Brazil **126** 19 55 S 57 48W
Coimbra, Port. **30** 40 15N 8 27W
Coimbra □ **30** 40 12N 8 25W
Coín **31** 36 40N 4 48W
Cojimies **126** 0 20N 80 0W
Cojocna **46** 46 45N 23 50 E
Cojutepequé **120** 13 41N 88 54W
Čoka **42** 45 57N 20 12 E
Cokeville **118** 42 4N 111 0W
Col di Tenda **38** 44 7N 7 36 E
Colaba Pt. **70** 18 54N 72 47 E
Colac **97** 38 21 S 143 35 E
Colachel **70** 8 10N 77 15 E
Colares **31** 38 48N 9 30W
Colbeck, C. **5** 77 6 S 157 48W
Colbinabbin **99** 36 38 S 144 48 E
Colborne **112** 44 0N 77 53W
Colby **116** 39 27N 101 2W
Colchagua □ **124** 34 30 S 71 0W
Colchester **13** 51 54N 0 55 E
Coldstream **14** 55 39N 2 14W
Coldwater, Can. **112** 44 42N 79 40W
Coldwater, U.S.A. **117** 37 18N 99 24W
Colebrook, Austral. **99** 42 31 S 147 21 E
Colebrook, U.S.A. **114** 44 54N 71 29W
Coleman, Can. **108** 49 40N 114 30W
Coleman, U.S.A. **117** 31 52N 99 30W
Coleman → **97** 15 6 S 141 38 E
Colenso **93** 28 44 S 29 50 E
Coleraine, Austral. **99** 37 36 S 141 40 E
Coleraine, U.K. **15** 55 8N 6 40 E
Coleraine □ **15** 55 8N 6 40 E
Coleridge, L. **101** 43 17 S 171 30 E
Coleroon → **70** 11 25N 79 50 E
Colesberg **92** 30 45 S 25 5 E
Colfax, La., U.S.A. **117** 31 35N 92 39W
Colfax, Wash., U.S.A. **118** 46 57N 117 28W
Colhué Huapi, L. **128** 45 30 S 69 0W
Cólico **38** 46 8N 9 22 E
Coligny **93** 26 17 S 26 15 E
Colima **120** 19 10N 103 40W
Colima □ **120** 19 10N 103 40W
Colima, Nevado de **120** 19 35N 103 45W
Colina **124** 33 13 S 70 45W
Colina do Norte **84** 12 28N 15 0W
Colinas **127** 6 0 S 44 10W
Colinton **100** 35 50 S 149 10 E
Coll **14** 56 40N 6 35W
Collaguasi **124** 21 5 S 68 45W
Collarada, Peña **32** 42 43N 0 29W
Collarenebri **99** 29 33 S 148 34 E
Collbran **119** 39 16N 107 58W
Colle di Val d'Elsa **39** 43 25N 11 7 E
Colle Salvetti **38** 43 34N 10 27 E
Colle Sannita **41** 41 22N 14 48 E
Collécchio **38** 44 45N 10 10 E
Colleen Bawn **91** 21 0 S 29 12 E
College Park **115** 33 42N 84 27W
Collette **107** 46 40N 65 30W
Collie **96** 33 22 S 116 8 E
Collier B. **96** 16 10 S 124 15 E
Colline Metallifere **38** 43 10N 11 0 E
Collingwood, Austral. **98** 22 20 S 142 31 E
Collingwood, Can. **106** 44 29N 80 13W
Collingwood, N.Z. **101** 40 41 S 172 40 E
Collins **106** 50 17N 89 27W
Collinsville **97** 20 30 S 147 56 E
Collipulli **124** 37 55 S 72 30W
Collo **83** 36 58N 6 37 E
Collonges **21** 46 9N 5 52 E
Collooney **15** 54 11N 8 28W
Colmar **19** 48 5N 7 20 E
Colmars **21** 44 11N 6 39 E
Colmenar **31** 36 54N 4 20W
Colmenar de Oreja **32** 40 6N 3 25W
Colmenar Viejo **30** 40 39N 3 47W
Colne **12** 53 51N 2 11W
Colo → **99** 33 25 S 150 52 E
Cologna Véneta **39** 45 19N 11 21 E
Cologne = Köln **24** 50 56N 9 58 E
Colomb-Béchar = Béchar **82** 31 38N 2 18W
Colombey-les-Belles **19** 48 32N 5 54 E
Colombey-les-Deux-Églises **19** 48 13N 4 50 E
Colômbia **127** 20 10 S 48 40W
Colombia ■ **126** 3 45N 73 0W
Colombo **70** 6 56N 79 58 E
Colombus **119** 31 54N 107 43W
Colome **116** 43 20N 99 44W
Colón, Argent. **124** 32 12 S 58 10W
Colón, Cuba **121** 22 42N 80 54W
Colón, Panama **120** 9 20N 79 54W
Colonella **39** 42 52N 13 50 E
Colonia **124** 34 25 S 57 50W
Colonia Dora **124** 28 34 S 62 59W
Colonial Hts. **114** 37 19N 77 25W
Colonne, C. delle **41** 39 2N 17 11 E
Colonsay, Can. **109** 51 59N 105 52W
Colonsay, U.K. **14** 56 4N 6 12W
Colorado □ **110** 37 40N 106 0W
Colorado →, Argent. **128** 39 50 S 62 8W
Colorado →, Calif., U.S.A. **119** 34 45N 114 40W
Colorado →, Tex., U.S.A. **117** 28 36N 95 58W
Colorado City **117** 32 25N 100 50W
Colorado Desert **110** 34 20N 116 0W
Colorado, I. **120** 9 12N 79 50W
Colorado Plateau **119** 36 40N 110 30W
Colorado R. Aqueduct **119** 34 17N 114 10W
Colorado Springs **116** 38 55N 104 50W
Colorno **38** 44 55N 10 21 E
Colton, N.Y., U.S.A. **113** 44 34N 74 58W
Colton, Wash., U.S.A. **118** 46 41N 117 6W
Columbia, La., U.S.A. **117** 32 7N 92 5W
Columbia, Miss., U.S.A. **117** 31 16N 89 50W
Columbia, Mo., U.S.A. **116** 38 58N 92 20W
Columbia, Pa., U.S.A. **114** 40 2N 76 30W
Columbia, S.C., U.S.A. **115** 34 0N 81 0W
Columbia, Tenn., U.S.A. **115** 35 40N 87 0W
Columbia → **118** 46 15N 124 5W
Columbia Basin **118** 47 30N 118 30W
Columbia, C. **4** 83 0N 70 0W
Columbia City **114** 41 8N 85 30W
Columbia, District of □ **114** 38 55N 77 0W
Columbia Falls **118** 48 25N 114 16W
Columbia Heights **116** 45 5N 93 10W
Columbia, Mt. **108** 52 8N 117 20W
Columbiana **112** 40 53N 80 40W
Columbretes, Is. **32** 39 50N 0 50 E
Columbus, Ga., U.S.A. **115** 32 30N 84 58W
Columbus, Ind., U.S.A. **114** 39 14N 85 55W
Columbus, Kans., U.S.A. **117** 37 15N 94 30W
Columbus, Miss., U.S.A. **115** 33 30N 88 26W
Columbus, Mont., U.S.A. **118** 45 38N 109 14W
Columbus, N.D., U.S.A. **116** 48 52N 102 48W
Columbus, Nebr., U.S.A. **116** 41 30N 97 25W
Columbus, Ohio, U.S.A. **114** 39 57N 83 1W
Columbus, Tex., U.S.A. **117** 29 42N 96 33W
Columbus, Wis., U.S.A. **116** 43 20N 89 2W

Colunga Cradock

Colunga **30** 43 29N 5 16W
Colusa **118** 39 15N 122 1W
Colville **118** 48 33N 117 54W
Colville → **104** 70 25N 151 0W
Colville, C. **101** 36 29 S 175 21 E
Colwyn Bay **12** 53 17N 3 44W
Coma **87** 8 29N 36 53 E
Comácchio **39** 44 41N 12 10 E
Comallo **128** 41 0 S 70 5W
Comana **46** 44 10N 26 10 E
Comanche, Okla., U.S.A. **117** 34 27N 97 58W
Comanche, Tex., U.S.A. **117** 31 55N 98 35W
Comăneşti **46** 46 25N 26 26 E
Combahee → **115** 32 30N 80 31W
Combeaufontaine **19** 47 38N 5 54 E
Comber **112** 42 14N 82 33W
Comblain-au-Pont **16** 50 29N 5 35 E
Combles **19** 50 0N 2 50 E
Combourg **18** 48 25N 1 46W
Combronde **20** 45 58N 3 5 E
Comeragh Mts. **15** 52 17N 7 35W
Comet **98** 23 36 S 148 38 E
Comilla **69** 23 28N 91 10 E
Comino, C. **40** 40 28N 9 47 E
Comino I. **36** 36 0N 14 20 E
Cómiso **41** 36 57N 14 35 E
Comitán **120** 16 18N 92 9W
Commentry **20** 46 20N 2 46 E
Commerce, Ga., U.S.A. **115** 34 10N 83 25W
Commerce, Tex., U.S.A. **117** 33 15N 95 50W
Commercy **19** 48 46N 5 34 E
Committee B. **105** 68 30N 86 30W
Commonwealth B. **5** 67 0 S 144 0 E
Commoron Cr. → **99** 28 22 S 150 8 E
Communism Pk. = Kommunisma, Pic **65** 38 40N 72 0 E
Como **38** 45 48N 9 5 E
Como, L. di **38** 46 5N 9 17 E
Comodoro Rivadavia **128** 45 50 S 67 40W
Comorin, C. **70** 8 3N 77 40 E
Comorişte **42** 45 10N 21 35 E
Comoro Is. **3** 12 10 S 44 15 E
Comox **108** 49 42N 124 55W
Compiègne **19** 49 24N 2 50 E
Compíglia Maríttima **38** 43 4N 10 37 E
Comporta **31** 38 22N 8 46W
Comprida, I. **125** 24 50 S 47 42W
Compton Downs **99** 30 28 S 146 30 E
Côn Dao **71** 8 45N 106 45 E
Conakry **84** 9 29N 13 49W
Conara Junction **99** 41 50 S 147 26 E
Concarneau **18** 47 52N 3 56W
Conceição **91** 18 47 S 36 7 E
Conceição da Barra **127** 18 35 S 39 45W
Conceição do Araguaia **127** 8 0 S 49 2W
Concepción, Argent. **124** 27 20 S 65 35W
Concepción, Boliv. **126** 16 15 S 62 8W
Concepción, Chile **124** 36 50 S 73 0W
Concepción, Parag. **124** 23 22 S 57 26W
Concepción □ **124** 37 0 S 72 30W
Concepción → **120** 30 32N 113 2W
Concepción del Oro **120** 24 40N 101 30W
Concepción del Uruguay **124** 32 35 S 58 20W
Concepción, L. **126** 17 20 S 61 20W
Concepción, La = Ri-Aba **85** 3 28N 8 40 E
Concepcion, Pt. **119** 34 27N 120 27W
Concepción, Punta **120** 26 55N 111 59W
Conception B. **92** 23 55 S 14 22 E
Conception I. **121** 23 52N 75 9W
Conception, Pt. **119** 34 30N 120 34W
Concession **91** 17 27 S 30 56 E
Conchas Dam **117** 35 25N 104 10W
Conche **107** 50 55N 55 58W
Conches **18** 48 51N 2 43 E
Concho **119** 34 32N 109 43W
Concho → **117** 31 30N 99 45W
Conchos → **120** 29 32N 104 25W
Concord, N.C., U.S.A. **115** 35 28N 80 35W
Concord, N.H., U.S.A. **114** 43 12N 71 30W
Concordia **124** 31 20 S 58 2W
Concórdia **126** 4 36 S 66 36W
Concordia **116** 39 35N 97 40W
Concordia, La **120** 16 8N 92 38W
Concots **20** 44 26N 1 40 E
Concrete **118** 48 35N 121 49W
Condamine → **97** 27 7 S 149 48 E
Condat **20** 45 21N 2 46 E
Condé **19** 50 26N 3 34 E
Conde **116** 45 13N 98 5W
Condé-sur-Noireau **18** 48 51N 0 33W
Condeúba **127** 14 52 S 42 0W
Condobolin **99** 33 4 S 147 6 E
Condom **20** 43 57N 0 22 E
Condon **118** 45 15N 120 8W
Condove **38** 45 8N 7 19 E
Conegliano **39** 45 53N 12 18 E
Conejera, I. **33** 39 11N 2 58 E
Conflans-en-Jarnisy **19** 49 10N 5 52 E
Confolens **20** 46 2N 0 40 E
Confuso → **124** 25 9 S 57 34W
Congleton **12** 53 10N 2 12W
Congo = Zaïre → **88** 1 30N 28 0 E
Congo ■ **88** 1 0 S 16 0 E
Congo Basin **78** 0 10 S 24 30 E
Congonhas **125** 20 30 S 43 52W
Congress **119** 34 11N 112 56W
Conil **31** 36 17N 6 10W
Coniston **106** 46 29N 80 51W
Conjeevaram = Kanchipuram **70** 12 52N 79 45 E
Conjuboy **98** 18 35 S 144 35 E
Conklin **109** 55 38N 111 5W
Conlea **99** 30 7 S 144 35 E
Conn, L. **15** 54 3N 9 15W
Connacht **15** 53 23N 8 40W
Conneaut **114** 41 55N 80 32W
Connecticut □ **114** 41 40N 72 40W
Connecticut → **114** 41 17N 72 21W
Connell **118** 46 36N 118 51W
Connellsville **114** 40 3N 79 32W
Connemara **15** 53 29N 9 45W
Connemaugh → **112** 40 38N 79 42W
Conner, La **118** 48 22N 122 27W
Connerré **18** 48 3N 0 30 E
Connersville **114** 39 40N 85 10W
Connors Ra. **98** 21 40 S 149 10 E
Conoble **99** 32 55 S 144 33 E
Conon → **14** 57 33N 4 28W
Cononaco → **126** 1 32 S 75 35W
Cononbridge **14** 57 32N 4 30W
Conquest **109** 51 32N 107 14W
Conquet, Le **18** 48 21N 4 46W
Conrad **118** 48 11N 112 0W
Conran, C. **99** 37 49 S 148 44 E
Conroe **117** 30 15N 95 28W
Conselheiro Lafaiete **125** 20 40 S 43 48W
Conshohocken **113** 40 5N 75 18W
Consort **109** 52 1N 110 46W
Constance = Konstanz **25** 47 39N 9 10 E
Constance, L. = Bodensee **25** 47 35N 9 25 E
Constanţa **46** 44 14N 28 38 E
Constanţa □ **46** 44 15N 28 15 E
Constantina **31** 37 51N 5 40W
Constantine **83** 36 25N 6 42 E
Constitución, Chile **124** 35 20 S 72 30W
Constitución, Uruguay **124** 42 0 S 57 50W
Consuegra **31** 39 28N 3 36W
Consul **109** 49 20N 109 30W
Contact **118** 41 50N 114 56W
Contai **69** 21 54N 87 46 E
Contamana **126** 7 19 S 74 55W
Contarina **39** 45 2N 12 13 E
Contas → **127** 14 17 S 39 1W
Contes **21** 43 49N 7 19 E
Contoocook **113** 43 13N 71 45W
Contra Costa **93** 25 9 S 33 30 E
Contres **18** 47 24N 1 26 E
Contrexéville **19** 48 6N 5 53 E
Conversano **41** 40 57N 17 8 E
Conway, Ark., U.S.A. **117** 35 5N 92 30W
Conway, N.H., U.S.A. **114** 43 58N 71 8W
Conway, S.C., U.S.A. **115** 33 49N 79 2W
Conway = Conwy **12** 53 17N 3 50W
Conwy **12** 53 17N 3 50W
Conwy → **12** 53 18N 3 50W
Coober Pedy **96** 29 1 S 134 43 E
Cooch Behar **69** 26 22N 89 29 E
Cook **116** 47 49N 92 39W
Cook, Bahía **128** 55 10 S 70 0W
Cook Inlet **104** 59 0N 151 0W
Cook Is. **95** 17 0 S 160 0W
Cook, Mt. **101** 43 36 S 170 9 E
Cook Strait **101** 41 15 S 174 29 E
Cookeville **115** 36 12N 85 30W
Cookhouse **92** 32 44 S 25 47 E
Cookshire **113** 45 25N 71 38W
Cookstown **15** 54 40N 6 43W
Cookstown □ **15** 54 40N 6 43W
Cooksville **112** 43 36N 79 35W
Cooktown **97** 15 30 S 145 16 E
Coolabah **99** 31 1 S 146 43 E
Cooladdi **99** 26 37 S 145 23 E
Coolah **99** 31 48 S 149 41 E
Coolamon **99** 34 46 S 147 8 E
Coolangatta **99** 28 11 S 153 29 E
Coolgardie **96** 30 55 S 121 8 E
Coolidge **119** 33 1N 111 35W
Coolidge Dam **119** 33 10N 110 30W
Cooma **97** 36 12 S 149 8 E
Coonabarabran **99** 31 14 S 149 18 E
Coonamble **97** 30 56 S 148 27 E
Coondapoor **70** 13 42N 74 40 E
Coongie **99** 27 9 S 140 8 E
Coongoola **99** 27 43 S 145 51 E
Cooninie, L. **99** 26 4 S 139 59 E
Coonoor **70** 11 21N 76 45 E
Cooper **117** 33 20N 95 40W
Cooper → **115** 33 0N 79 55W
Coopers Cr. → **97** 28 29 S 137 46 E
Cooperstown, N.D., U.S.A. **116** 47 30N 98 6W
Cooperstown, N.Y., U.S.A. **114** 42 42N 74 57W
Coorabulka **98** 23 41 S 140 20 E
Coorong, The **97** 35 50 S 139 20 E
Cooroy **99** 26 22 S 152 54 E
Coos Bay **118** 43 26N 124 7W
Cootamundra **97** 34 36 S 148 1 E
Cootehill **15** 54 5N 7 5W
Cooyar **99** 26 59 S 151 51 E
Cooyeana **98** 24 29 S 138 45 E
Copahue Paso **124** 37 49 S 71 8W
Copainalá **120** 17 8N 93 11W
Cope **116** 39 44N 102 50W
Cope, Cabo **33** 37 26N 1 28W
Copenhagen = København **49** 55 41N 12 34 E
Copertino **41** 40 17N 18 2 E
Copiapó **124** 27 30 S 70 20W
Copiapó → **124** 27 19 S 70 56W
Copley **99** 30 36 S 138 26 E
Copp L. **108** 60 14N 114 40W
Copparo **39** 44 52N 11 49 E
Copper Center **104** 62 10N 145 25W
Copper Cliff **106** 46 28N 81 4W
Copper Harbor **114** 47 31N 87 55W
Copper Queen **91** 17 29 S 29 18 E
Copperbelt □ **91** 13 15 S 27 30 E
Coppermine **104** 67 50N 115 5W
Coppermine → **104** 67 49N 116 4W
Coquet → **12** 55 18N 1 45W
Coquilhatville = Mbandaka **88** 0 1N 18 18 E
Coquille **118** 43 15N 124 12W
Coquimbo **124** 30 0 S 71 20W
Coquimbo □ **124** 31 0 S 71 0W
Corabia **46** 43 48N 24 30 E
Coracora **126** 15 5 S 73 45W
Coradi, Is. **41** 40 27N 17 10 E
Coral Gables **115** 25 45N 80 16W
Coral Harbour **105** 64 8N 83 10W
Coral Sea **94** 15 0 S 150 0 E
Coral Sea Islands Terr. **97** 20 0 S 155 0 E
Corangamite, L. **100** 38 0 S 143 30 E
Coraopolis **112** 40 30N 80 10W
Corato **41** 41 12N 16 22 E
Corbeil-Essonnes **19** 48 36N 2 26 E
Corbie **19** 49 54N 2 30 E
Corbières **20** 42 55N 2 35 E
Corbigny **19** 47 16N 3 40 E
Corbin **114** 37 0N 84 3W
Corbones → **31** 37 36N 5 39W
Corby **13** 52 49N 0 31W
Corcoles → **33** 39 40N 3 18W
Corcoran **119** 36 6N 119 35W
Corcubión **30** 42 56N 9 12W
Cordele **115** 31 55N 83 49W
Cordell **117** 35 18N 99 0W
Cordenons **39** 45 59N 12 42 E
Cordes **20** 44 5N 1 57 E
Córdoba, Argent. **124** 31 20 S 64 10W
Córdoba, Mexico **120** 18 50N 97 0W
Córdoba, Spain **31** 37 50N 4 50W
Córdoba □, Argent. **124** 31 22 S 64 15W
Córdoba □, Spain **31** 38 5N 5 0W
Córdoba, Sierra de **124** 31 10 S 64 25W
Cordon **73** 16 42N 121 32 E
Cordova, Ala., U.S.A. **115** 33 45N 87 12W
Cordova, Alaska, U.S.A. **104** 60 36N 145 45W
Corella **32** 42 7N 1 48W
Corella → **98** 19 34 S 140 47 E
Corfield **98** 21 40 S 143 21 E
Corfu = Kérkira **44** 39 38N 19 50 E
Corgo **30** 42 56N 7 25W
Cori **40** 41 39N 12 53 E
Coria **30** 40 0N 6 33W
Coricudgy, Mt. **100** 32 51 S 150 24 E
Corigliano Cálabro **41** 39 36N 16 31 E
Corinna **99** 41 35 S 145 10 E
Corinth, Miss., U.S.A. **115** 34 54N 88 30W
Corinth, N.Y., U.S.A. **113** 43 15N 73 50W
Corinth = Kórinthos **45** 38 19N 22 24 E
Corinth Canal **45** 37 58N 23 0 E
Corinth, G. of = Korinthiakós **45** 38 16N 22 30 E
Corinto, Brazil **127** 18 20 S 44 30W
Corinto, Nic. **121** 12 30N 87 10W
Corj □ **46** 45 5N 23 25 E
Cork **15** 51 54N 8 30W
Cork □ **15** 51 50N 8 50W
Cork Harbour **15** 51 46N 8 16W
Corlay **18** 48 20N 3 5W
Corleone **40** 37 48N 13 16 E
Corleto Perticara **41** 40 23N 16 2 E
Çorlu **43** 41 11N 27 49 E
Cormack L. **108** 60 56N 121 37W
Cormóns **39** 45 58N 13 29 E
Cormorant **109** 54 14N 100 35W
Cormorant L. **109** 54 15N 100 50W
Corn Is. = Maiz, Is. del **121** 12 0N 83 0W
Cornélio Procópio **125** 23 7 S 50 40W
Cornell **116** 45 10N 91 8W
Corner Brook **107** 48 57N 57 58W
Corner Inlet **97** 38 45 S 146 20 E
Corníglio **38** 44 29N 10 5 E
Corning, Ark., U.S.A. **117** 36 27N 90 34W
Corning, Calif., U.S.A. **118** 39 56N 122 9W
Corning, Iowa, U.S.A. **116** 40 57N 94 40W
Corning, N.Y., U.S.A. **114** 42 10N 77 3W
Corno, Monte **39** 42 28N 13 34 E
Cornwall, Austral. **99** 41 33 S 148 7 E
Cornwall, Can. **106** 45 2N 74 44W
Cornwall □ **13** 50 26N 4 40W
Cornwallis I. **4** 75 8N 95 0W
Corny Pt. **99** 34 55 S 137 0 E
Coro **126** 11 25N 69 41W
Coroatá **127** 4 8 S 44 0W
Corocoro **126** 17 15 S 68 28W
Coroico **126** 16 0 S 67 50W
Coromandel **101** 36 45 S 175 31 E
Coromandel Coast **70** 12 30N 81 0 E
Corona, Austral. **99** 31 16 S 141 24 E
Corona, Calif., U.S.A. **119** 33 49N 117 36W
Corona, N. Mex., U.S.A. **119** 34 15N 105 32W
Coronada **119** 32 45N 117 9W
Coronado, Bahía de **121** 9 0N 83 40W
Coronation **108** 52 5N 111 27W
Coronation Gulf **104** 68 25N 110 0W
Coronation I., Antarct. **5** 60 45 S 46 0W
Coronation I., U.S.A. **108** 55 52N 134 20W
Coronda **124** 31 58 S 60 56W
Coronel **124** 37 0 S 73 10W
Coronel Bogado **124** 27 11 S 56 18W
Coronel Dorrego **124** 38 40 S 61 10W
Coronel Oviedo **124** 25 24 S 56 30W
Coronel Pringles **124** 38 0 S 61 30W
Coronel Suárez **124** 37 30 S 61 52W
Coronel Vidal **124** 37 28 S 57 45W
Çorovoda **44** 40 31N 20 14 E
Corowa **99** 35 58 S 146 21 E
Corozal, Belize **120** 18 23N 88 23W
Corozal, Panama **120** 8 59N 79 34W
Corps **21** 44 50N 5 56 E
Corpus **125** 27 10 S 55 30W
Corpus Christi **117** 27 50N 97 28W
Corpus Christi L. **117** 28 5N 97 54W
Corque **126** 18 20 S 67 41W
Corral de Almaguer **32** 39 45N 3 10W
Corréggio **38** 44 46N 10 47 E
Correntes, C. das **93** 24 6 S 35 34 E
Corrèze □ **20** 45 20N 1 45 E
Correze → **20** 45 10N 1 28 E
Corrib, L. **15** 53 5N 9 10W
Corrientes **124** 27 30 S 58 45W
Corrientes □ **124** 28 0 S 57 0W
Corrientes →, Argent. **124** 30 42 S 59 38W
Corrientes →, Peru **126** 3 43 S 74 35W
Corrientes, C., Colomb. **126** 5 30N 77 34W
Corrientes, C., Cuba **121** 21 43N 84 30W
Corrientes, C., Mexico **120** 20 25N 105 42W
Corrigan **117** 31 0N 94 48W
Corry **114** 41 55N 79 39W
Corse **21** 42 0N 9 0 E
Corse, C. **21** 43 1N 9 25 E
Corse-du-Sud □ **21** 41 45N 9 0 E
Corsica = Corse **21** 42 0N 9 0 E
Corsicana **117** 32 5N 96 30W
Corté **21** 42 19N 9 11 E
Corte do Pinto **31** 37 42N 7 29W
Cortegana **31** 37 52N 6 49W
Cortez **119** 37 24N 108 35W
Cortina d'Ampezzo **39** 46 32N 12 9 E
Cortland **114** 42 35N 76 11W
Cortona **39** 43 16N 12 0 E
Coruche **31** 38 57N 8 30W
Çorum **64** 40 30N 34 57 E
Corumbá **126** 19 0 S 57 30W
Corumbá de Goiás **127** 16 0 S 48 50W
Coruña, La **30** 43 20N 8 25W
Coruña, La □ **30** 43 10N 8 30W
Corund **46** 46 30N 25 13 E
Corunna = La Coruña **30** 43 20N 8 25W
Corvallis **118** 44 36N 123 15W
Corvette, L. de la **106** 53 25N 74 3W
Corydon **116** 40 42N 93 22W
Cosalá **120** 24 28N 106 40W
Cosamaloapan **120** 18 23N 95 50W
Cosenza **41** 39 17N 16 14 E
Coşereni **46** 44 38N 26 35 E
Coshocton **114** 40 17N 81 51W
Cosne-sur-Loire **19** 47 24N 2 54 E
Cospeito **30** 43 12N 7 34W
Cosquín **124** 31 15 S 64 30W
Cossato **38** 45 34N 8 10 E
Cossé-le-Vivien **18** 47 57N 0 54W
Cosson → **19** 47 30N 1 15 E
Costa Blanca **33** 38 25N 0 10W
Costa Brava **32** 41 30N 3 0 E
Costa del Sol **31** 36 30N 4 30W
Costa Dorada **32** 40 45N 1 15 E
Costa Rica ■ **121** 10 0N 84 0W
Costa Smeralda **40** 41 5N 9 35 E
Costigliole d'Asti **38** 44 48N 8 11 E
Costilla **119** 37 0N 105 30W
Coştiui **46** 47 53N 24 2 E
Coswig **24** 51 52N 12 31 E
Cotabato **73** 7 14N 124 15 E
Cotagaita **124** 20 45 S 65 40W
Côte d'Azur **21** 43 25N 6 50 E
Côte d'Or **19** 47 10N 4 50 E
Côte-d'Or □ **19** 47 30N 4 50 E
Côte-St.-André, La **21** 45 24N 5 15 E
Coteau des Prairies **116** 44 30N 97 0W
Coteau du Missouri, Plat. du **116** 47 0N 101 0W
Coteau Landing **113** 45 15N 74 13W
Cotentin **18** 49 30N 1 30W
Côtes de Meuse **19** 49 15N 5 22 E
Côtes-du-Nord □ **18** 48 25N 2 40W
Cotiella **32** 42 31N 0 19 E
Cotina → **42** 43 36N 18 50 E
Cotonou **85** 6 20N 2 25 E
Cotopaxi, Vol. **126** 0 40 S 78 30W
Cotronei **41** 39 9N 16 45 E
Cotswold Hills **13** 51 42N 2 10W
Cottage Grove **118** 43 48N 123 2W
Cottbus **24** 51 44N 14 20 E
Cottbus □ **24** 51 43N 13 30 E
Cottonwood **119** 34 48N 112 1W
Cotulla **117** 28 26N 99 14W
Coubre, Pte. de la **20** 45 42N 1 15W
Couches **19** 46 53N 4 30 E
Couço **31** 38 59N 8 17W
Coudersport **114** 41 45N 77 40W
Couëron **18** 47 13N 1 44W
Couesnon → **18** 48 38N 1 32W
Couhe-Vérac **20** 46 18N 0 12 E
Coulanges **19** 47 30N 3 30 E
Coulee City **118** 47 36N 119 18W
Coulman I. **5** 73 35 S 170 0 E
Coulommiers **19** 48 50N 3 3 E
Coulon → **21** 43 51N 5 0 E
Coulonge → **106** 45 52N 76 46W
Coulonges **20** 46 28N 0 35W
Council, Alaska, U.S.A. **104** 64 55N 163 45W
Council, Idaho, U.S.A. **118** 44 44N 116 26W
Council Bluffs **116** 41 20N 95 50W
Council Grove **116** 38 41N 96 30W
Courantyne → **126** 5 55N 57 5W
Courçon **20** 46 15N 0 50W
Couronne, C. **21** 43 19N 5 3 E
Cours **21** 46 7N 4 19 E
Coursan **20** 43 14N 3 4 E
Courseulles **18** 49 20N 0 29W
Courtenay **108** 49 45N 125 0W
Courtine, La **20** 45 43N 2 16 E
Courtrai = Kortrijk **16** 50 50N 3 17 E
Courtright **112** 42 49N 82 28W
Courville **18** 48 28N 1 15 E
Coushatta **117** 32 0N 93 21W
Coutances **18** 49 3N 1 28W
Couterne **18** 48 30N 0 25W
Coutras **20** 45 3N 0 8W
Coutts **108** 49 0N 111 57W
Covarrubias **32** 42 4N 3 31W
Covasna **46** 45 50N 26 10 E
Covasna □ **46** 45 50N 26 0 E
Coventry **13** 52 25N 1 31W
Coventry L. **109** 61 15N 106 15W
Covilhã **30** 40 17N 7 31W
Covington, Ga., U.S.A. **115** 33 36N 83 50W
Covington, Ky., U.S.A. **114** 39 5N 84 30W
Covington, Okla., U.S.A. **117** 36 21N 97 36W
Covington, Tenn., U.S.A. **117** 35 34N 89 39W
Cowal, L. **97** 33 40 S 147 25 E
Cowan **109** 52 5N 100 45W
Cowan, L. **96** 31 45 S 121 45 E
Cowan L. **109** 54 0N 107 15W
Cowangie **99** 35 12 S 141 26 E
Cowansville **113** 45 14N 72 46W
Cowarie **99** 27 45 S 138 15 E
Cowdenbeath **14** 56 7N 3 20W
Cowes **13** 50 45N 1 18W
Cowra **97** 33 49 S 148 42 E
Coxim **127** 18 30 S 54 55W
Cox's Bazar **67** 21 26N 91 59 E
Cox's Cove **107** 49 7N 58 5W
Coyuca de Benítez **120** 17 1N 100 8W
Coyuca de Catalan **120** 18 18N 100 41W
Cozad **116** 40 55N 99 57W
Cozumel, Isla de **120** 20 30N 86 40W
Craboon **99** 32 3 S 149 30 E
Cracow **99** 25 17 S 150 17 E
Cracow = Kraków **27** 50 4N 19 57 E
Cradock **92** 32 8 S 25 36 E

Craig Damba

Craig, Alaska, U.S.A. **108** 55 30N 133 5W
Craig, Colo., U.S.A. **118** 40 32N 107 33W
Craigavon = Lurgan **15** 54 28N 6 20W
Craigmore **91** 20 28 S 32 50 E
Crailsheim **25** 49 7N 10 5 E
Craiova **46** 44 21N 23 48 E
Cramsie **98** 23 20 S 144 15 E
Cranberry Portage **109** 54 35N 101 23W
Cranbrook, Austral. **99** 42 0 S 148 5 E
Cranbrook, Can. **108** 49 30N 115 46W
Crandon **116** 45 32N 88 52W
Crane, Oregon, U.S.A. **118** 43 21N 118 39W
Crane, Texas, U.S.A. **117** 31 26N 102 27W
Cranston **113** 41 47N 71 27W
Craon **18** 47 50N 0 58W
Craonne **19** 49 27N 3 46 E
Craponne **20** 45 20N 3 51 E
Crasna **46** 46 32N 27 51 E
Crasna → **46** 47 44N 22 35 E
Crasnei, Munţii **46** 47 0N 23 20 E
Crater, L. **118** 42 55N 122 3W
Crater Pt. **98** 5 25 S 152 9 E
Crateús **127** 5 10 S 40 39W
Crati → **41** 39 41N 16 30 E
Crato, Brazil **127** 7 10 S 39 25W
Crato, Port. **31** 39 16N 7 39W
Crau **21** 43 32N 4 40 E
Crawford **116** 42 40N 103 25W
Crawfordsville **114** 40 2N 86 51W
Crawley **13** 51 7N 0 10W
Crazy Mts. **118** 46 14N 110 30W
Crean L. **109** 54 5N 106 9W
Crécy-en-Brie **19** 48 50N 2 53 E
Crécy-en-Ponthieu **19** 50 15N 1 53 E
Crediton **112** 43 17N 81 33W
Cree →, Can. **109** 58 57N 105 47W
Cree →, U.K. **14** 54 51N 4 24W
Cree L. **109** 57 30N 106 30W
Creede **119** 37 56N 106 59W
Creel **120** 27 45N 107 38W
Creighton **116** 42 30N 97 52W
Creil **19** 49 15N 2 34 E
Crema **38** 45 21N 9 40 E
Cremona **38** 45 8N 10 2 E
Crepaja **42** 45 1N 20 38 E
Crépy **19** 49 37N 3 32 E
Crépy-en-Valois **19** 49 14N 2 54 E
Cres **39** 44 58N 14 25 E
Cresbard **116** 45 13N 98 57W
Crescent, Okla., U.S.A. **117** 35 58N 97 36W
Crescent, Oreg., U.S.A. **118** 43 30N 121 37W
Crescent City **118** 41 45N 124 12W
Crescentino **38** 45 11N 8 7 E
Crespino **39** 44 59N 11 51 E
Crespo **124** 32 2 S 60 19W
Cressy **99** 38 2 S 143 40 E
Crest **21** 44 44N 5 2 E
Crested Butte **119** 38 57N 107 0W
Crestline **112** 40 46N 82 45W
Creston, Can. **108** 49 10N 116 31W
Creston, Iowa, U.S.A. **116** 41 0N 94 20W
Creston, Wash., U.S.A. **118** 47 47N 118 36W
Creston, Wyo., U.S.A. **118** 41 46N 107 50W
Crestview **115** 30 45N 86 35W
Creswick **100** 37 25 S 143 58 E
Crete **116** 40 38N 96 58W
Crete = Kríti **45** 35 15N 25 0 E
Crete, La **108** 58 11N 116 24W
Crete, Sea of **45** 36 0N 25 0 E
Cretin, C. **98** 6 40 S 147 53 E
Creus, C. **32** 42 20N 3 19 E
Creuse □ **20** 46 0N 2 0 E
Creuse → **20** 47 0N 0 34 E
Creusot, Le **19** 46 50N 4 24 E
Creuzburg **24** 51 3N 10 15 E
Crevalcore **39** 44 41N 11 10 E
Crèvecœur-le-Grand **19** 49 37N 2 5 E
Crevillente **33** 38 12N 0 48W
Crewe **12** 53 6N 2 28W
Crib Point **99** 38 22 S 145 13 E
Criciúma **125** 28 40 S 49 23W
Crieff **14** 56 22N 3 50W
Crikvenica **39** 45 11N 14 40 E
Crimea = Krymskaya **56** 45 0N 34 0 E
Crimmitschau **24** 50 48N 12 23 E
Crinan **14** 56 6N 5 34W
Cristeşti **46** 47 15N 26 33 E
Cristóbal **120** 9 19N 79 54W
Crişul Alb → **42** 46 42N 21 17 E
Crişul Negru → **46** 46 38N 22 26 E
Crişul Repede → **46** 46 55N 20 59 E
Crivitz **24** 53 35N 11 39 E
Crna Gora **42** 42 10N 21 30 E
Crna Gora □ **42** 42 40N 19 20 E
Crna Reka → **42** 41 33N 21 59 E
Crna Trava **42** 42 49N 22 19 E
Crni Drim → **42** 41 17N 20 40 E
Crni Timok → **42** 43 53N 22 15 E
Črnoljeva Planina **42** 42 20N 21 0 E
Črnomelj **39** 45 33N 15 10 E
Croaghpatrick **15** 53 46N 9 40W
Croatia = Hrvatska □ **39** 45 20N 16 0 E
Crocker, Barisan **72** 5 40N 116 30 E
Crocker I. **96** 11 12 S 132 32 E
Crockett **117** 31 20N 95 30W
Crocodile = Krokodil → **93** 25 26 S 32 0 E
Crocodile Is. **96** 12 3 S 134 58 E
Crocq **20** 45 52N 2 21 E
Croisette, C. **21** 43 13N 5 20 E
Croisic, Le **18** 47 18N 2 30W
Croisic, Pte. du **18** 47 19N 2 31W
Croix, La, L. **106** 48 20N 92 15W
Cromarty, Can. **109** 58 3N 94 9W
Cromarty, U.K. **14** 57 40N 4 2W
Cromer **12** 52 56N 1 18 E
Cromwell **101** 45 3 S 169 14 E
Cronat **19** 46 43N 3 40 E
Cronulla **100** 34 3 S 151 8 E
Crooked →, Can. **108** 54 50N 122 54W
Crooked →, U.S.A. **118** 44 30N 121 16W
Crooked I. **121** 22 50N 74 10W
Crookston, Minn., U.S.A. **116** 47 50N 96 40W
Crookston, Nebr., U.S.A. **116** 42 56N 100 45W
Crooksville **114** 39 45N 82 8W
Crookwell **99** 34 28 S 149 24 E
Crosby, Minn., U.S.A. **116** 46 28N 93 57W
Crosby, N.D., U.S.A. **109** 48 55N 103 18W
Crosby, Pa., U.S.A. **112** 41 45N 78 23W
Crosbyton **117** 33 37N 101 12W
Cross → **85** 4 42N 8 21 E
Cross City **115** 29 35N 83 5W
Cross Fell **12** 54 44N 2 29W
Cross L. **109** 54 45N 97 30W
Cross Plains **117** 32 8N 99 7W
Cross River □ **85** 6 0N 8 0 E
Cross Sound **104** 58 20N 136 30W
Crosse, La, Kans., U.S.A. **116** 38 33N 99 20W
Crosse, La, Wis., U.S.A. **116** 43 48N 91 13W
Crossett **117** 33 10N 91 57W
Crossfield **108** 51 25N 114 0W
Crosshaven **15** 51 48N 8 19W
Croton-on-Hudson **113** 41 12N 73 55W
Crotone **41** 39 5N 17 6 E
Crow → **108** 59 41N 124 20W
Crow Agency **118** 45 40N 107 30W
Crow Hd. **15** 51 34N 10 9W
Crowell **117** 33 59N 99 45W
Crowley **117** 30 15N 92 20W
Crown Point **114** 41 24N 87 23W
Crows Nest **99** 27 16 S 152 4 E
Crowsnest Pass **108** 49 40N 114 40W
Croydon, Austral. **97** 18 13 S 142 14 E
Croydon, U.K. **13** 51 18N 0 5W
Crozet Is. **3** 46 27 S 52 0 E
Crozon **18** 48 15N 4 30W
Cruz Alta **125** 28 45 S 53 40W
Cruz, C. **121** 19 50N 77 50W
Cruz del Eje **124** 30 45 S 64 50W
Cruz, La **120** 23 55N 106 54W
Cruzeiro **125** 22 33 S 45 0W
Cruzeiro do Oeste **125** 23 46 S 53 4W
Cruzeiro do Sul **126** 7 35 S 72 35W
Cry L. **108** 58 45N 129 0W
Crystal Brook **99** 33 21 S 138 12 E
Crystal City, Mo., U.S.A. **116** 38 15N 90 23W
Crystal City, Tex., U.S.A. **117** 28 40N 99 50W
Crystal Falls **114** 46 9N 88 11W
Crystal River **115** 28 54N 82 35W
Crystal Springs **117** 31 59N 90 25W
Csongrád **27** 46 43N 20 12 E
Csongrád □ **27** 46 32N 20 15 E
Csorna **27** 47 38N 17 18 E
Csurgo **27** 46 16N 17 9 E
Cu Lao Hon **71** 10 54N 108 18 E
Cuácua → **91** 17 54 S 37 0 E
Cuamato **92** 17 2 S 15 7 E
Cuamba **91** 14 45 S 36 22 E
Cuando → **89** 14 0 S 19 30 E
Cuando Cubango □ **92** 16 25 S 20 0 E
Cuangar **92** 17 36 S 18 39 E
Cuarto → **124** 33 25 S 63 2W
Cuba, Port. **31** 38 10N 7 54W
Cuba, N. Mex., U.S.A. **119** 36 0N 107 0W
Cuba, N.Y., U.S.A. **112** 42 12N 78 18W
Cuba ■ **121** 22 0N 79 0W
Cubango → **92** 18 50 S 22 25 E
Cuchi **89** 14 37 S 16 58 E
Cúcuta **126** 7 54N 72 31W
Cudahy **114** 42 54N 87 50W
Cudalbi **46** 45 46N 27 41 E
Cuddalore **70** 11 46N 79 45 E
Cuddapah **70** 14 30N 78 47 E
Cuddapan, L. **99** 25 45 S 141 26 E
Cudgewa **99** 36 10 S 147 42 E
Cudillero **30** 43 33N 6 9W
Cue **96** 27 25 S 117 54 E
Cuéllar **30** 41 23N 4 21W
Cuenca, Ecuador **126** 2 50 S 79 9W
Cuenca, Spain **32** 40 5N 2 10W
Cuenca □ **32** 40 0N 2 0W
Cuenca, Serranía de **32** 39 55N 1 50W
Cuerda del Pozo, Pantano de la **32** 41 51N 2 44W
Cuernavaca **120** 18 50N 99 20W
Cuero **117** 29 5N 97 17W
Cuers **21** 43 14N 6 5 E
Cuervo **117** 35 5N 104 25W
Cuevas del Almanzora **33** 37 18N 1 58W
Cuevo **126** 20 15 S 63 30W
Cugir **46** 45 48N 23 25 E
Cuiabá **127** 15 30 S 56 0W
Cuiabá → **127** 17 5 S 56 36W
Cuillin Hills **14** 57 14N 6 15W
Cuillin Sd. **14** 57 4N 6 20W
Cuiluan **76** 47 51N 128 32 E
Cuima **89** 13 25 S 15 45 E
Cuiseaux **21** 46 30N 5 22 E
Cuito → **92** 18 1 S 20 48 E
Cuitzeo, L. de **120** 19 55N 101 5W
Cujmir **46** 44 13N 22 57 E
Culan **20** 46 34N 2 20 E
Culbertson **116** 48 9N 104 30W
Culcairn **99** 35 41 S 147 3 E
Culebra, Sierra de la **30** 41 55N 6 20W
Culgoa → **99** 29 56 S 146 20 E
Culiacán **120** 24 50N 107 23W
Culion **73** 11 54N 120 1 E
Cúllar de Baza **33** 37 35N 2 34W
Cullarin Range **99** 34 30 S 149 30 E
Cullen **14** 57 45N 2 50W
Cullen Pt. **98** 11 57 S 141 54 E
Cullera **33** 39 9N 0 17W
Cullman **115** 34 13N 86 50W
Culloden Moor **14** 57 29N 4 7W
Culoz **21** 45 47N 5 46 E
Culpeper **114** 38 29N 77 59W
Culuene → **127** 12 56 S 52 51W
Culver, Pt. **96** 32 54 S 124 43 E
Culverden **101** 42 47 S 172 49 E
Cumali **45** 36 42N 27 28 E
Cumaná **126** 10 30N 64 5W
Cumberland, B.C., Can. **108** 49 40N 125 0W
Cumberland, Qué., Can. **113** 45 30N 75 24W
Cumberland, Md., U.S.A. **114** 39 40N 78 43W
Cumberland, Wis., U.S.A. **116** 45 32N 92 3W
Cumberland → **115** 36 15N 87 0W
Cumberland I. **115** 30 52N 81 30W
Cumberland Is. **97** 20 35 S 149 10 E
Cumberland L. **109** 54 3N 102 18W
Cumberland Pen. **105** 67 0N 64 0W
Cumberland Plat. **115** 36 0N 84 30W
Cumberland Sd. **105** 65 30N 66 0W
Cumborah **99** 29 40 S 147 45 E
Cumbres Mayores **31** 38 4N 6 39W
Cumbria □ **12** 54 35N 2 55W
Cumbrian Mts. **12** 54 30N 3 0W
Cumbum **70** 15 40N 79 10 E
Cumnock, Austral. **99** 32 59 S 148 46 E
Cumnock, U.K. **14** 55 27N 4 18W
Cuncumén **124** 31 53 S 70 38W
Cunene → **92** 17 20 S 11 50 E
Cúneo **38** 44 23N 7 31 E
Cunillera, I. **33** 38 59N 1 13 E
Cunlhat **20** 45 38N 3 32 E
Cunnamulla **97** 28 2 S 145 38 E
Cuorgnè **38** 45 23N 7 39 E
Cupar, Can. **109** 50 57N 104 10W
Cupar, U.K. **14** 56 20N 3 0W
Cupica, Golfo de **126** 6 25N 77 30W
Ćuprija **42** 43 57N 21 26 E
Curaçao **121** 12 10N 69 0W
Curanilahue **124** 37 29 S 73 28W
Curaray → **126** 2 20 S 74 5W
Cure → **19** 47 40N 3 41 E
Curepto **124** 35 8 S 72 1W
Curiapo **126** 8 33N 61 5W
Curicó **124** 34 55 S 71 20W
Curicó □ **124** 34 50 S 71 15W
Curitiba **125** 25 20 S 49 10W
Currabubula **99** 31 16 S 150 44 E
Currais Novos **127** 6 13 S 36 30W
Curralinho **127** 1 45 S 49 46W
Currant **118** 38 51N 115 32W
Curraweena **99** 30 47 S 145 54 E
Currawilla **99** 25 10 S 141 20 E
Current → **117** 37 15N 91 10W
Currie, Austral. **99** 39 56 S 143 53 E
Currie, U.S.A. **118** 40 16N 114 45W
Currie, Mt. **93** 30 29 S 29 21 E
Currituck Sd. **115** 36 20N 75 50W
Currockbilly Mt. **100** 35 25 S 150 0 E
Curtea de Argeş **46** 45 12N 24 42 E
Curtis, Spain **30** 43 7N 8 4W
Curtis, U.S.A. **116** 40 41N 100 32W
Curtis I. **97** 23 35 S 151 10 E
Curuápanema → **127** 2 25 S 55 2W
Curuçá **127** 0 43 S 47 50W
Curuguaty **125** 24 31 S 55 42W
Çürüksu Çayi → **53** 37 27N 27 11 E
Curundu **120** 8 59N 79 38W
Curup **72** 4 26 S 102 13 E
Cururupu **127** 1 50 S 44 50W
Curuzú Cuatiá **124** 29 50 S 58 5W
Curvelo **127** 18 45 S 44 27W
Cushing **117** 35 59N 96 46W
Cushing, Mt. **108** 57 35N 126 57W
Cusihuiriáchic **120** 28 10N 106 50W
Cusna, Monte **38** 44 13N 10 25 E
Cusset **20** 46 8N 3 28 E
Custer **116** 43 45N 103 38W
Cut Bank **118** 48 40N 112 15W
Cuthbert **115** 31 47N 84 47W
Cutro **41** 39 1N 16 58 E
Cuttaburra → **99** 29 43 S 144 22 E
Cuttack **69** 20 25N 85 57 E
Cuvier, C. **96** 23 14 S 113 22 E
Cuvier I. **101** 36 27 S 175 50 E
Cuxhaven **24** 53 51N 8 41 E
Cuyahoga Falls **114** 41 8N 81 30W
Cuyo **73** 10 50N 121 5 E
Cuzco, Boliv. **126** 20 0 S 66 50W
Cuzco, Peru **126** 13 32 S 72 0W
Čvrsnica **42** 43 36N 17 35 E
Cwmbran **13** 51 39N 3 0W
Cyangugu **90** 2 29 S 28 54 E
Cybinka **28** 52 12N 14 46 E
Cyclades = Kikladhes **45** 37 20N 24 30 E
Cygnet **99** 43 8 S 147 1 E
Cynthiana **114** 38 23N 84 10W
Cypress Hills **109** 49 40N 109 30W
Cyprus ■ **64** 35 0N 33 0 E
Cyrenaica **81** 27 0N 23 0 E
Cyrene = Shaḥḥāt **81** 32 40N 21 35 E
Czaplinek **28** 53 34N 16 14 E
Czar **109** 52 27N 110 50W
Czarna →, Piotrkow Trybunalski, Poland **28** 51 18N 19 55 E
Czarna →, Tarnobrzeg, Poland **28** 50 3N 21 21 E
Czarna Woda **28** 53 51N 18 6 E
Czarne **28** 53 42N 16 58 E
Czarnków **28** 52 55N 16 38 E
Czechoslovakia ■ **27** 49 0N 17 0 E
Czechowice-Dziedzice **27** 49 54N 18 59 E
Czeladz **28** 50 16N 19 2 E
Czempiń **28** 52 9N 16 33 E
Czeremcha **28** 52 31N 23 21 E
Czersk **28** 53 46N 17 58 E
Czerwieńsk **28** 52 1N 15 13 E
Czerwionka **27** 50 7N 18 37 E
Częstochowa **28** 50 49N 19 7 E
Częstochowa □ **28** 50 45N 19 0 E
Człopa **28** 53 6N 16 6 E
Człuchów **28** 53 41N 17 22 E
Czyzew **28** 52 48N 22 19 E

D

Da → **71** 21 15N 105 20 E
Da Hinggan Ling **75** 48 0N 121 0 E
Da Lat **71** 11 56N 108 25 E
Da Nang **71** 16 4N 108 13 E
Da Qaidam **75** 37 50N 95 15 E
Da Yunhe, Jiangsu, China **77** 34 25N 120 5 E
Da Yunhe, Zhejiang, China **77** 30 45N 120 35 E
Da'an **76** 45 30N 124 7 E
Dab'a, Râs el **86** 31 3N 28 31 E
Daba Shan **75** 32 0N 109 0 E
Dabai **85** 11 25N 5 15 E
Dabakala **84** 8 15N 4 20W
Dabbūrīya **62** 32 42N 35 22 E
Dabhoi **68** 22 10N 73 20 E
Dąbie, Poland **28** 53 27N 14 45 E
Dąbie, Poland **28** 52 5N 18 50 E
Dabo **72** 0 30 S 104 33 E
Dabola **84** 10 50N 11 5W
Dabou **84** 5 20N 4 23W
Daboya **85** 9 30N 1 20W
Dabrowa Górnicza **28** 50 15N 19 10 E
Dabrowa Tarnówska **27** 50 10N 20 59 E
Dąbrówno **28** 53 27N 20 2 E
Dabus → **87** 10 48N 35 10 E
Dacato → **87** 7 25N 42 40 E
*Dacca **69** 23 43N 90 26 E
*Dacca □ **69** 24 25N 90 25 E
Dachau **25** 48 16N 11 27 E
Dadanawa **126** 2 50N 59 30W
Daday **56** 41 28N 33 27 E
Dade City **115** 28 20N 82 12W
Dades, Oued → **82** 30 58N 6 44W
Dadiya **85** 9 35N 11 24 E
Dadra and Nagar Haveli □ **68** 20 5N 73 0 E
Dadri = Charkhi Dadri **68** 28 37N 76 17 E
Dadu **68** 26 45N 67 45 E
Dăeni **46** 44 51N 28 10 E
Daet **73** 14 2N 122 55 E
Dafang **77** 27 9N 105 39 E
Dagana **84** 16 30N 15 35W
Dagash **86** 19 19N 33 25 E
Dagestan A.S.S.R. □ **57** 42 30N 47 0 E
Dagestanskiye Ogni **57** 42 6N 48 12 E
Daghfeli **86** 19 18N 32 40 E
Dagö = Hiiumaa **54** 58 50N 22 45 E
Dagupan **73** 16 3N 120 20 E
Dahab **86** 28 30N 34 31 E
Dahlak Kebir **87** 15 50N 40 10 E
Dahlenburg **24** 53 11N 10 43 E
Dahlonega **115** 34 35N 83 59W
Dahme, Germ., E. **24** 51 51N 13 25 E
Dahme, Germ., W. **24** 54 13N 11 5 E
Dahomey = Benin ■ **85** 10 0N 2 0 E
Dahra **84** 15 22N 15 30W
Dahra, Massif de **82** 36 7N 1 21 E
Dai Shan **77** 30 25N 122 10 E
Dai Xian **76** 39 4N 112 58 E
Daimiel **33** 39 5N 3 35W
Daingean **15** 53 18N 7 15W
Daintree **98** 16 20 S 145 20 E
Daiō-Misaki **74** 34 15N 136 45 E
Dairût **86** 27 34N 30 43 E
Daitari **69** 21 10N 85 46 E
Dajarra **97** 21 42 S 139 30 E
Dakar **84** 14 34N 17 29W
Dakhla **80** 23 50N 15 53W
Dakhla, El Wâhât el- **86** 25 30N 28 50 E
Dakhovskaya **57** 44 13N 40 13 E
Dakingari **85** 11 37N 4 1 E
Dakor **68** 22 45N 73 11 E
Dakoro **85** 14 31N 6 46 E
Dakota City **116** 42 27N 96 28W
Đakovica **42** 42 22N 20 26 E
Đakovo **42** 45 19N 18 24 E
Dalaba **84** 10 42N 12 15W
Dalachi **76** 36 48N 105 0 E
Dalai Nur **76** 43 20N 116 45 E
Dalandzadgad **75** 43 27N 104 30 E
Dalbandin **65** 29 0N 64 23 E
Dalbeattie **14** 54 55N 3 50W
Dalbosjön **49** 58 40N 12 45 E
Dalby, Austral. **97** 27 10 S 151 17 E
Dalby, Sweden **49** 55 40N 13 22 E
Dale **47** 61 22N 5 23 E
Dalen **47** 59 26N 8 0 E
Dalga **86** 27 39N 30 41 E
Dalhart **117** 36 10N 102 30W
Dalhousie, Can. **107** 48 5N 66 26W
Dalhousie, India **68** 32 38N 76 0 E
Dali, Shaanxi, China **77** 34 48N 109 58 E
Dali, Yunnan, China **75** 25 40N 100 10 E
Daliang Shan **75** 28 0N 102 45 E
Dalias **33** 36 49N 2 52W
Dāliyat el Karmel **62** 32 43N 35 2 E
Dalj **42** 45 29N 18 59 E
Dalkeith **14** 55 54N 3 5W
Dall I. **108** 54 59N 133 25W
Dallarnil **99** 25 19 S 152 2 E
Dallas, Oregon, U.S.A. **118** 45 0N 123 15W
Dallas, Texas, U.S.A. **117** 32 50N 96 50W
Dallol **87** 14 14N 40 17 E
Dalmacija □ **42** 43 20N 17 0 E
Dalmatia = Dalmacija □ **42** 43 20N 17 0 E
Dalmellington **14** 55 20N 4 25W
Dalneretchensk **59** 45 50N 133 40 E
Daloa **84** 7 0N 6 30W
Dalrymple, Mt. **97** 21 1 S 148 39 E
Dalsjöfors **49** 57 46N 13 5 E
Dalskog **49** 58 44N 12 18 E
Dalton, Can. **106** 48 11N 84 1W
Dalton, Ga., U.S.A. **115** 34 47N 84 58W
Dalton, Mass., U.S.A. **113** 42 28N 73 11W
Dalton, Nebr., U.S.A. **116** 41 27N 103 0W
Dalton Iceberg Tongue **5** 66 15 S 121 30 E
Daltonganj **69** 24 0N 84 4 E
Dalvik **50** 65 58N 18 32W
Daly → **96** 13 35 S 130 19 E
Daly L. **109** 56 32N 105 39W
Daly Waters **96** 16 15 S 133 24 E
Dama, Wadi → **86** 27 12N 35 50 E
Daman **68** 20 25N 72 57 E
Daman □ **68** 20 25N 72 58 E
Damanhûr **86** 31 0N 30 30 E
Damar **73** 7 7 S 128 40 E
Damaraland **92** 21 0 S 17 0 E
Damascus = Dimashq **64** 33 30N 36 18 E
Damaturu **85** 11 45N 11 55 E
Damāvand **65** 35 47N 52 0 E
Damāvand, Qolleh-ye **65** 35 56N 52 10 E
Damba **88** 6 44 S 15 20 E

*Renamed Dhaka

Dāmghān Dessye

Dāmghān 65 36 10N 54 17 E
Dâmienesti 46 46 44N 27 1 E
Damietta = Dumyât 86 31 24N 31 48 E
Daming 76 36 15N 115 6 E
Dāmīya 62 32 6N 35 34 E
Dammarie 19 48 20N 1 30 E
Dammartin 19 49 3N 2 41 E
Damme 24 52 32N 8 12 E
Damodar → 69 23 17N 87 35 E
Damoh 69 23 50N 79 28 E
Damous 82 36 31N 1 42 E
Dampier 96 20 41 S 116 42 E
Dampier Arch. 96 20 38 S 116 32 E
Dampier Downs 96 18 24 S 123 5 E
Dampier, Selat 73 0 40 S 131 0 E
Dampier Str. 98 5 50 S 148 0 E
Damville 18 48 51N 1 5 E
Damvillers 19 49 20N 5 21 E
Dan-Gulbi 85 11 40N 6 15 E
Dan Xian 77 19 31N 109 33 E
Dana 73 11 0 S 122 52 E
Dana, Lac 106 50 53N 77 20W
Danakil Depression 87 12 45N 41 0 E
Danao 73 10 31N 124 1 E
Danbury 114 41 23N 73 29W
Danby L. 119 34 17N 115 0W
Dandeldhura 69 29 20N 80 35 E
Dandenong 99 38 0 S 145 15 E
Dandong 76 40 10N 124 20 E
Danforth 107 45 39N 67 57W
* Danger Is. 95 10 53 S 165 49W
Danger Pt. 92 34 40 S 19 17 E
Dangla 87 11 18N 36 56 E
Dangora 85 11 30N 8 7 E
Dangshan 77 34 27N 116 22 E
Dangtu 77 31 32N 118 25 E
Dangyang 77 30 52N 111 44 E
Daniel 118 42 56N 110 2W
Daniel's Harbour 107 50 13N 57 35W
Danielskull 92 28 11 S 23 33 E
Danielson 113 41 50N 71 52W
Danilov 55 58 16N 40 13 E
Danilovgrad 42 42 38N 19 9 E
Danilovka 55 50 25N 44 12 E
Danissa 90 3 15N 40 58 E
Danja 85 11 21N 7 30 E
Dankalwa 85 11 52N 12 12 E
Dankama 85 13 20N 7 44 E
Dankov 55 53 20N 39 5 E
Danlí 121 14 4N 86 35W
Dannemora, Sweden 48 60 12N 17 51 E
Dannemora, U.S.A. 114 44 41N 73 44W
Dannenberg 24 53 7N 11 4 E
Dannevirke 101 40 12 S 176 8 E
Dannhauser 93 28 0 S 30 3 E
Danshui 77 25 12N 121 25 E
Dansville 114 42 32N 77 41W
Dantan 69 21 57N 87 20 E
Dante 63 10 25N 51 26 E
Danube → 43 45 20N 29 40 E
Danukandi 69 23 32N 90 43 E
Danvers 113 42 34N 70 55W
Danville, Ill., U.S.A. 114 40 10N 87 40W
Danville, Ky., U.S.A. 114 37 40N 84 45W
Danville, Va., U.S.A. 115 36 40N 79 20W
Danzhai 77 26 11N 107 48 E
Danzig = Gdańsk 28 54 22N 18 40 E
Dao 73 10 30N 121 57 E
Dão → 30 40 20N 8 11W
Dao Xian 77 25 36N 111 31 E
Daosa 68 26 52N 76 20 E
Daoud = Aïn Beida 83 35 44N 7 22 E
Daoulas 18 48 22N 4 17W
Dapong 85 10 55N 0 16 E
Daqing Shan 76 40 40N 111 0 E
Daqu Shan 77 30 25N 122 20 E
Dar al Hamrā, Ad 64 27 22N 37 43 E
Dar es Salaam 90 6 50 S 39 12 E
Dar'ā 62 32 36N 36 7 E
Dārāb 65 28 50N 54 30 E
Darabani 46 48 10N 26 39 E
Daraj 83 30 10N 10 28 E
Daravica 42 42 32N 20 8 E
Daraw 86 24 22N 32 51 E
Darazo 85 11 1N 10 24 E
Darband 66 34 20N 72 50 E
Darbhanga 69 26 15N 85 55 E
Darby 118 46 2N 114 7W
Darda 42 45 40N 18 41 E
Dardanelle 117 35 12N 93 9W
Dardanelles = Canakkale Boğazi 44 40 0N 26 0 E
Darfo 38 45 52N 10 11 E
Dargai 66 34 25N 71 55 E
Dargan Ata 58 40 29N 62 10 E
Dargaville 101 35 57 S 173 52 E
Darhan Muminggan Lianheqi 76 41 40N 110 28 E
Dari 87 5 48N 30 26 E
Darien 120 9 7N 79 46W
Darién, G. del 126 9 0N 77 0W
Darjeeling 69 27 3N 88 18 E
Dark Cove 107 48 47N 54 13W
Darling → 97 34 4 S 141 54 E
Darling Downs 99 27 30 S 150 30 E
Darling Ra. 96 32 30 S 116 0 E
Darlington, U.K. 12 54 33N 1 33W
Darlington, S.C., U.S.A. 115 34 18N 79 50W
Darlington, Wis., U.S.A. 116 42 43N 90 7W
Darlington Point 100 34 37 S 146 1 E
Darłowo 28 54 25N 16 25 E
Dărmăneşti 46 46 21N 26 33 E
Darmstadt 25 49 51N 8 40 E
Darnah 81 32 40N 22 35 E
Darnall 93 29 23 S 31 18 E
Darnétal 18 49 25N 1 10 E
Darney 19 48 5N 6 0 E
Darnick 100 32 48 S 143 38 E
Darnley B. 104 69 30N 123 30W
Darnley, C. 5 68 0 S 69 0 E
Daroca 32 41 9N 1 25W
Darr 98 23 13 S 144 7 E
Darr → 98 23 39 S 143 50 E
Darrington 118 48 14N 121 37W
Darror → 63 10 30N 50 0 E
Darsana 69 23 35N 88 48 E
Darsi 70 15 46N 79 44 E
Darsser Ort 24 54 29N 12 31 E
Dart → 13 50 24N 3 36W
Dart, C. 5 73 6 S 126 20W
Dartmoor 13 50 36N 4 0W
Dartmouth, Austral. 98 23 31 S 144 44 E
Dartmouth, Can. 107 44 40N 63 30W
Dartmouth, U.K. 13 50 21N 3 35W
Dartmouth, L. 99 26 4 S 145 18 E
Dartuch, C. 32 39 55N 3 49 E
Daru 98 9 3 S 143 13 E
Daruvar 42 45 35N 17 14 E
Darvaza 58 40 11N 58 24 E
Darwha 68 20 15N 77 45 E
Darwin 96 12 25 S 130 51 E
Darwin Glacier 5 79 53 S 159 0 E
Daryacheh-ye-Sistan 65 31 0N 61 0 E
Daryapur 68 20 55N 77 20 E
Das 65 25 20N 53 30 E
Dashkesan 57 40 40N 46 0 E
Dasht → 65 25 10N 61 40 E
Dasht-e Kavīr 65 34 30N 55 0 E
Dasht-e Lūt 65 31 30N 58 0 E
Dasht-e Mārgow 65 30 40N 62 30 E
Daska 68 32 20N 74 20 E
Dassa-Zoume 85 7 46N 2 14 E
Dasseneiland 92 33 25 S 18 3 E
Datça 45 36 46N 27 40 E
Datia 68 25 39N 78 27 E
Datian 77 25 40N 117 50 E
Datong, Anhui, China 77 30 48N 117 44 E
Datong, Shanxi, China 76 40 6N 113 18 E
Dattapur 68 20 45N 78 15 E
Datu Piang 73 7 2N 124 30 E
Datu, Tanjung 72 2 5N 109 39 E
Daugava → 54 57 4N 24 3 E
Daugavpils 54 55 53N 26 32 E
Daulatabad 70 19 57N 75 15 E
Daun 25 50 10N 6 53 E
Dauphin 109 51 9N 100 5W
Dauphin I. 115 30 16N 88 10W
Dauphin L. 109 51 20N 99 45W
Dauphiné 21 45 15N 5 25 E
Dauqa 86 19 30N 41 0 E
Daura, Borno, Nigeria 85 11 31N 11 24 E
Daura, Kaduna, Nigeria 85 13 2N 8 21 E
Davangere 70 14 25N 75 55 E
Davao 73 7 0N 125 40 E
Davao, G. of 73 6 30N 125 48 E
Dāvar Panāh 65 27 25N 62 15 E
Davenport, Iowa, U.S.A. 116 41 30N 90 40W
Davenport, Wash., U.S.A. 118 47 40N 118 5W
Davenport Downs 98 24 8 S 141 7 E
Davenport Ra. 96 20 28 S 134 0 E
David 121 8 30N 82 30W
David City 116 41 18N 97 10W
David Gorodok 54 52 4N 27 8 E
Davidson 109 51 16N 105 59W
Davis, Antarct. 5 68 34 S 17 55 E
Davis, U.S.A. 118 38 33N 121 44W
Davis Dam 119 35 11N 114 35W
Davis Inlet 107 55 50N 60 59W
Davis Mts. 117 30 42N 104 15W
Davis Sea 5 66 0 S 92 0 E
Davis Str. 105 65 0N 58 0W
Davos 25 46 48N 9 49 E
Davy L. 109 58 53N 108 18W
Dawa → 87 4 11N 42 6 E
Dawaki, Bauchi, Nigeria 85 9 25N 9 33 E
Dawaki, Kano, Nigeria 85 12 5N 8 23 E
Dawes Ra. 98 24 40 S 150 40 E
Dawson, Can. 104 64 10N 139 30W
Dawson, Ga., U.S.A. 115 31 45N 84 28W
Dawson, N.D., U.S.A. 116 46 56N 99 45W
Dawson → 97 23 25 S 149 45 E
Dawson Creek 108 55 45N 120 15W
Dawson, I. 128 53 50 S 70 50W
Dawson Inlet 109 61 50N 93 25W
Dawson Range 98 24 30 S 149 48 E
Dax 20 43 44N 1 3W
Daxian 75 31 15N 107 23 E
Daxin 77 22 50N 107 11 E
Daxue Shan 75 30 30N 101 30 E
Daye 77 30 6N 114 58 E
Daylesford 100 37 21 S 144 9 E
Dayong 77 29 11N 110 30 E
Dayr Abū Sa'īd 62 32 30N 35 42 E
Dayr al-Ghuşūn 62 32 21N 35 4 E
Dayr az Zawr 64 35 20N 40 5 E
Dayr Dirwān 62 31 55N 35 15 E
Daysland 108 52 50N 112 20W
Dayton, Ohio, U.S.A. 114 39 45N 84 10W
Dayton, Pa., U.S.A. 112 40 54N 79 18W
Dayton, Tenn., U.S.A. 115 35 30N 85 1W
Dayton, Wash., U.S.A. 118 46 20N 118 0W
Daytona Beach 115 29 14N 81 0W
Dayu 77 25 24N 114 22 E
Dayville 118 44 33N 119 37W
Dazhu 77 30 41N 107 15 E
Dazu 77 29 40N 105 42 E
De Aar 92 30 39 S 24 0 E
De Funiak Springs 115 30 42N 86 10W
De Grey 96 20 12 S 119 12 E
De Land 115 29 1N 81 19W
De Leon 117 32 9N 98 35W
De Pere 114 44 28N 88 1W
De Queen 117 34 3N 94 24W
De Quincy 117 30 30N 93 27W
De Ridder 117 30 48N 93 15W
De Smet 116 44 25N 97 35W
De Soto 116 38 7N 90 33W
De Tour 114 45 59N 83 56W
De Witt 117 34 19N 91 20W
Dead Sea = Miyet, Bahr el 64 31 30N 35 30 E
Deadwood 116 44 23N 103 44W
Deadwood L. 108 59 10N 128 30W
Deakin 96 30 46 S 128 0 E
Deal 13 51 13N 1 25 E
Dealesville 92 28 41 S 25 44 E
Dean, Forest of 13 51 50N 2 35W
Deán Funes 124 30 20 S 64 20W
Dearborn 106 42 18N 83 15W
Dease → 108 59 56N 128 32W
Dease L. 108 58 40N 130 5W
Dease Lake 108 58 25N 130 6W
Death Valley 119 36 19N 116 52W
Death Valley Junc. 119 36 21N 116 30W
Death Valley Nat. Monument 119 36 30N 117 0W
Deauville 18 49 23N 0 2 E
Deba Habe 85 10 14N 11 20 E
Debaltsevo 56 48 22N 38 26 E
Debao 77 23 21N 106 46 E
Debar 42 41 31N 20 30 E
Debden 109 53 30N 106 50W
Debdou 82 33 59N 3 0W
Dębica 27 50 2N 21 25 E
Dęblin 28 51 34N 21 50 E
Debno 28 52 44N 14 41 E
Débo, L. 84 15 14N 4 15W
Debolt 108 55 12N 118 1W
Debrc 42 44 38N 19 53 E
Debre Birhan 87 9 41N 39 31 E
Debre Markos 87 10 20N 37 40 E
Debre May 87 11 20N 37 25 E
Debre Sina 87 9 51N 39 50 E
Debre Tabor 87 11 50N 38 26 E
Debre Zebit 87 11 48N 38 30 E
Debrecen 27 47 33N 21 42 E
Dečani 42 42 30N 20 10 E
Decatur, Ala., U.S.A. 115 34 35N 87 0W
Decatur, Ga., U.S.A. 115 33 47N 84 17W
Decatur, Ill., U.S.A. 116 39 50N 89 0W
Decatur, Ind., U.S.A. 114 40 50N 84 56W
Decatur, Texas, U.S.A. 117 33 15N 97 35W
Decazeville 20 44 34N 2 15 E
Deccan 70 18 0N 79 0 E
Deception I. 5 63 0 S 60 15W
Deception L. 109 56 33N 104 13W
Děčín 26 50 47N 14 12 E
Decize 19 46 50N 3 28 E
Deckerville 112 43 33N 82 46W
Decollatura 41 39 2N 16 21 E
Decorah 116 43 20N 91 50W
Deda 46 46 56N 24 50 E
Dedéagach = Alexandroúpolis 44 40 50N 25 54 E
Dedham 113 42 14N 71 10W
Dedilovo 55 53 59N 37 50 E
Dédougou 84 12 30N 3 25W
Deduru Oya 70 7 32N 79 50 E
Dedza 91 14 20 S 34 20 E
Dee →, Scot., U.K. 14 57 4N 2 7W
Dee →, Wales, U.K. 12 53 15N 3 7W
Deep B. 108 61 15N 116 35W
Deepdale 96 21 42 S 116 10 E
Deepwater 99 29 25 S 151 51 E
Deer → 109 58 23N 94 13W
Deer Lake, Newf., Can. 107 49 11N 57 27W
Deer Lake, Ontario, Can. 109 52 36N 94 20W
Deer Lodge 118 46 25N 112 40W
Deer Park 118 47 55N 117 21W
Deer River 116 47 21N 93 44W
Deeral 98 17 14 S 145 55 E
Deerdepoort 92 24 37 S 26 27 E
Deesa 68 24 18N 72 10 E
Deferiet 113 44 2N 75 41W
Defiance 114 41 20N 84 20W
Deganya 62 32 43N 35 34 E
Degebe → 31 38 13N 7 29W
Degeh Bur 63 8 11N 43 31 E
Degema 85 4 50N 6 48 E
Deggendorf 25 48 49N 12 59 E
Degloor 70 18 34N 77 33 E
Deh Bīd 65 30 39N 53 11 E
Deh Kheyr 65 28 45N 54 40 E
Dehibat 83 32 0N 10 47 E
Dehiwala 70 6 50N 79 51 E
Dehkareqan 64 37 43N 45 55 E
Dehra Dun 68 30 20N 78 4 E
Dehri 69 24 50N 84 15 E
Dehui 76 44 30N 125 40 E
Deinze 16 50 59N 3 32 E
Dej 46 47 10N 23 52 E
Deje 48 59 35N 13 29 E
Dekalb 116 41 55N 88 45W
Dekemhare 87 15 6N 39 0 E
Dekese 88 3 24 S 21 24 E
Del Norte 119 37 40N 106 27W
Del Rio 117 29 23N 100 50W
Delagua 117 37 21N 104 35W
Delai 86 17 21N 36 6 E
Delano 119 35 48N 119 13W
Delareyville 92 26 41 S 25 26 E
Delavan 116 42 40N 88 39W
Delaware 114 40 20N 83 0W
Delaware □ 114 39 0N 75 40W
Delaware → 114 39 20N 75 25W
Delčevo 42 41 58N 22 46 E
Delegate 99 37 4 S 148 56 E
Delémont 25 47 22N 7 20 E
Delft 16 52 1N 4 22 E
Delft I. 70 9 30N 79 40 E
Delfzijl 16 53 20N 6 55 E
Delgado, C. 91 10 45 S 40 40 E
Delgo 86 20 6N 30 40 E
Delhi, Can. 112 42 51N 80 30W
Delhi, India 68 28 38N 77 17 E
Delhi, U.S.A. 113 42 17N 74 56W
Deli Jovan 42 44 13N 22 9 E
Delia 108 51 38N 112 23W
Delice → 64 39 45N 34 15 E
Delicias 120 28 10N 105 30W
Delitzsch 24 51 32N 12 22 E
Dell City 119 31 58N 105 19W
Dell Rapids 116 43 53N 96 44W
Delle 19 47 30N 7 2 E
Dellys 83 36 57N 3 57 E
Delmar 113 42 37N 73 47W
Delmenhorst 24 53 3N 8 37 E
Delmiro Gouveia 127 9 24 S 38 6W
Delnice 39 45 23N 14 50 E
Delong, Ostrova 59 76 40N 149 20 E
Deloraine, Austral. 99 41 30 S 146 40 E
Deloraine, Can. 109 49 15N 100 29W
Delorme, L. 107 54 31N 69 52W
Delphi, Greece 45 38 28N 22 30 E
Delphi, U.S.A. 114 40 37N 86 40W
Delphos 114 40 51N 84 17W
Delportshoop 92 28 22 S 24 20 E
Delray Beach 115 26 27N 80 4W
Delsbo 48 61 48N 16 32 E
Delta, Colo., U.S.A. 119 38 44N 108 5W
Delta, Utah, U.S.A. 118 39 21N 112 29W
Delungra 99 29 39 S 150 51 E
Delvina 44 39 59N 20 4 E
Delvinákion 44 39 57N 20 32 E
Demanda, Sierra de la 32 42 15N 3 0W
Demba 88 5 28 S 22 15 E
Dembecha 87 10 32N 37 30 E
Dembi 87 8 5N 36 25 E
Dembia 90 3 33N 25 48 E
Dembidolo 87 8 34N 34 50 E
Demer → 16 50 57N 4 42 E
Demetrias 44 39 22N 23 1 E
Demidov 54 55 16N 31 30 E
Deming 119 32 10N 107 50W
Demini → 126 0 46 S 62 56W
Demmin 24 53 54N 13 2 E
Demnate 82 31 44N 6 59W
Demonte 38 44 18N 7 18 E
Demopolis 115 32 30N 87 48W
Dempo, Mt. 72 4 2 S 103 15 E
Demyansk 54 57 40N 32 27 E
Den Burg 16 53 3N 4 47 E
Den Haag = 's Gravenhage 16 52 7N 4 17 E
Den Helder 16 52 57N 4 45 E
Den Oever 16 52 56N 5 2 E
Denain 19 50 20N 3 22 E
Denau 58 38 16N 67 54 E
Denbigh 12 53 12N 3 26W
Dendang 72 3 7 S 107 56 E
Dendermonde 16 51 2N 4 5 E
Deneba 87 9 47N 39 10 E
Deng Xian 77 32 34N 112 4 E
Denge 85 12 52N 5 21 E
Dengi 85 9 25N 9 55 E
Denham 96 25 56 S 113 31 E
Denham Ra. 97 21 55 S 147 46 E
Denia 33 38 49N 0 8 E
Deniliquin 97 35 30 S 144 58 E
Denison, Iowa, U.S.A. 116 42 0N 95 18W
Denison, Texas, U.S.A. 117 33 50N 96 40W
Denison Range 97 28 30 S 136 5 E
Denizli 64 37 42N 29 2 E
Denman Glacier 5 66 45 S 99 25 E
Denmark 96 34 59 S 117 25 E
Denmark ■ 49 55 30N 9 0 E
Denmark Str. 6 66 0N 30 0W
Dennison 112 40 21N 81 21W
Denpasar 72 8 45 S 115 14 E
Denton, Mont., U.S.A. 118 47 25N 109 56W
Denton, Texas, U.S.A. 117 33 12N 97 10W
D'Entrecasteaux Is. 98 9 0 S 151 0 E
D'Entrecasteaux Pt. 96 34 50 S 115 57 E
Denu 85 6 4N 1 8 E
Denver 116 39 45N 105 0W
Denver City 117 32 58N 102 48W
Deoband 68 29 42N 77 43 E
Deobhog 70 19 53N 82 44 E
Deogarh 69 21 32N 84 45 E
Deoghar 69 24 30N 86 42 E
Deolali 70 19 58N 73 50 E
Deoli 68 25 50N 75 20 E
Deoria 69 26 31N 83 48 E
Deosai Mts. 69 35 40N 75 0 E
Depew 112 42 55N 78 43W
Deping 76 37 25N 116 58 E
Deposit 113 42 5N 75 23W
Deputatskiy 59 69 18N 139 54 E
Dêqên 75 28 34N 98 51 E
Deqing 77 23 8N 111 42 E
Dera Ghazi Khan 68 30 5N 70 43 E
Dera Ismail Khan 68 31 50N 70 50 E
* Dera Ismail Khan □ 68 32 30N 70 0 E
Derbent 56 42 5N 48 4 E
Derby, Austral. 96 17 18 S 123 38 E
Derby, U.K. 12 52 55N 1 28W
Derby, Conn., U.S.A. 113 41 20N 73 5W
Derby, N.Y., U.S.A. 112 42 40N 78 59W
Derby □ 12 52 55N 1 28W
Derecske 27 47 20N 21 33 E
Derg → 15 54 42N 7 26W
Derg, L. 15 53 0N 8 20W
Dergachi 55 50 9N 36 11 E
Dergaon 67 26 45N 94 0 E
Dermantsi 43 43 8N 24 17 E
Dernieres Isles 117 29 0N 90 45W
Derryveagh Mts. 15 55 0N 8 40W
Derudub 86 17 31N 36 7 E
Derval 18 47 40N 1 41W
Dervéni 45 38 8N 22 25 E
Derventa 42 44 59N 17 55 E
Derwent 109 53 41N 110 58W
Derwent →, Derby, U.K. 12 52 53N 1 17W
Derwent →, N. Yorks., U.K. 12 53 45N 0 57W
Derwentwater, L. 12 54 35N 3 9W
Des Moines, Iowa, U.S.A. 116 41 35N 93 37W
Des Moines, N. Mex., U.S.A. 117 36 50N 103 51W
Des Moines → 116 40 23N 91 25W
Desaguadero →, Argent. 124 34 30 S 66 46W
Desaguadero →, Boliv. 126 18 24 S 67 5W
Deschaillons 107 46 32N 72 7W
Descharme → 109 56 51N 109 13W
Deschutes → 118 45 30N 121 0W
Dese 87 11 5N 39 40 E
Desenzano del Gardo 38 45 28N 10 32 E
Desert Center 119 33 45N 115 27W
Deskenatlata L. 108 60 55N 112 3W
Desna → 54 50 33N 30 32 E
Desnătui → 46 44 15N 23 27 E
Desolación, I. 128 53 0 S 74 0W
Despeñaperros, Paso 33 38 24N 3 30W
Despotovac 42 44 6N 21 30 E
Dessau 24 51 49N 12 15 E
Dessye = Dese 87 11 5N 39 40 E

* Renamed Pakapuka

* Now part of North West Frontier □

D'Estrees B. Donja Stubica

D'Estrees B. **99** 35 55 S 137 45 E
Desuri **68** 25 18N 73 35 E
Desvrès **19** 50 40N 1 48 E
Deta **42** 45 24N 21 13 E
Detinja → **42** 43 51N 19 45 E
Detmold **24** 51 55N 8 50 E
Detour Pt. **114** 45 37N 86 35W
Detroit, Mich., U.S.A. **106** 42 23N 83 5W
Detroit, Tex., U.S.A. **117** 33 40N 95 10W
Detroit Lakes **116** 46 50N 95 50W
Dett **91** 18 38 S 26 50 E
Deurne, Belg. **16** 51 12N 4 24 E
Deurne, Neth. **16** 51 27N 5 49 E
Deutsche Bucht **24** 54 10N 7 51 E
Deutschlandsberg **26** 46 49N 15 14 E
Deux-Sèvres □ **18** 46 35N 0 20W
Deva **46** 45 53N 22 55 E
Devakottai **70** 9 55N 78 45 E
Devaprayag **68** 30 13N 78 35 E
Dévaványa **27** 47 2N 20 59 E
Deveci Daği **56** 40 10N 36 0 E
Devecser **27** 47 6N 17 26 E
Deventer **16** 52 15N 6 10 E
Deveron → **14** 57 40N 2 31W
Devesel **46** 44 28N 22 41 E
Devgad Baria **68** 22 40N 73 55 E
Devgad, I. **70** 14 48N 74 5 E
Devils Lake **116** 48 5N 98 50W
Devils Paw **108** 58 47N 134 0W
Devil's Pt. **70** 9 26N 80 6 E
Devin **43** 41 44N 24 24 E
Devizes **13** 51 21N 2 0W
Devnya **43** 43 13N 27 33 E
Devolii → **44** 40 57N 20 15 E
Devon **108** 53 24N 113 44W
Devon I. **4** 75 10N 85 0W
Devonport, Austral. **97** 41 10 S 146 22 E
Devonport, N.Z. **101** 36 49 S 174 49 E
Devonport, U.K. **13** 50 23N 4 11W
Devonshire □ **13** 50 50N 3 40W
Dewas **68** 22 59N 76 3 E
Dewetsdorp **92** 29 33 S 26 39 E
Dewsbury **12** 53 42N 1 38W
Dexter, Mo., U.S.A. **117** 36 50N 90 0W
Dexter, N. Mex., U.S.A. **117** 33 15N 104 25W
Deyhūk **65** 33 15N 57 30 E
Deyyer **65** 27 55N 51 55 E
Dezadeash L. **108** 60 28N 136 58W
Dezfūl **64** 32 20N 48 30 E
Dezh Shāhpūr **64** 35 30N 46 25 E
Dezhneva, Mys **59** 66 5N 169 40W
Dezhou **76** 37 26N 116 18 E
Dháfni **45** 37 48N 22 1 E
Dhafra **65** 23 20N 54 0 E
Dhahaban **86** 21 58N 39 3 E
Dhahira **65** 23 40N 57 0 E
Dhahiriya = Az Zāhirīyah **62** 31 25N 34 58 E
Dhahran = Az Zahrān **64** 26 18N 50 10 E
Dhamar **63** 14 30N 44 20 E
Dhamási **44** 39 43N 22 11 E
Dhampur **68** 29 19N 78 33 E
Dhamtari **69** 20 42N 81 35 E
Dhanbad **69** 23 50N 86 30 E
Dhankuta **69** 26 55N 87 40 E
Dhanora **69** 20 20N 80 22 E
Dhar **68** 22 35N 75 26 E
Dharampur, Gujarat, India **70** 20 32N 73 17 E
Dharampur, Mad. P., India **68** 22 13N 75 18 E
Dharapuram **70** 10 45N 77 34 E
Dharmapuri **70** 12 10N 78 10 E
Dharmavaram **70** 14 29N 77 44 E
Dharmsala (Dharamsala) **68** 32 16N 76 23 E
Dhaulagiri **69** 28 39N 83 28 E
Dhebar, L. **68** 24 10N 74 0 E
Dhenkanal **69** 20 45N 85 35 E
Dhenoúsa **45** 37 8N 25 48 E
Dheskáti **44** 39 55N 21 49 E
Dhespotikó **45** 36 57N 24 58 E
Dhestina **45** 38 25N 22 31 E
Dhidhimótikhon **44** 41 22N 26 29 E
Dhikti **45** 35 8N 25 22 E
Dhilianáta **45** 38 15N 20 34 E
Dhílos **45** 37 23N 25 15 E
Dhimitsána **45** 37 36N 22 3 E
Dhirfis **45** 38 40N 23 54 E
Dhodhekánisos **45** 36 35N 27 0 E
Dhokós **45** 37 20N 23 20 E
Dholiana **44** 39 54N 20 32 E
Dholka **68** 22 44N 72 29 E
Dholpur **68** 26 45N 77 59 E
Dhomokós **45** 39 10N 22 18 E
Dhond **70** 18 26N 74 40 E
Dhoraji **68** 21 45N 70 37 E
Dhoxáton **44** 41 9N 24 16 E
Dhragonísi **45** 37 27N 25 29 E
Dhrangadhra **68** 22 59N 71 31 E
Dhriopís **45** 37 25N 24 35 E
Dhrol **68** 22 33N 70 25 E
Dhubaibah **65** 23 25N 54 35 E
Dhubri **69** 26 2N 89 59 E
Dhula **63** 15 10N 47 30 E
Dhulia **68** 20 58N 74 50 E
Dhurm → **86** 20 18N 42 53 E
Di Linh, Cao Nguyen **71** 11 30N 108 0 E
Dia **45** 35 26N 25 13 E
Diablo Heights **120** 8 58N 79 34W
Diafarabé **84** 14 9N 4 57W
Diala **84** 14 10N 10 0W
Dialakoro **84** 12 18N 7 54W
Diallassagou **84** 13 47N 3 41W
Diamante **124** 32 5 S 60 40W
Diamante → **124** 34 30 S 66 46W
Diamantina **127** 18 17 S 43 40W
Diamantina → **97** 26 45 S 139 10 E
Diamantino **127** 14 30 S 56 30W
Diamond Harbour **69** 22 11N 88 14 E
Diamond Mts. **118** 40 0N 115 58W
Diamondville **118** 41 51N 110 30W
Diancheng **77** 21 30N 111 4 E
Diano Marina **38** 43 55N 8 3 E
Dianra **84** 8 45N 6 14W
Diapaga **85** 12 5N 1 46 E
Diapangou **85** 12 5N 0 10 E
Diariguila **84** 10 35N 10 2W
Dibaya **88** 6 30 S 22 57 E
Dibaya-Lubue **88** 4 12 S 19 54 E
Dibbi **87** 4 10N 41 52 E
Dibble Glacier Tongue **5** 66 8 S 134 32 E
Dibete **92** 23 45 S 26 32 E
Dibrugarh **67** 27 29N 94 55 E
Dickinson **116** 46 50N 102 48W
Dickson **115** 36 5N 87 22W
Dickson City **113** 41 29N 75 40W
Dickson (Dikson) **58** 73 40N 80 5 E
Dicomano **39** 43 53N 11 30 E
Didesa, W. → **87** 10 2N 35 32 E
Didiéni **84** 13 53N 8 6W
Didsbury **108** 51 35N 114 10W
Didwana **68** 27 23N 17 36 E
Die **21** 44 47N 5 22 E
Diébougou **84** 11 0N 3 15W
Diefenbaker L. **109** 51 0N 106 55W
Diego Garcia **3** 7 50 S 72 50 E
Diekirch **16** 49 52N 6 10 E
Diélette **18** 49 33N 1 52W
Diéma **84** 14 32N 9 12W
Diémbéring **84** 12 29N 16 47W
Dien Bien **71** 21 20N 103 0 E
Diepholz **24** 52 37N 8 22 E
Dieppe **18** 49 54N 1 4 E
Dieren **16** 52 3N 6 6 E
Dierks **117** 34 9N 94 0W
Diest **16** 50 58N 5 4 E
Dieulefit **21** 44 32N 5 4 E
Dieuze **19** 48 49N 6 43 E
Differdange **16** 49 31N 5 54 E
Dig **68** 27 28N 77 20 E
Digba **90** 4 25N 25 48 E
Digby **107** 44 38N 65 50W
Digges **109** 58 40N 94 0W
Digges Is. **105** 62 40N 77 50W
Dighinala **67** 23 15N 92 5 E
Dighton **116** 38 30N 100 26W
Digne **21** 44 5N 6 12 E
Digoin **20** 46 29N 3 58 E
Digos **73** 6 45N 125 20 E
Digranes **50** 66 4N 14 44 E
Digras **70** 20 6N 77 45 E
Digul → **73** 7 7 S 138 42 E
Dihang → **67** 27 48N 95 30 E
Dijlah, Nahr → **64** 31 0N 47 25 E
Dijon **19** 47 20N 5 0 E
Dikala **87** 4 45N 31 28 E
Dikkil **87** 11 8N 42 20 E
Dikomu di Kai **92** 24 58 S 24 36 E
Diksmuide **16** 51 2N 2 52 E
Dikwa **85** 12 4N 13 30 E
Dila **87** 6 21N 38 22 E
Dili **73** 8 39 S 125 34 E
Dilizhan **57** 40 46N 44 57 E
Dilj **42** 45 29N 18 1 E
Dillenburg **24** 50 44N 8 17 E
Dilley **117** 28 40N 99 12W
Dilling **87** 12 3N 29 35 E
Dillingen **25** 48 32N 10 29 E
Dillon, Can. **109** 55 56N 108 35W
Dillon, Mont., U.S.A. **118** 45 9N 112 36W
Dillon, S.C., U.S.A. **115** 34 26N 79 20W
Dillon → **109** 55 56N 108 56W
Dilston **99** 41 22 S 147 10 E
Dimashq **64** 33 30N 36 18 E
Dimbokro **84** 6 45N 4 46W
Dimboola **99** 36 28 S 142 7 E
Dîmboviţa □ **46** 45 0N 25 30 E
Dîmboviţa → **46** 44 14N 26 13 E
Dîmbovnic → **46** 44 28N 25 18 E
Dimbulah **98** 17 8 S 145 4 E
Dimitrovgrad, Bulg. **43** 42 5N 25 35 E
Dimitrovgrad, U.S.S.R. **55** 54 14N 49 39 E
Dimitrovgrad, Yugo. **42** 43 0N 22 48 E
Dimitrovo = Pernik **42** 42 35N 23 2 E
Dimmitt **117** 34 36N 102 16W
Dimo **87** 5 19N 29 10 E
Dimona **62** 31 2N 35 1 E
Dimovo **42** 43 43N 22 50 E
Dinagat **73** 10 10N 125 40 E
Dinajpur **69** 25 33N 88 43 E
Dinan **18** 48 28N 2 2W
Dinant **16** 50 16N 4 55 E
Dinapur **69** 25 38N 85 5 E
Dinar **64** 38 5N 30 15 E
Dinara Planina **39** 43 50N 16 35 E
Dinard **18** 48 38N 2 6W
Dinaric Alps = Dinara Planina **39** 43 50N 16 35 E
Dinder, Nahr ed → **87** 14 6N 33 40 E
Dindi → **70** 16 24N 78 15 E
Dindigul **70** 10 25N 78 0 E
Ding Xian **76** 38 30N 114 59 E
Dingbian **76** 37 35N 107 32 E
Dingelstädt **24** 51 19N 10 19 E
Dinghai **77** 30 1N 122 6 E
Dingle **15** 52 9N 10 17W
Dingle B. **15** 52 3N 10 20W
Dingmans Ferry **113** 41 13N 74 55W
Dingnan **77** 24 45N 115 0 E
Dingo **98** 23 38 S 149 19 E
Dingolfing **25** 48 38N 12 30 E
Dingtao **77** 35 5N 115 35 E
Dinguiraye **84** 11 18N 10 49W
Dingwall **14** 57 36N 4 26W
Dingxi **76** 35 30N 104 33 E
Dingxiang **76** 38 30N 112 58 E
Dinokwe (Palla Road) **92** 23 29 S 26 37 E
Dinosaur National Monument **118** 40 30N 108 58W
Dinuba **119** 36 31N 119 22W
Dio **49** 56 37N 14 15 E
Diósgyör **27** 48 7N 20 43 E
Diosig **46** 47 18N 22 2 E
Diourbel **84** 14 39N 16 12W
Diplo **68** 24 35N 69 35 E
Dipolog **73** 8 36N 123 20 E
Dipşa **46** 46 58N 24 27 E
Dir **66** 35 08N 71 59 E
Diré **84** 16 20N 3 25W
Dire Dawa **87** 9 35N 41 45 E
Direction, C. **97** 12 51 S 143 32 E
Diriamba **121** 11 51N 86 19W
Dirk Hartog I. **96** 25 50 S 113 5 E
Dirranbandi **97** 28 33 S 148 17 E
Disa **87** 12 5N 34 15 E
Disappointment, C. **118** 46 20N 124 0W
Disappointment L. **96** 23 20 S 122 40 E
Disaster B. **97** 37 15 S 150 0 E
Discovery B. **97** 38 10 S 140 40 E
Disentis **25** 46 42N 8 50 E
Dishna **86** 26 9N 32 32 E
Disina **85** 11 35N 9 50 E
Disko **4** 69 45N 53 30W
Disko Bugt **4** 69 10N 52 0W
Disna **54** 55 32N 28 11 E
Disna → **54** 55 34N 28 12 E
Distrito Federal □ **127** 15 45 S 47 45W
Disûq **86** 31 8N 30 35 E
Diu **68** 20 45N 70 58 E
Dives → **18** 49 18N 0 7W
Dives-sur-Mer **18** 49 18N 0 8W
Divi Pt. **70** 15 59N 81 9 E
Divichi **57** 41 15N 48 57 E
Divide **118** 45 48N 112 47W
Divinópolis **127** 20 10 S 44 54W
Divnoye **57** 45 55N 43 21 E
Divo **84** 5 48N 5 15W
Diwal Kol **66** 34 23N 67 52 E
Dixie **118** 45 37N 115 27W
Dixon, Ill., U.S.A. **116** 41 50N 89 30W
Dixon, Mont., U.S.A. **118** 47 19N 114 25W
Dixon, N. Mex., U.S.A. **119** 36 15N 105 57W
Dixon Entrance **108** 54 30N 132 0W
Dixonville **108** 56 32N 117 40W
Diyarbakir **64** 37 55N 40 18 E
Diz Chah **65** 35 30N 55 30 E
Djado **83** 21 4N 12 14 E
Djado, Plateau du **83** 21 29N 12 21 E
Djakarta = Jakarta **73** 6 9 S 106 49 E
Djamâa **83** 33 32N 5 59 E
Djamba **92** 16 45 S 13 58 E
Djambala **88** 2 32 S 14 30 E
Djanet **83** 24 35N 9 32 E
Djaul I. **98** 2 58 S 150 57 E
Djawa = Jawa **73** 7 0 S 110 0 E
Djebiniana **83** 35 1N 11 0 E
Djelfa **82** 34 40N 3 15 E
Djema **90** 6 3N 25 15 E
Djendel **82** 36 15N 2 25 E
Djeneïene **83** 31 45N 10 9 E
Djenné **84** 14 0N 4 30W
Djenoun, Garet el **83** 25 4N 5 31 E
Djerba **83** 33 52N 10 51 E
Djerba, Île de **83** 33 56N 11 0 E
Djerid, Chott **83** 33 42N 8 30 E
Djibo **85** 14 9N 1 35W
Djibouti **87** 11 30N 43 5 E
Djibouti ■ **63** 12 0N 43 0 E
Djolu **88** 0 35N 22 5 E
Djorong **72** 3 58 S 114 56 E
Djougou **85** 9 40N 1 45 E
Djoum **88** 2 41N 12 35 E
Djourab **81** 16 40N 18 50 E
Djugu **90** 1 55N 30 35 E
Djúpivogur **50** 64 39N 14 17W
Djursholm **48** 59 25N 18 6 E
Djursland **49** 56 27N 10 45 E
Dmitriev-Lgovskiy **54** 52 10N 35 0 E
Dmitriya Lapteva, Proliv **59** 73 0N 140 0 E
Dmitrov **55** 56 25N 37 32 E
Dmitrovsk-Orlovskiy **54** 52 29N 35 10 E
Dneiper = Dnepr → **56** 46 30N 32 18 E
Dnepr → **56** 46 30N 32 18 E
Dneprodzerzhinsk **56** 48 32N 34 37 E
Dneprodzerzhinskoye Vdkhr. **56** 49 0N 34 0 E
Dnepropetrovsk **56** 48 30N 35 0 E
Dneprorudnoye **56** 47 21N 34 58 E
Dnestr → **56** 46 18N 30 17 E
Dnestrovski = Belgorod **56** 50 35N 36 35 E
Dniester = Dnestr → **56** 46 18N 30 17 E
Dno **54** 57 50N 29 58 E
Doba **81** 8 40N 16 50 E
Dobbiaco **39** 46 44N 12 13 E
Dobbyn **97** 19 44 S 139 59 E
Dobczyce **27** 49 52N 20 25 E
Döbeln **24** 51 7N 13 10 E
Doberai, Jazirah **73** 1 25 S 133 0 E
Dobiegniew **28** 52 59N 15 45 E
Doblas **124** 37 5 S 64 0W
Dobo **73** 5 45 S 134 15 E
Doboj **42** 44 46N 18 6 E
Dobra, Konin, Poland **28** 51 55N 18 37 E
Dobra, Szczecin, Poland **28** 53 34N 15 20 E
Dobra, Dîmbovita, Romania **43** 44 52N 25 40 E
Dobra, Hunedoara, Romania **46** 45 54N 22 36 E
Dobre Miasto **28** 53 58N 20 26 E
Dobrinishta **43** 41 49N 23 34 E
Dobřiš **26** 49 46N 14 10 E
Dobrodzień **28** 50 45N 18 25 E
Dobropole **56** 48 25N 37 2 E
Dobruja **46** 44 30N 28 15 E
Dobrush **55** 52 28N 30 19 E
Dobrzyń nad Wisłą **28** 52 39N 19 22 E
Dobtong **87** 6 25N 31 40 E
Dodecanese = Dhodhekánisos **45** 36 35N 27 0 E
Dodge Center **116** 44 1N 92 50W
Dodge City **117** 37 42N 100 0W
Dodge L. **109** 59 50N 105 36W
Dodgeville **116** 42 55N 90 8W
Dodo **87** 5 10N 29 57 E
Dodola **87** 6 59N 39 11 E
Dodoma **90** 6 8 S 35 45 E
Dodoma □ **90** 6 0 S 36 0 E
Dodona **44** 39 40N 20 46 E
Dodsland **109** 51 50N 108 45W
Dodson **118** 48 23N 108 16W
Doetinchem **16** 51 59N 6 18 E
Doftana **46** 45 11N 25 45 E
Dog Creek **108** 51 35N 122 14W
Dog L., Man., Can. **109** 51 2N 98 31W
Dog L., Ont., Can. **106** 48 18N 89 30W
Doğanbey **45** 37 40N 27 10 E
Dogliani **38** 44 35N 7 55 E
Dogondoutchi **85** 13 38N 4 2 E
Dogran **68** 31 48N 73 35 E
Doguéraoua **85** 14 0N 5 31 E
Dohad **68** 22 50N 74 15 E
Dohazari **67** 22 10N 92 5 E
Doi **73** 2 14N 127 49 E
Doi Luang **71** 18 30N 101 0 E
Doig → **108** 56 25N 120 40W
Dois Irmãos, Sa. **127** 9 0 S 42 30W
Dojransko Jezero **42** 41 13N 22 44 E
Dokka **47** 60 49N 10 7 E
Dokka → **47** 61 7N 10 0 E
Dokkum **16** 53 20N 5 59 E
Dokri **68** 27 25N 68 7 E
Dol-de-Bretagne **18** 48 34N 1 47W
Doland **116** 44 55N 98 5W
Dolbeau **107** 48 53N 72 18W
Dole **19** 47 7N 5 31 E
Doleib, Wadi → **87** 12 10N 33 15 E
Dolgellau **12** 52 44N 3 53W
Dolgelley = Dolgellau **12** 52 44N 3 53W
Dolginovo **54** 54 39N 27 29 E
Dolianova **40** 39 23N 9 11 E
Dolinskaya **56** 48 6N 32 46 E
Dolj □ **46** 44 10N 23 30 E
Dollart **16** 53 20N 7 10 E
Dolna Banya **43** 42 18N 23 44 E
Dolni Dŭbnik **43** 43 24N 24 26 E
Dolo, Ethiopia **87** 4 11N 42 3 E
Dolo, Italy **39** 45 25N 12 4 E
Dolomites = Dolomiti **39** 46 30N 11 40 E
Dolomiti **39** 46 30N 11 40 E
Dolores, Argent. **124** 36 20 S 57 40W
Dolores, Uruguay **124** 33 34 S 58 15W
Dolores, Colo., U.S.A. **119** 37 30N 108 30W
Dolores, Tex., U.S.A. **117** 27 40N 99 38W
Dolores → **119** 38 49N 108 17W
Đolovo **42** 44 55N 20 52 E
Dolphin and Union Str. **104** 69 5N 114 45W
Dolphin C. **128** 51 10 S 59 0W
Dolsk **28** 51 59N 17 3 E
Dom Pedrito **125** 31 0 S 54 40W
Doma **85** 8 25N 8 18 E
Domasi **91** 15 15 S 35 22 E
Domazlice **26** 49 28N 13 0 E
Dombarovskiy **58** 50 46N 59 32 E
Dombasle **19** 48 38N 6 21 E
Dombes **21** 46 3N 5 0 E
Dombóvár **27** 46 21N 18 9 E
Dombrád **27** 48 13N 21 54 E
Domburg **16** 51 34N 3 30 E
Domel I. = Letsok-aw Kyun **71** 11 30N 98 25 E
Domérat **20** 46 21N 2 32 E
Domeyko **124** 29 0 S 71 0W
Domeyko, Cordillera **124** 24 30 S 69 0W
Domfront **18** 48 37N 0 40W
Dominador **124** 24 21 S 69 20W
Dominica ■ **121** 15 20N 61 20W
Dominican Rep. ■ **121** 19 0N 70 30W
Dömitz **24** 53 9N 11 13 E
Domme **20** 44 48N 1 12 E
Domo **63** 7 50N 47 10 E
Domodóssola **38** 46 6N 8 19 E
Dompaire **19** 48 14N 6 14 E
Dompierre-sur-Besbre **20** 46 31N 3 41 E
Dompim **84** 5 10N 2 5W
Domrémy **19** 48 26N 5 40 E
Domsjö **48** 63 16N 18 41 E
Domville, Mt. **99** 28 1 S 151 15 E
Domvraína **45** 38 15N 22 59 E
Domžale **39** 46 9N 14 35 E
Don →, India **70** 16 20N 76 15 E
Don →, Eng., U.K. **12** 53 41N 0 51W
Don →, Scot., U.K. **14** 57 14N 2 5W
Don →, U.S.S.R. **57** 47 4N 39 18 E
Don Benito **31** 38 53N 5 51W
Don Martín, Presa de **120** 27 30N 100 50W
Dona Ana **91** 17 25 S 35 5 E
Donaghadee **15** 54 38N 5 32W
Donald **99** 36 23 S 143 0 E
Donalda **108** 52 35N 112 34W
Donaldsonville **117** 30 2N 91 0W
Donalsonville **115** 31 3N 84 52W
Donau → **23** 48 10N 17 0 E
Donaueschingen **25** 47 57N 8 30 E
Donauwörth **25** 48 42N 10 47 E
Donawitz **26** 47 22N 15 4 E
Doncaster **12** 53 31N 1 9W
Dondo, Angola **88** 9 45 S 14 25 E
Dondo, Mozam. **91** 19 33 S 34 46 E
Dondo, Teluk **73** 0 29N 120 30 E
Dondra Head **70** 5 55N 80 40 E
Donegal **15** 54 39N 8 8W
Donegal □ **15** 54 53N 8 0W
Donegal B. **15** 54 30N 8 35W
Donets → **57** 47 33N 40 55 E
Donetsk **56** 48 0N 37 45 E
Donga **85** 7 45N 10 2 E
Dongara **96** 29 14 S 114 57 E
Dongargarh **69** 21 10N 80 40 E
Donges **18** 47 18N 2 4W
Dongfang **77** 18 50N 108 33 E
Donggala **73** 0 30 S 119 40 E
Donggou **76** 39 52N 124 10 E
Dongguan **77** 22 58N 113 44 E
Dongguang **76** 37 50N 116 30 E
Dongjingcheng **76** 44 0N 129 10 E
Donglan **77** 24 30N 107 21 E
Dongliu **77** 30 13N 116 55 E
Dongola **86** 19 9N 30 22 E
Dongou **88** 2 0N 18 5 E
Dongping **76** 35 55N 116 20 E
Dongshan **77** 23 43N 117 30 E
Dongsheng **76** 39 50N 110 0 E
Dongtai **77** 32 51N 120 21 E
Dongting Hu **75** 29 18N 112 45 E
Dongxing **75** 21 34N 108 0 E
Dongyang **77** 29 13N 120 15 E
Doniphan **117** 36 40N 90 50W
Donja Stubica **39** 45 59N 16 0 E

Donji Dušnik
Dzhelinde

Donji Dušnik **42** 43 12N 22 5 E
Donji Miholjac **42** 45 45N 18 10 E
Donji Milanovac **42** 44 28N 22 6 E
Donji Vakuf **42** 44 8N 17 24 E
Donjon, Le **20** 46 22N 3 48 E
Dønna **50** 66 6N 12 30 E
Donna **117** 26 12N 98 2W
Donnaconna **107** 46 41N 71 41W
Donnelly's Crossing **101** 35 42 S 173 38 E
Donora **112** 40 11N 79 50W
Donor's Hills **98** 18 42 S 140 33 E
Donskoy **55** 53 55N 38 15 E
Donya Lendava **39** 46 35N 16 25 E
Donzère-Mondragon **21** 44 28N 4 43 E
Donzère-Mondragon, Barrage de **21** 44 13N 4 42 E
Donzy **19** 47 20N 3 6 E
Doon → **14** 55 26N 4 41W
Dor (Tantûra) **62** 32 37N 34 55 E
Dora Báltea → **38** 45 11N 8 5 E
Dora, L. **96** 22 0 S 123 0 E
Dora Riparia → **38** 45 5N 7 44 E
Dorada, La **126** 5 30N 74 40W
Doran L. **109** 61 13N 108 6W
Dorat, Le **20** 46 14N 1 5 E
Dorchester **13** 50 42N 2 28W
Dorchester, C. **105** 65 27N 77 27W
Dordogne ☐ **20** 45 5N 0 40 E
Dordogne → **20** 45 2N 0 36W
Dordrecht, Neth. **16** 51 48N 4 39 E
Dordrecht, S. Afr. **92** 31 20 S 27 3 E
Dore → **20** 45 50N 3 35 E
Doré L. **109** 54 46N 107 17W
Doré Lake **109** 54 38N 107 36W
Dore, Mt. **20** 45 32N 2 50 E
Dorfen **25** 48 16N 12 10 E
Dorgali **40** 40 18N 9 35 E
Dori **85** 14 3N 0 2W
Doring → **92** 31 54 S 18 39 E
Dorion **106** 45 23N 74 3W
Dormaa-Ahenkro **84** 7 15N 2 52W
Dormo, Ras **87** 13 14N 42 35 E
Dornberg **39** 55 45N 13 50 E
Dornbirn **26** 47 25N 9 45 E
Dornes **19** 46 48N 3 18 E
Dornoch **14** 57 52N 4 0W
Dornoch Firth **14** 57 52N 4 0W
Doro **85** 16 9N 0 51W
Dorog **27** 47 42N 18 45 E
Dorogobuzh **54** 54 50N 33 18 E
Dorohoi **46** 47 56N 26 30 E
Döröö Nuur **75** 48 0N 93 0 E
Dorre I. **96** 25 13 S 113 12 E
Dorrigo **99** 30 20 S 152 44 E
Dorris **118** 41 59N 121 58W
Dorset, Can. **112** 45 14N 78 54W
Dorset, U.S.A. **112** 41 4N 80 40W
Dorset ☐ **13** 50 48N 2 25W
Dorsten **24** 51 40N 6 55 E
Dortmund **24** 51 32N 7 28 E
Dörtyol **64** 36 52N 36 12 E
Dorum **24** 53 40N 8 33 E
Doruma **90** 4 42N 27 33 E
Dos Bahías, C. **128** 44 58 S 65 32W
Dos Cabezas **119** 32 10N 109 37W
Dos Hermanas **31** 37 16N 5 55W
Dosso **85** 13 0N 3 13 E
Dothan **115** 31 10N 85 25W
Douai **19** 50 21N 3 4 E
Douala **88** 4 0N 9 45 E
Douaouir **82** 20 45N 3 0W
Douarnenez **18** 48 6N 4 21W
Douăzeci Şi Trei August **46** 43 55N 28 40 E
Double Island Pt. **99** 25 56 S 153 11 E
Doubrava → **26** 49 40N 15 30 E
Doubs ☐ **19** 47 10N 6 20 E
Doubs → **19** 46 53N 5 1 E
Doubtful B. **96** 34 15 S 119 28 E
Doubtful Sd. **101** 45 20 S 166 49 E
Doubtless B. **101** 34 55 S 173 26 E
Doudeville **18** 49 43N 0 47 E
Doué **18** 47 11N 0 20W
Douentza **84** 14 58N 2 48W
Douglas, S. Afr. **92** 29 4 S 23 46 E
Douglas, U.K. **12** 54 9N 4 29W
Douglas, Alaska, U.S.A. **108** 58 23N 134 24W
Douglas, Ariz., U.S.A. **119** 31 21N 109 30W
Douglas, Ga., U.S.A. **115** 31 32N 82 52W
Douglas, Wyo., U.S.A. **116** 42 45N 105 20W
Douglastown **107** 48 46N 64 24W
Douglasville **115** 33 46N 84 43W
Douirat **82** 33 2N 4 11W
Doukáton, Ákra **45** 38 34N 20 30 E
Doulevant **19** 48 22N 4 53 E
Doullens **19** 50 10N 2 20 E
Doumé **88** 4 15N 13 25 E
Douna **84** 13 13N 6 0W
Dounreay **14** 58 34N 3 44W
Dourados **125** 22 9 S 54 50W
Dourados → **125** 21 58 S 54 18W
Dourdan **19** 48 30N 2 0 E
Douro → **30** 41 8N 8 40W
Douvaine **21** 46 19N 6 16 E
Douz **83** 33 25N 9 0 E
Douze → **20** 43 54N 0 30W
Dove → **12** 52 51N 1 36W
Dove Creek **119** 37 46N 108 59W
Dover, Austral. **99** 43 18 S 147 2 E
Dover, U.K. **13** 51 7N 1 19 E
Dover, Del., U.S.A. **114** 39 10N 75 31W
Dover, N.H., U.S.A. **114** 43 12N 70 51W
Dover, N.J., U.S.A. **113** 40 53N 74 34W
Dover, Ohio, U.S.A. **114** 40 32N 81 30W
Dover-Foxcroft **107** 45 14N 69 14W
Dover Plains **113** 41 43N 73 35W
Dover, Pt. **96** 32 32 S 125 32 E
Dover, Str. of **18** 51 0N 1 30 E
Dovey → **13** 52 32N 4 0W
Dovrefjell **47** 62 15N 9 33 E
Dowa **91** 13 38 S 33 58 E
Dowagiac **114** 42 0N 86 8W
Dowlat Yār **65** 34 30N 65 45 E
Dowlatabad **65** 28 20N 56 40W
Down ☐ **15** 54 20N 6 0W
Downey **118** 42 29N 112 3W
Downham Market **13** 52 36N 0 22 E
Downieville **118** 39 34N 120 50W
Downpatrick **15** 54 20N 5 43W
Downpatrick Hd. **15** 54 20N 9 21W
Dowshī **65** 35 35N 68 43 E
Doylestown **113** 40 21N 75 10W
Draa, C. **82** 28 47N 11 0W
Draa, Oued → **82** 30 29N 6 1W
Drac → **21** 45 13N 5 41 E
Drachten **16** 53 7N 6 5 E
Drăgăneşti **46** 44 9N 24 32 E
Drăgăneşti-Viaşca **46** 44 5N 25 33 E
Dragaš **42** 42 5N 20 35 E
Drăgăsani **46** 44 39N 24 17 E
Dragina **42** 44 30N 19 25 E
Dragocvet **42** 44 0N 21 15 E
Dragoman, Prokhod **42** 43 0N 22 53 E
Dragonera, I. **32** 39 35N 2 19 E
Dragovishtitsa (Perivol) **42** 42 22N 22 39 E
Draguignan **21** 43 30N 6 27 E
Drain **118** 43 45N 123 17W
Drake, Austral. **99** 28 55 S 152 25 E
Drake, U.S.A. **116** 47 56N 100 21W
Drake Passage **5** 58 0 S 68 0W
Drakensberg **93** 31 0 S 28 0 E
Dráma **44** 41 9N 24 10 E
Dráma ☐ **44** 41 20N 24 0 E
Drammen **47** 59 42N 10 12 E
Drangajökull **50** 66 9N 22 15W
Drangedal **47** 59 6N 9 3 E
Dranov, Ostrov **46** 44 55N 29 30 E
Drau = Drava → **26** 46 32N 14 58 E
Drava → **42** 45 33N 18 55 E
Draveil **19** 48 41N 2 25 E
Dravograd **39** 46 36N 15 5 E
Drawa → **28** 52 52N 15 59 E
Drawno **28** 53 13N 15 46 E
Drawsko Pomorskie **28** 53 35N 15 50 E
Drayton Valley **108** 53 12N 114 58W
Dren **42** 43 8N 20 44 E
Drenthe ☐ **16** 52 52N 6 40 E
Dresden, Can. **112** 42 35N 82 11W
Dresden, Ger. **24** 51 2N 13 45 E
Dresden ☐ **24** 51 12N 14 0 E
Dreux **18** 48 44N 1 23 E
Drezdenko **28** 52 50N 15 49 E
Driffield **12** 54 0N 0 25W
Driftwood **112** 41 22N 78 9W
Driggs **118** 43 50N 111 8W
Drin i zi → **44** 41 37N 20 28 E
Drina → **42** 44 53N 19 21 E
Drincea → **46** 44 20N 22 55 E
Drînceni **46** 46 49N 28 10 E
Drini → **44** 42 20N 20 0 E
Drinjača → **42** 44 15N 19 8 E
Driva → **47** 62 33N 9 38 E
Drivstua **47** 62 26N 9 47 E
Drniš **39** 43 51N 16 10 E
Drøbak **47** 59 39N 10 39 E
Drobin **28** 52 42N 19 58 E
Drogheda **15** 53 45N 6 20W
Drogichin **54** 52 15N 25 8 E
Drogobych **54** 49 20N 23 30 E
Drohiczyn **28** 52 24N 22 39 E
Droichead Nua **15** 53 11N 6 50W
Droitwich **13** 52 16N 2 10W
Drôme ☐ **21** 44 38N 5 15 E
Drôme → **21** 44 46N 4 46 E
Dromedary, C. **99** 36 17 S 150 10 E
Dronero **38** 44 29N 7 22 E
Dronfield **98** 21 12 S 140 3 E
Dronne → **20** 45 2N 0 9W
Dronning Maud Land **5** 72 30 S 12 0 E
Dronninglund **49** 57 10N 10 19 E
Dropt → **20** 44 35N 0 6W
Drosendorf **26** 48 52N 15 37 E
Drouzhba **43** 43 15N 28 0 E
Drumbo **112** 43 16N 80 35W
Drumheller **108** 51 25N 112 40W
Drummond **118** 46 40N 113 4W
Drummond I. **106** 46 0N 83 40W
Drummond Ra. **97** 23 45 S 147 10 E
Drummondville **106** 45 55N 72 25W
Drumright **117** 35 59N 96 38W
Druskininkai **54** 54 3N 23 58 E
Drut → **54** 53 3N 30 42 E
Druya **54** 55 45N 27 28 E
Druzhina **59** 68 14N 145 18 E
Drvar **39** 44 21N 16 23 E
Drvenik **39** 43 27N 16 3 E
Drwęca → **28** 53 0N 18 42 E
Dry Tortugas **121** 24 38N 82 55W
Dryanovo **43** 42 59N 25 28 E
Dryden, Can. **109** 49 47N 92 50W
Dryden, U.S.A. **117** 30 3N 102 3W
Drygalski I. **5** 66 0 S 92 0 E
Drysdale → **96** 13 59 S 126 51 E
Drzewiczka → **28** 51 36N 20 36 E
Dschang **85** 5 32N 10 3 E
Du Bois **114** 41 8N 78 46W
Du Quoin **116** 38 0N 89 10W
Duanesburg **113** 42 45N 74 11W
Duaringa **98** 23 42 S 149 42 E
Ḑubā **64** 27 10N 35 40 E
Dubai = Dubayy **65** 25 18N 55 20 E
Dubawnt → **109** 64 33N 100 6W
Dubawnt, L. **109** 63 4N 101 42W
Dubayy **65** 25 18N 55 20 E
Dubbo **97** 32 11 S 148 35 E
Dubele **90** 2 56N 29 35 E
Dubica **39** 45 11N 16 48 E
Dublin, Ireland **15** 53 20N 6 18W
Dublin, Ga., U.S.A. **115** 32 30N 82 34W
Dublin, Tex., U.S.A. **117** 32 0N 98 20W
Dublin ☐ **15** 53 24N 6 20W
Dublin B. **15** 53 18N 6 5W
Dubna, U.S.S.R. **55** 54 8N 36 59 E
Dubna, U.S.S.R. **55** 56 44N 37 10 E
Dubno **54** 50 25N 25 45 E
Dubois **118** 44 7N 112 9W
Dubossary **56** 47 15N 29 10 E
Dubossasy Vdkhr. **56** 47 30N 29 0 E
Dubovka **57** 49 5N 44 50 E
Dubovskoye **57** 47 28N 42 46 E
Dubrajpur **69** 23 48N 87 25 E
Dubréka **84** 9 46N 13 31W
Dubrovitsa **54** 51 31N 26 35 E
Dubrovnik **42** 42 39N 18 6 E
Dubrovskoye **59** 58 55N 111 10 E
Dubuque **116** 42 30N 90 41W
Duchang **77** 29 18N 116 12 E
Duchesne **118** 40 14N 110 22W
Duchess **97** 21 20 S 139 50 E
Ducie I. **95** 24 40 S 124 48W
Duck Lake **109** 52 50N 106 16W
Duck Mt. Prov. Parks **109** 51 45N 101 0W
Duderstadt **24** 51 30N 10 15 E
Dudinka **59** 69 30N 86 13 E
Dudley **13** 52 30N 2 5W
Dudna → **70** 19 17N 76 54 E
Dueñas **30** 41 52N 4 33W
Dueodde **49** 54 59N 15 4 E
Duero → **30** 41 8N 8 40W
Duff Is. **94** 9 53 S 167 8 E
Dufftown **14** 57 26N 3 9W
Dugi **39** 44 0N 15 0 E
Dugo Selo **39** 45 51N 16 18 E
Duifken Pt. **97** 12 33 S 141 38 E
Duisburg **24** 51 27N 6 42 E
Duiwelskloof **93** 23 42 S 30 10 E
Dukati **44** 40 16N 19 32 E
Duke I. **108** 54 50N 131 20W
Dukelsky průsmyk **27** 49 25N 21 42 E
Dukhān **65** 25 25N 50 50 E
Dukhovshchina **54** 55 15N 32 27 E
Dukla **27** 49 30N 21 35 E
Duku, Bauchi, Nigeria **85** 10 43N 10 43 E
Duku, Sokoto, Nigeria **85** 11 11N 4 55 E
Dulce → **124** 30 32 S 62 33W
Dulce, Golfo **121** 8 40N 83 20W
Dŭlgopol **43** 43 3N 27 22 E
Dullewala **68** 31 50N 71 25 E
Dülmen **24** 51 49N 7 18 E
Dulovo **43** 43 48N 27 9 E
Dululu **98** 23 48 S 150 15 E
Duluth **116** 46 48N 92 10W
Dum Dum **69** 22 39N 88 33 E
Dum Duma **67** 27 40N 95 40 E
Dum Hadjer **81** 13 18N 19 41 E
Dumaguete **73** 9 17N 123 15 E
Dumai **72** 1 35N 101 28 E
Dumaran **73** 10 33N 119 50 E
Dumaring **73** 1 46N 118 10 E
Dumas, Ark., U.S.A. **117** 33 52N 91 30W
Dumas, Tex., U.S.A. **117** 35 50N 101 58W
Dumbarton **14** 55 58N 4 35W
Dumbrăveni **46** 46 14N 24 34 E
Dumfries **14** 55 4N 3 37W
Dumfries & Galloway ☐ **14** 55 0N 4 0W
Dumka **69** 24 12N 87 15 E
Dümmersee **24** 52 30N 8 21 E
Dumoine → **106** 46 13N 77 51W
Dumoine L. **106** 46 55N 77 55W
Dumraon **69** 25 33N 84 8 E
Dumyât **86** 31 24N 31 48 E
Dumyât, Masabb **86** 31 28N 31 51 E
Dun Laoghaire **15** 53 17N 6 9W
Dun-le-Palestel **20** 46 18N 1 39 E
Dun-sur-Auron **19** 46 53N 2 33 E
Duna → **27** 45 51N 18 48 E
Dunaföldvár **27** 46 50N 18 57 E
Dunaj → **27** 48 5N 17 10 E
Dunajec → **27** 50 15N 20 44 E
Dunajska Streda **27** 48 0N 17 37 E
Dunapatai **27** 46 39N 19 4 E
Dunărea → **46** 45 30N 8 15 E
Dunaszekcsö **27** 46 6N 18 45 E
Dunaújváros **27** 47 0N 18 57 E
Dunav → **42** 44 47N 21 20 E
Dunavtsi **42** 43 57N 22 53 E
Dunback **101** 45 23 S 170 36 E
Dunbar, Austral. **98** 16 0 S 142 22 E
Dunbar, U.K. **14** 56 0N 2 32W
Dunblane **14** 56 10N 3 58W
Duncan, Can. **108** 48 45N 123 40W
Duncan, Ariz., U.S.A. **119** 32 46N 109 6W
Duncan, Okla., U.S.A. **117** 34 25N 98 0W
Duncan L. **108** 62 51N 113 58W
Duncan, L. **106** 53 29N 77 58W
Duncan Pass. **71** 11 0N 92 30 E
Duncan Town **121** 22 15N 75 45W
Duncannon **112** 40 23N 77 2W
Dundalk, Can. **112** 44 10N 80 24W
Dundalk, Ireland **15** 54 1N 6 25W
Dundalk Bay **15** 53 55N 6 15W
Dundas **106** 43 17N 79 59W
Dundas I. **108** 54 30N 130 50W
Dundas, L. **96** 32 35 S 121 50 E
Dundas Str. **96** 11 15 S 131 35 E
Dundee, S. Afr. **93** 28 11 S 30 15 E
Dundee, U.K. **14** 56 29N 3 0W
Dundoo **99** 27 40 S 144 37 E
Dundrum **15** 54 17N 5 50W
Dundrum B. **15** 54 12N 5 40W
Dundwara **68** 27 48N 79 9 E
Dunedin, N.Z. **101** 45 50 S 170 33 E
Dunedin, U.S.A. **115** 28 1N 82 45W
Dunedin → **108** 59 30N 124 5W
Dunfermline **14** 56 5N 3 28W
Dungannon, Can. **112** 43 51N 81 36W
Dungannon, U.K. **15** 54 30N 6 47W
Dungannon ☐ **15** 54 30N 6 55W
Dungarpur **68** 23 52N 73 45 E
Dungarvan **15** 52 6N 7 40W
Dungarvan Bay **15** 52 5N 7 35W
Dungeness **13** 50 54N 0 59 E
Dungo, L. do **92** 17 15 S 19 0 E
Dungog **99** 32 22 S 151 46 E
Dungu **90** 3 40N 28 32 E
Dungunâb **86** 21 10N 37 9 E
Dungunâb, Khalij **86** 21 5N 37 12 E
Dunhinda Falls **70** 7 5N 81 6 E
Dunhua **76** 43 20N 128 14 E
Dunhuang **75** 40 8N 94 36 E
Dunières **21** 45 13N 4 20 E
Dunk I. **98** 17 59 S 146 29 E
Dunkeld **14** 56 34N 3 36W
Dunkerque **19** 51 2N 2 20 E
Dunkery Beacon **13** 51 15N 3 37W
Dunkirk **114** 42 30N 79 18W
Dunkirk = Dunkerque **19** 51 2N 2 20 E
Dunkuj **87** 12 50N 32 49 E
Dunkwa, Central, Ghana **84** 6 0N 1 47W
Dunkwa, Central, Ghana **85** 5 30N 1 0W
Dunlap **116** 41 50N 95 36W
Dunmanus B. **15** 51 31N 9 50W
Dunmore **114** 41 27N 75 38W
Dunmore Hd. **15** 52 10N 10 35W
Dunn **115** 35 18N 78 36W
Dunnellon **115** 29 4N 82 28W
Dunnet Hd. **14** 58 38N 3 22W
Dunning **116** 41 52N 100 4W
Dunnville **112** 42 54N 79 36W
Dunolly **99** 36 51 S 143 44 E
Dunoon **14** 55 57N 4 56W
Dunqul **86** 23 26N 31 37 E
Duns **14** 55 47N 2 20W
Dunseith **116** 48 49N 100 2W
Dunsmuir **118** 41 10N 122 18W
Dunstable **13** 51 53N 0 31W
Dunstan Mts. **101** 44 53 S 169 35 E
Dunster **108** 53 8N 119 50W
Dunvegan L. **109** 60 8N 107 10W
Duolun **76** 42 12N 116 28 E
Dupree **116** 45 4N 101 35W
Dupuyer **118** 48 11N 112 31W
Duque de Caxias **125** 22 45 S 43 19W
Duquesne **112** 40 22N 79 55W
Dūrā **62** 31 31N 35 1 E
Durack Range **96** 16 50 S 127 40 E
Durance → **21** 43 55N 4 45 E
Durand **114** 42 54N 83 58W
Durango, Mexico **120** 24 3N 104 39W
Durango, Spain **32** 43 13N 2 40W
Durango, U.S.A. **119** 37 16N 107 50W
Durango ☐ **120** 25 0N 105 0W
Durant **117** 34 0N 96 25W
Duratón → **30** 41 37N 4 7W
Durazno **124** 33 25 S 56 31W
Durazzo = Durrësi **44** 41 19N 19 28 E
Durban, France **20** 43 0N 2 49 E
Durban, S. Afr. **93** 29 49 S 31 1 E
Dúrcal **31** 37 0N 3 34W
Đurđevac **42** 46 2N 17 3 E
Düren **24** 50 48N 6 30 E
Durg **69** 21 15N 81 22 E
Durgapur **69** 23 30N 87 20 E
Durham, Can. **106** 44 10N 80 49W
Durham, U.K. **12** 54 47N 1 34W
Durham, U.S.A. **115** 36 0N 78 55W
Durham ☐ **12** 54 42N 1 45W
Durmitor **34** 43 10N 19 0 E
Durness **14** 58 34N 4 45W
Durrës **44** 41 19N 19 28 E
Durrësi **44** 41 19N 19 28 E
Durrie **99** 25 40 S 140 15 E
Durtal **18** 47 40N 0 18W
Duru **90** 4 14N 28 50 E
D'Urville I. **101** 40 50 S 173 55 E
D'Urville, Tanjung **73** 1 28 S 137 54 E
Duryea **113** 41 20N 75 45W
Dusa Mareb **63** 5 30N 46 15 E
Dûsh **86** 24 35N 30 41 E
Dushak **58** 37 13N 60 1 E
Dushan **77** 25 48N 107 30 E
Dushanbe **58** 38 33N 68 48 E
Dusheti **57** 42 10N 44 42 E
Dusky Sd. **101** 45 47 S 166 30 E
Düsseldorf **24** 51 15N 6 46 E
Duszniki-Zdrój **28** 50 24N 16 24 E
Dutch Harbor **104** 53 54N 166 35W
Dutlhe **92** 23 58 S 23 46 E
Dutsan Wai **85** 10 50N 8 10 E
Dutton **112** 42 39N 81 30W
Dutton → **98** 20 44 S 143 10 E
Duved **48** 63 24N 12 55 E
Duvno **42** 43 42N 17 13 E
Duwādimi **64** 24 35N 44 15 E
Duyun **77** 26 18N 107 29 E
Duzce **64** 40 50N 31 10 E
Duzdab = Zāhedān **65** 29 30N 60 50 E
Dve Mogili **43** 43 35N 25 55 E
Dvina, Sev. **52** 64 32N 40 30 E
Dvinsk = Daugavpils **54** 55 53N 26 32 E
Dvinskaya Guba **52** 65 0N 39 0 E
Dvor **39** 45 4N 16 22 E
Dvorce **27** 49 50N 17 34 E
Dvur Králové **26** 50 27N 15 50 E
Dwarka **68** 22 18N 69 8 E
Dwight, Can. **112** 45 20N 79 1W
Dwight, U.S.A. **114** 41 5N 88 25W
Dyakovskoya **55** 60 5N 41 12 E
Dyatkovo **54** 53 40N 34 27 E
Dyatlovo **54** 53 28N 25 28 E
Dyer, C. **105** 66 40N 61 0W
Dyer Plateau **5** 70 45 S 65 30W
Dyersburg **117** 36 2N 89 20W
Dyfed ☐ **13** 52 0N 4 30W
Dyje → **27** 48 37N 16 56 E
Dynevor Downs **99** 28 10 S 144 20 E
Dynów **27** 49 50N 22 11 E
Dysart **109** 50 57N 104 2W
Dzamin Üüd **75** 43 50N 111 58 E
Dzerzhinsk, Byelorussian S.S.R., U.S.S.R. **54** 53 40N 27 1 E
Dzerzhinsk, R.S.F.S.R., U.S.S.R. **55** 56 14N 43 30 E
Dzhalal-Abad **58** 40 56N 73 0 E
Dzhalinda **59** 53 26N 124 0 E
Dzhambeyty **57** 50 15N 52 30 E
Dzhambul **58** 42 54N 71 22 E
Dzhankoi **56** 45 40N 34 20 E
Dzhanybek **57** 49 25N 46 50 E
Dzhardzhan **59** 68 10N 124 10 E
Dzhelinde **59** 70 0N 114 20 E

Dzhetygara Elbow

Dzhetygara	**58**	52 11N	61 12 E
Dzhezkazgan	**58**	47 44N	67 40 E
Dzhikimde	**59**	59 1N	121 47 E
Dzhizak	**58**	40 6N	67 50 E
Dzhugdzur, Khrebet	**59**	57 30N	138 0 E
Dzhungarskiye Vorota	**58**	45 0N	82 0 E
Dzhvari	**57**	42 42N	42 4 E
Działdowo	**28**	53 15N	20 15 E
Działoszyce	**28**	50 22N	20 20 E
Działoszyn	**28**	51 6N	18 50 E
Dzierzgoń	**28**	53 58N	19 20 E
Dzierzoniów	**28**	50 45N	16 39 E
Dzioua	**83**	33 14N	5 14 E
Dziwnów	**28**	54 2N	14 45 E
Dzungarian Gate = Alataw Shankou	**75**	45 5N	81 57 E
Dzuumod	**75**	47 45N	106 58 E
E			
Eabamet, L.	**106**	51 30N	87 46W
Eads	**116**	38 30N	102 46W
Eagle, Alaska, U.S.A.	**104**	64 44N	141 7W
Eagle, Colo., U.S.A.	**118**	39 39N	106 55W
Eagle →	**107**	53 36N	57 26W
Eagle Butt	**116**	45 1N	101 12W
Eagle Grove	**116**	42 37N	93 53W
Eagle L., Calif., U.S.A.	**118**	40 35N	120 50W
Eagle L., Me., U.S.A.	**107**	46 23N	69 22W
Eagle Lake	**117**	29 35N	96 21W
Eagle Nest	**119**	36 33N	105 13W
Eagle Pass	**117**	28 45N	100 35W
Eagle River	**116**	45 55N	89 17W
Eaglehawk	**99**	36 39 S	144 16 E
Ealing	**13**	51 30N	0 19W
Earl Grey	**109**	50 57N	104 43W
Earle	**117**	35 18N	90 26W
Earlimart	**119**	35 53N	119 16W
Earn →	**14**	56 20N	3 19W
Earn, L.	**14**	56 23N	4 14W
Earnslaw, Mt.	**101**	44 32 S	168 27 E
Earth	**117**	34 18N	102 30W
Easley	**115**	34 52N	82 35W
East Angus	**107**	45 30N	71 40W
East Aurora	**112**	42 46N	78 38W
East B.	**117**	29 2N	89 16W
East Bengal	**67**	24 0N	90 0 E
East Beskids = Vychodné Beskydy	**27**	49 30N	22 0 E
East Brady	**112**	40 59N	79 36W
East C.	**101**	37 42 S	178 35 E
East Chicago	**114**	41 40N	87 30W
East China Sea	**75**	30 5N	126 0 E
East Coulee	**108**	51 23N	112 27W
East Falkland	**128**	51 30 S	58 30W
East Grand Forks	**116**	47 55N	97 5W
East Greenwich	**113**	41 39N	71 27W
East Hartford	**113**	41 45N	72 39W
East Helena	**118**	46 37N	111 58W
East Indies	**72**	0 0	120 0 E
East Jordan	**114**	45 10N	85 7W
East Kilbride	**14**	55 46N	4 10W
East Lansing	**114**	42 44N	84 29W
East Liverpool	**114**	40 39N	80 35W
East London	**93**	33 0 S	27 55 E
East Orange	**114**	40 46N	74 13W
East Pacific Ridge	**95**	15 0 S	110 0W
East Pakistan = Bangladesh ■	**67**	24 0N	90 0 E
East Palestine	**112**	40 50N	80 32W
East Pine	**108**	55 48N	120 12W
East Pt.	**107**	46 27N	61 58W
East Point	**115**	33 40N	84 28W
East Providence	**113**	41 48N	71 22W
East Retford	**12**	53 19N	0 55W
East St. Louis	**116**	38 37N	90 4W
East Schelde → = Oosterschelde	**16**	51 38N	3 40 E
East Siberian Sea	**59**	73 0N	160 0 E
East Stroudsburg	**113**	41 1N	75 11W
East Sussex □	**13**	51 0N	0 20 E
East Tawas	**114**	44 17N	83 31W
Eastbourne, N.Z.	**101**	41 19 S	174 55 E
Eastbourne, U.K.	**13**	50 46N	0 18 E
Eastend	**109**	49 32N	108 50W
Easter I.	**95**	27 8 S	109 23W
Easter Islands	**95**	27 0 S	109 0W
Eastern □, Kenya	**90**	0 0 S	38 30 E
Eastern □, Uganda	**90**	1 50N	33 45 E
Eastern Cr. →	**98**	20 40 S	141 35 E
Eastern Ghats	**70**	14 0N	78 50 E
Eastern Province □	**84**	8 15N	11 0W
Easterville	**109**	53 8N	99 49W
Easthampton	**113**	42 15N	72 41W
Eastland	**117**	32 26N	98 45W
Eastleigh	**13**	50 58N	1 21W
Eastmain →	**106**	52 27N	78 26W
Eastmain (East Main)	**106**	52 10N	78 30W
Eastman, Can.	**113**	45 18N	72 19W
Eastman, U.S.A.	**115**	32 13N	83 20W
Easton, Md., U.S.A.	**114**	38 47N	76 7W
Easton, Pa., U.S.A.	**114**	40 41N	75 15W
Easton, Wash., U.S.A.	**118**	47 14N	121 8W
Eastport	**107**	44 57N	67 0W
Eaton	**116**	40 35N	104 42W
Eatonia	**109**	51 13N	109 25W
Eatonton	**115**	33 22N	83 24W
Eatontown	**113**	40 18N	74 7W
Eau Claire, S.C., U.S.A.	**115**	34 5N	81 2W
Eau Claire, Wis., U.S.A.	**116**	44 46N	91 30W
Eauze	**20**	43 53N	0 7 E
Ebagoola	**98**	14 15 S	143 12 E
Eban	**85**	9 40N	4 50 E
Ebbw Vale	**13**	51 47N	3 12W
Ebeggui	**83**	26 2N	6 0 E
Ebensburg	**112**	40 29N	78 43W
Ebensee	**26**	47 48N	13 46 E
Eberbach	**25**	49 27N	8 59 E
Eberswalde	**24**	52 49N	13 50 E
Ebingen	**25**	48 13N	9 1 E
Eboli	**41**	40 39N	15 2 E
Ebolowa	**88**	2 55N	11 10 E
Ebrach	**25**	49 50N	10 30 E
Ébrié, Lagune	**84**	5 12N	4 26W
Ebro →	**32**	40 43N	0 54 E
Ebro, Pantano del	**30**	43 0N	3 58W
Ebstorf	**24**	53 2N	10 23 E
Eceabat	**44**	40 11N	26 21 E
Éceuillé	**18**	47 10N	1 19 E
Echelles, Les	**21**	45 27N	5 45 E
Echmiadzin	**57**	40 12N	44 19 E
Echo Bay	**106**	46 29N	84 4W
Echo Bay (Port Radium)	**104**	66 05N	117 55W
Echoing →	**109**	55 51N	92 5W
Echternach	**16**	49 49N	6 25 E
Echuca	**100**	36 10 S	144 20 E
Ecija	**31**	37 30N	5 10W
Eckernförde	**24**	54 26N	9 50 E
Écommoy	**18**	47 50N	0 17 E
Écos	**19**	49 9N	1 35 E
Écouché	**18**	48 42N	0 10W
Ecuador ■	**126**	2 0 S	78 0W
Ed	**49**	58 55N	11 55 E
Ed Dabbura	**86**	17 40N	34 15 E
Ed Dâmer	**86**	17 27N	34 0 E
Ed Debba	**86**	18 0N	30 51 E
Ed-Déffa	**86**	30 40N	26 30 E
Ed Deim	**87**	10 10N	28 20 E
Ed Dueim	**87**	14 0N	32 10 E
Edam, Can.	**109**	53 11N	108 46W
Edam, Neth.	**16**	52 31N	5 3 E
Edapally	**70**	11 19N	78 3 E
Eday	**14**	59 11N	2 47W
Edd	**87**	14 0N	41 38 E
Eddrachillis B.	**14**	58 16N	5 10W
Eddystone	**13**	50 11N	4 16W
Eddystone Pt.	**99**	40 59 S	148 20 E
Ede, Neth.	**16**	52 4N	5 40 E
Ede, Nigeria	**85**	7 45N	4 29 E
Édea	**88**	3 51N	10 9 E
Edehon L.	**109**	60 25N	97 15W
Edekel, Adrar	**83**	23 56N	6 47 E
Eden, Austral.	**99**	37 3 S	149 55 E
Eden, N.C., U.S.A.	**115**	36 29N	79 53W
Eden, N.Y., U.S.A.	**112**	42 39N	78 55W
Eden, Tex., U.S.A.	**117**	31 16N	99 50W
Eden, Wyo., U.S.A.	**118**	42 2N	109 27W
Eden →	**12**	54 57N	3 2W
Eden L.	**109**	56 38N	100 15W
Edenburg	**92**	29 43 S	25 58 E
Edenderry	**15**	53 21N	7 3W
Edenton	**115**	36 5N	76 36W
Edenville	**93**	27 37 S	27 34 E
Eder →	**24**	51 15N	9 25 E
Ederstausee	**24**	51 11N	9 0 E
Edgar	**116**	40 25N	98 0W
Edgartown	**113**	41 22N	70 28W
Edge Hill	**13**	52 7N	1 28W
Edgefield	**115**	33 50N	81 59W
Edgeley	**116**	46 27N	98 41W
Edgemont	**116**	43 15N	103 53W
Edgeøya	**4**	77 45N	22 30 E
Edhessa	**44**	40 48N	22 5 E
Edievale	**101**	45 49 S	169 22 E
Edina, Liberia	**84**	6 0N	10 10W
Edina, U.S.A.	**116**	40 6N	92 10W
Edinburg	**117**	26 22N	98 10W
Edinburgh	**14**	55 57N	3 12W
Edirne	**43**	41 40N	26 34 E
Edithburgh	**99**	35 5 S	137 43 E
Edjeleh	**83**	28 38N	9 50 E
Edmeston	**113**	42 42N	75 15W
Edmond	**117**	35 37N	97 30W
Edmonds	**118**	47 47N	122 22W
Edmonton, Austral.	**98**	17 2 S	145 46 E
Edmonton, Can.	**108**	53 30N	113 30W
Edmund L.	**109**	54 45N	93 17W
Edmundston	**107**	47 23N	68 20W
Edna	**117**	29 0N	96 40W
Edna Bay	**108**	55 55N	133 40W
Edolo	**38**	46 10N	10 21 E
Edremit	**64**	39 34N	27 0 E
Edsbyn	**48**	61 23N	15 49 E
Edsel Ford Ra.	**5**	77 0 S	143 0W
Edsele	**48**	63 25N	16 32 E
Edson	**108**	53 35N	116 28W
Eduardo Castex	**124**	35 50 S	64 18W
Edward →	**99**	35 0 S	143 30 E
Edward I.	**106**	48 22N	88 37W
Edward, L.	**90**	0 25 S	29 40 E
Edward VII Pen.	**5**	80 0 S	150 0W
Edwards Plat.	**117**	30 30N	101 5W
Edwardsville	**113**	41 15N	75 56W
Edzo	**108**	62 49N	116 4W
Eekloo	**16**	51 11N	3 33 E
Ef'e, Nahal	**62**	31 9N	35 13 E
Eferding	**26**	48 18N	14 1 E
Eferi	**83**	24 30N	9 28 E
Effingham	**114**	39 8N	88 30W
Eforie Sud	**46**	44 1N	28 37 E
Ega →	**32**	42 19N	1 55W
Égadi, Ísole	**40**	37 55N	12 16 E
Eganville	**106**	45 32N	77 5W
Egeland	**116**	48 42N	99 6W
Egenolf L.	**109**	59 3N	100 0W
Eger	**27**	47 53N	20 27 E
Eger →	**27**	47 38N	20 50 E
Egersund	**47**	58 26N	6 1 E
Egerton, Mt.	**96**	24 42 S	117 44 E
Egg L.	**109**	55 5N	105 30W
Eggenburg	**26**	48 38N	15 50 E
Eggenfelden	**25**	48 24N	12 46 E
Égletons	**20**	45 24N	2 3 E
Egmont, C.	**101**	39 16 S	173 45 E
Egmont, Mt.	**101**	39 17 S	174 5 E
Eğridir	**64**	37 52N	30 51 E
Eğridir Gölü	**64**	37 53N	30 50 E
Egtved	**49**	55 38N	9 18 E
Egume	**85**	7 30N	7 14 E
Éguzon	**20**	46 27N	1 33 E
Egvekinot	**59**	66 19N	179 50W
Egyek	**27**	47 39N	20 52 E
Egypt ■	**86**	28 0N	31 0 E
Eha Amufu	**85**	6 30N	7 46 E
Ehime □	**74**	33 30N	132 40 E
Ehingen	**25**	48 16N	9 43 E
Ehrwald	**26**	47 24N	10 56 E
Eibar	**32**	43 11N	2 28W
Eichstatt	**25**	48 53N	11 12 E
Eida	**47**	60 32N	6 43 E
Eider →	**24**	54 19N	8 58 E
Eidsvold	**99**	25 25 S	151 12 E
Eifel	**25**	50 10N	6 45 E
Eiffel Flats	**91**	18 20 S	30 0 E
Eigg	**14**	56 54N	6 10W
Eighty Mile Beach	**96**	19 30 S	120 40 E
Eil	**63**	8 0N	49 50 E
Eil, L.	**14**	56 50N	5 15W
Eildon, L.	**99**	37 10 S	146 0 E
Eileen L.	**109**	62 16N	107 37W
Eilenburg	**24**	51 28N	12 38 E
Ein el Luweiqa	**87**	14 5N	33 50 E
Einasleigh	**97**	18 32 S	144 5 E
Einasleigh →	**98**	17 30 S	142 17 E
Einbeck	**24**	51 48N	9 50 E
Eindhoven	**16**	51 26N	5 30 E
Einsiedeln	**25**	47 7N	8 46 E
Eiríksjökull	**50**	64 46N	20 24W
Eirunepé	**126**	6 35 S	69 53W
Eisenach	**24**	50 58N	10 18 E
Eisenberg	**24**	50 59N	11 50 E
Eisenerz	**26**	47 32N	14 54 E
Eisenhüttenstadt	**24**	52 9N	14 41 E
Eisenkappel	**26**	46 29N	14 36 E
Eisenstadt	**27**	47 51N	16 31 E
Eiserfeld	**24**	50 50N	7 59 E
Eisfeld	**24**	50 25N	10 54 E
Eisleben	**24**	51 31N	11 31 E
Ejby	**49**	55 25N	9 56 E
Eje, Sierra del	**30**	42 24N	6 54W
Ejea de los Caballeros	**32**	42 7N	1 9W
Ekalaka	**116**	45 55N	104 30W
Eket	**85**	4 38N	7 56 E
Eketahuna	**101**	40 38 S	175 43 E
Ekhínos	**44**	41 16N	25 1 E
Ekibastuz	**58**	51 50N	75 10 E
Ekimchan	**59**	53 0N	133 0W
Ekoli	**90**	0 23 S	24 13 E
Eksjö	**49**	57 40N	14 58W
Ekwan →	**106**	53 12N	82 15W
Ekwan Pt.	**106**	53 16N	82 7W
El Aaiún	**80**	27 9N	13 12W
El Aat	**62**	32 50N	35 45 E
El Abiodh-Sidi-Cheikh	**82**	32 53N	0 31 E
El Aïoun	**82**	34 33N	2 30W
El 'Aiyat	**86**	29 36N	31 15 E
El Alamein	**86**	30 48N	28 58 E
El 'Arag	**86**	28 40N	26 20 E
El Arahal	**31**	37 15N	5 33W
El Arba	**82**	36 37N	3 12 E
El Aricha	**82**	34 13N	1 10W
El Arīhā	**62**	31 52N	35 27 E
El Arish	**98**	17 35 S	146 1 E
El 'Arîsh	**86**	31 8N	33 50 E
El Arrouch	**83**	36 37N	6 53 E
* El Asnam	**82**	36 10N	1 20 E
El Astillero	**30**	43 24N	3 49W
El Badâri	**86**	27 4N	31 25 E
El Bahrein	**86**	28 30N	26 25 E
El Ballâs	**86**	26 2N	32 43 E
El Balyana	**86**	26 10N	32 3 E
El Baqeir	**86**	18 40N	33 40 E
El Barco de Ávila	**30**	40 21N	5 31W
El Barco de Valdeorras	**30**	42 23N	7 0W
El Bauga	**86**	18 18N	33 52 E
El Bawiti	**86**	28 25N	28 45 E
El Bayadh	**82**	33 40N	1 1 E
El Bierzo	**30**	42 45N	6 30W
El Bluff	**121**	11 59N	83 40W
El Bonillo	**33**	38 57N	2 35W
El Cajon	**119**	32 49N	117 0W
El Callao	**126**	7 18N	61 50W
El Camp	**32**	41 5N	1 10 E
El Campo	**117**	29 10N	96 20W
El Castillo	**31**	37 41N	6 19W
El Centro	**119**	32 50N	115 40W
El Cerro, Boliv.	**126**	17 30 S	61 40W
El Cerro, Spain	**31**	37 45N	6 57W
El Coronil	**31**	37 5N	5 38W
El Cuy	**128**	39 55 S	68 25W
El Cuyo	**120**	21 30N	87 40W
El Dab'a	**86**	31 0N	28 27 E
El Deir	**86**	25 25N	32 20 E
El Dere	**63**	3 50N	47 8 E
El Días	**120**	20 40N	87 20W
El Dilingat	**86**	30 50N	30 31 E
El Diviso	**126**	1 22N	78 14W
El Djem	**83**	35 18N	10 42 E
El Djouf	**84**	20 0N	11 30 E
El Dorado, Ark., U.S.A.	**117**	33 10N	92 40W
El Dorado, Kans., U.S.A.	**117**	37 55N	96 56W
El Dorado, Venez.	**126**	6 55N	61 37W
El Dorado Springs	**117**	37 54N	93 59W
El Eglab	**82**	26 20N	4 30W
El Escorial	**30**	40 35N	4 7W
El Eulma	**83**	36 9N	5 42 E
El Faiyûm	**86**	29 19N	30 50 E
El Fâsher	**87**	13 33N	25 26 E
El Fashn	**86**	28 50N	30 54 E
El Ferrol	**30**	43 29N	8 15W
El Fifi	**87**	10 4N	25 0 E
El Fuerte	**120**	26 30N	108 40W
El Gal	**63**	10 58N	50 20 E
El Gebir	**87**	13 40N	29 40 E
El Gedida	**86**	25 40N	28 30 E
El Geteina	**87**	14 50N	32 27 E
El Gezira □	**87**	15 0N	33 0 E
El Gîza	**86**	30 0N	31 10 E
El Goléa	**82**	30 30N	2 50 E
El Guettar	**83**	34 5N	4 38 E
El Hadjira	**83**	32 36N	5 30 E
El Hagiz	**87**	15 15N	35 50 E
El Hajeb	**82**	33 43N	5 13W
El Hammam	**86**	30 52N	29 25 E
El Hank	**82**	24 30N	7 0W
El Harrache	**80**	36 45N	3 5 E
El Hawata	**87**	13 25N	34 42 E
El Heiz	**86**	27 50N	28 40 E
El 'Idisât	**86**	25 30N	32 35 E
El Iskandarîya	**86**	31 0N	30 0 E
El Istwâ'ya □	**87**	5 0N	30 0 E
El Jadida	**80**	33 11N	8 17W
El Jebelein	**81**	12 40N	32 55 E
El Kab	**86**	19 27N	32 46 E
El Kala	**83**	36 50N	8 30 E
El Kalâa	**82**	32 4N	7 27W
El Kamlin	**87**	15 3N	33 11 E
El Kantara, Alg.	**83**	35 14N	5 45 E
El Kantara, Tunisia	**83**	33 45N	10 58 E
El Karaba	**86**	18 32N	33 41 E
El Kef	**83**	36 12N	8 47 E
El Khandaq	**86**	18 30N	30 30 E
El Khârga	**86**	25 30N	30 33 E
El Khartûm	**87**	15 31N	32 35 E
El Khartûm □	**87**	16 0N	33 0 E
El Khartûm Bahrî	**87**	15 40N	32 31 E
El-Khroubs	**83**	36 10N	6 55 E
El Khureiba	**86**	28 3N	35 10 E
El Kseur	**83**	36 46N	4 49 E
El Ksiba	**82**	32 45N	6 1W
El Kuntilla	**86**	30 1N	34 45 E
El Laqâwa	**81**	11 25N	29 1 E
El Laqeita	**86**	25 50N	33 15 E
El Leiya	**87**	16 15N	35 28 E
El Mafâza	**87**	13 38N	34 30 E
El Mahalla el Kubra	**86**	31 0N	31 0 E
El Mahârîq	**86**	25 35N	30 35 E
El Mahmûdîya	**86**	31 10N	30 32 E
El Maiz	**82**	28 19N	0 9W
El-Maks el-Bahari	**86**	24 30N	30 40 E
El Manshâh	**86**	26 26N	31 50 E
El Mansour	**82**	27 47N	0 14W
El Mansûra	**86**	31 0N	31 19 E
El Manzala	**86**	31 10N	31 50 E
El Marâgha	**86**	26 35N	31 10 E
El Masid	**87**	15 15N	33 0 E
El Matariya	**86**	31 15N	32 0 E
El Meghaier	**83**	33 55N	5 58 E
El Meraguen	**82**	28 0N	0 7W
El Metemma	**87**	16 50N	33 10 E
El Milagro	**124**	30 59 S	65 59W
El Milia	**83**	36 51N	6 13 E
El Minyâ	**86**	28 7N	30 33 E
El Molar	**32**	40 42N	3 45W
El Mreyye	**84**	18 0N	6 0W
El Obeid	**87**	13 8N	30 10 E
El Odaiya	**81**	12 8N	28 12 E
El Oro	**120**	19 48N	100 8W
El Oro = Sta. María del Oro	**120**	25 50N	105 20W
El Oued	**83**	33 20N	6 58 E
El Palmito, Presa	**120**	25 40N	105 30W
El Panadès	**32**	41 10N	1 30 E
El Pardo	**30**	40 31N	3 47W
El Paso	**119**	31 50N	106 30W
El Pedernoso	**33**	39 29N	2 45W
El Pedroso	**31**	37 51N	5 45W
El Pobo de Dueñas	**32**	40 46N	1 39W
El Portal	**119**	37 44N	119 49W
El Prat de Llobregat	**32**	41 18N	2 3 E
El Progreso	**120**	15 26N	87 51W
El Provencío	**33**	39 23N	2 35W
El Pueblito	**120**	29 3N	105 4W
El Qâhira	**86**	30 1N	31 14 E
El Qantara	**86**	30 51N	32 20 E
El Qasr	**86**	25 44N	28 42 E
El Quseima	**86**	30 40N	34 15 E
El Qusîya	**86**	27 29N	30 44 E
El Râshda	**86**	25 36N	28 57 E
El Reno	**117**	35 30N	98 0W
El Ribero	**30**	42 30N	8 30W
El Rîdisiya	**86**	24 56N	32 51 E
El Ronquillo	**31**	37 44N	6 10W
El Rubio	**31**	37 22N	5 0W
El Saff	**86**	29 34N	31 16 E
El Salvador ■	**120**	13 50N	89 0W
El Sancejo	**31**	37 4N	5 6W
El Sauce	**121**	13 0N	86 40W
El Shallal	**86**	24 0N	32 53 E
El Simbillawein	**86**	30 48N	31 13 E
El Suweis	**86**	29 58N	32 31 E
El Thamad	**86**	29 40N	34 28 E
El Tigre	**126**	8 44N	64 15W
El Tocuyo	**126**	9 47N	69 48W
El Tofo	**124**	29 22 S	71 18W
El Tránsito	**124**	28 52 S	70 17W
El Tûr	**86**	28 14N	33 36 E
El Turbio	**128**	51 45 S	72 5W
El Uqsur	**86**	25 41N	32 38 E
El Vado	**32**	41 2N	3 18W
El Vallés	**32**	41 35N	2 20 E
El Vigía	**126**	8 38N	71 39W
El Wak	**90**	2 49N	40 56 E
El Waqf	**86**	25 45N	32 15 E
El Wâsta	**86**	29 19N	31 12 E
El Weguet	**87**	5 28N	42 17 E
El Wuz	**81**	15 0N	30 7 E
Elafónisos	**45**	36 29N	22 56 E
Elamanchili = Yellamanchilli	**70**	17 26N	82 50 E
Elandsvlei	**92**	32 19 S	19 31 E
Élassa	**45**	35 18N	26 21 E
Elassón	**44**	39 53N	22 12 E
Elat	**62**	29 30N	34 56 E
Eláthia	**45**	38 37N	22 46 E
Elâzığ	**64**	38 37N	39 14 E
Elba, Italy	**38**	42 48N	10 15 E
Elba, U.S.A.	**115**	31 27N	86 4W
Elbasani	**44**	41 9N	20 9 E
Elbasani-Berati □	**44**	40 58N	20 0 E
Elbe →	**24**	53 50N	9 0 E
Elbert, Mt.	**119**	39 5N	106 27W
Elberta	**114**	44 35N	86 14W
Elberton	**115**	34 7N	82 51W
Elbeuf	**18**	49 17N	1 2 E
Elbidtan	**64**	38 13N	37 12 E
Elbing = Elbląg	**28**	54 10N	19 25 E
Elbląg	**28**	54 10N	19 25 E
Elbląg □	**28**	54 15N	19 30 E
Elbow	**109**	51 7N	106 35W

* *Renamed Ech Cheliff*

Elbrus Estevan

Elbrus **57** 43 21N 42 30 E
Elburg **16** 52 26N 5 50 E
Elburz Mts. = Alborz **65** 36 0N 52 0 E
Elche **33** 38 15N 0 42 W
Elche de la Sierra **33** 38 27N 2 3W
Elcho I. **97** 11 55 S 135 45 E
Elda **33** 38 29N 0 47W
Eldon **116** 38 20N 92 38W
Eldora **116** 42 20N 93 5W
Eldorado, Argent. **125** 26 28 S 54 43W
Eldorado, Can. **109** 59 35N 108 30W
Eldorado, Mexico **120** 24 20N 107 22W
Eldorado, Ill., U.S.A. **114** 37 50N 88 25W
Eldorado, Tex., U.S.A. **117** 30 52N 100 35W
Eldoret **90** 0 30N 35 17 E
Eldred **112** 41 57N 78 24W
Electra **117** 34 0N 99 0W
Elefantes → **93** 24 10 S 32 40 E
Elektrogorsk **55** 55 56N 38 50 E
Elektrostal **55** 55 41N 38 32 E
Elele **85** 5 5N 6 50 E
Elena **43** 42 55N 25 53 E
Elephant Butte Res. **119** 33 45N 107 30W
Elephant I. **5** 61 0 S 55 0W
Elephant Pass **70** 9 35N 80 25 E
Eleshnitsa **43** 41 52N 23 36 E
Eleuthera **121** 25 0N 76 20W
Elevsís **45** 38 4N 23 26 E
Elevtheroúpolis **44** 40 52N 24 20 E
Elgepiggen **47** 62 10N 11 21 E
Elgeyo-Marakwet □ **90** 0 45N 35 30 E
Elgin, N.B., Can. **107** 45 48N 65 10W
Elgin, Ont., Can. **113** 44 36N 76 13W
Elgin, U.K. **14** 57 39N 3 20W
Elgin, Ill., U.S.A. **114** 42 0N 88 20W
Elgin, N.D., U.S.A. **116** 46 24N 101 46W
Elgin, Nebr., U.S.A. **116** 41 58N 98 3W
Elgin, Nev., U.S.A. **119** 37 21N 114 20W
Elgin, Oreg., U.S.A. **118** 45 37N 118 0W
Elgin, Texas, U.S.A. **117** 30 21N 97 22W
Elgon, Mt. **90** 1 10N 34 30 E
Eliase **73** 8 21 S 130 48 E
Elida **117** 33 56N 103 41W
Elikón, Mt. **45** 38 18N 22 45 E
Elin Pelin **43** 42 40N 23 36 E
Elisabethville = Lubumbashi **91** 11 40 S 27 28 E
Elista **57** 46 16N 44 14 E
Elizabeth, Austral. **97** 34 42 S 138 41 E
Elizabeth, U.S.A. **114** 40 37N 74 12W
Elizabeth City **115** 36 18N 76 16W
Elizabethton **115** 36 20N 82 13W
Elizabethtown, Ky., U.S.A. **114** 37 40N 85 54W
Elizabethtown, N.Y., U.S.A. **113** 44 13N 73 36W
Elizabethtown, Pa., U.S.A. **113** 40 8N 76 36W
Elizondo **32** 43 12N 1 30W
Ełk **28** 53 50N 22 21 E
Ełk → **28** 53 41N 22 28 E
Elk City **117** 35 25N 99 25W
Elk Island Nat. Park **108** 53 35N 112 59W
Elk Lake **106** 47 40N 80 25W
Elk Point **109** 53 54N 110 55W
Elk River, Idaho, U.S.A. **118** 46 50N 116 8W
Elk River, Minn., U.S.A. **116** 45 17N 93 34W
Elkhart, Ind., U.S.A. **114** 41 42N 85 55W
Elkhart, Kans., U.S.A. **117** 37 3N 101 54W
Elkhorn **109** 49 59N 101 14W
Elkhorn → **116** 41 7N 98 15W
Elkhotovo **57** 43 19N 44 15 E
Elkhovo **43** 42 10N 26 40 E
Elkin **115** 36 17N 80 50W
Elkins **114** 38 53N 79 53W
Elko, Can. **108** 49 20N 115 10W
Elko, U.S.A. **118** 40 50N 115 50W
Ellef Ringnes I. **4** 78 30N 102 2W
Ellen, Mt. **119** 38 4N 110 56W
Ellendale **116** 46 3N 98 30W
Ellensburg **118** 47 0N 120 30W
Ellenville **114** 41 42N 74 23W
Ellery, Mt. **99** 37 28 S 148 47 E
Ellesmere I. **4** 79 30N 80 0W
Ellesworth Land **5** 76 0 S 89 0W
Ellice Is. = Tuvalu ■ **94** 8 0 S 176 0 E
Ellinwood **116** 38 27N 98 37W
Elliot **93** 31 22 S 27 48 E
Elliot Lake **106** 46 25N 82 35W
Ellis **116** 39 0N 99 39W
Ellisville **117** 31 38N 89 12W
Ellon **14** 57 21N 2 5W
Ellore = Eluru **70** 16 48N 81 8 E
Ells → **108** 57 18N 111 40W
Ellsworth **116** 38 47N 98 15W
Ellsworth Land **5** 76 0 S 89 0W
Ellsworth Mts. **5** 78 30 S 85 0W
Ellwangen **25** 48 57N 10 9 E
Ellwood City **114** 40 52N 80 19W
Elm **25** 46 54N 9 10 E
Elma, Can. **109** 49 52N 95 55W
Elma, U.S.A. **118** 47 0N 123 30 E
Elmalı **64** 36 44N 29 56 E
Elmhurst **114** 41 52N 87 58W
Elmina **85** 5 5N 1 21W
Elmira, Can. **112** 43 36N 80 33W
Elmira, U.S.A. **114** 42 8N 76 49W
Elmore **99** 36 30 S 144 37 E
Elmshorn **24** 53 44N 9 40 E
Elmvale **112** 44 35N 79 52W
Elne **20** 42 36N 2 58 E
Elora **112** 43 41N 80 26W
Elos **45** 36 46N 22 43 E
Eloy **119** 32 46N 111 33W
Éloyes **19** 48 6N 6 36 E
Elrose **109** 51 12N 108 0W
Elsas **106** 48 32N 82 55W
Elsinore, Cal., U.S.A. **119** 33 40N 117 15W
Elsinore, Utah, U.S.A. **119** 38 40N 112 2W
Elspe **24** 51 10N 8 1 E
Elster → **24** 51 25N 11 57 E
Elsterwerda **24** 51 27N 13 32 E
Eltham **101** 39 26 S 174 19 E
Elton **57** 49 5N 46 52 E
Eluru **70** 16 48N 81 8 E
Elvas **31** 38 50N 7 10W
Elven **18** 47 44N 2 36W
Elverum **47** 60 53N 11 34 E
Elvo → **38** 45 23N 8 21 E
Elvran **47** 63 24N 11 3 E
Elwood, Ind., U.S.A. **114** 40 20N 85 50W
Elwood, Nebr., U.S.A. **116** 40 38N 99 51W
Ely, U.K. **13** 52 24N 0 16 E
Ely, Minn., U.S.A. **116** 47 54N 91 52W
Ely, Nev., U.S.A. **118** 39 10N 114 50W
Elyashiv **62** 32 23N 34 55 E
Elyria **114** 41 22N 82 8W
Elyrus **45** 35 15N 23 45 E
Elz → **25** 48 21N 7 45 E
Emådalen **48** 61 20N 14 44 E
Emba **58** 48 50N 58 8 E
Emba → **58** 45 25N 52 30 E
Embarcación **124** 23 10 S 64 0W
Embarras Portage **109** 58 27N 111 28W
Embóna **45** 36 13N 27 51 E
Embrun **21** 44 34N 6 30 E
Embu **90** 0 32 S 37 38 E
Embu □ **90** 0 30 S 37 35 E
Emden **24** 53 22N 7 12 E
'Emeq Yizre'el **62** 32 35N 35 12 E
Emerald **97** 23 32 S 148 10 E
Emerson **109** 49 0N 97 10W
Emery **119** 38 59N 111 17W
Emery Park **119** 32 10N 110 59W
Emi Koussi **83** 20 0N 18 55 E
Emilia-Romagna □ **38** 44 33N 10 40 E
Emilius, Mte. **38** 45 41N 7 23 E
Eminabad **68** 32 2N 74 8 E
Emine, Nos **43** 42 40N 27 56 E
Emlenton **112** 41 11N 79 41W
Emlichheim **24** 52 37N 6 51 E
Emmaboda **49** 56 37N 15 32 E
Emme → **25** 47 0N 7 42 E
Emmeloord **16** 52 44N 5 46 E
Emmen **16** 52 48N 6 57 E
Emmendingen **25** 48 7N 7 51 E
Emmental **25** 47 0N 7 35 E
Emmerich **24** 51 50N 6 12 E
Emmet **98** 24 45 S 144 30 E
Emmetsburg **116** 43 3N 94 40W
Emmett **118** 43 51N 116 33W
Emöd **27** 47 57N 20 47 E
Emona **43** 42 43N 27 53 E
Empalme **120** 28 1N 110 49W
Empangeni **93** 28 50 S 31 52 E
Empedrado **124** 28 0 S 58 46W
Emperor Seamount Chain **94** 40 0N 170 0 E
Empoli **38** 43 43N 10 57 E
Emporia, Kans., U.S.A. **116** 38 25N 96 10W
Emporia, Va., U.S.A. **115** 36 41N 77 32W
Emporium **114** 41 30N 78 17W
Empress **109** 50 57N 110 0W
Ems → **24** 52 37N 9 26 E
Emsdale **112** 45 32N 79 19W
Emsdetten **24** 52 11N 7 31 E
Emu **76** 43 40N 128 6 E
Emu Park **98** 23 13 S 150 50 E
En Gedi **62** 31 28N 35 25 E
En Gev **62** 32 47N 35 38 E
En Harod **62** 32 33N 35 22 E
'En Kerem **62** 31 47N 35 6 E
En Nahud **87** 12 45N 28 25 E
Enafors **48** 63 17N 12 20 E
Enana **92** 17 30 S 16 23 E
Enånger **48** 61 30N 17 9 E
Enaratoli **73** 3 55 S 136 21 E
Enard B. **14** 58 5N 5 20W
Encantadas, Serra **125** 30 40 S 53 0W
Encanto, C. **73** 15 45N 121 38 E
Encarnación **125** 27 15 S 55 50W
Encarnación de Diaz **120** 21 30N 102 13W
Enchi **84** 5 53N 2 48W
Encinal **117** 28 3N 99 25W
Encino **119** 34 38N 105 40W
Encounter B. **97** 35 45 S 138 45 E
Endau **71** 2 40N 103 38 E
Endau → **71** 2 30N 103 30 E
Ende **73** 8 45 S 121 40 E
Endeavour **109** 52 10N 102 39W
Endeavour Str. **97** 10 45 S 142 0 E
Endelave **49** 55 46N 10 18 E
Enderbury I. **94** 3 8 S 171 5W
Enderby **108** 50 35N 119 10W
Enderby Land **5** 66 0 S 53 0 E
Enderlin **116** 46 37N 97 41W
Endicott, N.Y., U.S.A. **114** 42 6N 76 2W
Endicott, Wash., U.S.A. **118** 47 0N 117 45W
Endröd **27** 46 55N 20 47 E
Enez **44** 40 45N 26 5 E
Enfida **83** 36 6N 10 28 E
Enfield **13** 51 39N 0 4W
Engadin = Engiadina **25** 46 51N 10 18 E
Engaño, C., Dom. Rep. **121** 18 30N 68 20W
Engaño, C., Phil. **73** 18 35N 122 23 E
Engelberg **25** 46 48N 8 26 E
Engels **55** 51 28N 46 6 E
Engemann L. **109** 58 0N 106 55W
Enger **47** 60 35N 10 20 E
Enggano **72** 5 20 S 102 40 E
Enghien **16** 50 37N 4 2 E
Engiadina **25** 46 51N 10 18 E
Engil **82** 33 12N 4 32W
Engkilili **72** 1 3N 111 42 E
England **117** 34 30N 91 58W
England □ **11** 53 0N 2 0W
Englee **107** 50 45N 56 5W
Englehart **106** 47 49N 79 52W
Engler L. **109** 59 8N 106 52W
Englewood, Colo., U.S.A. **116** 39 40N 105 0W
Englewood, Kans., U.S.A. **117** 37 7N 99 59W
Englewood, N.J., U.S.A. **113** 40 54N 73 59W
English → **109** 50 35N 93 30W
English Bazar **69** 24 58N 88 10 E
English Channel **18** 50 0N 2 0W
English River **106** 49 14N 91 0W
Enid **117** 36 26N 97 52W
Enipévs → **44** 39 22N 22 17 E
Eniwetok **94** 11 30N 162 15 E
Enkeldoorn **91** 19 2 S 30 52 E
Enkhuizen **16** 52 42N 5 17 E
Enköping **48** 59 37N 17 4 E
Enna **41** 37 34N 14 15 E
Ennadai **109** 61 8N 100 53W
Ennadai L. **109** 61 0N 101 0W
Ennedi **81** 17 15N 22 0 E
Enngonia **99** 29 21 S 145 50 E
Ennis, Ireland **15** 52 51N 8 59W
Ennis, Mont., U.S.A. **118** 45 20N 111 42W
Ennis, Texas, U.S.A. **117** 32 15N 96 40W
Enniscorthy **15** 52 30N 6 35W
Enniskillen **15** 54 20N 7 40W
Ennistimon **15** 52 56N 9 18W
Enns **26** 48 12N 14 28 E
Enns → **26** 48 14N 14 32 E
Enontekiö **50** 68 23N 23 37 E
Enping **77** 22 16N 112 21 E
Enriquillo, L. **121** 18 20N 72 5W
Enschede **16** 52 13N 6 53 E
Ensenada, Argent. **124** 34 55 S 57 55W
Ensenada, Mexico **120** 31 50N 116 50W
Enshi **77** 30 18N 109 29 E
Ensisheim **19** 47 50N 7 20 E
Entebbe **90** 0 4N 32 28 E
Enterprise, Can. **108** 60 47N 115 45W
Enterprise, Oreg., U.S.A. **118** 45 30N 117 18W
Enterprise, Utah, U.S.A. **119** 37 37N 113 36W
Entre Ríos, Boliv. **124** 21 30 S 64 25W
Entre Rios, Mozam. **91** 14 57 S 37 20 E
Entre Ríos □ **124** 30 30 S 58 30W
Entrecasteaux, Pt. d' **96** 34 50 S 115 56 E
Entrepeñas, Pantano de **32** 40 34N 2 42W
Enugu **85** 6 20N 7 30 E
Enugu Ezike **85** 7 0N 7 29 E
Enumclaw **118** 47 12N 122 0W
Envermeières **18** 49 54N 1 16 E
Envermeu **18** 49 53N 1 15 E
Enz → **25** 49 1N 9 6 E
Enza → **38** 44 54N 10 31 E
Eólie, I. **41** 38 30N 14 50 E
Epanomí **44** 40 25N 22 59 E
Epe, Neth. **16** 52 21N 5 59 E
Epe, Nigeria **85** 6 36N 3 59 E
Épernay **19** 49 3N 3 56 E
Épernon **19** 48 35N 1 40 E
Ephesus, Turkey **45** 37 50N 27 33 E
Ephesus, Turkey **64** 38 0N 27 19 E
Ephraim **118** 39 21N 111 37W
Ephrata **118** 47 20N 119 32W
Epidaurus Limera **45** 36 46N 23 0 E
Epila **32** 41 36N 1 17W
Épinac-les-Mines **19** 46 59N 4 31 E
Épinal **19** 48 10N 6 27 E
Episcopia Bihorului **46** 47 12N 21 55 E
Epitálion **45** 37 37N 21 30 E
Epping **13** 51 42N 0 8 E
Epukiro **92** 21 40 S 19 9 E
Equatorial Guinea ■ **88** 2 0 S 8 0 E
Er Rahad **87** 12 45N 30 32 E
Er Rif **82** 35 1N 4 1W
Er Roseires **87** 11 55N 34 30 E
Er Yébigué **83** 22 30N 17 30 E
Erandol **68** 20 56N 75 20 E
Erāwadī Myit = Irrawaddy → **67** 15 50N 95 6 E
Erba, Italy **38** 45 49N 9 12 E
Erba, Sudan **86** 19 5N 36 51 E
Ercha **59** 69 45N 147 20 E
Erciyaş Dağı **64** 38 30N 35 30 E
Erdao Jiang → **76** 43 0N 127 0 E
Erding **25** 48 18N 11 55 E
Erdre → **18** 47 13N 1 32W
Erebus, Mt. **5** 77 35 S 167 0 E
Erechim **125** 27 35 S 52 15W
Ereğli, Turkey **64** 41 15N 31 30 E
Ereğli, Turkey **64** 37 31N 34 4 E
Erei, Monti **41** 37 20N 14 20 E
Erenhot **76** 43 48N 111 59 E
Eresma → **30** 41 26N 40 45W
Eressós **45** 39 11N 25 57 E
Erfenis Dam **92** 28 30 S 26 50 E
Erfjord **47** 59 20N 6 14 E
Erfoud **82** 31 30N 4 15W
Erft → **24** 51 11N 6 44 E
Erfurt **24** 50 58N 11 2 E
Erfurt □ **24** 51 10N 10 30 E
Ergani **64** 38 17N 39 49 E
Ergene → **43** 41 1N 26 22 E
Ergeni Vozyshennost **57** 47 0N 44 0 E
Ergli **54** 56 54N 25 38 E
Ergun Zuoqi **76** 50 47N 121 31 E
Eria → **30** 42 3N 5 44W
Eriba **87** 16 40N 36 10 E
Eriboll, L. **14** 58 28N 4 41W
Érice **40** 38 4N 12 34 E
Erie **114** 42 10N 80 7W
Erie Canal **112** 43 15N 78 0W
Erie, L. **112** 42 15N 81 0W
Erieau **112** 42 16N 81 57W
Erigavo **63** 10 35N 47 20 E
Erikoúsa **44** 39 55N 19 14 E
Eriksdale **109** 50 52N 98 7W
Erikslund **48** 62 31N 15 54 E
Erimanthos **45** 37 57N 21 50 E
Erimo-misaki **74** 41 50N 143 15 E
Erithraí **45** 38 13N 23 20 E
Eritrea □ **87** 14 0N 41 0 E
Erjas → **31** 39 40N 7 1W
Erlangen **25** 49 35N 11 0 E
Ermelo, Neth. **16** 52 18N 5 35 E
Ermelo, S. Afr. **93** 26 31 S 29 59 E
Ermenak **64** 36 38N 33 0 E
Ermióni **45** 37 23N 23 15 E
Ermoúpolis = Síros **45** 37 28N 24 57 E
Ernakulam = Cochin **70** 9 59N 76 22 E
Erne → **15** 54 30N 8 16W
Erne, Lough **15** 54 26N 7 46W
Ernée **18** 48 18N 0 56W
Ernstberg **25** 50 14N 6 46 E
Erode **70** 11 24N 77 45 E
Eromanga **99** 26 40 S 143 11 E
Erongo **92** 21 39 S 15 58 E
Erquy **18** 48 38N 2 29W
Erquy, Cap d' **18** 48 39N 2 29W
Erramala Hills **70** 15 30N 78 15 E
Errer → **87** 7 32N 42 35 E
Errigal, Mt. **15** 55 2N 8 8W
Erris Hd. **15** 54 19N 10 0W
Erseka **44** 40 22N 20 40 E
Erskine **116** 47 37N 96 0W
Erstein **19** 48 25N 7 38 E
Ertil **55** 51 55N 40 50 E
Ertvågøy **47** 63 13N 8 26 E
Eruwa **85** 7 33N 3 26 E
Ervy-le-Châtel **19** 48 2N 3 55 E
Erwin **115** 36 10N 82 28W
Erzgebirge **24** 50 25N 13 0 E
Erzin **59** 50 15N 95 10 E
Erzincan **64** 39 46N 39 30 E
Erzurum **64** 39 57N 41 15 E
Es Sahrâ' Esh Sharqîya **86** 26 0N 33 30 E
Es Sînâ' **86** 29 0N 34 0 E
Es Sûkî **87** 13 20N 33 58 E
Esambo **90** 3 48 S 23 30 E
Esan-Misaki **74** 41 40N 141 10 E
Esbjerg **49** 55 29N 8 29 E
Escalante **119** 37 47N 111 37W
Escalante → **119** 37 17N 110 53W
Escalón **120** 26 46N 104 20W
Escalona **30** 40 9N 4 29W
Escambia → **115** 30 32N 87 15W
Escanaba **114** 45 44N 87 5W
Esch-sur-Alzette **16** 49 32N 6 0 E
Eschallens **25** 46 39N 6 38 E
Eschede **24** 52 44N 10 13 E
Eschwege **24** 51 10N 10 3 E
Eschweiler **24** 50 49N 6 14 E
Escobal **120** 9 6N 80 1W
Escondido **119** 33 9N 117 4W
Escuinapa **120** 22 50N 105 50W
Escuintla **120** 14 20N 90 48W
Eséka **85** 3 41N 10 44 E
Esens **24** 53 40N 7 35 E
Esera → **32** 42 6N 0 15 E
Eşfahān **65** 33 0N 53 0 E
Esgueva → **30** 41 40N 4 43W
Esh Sham = Dimashq **64** 33 30N 36 18 E
Esh Shamâlîya □ **86** 19 0N 29 0 E
Eshowe **93** 28 50 S 31 30 E
Eshta' ol **62** 31 47N 35 0 E
Esiama **84** 4 56N 2 25W
Esino → **39** 43 39N 13 22 E
Esk →, Dumfries, U.K. **14** 54 58N 3 4W
Esk →, N. Yorks., U.K. **12** 54 27N 0 36W
Eskifjörður **50** 65 3N 13 55W
Eskilstuna **48** 59 22N 16 32 E
Eskimo Pt. **109** 61 10N 94 15W
Eskişehir **64** 39 50N 30 35 E
Esla → **30** 41 29N 6 3W
Esla, Pantano del **30** 41 29N 6 3W
Eslöv **49** 55 50N 13 20 E
Esmeralda, La **124** 22 16 S 62 33W
Esmeraldas **126** 1 0N 79 40W
Espalion **20** 44 32N 2 47 E
Espalmador, I. **33** 38 47N 1 26 E
Espanola **106** 46 15N 81 46W
Espardell, I. del **33** 38 48N 1 29 E
Esparraguera **32** 41 33N 1 52 E
Espejo **31** 37 40N 4 34W
Esperance **96** 33 45 S 121 55 E
Esperance B. **96** 33 48 S 121 55 E
Esperanza **124** 31 29 S 61 3W
Espéraza **20** 42 56N 2 14 E
Espevær **47** 59 35N 5 7 E
Espichel, C. **31** 38 22N 9 16W
Espiel **31** 38 11N 5 1W
Espigão, Serra do **125** 26 35 S 50 30W
Espinal **126** 4 9N 74 53W
Espinhaço, Serra do **127** 17 30 S 43 30W
Espinho **30** 41 1N 8 38W
Espinilho, Serra do **125** 28 30 S 55 0W
Espinosa de los Monteros **30** 43 5N 3 34W
Espírito Santo □ **127** 20 0 S 40 45W
Espíritu Santo, B. del **120** 19 15N 87 0W
Espíritu Santo, I. **120** 24 30N 110 23W
Espluga de Francolí **32** 41 24N 1 7 E
Espuña, Sierra **33** 37 51N 1 35W
Espungabera **93** 20 29 S 32 45 E
Esquel **128** 42 55 S 71 20W
Esquina **124** 30 0 S 59 30W
Essaouira (Mogador) **82** 31 32N 9 48W
Essarts, Les **18** 46 47N 1 12W
Essebie **90** 2 58N 30 40 E
Essen, Belg. **16** 51 28N 4 28 E
Essen, Ger. **24** 51 28N 6 59 E
Essequibo → **126** 6 50N 58 30W
Essex, Can. **112** 42 10N 82 49W
Essex, U.S.A. **113** 44 17N 73 21W
Essex □ **13** 51 48N 0 30 E
Esslingen **25** 48 43N 9 19 E
Essonne □ **19** 48 30N 2 20 E
Essvik **48** 62 18N 17 24 E
Estaca, Pta. del **30** 43 46N 7 42W
Estadilla **32** 42 4N 0 16 E
Estados, I. de Los **128** 54 40 S 64 30W
Estagel **20** 42 47N 2 40 E
Estância **127** 11 16 S 37 26W
Estancia **119** 34 50N 106 1W
Estarreja **30** 40 45N 8 35W
Estats, Pic d' **32** 42 40N 1 24 E
Estcourt **93** 28 58 S 29 53 E
Este **39** 45 12N 11 40 E
Esteban **30** 43 33N 6 5W
Estelí **121** 13 9N 86 22W
Estella **32** 42 40N 2 0W
Estelline, S.D., U.S.A. **116** 44 39N 96 52W
Estelline, Texas, U.S.A. **117** 34 35N 100 27W
Estena → **31** 39 23N 4 44W
Estepa **31** 37 17N 4 52W
Estepona **31** 36 24N 5 7W
Esterhazy **109** 50 37N 102 5W
Esternay **19** 48 44N 3 33 E
Esterri de Aneu **32** 42 38N 1 5 E
Estevan **109** 49 10N 102 59W

Estevan Group Ferland

Estevan Group **108** 53 3N 129 38W
Estherville **116** 43 25N 94 50W
Estissac **19** 48 16N 3 48 E
Eston **109** 51 8N 108 40W
Estonian S.S.R. □ **54** 58 30N 25 30 E
Estoril **31** 38 42N 9 23W
Estouk **85** 18 14N 1 2 E
Estrada, La **30** 42 43N 8 27W
Estrêla, Serra da **30** 40 10N 7 45W
Estrella **33** 38 25N 3 35W
Estremoz **31** 38 51N 7 39W
Estrondo, Serra do **127** 7 20 S 48 0W
Esztergom **27** 47 47N 18 44 E
Et Tîdra **84** 19 45N 16 20W
Eţ Ţīra **62** 32 14N 34 56 E
Étables-sur-Mer **18** 48 38N 2 51W
Etah **68** 27 35N 78 40 E
Étain **19** 49 13N 5 38 E
Etamamu **107** 50 18N 59 59W
Étampes **19** 48 26N 2 10 E
Étang **19** 46 52N 4 10 E
Etanga **92** 17 55 S 13 00 E
Étaples **19** 50 30N 1 39 E
Etawah **68** 26 48N 79 6 E
Etawah → **115** 34 20N 84 15W
Etawney L. **109** 57 50N 96 50W
Eteh **85** 7 2N 7 28 E
Ethel, Oued el → **82** 28 31N 3 37W
Ethelbert **109** 51 32N 100 25W
Ethiopia ■ **63** 8 0N 40 0 E
Ethiopian Highlands **78** 10 0N 37 0 E
Etive, L. **14** 56 30N 5 12W
Etna, Mt. **41** 37 45N 15 0 E
Etne **47** 59 40N 5 56 E
Etoile **91** 11 33 S 27 30 E
Etolin I. **108** 56 5N 132 20W
Etosha Pan **92** 18 40 S 16 30 E
Etowah **115** 35 20N 84 30W
Étrépagny **18** 49 18N 1 36 E
Étretat **18** 49 42N 0 12 E
Étroits, Les **107** 47 24N 68 54W
Etropole **43** 42 50N 24 0 E
Ettlingen **25** 48 58N 8 25 E
Ettrick Water **14** 55 31N 2 55W
Etuku **90** 3 42 S 25 45 E
Etzatlán **120** 20 48N 104 5W
Eu **18** 50 3N 1 26 E
Euabalong West **100** 33 3 S 146 23 E
Euboea = Évvoia **45** 38 40N 23 40 E
Eucla Basin **96** 31 19 S 126 9 E
Euclid **114** 41 32N 81 31W
Eucumbene, L. **99** 36 2 S 148 40 E
Eudora **117** 33 5N 91 17W
Eufaula, Ala., U.S.A. **115** 31 55N 85 11W
Eufaula, Okla., U.S.A. **117** 35 20N 95 33W
Eufaula, L. **117** 35 15N 95 28W
Eugene **118** 44 0N 123 8W
Eugenia, Punta **120** 27 50N 115 5W
Eugowra **99** 33 22 S 148 24 E
Eulo **99** 28 10 S 145 3 E
Eunice, La., U.S.A. **117** 30 35N 92 28W
Eunice, N. Mex., U.S.A. **117** 32 30N 103 10W
Eupen **16** 50 37N 6 3 E
Euphrates = Furāt, Nahr al → **64** 31 0N 47 25 E
Eure □ **18** 49 6N 1 0 E
Eure → **18** 49 18N 1 12 E
Eure-et-Loir □ **18** 48 22N 1 30 E
Eureka, Can. **4** 80 0N 85 56W
Eureka, Calif., U.S.A. **118** 40 50N 124 0W
Eureka, Kans., U.S.A. **117** 37 50N 96 20W
Eureka, Mont., U.S.A. **118** 48 53N 115 6W
Eureka, Nev., U.S.A. **118** 39 32N 116 2W
Eureka, S.D., U.S.A. **116** 45 49N 99 38W
Eureka, Utah, U.S.A. **118** 40 0N 112 9W
Euroa **99** 36 44 S 145 35 E
Europa, Picos de **30** 43 10N 4 49W
Europa Pt. = Europa, Pta. de **31** 36 3N 5 21W
Europa, Pta. de **31** 36 3N 5 21W
Europe **8** 50 0N 20 0 E
Europoort **16** 51 57N 4 10 E
Euskirchen **24** 50 40N 6 45 E
Eustis **115** 28 54N 81 36W
Eutin **24** 54 7N 10 38 E
Eutsuk L. **108** 53 20N 126 45W
Eval **62** 32 15N 35 15 E
Evale **92** 16 33 S 15 44 E
Evanger **47** 60 39N 6 7 E
Evans **116** 40 25N 104 43W
Evans Head **99** 29 7 S 153 27 E
Evans L. **106** 50 50N 77 0W
Evans Mills **113** 44 6N 75 48W
Evans Pass **116** 41 0N 105 35W
Evanston, Ill., U.S.A. **114** 42 0N 87 40W
Evanston, Wyo., U.S.A. **118** 41 10N 111 0W
Evansville, Ind., U.S.A. **114** 38 0N 87 35W
Evansville, Wis., U.S.A. **116** 42 47N 89 18W
Évaux-les-Bains **20** 46 12N 2 29 E
Eveleth **116** 47 29N 92 46W
Even Yahuda **62** 32 16N 34 53 E
Evensk **59** 62 12N 159 30 E
Evenstad **47** 61 25N 11 7 E
Everard, L. **96** 31 30 S 135 0 E
Everard Ras. **96** 27 5 S 132 28 E
Everest, Mt. **69** 28 5N 86 58 E
Everett, Pa., U.S.A. **112** 40 2N 78 24W
Everett, Wash., U.S.A. **118** 48 0N 122 10W
Everglades, Fla., U.S.A. **115** 26 0N 80 30W
Everglades, Fla., U.S.A. **115** 25 52N 81 23W
Everglades Nat. Park. **115** 25 27N 80 53W
Evergreen **115** 31 28N 86 55W
Everson **118** 48 57N 122 22W
Evesham **13** 52 6N 1 57W
Evian-les-Bains **21** 46 24N 6 35 E
Evinayong **88** 1 26N 10 35 E
Évinos → **45** 38 27N 21 40 E
Evisa **21** 42 15N 8 48 E
Evje **47** 58 36N 7 51 E
Évora **31** 38 33N 7 57W
Évora □ **31** 38 33N 7 50W
Évreux **18** 49 0N 1 8 E
Evritania □ **45** 39 5N 21 30 E
Évron **18** 48 10N 0 24W
Évros □ **44** 41 10N 26 0 E
Evrótas → **45** 36 50N 22 40 E
Évvoia **45** 38 30N 24 0 E
Évvoia □ **45** 38 40N 23 40 E
Ewe, L. **14** 57 49N 5 38W
Ewing **116** 42 18N 98 22W
Ewo **88** 0 48 S 14 45 E
Exaltación **126** 13 10 S 65 20W
Excelsior Springs **116** 39 20N 94 10W
Excideuil **20** 45 20N 1 4 E
Exe → **13** 50 38N 3 27W
Exeter, Can. **112** 43 21N 81 29W
Exeter, U.K. **13** 50 43N 3 31W
Exeter, Calif., U.S.A. **119** 36 17N 119 9W
Exeter, N.H., U.S.A. **113** 43 0N 70 58W
Exeter, Nebr., U.S.A. **116** 40 43N 97 30W
Exmes **18** 48 45N 0 10 E
Exmoor **13** 51 10N 3 59W
Exmouth, Austral. **96** 21 54 S 114 10 E
Exmouth, U.K. **13** 50 37N 3 26W
Exmouth G. **96** 22 15 S 114 15 E
Expedition Range **97** 24 30 S 149 12 E
Extremadura **31** 39 30N 6 5W
Exuma Sound **121** 24 30N 76 20W
Eyasi, L. **90** 3 30 S 35 0 E
Eyeberry L. **109** 63 8N 104 43W
Eyemouth **14** 55 53N 2 5W
Eygurande **20** 45 40N 2 26 E
Eyjafjörður **50** 66 15N 18 30W
Eymet **20** 44 40N 0 25 E
Eymoutiers **20** 45 40N 1 45 E
Eyrarbakki **50** 63 52N 21 9W
Eyre **96** 32 15 S 126 18 E
Eyre Cr. → **97** 26 40 S 139 0 E
Eyre, L. **97** 29 30 S 137 26 E
Eyre Mts. **101** 45 25 S 168 25 E
Eyre (North), L. **97** 28 30 S 137 20 E
Eyre Pen. **96** 33 30 S 137 17 E
Eyre (South), L. **99** 29 18 S 137 25 E
Eyzies, Les **20** 44 56N 1 1 E
Ez Zeidab **86** 17 25N 33 55 E
Ezcaray **32** 42 19N 3 0W
Ezine **44** 39 48N 26 12 E

F

Fabens **119** 31 30N 106 8W
Fåborg **49** 55 6N 10 15 E
Fabriano **39** 43 20N 12 52 E
Făcăeni **46** 44 32N 27 53 E
Facatativá **126** 4 49N 74 22W
Fachi **80** 18 6N 11 34 E
Facture **20** 44 39N 0 58W
Fada **81** 17 13N 21 34 E
Fada-n-Gourma **85** 12 10N 0 30 E
Fadd **27** 46 28N 18 49 E
Faddeyevskiy, Ostrov **59** 76 0N 150 0 E
Fāḑilī **64** 26 55N 49 10 E
Fadlab **86** 17 42N 34 2 E
Faenza **39** 44 17N 11 53 E
Fafa **85** 15 22N 0 48 E
Fafe **30** 41 27N 8 11W
Fagam **85** 11 1N 10 1 E
Făgăras **46** 45 48N 24 58 E
Făgăras, Munţii **46** 45 40N 24 40 E
Fågelsjö **48** 61 50N 14 35 E
Fagerhult **49** 57 8N 15 40 E
Fagersta **48** 60 1N 15 46 E
Făget **46** 45 52N 22 10 E
Făget, Munţii **46** 47 40N 23 10 E
Fagnano Castello **41** 39 31N 16 4 E
Fagnano, L. **128** 54 30 S 68 0W
Fagnières **19** 48 58N 4 20 E
Fahraj **65** 29 0N 59 0 E
Fahūd **65** 22 18N 56 28 E
Fair Hd. **15** 55 14N 6 10W
Fair Isle **11** 59 30N 1 40W
Fairbank **119** 31 44N 110 12W
Fairbanks **104** 64 50N 147 50W
Fairbury **116** 40 5N 97 5W
Fairfax **117** 36 37N 96 45W
Fairfield, Austral. **100** 33 53 S 150 57 E
Fairfield, Ala., U.S.A. **115** 33 30N 87 0W
Fairfield, Calif., U.S.A. **118** 38 14N 122 1W
Fairfield, Conn., U.S.A. **113** 41 8N 73 16W
Fairfield, Idaho, U.S.A. **118** 43 21N 114 46W
Fairfield, Ill., U.S.A. **114** 38 20N 88 20W
Fairfield, Iowa, U.S.A. **116** 41 0N 91 58W
Fairfield, Mont., U.S.A. **118** 47 40N 112 0W
Fairfield, Texas, U.S.A. **117** 31 40N 96 0W
Fairford **109** 51 37N 98 38W
Fairhope **115** 30 35N 87 50W
Fairlie **101** 44 5 S 170 49 E
Fairmont, Minn., U.S.A. **116** 43 37N 94 30W
Fairmont, W. Va., U.S.A. **114** 39 29N 80 10W
Fairmont Hot Springs **108** 50 20N 115 56W
Fairplay **119** 39 9N 105 40W
Fairport, N.Y., U.S.A. **114** 43 8N 77 29W
Fairport, Ohio, U.S.A. **112** 41 45N 81 17W
Fairview, Austral. **98** 15 31 S 144 17 E
Fairview, Can. **108** 56 5N 118 25W
Fairview, N. Dak., U.S.A. **116** 47 49N 104 7W
Fairview, Okla., U.S.A. **117** 36 19N 98 30W
Fairview, Utah, U.S.A. **118** 39 50N 111 0W
Fairweather, Mt. **104** 58 55N 137 45W
Faith **116** 45 2N 102 4W
Faizabad **69** 26 45N 82 10 E
Faizpur **68** 21 14N 75 49 E
Fajardo **121** 18 20N 65 39W
Fakfak **73** 3 0 S 132 15 E
Fakiya **43** 42 10N 27 6 E
Fakobli **84** 7 23N 7 23W
Fakse **49** 55 15N 12 8 E
Fakse B. **49** 55 11N 12 15 E
Fakse Ladeplads **49** 55 11N 12 9 E
Faku **76** 42 32N 123 21 E
Falaise **18** 48 54N 0 12W
Falakrón Óros **44** 41 15N 23 58 E
Falam **67** 23 0N 93 45 E
Falces **32** 42 24N 1 48W
Fălciu **46** 46 17N 28 7 E
Falcon, C. **82** 35 50N 0 50W
Falcon Dam **117** 26 50N 99 20W
Falconara Marittima **39** 43 37N 13 23 E
Falconer **112** 42 7N 79 13W
Faléa **84** 12 16N 11 17W
Falenki **55** 58 22N 51 35 E
Faleshty **56** 47 32N 27 44 E
Falfurrias **117** 27 14N 98 8W
Falher **108** 55 44N 117 15W
Falkenberg, Ger. **24** 51 34N 13 13 E
Falkenberg, Sweden **49** 56 54N 12 30 E
Falkensee **24** 52 35N 13 6 E
Falkenstein **24** 50 27N 12 24 E
Falkirk **14** 56 0N 3 47W
Falkland Is. **128** 51 30 S 59 0W
Falkland Is. Dependency □ **5** 57 0 S 40 0W
Falkland Sd. **128** 52 0 S 60 0W
Falkonéra **45** 36 50N 23 52 E
Falköping **49** 58 12N 13 33 E
Fall Brook **119** 33 25N 117 12W
Fall River **114** 41 45N 71 5W
Fall River Mills **118** 41 1N 121 30W
Fallon, Mont., U.S.A. **116** 46 52N 105 8W
Fallon, Nev., U.S.A. **118** 39 31N 118 51W
Falls City, Nebr., U.S.A. **116** 40 0N 95 40W
Falls City, Oreg., U.S.A. **118** 44 54N 123 29W
Falls Creek **112** 41 8N 78 49W
Falmouth, Jamaica **121** 18 30N 77 40W
Falmouth, U.K. **13** 50 9N 5 5W
Falmouth, U.S.A. **114** 38 40N 84 20W
False Divi Pt. **70** 15 43N 80 50 E
Falset **32** 41 7N 0 50 E
Falso, C. **121** 15 12N 83 21W
Falster **49** 54 45N 11 55 E
Falsterbo **49** 55 23N 12 50 E
Fălticeni **46** 47 21N 26 20 E
Falun **48** 60 37N 15 37 E
Famagusta **64** 35 8N 33 55 E
Famatina, Sierra, de **124** 27 30 S 68 0W
Family L. **109** 51 54N 95 27W
Fan Xian **76** 35 55N 115 38 E
Fana, Mali **84** 13 0N 6 56W
Fana, Norway **47** 60 16N 5 20 E
Fanárion **44** 39 24N 21 47 E
Fandriana **93** 20 14 S 47 21 E
Fang Xian **77** 32 3N 110 40 E
Fangchang **77** 31 5N 118 4 E
Fangcheng **77** 33 18N 112 59 E
Fangliao **77** 22 22N 120 38 E
Fangzheng **76** 49 50N 128 48 E
Fani i Madh → **44** 41 56N 20 16 E
Fanjiatun **76** 43 40N 125 0 E
Fannich, L. **14** 57 40N 5 0W
* Fanning I. **95** 3 51N 159 22W
Fanny Bay **108** 49 27N 124 48W
Fanø **49** 55 25N 8 25 E
Fano **39** 43 50N 13 0 E
Fanshaw **108** 57 11N 133 30W
Fao (Al Fāw) **64** 30 0N 48 30 E
Faqirwali **68** 29 27N 73 0 E
Fara in Sabina **39** 42 13N 12 44 E
Faradje **90** 3 50N 29 45 E
Faradofay **93** 25 2 S 47 0 E
Farafangana **93** 22 49 S 47 50 E
Farâfra, El Wâhât el- **86** 27 15N 28 20 E
Farāh **65** 32 20N 62 7 E
Farāh □ **65** 32 25N 62 10 E
Farahalana **93** 14 26 S 50 10 E
Faraid, Gebel **86** 23 33N 35 19 E
Faramana **84** 11 56N 4 45W
Faranah **84** 10 3N 10 45W
Farasān, Jazā'ir **63** 16 45N 41 55 E
Faratsiho **93** 19 24 S 46 57 E
Fardes → **33** 37 35N 3 0W
Fareham **13** 50 52N 1 11W
Farewell, C. **101** 40 29 S 172 43 E
Farewell C. = Farvel, K. **4** 59 48N 43 55W
Fargo **116** 46 52N 96 40W
Fari'a → **62** 32 12N 35 27 E
Faribault **116** 44 15N 93 19W
Faridkot **68** 30 44N 74 45 E
Faridpur **69** 23 15N 89 55 E
Färila **48** 61 48N 15 50 E
Farim **84** 12 27N 15 9W
Farīmān **65** 35 40N 59 49 E
Farina **99** 30 3 S 138 15 E
Faringe **48** 59 55N 18 7 E
Fâriskûr **86** 31 20N 31 43 E
Farmakonisi **45** 37 17N 27 8 E
Farmerville **117** 32 48N 92 23W
Farmington, N. Mex., U.S.A. **119** 36 45N 108 28W
Farmington, N.H., U.S.A. **113** 43 25N 71 7W
Farmington, Utah, U.S.A. **118** 41 0N 111 12W
Farmington → **113** 41 51N 72 38W
Farmville **114** 37 19N 78 22W
Farnborough **13** 51 17N 0 46W
Farne Is. **12** 55 38N 1 37W
Farnham **113** 45 17N 72 59W
Faro, Brazil **127** 2 10 S 56 39W
Faro, Port. **31** 37 2N 7 55W
Faro □ **31** 37 12N 8 10W
Faroe Is. **8** 62 0N 7 0W
Farquhar, C. **96** 23 50 S 113 36 E
Farrar → **14** 57 30N 4 30W
Farrars, Cr. → **98** 25 35 S 140 43 E
Farrāshband **65** 28 57N 52 5 E
Farrell **114** 41 13N 80 29W
Farrell Flat **99** 33 48 S 138 48 E
Farrukhabad-cum-Fatehgarh **69** 27 30N 79 32 E
Fars □ **65** 29 30N 55 0 E
Farsala **44** 39 17N 22 23 E
Farsø **49** 56 46N 9 19 E
Farsund **47** 58 5N 6 55 E
Fartak, Râs **64** 28 5N 34 34 E
Fartura, Serra da **125** 26 21 S 52 52W
Faru **85** 12 48N 6 12 E
Farum **49** 55 49N 12 21 E
Farvel, Kap **4** 59 48N 43 55W
Farwell **117** 34 25N 103 0W
Faryab □ **65** 36 0N 65 0 E
Fasā **65** 29 0N 53 39 E

* *Renamed Tabuaeran*

Fasano **41** 40 50N 17 20 E
Fashoda **87** 9 50N 32 2 E
Fastnet Rock **15** 51 22N 9 37W
Fastov **54** 50 7N 29 57 E
Fatagar, Tanjung **73** 2 46 S 131 57 E
Fatehgarh **69** 27 25N 79 35 E
Fatehpur, Raj., India **68** 28 0N 74 40 E
Fatehpur, Ut. P., India **69** 25 56N 81 13 E
Fatesh **55** 52 8N 35 57 E
Fatick **84** 14 19N 16 27W
Fatima **107** 47 24N 61 53W
Fátima **31** 39 37N 8 39W
Fatoya **84** 11 37N 9 10W
Faucille, Col de la **21** 46 22N 6 2 E
Faucilles, Monts **19** 48 5N 5 50 E
Faulkton **116** 45 4N 99 8W
Faulquemont **19** 49 3N 6 36 E
Fauquembergues **19** 50 36N 2 5 E
Făurei **46** 45 6N 27 19 E
Fauresmith **92** 29 44 S 25 17 E
Fauske **50** 67 17N 15 25 E
Fåvang **47** 61 27N 10 11 E
Favara **40** 37 19N 13 39 E
Favignana **40** 37 56N 12 18 E
Favignana, I. **40** 37 56N 12 18 E
Favone **21** 41 47N 9 26 E
Favourable Lake **106** 52 50N 93 39W
Fawn → **106** 52 22N 88 20W
Faxaflói **50** 64 29N 23 0W
Faya-Largeau **81** 17 58N 19 6 E
Fayd **64** 27 1N 42 52 E
Fayence **21** 43 38N 6 42 E
Fayette, Ala., U.S.A. **115** 33 40N 87 50W
Fayette, Mo., U.S.A. **116** 39 10N 92 40W
Fayette, La **114** 40 22N 86 52W
Fayetteville, Ark., U.S.A. **117** 36 0N 94 5W
Fayetteville, N.C., U.S.A. **115** 35 0N 78 58W
Fayetteville, Tenn., U.S.A. **115** 35 8N 86 30W
Fayón **32** 41 15N 0 20 E
Fazilka **68** 30 27N 74 2 E
Fazilpur **68** 29 18N 70 29 E
Fdérik **80** 22 40N 12 45W
Feale → **15** 52 26N 9 40W
Fear, C. **115** 33 51N 78 0W
Feather → **118** 38 47N 121 36W
Featherston **101** 41 6 S 175 20 E
Featherstone **91** 18 42 S 30 55 E
Fécamp **18** 49 45N 0 22 E
Fedala = Mohammedia **82** 33 44N 7 21W
Federación **124** 31 0 S 57 55W
Fedjadj, Chott el **83** 33 52N 9 14 E
Fedje **47** 60 47N 4 43 E
Fehérgyarmat **27** 48 0N 22 30 E
Fehmarn **24** 54 26N 11 10 E
Fei Xian **77** 35 18N 117 59 E
Feilding **101** 40 13 S 175 35 E
Feira de Santana **127** 12 15 S 38 57W
Fejér □ **27** 47 9N 18 30 E
Fejø **49** 54 55N 11 30 E
Fekete → **27** 45 47N 18 15 E
Felanitx **33** 39 28N 3 9 E
Feldbach **26** 46 57N 15 52 E
Feldberg, Germ., E. **24** 53 20N 13 26 E
Feldberg, Germ., W. **25** 47 51N 7 58 E
Feldkirch **26** 47 15N 9 37 E
Feldkirchen **26** 46 44N 14 6 E
Felipe Carrillo Puerto **120** 19 38N 88 3W
Felixstowe **13** 51 58N 1 22 E
Felletin **20** 45 53N 2 11 E
Feltre **39** 46 1N 11 55 E
Femø **49** 54 58N 11 53 E
Femunden **47** 62 10N 11 53 E
Fen He → **76** 35 36N 110 42 E
Fenelon Falls **112** 44 32N 78 45W
Feneroa **87** 13 5N 39 3 E
Feng Xian, Jiangsu, China **77** 34 43N 116 35 E
Feng Xian, Shaanxi, China **77** 33 54N 106 40 E
Fengári **44** 40 25N 25 32 E
Fengcheng, Jiangxi, China **77** 28 12N 115 48 E
Fengcheng, Liaoning, China **76** 40 28N 124 5 E
Fengdu **77** 29 55N 107 41 E
Fengfeng **76** 36 28N 114 8 E
Fenghua **77** 29 40N 121 25 E
Fenghuang **77** 27 57N 109 29 E
Fengjie **75** 31 5N 109 36 E
Fengkai **77** 23 24N 111 30 E
Fengle **77** 31 29N 112 29 E
Fengning **76** 41 10N 116 33 E
Fengtai **76** 39 50N 116 18 E
Fengxian **77** 30 55N 121 26 E
Fengxiang **77** 34 29N 107 25 E
Fengxin **77** 28 41N 115 18 E
Fengyang **77** 32 51N 117 29 E
Fengzhen **76** 40 25N 113 2 E
Feni Is. **98** 4 0 S 153 40 E
Fenit **15** 52 17N 9 51W
Fennimore **116** 42 58N 90 41W
Fenny **69** 22 55N 91 32 E
Feno, C. de **21** 41 58N 8 33 E
Fenoarivo Afovoany **93** 18 26 S 46 34 E
Fenoarivo Atsinanana **93** 17 22 S 49 25 E
Fens, The **12** 52 45N 0 2 E
Fenton **114** 42 47N 83 44W
Fenyang **76** 37 18N 111 48 E
Feodosiya **56** 45 2N 35 28 E
Fer, C. de **83** 37 3N 7 10 E
Ferdow **65** 33 58N 58 2 E
Fère-Champenoise **19** 48 45N 4 0 E
Fère-en-Tardenois **19** 49 10N 3 30 E
Fère, La **19** 49 40N 3 20 E
Ferentino **40** 41 42N 13 14 E
Ferfer **63** 5 4N 45 9 E
Fergana **58** 40 23N 71 19 E
Fergus **106** 43 43N 80 24W
Fergus Falls **116** 46 18N 96 7W
Fergusson I. **98** 9 30 S 150 45 E
Fériana **83** 34 59N 8 33 E
Feričanci **42** 45 32N 18 0 E
Ferkane **83** 34 37N 7 26 E
Ferkéssédougou **84** 9 35N 5 6W
Ferlach **26** 46 32N 14 18 E
Ferland **106** 50 19N 88 27W

Ferlo, Vallée du | Fortuna

Ferlo, Vallée du	**84**	15 15N	14 15W
Fermanagh □	**15**	54 21N	7 40W
Fermo	**39**	43 10N	13 42 E
Fermoselle	**30**	41 19N	6 27W
Fermoy	**15**	52 4N	8 18W
Fernán Nuñéz	**31**	37 40N	4 44W
Fernández	**124**	27 55 S	63 50W
Fernandina Beach	**115**	30 40N	81 30W
Fernando de Noronha	**127**	4 0 S	33 10W
Fernando Póo = Bioko	**85**	3 30N	8 40 E
Ferndale, Calif., U.S.A.	**118**	40 37N	124 12W
Ferndale, Wash., U.S.A.	**118**	48 51N	122 41W
Fernie	**108**	49 30N	115 5W
Fernlees	**98**	23 51 S	148 7 E
Fernley	**118**	39 36N	119 14W
Feroke	**70**	11 9N	75 46 E
Ferozepore	**68**	30 55N	74 40 E
Férrai	**44**	40 53N	26 10 E
Ferrandina	**41**	40 30N	16 28 E
Ferrara	**39**	44 50N	11 36 E
Ferrato, C.	**40**	39 18N	9 39 E
Ferreira do Alentejo	**31**	38 4N	8 6W
Ferreñafe	**126**	6 42 S	79 50W
Ferret, C.	**20**	44 38N	1 15W
Ferrette	**19**	47 30N	7 20 E
Ferriday	**117**	31 35N	91 33W
Ferrières	**19**	48 5N	2 48 E
Ferriete	**38**	44 40N	9 30 E
Ferron	**119**	39 3N	111 3W
Ferryland	**107**	47 2N	52 53W
Ferté-Bernard, La	**18**	48 10N	0 40 E
Ferté, La	**19**	48 57N	3 6 E
Ferté-Mace, La	**18**	48 35N	0 21W
Ferté-St.-Aubin, La	**19**	47 42N	1 57 E
Ferté-Vidame, La	**18**	48 37N	0 53 E
Fertile	**116**	47 31N	96 18W
Fertília	**40**	40 37N	8 13 E
Fertöszentmiklós	**27**	47 35N	16 53 E
Fès	**82**	34 0N	5 0W
Feshi	**88**	6 8 S	18 10 E
Fessenden	**116**	47 42N	99 38W
Feteşti	**46**	44 22N	27 51 E
Fethiye	**64**	36 36N	29 10 E
Fetlar	**14**	60 36N	0 52W
Feuilles →	**105**	58 47N	70 4W
Feurs	**21**	45 45N	4 13 E
Feyzābād	**65**	37 7N	70 33 E
Fezzan	**81**	27 0N	15 0 E
Ffestiniog	**12**	52 58N	3 56W
Fiambalá	**124**	27 45 S	67 37W
Fianarantsoa	**93**	21 26 S	47 5 E
Fianarantsoa □	**93**	19 30 S	47 0 E
Fianga	**81**	9 55N	15 9 E
Fibiş	**42**	45 57N	21 26 E
Fichtelgebirge	**25**	50 10N	12 0 E
Ficksburg	**93**	28 51 S	27 53 E
Fidenza	**38**	44 51N	10 3 E
Field	**106**	46 31N	80 1W
Field →	**98**	23 48 S	138 0 E
Fieri	**44**	40 43N	19 33 E
Fife □	**14**	56 13N	3 2W
Fife Ness	**14**	56 17N	2 35W
Fifth Cataract	**86**	18 22N	33 50 E
Figeac	**20**	44 37N	2 2 E
Figline Valdarno	**39**	43 37N	11 28 E
Figtree	**91**	20 22 S	28 20 E
Figueira Castelo Rodrigo	**30**	40 57N	6 58W
Figueira da Foz	**30**	40 7N	8 54W
Figueiró dos Vinhos	**30**	39 55N	8 16W
Figueras	**32**	42 18N	2 58 E
Figuig	**82**	32 5N	1 11W
Fihaonana	**93**	18 36 S	47 12 E
Fiherenana	**93**	18 29 S	48 24 E
Fiherenana →	**93**	23 19 S	43 37 E
Fiji ■	**101**	17 20 S	179 0 E
Fika	**85**	11 15N	11 13 E
Filabres, Sierra de los	**33**	37 13N	2 20W
Filadélfia	**41**	38 47N	16 17 E
Fil'akovo	**27**	48 17N	19 50 E
Filchner Ice Shelf	**5**	78 0 S	60 0W
Filer	**118**	42 30N	114 35W
Filey	**12**	54 13N	0 18W
Filiaşi	**46**	44 32N	23 31 E
Filiátes	**44**	39 38N	20 16 E
Filiatrá	**45**	37 9N	21 35 E
Filicudi	**41**	38 35N	14 33 E
Filiourí →	**44**	41 15N	25 40 E
Filipów	**28**	54 11N	22 37 E
Filipstad	**48**	59 43N	14 9 E
Filisur	**25**	46 41N	9 40 E
Fillmore, Can.	**109**	49 50N	103 25W
Fillmore, Calif., U.S.A.	**119**	34 23N	118 58W
Fillmore, Utah, U.S.A.	**119**	38 58N	112 20W
Filottrano	**39**	43 28N	13 20 E
Filyos	**56**	41 34N	32 4 E
Filyos →	**64**	41 35N	32 10 E
Finale Lígure	**38**	44 10N	8 21 E
Finale nell' Emília	**39**	44 50N	11 18 E
Fiñana	**33**	37 10N	2 50W
Finch	**113**	45 11N	75 7W
Findhorn →	**14**	57 38N	3 38W
Findlay	**114**	41 0N	83 41W
Finger L.	**109**	53 33N	124 18W
Fíngõe	**91**	15 12 S	31 50 E
Finike	**64**	36 21N	30 10 E
Finistère □	**18**	48 20N	4 0W
Finisterre	**30**	42 54N	9 16W
Finisterre, C.	**30**	42 50N	9 19W
Finisterre Ra.	**98**	6 0 S	146 30 E
Finke →	**96**	27 0 S	136 10 E
Finland ■	**52**	63 0N	27 0 E
Finland, G. of	**52**	60 0N	26 0 E
Finlay →	**108**	57 0N	125 10W
Finley, Austral.	**99**	35 38 S	145 35 E
Finley, U.S.A.	**116**	47 35N	97 50W
Finn →	**15**	54 50N	7 55W
Finnigan, Mt.	**98**	15 49 S	145 17 E
Finnmark fylke □	**50**	69 30N	25 0 E
Finschhafen	**98**	6 33 S	147 50 E
Finse	**47**	60 36N	7 30 E
Finsteraarhorn	**25**	46 31N	8 10 E
Finsterwalde	**24**	51 37N	13 42 E
Finucane I.	**96**	20 19 S	118 30 E
Fiora →	**39**	42 20N	11 35 E
Fiorenzuola d'Arda	**38**	44 56N	9 54 E
Fīq	**62**	32 46N	35 41 E
Fire River	**106**	48 47N	83 21W
Firebag →	**109**	57 45N	111 21W
Firedrake L.	**109**	61 25N	104 30W
Firenze	**39**	43 47N	11 15 E
Firminy, Aveyron, France	**20**	44 32N	2 19 E
Firminy, Loire, France	**21**	45 23N	4 18 E
Firozabad	**68**	27 10N	78 25 E
Fīrūzābād	**65**	28 52N	52 35 E
Fīrūzkūh	**65**	35 50N	52 50 E
Firvale	**108**	52 27N	126 13W
Fish →	**92**	28 7 S	17 45 E
Fisher B.	**109**	51 35N	97 13W
Fishguard	**13**	51 59N	4 59W
Fishing L.	**109**	52 10N	95 24W
Fismes	**19**	49 20N	3 40 E
Fitchburg	**114**	42 35N	71 47W
Fitero	**32**	42 4N	1 52W
Fitjar	**47**	59 55N	5 17 E
Fitri, L.	**81**	12 50N	17 28 E
Fitz Roy	**128**	47 0 S	67 0W
Fitzgerald, Can.	**108**	59 51N	111 36W
Fitzgerald, U.S.A.	**115**	31 45N	83 16W
Fitzroy →, Queens., Austral.	**98**	23 32 S	150 52 E
Fitzroy →, W. Australia, Austral.	**96**	17 31 S	123 35 E
Fitzroy Crossing	**96**	18 9 S	125 38 E
Fitzwilliam I.	**112**	45 30N	81 45W
Fiume = Rijeka	**39**	45 20N	14 27 E
Fiumefreddo Brúzio	**41**	39 14N	16 4 E
Fivizzano	**38**	44 12N	10 11 E
Fizi	**90**	4 17 S	28 55 E
Fjæra	**47**	59 52N	6 22 E
Fjellerup	**49**	56 29N	10 34 E
Fjerritslev	**49**	57 5N	9 15 E
Fkih ben Salah	**82**	32 32N	6 45W
Flå, Buskerud, Norway	**47**	60 25N	9 28 E
Flå, Sør-Trøndelag, Norway	**47**	63 13N	10 18 E
Flagler	**116**	39 20N	103 4W
Flagstaff	**119**	35 10N	111 40W
Flaherty I.	**106**	56 15N	79 15W
Flambeau →	**116**	45 18N	91 15W
Flamborough Hd.	**12**	54 8N	0 4W
Flaming Gorge Dam	**118**	40 50N	109 46W
Flaming Gorge L.	**118**	41 15N	109 30W
Flamingo, Teluk	**73**	5 30 S	138 0 E
Flanders = Flandres	**16**	51 10N	3 15 E
Flandre Occidental □	**16**	51 0N	3 0 E
Flandre Orientale □	**16**	51 0N	4 0 E
Flandreau	**116**	44 5N	96 38W
Flandres, Plaines des	**16**	51 10N	3 15 E
Flannan Is.	**11**	58 9N	7 52W
Flåsjön	**50**	64 5N	15 40 E
Flat →	**108**	61 51N	128 0W
Flat River	**117**	37 50N	90 30W
Flatey, Barðastrandarsýsla, Iceland	**50**	66 10N	17 52W
Flatey, Suöur-Þingeyjarsýsla, Iceland	**50**	65 22N	22 56W
Flathead L.	**118**	47 50N	114 0W
Flattery, C., Austral.	**98**	14 58 S	145 21 E
Flattery, C., U.S.A.	**118**	48 21N	124 43W
Flavy-le-Martel	**19**	49 43N	3 12 E
Flaxton	**116**	48 52N	102 24W
Flèche, La	**18**	47 42N	0 5W
Fleetwood	**12**	53 55N	3 1W
Flekkefjord	**47**	58 18N	6 39 E
Flemington	**112**	41 7N	77 28W
Flensborg Fjord	**49**	54 50N	9 40 E
Flensburg	**24**	54 46N	9 28 E
Flers	**18**	48 47N	0 33W
Flesherton	**112**	44 16N	80 33W
Flesko, Tanjung	**73**	0 29N	124 30 E
Fletton	**13**	52 34N	0 13W
Fleurance	**20**	43 52N	0 40 E
Fleurier	**25**	46 54N	6 35 E
Flin Flon	**109**	54 46N	101 53W
Flinders →	**97**	17 36 S	140 36 E
Flinders B.	**96**	34 19 S	115 19 E
Flinders Group	**98**	14 11 S	144 15 E
Flinders I.	**97**	40 0 S	148 0 E
Flinders Ranges	**97**	31 30 S	138 30 E
Flint, U.K.	**12**	53 15N	3 7W
Flint, U.S.A.	**114**	43 5N	83 40W
Flint →	**115**	30 52N	84 38W
Flint, I.	**95**	11 26 S	151 48W
Flinton	**99**	27 55 S	149 32 E
Fliseryd	**49**	57 6N	16 15 E
Flix	**32**	41 14N	0 32 E
Flixecourt	**19**	50 0N	2 5 E
Flodden	**12**	55 37N	2 8W
Floodwood	**116**	46 55N	92 55W
Flora, Norway	**47**	63 27N	11 22 E
Flora, U.S.A.	**114**	38 40N	88 30W
Florac	**20**	44 20N	3 37 E
Florala	**115**	31 0N	86 20W
Florence, Ala., U.S.A.	**115**	34 50N	87 40W
Florence, Ariz., U.S.A.	**119**	33 0N	111 25W
Florence, Colo., U.S.A.	**116**	38 26N	105 0W
Florence, Oreg., U.S.A.	**118**	44 0N	124 3W
Florence, S.C., U.S.A.	**115**	34 12N	79 44W
Florence = Firenze	**39**	43 47N	11 15 E
Florence, L.	**99**	28 53 S	138 9 E
Florennes	**16**	50 15N	4 35 E
Florensac	**20**	43 23N	3 28 E
Florenville	**16**	49 40N	5 19 E
Flores, Azores	**8**	39 13N	31 13W
Flores, Guat.	**120**	16 59N	89 50W
Flores, Indon.	**73**	8 35 S	121 0 E
Flores I.	**108**	49 20N	126 10W
Flores Sea	**72**	6 30 S	124 0 E
Floresville	**117**	29 10N	98 10W
Floriano	**127**	6 50 S	43 0W
Florianópolis	**125**	27 30 S	48 30W
Florida, Cuba	**121**	21 32N	78 14W
Florida, Uruguay	**125**	34 7 S	56 10W
Florida □	**115**	28 30N	82 0W
Florida B.	**121**	25 0N	81 20W
Florida Keys	**121**	25 0N	80 40W
Florida, Straits of	**121**	25 0N	80 0W
Florídia	**41**	37 6N	15 9 E
Floridsdorf	**27**	48 14N	16 22 E
Flórina	**44**	40 48N	21 26 E
Flórina □	**44**	40 45N	21 20 E
Florø	**47**	61 35N	5 1 E
Flower Sta.	**113**	45 10N	76 41W
Flower's Cove	**107**	51 14N	56 46W
Floydada	**117**	33 58N	101 18W
Fluk	**73**	1 42 S	127 44 E
Flumen →	**32**	41 43N	0 9W
Flumendosa →	**40**	39 26N	9 38 E
Fluminimaggiore	**40**	39 25N	8 30 E
Flushing = Vlissingen	**16**	51 26N	3 34 E
Fluviá →	**32**	42 12N	3 7 E
Fly →	**94**	8 25 S	143 0 E
Flying Fish, C.	**5**	72 6 S	102 29W
Foam Lake	**109**	51 40N	103 32W
Foča	**42**	43 31N	18 47 E
Focşani	**46**	45 41N	27 15 E
Fogang	**77**	23 52N	113 30 E
Foggaret el Arab	**82**	27 13N	2 49 E
Foggaret ez Zoua	**82**	27 20N	2 53 E
Fóggia	**41**	41 28N	15 31 E
Foggo	**85**	11 21N	9 57 E
Foglia →	**39**	43 55N	12 54 E
Fogo	**107**	49 43N	54 17W
Fogo I.	**107**	49 40N	54 5W
Fohnsdorf	**26**	47 12N	14 40 E
Föhr	**24**	54 40N	8 30 E
Foia	**31**	37 19N	8 37W
Foix	**20**	42 58N	1 38 E
Foix □	**20**	43 0N	1 30 E
Fojnica	**42**	43 59N	17 51 E
Fokino	**54**	53 30N	34 22 E
Fokís □	**45**	38 30N	22 15 E
Fokstua	**47**	62 7N	9 17 E
Folda, Nord-Trøndelag, Norway	**50**	64 41N	10 50 E
Folda, Nordland, Norway	**50**	67 38N	14 50 E
Földeák	**27**	46 19N	20 30 E
Folégandros	**45**	36 40N	24 55 E
Folette, La	**115**	36 23N	84 9W
Foleyet	**106**	48 15N	82 25W
Folgefonn	**47**	60 3N	6 23 E
Foligno	**39**	42 58N	12 40 E
Folkestone	**13**	51 5N	1 11 E
Folkston	**115**	30 55N	82 0W
Follett	**117**	36 30N	100 12W
Follónica	**38**	42 55N	10 45 E
Follónica, Golfo di	**38**	42 50N	10 40 E
Folsom	**118**	38 41N	121 7W
Fond-du-Lac	**109**	59 19N	107 12W
Fond du Lac	**116**	43 46N	88 26W
Fond-du-Lac →	**109**	59 17N	106 0W
Fonda	**113**	42 57N	74 23W
Fondi	**40**	41 21N	13 25 E
Fonfría	**30**	41 37N	6 9W
Fongen	**47**	63 11N	11 38 E
Fonni	**40**	40 5N	9 16 E
Fonsagrada	**30**	43 8N	7 4W
Fonseca, G. de	**120**	13 10N	87 40W
Fontaine-Française	**19**	47 32N	5 21 E
Fontainebleau	**19**	48 24N	2 40 E
Fontas →	**108**	58 14N	121 48W
Fonte Boa	**126**	2 33 S	66 0W
Fontem	**85**	5 32N	9 52 E
Fontenay-le-Comte	**20**	46 28N	0 48W
Fontur	**50**	66 23N	14 32W
Fonyód	**27**	46 44N	17 33 E
Foochow = Fuzhou	**75**	26 5N	119 16 E
Foping	**77**	33 41N	108 0 E
Foppiano	**38**	46 21N	8 24 E
Föra	**49**	57 1N	16 51 E
Forbach	**19**	49 10N	6 52 E
Forbes	**97**	33 22 S	148 0 E
Forbesganj	**69**	26 17N	87 18 E
Forcados	**85**	5 26N	5 26 E
Forcados →	**85**	5 25N	5 19 E
Forcall →	**32**	40 51N	0 16W
Forcalquier	**21**	43 58N	5 47 E
Forchheim	**25**	49 42N	11 4 E
Ford City	**112**	40 47N	79 31W
Førde	**47**	61 27N	5 53 E
Ford's Bridge	**99**	29 41 S	145 29 E
Fordyce	**117**	33 50N	92 20W
Forécariah	**84**	9 28N	13 10W
Forel, Mt.	**4**	66 52N	36 55W
Foremost	**108**	49 26N	111 34W
Forenza	**41**	40 50N	15 50 E
Forest, Can.	**112**	43 6N	82 0W
Forest, U.S.A.	**117**	32 21N	89 27W
Forest City, Iowa, U.S.A.	**116**	43 12N	93 39W
Forest City, N.C., U.S.A.	**115**	35 23N	81 50W
Forest City, Pa., U.S.A.	**113**	41 39N	75 29W
Forest Grove	**118**	45 31N	123 4W
Forestburg	**108**	52 35N	112 1W
Forestier Pen.	**99**	43 0 S	148 0 E
Forestville, Can.	**107**	48 48N	69 2W
Forestville, U.S.A.	**114**	44 41N	87 29W
Forez, Mts. du	**20**	45 40N	3 50 E
Forfar	**14**	56 40N	2 53W
Forges-les-Eaux	**19**	49 37N	1 30 E
Forks	**118**	47 56N	124 23W
Forlì	**39**	44 14N	12 2 E
Forman	**116**	46 9N	97 43W
Formazza	**38**	46 23N	8 26 E
Formby Pt.	**12**	53 33N	3 7W
Formentera	**33**	38 43N	1 27 E
Formentor, C. de	**32**	39 58N	3 13 E
Fórmia	**40**	41 15N	13 34 E
Formigine	**38**	44 37N	10 51 E
Formiguères	**20**	42 37N	2 5 E
Formosa	**124**	26 15 S	58 10W
Formosa = Taiwan ■	**75**	24 0N	121 0 E
Formosa □	**124**	25 0 S	60 0W
Formosa Bay	**90**	2 40 S	40 20 E
Formosa, Serra	**127**	12 0 S	55 0W
Fornells	**32**	40 3N	4 7 E
Fornos de Algodres	**30**	40 38N	7 32W
Fornovo di Taro	**38**	44 42N	10 7 E
Forres	**14**	57 37N	3 38W
Forrest	**99**	38 33 S	143 47 E
Forrest City	**117**	35 0N	90 50W
Fors	**48**	60 14N	16 20 E
Forsa	**48**	61 44N	16 55 E
Forsand	**47**	58 54N	6 5 E
Forsayth	**97**	18 33 S	143 34 E
Forserum	**49**	57 42N	14 30 E
Forshaga	**48**	59 33N	13 29 E
Forskacka	**48**	60 39N	16 54 E
Forsmo	**48**	63 16N	17 11 E
Forst	**24**	51 43N	14 37 E
Forster	**99**	32 12 S	152 31 E
Forsyth, Ga., U.S.A.	**115**	33 4N	83 55W
Forsyth, Mont., U.S.A.	**118**	46 14N	106 37W
Fort Albany	**106**	52 15N	81 35W
Fort Amador	**120**	8 56N	79 32W
Fort Apache	**119**	33 50N	110 0W
Fort Assiniboine	**108**	54 20N	114 45W
Fort Augustus	**14**	57 9N	4 40W
Fort Beaufort	**92**	32 46 S	26 40 E
Fort Benton	**118**	47 50N	110 40W
Fort Bragg	**118**	39 28N	123 50W
Fort Bridger	**118**	41 22N	110 20W
Fort Chimo	**105**	58 6N	68 15W
Fort Chipewyan	**109**	58 42N	111 8W
Fort Clayton	**120**	9 0N	79 35W
Fort Collins	**116**	40 30N	105 4W
Fort-Coulonge	**106**	45 50N	76 45W
Fort Davis, Panama	**120**	9 17N	79 56W
Fort Davis, U.S.A.	**117**	30 38N	103 53W
Fort-de-France	**121**	14 36N	61 2W
Fort de Possel = Possel	**88**	5 5N	19 10 E
Fort Defiance	**119**	35 47N	109 4W
Fort Dodge	**116**	42 29N	94 10W
Fort Edward	**113**	43 16N	73 35W
Fort Frances	**109**	48 36N	93 24W
Fort Franklin	**104**	65 10N	123 30W
Fort Garland	**119**	37 28N	105 30W
Fort George	**106**	53 50N	79 0W
Fort Good-Hope	**104**	66 14N	128 40W
Fort Hancock	**119**	31 19N	105 56W
Fort Hertz (Putao)	**67**	27 28N	97 30 E
Fort Hope	**106**	51 30N	88 0W
Fort Huachuca	**119**	31 32N	110 30W
Fort Jameson = Chipata	**91**	13 38 S	32 28 E
Fort Kent	**107**	47 12N	68 30W
Fort Klamath	**118**	42 45N	122 0W
Fort Lallemand	**83**	31 13N	6 17 E
Fort-Lamy = Ndjamena	**81**	12 4N	15 8 E
Fort Laramie	**116**	42 15N	104 30W
Fort Lauderdale	**115**	26 10N	80 5W
Fort Liard	**108**	60 14N	123 30W
Fort Liberté	**121**	19 42N	71 51W
Fort Lupton	**116**	40 8N	104 48W
Fort Mackay	**108**	57 12N	111 41W
Fort McKenzie	**107**	57 20N	69 0W
Fort Macleod	**108**	49 45N	113 30W
Fort MacMahon	**82**	29 43N	1 45 E
Fort McMurray	**108**	56 44N	111 7W
Fort McPherson	**104**	67 30N	134 55W
Fort Madison	**116**	40 39N	91 20W
Fort Meade	**115**	27 45N	81 45W
Fort Miribel	**82**	29 25N	2 55 E
Fort Morgan	**116**	40 10N	103 50W
Fort Myers	**115**	26 39N	81 51W
Fort Nelson	**108**	58 50N	122 44W
Fort Nelson →	**108**	59 32N	124 0W
Fort Norman	**104**	64 57N	125 30W
Fort Payne	**115**	34 25N	85 44W
Fort Peck	**118**	48 1N	106 30W
Fort Peck Dam	**118**	48 0N	106 38W
Fort Peck L.	**118**	47 40N	107 0W
Fort Pierce	**115**	27 29N	80 19W
Fort Pierre	**116**	44 25N	100 25W
Fort Pierre Bordes = Ti-n-Zaouatene	**82**	20 0N	2 55 E
Fort Plain	**113**	42 56N	74 39W
Fort Portal	**90**	0 40N	30 20 E
Fort Providence	**108**	61 3N	117 40W
Fort Qu'Appelle	**109**	50 45N	103 50W
Fort Randolph	**120**	9 23N	79 53W
Fort Resolution	**108**	61 10N	113 40W
Fort Rixon	**91**	20 2 S	29 17 E
Fort Roseberry = Mansa	**91**	11 10 S	28 50 E
Fort Rupert (Rupert House)	**106**	51 30N	78 40W
Fort Saint	**83**	30 19N	9 31 E
Fort St. James	**108**	54 30N	124 10W
Fort St. John	**108**	56 15N	120 50W
Fort Sandeman	**68**	31 20N	69 31 E
Fort Saskatchewan	**108**	53 40N	113 15W
Fort Scott	**117**	37 50N	94 40W
Fort Severn	**106**	56 0N	87 40W
Fort Sherman	**120**	9 22N	79 56W
Fort Shevchenko	**57**	43 40N	51 20 E
Fort-Sibut	**88**	5 46N	19 10 E
Fort Simpson	**108**	61 45N	121 15W
Fort Smith, Can.	**108**	60 0N	111 51W
Fort Smith, U.S.A.	**117**	35 25N	94 25W
Fort Stanton	**119**	33 33N	105 36W
Fort Stockton	**117**	30 54N	102 54W
Fort Sumner	**117**	34 24N	104 16W
Fort Thomas	**119**	33 2N	109 59W
Fort Trinquet = Bir Mogrein	**80**	25 10N	11 35W
Fort Valley	**115**	32 33N	83 52W
Fort Vermilion	**108**	58 24N	116 0W
* Fort Victoria	**91**	20 8 S	30 49 E
Fort Walton Beach	**115**	30 25N	86 40W
Fort Wayne	**114**	41 5N	85 10W
Fort William	**14**	56 48N	5 8W
Fort Worth	**117**	32 45N	97 25W
Fort Yates	**116**	46 8N	100 38W
Fort Yukon	**104**	66 35N	145 20W
Fortaleza	**127**	3 45 S	38 35W
Forteau	**107**	51 28N	56 58W
Fortescue →	**96**	21 20 S	116 5 E
Forth, Firth of	**14**	56 5N	2 55W
Forthassa Rharbia	**82**	32 52N	1 18W
Fortore →	**39**	41 55N	15 17 E
Fortrose	**14**	57 35N	4 10W
Fortuna, Spain	**33**	38 11N	1 7W
Fortuna, Cal., U.S.A.	**118**	40 38N	124 8W
Fortuna, N.D., U.S.A.	**116**	48 55N	103 48W

* *Renamed Masvingo*

Fortune B. Galley Hd.

Name	Page	Lat.	Long.
Fortune B.	**107**	47 30N	55 22W
Forūr	**65**	26 20N	54 30 E
Fos	**21**	43 26N	4 56 E
Foshan	**75**	23 4N	113 5 E
Fossacesia	**39**	42 15N	14 30 E
Fossano	**38**	44 33N	7 40 E
Fossil	**118**	45 0N	120 9W
Fossilbrook P.O.	**98**	17 47 S	144 29 E
Fossombrone	**39**	43 41N	12 49 E
Fosston	**116**	47 33N	95 39W
Foster	**113**	45 17N	72 30W
Foster ⤳	**109**	55 47N	105 49W
Fostoria	**114**	41 8N	83 25W
Fougamou	**88**	1 16 S	10 30 E
Fougères	**18**	48 21N	1 14W
Foul Pt.	**70**	8 35N	81 18 E
Foulness I.	**13**	51 36N	0 55 E
Foulness Pt.	**13**	51 36N	0 59 E
Foulpointe	**93**	17 41 S	49 31 E
Foum Assaka	**82**	29 8N	10 24W
Foum Zguid	**82**	30 2N	6 59W
Foumban	**85**	5 45N	10 50 E
Foundiougne	**84**	14 5N	16 32W
Fountain, Colo., U.S.A.	**116**	38 42N	104 40W
Fountain, Utah, U.S.A.	**118**	39 41N	111 37W
Fourchambault	**19**	47 0N	3 3 E
Fourchu	**107**	45 43N	60 17W
Fourmies	**19**	50 1N	4 2 E
Fournás	**45**	39 3N	21 52 E
Foúrnoi, Greece	**45**	37 36N	26 32 E
Foúrnoi, Greece	**45**	37 36N	26 28 E
Fours	**19**	46 50N	3 42 E
Fouta Djalon	**84**	11 20N	12 10W
Foux, Cap-à-	**121**	19 43N	73 27W
Foveaux Str.	**101**	46 42 S	168 10 E
Fowey	**13**	50 20N	4 39W
Fowler, Calif., U.S.A.	**119**	36 41N	119 41W
Fowler, Colo., U.S.A.	**116**	38 10N	104 0W
Fowler, Kans., U.S.A.	**117**	37 28N	100 7W
Fowlerton	**117**	28 26N	98 50W
Fownhope	**13**	52 0N	2 37W
Fox ⤳	**109**	56 3N	93 18W
Fox Valley	**109**	50 30N	109 25W
Foxe Basin	**105**	68 30N	77 0W
Foxe Channel	**105**	66 0N	80 0W
Foxe Pen.	**105**	65 0N	76 0W
Foxen, L.	**48**	59 25N	11 55 E
Foxpark	**118**	41 4N	106 6W
Foxton	**101**	40 29 S	175 18 E
Foyle, Lough	**15**	55 6N	7 8W
Foynes	**15**	52 37N	9 5W
Foz	**30**	43 33N	7 20W
Fóz do Cunene	**92**	17 15 S	11 48 E
Foz do Gregório	**126**	6 47 S	70 44W
Foz do Iguaçu	**125**	25 30 S	54 30W
Frackville	**113**	40 46N	76 15W
Fraga	**32**	41 32N	0 21 E
Framingham	**113**	42 18N	71 26W
Frampol	**28**	50 41N	22 40 E
Franca	**127**	20 33 S	47 30W
Francavilla al Mare	**39**	42 25N	14 16 E
Francavilla Fontana	**41**	40 32N	17 35 E
France ■	**17**	47 0N	3 0 E
Frances	**99**	36 41 S	140 55 E
Frances ⤳	**108**	60 16N	129 10W
Frances L.	**108**	61 23N	129 30W
Franceville	**88**	1 40 S	13 32 E
Franche-Comté	**19**	46 30N	5 50 E
Francisco I. Madero, Coahuila, Mexico	**120**	25 48N	103 18W
Francisco I. Madero, Durango, Mexico	**120**	24 32N	104 22W
Francofonte	**41**	37 13N	14 50 E
François, Can.	**107**	47 35N	56 45W
François, Mart.	**121**	14 38N	60 57W
François L.	**108**	54 0N	125 30W
Franeker	**16**	53 12N	5 33 E
Frankado	**87**	12 30N	43 12 E
Frankenberg	**24**	51 3N	8 47 E
Frankenthal	**25**	49 32N	8 21 E
Frankenwald	**25**	50 18N	11 36 E
Frankfort, Madag.	**93**	27 17 S	28 30 E
Frankfort, Ind., U.S.A.	**114**	40 20N	86 33W
Frankfort, Kans., U.S.A.	**116**	39 42N	96 26W
Frankfort, Ky., U.S.A.	**114**	38 12N	84 52W
Frankfort, Mich., U.S.A.	**114**	44 38N	86 14W
Frankfurt □	**24**	52 30N	14 0 E
Frankfurt am Main	**25**	50 7N	8 40 E
Frankfurt an der Oder	**24**	52 50N	14 31 E
Fränkische Alb	**25**	49 20N	11 30 E
Fränkische Rezal ⤳	**25**	49 11N	11 1 E
Fränkische Saale ⤳	**25**	50 30N	9 42 E
Fränkische Schweiz	**25**	49 45N	11 10 E
Franklin, Ky., U.S.A.	**115**	36 40N	86 30W
Franklin, La., U.S.A.	**117**	29 45N	91 30W
Franklin, Mass., U.S.A.	**113**	42 4N	71 23W
Franklin, N.H., U.S.A.	**114**	43 28N	71 39W
Franklin, N.J., U.S.A.	**113**	41 9N	74 38W
Franklin, Nebr., U.S.A.	**116**	40 9N	98 55W
Franklin, Pa., U.S.A.	**114**	41 22N	79 45W
Franklin, Tenn., U.S.A.	**115**	35 54N	86 53W
Franklin, Va., U.S.A.	**115**	36 40N	76 58W
Franklin, W. Va., U.S.A.	**114**	38 38N	79 21W
* Franklin □	**105**	71 0N	99 0W
Franklin B.	**104**	69 45N	126 0W
Franklin D. Roosevelt L.	**118**	48 30N	118 16W
Franklin I.	**5**	76 10 S	168 30 E
Franklin, L.	**118**	40 20N	115 26W
Franklin Mts.	**104**	65 0N	125 0W
Franklin Str.	**104**	72 0N	96 0W
Franklinton	**117**	30 53N	90 10W
Franklinville	**112**	42 21N	78 28W
Franks Peak	**118**	43 50N	109 5W
Frankston	**99**	38 8 S	145 8 E
Fränsta	**48**	62 30N	16 11 E
Frantsa Josifa, Zemlya	**58**	82 0N	55 0 E
Franz	**106**	48 25N	84 30W
Franz Josef Land = Frantsa Josifa	**58**	79 0N	62 0 E
Franzburg	**24**	54 9N	12 52 E
Frascati	**40**	41 48N	12 41 E
Fraser ⤳, B.C., Can.	**108**	49 7N	123 11W
Fraser ⤳, Newf., Can.	**107**	56 39N	62 10W
Fraser I.	**97**	25 15 S	153 10 E
Fraser Lake	**108**	54 0N	124 50W
Fraserburg	**92**	31 55 S	21 30 E
Fraserburgh	**14**	57 41N	2 0W
Fraserdale	**106**	49 55N	81 37W
Frashëri	**44**	40 23N	20 26 E
Frasne	**19**	46 50N	6 10 E
Frauenfeld	**25**	47 34N	8 54 E
Fray Bentos	**124**	33 10 S	58 15W
Frechilla	**30**	42 8N	4 50W
Fredericia	**49**	55 34N	9 45 E
Frederick, Md., U.S.A.	**114**	39 25N	77 23W
Frederick, Okla., U.S.A.	**117**	34 22N	99 0W
Frederick, S.D., U.S.A.	**116**	45 55N	98 29W
Frederick Reef	**97**	20 58 S	154 23 E
Frederick Sd.	**108**	57 10N	134 0W
Fredericksburg, Tex., U.S.A.	**117**	30 17N	98 55W
Fredericksburg, Va., U.S.A.	**114**	38 16N	77 29W
Frederickstown	**117**	37 35N	90 15W
Fredericton	**107**	45 57N	66 40W
Fredericton Junc.	**107**	45 41N	66 40W
Frederikshavn	**49**	57 28N	10 31 E
Frederikssund	**49**	55 50N	12 3 E
Fredonia, Ariz., U.S.A.	**119**	36 59N	112 36W
Fredonia, Kans., U.S.A.	**117**	37 34N	95 50W
Fredonia, N.Y., U.S.A.	**114**	42 26N	79 20W
Fredrikstad	**47**	59 13N	10 57 E
Freehold	**113**	40 15N	74 18W
Freeland	**113**	41 3N	75 48W
Freeling, Mt.	**96**	22 35 S	133 06 E
Freels, C.	**107**	49 15N	53 30W
Freeman	**116**	43 25N	97 20W
Freeport, Bahamas	**121**	26 30N	78 47W
Freeport, Can.	**107**	44 15N	66 20W
Freeport, Ill., U.S.A.	**116**	42 18N	89 40W
Freeport, N.Y., U.S.A.	**114**	40 39N	73 35W
Freeport, Tex., U.S.A.	**117**	28 55N	95 22W
Freetown	**84**	8 30N	13 17W
Frégate, L.	**106**	53 15N	74 45W
Fregenal de la Sierra	**31**	38 10N	6 39W
Fregene	**40**	41 50N	12 12 E
Fregeneda, La	**30**	40 58N	6 54W
Fréhel, C.	**18**	48 40N	2 20W
Frei	**47**	63 4N	7 48 E
Freiberg	**24**	50 55N	13 20 E
Freibourg = Fribourg	**25**	46 49N	7 9 E
Freiburg, Baden, Ger.	**25**	48 0N	7 52 E
Freiburg, Niedersachsen, Ger.	**24**	53 49N	9 17 E
Freire	**128**	38 54 S	72 38W
Freirina	**124**	28 30 S	71 10W
Freising	**25**	48 24N	11 47 E
Freistadt	**26**	48 30N	14 30 E
Freital	**24**	51 0N	13 40 E
Fréjus	**21**	43 25N	6 44 E
Fremantle	**96**	32 7 S	115 47 E
Fremont, Mich., U.S.A.	**114**	43 29N	85 59W
Fremont, Nebr., U.S.A.	**116**	41 30N	96 30W
Fremont, Ohio, U.S.A.	**114**	41 20N	83 5W
Fremont ⤳	**119**	38 15N	110 20W
Fremont, L.	**118**	43 0N	109 50W
French ⤳	**114**	41 30N	80 2W
French Guiana ■	**127**	4 0N	53 0W
French I.	**100**	38 20 S	145 22 E
French Terr. of Afars & Issas = Djibouti ■	**87**	11 30N	42 15 E
Frenchglen	**118**	42 48N	119 0W
Frenchman ⤳	**118**	48 24N	107 5W
Frenchman Butte	**109**	53 35N	109 38W
Frenchman Creek ⤳	**116**	40 13N	100 50W
Frenda	**82**	35 2N	1 1 E
Fresco ⤳	**127**	7 15 S	51 30W
Freshfield, C.	**5**	68 25 S	151 10 E
Fresnay	**18**	48 17N	0 1 E
Fresnillo	**120**	23 10N	103 0W
Fresno	**119**	36 47N	119 50W
Fresno Alhandiga	**30**	40 42N	5 37W
Fresno Res.	**118**	48 40N	110 0W
Freudenstadt	**25**	48 27N	8 25 E
Frévent	**19**	50 15N	2 17 E
Freycinet Pen.	**97**	42 10 S	148 25 E
Freyung	**25**	48 48N	13 33 E
Fria	**84**	10 27N	13 38W
Fria, C.	**92**	18 0 S	12 0 E
Frías	**124**	28 40 S	65 5W
Fribourg	**25**	46 49N	7 9 E
Fribourg □	**25**	46 40N	7 0 E
Fridafors	**49**	56 25N	14 39 E
Friedberg, Bayern, Ger.	**25**	48 21N	10 59 E
Friedberg, Hessen, Ger.	**25**	50 21N	8 46 E
Friedland	**24**	53 40N	13 33 E
Friedrichshafen	**25**	47 39N	9 29 E
Friedrichskoog	**24**	54 1N	8 52 E
Friedrichsort	**24**	54 24N	10 11 E
Friedrichstadt	**24**	54 23N	9 6 E
Friendly (Tonga) Is.	**101**	22 0 S	173 0W
Friesach	**26**	46 57N	14 24 E
Friesack	**24**	52 43N	12 35 E
Friesland □	**16**	53 5N	5 50 E
Friesoythe	**24**	53 1N	7 51 E
Frijoles	**120**	9 11N	79 48W
Frillesås	**49**	57 20N	12 12 E
Frinnaryd	**49**	57 55N	14 50 E
Frio ⤳	**117**	28 30N	98 10W
Friona	**117**	34 40N	102 42W
Frisian Is.	**24**	53 30N	6 0 E
Fristad	**49**	57 50N	13 0 E
Fritch	**117**	35 40N	101 35W
Fritsla	**49**	57 33N	12 47 E
Fritzlar	**24**	51 8N	9 19 E
Friuli-Venezia Giulia □	**39**	46 0N	13 0 E
Friville-Escarbotin	**19**	50 5N	1 33 E
Frobisher B.	**105**	62 30N	66 0W
Frobisher Bay	**105**	63 44N	68 31W
Frobisher L.	**109**	56 20N	108 15W
Frohavet	**50**	63 50N	9 35 E
Froid	**116**	48 20N	104 29W
Frolovo	**57**	49 45N	43 40 E
Fromberg	**118**	42 25N	108 58W
Frombork	**28**	54 21N	19 41 E
Frome	**13**	51 16N	2 17W
Frome, L.	**97**	30 45 S	139 45 E
Fromentine	**18**	46 53N	2 9W
Frómista	**30**	42 16N	4 25W
Front Range	**118**	40 0N	105 40W
Front Royal	**114**	38 55N	78 10W
Fronteira	**31**	39 3N	7 39W
Frontera	**120**	18 30N	92 40W
Frontignan	**20**	43 27N	3 45 E
Frosinone	**40**	41 38N	13 20 E
Frosolone	**41**	41 34N	14 27 E
Frostburg	**114**	39 43N	78 57W
Frostisen	**50**	68 14N	17 10 E
Frouard	**19**	48 47N	6 8 E
Frövi	**48**	59 28N	15 24 E
Frøya	**47**	63 43N	8 40 E
Fruges	**19**	50 30N	2 8 E
Frumoasa	**46**	46 28N	25 48 E
Frunze	**58**	42 54N	74 46 E
Fruška Gora	**42**	45 7N	19 30 E
Frutal	**127**	20 0 S	49 0W
Frutigen	**25**	46 35N	7 38 E
Frýdek-Místek	**27**	49 40N	18 20 E
Frýdlant, Severočeský, Czech.	**26**	50 56N	15 9 E
Frýdlant, Severomoravsky, Czech.	**27**	49 35N	18 20 E
Fryvaldov = Jeseník	**27**	50 0N	17 8 E
Fthiótis □	**45**	38 50N	22 25 E
Fu Xian, Liaoning, China	**76**	39 38N	121 58 E
Fu Xian, Shaanxi, China	**76**	36 0N	109 20 E
Fucécchio	**38**	43 44N	10 51 E
Fucheng	**76**	37 50N	116 10 E
Fuchou = Fuzhou	**75**	26 5N	119 16 E
Fuchuan	**77**	24 50N	111 5 E
Fuchun Jiang ⤳	**77**	30 5N	120 5 E
Fúcino, Conca del	**39**	42 1N	13 31 E
Fuding	**77**	27 20N	120 12 E
Fuencaliente	**31**	38 25N	4 18W
Fuengirola	**31**	36 32N	4 41W
Fuente Alamo	**33**	38 44N	1 24W
Fuente Álamo	**33**	37 42N	1 6W
Fuente de Cantos	**31**	38 15N	6 18W
Fuente de San Esteban, La	**30**	40 49N	6 15W
Fuente del Maestre	**31**	38 31N	6 28W
Fuente el Fresno	**31**	39 14N	3 46W
Fuente Ovejuna	**31**	38 15N	5 25W
Fuentes de Andalucía	**31**	37 28N	5 20W
Fuentes de Ebro	**32**	41 31N	0 38W
Fuentes de León	**31**	38 5N	6 32W
Fuentes de Oñoro	**30**	40 33N	6 52W
Fuentesaúco	**30**	41 15N	5 30W
Fuerte ⤳	**120**	25 50N	109 25W
Fuerte Olimpo	**124**	21 0 S	57 51W
Fuerteventura	**80**	28 30N	14 0W
Fŭget, Munţii	**46**	45 50N	22 9 E
Fugløysund	**50**	70 15N	20 20 E
Fugou	**77**	34 3N	114 25 E
Fuhai	**75**	47 2N	87 25 E
Fuji-no-miya	**74**	35 10N	138 40 E
Fuji-San	**74**	35 22N	138 44 E
Fujian □	**75**	26 0N	118 0 E
Fujin	**76**	47 16N	132 1 E
Fujisawa	**74**	35 22N	139 29 E
Fukien = Fujian □	**75**	26 0N	118 0 E
Fukuchiyama	**74**	35 19N	135 9 E
Fukui	**74**	36 0N	136 10 E
Fukui □	**74**	36 0N	136 12 E
Fukuoka	**74**	33 39N	130 21 E
Fukuoka □	**74**	33 30N	131 0 E
Fukushima	**74**	37 44N	140 28 E
Fukushima □	**74**	37 30N	140 15 E
Fukuyama	**74**	34 35N	133 20 E
Fulda	**24**	50 32N	9 41 E
Fulda ⤳	**24**	51 27N	9 40 E
Fuling	**77**	29 40N	107 20 E
Fullerton, Calif., U.S.A.	**119**	33 52N	117 58W
Fullerton, Nebr., U.S.A.	**116**	41 25N	98 0W
Fulton, Mo., U.S.A.	**116**	38 50N	91 55W
Fulton, N.Y., U.S.A.	**114**	43 20N	76 22W
Fulton, Tenn., U.S.A.	**115**	36 31N	88 53W
Fuluälven	**48**	61 18N	13 4 E
Fulufjället	**48**	61 32N	12 41 E
Fumay	**19**	50 0N	4 40 E
Fumel	**20**	44 30N	0 58 E
Funabashi	**74**	35 45N	140 0 E
Funafuti	**94**	8 30 S	179 0 E
Funchal	**80**	32 38N	16 54W
Fundación	**126**	10 31N	74 11W
Fundão	**30**	40 8N	7 30W
Fundy, B. of	**107**	45 0N	66 0W
Funing, Jiangsu, China	**77**	33 45N	119 50 E
Funing, Yunnan, China	**77**	23 35N	105 45 E
Funiu Shan	**77**	33 30N	112 20 E
Funsi	**84**	10 21N	1 54W
Funtua	**85**	11 30N	7 18 E
Fuping	**76**	38 48N	114 12 E
Fuqing	**77**	25 41N	119 21 E
Fur	**49**	56 50N	9 0 E
Furāt, Nahr al ⤳	**64**	31 0N	47 25 E
Furmanov	**55**	57 10N	41 9 E
Furmanovo	**57**	49 42N	49 25 E
Furnas, Reprêsa de	**125**	20 50 S	45 0W
Furneaux Group	**97**	40 10 S	147 50 E
Furness, Pen.	**12**	54 12N	3 10W
Fürstenau	**24**	52 32N	7 40 E
Fürstenberg	**24**	53 11N	13 9 E
Fürstenfeld	**26**	47 3N	16 3 E
Fürstenfeldbruck	**25**	48 10N	11 15 E
Fürstenwalde	**24**	52 20N	14 3 E
Fürth	**25**	49 29N	11 0 E
Furth im Wald	**25**	49 19N	12 51 E
Furtwangen	**25**	48 3N	8 14 E
Furudal	**48**	61 10N	15 11 E
Furusund	**48**	59 40N	18 55 E
Fury and Hecla Str.	**105**	69 56N	84 0W
Fusa	**47**	60 12N	5 37 E
Fusagasuga	**126**	4 21N	74 22W
Fuscaldo	**41**	39 25N	16 1 E
Fushan	**76**	37 30N	121 15 E
Fushë Arrëzi	**44**	42 4N	20 2 E
Fushun	**76**	41 50N	123 56 E
Fusong	**76**	42 20N	127 15 E
Füssen	**25**	47 35N	10 43 E
Fusui	**77**	22 40N	107 56 E
Futuna	**94**	14 25 S	178 20 E
Fuwa	**86**	31 12N	30 33 E
Fuxin	**76**	42 5N	121 48 E
Fuyang, Anhui, China	**77**	33 0N	115 48 E
Fuyang, Zhejiang, China	**77**	30 5N	119 57 E
Fuyu	**76**	45 12N	124 43 E
Fuyuan	**75**	48 20N	134 5 E
Füzesgyarmat	**27**	47 6N	21 14 E
Fuzhou, Fujian, China	**75**	26 5N	119 16 E
Fuzhou, Jiangxi, China	**75**	28 0N	116 25 E
Fylde	**12**	53 50N	2 58W
Fyn	**49**	55 20N	10 30 E
Fyne, L.	**14**	56 0N	5 20W
Fyns Amtskommune □	**49**	55 15N	10 30 E
Fyresvatn	**47**	59 6N	8 10 E

G

Name	Page	Lat.	Long.
Gaanda	**85**	10 10N	12 27 E
Gabarin	**85**	11 8N	10 27 E
Gabas ⤳	**20**	43 46N	0 42W
Gabela	**88**	11 0 S	14 24 E
Gabès	**83**	33 53N	10 2 E
Gabès, Golfe de	**83**	34 0N	10 30 E
Gabgaba, W.	**86**	22 10N	33 5 E
Gabin	**28**	52 23N	19 41 E
Gabon ■	**88**	0 10 S	10 0 E
Gaborone	**92**	24 45 S	25 57 E
Gabriels	**113**	44 26N	74 12W
Gabrovo	**43**	42 52N	25 19 E
Gacé	**18**	48 49N	0 20 E
Gach Sārān	**65**	30 15N	50 45 E
Gacko	**42**	43 10N	18 33 E
Gadag-Batgeri	**70**	15 30N	75 45 E
Gadamai	**87**	17 11N	36 10 E
Gadap	**68**	25 5N	67 28 E
Gadarwara	**68**	22 50N	78 50 E
Gadebusch	**24**	53 41N	11 6 E
Gadein	**87**	8 10N	28 45 E
Gadhada	**68**	22 0N	71 35 E
Gádor, Sierra de	**33**	36 57N	2 45W
Gadsden, Ala., U.S.A.	**115**	34 1N	86 0W
Gadsden, Ariz., U.S.A.	**119**	32 35N	114 47W
Gadwal	**70**	16 10N	77 50 E
Gadyach	**54**	50 21N	34 0 E
Găeşti	**46**	44 48N	25 19 E
Gaeta	**40**	41 12N	13 35 E
Gaeta, G. di	**40**	41 0N	13 25 E
Gaffney	**115**	35 3N	81 40W
Gafsa	**83**	32 24N	8 43 E
Gagarin (Gzhatsk)	**54**	55 38N	35 0 E
Gagetown	**107**	45 46N	66 10W
Gagino	**55**	55 15N	45 1 E
Gagliano del Capo	**41**	39 50N	18 23 E
Gagnef	**48**	60 36N	15 5 E
Gagnoa	**84**	6 56N	5 16W
Gagnon	**107**	51 50N	68 5W
Gagnon, L.	**109**	62 3N	110 27W
Gagra	**57**	43 20N	40 10 E
Gahini	**90**	1 50 S	30 30 E
Gahmar	**69**	25 27N	83 49 E
Gai Xian	**76**	40 22N	122 20 E
Gaibanda	**69**	25 20N	89 36 E
Gaïdhouronísi	**45**	34 53N	25 41 E
Gail	**117**	32 48N	101 25W
Gail ⤳	**26**	46 36N	13 53 E
Gaillac	**20**	43 54N	1 54 E
Gaillon	**18**	49 10N	1 20 E
Gaines	**112**	41 46N	77 35W
Gainesville, Fla., U.S.A.	**115**	29 38N	82 20W
Gainesville, Ga., U.S.A.	**115**	34 17N	83 47W
Gainesville, Mo., U.S.A.	**117**	36 35N	92 26W
Gainesville, Tex., U.S.A.	**117**	33 40N	97 10W
Gainsborough	**12**	53 23N	0 46W
Gairdner L.	**96**	31 30 S	136 0 E
Gairloch, L.	**14**	57 43N	5 45W
Gaj	**42**	45 28N	17 3 E
Gal Oya Res.	**70**	7 5N	81 30 E
Galachipa	**69**	22 8N	90 26 E
Galán, Cerro	**124**	25 55 S	66 52W
Galana ⤳	**90**	3 9 S	40 8 E
Galangue	**89**	13 42 S	16 9 E
Galanta	**27**	48 11N	17 45 E
Galápagos	**95**	0 0	89 0W
Galas ⤳	**71**	4 55N	101 57 E
Galashiels	**14**	55 37N	2 50W
Galatás	**45**	37 30N	23 26 E
Galaţi	**46**	45 27N	28 2 E
Galaţi □	**46**	45 45N	27 30 E
Galatina	**41**	40 10N	18 10 E
Galátone	**41**	40 8N	18 3 E
Galax	**115**	36 42N	80 57W
Galaxídhion	**45**	38 22N	22 23 E
Galbraith	**98**	16 25 S	141 30 E
Galcaio	**63**	6 30N	47 30 E
Galdhøpiggen	**47**	61 38N	8 18 E
Galela	**73**	1 50N	127 49 E
Galera	**33**	37 45N	2 33W
Galesburg	**116**	40 57N	90 23W
Galeton	**112**	41 43N	77 40W
Gali	**57**	42 37N	41 46 E
Galicea Mare	**46**	44 4N	23 19 E
Galich	**55**	58 23N	42 12 E
Galiche	**43**	43 34N	23 50 E
Galicia	**30**	42 43N	7 45W
Galilee = Hagalil	**62**	32 53N	35 18 E
Galilee, L.	**98**	22 20 S	145 50 E
Galion	**112**	40 43N	82 48W
Galite, Is. de la	**83**	37 30N	8 59 E
Galiuro Mts.	**119**	32 40N	110 30W
Gallabat	**81**	12 58N	36 11 E
Gallarate	**38**	45 40N	8 48 E
Gallardon	**19**	48 32N	1 47 E
Gallatin	**115**	36 24N	86 27W
Galle	**70**	6 5N	80 10 E
Gállego ⤳	**32**	41 39N	0 51W
Gallegos ⤳	**128**	51 35 S	69 0W
Galley Hd.	**15**	51 32N	8 56W

* *Now part of Central Arctic and Baffin □*

Galliate

Ghayl

Galliate	**38**	45 27N	8 44 E
Gallinas, Pta.	**126**	12 28N	71 40W
Gallípoli	**41**	40 8N	18 0 E
Gallipoli = Gelibolu	**44**	40 28N	26 43 E
Gallipolis	**114**	38 50N	82 10W
Gällivare	**50**	67 9N	20 40 E
Gallo, C.	**40**	38 13N	13 19 E
Gallocanta, Laguna de	**32**	40 58N	1 30W
Galloway	**14**	55 0N	4 25W
Galloway, Mull of	**14**	54 38N	4 50W
Gallup	**119**	35 30N	108 45W
Gallur	**32**	41 52N	1 19W
Gal'on	**62**	31 38N	34 51 E
Galong	**99**	34 37 S	148 34 E
Galtström	**48**	62 10N	17 30 E
Galtür	**26**	46 58N	10 11 E
Galty Mts.	**15**	52 22N	8 10W
Galtymore	**15**	52 22N	8 12W
Galva	**116**	41 10N	90 0W
Galve de Sorbe	**32**	41 13N	3 10W
Galveston	**117**	29 15N	94 48W
Galveston B.	**117**	29 30N	94 50W
Gálvez, Argent.	**124**	32 0 S	61 14W
Gálvez, Spain	**31**	39 42N	4 16W
Galway	**15**	53 16N	9 4W
Galway □	**15**	53 16N	9 3W
Galway B.	**15**	53 10N	9 20W
Gamari, L.	**87**	11 32N	41 40 E
Gamawa	**85**	12 10N	10 31 E
Gambaga	**85**	10 30N	0 28W
Gambat	**68**	27 17N	68 26 E
Gambela	**87**	8 14N	34 38 E
Gambia ■	**84**	13 25N	16 0W
Gambia →	**84**	13 28N	16 34W
Gamboa	**120**	9 8N	79 42W
Gamboli	**68**	29 53N	68 24 E
* Gambos	**89**	14 37 S	14 40 E
Gamerco	**119**	35 33N	108 56W
Gammon →	**109**	51 24N	95 44W
Gammouda	**83**	35 3N	9 39 E
Gan	**20**	43 12N	0 27W
Gan Goriama, Mts.	**85**	7 44N	12 45 E
Gan Jiang →	**75**	29 15N	116 0 E
Gan Shemu'el	**62**	32 28N	34 56 E
Gan Yavne	**62**	31 48N	34 42 E
Ganado, Ariz., U.S.A.	**119**	35 46N	109 41W
Ganado, Tex., U.S.A.	**117**	29 4N	96 31W
Gananoque	**106**	44 20N	76 10W
Ganaveh	**65**	29 35N	50 35 E
Gancheng	**77**	18 51N	108 37 E
Gand = Gent	**16**	51 2N	3 42 E
Ganda	**89**	13 3 S	14 35 E
Gandak →	**69**	25 39N	85 13 E
Gandava	**68**	28 32N	67 32 E
Gander	**107**	48 58N	54 35W
Gander L.	**107**	48 58N	54 35W
Ganderowe Falls	**91**	17 20 S	29 10 E
Gandesa	**32**	41 3N	0 26 E
Gandhi Sagar	**68**	24 40N	75 40 E
Gandi	**85**	12 55N	5 49 E
Gandía	**33**	38 58N	0 9W
Gandino	**38**	45 50N	9 52 E
Gandole	**85**	8 28N	11 35 E
Ganedidalem = Gani	**73**	0 48 S	128 14 E
Ganetti	**86**	18 0N	31 10 E
Ganga →	**69**	23 20N	90 30 E
Ganga, Mouths of the	**69**	21 30N	90 0 E
Ganganagar	**68**	29 56N	73 56 E
Gangapur	**68**	26 32N	76 49 E
Gangara	**85**	14 35N	8 29 E
Gangavati	**70**	15 30N	76 36 E
Gangaw	**67**	22 5N	94 5 E
Gangdisê Shan	**67**	31 20N	81 0 E
Ganges	**20**	43 56N	3 42 E
Ganges = Ganga →	**69**	23 20N	90 30 E
Gangoh	**68**	29 46N	77 18 E
Gangtok	**69**	27 20N	88 37 E
Gani	**73**	0 48 S	128 14 E
Ganj	**68**	27 45N	78 57 E
Gannat	**20**	46 7N	3 11 E
Gannett Pk.	**118**	43 15N	109 38W
Gannvalley	**116**	44 3N	98 57W
Ganquan	**76**	36 20N	109 20 E
Gänserdorf	**27**	48 20N	16 43 E
Gansu □	**75**	36 0N	104 0 E
Ganta (Gompa)	**84**	7 15N	8 59W
Gantheaume B.	**96**	27 40 S	114 10 E
Gantheaume, C.	**99**	36 4 S	137 32 E
Gantsevichi	**54**	52 49N	26 30 E
Ganyu	**77**	34 50N	119 8 E
Ganyushkino	**57**	46 35N	49 20 E
Ganzhou	**75**	25 51N	114 56 E
Gao □	**85**	18 0N	1 0 E
Gao Bang	**71**	22 37N	106 18 E
Gao'an	**77**	28 26N	115 17 E
Gaomi	**76**	36 20N	119 42 E
Gaoping	**76**	35 45N	112 55 E
Gaoua	**84**	10 20N	3 8W
Gaoual	**84**	11 45N	13 25W
Gaoxiong	**75**	22 38N	120 18 E
Gaoyou	**77**	32 47N	119 26 E
Gaoyou Hu	**77**	32 45N	119 20 E
Gaoyuan	**76**	37 8N	117 58 E
Gap	**21**	44 33N	6 5 E
Gar	**75**	32 10N	79 58 E
Garachiné	**121**	8 0N	78 12W
Garanhuns	**127**	8 50 S	36 30W
Garawe	**84**	4 35N	8 0W
Garba Tula	**90**	0 30N	38 32 E
Garber	**117**	36 30N	97 36W
Garberville	**118**	40 11N	123 50W
Gard	**63**	9 30N	49 6 E
Gard □	**21**	44 2N	4 10 E
Gard →	**21**	43 51N	4 37 E
Garda, L. di	**38**	45 40N	10 40 E
Gardala	**81**	5 40N	37 25 E
Gardanne	**21**	43 27N	5 27 E
Garde L.	**109**	62 50N	106 13W
Gardelegen	**24**	52 32N	11 21 E
Garden City, Kans., U.S.A.	**117**	38 0N	100 45W
Garden City, Tex., U.S.A.	**117**	31 52N	101 28W
Gardez	**66**	33 37N	69 9 E

* *Renamed Kipungo*

Gardhíki	**45**	38 50N	21 55 E
Gardiner	**118**	45 3N	110 42W
Gardiners I.	**113**	41 4N	72 5W
Gardner	**114**	42 35N	72 0W
Gardner Canal	**108**	53 27N	128 8W
Gardnerville	**118**	38 59N	119 47W
Gardno, Jezioro	**28**	54 40N	17 7 E
Garešnica	**42**	45 36N	16 56 E
Garéssio	**38**	44 12N	8 1 E
Garfield	**118**	47 3N	117 8W
Gargaliánoi	**45**	37 4N	21 38 E
Gargano, Mte.	**41**	41 43N	15 43 E
Gargans, Mt.	**20**	45 37N	1 39 E
Gargouna	**85**	15 56N	0 13 E
Garhshankar	**68**	31 13N	76 11 E
Garibaldi Prov. Park	**108**	49 50N	122 40W
Garies	**92**	30 32 S	17 59 E
Garigliano →	**40**	41 13N	13 44 E
Garissa	**90**	0 25 S	39 40 E
Garissa □	**90**	0 20 S	40 0 E
Garkida	**85**	10 27N	12 36 E
Garko	**85**	11 45N	8 53 E
Garland	**118**	41 47N	112 10W
Garlasco	**38**	45 11N	8 55 E
Garm	**58**	39 0N	70 20 E
Garmisch-Partenkirchen	**25**	47 30N	11 5 E
Garmsār	**65**	35 20N	52 25 E
Garner	**116**	43 4N	93 37W
Garnett	**116**	38 18N	95 12W
Garo Hills	**69**	25 30N	90 30 E
Garob	**92**	26 37 S	16 0 E
Garoe	**63**	8 25N	48 33 E
Garonne →	**20**	45 2N	0 36W
Garoua (Garwa)	**85**	9 19N	13 21 E
Garrel	**24**	52 58N	7 59 E
Garrigues	**20**	43 40N	3 30 E
Garrison, Mont., U.S.A.	**118**	46 30N	112 56W
Garrison, N.D., U.S.A.	**116**	47 39N	101 27W
Garrison, Tex., U.S.A.	**117**	31 50N	94 28W
Garrison Res.	**116**	47 30N	102 0W
Garrovillas	**31**	39 40N	6 33W
Garrucha	**33**	37 11N	1 49W
Garry →	**14**	56 47N	3 47W
Garry L.	**104**	65 58N	100 18W
Garsen	**90**	2 20 S	40 5 E
Garson →	**109**	56 20N	110 1W
Garson L.	**109**	56 19N	110 2W
Gartempe →	**20**	46 47N	0 49 E
Gartz	**24**	53 12N	14 23 E
Garu	**85**	10 55N	0 11W
Garut	**73**	7 14 S	107 53 E
Garvão	**31**	37 42N	8 21W
Garvie Mts.	**101**	45 30 S	168 50 E
Garwa	**69**	24 11N	83 47 E
Garwolin	**28**	51 55N	21 38 E
Gary	**114**	41 35N	87 20W
Garz	**24**	54 17N	13 21 E
Garzê	**75**	31 39N	99 58 E
Garzón	**126**	2 10N	75 40W
Gasan Kuli	**58**	37 40N	54 20 E
Gascogne	**20**	43 45N	0 20 E
Gascogne, G. de	**32**	44 0N	2 0W
Gascony = Gascogne	**20**	43 45N	0 20 E
Gascoyne →	**96**	24 52 S	113 37 E
Gascueña	**32**	40 18N	2 31W
Gash, Wadi →	**87**	16 48N	35 51 E
Gashaka	**85**	7 20N	11 29 E
Gashua	**85**	12 54N	11 0 E
Gaspé	**107**	48 52N	64 30W
Gaspé, C.	**107**	48 48N	64 7W
Gaspé, Pén. de	**107**	48 45N	65 40W
Gaspésie, Parc Prov. de la	**107**	48 55N	65 50W
Gassaway	**114**	38 42N	80 43W
Gássino Torinese	**38**	45 8N	7 50 E
Gassol	**85**	8 34N	10 25 E
Gastonia	**115**	35 17N	81 10W
Gastoúni	**45**	37 51N	21 15 E
Gastoúri	**44**	39 34N	19 54 E
Gastre	**128**	42 20 S	69 15W
Gata, C. de	**33**	36 41N	2 13W
Gata, Sierra de	**30**	40 20N	6 45W
Gataga →	**108**	58 35N	126 59W
Gătaia	**42**	45 26N	21 30 E
Gatchina	**54**	59 35N	30 9 E
Gateshead	**12**	54 57N	1 37W
Gatesville	**117**	31 29N	97 45W
Gaths	**91**	20 2 S	30 32 E
Gatico	**124**	22 29 S	70 20W
Gâtinais	**19**	48 5N	2 40 E
Gâtine, Hauteurs de	**20**	46 35N	0 45W
Gatineau	**113**	45 29N	75 39W
Gatineau →	**106**	45 27N	75 42W
Gatineau, Parc de la	**106**	45 40N	76 0W
* Gatooma	**91**	18 20 S	29 52 E
Gattinara	**38**	45 37N	8 22 E
Gatun	**120**	9 16N	79 55W
Gatun Dam	**120**	9 16N	79 55W
Gatun, L.	**120**	9 7N	79 56W
Gatun Locks	**120**	9 16N	79 55W
Gaucín	**31**	36 31N	5 19W
Gauer L.	**109**	57 0N	97 50W
Gauhati	**67**	26 10N	91 45 E
Gauja →	**54**	57 10N	24 16 E
Gaula →	**47**	63 21N	10 14 E
Gaussberg	**5**	66 45 S	89 0 E
Gausta	**47**	59 50N	8 37 E
Gavá	**32**	41 18N	2 0 E
Gavarnie	**20**	42 44N	0 3W
Gavāter	**65**	25 10N	61 31 E
Gavdhopoúla	**45**	34 56N	24 0 E
Gávdhos	**45**	34 50N	24 5 E
Gavião	**31**	39 28N	7 56W
Gävle	**48**	60 40N	17 9 E
Gävleborgs län □	**48**	61 30N	16 15 E
Gavorrano	**38**	42 55N	10 49 E
Gavray	**18**	48 55N	1 20W
Gavrilov Yam	**55**	57 18N	39 49 E
Gávrion	**45**	37 54N	24 44 E
Gawachab	**92**	27 4 S	17 55 E
Gawilgarh Hills	**68**	21 15N	76 45 E
Gawler	**97**	34 30 S	138 42 E
Gawler Ranges	**96**	32 30 S	135 45 E

* *Renamed Kadoma*

Gaxun Nur	**75**	42 22N	100 30 E
Gay	**52**	51 27N	58 27 E
Gaya, India	**69**	24 47N	85 4 E
Gaya, Niger	**85**	11 52N	3 28 E
Gaya, Nigeria	**85**	11 57N	9 0 E
Gaylord	**114**	45 1N	84 41W
Gayndah	**97**	25 35 S	151 32 E
Gaysin	**56**	48 57N	28 25 E
Gayvoron	**56**	48 22N	29 52 E
Gaza	**62**	31 30N	34 28 E
Gaza □	**93**	23 10 S	32 45 E
Gaza Strip	**62**	31 29N	34 25 E
Gazaoua	**85**	13 32N	7 55 E
Gazelle Pen.	**98**	4 40 S	152 0 E
Gazi	**90**	1 3N	24 30 E
Gaziantep	**64**	37 6N	37 23 E
Gazli	**58**	40 14N	63 24 E
Gbarnga	**84**	7 19N	9 13W
Gbekebo	**85**	6 20N	4 56 E
Gboko	**85**	7 17N	9 4 E
Gbongan	**85**	7 28N	4 20 E
Gcuwa	**93**	32 20 S	28 11 E
Gdańsk	**28**	54 22N	18 40 E
Gdańsk □	**28**	54 10N	18 30 E
Gdańska, Zatoka	**28**	54 30N	19 20 E
Gdov	**54**	58 48N	27 55 E
Gdynia	**28**	54 35N	18 33 E
Ge'a	**62**	31 38N	34 37 E
Gebe	**73**	0 5N	129 25 E
Gebeit Mine	**86**	21 3N	36 29 E
Gebel Mûsa	**86**	28 32N	33 59 E
Gecha	**87**	7 30N	35 18 E
Gedaref	**87**	14 2N	35 28 E
Gede, Tanjung	**72**	6 46 S	105 12 E
Gedera	**62**	31 49N	34 46 E
Gedo	**87**	9 2N	37 25 E
Gèdre	**20**	42 47N	0 2 E
Gedser	**49**	54 35N	11 55 E
Gedser Odde	**49**	54 30N	11 58 E
Geelong	**97**	38 10 S	144 22 E
Geestenseth	**24**	53 31N	8 51 E
Geesthacht	**24**	53 25N	10 20 E
Geidam	**85**	12 57N	11 57 E
Geikie →	**109**	57 45N	103 52W
Geili	**87**	16 1N	32 37 E
Geilo	**47**	60 32N	8 14 E
Geinica	**27**	48 51N	20 55 E
Geisingen	**25**	47 55N	8 37 E
Geislingen	**25**	48 37N	9 51 E
Geita	**90**	2 48 S	32 12 E
Geita □	**90**	2 50 S	32 10 E
Gejiu	**75**	23 20N	103 10 E
Gel →	**87**	7 5N	29 10 E
Gel River	**87**	7 5N	29 10 E
Gela	**41**	37 6N	14 18 E
Gela, Golfo di	**41**	37 0N	14 8 E
Geladi	**63**	6 59N	46 30 E
Gelderland □	**16**	52 5N	6 10 E
Geldermalsen	**16**	51 53N	5 17 E
Geldern	**24**	51 32N	6 18 E
Geldrop	**16**	51 25N	5 32 E
Geleen	**16**	50 57N	5 49 E
Gelehun	**84**	8 20N	11 40W
Gelendzhik	**56**	44 33N	38 10 E
Gelibolu	**44**	40 28N	26 43 E
Gelnhausen	**25**	50 12N	9 12 E
Gelsenkirchen	**24**	51 30N	7 5 E
Gelting	**24**	54 43N	9 53 E
Gemas	**71**	2 37N	102 36 E
Gembloux	**16**	50 34N	4 43 E
Gemena	**88**	3 13N	19 48 E
Gemerek	**64**	39 15N	36 10 E
Gemona del Friuli	**39**	46 16N	13 7 E
Gemsa	**86**	27 39N	33 35 E
Gemu-Gofa □	**87**	5 40N	36 40 E
Gemünden	**25**	50 3N	9 43 E
Gen He →	**76**	50 16N	119 32 E
Genale	**87**	6 0N	39 30 E
Gençay	**20**	46 23N	0 23 E
Gendringen	**16**	51 52N	6 21 E
Geneina, Gebel	**86**	29 2N	33 55 E
General Acha	**124**	37 20 S	64 38W
General Alvear, Buenos Aires, Argent.	**124**	36 0 S	60 0W
General Alvear, Mendoza, Argent.	**124**	35 0 S	67 40W
General Artigas	**124**	26 52 S	56 16W
General Belgrano	**124**	36 35 S	58 47W
General Cabrera	**124**	32 53 S	63 52W
General Guido	**124**	36 40 S	57 50W
General Juan Madariaga	**124**	37 0 S	57 0W
General La Madrid	**124**	37 17 S	61 20W
General MacArthur	**73**	11 18N	125 28 E
General Martin Miguel de Güemes	**124**	24 35 S	65 0W
General Paz	**124**	27 45 S	57 36W
General Pico	**124**	35 45 S	63 50W
General Pinedo	**124**	27 15 S	61 20W
General Pinto	**124**	34 45 S	61 50W
General Santos	**73**	6 5N	125 14 E
General Toshevo	**43**	43 42N	28 6 E
General Trías	**120**	28 21N	106 22W
General Viamonte	**124**	35 1 S	61 3W
General Villegas	**124**	35 0 S	63 0W
Genesee, Idaho, U.S.A.	**118**	46 31N	116 59W
Genesee, Pa., U.S.A.	**112**	42 0N	77 54W
Genesee →	**114**	42 35N	78 0W
Geneseo, Ill., U.S.A.	**116**	41 25N	90 10W
Geneseo, Kans., U.S.A.	**116**	38 32N	98 8W
Geneseo, N.Y., U.S.A.	**112**	42 49N	77 49W
Geneva, Ala., U.S.A.	**115**	31 2N	85 52W
Geneva, N.Y., U.S.A.	**114**	42 53N	77 0W
Geneva, Nebr., U.S.A.	**116**	40 35N	97 35W
Geneva, Ohio, U.S.A.	**114**	41 49N	80 58W
Geneva = Genève	**25**	46 12N	6 9 E
Geneva, L.	**114**	42 38N	88 30W
Geneva, L. = Léman, Lac	**25**	46 26N	6 30 E
Genève	**25**	46 12N	6 9 E
Genève □	**25**	46 10N	6 10 E
Gengenbach	**25**	48 25N	8 0 E
Genichesk	**56**	46 12N	34 50 E
Genil →	**31**	37 42N	5 19W

Génissiat, Barrage de	**21**	46 1N	5 48 E
Genjem	**73**	2 46 S	140 12 E
Genk	**16**	50 58N	5 32 E
Genlis	**19**	47 15N	5 12 E
Gennargentu, Mti. del	**40**	40 0N	9 10 E
Gennep	**16**	51 41N	5 59 E
Gennes	**18**	47 20N	0 17W
Genoa, Austral.	**99**	37 29 S	149 35 E
Genoa, N.Y., U.S.A.	**113**	42 40N	76 32W
Genoa, Nebr., U.S.A.	**116**	41 31N	97 44W
Genoa = Génova	**38**	44 24N	8 57 E
Génova	**38**	44 24N	8 56 E
Génova, Golfo di	**38**	44 0N	9 0 E
Gent	**16**	51 2N	3 42 E
Genthin	**24**	52 24N	12 10 E
Geographe B.	**96**	33 30 S	115 15 E
Geographe Chan.	**96**	24 30 S	113 0 E
Geokchay	**57**	40 42N	47 43 E
Georga, Zemlya	**58**	80 30N	49 0 E
George	**92**	33 58 S	22 29 E
George →	**107**	58 49N	66 10W
George, L., N.S.W., Austral.	**99**	35 10 S	149 25 E
George, L., S. Austral., Austral.	**99**	37 25 S	140 0 E
George, L., Uganda	**90**	0 5N	30 10 E
George, L., Fla., U.S.A.	**115**	29 15N	81 35W
George, L., N.Y., U.S.A.	**113**	43 30N	73 30W
George River = Port Nouveau	**105**	58 30N	65 50W
George Sound	**101**	44 52 S	167 25 E
George Town, Austral.	**99**	41 5 S	146 49 E
George Town, Bahamas	**121**	23 33N	75 47W
George Town, Malay.	**71**	5 25N	100 15 E
George V Coast	**5**	69 0 S	148 0 E
George VI Sound	**5**	71 0 S	68 0W
George West	**117**	28 18N	98 5W
Georgetown, Austral.	**97**	18 17 S	143 33 E
Georgetown, Ont., Can.	**106**	43 40N	79 56W
Georgetown, P.E.I., Can.	**107**	46 13N	62 24W
Georgetown, Gambia	**84**	13 30N	14 47W
Georgetown, Guyana	**126**	6 50N	58 12W
Georgetown, Colo., U.S.A.	**118**	39 46N	105 49W
Georgetown, Ky., U.S.A.	**114**	38 13N	84 33W
Georgetown, Ohio, U.S.A.	**114**	38 50N	83 50W
Georgetown, S.C., U.S.A.	**115**	33 22N	79 15W
Georgetown, Tex., U.S.A.	**117**	30 40N	97 45W
Georgi Dimitrov	**43**	42 15N	23 54 E
Georgi Dimitrov, Yazovir	**43**	42 37N	25 18 E
Georgia □	**115**	32 0N	82 0W
Georgia, Str. of	**108**	49 25N	124 0W
Georgian B.	**106**	45 15N	81 0W
Georgian S.S.R. □	**57**	42 0N	43 0 E
Georgievsk	**57**	44 12N	43 28 E
Georgina →	**97**	23 30 S	139 47 E
Georgiu-Dezh	**55**	51 3N	39 30 E
Gera	**24**	50 53N	12 11 E
Gera □	**24**	50 45N	11 45 E
Geraardsbergen	**16**	50 45N	3 53 E
Geral de Goiás, Serra	**127**	12 0 S	46 0W
Geral, Serra	**125**	26 25 S	50 0W
Geraldine	**118**	47 36N	110 18W
Geraldton, Austral.	**96**	28 48 S	114 32 E
Geraldton, Can.	**106**	49 44N	86 59W
Gérardmer	**19**	48 3N	6 50 E
Gerede	**56**	40 45N	32 10 E
Gereshk	**65**	31 47N	64 35 E
Gérgal	**33**	37 7N	2 31W
Gerik	**71**	5 25N	101 0 E
Gering	**116**	41 51N	103 30W
Gerizim	**62**	32 13N	35 15 E
Gerlach	**118**	40 43N	119 27W
Gerlachovka	**27**	49 11N	20 7 E
Gerlogubi	**63**	6 53N	45 3 E
German Planina	**42**	42 20N	22 0 E
Germansen Landing	**108**	55 43N	124 40W
Germany, East ■	**24**	52 0N	12 0 E
Germany, West ■	**24**	52 0N	9 0 E
Germersheim	**25**	49 13N	8 20 E
Germiston	**93**	26 15 S	28 10 E
Gernsheim	**25**	49 44N	8 29 E
Gerolstein	**25**	50 12N	6 40 E
Gerolzhofen	**25**	49 54N	10 21 E
Gerona	**32**	41 58N	2 46 E
Gerona □	**32**	42 11N	2 30 E
Gerrard	**108**	50 30N	117 17W
Gers □	**20**	43 35N	0 38 E
Gers →	**20**	44 9N	0 39 E
Gersfeld	**24**	50 27N	9 57 E
Gersoppa Falls	**70**	14 12N	74 46 E
Gerufa	**92**	19 17 S	26 0 E
Geseke	**24**	51 38N	8 29 E
Geser	**73**	3 50 S	130 54 E
Gesso →	**38**	44 24N	7 33 E
Gestro, Wabi →	**87**	4 12N	42 2 E
Getafe	**30**	40 18N	3 44W
Gethsémani	**107**	50 13N	60 40W
Gettysburg, Pa., U.S.A.	**114**	39 47N	77 18W
Gettysburg, S.D., U.S.A.	**116**	45 3N	99 56W
Getz Ice Shelf	**5**	75 0 S	130 0W
Gévaudan	**20**	44 40N	3 40 E
Gevgelija	**42**	41 9N	22 30 E
Gévora →	**31**	38 53N	6 57W
Gex	**21**	46 21N	6 3 E
Geyiklı	**44**	39 50N	26 12 E
Geyser	**118**	47 17N	110 30W
Geysir	**50**	64 19N	20 18W
Ghaghara →	**69**	25 45N	84 40 E
Ghalla, Wadi el →	**87**	10 25N	27 32 E
Ghana ■	**85**	6 0N	1 0W
Ghansor	**69**	22 39N	80 1 E
Ghanzi	**92**	21 50 S	21 34 E
Ghanzi □	**92**	21 50 S	21 45 E
Gharbîya, Es Sahrâ el	**86**	27 40N	26 30 E
Ghard Abû Muharik	**86**	26 50N	30 0 E
Ghardaïa	**82**	32 20N	3 37 E
Ghârib, G.	**86**	28 6N	32 54 E
Ghârib, Râs	**86**	28 6N	33 18 E
Gharyān	**83**	32 10N	13 0 E
Gharyān □	**83**	30 35N	12 0 E
Ghat	**83**	24 59N	10 11 E
Ghatal	**69**	22 40N	87 46 E
Ghatampur	**69**	26 8N	80 13 E
Ghatprabha →	**70**	16 15N	75 20 E
Ghayl	**64**	21 40N	46 20 E

Ghazal, Bahr el
Gorki

Ghazal, Bahr el → **81** 15 0N 17 0 E
Ghazâl, Bahr el → **87** 9 31N 30 25 E
Ghazaouet **82** 35 8N 1 50W
Ghaziabad **68** 28 42N 77 26 E
Ghazipur **69** 25 38N 83 35 E
Ghazni **66** 33 30N 68 28 E
Ghaznī □ **65** 33 0N 68 0 E
Ghedi **38** 45 24N 10 16 E
Ghelari **46** 45 38N 22 45 E
Ghèlinsor **63** 6 28N 46 39 E
Ghent = Gand **16** 51 2N 3 42 E
Gheorghe Gheorghiu-Dej **46** 46 17N 26 47 E
Gheorgheni **46** 46 43N 25 41 E
Ghergani **46** 44 37N 25 37 E
Gherla **46** 47 0N 23 57 E
Ghilarza **40** 40 8N 8 50 E
Ghisonaccia **21** 42 1N 9 26 E
Ghod → **70** 18 30N 74 35 E
Ghot Ogrein **86** 31 10N 25 20 E
Ghotaru **68** 27 20N 70 1 E
Ghotki **68** 28 5N 69 21 E
Ghowr □ **65** 34 0N 64 20 E
Ghudāmis **83** 30 11N 9 29 E
Ghugri **69** 22 39N 80 41 E
Ghugus **70** 19 58N 79 12 E
Ghulam Mohammad Barrage **68** 25 30N 68 20 E
Ghūrīān **65** 34 17N 61 25 E
Gia Nghia **71** 12 0N 107 42 E
Gian **73** 5 45N 125 20 E
Giannutri **38** 42 16N 11 5 E
Giant Mts. = Krkonoše **26** 50 50N 16 10 E
Giant's Causeway **15** 55 15N 6 30W
Giarre **41** 37 44N 15 10 E
Giaveno **38** 45 3N 7 20 E
Gibara **121** 21 9N 76 11W
Gibbon **116** 40 49N 98 45W
Gibe → **87** 7 20N 37 36 E
Gibellina **40** 37 48N 13 0 E
Gibeon **92** 25 7 S 17 45 E
Gibraléon **31** 37 23N 6 58W
Gibraltar **31** 36 7N 5 22W
Gibraltar, Str. of **31** 35 55N 5 40W
Gibson Des. **96** 24 0 S 126 0 E
Gibsons **108** 49 24N 123 32W
Giddalur **70** 15 20N 78 57 E
Giddings **117** 30 11N 96 58W
Gidole **87** 5 40N 37 25 E
Gien **19** 47 40N 2 36 E
Giessen **24** 50 34N 8 40 E
Gifatin, Geziret **86** 27 10N 33 50 E
Gifhorn **24** 52 29N 10 32 E
Gifu **74** 35 30N 136 45 E
Gifu □ **74** 35 40N 137 0 E
Gigant **57** 46 28N 41 20 E
Giganta, Sa. de la **120** 25 30N 111 30W
Gigen **43** 43 40N 24 28 E
Gigha **14** 55 42N 5 45W
Giglio **38** 42 20N 10 52 E
Gignac **20** 43 39N 3 32 E
Gigüela → **33** 39 8N 3 44W
Gijón **30** 43 32N 5 42W
Gil I. **108** 53 12N 129 15W
Gila → **119** 32 43N 114 33W
Gila Bend **119** 33 0N 112 46W
Gila Bend Mts. **119** 33 15N 113 0W
Gilan □ **64** 37 0N 48 0 E
Gilău **46** 46 45N 23 23 E
Gilbert → **97** 16 35 S 141 15 E
Gilbert Is. **94** 1 0N 176 0 E
Gilbert Plains **109** 51 9N 100 28W
Gilbert River **98** 18 9 S 142 52 E
Gilberton **98** 19 16 S 143 35 E
Gilf el Kebîr, Hadabat el **86** 23 50N 25 50 E
Gilford I. **108** 50 40N 126 30W
Gilgandra **97** 31 43 S 148 39 E
Gilgil **90** 0 30 S 36 20 E
Gilgit **69** 35 50N 74 15 E
Giljeva Planina **42** 43 9N 20 0 E
Gillam **109** 56 20N 94 40W
Gilleleje **49** 56 8N 12 19 E
Gillette **116** 44 20N 105 30W
Gilliat **98** 20 40 S 141 28 E
Gillingham **13** 51 23N 0 34 E
Gilmer **117** 32 44N 94 55W
Gilmore **99** 35 20 S 148 12 E
Gilmour **106** 44 48N 77 37W
Gilo → **87** 8 10N 33 15 E
Gilort → **46** 44 38N 23 32 E
Gilroy **119** 37 1N 121 37W
Gimbi **87** 9 3N 35 42 E
Gimigliano **41** 38 58N 16 32 E
Gimli **109** 50 40N 97 0W
Gimo **48** 60 11N 18 12 E
Gimone → **20** 44 0N 1 6 E
Gimont **20** 43 38N 0 52 E
Gimzo **62** 31 56N 34 56 E
Gin → **70** 6 5N 80 7 E
Gin Gin **99** 25 0 S 151 58 E
Ginâh **86** 25 21N 30 30 E
Gindie **98** 23 44 S 148 8 E
Gineta, La **33** 39 8N 2 1W
Gîngiova **46** 43 54N 23 50 E
Ginir **87** 7 6N 40 40 E
Ginosa **41** 40 35N 16 45 E
Ginzo de Limia **30** 42 3N 7 47W
Giohar **63** 2 48N 45 30 E
Gióia del Colle **41** 40 49N 16 55 E
Gióia, G. di **41** 38 30N 15 50 E
Gióia Táuro **41** 38 26N 15 53 E
Gioiosa Iónica **41** 38 20N 16 19 E
Gióna, Óros **45** 38 38N 22 14 E
Giong, Teluk **73** 4 50N 118 20 E
Giovi, Passo dei **38** 44 33N 8 57 E
Giovinazzo **41** 41 10N 16 40 E
Gippsland **97** 37 45 S 147 15 E
Gir Hills **68** 21 0N 71 0 E
Girab **68** 26 2N 70 38 E
Giraltovce **27** 49 7N 21 32 E
Girard, Kans., U.S.A. **117** 37 30N 94 50W
Girard, Ohio, U.S.A. **112** 41 10N 80 42W
Girard, Pa., U.S.A. **112** 42 1N 80 21W
Girardot **126** 4 18N 74 48W
Girdle Ness **14** 57 9N 2 2W
Giresun **64** 40 55N 38 30 E
Girga **86** 26 17N 31 55 E
Giridih **69** 24 10N 86 21 E
Girifalco **41** 38 49N 16 25 E
Girilambone **99** 31 16 S 146 57 E
Giro **85** 11 7N 4 42 E
Giromagny **19** 47 44N 6 50 E
Gironde □ **20** 44 45N 0 30W
Gironde → **20** 45 32N 1 7W
Gironella **32** 42 2N 1 53 E
Giru **98** 19 30 S 147 5 E
Girvan **14** 55 15N 4 50W
Gisborne **101** 38 39 S 178 5 E
Gisenyi **90** 1 41 S 29 15 E
Giske **47** 62 30N 6 3 E
Gislaved **49** 57 19N 13 32 E
Gisors **19** 49 15N 1 47 E
Gitega (Kitega) **90** 3 26 S 29 56 E
Giuba → **63** 1 30N 42 35 E
Giugliano in Campania **41** 40 55N 14 12 E
Giulianova **39** 42 45N 13 58 E
Giurgeni **46** 44 45N 27 48 E
Giurgiu **46** 43 52N 25 57 E
Giv'at Brenner **62** 31 52N 34 47 E
Giv'atayim **62** 32 4N 34 49 E
Give **49** 55 51N 9 13 E
Givet **19** 50 8N 4 49 E
Givors **21** 45 35N 4 45 E
Givry **19** 46 41N 4 46 E
Giyon **87** 8 33N 38 1 E
Giza = El Gîza **86** 30 1N 31 11 E
Gizhiga **59** 62 3N 160 30 E
Gizhiginskaya, Guba **59** 61 0N 158 0 E
Giżycko **28** 54 2N 21 48 E
Gizzeria **41** 38 57N 16 10 E
Gjegjan **44** 41 58N 20 3 E
Gjerstad **47** 58 54N 9 0 E
Gjirokastra **44** 40 7N 20 10 E
Gjoa Haven **104** 68 20N 96 8W
Gjøl **49** 57 4N 9 42 E
Gjøvik **47** 60 47N 10 43 E
Glace Bay **107** 46 11N 59 58W
Glacier B. **108** 58 30N 136 10W
Glacier Nat. Park, Can. **108** 51 15N 117 30W
Glacier Nat. Park, U.S.A. **118** 48 35N 113 40W
Glacier Park **118** 48 30N 113 18W
Glacier Peak Mt. **118** 48 7N 121 7W
Gladewater **117** 32 30N 94 58W
Gladstone, Austral. **99** 33 15 S 138 22 E
Gladstone, Can. **109** 50 13N 98 57W
Gladstone, U.S.A. **114** 45 52N 87 1W
Gladwin **114** 43 59N 84 29W
Gladys L. **108** 59 50N 133 0W
Glafsfjorden **48** 59 30N 12 37 E
Głagów Małapolski **27** 50 10N 21 56 E
Gláma **50** 65 48N 23 0W
Glåma → **47** 59 12N 10 57 E
Glamoč **39** 44 3N 16 51 E
Glan **49** 58 37N 16 0 E
Glarus **25** 47 3N 9 4 E
Glasco, Kans., U.S.A. **116** 39 25N 97 50W
Glasco, N.Y., U.S.A. **113** 42 3N 73 57W
Glasgow, U.K. **14** 55 52N 4 14W
Glasgow, Ky., U.S.A. **114** 37 2N 85 55W
Glasgow, Mont., U.S.A. **118** 48 12N 106 35W
Glastonbury, U.K. **13** 51 9N 2 42W
Glastonbury, U.S.A. **113** 41 42N 72 27W
Glauchau **24** 50 50N 12 33 E
Glazov **55** 58 9N 52 40 E
Gleisdorf **26** 47 6N 15 44 E
Gleiwitz = Gliwice **28** 50 22N 18 41 E
Glen **113** 44 7N 71 10W
Glen Affric **14** 57 15N 5 0W
Glen Canyon Dam **119** 37 0N 111 25W
Glen Canyon Nat. Recreation Area **119** 37 30N 111 0W
Glen Coe **12** 56 40N 5 0W
Glen Cove **113** 40 51N 73 37W
Glen Garry **14** 57 3N 5 7W
Glen Innes **97** 29 44 S 151 44 E
Glen Lyon **113** 41 10N 76 7W
Glen Mor **14** 57 12N 4 37 E
Glen Moriston **14** 57 10N 4 58W
Glen Orchy **14** 56 27N 4 52W
Glen Spean **14** 56 53N 4 40W
Glen Ullin **116** 46 48N 101 46W
Glénans, Îles. de **18** 47 42N 4 0W
Glenburnie **100** 37 51 S 140 50 E
Glencoe, Can. **112** 42 45N 81 43W
Glencoe, S. Afr. **93** 28 11 S 30 11 E
Glencoe, U.S.A. **116** 44 45N 94 10W
Glendale, Ariz., U.S.A. **119** 33 40N 112 8W
Glendale, Calif., U.S.A. **119** 34 7N 118 18W
Glendale, Oreg., U.S.A. **118** 42 44N 123 29W
Glendale, Zimb. **91** 17 22 S 31 5 E
Glendive **116** 47 7N 104 40W
Glendo **116** 42 30N 105 0W
Glenelg **99** 34 58 S 138 31 E
Glenelg → **99** 38 4 S 140 59 E
Glengarriff **15** 51 45N 9 33W
Glengyle **98** 24 48 S 139 37 E
Glenmora **117** 31 1N 92 34W
Glenmorgan **99** 27 14 S 149 42 E
Glenns Ferry **118** 43 0N 115 15W
Glenorchy **99** 42 49 S 147 18 E
Glenore **98** 17 50 S 141 12 E
Glenormiston **98** 22 55 S 138 50 E
Glenreagh **99** 30 2 S 153 1 E
Glenrock **118** 42 53N 105 55W
Glenrothes **14** 56 12N 3 11W
Glens Falls **114** 43 20N 73 40W
Glenties **15** 54 48N 8 18W
Glenville **114** 38 56N 80 50W
Glenwood, Alta., Can. **108** 49 21N 113 31W
Glenwood, Newf., Can. **107** 49 0N 54 58W
Glenwood, Ark., U.S.A. **117** 34 20N 93 30W
Glenwood, Hawaii, U.S.A. **110** 19 29N 155 10W
Glenwood, Iowa, U.S.A. **116** 41 7N 95 41W
Glenwood, Minn., U.S.A. **116** 45 38N 95 21W
Glenwood Sprs. **118** 39 39N 107 21W
Glina **39** 45 20N 16 6 E
Glinojeck **28** 52 49N 20 21 E
Glittertind **47** 61 40N 8 32 E
Gliwice **28** 50 22N 18 41 E
Globe **119** 33 25N 110 53W
Glodeanu Siliştea **46** 44 50N 26 48 E
Glödnitz **26** 46 53N 14 7 E
Glodyany **46** 47 45N 27 31 E
Gloggnitz **26** 47 41N 15 56 E
Głogów **28** 51 37N 16 5 E
Głogowek **28** 50 21N 17 53 E
Glorieuses, Îles **93** 11 30 S 47 20 E
Glossop **12** 53 27N 1 56W
Gloucester, Austral. **99** 32 0 S 151 59 E
Gloucester, U.K. **13** 51 52N 2 15W
Gloucester, U.S.A. **113** 42 38N 70 39W
Gloucester, C. **98** 5 26 S 148 21 E
Gloucester I. **98** 20 0 S 148 30 E
Gloucestershire □ **13** 51 44N 2 10W
Gloversville **114** 43 5N 74 18W
Glovertown **107** 48 40N 54 03W
Główno **28** 51 59N 19 42 E
Głubczyce **27** 50 13N 17 52 E
Glubokiy **57** 48 35N 40 25 E
Glubokoye **54** 55 10N 27 45 E
Glŭbovo **43** 42 8N 25 55 E
Głuchołazy **28** 50 19N 17 24 E
Glücksburg **24** 54 48N 9 34 E
Glückstadt **24** 53 46N 9 28 E
Glukhov **54** 51 40N 33 58 E
Glussk **54** 52 53N 28 41 E
Glyngøre **49** 56 46N 8 52 E
Gmünd, Kärnten, Austria **26** 46 54N 13 31 E
Gmünd, Niederösterreich, Austria **26** 48 45N 15 0 E
Gmunden **26** 47 55N 13 48 E
Gnarp **48** 62 3N 17 16 E
Gnesta **48** 59 3N 17 17 E
Gniew **28** 53 50N 18 50 E
Gniewkowo **28** 52 54N 18 25 E
Gniezno **28** 52 30N 17 35 E
Gnjilane **42** 42 28N 21 29 E
Gnoien **24** 53 58N 12 41 E
Gnosjö **49** 57 22N 13 43 E
Gnowangerup **96** 33 58 S 117 59 E
Go Cong **71** 10 22N 106 40 E
Goa **70** 15 33N 73 59 E
Goa □ **70** 15 33N 73 59 E
Goageb **92** 26 49 S 17 15 E
Goalen Hd. **99** 36 33 S 150 4 E
Goalpara **69** 26 10N 90 40 E
Goalundo Ghat **69** 23 50N 89 47 E
Goaso **84** 6 48N 2 30W
Goat Fell **14** 55 37N 5 11W
Goba **87** 7 1N 39 59 E
Gobabis **92** 22 30 S 19 0 E
Gobi **75** 44 0N 111 0 E
Gobichettipalayam **70** 11 31N 77 21 E
Gobo **87** 5 40N 31 10 E
Goch **24** 51 40N 6 9 E
Gochas **92** 24 59 S 18 55 E
Godavari → **70** 16 25N 82 18 E
Godavari Point **70** 17 0N 82 20 E
Godbout **107** 49 20N 67 38W
Godda **69** 24 50N 87 13 E
Goddua **83** 26 26N 14 19 E
Godech **42** 43 1N 23 4 E
Godegård **49** 58 43N 15 8 E
Goderich **106** 43 45N 81 41W
Goderville **18** 49 38N 0 22 E
Godhavn **4** 69 15N 53 38W
Godhra **68** 22 49N 73 40 E
Gödöllö **27** 47 38N 19 25 E
Godoy Cruz **124** 32 56 S 68 52W
Gods → **109** 56 22N 92 51W
Gods L. **109** 54 40N 94 15W
Godthåb **4** 64 10N 51 35W
Godwin Austen (K2) **69** 36 0N 77 0 E
Goeie Hoop, Kaap die **92** 34 24 S 18 30 E
Goéland, L. au **106** 49 50N 76 48W
Goeree **16** 51 50N 4 0 E
Goes **16** 51 30N 3 55 E
Gogama **106** 47 35N 81 43W
Gogango **98** 23 40 S 150 2 E
Gogebic, L. **116** 46 20N 89 34W
Gogha **68** 21 40N 72 20 E
Gogolin **28** 50 30N 18 0 E
Gogra = Ghaghara → **67** 26 0N 84 20 E
Gogriâl **87** 8 30N 28 8 E
Goiânia **127** 16 43 S 49 20W
Goiás **127** 15 55 S 50 10W
Goiás □ **127** 12 10 S 48 0W
Góis **30** 40 10N 8 6W
Goisern **26** 47 38N 13 38 E
Gojam □ **87** 10 55N 36 30 E
Gojeb, Wabi → **87** 7 12N 36 40 E
Gojra **68** 31 10N 72 40 E
Gokak **70** 16 11N 74 52 E
Gokarannath **69** 27 57N 80 39 E
Gokarn **70** 14 33N 74 17 E
Gökçeada **44** 40 10N 25 50 E
Gokteik **67** 22 26N 97 0 E
Gokurt **68** 29 40N 67 26 E
Gola **69** 28 3N 80 32 E
Golakganj **69** 26 8N 89 52 E
Golaya Pristen **56** 46 29N 32 32 E
Golchikha **4** 71 45N 83 30 E
Golconda **118** 40 58N 117 32W
Gold Beach **118** 42 25N 124 25W
Gold Coast, Austral. **99** 28 0 S 153 25 E
Gold Coast, W. Afr. **85** 4 0N 1 40W
Gold Hill **118** 42 28N 123 2W
Gold River **108** 49 46N 126 3 E
Gołdap **28** 54 19N 22 18 E
Goldberg **24** 53 34N 12 6 E
Golden, Can. **108** 51 20N 117 59W
Golden, U.S.A. **116** 39 42N 105 15W
Golden Bay **101** 40 40 S 172 50 E
Golden Gate **118** 37 54N 122 30W
Golden Hinde **108** 49 40N 125 44W
Golden Lake **112** 45 34N 77 21W
Golden Prairie **109** 50 13N 109 37W
Golden Rock **70** 10 45N 78 48 E
Golden Vale **15** 52 33N 8 17W
Goldendale **118** 45 53N 120 48W
Goldfield **119** 37 45N 117 13W
Goldfields **109** 59 28N 108 29W
Goldsand L. **109** 57 2N 101 8W
Goldsboro **115** 35 24N 77 59W
Goldsmith **117** 32 0N 102 40W
Goldthwaite **117** 31 25N 98 32W
Golegã **31** 39 24N 8 29W
Golęniów **28** 53 35N 14 50 E
Golfito **121** 8 41N 83 5W
Golfo Aranci **40** 41 0N 9 35 E
Goliad **117** 28 40N 97 22W
Golija, Crna Gora, Yugo. **42** 43 5N 18 45 E
Golija, Srbija, Yugo. **42** 43 22N 20 15 E
Golina **28** 52 15N 18 4 E
Göllersdorf **27** 48 29N 16 7 E
Golo → **21** 42 31N 9 32 E
Golovanevsk **56** 48 25N 30 30 E
Golspie **14** 57 58N 3 58W
Golub Dobrzyń **28** 53 7N 19 2 E
Golubac **42** 44 38N 21 38 E
Golyam Perelik **43** 41 36N 24 33 E
Golyama Kamchiya → **43** 43 10N 27 55 E
Goma, Rwanda **90** 2 11 S 29 18 E
Goma, Zaîre **90** 1 37 S 29 10 E
Gomare **92** 19 25 S 22 8 E
Gomati → **69** 25 32N 83 11 E
Gombari **90** 2 45N 29 3 E
Gombe **85** 10 19N 11 2 E
Gombe → **90** 4 38 S 31 40 E
Gombi **85** 10 12N 12 30 E
Gomel **54** 52 28N 31 0 E
Gomera **80** 28 7N 17 14W
Gómez Palacio **120** 25 40N 104 0W
Gommern **24** 52 5N 11 47 E
Gomogomo **73** 6 39 S 134 43 E
Gomotartsi **42** 44 6N 22 57 E
Gomphoi **44** 39 31N 21 27 E
Gonābād **65** 34 15N 58 45 E
Gonaïves **121** 19 20N 72 42W
Gonâve, G. de la **121** 19 29N 72 42W
Gonbab-e Kāvūs **65** 37 20N 55 25 E
Gönc **27** 48 28N 21 14 E
Gonda **69** 27 9N 81 58 E
Gondal **68** 21 58N 70 52 E
Gonder **87** 12 39N 37 30 E
Gondia **69** 21 23N 80 10 E
Gondola **91** 19 10 S 33 37 E
Gondomar, Port. **30** 41 10N 8 35W
Gondomar, Spain **30** 42 7N 8 45W
Gondrecourt-le-Château **19** 48 26N 5 30 E
Gonghe **75** 36 18N 100 32 E
Gongola □ **85** 8 0N 12 0 E
Gongola → **85** 9 30N 12 4 E
Goniadz **28** 53 30N 22 44 E
Goniri **85** 11 30N 12 15 E
Gonnesa **40** 39 17N 8 27 E
Gónnos **44** 39 52N 22 29 E
Gonnosfanadiga **40** 39 30N 8 39 E
Gonzales, Calif., U.S.A. **119** 36 35N 121 30W
Gonzales, Tex., U.S.A. **117** 29 30N 97 30W
González Chaves **124** 38 02 S 60 05W
Good Hope, C. of = Goeie Hoop, K. die **92** 34 24 S 18 30 E
Goodenough I. **98** 9 20 S 150 15 E
Gooderham **106** 44 54N 78 21W
Goodeve **109** 51 4N 103 10W
Gooding **118** 43 0N 114 44W
Goodland **116** 39 22N 101 44W
Goodnight **117** 35 4N 101 13W
Goodooga **99** 29 3 S 147 28 E
Goodsoil **109** 54 24N 109 13W
Goodsprings **119** 35 51N 115 30W
Goole **12** 53 42N 0 52W
Goolgowi **99** 33 58 S 145 41 E
Goombalie **99** 29 59 S 145 26 E
Goonda **91** 19 48 S 33 57 E
Goondiwindi **97** 28 30 S 150 21 E
Goor **16** 52 13N 6 33 E
Gooray **99** 28 25 S 150 2 E
Goose → **107** 53 20N 60 35W
Goose Bay **107** 53 15N 60 20W
Goose L. **118** 42 0N 120 30W
Gooty **70** 15 7N 77 41 E
Gopalganj, Bangla. **69** 23 1N 89 50 E
Gopalganj, India **69** 26 28N 84 30 E
Göppingen **25** 48 42N 9 40 E
Gor **33** 37 23N 2 58W
Góra, Leszno, Poland **28** 51 40N 16 31 E
Góra, Płock, Poland **28** 52 39N 20 6 E
Góra Kalwaria **28** 51 59N 21 14 E
Gorakhpur **69** 26 47N 83 23 E
Goražde **42** 43 38N 18 58 E
Gorbatov **55** 56 12N 43 2 E
Gorbea, Peña **32** 43 1N 2 50W
Gorda, Punta **121** 14 20N 83 10W
Gordon, Austral. **99** 32 7 S 138 20 E
Gordon, U.S.A. **116** 42 49N 102 12W
Gordon → **99** 42 27 S 145 30 E
Gordon Downs **96** 18 48 S 128 33 E
Gordon L., Alta., Can. **109** 56 30N 110 25W
Gordon L., N.W.T., Can. **108** 63 5N 113 11W
Gordonia **92** 28 13 S 21 10 E
Gordonvale **98** 17 5 S 145 50 E
Gore **99** 28 17 S 151 30 E
Goré **81** 7 59N 16 31 E
Gore, Ethiopia **87** 8 12N 35 32 E
Gore, N.Z. **101** 46 5 S 168 58 E
Gore Bay **106** 45 57N 82 28W
Gorey **15** 52 41N 6 18W
Gorgān **65** 36 55N 54 30 E
Gorgona **38** 43 27N 9 52 E
Gorgona, I. **126** 3 0N 78 10W
Gorgora **87** 12 15N 37 17 E
Gorham **113** 44 23N 71 10W
Gori **57** 42 0N 44 7 E
Gorinchem **16** 51 50N 4 59 E
Goritsy **55** 57 4N 36 43 E
Gorízia **39** 45 56N 13 37 E
Górka **28** 51 39N 16 58 E
Gorki **54** 54 17N 30 59 E

Gorki Grindsted

Gorki = Gorkiy	55	56 20N	44 0 E
Gorkiy	55	56 20N	44 0 E
Gorkovskoye Vdkhr.	55	57 2N	43 4 E
Gorlev	49	55 30N	11 15 E
Gorlice	27	49 35N	21 11 E
Görlitz	24	51 10N	14 59 E
Gorlovka	56	48 19N	38 5 E
Gorman	117	32 15N	98 43W
Gorna Oryakhovitsa	43	43 7N	25 40 E
Gornja Radgona	39	46 40N	16 2 E
Gornja Tuzla	42	44 35N	18 46 E
Gornji Grad	39	46 20N	14 52 E
Gornji Milanovac	42	44 00N	20 29 E
Gornji Vakuf	42	43 57N	17 34 E
Gorno Ablanovo	43	43 37N	25 43 E
Gorno-Altaysk	58	51 50N	86 5 E
Gorno Slinkino	58	60 5N	70 0 E
Gornyatski	52	67 32N	64 3 E
Gornyy	55	51 50N	48 30 E
Gorodenka	56	48 41N	25 29 E
Gorodets	55	56 38N	43 28 E
Gorodische	55	53 13N	45 40 E
Gorodishche	56	49 17N	31 27 E
Gorodnitsa	54	50 46N	27 19 E
Gorodnya	54	51 55N	31 33 E
Gorodok, Byelorussia, U.S.S.R.	54	55 30N	30 3 E
Gorodok, Ukraine, U.S.S.R.	54	49 46N	23 32 E
Goroka	98	6 7S	145 25 E
Gorokhov	54	50 30N	24 45 E
Gorokhovets	55	56 13N	42 39 E
Gorom Gorom	85	14 26N	0 14W
Goromonzi	91	17 52S	31 22 E
Gorong, Kepulauan	73	4 5S	131 25 E
Gorongosa, Sa. da	91	18 27S	34 2 E
Gorongose →	93	20 30S	34 40 E
Gorontalo	73	0 35N	123 5 E
Goronyo	85	13 29N	5 39 E
Górowo Iławeckie	28	54 17N	20 30 E
Gorron	18	48 25N	0 50W
Gort	15	53 4N	8 50W
Gorumahisani	69	22 20N	86 24 E
Gorzkowice	28	51 13N	19 36 E
Gorzno	28	53 12N	19 38 E
Gorzów Śląski	28	51 3N	18 22 E
Gorzów Wielkopolski	28	52 43N	15 15 E
Gorzów Wielkopolski □	28	52 45N	15 30 E
Gosford	99	33 23S	151 18 E
Goshen, S. Afr.	92	25 50S	25 0 E
Goshen, Ind., U.S.A.	114	41 36N	85 46W
Goshen, N.Y., U.S.A.	113	41 23N	74 21W
Goslar	24	51 55N	10 23 E
Gospič	39	44 35N	15 23 E
Gosport	13	50 48N	1 8W
Gostivar	42	41 48N	20 57 E
Gostyń	28	51 50N	17 3 E
Gostynin	28	52 26N	19 29 E
Göta älv →	49	57 42N	11 54 E
Göteborg	49	57 43N	11 59 E
Götene	49	58 32N	13 30 E
Gotha	24	50 56N	10 42 E
Gothenburg	116	40 58N	100 8W
Gotland	49	57 30N	18 33 E
Gotō-Rettō	74	32 55N	129 5 E
Gotse Delchev (Nevrokop)	43	41 43N	23 46 E
Göttingen	24	51 31N	9 55 E
Gottwaldov (Zlin)	27	49 14N	17 40 E
Goubangzi	76	41 20N	121 52 E
Gouda	16	52 1N	4 42 E
Goudiry	84	14 15N	12 45W
Gough I.	7	40 10S	9 45W
Gouin Rés.	106	48 35N	74 40W
Gouitafla	84	7 30N	5 53W
Goula Touila	82	21 50N	1 57W
Goulburn	97	34 44S	149 44 E
Goulburn →	100	36 6S	144 55 E
Goulburn Is.	96	11 40S	133 20 E
Goulia	84	10 1N	7 11W
Goulimine	82	28 56N	10 0W
Goulmina	82	31 41N	4 57W
Gouménissa	44	40 56N	22 37 E
Gounou-Gaya	81	9 38N	15 31 E
Goûra	45	37 56N	22 20 E
Gourara	82	29 0N	0 30 E
Gouraya	82	36 31N	1 56 E
Gourdon	20	44 44N	1 23 E
Gouré	85	14 0N	10 10 E
Gouri	81	19 36N	19 36 E
Gourits →	92	34 21S	21 52 E
Gourma Rharous	85	16 55N	1 50W
Gournay-en-Bray	19	49 29N	1 44 E
Gourock Ra.	99	36 0S	149 25 E
Goursi	84	12 42N	2 37W
Gouverneur	113	44 18N	75 30W
Gouzon	20	46 12N	2 14 E
Govan	109	51 20N	105 0W
Gove	97	12 25S	136 55 E
Governador Valadares	127	18 15S	41 57W
Gowan Ra.	98	25 0S	145 0 E
Gowanda	114	42 29N	78 58W
Gowd-e Zirreh	65	29 45N	62 0 E
Gower, The	13	51 35N	4 10W
Gowna, L.	15	53 52N	7 35W
Gowrie, Carse of	14	56 30N	3 10W
Goya	124	29 10S	59 10W
Goyllarisquisga	126	10 31S	76 24W
Goz Beïda	81	12 10N	21 20 E
Goz Regeb	87	16 3N	35 33 E
Gozdnica	28	51 28N	15 4 E
Gozo (Ghawdex)	36	36 0N	14 13 E
Graaff-Reinet	92	32 13S	24 32 E
Grabow	24	53 17N	11 31 E
Grabów	28	51 31N	18 7 E
Gračac	39	44 18N	15 57 E
Gračanica	42	44 43N	18 18 E
Graçay	19	47 10N	1 50 E
Grace	118	42 38N	111 46W
Graceville	116	45 36N	96 23W
Gracias a Dios, C.	121	15 0N	83 10W
Gradačac	42	44 52N	18 26 E
Gradeška Planina	42	41 30N	22 15 E
Gradets	43	42 46N	26 30 E
Grado, Italy	39	45 40N	13 20 E
Grado, Spain	30	43 23N	6 4W
Gradule	99	28 32S	149 15 E
Grady	117	34 52N	103 15W
Graeca, Lacul	46	44 5N	26 10 E
Graënalon, L.	50	64 10N	17 20W
Grafenau	25	48 51N	13 24 E
Gräfenberg	25	49 39N	11 15 E
Grafton, Austral.	97	29 38S	152 58 E
Grafton, U.S.A.	116	48 30N	97 25W
Grafton, C.	97	16 51S	146 0 E
Gragnano	41	40 42N	14 30 E
Graham, Can.	106	49 20N	90 30W
Graham, N.C., U.S.A.	115	36 5N	79 22W
Graham, Tex., U.S.A.	117	33 7N	98 38W
Graham →	108	56 31N	122 17W
Graham Bell, Os.	58	80 5N	70 0 E
Graham I.	108	53 40N	132 30W
Graham Land	5	65 0S	64 0W
Graham Mt.	119	32 46N	109 58W
Grahamdale	109	51 23N	98 30W
Grahamstown	92	33 19S	26 31 E
Grahovo	42	42 40N	18 40 E
Graïba	83	34 30N	10 13 E
Graie, Alpi	38	45 30N	7 10 E
Grain Coast	84	4 20N	10 0W
Grajaú	127	5 50S	46 4W
Grajaú →	127	3 41S	44 48W
Grajewo	28	53 39N	22 30 E
Gral. Martin Miguel de Güemes	124	24 50S	65 0W
Gramada	42	43 49N	22 39 E
Gramat	20	44 48N	1 43 E
Grammichele	41	37 12N	14 37 E
Grámmos, Óros	44	40 18N	20 47 E
Grampian □	14	57 0N	3 0W
Grampian Mts.	14	56 50N	4 0W
Grampians, Mts.	99	37 0S	142 20 E
Gran Canaria	80	27 55N	15 35W
Gran Chaco	124	25 0S	61 0W
Gran Paradiso	38	45 33N	7 17 E
Gran Sasso d'Italia	39	42 25N	13 30 E
Granada, Nic.	121	11 58N	86 0W
Granada, Spain	33	37 10N	3 35W
Granada, U.S.A.	117	38 5N	102 20W
Granada □	31	37 18N	3 0W
Granard	15	53 47N	7 30W
Granbury	117	32 28N	97 48W
Granby	106	45 25N	72 45W
Grand →, Mo., U.S.A.	116	39 23N	93 6W
Grand →, Mo., U.S.A.	116	39 23N	93 6W
Grand →, S.D., U.S.A.	116	45 40N	100 32W
Grand Bahama	121	26 40N	78 30W
Grand Bank	107	47 6N	55 48W
Grand Bassam	84	5 10N	3 49W
Grand Béréby	84	4 38N	6 55W
Grand-Bourge	121	15 53N	61 19W
Grand Canyon	119	36 3N	112 9W
Grand Canyon National Park	119	36 15N	112 20W
Grand Cayman	121	19 20N	81 20W
Grand Cess	84	4 40N	8 12W
Grand-Combe, La	21	44 13N	4 2 E
Grand Coulee	118	47 48N	119 1W
Grand Coulee Dam	118	48 0N	118 50W
Grand Erg Occidental	82	30 20N	1 0 E
Grand Erg Oriental	83	30 0N	6 30 E
Grand Falls	107	48 56N	55 40W
Grand Forks, Can.	108	49 0N	118 30W
Grand Forks, U.S.A.	116	48 0N	97 3W
Grand-Fougeray	18	47 44N	1 43W
Grand Haven	114	43 3N	86 13W
Grand I.	106	46 30N	86 40W
Grand Island	116	40 59N	98 25W
Grand Isle	117	29 15N	89 58W
Grand Junction	119	39 0N	108 30W
Grand L., N.B., Can.	107	45 57N	66 7W
Grand L., Newf., Can.	107	53 40N	60 30W
Grand L., Newf., Can.	107	49 0N	57 30W
Grand L., U.S.A.	117	29 55N	92 45W
Grand Lac Victoria	106	47 35N	77 35W
Grand Lahou	84	5 10N	5 0W
Grand Lake	118	40 20N	105 54W
Grand-Lieu, Lac de	18	47 6N	1 40W
Grand-Luce, Le	18	47 52N	0 28 E
Grand Manan I.	107	44 45N	66 52W
Grand Marais, Can.	116	47 45N	90 25W
Grand Marais, U.S.A.	114	46 39N	85 59W
Grand Mère	106	46 36N	72 40W
Grand Popo	85	6 15N	1 57 E
Grand Portage	106	47 58N	89 41W
Grand-Pressigny, Le	18	46 55N	0 48 E
Grand Rapids, Can.	109	53 12N	99 19W
Grand Rapids, Mich., U.S.A.	114	42 57N	86 40W
Grand Rapids, Minn., U.S.A.	116	47 15N	93 29W
Grand St.-Bernard, Col. du	25	45 53N	7 11 E
Grand Teton	118	43 54N	111 50W
Grand Valley	118	39 30N	108 2W
Grand View	109	51 10N	100 42W
Grandas de Salime	30	43 13N	6 53W
Grande →, Jujuy, Argent.	124	24 20S	65 2W
Grande →, Mendoza, Argent.	124	36 52S	69 45W
Grande →, Boliv.	126	15 51S	64 39W
Grande →, Bahia, Brazil	127	11 30S	44 30W
Grande →, Minas Gerais, Brazil	127	20 6S	51 4W
Grande →, Spain	33	39 6N	0 48W
Grande →, U.S.A.	117	25 57N	97 9W
Grande, B.	128	50 30S	68 20W
Grande Baie	107	48 19N	70 52W
Grande Baleine →	106	55 20N	77 50W
Grande Cache	108	53 53N	119 8W
Grande, Coxilha	125	28 18S	51 30W
Grande de Santiago →	120	21 20N	105 50W
Grande-Entrée	107	47 30N	61 40W
Grande, La	118	45 15N	118 0W
Grande-Motte, La	21	43 23N	4 3 E
Grande Prairie	108	55 10N	118 50W
Grande-Rivière	107	48 26N	64 30W
Grande-Saulde →	19	47 22N	1 55 E
Grande-Vallée	107	49 14N	65 8W
Grandes-Bergeronnes	107	48 16N	69 35W
Grandfalls	117	31 21N	102 51W
Grandoe Mines	108	56 29N	129 54W
Grândola	31	38 12N	8 35W
Grandpré	19	49 20N	4 50 E
Grandview	118	46 13N	119 58W
Grandvilliers	19	49 40N	1 57 E
Graneros	124	34 5S	70 45W
Grange, La, Ga., U.S.A.	115	33 4N	85 0W
Grange, La, Ky., U.S.A.	114	38 20N	85 20W
Grange, La, Tex., U.S.A.	117	29 54N	96 52W
Grangemouth	14	56 1N	3 43W
Granger, U.S.A.	118	46 25N	120 5W
Granger, Wyo., U.S.A.	118	41 35N	109 58W
Grängesberg	48	60 6N	15 1 E
Grangeville	118	45 57N	116 4W
Granite City	116	38 45N	90 3W
Granite Falls	116	44 45N	95 35W
Granite Pk.	118	45 8N	109 52W
Granity	101	41 39S	171 51 E
Granja	127	3 7S	40 50W
Granja de Moreruela	30	41 48N	5 44W
Granja de Torrehermosa	31	38 19N	5 35W
Gränna	49	58 1N	14 28 E
Granollers	32	41 39N	2 18 E
Gransee	24	53 0N	13 10 E
Grant	116	40 53N	101 42W
Grant City	116	40 30N	94 25W
Grant, Mt.	118	38 34N	118 48W
Grant, Pt.	100	38 32S	145 6 E
Grant Range Mts.	119	38 30N	115 30W
Grantham	12	52 55N	0 39W
Grantown-on-Spey	14	57 19N	3 36W
Grants	119	35 14N	107 51W
Grants Pass	118	42 30N	123 22W
Grantsburg	116	45 46N	92 44W
Grantsville	118	40 35N	112 32W
Granville, France	18	48 50N	1 35W
Granville, N.D., U.S.A.	116	48 18N	100 48W
Granville, N.Y., U.S.A.	114	43 24N	73 16W
Granville L.	109	56 18N	100 30W
Grao de Gandia	33	39 0N	0 7W
Grapeland	117	31 30N	95 31W
Gras, L. de	104	64 30N	110 30W
Graskop	93	24 56S	30 49 E
Gräsö	48	60 28N	18 35 E
Grass →	109	56 3N	96 33W
Grass Range	118	47 0N	109 0W
Grass River Prov. Park	109	54 40N	100 50W
Grass Valley, Calif., U.S.A.	118	39 18N	121 0W
Grass Valley, Oreg., U.S.A.	118	45 22N	120 48W
Grassano	41	40 38N	16 17 E
Grasse	21	43 38N	6 56 E
Graubünden (Grisons) □	25	46 45N	9 30 E
Graulhet	20	43 45N	1 58 E
Graus	32	42 11N	0 20 E
Grave, Pte. de	20	45 34N	1 4W
Gravelbourg	109	49 50N	106 35W
Gravelines	19	51 0N	2 10 E
's-Gravenhage	16	52 7N	4 17 E
Gravenhurst	112	44 52N	79 20W
Gravesend, Austral.	99	29 35S	150 20 E
Gravesend, U.K.	13	51 25N	0 22 E
Gravina di Púglia	41	40 48N	16 25 E
Gravois, Pointe-à-	121	16 15N	73 56W
Gravone →	21	41 58N	8 45 E
Gray	19	47 27N	5 35 E
Grayling	114	44 40N	84 42W
Grayling →	108	59 21N	125 0W
Grays Harbor	118	46 55N	124 8W
Grays L.	118	43 8N	111 30W
Grayson	109	50 45N	102 40W
Graz	26	47 4N	15 27 E
Grazalema	31	36 46N	5 23W
Grdelica	42	42 55N	22 3 E
Greasy L.	108	62 55N	122 12W
Great Abaco I.	121	26 25N	77 10W
Great Australia Basin	97	26 0S	140 0 E
Great Australian Bight	96	33 30S	130 0 E
Great Bahama Bank	121	23 15N	78 0W
Great Barrier I.	101	36 11S	175 25 E
Great Barrier Reef	97	18 0S	146 50 E
Great Barrington	113	42 11N	73 22W
Great Basin	118	40 0N	116 30W
Great Bear →	104	65 0N	124 0W
Great Bear L.	104	65 30N	120 0W
Great Bena	113	41 57N	75 45W
Great Bend	116	38 25N	98 55W
Great Blasket I.	15	52 5N	10 30W
Great Britain	8	54 0N	2 15W
Great Bushman Land	92	29 20S	19 20 E
Great Central	108	49 20N	125 10W
Great Divide, The	100	35 0S	149 17 E
Great Dividing Ra.	97	23 0S	146 0 E
Great Exuma I.	121	23 30N	75 50W
Great Falls, Can.	109	50 27N	96 1W
Great Falls, U.S.A.	118	47 27N	111 12W
Great Fish →, C. Prov., S. Afr.	92	31 30S	20 16 E
Great Fish →, C. Prov., S. Afr.	92	33 28S	27 5 E
Great Guana Cay	121	24 0N	76 20W
Great Harbour Deep	107	50 25N	56 32W
Great I.	109	58 53N	96 35W
Great Inagua I.	121	21 0N	73 20W
Great Indian Desert = Thar Desert	68	28 0N	72 0 E
Great Lake	97	41 50S	146 40 E
Great Orme's Head	12	53 20N	3 52W
Great Ouse →	12	52 47N	0 22 E
Great Palm I.	98	18 45S	146 40 E
Great Plains	102	47 0N	105 0W
Great Ruaha →	90	7 56S	37 52 E
Great Salt Lake	102	41 0N	112 30W
Great Salt Lake Desert	118	40 20N	113 50W
Great Salt Plains Res.	117	36 40N	98 15W
Great Sandy Desert	96	21 0S	124 0 E
Great Scarcies →	84	9 0N	13 0W
Great Slave L.	108	61 23N	115 38W
Great Smoky Mt. Nat. Park	115	35 39N	83 30W
Great Stour →	13	51 15N	1 20 E
Great Victoria Des.	96	29 30S	126 30 E
Great Wall	76	38 30N	109 30 E
Great Whernside	12	54 9N	1 59W
Great Winterhoek	92	33 07S	19 10 E
Great Yarmouth	12	52 40N	1 45 E
Greater Antilles	121	17 40N	74 0W
Greater London □	13	51 30N	0 5W
Greater Manchester □	12	53 30N	2 15W
Greater Sunda Is.	72	7 0S	112 0 E
Grebbestad	49	58 42N	11 15 E
Grebenka	54	50 9N	32 22 E
Greco, Mte.	40	41 48N	14 0 E
Gredos, Sierra de	30	40 20N	5 0W
Greece ■	44	40 0N	23 0 E
Greeley, Colo., U.S.A.	116	40 30N	104 40W
Greeley, Nebr., U.S.A.	116	41 36N	98 32W
Green →, Ky., U.S.A.	114	37 54N	87 30W
Green →, Utah, U.S.A.	119	38 11N	109 53W
Green B.	114	45 0N	87 30W
Green Bay	114	44 30N	88 0W
Green C.	99	37 13S	150 1 E
Green Cove Springs	115	29 59N	81 40W
Green Is.	98	4 35S	154 10 E
Green Island	101	45 55S	170 26 E
Green River	119	38 59N	110 10W
Greenbush, Mich., U.S.A.	112	44 35N	83 19W
Greenbush, Minn., U.S.A.	116	48 46N	96 10W
Greencastle	114	39 40N	86 48W
Greene	113	42 20N	75 45W
Greenfield, Ind., U.S.A.	114	39 47N	85 51W
Greenfield, Iowa, U.S.A.	116	41 18N	94 28W
Greenfield, Mass., U.S.A.	114	42 38N	72 38W
Greenfield, Miss., U.S.A.	117	37 28N	93 50W
Greenfield Park	113	45 29N	73 29W
Greenland □	4	66 0N	45 0W
Greenland Sea	4	73 0N	10 0W
Greenock	14	55 57N	4 46W
Greenore	15	54 2N	6 8W
Greenore Pt.	15	52 15N	6 20W
Greenport	113	41 5N	72 23W
Greensboro, Ga., U.S.A.	115	33 34N	83 12W
Greensboro, N.C., U.S.A.	115	36 7N	79 46W
Greensburg, Ind., U.S.A.	114	39 20N	85 30W
Greensburg, Kans., U.S.A.	117	37 38N	99 20W
Greensburg, Pa., U.S.A.	114	40 18N	79 31W
Greenville, Liberia	84	5 1N	9 6W
Greenville, Ala., U.S.A.	115	31 50N	86 37W
Greenville, Calif., U.S.A.	118	40 8N	121 0W
Greenville, Ill., U.S.A.	116	38 53N	89 22W
Greenville, Me., U.S.A.	107	45 30N	69 32W
Greenville, Mich., U.S.A.	114	43 12N	85 14W
Greenville, Miss., U.S.A.	117	33 25N	91 0W
Greenville, N.C., U.S.A.	115	35 37N	77 26W
Greenville, Ohio, U.S.A.	114	40 5N	84 38W
Greenville, Pa., U.S.A.	114	41 23N	80 22W
Greenville, S.C., U.S.A.	115	34 54N	82 24W
Greenville, Tenn., U.S.A.	115	36 13N	82 51W
Greenville, Tex., U.S.A.	117	33 5N	96 5W
Greenwater Lake Prov. Park	109	52 32N	103 30W
Greenwich, U.K.	13	51 28N	0 0
Greenwich, Conn., U.S.A.	113	41 1N	73 38W
Greenwich, N.Y., U.S.A.	113	43 2N	73 36W
Greenwich, Ohio, U.S.A.	112	41 1N	82 32W
Greenwood, Can.	108	49 10N	118 40W
Greenwood, Miss., U.S.A.	117	33 30N	90 4W
Greenwood, S.C., U.S.A.	115	34 13N	82 13W
Gregory	116	43 14N	99 20W
Gregory →	98	17 53S	139 17 E
Gregory Downs	98	18 35S	138 45 E
Gregory, L.	97	28 55S	139 0 E
Gregory Lake	96	20 10S	127 30 E
Gregory Ra.	97	19 30S	143 40 E
Greiffenberg	24	53 6N	13 57 E
Greifswald	24	54 6N	13 23 E
Greifswalder Bodden	24	54 12N	13 35 E
Greifswalder Oie	24	54 15N	13 55 E
Grein	26	48 14N	14 51 E
Greiner Wald	26	48 30N	15 0 E
Greiz	24	50 39N	12 12 E
Gremikha	52	67 50N	39 40 E
Grenå	49	56 25N	10 53 E
Grenada	117	33 45N	89 50W
Grenada ■	121	12 10N	61 40W
Grenade	20	43 47N	1 17 E
Grenadines	121	12 40N	61 20W
Grenen	49	57 44N	10 40 E
Grenfell, Austral.	99	33 52S	148 8 E
Grenfell, Can.	109	50 30N	102 56W
Grenoble	21	45 12N	5 42 E
Grenora	116	48 38N	103 54W
Grenville, C.	97	12 0S	143 13 E
Grenville Chan.	108	53 40N	129 46W
Gréoux-les-Bains	21	43 45N	5 52 E
Gresham	118	45 30N	122 25W
Gresik	73	7 13S	112 38 E
Grëssoney St. Jean	38	45 49N	7 47 E
Gretna Green	14	55 0N	3 3W
Greven	24	52 7N	7 36 E
Grevená	44	40 4N	21 25 E
Grevená □	44	40 2N	21 25 E
Grevenbroich	24	51 6N	6 32 E
Grevenmacher	16	49 41N	6 26 E
Grevesmühlen	24	53 51N	11 10 E
Grevie	49	56 22N	12 46 E
Grey →	101	42 27S	171 12 E
Grey, C.	97	13 0S	136 35 E
Grey Range	97	27 0S	143 30 E
Grey Res.	107	48 20N	56 30W
Greybull	118	44 30N	108 3W
Greytown, N.Z.	101	41 5S	175 29 E
Greytown, S. Afr.	93	29 1S	30 36 E
Gribanovskiy	55	51 28N	41 50 E
Gribbell I.	108	53 23N	129 0W
Gridley	118	39 27N	121 47W
Griekwastad	92	28 49S	23 15 E
Griffin	115	33 17N	84 14W
Griffith	97	34 18S	146 2 E
Grillby	48	59 38N	17 15 E
Grim, C.	97	40 45S	144 45 E
Grimari	88	5 43N	20 6 E
Grimaylov	54	49 20N	26 5 E
Grimma	24	51 14N	12 44 E
Grimmen	24	54 6N	13 2 E
Grimsby	112	43 12N	79 34W
Grimsby, Greater	12	53 35N	0 5W
Grimsey	50	66 33N	18 0W
Grimshaw	108	56 10N	117 40W
Grimstad	47	58 22N	8 35 E
Grindelwald	25	46 38N	8 2 E
Grindsted	49	55 46N	8 55 E

Grindu Haifeng

Grindu **46** 44 44N 26 50 E
Grinnell **116** 41 45N 92 43W
Griñón **30** 40 13N 3 51W
Grintavec **39** 46 22N 14 32 E
Grip **47** 63 16N 7 37 E
Griqualand East **93** 30 30 S 29 0 E
Griqualand West **92** 28 40 S 23 30 E
Grisolles **20** 43 49N 1 19 E
Grisslehamn **48** 60 5N 18 49 E
Griz Nez, C. **19** 50 50N 1 35 E
Grmeč Planina **39** 44 43N 16 16 E
Groais I. **107** 50 55N 55 35W
Groblersdal **93** 25 15 S 29 25 E
Grobming **26** 47 27N 13 54 E
Grocka **42** 44 40N 20 42 E
Gródek **28** 53 6N 23 40 E
Grodkow **28** 50 43N 17 21 E
Grodno **54** 53 42N 23 52 E
Grodzisk Mázowiecki **28** 52 7N 20 37 E
Grodzisk Wielkopolski **28** 52 15N 16 22 E
Grodzyanka **54** 53 31N 28 42 E
Groesbeck **117** 31 32N 96 34W
Groix **18** 47 38N 3 29W
Groix, I. de **18** 47 38N 3 28W
Grójec **28** 51 50N 20 58 E
Gronau, Niedersachsen, Ger. **24** 52 5N 9 47 E
Gronau, Nordrhein-Westfalen, Ger. **24** 52 13N 7 2 E
Grong **50** 64 25N 12 8 E
Groningen **16** 53 15N 6 35 E
Groningen □ **16** 53 16N 6 40 E
Grönskåra **49** 57 5N 15 43 E
Groom **117** 35 12N 100 59W
Groot → **92** 33 45 S 24 36 E
Groot Berg → **92** 32 47 S 18 8 E
Groot-Brakrivier **92** 34 2 S 22 18 E
Groot Karoo **92** 32 35 S 23 0 E
Groote Eylandt **97** 14 0 S 136 40 E
Grootfontein **92** 19 31 S 18 6 E
Grootlaagte → **92** 20 55 S 21 27 E
Gros C. **108** 61 59N 113 32W
Grosa, P. **33** 39 6N 1 36 E
Grósio **38** 46 18N 10 17 E
Grosne → **21** 46 42N 4 56 E
Gross Glockner **26** 47 5N 12 40 E
Gross Ottersleben **24** 52 5N 11 33 E
Grossenbrode **24** 54 21N 11 4 E
Grossenhain **24** 51 17N 13 32 E
Grosseto **38** 42 45N 11 7 E
Grossgerungs **26** 48 34N 14 57 E
Groswater B. **107** 54 20N 57 40W
Groton, Conn., U.S.A. **113** 41 22N 72 12W
Groton, S.D., U.S.A. **116** 45 27N 98 6W
Grottáglie **41** 40 32N 17 25 E
Grottaminarda **41** 41 5N 15 4 E
Grottammare **39** 42 59N 13 52 E
Grouard Mission **108** 55 33N 116 9W
Grouin, Pointe du **18** 48 43N 1 51W
Groundhog → **106** 48 45N 82 58W
Grouse Creek **118** 41 44N 113 57W
Grove City **112** 41 10N 80 5W
Groveton, N.H., U.S.A. **114** 44 34N 71 30W
Groveton, Tex., U.S.A. **117** 31 5N 95 4W
Groznjan **39** 45 22N 13 43 E
Groznyy **57** 43 20N 45 45 E
Grubišno Polje **42** 45 44N 17 12 E
Grudovo **43** 42 21N 27 10 E
Grudusk **28** 53 3N 20 38 E
Grudziądz **28** 53 30N 18 47 E
Gruissan **20** 43 8N 3 7 E
Grumo Áppula **41** 41 2N 16 43 E
Grums **48** 59 22N 13 5 E
Grünberg **24** 50 37N 8 55 E
Grundy Center **116** 42 22N 92 45W
Grungedal **47** 59 44N 7 43 E
Gruver **117** 36 19N 101 20W
Gruyères **25** 46 35N 7 4 E
Gruža **42** 43 54N 20 46 E
Gryazi **55** 52 30N 39 58 E
Gryazovets **55** 58 50N 40 10 E
Grybów **27** 49 36N 20 55 E
Grycksbo **48** 60 40N 15 29 E
Gryfice **28** 53 55N 15 13 E
Gryfino **28** 53 16N 14 29 E
Gryfow Sl. **28** 51 2N 15 24 E
Grythyttan **48** 59 41N 14 32 E
Grytviken **5** 53 50 S 37 10W
Gstaad **25** 46 28N 7 18 E
Guacanayabo, G. de **121** 20 40N 77 20W
Guachípas → **124** 25 40 S 65 30W
Guadajoz → **31** 37 50N 4 51W
Guadalajara, Mexico **120** 20 40N 103 20W
Guadalajara, Spain **32** 40 37N 3 12W
Guadalajara □ **32** 40 47N 3 0W
Guadalcanal, Solomon Is. **94** 9 32 S 160 12 E
Guadalcanal, Spain **31** 38 5N 5 52W
Guadalén → **31** 38 5N 3 32W
Guadales **124** 34 30 S 67 55W
Guadalete → **31** 36 35N 6 13W
Guadalhorce → **31** 36 41N 4 27W
Guadalimar → **33** 38 5N 3 28W
Guadalmena → **33** 38 19N 2 56W
Guadalmez → **31** 38 46N 5 4W
Guadalope → **32** 41 15N 0 3W
Guadalquivir → **31** 36 47N 6 22W
Guadalupe, Spain **31** 39 27N 5 17W
Guadalupe, U.S.A. **119** 34 59N 120 33W
Guadalupe → **117** 28 30N 96 53W
Guadalupe Bravos **120** 31 20N 106 10W
Guadalupe I. **95** 21 20N 118 50W
Guadalupe Pk. **119** 31 50N 105 30W
Guadalupe, Sierra de **31** 39 28N 5 30W
Guadarrama, Sierra de **30** 41 0N 4 0W
Guadeloupe **121** 16 20N 61 40W
Guadeloupe Passage **121** 16 50N 62 15W
Guadiamar → **31** 36 55N 6 24W
Guadiana → **31** 37 14N 7 22W
Guadiana Menor → **33** 37 56N 3 15W
Guadiaro → **31** 36 17N 5 17W
Guadiato → **31** 37 48N 5 5W
Guadiela → **32** 40 22N 2 49W
Guadix **33** 37 18N 3 11W
Guafo, Boca del **128** 43 35 S 74 0W
Guaíra **125** 24 5 S 54 10W
Guaira, La **126** 10 36N 66 56W
Guaitecas, Islas **128** 44 0 S 74 30W
Guajará-Mirim **126** 10 50 S 65 20W
Guajira, Pen. de la **126** 12 0N 72 0W
Gualdo Tadino **39** 43 14N 12 46 E
Gualeguay **124** 33 10 S 59 14W
Gualeguaychú **124** 33 3 S 59 31W
Guam **94** 13 27N 144 45 E
Guaminí **124** 37 1 S 62 28W
Guamúchil **120** 25 25N 108 3W
Guan Xian **75** 31 2N 103 38 E
Guanabacoa **121** 23 8N 82 18W
Guanacaste, Cordillera del **121** 10 40N 85 4W
Guanaceví **120** 25 40N 106 0W
Guanahani = San Salvador, I. **121** 24 0N 74 40W
Guanajay **121** 22 56N 82 42W
Guanajuato **120** 21 0N 101 20W
Guanajuato □ **120** 20 40N 101 20W
Guanare **126** 8 42N 69 12W
Guandacol **124** 29 30 S 68 40W
Guane **121** 22 10N 84 7W
Guang'an **77** 30 28N 106 35 E
Guangde **77** 30 54N 119 25 E
Guangdong □ **75** 23 0N 113 0 E
Guanghua **75** 32 22N 111 38 E
Guangshun **77** 26 8N 106 21 E
Guangxi Zhuangzu Zizhiqu □ **75** 24 0N 109 0 E
Guangyuan **77** 32 26N 105 51 E
Guangze **77** 27 30N 117 12 E
Guangzhou **75** 23 5N 113 10 E
Guanipa → **126** 9 56N 62 26W
Guantánamo **121** 20 10N 75 14W
Guantao **76** 36 42N 115 25 E
Guanyun **77** 34 20N 119 18 E
Guápiles **121** 10 10N 83 46W
Guaporé → **126** 11 55 S 65 4W
Guaqui **126** 16 41 S 68 54W
Guara, Sierra de **32** 42 19N 0 15W
Guarapari **125** 20 40 S 40 30W
Guarapuava **125** 25 20 S 51 30W
Guaratinguetá **125** 22 49 S 45 9W
Guaratuba **125** 25 53 S 48 38W
Guarda **30** 40 32N 7 20W
Guarda □ **30** 40 40N 7 20W
Guardafui, C. = Asir, Ras **63** 11 55N 51 16 E
Guardamar del Segura **33** 38 5N 0 39W
Guardavalle **41** 38 31N 16 30 E
Guardia, La **30** 41 56N 8 52W
Guardiagrele **39** 42 11N 14 11 E
Guardo **30** 42 47N 4 50W
Guareña **31** 38 51N 6 6W
Guareña → **30** 41 29N 5 23W
Guaria □ **124** 25 45 S 56 30W
Guarujá **125** 24 2 S 46 25W
Guarus **125** 21 44 S 41 20W
Guasdualito **126** 7 15N 70 44W
Guasipati **126** 7 28N 61 54W
Guastalla **38** 44 55N 10 40 E
Guatemala **120** 14 40N 90 22W
Guatemala ■ **120** 15 40N 90 30W
Guatire **126** 10 28N 66 32W
Guaviare → **126** 4 3N 67 44W
Guaxupé **125** 21 10 S 47 5W
Guayama **121** 17 59N 66 7W
Guayaquil **126** 2 15 S 79 52W
Guayaquil, G. de **126** 3 10 S 81 0W
Guaymas **120** 27 59N 110 54W
Guazhou **77** 32 17N 119 21 E
Guba **91** 10 38 S 26 27 E
Gûbâl **86** 27 30N 34 0 E
Gúbbio **39** 43 20N 12 34 E
Gubin **28** 51 57N 14 43 E
Gubio **85** 12 30N 12 42 E
Gubkin **55** 51 17N 37 32 E
Guča **42** 43 46N 20 15 E
Guchil **71** 5 35N 102 10 E
Gudalur **70** 11 30N 76 29 E
Gudata **57** 43 7N 40 10 E
Gudenå **49** 56 27N 9 40 E
Gudermes **57** 43 24N 46 5 E
Gudhjem **49** 55 12N 14 58 E
Gudiña, La **30** 42 4N 7 8W
Gudivada **70** 16 30N 81 3 E
Gudiyatam **70** 12 57N 78 55 E
Gudur **70** 14 12N 79 55 E
Guebwiller **19** 47 55N 7 12 E
Guecho **32** 43 21N 2 59W
Guékédou **84** 8 40N 10 5W
Guelma **83** 36 25N 7 29 E
Guelph **106** 43 35N 80 20W
Guelt es Stel **82** 35 12N 3 1 E
Guelttara **82** 29 23N 2 10W
Guemar **83** 33 30N 6 49 E
Guéméné-Penfao **18** 47 38N 1 50W
Guéméné-sur-Scorff **18** 48 4N 3 13W
Guéné **85** 11 44N 3 16 E
Guer **18** 47 54N 2 8W
Güera, La **80** 20 51N 17 0W
Guérande **18** 47 20N 2 26W
Guerche, La **18** 47 57N 1 16W
Guerche-sur-l'Aubois, La **19** 46 58N 2 56 E
Guercif **82** 34 14N 3 21W
Guéréda **81** 14 31N 22 5 E
Guéret **20** 46 11N 1 51 E
Guérigny **19** 47 6N 3 10 E
Guernica **32** 43 19N 2 40W
Guernsey, Chan. Is. **18** 49 30N 2 35W
Guernsey, U.S.A. **116** 42 19N 104 45W
Guerrara, Oasis, Alg. **83** 32 51N 4 22 E
Guerrara, Saoura, Alg. **82** 28 5N 0 8W
Guerrero □ **120** 17 30N 100 0W
Guerzim **82** 29 39N 1 40W
Guest I. **5** 76 18 S 148 0W
Gueugnon **21** 46 36N 4 4 E
Gueydan **117** 30 3N 92 30W
Guglionesi **41** 41 55N 14 54 E
Gui Jiang → **77** 23 30N 111 15 E
Gui Xian **77** 23 8N 109 35 E
Guia Lopes da Laguna **125** 21 26 S 56 7W
Guichi **77** 30 39N 117 27 E
Guider **85** 9 56N 13 57 E
Guidimouni **85** 13 42N 9 31 E
Guidong **77** 26 7N 113 57 E
Guiglo **84** 6 45N 7 30W
Guijo de Coria **30** 40 6N 6 28W
Guildford **13** 51 14N 0 34W
Guilford **107** 45 12N 69 25W
Guilin **75** 25 18N 110 15 E
Guillaumes **21** 44 5N 6 52 E
Guillestre **21** 44 39N 6 40 E
Guilvinec **18** 47 48N 4 17W
Guimarães, Braz. **127** 2 9 S 44 42W
Guimarães, Port. **30** 41 28N 8 24W
Guimaras **73** 10 35N 122 37 E
Guinea ■ **84** 10 20N 10 0W
Guinea-Bissau ■ **84** 12 0N 15 0W
Guinea, Gulf of **85** 3 0N 2 30 E
Güines **121** 22 50N 82 0W
Guingamp **18** 48 34N 3 10W
Guipavas **18** 48 26N 4 29W
Guiping **75** 23 21N 110 2 E
Guipúzcoa □ **32** 43 12N 2 15W
Guir, O. → **82** 31 29N 2 17W
Güiria **126** 10 32N 62 18W
Guiscard **19** 49 40N 3 0 E
Guise **19** 49 52N 3 35 E
Guitiriz **30** 43 11N 7 50W
Guiuan **73** 11 5N 125 55 E
Guixi **77** 28 16N 117 15 E
Guiyang, Guizhou, China **75** 26 32N 106 40 E
Guiyang, Hunan, China **77** 25 46N 112 42 E
Guizhou □ **75** 27 0N 107 0 E
Gujan-Mestras **20** 44 38N 1 4W
Gujarat □ **68** 23 20N 71 0 E
Gujranwala **68** 32 10N 74 12 E
Gujrat **68** 32 40N 74 2 E
Gukovo **57** 48 1N 39 58 E
Gulargambone **100** 31 20 S 148 30 E
Gulbarga **70** 17 20N 76 50 E
Gulbene **54** 57 8N 26 52 E
Guledgud **70** 16 3N 75 48 E
Gulf Basin **96** 15 20 S 129 0 E
Gulfport **117** 30 21N 89 3W
Gulgong **99** 32 20 S 149 49 E
Gulistan **68** 30 30N 66 35 E
Gull Lake **109** 50 10N 108 29W
Gullringen **49** 57 48N 15 44 E
Gulma **85** 12 40N 4 23 E
Gülpinar **44** 39 32N 26 10 E
Gulshad **58** 46 45N 74 25 E
Gulsvik **47** 60 24N 9 38 E
Gulu **90** 2 48N 32 17 E
Gulwe **90** 6 30 S 36 25 E
Gulyaypole **56** 47 45N 36 21 E
Gum Lake **99** 32 42 S 143 9 E
Gumal → **68** 31 40N 71 50 E
Gumbaz **68** 30 2N 69 0 E
Gumel **85** 12 39N 9 22 E
Gumiel de Hizán **32** 41 46N 3 41W
Gumlu **98** 19 53 S 147 41 E
Gumma □ **74** 36 30N 138 20 E
Gummersbach **24** 51 2N 7 32 E
Gummi **85** 12 4N 5 9 E
Gümüsane **64** 40 30N 39 30 E
Gümüşhaciköy **56** 40 50N 35 18 E
Gumzai **73** 5 28 S 134 42 E
Guna **68** 24 40N 77 19 E
Guna Mt. **87** 11 50N 37 40 E
Gundagai **99** 35 3 S 148 6 E
Gundelfingen **25** 48 33N 10 22 E
Gundih **73** 7 10 S 110 56 E
Gundlakamma → **70** 15 30N 80 15 E
Gungu **88** 5 43 S 19 20 E
Gunisao → **109** 53 56N 97 53W
Gunisao L. **109** 53 33N 96 15W
Gunnedah **97** 30 59 S 150 15 E
Gunning **100** 34 47 S 149 14 E
Gunnison, Colo., U.S.A. **119** 38 32N 106 56W
Gunnison, Utah, U.S.A. **118** 39 11N 111 48W
Gunnison → **119** 39 3N 108 30W
Guntakal **70** 15 11N 77 27 E
Guntersville **115** 34 18N 86 16W
Guntur **70** 16 23N 80 30 E
Gunung-Sitoli **72** 1 15N 97 30 E
Gunungapi **73** 6 45 S 126 30 E
Gunupur **70** 19 5N 83 50 E
Günz → **25** 48 27N 10 16 E
Gunza **88** 10 50 S 13 50 E
Günzburg **25** 48 27N 10 16 E
Gunzenhausen **25** 49 6N 10 45 E
Guo He → **77** 32 59N 117 10 E
Guoyang **77** 33 32N 116 12 E
Gupis **69** 36 15N 73 20 E
Gura **68** 25 12N 71 39 E
Gura Humorului **46** 47 35N 25 53 E
Gura-Teghii **46** 45 30N 26 25 E
Gurag **87** 8 20N 38 20 E
Gürchañ **64** 34 55N 49 25 E
Gurdaspur **68** 32 5N 75 31 E
Gurdon **117** 33 55N 93 10W
Gurdzhaani **57** 41 43N 45 52 E
Gurgaon **68** 28 27N 77 1 E
Gurghiu, Munţii **46** 46 41N 25 15 E
Gurk → **26** 46 35N 14 31 E
Gurkha **69** 28 5N 84 40 E
Gurley **99** 29 45 S 149 48 E
Gurun **71** 5 49N 100 27 E
Gurupá **127** 1 25 S 51 35W
Gurupá, I. Grande de **127** 1 25 S 51 45W
Gurupi → **127** 1 13 S 46 6W
Guryev **57** 47 5N 52 0 E
Gus-Khrustalnyy **55** 55 42N 40 44 E
Gusau **85** 12 12N 6 40 E
Gusev **54** 54 35N 22 10 E
Gushan **76** 39 50N 123 35 E
Gushi **77** 32 11N 115 41 E
Gushiago **85** 9 55N 0 15W
Gusinje **42** 42 35N 19 50 E
Gúspini **40** 39 32N 8 38 E
Gusselby **48** 59 38N 15 14 E
Güssing **27** 47 3N 16 20 E
Gustanj **39** 46 36N 14 49 E
Gustine **119** 37 14N 121 0 E
Güstrow **24** 53 47N 12 12 E
Gusum **49** 58 16N 16 30 E
Guta = Kalárovo **27** 47 54N 18 0 E
Gütersloh **24** 51 54N 8 25 E
Guthalongra **98** 19 52 S 147 50 E
Guthega Dam **100** 36 20 S 148 27 E
Guthrie **117** 35 55N 97 30W
Guttenberg **116** 42 46N 91 10W
Guyana ■ **126** 5 0N 59 0W
Guyang **76** 41 0N 110 5 E
Guyenne **20** 44 30N 0 40 E
Guymon **117** 36 45N 101 30W
Guyra **99** 30 15 S 151 40 E
Guyuan **76** 36 0N 106 20 E
Guzhen **77** 33 22N 117 18 E
Guzmán, Laguna de **120** 31 25N 107 25W
Gwa **67** 17 36N 94 34 E
Gwaai **91** 19 15 S 27 45 E
Gwabegar **99** 30 31 S 149 0 E
Gwadabawa **85** 13 28N 5 15 E
Gwādar **66** 25 10N 62 18 E
Gwagwada **85** 10 15N 7 15 E
Gwalior **68** 26 12N 78 10 E
Gwanda **91** 20 55 S 29 0 E
Gwandu **85** 12 30N 4 41 E
Gwane **90** 4 45N 25 48 E
Gwaram **85** 10 15N 10 25 E
Gwarzo **85** 12 20N 8 55 E
Gwda → **28** 53 3N 16 44 E
Gweebarra B. **15** 54 52N 8 21W
Gweedore **15** 55 4N 8 15W
* Gwelo **91** 19 28 S 29 45 E
Gwent □ **13** 51 45N 2 55W
Gwi **85** 9 0N 7 10 E
Gwinn **114** 46 15N 87 29W
Gwio Kura **85** 12 40N 11 2 E
Gwol **84** 10 58N 1 59W
Gwoza **85** 11 5N 13 40 E
Gwydir → **97** 29 27 S 149 48 E
Gwynedd □ **12** 53 0N 4 0W
Gyaring Hu **75** 34 50N 97 40 E
Gydanskiy P-ov. **58** 70 0N 78 0 E
Gyland **47** 58 24N 6 45 E
Gympie **97** 26 11 S 152 38 E
Gyoda **74** 36 10N 139 30 E
Gyoma **27** 46 56N 20 50 E
Gyöngyös **27** 47 48N 20 0 E
Györ **27** 47 41N 17 40 E
Györ-Sopron □ **27** 47 40N 17 20 E
Gypsum Pt. **108** 61 53N 114 35W
Gypsumville **109** 51 45N 98 40W
Gyttorp **48** 59 31N 14 58 E
Gyula **27** 46 38N 21 17 E
Gzhatsk = Gagarin **54** 55 30N 35 0 E

H

Ha 'Arava **62** 30 50N 35 20 E
Haag **25** 48 11N 12 12 E
Haapamäki **50** 62 18N 24 28 E
Haapsalu **54** 58 56N 23 30 E
Haarlem **16** 52 23N 4 39 E
Haast → **101** 43 50 S 169 2 E
Hab Nadi Chauki **66** 25 0N 66 50 E
Habana, La **121** 23 8N 82 22W
Habaswein **90** 1 2N 39 30 E
Habay **108** 58 50N 118 44W
Habiganj **69** 24 24N 91 30 E
Hablingbo **49** 57 12N 18 16 E
Habo **49** 57 55N 14 6 E
Hachenburg **24** 50 40N 7 49 E
Hachijō-Jima **74** 33 5N 139 45 E
Hachinohe **74** 40 30N 141 29 E
Hachiōji **74** 35 40N 139 20 E
Hadali **68** 32 16N 72 11 E
Hadarba, Ras **86** 22 4N 36 51 E
Hadd, Ras al **65** 22 35N 59 50 E
Haddington **14** 55 57N 2 48W
Hadejia **85** 12 30N 10 5 E
Hadejia → **85** 12 50N 10 51 E
Haden **99** 27 13 S 151 54 E
Ḥadera **62** 32 27N 34 55 E
Ḥadera, N. → **62** 32 28N 34 52 E
Haderslev **49** 55 15N 9 30 E
Hadhra **86** 20 10N 41 5 E
Hadhramaut = Haḑramawt **63** 15 30N 49 30 E
Hadibu **63** 12 35N 54 2 E
Hadjeb El Aïoun **83** 35 21N 9 32 E
Haḑramawt **63** 15 30N 49 30 E
Hadrians Wall **12** 55 0N 2 30W
Hadsten **49** 56 19N 10 3 E
Hadsund **49** 56 44N 10 8 E
Haeju **76** 38 3N 125 45 E
Haerhpin = Harbin **76** 45 48N 126 40 E
Ḥafar al Baţin **64** 28 25N 46 0 E
Hafizabad **68** 32 5N 73 40 E
Haflong **67** 25 10N 93 5 E
Hafnarfjörður **50** 64 4N 21 57W
Haft-Gel **64** 31 30N 49 32 E
Hafun, Ras **63** 10 29N 51 30 E
Hagalil **62** 32 53N 35 18 E
Hagari → **70** 15 40N 77 0 E
Hagen **24** 51 21N 7 29 E
Hagenow **24** 53 25N 11 10 E
Hagerman **117** 33 5N 104 22W
Hagerstown **114** 39 39N 77 46W
Hagetmau **20** 43 39N 0 37W
Hagfors **48** 60 3N 13 45 E
Häggenås **48** 63 24N 14 55 E
Hagi, Iceland **50** 65 28N 23 25W
Hagi, Japan **74** 34 30N 131 22 E
Hagolan **62** 33 0N 35 45 E
Hags Hd. **15** 52 57N 9 30W
Hague, C. de la **18** 49 44N 1 56W
Hague, The = s'-Gravenhage **16** 52 7N 4 17 E
Haguenau **19** 48 49N 7 47 E
Hai □ **90** 3 10 S 37 10 E
Haicheng **76** 40 50N 122 45 E
Haifeng **77** 22 58N 115 10 E

* *Renamed Gweru*

Haiger Håverud

Name	Page	Lat.	Long.
Haiger	24	50 44N	8 12 E
Haikang	77	20 52N	110 8 E
Haikou	75	20 1N	110 16 E
Ḥā'il	64	27 28N	41 45 E
Hailar	75	49 10N	119 38 E
Hailar He →	76	49 30N	117 50 E
Hailey	118	43 30N	114 15W
Haileybury	106	47 30N	79 38W
Hailin	76	44 37N	129 30 E
Hailing Dao	77	21 35N	111 47 E
Hailong	76	42 32N	125 40 E
Hailun	75	47 28N	126 50 E
Hailuoto	50	65 3N	24 45 E
Haimen	77	31 52N	121 10 E
Hainan	77	19 0N	110 0 E
Hainan Dao	75	19 0N	109 30 E
Hainaut □	16	50 30N	4 0 E
Hainburg	27	48 9N	16 56 E
Haines	118	44 51N	117 59W
Haines City	115	28 6N	81 35W
Haines Junction	108	60 45N	137 30W
Hainfeld	26	48 3N	15 48 E
Haining	77	30 28N	120 40 E
Haiphong	71	20 47N	106 41 E
Haiti ■	121	19 0N	72 30W
Haiya Junction	86	18 20N	36 21 E
Haiyan	77	30 28N	120 58 E
Haiyang	76	36 47N	121 9 E
Haiyuan	76	36 35N	105 52 E
Haja	73	3 19 S	129 37 E
Hajar Bangar	81	10 40N	22 45 E
Hajar, Jabal	64	26 5N	39 10 E
Hajdú-Bihar □	27	47 30N	21 30 E
Hajdúböszörmény	27	47 40N	21 30 E
Hajdúdurog	27	47 48N	21 30 E
Hajdúhadház	27	47 40N	21 40 E
Hajdúnánás	27	47 50N	21 26 E
Hajdúsámson	27	47 37N	21 42 E
Hajdúszobaszló	27	47 27N	21 22 E
Hajipur	69	25 45N	85 13 E
Hajówka	28	52 47N	23 35 E
Hajr	65	24 0N	56 34 E
Hakansson, Mts.	91	8 40 S	25 45 E
Håkantorp	49	58 18N	12 55 E
Hakken-Zan	74	34 10N	135 54 E
Hakodate	74	41 45N	140 44 E
Ḥalab = Aleppo	64	36 10N	37 15 E
Ḥalabjah	64	35 10N	45 58 E
Halaib	86	22 12N	36 30 E
Halbe	86	19 40N	42 15 E
Halberstadt	24	51 53N	11 2 E
Halcombe	101	40 8 S	175 30 E
Halcyon, Mt.	73	13 0N	121 30 E
Halden	47	59 9N	11 23 E
Haldensleben	24	52 17N	11 30 E
Haldia	67	22 5N	88 3 E
Haldwani-cum-Kathgodam	69	29 31N	79 30 E
Haleakala Crater	110	20 43N	156 12W
Haleyville	115	34 15N	87 40W
Half Assini	84	5 1N	2 50W
Halfway	118	44 56N	117 8W
Halfway →	108	56 12N	121 32W
Ḥalḥul	62	31 35N	35 7 E
Hali, Si. Arab.	86	18 40N	41 15 E
Hali, Yemen	63	18 30N	41 30 E
Haliburton	106	45 3N	78 30W
Halicarnassus	45	37 3N	27 30 E
Halifax, Austral.	98	18 32 S	146 22 E
Halifax, Can.	107	44 38N	63 35W
Halifax, U.K.	12	53 43N	1 51W
Halifax B.	97	18 50 S	147 0 E
Halifax I.	92	26 38 S	15 4 E
Halīl Rūd →	65	27 40N	58 30 E
Hall	26	47 17N	11 30 E
Hall Beach	105	68 46N	81 12W
Hallabro	49	56 22N	15 5 E
Hallands län □	49	56 50N	12 50 E
Hallands Väderö	49	56 27N	12 34 E
Hallandsås	49	56 22N	13 0 E
Halle, Belg.	16	50 44N	4 13 E
Halle, Halle, Ger.	24	51 29N	12 0 E
Halle, Nordrhein-Westfalen, Ger.	24	52 4N	8 20 E
Halle □	24	51 28N	11 58 E
Hällefors	48	59 47N	14 31 E
Hallefors	49	59 46N	14 30 E
Hallein	26	47 40N	13 5 E
Hällekis	49	58 38N	13 27 E
Hallett	99	33 25 S	138 55 E
Hallettsville	117	29 28N	96 57W
Hällevadsholm	49	58 35N	11 33 E
Halley Bay	5	75 31 S	26 36W
Hallia →	70	16 55N	79 20 E
Halliday	116	47 20N	102 25W
Halliday L.	109	61 21N	108 56W
Hallingskeid	47	60 40N	7 17 E
Hällnäs	50	64 19N	19 36 E
Hallock	109	48 47N	97 0W
Halls Creek	96	18 16 S	127 38 E
Hallsberg	48	59 5N	15 7 E
Hallstahammar	48	59 38N	16 15 E
Hallstatt	26	47 33N	13 38 E
Hallstavik	48	60 5N	18 37 E
Hallstead	113	41 56N	75 45W
Halmahera	73	0 40N	128 0 E
Halmeu	46	47 57N	23 2 E
Halmstad	49	56 41N	12 52 E
Halq el Oued	83	36 53N	10 18 E
Hals	49	56 59N	10 18 E
Halsa	47	63 3N	8 14 E
Halsafjorden	47	63 5N	8 10 E
Hälsingborg = Helsingborg	49	56 3N	12 42 E
Halstad	116	47 21N	96 50W
Haltdalen	47	62 56N	11 8 E
Haltern	24	51 44N	7 10 E
Halul	65	25 40N	52 40 E
Ham	19	49 45N	3 4 E
Hamab	92	28 7 S	19 16 E
Hamad	87	15 20N	33 32 E
Hamada	74	34 56N	132 4 E
Hamadān	64	34 52N	48 32 E
Hamadān □	64	35 0N	49 0 E
Hamadia	82	35 28N	1 57 E
Hamāh	64	35 5N	36 40 E
Hamamatsu	74	34 45N	137 45 E
Hamar	47	60 48N	11 7 E
Hamarøy	50	68 5N	15 38 E
Hamâta, Gebel	86	24 17N	35 0 E
Hamber Prov. Park	108	52 20N	118 0W
Hamburg, Ger.	24	53 32N	9 59 E
Hamburg, Ark., U.S.A.	117	33 15N	91 47W
Hamburg, Iowa, U.S.A.	116	40 37N	95 38W
Hamburg, N.Y., U.S.A.	112	42 44N	78 50W
Hamburg, Pa., U.S.A.	113	40 33N	76 0W
Hamburg □	24	53 30N	10 0 E
Hamden	113	41 21N	72 56W
Hamdh, W. →	86	24 55N	36 20 E
Hämeen lääni □	51	61 24N	24 10 E
Hämeenlinna	50	61 0N	24 28 E
Hamélé	84	10 56N	2 45W
Hameln	24	52 7N	9 24 E
Hamer Koke	87	5 15N	36 45 E
Hamersley Ra.	96	22 0 S	117 45 E
Hamhung	76	39 54N	127 30 E
Hami	75	42 55N	93 25 E
Hamilton, Austral.	97	37 45 S	142 2 E
Hamilton, Berm.	121	32 15N	64 45W
Hamilton, Can.	106	43 15N	79 50W
Hamilton, N.Z.	101	37 47 S	175 19 E
Hamilton, U.K.	14	55 47N	4 2W
Hamilton, Mo., U.S.A.	116	39 45N	93 59W
Hamilton, Mont., U.S.A.	118	46 20N	114 6W
Hamilton, N.Y., U.S.A.	114	42 49N	75 31W
Hamilton, Ohio, U.S.A.	114	39 20N	84 35W
Hamilton, Tex., U.S.A.	117	31 40N	98 5W
Hamilton →	98	23 30 S	139 47 E
Hamilton Hotel	98	22 45 S	140 40 E
Hamilton Inlet	107	54 0N	57 30W
Hamiota	109	50 11N	100 38W
Hamlet	115	34 56N	79 40W
Hamley Bridge	99	34 17 S	138 35 E
Hamlin, N.Y., U.S.A.	112	43 17N	77 55W
Hamlin, Tex., U.S.A.	117	32 58N	100 8W
Hamm	24	51 40N	7 49 E
Hammam Bouhadjar	82	35 23N	0 58W
Hammamet	83	36 24N	10 38 E
Hammamet, G. de	83	36 10N	10 48 E
Hammarstrand	48	63 7N	16 20 E
Hammel	49	56 16N	9 52 E
Hammelburg	25	50 7N	9 54 E
Hammeren	49	55 18N	14 47 E
Hammerfest	50	70 39N	23 41 E
Hammond, Ind., U.S.A.	114	41 40N	87 30W
Hammond, La., U.S.A.	117	30 32N	90 30W
Hammonton	114	39 40N	74 47W
Hamneda	49	56 41N	13 51 E
Hamoyet, Jebel	86	17 33N	38 2 E
Hampden	101	45 18 S	170 50 E
Hampshire □	13	51 3N	1 20W
Hampshire Downs	13	51 10N	1 10W
Hampton, Ark., U.S.A.	117	33 35N	92 29W
Hampton, Iowa, U.S.A.	116	42 42N	93 12W
Hampton, N.H., U.S.A.	113	42 56N	70 48W
Hampton, S.C., U.S.A.	115	32 52N	81 2W
Hampton, Va., U.S.A.	114	37 4N	76 18W
Hampton Harbour	96	20 30 S	116 30 E
Hampton Tableland	96	32 0 S	127 0 E
Hamrat esh Sheykh	87	14 38N	27 55 E
Han Jiang →	77	23 25N	116 40 E
Han Shui →	77	30 35N	114 18 E
Hana	110	20 45N	155 59W
Hanak	86	25 32N	37 0 E
Hanang	90	4 30 S	35 25 E
Hanau	25	50 8N	8 56 E
Hancheng	76	35 31N	110 25 E
Hancock, Mich., U.S.A.	116	47 10N	88 40W
Hancock, Minn., U.S.A.	116	45 26N	95 46W
Hancock, Pa., U.S.A.	113	41 57N	75 19W
Handa, Japan	74	34 53N	137 0 E
Handa, Somalia	63	10 37N	51 2 E
Handan	76	36 35N	114 28 E
Handen	48	59 12N	18 12 E
Handeni	90	5 25 S	38 2 E
Handeni □	90	5 30 S	38 0 E
Handlová	27	48 45N	18 35 E
Handub	86	19 15N	37 16 E
Hanegev	62	30 50N	35 0 E
Haney	108	49 12N	122 40W
Hanford	119	36 23N	119 39W
Hangang →	76	37 50N	126 30 E
Hangayn Nuruu	75	47 30N	100 0 E
Hangchou = Hangzhou	75	30 18N	120 11 E
Hanggin Houqi	76	40 58N	107 4 E
Hangklip, K.	92	34 26 S	18 48 E
Hangö	51	59 50N	22 57 E
Hangu	76	39 18N	117 53 E
Hangzhou	75	30 18N	120 11 E
Hangzhou Wan	75	30 15N	120 45 E
Ḥanīsh J.	63	13 45N	42 46 E
Haniska	27	48 37N	21 15 E
Hanita	62	33 5N	35 10 E
Hankinson	116	46 9N	96 58W
Hanko	51	59 59N	22 57 E
Hankou	77	30 35N	114 30 E
Hanksville	119	38 19N	110 45W
Hanmer	101	42 32 S	172 50 E
Hann, Mt.	96	16 0 S	126 0 E
Hanna	108	51 40N	111 54W
Hannaford	116	47 23N	98 11W
Hannah	116	48 58N	98 42W
Hannah B.	106	51 40N	80 0W
Hannibal	116	39 42N	91 22W
Hannik	86	18 12N	32 20 E
Hannover	24	52 23N	9 43 E
Hanö	49	56 2N	14 50 E
Hanöbukten	49	55 35N	14 30 E
Hanoi	71	21 5N	105 55 E
Hanover, Can.	112	44 9N	81 2W
Hanover, S. Afr.	92	31 4 S	24 29 E
Hanover, N.H., U.S.A.	114	43 43N	72 17W
Hanover, Ohio, U.S.A.	112	40 5N	82 17W
Hanover, Pa., U.S.A.	114	39 46N	76 59W
Hanover = Hannover	24	52 23N	9 43 E
Hanover, I.	128	51 0 S	74 50W
Hansi	68	29 10N	75 57 E
Hansjö	48	61 10N	14 40 E
Hanson Range	96	27 0 S	136 30 E
Hanwood	100	34 22 S	146 2 E
Hanyang	77	30 35N	114 2 E
Hanyin	77	32 54N	108 28 E
Hanzhong	75	33 10N	107 1 E
Hanzhuang	77	34 33N	117 23 E
Haparanda	50	65 52N	24 8 E
Happy	117	34 47N	101 50W
Happy Camp	118	41 52N	123 22W
Happy Valley	107	53 15N	60 20W
Hapur	68	28 45N	77 45 E
Ḥaql	86	29 10N	35 0 E
Har	73	5 16 S	133 14 E
Har Hu	75	38 20N	97 38 E
Har Us Nuur	75	48 0N	92 0 E
Har Yehuda	62	31 35N	34 57 E
Ḥaraḍ	64	24 22N	49 0 E
Haraisan Plateau	64	23 0N	47 40 E
Haramsøya	47	62 39N	6 12 E
Harardera	63	4 33N	47 38 E
Harat	87	16 5N	39 26 E
Harazé, Chad	81	14 20N	19 12 E
Harazé, Chad	81	9 57N	20 48 E
Harbin	76	45 48N	126 40 E
Harboør	49	56 38N	8 10 E
Harbor Beach	114	43 50N	82 38W
Harbor Springs	114	45 28N	85 0W
Harbour Breton	107	47 29N	55 50W
Harbour Grace	107	47 40N	53 22W
Harburg	24	53 27N	9 58 E
Hårby	49	55 13N	10 7 E
Harcourt	98	24 17 S	149 55 E
Harda	68	22 27N	77 5 E
Hardangerfjorden	47	60 15N	6 0 E
Hardangerjøkulen	47	60 30N	7 0 E
Hardangervidda	47	60 20N	7 20 E
Hardap Dam	92	24 32 S	17 50 E
Hardenberg	16	52 34N	6 37 E
Harderwijk	16	52 21N	5 38 E
Hardin	118	45 44N	107 35W
Harding	93	30 35 S	29 55 E
Hardisty	108	52 40N	111 18W
Hardman	118	45 12N	119 40W
Hardoi	69	27 26N	80 6 E
Hardwar	68	29 58N	78 9 E
Hardwick	113	44 30N	72 20W
Hardy	117	36 20N	91 30W
Hardy, Pen.	128	55 30 S	68 20W
Hare B.	107	51 15N	55 45W
Hare Gilboa	62	32 31N	35 25 E
Hare Meron	62	32 59N	35 24 E
Haren	24	52 47N	7 18 E
Harer	87	9 20N	42 8 E
Harer □	87	7 12N	42 0 E
Hareto	87	9 23N	37 6 E
Harfleur	18	49 30N	0 10 E
Hargeisa	63	9 30N	44 2 E
Harghita □	46	46 30N	25 30 E
Harghita, Mţii	46	46 25N	25 35 E
Hargshamn	48	60 12N	18 30 E
Hari →	72	1 16 S	104 5 E
Haricha, Hamada el	82	22 40N	3 15W
Harihar	70	14 32N	75 44 E
Haringhata →	69	22 0N	89 58 E
Haripad	70	9 14N	76 28 E
Harīrūd	65	35 0N	61 0 E
Harīrūd →	65	34 20N	62 30 E
Harkat	86	20 25N	39 40 E
Harlan, Iowa, U.S.A.	116	41 37N	95 20W
Harlan, Tenn., U.S.A.	115	36 50N	83 20W
Harlech	12	52 52N	4 7W
Harlem	118	48 29N	108 47W
Harlingen, Neth.	16	53 11N	5 25 E
Harlingen, U.S.A.	117	26 20N	97 50W
Harlowton	118	46 30N	109 54W
Harmånger	48	61 55N	17 20 E
Harmil	87	16 30N	40 10 E
Harney Basin	118	43 30N	119 0W
Harney L.	118	43 0N	119 0W
Harney Pk.	116	43 52N	103 33W
Härnön	48	62 36N	18 0 E
Härnösand	48	62 38N	18 0 E
Haro	32	42 35N	2 55W
Haro, C.	120	27 50N	110 55W
Harp L.	107	55 5N	61 50W
Harpanahalli	70	14 47N	76 2 E
Harpe, La	116	40 30N	91 0W
Harper	84	4 25N	7 43W
Harplinge	49	56 45N	12 45 E
Harrand	68	29 28N	70 3 E
Ḥarrat al Kishb	64	22 30N	40 15 E
Harrat al 'Uwairidh	64	26 50N	38 0 E
Harrat Khaibar	86	25 45N	40 0 E
Harrat Nawāsīf	86	21 30N	42 0 E
Harriman	115	36 0N	84 35W
Harrington Harbour	107	50 31N	59 30W
Harris	14	57 50N	6 55W
Harris L.	96	31 10 S	135 10 E
Harris, Sd. of	14	57 44N	7 6W
Harrisburg, Ill., U.S.A.	117	37 42N	88 30W
Harrisburg, Nebr., U.S.A.	116	41 36N	103 46W
Harrisburg, Oreg., U.S.A.	118	44 16N	123 10W
Harrisburg, Pa., U.S.A.	114	40 18N	76 52W
Harrismith	93	28 15 S	29 8 E
Harrison, Ark., U.S.A.	117	36 10N	93 4W
Harrison, Idaho, U.S.A.	118	47 30N	116 51W
Harrison, Nebr., U.S.A.	116	42 42N	103 52W
Harrison B.	104	70 25N	151 30W
Harrison, C.	107	54 55N	57 55W
Harrison L.	108	49 33N	121 50W
Harrisonburg	114	38 28N	78 52W
Harrisonville	116	38 39N	94 21W
Harriston	106	43 57N	80 53W
Harrisville	106	44 40N	83 19W
Harrogate	12	53 59N	1 32W
Harrow, Can.	112	42 2N	82 55W
Harrow, U.K.	13	51 35N	0 15W
Harsefeld	24	53 26N	9 31 E
Harstad	50	68 48N	16 30 E
Hart	114	43 42N	86 21W
Hartbees →	92	28 45 S	20 32 E
Hartberg	26	47 17N	15 58 E
Hartford, Conn., U.S.A.	114	41 47N	72 41W
Hartford, Ky., U.S.A.	114	37 26N	86 50W
Hartford, S.D., U.S.A.	116	43 40N	96 58W
Hartford, Wis., U.S.A.	116	43 18N	88 25W
Hartford City	114	40 22N	85 20W
Hartland	107	46 20N	67 32W
Hartland Pt.	13	51 2N	4 32W
Hartlepool	12	54 42N	1 11W
Hartley	91	18 10 S	30 14 E
Hartley Bay	108	53 25N	129 15W
Hartmannberge	92	17 0 S	13 0 E
Hartney	109	49 30N	100 35W
Hartselle	115	34 25N	86 55W
Hartshorne	117	34 51N	95 30W
Hartsville	115	34 23N	80 2W
Hartwell	115	34 21N	82 52W
Harunabad	68	29 35N	73 8 E
Harur	70	12 3N	78 29 E
Harvey, Ill., U.S.A.	114	41 40N	87 40W
Harvey, N.D., U.S.A.	116	47 50N	99 58W
Harwich	13	51 56N	1 18 E
Haryana □	68	29 0N	76 10 E
Harz	24	51 40N	10 40 E
Harzgerode	24	51 38N	11 8 E
Hasa	64	26 0N	49 0 E
Hasaheisa	87	14 44N	33 20 E
Hasani	86	25 0N	37 8 E
Hasanpur	68	28 43N	78 17 E
Haselünne	24	52 40N	7 30 E
Hasharon	62	32 12N	34 49 E
Hashefela	62	31 30N	34 43 E
Håsjö	48	63 1N	16 5 E
Haskell, Okla., U.S.A.	117	35 51N	95 40W
Haskell, Tex., U.S.A.	117	33 10N	99 45W
Haslach	25	48 16N	8 7 E
Hasle	49	55 11N	14 44 E
Haslev	49	55 18N	11 57 E
Hasparren	20	43 24N	1 18W
Hasselt	16	50 56N	5 21 E
Hassene, Ad.	82	21 0N	4 0 E
Hassfurt	25	50 2N	10 30 E
Hassi Berrekrem	83	33 45N	5 16 E
Hassi bou Khelala	82	30 17N	0 18W
Hassi Daoula	83	33 4N	5 38 E
Hassi Djafou	82	30 55N	3 35 E
Hassi el Abiod	82	31 47N	3 37 E
Hassi el Biod	83	28 30N	6 0 E
Hassi el Gassi	83	30 52N	6 5 E
Hassi el Hadjar	83	31 28N	4 45 E
Hassi er Rmel	82	32 56N	3 17 E
Hassi Imoulaye	83	29 54N	9 10 E
Hassi Inifel	82	29 50N	3 41 E
Hassi Marroket	82	30 10N	3 0 E
Hassi Messaoud	83	31 43N	6 8 E
Hassi Rhénami	83	31 50N	5 58 E
Hassi Tartrat	83	30 5N	6 28 E
Hassi Zerzour	82	30 51N	3 56W
Hastings, Can.	112	44 18N	77 57W
Hastings, N.Z.	101	39 39 S	176 52 E
Hastings, U.K.	13	50 51N	0 36 E
Hastings, Mich., U.S.A.	114	42 40N	85 20W
Hastings, Minn., U.S.A.	116	44 41N	92 51W
Hastings, Nebr., U.S.A.	116	40 34N	98 22W
Hastings Ra.	99	31 15 S	152 14 E
Hästveda	49	56 17N	13 55 E
Hat Nhao	71	14 46N	106 32 E
Hatch	119	32 45N	107 8W
Hatches Creek	96	20 56 S	135 12 E
Hatchet L.	109	58 36N	103 40W
Haţeg	46	45 36N	22 55 E
Haţeg, Mţii.	46	45 25N	23 0 E
Hatfield P.O.	99	33 54 S	143 49 E
Hatgal	75	50 26N	100 9 E
Hathras	68	27 36N	78 6 E
Hattah	99	34 48 S	142 17 E
Hatteras, C.	115	35 10N	75 30W
Hattiesburg	117	31 20N	89 20W
Hatvan	27	47 40N	19 45 E
Hau Bon = Cheo Reo	71	13 25N	108 28 E
Haug	47	60 23N	10 26 E
Haugastøl	47	60 30N	7 50 E
Haugesund	47	59 23N	5 13 E
Haultain →	109	55 51N	106 46W
Hauraki Gulf	101	36 35 S	175 5 E
Hauran	62	32 50N	36 15 E
Hausruck	26	48 6N	13 30 E
Haut Atlas	82	32 30N	5 0W
Haut-Rhin □	19	48 0N	7 15 E
Haut Zaïre □	90	2 20N	26 0 E
Hautah, Wahāt al	64	23 40N	47 0 E
Haute-Corse □	21	42 30N	9 30 E
Haute-Garonne □	20	43 28N	1 30 E
Haute-Loire □	20	45 5N	3 50 E
Haute-Marne □	19	48 10N	5 20 E
Haute-Saône □	19	47 45N	6 10 E
Haute-Savoie □	21	46 0N	6 20 E
Haute-Vienne □	20	45 50N	1 10 E
Hauterive	107	49 10N	68 16W
Hautes-Alpes □	21	44 42N	6 20 E
Hautes-Pyrénées □	20	43 0N	0 10 E
Hauteville	21	45 58N	5 36 E
Hautmont	19	50 15N	3 55 E
Hauts-de-Seine □	19	48 52N	2 15 E
Hauts Plateaux	82	34 14N	1 0 E
Hauzenberg	25	48 39N	13 38 E
Havana	116	40 19N	90 3W
Havana = La Habana	121	23 8N	82 22W
Havasu, L.	119	34 18N	114 28W
Havdhem	49	57 10N	18 20 E
Havelange	16	50 23N	5 15 E
Havelock, N.B., Can.	107	46 2N	65 24W
Havelock, Ont., Can.	106	44 26N	77 53W
Havelock, N.Z.	101	41 17 S	173 48 E
Havelock I.	71	11 55N	93 2 E
Haverfordwest	13	51 48N	4 59W
Haverhill	114	42 50N	71 2W
Haveri	70	14 53N	75 24 E
Havering	13	51 33N	0 20 E
Haverstraw	113	41 12N	73 58W
Håverud	49	58 50N	12 28 E

Havîrna Hogansville

Havîrna 46 48 4N 26 43 E
Havlíčkův Brod 26 49 36N 15 33 E
Havneby 49 55 5N 8 34 E
Havre 118 48 34N 109 40W
Havre -St.-Pierre 107 50 18N 63 33W
Havre-Aubert 107 47 12N 61 56W
Havre, Le 18 49 30N 0 5 E
Havza 64 41 0N 35 35 E
Haw → 115 35 36N 79 3W
Hawaii □ 110 20 30N 157 0W
Hawaii 110 20 0N 155 0W
Hawaiian Is. 110 20 30N 156 0W
Hawaiian Ridge 95 24 0N 165 0W
Hawarden, Can. 109 51 25N 106 36W
Hawarden, U.S.A. 116 43 2N 96 28W
Hawea Lake 101 44 28 S 169 19 E
Hawera 101 39 35 S 174 19 E
Hawick 14 55 25N 2 48W
Hawk Junction 106 48 5N 84 38W
Hawke B. 101 39 25 S 177 20 E
Hawke, C. 100 32 13 S 152 34 E
Hawker 97 31 59 S 138 22 E
Hawke's Bay □ 101 39 45 S 176 35 E
Hawkesbury 106 45 37N 74 37W
Hawkesbury → 97 33 30 S 151 10 E
Hawkesbury I. 108 53 37N 129 3W
Hawkinsville 115 32 17N 83 30W
Hawkwood 99 25 45 S 150 50 E
Hawley 116 46 58N 96 20W
Hawrān 62 32 45N 36 15 E
Hawthorne 118 38 31N 118 37W
Hawzen 87 13 58N 39 28 E
Haxtun 116 40 40N 102 39W
Hay, Austral. 97 34 30 S 144 51 E
Hay, U.K. 13 52 4N 3 9W
Hay →, Austral. 97 25 14 S 138 0 E
Hay →, Can. 108 60 50N 116 26W
Hay L. 108 58 50N 118 50W
Hay Lakes 108 53 12N 113 2W
Hay River 108 60 51N 115 44W
Hay Springs 116 42 40N 102 38W
Hayange 19 49 20N 6 2 E
Hayden, Ariz., U.S.A. 119 33 2N 110 48W
Hayden, Colo., U.S.A. 118 40 30N 107 22W
Haydon 98 18 0 S 141 30 E
Haye-Descartes, La 18 46 58N 0 42 E
Haye-du-Puits, La 18 49 17N 1 33W
Hayes 116 44 22N 101 1W
Hayes → 109 57 3N 92 12W
Haynesville 117 33 0N 93 7W
Hays, Can. 108 50 6N 111 48W
Hays, U.S.A. 116 38 55N 99 25W
Hayward 116 46 2N 91 30W
Hayward's Heath 13 51 0N 0 5W
Hazard 114 37 18N 83 10W
Hazaribagh 69 23 58N 85 26 E
Hazaribagh Road 69 24 12N 85 57 E
Hazebrouck 19 50 42N 2 31 E
Hazelton, Can. 108 55 20N 127 42W
Hazelton, U.S.A. 116 46 30N 100 15W
Hazen, N.D., U.S.A. 116 47 18N 101 38W
Hazen, Nev., U.S.A. 118 39 37N 119 2W
Hazlehurst, Ga., U.S.A. 115 31 50N 82 35W
Hazlehurst, Miss., U.S.A. 117 31 52N 90 24W
Hazleton 114 40 58N 76 0W
Ḩazor 62 33 2N 35 32 E
He Xian 77 24 27N 111 30 E
Head of Bight 96 31 30 S 131 25 E
Headlands 91 18 15 S 32 2 E
Healdsburg 118 38 33N 122 51W
Healdton 117 34 16N 97 31W
Healesville 99 37 35 S 145 30 E
Heanor 12 53 1N 1 20W
Heard I. 3 53 0 S 74 0 E
Hearne 117 30 54N 96 35W
Hearne B. 109 60 10N 99 10W
Hearne L. 108 62 20N 113 10W
Hearst 106 49 40N 83 41W
Heart → 116 46 40N 100 51W
Heart's Content 107 47 54N 53 27W
Heath Pt. 107 49 8N 61 40W
Heath Steele 107 47 17N 66 5W
Heavener 117 34 54N 94 36W
Hebbronville 117 27 20N 98 40W
Hebei □ 76 39 0N 116 0 E
Hebel 99 28 58 S 147 47 E
Heber Springs 117 35 29N 91 59W
Hebert 109 50 30N 107 10W
Hebgen, L. 118 44 50N 111 15W
Hebi 76 35 57N 114 7 E
Hebrides 14 57 30N 7 0W
Hebrides, Inner Is. 14 57 20N 6 40W
Hebrides, Outer Is. 14 57 30N 7 40W
Hebron, Can. 105 58 5N 62 30W
Hebron, N.D., U.S.A. 116 46 56N 102 2W
Hebron, Nebr., U.S.A. 116 40 15N 97 33W
Hebron = Al Khalil 62 31 32N 35 6 E
Heby 48 59 56N 16 53 E
Hecate Str. 108 53 10N 130 30W
Hechi 75 24 40N 108 2 E
Hechingen 25 48 20N 8 58 E
Hechuan 75 30 2N 106 12 E
Hecla 116 45 56N 98 8W
Hecla I. 109 51 10N 96 43W
Heddal 47 59 36N 9 9 E
Hédé 18 48 18N 1 49W
Hede 48 62 23N 13 30 E
Hedemora 48 60 18N 15 58 E
Hedley 117 34 53N 100 39W
Hedmark fylke □ 47 61 17N 11 40 E
Hedrum 47 59 7N 10 5 E
Heemstede 16 52 22N 4 37 E
Heerde 16 52 24N 6 2 E
Heerenveen 16 52 57N 5 55 E
Heerlen 16 50 55N 6 0 E
Ḩefa 62 32 46N 35 0 E
Hefei 75 31 52N 117 18 E
Hegang 75 47 20N 130 19 E
Hegyalja 27 48 25N 21 25 E
Heide 24 54 10N 9 7 E
Heidelberg, Ger. 25 49 23N 8 41 E
Heidelberg, C. Prov., S. Afr. 92 34 6 S 20 59 E
Heidelberg, Trans., S. Afr. 93 26 30 S 28 23 E
Heidenheim 25 48 40N 10 10 E
Heilbron 93 27 16 S 27 59 E
Heilbronn 25 49 8N 9 13 E
Heiligenblut 26 47 2N 12 51 E
Heiligenhafen 24 54 21N 10 58 E
Heiligenstadt 24 51 22N 10 9 E
Heilongjiang □ 75 48 0N 126 0 E
Heilunkiang = Heilongjiang □ 75 48 0N 126 0 E
Heim 47 63 26N 9 5 E
Heinola 51 61 13N 26 2 E
Heinze Is. 71 14 25N 97 45 E
Hejaz = Ḩijāz 64 26 0N 37 30 E
Hejian 76 38 25N 116 5 E
Hejiang 77 28 43N 105 46 E
Hekimhan 64 38 50N 38 0 E
Hekla 50 63 56N 19 35W
Hekou 75 22 30N 103 59 E
Hel 28 54 37N 18 47 E
Helagsfjället 48 62 54N 12 25 E
Helan Shan 76 39 0N 105 55 E
Helechosa 31 39 22N 4 53W
Helena, Ark., U.S.A. 117 34 30N 90 35W
Helena, Mont., U.S.A. 118 46 40N 112 0W
Helensburgh, Austral. 100 34 11 S 151 1 E
Helensburgh, U.K. 14 56 0N 4 44W
Helensville 101 36 41 S 174 29 E
Ḩelez 62 31 36N 34 39 E
Helgasjön 49 57 0N 14 50 E
Helgeroa 47 59 0N 9 45 E
Helgoland 24 54 10N 7 51 E
Heligoland = Helgoland 24 54 10N 7 51 E
Heliopolis 86 30 6N 31 17 E
Hell-Ville 93 13 25 S 48 16 E
Hellebæk 49 56 4N 12 32 E
Helleland 47 58 33N 6 7 E
Hellendoorn 16 52 24N 6 27 E
Hellevoetsluis 16 51 50N 4 8 E
Hellín 33 38 31N 1 40W
Helmand □ 65 31 20N 64 0 E
Helmand → 66 31 12N 61 34 E
Helmand, Hamun 65 31 15N 61 15 E
Helme → 24 51 40N 11 20 E
Helmond 16 51 29N 5 41 E
Helmsdale 14 58 7N 3 40W
Helmstedt 24 52 16N 11 0 E
Helnæs 49 55 9N 10 0 E
Helper 118 39 44N 110 56W
Helsingborg 49 56 3N 12 42 E
Helsinge 49 56 2N 12 12 E
Helsingfors 51 60 15N 25 3 E
Helsingør 49 56 2N 12 35 E
Helsinki 51 60 15N 25 3 E
Helska, Mierzeja 28 54 45N 18 40 E
Helston 13 50 7N 5 17W
Helvellyn 12 54 31N 3 1W
Helwân 86 29 50N 31 20 E
Hemavati → 70 12 30N 76 20 E
Hemet 119 33 45N 116 59W
Hemingford 116 42 21N 103 4W
Hemphill 117 31 21N 93 49W
Hempstead 117 30 5N 96 5W
Hemse 49 57 15N 18 22 E
Hemsö 48 62 43N 18 5 E
Henan □ 75 34 0N 114 0 E
Henares → 32 40 24N 3 30W
Hendaye 20 43 23N 1 47W
Henderson, Argent. 124 36 18 S 61 43W
Henderson, Ky., U.S.A. 114 37 50N 87 38W
Henderson, N.C., U.S.A. 115 36 20N 78 25W
Henderson, Nev., U.S.A. 119 36 2N 115 0W
Henderson, Pa., U.S.A. 115 35 25N 88 40W
Henderson, Tex., U.S.A. 117 32 5N 94 49W
Hendersonville 115 35 21N 82 28W
Hendon 99 28 5 S 151 50 E
Hendorf 46 46 4N 24 55 E
Heng Xian 77 22 40N 109 17 E
Hengdaohezi 76 44 52N 129 0 E
Hengelo 16 52 3N 6 19 E
Hengshan, Hunan, China 77 27 16N 112 45 E
Hengshan, Shaanxi, China 76 37 58N 109 5 E
Hengshui 76 37 41N 115 40 E
Hengyang 75 26 52N 112 33 E
Hénin-Beaumont 19 50 25N 2 58 E
Henlopen, C. 114 38 48N 75 5W
Hennan, L. 48 62 3N 55 46 E
Hennebont 18 47 49N 3 19W
Hennenman 92 27 59 S 27 1 E
Hennessy 117 36 8N 97 53W
Hennigsdorf 24 52 38N 13 13 E
Henrichemont 19 47 20N 2 30 E
Henrietta 117 33 50N 98 15W
Henrietta Maria C. 106 55 9N 82 20W
Henrietta, Ostrov 59 77 6N 156 30 E
Henry 116 41 5N 89 20W
Henryetta 117 35 30N 96 0W
Hensall 112 43 26N 81 30W
Hentiyn Nuruu 75 48 30N 108 30 E
Henty 99 35 30 S 147 0 E
Henzada 67 17 38N 95 26 E
Hephaestia 44 39 55N 25 14 E
Heping 77 24 29N 115 0 E
Heppner 118 45 21N 119 34W
Hepu 77 21 40N 109 12 E
Hepworth 112 44 37N 81 9W
Herad 47 58 8N 6 47 E
Héraðsflói 50 65 42N 14 12W
Héraðsvötn → 50 65 45N 19 25W
Herāt 65 34 20N 62 7 E
Herāt □ 65 35 0N 62 0 E
Hérault □ 20 43 34N 3 15 E
Hérault → 20 43 17N 3 26 E
Herbault 18 47 36N 1 8 E
Herbert → 98 18 31 S 146 17 E
Herbert Downs 98 23 7 S 139 9 E
Herberton 98 17 20 S 145 25 E
Herbiers, Les 18 46 52N 1 0W
Herbignac 18 47 27N 2 18W
Herborn 24 50 40N 8 19 E
Herby 28 50 45N 18 50 E
Hercegnovi 42 42 30N 18 33 E
Herðubreið 50 65 11N 16 21W
Hereford, U.K. 13 52 4N 2 42W
Hereford, U.S.A. 117 34 50N 102 28W
Hereford and Worcester □ 13 52 10N 2 30W
Herefoss 47 58 32N 8 23 E
Herentals 16 51 12N 4 51 E
Herfølge 49 55 26N 12 9 E
Herford 24 52 7N 8 40 E
Héricourt 19 47 32N 6 45 E
Herington 116 38 43N 97 0W
Herisau 25 47 22N 9 17 E
Hérisson 20 46 32N 2 42 E
Herkimer 114 43 0N 74 59W
Herm 18 49 30N 2 28W
Hermagor 26 46 38N 13 23 E
Herman 116 45 51N 96 8W
Hermann 116 38 40N 91 25W
Hermannsburg 24 52 49N 10 6 E
Hermanus 92 34 27 S 19 12 E
Herment 20 45 45N 2 24 E
Hermidale 99 31 30 S 146 42 E
Hermiston 118 45 50N 119 16W
Hermitage 101 43 44 S 170 5 E
Hermite, I. 128 55 50 S 68 0W
Hermon, Mt. = Ash Shaykh, J. 64 33 20N 35 51 E
Hermosillo 120 29 10N 111 0W
Hernad → 27 47 56N 21 8 E
Hernandarias 125 25 20 S 54 40W
Hernando, Argent. 124 32 28 S 63 40W
Hernando, U.S.A. 117 34 50N 89 59W
Herne 24 51 33N 7 12 E
Herne Bay 13 51 22N 1 8 E
Herning 49 56 8N 8 58 E
Heroica Nogales = Nogales 120 31 20N 110 56W
Heron Bay 106 48 40N 86 25W
Herowābād 64 38 37N 48 32 E
Herreid 116 45 53N 100 5W
Herrera 31 37 26N 4 55W
Herrera de Alcántar 31 39 39N 7 25W
Herrera de Pisuerga 30 42 35N 4 20W
Herrera del Duque 31 39 10N 5 3W
Herrick 99 41 5 S 147 55 E
Herrin 117 37 50N 89 0W
Herrljunga 49 58 5N 13 1 E
Hersbruck 25 49 30N 11 25 E
Herstal 16 50 40N 5 38 E
Hersvik 47 61 10N 4 53 E
Hertford 13 51 47N 0 4W
Hertford □ 13 51 51N 0 5W
's-Hertogenbosch 16 51 42N 5 17 E
Hertzogville 92 28 9 S 25 30 E
Hervás 30 40 16N 5 52W
Hervey B. 97 25 0 S 152 52 E
* Hervey Is. 95 19 30 S 159 0W
Herzberg, Cottbus, Ger. 24 51 40N 13 13 E
Herzberg, Niedersachsen, Ger. 24 51 38N 10 20 E
Herzliyya 62 32 10N 34 50 E
Herzogenburg 26 48 17N 15 41 E
Hesdin 19 50 21N 2 0 E
Hesel 24 53 18N 7 36 E
Heskestad 47 58 28N 6 22 E
Hespeler 112 43 26N 80 19W
Hesse = Hessen 24 50 40N 9 20 E
Hessen □ 24 50 40N 9 20 E
Hettinger 116 46 0N 102 38W
Hettstedt 24 51 39N 11 30 E
Hève, C. de la 18 49 30N 0 5 E
Heves □ 27 47 50N 20 0 E
Hevron → 62 31 12N 34 42 E
Hewett, C. 105 70 16N 67 45W
Hex River 92 33 30 S 19 35 E
Hexham 12 54 58N 2 7W
Hexigten Qi 76 43 18N 117 30 E
Heyfield 100 37 59 S 146 47 E
Heysham 12 54 5N 2 53W
Heywood 99 38 8 S 141 37 E
Hi-no-Misaki 74 35 26N 132 38 E
Hialeach 115 25 49N 80 17W
Hiawatha, Kans., U.S.A. 116 39 55N 95 33W
Hiawatha, Utah, U.S.A. 118 39 29N 111 1W
Hibbing 116 47 30N 93 0W
Hickman 117 36 35N 89 8W
Hickory 115 35 46N 81 17W
Hicks Pt. 97 37 49 S 149 17 E
Hicksville 113 40 46N 73 30W
Hida 46 47 10N 23 19 E
Hida-Sammyaku 74 36 30N 137 40 E
Hidalgo 120 24 15N 99 26W
Hidalgo del Parral 120 26 58N 105 40W
Hidalgo, Presa M. 120 26 30N 108 35W
Hiddensee 24 54 30N 13 6 E
Hieflau 26 47 36N 14 46 E
Hiendelaencina 32 41 5N 3 0W
Hierro 80 27 44N 18 0 E
Higashiōsaka 74 34 40N 135 37 E
Higgins 117 36 9N 100 1W
High Atlas = Haut Atlas 82 32 30N 5 0W
High I. 107 56 40N 61 10W
High Island 117 29 32N 94 22W
High Level 108 58 31N 117 8W
High Point 115 35 57N 79 58W
High Prairie 108 55 30N 116 30W
High River 108 50 30N 113 50W
High Springs 115 29 50N 82 40W
High Tatra 27 49 30N 20 00 E
High Wycombe 13 51 37N 0 45W
Highbury 98 16 25 S 143 9 E
Highland □ 14 57 30N 5 0W
Highland Park 114 42 10N 87 50W
Highmore 116 44 35N 99 26W
Highrock L. 109 57 5N 105 32W
Higley 119 33 27N 111 46W
Hihya 86 30 40N 31 36 E
Hiiumaa 54 58 50N 22 45 E
Híjar 32 41 10N 0 27W
Ḩijārah, Şaḩrā' al 64 30 25N 44 30 E
Hiko 119 37 30N 115 13W
Hikone 74 35 15N 136 10 E
Hildburghhausen 25 50 24N 10 43 E
Hildesheim 24 52 9N 9 55 E
Hill City, Idaho, U.S.A. 118 43 20N 115 2W
Hill City, Kans., U.S.A. 116 39 25N 99 51W
Hill City, Minn., U.S.A. 116 46 57N 93 35W
Hill City, S.D., U.S.A. 116 43 58N 103 35W
Hill Island L. 109 60 30N 109 50W
Hillared 49 57 37N 13 10 E
Hillegom 16 52 18N 4 35 E
Hillerød 49 55 56N 12 19 E
Hillerstorp 49 57 20N 13 52 E
Hillingdon 13 51 33N 0 29W
Hillman 114 45 5N 83 52W
Hillmond 109 53 26N 109 41W
Hillsboro, Kans., U.S.A. 116 38 22N 97 10W
Hillsboro, N. Mex., U.S.A. 119 33 0N 107 35W
Hillsboro, N.D., U.S.A. 116 47 23N 97 9W
Hillsboro, N.H., U.S.A. 114 43 8N 71 56W
Hillsboro, Oreg., U.S.A: 118 45 31N 123 0W
Hillsboro, Tex., U.S.A. 117 32 0N 97 10W
Hillsdale, Mich., U.S.A. 114 41 55N 84 40W
Hillsdale, N.Y., U.S.A. 113 42 11N 73 30W
Hillsport 106 49 27N 85 34W
Hillston 97 33 30 S 145 31 E
Hilo 110 19 44N 155 5W
Hilonghilong 73 9 10N 125 45 E
Hilton 112 43 16N 77 48W
Hilversum 16 52 14N 5 10 E
Himachal Pradesh □ 68 31 30N 77 0 E
Himalaya 67 29 0N 84 0 E
Himara 44 40 8N 19 43 E
Himeji 74 34 50N 134 40 E
Himi 74 36 50N 137 0 E
Himmerland 49 56 45N 9 30 E
Ḩimş 64 34 40N 36 45 E
Hinako, Kepulauan 72 0 50N 97 20 E
Hinchinbrook I. 97 18 20 S 146 15 E
Hinckley, U.K. 13 52 33N 1 21W
Hinckley, U.S.A. 118 39 18N 112 41W
Hindås 49 57 42N 12 27 E
Hindaun 68 26 44N 77 5 E
Hindmarsh L. 99 36 5 S 141 55 E
Hindol 69 20 40N 85 10 E
Hindsholm 49 55 30N 10 40 E
Hindu Bagh 68 30 56N 67 50 E
Hindu Kush 65 36 0N 71 0 E
Hindupur 70 13 49N 77 32 E
Hines Creek 108 56 20N 118 40W
Hinganghat 68 20 30N 78 52 E
Hingham 118 48 34N 110 29W
Hingoli 70 19 41N 77 15 E
Hinlopenstretet 4 79 35N 18 40 E
Hinna 85 10 25N 11 35 E
Hinojosa del Duque 31 38 30N 5 9W
Hinsdale 118 48 26N 107 2W
Hinterrhein → 25 46 40N 9 25 E
Hinton, Can. 108 53 26N 117 34W
Hinton, U.S.A. 114 37 40N 80 51W
Hippolytushoef 16 52 54N 4 58 E
Hirakud 69 21 32N 83 51 E
Hirakud Dam 69 21 32N 83 45 E
Hiratsuka 74 35 19N 139 21 E
Hirhafok 83 23 49N 5 45 E
Hîrlău 46 47 23N 27 0 E
Hirosaki 74 40 34N 140 28 E
Hiroshima 74 34 24N 132 30 E
Hiroshima □ 74 34 50N 133 0 E
Hirsoholmene 49 57 30N 10 36 E
Hirson 19 49 55N 4 4 E
Hîrşova 46 44 40N 27 59 E
Hirtshals 49 57 36N 9 57 E
Ḩişn Dibā 65 25 45N 56 16 E
Hispaniola 121 19 0N 71 0W
Hissar 68 29 12N 75 45 E
Hita 74 33 20N 130 58 E
Hitachi 74 36 36N 140 39 E
Hitchin 13 51 57N 0 16W
Hitoyoshi 74 32 13N 130 45 E
Hitra 47 63 30N 8 45 E
Hitzacker 24 53 9N 11 1 E
Ḩiyyon, N. → 62 30 25N 35 10 E
Hjalmar L. 109 61 33N 109 25W
Hjälmare kanal 48 59 20N 15 59 E
Hjälmaren 48 59 18N 15 40 E
Hjartdal 47 59 37N 8 41 E
Hjerkinn 47 62 13N 9 33 E
Hjørring 49 57 29N 9 59 E
Hjorted 49 57 37N 16 19 E
Hjortkvarn 49 58 54N 15 26 E
Hlinsko 26 49 45N 15 54 E
Hlohovec 27 48 26N 17 49 E
Hńak 4 70 40N 52 10W
Ho 85 6 37N 0 27 E
Ho Chi Minh, Phanh Bho 71 10 58N 106 40 E
Hoa Binh 71 20 50N 105 20 E
Hoai Nhon (Bon Son) 71 14 28N 109 1 E
Hoare B. 105 65 17N 62 30W
Hobart, Austral. 97 42 50 S 147 21 E
Hobart, U.S.A. 117 35 0N 99 5W
Hobbs 117 32 40N 103 3W
Hobbs Coast 5 74 50 S 131 0W
Hoboken, Belg. 16 51 11N 4 21 E
Hoboken, U.S.A. 113 40 45N 74 4W
Hobro 49 56 39N 9 46 E
Hoburgen 49 56 55N 18 7 E
Hochatown 117 34 11N 94 39W
Hochschwab 26 47 35N 15 0 E
Höchst 25 50 6N 8 33 E
Höchstadt 25 49 42N 10 48 E
Hockenheim 25 49 18N 8 33 E
Hodgson 109 51 13N 97 36W
Hódmezövásárhely 27 46 28N 20 22 E
Hodna, Chott el 83 35 30N 5 0 E
Hodna, Monts du 83 35 52N 4 42 E
Hodonín 27 48 50N 17 10 E
Hoëdic 18 47 21N 2 52W
Hoek van Holland 16 52 0N 4 7 E
Hoëveld 93 26 30 S 30 0 E
Hof, Ger. 25 50 18N 11 55 E
Hof, Iceland 50 64 33N 14 40W
Höfðakaupstaður 50 65 50N 20 19W
Hofgeismar 24 51 29N 9 23 E
Hofors 48 60 31N 16 15 E
Hofsjökull 50 64 49N 18 48W
Hofsós 50 65 53N 19 26W
Hōfu 74 34 3N 131 34 E
Hogansville 115 33 14N 84 50W

* *Renamed Manuae*

Hogeland Hunterville

Hogeland 118 48 51N 108 40W
Hogenakai Falls 70 12 6N 77 50 E
Högfors 48 59 58N 15 3 E
Högsäter 49 58 38N 12 5 E
Högsby 49 57 10N 16 1 E
Högsjö 48 59 4N 15 44 E
Hoh Xil Shan 75 35 0N 89 0 E
Hohe Rhön 25 50 24N 9 58 E
Hohe Tauern 26 47 11N 12 40 E
Hohe Venn 16 50 30N 6 5 E
Hohenau 27 48 36N 16 55 E
Hohenems 26 47 22N 9 42 E
Hohenstein Ernstthal 24 50 48N 12 43 E
Hohenwald 115 35 35N 87 30W
Hohenwestedt 24 54 6N 9 30 E
Hohhot 76 40 52N 111 40 E
Hohoe 85 7 8N 0 32 E
Hoi An 71 15 30N 108 19 E
Hoi Xuan 71 20 25N 105 9 E
Hoisington 116 38 33N 98 50W
Højer 49 54 58N 8 42 E
Hok 49 57 31N 14 16 E
Hökensås 49 58 0N 14 5 E
Hökerum 49 57 51N 13 16 E
Hokianga Harbour 101 35 31 S 173 22 E
Hokitika 101 42 42 S 171 0 E
Hokkaidō □ 74 43 30N 143 0 E
Hokksund 47 59 44N 9 59 E
Hol-Hol 87 11 20N 42 50 E
Holbæk 49 55 43N 11 43 E
Holbrook, Austral. 99 35 42 S 147 18 E
Holbrook, U.S.A. 119 35 54N 110 10W
Holden, Can. 108 53 13N 112 11W
Holden, U.S.A. 118 39 0N 112 26W
Holdenville 117 35 5N 96 25W
Holderness 12 53 45N 0 5W
Holdfast 109 50 58N 105 25W
Holdrege 116 40 26N 99 22W
Hole 47 60 6N 10 12 E
Hole-Narsipur 70 12 48N 76 16 E
Holešov 27 49 20N 17 35 E
Holguín 121 20 50N 76 20W
Holič 27 48 49N 17 10 E
Hollabrunn 26 48 34N 16 5 E
Hollams Bird I. 92 24 40 S 14 30 E
Holland 114 42 47N 86 7W
Hollandia = Jayapura 73 2 28 S 140 38 E
Höllen 47 58 6N 7 49 E
Hollfeld 25 49 56N 11 18 E
Hollick Kenyon Plateau 5 82 0 S 110 0W
Hollidaysburg 114 40 26N 78 25W
Hollis 117 34 45N 99 55W
Hollister, Calif., U.S.A. 119 36 51N 121 24W
Hollister, Idaho, U.S.A. 118 42 21N 114 40W
Holly 116 38 7N 102 7W
Holly Hill 115 29 15N 81 3W
Holly Springs 117 34 45N 89 25W
Hollywood, Calif., U.S.A. 110 34 7N 118 25W
Hollywood, Fla., U.S.A. 115 26 0N 80 9W
Holm 48 62 40N 16 40 E
Holman Island 104 70 42N 117 41W
Hólmavík 50 65 42N 21 40W
Holmedal 47 61 22N 5 11 E
Holmegil 48 59 10N 11 44 E
Holmestrand 47 59 31N 10 14 E
Holmsbu 47 59 32N 10 27 E
Holmsjön 48 62 26N 15 20 E
Holmsland Klit 49 56 0N 8 5 E
Holmsund 50 63 41N 20 20 E
Holod 46 46 49N 22 8 E
Holon 62 32 2N 34 47 E
Holroyd → 97 14 10 S 141 36 E
Holstebro 49 56 22N 8 37 E
Holsworthy 13 50 48N 4 21W
Holt 50 63 33N 19 48W
Holte 49 55 50N 12 29 E
Holton, Can. 107 54 31N 57 12W
Holton, U.S.A. 116 39 28N 95 44W
Holtville 119 32 50N 115 27W
Holum 47 58 6N 7 32 E
Holwerd 16 53 22N 5 54 E
Holy Cross 104 62 10N 159 52W
Holy I., England, U.K. 12 55 42N 1 48W
Holy I., Wales, U.K. 12 53 17N 4 37W
Holyhead 12 53 18N 4 38W
Holyoke, Colo., U.S.A. 116 40 39N 102 18W
Holyoke, Mass., U.S.A. 114 42 14N 72 37W
Holyrood 107 47 27N 53 8W
Holzkirchen 25 47 53N 11 42 E
Holzminden 24 51 49N 9 31 E
Homa Bay 90 0 36 S 34 30 E
* Homa Bay □ 90 0 50 S 34 30 E
Homalin 67 24 55N 95 0 E
Homberg 24 51 2N 9 20 E
Hombori 85 15 20N 1 38W
Homburg 25 49 19N 7 21 E
Home B. 105 68 40N 67 10W
Home Hill 97 19 43 S 147 25 E
Homedale 118 43 42N 116 59W
Homer, Alaska, U.S.A. 104 59 40N 151 35W
Homer, La., U.S.A. 117 32 50N 93 4W
Homestead, Austral. 98 20 20 S 145 40 E
Homestead, Fla., U.S.A. 115 25 29N 80 27W
Homestead, Oreg., U.S.A. 118 45 5N 116 57W
Hominy 117 36 26N 96 24W
Homnabad 70 17 45N 77 11 E
Homoine 93 23 55 S 35 8 E
Homoljske Planina 42 44 10N 21 45 E
Homorod 46 46 5N 25 15 E
Homs = Ḥimş 64 34 40N 36 45 E
Hon Chong 71 10 25N 104 30 E
Honan = Henan □ 75 34 0N 114 0 E
Honda 126 5 12N 74 45W
Hondeklipbaai 92 30 19 S 17 17 E
Hondo 117 29 22N 99 6W
Hondo → 120 18 25N 88 21W
Honduras ■ 121 14 40N 86 30W
Honduras, Golfo de 120 16 50N 87 0W
Honesdale 113 41 34N 75 17W
Honey L. 118 40 13N 120 14W
Honfleur 18 49 25N 0 13 E
Hong Kong ■ 75 22 11N 114 14 E
Hong'an 77 31 20N 114 40 E
Hongha → 71 22 0N 104 0 E
Honghai Wan 77 22 40N 115 0 E
Honghu 77 29 50N 113 30 E
Hongjiang 75 27 7N 109 59 E
Hongshui He → 75 23 48N 109 30 E
Hongtong 76 36 16N 111 40 E
Honguedo, Détroit d' 107 49 15N 64 0W
Hongze Hu 75 33 15N 118 35 E
Honiara 94 9 27 S 159 57 E
Honiton 13 50 48N 3 11W
Honkorâb, Ras 86 24 35N 35 10 E
Honolulu 110 21 19N 157 52W
Honshū 74 36 0N 138 0 E
Hontoria del Pinar 32 41 50N 3 10W
Hood Mt. 118 45 24N 121 41W
Hood, Pt. 96 34 23 S 119 34 E
Hood River 118 45 45N 121 31W
Hoodsport 118 47 24N 123 7W
Hooge 24 54 31N 8 36 E
Hoogeveen 16 52 44N 6 30 E
Hoogezand 16 53 11N 6 45 E
Hooghly → 69 21 56N 88 4 E
Hooghly-Chinsura 69 22 53N 88 27 E
Hook Hd. 15 52 8N 6 57W
Hook I. 98 20 4 S 149 0 E
Hook of Holland = Hoek van Holland 16 52 0N 4 7 E
Hooker 117 36 55N 101 10W
Hoopeston 114 40 30N 87 40W
Hoopstad 92 27 50 S 25 55 E
Hoorn 16 52 38N 5 4 E
Hoover Dam 119 36 0N 114 45W
Hooversville 112 40 8N 78 57W
Hop Bottom 113 41 41N 75 47W
Hopà 57 41 28N 41 30 E
Hope, Can. 108 49 25N 121 25 E
Hope, Ark., U.S.A. 117 33 40N 93 36W
Hope, N.D., U.S.A. 116 47 21N 97 42W
Hope Bay 5 65 0 S 55 0W
Hope, L. 99 28 24 S 139 18 E
Hope Pt. 104 68 20N 166 50W
Hope Town 121 26 35N 76 57W
Hopedale 107 55 28N 60 13W
Hopefield 92 33 3 S 18 22 E
Hopei = Hebei □ 76 39 0N 116 0 E
Hopelchén 120 19 46N 89 50W
Hopen 47 63 27N 8 2 E
Hopetoun, Vic., Austral. 99 35 42 S 142 22 E
Hopetoun, W. Australia, Austral. 100 33 57 S 120 7 E
Hopetown 92 29 34 S 24 3 E
Hopkins 116 40 31N 94 45W
Hopkins → 100 38 25 S 142 30 E
Hopkinsville 115 36 52N 87 26W
Hopland 118 39 0N 123 7W
Hoptrup 49 55 11N 9 28 E
Hoquiam 118 46 50N 123 55W
Horazdovice 26 49 19N 13 42 E
Horcajo de Santiago 32 39 50N 3 1W
Hordaland fylke □ 47 60 25N 6 15 E
Horden Hills 96 20 40 S 130 20 E
Horezu 46 45 6N 24 0 E
Horgen 25 47 15N 8 35 E
Horgoš 42 46 10N 20 0 E
Horice 26 50 21N 15 39 E
Horlick Mts. 5 84 0 S 102 0W
Hormoz 65 27 35N 55 0 E
Hormoz, Jaz. ye 65 27 8N 56 28 E
Hormuz Str. 65 26 30N 56 30 E
Horn, Austria 26 48 39N 15 40 E
Horn, Ísafjarðarsýsla, Iceland 50 66 28N 22 28W
Horn, Suður-Múlasýsla, Iceland 50 65 10N 13 31W
Horn → 108 61 30N 118 1W
Horn, Cape = Hornos, Cabo de 128 55 50 S 67 30W
Horn Head 15 55 13N 8 0W
Horn, I. 115 30 17N 88 40W
Horn Mts. 108 62 15N 119 15W
Hornachuelos 31 37 50N 5 14W
Hornavan 50 66 15N 17 30 E
Hornbæk 49 56 5N 12 26 E
Hornbeck 117 31 22N 93 20W
Hornbrook 118 41 58N 122 37W
Hornburg 24 52 2N 10 36 E
Horncastle 12 53 13N 0 8W
Horndal 48 60 18N 16 23 E
Hornell 114 42 23N 77 41W
Hornell L. 108 62 20N 119 25W
Hornepayne 106 49 14N 84 48W
Hornindal 47 61 58N 6 30 E
Hornnes 47 58 34N 7 45 E
Hornos, Cabo de 128 55 50 S 67 30W
Hornoy 19 49 50N 1 54 E
Hornsby 99 33 42 S 151 2 E
Hornsea 12 53 55N 0 10W
Hornslandet 48 61 35N 17 37 E
Hornslet 49 56 18N 10 19 E
Hörnum 24 54 44N 8 18 E
Horovice 26 49 48N 13 53 E
Horqin Youyi Qianqi 75 46 5N 122 3 E
Horqueta 124 23 15 S 56 55W
Horra, La 30 41 44N 3 53W
Horred 49 57 22N 12 28 E
Horse Cr. → 116 41 57N 103 58W
Horse Is. 107 50 15N 55 50W
Horsefly L. 108 52 25N 121 0W
Horsens 49 55 52N 9 51 E
Horsens Fjord 49 55 50N 10 0 E
Horseshoe Dam 119 33 45N 111 35W
Horsham, Austral. 97 36 44 S 142 13 E
Horsham, U.K. 13 51 4N 0 20W
Horšovský Týn 26 49 31N 12 58 E
Horten 47 59 25N 10 32 E
Hortobágy → 27 47 30N 21 6 E
Horton 116 39 42N 95 30W
Horton → 104 69 56N 126 52W
Hörvik 49 56 2N 14 45 E
Horwood, L. 106 48 5N 82 20W
Hosaina 87 7 30N 37 47 E
Hosdurga 70 13 49N 76 17 E
Hose, Pegunungan 72 2 5N 114 6 E
Hoshangabad 68 22 45N 77 45 E
Hoshiarpur 68 31 30N 75 58 E
Hosmer 116 45 36N 99 29W
Hospet 70 15 15N 76 20 E
Hospitalet de Llobregat 32 41 21N 2 6 E
Hospitalet, L' 20 42 36N 1 47 E
Hoste, I. 128 55 0 S 69 0W
Hostens 20 44 30N 0 40W
Hot 71 18 8N 98 29 E
Hot Creek Ra. 118 39 0N 116 0W
Hot Springs, Ari., U.S.A. 117 34 30N 93 0W
Hot Springs, S.D., U.S.A. 116 43 25N 103 30W
Hotagen 50 63 50N 14 30 E
Hotan 75 37 25N 79 55 E
Hotazel 92 27 17 S 23 00 E
Hotchkiss 119 38 47N 107 47W
Hoting 50 64 8N 16 15 E
Hotolishti 44 41 10N 20 25 E
Hottentotsbaai 92 26 8 S 14 59 E
Houat 18 47 24N 2 58W
Houck 119 35 15N 109 15W
Houdan 19 48 48N 1 35 E
Houffalize 16 50 8N 5 48 E
Houghton 116 47 9N 88 39W
Houghton L. 114 44 20N 84 40W
Houghton-le-Spring 12 54 51N 1 28W
Houhora 101 34 49 S 173 9 E
Houlton 107 46 5N 67 50W
Houma 117 29 35N 90 44W
Houndé 84 11 34N 3 31W
Hourtin 20 45 11N 1 4W
Hourtin, Étang d' 20 45 10N 1 6W
Houston, Can. 108 54 25N 126 39W
Houston, Mo., U.S.A. 117 37 20N 92 0W
Houston, Tex., U.S.A. 117 29 50N 95 20W
Houtman Abrolhos 96 28 43 S 113 48 E
Hov 49 55 55N 10 15 E
Hova 49 58 53N 14 14 E
Høvåg 47 58 10N 8 16 E
Hovd (Jargalant) 75 48 2N 91 37 E
Hovden 47 59 33N 7 22 E
Hove 13 50 50N 0 10W
Hovmantorp 49 56 47N 15 7 E
Hövsgöl Nuur 75 51 0N 100 30 E
Hovsta 48 59 22N 15 15 E
Howakil 87 15 10N 40 16 E
Howar, Wadi → 87 17 30N 27 8 E
Howard, Austral. 99 25 16 S 152 32 E
Howard, Kans., U.S.A. 117 37 30N 96 16W
Howard, Pa., U.S.A. 112 41 0N 77 40W
Howard, S.D., U.S.A. 116 44 2N 97 30W
Howard L. 109 62 15N 105 57W
Howe 118 43 48N 113 0W
Howe, C. 97 37 30 S 150 0 E
Howell 114 42 38N 83 56W
Howick, Can. 113 45 11N 73 51W
Howick, S. Afr. 93 29 28 S 30 14 E
Howick Group 98 14 20 S 145 30 E
Howitt, L. 99 27 40 S 138 40 E
Howley 107 49 12N 57 2W
Howrah 69 22 37N 88 20 E
Howth Hd. 15 53 21N 6 0W
Höxter 24 51 45N 9 26 E
Hoy I. 14 58 50N 3 15W
Hoya 24 52 47N 9 10 E
Hoyerswerda 24 51 26N 14 14 E
Hoyos 30 40 9N 6 45W
Hpungan Pass 67 27 30N 96 55 E
Hrádec Králové 26 50 15N 15 50 E
Hrádek 27 48 46N 16 16 E
Hranice 27 49 34N 17 45 E
Hron → 27 47 49N 18 45 E
Hrubieszów 28 50 49N 23 51 E
Hrubý Nizký Jeseník 27 50 7N 17 10 E
Hrvatska 39 45 20N 16 0 E
Hrvatska □ 42 45 20N 18 0 E
Hsenwi 67 23 22N 97 55 E
Hsiamen = Xiamen 75 24 25N 118 4 E
Hsian = Xi'an 77 34 15N 109 0 E
Hsinhailien = Lianyungang 77 34 40N 119 11 E
Hsüchou = Xuzhou 77 34 18N 117 18 E
Hua Hin 71 12 34N 99 58 E
Hua Xian, Henan, China 77 35 30N 114 30 E
Hua Xian, Shaanxi, China 77 34 30N 109 48 E
Huacheng 77 24 4N 115 37 E
Huacho 126 11 10 S 77 35W
Huachón 126 10 35 S 76 0W
Huachuan 76 46 50N 130 21 E
Huade 76 41 55N 113 59 E
Huadian 76 43 0N 126 40 E
Huai He → 75 33 0N 118 30 E
Huai'an 77 33 30N 119 10 E
Huaide 76 43 30N 124 40 E
Huainan 75 32 38N 116 58 E
Huaiyang 77 33 40N 114 52 E
Huaiyuan 77 24 31N 108 22 E
Huajianzi 76 41 23N 125 20 E
Huajuapan de Leon 120 17 50N 97 48W
Hualian 77 23 59N 121 37 E
Huallaga → 126 5 0 S 75 30W
Hualpai Pk. 119 35 8N 113 58W
Huambo 89 12 42 S 15 54 E
Huan Jiang → 76 34 28N 109 0 E
Huan Xian 76 36 33N 107 7 E
Huancabamba 126 5 10 S 79 15W
Huancane 126 15 10 S 69 44W
Huancapi 126 13 40 S 74 0W
Huancavelica 126 12 50 S 75 5W
Huancayo 126 12 5 S 75 12W
Huang He 75 37 55N 118 50 E
Huangchuan 77 32 15N 115 10 E
Huangliu 75 18 20N 108 50 E
Huanglong 76 35 30N 109 59 E
Huangshi 75 30 10N 115 3 E
Huangyan 77 28 38N 121 19 E
Huánuco 126 9 55 S 76 15W
Huaraz 126 9 30 S 77 32W
Huarmey 126 10 5 S 78 5W
Huascarán 126 9 8 S 77 36W
Huasco 124 28 30 S 71 15W
Huasco → 124 28 27 S 71 13W
Huatabampo 120 26 50N 109 50W
Huay Namota 120 21 56N 104 30W
Huayllay 126 11 03 S 76 21W
Hubbard 117 31 50N 96 50W
Hubbart Pt. 109 59 21N 94 41W
Hubei □ 75 31 0N 112 0 E
Hubli 70 15 22N 75 15 E
Hückelhoven-Ratheim 24 51 6N 6 13 E
Huczwa → 28 50 49N 23 58 E
Huddersfield 12 53 38N 1 49W
Hudi 86 17 43N 34 18 E
Hudiksvall 48 61 43N 17 10 E
Hudson, Can. 109 50 6N 92 09W
Hudson, Mass., U.S.A. 113 42 23N 71 35W
Hudson, Mich., U.S.A. 114 41 50N 84 20W
Hudson, N.Y., U.S.A. 114 42 15N 73 46W
Hudson, Wis., U.S.A. 116 44 57N 92 45W
Hudson, Wyo., U.S.A. 118 42 54N 108 37W
Hudson → 114 40 42N 74 2W
Hudson Bay, Can. 105 60 0N 86 0W
Hudson Bay, Sask., Can. 109 52 51N 102 23W
Hudson Falls 114 43 18N 73 34W
Hudson Hope 108 56 0N 121 54W
Hudson Mts. 5 74 32 S 99 20W
Hudson Str. 105 62 0N 70 0W
Hue 71 16 30N 107 35 E
Huebra → 30 41 2N 6 48W
Huedin 46 46 52N 23 2 E
Huelgoat 18 48 22N 3 46W
Huelma 33 37 39N 3 28W
Huelva 31 37 18N 6 57W
Huelva □ 31 37 40N 7 0W
Huelva → 31 37 27N 6 0W
Huentelauquén 124 31 38 S 71 33W
Huércal Overa 33 37 23N 1 57W
Huerta, Sa. de la 124 31 10 S 67 30W
Huertas, C. de las 33 38 21N 0 24W
Huerva → 32 41 39N 0 52W
Huesca 32 42 8N 0 25W
Huesca □ 32 42 20N 0 1 E
Huéscar 33 37 44N 2 35W
Huetamo 120 18 36N 100 54W
Huete 32 40 10N 2 43W
Hugh → 96 25 1 S 134 1 E
Hughenden 97 20 52 S 144 10 E
Hughes 104 66 0N 154 20W
Hugo 116 39 12N 103 27W
Hugoton 117 37 11N 101 22W
Hui Xian 76 35 27N 113 12 E
Hui'an 77 25 1N 118 43 E
Huichang 77 25 32N 115 45 E
Huichapán 120 20 24N 99 40W
Huihe 76 48 12N 119 17 E
Huila, Nevado del 126 3 0N 76 0W
Huilai 77 23 0N 116 18 E
Huimin 76 37 27N 117 28 E
Huinan 76 42 40N 126 2 E
Huinca Renancó 124 34 51 S 64 22W
Huining 76 35 38N 105 0 E
Huinong 76 39 5N 106 35 E
Huisne → 18 47 59N 0 11 E
Huize 75 26 24N 103 15 E
Huizhou 77 23 0N 114 23 E
Hukawng Valley 67 26 30N 96 30 E
Hukou 77 29 45N 116 21 E
Hukuntsi 92 23 58 S 21 45 E
Hula 87 6 33N 38 30 E
Hulan 75 46 1N 126 37 E
Ḩulayfā' 64 25 58N 40 45 E
Huld 75 45 5N 105 30 E
Ḩulda 62 31 50N 34 51 E
Hulin 76 45 48N 132 59 E
Hull, Can. 106 45 25N 75 44W
Hull, U.K. 12 53 45N 0 20W
Hull → 12 53 43N 0 25W
Hulst 16 51 17N 4 2 E
Hultsfred 49 57 30N 15 52 E
Hulun Nur 75 49 0N 117 30 E
Huma 76 51 43N 126 38 E
Huma He → 76 51 42N 126 42 E
Humahuaca 124 23 10 S 65 25W
Humaitá, Brazil 126 7 35 S 63 1W
Humaitá, Parag. 124 27 2 S 58 31W
Humansdorp 92 34 2 S 24 46 E
Humbe 92 16 40 S 14 55 E
Humber → 12 53 40N 0 10W
Humberside □ 12 53 50N 0 30W
Humble 117 29 59N 93 18W
Humboldt, Can. 109 52 15N 105 9W
Humboldt, Iowa, U.S.A. 116 42 42N 94 15W
Humboldt, Tenn., U.S.A. 117 35 50N 88 55W
Humboldt → 118 40 2N 118 31W
Humboldt Gletscher 4 79 30N 62 0W
Hume, L. 97 36 0 S 147 0 E
Humenné 27 48 55N 21 50 E
Humphreys Pk. 119 35 24N 111 38W
Humpolec 26 49 31N 15 20 E
Hūn 83 29 2N 16 0 E
Húnaflói 50 65 50N 20 50W
Hunan □ 75 27 30N 112 0 E
Hunchun 76 42 52N 130 28 E
Hundested 49 55 58N 11 52 E
Hundred Mile House 108 51 38N 121 18W
Hunedoara 46 45 40N 22 50 E
Hunedoara □ 46 45 50N 22 54 E
Hünfeld 24 50 40N 9 47 E
Hungary ■ 27 47 20N 19 20 E
Hungary, Plain of 9 47 0N 20 0 E
Hungerford 99 28 58 S 144 24 E
Hŭngnam 76 39 49N 127 45 E
Huni Valley 84 5 33N 1 56W
Hunsberge 92 27 45 S 17 12 E
Hunsrück 25 49 30N 7 0 E
Hunstanton 12 52 57N 0 30 E
Hunsur 70 12 16N 76 16 E
Hunte → 24 52 30N 8 19 E
Hunter, N.D., U.S.A. 116 47 12N 97 17W
Hunter, N.Y., U.S.A. 113 42 13N 74 13W
Hunter → 100 32 52 S 151 46 E
Hunter I., Austral. 97 40 30 S 144 45 E
Hunter I., Can. 108 51 55N 128 0W
Hunter Ra. 99 32 45 S 150 15 E
Hunters Road 91 19 9 S 29 49 E
Hunterton 99 26 12 S 148 30 E
Hunterville 101 39 56 S 175 35 E

* *Renamed South Nyanza*

Huntingburg Inthanon, Doi

Huntingburg 114 38 20N 86 58W
Huntingdon, Can. 106 45 6N 74 10W
Huntingdon, U.K. 13 52 20N 0 11W
Huntingdon, U.S.A. 114 40 28N 78 1W
Huntington, Ind., U.S.A. 114 40 52N 85 30W
Huntington, N.Y., U.S.A. 113 40 52N 73 25W
Huntington, Oreg., U.S.A. 118 44 22N 117 21W
Huntington, Ut., U.S.A. 118 39 24N 111 1W
Huntington, W. Va., U.S.A. 114 38 20N 82 30W
Huntington Beach 119 33 40N 118 0W
Huntington Park 119 33 58N 118 15W
Huntly, N.Z. 101 37 34S 175 11E
Huntly, U.K. 14 57 27N 2 48W
Huntsville, Can. 106 45 20N 79 14W
Huntsville, Ala., U.S.A. 115 34 45N 86 35W
Huntsville, Tex., U.S.A. 117 30 45N 95 35W
Hunyani → 91 15 57S 30 39E
Huo Xian 76 36 36N 111 42E
Huon, G. 98 7 0S 147 30E
Huonville 97 43 0S 147 5E
Huoqiu 77 32 20N 116 12E
Huoshao Dao 77 22 40N 121 30E
Hupeh □ = Hubei □ 75 31 0N 112 0E
Hurbanovo 27 47 51N 18 11E
Hure Qi 76 42 45N 121 45E
Hurezani 46 44 49N 23 40E
Hurghada 86 27 15N 33 50E
Hurley, N. Mex., U.S.A. 119 32 45N 108 7W
Hurley, Wis., U.S.A. 116 46 26N 90 10W
Huron, Ohio, U.S.A. 112 41 22N 82 34W
Huron, S.D., U.S.A. 116 44 22N 98 12W
Huron, L. 112 45 0N 83 0W
Hurricane 119 37 10N 113 12W
Hurso 87 9 35N 41 33E
Hurum, Buskerud, Norway 47 59 36N 10 23E
Hurum, Oppland, Norway 47 61 9N 8 46E
Hurunui → 101 42 54S 173 18E
Hurup 49 56 46N 8 25E
Húsavík 50 66 3N 17 21W
Huşi 46 46 41N 28 7E
Huskvarna 49 57 47N 14 15E
Husøy 47 61 3N 4 44E
Hussar 108 51 3N 112 41W
Hustopéce 27 48 57N 16 43E
Husum, Ger. 24 54 27N 9 3E
Husum, Sweden 48 63 21N 19 12E
Hutchinson, Kans., U.S.A. 117 38 3N 97 59W
Hutchinson, Minn., U.S.A. 116 44 50N 94 22W
Hutou 76 45 58N 133 38E
Huttenberg 26 46 56N 14 33E
Hüttental 24 50 52N 8 1E
Huttig 117 33 5N 92 10W
Hutton, Mt. 99 25 51S 148 20E
Huwun 87 4 23N 40 6E
Ḩuwwārah 62 32 9N 35 15E
Huy 16 50 31N 5 15E
Hvaler 47 59 4N 11 1E
Hvammur 50 65 13N 21 49W
Hvar 39 43 11N 16 28E
Hvarski Kanal 39 43 15N 16 35E
Hvítá 50 64 40N 21 5W
Hvítá → 50 64 0N 20 58W
Hvítárvatn 50 64 37N 19 50W
Hvitsten 47 59 35N 10 42E
Hwang Ho = Huang He → 76 37 50N 118 50E
Hyannis 116 42 0N 101 45W
Hyargas Nuur 75 49 0N 93 0E
Hyatts 114 38 59N 76 55W
Hybo 48 61 49N 16 15E
Hyderabad, India 70 17 22N 78 29E
Hyderabad, Pak. 68 25 23N 68 24E
* Hyderabad □ 68 25 3N 68 24E
Hyères 21 43 8N 6 9E
Hyères, Îles d' 21 43 0N 6 28E
Hyesan 76 41 20N 128 10E
Hyland → 108 59 52N 128 12W
Hylestad 47 59 6N 7 29E
Hyltebruk 49 56 59N 13 15E
Hyndman Pk. 118 43 50N 114 10W
Hyōgo □ 74 35 15N 135 0E
Hyrum 118 41 35N 111 56W
Hysham 118 46 21N 107 11W
Hythe 13 51 4N 1 5E
Hyvinkää 51 60 38N 24 50E

I

I-n-Azaoua 83 20 45N 7 31E
I-n-Échaï 82 20 10N 2 5W
I-n-Gall 85 16 51N 7 1E
I-n-Tabedog 82 19 48N 1 11E
Iabès, Erg 82 27 30N 2 2W
Iaco → 126 9 3S 68 34W
Iacobeni 46 47 25N 25 20E
Iakora 93 23 6S 46 40E
Ialomiţa □ 46 44 30N 27 30E
Ialomiţa → 46 44 42N 27 51E
Ianca 46 45 6N 27 29E
Iara 46 46 31N 23 35E
Iaşi 46 47 20N 27 0E
Iba 73 15 22N 120 0E
Ibadan 85 7 22N 3 58E
Ibagué 126 4 20N 75 20W
Iballja 44 42 12N 20 0E
Ibăneşti 46 46 45N 24 50E
Ibar → 42 43 43N 20 45E
Ibaraki □ 74 36 10N 140 10E
Ibarra 126 0 21N 78 7W
Ibba 87 4 49N 29 2E
Ibba, Bahr el 87 5 30N 28 55E
Ibbenbüren 24 52 16N 7 41E
Ibembo 90 2 35N 23 35E
Ibera, Laguna 124 28 30S 57 9W
Iberian Peninsula 8 40 0N 5 0W
Iberville 106 45 19N 73 17W
Iberville, Lac d' 106 55 55N 73 15W
Ibi 85 8 15N 9 44E
Ibiá 127 19 30S 46 30W
Ibicuy 124 33 55S 59 10W
Ibioapaba, Sa. da 127 4 0S 41 30W
Ibiza 33 38 54N 1 26E
Iblei, Monti 41 37 15N 14 45E
Ibo 91 12 22S 40 40E
Ibonma 73 3 29S 133 31E
Ibotirama 127 12 13S 43 12W
Ibriktepe 44 41 2N 26 33E
Ibshawâi 86 29 21N 30 40E
Ibu 73 1 35N 127 33E
Iburg 24 52 10N 8 3E
Icá 126 14 0S 75 48W
Iça → 126 2 55S 67 58W
Içana 126 0 21N 67 19W
Iceland ■ 50 65 0N 19 0W
Icha 59 55 30N 156 0E
Ich'ang = Yichang 75 30 40N 111 20E
Ichchapuram 70 19 10N 84 40E
Ichihara 74 35 28N 140 5E
Ichihawa 74 35 44N 139 55E
Ichilo → 126 15 57S 64 50W
Ichinomiya 74 35 18N 136 48E
Ichnya 54 50 52N 32 24E
Icht 82 29 6N 8 54W
Icy Str. 108 58 20N 135 30W
Ida Grove 116 42 20N 95 25W
Idabel 117 33 53N 94 50W
Idaga Hamus 87 14 13N 39 48E
Idah 85 7 5N 6 40E
Idaho □ 118 44 10N 114 0W
Idaho City 118 43 50N 115 52W
Idaho Falls 118 43 30N 112 1W
Idaho Springs 118 39 49N 105 30W
Idanha-a-Nova 30 39 50N 7 15W
Idar-Oberstein 25 49 43N 7 19E
Idd el Ghanam 81 11 30N 24 19E
Iddan 63 6 10N 48 55E
Idehan 83 27 10N 11 30E
Idehan Marzūq 83 24 50N 13 51E
Idelès 83 23 50N 5 53E
Idfû 86 25 0N 32 49E
Ídhi Óros 45 35 15N 24 45E
Ídhra 45 37 20N 23 28E
Idi 72 5 2N 97 37E
Idi Amin Dada, L. = Edward, L. 90 0 25S 29 40E
Idiofa 88 4 55S 19 42E
Idkerberget 48 60 22N 15 15E
Idku, Bahra el 86 31 18N 30 18E
Idlip 64 35 55N 36 38E
Idna 62 31 34N 34 58E
Idrija 39 46 0N 14 5E
Idritsa 54 56 25N 28 30E
Idstein 25 50 13N 8 17E
Idutywa 93 32 8S 28 18E
Ieper 16 50 51N 2 53E
Ierápetra 45 35 0N 25 44E
Ierissós 44 40 22N 23 52E
Ierissóu Kólpos 44 40 27N 23 57E
Ierzu 40 39 48N 9 32E
Iesi 39 43 32N 13 12E
Ifach, Punta 33 38 38N 0 5E
Ifanadiana 93 21 19S 47 39E
Ife 85 7 30N 4 31E
Iférouâne 85 19 5N 8 24E
Iffley 98 18 53S 141 12E
Ifni 82 29 29N 10 12W
Ifon 85 6 58N 5 40E
Iforas, Adrar des 85 19 40N 1 40E
Ifrane 82 33 33N 5 7W
Iganga 90 0 37N 33 28E
Igarapava 127 20 3S 47 47W
Igarapé Açu 127 1 4S 47 33W
Igarka 59 67 30N 86 33E
Igatimi 125 24 5S 55 40W
Igatpuri 70 19 40N 73 35E
Igbetti 85 8 44N 4 8E
Igbo-Ora 85 7 29N 3 15E
Igboho 85 8 53N 3 50E
Iggesund 48 61 39N 17 10E
Ighil Izane 82 35 44N 0 31E
Iglene 82 22 57N 4 58E
Iglésias 40 39 19N 8 27E
Igli 82 30 25N 2 19W
Igloolik 105 69 20N 81 49W
Igma 82 29 9N 6 24W
Igma, Gebel el 86 28 55N 34 0E
Ignace 106 49 30N 91 40W
Igoshevo 55 59 25N 42 35E
Igoumenítsa 44 39 32N 20 18E
Iguaçu → 125 25 36S 54 36W
Iguaçu, Cat. del 125 25 41S 54 26W
Iguala 120 18 20N 99 40W
Igualada 32 41 37N 1 37E
Iguassu = Iguaçu 125 25 41N 54 26W
Iguatu 127 6 20S 39 18W
Iguéla 88 2 0S 9 16E
Igunga □ 90 4 20S 33 45E
Ihiala 85 5 51N 6 55E
Ihosy 93 22 24S 46 8E
Ihotry, L. 93 21 56S 43 41E
Ii 50 65 19N 25 22E
Iida 74 35 35N 137 50E
Iijoki → 50 65 20N 25 20E
Iisalmi 50 63 32N 27 10E
Iizuka 74 33 38N 130 42E
Ijebu-Igbo 85 6 56N 4 1E
Ijebu-Ode 85 6 47N 3 58E
IJmuiden 16 52 28N 4 35E
IJssel → 16 52 35N 5 50E
IJsselmeer 16 52 45N 5 20E
Ijuí → 125 27 58S 55 20W
Ikale 85 7 40N 5 37E
Ikare 85 7 32N 5 40E
Ikaría 45 37 35N 26 10E
Ikast 49 56 8N 9 10E
Ikeja 85 6 36N 3 23E
Ikela 88 1 6S 23 6E
Ikerre-Ekiti 85 7 25N 5 19E
Ikhtiman 43 42 27N 23 48E
Iki 74 33 45N 129 42E
Ikimba L. 90 1 30S 31 20E
Ikire 85 7 23N 4 15E
Ikom 85 6 0N 8 42E
Ikopa → 93 16 45S 46 40E
Ikot Ekpene 85 5 12N 7 40E
Ikungu 90 1 33S 33 42E
Ikurun 85 7 54N 4 40E
Ila 85 8 0N 4 39E
Ilagan 73 17 7N 121 53E
Ilam 69 26 58N 87 58E
Ilanskiy 59 56 14N 96 3E
Ilaro 85 6 53N 3 3E
Iława 28 53 36N 19 34E
Ilayangudi 70 9 34N 78 37E
Ilbilbie 98 21 45S 149 20E
Île-à-la Crosse 109 55 27N 107 53W
Île-à-la-Crosse, Lac 109 55 40N 107 45W
Île-Bouchard, L' 18 47 7N 0 26E
Île-de-France 19 49 0N 2 20E
Île-sur-le-Doubs, L' 19 47 26N 6 34E
Ilebo 88 4 17S 20 55E
Ileje □ 91 9 30S 33 25E
Ilek 58 51 32N 53 21E
Ilek → 52 51 30N 53 22E
Ilero 85 8 0N 3 20E
Ilesha, Oyo, Nigeria 85 7 37N 4 40E
Ilesha, Oyo, Nigeria 85 8 57N 3 28E
Ilford 109 56 4N 95 35W
Ilfov □ 46 44 20N 26 0E
Ilfracombe, Austral. 97 23 30S 144 30E
Ilfracombe, U.K. 13 51 13N 4 8W
Ílhavo 30 40 33N 8 43W
Ilhéus 127 14 49S 39 2W
Ilia 46 45 57N 22 40E
Ilia □ 45 37 45N 21 35E
Ilich 58 40 50N 68 27E
Iliff 116 40 50N 103 3W
Iligan 73 8 12N 124 13E
Ilíki, L. 45 38 24N 23 15E
Iliodhrómia 44 39 12N 23 50E
Ilion 114 43 0N 75 3W
Ilirska-Bistrica 39 45 34N 14 14E
Ilkal 70 15 57N 76 8E
Ilkeston 12 52 59N 1 19W
Illana B. 73 7 35N 123 45E
Illapel 124 32 0S 71 10W
'Illār 62 32 23N 35 7E
Ille 20 42 40N 2 37E
Ille-et-Vilaine □ 18 48 10N 1 30W
Iller → 25 48 23N 9 58E
Illescas 30 40 8N 3 51W
Illiers 18 48 18N 1 15E
Illimani 126 16 30S 67 50W
Illinois □ 111 40 15N 89 30W
Illinois → 111 38 55N 90 28W
Illium = Troy 44 39 57N 26 12E
Illizi 83 26 31N 8 32E
Illora 31 37 17N 3 53W
Ilm → 24 51 7N 11 45E
Ilmen, Oz. 54 58 15N 31 10E
Ilmenau 24 50 41N 10 55E
Ilo 126 17 40S 71 20W
Ilobu 85 7 45N 4 25E
Iloilo 73 10 45N 122 33E
Ilok 42 45 15N 19 20E
Ilora 85 7 45N 3 50E
Ilorin 85 8 30N 4 35E
Iloulya 57 49 15N 44 2E
Ilovatka 55 50 30N 45 50E
Ilovlya → 57 49 14N 43 54E
Iłowa 28 51 30N 15 10E
Ilubabor □ 87 7 25N 35 0E
Ilukste 54 55 55N 26 20E
Ilva Mică 46 47 17N 24 40E
Ilwaki 73 7 55S 126 30E
Ilyichevsk 56 46 10N 30 35E
Iłża 28 51 10N 21 15E
Iłżanka → 28 51 14N 21 48E
Imabari 74 34 4N 133 0E
Imaloto → 93 23 27S 45 13E
Imandra, Oz. 52 67 30N 33 0E
Imari 74 33 15N 129 52E
Imasa 86 18 0N 36 12E
Imathía □ 44 40 30N 22 15E
Imbâbah 86 30 5N 31 12E
Imbler 118 45 31N 118 0W
Imdahane 82 32 8N 7 0W
imeni 26 Bakinskikh Komissarov (Neft-chala) 53 39 19N 49 12E
imeni 26 Bakinskikh Komissarov (Vyshzha) 53 39 22N 54 10E
Imeni Poliny Osipenko 59 52 30N 136 29E
Imeri, Serra 126 0 50N 65 25W
Imerimandroso 93 17 26S 48 35E
Imi (Hinna) 87 6 28N 42 10E
Imishly 57 39 49N 48 4E
Imitek 82 29 43N 8 10W
Imlay 118 40 45N 118 9W
Imlay City 112 43 0N 83 2W
Immenstadt 25 47 34N 10 13E
Immingham 12 53 37N 0 12W
Immokalee 115 26 25N 81 26W
Imo □ 85 5 15N 7 20E
Imola 39 44 20N 11 42E
Imotski 42 43 27N 17 12E
Imperatriz 127 5 30S 47 29W
Impéria 38 43 52N 8 0E
Imperial, Can. 109 51 21N 105 28W
Imperial, Calif., U.S.A. 119 32 52N 115 34W
Imperial, Nebr., U.S.A. 116 40 38N 101 39W
Imperial Dam 119 32 50N 114 30W
Impfondo 88 1 40N 18 0E
Imphal 67 24 48N 93 56E
Imphy 19 46 56N 3 15E
İmroz = Gökçeada 44 40 10N 25 50E
Imst 26 47 15N 10 44E
Imuruan B. 73 10 40N 119 10E
In Belbel 82 27 55N 1 12E
In Delimane 85 15 52N 1 31E
In Rhar 82 27 10N 1 59E
In Salah 82 27 10N 2 32E
In Tallak 85 16 19N 3 15E
Ina 74 35 50N 138 0E
Ina-Bonchi 74 35 45N 137 58E
Inangahua Junc. 101 41 52S 171 59E
Inanwatan 73 2 10S 132 14E
Iñapari 126 11 0S 69 40W
Inari 50 68 54N 27 5E
Inarijärvi 50 69 0N 28 0E
Inawashiro-Ko 74 37 29N 140 6E
Inca 32 39 43N 2 54E
Incaguasi 124 29 12S 71 5W
İnce-Burnu 56 42 7N 34 56E
Inchon 76 37 27N 126 40E
Incio 30 42 39N 7 21W
Incomáti → 93 25 46S 32 43E
Incudine, L' 21 41 50N 9 12E
Inda Silase 87 14 10N 38 15E
Indalsälven → 48 62 36N 17 30E
Indaw 67 24 15N 96 5E
Indbir 87 8 7N 37 52E
Independence, Calif., U.S.A. 119 36 51N 118 14W
Independence, Iowa, U.S.A. 116 42 27N 91 52W
Independence, Kans., U.S.A. 117 37 10N 95 43W
Independence, Mo., U.S.A. 116 39 3N 94 25W
Independence, Oreg., U.S.A. 118 44 53N 123 12W
Independence Fjord 4 82 10N 29 0W
Independence Mts. 118 41 30N 116 2W
Independenţa 46 45 25N 27 42E
Inderborskiy 57 48 30N 51 42E
India ■ 3 20 0N 78 0E
Indian → 115 27 59N 80 34W
Indian-Antarctic Ridge 94 49 0S 120 0E
Indian Cabins 108 59 52N 117 40W
Indian Harbour 107 54 27N 57 13W
Indian Head 109 50 30N 103 41W
Indian Ocean 3 5 0S 75 0E
Indiana 114 40 38N 79 9W
Indiana □ 114 40 0N 86 0W
Indianapolis 114 39 42N 86 10W
Indianola, Iowa, U.S.A. 116 41 20N 93 32W
Indianola, Miss., U.S.A. 117 33 27N 90 40W
Indiga 52 67 50N 48 50E
Indigirka → 59 70 48N 148 54E
Inđija 42 45 6N 20 7E
Indio 119 33 46N 116 15W
Indonesia ■ 72 5 0S 115 0E
Indore 68 22 42N 75 53E
Indramayu 73 6 21S 108 20E
Indramayu, Tg. 73 6 20S 108 20E
Indravati → 70 19 20N 80 20E
Indre □ 19 46 50N 1 39E
Indre → 18 47 16N 0 19E
Indre-et-Loire □ 18 47 12N 0 40E
Indus → 68 24 20N 67 47E
Indus, Mouth of the 68 24 00N 68 00E
İnebolu 64 41 55N 33 40E
İnegöl 64 40 5N 29 31E
Ineu 42 46 26N 21 51E
Inezgane 82 30 25N 9 29W
Infante, Kaap 92 34 27S 20 51E
Infantes 33 38 43N 3 1W
Infiernillo, Presa del 120 18 9N 102 0W
Infiesto 30 43 21N 5 21W
Ingende 88 0 12S 18 57E
Ingenio Santa Ana 124 27 25S 65 40W
Ingersoll 112 43 4N 80 55W
Ingham 97 18 43S 146 10E
Ingleborough 12 54 11N 2 23W
Inglewood, Queensland, Austral. 99 28 25S 151 2E
Inglewood, Vic., Austral. 99 36 29S 143 53E
Inglewood, N.Z. 101 39 9S 174 14E
Inglewood, U.S.A. 119 33 58N 118 21W
Ingólfshöfði 50 63 48N 16 39W
Ingolstadt 25 48 45N 11 26E
Ingomar 118 46 35N 107 21W
Ingonish 107 46 42N 60 18W
Ingore 84 12 24N 15 48W
Ingrid Christensen Coast 5 69 30S 76 0E
Ingul → 56 46 50N 32 15E
Ingulec 56 47 42N 33 14E
Ingulets → 56 46 41N 32 48E
Inguri →, U.S.S.R. 57 42 38N 41 35E
Inguri →, U.S.S.R. 57 42 15N 41 48E
Inhaca, I. 93 26 1S 32 57E
Inhafenga 93 20 36S 33 53E
Inhambane 93 23 54S 35 30E
Inhambane □ 93 22 30S 34 20E
Inhaminga 91 18 26S 35 0E
Inharrime 93 24 30S 35 0E
Inharrime → 93 24 30S 35 0E
Iniesta 33 39 27N 1 45W
Ining = Yining 75 43 58N 81 10E
Inírida → 126 3 55N 67 52W
Inishbofin 15 53 35N 10 12W
Inishmore 15 53 8N 9 45W
Inishowen 15 55 14N 7 15W
Injune 97 25 53S 148 32E
Inklin 108 58 56N 133 5W
Inklin → 108 58 50N 133 10W
Inkom 118 42 51N 112 15W
Inle L. 67 20 30N 96 58E
Inn → 25 48 35N 13 28E
Innamincka 99 27 44S 140 46E
Inner Hebrides 14 57 0N 6 30W
Inner Mongolia = Nei Monggol Zizhiqu □ 76 42 0N 112 0E
Inner Sound 14 57 30N 5 55W
Innerkip 112 43 13N 80 42W
Innerste → 24 52 45N 9 40E
Innetalling I. 106 56 0N 79 0W
Innisfail, Austral. 97 17 33S 146 5E
Innisfail, Can. 108 52 0N 113 57W
Innsbruck 26 47 16N 11 23E
Inny → 15 53 30N 7 50W
Inongo 88 1 55S 18 30E
Inoucdjouac (Port Harrison) 105 58 25N 78 15W
Inowrocław 28 52 50N 18 12E
Inquisivi 126 16 50S 67 10W
Insein 67 16 50N 96 5E
Însurăţei 46 44 50N 27 40E
Inta 52 66 5N 60 8E
Intendente Alvear 124 35 12S 63 32W
Interior 116 43 46N 101 59W
Interlaken 25 46 41N 7 50E
International Falls 116 48 36N 93 25W
Interview I. 71 12 55N 92 42E
Inthanon, Doi 71 18 35N 98 29E

* Now part of Sind □

Intiyaco Janikowo

Intiyaco	124	28 43 S	60 5W
Inútil, B.	128	53 30 S	70 15W
Inuvik	104	68 16N	133 40W
Inveraray	14	56 13N	5 5W
Inverbervie	14	56 50N	2 17W
Invercargill	101	46 24 S	168 24 E
Inverell	97	29 45 S	151 8 E
Invergordon	14	57 41N	4 10W
Invermere	108	50 30N	116 2W
Inverness, Can.	107	46 15N	61 19W
Inverness, U.K.	14	57 29N	4 12W
Inverness, U.S.A.	115	28 50N	82 20W
Inverurie	14	57 15N	2 21W
Investigator Group	96	34 45 S	134 20 E
Investigator Str.	97	35 30 S	137 0 E
Invona	112	40 46N	78 35W
Inya	58	50 28N	86 37 E
Inyanga	91	18 12 S	32 40 E
Inyangani	91	18 5 S	32 50 E
Inyantue	91	18 30 S	26 40 E
Inyazura	91	18 40 S	32 16 E
Inyo Range	119	37 0N	118 0W
Inyokern	119	35 38N	117 48W
Inza	55	53 55N	46 25 E
Inzhavino	55	52 22N	42 30 E
Ioánnina	44	39 42N	20 47 E
Ioánnina (Janinà) □	44	39 39N	20 57 E
Iola	117	38 0N	95 20W
Ion Corvin	46	44 7N	27 50 E
Iona	14	56 20N	6 25W
Ione, Calif., U.S.A.	118	38 20N	120 56W
Ione, Wash., U.S.A.	118	48 44N	117 29W
Ionia	114	42 59N	85 7W
Ionian Is. = Iónioi Nísoi	45	38 40N	20 0 E
Ionian Sea	35	37 30N	17 30 E
Iónioi Nísoi	45	38 40N	20 0 E
Iori →	57	41 3N	46 17 E
Íos	45	36 41N	25 20 E
Iowa □	116	42 18N	93 30W
Iowa City	116	41 40N	91 35W
Iowa Falls	116	42 30N	93 15W
Ipala	90	4 30 S	32 52 E
Ipameri	127	17 44 S	48 9W
Ipáti	45	38 52N	22 14 E
Ipatovo	57	45 45N	42 50 E
Ipel →	27	48 10N	19 35 E
Ipiales	126	0 50N	77 37W
Ipin = Yibin	75	28 45N	104 32 E
Ípiros □	44	39 30N	20 30 E
Ipixuna	126	7 0 S	71 40W
Ipoh	71	4 35N	101 5 E
Ippy	88	6 5N	21 7 E
Ipsala	44	40 55N	26 23 E
Ipsárion Óros	44	40 40N	24 40 E
Ipswich, Austral.	97	27 35 S	152 40 E
Ipswich, U.K.	13	52 4N	1 9 E
Ipswich, Mass., U.S.A.	113	42 40N	70 50W
Ipswich, S.D., U.S.A.	116	45 28N	99 1W
Ipu	127	4 23 S	40 44W
Iput →	54	52 26N	31 2 E
Iquique	126	20 19 S	70 5W
Iquitos	126	3 45 S	73 10W
Iracoubo	127	5 30N	53 10W
Iráklia	45	36 50N	25 28 E
Iráklion	45	35 20N	25 12 E
Iráklion □	45	35 10N	25 10 E
Irala	125	25 55 S	54 35W
Iramba □	90	4 30 S	34 30 E
Iran ■	65	33 0N	53 0 E
Iran, Pegunungan	72	2 20N	114 50 E
Iranamadu Tank	70	9 23N	80 29 E
Īrānshahr	65	27 15N	60 40 E
Irapuato	120	20 40N	101 30W
Iraq ■	64	33 0N	44 0 E
Irarrar, O. →	82	20 0N	1 30 E
Irati	125	25 25 S	50 38W
Irbid	62	32 35N	35 48 E
Irebu	88	0 40 S	17 46 E
Iregua →	32	42 27N	2 24 E
Ireland ■	15	53 0N	8 0W
Ireland I.	121	32 16N	64 50W
Ireland's Eye	15	53 25N	6 4W
Irele	85	7 40N	5 40 E
Iret	59	60 3N	154 20 E
Irgiz, Bol.	55	52 10N	49 10 E
Irhârharene	83	27 37N	7 30 E
Irharrhar, O. →	83	28 3N	6 15 E
Irherm	82	30 7N	8 18W
Irhil Mgoun	82	31 30N	6 28W
Irian Jaya □	73	4 0 S	137 0 E
Irié	84	8 15N	9 10W
Iringa	90	7 48 S	35 43 E
Iringa □	90	7 48 S	35 43 E
Irinjalakuda	70	10 21N	76 14 E
Iriri →	127	3 52 S	52 37W
Irish Sea	12	54 0N	5 0W
Irkineyeva	59	58 30N	96 49 E
Irkutsk	59	52 18N	104 20 E
Irma	109	52 55N	111 14W
Iroise, Mer d'	18	48 15N	4 45W
Iron Baron	99	32 58 S	137 11 E
Iron Gate = Portile de Fier	46	44 42N	22 30 E
Iron Knob	97	32 46 S	137 8 E
Iron Mountain	114	45 49N	88 4W
Iron River	116	46 6N	88 40W
Ironbridge	13	52 38N	2 29W
Ironstone Kopje	92	25 17 S	24 5 E
Ironton, Mo., U.S.A.	117	37 40N	90 40W
Ironton, Ohio, U.S.A.	114	38 35N	82 40W
Ironwood	116	46 30N	90 10W
Iroquois Falls	106	48 46N	80 41W
Irpen	54	50 30N	30 15 E
Irrara Cr. →	99	29 35 S	145 31 E
Irrawaddy □	67	17 0N	95 0 E
Irrawaddy →	67	15 50N	95 6 E
Irsina	41	40 45N	16 15 E
Irtysh →	58	61 4N	68 52 E
Irumu	90	1 32N	29 53 E
Irún	32	43 20N	1 52W
Irurzun	32	42 55N	1 50W
Irvine, Can.	109	49 57N	110 16W
Irvine, U.K.	14	55 37N	4 40W
Irvine, U.S.A.	114	37 42N	83 58W
Irvinestown	15	54 28N	7 38W
Irymple	99	34 14 S	142 8 E
Is-sur-Tille	19	47 30N	5 10 E
Isa	85	13 14N	6 24 E
Isaac →	97	22 55 S	149 20 E
Isabel	116	45 27N	101 22W
Isabela, I.	120	21 51N	105 55W
Isabella, Cord.	121	13 30N	85 25W
Ísafjarðardjúp	50	66 10N	23 0W
Ísafjörður	50	66 5N	23 9W
Isagarh	68	24 48N	77 51 E
Isaka	90	3 56 S	32 59 E
Isangi	88	0 52N	24 10 E
Isar →	25	48 49N	12 58 E
Isarco →	39	46 57N	11 18 E
Ísari	45	37 22N	22 0 E
Isbergues	19	50 36N	2 24 E
Isbiceni	46	43 45N	24 40 E
Íschia	40	40 45N	13 51 E
Ise	74	34 25N	136 45 E
Ise-Wan	74	34 43N	136 43 E
Isefjord	49	55 53N	11 50 E
Iseo	38	45 40N	10 3 E
Iseo, L. d'	38	45 45N	10 3 E
Iseramagazi	90	4 37 S	32 10 E
Isère □	21	45 15N	5 40 E
Isère →	21	44 59N	4 51 E
Iserlohn	24	51 22N	7 40 E
Isérnia	41	41 35N	14 12 E
Iseyin	85	8 0N	3 36 E
Ishikari-Wan (Otaru-Wan)	74	43 25N	141 1 E
Ishikawa □	74	36 30N	136 30 E
Ishim	58	56 10N	69 30 E
Ishim →	58	57 45N	71 10 E
Ishinomaki	74	38 32N	141 20 E
Ishmi	44	41 33N	19 34 E
Ishpeming	114	46 30N	87 40W
Isigny-sur-Mer	18	49 19N	1 6W
Isil Kul	58	54 55N	71 16 E
Isiolo	90	0 24N	37 33 E
Isiolo □	90	2 30N	37 30 E
Isipingo Beach	93	30 00 S	30 57 E
Isiro	90	2 53N	27 40 E
Isisford	98	24 15 S	144 21 E
İskenderun	64	36 32N	36 10 E
İskilip	56	40 50N	34 20 E
Iskŭr →	43	43 45N	24 25 E
Iskŭr, Yazovir	43	42 23N	23 30 E
Iskut →	108	56 45N	131 49W
Isla →	14	56 32N	3 20W
Isla Cristina	31	37 13N	7 17W
Islamabad	66	33 40N	73 10 E
Islamkot	68	24 42N	70 13 E
Islampur	70	17 2N	74 20 E
Island →	108	60 25N	121 12W
Island Falls, Can.	106	49 35N	81 20W
Island Falls, U.S.A.	107	46 0N	68 16W
Island L.	109	53 47N	94 25W
Island Pond	114	44 50N	71 50W
Islands, B. of, Can.	107	49 11N	58 15W
Islands, B. of, N.Z.	101	35 20 S	174 20 E
Islay	14	55 46N	6 10W
Isle →	20	44 55N	0 15W
Isle-Adam, L'	19	49 6N	2 14 E
Isle aux Morts	107	47 35N	59 0W
Isle-Jourdain, L', Gers, France	20	43 36N	1 5 E
Isle-Jourdain, L', Vienne, France	20	46 13N	0 31 E
Isle of Wight □	13	50 40N	1 20W
Isle Royale	116	48 0N	88 50W
Isleta	119	34 58N	106 46W
Ismail	56	45 22N	28 46 E
Ismâ'ilîya	86	30 37N	32 18 E
Ismaning	25	48 14N	11 41 E
Ismay	116	46 33N	104 44W
Isna	86	25 17N	32 30 E
Isola del Gran Sasso d'Italia	39	42 30N	13 40 E
Ísola del Liri	40	41 39N	13 32 E
Ísola della Scala	38	45 16N	11 0 E
Ísola di Capo Rizzuto	41	38 56N	17 5 E
Isparta	64	37 47N	30 30 E
Isperikh	43	43 43N	26 50 E
Íspica	41	36 47N	14 53 E
İspir	57	40 40N	40 50 E
Israel ■	62	32 0N	34 50 E
Issia	84	6 33N	6 33W
Issoire	20	45 32N	3 15 E
Issoudun	19	46 57N	2 0 E
Issyk-Kul, Ozero	58	42 25N	77 15 E
Ist	39	44 17N	14 47 E
İstanbul	64	41 0N	29 0 E
Istiaía	45	38 57N	23 9 E
Istok	42	42 45N	20 24 E
Istokpoga, L.	115	27 22N	81 14W
Istra, U.S.S.R.	55	55 55N	36 50 E
Istra, Yugo.	39	45 10N	14 0 E
Istranca Dağları	43	41 48N	27 30 E
Istres	21	43 31N	4 59 E
Istria = Istra	39	45 10N	14 0 E
Itá	124	25 29 S	57 21W
Itabaiana	127	7 18 S	35 19W
Itaberaba	127	12 32 S	40 18W
Itabira	127	19 37 S	43 13W
Itabirito	125	20 15 S	43 48W
Itabuna	127	14 48 S	39 16W
Itaituba	127	4 10 S	55 50W
Itajaí	125	27 50 S	48 39W
Itajubá	125	22 24 S	45 30W
Itaka	91	8 50 S	32 49 E
Italy ■	36	42 0N	13 0 E
Itampolo	93	24 41 S	43 57 E
Itapecuru-Mirim	127	3 24 S	44 20W
Itaperuna	127	21 10 S	41 54W
Itapetininga	125	23 36 S	48 7W
Itapeva	125	23 59 S	48 59W
Itapicuru →, Bahia, Brazil	127	11 47 S	37 32W
Itapicuru →, Maranhão, Brazil	127	2 52 S	44 12W
Itapuá □	125	26 40 S	55 40W
Itaquari	125	20 20 S	40 25W
Itaquatiara	126	2 58 S	58 30W
Itaquí	124	29 8 S	56 30W
Itararé	125	24 6 S	49 23W
Itarsi	68	22 36N	77 51 E
Itatí	124	27 16 S	58 15W
Itatuba	126	5 46 S	63 20W
Itchen →	13	50 57N	1 20W
Itéa	45	38 25N	22 25 E
Ithaca	114	42 25N	76 30W
Ithaca = Itháki	45	38 25N	20 43 E
Itháki	45	38 25N	20 40 E
Ito	74	34 58N	139 5 E
Itoman	77	26 7N	127 40 E
Iton →	18	49 9N	1 12 E
Itonamas →	126	12 28 S	64 24W
Itsa	86	29 15N	30 47 E
Íttiri	40	40 38N	8 32 E
Itu, Brazil	125	23 17 S	47 15W
Itu, Nigeria	85	5 10N	7 58 E
Ituaçu	127	13 50 S	41 18W
Ituiutaba	127	19 0 S	49 25W
Itumbiara	127	18 20 S	49 10W
Ituna	109	51 10N	103 24W
Itunge Port	91	9 40 S	33 55 E
Iturbe	124	23 0 S	65 25W
Ituri →	90	1 40N	27 1 E
Iturup, Ostrov	59	45 0N	148 0 E
Ituyuro →	124	22 40 S	63 50W
Itzehoe	24	53 56N	9 31 E
Ivaí →	125	23 18 S	53 42W
Ivalo	50	68 38N	27 35 E
Ivalojoki →	50	68 40N	27 40 E
Ivangorod	54	59 37N	28 40 E
Ivangrad	42	42 51N	19 52 E
Ivanhoe	97	32 56 S	144 20 E
Ivanhoe L.	109	60 25N	106 30W
Ivanić Grad	39	45 41N	16 25 E
Ivanjica	42	43 35N	20 12 E
Ivanjšcice	39	46 12N	16 13 E
Ivankoyskoye Vdkhr.	55	56 37N	36 32 E
Ivano-Frankovsk	56	48 56N	24 43 E
Ivano-Frankovsk (Stanislav)	54	48 40N	24 40 E
Ivanovo, Byelorussia, U.S.S.R.	54	52 7N	25 29 E
Ivanovo, R.S.F.S.R., U.S.S.R.	55	57 5N	41 0 E
Ivato	93	20 37 S	47 10 E
Ivaylovgrad	43	41 32N	26 8 E
Ivdel	52	60 42N	60 24 E
Ivinheima →	125	23 14 S	53 42W
Iviza = Ibiza	33	39 0N	1 30 E
Ivohibe	93	22 31 S	46 57 E
Ivory Coast ■	84	7 30N	5 0W
Ivösjön	49	56 8N	14 25 E
Ivrea	38	45 30N	7 52 E
Ivugivik, (N.D. d'Ivugivic)	105	62 24N	77 55W
Iwahig	72	8 35N	117 32 E
Iwaki	74	37 3N	140 55 E
Iwakuni	74	34 15N	132 8 E
Iwata	74	34 42N	137 51 E
Iwate □	74	39 30N	141 30 E
Iwate-San	74	39 51N	141 0 E
Iwo	85	7 39N	4 9 E
IwoniczZdrój	27	49 37N	21 47 E
Ixiamas	126	13 50 S	68 5W
Ixopo	93	30 11 S	30 5 E
Ixtepec	120	16 32N	95 10W
Ixtlán de Juárez	120	17 23N	96 28W
Ixtlán del Río	120	21 5N	104 21W
Izabal, L. de	120	15 30N	89 10W
Izamal	120	20 56N	89 1W
Izberbash	57	42 35N	47 52 E
Izbica	28	50 53N	23 10 E
Izbica Kujawska	28	52 25N	18 30 E
Izegem	16	50 55N	3 12 E
Izgrev	43	43 36N	26 58 E
*Izhevsk	52	56 51N	53 14 E
İzmir (Smyrna)	53	38 25N	27 8 E
İzmit	64	40 45N	29 50 E
Iznajar	31	37 15N	4 19W
Iznalloz	33	37 24N	3 30W
Izobil'nyy	57	45 25N	41 44 E
Izola	39	45 32N	13 39 E
Izra	62	32 51N	36 15 E
Izra'	62	32 52N	36 5 E
Iztochni Rodopi	43	41 45N	25 30 E
Izumi-sano	74	34 23N	135 18 E
Izumo	74	35 20N	132 46 E
Izyaslav	54	50 5N	26 50 E
Izyum	56	49 12N	37 19 E

J

Jaba	87	6 20N	35 7 E
Jaba'	62	32 20N	35 13 E
Jabal el Awlîya	87	15 10N	32 31 E
Jabalón →	31	38 53N	4 5W
Jabalpur	69	23 9N	79 58 E
Jabālyah	62	31 32N	34 27 E
Jablah	64	35 20N	36 0 E
Jablanac	39	44 42N	14 56 E
Jablonec	26	50 43N	15 10 E
Jablonica	27	48 37N	17 26 E
Jabłonowo	28	53 23N	19 10 E
Jaboticabal	125	21 15 S	48 17W
Jabukovac	42	44 22N	22 21 E
Jaburu	126	5 30 S	64 0W
Jaca	32	42 35N	0 33W
Jacareí	125	23 20 S	46 0W
Jacarèzinho	125	23 5 S	50 0W
Jáchymov	26	50 22N	12 55 E
Jackman	107	45 35N	70 17W
Jacksboro	117	33 14N	98 15W
Jackson, Austral.	99	26 39 S	149 39 E
Jackson, Ala., U.S.A.	115	31 32N	87 53W
Jackson, Calif., U.S.A.	118	38 19N	120 47W
Jackson, Ky., U.S.A.	114	37 35N	83 22W
Jackson, Mich., U.S.A.	114	42 18N	84 25W
Jackson, Minn., U.S.A.	116	43 35N	95 0W
Jackson, Miss., U.S.A.	117	32 20N	90 10W
Jackson, Mo., U.S.A.	117	37 25N	89 42W
Jackson, Ohio, U.S.A.	114	39 0N	82 40W
Jackson, Tenn., U.S.A.	115	35 40N	88 50W
Jackson, Wyo., U.S.A.	118	43 30N	110 49W
Jackson Bay	101	43 58 S	168 42 E
Jackson, L.	118	43 55N	110 40W
Jacksons	101	42 46 S	171 32 E
Jacksonville, Ala., U.S.A.	115	33 49N	85 45W
Jacksonville, Fla., U.S.A.	115	30 15N	81 38W
Jacksonville, Ill., U.S.A.	116	39 42N	90 15W
Jacksonville, N.C., U.S.A.	115	34 50N	77 29W
Jacksonville, Oreg., U.S.A.	118	42 19N	122 56W
Jacksonville, Tex., U.S.A.	117	31 58N	95 19W
Jacksonville Beach	115	30 19N	81 26W
Jacmel	121	18 14N	72 32W
Jacob Lake	119	36 45N	112 12W
Jacobabad	68	28 20N	68 29 E
Jacobina	127	11 11 S	40 30W
Jacob's Well	62	32 13N	35 13 E
Jacques-Cartier, Mt.	107	48 57N	66 0W
Jacqueville	84	5 12N	4 25W
Jacuí →	125	30 2 S	51 15W
Jacundá →	127	1 57 S	50 26W
Jade	24	53 22N	8 14 E
Jadebusen	24	53 30N	8 15 E
Jadotville = Likasi	91	10 55 S	26 48 E
Jadovnik	42	43 20N	19 45 E
Jadów	28	52 28N	21 38 E
Jadraque	32	40 55N	2 55W
Jādū	83	32 0N	12 0 E
Jaén, Peru	126	5 25 S	78 40W
Jaén, Spain	31	37 44N	3 43W
Jaén □	31	37 50N	3 30W
Jaerens Rev	47	58 45N	5 45 E
Jafène	82	20 35N	5 30W
Jaffa = Tel Aviv-Yafo	62	32 4N	34 48 E
Jaffa, C.	99	36 58 S	139 40 E
Jaffna	70	9 45N	80 2 E
Jagadhri	68	30 10N	77 20 E
Jagadishpur	69	25 30N	84 21 E
Jagdalpur	70	19 3N	82 0 E
Jagersfontein	92	29 44 S	25 27 E
Jagst →	25	49 14N	9 11 E
Jagtial	70	18 50N	79 0 E
Jaguariaíva	125	24 10 S	49 50W
Jaguaribe →	127	4 25 S	37 45W
Jagüey Grande	121	22 35N	81 7W
Jahangirabad	68	28 19N	78 4 E
Jahrom	65	28 30N	53 31 E
Jailolo	73	1 5N	127 30 E
Jailolo, Selat	73	0 5N	129 5 E
Jainti	69	26 45N	89 40 E
Jaipur	68	27 0N	75 50 E
Jajce	42	44 19N	17 17 E
Jajpur	69	20 53N	86 22 E
Jakarta	73	6 9 S	106 49 E
Jakobstad (Pietarsaari)	50	63 40N	22 43 E
Jakupica	42	41 45N	21 22 E
Jal	117	32 8N	103 8W
Jalai Nur	76	49 27N	117 42 E
Jalalabad, Afghan.	66	34 30N	70 29 E
Jalalabad, India	69	27 41N	79 42 E
Jalalpur Jattan	68	32 38N	74 11 E
Jalapa, Guat.	120	14 39N	89 59W
Jalapa, Mexico	120	19 32N	96 56W
Jalas, Jabal al	64	27 30N	36 30 E
Jalaun	69	26 8N	79 25 E
Jaleswar	69	26 38N	85 48 E
Jalgaon, Maharashtra, India	68	21 0N	75 42 E
Jalgaon, Maharashtra, India	68	21 2N	76 31 E
Jalingo	85	8 55N	11 25 E
Jalisco □	120	20 0N	104 0W
Jallas →	30	42 54N	9 8W
Jalna	70	19 48N	75 38 E
Jalón →	32	41 47N	1 4W
Jalpa	120	21 38N	102 58W
Jalpaiguri	69	26 32N	88 46 E
Jalq	65	27 35N	62 46 E
Jaluit I.	94	6 0N	169 30 E
Jamaari	85	11 44N	9 53 E
Jamaica ■	121	18 10N	77 30W
Jamalpur, Bangla.	69	24 52N	89 56 E
Jamalpur, India	69	25 18N	86 28 E
Jamalpurganj	69	23 2N	88 1 E
Jamanxim →	127	4 43 S	56 18W
Jambe	73	1 15 S	132 10 E
Jambi	72	1 38 S	103 30 E
Jambi □	72	1 30 S	102 30 E
Jambusar	68	22 3N	72 51 E
James →	116	42 52N	97 18W
James B.	106	51 30N	80 0W
James Range	96	24 10 S	132 30 E
James Ross I.	5	63 58 S	57 50W
Jamestown, Austral.	97	33 10 S	138 32 E
Jamestown, S. Afr.	92	31 6 S	26 45 E
Jamestown, Ky., U.S.A.	114	37 0N	85 5W
Jamestown, N.D., U.S.A.	116	46 54N	98 42W
Jamestown, N.Y., U.S.A.	114	42 5N	79 18W
Jamestown, Pa., U.S.A.	112	41 32N	80 27W
Jamestown, Tenn., U.S.A.	115	36 25N	85 0W
Jamkhaudi	70	16 30N	75 15 E
Jammā'īn	62	32 8N	35 12 E
Jammalamadugu	70	14 51N	78 25 E
Jammerbugt	49	57 15N	9 20 E
Jammu	68	32 43N	74 54 E
Jammu & Kashmir □	66	34 25N	77 0 E
Jamnagar	68	22 30N	70 6 E
Jamner	68	20 45N	75 52 E
Jampur	68	29 39N	70 40 E
Jamrud Fort	66	33 59N	71 24 E
Jamshedpur	69	22 44N	86 12 E
Jamtara	69	23 59N	86 49 E
Jämtlands län □	48	62 40N	13 50 E
Jan Kemp	92	27 55 S	24 51 E
Jan L.	109	54 56N	102 55W
Jan Mayen Is.	4	71 0N	9 0W
Jand	66	33 30N	72 6 E
Janda, Laguna de la	31	36 15N	5 45W
Jandaq	65	34 3N	54 22 E
Jandola	68	32 20N	70 9 E
Jandowae	99	26 45 S	151 7 E
Jándula →	31	38 3N	4 6W
Janesville	116	42 39N	89 1W
Janga	85	10 5N	1 0W
Jangaon	70	17 44N	79 5 E
Jangeru	72	2 20 S	116 29 E
Janikowo	28	52 45N	18 7 E

*Renamed Ustinov

Janīn Jyväskylä

Janīn 62 32 28N 35 18 E
Janja 42 44 40N 19 17 E
Janjevo 42 42 35N 21 19 E
Janjina 42 42 58N 17 25 E
Jánoshalma 27 46 18N 19 21 E
Jánosháza 27 47 8N 17 12 E
Jánossomorja 27 47 47N 17 11 E
Janów 28 50 44N 19 27 E
Janów Lubelski 28 50 48N 22 23 E
Janów Podlaski 28 52 11N 23 11 E
Janowiec Wielkopolski 28 52 45N 17 30 E
Januária 127 15 25 S 44 25W
Janub Dârfûr □ 87 11 0N 25 0 E
Janub Kordofân □ 87 12 0N 30 0 E
Janville 19 48 10N 1 50 E
Janzé 18 47 55N 1 28W
Jaora 68 23 40N 75 10 E
Japan ■ 74 36 0N 136 0 E
Japan, Sea of 74 40 0N 135 0 E
Japan Trench 94 32 0N 142 0 E
Japara 73 6 30 S 110 40 E
Japen = Yapen 73 1 50 S 136 0 E
Japurá → 126 3 8 S 64 46W
Jaque 126 7 27N 78 8W
Jara, La 119 37 16N 106 0W
Jaraicejo 31 39 40N 5 49W
Jaraiz 30 40 4N 5 45W
Jarales 119 34 39N 106 51W
Jarama → 32 40 2N 3 39W
Jarandilla 30 40 8N 5 39W
Jaranwala 68 31 15N 73 26 E
Jarash 62 32 17N 35 54 E
Jarbidge 118 41 56N 115 27W
Jardim 124 21 28 S 56 2W
Jardín → 33 38 50N 2 10W
Jardines de la Reina, Is. 121 20 50N 78 50W
Jargalant (Kobdo) 75 48 2N 91 37 E
Jargeau 19 47 50N 2 1 E
Jarmen 24 53 56N 13 20 E
Jarnac 20 45 40N 0 11W
Jarny 19 49 9N 5 53 E
Jarocin 28 51 59N 17 29 E
Jaroměr 26 50 22N 15 52 E
Jarosław 27 50 2N 22 42 E
Järpås 49 58 23N 12 57 E
Järpen 48 63 21N 13 26 E
Jarso 87 5 15N 37 30 E
Jarvis 112 42 53N 80 6W
Jarvis I. 95 0 15 S 159 55W
Jarvornik 27 50 23N 17 2 E
Jarwa 69 27 38N 82 30 E
Jaša Tomić 42 45 26N 20 50 E
Jasien 28 51 46N 15 0 E
Jasin 71 2 20N 102 26 E
Jäsk 65 25 38N 57 45 E
Jasło 27 49 45N 21 30 E
Jasper, Alta., Can. 108 52 55N 118 5W
Jasper, Ont., Can. 113 44 52N 75 57W
Jasper, Ala., U.S.A. 115 33 48N 87 16W
Jasper, Fla., U.S.A. 115 30 31N 82 58W
Jasper, Minn., U.S.A. 116 43 52N 96 22W
Jasper, Tex., U.S.A. 117 30 59N 93 58W
Jasper Nat. Park 108 52 50N 118 8W
Jassy = Iaşi 46 47 10N 27 40 E
Jastrebarsko 39 45 41N 15 39 E
Jastrowie 28 53 26N 16 49 E
Jastrzębie Zdrój 27 49 57N 18 35 E
Jászapáti 27 47 32N 20 10 E
Jászárokszállás 27 47 39N 20 1 E
Jászberény 27 47 30N 19 55 E
Jászkiser 27 47 27N 20 20 E
Jászladány 27 47 23N 20 10 E
Jataí 127 17 58 S 51 48W
Jati 68 24 20N 68 19 E
Jatibarang 73 6 28 S 108 18 E
Jatinegara 73 6 13 S 106 52 E
Játiva 33 39 0N 0 32W
Jatobal 127 4 35 S 49 33W
Jatt 62 32 24N 35 2 E
Jaú 125 22 10 S 48 30W
Jauja 126 11 45 S 75 15W
Jaunjelgava 54 56 35N 25 0 E
Jaunpur 69 25 46N 82 44 E
Java = Jawa 73 7 0 S 110 0 E
Java Sea 72 4 35 S 107 15 E
Java Trench 94 10 0 S 110 0W
Javadi Hills 70 12 40N 78 40 E
Jávea 33 38 48N 0 10 E
Javhlant = Ulyasutay 75 47 56N 97 28 E
Javla 70 17 18N 75 9 E
Javron 18 48 25N 0 25W
Jawa 73 7 0 S 110 0 E
Jawor 28 51 4N 16 11 E
Jaworzno 27 50 13N 19 11 E
Jay 117 36 25N 94 46W
Jaya, Puncak 73 3 57 S 137 17 E
Jayapura 73 2 28 S 140 38 E
Jayawijaya, Pegunungan 73 5 0 S 139 0 E
Jayton 117 33 17N 100 35W
Jean 119 35 47N 115 20W
Jean Marie River 104 61 32N 120 38W
Jean Rabel 121 19 50N 73 5W
Jeanerette 117 29 52N 91 38W
Jeanette, Ostrov 59 76 43N 158 0 E
Jeannette 112 40 20N 79 36W
Jebba, Moroc. 82 35 11N 4 43W
Jebba, Nigeria 85 9 9N 4 48 E
Jebel, Bahr el → 81 15 38N 32 31 E
Jebel Qerri 87 16 16N 32 50 E
Jedburgh 14 55 28N 2 33W
Jedlicze 27 49 43N 21 40 E
Jedlnia-Letnisko 28 51 25N 21 19 E
Jędrzejów 28 50 35N 20 15 E
Jedwabne 28 53 17N 22 18 E
Jedway 108 52 17N 131 14W
Jeetze → 24 53 9N 11 6 E
Jefferson, Iowa, U.S.A. 116 42 3N 94 25W
Jefferson, Ohio, U.S.A. 112 41 40N 80 46W
Jefferson, Tex., U.S.A. 117 32 45N 94 23W
Jefferson, Wis., U.S.A. 116 43 0N 88 49W
Jefferson City, Mo., U.S.A. 116 38 34N 92 10W
Jefferson City, Tenn., U.S.A. 115 36 8N 83 30W
Jefferson, Mt., Nev., U.S.A. 118 38 51N 117 0W
Jefferson, Mt., Oreg., U.S.A. 118 44 45N 121 50W
Jeffersonville 114 38 20N 85 42W
Jega 85 12 15N 4 23 E
Jekabpils 54 56 29N 25 57 E
Jelenia Góra 28 50 50N 15 45 E
Jelenia Góra □ 28 51 0N 15 30 E
Jelgava 54 56 41N 23 49 E
Jelica 42 43 50N 20 17 E
Jelli 87 5 25N 31 45 E
Jellicoe 106 49 40N 87 30W
Jelšava 27 48 37N 20 15 E
Jemaja 72 3 5N 105 45 E
Jember 73 8 11 S 113 41 E
Jembongan 72 6 45N 117 20 E
Jemeppe 16 50 37N 5 30 E
Jemnice 26 49 1N 15 34 E
Jena, Ger. 24 50 56N 11 33 E
Jena, U.S.A. 117 31 41N 92 7W
Jenbach 26 47 24N 11 47 E
Jendouba 83 36 29N 8 47 E
Jenkins 114 37 13N 82 41W
Jennings 117 30 10N 92 45W
Jennings → 108 59 38N 132 5W
Jenny 49 57 47N 16 35 E
Jeparit 99 36 8 S 142 1 E
Jequié 127 13 51 S 40 5W
Jequitinhonha 127 16 30 S 41 0W
Jequitinhonha → 127 15 51 S 38 53W
Jerada 82 34 17N 2 10W
Jerantut 71 3 56N 102 22 E
Jérémie 121 18 40N 74 10W
Jerez de García Salinas 120 22 39N 103 0W
Jerez de la Frontera 31 36 41N 6 7W
Jerez de los Caballeros 31 38 20N 6 45W
Jerez, Punta 120 22 58N 97 40W
Jericho 98 23 38 S 146 6 E
Jericho = El Arīhā 62 31 52N 35 27 E
Jerichow 24 52 30N 12 2 E
Jerilderie 99 35 20 S 145 41 E
Jermyn 113 41 31N 75 31W
Jerome 119 34 50N 112 0W
Jerrobert 109 51 56N 109 8W
Jersey City 114 40 41N 74 8W
Jersey, I. 18 49 13N 2 7W
Jersey Shore 114 41 17N 77 18W
Jerseyville 116 39 5N 90 20W
Jerusalem 62 31 47N 35 10 E
Jervis B. 97 35 8 S 150 46 E
Jesenice 39 46 28N 14 3 E
Jeseník 27 50 0N 17 8 E
Jesenske 27 48 20N 20 10 E
Jesselton = Kota Kinabalu 72 6 0N 116 4 E
Jessnitz 24 51 42N 12 19 E
Jessore 69 23 10N 89 10 E
Jesup 115 31 36N 81 54W
Jesús María 124 30 59 S 64 5W
Jetmore 117 38 10N 99 57W
Jetpur 68 21 45N 70 10 E
Jevnaker 47 60 15N 10 26 E
Jewett, Ohio, U.S.A. 112 40 22N 81 2W
Jewett, Tex., U.S.A. 117 31 20N 96 8W
Jewett City 113 41 36N 72 0W
Jeypore 70 18 50N 82 38 E
Jeziorak, Jezioro 28 53 40N 19 35 E
Jeziorany 28 53 58N 20 46 E
Jeziorka → 28 51 59N 20 57 E
Jhajjar 68 28 37N 76 42 E
Jhal Jhao 66 26 20N 65 35 E
Jhalawar 68 24 40N 76 10 E
Jhang Maghiana 68 31 15N 72 22 E
Jhansi 68 25 30N 78 36 E
Jharia 69 23 45N 86 26 E
Jharsuguda 69 21 56N 84 5 E
Jhelum 68 33 0N 73 45 E
Jhelum → 68 31 20N 72 10 E
Jhunjhunu 68 28 10N 75 30 E
Ji Xian 76 36 7N 110 40 E
Jia Xian 76 38 12N 110 28 E
Jiamusi 75 46 40N 130 26 E
Ji'an 75 27 6N 114 59 E
Jianchuan 75 26 38N 99 55 E
Jiande 77 29 23N 119 15 E
Jiangbei 77 29 40N 106 34 E
Jiange 77 32 4N 105 32 E
Jiangjin 77 29 14N 106 14 E
Jiangling 75 30 25N 112 12 E
Jiangmen 75 22 32N 113 0 E
Jiangshan 77 28 40N 118 37 E
Jiangsu □ 75 33 0N 120 0 E
Jiangxi □ 75 27 30N 116 0 E
Jiangyin 77 31 54N 120 17 E
Jiangyong 77 25 20N 111 22 E
Jiangyou 77 31 44N 104 43 E
Jianning 77 26 50N 116 50 E
Jian'ou 75 27 3N 118 17 E
Jianshi 77 30 37N 109 38 E
Jianshui 75 23 36N 102 43 E
Jianyang 77 27 20N 118 5 E
Jiao Xian 76 36 18N 120 1 E
Jiaohe 76 38 2N 116 20 E
Jiaozhou Wan 76 36 5N 120 10 E
Jiaozuo 77 35 16N 113 12 E
Jiawang 77 34 28N 117 26 E
Jiaxing 75 30 49N 120 45 E
Jiayi 75 23 30N 120 24 E
Jibāl 63 22 10N 56 8 E
Jibiya 85 13 5N 7 12 E
Jibou 46 47 15N 23 17 E
Jibuti = Djibouti ■ 63 12 0N 43 0 E
Jičín 26 50 25N 15 28 E
Jiddah 64 21 29N 39 10 E
Jido 67 29 2N 94 58 E
Jifnā 62 31 58N 35 13 E
Jihlava 26 49 28N 15 35 E
Jihlava → 26 48 55N 16 36 E
Jihočeský □ 26 49 8N 14 35 E
Jihomoravský □ 27 49 5N 16 30 E
Jijel 83 36 52N 5 50 E
Jijiga 63 9 20N 42 50 E
Jijona 33 38 34N 0 30W
Jikamshi 85 12 12N 7 45 E
Jilin 76 43 44N 126 30 E
Jilin □ 76 44 0N 124 0 E
Jiloca → 32 41 21N 1 39W
Jilong 75 25 8N 121 42 E
Jílové 26 49 52N 14 29 E
Jima 87 7 40N 36 47 E
Jimbolia 42 45 47N 20 43 E
Jimena de la Frontera 31 36 27N 5 24W
Jiménez 120 27 10N 104 54W
Jimo 76 36 23N 120 30 E
Jin Xian 76 38 55N 121 42 E
Jinan 76 36 38N 117 1 E
Jincheng 76 35 29N 112 50 E
Jind 68 29 19N 76 22 E
Jindabyne 99 36 25 S 148 35 E
Jindabyne L. 100 36 20 S 148 38 E
Jindrichuv Hradeç 26 49 10N 15 2 E
Jing He → 77 34 27N 109 4 E
Jing Xian 77 26 33N 109 40 E
Jingchuan 76 35 20N 107 20 E
Jingdezhen 75 29 20N 117 11 E
Jinggu 75 23 35N 100 41 E
Jinghai 76 38 55N 116 55 E
Jingle 76 38 20N 111 55 E
Jingmen 77 31 0N 112 10 E
Jingning 76 35 30N 105 43 E
Jingshan 77 31 1N 113 7 E
Jingtai 76 37 10N 104 6 E
Jingxi 75 23 8N 106 27 E
Jingyu 76 42 25N 126 45 E
Jingyuan 76 36 30N 104 40 E
Jingziguan 77 33 15N 111 0 E
Jinhe 76 51 18N 121 32 E
Jinhua 75 29 8N 119 38 E
Jining, Nei Mongol Zizhiqu, China 76 41 5N 113 0 E
Jining, Shandong, China 77 35 22N 116 34 E
Jinja 90 0 25N 33 12 E
Jinjini 84 7 26N 3 42W
Jinmen Dao 77 24 25N 118 25 E
Jinnah Barrage 65 32 58N 71 33 E
Jinotega 121 13 6N 85 59W
Jinotepe 121 11 50N 86 10W
Jinshi 75 29 40N 111 50 E
Jinxiang 77 35 5N 116 22 E
Jinzhou 76 41 5N 121 3 E
Jiparaná (Machado) → 126 8 3 S 62 52W
Jipijapa 126 1 0 S 80 40W
Jiquilpan 120 19 57N 102 42W
Jishou 77 28 21N 109 43 E
Jisr al Ḩusayn (Allenby) Br. 62 31 53N 35 33 E
Jisr ash Shughūr 64 35 49N 36 18 E
Jitra 71 6 16N 100 25 E
Jiu → 46 44 40N 23 25 E
Jiudengkou 76 39 56N 106 40 E
Jiujiang 75 29 42N 115 58 E
Jiuling Shan 77 28 40N 114 40 E
Jiuquan 75 39 50N 98 20 E
Jixi 75 45 20N 130 50 E
Jizera → 26 50 10N 14 43 E
Jizl Wadi 86 25 30N 38 30 E
Joaçaba 125 27 5 S 51 31W
João Pessoa 127 7 10 S 34 52W
Joaquín V. González 124 25 10 S 64 0W
Jobourg, Nez de 18 49 41N 1 57W
Jódar 33 37 50N 3 21W
Jodhpur 68 26 23N 73 8 E
Joensuu 52 62 37N 29 49 E
Jœuf 19 49 12N 6 1 E
Joggins 107 45 42N 64 27W
Jogjakarta = Yogyakarta 73 7 49 S 110 22 E
Johannesburg 93 26 10 S 28 2 E
Johansfors 49 56 42N 15 32 E
John Day 118 44 25N 118 57W
John Day → 118 45 44N 120 39W
John H. Kerr Res. 115 36 20N 78 30W
John o' Groats 14 58 39N 3 3W
Johnson 117 37 35N 101 48W
Johnson City, N.Y., U.S.A. 114 42 7N 75 57W
Johnson City, Tenn., U.S.A. 115 36 18N 82 21W
Johnson City, Tex., U.S.A. 117 30 15N 98 24W
Johnsonburg 112 41 30N 78 40W
Johnson's Crossing 108 60 29N 133 18W
Johnston Falls = Mambilima Falls 91 10 31 S 28 45 E
Johnston I. 95 17 10N 169 8W
Johnstone Str. 108 50 28N 126 0W
Johnstown, N.Y., U.S.A. 114 43 1N 74 20W
Johnstown, Pa., U.S.A. 114 40 19N 78 53W
Johor □ 71 2 5N 103 20 E
Joigny 19 48 0N 3 20 E
Joinvile 125 26 15 S 48 55 E
Joinville 19 48 27N 5 10 E
Joinville I. 5 65 0 S 55 30W
Jokkmokk 50 66 35N 19 50 E
Jökulsá á Brú → 50 65 40N 14 16W
Jökulsá Fjöllum → 50 66 10N 16 30W
Joliet 114 41 30N 88 0W
Joliette 106 46 3N 73 24W
Jolo 73 6 0N 121 0 E
Jombang 73 7 33 S 112 14 E
Jome 73 1 16 S 127 30 E
Jomfruland 49 58 52N 9 36 E
Jönåker 49 58 44N 16 40 E
Jonava 54 55 8N 24 12 E
Jones Sound 4 76 0N 85 0W
Jonesboro, Ark., U.S.A. 117 35 50N 90 45W
Jonesboro, Ill., U.S.A. 117 37 26N 89 18W
Jonesboro, La., U.S.A. 117 32 15N 92 41W
Jonesport 107 44 32N 67 38W
Jonglei 87 6 25N 30 50 E
Joniskis 54 56 13N 23 35 E
Jönköping 49 57 45N 14 10 E
Jönköpings län □ 49 57 30N 14 30 E
Jonquière 107 48 27N 71 14W
Jonsberg 49 58 30N 16 48 E
Jonsered 49 57 45N 12 10 E
Jonzac 20 45 27N 0 28W
Joplin 117 37 0N 94 31W
Jordan, Phil. 73 10 41N 122 38 E
Jordan, U.S.A. 118 47 25N 106 58W
Jordan ■ 64 31 0N 36 0 E
Jordan → 62 31 48N 35 32 E
Jordan Valley 118 43 0N 117 2W
Jordanów 27 49 41N 19 49 E
Jorhat 67 26 45N 94 12 E
Jorm 65 36 50N 70 52 E
Jörn 50 65 4N 20 1 E
Jørpeland 47 59 3N 6 1 E
Jorquera → 124 28 3 S 69 58W
Jos 85 9 53N 8 51 E
Jošanička Banja 42 43 24N 20 47 E
José Batlle y Ordóñez 125 33 20 S 55 10W
Joseni 46 46 42N 25 29 E
Joseph 118 45 27N 117 13W
Joseph Bonaparte G. 96 14 35 S 128 50 E
Joseph City 119 35 0N 110 16W
Joseph, L., Newf., Can. 107 52 45N 65 18W
Joseph, L., Ont., Can. 112 45 10N 79 44W
Josselin 18 47 57N 2 33W
Jostedal 47 61 35N 7 15 E
Jotunheimen 47 61 35N 8 25 E
Jourdanton 117 28 54N 98 32W
Joussard 108 55 22N 115 50W
Jovellanos 121 22 40N 81 10W
Jowzjān □ 65 36 10N 66 0 E
Joyeuse 21 44 29N 4 16 E
Józefów 28 52 10N 21 11 E
Ju Xian 77 36 35N 118 20 E
Juan Aldama 120 24 20N 103 23W
Juan Bautista 119 36 55N 121 33W
Juan Bautista Alberdi 124 34 26 S 61 48W
Juan de Fuca Str. 118 48 15N 124 0W
Juan de Nova 93 17 3 S 43 45 E
Juan Fernández, Arch. de 95 33 50 S 80 0W
Juan José Castelli 124 25 27 S 60 57W
Juan L. Lacaze 124 34 26 S 57 25W
Juárez 124 37 40 S 59 43W
Juárez, Sierra de 120 32 0N 116 0W
Juàzeiro 127 9 30 S 40 30W
Juàzeiro do Norte 127 7 10 S 39 18W
Jubbulpore = Jabalpur 69 23 9N 79 58 E
Jübek 24 54 31N 9 24 E
Jubga 57 44 19N 38 48 E
Juby, C. 80 28 0N 12 59W
Júcar → 33 39 5N 0 10W
Juchitán 120 16 27N 95 5W
Judaea = Yehuda 62 31 35N 34 57 E
Judenburg 26 47 12N 14 38 E
Judith → 118 47 44N 109 38W
Judith Gap 118 46 40N 109 46W
Judith Pt. 113 41 20N 71 30W
Jugoslavia = Yugoslavia ■ 37 44 0N 20 0 E
Juigalpa 121 12 6N 85 26W
Juillac 20 45 20N 1 19 E
Juist 24 53 40N 7 0 E
Juiz de Fora 127 21 43 S 43 19W
Jujuy □ 124 23 20 S 65 40W
Julesberg 116 41 0N 102 20W
Juli 126 16 10 S 69 25W
Julia Cr. → 98 20 0 S 141 11 E
Julia Creek 97 20 39 S 141 44 E
Juliaca 126 15 25 S 70 10W
Julian 119 33 4N 116 38W
Julian Alps = Julijske Alpe 39 46 15N 14 1 E
Julianehåb 4 60 43N 46 0W
Jülich 24 50 55N 6 20 E
Julijske Alpe 39 46 15N 14 1 E
Jullundur 68 31 20N 75 40 E
Julu 76 37 15N 115 2 E
Jumbo 91 17 30 S 30 58 E
Jumentos Cays 121 23 0N 75 40 E
Jumet 16 50 27N 4 25 E
Jumilla 33 38 28N 1 19W
Jumla 69 29 15N 82 13 E
Jumna = Yamuna → 68 25 30N 81 53 E
Junagadh 68 21 30N 70 30 E
Junction, Tex., U.S.A. 117 30 29N 99 48W
Junction, Utah, U.S.A. 119 38 10N 112 15W
Junction B. 96 11 52 S 133 55 E
Junction City, Kans., U.S.A. 116 39 4N 96 55W
Junction City, Oreg., U.S.A. 118 44 14N 123 12W
Jundah 97 24 46 S 143 2 E
Jundiaí 125 24 30 S 47 0W
Juneau 104 58 20N 134 20W
Junee 97 34 53 S 147 35 E
Jungfrau 25 46 32N 7 58 E
Junggar Pendi 75 44 30N 86 0 E
Jungshahi 68 24 52N 67 44 E
Juniata → 112 40 30N 77 40W
Junín 124 34 33 S 60 57W
Junín de los Andes 128 39 45 S 71 0W
Jūniyah 64 33 59N 35 38 E
Junnar 70 19 12N 73 58 E
Junquera, La 32 42 25N 2 53 E
Junta, La 117 38 0N 103 30W
Juntura 118 43 44N 118 4W
Jupiter → 107 49 29N 63 37W
Jur, Nahr el → 87 8 45N 29 15 E
Jura, France 19 46 35N 6 5 E
Jura, U.K. 14 56 0N 5 50W
Jura □ 19 46 47N 5 45 E
Jura, Sd. of 14 55 57N 5 45W
Jura Suisse 25 47 10N 7 0 E
Jurado 126 7 7N 77 46W
Jurien B. 96 30 17 S 115 0 E
Jurilovca 46 44 46N 28 52 E
Juruá → 126 2 37 S 65 44W
Juruena → 126 7 20 S 58 3W
Juruti 127 2 9 S 56 4W
Jussey 19 47 50N 5 55 E
Justo Daract 124 33 52 S 65 12W
Jüterbog 24 52 0N 13 6 E
Juticalpa 121 14 40N 86 12W
Jutland = Jylland 8 56 25N 9 30 E
Juvigny-sous-Andaine 18 48 32N 0 30W
Juvisy 19 48 43N 2 23 E
Juwain 65 31 45N 61 30 E
Juzennecourt 19 48 10N 4 58 E
Jylland 8 56 25N 9 30 E
Jyväskylä 72 62 14N 25 50 E

K2 Kaputir

K

K2	**66**	35 58N	76 32 E
Kaalasin	**71**	16 26N	103 30 E
Kaap die Goeie Hoop	**92**	34 24 S	18 30 E
Kaap Plato	**92**	28 30 S	24 0 E
Kaapkruis	**92**	21 43 S	14 0 E
Kaapstad = Cape Town	**92**	33 55 S	18 22 E
Kabaena	**73**	5 15 S	122 0 E
Kabala	**84**	9 38N	11 37W
Kabale	**90**	1 15 S	30 0 E
Kabalo	**90**	6 0 S	27 0 E
Kabambare	**90**	4 41 S	27 39 E
Kabango	**91**	8 35 S	28 30 E
Kabanjahe	**72**	3 6N	98 30 E
Kabara	**84**	16 40N	2 50W
Kabardinka	**56**	44 40N	37 57 E
Kabardino-Balkar-A.S.S.R. □	**57**	43 30N	43 30 E
Kabare	**73**	0 4 S	130 58 E
Kabarega Falls	**90**	2 15N	31 30 E
Kabasalan	**73**	7 47N	122 44 E
Kabba	**85**	7 50N	6 3 E
Kabi	**85**	13 30N	12 35 E
Kabinakagami L.	**106**	48 54N	84 25W
Kabīr Kūh	**64**	33 0N	47 30 E
Kabīr, Zab al	**64**	36 0N	43 0 E
Kabkabīyah	**81**	13 50N	24 0 E
Kabna	**86**	19 6N	32 40 E
Kabompo	**91**	13 36 S	24 14 E
Kabompo →	**89**	14 10 S	23 11 E
Kabondo	**91**	8 58 S	25 40 E
Kabongo	**90**	7 22 S	25 33 E
Kabou	**85**	9 28N	0 55 E
Kaboudia, Rass	**83**	35 13N	11 10 E
Kabra	**98**	23 25 S	150 25 E
Kabūd Gonbad	**65**	37 5N	59 45 E
Kabul	**66**	34 28N	69 11 E
Kabúl □	**65**	34 30N	69 0 E
Kabul →	**66**	33 55N	72 14 E
Kabunga	**90**	1 38 S	28 3 E
Kaburuang	**73**	3 50N	126 30 E
Kabushiya	**87**	16 54N	33 41 E
Kabwe	**91**	14 30 S	28 29 E
Kačanik	**42**	42 13N	21 12 E
Kachanovo	**54**	57 25N	27 38 E
Kachebera	**91**	13 50 S	32 50 E
Kachin □	**67**	26 0N	97 30 E
Kachira, L.	**90**	0 40 S	31 7 E
Kachiry	**58**	53 10N	75 50 E
Kachisi	**87**	9 40N	37 50 E
Kackar	**57**	40 45N	41 10 E
Kadan Kyun	**72**	12 30N	98 20 E
Kadarkút	**27**	46 13N	17 39 E
Kadayanallur	**70**	9 3N	77 22 E
Kade	**85**	6 7N	0 56W
Kadi	**68**	23 18N	72 23 E
Kadina	**97**	34 0 S	137 43 E
Kadiri	**70**	14 12N	78 13 E
Kadirli	**64**	37 23N	36 5 E
Kadiyevka	**57**	48 35N	38 40 E
Kadoka	**116**	43 50N	101 31W
Kadom	**55**	54 37N	42 30 E
Kâdugli	**81**	11 0N	29 45 E
Kaduna	**85**	10 30N	7 21 E
Kaduna □	**85**	11 0N	7 30 E
Kaédi	**84**	16 9N	13 28W
Kaelé	**85**	10 7N	14 27 E
Kaesŏng	**76**	37 58N	126 35 E
Kāf	**64**	31 25N	37 29 E
Kafakumba	**88**	9 38 S	23 46 E
Kafan	**53**	39 18N	46 15 E
Kafanchan	**85**	9 40N	8 20 E
Kafareti	**85**	10 25N	11 12 E
Kaffrine	**84**	14 8N	15 36W
Kafia Kingi	**81**	9 20N	24 25 E
Kafinda	**91**	12 32 S	30 20 E
Kafirévs, Ákra	**45**	38 9N	24 38 E
Kafr 'Ayn	**62**	32 3N	35 7 E
Kafr el Dauwâr	**86**	31 8N	30 8 E
Kafr el Sheikh	**86**	31 15N	30 50 E
Kafr Kammā	**62**	32 44N	35 26 E
Kafr Kannā	**62**	32 45N	35 20 E
Kafr Mālik	**62**	32 0N	35 18 E
Kafr Mandā	**62**	32 49N	35 15 E
Kafr Quaddūm	**62**	32 14N	35 7 E
Kafr Rā'ī	**62**	32 23N	35 9 E
Kafr Şīr	**62**	33 19N	35 23 E
Kafr Yāsīf	**62**	32 58N	35 10 E
Kafue	**91**	15 46 S	28 9 E
Kafue Flats	**91**	15 40 S	27 25 E
Kafulwe	**91**	9 0 S	29 1 E
Kaga Bandoro	**88**	7 0N	19 10 E
Kagan	**58**	39 43N	64 33 E
Kagawa □	**74**	34 15N	134 0 E
Kagera →	**90**	0 57 S	31 47 E
Kağizman	**64**	40 5N	43 10 E
Kagoshima	**74**	31 35N	130 33 E
Kagoshima □	**74**	31 30N	130 30 E
Kagoshima-Wan	**74**	31 25N	130 40 E
Kagul	**56**	45 50N	28 15 E
Kahajan →	**72**	3 40 S	114 0 E
Kahama	**90**	4 8 S	32 30 E
Kahama □	**90**	3 50 S	32 0 E
Kahe	**90**	3 30 S	37 25 E
Kahemba	**88**	7 18 S	18 55 E
Kahil, Djebel bou	**83**	34 26N	4 0 E
Kahniah →	**108**	58 15N	120 55W
Kahnūj	**65**	27 55N	57 40 E
Kahoka	**116**	40 25N	91 42W
Kahoolawe	**110**	20 33N	156 35W
Kai Besar	**73**	5 35 S	133 0 E
Kai Kai	**92**	19 52 S	21 15 E
Kai, Kepulauan	**73**	5 55 S	132 45W
Kai-Ketjil	**73**	5 45 S	132 40 E
Kaiama	**85**	9 36N	4 1 E
Kaiapoi	**101**	42 24 S	172 40 E
Kaieteur Falls	**126**	5 1N	59 10W
Kaifeng	**77**	34 48N	114 21 E
Kaihua	**77**	29 12N	118 20 E
Kaiingveld	**92**	30 0 S	22 0 E
Kaikohe	**101**	35 25 S	173 49 E
Kaikoura	**101**	42 25 S	173 43 E
Kaikoura Pen.	**101**	42 25 S	173 43 E
Kaikoura Ra.	**101**	41 59 S	173 41 E
Kailahun	**84**	8 18N	10 39W
Kaili	**77**	26 33N	107 59 E
Kailu	**76**	43 38N	121 18 E
Kailua	**110**	19 39N	156 0W
Kaimana	**73**	3 39 S	133 45 E
Kaimanawa Mts.	**101**	39 15 S	175 56 E
Kaimganj	**69**	27 33N	79 24 E
Kaimur Hill	**69**	24 30N	82 0 E
Kainantu	**98**	6 18 S	145 52 E
Kaingaroa Forest	**101**	38 24 S	176 30 E
Kainji Res.	**85**	10 1N	4 40 E
Kaipara Harbour	**101**	36 25 S	174 14 E
Kaiping	**77**	22 23N	112 42 E
Kaipokok B.	**107**	54 54N	59 47W
Kairana	**68**	29 24N	77 15 E
Kaironi	**73**	0 47 S	133 40 E
Kairouan	**83**	35 45N	10 5 E
Kairuku	**98**	8 51 S	146 35 E
Kaiserslautern	**25**	49 30N	7 43 E
Kaitaia	**101**	35 8 S	173 17 E
Kaitangata	**101**	46 17 S	169 51 E
Kaithal	**68**	29 48N	76 26 E
Kaiwi Channel	**110**	21 13N	157 30W
Kaiyuan	**76**	42 28N	124 1 E
Kajaani	**50**	64 17N	27 46 E
Kajabbi	**97**	20 0 S	140 1 E
Kajan →	**72**	2 55N	117 35 E
Kajang	**71**	2 59N	101 48 E
Kajiado	**90**	1 53 S	36 48 E
Kajiado □	**90**	2 0 S	36 30 E
Kajo Kaji	**87**	3 58N	31 40 E
Kajoa	**73**	0 1N	127 28 E
Kaka	**81**	10 38N	32 10 E
Kakabeka Falls	**106**	48 24N	89 37W
Kakamega	**90**	0 20N	34 46 E
Kakamega □	**90**	0 20N	34 46 E
Kakanj	**42**	44 9N	18 7 E
Kakanui Mts.	**101**	45 10 S	170 30 E
Kakegawa	**74**	34 45N	138 1 E
Kakhib	**57**	42 28N	46 34 E
Kakhovka	**56**	46 40N	33 15 E
Kakhovskoye Vdkhr.	**56**	47 5N	34 16 E
Kakinada (Cocanada)	**70**	16 57N	82 11 E
Kakisa →	**108**	61 3N	118 10W
Kakisa L.	**108**	60 56N	117 43W
Kakwa →	**108**	54 37N	118 28W
Kala	**85**	12 2N	14 40 E
Kala Oya →	**70**	8 20N	79 45 E
Kalaa-Kebira	**83**	35 59N	10 32 E
Kalabagh	**68**	33 0N	71 28 E
Kalabahi	**73**	8 13 S	124 31 E
Kalabáka	**44**	39 42N	21 39 E
Kalabo	**89**	14 58 S	22 40 E
Kalach	**55**	50 22N	41 0 E
Kalach na Donu	**57**	48 43N	43 32 E
Kaladan →	**67**	20 20N	93 5 E
Kaladar	**112**	44 37N	77 5W
Kalahari	**92**	24 0 S	21 30 E
Kalahari Gemsbok Nat. Park	**92**	25 30 S	20 30 E
Kalahasti	**70**	13 45N	79 44 E
Kalakamati	**93**	20 40 S	27 25 E
Kalakan	**59**	55 15N	116 45 E
Kalama, U.S.A.	**118**	46 0N	122 55W
Kalama, Zaïre	**90**	2 52 S	28 35 E
Kalamariá	**44**	40 33N	22 55 E
Kalamata	**45**	37 3N	22 10 E
Kalamazoo	**114**	42 20N	85 35W
Kalamazoo →	**114**	42 40N	86 12W
Kalamb	**70**	18 3N	74 48 E
Kalambo Falls	**91**	8 37 S	31 35 E
Kálamos, Greece	**45**	38 37N	20 55 E
Kálamos, Greece	**45**	38 17N	23 52 E
Kalamoti	**45**	38 15N	26 4 E
Kalan	**64**	39 7N	39 32 E
Kalao	**73**	7 21 S	121 0 E
Kalaotoa	**73**	7 20 S	121 50 E
Kälarne	**48**	62 59N	16 8 E
Kalárovo	**27**	47 54N	18 0 E
Kalasin	**71**	16 26N	103 30 E
Kalat	**66**	29 8N	66 31 E
* Kalat □	**68**	27 30N	66 0 E
Kálathos (Calato)	**45**	36 9N	28 8 E
Kalaus →	**57**	45 40N	44 7 E
Kalávrita	**45**	38 3N	22 8 E
Kalecik	**56**	40 4N	33 26 E
Kalegauk Kyun	**67**	15 33N	97 35 E
Kalehe	**90**	2 6 S	28 50 E
Kalema	**90**	1 12 S	31 55 E
Kalemie	**90**	5 55 S	29 9 E
Kalety	**28**	50 35N	18 52 E
Kalewa	**67**	23 10N	94 15 E
Kálfafellsstaður	**50**	64 11N	15 53W
Kalgan = Zhangjiakou	**76**	40 48N	114 55 E
Kalgoorlie	**96**	30 40 S	121 22 E
Kaliakra, Nos	**43**	43 21N	28 30 E
Kalianda	**72**	5 50 S	105 45 E
Kalibo	**73**	11 43N	122 22 E
Kaliganj Town	**69**	22 25N	89 8 E
Kalima	**90**	2 33 S	26 32 E
Kalimantan Barat □	**72**	0 0	110 30 E
Kalimantan Selatan □	**72**	2 30 S	115 30 E
Kalimantan Tengah □	**72**	2 0 S	113 30 E
Kalimantan Timur □	**72**	1 30N	116 30 E
Kálimnos	**45**	37 0N	27 0 E
Kalimpong	**69**	27 4N	88 35 E
Kalinadi →	**70**	14 50N	74 7 E
Kalinin	**55**	56 55N	35 55 E
Kaliningrad	**54**	54 42N	20 32 E
Kalinkovichi	**54**	52 12N	29 20 E
Kalinovik	**42**	43 31N	18 29 E
Kalipetrovo (Stančevo)	**43**	44 5N	27 14 E
Kaliro	**90**	0 56N	33 30 E
Kalirrákhi	**44**	40 40N	24 35 E
Kalispell	**118**	48 10N	114 22W
Kalisz	**28**	51 45N	18 8 E
Kalisz □	**28**	51 30N	18 0 E
Kalisz Pomorski	**28**	53 17N	15 55 E
Kaliua	**90**	5 5 S	31 48 E
Kaliveli Tank	**70**	12 5N	79 50 E

* *Now part of Baluchistan* □

Kalix, →	**50**	65 50N	23 11 E
Kalka	**68**	30 46N	76 57 E
Kalkaska	**106**	44 44N	85 11W
Kalkfeld	**92**	20 57 S	16 14 E
Kalkfontein	**92**	22 4 S	20 57 E
Kalkrand	**92**	24 1 S	17 35 E
Kallakurichi	**70**	11 44N	79 1 E
Kållandsö	**49**	58 40N	13 5 E
Kallia	**62**	31 46N	35 30 E
Kallidaikurichi	**70**	8 38N	77 31 E
Kallinge	**49**	56 15N	15 18 E
Kallithéa	**45**	37 55N	23 41 E
Kallmeti	**44**	41 51N	19 41 E
Kallonís, Kólpos	**45**	39 10N	26 10 E
Kallsjön	**50**	63 38N	13 0 E
Kalmalo	**85**	13 40N	5 20 E
Kalmar	**49**	56 40N	16 20 E
Kalmar län □	**49**	57 25N	16 0 E
Kalmar sund	**49**	56 40N	16 25 E
Kalmyk A.S.S.R. □	**57**	46 5N	46 1 E
Kalmykovo	**57**	49 0N	51 47 E
Kalna	**69**	23 13N	88 25 E
Kalo	**98**	10 1 S	147 48 E
Kalocsa	**27**	46 32N	19 0 E
Kalofer	**43**	42 37N	24 59 E
Kaloko	**90**	6 47 S	25 48 E
Kalol, Gujarat, India	**68**	23 15N	72 33 E
Kalol, Gujarat, India	**68**	22 37N	73 31 E
Kalolímnos	**45**	37 4N	27 8 E
Kalomo	**91**	17 0 S	26 30 E
Kalonerón	**45**	37 20N	21 38 E
Kalpi	**69**	26 8N	79 47 E
Kalrayan Hills	**70**	11 45N	78 40 E
Kalsubai	**70**	19 35N	73 45 E
Kaltungo	**85**	9 48N	11 19 E
Kalu	**68**	25 5N	67 39 E
Kaluga	**55**	54 35N	36 10 E
Kalulushi	**91**	12 50 S	28 3 E
Kalundborg	**49**	55 41N	11 5 E
Kalush	**54**	49 3N	24 23 E
Kałuszyn	**28**	52 13N	21 52 E
Kalutara	**70**	6 35N	80 0 E
Kalwaria	**27**	49 53N	19 41 E
Kalya	**52**	60 15N	59 59 E
Kalyan	**68**	20 30N	74 3 E
Kalyazin	**55**	57 15N	37 55 E
Kam Keut	**71**	18 20N	104 48 E
Kama	**90**	3 30 S	27 5 E
Kama →	**52**	55 45N	52 0 E
Kamachumu	**90**	1 37 S	31 37 E
Kamaishi	**74**	39 20N	142 0 E
Kamalia	**68**	30 44N	72 42 E
Kamandorskiye Ostrava	**59**	55 0N	167 0 E
Kamapanda	**91**	12 5 S	24 0 E
Kamaran	**63**	15 21N	42 35 E
Kamativi	**91**	18 15 S	27 27 E
Kamba	**85**	11 50N	3 45 E
Kambam	**70**	9 45N	77 16 E
Kambar	**68**	27 37N	68 1 E
Kambarka	**52**	56 15N	54 11 E
Kambia	**84**	9 3N	12 53W
Kambolé	**91**	8 47 S	30 48 E
Kambove	**91**	10 51 S	26 33 E
Kamchatka, P-ov.	**59**	57 0N	160 0 E
Kamen	**58**	53 50N	81 30 E
Kamen Kashirskiy	**54**	51 39N	24 56 E
Kamenica, Srbija, Yugo.	**42**	44 25N	19 40 E
Kamenica, Srbija, Yugo.	**42**	43 27N	22 27 E
Kamenice	**26**	49 18N	15 2 E
Kamenjak, Rt	**39**	44 47N	13 55 E
Kamenka, R.S.F.S.R., U.S.S.R.	**52**	65 58N	44 0 E
Kamenka, R.S.F.S.R., U.S.S.R.	**55**	50 47N	39 20 E
Kamenka, R.S.F.S.R., U.S.S.R.	**55**	53 10N	44 5 E
Kamenka, Ukraine S.S.R., U.S.S.R.	**56**	49 3N	32 6 E
Kamenka Bugskaya	**54**	50 8N	24 16 E
Kamenka Dneprovskaya	**56**	47 29N	34 14 E
Kameno	**43**	42 34N	27 18 E
Kamenolomini	**57**	47 40N	40 14 E
Kamensk-Shakhtinskiy	**57**	48 23N	40 20 E
Kamensk Uralskiy	**58**	56 25N	62 2 E
Kamenskiy, R.S.F.S.R., U.S.S.R.	**55**	50 48N	45 25 E
Kamenskiy, R.S.F.S.R., U.S.S.R.	**57**	49 20N	41 15 E
Kamenskoye	**59**	62 45N	165 30 E
Kamenyak	**43**	43 24N	26 57 E
Kamenz	**24**	51 17N	14 7 E
Kami	**44**	42 17N	20 18 E
Kamiah	**118**	46 12N	116 2W
Kamień Krajeński	**28**	53 32N	17 32 E
Kamień Pomorski	**28**	53 57N	14 43 E
Kamienna →	**28**	51 6N	21 47 E
Kamienna Góra	**28**	50 47N	16 2 E
Kamiensk	**28**	51 12N	19 29 E
Kamilukuak, L.	**109**	62 22N	101 40W
Kamina	**91**	8 45 S	25 0 E
Kaminak L.	**109**	62 10N	95 0W
Kamituga	**90**	3 2 S	28 10 E
Kamloops	**108**	50 40N	120 20W
Kamloops L.	**108**	50 45N	120 40W
Kamnik	**39**	46 14N	14 37 E
Kamo	**57**	40 21N	45 7 E
Kamoke	**68**	32 4N	74 4 E
Kamp →	**26**	48 23N	15 42 E
Kampala	**90**	0 20N	32 30 E
Kampar	**71**	4 18N	101 9 E
Kampar →	**72**	0 30N	103 8 E
Kampen	**16**	52 33N	5 53 E
Kampolombo, L.	**91**	11 37 S	29 42 E
Kampot	**71**	10 36N	104 10 E
Kamptee	**68**	21 9N	79 19 E
Kampti	**84**	10 7N	3 25W
Kampuchea = Cambodia ■	**71**	13 0N	105 0 E
Kampung →	**73**	5 44 S	138 24 E
Kampungbaru = Tolitoli	**73**	1 5N	120 50 E
Kamrau, Teluk	**73**	3 30 S	133 36 E
Kamsack	**109**	51 34N	101 54W
Kamskoye Ustye	**55**	55 10N	49 20 E
Kamskoye Vdkhr.	**52**	58 0N	56 0 E
Kamuchawie L.	**109**	56 18N	101 59W
Kamyshin	**55**	50 10N	45 24 E
Kamyzyak	**57**	46 4N	48 10 E
Kanaaupscow	**106**	54 2N	76 30W
Kanab	**119**	37 3N	112 29W
Kanab Creek	**119**	37 0N	112 40W
Kanagawa □	**74**	35 20N	139 20 E
Kanairiktok →	**107**	55 2N	60 18W
Kanakapura	**70**	12 33N	77 28 E
Kanália	**44**	39 30N	22 53 E
Kananga	**88**	5 55 S	22 18 E
Kanarraville	**119**	37 34N	113 12W
Kanash	**55**	55 30N	47 32 E
Kanastraíon, Ákra	**44**	39 57N	23 45 E
Kanawha →	**114**	38 50N	82 8W
Kanazawa	**74**	36 30N	136 38 E
Kanchanaburi	**71**	14 2N	99 31 E
Kanchenjunga	**69**	27 50N	88 10 E
Kanchipuram (Conjeeveram)	**70**	12 52N	79 45 E
Kańczuga	**27**	49 59N	22 25 E
Kanda Kanda	**88**	6 52 S	23 48 E
Kandahar	**65**	31 32N	65 30 E
Kandalaksha	**52**	67 9N	32 30 E
Kandalakshkiy Zaliv	**52**	66 0N	35 0 E
Kandangan	**72**	2 50 S	115 20 E
Kandanos	**45**	35 19N	23 44 E
Kandhíla	**45**	37 46N	22 22 E
Kandhkot	**68**	28 16N	69 8 E
Kandhla	**68**	29 18N	77 19 E
Kandi, Benin	**85**	11 7N	2 55 E
Kandi, India	**69**	23 58N	88 5 E
Kandla	**68**	23 0N	70 10 E
Kandos	**99**	32 45 S	149 58 E
Kandukur	**70**	15 12N	79 57 E
Kandy	**70**	7 18N	80 43 E
Kane	**114**	41 39N	78 53W
Kane Bassin	**4**	79 30N	68 0W
Kanevskaya	**57**	46 3N	39 3 E
Kanfanar	**39**	45 7N	13 50 E
Kangaba	**84**	11 56N	8 25W
Kangar	**71**	6 27N	100 12 E
Kangaroo I.	**97**	35 45 S	137 0 E
Kangaroo Mts.	**98**	23 25 S	142 0 E
Kangavar	**64**	34 40N	48 0 E
Kangean, Kepulauan	**72**	6 55 S	115 23 E
Kangerdlugsuak	**4**	68 10N	32 20W
Kanggyee	**76**	41 0N	126 35 E
Kangnŭng	**76**	37 45N	128 54 E
Kango	**88**	0 11N	10 5 E
Kangto	**67**	27 50N	92 35 E
Kanhangad	**70**	12 21N	74 58 E
Kanheri	**70**	19 13N	72 50 E
Kani	**84**	8 29N	6 36W
Kaniama	**90**	7 30 S	24 12 E
Kaniapiskau →	**107**	56 40N	69 30W
Kaniapiskau L.	**107**	54 10N	69 55W
Kanin Nos, Mys	**52**	68 45N	43 20 E
Kanin, P-ov.	**52**	68 0N	45 0 E
Kanina	**44**	40 23N	19 30 E
Kaniva	**99**	36 22 S	141 18 E
Kanjiža	**42**	46 3N	20 4 E
Kankakee	**114**	41 6N	87 50W
Kankakee →	**114**	41 23N	88 16W
Kankan	**84**	10 23N	9 15W
Kanker	**70**	20 10N	81 40 E
Kankunskiy	**59**	57 37N	126 8 E
Kannapolis	**115**	35 32N	80 37W
Kannauj	**69**	27 3N	79 56 E
Kano	**85**	12 2N	8 30 E
Kano □	**85**	11 45N	9 0 E
Kanoroba	**84**	9 7N	6 8W
Kanowit	**72**	2 14N	112 20 E
Kanowna	**96**	30 32 S	121 31 E
Kanoya	**74**	31 25N	130 50 E
Kanpetlet	**67**	21 10N	93 59 E
Kanpur	**69**	26 28N	80 20 E
Kansas □	**116**	38 40N	98 0W
Kansas →	**116**	39 7N	94 36W
Kansas City, Kans., U.S.A.	**116**	39 0N	94 40W
Kansas City, Mo., U.S.A.	**116**	39 3N	94 30W
Kansenia	**91**	10 20 S	26 0 E
Kansk	**59**	56 20N	95 37 E
Kansu = Gansu □	**75**	37 0N	103 0 E
Kantang	**71**	7 25N	99 31 E
Kantché	**85**	13 31N	8 30 E
Kanté	**85**	9 57N	1 3 E
Kantemirovka	**57**	49 43N	39 55 E
Kanturk	**15**	52 10N	8 55W
Kanuma	**74**	36 34N	139 42 E
Kanus	**92**	27 50 S	18 39 E
Kanye	**92**	25 0 S	25 28 E
Kanyu	**92**	20 7 S	24 37 E
Kanzenze	**91**	10 30 S	25 12 E
Kanzi, Ras	**90**	7 1 S	39 33 E
Kaohsiung = Gaoxiong	**75**	22 38N	120 18 E
Kaokoveld	**92**	18 20 S	13 37 E
Kaolack	**84**	14 5N	16 8W
Kapadvanj	**68**	23 5N	73 0 E
Kapanga	**88**	8 30 S	22 40 E
Kapchagai	**58**	43 50N	77 10 E
Kapéllo, Ákra	**45**	36 9N	23 3 E
Kapema	**91**	10 45 S	28 22 E
Kapfenberg	**26**	47 26N	15 18 E
Kapiri Mposhi	**91**	13 59 S	28 43 E
Kapisa □	**65**	35 0N	69 20 E
Kapiskau →	**106**	52 47N	81 55W
Kapit	**72**	2 0N	112 55 E
Kapiti I.	**101**	40 50 S	174 56 E
Kaplice	**26**	48 42N	14 30 E
Kapoeta	**87**	4 50N	33 35 E
Kápolnásnyék	**27**	47 16N	18 41 E
Kapos →	**27**	46 44N	18 30 E
Kaposvár	**27**	46 25N	17 47 E
Kappeln	**24**	54 37N	9 56 E
Kapps	**92**	22 32 S	17 18 E
Kaprije	**39**	43 42N	15 43 E
Kapsukas	**54**	54 33N	23 19 E
Kapuas →	**72**	0 25 S	109 20 E
Kapuas Hulu, Pegunungan	**72**	1 30N	113 30 E
Kapulo	**91**	8 18 S	29 15 E
Kapunda	**99**	34 20 S	138 56 E
Kapurthala	**68**	31 23N	75 25 E
Kapuskasing	**106**	49 25N	82 30W
Kapuskasing →	**106**	49 49N	82 0W
Kapustin Yar	**57**	48 37N	45 40 E
Kaputir	**90**	2 5N	35 28 E

Kapuvár Kent

Kapuvár	**27**	47 36N	17 1 E
Kara, Turkey	**45**	36 58N	27 30 E
Kara, U.S.S.R.	**58**	69 10N	65 0 E
Kara Bogaz Gol, Zaliv	**53**	41 0N	53 30 E
Kara Burun	**45**	38 41N	26 28 E
Kara Kalpak A.S.S.R. □	**58**	43 0N	60 0 E
Kara Sea	**58**	75 0N	70 0 E
Kara, Wadi	**86**	20 0N	41 25 E
Karabük	**64**	41 12N	32 37 E
Karaburuni	**44**	40 25N	19 20 E
Karabutak	**58**	49 59N	60 14 E
Karachala	**57**	39 45N	48 53 E
Karachayevsk	**57**	43 50N	42 0 E
Karachev	**54**	53 10N	35 5 E
Karachi	**68**	24 53N	67 0 E
Karachi □	**68**	25 30N	67 0 E
Karád	**27**	46 41N	17 51 E
Karad	**70**	17 15N	74 10 E
Karadeniz Boğazı	**64**	41 10N	29 10 E
Karaga	**85**	9 58N	0 28W
Karaganda	**58**	49 50N	73 10 E
Karagayly	**58**	49 26N	76 0 E
Karaginskiy, Ostrov	**59**	58 45N	164 0 E
Karagiye Depression	**53**	43 27N	51 45 E
Karagwe □	**90**	2 0 S	31 0 E
Karaikkudi	**70**	10 0N	78 45 E
Karaitivu I.	**70**	9 45N	79 52 E
Karaitivu, I.	**70**	8 22N	79 47 E
Karaj	**65**	35 48N	51 0 E
Karakas	**58**	48 20N	83 30 E
Karakitang	**73**	3 14N	125 28 E
Karakoram Pass	**66**	35 33N	77 50 E
Karakoram Ra.	**66**	35 30N	77 0 E
Karakum, Peski	**58**	39 30N	60 0 E
Karalon	**59**	57 5N	115 50 E
Karaman	**64**	37 14N	33 13 E
Karamay	**75**	45 30N	84 58 E
Karambu	**72**	3 53 S	116 6 E
Karamea Bight	**101**	41 22 S	171 40 E
Karamoja □	**90**	3 0N	34 15 E
Karamsad	**68**	22 35N	72 50 E
Karanganjar	**73**	7 38 S	109 37 E
Karanja	**68**	20 29N	77 31 E
Karasburg	**92**	28 0 S	18 44 E
Karasino	**58**	66 50N	86 50 E
Karasjok	**50**	69 27N	25 30 E
Karasuk	**58**	53 44N	78 2 E
Karatau	**58**	43 10N	70 28 E
Karatau, Khrebet	**58**	43 30N	69 30 E
Karauli	**68**	26 30N	77 4 E
Karávi	**45**	36 49N	23 37 E
Karawanken	**26**	46 30N	14 40 E
Karazhal	**58**	48 2N	70 49 E
Karbalā	**64**	32 36N	44 3 E
Kårböle	**48**	61 59N	15 22 E
Karcag	**27**	47 19N	20 57 E
Karda	**59**	55 0N	103 16 E
Kardhámila	**45**	38 35N	26 5 E
Kardhítsa	**44**	39 23N	21 54 E
Kardhítsa □	**44**	39 15N	21 50 E
Kärdla	**54**	58 50N	22 40 E
Kareeberge	**92**	30 50 S	22 0 E
Kareima	**86**	18 30N	31 49 E
Karelian A.S.S.R. □	**52**	65 30N	32 30 E
Karen	**71**	12 49N	92 53 E
Kargānrūd	**64**	37 55N	49 0 E
Kargasok	**58**	59 3N	80 53 E
Kargat	**58**	55 10N	80 15 E
Kargı	**56**	41 11N	34 30 E
Kargil	**69**	34 32N	76 12 E
Kargopol	**52**	61 30N	38 58 E
Kargowa	**28**	52 5N	15 51 E
Karguéri	**85**	13 27N	10 30 E
Karia ba Mohammed	**82**	34 22N	5 12W
Kariaí	**44**	40 14N	24 19 E
Kariba	**91**	16 28 S	28 50 E
Kariba Gorge	**91**	16 30 S	28 50 E
Kariba Lake	**91**	16 40 S	28 25 E
Karibib	**92**	21 0 S	15 56 E
Karikal	**70**	10 59N	79 50 E
Karimata, Kepulauan	**72**	1 25 S	109 0 E
Karimata, Selat	**72**	2 0 S	108 40 E
Karimnagar	**70**	18 26N	79 10 E
Karimunjawa, Kepulauan	**72**	5 50 S	110 30 E
Karin	**63**	10 50N	45 52 E
Káristos	**45**	38 1N	24 29 E
Kariya	**74**	34 58N	137 1 E
Karkal	**70**	13 15N	74 56 E
Karkar I.	**98**	4 40 S	146 0 E
Karkaralinsk	**58**	49 26N	75 30 E
Karkinitskiy Zaliv	**56**	45 56N	33 0 E
Karkur	**62**	32 29N	34 57 E
Karkur Tohl	**86**	22 5N	25 5 E
Karl Libknekht	**54**	51 40N	35 35 E
Karl-Marx-Stadt	**24**	50 50N	12 55 E
Karl-Marx-Stadt □	**24**	50 45N	13 0 E
Karla, L. = Voiviïs, L.	**44**	39 30N	22 45 E
Karlino	**28**	54 3N	15 53 E
Karlobag	**39**	44 32N	15 5 E
Karlovac	**39**	45 31N	15 36 E
Karlovka	**56**	49 29N	35 8 E
Karlovy Vary	**26**	50 13N	12 51 E
Karlsborg	**49**	58 33N	14 33 E
Karlshamn	**49**	56 10N	14 51 E
Karlskoga	**48**	59 22N	14 33 E
Karlskrona	**49**	56 10N	15 35 E
Karlsruhe	**25**	49 3N	8 23 E
Karlstad, Sweden	**48**	59 23N	13 30 E
Karlstad, U.S.A.	**116**	48 38N	96 30W
Karlstadt	**25**	49 57N	9 46 E
Karmøy	**47**	59 15N	5 15 E
Karnal	**68**	29 42N	77 2 E
Karnali →	**69**	29 0N	83 20 E
Karnaphuli Res.	**67**	22 40N	92 20 E
Karnataka □	**70**	14 15N	76 0 E
Karnes City	**117**	28 53N	97 53W
Karnische Alpen	**26**	46 36N	13 0 E
Kärnten □	**26**	46 52N	13 30 E
Karo	**84**	12 16N	3 18W
Karoi	**91**	16 48 S	29 45 E
Karonga	**91**	9 57 S	33 55 E
Karoonda	**99**	35 1 S	139 59 E
Káros	**45**	36 54N	25 40 E
Karousádhes	**44**	39 47N	19 45 E
Kárpathos	**45**	35 37N	27 10 E
Karpáthos, Stenón	**45**	36 0N	27 30 E
Karpinsk	**52**	59 45N	60 1 E
Karpogory	**52**	63 59N	44 27 E
Karrebæk	**49**	55 12N	11 39 E
Kars, Turkey	**64**	40 40N	43 5 E
Kars, U.S.S.R.	**56**	40 36N	43 5 E
Karsakpay	**58**	47 55N	66 40 E
Karsha	**57**	49 45N	51 35 E
Karshi	**58**	38 53N	65 48 E
Karst	**39**	45 35N	14 0 E
Karsun	**55**	54 14N	46 57 E
Kartál Óros	**44**	41 15N	25 13 E
Kartaly	**58**	53 3N	60 40 E
Kartapur	**68**	31 27N	75 32 E
Karthaus	**112**	41 8N	78 9W
Kartuzy	**28**	54 22N	18 10 E
Karufa	**73**	3 50 S	133 20 E
Karumba	**98**	17 31 S	140 50 E
Karumo	**90**	2 25 S	32 50 E
Karumwa	**90**	3 12 S	32 38 E
Karungu	**90**	0 50 S	34 10 E
Karup	**49**	56 19N	9 10 E
Karur	**70**	10 59N	78 2 E
Karviná	**27**	49 53N	18 25 E
Karwi	**69**	25 12N	80 57 E
Kas Kong	**71**	11 27N	102 12 E
Kasache	**91**	13 25 S	34 20 E
Kasai →	**88**	3 30 S	16 10 E
Kasai Oriental □	**90**	5 0 S	24 30 E
Kasaji	**91**	10 25 S	23 27 E
Kasama	**91**	10 16 S	31 9 E
Kasane	**92**	17 34 S	24 50 E
Kasanga	**91**	8 30 S	31 10 E
Kasangulu	**88**	4 33 S	15 15 E
Kasaragod	**70**	12 30N	74 58 E
Kasba L.	**109**	60 20N	102 10W
Kasba Tadla	**82**	32 36N	6 17W
Kasempa	**91**	13 30 S	25 44 E
Kasenga	**91**	10 20 S	28 45 E
Kasese	**90**	0 13N	30 3 E
Kasewa	**91**	14 28 S	28 53 E
Kasganj	**68**	27 48N	78 42 E
Kashabowie	**106**	48 40N	90 26W
Kāshān	**65**	34 5N	51 30 E
Kashi	**75**	39 30N	76 2 E
Kashimbo	**91**	11 12 S	26 19 E
Kashin	**55**	57 20N	37 36 E
Kashipur, Orissa, India	**70**	19 16N	83 3 E
Kashipur, Ut. P., India	**68**	29 15N	79 0 E
Kashira	**55**	54 45N	38 10 E
Kāshmar	**65**	35 16N	58 26 E
Kashmir	**69**	34 0N	76 0 E
Kashmor	**68**	28 28N	69 32 E
Kashpirovka	**55**	53 0N	48 30 E
Kashun Noerh = Gaxun Nur	**75**	42 22N	100 30 E
Kasimov	**55**	54 55N	41 20 E
Kasinge	**90**	6 15 S	26 58 E
Kasiruta	**73**	0 25 S	127 12 E
Kaskaskia →	**116**	37 58N	89 57W
Kaskattama →	**109**	57 3N	90 4W
Kaskinen	**50**	62 22N	21 15 E
Kaskö	**50**	62 22N	21 15 E
Kaslo	**108**	49 55N	116 55W
Kasmere L.	**109**	59 34N	101 10W
Kasongo	**90**	4 30 S	26 33 E
Kasongo Lunda	**88**	6 35 S	16 49 E
Kásos	**45**	35 20N	26 55 E
Kasos, Stenón	**45**	35 30N	26 30 E
Kaspi	**57**	41 54N	44 17 E
Kaspichan	**43**	43 18N	27 11 E
Kaspiysk	**57**	42 52N	47 40 E
Kaspiyskiy	**57**	45 22N	47 23 E
Kassab ed Doleib	**87**	13 30N	33 35 E
Kassaba	**86**	22 40N	29 55 E
Kassala	**87**	16 0N	36 0 E
Kassalâ □	**87**	15 20N	36 26 E
Kassándra	**44**	40 0N	23 30 E
Kassel	**24**	51 19N	9 32 E
Kassinga	**89**	15 5 S	16 4 E
Kassinger	**86**	18 46N	31 51 E
Kassue	**73**	6 58 S	139 21 E
Kastamonu	**64**	41 25N	33 43 E
Kastav	**39**	45 22N	14 20 E
Kastélli	**45**	35 29N	23 38 E
Kastéllion	**45**	35 12N	25 20 E
Kastellorizon = Megiste	**35**	36 8N	29 34 E
Kastellou, Ákra	**45**	35 30N	27 15 E
Kastlösa	**49**	56 26N	16 25 E
Kastóri	**45**	37 10N	22 17 E
Kastoría	**44**	40 30N	21 19 E
Kastoría □	**44**	40 30N	21 15 E
Kastorías, L.	**44**	40 30N	21 20 E
Kastornoye	**55**	51 55N	38 2 E
Kastós	**45**	38 35N	20 55 E
Kástron	**44**	39 50N	25 2 E
Kastrosikiá	**45**	39 6N	20 36 E
Kasulu	**90**	4 37 S	30 5 E
Kasulu □	**90**	4 37 S	30 5 E
Kasumkent	**57**	41 47N	48 15 E
Kasungu	**91**	13 0 S	33 29 E
Kasur	**68**	31 5N	74 25 E
Kata	**59**	58 46N	102 40 E
Kataba	**91**	16 5 S	25 10 E
Katako Kombe	**90**	3 25 S	24 20 E
Katákolon	**45**	37 38N	21 19 E
Katale	**90**	4 52 S	31 7 E
Katamatite	**99**	36 6 S	145 41 E
Katanda, Zaïre	**90**	0 55 S	29 21 E
Katanda, Zaïre	**90**	7 52 S	24 13 E
Katangi	**69**	21 56N	79 50 E
Katangli	**59**	51 42N	143 14 E
Katanning	**96**	33 40 S	117 33 E
Katastári	**45**	37 50N	20 45 E
Katavi Swamp	**90**	6 50 S	31 10 E
Kateríni	**44**	40 18N	22 37 E
Katha	**67**	24 10N	96 30 E
Katherîna, Gebel	**86**	28 30N	33 57 E
Katherine	**96**	14 27 S	132 20 E
Kathiawar	**68**	22 20N	71 0 E
Kati	**84**	12 41N	8 4W
Katiet	**72**	2 21 S	99 54 E
Katihar	**69**	25 34N	87 36 E
Katima Mulilo	**92**	17 28 S	24 13 E
Katimbira	**91**	12 40 S	34 0 E
Katiola	**84**	8 10N	5 10W
Katkopberg	**92**	30 0 S	20 0 E
Katlanovo	**42**	41 52N	21 40 E
Katmandu	**69**	27 45N	85 20 E
Kato Akhaïa	**45**	38 8N	21 33 E
Káto Stavros	**44**	40 39N	23 43 E
Katol	**68**	21 17N	78 38 E
Katompe	**90**	6 2 S	26 23 E
Katonga →	**90**	0 34N	31 50 E
Katoomba	**97**	33 41 S	150 19 E
Katowice	**28**	50 17N	19 5 E
Katowice □	**28**	50 10N	19 0 E
Katrine, L.	**14**	56 15N	4 30W
Katrineholm	**48**	59 9N	16 12 E
Katsepe	**93**	15 45 S	46 15 E
Katsina Ala →	**85**	7 10N	9 20 E
Katsuura	**74**	35 10N	140 20 E
Kattawaz-Urgun □	**65**	32 10N	68 20 E
Kattegatt	**49**	57 0N	11 20 E
Katumba	**90**	7 40 S	25 17 E
Katungu	**90**	2 55 S	40 3 E
Katwa	**69**	23 30N	88 5 E
Katwijk-aan-Zee	**16**	52 12N	4 24 E
Katy	**28**	51 2N	16 45 E
Kauai	**110**	22 0N	159 30W
Kauai Chan.	**110**	21 45N	158 50W
Kaub	**25**	50 5N	7 46 E
Kaufbeuren	**25**	47 50N	10 37 E
Kaufman	**117**	32 35N	96 20W
Kaukauna	**114**	44 20N	88 13W
Kaukauveld	**92**	20 0 S	20 15 E
Kaukonen	**50**	67 31N	24 53 E
Kauliranta	**50**	66 27N	23 41 E
Kaunas	**54**	54 54N	23 54 E
Kaura Namoda	**85**	12 37N	6 33 E
Kautokeino	**50**	69 0N	23 4 E
Kavacha	**59**	60 16N	169 51 E
Kavadarci	**42**	41 26N	22 3 E
Kavaja	**44**	41 11N	19 33 E
Kavali	**70**	14 55N	80 1 E
Kaválla	**44**	40 57N	24 28 E
Kaválla □	**44**	41 5N	24 30 E
Kaválla Kólpos	**44**	40 50N	24 25 E
Kavarna	**43**	43 26N	28 22 E
Kavieng	**98**	2 36 S	150 51 E
Kavkaz, Bolshoi	**57**	42 50N	44 0 E
Kavoúsi	**45**	35 7N	25 51 E
Kaw = Caux	**127**	4 30N	52 15W
Kawa	**87**	13 42N	32 34 E
Kawagama L.	**112**	45 18N	78 45W
Kawagoe	**74**	35 55N	139 29 E
Kawaguchi	**74**	35 52N	139 45 E
Kawaihae	**110**	20 3N	155 50W
Kawambwa	**91**	9 48 S	29 3 E
Kawardha	**69**	22 0N	81 17 E
Kawasaki	**74**	35 35N	139 42 E
Kawene	**106**	48 45N	91 15W
Kawerau	**101**	38 7 S	176 42 E
Kawhia Harbour	**101**	38 5 S	174 51 E
Kawio, Kepulauan	**73**	4 30N	125 30 E
Kawnro	**67**	22 48N	99 8 E
Kawthaung	**71**	10 5N	98 36 E
Kawthoolei □ = Kawthule	**67**	18 0N	97 30 E
Kawthule □	**67**	18 0N	97 30 E
Kaya	**85**	13 4N	1 10W
Kayah □	**67**	19 15N	97 15 E
Kayangulam	**70**	9 10N	76 33 E
Kaycee	**118**	43 45N	106 46W
Kayeli	**73**	3 20 S	127 10 E
Kayenta	**119**	36 46N	110 15W
Kayes	**84**	14 25N	11 30W
Kayima	**84**	8 54N	11 15W
Kayomba	**91**	13 11 S	24 2 E
Kayoro	**85**	11 0N	1 28W
Kayrunnera	**99**	30 40 S	142 30 E
Kaysatskoye	**57**	49 47N	46 49 E
Kayseri	**64**	38 45N	35 30 E
Kaysville	**118**	41 2N	111 58W
Kayuagung	**72**	3 24 S	104 50 E
Kazachinskoye	**59**	56 16N	107 36 E
Kazachye	**59**	70 52N	135 58 E
Kazakh S.S.R. □	**58**	50 0N	70 0 E
Kazan	**55**	55 48N	49 3 E
Kazanlúk	**43**	42 38N	25 20 E
Kazanskaya	**57**	49 50N	41 10 E
Kazatin	**56**	49 45N	28 50 E
Kazbek	**57**	42 42N	44 30 E
Kāzerūn	**65**	29 38N	51 40 E
Kazi Magomed	**57**	40 3N	49 0 E
Kazimierz Dolny	**28**	51 19N	21 57 E
Kazimierza Wielka	**28**	50 15N	20 30 E
Kazincbarcika	**27**	48 17N	20 36 E
Kaztalovka	**57**	49 47N	48 43 E
Kazumba	**88**	6 25 S	22 5 E
Kazym →	**58**	63 54N	65 50 E
Kcynia	**28**	53 0N	17 30 E
Ké-Macina	**84**	13 58N	5 22W
Kéa	**45**	37 35N	24 22 E
Kea	**45**	37 30N	24 22 E
Keams Canyon	**119**	35 53N	110 9W
Kearney	**116**	40 45N	99 3W
Keban	**64**	38 50N	38 50 E
Kébi	**84**	9 18N	6 37W
Kebili	**83**	33 47N	9 0 E
Kebnekaise	**50**	67 53N	18 33 E
Kebri Dehar	**63**	6 45N	44 17 E
Kebumen	**73**	7 42 S	109 40 E
Kecel	**27**	46 31N	19 16 E
Kechika →	**108**	59 41N	127 12W
Kecskemét	**27**	46 57N	19 42 E
Kedada	**87**	5 25N	35 58 E
Kedah □	**71**	5 50N	100 40 E
Kedainiai	**54**	55 15N	24 2 E
Kedgwick	**107**	47 40N	67 20W
Kedia Hill	**92**	21 28 S	24 37 E
Kediri	**73**	7 51 S	112 1 E
Kédougou	**84**	12 35N	12 10W
Kedzierzyn	**28**	50 20N	18 12 E
Keefers	**108**	50 0N	121 40W
Keeley L.	**109**	54 54N	108 8W
Keeling Is. = Cocos Is.	**94**	12 12 S	96 55 E
Keene	**114**	42 57N	72 17W
Keeper Hill	**15**	52 46N	8 17W
Keer-Weer, C.	**97**	14 0 S	141 32 E
Keeseville	**113**	44 29N	73 30W
Keetmanshoop	**92**	26 35 S	18 8 E
Keewatin	**116**	47 23N	93 0W
Keewatin □	**109**	63 20N	95 0W
Keewatin →	**109**	56 29N	100 46W
Kefa □	**87**	6 55N	36 30 E
Kefallinía	**45**	38 20N	20 30 E
Kefamenanu	**73**	9 28 S	124 29 E
Kefar 'Eqron	**62**	31 52N	34 49 E
Kefar Hasīdim	**62**	32 47N	35 5 E
Kefar Naḥum	**62**	32 54N	35 34 E
Kefar Sava	**62**	32 11N	34 54 E
Kefar Szold	**62**	33 11N	35 39 E
Kefar Vitkin	**62**	32 22N	34 53 E
Kefar Yehezqel	**62**	32 34N	35 22 E
Kefar Yona	**62**	32 20N	34 54 E
Kefar Zekharya	**62**	31 43N	34 57 E
Kefar Zetim	**62**	32 48N	35 27 E
Keffi	**85**	8 55N	7 43 E
Keflavík	**50**	64 2N	22 35W
Keg River	**108**	57 54N	117 55W
Kegahka	**107**	50 9N	61 18W
Kegalla	**70**	7 15N	80 21 E
Kehl	**25**	48 34N	7 50 E
Keighley	**12**	53 52N	1 54W
Keimoes	**92**	28 41 S	21 0 E
Keita	**85**	14 46N	5 56 E
Keith, Austral.	**99**	36 6 S	140 20 E
Keith, U.K.	**14**	57 33N	2 58W
Keith Arm	**104**	64 20N	122 15W
Kekri	**68**	26 0N	75 10 E
Këł	**59**	69 30N	124 10 E
Kelamet	**87**	16 0N	38 30 E
Kelan	**76**	38 43N	111 31 E
Kelang	**71**	3 2N	101 26 E
Kelani Ganga →	**70**	6 58N	79 50 E
Kelantan □	**71**	5 10N	102 0 E
Kelantan →	**71**	6 13N	102 14 E
Këlcyra	**44**	40 22N	20 12 E
Kelheim	**25**	48 58N	11 57 E
Kelibia	**83**	36 50N	11 3 E
Kellé	**88**	0 8 S	14 38 E
Keller	**118**	48 2N	118 44W
Kellerberrin	**96**	31 36 S	117 38 E
Kellett C.	**4**	72 0N	126 0W
Kelleys I.	**112**	41 35N	82 42W
Kellogg	**118**	47 30N	116 5W
Kelloselkä	**50**	66 56N	28 53 E
Kells = Ceanannus Mor	**15**	53 42N	6 53W
Kélo	**81**	9 10N	15 45 E
Kelowna	**108**	49 50N	119 25W
Kelsey Bay	**108**	50 25N	126 0W
Kelso, N.Z.	**101**	45 54 S	169 15 E
Kelso, U.K.	**14**	55 36N	2 27W
Kelso, U.S.A.	**118**	46 10N	122 57W
Keluang	**71**	2 3N	103 18 E
Kelvington	**109**	52 10N	103 30W
Kem	**52**	65 0N	34 38 E
Kem →	**52**	64 57N	34 41 E
Kem-Kem	**82**	30 40N	4 30W
Kema	**73**	1 22N	125 8 E
Kemah	**54**	39 32N	39 5 E
Kemano	**108**	53 35N	128 0W
Kembolcha	**87**	11 2N	39 42 E
Kemenets-Podolskiy	**56**	48 40N	26 40 E
Kemerovo	**58**	55 20N	86 5 E
Kemi	**50**	65 44N	24 34 E
Kemi älv = Kemijoki →	**50**	65 47N	24 32 E
Kemijärvi	**50**	66 43N	27 22 E
Kemijoki →	**50**	65 47N	24 32 E
Kemmerer	**118**	41 52N	110 30W
Kemp Coast	**5**	69 0 S	55 0 E
Kemp L.	**117**	33 45N	99 15W
Kempsey	**97**	31 1 S	152 50 E
Kempt, L.	**106**	47 25N	74 22W
Kempten	**25**	47 42N	10 18 E
Kemptville	**106**	45 0N	75 38W
Kenadsa	**82**	31 48N	2 26W
Kendal, Indon.	**72**	6 56 S	110 14 E
Kendal, U.K.	**12**	54 19N	2 44W
Kendall	**99**	31 35 S	152 44 E
Kendall →	**98**	14 4 S	141 35 E
Kendallville	**114**	41 25N	85 15W
Kendari	**73**	3 50 S	122 30 E
Kendawangan	**72**	2 32 S	110 17 E
Kende	**85**	11 30N	4 12 E
Kendervicës, m. e.	**44**	40 15N	19 52 E
Kendrapara	**69**	20 35N	86 30 E
Kendrick	**118**	46 43N	116 41W
Kenedy	**117**	28 49N	97 51W
Kenema	**84**	7 50N	11 14W
Keng Tung	**67**	21 0N	99 30 E
Kenge	**88**	4 50 S	17 4 E
Kengeja	**90**	5 26 S	39 45 E
Kenhardt	**92**	29 19 S	21 12 E
Kénitra (Port Lyautey)	**82**	34 15N	6 40W
Kenmare, Ireland	**15**	51 52N	9 35W
Kenmare, U.S.A.	**116**	48 40N	102 4W
Kenmare →	**15**	51 40N	10 0W
Kenmore	**100**	34 44 S	149 45 E
Kenn Reef	**97**	21 12 S	155 46 E
Kennebec	**116**	43 56N	99 54W
Kennedy	**91**	18 52 S	27 10 E
Kennedy Taungdeik	**67**	23 15N	93 45 E
Kennet →	**13**	51 24N	0 58W
Kennett	**117**	36 7N	90 0W
Kennewick	**118**	46 11N	119 2W
Kénogami	**107**	48 25N	71 15W
Kenogami →	**106**	51 6N	84 28W
Kenora	**109**	49 47N	94 29W
Kenosha	**114**	42 33N	87 48W
Kensington, Can.	**107**	46 28N	63 34W
Kensington, U.S.A.	**116**	39 48N	99 2W
Kensington Downs	**98**	22 31 S	144 19 E
Kent, Ohio, U.S.A.	**114**	41 8N	81 20W

Kent Kiparissía

Kent, Oreg., U.S.A.	118	45 11N	120 45W
Kent, Tex., U.S.A.	117	31 5N	104 12W
Kent □	13	51 12N	0 40 E
Kent Group	99	39 30 S	147 20 E
Kent Pen.	104	68 30N	107 0W
Kentau	58	43 32N	68 36 E
Kentland	114	40 45N	87 25W
Kenton	114	40 40N	83 35W
Kentucky □	114	37 20N	85 0W
Kentucky →	114	38 41N	85 11W
Kentucky Dam	114	37 2N	88 15W
Kentucky L.	115	36 25N	88 0W
Kentville	107	45 6N	64 29W
Kentwood	117	31 0N	90 30W
Kenya ■	90	1 0N	38 0 E
Kenya, Mt.	90	0 10 S	37 18 E
Keokuk	116	40 25N	91 24W
Kep-i-Gjuhës	44	40 28N	19 15 E
Kepi	73	6 32 S	139 19 E
Kepice	28	54 16N	16 51 E
Kępno	28	51 18N	17 58 E
Keppel B.	97	23 21 S	150 55 E
Kepsut	64	39 40N	28 9 E
Kerala □	70	11 0N	76 15 E
Kerang	97	35 40 S	143 55 E
Keratéa	45	37 48N	23 58 E
Keraudren, C.	99	19 58 S	119 45 E
Keray	65	26 15N	57 30 E
Kerch	56	45 20N	36 20 E
Kerchenskiy Proliv	56	45 10N	36 30 E
Kerchoual	85	17 12N	0 20 E
Kerem Maharal	62	32 39N	34 59 E
Kerema	98	7 58 S	145 50 E
Keren	87	15 45N	38 28 E
Kerewan	84	13 29N	16 10W
Kerguelen	3	48 15 S	69 10 E
Keri	45	37 40N	20 49 E
Keri Kera	87	12 21N	32 42 E
Kericho	90	0 22 S	35 15 E
Kericho □	90	0 30 S	35 15 E
Kerinci	72	1 40 S	101 15 E
Kerkenna, Iles	83	34 48N	11 11 E
Kerki	58	37 50N	65 12 E
Kerkinitis, Límni	44	41 12N	23 10 E
Kérkira	44	39 38N	19 50 E
Kerkrade	16	50 53N	6 4 E
Kerma	86	19 33N	30 32 E
Kermadec Is.	94	30 0 S	178 15W
Kermadec Trench	94	30 30 S	176 0W
Kermân	65	30 15N	57 1 E
Kermân □	65	30 0N	57 0 E
** Kermânshâh	64	34 23N	47 0 E
Kermânshâhân □	64	34 0N	46 30 E
Kerme Körfezi	45	36 55N	27 50 E
Kermen	43	42 30N	26 16 E
Kermit	117	31 56N	103 3W
Kern →	119	35 16N	119 18W
Kerrobert	109	52 0N	109 11W
Kerrville	117	30 1N	99 8W
Kerry □	15	52 7N	9 35W
Kerry Hd.	15	52 26N	9 56W
Kersa	87	9 28N	41 48 E
Kerteminde	49	55 28N	10 39 E
Kertosono	73	7 38 S	112 9 E
Kerulen →	75	48 48N	117 0 E
Kerzaz	82	29 29N	1 37W
Kesagami →	106	51 40N	79 45W
Kesagami L.	106	50 23N	80 15W
Keşan	44	40 49N	26 38 E
Keski-Suomen lääni □	50	62 0N	25 30 E
Kestell	93	28 17 S	28 42 E
Kestenga	52	66 0N	31 50 E
Keswick	12	54 35N	3 9W
Keszthely	27	46 50N	17 15 E
Ket →	58	58 55N	81 32 E
Keta	85	5 49N	1 0 E
Ketapang	72	1 55 S	110 0 E
Ketchikan	104	55 25N	131 40W
Ketchum	118	43 41N	114 27W
Kete Krachi	85	7 46N	0 1W
Ketef, Khalîg Umm el	86	23 40N	35 35 E
Keti Bandar	68	24 8N	67 27 E
Ketri	68	28 1N	75 50 E
Kętrzyn	28	54 7N	21 22 E
Kettering	13	52 24N	0 44W
Kettle →	109	56 40N	89 34W
Kettle Falls	118	48 41N	118 2W
Kety	27	49 51N	19 16 E
Kevin	118	48 45N	111 58W
Kewanee	116	41 18N	89 55W
Kewaunee	114	44 27N	87 30W
Keweenaw B.	114	46 56N	88 23W
Keweenaw Pen.	114	47 30N	88 0W
Keweenaw Pt.	114	47 26N	87 40W
Key Harbour	106	45 50N	80 45W
Key West	121	24 33N	82 0W
Keyport	113	40 26N	74 12W
Keyser	114	39 26N	79 0W
Keystone, S.D., U.S.A.	116	43 54N	103 27W
Keystone, W. Va., U.S.A.	114	37 30N	81 30W
Kezhma	59	58 59N	101 9 E
Kežmarok	27	49 10N	20 28 E
Khabarovo	58	69 30N	60 30 E
Khabarovsk	59	48 30N	135 5 E
Khâbûr →	64	35 0N	40 30 E
Khachmas	57	41 31N	48 42 E
Khachraud	68	23 25N	75 20 E
Khadari, W. el →	87	10 29N	27 15 E
Khadro	68	26 11N	68 50 E
Khadyzhensk	57	44 26N	39 32 E
Khagaria	69	25 30N	86 32 E
Khaibar	86	25 49N	39 16 E
Khaipur, Bahawalpur, Pak.	68	29 34N	72 17 E
Khaipur, Hyderabad, Pak.	68	27 32N	68 49 E
Khair	68	27 57N	77 46 E
Khairabad	69	27 33N	80 47 E
Khairagarh Raj	69	21 27N	81 2 E
* Khairpur □	68	27 20N	69 8 E
Khakhea	92	24 48 S	23 22 E
Khalfallah	82	34 20N	0 16 E
Khalij-e-Fars □	65	28 20N	51 45 E
Khalilabad	69	26 48N	83 5 E

Khálki	44	39 36N	22 30 E
Khalkidhiki □	44	40 25N	23 20 E
Khalkís	45	38 27N	23 42 E
Khalmer-Sede = Tazovskiy	58	67 30N	78 30 E
Khalmer Yu	58	67 58N	65 1 E
Khalturin	55	58 40N	48 50 E
Khamaria	69	23 10N	80 52 E
Khamas Country	92	21 45 S	26 30 E
Khambhalia	68	22 14N	69 41 E
Khamgaon	68	20 42N	76 37 E
Khamilonísion	45	35 50N	26 15 E
Khamir	63	16 0N	44 0 E
Khammam	70	17 11N	80 6 E
Khān Yūnis	62	31 21N	34 18 E
Khānābād	65	36 45N	69 5 E
Khānaqīn	64	34 23N	45 25 E
Khandrá	45	35 3N	26 8 E
Khandwa	68	21 49N	76 22 E
Khandyga	59	62 42N	135 35 E
Khanewal	68	30 20N	71 55 E
* Khanh Hung	71	9 37N	105 50 E
Khaniá	45	35 30N	24 4 E
Khaniá □	45	35 30N	24 0 E
Khanion Kólpos	45	35 33N	23 55 E
Khanka, Oz.	59	45 0N	132 30 E
Khanna	68	30 42N	76 16 E
Khanpur	68	28 42N	70 35 E
Khanty-Mansiysk	58	61 0N	69 0 E
Khapcheranga	59	49 42N	112 24 E
Kharagpur	69	22 20N	87 25 E
Kharaij	86	21 25N	41 0 E
Kharan Kalat	66	28 34N	65 21 E
Kharānaq	65	32 20N	54 45 E
Kharda	70	18 40N	75 34 E
Khârga, El Wâhât el	86	25 10N	30 35 E
Khargon	68	21 45N	75 40 E
Kharit, Wadi el →	86	24 26N	33 3 E
Khārk, Jazireh	64	29 15N	50 28 E
Kharkov	56	49 58N	36 20 E
Kharmanli	43	41 55N	25 55 E
Kharovsk	55	59 56N	40 13 E
Kharsānīya	64	27 10N	49 10 E
Khartoum = El Khartûm	87	15 31N	32 35 E
Khasab	65	26 14N	56 15 E
Khasavyurt	57	43 16N	46 40 E
Khasebake	92	20 42 S	24 29 E
Khāsh	65	28 15N	61 15 E
Khashm el Girba	87	14 59N	35 58 E
Khashuri	57	41 58N	43 35 E
Khasi Hills	69	25 30N	91 30 E
Khaskovo	43	41 56N	25 30 E
Khatanga	59	72 0N	102 20 E
Khatanga →	59	72 55N	106 0 E
Khatangskiy, Saliv	4	66 0N	112 0 E
Khatauli	68	29 17N	77 43 E
Khatyrka	59	62 3N	175 15 E
Khavār □	64	37 20N	47 0 E
Khaybar, Harrat	64	25 45N	40 0 E
Khazzân Jabal el Awliyâ	87	15 24N	32 20 E
Khed, Maharashtra, India	70	17 43N	73 27 E
Khed, Maharashtra, India	70	18 51N	73 56 E
Khekra	68	28 52N	77 20 E
Khemelnik	56	49 33N	27 58 E
Khemis Miliana	82	36 11N	2 14 E
Khemissèt	82	33 50N	6 1W
Khemmarat	71	16 10N	105 15 E
Khenchela	83	35 28N	7 11 E
Khenifra	82	32 58N	5 46W
Kherrata	83	36 27N	5 13 E
Khérson	44	41 5N	22 47 E
Kherson	56	46 35N	32 35 E
Khersónisos Akrotíri	45	35 30N	24 10 E
Kheta →	59	71 54N	102 6 E
Khiliomódhion	45	37 48N	22 51 E
Khilok	59	51 30N	110 45 E
Khimki	55	55 50N	37 20 E
Khíos	45	38 27N	26 9 E
Khisar-Momina Banya	43	42 30N	24 44 E
Khiuma = Hiiumaa	54	58 50N	22 45 E
Khiva	58	41 30N	60 18 E
Khīyāv	64	38 30N	47 45 E
Khlebarovo	43	43 37N	26 15 E
Khlong →	71	15 30N	98 50 E
Khmelnitskiy	56	49 23N	27 0 E
Khmer Rep. = Cambodia ■	71	12 15N	105 0 E
Khojak P.	65	30 55N	66 30 E
Khokholskiy	55	51 35N	38 40 E
Kholm, Afghan.	65	36 45N	67 40 E
Kholm, U.S.S.R.	54	57 10N	31 15 E
Kholmsk	59	47 40N	142 5 E
Khomas Hochland	92	22 40 S	16 0 E
Khomeyn	64	33 40N	50 7 E
Khomo	92	21 7 S	24 35 E
Khon Kaen	71	16 30N	102 47 E
Khong	71	14 5N	105 56 E
Khong →	71	15 0N	106 50 E
Khonu	59	66 30N	143 12 E
Khoper →	55	49 30N	42 20 E
Khor el 'Atash	87	13 20N	34 15 E
Khóra	45	37 3N	21 42 E
Khóra Sfakion	45	35 15N	24 9 E
Khorāsān □	65	34 0N	58 0 E
Khorat = Nakhon Ratchasima	71	14 59N	102 12 E
Khorat, Cao Nguyen	71	15 30N	102 50 E
Khorb el Ethel	82	28 30N	6 17W
Khorixas	92	20 16 S	14 59 E
Khorog	58	37 30N	71 36 E
Khorol	56	49 48N	33 15 E
Khorramābād	64	33 30N	48 25 E
Khorramshahr	64	30 29N	48 15 E
Khotin	56	48 31N	26 27 E
Khouribga	82	32 58N	6 57W
Khowai	67	24 5N	91 40 E
Khoyniki	54	51 54N	29 55 E
Khrami →	57	41 30N	45 0 E
Khrenovoye	55	51 4N	40 16 E
Khristianá	45	36 14N	25 13 E
Khtapodhiá	45	37 24N	25 34 E
Khu Khan	71	14 42N	104 12 E
Khulna	69	22 45N	89 34 E
Khulo	57	41 33N	42 19 E
Khumago	92	20 26 S	24 32 E

Khunzakh	57	42 35N	46 42 E
Khūr	65	32 55N	58 18 E
Khurai	68	24 3N	78 23 E
Khurayş	64	24 55N	48 5 E
Khurja	68	28 15N	77 58 E
Khūryān Mūryān, Jazā 'ir	63	17 30N	55 58 E
Khushab	68	32 20N	72 20 E
Khuzdar	66	27 52N	66 30 E
Khūzetān □	64	31 0N	50 0 E
Khvalynsk	55	52 30N	48 2 E
Khvatovka	55	52 24N	46 32 E
Khvor	65	33 45N	55 0 E
Khvormūj	65	28 40N	51 30 E
Khvoy	64	38 35N	45 0 E
Khvoynaya	54	58 58N	34 28 E
Khyber Pass	66	34 10N	71 8 E
Kiabukwa	91	8 40 S	24 48 E
Kiadho →	70	19 37N	77 40 E
Kiama	99	34 40 S	150 50 E
Kiamba	73	6 2N	124 46 E
Kiambi	90	7 15 S	28 0 E
Kiambu	90	1 8 S	36 50 E
Kiangsi = Jiangxi □	75	27 30N	116 0 E
Kiangsu = Jiangsu □	75	33 0N	120 0 E
Kiáton	45	38 2N	22 43 E
Kibæk	49	56 2N	8 51 E
Kibanga Port	90	0 10N	32 58 E
Kibangou	88	3 26 S	12 22 E
Kibara	90	2 8 S	33 30 E
Kibare, Mts.	90	8 25 S	27 10 E
Kibombo	90	3 57 S	25 53 E
Kibondo	90	3 35 S	30 45 E
Kibondo □	90	4 0 S	30 55 E
Kibumbu	90	3 32 S	29 45 E
Kibungu	90	2 10 S	30 32 E
Kibuye, Burundi	90	3 39 S	29 59 E
Kibuye, Rwanda	90	2 3 S	29 21 E
Kibwesa	90	6 30 S	29 58 E
Kibwezi	90	2 27 S	37 57 E
Kičevo	42	41 34N	20 59 E
Kichiga	59	59 50N	163 5 E
Kicking Horse Pass	108	51 28N	116 16W
Kidal	85	18 26N	1 22 E
Kidderminster	13	52 24N	2 13W
Kidete	90	6 25 S	37 17 E
Kidira	84	14 28N	12 13W
Kidnappers, C.	101	39 38 S	177 5 E
Kidston	98	18 52 S	144 8 E
Kidugallo	90	6 49 S	38 15 E
Kiel	24	54 16N	10 8 E
Kiel Kanal = Nord-Ostee-Kanal	24	54 15N	9 40 E
Kielce	28	50 52N	20 42 E
Kielce □	28	50 40N	20 40 E
Kieler Bucht	24	54 30N	10 30 E
Kienge	91	10 30 S	27 30 E
Kiessé	85	13 29N	4 1 E
Kiev = Kiyev	54	50 30N	30 28 E
Kifār 'Aşyūn	62	31 39N	35 7 E
Kiffa	84	16 37N	11 24W
Kifisiá	45	38 4N	23 49 E
Kifissós →	45	38 35N	23 20 E
Kifrī	64	34 45N	45 0 E
Kigali	90	1 59 S	30 4 E
Kigarama	90	1 1 S	31 50 E
Kigoma □	90	5 0 S	30 0 E
Kigoma-Ujiji	90	4 55 S	29 36 E
Kigomasha, Ras	90	4 58 S	38 58 E
Kihee	99	27 23 S	142 37 E
Kii-Suidō	74	33 40N	135 0 E
Kikinda	42	45 50N	20 30 E
Kikládhes	45	37 20N	24 30 E
Kikládhes □	45	37 0N	25 0 E
Kikori	98	7 25 S	144 15 E
Kikori →	98	7 38 S	144 20 E
Kikwit	88	5 5 S	18 45 E
Kilafors	48	61 14N	16 36 E
Kilakarai	70	9 12N	78 47 E
Kilalki	45	36 15N	27 35 E
Kilauea Crater	110	19 24N	155 17W
Kilcoy	99	26 59 S	152 30 E
Kildare	15	53 10N	6 50W
Kildare □	15	53 10N	6 50W
Kilgore	117	32 22N	94 55W
Kilifi	90	3 40 S	39 48 E
Kilifi □	90	3 30 S	39 40 E
Kilimanjaro	90	3 7 S	37 20 E
Kilimanjaro □	90	4 0 S	38 0 E
Kilindini	90	4 4 S	39 40 E
Kilis	64	36 50N	37 10 E
Kiliya	56	45 28N	29 16 E
Kilju	76	40 57N	129 25 E
Kilkee	15	52 41N	9 40W
Kilkenny	15	52 40N	7 17W
Kilkenny □	15	52 35N	7 15W
Kilkieran B.	15	53 18N	9 45W
Kilkís	44	40 58N	22 57 E
Kilkís □	44	41 5N	22 50 E
Killala	15	54 13N	9 12W
Killala B.	15	54 20N	9 12W
Killaloe	15	52 48N	8 28W
Killaloe Sta.	112	45 33N	77 25W
Killam	108	52 47N	111 51W
Killarney, Can.	106	45 55N	81 30W
Killarney, Ireland	15	52 2N	9 30W
Killarney, Lakes of	15	52 0N	9 30W
Killary Harbour	15	53 38N	9 52W
Killdeer, Can.	109	49 6N	106 22W
Killdeer, U.S.A.	116	47 26N	102 48W
Killeen	117	31 7N	97 45W
Killiecrankie, Pass of	14	56 44N	3 46W
Killin	14	56 28N	4 20W
Killíni, Ilía, Greece	45	37 55N	21 8 E
Killíni, Korinthía, Greece	45	37 54N	22 25 E
Killybegs	15	54 38N	8 26W
Kilmarnock	14	55 36N	4 30W
Kilmez	55	56 58N	50 55 E
Kilmez →	55	56 58N	50 28 E
Kilmore	99	37 25 S	144 53 E
Kilondo	91	9 45 S	34 20 E
Kilosa	90	6 48 S	37 0 E
Kilosa □	90	6 48 S	37 0 E
Kilrush	15	52 39N	9 30W

Kilsmo	48	59 6N	15 35 E
Kilwa □	91	9 0 S	39 0 E
Kilwa Kisiwani	91	8 58 S	39 32 E
Kilwa Kivinje	91	8 45 S	39 25 E
Kilwa Masoko	91	8 55 S	39 30 E
Kim	117	37 18N	103 20W
Kimaam	73	7 58 S	138 53 E
Kimamba	90	6 45 S	37 10 E
Kimba	97	33 8 S	136 23 E
Kimball, Nebr., U.S.A.	116	41 17N	103 40W
Kimball, S.D., U.S.A.	116	43 47N	98 57W
Kimbe	98	5 33 S	150 11 E
Kimbe B.	98	5 15 S	150 30 E
Kimberley, Austral.	96	16 20 S	127 0 E
Kimberley, Can.	108	49 40N	115 59W
Kimberley, S. Afr.	92	28 43 S	24 46 E
Kimberly	118	42 33N	114 25W
Kimchaek	76	40 40N	129 10 E
Kimchŏn	76	36 11N	128 4 E
Kími	45	38 38N	24 6 E
Kimolos	45	36 48N	24 37 E
Kimovsk	55	54 0N	38 29 E
Kimparana	84	12 48N	5 0W
Kimry	55	56 55N	37 15 E
Kimsquit	108	52 45N	126 57W
Kimstad	49	58 35N	15 58 E
Kinabalu	72	6 0N	116 0 E
Kínaros	45	36 59N	26 15 E
Kinaskan L.	108	57 38N	130 8W
Kincaid	109	49 40N	107 0W
Kincardine	106	44 10N	81 40W
Kinda	91	9 18 S	25 4 E
Kindersley	109	51 30N	109 10W
Kindia	84	10 0N	12 52W
Kindu	90	2 55 S	25 50 E
Kinel	55	53 15N	50 40 E
Kineshma	55	57 30N	42 5 E
Kinesi	90	1 25 S	33 50 E
King City	119	36 11N	121 8W
King Cr. →	98	24 35 S	139 30 E
King Frederick VI Land = Kong Frederik VI.s. Kyst	4	63 0N	43 0W
King George B.	128	51 30 S	60 30W
King George I.	5	60 0 S	60 0W
King George Is.	105	57 20N	80 30W
King George Sd.	96	35 5 S	118 0 E
King I., Austral.	97	39 50 S	144 0 E
King I., Can.	108	52 10N	127 40W
King I. = Kadah Kyun	71	12 30N	98 20 E
King Leopold Ranges	96	17 30 S	125 45 E
King, Mt.	99	25 10 S	147 30 E
King Sd.	96	16 50 S	123 20 E
King William I.	104	69 10N	97 25W
King William's Town	92	32 51 S	27 22 E
Kingaroy	97	26 32 S	151 51 E
Kingfisher	117	35 50N	97 55W
Kingisepp	54	59 25N	28 40 E
Kingisepp (Kuressaare)	54	58 15N	22 30 E
Kingman, Ariz., U.S.A.	119	35 12N	114 2W
Kingman, Kans., U.S.A.	117	37 41N	98 9W
Kings →	119	36 10N	119 50W
Kings Canyon National Park	119	37 0N	118 35W
King's Lynn	12	52 45N	0 25 E
Kings Mountain	115	35 13N	81 20W
King's Peak	118	40 46N	110 27W
Kingsbridge	13	50 17N	3 46W
Kingsburg	119	36 35N	119 36W
Kingscote	99	35 40 S	137 38 E
Kingscourt	15	53 55N	6 48W
Kingsley	116	42 37N	95 58W
Kingsley Dam	116	41 20N	101 40W
Kingsport	115	36 33N	82 36W
Kingston, Can.	106	44 14N	76 30W
Kingston, Jamaica	121	18 0N	76 50W
Kingston, N.Z.	101	45 20 S	168 43 E
Kingston, N.Y., U.S.A.	114	41 55N	74 0W
Kingston, Pa., U.S.A.	114	41 19N	75 58W
Kingston, R.I., U.S.A.	113	41 29N	71 30W
Kingston South East	97	36 51 S	139 55 E
Kingston-upon-Thames	13	51 23N	0 20W
Kingstown	121	13 10N	61 10W
Kingstree	115	33 40N	79 48W
Kingsville, Can.	106	42 2N	82 45W
Kingsville, U.S.A.	117	27 30N	97 53W
Kingussie	14	57 5N	4 2W
Kinistino	109	52 57N	105 2W
Kinkala	88	4 18 S	14 49 E
Kinleith	101	38 20 S	175 56 E
Kinmount	112	44 48N	78 45W
Kinn	47	61 34N	4 45 E
Kinna	49	57 32N	12 42 E
Kinnaird	108	49 17N	117 39W
Kinnairds Hd.	14	57 40N	2 0W
Kinnared	49	57 2N	13 7 E
Kinneret	62	32 44N	35 34 E
Kinneret, Yam	62	32 45N	35 35 E
Kinoje →	106	52 8N	81 25W
Kinoni	90	0 41 S	30 28 E
Kinross	14	56 13N	3 25W
Kinsale	15	51 42N	8 31W
Kinsale, Old Hd. of	15	51 37N	8 32W
Kinsarvik	47	60 22N	6 43 E
Kinshasa	88	4 20 S	15 15 E
Kinsley	117	37 57N	99 30W
Kinston	115	35 18N	77 35W
Kintampo	85	8 5N	1 41W
Kintap	72	3 51 S	115 13 E
Kintyre	14	55 30N	5 35W
Kintyre, Mull of	14	55 17N	5 55W
Kinushseo →	106	55 15N	83 45W
Kinuso	108	55 20N	115 25W
Kinyangiri	90	4 25 S	34 37 E
Kinzig →	25	48 37N	7 49 E
Kinzua	112	41 52N	78 58W
Kinzua Dam	112	41 53N	79 0W
Kíoni	45	38 27N	20 41 E
Kiosk	106	46 6N	78 53W
Kiowa, Kans., U.S.A.	117	37 3N	98 30W
Kiowa, Okla., U.S.A.	117	34 45N	95 50W
Kipahigan L.	109	55 20N	101 55W
Kipanga	90	6 15 S	35 20 E
Kiparissía	45	37 15N	21 40 E

* *Now part of Sind* □
** *Renamed Bakhtâran*

* *Renamed Soc Trang*

Kiparissiakós Kólpos Kopliku

Kiparissiakós Kólpos	**45**	37 25N	21 25 E
Kipembawe	**90**	7 38 S	33 27 E
Kipengere Ra.	**91**	9 12 S	34 15 E
Kipili	**90**	7 28 S	30 32 E
Kipini	**90**	2 30 S	40 32 E
Kipling	**109**	50 6N	102 38W
Kippure	**15**	53 11N	6 23W
Kipushi	**91**	11 48 S	27 12 E
Kirandul	**70**	18 33N	81 10 E
Kiratpur	**68**	29 32N	78 12 E
Kirchhain	**24**	50 49N	8 54 E
Kirchheim	**25**	48 38N	9 20 E
Kirchheim-Bolanden	**25**	49 40N	8 0 E
Kirchschlag	**27**	47 30N	16 19 E
Kirensk	**59**	57 50N	107 55 E
Kirgiz S.S.R. □	**58**	42 0N	75 0 E
Kirgiziya Steppe	**53**	50 0N	55 0 E
Kiri	**88**	1 29 S	19 0 E
Kiribati ■	**94**	1 0N	176 0 E
Kiriburu	**69**	22 0N	85 0 E
Kırıkkale	**64**	39 51N	33 32 E
Kirillov	**55**	59 51N	38 14 E
Kirin = Jilin	**76**	43 55N	126 30 E
Kirin = Jilin □	**76**	44 0N	126 0 E
Kirindi →	**70**	6 15N	81 20 E
Kirishi	**54**	59 28N	31 59 E
Kirkcaldy	**14**	56 7N	3 10W
Kirkcudbright	**14**	54 50N	4 3W
Kirkee	**70**	18 34N	73 56 E
Kirkenær	**47**	60 27N	12 3 E
Kirkenes	**50**	69 40N	30 5 E
Kirkintilloch	**14**	55 57N	4 10W
Kirkjubæjarklaustur	**50**	63 47N	18 4W
Kirkland	**119**	34 29N	112 46W
Kirkland Lake	**106**	48 9N	80 2W
Kırklareli	**43**	41 44N	27 15 E
Kirksville	**116**	40 8N	92 35W
Kirkūk	**64**	35 30N	44 21 E
Kirkwall	**14**	58 59N	2 59W
Kirkwood	**92**	33 22 S	25 15 E
Kirlampudi	**70**	17 12N	82 12 E
Kirn	**25**	49 46N	7 29 E
Kirov, R.S.F.S.R., U.S.S.R.	**54**	54 3N	34 20 E
Kirov, R.S.F.S.R., U.S.S.R.	**58**	58 35N	49 40 E
Kirovabad	**57**	40 45N	46 20 E
Kirovakan	**57**	40 48N	44 30 E
Kirovo-Chepetsk	**55**	58 28N	50 0 E
Kirovograd	**56**	48 35N	32 20 E
Kirovsk, R.S.F.S.R., U.S.S.R.	**52**	67 48N	33 50 E
Kirovsk, Turkmen S.S.R., U.S.S.R.	**58**	37 42N	60 23 E
Kirovsk, Ukraine S.S.R., U.S.S.R.	**57**	48 35N	38 30 E
Kirovski	**57**	45 51N	48 11 E
Kirovskiy	**59**	54 27N	155 42 E
Kirriemuir, Can.	**109**	51 56N	110 20W
Kirriemuir, U.K.	**14**	56 41N	3 0W
Kirsanov	**55**	52 35N	42 40 E
Kırşehir	**64**	39 14N	34 5 E
Kirstonia	**92**	25 30 S	23 45 E
Kirtachi	**85**	12 52N	2 30 E
Kīrteh	**65**	32 15N	63 0 E
Kirthar Range	**68**	27 0N	67 0 E
Kiruna	**50**	67 52N	20 15 E
Kirundu	**90**	0 50 S	25 35 E
Kirya	**55**	55 5N	46 45 E
Kiryū	**74**	36 24N	139 20 E
Kisa	**49**	58 0N	15 39 E
Kisaga	**90**	4 30 S	34 23 E
Kisámou, Kólpos	**45**	35 30N	23 38 E
Kisanga	**90**	2 30N	26 35 E
Kisangani	**90**	0 35N	25 15 E
Kisar	**73**	8 5 S	127 10 E
Kisaran	**72**	3 0N	99 37 E
Kisarawe	**90**	6 53 S	39 0 E
Kisarawe □	**90**	7 3 S	39 0 E
Kisarazu	**74**	35 23N	139 55 E
Kisbér	**27**	47 30N	18 0 E
Kiselevsk	**58**	54 5N	86 39 E
Kishanganj	**69**	26 3N	88 14 E
Kishangarh	**68**	27 50N	70 30 E
Kishi	**85**	9 1N	3 52 E
Kishinev	**56**	47 0N	28 50 E
Kishiwada	**74**	34 28N	135 22 E
Kishon	**62**	32 49N	35 2 E
Kishorganj	**69**	24 26N	90 40 E
Kishtwar	**69**	33 20N	75 48 E
Kisii	**90**	0 40 S	34 45 E
Kisii □	**90**	0 40 S	34 45 E
Kisiju	**90**	7 23 S	39 19 E
Kısır, Dağ	**57**	41 0N	43 5 E
Kisizi	**90**	1 0 S	29 58 E
Kiska I.	**104**	52 0N	177 30 E
Kiskatinaw →	**108**	56 8N	120 10W
Kiskittogisu L.	**109**	54 13N	98 20W
Kiskomárom = Zalakomár	**27**	46 33N	17 10 E
Kiskörös	**27**	46 37N	19 20 E
Kiskundorozsma	**27**	46 16N	20 5 E
Kiskunfelégyháza	**27**	46 42N	19 53 E
Kiskunhalas	**27**	46 28N	19 37 E
Kiskunmajsa	**27**	46 30N	19 48 E
Kislovodsk	**57**	43 50N	42 45 E
Kiso-Sammyaku	**74**	35 45N	137 45 E
Kisoro	**90**	1 17 S	29 48 E
Kispest	**27**	47 27N	19 9 E
Kissidougou	**84**	9 5N	10 0W
Kissimmee	**115**	28 18N	81 22W
Kissimmee →	**115**	27 20N	80 55W
Kississing L.	**109**	55 10N	101 20W
Kistanje	**39**	43 58N	15 55 E
Kisterenye	**27**	48 3N	19 50 E
Kisújszállás	**27**	47 12N	20 50 E
Kisumu	**90**	0 3 S	34 45 E
Kisvárda	**27**	48 14N	22 4 E
Kiswani	**90**	4 5 S	37 57 E
Kiswere	**91**	9 27 S	39 30 E
Kit Carson	**116**	38 48N	102 45W
Kita	**84**	13 5N	9 25W
Kitab	**58**	39 7N	66 52 E
Kitaibaraki	**74**	36 50N	140 45 E
Kitakami-Gawa →	**74**	38 25N	141 19 E
Kitakyūshū	**74**	33 50N	130 50 E
Kitale	**90**	1 0N	35 0 E
Kitangiri, L.	**90**	4 5 S	34 20 E
Kitaya	**91**	10 38 S	40 8 E
Kitchener	**106**	43 27N	80 29W
Kitega = Citega	**90**	3 30 S	29 58 E
Kitengo	**90**	7 26 S	24 8 E
Kiteto □	**90**	5 0 S	37 0 E
Kitgum	**90**	3 17N	32 52 E
Kíthira	**45**	36 9N	23 0 E
Kíthnos	**45**	37 26N	24 27 E
Kitimat	**108**	54 3N	128 38W
Kitinen →	**50**	67 34N	26 40 E
Kitiyab	**87**	17 13N	33 35 E
Kítros	**44**	40 22N	22 34 E
Kittakittaooloo, L.	**99**	28 3 S	138 14 E
Kittanning	**114**	40 49N	79 30W
Kittatinny Mts.	**113**	41 0N	75 0W
Kittery	**114**	43 7N	70 42W
Kitui	**90**	1 17 S	38 0 E
Kitui □	**90**	1 30 S	38 25 E
Kitwe	**91**	12 54 S	28 13 E
Kitzbühel	**26**	47 27N	12 24 E
Kitzingen	**25**	49 44N	10 9 E
Kivalo	**50**	66 18N	26 0 E
Kivarli	**68**	24 33N	72 46 E
Kivotós	**44**	40 13N	21 26 E
Kivu □	**90**	3 10 S	27 0 E
Kivu, L.	**90**	1 48 S	29 0 E
Kiyev	**54**	50 30N	30 28 E
Kiyevskoye Vdkhr.	**54**	51 0N	30 0 E
Kizel	**52**	59 3N	57 40 E
Kiziguru	**90**	1 46 S	30 23 E
Kızıl Irmak →	**56**	39 15N	36 0 E
Kizil Yurt	**57**	43 13N	46 54 E
Kızılcahamam	**56**	40 30N	32 30 E
Kizimkazi	**90**	6 28 S	39 30 E
Kizlyar	**57**	43 51N	46 40 E
Kizyl-Arvat	**58**	38 58N	56 15 E
Kjellerup	**49**	56 17N	9 25 E
Kladanj	**42**	44 14N	18 42 E
Kladnica	**42**	43 23N	20 2 E
Kladno	**26**	50 10N	14 7 E
Kladovo	**42**	44 36N	22 33 E
Klagenfurt	**26**	46 38N	14 20 E
Klagshamn	**49**	55 32N	12 53 E
Klagstorp	**49**	55 22N	13 23 E
Klaipeda	**54**	55 43N	21 10 E
Klamath →	**118**	41 40N	124 4W
Klamath Falls	**118**	42 20N	121 50W
Klamath Mts.	**118**	41 20N	123 0W
Klanjec	**39**	46 3N	15 45 E
Klappan →	**108**	58 0N	129 43W
Klaten	**73**	7 43 S	110 36 E
Klatovy	**26**	49 23N	13 18 E
Klawak	**108**	55 35N	133 0W
Klawer	**92**	31 44 S	18 36 E
Kłecko	**28**	52 38N	17 25 E
Kleczew	**28**	52 22N	18 9 E
Kleena Kleene	**108**	52 0N	124 59W
Klein	**118**	46 26N	108 31W
Klein-Karas	**92**	27 33 S	18 7 E
Klein Karoo	**92**	33 45 S	21 30 E
Klekovača	**39**	44 25N	16 32 E
Klemtu	**108**	52 35N	128 55W
Klenovec, Czech.	**27**	48 36N	19 54 E
Klenovec, Yugo.	**42**	41 32N	20 49 E
Klerksdorp	**92**	26 51 S	26 38 E
Kleszczele	**28**	52 35N	23 19 E
Kletnya	**54**	53 23N	33 12 E
Kletsk	**54**	53 5N	26 45 E
Kletskiy	**57**	49 20N	43 0 E
Kleve	**24**	51 46N	6 10 E
Klickitat	**118**	45 50N	121 10W
Klimovichi	**54**	53 36N	32 0 E
Klin	**55**	56 20N	36 48 E
Klinaklini →	**108**	51 21N	125 40W
Klintsey	**54**	52 50N	32 10 E
Klipplaat	**92**	33 0 S	24 22 E
Klisura	**43**	42 40N	24 28 E
Klitmøller	**49**	57 3N	8 30 E
Kljajićevo	**42**	45 45N	19 17 E
Ključ	**39**	44 32N	16 48 E
Kłobuck	**28**	50 55N	18 55 E
Kłodawa	**28**	52 15N	18 55 E
Kłodzko	**28**	50 28N	16 38 E
Klondike	**104**	64 0N	139 26W
Klosi	**44**	41 28N	20 10 E
Klosterneuburg	**27**	48 18N	16 19 E
Klosters	**25**	46 52N	9 52 E
Klötze	**24**	52 38N	11 9 E
Klouto	**85**	6 57N	0 44 E
Kluane L.	**104**	61 15N	138 40W
Kluczbork	**28**	50 58N	18 12 E
Klyuchevskaya, Guba	**59**	55 50N	160 30 E
Knaresborough	**12**	54 1N	1 29W
Knee L., Man., Can.	**109**	55 3N	94 45W
Knee L., Sask., Can.	**109**	55 51N	107 0W
Kneïss, I.	**83**	34 22N	10 18 E
Knezha	**43**	43 30N	24 5 E
Knić	**42**	43 53N	20 45 E
Knight Inlet	**108**	50 45N	125 40W
Knighton	**13**	52 21N	3 2W
Knight's Landing	**118**	38 50N	121 43W
Knin	**39**	44 1N	16 17 E
Knittelfeld	**26**	47 13N	14 51 E
Knjaževac	**42**	43 35N	22 18 E
Knob, C.	**96**	34 32 S	119 16 E
Knockmealdown Mts.	**15**	52 16N	8 0W
Knokke	**16**	51 20N	3 17 E
Knossos	**45**	35 16N	25 10 E
Knox	**114**	41 18N	86 36W
Knox, C.	**108**	54 11N	133 5W
Knox City	**117**	33 26N	99 49W
Knox Coast	**5**	66 30 S	108 0 E
Knoxville, Iowa, U.S.A.	**116**	41 20N	93 5W
Knoxville, Tenn., U.S.A.	**115**	35 58N	83 57W
Knurów	**27**	50 13N	18 38 E
Knutshø	**47**	62 18N	9 41 E
Knysna	**92**	34 2 S	23 2 E
Knyszyn	**28**	53 20N	22 56 E
Ko Chang	**71**	12 0N	102 20 E
Ko Kut	**71**	11 40N	102 32 E
Ko Phra Thong	**71**	9 6N	98 15 E
Ko Tao	**71**	10 6N	99 48 E
Koartac (Notre Dame de Koartac)	**105**	60 55N	69 40W
Koba, Aru, Indon.	**73**	6 37 S	134 37 E
Koba, Bangka, Indon.	**72**	2 26 S	106 14 E
Kobarid	**39**	46 15N	13 30 E
Kobayashi	**74**	31 56N	130 59 E
Kobdo = Hovd	**75**	48 2N	91 37 E
Kōbe	**74**	34 45N	135 10 E
Kobelyaki	**56**	49 11N	34 9 E
København	**49**	55 41N	12 34 E
Koblenz	**25**	50 21N	7 36 E
Kobo	**87**	12 2N	39 56 E
Kobrin	**54**	52 15N	24 22 E
Kobroor, Kepulauan	**73**	6 10 S	134 30 E
Kobuleti	**57**	41 55N	41 45 E
Kobylin	**28**	51 43N	17 12 E
Kobyłka	**28**	52 21N	21 10 E
Kobylkino	**55**	54 8N	43 56 E
Kobylnik	**54**	54 58N	26 39 E
Kočane	**42**	43 12N	21 52 E
Kočani	**42**	41 55N	22 25 E
Koçarlı	**45**	37 45N	27 43 E
Koceljevo	**42**	44 28N	19 50 E
Kočevje	**39**	45 39N	14 50 E
Kochas	**69**	25 15N	83 56 E
Kocher →	**25**	49 14N	9 12 E
Kocheya	**59**	52 32N	120 42 E
Kōchi	**74**	33 30N	133 35 E
Kōchi □	**74**	33 40N	133 30 E
Kochiu = Gejiu	**75**	23 20N	103 10 E
Kock	**28**	51 38N	22 27 E
Koddiyar Bay	**70**	8 33N	81 15 E
Kodiak	**104**	57 30N	152 45W
Kodiak I.	**104**	57 30N	152 45W
Kodiang	**71**	6 21N	100 18 E
Kodinar	**68**	20 46N	70 46 E
Kodori →	**57**	42 47N	41 10 E
Koes	**92**	26 0 S	19 15 E
Kofiau	**73**	1 11 S	129 50 E
Köflach	**26**	47 4N	15 5 E
Koforidua	**85**	6 3N	0 17W
Kōfu	**74**	35 40N	138 30 E
Kogaluk →	**107**	56 12N	61 44W
Kogin Baba	**85**	7 55N	11 35 E
Koh-i-Bābā	**65**	34 30N	67 0 E
Kohat	**66**	33 40N	71 29 E
Kohima	**67**	25 35N	94 10 E
Kohler Ra.	**5**	77 0 S	110 0W
Kohtla Järve	**54**	59 20N	27 20 E
Kojetin	**27**	49 21N	17 20 E
Koka	**86**	20 5N	30 35 E
Kokand	**58**	40 30N	70 57 E
Kokanee Glacier Prov. Park	**108**	49 47N	117 10W
Kokas	**73**	2 42 S	132 26 E
Kokava	**27**	48 35N	19 50 E
Kokchetav	**58**	53 20N	69 25 E
Kokemäenjoki →	**51**	61 32N	21 44 E
Kokhma	**55**	56 55N	41 18 E
Kokkola (Gamlakarleby)	**50**	63 50N	23 8 E
Koko	**85**	11 28N	4 29 E
Koko Kyunzu	**71**	14 10N	93 25 E
Kokoda	**98**	8 54 S	147 47 E
Kokolopozo	**84**	5 8N	6 5W
Kokomo	**114**	40 30N	86 6W
Kokonau	**73**	4 43 S	136 26 E
Kokopo	**98**	4 22 S	152 19 E
Kokoro	**85**	14 12N	0 55 E
Koksoak →	**105**	58 30N	68 10W
Kokstad	**93**	30 32 S	29 29 E
Kokuora	**59**	71 35N	144 50 E
Kola, Indon.	**73**	5 35 S	134 30 E
Kola, U.S.S.R.	**52**	68 45N	33 8 E
Kola Pen. = Kolskiy P-ov.	**52**	67 30N	38 0 E
Kolahun	**84**	8 15N	10 4W
Kolaka	**73**	4 3 S	121 46 E
Kolar	**70**	13 12N	78 15 E
Kolar Gold Fields	**70**	12 58N	78 16 E
Kolari	**50**	67 20N	23 48 E
Kolarovgrad	**43**	43 18N	26 55 E
Kolašin	**42**	42 50N	19 31 E
Kolby Kås	**49**	55 48N	10 32 E
Kolchugino	**55**	56 17N	39 22 E
Kolda	**84**	12 55N	14 57W
Kolding	**49**	55 30N	9 29 E
Kole	**88**	3 16 S	22 42 E
Koléa	**82**	36 38N	2 46 E
* Kolepom, Pulau	**73**	8 0 S	138 30 E
Kolguyev, Ostrov	**52**	69 20N	48 30 E
Kolhapur	**70**	16 43N	74 15 E
Kolia	**84**	9 46N	6 28W
Kolín	**26**	50 2N	15 9 E
Kolind	**49**	56 21N	10 34 E
Kölleda	**24**	51 11N	11 14 E
Kollegal	**70**	12 9N	77 9 E
Kolleru L.	**70**	16 40N	81 10 E
Kolmanskop	**92**	26 45 S	15 14 E
Köln	**24**	50 56N	6 58 E
Kolno	**28**	53 25N	21 56 E
Koło	**28**	52 14N	18 40 E
Kołobrzeg	**28**	54 10N	15 35 E
Kologriv	**55**	58 48N	44 25 E
Kolokani	**84**	13 35N	7 45W
Kolomna	**55**	55 8N	38 45 E
Kolomyya	**56**	48 31N	25 2 E
Kolondiéba	**84**	11 5N	6 54W
Kolonodale	**73**	2 3 S	121 25 E
Kolosib	**67**	24 15N	92 45 E
Kolpashevo	**58**	58 20N	83 5 E
Kolpino	**54**	59 44N	30 39 E
Kolpny	**55**	52 12N	37 10 E
Kolskiy Poluostrov	**52**	67 30N	38 0 E
Kolskiy Zaliv	**52**	69 23N	34 0 E
Kolubara →	**42**	44 35N	20 15 E
Kolumna	**28**	51 36N	19 14 E
Koluszki	**28**	51 45N	19 46 E
Kolwezi	**91**	10 40 S	25 25 E
Kolyberovo	**55**	55 15N	38 40 E
Kolyma →	**59**	69 30N	161 0 E
Kolymskoye, Okhotsko	**59**	63 0N	157 0 E
Kôm Ombo	**86**	24 25N	32 52 E
Komárno	**27**	47 49N	18 5 E
Komárom	**27**	47 43N	18 7 E
Komárom □	**27**	47 35N	18 20 E
Komarovo	**54**	58 38N	33 40 E
Komatipoort	**93**	25 25 S	31 55 E
Kombissiri	**85**	12 4N	1 20W
Kombori	**84**	13 26N	3 56W
Kombóti	**45**	39 6N	21 5 E
Komen	**39**	45 49N	13 45 E
Komenda	**85**	5 4N	1 28W
Komi A.S.S.R. □	**52**	64 0N	55 0 E
Komiža	**39**	43 3N	16 11 E
Komló	**27**	46 15N	18 16 E
Kommamur Canal	**70**	16 0N	80 25 E
Kommunarsk	**57**	48 30N	38 45 E
Kommunizma, Pik	**58**	39 0N	72 2 E
Komnes	**47**	59 30N	9 55 E
Komodo	**73**	8 37 S	119 20 E
Komoé	**84**	5 12N	3 44W
Komono	**88**	3 10 S	13 20 E
Komoran, Pulau	**73**	8 18 S	138 45 E
Komotini	**44**	41 9N	25 26 E
Komovi	**42**	42 41N	19 39 E
Kompong Cham	**71**	12 0N	105 30 E
Kompong Chhnang	**71**	12 20N	104 35 E
Kompong Speu	**71**	11 26N	104 32 E
Kompong Thom	**71**	12 35N	104 51 E
Komrat	**56**	46 18N	28 40 E
Komsberge	**92**	32 40 S	20 45 E
Komsomolets, Ostrov	**59**	80 30N	95 0 E
Komsomolsk, R.S.F.S.R., U.S.S.R.	**55**	57 2N	40 20 E
Komsomolsk, R.S.F.S.R., U.S.S.R.	**59**	50 30N	137 0 E
Komsomolskaya	**5**	66 33 S	93 1 E
Komsomolskiy	**55**	53 30N	49 30 E
Konakovo	**55**	56 52N	36 45 E
Konarhá □	**65**	35 30N	71 3 E
Konawa	**117**	34 59N	96 46W
Kondagaon	**70**	19 35N	81 35 E
Kondakovo	**59**	69 36N	152 0 E
Konde	**90**	4 57 S	39 45 E
Kondiá	**44**	39 49N	25 10 E
Kondoa	**90**	4 55 S	35 50 E
Kondoa □	**90**	5 0 S	36 0 E
Kondopaga	**52**	62 12N	34 17 E
Kondratyevo	**59**	57 22N	98 15 E
Konduga	**85**	11 35N	13 26 E
Konevo	**52**	62 8N	39 20 E
Kong	**84**	8 54N	4 36W
Kong Christian IX.s Land	**4**	68 0N	36 0W
Kong Christian X.s Land	**4**	74 0N	29 0W
Kong Franz Joseph Fd.	**4**	73 20N	24 30W
Kong Frederik IX.s Land	**4**	67 0N	52 0W
Kong Frederik VI.s Kyst	**4**	63 0N	43 0W
Kong Frederik VIII.s Land	**4**	78 30N	26 0W
Kong, Koh	**71**	11 20N	103 0 E
Kong Oscar Fjord	**4**	72 20N	24 0W
Konga	**49**	56 30N	15 6 E
Kongeå	**49**	55 24N	9 39 E
Kongju	**76**	36 30N	127 0 E
Konglu	**67**	27 13N	97 57 E
Kongolo, Kasai Or., Zaïre	**90**	5 26 S	24 49 E
Kongolo, Shaba, Zaïre	**90**	5 22 S	27 0 E
Kongor	**81**	7 1N	31 27 E
Kongoussi	**85**	13 19N	1 32W
Kongsberg	**47**	59 39N	9 39 E
Kongsvinger	**47**	60 12N	12 2 E
Kongwa	**90**	6 11 S	36 26 E
Koni	**91**	10 40 S	27 11 E
Koni, Mts.	**91**	10 36 S	27 10 E
Koniecpol	**28**	50 46N	19 40 E
Königsberg = Kaliningrad	**54**	54 42N	20 32 E
Königshofen	**25**	50 18N	10 29 E
Königslutter	**24**	52 14N	10 50 E
Königswusterhausen	**24**	52 19N	13 38 E
Konin	**28**	52 12N	18 15 E
Konin □	**28**	52 15N	18 30 E
Konispoli	**44**	39 42N	20 10 E
Kónitsa	**44**	40 5N	20 48 E
Konjic	**42**	43 42N	17 58 E
Konjice	**39**	46 20N	15 28 E
Konkouré →	**84**	9 50N	13 42W
Könnern	**24**	51 40N	11 45 E
Konnur	**70**	16 14N	74 49 E
Kono	**84**	8 30N	11 5W
Konongo	**85**	6 40N	1 15W
Konosha	**52**	61 0N	40 5 E
Konotop	**54**	51 12N	33 7 E
Konqi He →	**75**	40 45N	90 10 E
Końskie	**28**	51 15N	20 23 E
Konsmo	**47**	58 16N	7 23 E
Konstantinovka	**56**	48 32N	37 39 E
Konstantinovski	**57**	47 33N	41 10 E
Konstantynów Łódźki	**28**	51 45N	19 20 E
Konstanz	**25**	47 39N	9 10 E
Kontagora	**85**	10 23N	5 27 E
Kontum	**71**	14 24N	108 0 E
Konya	**64**	37 52N	32 35 E
Konya Ovasi	**64**	38 30N	33 0 E
Konz	**25**	49 41N	6 36 E
Konza	**90**	1 45 S	37 7 E
Koo-wee-rup	**100**	38 13 S	145 28 E
Koolan I.	**96**	16 0 S	123 45 E
Kooloonong	**99**	34 48 S	143 10 E
Koondrook	**99**	35 33 S	144 8 E
Koorawatha	**99**	34 2 S	148 33 E
Kooskia	**118**	46 9N	115 59W
Koostatak	**109**	51 26N	97 26W
Kootenai →	**118**	49 15N	117 39W
Kootenay L.	**108**	49 45N	116 50W
Kootenay Nat. Park	**108**	51 0N	116 0W
Kopanovka	**57**	47 28N	46 50 E
Kopaonik Planina	**42**	43 10N	21 50 E
Kopargaon	**70**	19 51N	74 28 E
Kópavogur	**50**	64 6N	21 55W
Koper	**39**	45 31N	13 44 E
Kopervik	**47**	59 17N	5 17 E
Kopeysk	**58**	55 7N	61 37 E
Köping	**48**	59 31N	16 3 E
Kopiste	**39**	42 48N	16 42 E
Kopliku	**44**	42 15N	19 25 E

* *Renamed Yos Sudarso, P.*

Köpmanholmen Kulen Vakuf

Köpmanholmen	48	63 10N	18 35 E
Koppal	70	15 23N	76 5 E
Koppang	47	61 34N	11 3 E
Kopparbergs län □	48	61 20N	14 15 E
Koppeh Dāgh	65	38 0N	58 0 E
Kopperå	47	63 24N	11 50 E
Koppom	48	59 43N	12 10 E
Koprivlen	43	41 36N	23 53 E
Koprivnica	39	46 12N	16 45 E
Koprivshtitsa	43	42 40N	24 19 E
Kopychintsy	54	49 7N	25 58 E
Kopys	54	54 20N	30 17 E
Korab	42	41 44N	20 40 E
Korakiána	44	39 42N	19 45 E
Koraput	70	18 50N	82 40 E
Korba	69	22 20N	82 45 E
Korbach	24	51 17N	8 50 E
Korça	44	40 37N	20 50 E
Korça □	44	40 40N	20 50 E
Korčula	39	42 57N	17 8 E
Korčulanski Kanal	39	43 3N	16 40 E
Kordestan	64	35 30N	42 0 E
Kordestān □	64	36 0N	47 0 E
Korea Bay	76	39 0N	124 0 E
Koregaon	70	17 40N	74 10 E
Korenevo	54	51 27N	34 55 E
Korenovsk	57	45 30N	39 22 E
Korets	54	50 40N	27 5 E
Korgus	86	19 16N	33 29 E
Korhogo	84	9 29N	5 28W
Koribundu	84	7 41N	11 46W
Korim	73	0 58 S	136 10 E
Korinthía □	45	37 50N	22 35 E
Korinthiakós Kólpos	45	38 16N	22 30 E
Kórinthos	45	37 56N	22 55 E
Korioumé	84	16 35N	3 0W
Kōriyama	74	37 24N	140 23 E
Körmend	27	47 5N	16 35 E
Kornat	39	43 50N	15 20 E
Korneshty	56	47 21N	28 1 E
Korneuburg	27	48 20N	16 20 E
Kornsjø	47	58 57N	11 39 E
Kornstad	47	62 59N	7 27 E
Koro, Fiji	101	17 19 S	179 23 E
Koro, Ivory C.	84	8 32N	7 30W
Koro, Mali	84	14 1N	2 58W
Koro Sea	101	17 30 S	179 45W
Korocha	55	50 55N	37 30 E
Korogwe	90	5 5 S	38 25 E
Korogwe □	90	5 0 S	38 20 E
Koroit	99	38 18 S	142 24 E
Koróni	45	36 48N	21 57 E
Korónia, Limni	44	40 47N	23 37 E
Koronís	45	37 12N	25 35 E
Koronowo	28	53 19N	17 55 E
Koror	73	7 20N	134 28 E
Körös →	27	46 43N	20 12 E
Köröstarcsa	27	46 53N	21 3 E
Korosten	54	50 57N	28 25 E
Korotoyak	55	51 1N	39 2 E
Korraraika, Helodranon' i	93	17 45 S	43 57 E
Korsakov	59	46 36N	142 42 E
Korshunovo	59	58 37N	110 10 E
Korsun Shevchenkovskiy	56	49 26N	31 16 E
Korsze	28	54 11N	21 9 E
Korti	86	18 6N	31 33 E
Kortrijk	16	50 50N	3 17 E
Korwai	68	24 7N	78 5 E
Koryakskiy Khrebet	59	61 0N	171 0 E
Kos	45	36 50N	27 15 E
Kosa	87	7 50N	36 50 E
Kosaya Gora	55	54 10N	37 30 E
Koschagyl	53	46 40N	54 0 E
Kościan	28	52 5N	16 40 E
Kościerzyna	28	54 8N	17 59 E
Kosciusko	117	33 3N	89 34W
Kosciusko I.	108	56 0N	133 40W
Kosciusko, Mt.	97	36 27 S	148 16 E
Kösély →	27	47 25N	21 5 E
Kosgi	70	16 58N	77 43 E
Kosha	86	20 50N	30 30 E
K'oshih = Kashi	75	39 30N	76 2 E
Koshk-e Kohneh	65	34 55N	62 30 E
Kosi	68	27 48N	77 29 E
Kosi-meer	93	27 0 S	32 50 E
Košice	27	48 42N	21 15 E
Kosjerić	42	44 0N	19 55 E
Koslan	52	63 28N	48 52 E
Kosŏng	76	38 40N	128 22 E
Kosovo, Pokrajina	42	42 40N	21 5 E
Kosovo, Soc. Aut. Pokrajina □	42	42 30N	21 0 E
Kosovska-Mitrovica	42	42 54N	20 52 E
Kostajnica	39	45 17N	16 30 E
Kostamuksa	52	62 34N	32 44 E
Kostanjevica	39	45 51N	15 27 E
Kostelec	27	50 14N	16 35 E
Kostenets	43	42 15N	23 52 E
Koster	92	25 52 S	26 54 E
Kôstî	87	13 8N	32 43 E
Kostolac	42	44 37N	21 15 E
Kostopol	54	50 51N	26 22 E
Kostroma	55	57 50N	40 58 E
Kostromskoye Vdkhr.	55	57 52N	40 49 E
Kostrzyn, Poland	28	52 24N	17 14 E
Kostrzyn, Poland	28	52 35N	14 39 E
Kostyukovichi	54	53 20N	32 4 E
Koszalin	28	53 50N	16 8 E
Koszalin □	28	53 40N	16 10 E
Köszeg	27	47 23N	16 33 E
Kot Adu	68	30 30N	71 0 E
Kot Moman	68	32 13N	73 0 E
Kota	68	25 14N	75 49 E
Kota Baharu	71	6 7N	102 14 E
Kota Belud	72	6 21N	116 26 E
Kota Kinabalu	72	6 0N	116 4 E
Kota Tinggi	71	1 44N	103 53 E
Kotaagung	72	5 38 S	104 29 E
Kotabaru	72	3 20 S	116 20 E
Kotabumi	72	4 49 S	104 54 E
Kotagede	73	7 54 S	110 26 E
Kotamobagu	73	0 57N	124 31 E
Kotaneelee →	108	60 11N	123 42W
Kotawaringin	72	2 28 S	111 27 E
Kotcho L.	108	59 7N	121 12W
Kotel	43	42 52N	26 26 E
Kotelnich	55	58 20N	48 10 E
Kotelnikovo	57	47 38N	43 8 E
Kotelnyy, Ostrov	59	75 10N	139 0 E
Kothagudam	70	17 30N	80 40 E
Kothapet	70	19 21N	79 28 E
Köthen	24	51 44N	11 59 E
Kothi	69	24 45N	80 40 E
Kotiro	68	26 17N	67 13 E
Kotka	51	60 28N	26 58 E
Kotlas	52	61 15N	47 0 E
Kotlenska Planina	43	42 56N	26 30 E
Kotli	66	33 30N	73 55 E
Kotonkoro	85	11 3N	5 58 E
Kotor	42	42 25N	18 47 E
Kotor Varoš	42	44 38N	17 22 E
Kotoriba	39	46 23N	16 48 E
Kotovo	55	50 22N	44 45 E
Kotovsk	56	47 45N	29 35 E
Kotputli	68	27 43N	76 12 E
Kotri	68	25 22N	68 22 E
Kotri →	70	19 15N	80 35 E
Kótronas	45	36 38N	22 29 E
Kötschach-Mauthen	26	46 41N	13 1 E
Kottayam	70	9 35N	76 33 E
Kottur	70	10 34N	76 56 E
Kotuy →	59	71 54N	102 6 E
Kotzebue	104	66 50N	162 40W
Kouango	88	5 0N	20 10 E
Koudougou	84	12 10N	2 20W
Koufonísi	45	34 56N	26 8 E
Koufonísia	45	36 57N	25 35 E
Kougaberge	92	33 48 S	23 50 E
Kouibli	84	7 15N	7 14W
Kouilou →	88	4 10 S	12 5 E
Kouki	88	7 22N	17 3 E
Koula Moutou	88	1 15 S	12 25 E
Koulen	71	13 50N	104 40 E
Koulikoro	84	12 40N	7 50W
Koumala	98	21 38 S	149 15 E
Koumankou	84	11 58N	6 6W
Koumbia, Guin.	84	11 48N	13 29W
Koumbia, Upp. Vol.	84	11 10N	3 50W
Koumboum	84	10 25N	13 0W
Koumpenntoum	84	13 59N	14 34W
Koumra	81	8 50N	17 35 E
Koundara	84	12 29N	13 18W
Kounradskiy	58	46 59N	75 0 E
Kountze	117	30 20N	94 22W
Koupéla	85	12 11N	0 21W
Kourizo, Passe de	83	22 28N	15 27 E
Kouroussa	84	10 45N	9 45W
Koussané	84	14 53N	11 14W
Kousseri	81	12 0N	14 55 E
Koutiala	84	12 25N	5 23W
Kouto	84	9 53N	6 25W
Kouvé	85	6 25N	1 25 E
Kovačica	42	45 5N	20 38 E
Kovdor	52	67 34N	30 24 E
Kovel	54	51 10N	24 20 E
Kovilpatti	70	9 10N	77 50 E
Kovin	42	44 44N	20 59 E
Kovrov	55	56 25N	41 25 E
Kovur, Andhra Pradesh, India	70	17 3N	81 39 E
Kovur, Andhra Pradesh, India	70	14 30N	80 1 E
Kowal	28	52 32N	19 7 E
Kowalewo Pomorskie	28	53 10N	18 52 E
Kowkash	106	50 20N	87 12W
Kowloon	75	22 20N	114 15 E
Koyabuti	73	2 36 S	140 37 E
Koyan, Pegunungan	72	3 15N	114 30 E
Koyuk	104	64 55N	161 20W
Koyukuk →	104	64 56N	157 30W
Koyulhisar	56	40 20N	37 52 E
Koza	77	26 19N	127 46 E
Kozan	64	37 35N	35 50 E
Kozáni	44	40 19N	21 47 E
Kozáni □	44	40 18N	21 45 E
Kozara	39	45 0N	17 0 E
Kozarac	39	44 58N	16 48 E
Kozelsk	54	54 2N	35 48 E
Kozhikode = Calicut	70	11 15N	75 43 E
Kozhva	52	65 10N	57 0 E
Koziegłowy	28	50 37N	19 8 E
Kozienice	28	51 35N	21 34 E
Kozje	39	46 5N	15 35 E
Kozle	28	50 20N	18 8 E
Kozloduy	43	43 45N	23 42 E
Kozlovets	43	43 30N	25 20 E
Koźmin	28	51 48N	17 27 E
Kozmodemyansk	55	56 20N	46 36 E
Kozuchów	28	51 45N	15 31 E
Kpabia	85	9 10N	0 20W
Kpalimé	85	6 57N	0 44 E
Kpandae	85	8 30N	0 2W
Kpessi	85	8 4N	1 16 E
Kra Buri	71	10 22N	98 46 E
Kra, Isthmus of = Kra, Kho Khot	71	10 15N	99 30 E
Kra, Kho Khot	71	10 15N	99 30 E
Kragan	73	6 43 S	111 38 E
Kragerø	47	58 52N	9 25 E
Kragujevac	42	44 2N	20 56 E
Krajenka	28	53 18N	16 59 E
Krakatau = Rakata, Pulau	72	6 10 S	105 20 E
Kraków	27	50 4N	19 57 E
Kraków □	27	50 0N	20 0 E
Kraksaan	73	7 43 S	113 23 E
Kråkstad	47	59 39N	10 55 E
Králiky	27	50 6N	16 45 E
Kraljevo	42	43 44N	20 41 E
Kralovice	26	49 59N	13 29 E
Královský Chlmec	27	48 27N	22 0 E
Kralupy	26	50 13N	14 20 E
Kramatorsk	56	48 50N	37 30 E
Kramer	119	35 0N	117 38W
Kramfors	48	62 55N	17 48 E
Kramis, C.	82	36 26N	0 45 E
Krångede	48	63 9N	16 10 E
Kraniá	44	39 53N	21 18 E
Kranídhion	45	37 20N	23 10 E
Kranj	39	46 16N	14 22 E
Kranjska Gora	39	46 29N	13 48 E
Krapina	39	46 10N	15 52 E
Krapina →	39	45 50N	15 50 E
Krapivna	55	53 58N	37 10 E
Krapkowice	28	50 29N	17 56 E
Krasavino	52	60 58N	46 29 E
Kraskino	59	42 44N	130 48 E
Kraslice	26	50 19N	12 31 E
Krasnaya Gorbatka	55	55 52N	41 45 E
Krasnaya Polyana	57	43 40N	40 13 E
Kraśnik	28	50 55N	22 5 E
Kraśnik Fabryczny	28	50 58N	22 11 E
Krasnoarmeisk	56	48 18N	37 11 E
Krasnoarmeysk, R.S.F.S.R., U.S.S.R.	55	51 0N	45 42 E
Krasnoarmeysk, R.S.F.S.R., U.S.S.R.	57	48 30N	44 25 E
Krasnodar	57	45 5N	39 0 E
Krasnodon	57	48 17N	39 44 E
Krasnodonetskaya	57	48 5N	40 50 E
Krasnogorskiy	55	56 10N	48 28 E
Krasnograd	56	49 27N	35 27 E
Krasnogvardeyskoye	57	45 52N	41 33 E
Krasnogvardyesk	56	45 32N	34 16 E
Krasnokamsk	52	58 4N	55 48 E
Krasnokutsk	54	50 10N	34 50 E
Krasnoperekopsk	56	46 0N	33 54 E
Krasnoselkupsk	58	65 20N	82 10 E
Krasnoslobodsk, R.S.F.S.R., U.S.S.R.	55	54 25N	43 45 E
Krasnoslobodsk, R.S.F.S.R., U.S.S.R.	57	48 42N	44 33 E
Krasnoturinsk	58	59 46N	60 12 E
Krasnoufimsk	52	56 57N	57 46 E
Krasnouralsk	52	58 21N	60 3 E
Krasnovishersk	52	60 23N	57 3 E
Krasnovodsk	53	40 0N	52 52 E
Krasnoyarsk	59	56 8N	93 0 E
Krasnoye, Kalmyk A.S.S.R., U.S.S.R.	57	46 16N	45 0 E
Krasnoye, R.S.F.S.R., U.S.S.R.	55	59 15N	47 40 E
Krasnoye = Krasnyy	54	54 25N	31 30 E
Krasnozavodsk	55	56 27N	38 25 E
Krasny Liman	56	48 58N	37 50 E
Krasny Sulin	57	47 52N	40 8 E
Krasnystaw	28	50 57N	23 5 E
Krasnyy	54	54 25N	31 30 E
Krasnyy Kholm	55	58 10N	37 10 E
Krasnyy Kut	55	50 50N	47 0 E
Krasnyy Luch	57	48 13N	39 0 E
Krasnyy Profintern	55	57 45N	40 27 E
Krasnyy Yar, Kalmyk A.S.S.R., U.S.S.R.	57	46 43N	48 23 E
Krasnyy Yar, R.S.F.S.R., U.S.S.R.	55	53 30N	50 22 E
Krasnyy Yar, R.S.F.S.R., U.S.S.R.	55	50 42N	44 45 E
Krasnyye Baki	55	57 8N	45 10 E
Krasnyyoskolskoye Vdkhr.	56	49 30N	37 30 E
Kraszna →	27	48 0N	22 20 E
Kratie	71	12 32N	106 10 E
Kratovo	42	42 6N	22 10 E
Krau	73	3 19 S	140 5 E
Kravanh, Chuor Phnum	71	12 0N	103 32 E
Krawang	73	6 19N	107 18 E
Krefeld	24	51 20N	6 32 E
Krémaston, Límni	45	38 52N	21 30 E
Kremenchug	56	49 5N	33 25 E
Kremenchugskoye Vdkhr.	56	49 20N	32 30 E
Kremenets	56	50 8N	25 43 E
Kremenica	42	40 55N	21 25 E
Kremennaya	56	49 1N	38 10 E
Kremges = Svetlovodsk	56	49 5N	33 15 E
Kremikovtsi	43	42 46N	23 28 E
Kremmen	24	52 45N	13 1 E
Kremmling	118	40 10N	106 30W
Kremnica	27	48 45N	18 50 E
Krems	26	48 25N	15 36 E
Kremsmünster	26	48 3N	14 8 E
Kretinga	54	55 53N	21 15 E
Krettamia	82	28 47N	3 27W
Krettsy	54	58 15N	32 30 E
Kreuzberg	25	50 22N	9 58 E
Kribi	88	2 57N	9 56 E
Krichem	43	42 8N	24 28 E
Krichev	54	53 45N	31 50 E
Krim	39	45 53N	14 30 E
Krionéri	45	38 20N	21 35 E
Krishna →	70	15 57N	80 59 E
Krishnagiri	70	12 32N	78 16 E
Krishnanagar	69	23 24N	88 33 E
Krishnaraja Sagara	70	12 20N	76 30 E
Kristiansand	47	58 9N	8 1 E
Kristianstad	49	56 2N	14 9 E
Kristiansund	47	63 7N	7 45 E
Kristiinankaupunki	50	62 16N	21 21 E
Kristinehamn	48	59 18N	14 13 E
Kristinestad	50	62 16N	21 21 E
Kríti	45	35 15N	25 0 E
Kritsá	45	35 10N	25 41 E
Kriva →	42	42 5N	21 47 E
Kriva Palanka	42	42 11N	22 19 E
Krivaja →	42	44 27N	18 9 E
Krivelj	42	44 8N	22 5 E
Krivoy Rog	56	47 51N	33 20 E
Križevci	39	46 3N	16 32 E
Krk	39	45 8N	14 40 E
Krka →	39	45 50N	15 30 E
Krkonoše	26	50 50N	15 35 E
Krnov	27	50 5N	17 40 E
Krobia	28	51 47N	16 59 E
Kročehlavy	26	50 8N	14 9 E
Krøderen	47	60 9N	9 49 E
Krokawo	28	54 47N	18 9 E
Krokeaí	45	36 53N	22 32 E
Krokom	48	63 20N	14 30 E
Krolevets	54	51 35N	33 20 E
Kroměríz	27	49 18N	17 21 E
Krompachy	27	48 54N	20 52 E
Kromy	54	52 40N	35 48 E
Kronach	25	50 14N	11 19 E
Kronobergs län □	49	56 45N	14 30 E
Kronprins Olav Kyst	5	69 0 S	42 0 E
Kronprinsesse Märtha Kyst	5	73 30 S	10 0 E
Kronshtadt	54	60 5N	29 45 E
Kroonstad	92	27 43 S	27 19 E
Kröpelin	24	54 4N	11 48 E
Kropotkin, R.S.F.S.R., U.S.S.R.	57	45 28N	40 28 E
Kropotkin, R.S.F.S.R., U.S.S.R.	59	59 0N	115 30 E
Kropp	24	54 24N	9 32 E
Krościenko	27	49 29N	20 25 E
Krośniewice	28	52 15N	19 11 E
Krosno	27	49 42N	21 46 E
Krosno □	27	49 35N	22 0 E
Krosno Odrzańskie	28	52 3N	15 7 E
Krotoszyn	28	51 42N	17 23 E
Krraba	44	41 13N	20 0 E
Krško	39	45 57N	15 30 E
Krstača	42	42 57N	20 8 E
Kruger Nat. Park	93	24 0 S	31 40 E
Krugersdorp	93	26 5 S	27 46 E
Kruis, Kaap	92	21 55 S	13 57 E
Kruja	44	41 32N	19 46 E
Krulevshchina	54	55 5N	27 45 E
Kruma	44	42 14N	20 28 E
Krumbach	25	48 15N	10 22 E
Krumovgrad	43	41 29N	25 38 E
Krung Thep	71	13 45N	100 35 E
Krupanj	42	44 25N	19 22 E
Krupina	27	48 22N	19 5 E
Krupinica →	27	48 15N	18 52 E
Kruševac	42	43 35N	21 28 E
Kruševo	42	41 23N	21 19 E
Kruszwica	28	52 40N	18 20 E
Kruzof I.	108	57 10N	135 40W
Krylbo	48	60 7N	16 15 E
Krymsk Abinsk	56	44 50N	38 0 E
Krymskiy P-ov.	56	45 0N	34 0 E
Krynica	27	49 25N	20 57 E
Krynica Morska	28	54 23N	19 28 E
Krynki	28	53 17N	23 43 E
Krzepice	28	50 58N	18 50 E
Krzeszów	28	50 24N	22 21 E
Krzeszowice	27	50 8N	19 37 E
Krzna →	28	51 59N	22 47 E
Krzywiń	28	51 58N	16 50 E
Krzyz	28	52 52N	16 0 E
Ksabi	82	32 51N	4 13W
Ksar Chellala	82	35 13N	2 19 E
Ksar el Boukhari	82	35 51N	2 52 E
Ksar el Kebir	82	35 0N	6 0W
Ksar es Souk = Ar Rachidiya	82	31 58N	4 20W
Ksar Rhilane	83	33 0N	9 39 E
Ksiba, El	82	32 46N	6 0W
Ksour, Mts. des	82	32 45N	0 30W
Kstovo	55	56 12N	44 13 E
Kuala	72	2 55N	105 47 E
Kuala Kangsar	71	4 46N	100 56 E
Kuala Kerai	71	5 30N	102 12 E
Kuala Kubu Baharu	71	3 34N	101 39 E
Kuala Lipis	71	4 10N	102 3 E
Kuala Lumpur	71	3 9N	101 41 E
Kuala Sedili Besar	71	1 55N	104 5 E
Kuala Terengganu	72	5 20N	103 8 E
Kualakapuas	72	2 55 S	114 20 E
Kualakurun	72	1 10 S	113 50 E
Kualapembuang	72	3 14 S	112 38 E
Kualasimpang	72	4 17N	98 3 E
Kuandang	73	0 56N	123 1 E
Kuandian	76	40 45N	124 45 E
Kuangchou = Guangzhou	75	23 5N	113 10 E
Kuantan	71	3 49N	103 20 E
Kuba	57	41 21N	48 32 E
Kubak	66	27 10N	63 10 E
Kuban →	56	45 20N	37 30 E
Kubenskoye, Oz.	55	59 40N	39 25 E
Kuberle	57	47 0N	42 20 E
Kubrat	43	43 49N	26 31 E
Kučevo	42	44 30N	21 40 E
Kuchaman	68	27 13N	74 47 E
Kuchenspitze	26	47 7N	10 12 E
Kuching	72	1 33N	110 25 E
Kuçove = Qytet Stalin	44	40 47N	19 57 E
Kücük Kuyu	44	39 35N	26 27 E
Kudalier →	70	18 35N	79 48 E
Kudat	72	6 55N	116 55 E
Kudremukh, Mt.	70	13 15N	75 20 E
Kudus	73	6 48 S	110 51 E
Kudymkar	58	59 1N	54 39 E
Kueiyang = Guiyang	75	26 32N	106 40 E
Kufrinjah	62	32 20N	35 41 E
Kufstein	26	47 35N	12 11 E
Kugong I.	106	56 18N	79 50W
Kūh-e 'Alijūq	65	31 30N	51 41 E
Kūh-e Dīnār	65	30 40N	51 0 E
Kūh-e-Hazārān	65	29 35N	57 20 E
Kūh-e-Jebāl Bārez	65	29 0N	58 0 E
Kūh-e Sorkh	65	35 30N	58 45 E
Kūh-e Taftān	65	28 40N	61 0 E
Kūhak	65	27 12N	63 10 E
Kūhhā-ye-Bashākerd	65	26 45N	59 0 E
Kūhhā-ye Sabalān	64	38 15N	47 45 E
Kuhnsdorf	26	46 37N	14 38 E
Kūhpāyeh	65	32 44N	52 20 E
Kuile He →	76	49 32N	124 42 E
Kuito	89	12 22 S	16 55 E
Kukavica	42	42 48N	21 57 E
Kukawa	85	12 58N	13 27 E
Kukësi	44	42 5N	20 20 E
Kukësi □	44	42 25N	20 15 E
Kukmor	55	56 11N	50 54 E
Kukvidze	55	50 40N	43 15 E
Kula, Bulg.	42	43 52N	22 36 E
Kula, Yugo.	42	45 37N	19 32 E
Kulai	71	1 44N	103 35 E
Kulal, Mt.	90	2 42N	36 57 E
Kulaly, O.	57	45 0N	50 0 E
Kulasekharapattanam	70	8 20N	78 0 E
Kuldiga	54	56 58N	21 59 E
Kuldja = Yining	75	43 58N	81 10 E
Kuldu	87	12 50N	28 30 E
Kulebaki	55	55 22N	42 25 E
Kulen Vakuf	39	44 35N	16 2 E

Kuli Lampang

Kuli 57 42 2N 47 12 E
Küllük 45 37 12N 27 36 E
Kulm 116 46 22N 98 58W
Kulmbach 25 50 6N 11 27 E
Kulsary 58 46 59N 54 1 E
Kultay 57 45 5N 51 40 E
Kulti 69 23 43N 86 50 E
Kulunda 58 52 35N 78 57 E
Kulwin 99 35 0 S 142 42 E
Kulyab 58 37 55N 69 50 E
Kum Tekei 58 43 10N 79 30 E
Kuma → 57 44 55N 47 0 E
Kumaganum 85 13 8N 10 38 E
Kumagaya 74 36 9N 139 22 E
Kumai 72 2 44 S 111 43 E
Kumamba, Kepulauan 73 1 36 S 138 45 E
Kumamoto 74 32 45N 130 45 E
Kumamoto □ 74 32 55N 130 55 E
Kumanovo 42 42 9N 21 42 E
Kumara 101 42 37 S 171 12 E
Kumasi 84 6 41N 1 38W
Kumba 88 4 36N 9 24 E
Kumbakonam 70 10 58N 79 25 E
Kumbarilla 99 27 15 S 150 55 E
Kumbo 85 6 15N 10 36 E
Kumbukkan Oya → 70 6 35N 81 40 E
Kumeny 55 58 10N 49 47 E
Kumertau 52 52 46N 55 47 E
Kumi 90 1 30N 33 58 E
Kumkale 44 40 0N 26 13 E
Kumla 48 59 8N 15 10 E
Kummerower See 24 53 47N 12 52 E
Kumo 85 10 1N 11 12 E
Kumon Bum 67 26 30N 97 15 E
Kumta 70 14 29N 74 25 E
Kumtorkala 57 43 2N 46 50 E
Kumylzhenskaya 57 49 51N 42 38 E
Kunágota 27 46 26N 21 3 E
Kunama 99 35 35 S 148 4 E
Kunashir, Ostrov 59 44 0N 146 0 E
Kunch 68 26 0N 79 10 E
Kunda 54 59 30N 26 34 E
Kundiawa 98 6 2 S 145 1 E
Kundla 68 21 21N 71 25 E
Kungala 99 29 58 S 153 7 E
Kungälv 49 57 53N 11 59 E
Kunghit I. 108 52 6N 131 3W
Kungrad 58 43 6N 58 54 E
Kungsbacka 49 57 30N 12 5 E
Kungur 52 57 25N 56 57 E
Kungurri 98 21 3 S 148 46 E
Kunhegyes 27 47 22N 20 36 E
Kuningan 73 6 59 S 108 29 E
Kunlong 67 23 20N 98 50 E
Kunlun Shan 75 36 0N 85 0 E
Kunmadaras 27 47 28N 20 45 E
Kunming 75 25 1N 102 41 E
Kunnamkulam 70 10 38N 76 7 E
Kunsan 76 35 59N 126 45 E
Kunshan 77 31 22N 120 58 E
Kunszentmárton 27 46 50N 20 20 E
Kununurra 96 15 40 S 128 50 E
Kunwarara 98 22 55 S 150 9 E
Kunya-Urgenoh 58 42 19N 59 10 E
Künzelsau 25 49 17N 9 41 E
Kuopio 50 62 53N 27 35 E
Kuopion lääni □ 50 63 25N 27 10 E
Kupa → 39 45 28N 16 24 E
Kupang 73 10 19 S 123 39 E
Kupres 42 44 1N 17 15 E
Kupyansk 56 49 52N 37 35 E
Kupyansk-Uzlovoi 56 49 45N 37 34 E
Kuqa 75 41 35N 82 30 E
Kura → 57 39 50N 49 20 E
Kuranda 98 16 48 S 145 35 E
Kurashiki 74 34 40N 133 50 E
Kurayoshi 74 35 26N 133 50 E
Kurduvadi 70 18 8N 75 29 E
Kŭrdzhali 43 41 38N 25 21 E
Kure 74 34 14N 132 32 E
Kuressaare = Kingisepp 54 58 15N 22 15 E
Kurgaldzhino 58 50 35N 70 20 E
Kurgan 58 55 26N 65 18 E
Kurganinsk 57 44 54N 40 34 E
Kurgannaya = Kurganinsk 57 44 54N 40 34 E
Kuria Maria I. = Khūryān Mūryān, Jazā 'ir 63 17 30N 55 58 E
Kurichchi 70 11 36N 77 35 E
Kuridala P.O 98 21 16 S 140 29 E
Kuril Is. = Kurilskiye Os. 59 45 0N 150 0 E
Kuril Trench 94 44 0N 153 0 E
Kurilsk 59 45 14N 147 53 E
Kurilskiye Ostrova 59 45 0N 150 0 E
Kuring Kuru 92 17 42 S 18 32 E
Kurkur 86 23 50N 32 0 E
Kurkūrah 83 31 30N 20 1 E
Kurla 70 19 5N 72 52 E
Kurlovskiy 55 55 25N 40 40 E
Kurmuk 87 10 33N 34 21 E
Kurnool 70 15 45N 78 0 E
Kurovskoye 55 55 35N 38 55 E
Kurow 101 44 44 S 170 29 E
Kurów 28 51 23N 22 12 E
Kurrajong 99 33 33 S 150 42 E
Kurri Kurri 99 32 50 S 151 28 E
Kursavka 57 44 29N 42 32 E
Kuršenai 54 56 1N 23 3 E
Kurseong 69 26 56N 88 18 E
Kursk 55 51 42N 36 11 E
Kuršumlija 42 43 9N 21 19 E
Kuršumlijska Banja 42 43 3N 21 11 E
Kuru (Chel), Bahr el 87 8 10N 26 50 E
Kuruktag 75 41 0N 89 0 E
Kuruman 92 27 28 S 23 28 E
Kurume 74 33 15N 130 30 E
Kurunegala 70 7 30N 80 23 E
Kurya 59 61 15N 108 10 E
Kuşada Körfezı 45 37 56N 27 0 E
Kuşadası 45 37 52N 27 15 E
Kusawa L. 108 60 20N 136 13W
Kusel 25 49 31N 7 25 E
Kushchevskaya 57 46 33N 39 35 E
Kushiro 74 43 0N 144 25 E
Kushiro → 74 42 59N 144 23 E
Kushka 58 35 20N 62 18 E
Kushtia 69 23 55N 89 5 E
Kushum → 57 49 0N 50 20 E
Kushva 52 58 18N 59 45 E
Kuskokwim → 104 60 17N 162 27W
Kuskokwim Bay 104 59 50N 162 56W
Kussharo-Ko 74 43 38N 144 21 E
Kustanay 58 53 10N 63 35 E
Kütahya 64 39 30N 30 2 E
Kutaisi 57 42 19N 42 40 E
Kutaraja = Banda Aceh 72 5 35N 95 20 E
Kutch, G. of 68 22 50N 69 15 E
Kutch, Rann of 68 24 0N 70 0 E
Kutina 39 45 29N 16 48 E
Kutiyana 68 21 36N 70 2 E
Kutjevo 42 45 23N 17 55 E
Kutkashen 57 40 58N 47 47 E
Kutná Hora 26 49 57N 15 16 E
Kutno 28 52 15N 19 23 E
Kuttabul 98 21 5 S 148 48 E
Kutu 88 2 40 S 18 11 E
Kutum 87 14 10N 24 40 E
Kúty 27 48 40N 17 3 E
Kuvshinovo 54 57 2N 34 11 E
Kuwait = Al Kuwayt 64 29 30N 47 30 E
Kuwait ■ 64 29 30N 47 30 E
Kuwana 74 35 0N 136 43 E
Kuybyshev 58 55 27N 78 19 E
Kuybyshev 58 53 8N 50 6 E
Kuybyshevskoye Vdkhr. 55 55 2N 49 30 E
Kūysanjaq 64 36 5N 44 38 E
Kuyto, Oz. 52 64 40N 31 0 E
Kuyumba 59 60 58N 96 59 E
Kuzey Anadolu Dağlari 64 41 30N 35 0 E
Kuzhithura 70 8 18N 77 11 E
Kuzmin 42 45 2N 19 25 E
Kuznetsk 55 53 12N 46 40 E
Kuzomen 52 66 22N 36 50 E
Kvænangen 50 70 5N 21 15 E
Kvam 47 61 40N 9 42 E
Kvamsøy 47 61 7N 6 28 E
Kvareli 57 41 27N 45 47 E
Kvarner 39 44 50N 14 10 E
Kvarnerič 39 44 43N 14 37 E
Kvernes 47 63 1N 7 44 E
Kvillsfors 49 57 24N 15 29 E
Kvine → 47 58 17N 6 56 E
Kvinesdal 47 58 19N 6 57 E
Kviteseid 47 59 24N 8 29 E
Kwabhaga 93 30 51 S 29 0 E
Kwadacha → 108 57 28N 125 38W
Kwakhanai 92 21 39 S 21 16 E
Kwakoegron 127 5 12N 55 25W
Kwale, Kenya 90 4 15 S 39 31 E
Kwale, Nigeria 85 5 46N 6 26 E
Kwale □ 90 4 15 S 39 10 E
Kwamouth 88 3 9 S 16 12 E
Kwando → 92 18 27 S 23 32 E
Kwangsi-Chuang = Guangxi Zhuangzu □ 75 24 0N 109 0 E
Kwangtung = Guangdong □ 75 23 0N 113 0 E
Kwara □ 85 8 0N 5 0 E
Kwataboahegan → 106 51 9N 80 50W
Kwatisore 73 3 18 S 134 50 E
Kweichow = Guizhou □ 75 27 0N 107 0 E
Kwidzyn 28 53 44N 18 55 E
Kwiguk 104 63 45N 164 35W
Kwimba □ 90 3 0 S 33 0 E
Kwinana 96 32 15 S 115 47 E
Kwisa → 28 51 34N 15 24 E
Kwoka 73 0 31 S 132 27 E
Kyabé 81 9 30N 19 0 E
Kyabra Cr. → 99 25 36 S 142 55 E
Kyabram 99 36 19 S 145 4 E
Kyaikto 71 17 20N 97 3 E
Kyakhta 59 50 30N 106 25 E
Kyangin 67 18 20N 95 20 E
Kyaukpadaung 67 20 52N 95 8 E
Kyaukpyu 67 19 28N 93 30 E
Kyaukse 67 21 36N 96 10 E
Kyenjojo 90 0 40N 30 37 E
Kyle Dam 91 20 15 S 31 0 E
Kyle of Lochalsh 14 57 17N 5 43W
Kyll → 25 49 48N 6 42 E
Kyllburg 25 50 2N 6 35 E
Kyneton 99 37 10 S 144 29 E
Kynuna 98 21 37 S 141 55 E
Kyō-ga-Saki 74 35 45N 135 15 E
Kyoga, L. 90 1 35N 33 0 E
Kyogle 99 28 40 S 153 0 E
Kyongju 76 35 51N 129 14 E
Kyongpyaw 67 17 12N 95 10 E
Kyōto 74 35 0N 135 45 E
Kyōto □ 74 35 15N 135 45 E
Kyren 59 51 45N 101 45 E
Kyrenia 64 35 20N 33 20 E
Kyritz 24 52 57N 12 25 E
Kystatyam 59 67 20N 123 10 E
Kytal Ktakh 59 65 30N 123 40 E
Kyulyunken 59 64 10N 137 5 E
Kyunhla 67 23 25N 95 15 E
Kyuquot 108 50 3N 127 25W
Kyurdamir 57 40 25N 48 3 E
Kyūshū 74 33 0N 131 0 E
Kyūshū-Sanchi 74 32 35N 131 17 E
Kyustendil 42 42 16N 22 41 E
Kyusyur 59 70 39N 127 15 E
Kywong 99 34 58 S 146 44 E
Kyzyl 59 51 50N 94 30 E
Kyzyl-Kiya 58 40 16N 72 8 E
Kyzylkum, Peski 58 42 30N 65 0 E
Kzyl-Orda 58 44 48N 65 28 E

L

Laa 27 48 43N 16 23 E
Laaber → 25 49 0N 12 3 E
Laage 24 53 55N 12 21 E
Laasphe 24 50 56N 8 23 E
Laba → 57 45 11N 39 42 E
Labastide 20 43 28N 2 39 E
Labastide-Murat 20 44 39N 1 33 E
Labbézenga 85 15 2N 0 48 E
Labdah = Leptis Magna 83 32 40N 14 12 E
Labé 84 11 24N 12 16W
Labe = Elbe → 26 50 50N 14 12 E
Laberec → 27 48 37N 21 58 E
Laberge, L. 108 61 11N 135 12W
Labin 39 45 5N 14 8 E
Labinsk 57 44 40N 40 48 E
Labis 71 2 22N 103 2 E
Labiszyn 28 52 57N 17 54 E
Laboe 24 54 25N 10 13 E
Labouheyre 20 44 13N 0 55W
Laboulaye 124 34 10 S 63 30W
Labra, Peña 30 43 3N 4 26W
Labrador City 107 52 57N 66 55W
Labrador, Coast of □ 105 53 20N 61 0W
Lábrea 126 7 15 S 64 51W
Labrède 20 44 41N 0 32W
Labuan 72 5 21N 115 13 E
Labuha 73 0 30 S 127 30 E
Labuhan 73 6 26 S 105 50 E
Labuhanbajo 73 8 28 S 120 1 E
Labuk, Telok 72 6 10N 117 50 E
Labytnangi 58 66 39N 66 21 E
Łabźenica 28 53 18N 17 15 E
Lac Allard 107 50 33N 63 24W
Lac Bouchette 107 48 16N 72 11W
Lac du Flambeau 116 46 1N 89 51W
Lac Édouard 106 47 40N 72 16W
Lac la Biche 108 54 45N 111 58W
Lac la Martre 104 63 8N 117 16W
Lac-Mégantic 107 45 35N 70 53W
Lac Seul 109 50 28N 92 0W
Lacanau, Étang de 20 44 58N 1 7W
Lacanau-Médoc 20 44 59N 1 5W
Lacantúm → 120 16 36N 90 40W
Lacara → 31 38 55N 6 25W
Lacaune 20 43 43N 2 40 E
Lacaune, Mts. de 20 43 43N 2 50 E
Laccadive Is. = Lakshadweep Is. 60 10 0N 72 30 E
Lacepede B. 99 36 40 S 139 40 E
Lacepede Is. 96 16 55 S 122 0 E
Lacerdónia 91 18 3 S 35 35 E
Lachine 106 45 30N 73 40W
Lachlan → 97 34 22 S 143 55 E
Lachmangarh 68 27 50N 75 4 E
Lachute 106 45 39N 74 21W
Lackawanna 114 42 49N 78 50W
Lacolle 113 45 5N 73 22W
Lacombe 108 52 30N 113 44W
Lacona 113 43 37N 76 5W
Láconi 40 39 54N 9 4 E
Laconia 114 43 32N 71 30W
Lacq 20 43 25N 0 35W
Lacrosse 118 46 51N 117 58W
Ladakh Ra. 69 34 0N 78 0 E
Lądekzdrój 28 50 21N 16 53 E
Ládhon → 45 37 40N 21 50 E
Ladik 56 40 57N 35 58 E
Ladismith 92 33 28 S 21 15 E
Lādīz 65 28 55N 61 15 E
Ladnun 68 27 38N 74 25 E
Ladoga, L. = Ladozhskoye Oz. 52 61 15N 30 30 E
Ladon 19 48 0N 2 30 E
Ladozhskoye Ozero 52 61 15N 30 30 E
Lady Grey 92 30 43 S 27 13 E
Ladybrand 92 29 9 S 27 29 E
Ladysmith, Can. 108 49 0N 123 49W
Ladysmith, S. Afr. 93 28 32 S 29 46 E
Ladysmith, U.S.A. 116 45 27N 91 4W
Lae 94 6 40 S 147 2 E
Læsø 49 57 15N 10 53 E
Læsø Rende 49 57 20N 10 45 E
Lafayette, Colo., U.S.A. 116 40 0N 105 2W
Lafayette, Ga., U.S.A. 115 34 44N 85 15W
Lafayette, La., U.S.A. 117 30 18N 92 0W
Lafayette, Tenn., U.S.A. 115 36 35N 86 0W
Laferte → 108 61 53N 117 44W
Lafia 85 8 30N 8 34 E
Lafiagi 85 8 52N 5 20 E
Lafleche 109 49 45N 106 40W
Lafon 87 5 5N 32 29 E
Laforsen 48 61 56N 15 3 E
Lagan →, Sweden 49 56 56N 13 58 E
Lagan →, U.K. 15 54 35N 5 55W
Lagarfljót → 50 65 40N 14 18W
Lage, Ger. 24 52 0N 8 47 E
Lage, Spain 30 43 13N 9 0W
Lågen →, Oppland, Norway 47 61 8N 10 25 E
Lågen →, Vestfold, Norway 47 59 3N 10 5 E
Lägerdorf 24 53 53N 9 35 E
Laggers Pt. 99 30 52 S 153 4 E
Laghán □ 65 34 20N 70 0 E
Laghouat 82 33 50N 2 59 E
Lagnieu 21 45 55N 5 20 E
Lagny 19 48 52N 2 40 E
Lago 41 39 9N 16 8 E
Lagôa 31 37 8N 8 27W
Lagoaça 30 41 11N 6 44W
Lagodekhi 57 41 50N 46 22 E
Lagónegro 41 40 8N 15 45 E
Lagonoy Gulf 73 13 50N 123 50 E
Lagos, Nigeria 85 6 25N 3 27 E
Lagos, Port. 31 37 5N 8 41W
Lagos de Moreno 120 21 21N 101 55W
Lagrange 96 18 45 S 121 43 E
Laguardia 32 42 33N 2 35W
Laguépie 20 44 8N 1 57 E
Laguna, Brazil 125 28 30 S 48 50W
Laguna, U.S.A. 119 35 3N 107 28W
Laguna Beach 119 33 31N 117 52W
Laguna Dam 119 32 55N 114 30W
Laguna de la Janda 31 36 15N 5 45W
Laguna Limpia 124 26 32 S 59 45W
Laguna Madre 120 27 0N 97 20W
Lagunas, Chile 124 21 0 S 69 45W
Lagunas, Peru 126 5 10 S 75 35W
Laha 76 48 12N 124 35 E
Lahad Datu 73 5 0N 118 20 E
Laharpur 69 27 43N 80 56 E
Lahat 72 3 45 S 103 30 E
Lahewa 72 1 22N 97 12 E
Lahijan 64 37 10N 50 6 E
Lahn → 25 50 52N 8 35 E
Laholm 49 56 30N 13 2 E
Laholmsbukten 49 56 30N 12 45 E
Lahontan Res. 118 39 28N 118 58W
Lahore 68 31 32N 74 22 E
Lahore □ 68 31 55N 74 5 E
* Lahr 25 48 20N 7 52 E
Lahti 51 60 58N 25 40 E
Laï 81 9 25N 16 18 E
Lai Chau 71 22 5N 103 3 E
Laibin 75 23 42N 109 14 E
Laidley 99 27 39 S 152 20 E
Laifeng 77 29 27N 109 20 E
Laignes 19 47 50N 4 20 E
Laikipia □ 90 0 30N 36 30 E
Laingsburg 92 33 9 S 20 52 E
Lairg 14 58 1N 4 24W
Lais 72 3 35 S 102 0 E
Laiyang 76 36 59N 120 45 E
Laizhou Wan 76 37 30N 119 30 E
Laja → 120 20 55N 100 46W
Lajere 85 11 58N 11 25 E
Lajes 125 27 48 S 50 20W
Lajkovac 42 44 27N 20 14 E
Lajosmizse 27 47 3N 19 32 E
Lakaband 68 31 2N 69 15 E
Lakar 73 8 15 S 128 17 E
Lake Andes 116 43 10N 98 32W
Lake Anse 114 46 42N 88 25W
Lake Arthur 117 30 8N 92 40W
Lake Cargelligo 97 33 15 S 146 22 E
Lake Charles 117 30 15N 93 10W
Lake City, Colo, U.S.A. 119 38 3N 107 27W
Lake City, Fla., U.S.A. 115 30 10N 82 40W
Lake City, Iowa, U.S.A. 116 42 12N 94 42W
Lake City, Mich., U.S.A. 114 44 20N 85 10W
Lake City, Minn., U.S.A. 116 44 28N 92 21W
Lake City, Pa., U.S.A. 112 42 2N 80 20W
Lake City, S.C., U.S.A. 115 33 51N 79 44W
Lake George 113 43 25N 73 43W
Lake Harbour 105 62 50N 69 50W
Lake Havasu City 119 34 25N 114 29W
Lake Lenore 109 52 24N 104 59W
Lake Louise 108 51 30N 116 10W
Lake Mead Nat. Rec. Area 119 36 0N 114 30W
Lake Mills 116 43 23N 93 33W
Lake Nash 98 20 57 S 138 0 E
Lake Providence 117 32 49N 91 12W
Lake River 106 54 30N 82 31W
Lake Superior Prov. Park 106 47 45N 84 45W
Lake Village 117 33 20N 91 19W
Lake Wales 115 27 55N 81 32W
Lake Worth 115 26 36N 80 3W
Lakefield 106 44 25N 78 16W
Lakeland 115 28 0N 82 0W
Lakemba 101 18 13 S 178 47W
Lakes Entrance 99 37 50 S 148 0 E
Lakeside, Ariz., U.S.A. 119 34 12N 109 59W
Lakeside, Nebr., U.S.A. 116 42 5N 102 24W
Lakeview 118 42 15N 120 22W
Lakewood, N.J., U.S.A. 114 40 5N 74 13W
Lakewood, Ohio, U.S.A. 114 41 28N 81 50W
Lakhaniá 45 35 58N 27 54 E
Lákhi 45 35 24N 23 57 E
Lakhpat 68 23 48N 68 47 E
Laki 50 64 4N 18 14W
Lakin 117 37 58N 101 18W
Lakitusaki → 106 54 21N 82 25W
Lakonía □ 45 36 55N 22 30 E
Lakonikós Kólpos 45 36 40N 22 40 E
Lakota, Ivory C. 84 5 50N 5 30W
Lakota, U.S.A. 116 48 0N 98 22W
Laksefjorden 50 70 45N 26 50 E
Lakselv 50 70 2N 24 56 E
Lakshmi Kantapur 69 22 5N 88 20 E
Lala Ghat 67 24 30N 92 40 E
Lala Musa 68 32 40N 73 57 E
Lalago 90 3 28 S 33 58 E
Lalapanzi 91 19 20 S 30 15 E
Lalganj 69 25 52N 85 13 E
Lalibela 87 12 2N 39 2 E
Lalin 76 45 12N 127 0 E
Lalín 30 42 40N 8 5W
Lalinde 20 44 50N 0 44 E
Lalitpur 68 24 42N 78 28 E
Lama Kara 85 9 30N 1 15 E
Lamaing 67 15 25N 97 53 E
Lamar, Colo., U.S.A. 116 38 9N 102 35W
Lamar, Mo., U.S.A. 117 37 30N 94 20W
Lamas 126 6 28 S 76 31W
Lamastre 21 44 59N 4 35 E
Lambach 26 48 6N 13 51 E
Lamballe 18 48 29N 2 31W
Lambaréné 88 0 41 S 10 12 E
Lambasa 101 16 30 S 179 10 E
Lambay I. 15 53 30N 6 0W
Lambert 116 47 44N 104 39W
Lambert Glacier 5 71 0 S 70 0 E
Lambesc 21 43 39N 5 16 E
Lambi Kyun (Sullivan I.) 71 10 50N 98 20 E
Lámbia 45 37 52N 21 53 E
Lambro → 38 45 8N 9 32 E
Lame 85 43 35N 106 40W
Lame Deer 118 45 45N 106 40W
Lamego 30 41 5N 7 52W
Lamèque 107 47 45N 64 38W
Lameroo 99 35 19 S 140 33 E
Lamesa 117 32 45N 101 57W
Lamía 45 38 55N 22 26 E
† Lamitan 73 6 40N 122 10 E
Lammermuir Hills 14 55 50N 2 40W
Lamoille 118 40 47N 115 31W
Lamon Bay 73 14 30N 122 20 E
Lamont 108 53 46N 112 50W
Lampa 126 15 22 S 70 22W
Lampang, Thai. 71 18 18N 99 31 E
Lampang, Thai. 71 18 16N 99 32 E

* *Now part of Punjab □*

† *Renamed Isabela*

Lampasas Lenora

Lampasas **117** 31 5N 98 10W
Lampaul **18** 48 28N 5 7W
Lampazos de Naranjo **120** 27 2N 100 32W
Lampedusa **36** 35 36N 12 40 E
Lampeter **13** 52 6N 4 6W
Lampione **83** 35 33N 12 20 E
Lampman **109** 49 25N 102 50W
Lamprechtshausen **26** 48 0N 12 58 E
Lamprey **109** 58 33N 94 8W
Lampung □ **72** 5 30 S 104 30 E
Lamu **90** 2 16 S 40 55 E
Lamu □ **90** 2 0 S 40 45 E
Lamut, Tg. **72** 3 50 S 105 58 E
Lamy **119** 35 30N 105 58W
Lan Xian **76** 38 15N 111 35 E
Lan Yu **77** 22 5N 121 35 E
Lanai I. **110** 20 50N 156 55W
Lanak La **69** 34 27N 79 32 E
Lanak'o Shank'ou = Lanak La **69** 34 27N 79 32 E
Lanao, L. **73** 7 52N 124 15 E
Lanark, Can. **113** 45 1N 76 22W
Lanark, U.K. **14** 55 40N 3 48W
Lancashire □ **12** 53 40N 2 30W
Lancaster, Can. **113** 45 10N 74 30W
Lancaster, U.K. **12** 54 3N 2 48W
Lancaster, Calif., U.S.A. **119** 34 47N 118 8W
Lancaster, Ky., U.S.A. **114** 37 40N 84 40W
Lancaster, N.H., U.S.A. **114** 44 27N 71 33W
Lancaster, N.Y., U.S.A. **112** 42 53N 78 43W
Lancaster, Pa., U.S.A. **114** 40 4N 76 19W
Lancaster, S.C., U.S.A. **115** 34 45N 80 47W
Lancaster, Wis., U.S.A. **116** 42 48N 90 43W
Lancaster Sd. **4** 74 13N 84 0W
Lancer **109** 50 48N 108 53W
Lanchow = Lanzhou **76** 36 1N 103 52 E
Lanciano **39** 42 15N 14 22 E
Łancut **27** 50 10N 22 13 E
Lándana **88** 5 11 S 12 5 E
Landau, Bayern, Ger. **25** 48 41N 12 41 E
Landau, Rhld-Pfz., Ger. **25** 49 12N 8 7 E
Landeck **26** 47 9N 10 34 E
Landen **16** 50 45N 5 5 E
Lander **118** 42 50N 108 49W
Landerneau **18** 48 28N 4 17W
Landeryd **49** 57 7N 13 15 E
Landes □ **20** 43 57N 0 48W
Landes, Les **20** 44 20N 1 0W
Landete **32** 39 56N 1 25W
Landi Kotal **66** 34 7N 71 6 E
Landivisiau **18** 48 31N 4 6W
Landquart **25** 46 58N 9 32 E
Landrecies **19** 50 7N 3 40 E
Land's End **13** 50 4N 5 43W
Landsberg **25** 48 3N 10 52 E
Landsborough Cr. → **98** 22 28 S 144 35 E
Landsbro **49** 57 24N 14 56 E
Landshut **25** 48 31N 12 10 E
Landskrona **49** 55 53N 12 50 E
Landstuhl **25** 49 25N 7 34 E
Landvetter **49** 57 41N 12 17 E
Lanesboro **113** 41 57N 75 34W
Lanett **115** 33 0N 85 15W
Lang Bay **108** 49 45N 124 21W
Lang Shan **76** 41 0N 106 30 E
Lang Son **71** 21 52N 106 42 E
La'nga Co **67** 30 45N 81 15 E
Lángadhás **44** 40 46N 23 2 E
Langádhia **45** 37 43N 22 1 E
Långan → **48** 63 19N 14 44 E
Langara I. **108** 54 14N 133 1W
Langdon **116** 48 47N 98 24W
Langeac **20** 45 7N 3 29 E
Langeais **18** 47 20N 0 24 E
Langeb Baraka → **86** 17 28N 36 50 E
Langeberge, C. Prov., S. Afr. **92** 33 55 S 21 40 E
Langeberge, C. Prov., S. Afr. **92** 28 15 S 22 33 E
Langeland **49** 54 56N 10 48 E
Langen **25** 49 59N 8 40 E
Langenburg **109** 50 51N 101 43W
Langeness **24** 54 34N 8 35 E
Langenlois **26** 48 29N 15 40 E
Langeoog **24** 53 44N 7 33 E
Langeskov **49** 55 22N 10 35 E
Langesund **47** 59 0N 9 45 E
Länghem **49** 57 36N 13 14 E
Langhirano **38** 44 39N 10 16 E
Langholm **14** 55 9N 2 59W
Langjökull **50** 64 39N 20 12W
Langkawi, P. **71** 6 25N 99 45 E
Langkon **72** 6 30N 116 40 E
Langlade **107** 46 50N 56 20W
Langlois **118** 42 54N 124 26W
Langnau **25** 46 56N 7 47 E
Langogne **20** 44 43N 3 50 E
Langon **20** 44 33N 0 16W
Langøya **50** 68 45N 14 50 E
Langpran, Gunong **72** 1 0N 114 23 E
Langres **19** 47 52N 5 20 E
Langres, Plateau de **19** 47 45N 5 3 E
Langsa **72** 4 30N 97 57 E
Långsele **48** 63 12N 17 4 E
Långshyttan **48** 60 27N 16 2 E
Langtry **117** 29 50N 101 33W
Languedoc **20** 43 58N 4 0 E
Langxiangzhen **76** 39 43N 116 8 E
Langzhong **75** 31 38N 105 58 E
Lanigan **109** 51 51N 105 2W
Lankao **77** 34 48N 114 50 E
Lannemezan **20** 43 8N 0 23 E
Lannilis **18** 48 35N 4 32W
Lannion **18** 48 46N 3 29W
Lanouaille **20** 45 24N 1 9 E
Lansdale **113** 40 14N 75 18W
Lansdowne, Austral. **99** 31 48 S 152 30 E
Lansdowne, Can. **113** 44 24N 76 1W
Lansdowne House **106** 52 14N 87 53W
Lansford **113** 40 48N 75 55W
Lansing **114** 42 47N 84 40W
Lanslebourg **21** 45 17N 6 52 E
Lant, Pulau **72** 4 10 S 116 0 E
Lanus **124** 34 44 S 58 27W
Lanusei **40** 39 53N 9 31 E
Lanxi **77** 29 13N 119 28 E
Lanzarote **80** 29 0N 13 40W
Lanzhou **76** 36 1N 103 52 E
Lanzo Torinese **38** 45 16N 7 29 E
Lao → **41** 39 45N 15 45 E
Lao Cai **71** 22 30N 103 57 E
Laoag **73** 18 7N 120 34 E
Laoang **73** 12 32N 125 8 E
Laoha He → **76** 43 25N 120 35 E
Laois □ **15** 53 0N 7 20W
Laon **19** 49 33N 3 35 E
Laona **114** 45 32N 88 41W
Laos ■ **71** 17 45N 105 0 E
Lapa **125** 25 46 S 49 44W
Lapalisse **20** 46 15N 3 38 E
Laparan Cap **73** 6 0N 120 0 E
Lapeer **114** 43 3N 83 20W
Lapi □ **50** 67 0N 27 0 E
Lapland = Lappland **50** 68 7N 24 0 E
Laporte **113** 41 27N 76 30W
Lapovo **42** 44 10N 21 2 E
Lappland **50** 68 7N 24 0 E
Laprairie **113** 45 20N 73 30W
Laprida **124** 37 34 S 60 45W
Laptev Sea **59** 76 0N 125 0 E
Lapuş, Munţii **46** 47 20N 23 50 E
Lapush **118** 47 56N 124 33W
Lăpusul → **46** 47 25N 23 40 E
Łapy **28** 52 59N 22 52 E
Lār **65** 27 40N 54 14 E
Larabanga **84** 9 16N 1 56W
Laracha **30** 43 15N 8 35W
Larache **82** 35 10N 6 5W
Laragne-Monteglin **21** 44 18N 5 49 E
Laramie **116** 41 20N 105 38W
Laramie Mts. **116** 42 0N 105 30W
Laranjeiras do Sul **125** 25 23 S 52 23W
Larantuka **73** 8 21 S 122 55 E
Larap **73** 14 18N 122 39 E
Larat **73** 7 0 S 132 0 E
Lårdal **47** 59 25N 8 10 E
Larde **91** 16 28 S 39 43 E
Larder Lake **106** 48 5N 79 40W
Lárdhos, Ákra **45** 36 4N 28 10 E
Laredo, Spain **32** 43 26N 3 28W
Laredo, U.S.A. **117** 27 34N 99 29W
Laredo Sd. **108** 52 30N 128 53W
Largentière **21** 44 34N 4 18 E
Largs **14** 55 48N 4 51W
Lari **38** 43 34N 10 35 E
Lariang **73** 1 26 S 119 17 E
Larimore **116** 47 55N 97 35W
Larino **41** 41 48N 14 54 E
Lárisa **44** 39 49N 22 28 E
Lárisa □ **44** 39 39N 22 24 E
Larkana **68** 27 32N 68 18 E
Larkollen **47** 59 20N 10 41 E
Larnaca **64** 35 0N 33 35 E
Larne **15** 54 52N 5 50W
Larned **116** 38 15N 99 10W
Larrimah **96** 15 35 S 133 12 E
Larsen Ice Shelf **5** 67 0 S 62 0W
Larvik **47** 59 4N 10 0 E
Laryak **58** 61 15N 80 0 E
Larzac, Causse du **20** 44 0N 3 17 E
Las Animas **117** 38 8N 103 18W
Las Anod **63** 8 26N 47 19 E
Las Blancos **33** 37 38N 0 49W
Las Brenãs **124** 27 5 S 61 7W
Las Cabezas de San Juan **31** 37 0N 5 58W
Las Cascadas **120** 9 5N 79 41W
Las Cruces **119** 32 18N 106 50W
Las Flores **124** 36 10 S 59 7W
Las Heras **124** 32 51 S 68 49W
Las Khoreh **63** 11 10N 48 20 E
Las Lajas **128** 38 30 S 70 25W
Las Lomitas **124** 24 43 S 60 35W
Las Marismas **31** 37 5N 6 20W
Las Navas de la Concepción **31** 37 56N 5 30W
Las Navas de Tolosa **31** 38 18N 3 38W
Las Palmas, Argent. **124** 27 8 S 58 45W
Las Palmas, Canary Is. **80** 28 7N 15 26W
Las Palmas □ **80** 28 10N 15 28W
Las Piedras **125** 34 44 S 56 14W
Las Pipinas **124** 35 30 S 57 19W
Las Plumas **128** 43 40 S 67 15W
Las Rosas **124** 32 30 S 61 35W
Las Tablas **121** 7 49N 80 14W
Las Termas **124** 27 29 S 64 52W
Las Varillas **124** 31 50 S 62 50W
Las Vegas, N. Mex., U.S.A. **119** 35 35N 105 10W
Las Vegas, Nev., U.S.A. **119** 36 10N 115 5W
Lascano **125** 33 35 S 54 12W
Lascaux **20** 45 5N 1 10 E
Lashburn **109** 53 10N 109 40W
Lashio **67** 22 56N 97 45 E
Lashkar **68** 26 10N 78 10 E
Łasin **28** 53 30N 19 2 E
Lasíthi □ **45** 35 5N 25 50 E
Lask **28** 51 34N 19 8 E
Łaskarzew **28** 51 48N 21 36 E
Laško **39** 46 10N 15 16 E
Lassay **18** 48 27N 0 30W
Lassen Pk. **118** 40 29N 121 31W
Last Mountain L. **109** 51 5N 105 14W
Lastoursville **88** 0 55 S 12 38 E
Lastovo **39** 42 46N 16 55 E
Lastovski Kanal **39** 42 50N 17 0 E
Latacunga **126** 0 50 S 78 35W
Latakia = Al Lādhiqīyah **64** 35 30N 35 45 E
Latchford **106** 47 20N 79 50W
Laterza **41** 40 38N 16 47 E
Lathen **24** 52 51N 7 21 E
Latiano **41** 40 33N 17 43 E
Latina **40** 41 26N 12 53 E
Latisana **39** 45 47N 13 1 E
Latium = Lazio **39** 42 10N 12 30 E
Latorica → **27** 48 28N 21 50 E
Latouche Treville, C. **96** 18 27 S 121 49 E
Latrobe **112** 40 19N 79 21W
Latrónico **41** 40 5N 16 0 E
Latrun **62** 31 50N 34 58 E
Latur **70** 18 25N 76 40 E
Latvian S.S.R. □ **54** 56 50N 24 0 E
Lau (Eastern) Group **101** 17 0 S 178 30W
Lauchhammer **24** 51 35N 13 48 E
Laudal **47** 58 15N 7 30 E
Lauenburg **24** 53 23N 10 33 E
Lauffen **25** 49 4N 9 9 E
Laugarbakki **50** 65 20N 20 55W
Laujar **33** 37 0N 2 54W
Launceston, Austral. **97** 41 24 S 147 8 E
Launceston, U.K. **13** 50 38N 4 21W
Laune → **15** 52 5N 9 40W
Launglon Bok **71** 13 50N 97 54 E
Laupheim **25** 48 13N 9 53 E
Laura **97** 15 32 S 144 32 E
Laureana di Borrello **41** 38 28N 16 5 E
Laurel, Miss., U.S.A. **117** 31 41N 89 9W
Laurel, Mont., U.S.A. **118** 45 46N 108 49W
Laurencekirk **14** 56 50N 2 30W
Laurens **115** 34 32N 82 2W
Laurentian Plat. **107** 52 0N 70 0W
Laurentides, Parc Prov. des **107** 47 45N 71 15W
Lauria **41** 40 3N 15 50 E
Laurie I. **5** 60 44 S 44 37W
Laurie L. **109** 56 35N 101 57W
Laurinburg **115** 34 50N 79 25W
Laurium **114** 47 14N 88 26W
Lausanne **25** 46 32N 6 38 E
Laut, Kepulauan **72** 4 45N 108 0 E
Laut Ketil, Kepulauan **72** 4 45 S 115 40 E
Lauterbach **24** 50 39N 9 23 E
Lauterecken **25** 49 38N 7 35 E
Lautoka **101** 17 37 S 177 27 E
Lauzon **107** 46 48N 71 10W
Lava Hot Springs **118** 42 38N 112 1W
Lavadores **30** 42 14N 8 41W
Lavagna **38** 44 18N 9 22 E
Laval **18** 48 4N 0 48W
Lavalle **124** 28 15 S 65 15W
Lavandou, Le **21** 43 8N 6 22 E
Lávara **44** 41 19N 26 22 E
Lavardac **20** 44 12N 0 20 E
Lavaur **20** 43 30N 1 49 E
Lavaveix **20** 46 5N 2 8 E
Lavelanet **20** 42 57N 1 51 E
Lavello **41** 41 4N 15 47 E
Laverendrye Prov. Park **106** 46 15N 17 15W
Laverne **117** 36 43N 99 58W
Laverton **96** 28 44 S 122 29 E
Lavi **62** 32 47N 35 25 E
Lavik **47** 61 6N 5 25 E
Lávkos **45** 39 9N 23 14 E
Lavos **30** 40 6N 8 49W
Lavras **125** 21 20 S 45 0W
Lavre **31** 38 46N 8 22W
Lavrentiya **59** 65 35N 171 0W
Lávrion **45** 37 40N 24 4 E
Lavumisa **93** 27 20 S 31 55 E
Lawas **72** 4 55N 115 25 E
Lawele **73** 5 16 S 123 3 E
Lawn Hill **98** 18 36 S 138 33 E
Lawng Pit **67** 25 30N 97 25 E
Lawra **84** 10 39N 2 51W
Lawrence, Kans., U.S.A. **116** 39 0N 95 10W
Lawrence, Mass., U.S.A. **114** 42 40N 71 9W
Lawrenceburg, Ind., U.S.A. **114** 39 5N 84 50W
Lawrenceburg, Tenn., U.S.A. **115** 35 12N 87 19W
Lawrenceville **115** 33 55N 83 59W
Lawton **117** 34 33N 98 25W
Lawu **73** 7 40 S 111 13 E
Laxford, L. **14** 58 25N 5 10W
Laxmeshwar **70** 15 9N 75 28 E
Laylá **64** 22 10N 46 40 E
Layon → **18** 47 20N 0 45W
Laysan I. **95** 25 30N 167 0W
Laytonville **118** 39 44N 123 29W
Lazarevac **42** 44 23N 20 17 E
Lazio □ **39** 42 10N 12 30 E
Łazy **28** 50 27N 19 24 E
Lea → **13** 51 30N 0 10W
Lead **116** 44 20N 103 40W
Leader **109** 50 50N 109 30W
Leadhills **14** 55 25N 3 47W
Leadville **119** 39 17N 106 23W
Leaf → **117** 31 0N 88 45W
Leakey **117** 29 45N 99 45W
Leamington, Can. **106** 42 3N 82 36W
Leamington, U.K. **13** 52 18N 1 32W
Leamington, U.S.A. **118** 39 37N 112 17W
Leandro Norte Alem **125** 27 34 S 55 15W
Learmonth **96** 22 13 S 114 10 E
Leask **109** 53 5N 106 45W
Leavenworth, Mo., U.S.A. **116** 39 25N 95 0W
Leavenworth, Wash., U.S.A. **118** 47 44N 120 37W
Łeba **28** 54 45N 17 32 E
Łeba → **28** 54 46N 17 33 E
Lebak **73** 6 32N 124 5 E
Lebane **42** 42 56N 21 44 E
Lebanon, Ind., U.S.A. **114** 40 3N 86 28W
Lebanon, Kans., U.S.A. **116** 39 50N 98 35W
Lebanon, Ky., U.S.A. **114** 37 35N 85 15W
Lebanon, Mo., U.S.A. **117** 37 40N 92 40W
Lebanon, Oreg., U.S.A. **118** 44 31N 122 57W
Lebanon, Pa., U.S.A. **114** 40 20N 76 28W
Lebanon, Tenn., U.S.A. **115** 36 15N 86 20W
Lebanon ■ **64** 34 0N 36 0 E
Lebec **119** 34 50N 118 59W
Lebedin **54** 50 35N 34 30 E
Lebedyan **55** 53 0N 39 10 E
Lebombo-berge **93** 24 30 S 32 0 E
Lębork **28** 54 33N 17 46 E
Lebrija **31** 36 53N 6 5W
Łebsko, Jezioro **28** 54 40N 17 25 E
Lebu **124** 37 40 S 73 47W
Lecce **41** 40 20N 18 10 E
Lecco **38** 45 50N 9 27 E
Lecco, L. di. **38** 45 51N 9 22 E
Lécera **32** 41 13N 0 43W
Lech **26** 47 13N 10 9 E
Lech → **25** 48 44N 10 56 E
Lechang **77** 25 10N 113 20 E
Lechtaler Alpen **26** 47 15N 10 30 E
Lectoure **20** 43 56N 0 38 E
Łeczna **28** 51 18N 22 53 E
Łeczyca **28** 52 5N 19 15 E
Ledbury **13** 52 3N 2 25W
Ledeč **26** 49 41N 15 18 E
Ledesma **30** 41 6N 5 59W
Ledong **77** 18 41N 109 5 E
Leduc **108** 53 15N 113 30W
Ledyczek **28** 53 33N 16 59 E
Lee, Mass., U.S.A. **113** 42 17N 73 18W
Lee, Nev., U.S.A. **118** 40 35N 115 36W
Lee → **15** 51 50N 8 30W
Leech L. **116** 47 9N 94 23W
Leedey **117** 35 53N 99 24W
Leeds, U.K. **12** 53 48N 1 34W
Leeds, U.S.A. **115** 33 32N 86 30W
Leek **12** 53 7N 2 2W
Leer **24** 53 13N 7 29 E
Leesburg **115** 28 47N 81 52W
Leesville **117** 31 12N 93 15W
Leeton **97** 34 33 S 146 23 E
Leetonia **112** 40 53N 80 45W
Leeuwarden **16** 53 15N 5 48 E
Leeuwin, C. **96** 34 20 S 115 9 E
Leeward Is., Atl. Oc. **121** 16 30N 63 30W
Leeward Is., Pac. Oc. **95** 16 0 S 147 0W
Lefors **117** 35 30N 100 50W
Lefroy, L. **96** 31 21 S 121 40 E
Łeg → **28** 50 42N 21 50 E
Legal **108** 53 55N 113 35W
Legazpi **73** 13 10N 123 45 E
Leghorn = Livorno **38** 43 32N 10 18 E
Legion **91** 21 25 S 28 30 E
Legionowo **28** 52 25N 20 50 E
Legnago **39** 45 10N 11 19 E
Legnano **38** 45 35N 8 55 E
Legnica **28** 51 12N 16 10 E
Legnica □ **28** 51 30N 16 0 E
Legrad **39** 46 17N 16 51 E
Legume **99** 28 20 S 152 19 E
Leh **69** 34 9N 77 35 E
Lehi **118** 40 20N 111 51W
Lehighton **113** 40 50N 75 44W
Lehliu **46** 44 29N 26 20 E
Lehrte **24** 52 22N 9 58 E
Lehututu **92** 23 54 S 21 55 E
Leiah **68** 30 58N 70 58 E
Leibnitz **26** 46 47N 15 34 E
Leicester **13** 52 39N 1 9W
Leicester □ **13** 52 40N 1 10W
Leichhardt → **97** 17 35 S 139 48 E
Leichhardt Ra. **98** 20 46 S 147 40 E
Leiden **16** 52 9N 4 30 E
Leie → **16** 51 2N 3 45 E
Leigh Creek **97** 30 28 S 138 24 E
Leikanger **47** 61 10N 6 52 E
Leine → **24** 52 20N 9 50 E
Leinster □ **15** 53 0N 7 10W
Leinster, Mt. **15** 52 38N 6 47W
Leipzig **24** 51 20N 12 23 E
Leipzig □ **24** 51 20N 12 30 E
Leiria **31** 39 46N 8 53W
Leiria □ **31** 39 46N 8 53W
Leith **14** 55 59N 3 10W
Leith Hill **13** 51 10N 0 23W
Leitha → **27** 48 0N 16 35 E
Leitrim **15** 54 0N 8 5W
Leitrim □ **15** 54 8N 8 0W
Leiyang **77** 26 27N 112 45 E
Leiza **32** 43 5N 1 55W
Leizhou Bandao **77** 21 0N 110 0 E
Leizhou Wan **77** 20 50N 110 20 E
Lek → **16** 52 0N 6 0 E
Lekáni **44** 41 10N 24 35 E
Lekhainá **45** 37 57N 21 16 E
Leksula **73** 3 46 S 126 31 E
Leland **117** 33 25N 90 52W
Leland Lakes **109** 60 0N 110 59W
Leleque **128** 42 28 S 71 0W
Lelystad **16** 52 30N 5 25 E
Lema **85** 12 58N 4 13 E
Léman, Lac **25** 46 26N 6 30 E
Lemera **90** 3 0 S 28 55 E
Lemery **73** 13 51N 120 56 E
Lemgo **24** 52 2N 8 52 E
Lemhi Ra. **118** 44 30N 113 30W
Lemmer **16** 52 51N 5 43 E
Lemmon **116** 45 59N 102 10W
Lemoore **119** 36 23N 119 46W
Lempdes **20** 45 22N 3 17 E
Lemvig **49** 56 33N 8 20 E
Lena → **59** 72 52N 126 40 E
Lenartovce **27** 48 18N 20 19 E
Lencloître **18** 46 50N 0 20 E
Lendinara **39** 45 4N 11 37 E
Lengau de Vaca, Pta. **124** 30 14 S 71 38W
Lengerich **24** 52 12N 7 50 E
Lenggong **71** 5 6N 100 58 E
Lenggries **25** 47 41N 11 34 E
Lengyeltóti **27** 46 40N 17 40 E
Lenhovda **49** 57 0N 15 16 E
Lenin **57** 48 20N 40 56 E
Leninabad **58** 40 17N 69 37 E
Leninakan **57** 40 47N 43 50 E
Leningrad **54** 59 55N 30 20 E
Lenino **56** 45 17N 35 46 E
Leninogorsk **58** 50 20N 83 30 E
Leninsk, R.S.F.S.R., U.S.S.R. **57** 48 40N 45 15 E
Leninsk, R.S.F.S.R., U.S.S.R. **57** 46 10N 43 46 E
Leninsk-Kuznetskiy **58** 54 44N 86 10 E
Leninskaya Sloboda **55** 56 7N 44 29 E
Leninskoye, R.S.F.S.R., U.S.S.R. **55** 58 23N 47 3 E
Leninskoye, R.S.F.S.R., U.S.S.R. **59** 47 56N 132 38 E
Lenk **25** 46 27N 7 28 E
Lenkoran **53** 39 45N 48 50 E
Lenmalu **73** 1 45 S 130 15 E
Lenne → **24** 51 25N 7 30 E
Lennoxville **113** 45 22N 71 51W
Leno **38** 45 24N 10 14 E
Lenoir **115** 35 55N 81 36W
Lenoir City **115** 35 40N 84 20W
Lenora **116** 39 39N 100 1W

Lenore L. Liteni

Lenore L.	**109**	52 30N	104 59W
Lenox	**113**	42 20N	73 18W
Lens	**19**	50 26N	2 50 E
Lensk (Mukhtuya)	**59**	60 48N	114 55 E
Lenskoye	**56**	45 3N	34 1 E
Lenti	**27**	46 37N	16 33 E
Lentini	**41**	37 18N	15 0 E
Lentvaric	**54**	54 39N	25 3 E
Lenzen	**24**	53 6N	11 26 E
Léo	**84**	11 3N	2 2W
Leoben	**26**	47 22N	15 5 E
Leola	**116**	45 47N	98 58W
Leominster, U.K.	**13**	52 15N	2 43W
Leominster, U.S.A.	**114**	42 32N	71 45W
Léon	**20**	43 53N	1 18W
León, Mexico	**120**	21 7N	101 30W
León, Nic.	**121**	12 20N	86 51W
León, Spain	**30**	42 38N	5 34W
Leon	**116**	40 40N	93 40W
León □	**30**	42 40N	5 55W
León, Montañas de	**30**	42 30N	6 18W
Leonardtown	**114**	38 19N	76 39W
Leonforte	**41**	37 39N	14 22 E
Leongatha	**99**	38 30 S	145 58 E
Leonidhion	**45**	37 9N	22 52 E
Leonora	**96**	28 49 S	121 19 E
Léopold II, Lac = Mai-Ndombe	**88**	2 0 S	18 20 E
Leopoldina	**125**	21 28 S	42 40W
Leopoldsburg	**16**	51 7N	5 13 E
Léopoldville = Kinshasa	**88**	4 20 S	15 15 E
Leoti	**116**	38 31N	101 19W
Leoville	**109**	53 39N	107 33W
Lépa, L. do	**92**	17 0 S	19 0 E
Lepe	**31**	37 15N	7 12W
Lepel	**54**	54 50N	28 40 E
Lepikha	**59**	64 45N	125 55 E
Leping	**77**	28 47N	117 7 E
Lepontino, Alpi	**38**	46 22N	8 27 E
Lepsény	**27**	47 0N	18 15 E
Leptis Magna	**83**	32 40N	14 12 E
Lequeitio	**32**	43 20N	2 32W
Lercara Friddi	**40**	37 42N	13 36 E
Léré	**81**	9 39N	14 13 E
Lere	**85**	9 43N	9 18 E
Leribe	**93**	28 51 S	28 3 E
Lérici	**38**	44 4N	9 58 E
Lérida	**32**	41 37N	0 39 E
Lérida □	**32**	42 6N	1 0 E
Lérins, Is. de	**21**	43 31N	7 3 E
Lerma	**30**	42 0N	3 47W
Léros	**45**	37 10N	26 50 E
Lérouville	**19**	48 50N	5 30 E
Lerwick	**14**	60 10N	1 10W
Les	**46**	46 58N	21 50 E
Lesbos, I. = Lésvos	**45**	39 10N	26 20 E
Leshukonskoye	**52**	64 54N	45 46 E
Lésina, L. di	**39**	41 53N	15 25 E
Lesja	**47**	62 7N	8 51 E
Lesjaverk	**47**	62 12N	8 34 E
Lesko	**27**	49 30N	22 23 E
Leskov I.	**5**	56 0 S	28 0W
Leskovac	**42**	43 0N	21 58 E
Leskoviku	**44**	40 10N	20 34 E
Leslie	**117**	35 50N	92 35W
Lesna	**28**	51 0N	15 15 E
Lesneven	**18**	48 35N	4 20W
Lešnica	**42**	44 39N	19 20 E
Lesnoye	**54**	58 15N	35 18 E
Lesotho ■	**93**	29 40 S	28 0 E
Lesozavodsk	**59**	45 30N	133 29 E
Lesparre-Médoc	**20**	45 18N	0 57W
Lessay	**18**	49 14N	1 30W
Lesse →	**16**	50 15N	4 54 E
Lesser Antilles	**121**	15 0N	61 0W
Lesser Slave L.	**108**	55 30N	115 25W
Lessines	**16**	50 42N	3 50 E
Lestock	**109**	51 19N	103 59W
Lésvos	**45**	39 10N	26 20 E
Leszno	**28**	51 50N	16 30 E
Leszno □	**28**	51 45N	16 30 E
Letchworth	**13**	51 58N	0 13W
Letea, Ostrov	**46**	45 18N	29 20 E
Lethbridge	**108**	49 45N	112 45W
Leti	**73**	8 10 S	127 40 E
Leti, Kepulauan	**73**	8 10 S	128 0 E
Letiahau →	**92**	21 16 S	24 0 E
Leticia	**126**	4 9 S	70 0W
Leting	**76**	39 23N	118 55 E
Letlhakeng	**92**	24 0 S	24 59 E
Letpadan	**67**	17 45N	95 45 E
Letpan	**67**	19 28N	94 10 E
Letsôk-aw Kyun (Domel I.)	**71**	11 30N	98 25 E
Letterkenny	**15**	54 57N	7 42W
Leu	**46**	44 10N	24 0 E
Leucate	**20**	42 56N	3 3 E
Leucate, Étang de	**20**	42 50N	3 0 E
Leuk	**25**	46 19N	7 37 E
Leuser, G.	**72**	3 46N	97 12 E
Leutkirch	**25**	47 49N	10 1 E
Leuven (Louvain)	**16**	50 52N	4 42 E
Leuze, Hainaut, Belg.	**16**	50 36N	3 37 E
Leuze, Namur, Belg.	**16**	50 33N	4 54 E
Lev Tolstoy	**55**	53 13N	39 29 E
Levádhia	**45**	38 27N	22 54 E
Levan	**118**	39 37N	111 52W
Levanger	**47**	63 45N	11 19 E
Levani	**44**	40 40N	19 28 E
Levant, I. du	**21**	43 3N	6 28 E
Lévanto	**38**	44 10N	9 37 E
Levanzo	**40**	38 0N	12 19 E
Levelland	**117**	33 38N	102 23W
Leven	**14**	56 12N	3 0W
Leven, L.	**14**	56 12N	3 22W
Leven, Toraka	**93**	12 30 S	47 45 E
Levens	**21**	43 50N	7 12 E
Leveque C.	**96**	16 20 S	123 0 E
Leverano	**41**	40 16N	18 0 E
Leverkusen	**24**	51 2N	6 59 E
Levet	**19**	46 56N	2 22 E
Levice	**27**	48 13N	18 35 E
Levick, Mt.	**5**	75 0 S	164 0 E
Levico	**39**	46 0N	11 18 E
Levie	**21**	41 40N	9 7 E
Levier	**19**	46 58N	6 8 E
Levin	**101**	40 37 S	175 18 E
Lévis	**107**	46 48N	71 9W
Levis, L.	**108**	62 37N	117 58W
Levitha	**45**	37 0N	26 28 E
Levittown, N.Y., U.S.A.	**113**	40 41N	73 31W
Levittown, Pa., U.S.A.	**113**	40 10N	74 51W
Levka	**43**	41 52N	26 15 E
Lévka	**45**	35 18N	24 3 E
Levkás	**45**	38 40N	20 43 E
Levkímmi	**44**	39 25N	20 3 E
Levkôsia = Nicosia	**64**	35 10N	33 25 E
Levoča	**27**	49 2N	20 35 E
Levroux	**19**	47 0N	1 38 E
Levski	**43**	43 21N	25 10 E
Levskigrad	**43**	42 38N	24 47 E
Lewellen	**116**	41 22N	102 5W
Lewes, U.K.	**13**	50 53N	0 2 E
Lewes, U.S.A.	**114**	38 45N	75 8W
Lewin Brzeski	**28**	50 45N	17 37 E
Lewis	**14**	58 10N	6 40W
Lewis, Butt of	**14**	58 30N	6 12W
Lewis Ra.	**118**	48 0N	113 15W
Lewisburg, Pa., U.S.A.	**112**	40 57N	76 57W
Lewisburg, Tenn., U.S.A.	**115**	35 29N	86 46W
Lewisporte	**107**	49 15N	55 3W
Lewiston, Idaho, U.S.A.	**118**	46 25N	117 0W
Lewiston, Utah, U.S.A.	**118**	41 58N	111 56W
Lewistown, Mont., U.S.A.	**118**	47 0N	109 25W
Lewistown, Pa., U.S.A.	**114**	40 37N	77 33W
Lexington, Ill., U.S.A.	**116**	40 37N	88 47W
Lexington, Ky., U.S.A.	**114**	38 6N	84 30W
Lexington, Miss., U.S.A.	**117**	33 8N	90 2W
Lexington, Mo., U.S.A.	**116**	39 7N	93 55W
Lexington, N.C., U.S.A.	**115**	35 50N	80 13W
Lexington, Nebr., U.S.A.	**116**	40 48N	99 45W
Lexington, Ohio, U.S.A.	**112**	40 39N	82 35W
Lexington, Oreg., U.S.A.	**118**	45 29N	119 46W
Lexington, Tenn., U.S.A.	**115**	35 38N	88 25W
Lexington Park	**114**	38 16N	76 27W
Leyre →	**20**	44 39N	1 1W
Leyte	**73**	11 0N	125 0 E
Lezajsk	**28**	50 16N	22 25 E
Lezay	**20**	46 17N	0 0 E
Lezha	**44**	41 47N	19 42 E
Lézignan-Corbières	**20**	43 13N	2 43 E
Lezoux	**20**	45 49N	3 21 E
Lgov	**54**	51 42N	35 16 E
Lhasa	**75**	29 25N	90 58 E
Lhazê	**75**	29 5N	87 38 E
Lhokseumawe	**72**	5 10N	97 10 E
Lhuntsi Dzong	**67**	27 39N	91 10 E
Li Shui →	**77**	29 24N	112 1 E
Li Xian, Gansu, China	**77**	34 10N	105 5 E
Li Xian, Hunan, China	**77**	29 36N	111 42 E
Liádhoi	**45**	36 50N	26 11 E
Lianga	**73**	8 38N	126 6 E
Liangdang	**77**	33 56N	106 18 E
Lianhua	**77**	27 3N	113 54 E
Lianjiang	**77**	26 12N	119 27 E
Lianping	**77**	24 26N	114 30 E
Lianshanguan	**76**	40 53N	123 43 E
Lianyungang	**77**	34 40N	119 11 E
Liao He →	**76**	41 0N	121 50 E
Liaocheng	**76**	36 28N	115 58 E
Liaodong Bandao	**76**	40 0N	122 30 E
Liaodong Wan	**76**	40 20N	121 10 E
Liaoning □	**76**	42 0N	122 0 E
Liaoyang	**76**	41 15N	122 58 E
Liaoyuan	**76**	42 58N	125 2 E
Liaozhong	**76**	41 23N	122 50 E
Liapádhes	**44**	39 42N	19 40 E
Liard →	**108**	61 51N	121 18W
Libau = Liepaja	**54**	56 30N	21 0 E
Libby	**118**	48 20N	115 33W
Libenge	**88**	3 40N	18 55 E
Liberal, Kans., U.S.A.	**117**	37 4N	101 0W
Liberal, Mo., U.S.A.	**117**	37 35N	94 30W
Liberec	**26**	50 47N	15 7 E
Liberia	**121**	10 40N	85 30W
Liberia ■	**84**	6 30N	9 30W
Liberty, Mo., U.S.A.	**116**	39 15N	94 24W
Liberty, Tex., U.S.A.	**117**	30 5N	94 50W
Libiaz	**27**	50 7N	19 21 E
Libo	**77**	25 22N	107 53 E
Libobo, Tanjung	**73**	0 54 S	128 28 E
Libohava	**44**	40 3N	20 10 E
Libonda	**89**	14 28 S	23 12 E
Libourne	**20**	44 55N	0 14W
Libramont	**16**	49 55N	5 23 E
Librazhdi	**44**	41 12N	20 22 E
Libreville	**88**	0 25N	9 26 E
Libya ■	**81**	27 0N	17 0 E
Libyan Plateau = Ed-Déffa	**86**	30 40N	26 30 E
Licantén	**124**	35 55 S	72 0W
Licata	**40**	37 6N	13 55 E
Lichfield	**12**	52 40N	1 50W
Lichinga	**91**	13 13 S	35 11 E
Lichtenburg	**92**	26 8 S	26 8 E
Lichtenfels	**25**	50 7N	11 4 E
Lichuan	**77**	30 18N	108 57 E
Licosa, Punta	**41**	40 15N	14 53 E
Lida, U.S.A.	**119**	37 30N	117 30W
Lida, U.S.S.R.	**54**	53 53N	25 15 E
Lidhult	**49**	56 50N	13 27 E
Lidingö	**48**	59 22N	18 8 E
Lidköping	**49**	58 31N	13 14 E
Lido, Italy	**39**	45 25N	12 23 E
Lido, Niger	**85**	12 54N	3 44 E
Lido di Ostia	**40**	41 44N	12 14 E
Lidzbark	**28**	53 15N	19 49 E
Lidzbark Warminski	**28**	54 7N	20 34 E
Liebenwalde	**24**	52 51N	13 23 E
Lieberose	**24**	51 59N	14 18 E
Liebling	**42**	45 36N	21 20 E
Liechtenstein ■	**25**	47 8N	9 35 E
Liège	**16**	50 38N	5 35 E
Liège □	**16**	50 32N	5 35 E
Liegnitz = Legnica	**28**	51 12N	16 10 E
Lienart	**90**	3 3N	25 31 E
Lienyünchiangshih = Lianyungang	**77**	34 40N	119 11 E
Lienz	**26**	46 50N	12 46 E
Liepaja	**54**	56 30N	21 0 E
Lier	**16**	51 7N	4 34 E
Liesta	**46**	45 38N	27 34 E
Liévin	**19**	50 24N	2 47 E
Lièvre →	**106**	45 31N	75 26W
Liezen	**26**	47 34N	14 15 E
Liffey →	**15**	53 21N	6 20W
Lifford	**15**	54 50N	7 30W
Liffré	**18**	48 12N	1 30W
Lifjell	**47**	59 27N	8 45 E
Lightning Ridge	**99**	29 22 S	148 0 E
Lignano	**39**	45 42N	13 8 E
Ligny-en-Barrois	**19**	48 36N	5 20 E
Ligny-le-Châtel	**19**	47 54N	3 45 E
Ligoúrion	**45**	37 37N	23 2 E
Ligua, La	**124**	32 30 S	71 16W
Ligueil	**18**	47 2N	0 49 E
Liguria □	**38**	44 30N	9 0 E
Ligurian Sea	**38**	43 20N	9 0 E
Lihir Group	**98**	3 0 S	152 35 E
Lihou Reefs and Cays	**97**	17 25 S	151 40 E
Lihue	**110**	21 59N	159 24W
Lijiang	**75**	26 55N	100 20 E
Likasi	**91**	10 55 S	26 48 E
Likati	**88**	3 20N	24 0 E
Likhoslavl	**54**	57 12N	35 30 E
Likhovski	**57**	48 10N	40 10 E
Likoma I.	**91**	12 3 S	34 45 E
Likumburu	**91**	9 43 S	35 8 E
Liling	**77**	27 42N	113 29 E
Lille	**19**	50 38N	3 3 E
Lille Bælt	**49**	55 20N	9 45 E
Lillebonne	**18**	49 30N	0 32 E
Lillehammer	**47**	61 8N	10 30 E
Lillers	**19**	50 35N	2 28 E
Lillesand	**47**	58 15N	8 23 E
Lilleshall	**13**	52 45N	2 22W
Lillestrøm	**47**	59 58N	11 5 E
Lillo	**32**	39 45N	3 20W
Lillooet →	**108**	49 15N	121 57W
Lilongwe	**91**	14 0 S	33 48 E
Liloy	**73**	8 4N	122 39 E
Lim →	**42**	43 0N	19 40 E
Lima, Indon.	**73**	3 37 S	128 4 E
Lima, Peru	**126**	12 0 S	77 0W
Lima, Sweden	**48**	60 55N	13 20 E
Lima, Mont., U.S.A.	**118**	44 41N	112 38W
Lima, Ohio, U.S.A.	**114**	40 42N	84 5W
Lima →	**30**	41 41N	8 50W
Limages	**113**	45 20N	75 16W
Liman	**57**	45 45N	47 12 E
Limanowa	**27**	49 42N	20 22 E
Limassol	**64**	34 42N	33 1 E
Limavady	**15**	55 3N	6 58W
Limavady □	**15**	55 0N	6 55W
Limay →	**128**	39 0 S	68 0W
Limay Mahuida	**124**	37 10 S	66 45W
Limbang	**72**	4 42N	115 6 E
Limbara, Monti	**40**	40 50N	9 10 E
Limbdi	**68**	22 34N	71 51 E
Limbri	**99**	31 3 S	151 5 E
Limburg	**25**	50 22N	8 4 E
Limburg □, Belg.	**16**	51 2N	5 25 E
Limburg □, Neth.	**16**	51 20N	5 55 E
Limedsforsen	**48**	60 52N	13 25 E
Limeira	**125**	22 35 S	47 28W
Limenária	**44**	40 38N	24 32 E
Limerick	**15**	52 40N	8 38W
Limerick □	**15**	52 30N	8 50W
Limestone	**112**	42 2N	78 39W
Limestone →	**109**	56 31N	94 7W
Limfjorden	**49**	56 55N	9 0 E
Limia →	**30**	41 41N	8 50W
Limmared	**49**	57 34N	13 20 E
Limmen Bight	**96**	14 40 S	135 35 E
Límni	**45**	38 43N	23 18 E
Límnos	**44**	39 50N	25 5 E
Limoeiro do Norte	**127**	5 5 S	38 0W
Limoges	**20**	45 50N	1 15 E
Limón	**121**	10 0N	83 2W
Limon, Panama	**120**	9 17N	79 45W
Limon, U.S.A.	**116**	39 18N	103 38W
Limon B.	**120**	9 22N	79 56W
Limone Piemonte	**38**	44 12N	7 32 E
Limousin	**20**	46 0N	1 0 E
Limousin, Plateaux du	**20**	46 0N	1 0 E
Limoux	**20**	43 4N	2 12 E
Limpopo →	**93**	25 15 S	33 30 E
Limuru	**90**	1 2 S	36 35 E
Linares, Chile	**124**	35 50 S	71 40W
Linares, Mexico	**120**	24 50N	99 40W
Linares, Spain	**33**	38 10N	3 40W
Linares □	**124**	36 0 S	71 0W
Línas Mte.	**40**	39 25N	8 38 E
Lincheng	**76**	37 25N	114 30 E
Linchuan	**75**	27 57N	116 15 E
Lincoln, Argent.	**124**	34 55 S	61 30W
Lincoln, N.Z.	**101**	43 38 S	172 30 E
Lincoln, U.K.	**12**	53 14N	0 32W
Lincoln, Ill., U.S.A.	**116**	40 10N	89 20W
Lincoln, Kans., U.S.A.	**116**	39 6N	98 9W
Lincoln, Maine, U.S.A.	**107**	45 27N	68 29W
Lincoln, N. Mex., U.S.A.	**119**	33 30N	105 26W
Lincoln, N.H., U.S.A.	**113**	44 3N	71 40W
Lincoln, Nebr., U.S.A.	**116**	40 50N	96 42W
Lincoln □	**12**	53 14N	0 32W
Lincoln Sea	**4**	84 0N	55 0W
Lincoln Wolds	**12**	53 20N	0 5W
Lincolnton	**115**	35 30N	81 15W
Lind	**118**	47 0N	118 33W
Lindås, Norway	**47**	60 44N	5 9 E
Lindås, Sweden	**49**	56 38N	15 35 E
Lindau	**25**	47 33N	9 41 E
Linden, Guyana	**126**	6 0N	58 10W
Linden, U.S.A.	**117**	33 0N	94 20W
Linderöd	**49**	55 56N	13 47 E
Linderödsåsen	**49**	55 53N	13 53 E
Lindesberg	**48**	59 36N	15 15 E
Lindesnes	**47**	57 58N	7 3 E
Lindi	**91**	9 58 S	39 38 E
Lindi □	**91**	9 40 S	38 30 E
Lindi →	**90**	0 33N	25 5 E
Lindian	**76**	47 11N	124 52 E
Lindoso	**30**	41 52N	8 11W
Lindow	**24**	52 58N	12 58 E
Lindsay, Can.	**106**	44 22N	78 43W
Lindsay, Calif., U.S.A.	**119**	36 14N	119 6W
Lindsay, Okla., U.S.A.	**117**	34 51N	97 37W
Lindsborg	**116**	38 35N	97 40W
Línea de la Concepción, La	**31**	36 15N	5 23W
Linfen	**76**	36 3N	111 30 E
Ling Xian	**76**	37 22N	116 30 E
Lingao	**77**	19 56N	109 42 E
Lingayen	**73**	16 1N	120 14 E
Lingayen G.	**73**	16 10N	120 15 E
Lingchuan	**77**	25 26N	110 21 E
Lingen	**24**	52 32N	7 21 E
Lingga	**72**	0 12 S	104 37 E
Lingga, Kepulauan	**72**	0 10 S	104 30 E
Linghed	**48**	60 48N	15 55 E
Lingle	**116**	42 10N	104 18W
Lingling	**77**	26 17N	111 37 E
Lingshan	**77**	22 25N	109 18 E
Lingshi	**76**	36 48N	111 48 E
Lingshui	**77**	18 27N	110 0 E
Lingtai	**77**	35 0N	107 40 E
Linguéré	**84**	15 25N	15 5W
Lingyuan	**76**	41 10N	119 15 E
Lingyun	**75**	25 2N	106 35 E
Linh Cam	**71**	18 31N	105 31 E
Linhai	**75**	28 50N	121 8 E
Linhe	**76**	40 48N	107 20 E
Linjiang	**76**	41 50N	127 0 E
Linköping	**49**	58 28N	15 36 E
Linkou	**76**	45 15N	130 18 E
Linlithgow	**14**	55 58N	3 38W
Linn, Mt.	**118**	40 0N	123 0W
Linnhe, L.	**14**	56 36N	5 25W
Linosa, I.	**83**	35 51N	12 50 E
Linqing	**76**	36 50N	115 42 E
Lins	**125**	21 40 S	49 44W
Lintao	**76**	35 18N	103 52 E
Linth →	**25**	47 7N	9 7W
Linthal	**25**	46 54N	9 0 E
Lintlaw	**109**	52 4N	103 14W
Linton, Can.	**107**	47 15N	72 16W
Linton, Ind., U.S.A.	**114**	39 0N	87 10W
Linton, N. Dak., U.S.A.	**116**	46 21N	100 12W
Linville	**99**	26 50 S	152 11 E
Linwood	**112**	43 35N	80 43W
Linwu	**77**	25 19N	112 31 E
Linxe	**20**	43 56N	1 13W
Linxi	**76**	43 36N	118 2 E
Linxia	**75**	35 36N	103 10 E
Linyanti →	**92**	17 50 S	25 5 E
Linyi	**77**	35 5N	118 21 E
Linz, Austria	**26**	48 18N	14 18 E
Linz, Ger.	**24**	50 33N	7 18 E
Lion-d'Angers, Le	**18**	47 37N	0 43W
Lion, G. du	**20**	43 0N	4 0 E
Lioni	**41**	40 52N	15 10 E
Lion's Den	**91**	17 15 S	30 5 E
Lion's Head	**106**	44 58N	81 15W
Liozno	**54**	55 0N	30 50 E
Lipali	**91**	15 50 S	35 50 E
Lípari	**41**	38 26N	14 58 E
Lípari, Is.	**41**	38 30N	14 50 E
Lipetsk	**55**	52 37N	39 35 E
Lipiany	**28**	53 2N	14 58 E
Liping	**77**	26 15N	109 7 E
Lipkany	**56**	48 14N	26 48 E
Lipljan	**42**	42 31N	21 7 E
Lipnik	**27**	49 32N	17 36 E
Lipno	**28**	52 49N	19 15 E
Lipova	**42**	46 8N	21 42 E
Lipovets	**56**	49 12N	29 1 E
Lippe →	**24**	51 39N	6 38 E
Lippstadt	**24**	51 40N	8 19 E
Lipscomb	**117**	36 16N	100 16W
Lipsko	**28**	51 9N	21 40 E
Lipsói	**45**	37 19N	26 50 E
Liptovsky Svaty Milkulaš	**27**	49 6N	19 35 E
Liptrap C.	**99**	38 50 S	145 55 E
Lira	**90**	2 17N	32 57 E
Liri →	**40**	41 25N	13 52 E
Liria	**32**	39 37N	0 35W
Lisala	**88**	2 12N	21 38 E
Lisboa	**31**	38 42N	9 10W
Lisboa □	**31**	39 0N	9 12W
Lisbon, N. Dak., U.S.A.	**116**	46 30N	97 46W
Lisbon, N.H., U.S.A.	**113**	44 13N	71 52W
Lisbon, Ohio, U.S.A.	**112**	40 45N	80 42W
Lisbon = Lisboa	**31**	38 42N	9 10W
Lisburn	**15**	54 30N	6 9W
Lisburne, C.	**104**	68 50N	166 0W
Liscannor, B.	**15**	52 57N	9 24W
Liscia →	**40**	41 11N	9 9 E
Lishi	**76**	37 31N	111 8 E
Lishui	**75**	28 28N	119 54 E
Lisianski I.	**94**	26 2N	174 0W
Lisichansk	**56**	48 55N	38 30 E
Lisieux	**18**	49 10N	0 12 E
Lisle-sur-Tarn	**20**	43 52N	1 49 E
Lismore, Austral.	**97**	28 44 S	153 21 E
Lismore, Ireland	**15**	52 8N	7 58W
Lisse	**16**	52 16N	4 33 E
List	**24**	55 1N	8 26 E
Lista	**47**	58 7N	6 39 E
Lister, Mt.	**5**	78 0 S	162 0 E
Liston	**99**	28 39 S	152 6 E
Listowel, Can.	**106**	43 44N	80 58W
Listowel, Ireland	**15**	52 27N	9 30W
Lit-et-Mixe	**20**	44 2N	1 15W
Litang, China	**77**	23 12N	109 8 E
Litang, Malay.	**73**	5 27N	118 31 E
Litani →, Leb.	**62**	33 20N	35 14 E
Litani →, Surinam	**62**	3 40N	54 0W
Litchfield, Conn., U.S.A.	**113**	41 44N	73 12W
Litchfield, Ill., U.S.A.	**116**	39 10N	89 40W
Litchfield, Minn., U.S.A.	**116**	45 5N	94 31W
Liteni	**46**	47 32N	26 32 E

Lithgow Low Rocky Pt.

Place	Page	Lat.	Long.
Lithgow	97	33 25 S	150 8 E
Lithinon, Ákra	45	34 55N	24 44 E
Lithuanian S.S.R. □	54	55 30N	24 0 E
Litija	39	46 3N	14 50 E
Litókhoron	44	40 8N	22 34 E
Litoměřice	26	50 33N	14 10 E
Litomysl	27	49 52N	16 20 E
Litschau	26	48 58N	15 4 E
Little Abaco I.	121	26 50N	77 30W
Little America	5	79 0 S	160 0W
Little Andaman I.	71	10 40N	92 15 E
Little Barrier I.	101	36 12 S	175 8 E
Little Belt Mts.	118	46 50N	111 0W
Little Blue →	116	39 41N	96 40W
Little Bushman Land	92	29 10 S	18 10 E
Little Cadotte →	108	56 41N	117 6W
Little Churchill →	109	57 30N	95 22W
Little Colorado →	119	36 11N	111 48W
Little Current	106	45 55N	82 0W
Little Current →	106	50 57N	84 36W
Little Falls, Minn., U.S.A.	116	45 58N	94 19W
Little Falls, N.Y., U.S.A.	114	43 3N	74 50W
Little Fork →	116	48 31N	93 35W
Little Grand Rapids	109	52 0N	95 29W
Little Humboldt →	118	41 0N	117 43W
Little Inagua I.	121	21 40N	73 50W
Little Lake	119	35 58N	117 58W
Little Marais	116	47 24N	91 8W
Little Minch	14	57 35N	6 45W
Little Missouri →	116	47 30N	102 25W
Little Namaqualand	92	29 0 S	17 9 E
Little Ouse →	13	52 25N	0 50 E
Little Rann of Kutch	68	23 25N	71 25 E
Little Red →	117	35 11N	91 27W
Little River	101	43 45 S	172 49 E
Little Rock	117	34 41N	92 10W
Little Ruaha →	90	7 57 S	37 53 E
Little Sable Pt.	114	43 40N	86 32W
Little Sioux →	116	41 49N	96 4W
Little Smoky →	108	54 44N	117 11W
Little Snake →	118	40 27N	108 26W
Little Valley	112	42 15N	78 48W
Little Wabash →	114	37 54N	88 5W
Littlefield	117	33 57N	102 17W
Littlefork	116	48 24N	93 35W
Littlehampton	13	50 48N	0 32W
Littleton	114	44 19N	71 47W
Liuba	77	33 38N	106 55 E
Liucheng	77	24 38N	109 14 E
Liukang Tenggaja	73	6 45 S	118 50 E
Liuli	91	11 3 S	34 38 E
Liuwa Plain	89	14 20 S	22 30 E
Liuyang	77	28 10N	113 37 E
Liuzhou	75	24 22N	109 22 E
Livada	46	47 52N	23 5 E
Livadherón	44	40 2N	21 57 E
Livarot	18	49 0N	0 9 E
Live Oak	115	30 17N	83 0W
Livermore, Mt.	117	30 45N	104 8W
Liverpool, Austral.	97	33 54 S	150 58 E
Liverpool, Can.	107	44 5N	64 41W
Liverpool, U.K.	12	53 25N	3 0W
Liverpool Plains	97	31 15 S	150 15 E
Liverpool Ra.	97	31 50 S	150 30 E
Livingston, Guat.	120	15 50N	88 50W
Livingston, U.S.A.	118	45 40N	110 40W
Livingstone, U.S.A.	117	30 44N	94 54W
Livingstone, Zambia	91	17 46 S	25 52 E
Livingstone I.	5	63 0 S	60 15W
Livingstone Memorial	91	12 20 S	30 18 E
Livingstone Mts.	91	9 40 S	34 20 E
Livingstonia	91	10 38 S	34 5 E
Livno	42	43 50N	17 0 E
Livny	55	52 30N	37 30 E
Livorno	38	43 32N	10 18 E
Livramento	125	30 55 S	55 30W
Livron-sur-Drôme	21	44 46N	4 51 E
Liwale	91	9 48 S	37 58 E
Liwale □	91	9 0 S	38 0 E
Liwiec →	28	52 36N	21 34 E
Lixoúrion	45	38 14N	20 24 E
Lizard I.	98	14 42 S	145 30 E
Lizard Pt.	13	49 57N	5 11W
Lizzano	41	40 23N	17 25 E
Ljig	42	44 13N	20 18 E
Ljubija	39	44 55N	16 35 E
Ljubinje	42	42 58N	18 5 E
Ljubljana	39	46 4N	14 33 E
Ljubno	39	46 25N	14 46 E
Ljubovija	42	44 11N	19 22 E
Ljubuški	42	43 12N	17 34 E
Ljung	49	58 1N	13 3 E
Ljungan →	48	62 18N	17 23 E
Ljungaverk	48	62 30N	16 5 E
Ljungby	49	56 49N	13 55 E
Ljusdal	48	61 46N	16 3 E
Ljusnan →	48	61 12N	17 8 E
Ljusne	48	61 13N	17 7 E
Ljutomer	39	46 31N	16 11 E
Llagostera	32	41 50N	2 54 E
Llancanelo, Salina	124	35 40 S	69 8W
Llandeilo	13	51 53N	4 0W
Llandovery	13	51 59N	3 49W
Llandrindod Wells	13	52 15N	3 23W
Llandudno	12	53 19N	3 51W
Llanelli	13	51 41N	4 11W
Llanes	30	43 25N	4 50W
Llangollen	12	52 58N	3 10W
Llanidloes	13	52 28N	3 31W
Llano	117	30 45N	98 41W
Llano →	117	30 50N	98 25W
Llano Estacado	117	34 0N	103 0W
Llanos	126	5 0N	71 35W
Llera	120	23 19N	99 1W
Llerena	31	38 17N	6 0W
Llico	124	34 46 S	72 5W
Llobregat →	32	41 19N	2 9 E
Lloret de Mar	32	41 41N	2 53 E
Lloyd B.	98	12 45 S	143 27 E
Lloyd L.	109	57 22N	108 57W
Lloydminster	109	53 17N	110 0W
Lluchmayor	33	39 29N	2 53 E
Llullaillaco, volcán	124	24 43 S	68 30W
Loa	119	38 18N	111 40W
Loa →	124	21 26 S	70 41W
Loano	38	44 8N	8 14 E
Lobatse	92	25 12 S	25 40 E
Löbau	24	51 5N	14 42 E
Lobenstein	24	50 25N	11 39 E
Lobería	124	38 10 S	58 40W
Łobez	28	53 38N	15 39 E
Lobito	89	12 18 S	13 35 E
Lobón, Canal de	31	38 50N	6 55W
Lobos	124	35 10 S	59 0W
Lobos, I.	120	27 15N	110 30W
Lobos, Is.	122	6 57 S	80 45W
Lobstick L.	107	54 0N	65 0W
Loc Binh	71	21 46N	106 54 E
Loc Ninh	71	11 50N	106 34 E
Locarno	25	46 10N	8 47 E
Lochaber	14	56 55N	5 0W
Lochcarron	14	57 25N	5 30W
Loche, La	109	56 29N	109 26W
Lochem	16	52 9N	6 26 E
Loches	18	47 7N	1 0 E
Lochgelly	14	56 7N	3 18W
Lochgilphead	14	56 2N	5 37W
Lochinver	14	58 9N	5 15W
Lochnagar, Austral.	98	23 33 S	145 38 E
Lochnagar, U.K.	14	56 57N	3 14W
Łochów	28	52 33N	21 42 E
Lochy →	14	56 52N	5 3W
Lock	99	33 34 S	135 46 E
Lock Haven	114	41 7N	77 31W
Lockeport	107	43 47N	65 4W
Lockerbie	14	55 7N	3 21W
Lockhart, Austral.	99	35 14 S	146 40 E
Lockhart, U.S.A.	117	29 55N	97 40W
Lockney	117	34 7N	101 27W
Lockport	114	43 12N	78 42W
Locle, Le	25	47 3N	6 44 E
Locminé	18	47 54N	2 51W
Locri	41	38 14N	16 14 E
Locronan	18	48 7N	4 15W
Loctudy	18	47 50N	4 12W
Lod	62	31 57N	34 54 E
Lodalskåpa	47	61 47N	7 13 E
Loddon →	100	35 31 S	143 51 E
Lodeinoye Pole	52	60 44N	33 33 E
Lodève	20	43 44N	3 19 E
Lodge Grass	118	45 21N	107 20W
Lodgepole	116	41 12N	102 40W
Lodgepole Cr. →	116	41 20N	104 30W
Lodhran	68	29 32N	71 30 E
Lodi, Italy	38	45 19N	9 30 E
Lodi, U.S.A.	118	38 12N	121 16W
Lodja	90	3 30 S	23 23 E
Lodosa	32	42 25N	2 4W
Lödöse	49	58 2N	12 9 E
Lodwar	90	3 10N	35 40 E
Łódź	28	51 45N	19 27 E
Łódź □	28	51 45N	19 27 E
Loengo	90	4 48 S	26 30 E
Lofer	26	47 35N	12 41 E
Lofoten	50	68 30N	15 0 E
Lofsdalen	48	62 10N	13 20 E
Lofsen →	48	62 7N	13 57 E
Loftahammar	49	57 54N	16 41 E
Logan, Kans., U.S.A.	116	39 40N	99 35W
Logan, Ohio, U.S.A.	114	39 25N	82 22W
Logan, Utah, U.S.A.	118	41 45N	111 50W
Logan, W. Va., U.S.A.	114	37 51N	81 59W
Logan, Mt.	104	60 31N	140 22W
Logan Pass	108	48 41N	113 44W
Logansport, Ind., U.S.A.	114	40 45N	86 21W
Logansport, La., U.S.A.	117	31 58N	93 58W
Logar □	65	34 0N	69 0 E
Logo	87	5 20N	30 18 E
Logroño	32	42 28N	2 27W
* Logroño □	32	42 28N	2 27W
Logrosán	31	39 20N	5 32W
Løgstør	49	56 58N	9 14 E
Lohardaga	69	23 27N	84 45 E
Lohja	51	60 12N	24 5 E
Lohr	25	50 0N	9 35 E
Loi-kaw	67	19 40N	97 17 E
Loimaa	51	60 50N	23 5 E
Loir →	18	47 33N	0 32W
Loir-et-Cher □	18	47 40N	1 20 E
Loire □	21	45 40N	4 5 E
Loire →	18	47 16N	2 10W
Loire-Atlantique □	18	47 25N	1 40W
Loiret □	19	47 58N	2 10 E
Loitz	24	53 58N	13 8 E
Loja, Ecuador	126	3 59 S	79 16W
Loja, Spain	31	37 10N	4 10W
Loji	73	1 38 S	127 28 E
Loka	87	4 13N	31 0 E
Lokandu	90	2 30 S	25 45 E
Løken	47	59 48N	11 29 E
Lokeren	16	51 6N	3 59 E
Lokhvitsa	54	50 25N	33 18 E
Lokichokio	90	4 19N	34 13 E
Lokitaung	90	4 12N	35 48 E
Lokka	50	67 49N	27 45 E
Løkken	49	57 22N	9 41 E
Løkkenverk	47	63 8N	9 45 E
Loknya	54	56 49N	30 4 E
Lokoja	85	7 47N	6 45 E
Lokolama	88	2 35 S	19 50 E
Lokwei	77	19 5N	110 31 E
Lol →	87	9 13N	26 30 E
Lola	84	7 52N	8 29W
Lolibai, Gebel	87	3 50N	33 0 E
Lolimi	87	4 35N	34 0 E
Loliondo	90	2 2 S	35 39 E
Lolland	49	54 45N	11 30 E
Lollar	24	50 39N	8 43 E
Lolo	118	46 50N	114 8W
Lolodorf	85	3 16N	10 49 E
Lom	43	43 48N	23 12 E
Lom →	42	43 45N	23 15 E
Loma	118	47 59N	110 29W
Lomami →	90	0 46N	24 16 E
Lomas de Zamóra	124	34 45 S	58 25W
Lombard	118	46 7N	111 28W
Lombardia □	38	45 35N	9 45 E
Lombardy = Lombardia	38	45 35N	9 45 E
Lombez	20	43 29N	0 55 E
Lomblen	73	8 30 S	123 32 E
Lombok	72	8 45 S	116 30 E
Lomé	85	6 9N	1 20 E
Lomela	88	2 19 S	23 15 E
Lomela →	88	1 30 S	22 50 E
Lomello	38	45 5N	8 46 E
Lometa	117	31 15N	98 25W
Lomié	88	3 13N	13 38 E
Lomma	49	55 43N	13 6 E
Lomond	108	50 24N	112 36W
Lomond, L.	14	56 8N	4 38W
Lomonosov	54	59 57N	29 53 E
Lompobatang	73	5 24 S	119 56 E
Lompoc	119	34 41N	120 32W
Lomsegga	47	61 49N	8 21 E
Łomża	28	53 10N	22 2 E
Łomża □	28	53 0N	22 30 E
Lonavla	70	18 46N	73 29 E
Loncoche	128	39 20 S	72 50W
Londa	70	15 30N	74 30 E
Londe, La	21	43 8N	6 14 E
Londiani	90	0 10 S	35 33 E
Londinières	18	49 50N	1 25 E
London, Can.	106	42 59N	81 15W
London, U.K.	13	51 30N	0 5W
London, Ky., U.S.A.	114	37 11N	84 5W
London, Ohio, U.S.A.	114	39 54N	83 28W
London, Greater □	13	51 30N	0 5W
Londonderry	15	55 0N	7 20W
Londonderry □	15	55 0N	7 20W
Londonderry, C.	96	13 45 S	126 55 E
Londonderry, I.	128	55 0 S	71 0W
Londrina	125	23 18 S	51 10W
Lone Pine	119	36 35N	118 2W
Long Beach, Calif., U.S.A.	119	33 46N	118 12W
Long Beach, N.Y., U.S.A.	113	40 35N	73 40W
Long Beach, Wash., U.S.A.	118	46 20N	124 1W
Long Branch	114	40 19N	74 0W
Long Creek	118	44 43N	119 6W
Long Eaton	12	52 54N	1 16W
Long I., Austral.	98	22 8 S	149 53 E
Long I., Bahamas	121	23 20N	75 10W
Long I., P.N.G.	98	5 20 S	147 5 E
Long I., U.S.A.	114	40 50N	73 20W
Long I. Sd.	113	41 10N	73 0W
Long L.	106	49 30N	86 50W
Long Lake	113	43 57N	74 25W
Long Pine	116	42 33N	99 41W
Long Pt., Newf., Can.	107	48 47N	58 46W
Long Pt., Ont., Can.	112	42 35N	80 2W
Long Point B.	112	42 40N	80 10W
Long Range Mts.	107	49 30N	57 30W
Long Str.	4	70 0N	175 0 E
Long Xian	77	34 55N	106 55 E
Long Xuyen	71	10 19N	105 28 E
Longá	45	36 53N	21 55 E
Long'an	77	23 10N	107 40 E
Longarone	39	46 15N	12 18 E
Longchuan	77	24 5N	115 17 E
Longde	76	35 30N	106 20 E
Longeau	19	47 47N	5 20 E
Longford, Austral.	99	41 32 S	147 3 E
Longford, Ireland	15	53 43N	7 50W
Longford □	15	53 42N	7 45W
Longhua	76	41 18N	117 45 E
Longido	90	2 43 S	36 42 E
Longiram	72	0 5 S	115 45 E
Longjiang	76	47 20N	123 12 E
Longkou	76	37 40N	120 18 E
Longlac	106	49 45N	86 25W
Longlin	77	24 47N	105 20 E
Longmen	77	23 40N	114 18 E
Longmont	116	40 10N	105 4W
Longnan	77	24 55N	114 47 E
Longnawan	72	1 51N	114 55 E
Longobucco	41	39 27N	16 37 E
Longone →	81	10 0N	15 40 E
Longquan	77	28 7N	119 10 E
Longreach	97	23 28 S	144 14 E
Longs Peak	118	40 20N	105 37W
Longshan	77	29 29N	109 25 E
Longsheng	77	25 48N	110 0 E
Longton	98	20 58 S	145 55 E
Longtown	13	51 58N	2 59W
Longué	18	47 22N	0 8W
Longueau	19	49 52N	2 21 E
Longueuil	113	45 32N	73 28W
Longuyon	19	49 27N	5 35 E
Longview, Can.	108	50 32N	114 10W
Longview, Tex., U.S.A.	117	32 30N	94 45W
Longview, Wash., U.S.A.	118	46 9N	122 58W
Longwy	19	49 30N	5 45 E
Longxi	76	34 53N	104 40 E
Longzhou	77	22 22N	106 50 E
Lonigo	39	45 23N	11 22 E
Löningen	24	52 43N	7 44 E
Lonja →	39	45 30N	16 40 E
Lonoke	117	34 48N	91 57W
Lons-le-Saunier	19	46 40N	5 31 E
Lønstrup	49	57 29N	9 47 E
Looc	73	12 20N	112 5 E
Lookout, C., Can.	106	55 18N	83 56W
Lookout, C., U.S.A.	115	34 30N	76 30W
Loolmalasin	90	3 0 S	35 53 E
Loon →, Alta., Can.	108	57 8N	115 3W
Loon →, Man., Can.	109	55 53N	101 59W
Loon Lake	109	54 2N	109 10W
Loop Hd.	15	52 34N	9 55W
Lop Nor = Lop Nur	75	40 20N	90 10 E
Lop Nur	75	40 20N	90 10 E
Lopare	42	44 39N	18 46 E
Lopatin	57	43 50N	47 35 E
Lopatina, G.	59	50 47N	143 10 E
Lopaye	87	6 37N	33 40 E
Lopera	31	37 56N	4 14W
Lopez, C.	88	0 47 S	8 40 E
Lopphavet	50	70 27N	21 15 E
Lora →, Afghan.	65	32 0N	67 15 E
Lora →, Norway	47	62 8N	8 42 E
Lora del Río	31	37 39N	5 33W
Lora, Hamun-i-	66	29 38N	64 58 E
Lora, La	30	42 45N	4 0W
Lorain	114	41 28N	82 55W
Loralai	68	30 20N	68 41 E
Lorca	33	37 41N	1 42W
Lord Howe I.	94	31 33 S	159 6 E
Lord Howe Ridge	94	30 0 S	162 30 E
Lordsburg	119	32 22N	108 45W
Lorengau	98	2 1 S	147 15 E
Loreto, Brazil	127	7 5 S	45 10W
Loreto, Italy	39	43 26N	13 36 E
Loreto Aprutina	39	42 24N	13 59 E
Lorgues	21	43 28N	6 22 E
Lorient	18	47 45N	3 23W
Loristān □	64	33 20N	47 0 E
Lorn	14	56 26N	5 10W
Lorn, Firth of	14	56 20N	5 40W
Lorne	99	38 33 S	143 59 E
Lörrach	25	47 36N	7 38 E
Lorraine	19	49 0N	6 0 E
Lorrainville	106	47 21N	79 23W
Los Alamos	119	35 57N	106 17W
Los Andes	124	32 50 S	70 40W
Los Angeles, Chile	124	37 28 S	72 23W
Los Angeles, U.S.A.	119	34 0N	118 10W
Los Angeles Aqueduct	119	35 25N	118 0W
Los Banos	119	37 8N	120 56W
Los Barrios	31	36 11N	5 30W
Los Blancos	124	23 40 S	62 30W
Los Gatos	119	37 15N	121 59W
Los Hermanos	126	11 45N	84 25W
Los, Îles de	84	9 30N	13 50W
Los Lamentos	120	30 36N	105 50W
Los Lunas	119	34 48N	106 47W
Los Mochis	120	25 45N	109 5W
Los Monegros	32	41 29N	0 13W
Los Olivos	119	34 40N	120 7W
Los Palacios y Villafranca	31	37 10N	5 55W
Los Roques	126	11 50N	66 45W
Los Santos de Maimona	31	38 27N	6 22W
Los Testigos	126	11 23N	63 6W
Los Vilos	124	32 10 S	71 30W
Los Yébenes	31	39 36N	3 55W
Loshkalakh	59	62 45N	147 20 E
Łosice	28	52 13N	22 43 E
Lošinj	39	44 30N	14 30 E
Lossiemouth	14	57 43N	3 17W
Losuia	98	8 30 S	151 4 E
Lot □	20	44 39N	1 40 E
Lot →	20	44 18N	0 20 E
Lot-et-Garonne □	20	44 22N	0 30 E
Lota	124	37 5 S	73 10W
Løten	47	60 51N	11 21 E
Lothian □	14	55 50N	3 0W
Lothiers	19	46 42N	1 33 E
Lotschbergtunnel	25	46 26N	7 43 E
Lottefors	48	61 25N	16 24 E
Loubomo	88	4 9 S	12 47 E
Loudéac	18	48 11N	2 47W
Loudon	115	35 35N	84 22W
Loudonville	112	40 40N	82 15W
Loudun	18	47 0N	0 5 E
Loué	18	47 59N	0 9W
Loue →	19	47 1N	5 27 E
Louga	84	15 45N	16 5W
Loughborough	12	52 46N	1 11W
Loughrea	15	53 11N	8 33W
Loughros More B.	15	54 48N	8 30W
Louhans	21	46 38N	5 12 E
Louis Trichardt	93	23 0 S	29 43 E
Louis XIV, Pte.	106	54 37N	79 45W
Louisa	114	38 5N	82 40W
Louisbourg	107	45 55N	60 0W
Louise I.	108	52 55N	131 50W
Louiseville	106	46 20N	72 56W
Louisiade Arch.	94	11 10 S	153 0 E
Louisiana	116	39 25N	91 0W
Louisiana □	117	30 50N	92 0W
Louisville, Ky., U.S.A.	114	38 15N	85 45W
Louisville, Miss., U.S.A.	117	33 7N	89 3W
Loulay	20	46 3N	0 30W
Loulé	31	37 9N	8 0W
Lount L.	109	50 10N	94 20W
Louny	26	50 20N	13 48 E
Loup City	116	41 19N	98 57W
Loupe, La	18	48 29N	1 1 E
Lourdes	20	43 6N	0 3W
Lourdes-du-Blanc-Sablon	107	51 24N	57 12W
Lourenço-Marques = Maputo	93	25 58 S	32 32 E
Loures	31	38 50N	9 9W
Lourinhã	31	39 14N	9 17W
Louroux-Béconnais, Le	18	47 30N	0 55W
Lousã	30	40 7N	8 14W
Louth, Austral.	99	30 30 S	145 8 E
Louth, Ireland	15	53 47N	6 33W
Louth, U.K.	12	53 23N	0 0W
Louth □	15	53 55N	6 30W
Loutrá Aidhipsoú	45	38 54N	23 2 E
Loutráki	45	38 0N	22 57 E
Louvière, La	16	50 27N	4 10 E
Louviers	18	49 12N	1 10 E
Lovat →	54	58 14N	30 28 E
Lovćen	42	42 23N	18 51 E
Love	109	53 29N	104 10W
Lovech	43	43 8N	24 42 E
Loveland	116	40 27N	105 4W
Lovell	118	44 51N	108 20W
Lovelock	118	40 17N	118 25W
Lóvere	38	45 50N	10 4 E
Loviisa	51	60 28N	26 12 E
Loving	117	32 17N	104 4W
Lovington	117	33 0N	103 20W
Lovios	30	41 55N	8 4W
Lovisa	51	60 28N	26 12 E
Lovosice	26	50 30N	14 2 E
Lovran	39	45 18N	14 15 E
Lovrin	42	45 58N	20 48 E
Lövstabukten	48	60 35N	17 45 E
Low Rocky Pt.	97	42 59 S	145 29 E

* Renamed La Rioja □

Lowa McLure

Lowa 90 1 25 S 25 47 E
Lowa → 90 1 24 S 25 51 E
Lowell 114 42 38N 71 19W
Lower Arrow L. 108 49 40N 118 5W
Lower Austria = Niederösterreich □ 26 48 25N 15 40 E
Lower Hutt 101 41 10 S 174 55 E
Lower L. 118 41 17N 120 3W
Lower Lake 118 38 56N 122 36W
Lower Neguac 107 47 20N 65 10W
Lower Post 108 59 58N 128 30W
Lower Red L. 116 47 58N 95 0W
Lower Saxony = Niedersachsen □ 24 52 45N 9 0 E
Lowestoft 13 52 29N 1 44 E
Łowicz 28 52 6N 19 55 E
Lowville 114 43 48N 75 30W
Loxton 97 34 28 S 140 31 E
Loyalty Is. = Loyauté, Is. 94 21 0 S 167 30 E
Loyang = Luoyang 77 34 40N 112 26 E
Loyev, U.S.S.R. 54 51 55N 30 40 E
Loyev, U.S.S.R. 54 51 56N 30 46 E
Loyoro 90 3 22N 34 14 E
Lož 39 45 43N 30 14 E
Lozère □ 20 44 35N 3 30 E
Loznica 42 44 32N 19 14 E
Lozovaya 56 49 0N 36 20 E
Luachimo 88 7 23 S 20 48 E
Luacono 88 11 15 S 21 37 E
Lualaba → 90 0 26N 25 20 E
Luampa 91 15 4 S 24 20 E
Lu'an 77 31 45N 116 29 E
Luan Chau 71 21 38N 103 24 E
Luan Xian 76 39 40N 118 40 E
Luanda 88 8 50 S 13 15 E
Luang Prabang 71 19 52N 102 10 E
Luangwa Valley 91 13 30 S 31 30 E
Luanping 76 40 53N 117 23 E
Luanshya 91 13 3 S 28 28 E
Luapula □ 91 11 0 S 29 0 E
Luapula → 91 9 26 S 28 33 E
Luarca 30 43 32N 6 32W
Luashi 91 10 50 S 23 36 E
Luau 88 10 40 S 22 10 E
Lubaczów 28 50 10N 23 8 E
Lubalo 88 9 10 S 19 15 E
Lubań 28 51 5N 15 15 E
Lubana, Ozero 54 56 45N 27 0 E
Lubang Is. 73 13 50N 120 12 E
Lubartów 28 51 28N 22 42 E
Lubawa 28 53 30N 19 48 E
Lübben 24 51 56N 13 54 E
Lübbenau 24 51 49N 13 59 E
Lubbock 117 33 40N 101 53W
Lübeck 24 53 52N 10 41 E
Lübecker Bucht 24 54 3N 11 0 E
Lubefu 90 4 47 S 24 27 E
Lubefu → 90 4 10 S 23 0 E
Lubero = Luofu 90 0 1 S 29 15 E
Lubicon L. 108 56 23N 115 56W
Lubień Kujawski 28 52 23N 19 9 E
Lubin 28 51 24N 16 11 E
Lublin 28 51 12N 22 38 E
Lublin □ 28 51 5N 22 30 E
Lubliniec 28 50 43N 18 45 E
Lubny 54 50 3N 32 58 E
Lubok Antu 72 1 3N 111 50 E
Lubon 28 52 21N 16 51 E
Lubongola 90 2 35 S 27 50 E
Lubotin 27 49 17N 20 53 E
Lubran 64 34 0N 36 0 E
Lubraniec 28 52 33N 18 50 E
Lubsko 28 51 45N 14 57 E
Lübtheen 24 53 18N 11 4 E
Lubuagan 73 17 21N 121 10 E
Lubudi → 91 9 0 S 25 35 E
Lubuklinggau 72 3 15 S 102 55 E
Lubuksikaping 72 0 10N 100 15 E
Lubumbashi 91 11 40 S 27 28 E
Lubunda 90 5 12 S 26 41 E
Lubungu 91 14 35 S 26 24 E
Lubutu 90 0 45 S 26 30 E
Luc-en-Diois 21 44 36N 5 28 E
Luc, Le 21 43 23N 6 21 E
Lucan 112 43 11N 81 24W
Lucca 38 43 50N 10 30 E
Luce Bay 14 54 45N 4 48W
Lucea 121 18 25N 78 10W
Lucedale 115 30 55N 88 34W
Lucena, Phil. 73 13 56N 121 37 E
Lucena, Spain 31 37 27N 4 31W
Lucena del Cid 32 40 9N 0 17W
Lučenec 27 48 18N 19 42 E
Lucera 41 41 30N 15 20 E
Lucerne = Luzern 25 47 3N 8 18 E
Luchena → 33 37 44N 1 50W
Lucheringo → 91 11 43 S 36 17 E
Lüchow 24 52 58N 11 8 E
Lucira 89 14 0 S 12 35 E
Luckau 24 51 50N 13 43 E
Luckenwalde 24 52 5N 13 11 E
Lucknow 69 26 50N 81 0 E
Luçon 20 46 28N 1 10W
Lüda 76 38 50N 121 40 E
Luda Kamchiya → 43 43 3N 27 29 E
Ludbreg 39 46 15N 16 38 E
Lüdenscheid 24 51 13N 7 37 E
Lüderitz 92 26 41 S 15 8 E
Ludewe □ 91 10 0 S 34 50 E
Ludhiana 68 30 57N 75 56 E
Lüdinghausen 24 51 46N 7 28 E
Ludington 114 43 58N 86 27W
Ludlow, U.K. 13 52 23N 2 42W
Ludlow, Calif., U.S.A. 119 34 43N 116 10W
Ludlow, Vt., U.S.A. 113 43 25N 72 40W
Ludus 46 46 29N 24 5 E
Ludvika 48 60 8N 15 14 E
Ludwigsburg 25 48 53N 9 11 E
Ludwigshafen 25 49 27N 8 27 E
Ludwigslust 24 53 19N 11 28 E
Ludza 54 56 32N 27 43 E
Luebo 88 5 21 S 21 23 E
Lueki 90 3 20 S 25 48 E
Luena, Zaîre 91 9 28 S 25 43 E
Luena, Zambia 91 10 40 S 30 25 E
Lüeyang 77 33 22N 106 10 E
Lufeng 77 22 57N 115 38 E
Lufkin 117 31 25N 94 40W
Lufupa 91 10 37 S 24 56 E
Luga 54 58 40N 29 55 E
Luga → 54 59 40N 28 18 E
Lugang 77 24 4N 120 23 E
Lugano 25 46 0N 8 57 E
Lugano, L. di 25 46 0N 9 0 E
Lugansk = Voroshilovgrad 57 48 35N 39 20 E
Lugard's Falls 90 3 6 S 38 41 E
Lugela 91 16 25 S 36 43 E
Lugenda → 91 11 25 S 38 33 E
Lugh Ganana 63 3 48N 42 34 E
Lugnaquilla 15 52 58N 6 28W
Lugnvik 48 62 56N 17 55 E
Lugo, Italy 39 44 25N 11 53 E
Lugo, Spain 30 43 2N 7 35W
Lugo □ 30 43 0N 7 30W
Lugoj 42 45 42N 21 57 E
Lugones 30 43 26N 5 50W
Lugovoy 58 42 54N 72 45 E
Luhe → 24 53 18N 10 11 E
Luiana 92 17 25 S 22 59 E
Luino 38 46 0N 8 42 E
Luís Correia 127 3 0 S 41 35W
Luitpold Coast 5 78 30 S 32 0W
Luize 88 7 40 S 22 30 E
Luizi 90 6 0 S 27 25 E
Luján 124 34 45 S 59 5W
Lukanga Swamps 91 14 30 S 27 40 E
Lukenie → 88 3 0 S 18 50 E
Lukhisaral 69 25 11N 86 5 E
Lŭki 43 41 50N 24 43 E
Lukolela, Equateur, Zaîre 88 1 10 S 17 12 E
Lukolela, Kasai Or., Zaîre 90 5 23 S 24 32 E
Lukosi 91 18 30 S 26 30 E
Lukovit 43 43 13N 24 11 E
Łuków 28 51 55N 22 23 E
Lukoyanov 55 55 2N 44 29 E
Lule älv → 50 65 35N 22 10 E
Luleå 50 65 35N 22 10 E
Lüleburgaz 43 41 23N 27 22 E
Luling 117 29 45N 97 40W
Lulong 76 39 53N 118 51 E
Lulonga → 88 1 0N 19 0 E
Lulua → 88 6 30 S 22 50 E
Luluabourg = Kananga 88 5 55 S 22 26 E
Lumai 89 13 13 S 21 25 E
Lumajang 73 8 8 S 113 16 E
Lumbala 89 14 18 S 21 18 E
Lumberton, Miss., U.S.A. 117 31 4N 89 28W
Lumberton, N. Mex., U.S.A. 119 36 58N 106 57W
Lumberton, N.C., U.S.A. 115 34 37N 78 59W
Lumbres 19 50 40N 2 5 E
Lumbwa 90 0 12 S 35 28 E
Lumby 108 50 10N 118 50W
Lumsden 101 45 44 S 168 27 E
Lumut 71 4 13N 100 37 E
Lunavada 68 23 8N 73 37 E
Lunca 46 47 22N 25 1 E
Lund, Sweden 49 55 44N 13 12 E
Lund, U.S.A. 118 38 53N 115 0W
Lundazi 91 12 20 S 33 7 E
Lunde 47 59 17N 9 5 E
Lunderskov 49 55 29N 9 19 E
Lundi → 91 21 43 S 32 34 E
Lundu 72 1 40N 109 50 E
Lundy 13 51 10N 4 41W
Lune → 12 54 0N 2 51W
Lüneburg 24 53 15N 10 23 E
Lüneburg Heath = Lüneburger Heide 24 53 0N 10 0 E
Lüneburger Heide 24 53 0N 10 0 E
Lunel 21 43 39N 4 9 E
Lünen 24 51 36N 7 31 E
Lunenburg 107 44 22N 64 18W
Lunéville 19 48 36N 6 30 E
Lunga → 91 14 34 S 26 25 E
Lungi Airport 84 8 40N 13 17W
Lungleh 67 22 55N 92 45 E
Luni 68 26 0N 73 6 E
Lūni → 68 24 41N 71 14 E
Luninets 54 52 15N 26 50 E
Luning 118 38 30N 118 10W
Lunino 55 53 35N 45 6 E
Lunner 47 60 19N 10 35 E
Lunsemfwa → 91 14 54 S 30 12 E
Lunsemfwa Falls 91 14 30 S 29 6 E
Luo He → 77 34 35N 110 20 E
Luobei 76 47 35N 130 50 E
Luocheng 77 24 48N 108 53 E
Luochuan 76 35 45N 109 26 E
Luoding 77 22 45N 111 40 E
Luodong 77 24 41N 121 46 E
Luofu 90 0 10 S 29 15 E
Luoning 77 34 35N 111 40 E
Luoyang 77 34 40N 112 26 E
Luoyuan 77 26 28N 119 30 E
Luozi 88 4 54 S 14 0 E
Lupeni 46 45 21N 23 13 E
Łupków 27 49 15N 22 4 E
Luque, Parag. 124 25 19 S 57 25W
Luque, Spain 31 37 35N 4 16W
Luray 114 38 39N 78 26W
Lure 19 47 40N 6 30 E
Luremo 88 8 30 S 17 50 E
Lurgan 15 54 28N 6 20W
Lusaka 91 15 28 S 28 16 E
Lusambo 90 4 58 S 23 28 E
Lusangaye 90 4 54 S 26 0 E
Luseland 109 52 5N 109 24W
Lushan 77 33 45N 112 55 E
Lushih 77 34 3N 111 3 E
Lushnja 44 40 55N 19 41 E
Lushoto 90 4 47 S 38 20 E
Lushoto □ 90 4 45 S 38 20 E
Lüshun 76 38 45N 121 15 E
Lusignan 20 46 26N 0 8 E
Lusigny-sur-Barse 19 48 16N 4 15 E
Lusk 116 42 47N 104 27W
Lussac-les-Châteaux 20 46 24N 0 43 E
Luta = Lüda 76 38 50N 121 40 E
Luton 13 51 53N 0 24W
Lutong 72 4 30N 114 0 E
Lutsk 54 50 50N 25 15 E
Lützow Holmbukta 5 69 10 S 37 30 E
Luverne 116 43 35N 96 12W
Luvua 91 8 48 S 25 17 E
Luwegu → 91 8 31 S 37 23 E
Luwuk 73 0 56 S 122 47 E
Luxembourg 16 49 37N 6 9 E
Luxembourg ■ 16 50 0N 6 0 E
Luxembourg □ 16 49 58N 5 30 E
Luxeuil-les-Bains 19 47 49N 6 24 E
Luxi 77 28 20N 110 7 E
Luxor = El Uqsur 86 25 41N 32 38 E
Luy → 20 43 39N 1 9W
Luy-de-Béarn → 20 43 39N 0 48W
Luy-de-France → 20 43 39N 0 48W
Luz-St-Sauveur 20 42 53N 0 1 E
Luza 52 60 39N 47 10 E
Luzern 25 47 3N 8 18 E
Luzern □ 25 47 2N 7 55 E
Luzhai 77 24 29N 109 42 E
Luzhou 75 28 52N 105 20 E
Luziânia 127 16 20 S 48 0W
Luzon 73 16 0N 121 0 E
Luzy 19 46 47N 3 58 E
Luzzi 41 39 28N 16 17 E
Lvov 54 49 50N 24 0 E
Lwówek 28 52 28N 16 10 E
Lwówek Šlaşki 28 51 7N 15 38 E
Lyakhovichi 54 53 2N 26 32 E
Lyakhovskiye, Ostrova 59 73 40N 141 0 E
Lyaki 57 40 34N 47 22 E
Lyallpur = Faisalabad 68 31 30N 73 5 E
Lyaskovets 43 43 6N 25 44 E
Lychen 24 53 13N 13 20 E
Lyckeby 49 56 12N 15 37 E
Lycksele 50 64 38N 18 40 E
Lycosura 45 37 20N 22 3 E
Lydda = Lod 62 31 57N 34 54 E
Lydenburg 93 25 10 S 30 29 E
Lyell 101 41 48 S 172 4 E
Lyell I. 108 52 40N 131 35W
Lyell Range 101 41 38 S 172 20 E
Lygnern 49 57 30N 12 15 E
Lykling 47 59 42N 5 12 E
Lyman 118 41 24N 110 15W
Lyme Regis 13 50 44N 2 57W
Lymington 13 50 46N 1 32W
Łyńa → 28 54 37N 21 14 E
Lynchburg 114 37 23N 79 10W
Lynd → 98 16 28 S 143 18 E
Lynd Ra. 99 25 30 S 149 20 E
Lynden, Can. 112 43 14N 80 9W
Lynden, U.S.A. 118 48 56N 122 32W
Lyndhurst 99 30 15 S 138 18 E
Lyndonville, N.Y., U.S.A. 112 43 19N 78 25W
Lyndonville, Vt., U.S.A. 113 44 32N 72 1W
Lyngdal, Aust-Agder, Norway 47 58 8N 7 7 E
Lyngdal, Buskerud, Norway 47 59 54N 9 32 E
Lynn 114 42 28N 70 57W
Lynn Canal 108 58 50N 135 20W
Lynn Lake 109 56 51N 101 3W
Lynton 13 51 14N 3 50W
Lyntupy 54 55 4N 26 23 E
Lynx L. 109 62 25N 106 15W
Lyø 49 55 3N 10 9 E
Lyon 21 45 46N 4 50 E
Lyonnais 21 45 45N 4 15 E
Lyons, Colo., U.S.A. 116 40 17N 105 15W
Lyons, Ga., U.S.A. 115 32 10N 82 15W
Lyons, Kans., U.S.A. 116 38 24N 98 13W
Lyons, N.Y., U.S.A. 114 43 3N 77 0W
Lyons = Lyon 21 45 46N 4 50 E
Lyrestad 49 58 48N 14 4 E
Lys → 19 50 39N 2 24 E
Lysá 26 50 11N 14 51 E
Lysekil 49 58 17N 11 26 E
Lyskovo 55 56 0N 45 3 E
Lysva 52 58 07N 57 49 E
Lysvik 48 60 1N 13 9 E
Lytle 117 29 14N 98 46W
Lyttelton 101 43 35 S 172 44 E
Lytton 108 50 13N 121 31W
Lyuban 54 59 16N 31 18 E
Lyubcha 54 53 46N 26 1 E
Lyubertsy 55 55 39N 37 50 E
Lyubim 55 58 20N 40 39 E
Lyubimets 43 41 50N 26 5 E
Lyuboml, U.S.S.R. 54 51 10N 24 2 E
Lyuboml, U.S.S.R. 54 51 11N 24 4 E
Lyubotin 56 50 0N 36 0 E
Lyubytino 54 58 50N 33 16 E
Lyudinovo 54 53 52N 34 28 E

M

Mā'ad 62 32 37N 35 36 E
Ma'alah 64 26 31N 47 20 E
Maamba 92 17 17 S 26 28 E
Ma'ānn 64 30 12N 35 44 E
Ma'anshan 77 31 44N 118 29 E
Ma'arrat un Nu'man 64 35 38N 36 40 E
Maas → 16 51 45N 4 32 E
Maaseik 16 51 6N 5 45 E
Maassluis 16 51 56N 4 16 E
Maastricht 16 50 50N 5 40 E
Maave 93 21 4 S 34 47 E
Mabel L. 108 50 35N 118 43W
Mabenge 90 4 15N 24 12 E
Mablethorpe 12 53 21N 0 14 E
Maboma 90 2 30N 28 10 E
Mabrouk 85 19 29N 1 15W
Mabton 118 46 15N 120 12W
Mac Nutt 109 51 5N 101 36W
Mac Tier 112 45 9N 79 46W
Macachín 124 37 10 S 63 43W
Macaé 125 22 20 S 41 43W
McAlester 117 34 57N 95 46W
McAllen 117 26 12N 98 15W
Macallister → 100 38 2 S 146 59 E
Macamic 106 48 45N 79 0W
Macão 31 39 35N 7 59W
Macao = Macau ■ 75 22 16N 113 35 E
Macapá 127 0 5N 51 4W
McArthur → 97 15 54 S 136 40 E
McArthur River 97 16 27 S 136 7 E
Macau 127 5 0 S 36 40W
Macau ■ 75 22 16N 113 35 E
McBride 108 53 20N 120 19W
McCall 118 44 55N 116 6W
McCamey 117 31 8N 102 15W
McCammon 118 42 41N 112 11W
McCauley I. 108 53 40N 130 15W
Macclesfield 12 53 16N 2 9W
McClintock 109 57 50N 94 10W
McCloud 118 41 14N 122 5W
McClure 112 40 42N 77 20W
McClure Str. 4 75 0N 119 0W
McClusky 116 47 30N 100 31W
McComb 117 31 13N 90 30W
McCook 116 40 15N 100 35W
McCusker → 109 55 32N 108 39W
McDame 108 59 44N 128 59W
McDermitt 118 42 0N 117 45W
Macdonald → 100 33 22 S 151 0 E
McDonald Is. 3 54 0 S 73 0 E
Macdonald L. 96 23 30 S 129 0 E
Macdonnell Ranges 96 23 40 S 133 0 E
Macdougall L. 104 66 0N 98 27W
MacDowell L. 106 52 15N 92 45W
Macduff 14 57 40N 2 30W
Maceda 30 42 16N 7 39W
* Macedo de Cavaleiros 88 11 25 S 16 45 E
Macedonia = Makedhonía 44 40 39N 22 0 E
Macedonia = Makedonija 42 41 53N 21 40 E
Maceió 127 9 40 S 35 41W
Maceira 31 39 41N 8 55W
Macenta 84 8 35N 9 32W
Macerata 39 43 19N 13 28 E
McFarlane → 109 59 12N 107 58W
Macfarlane, L. 97 32 0 S 136 40 E
McGehee 117 33 40N 91 25W
McGill 118 39 27N 114 50W
Macgillycuddy's Reeks 15 52 2N 9 45W
MacGregor 109 49 57N 98 48W
McGregor, Iowa, U.S.A. 116 42 58N 91 15W
McGregor, Minn., U.S.A. 116 46 37N 93 17W
McGregor → 108 55 10N 122 0W
McGregor Ra. 99 27 0 S 142 45 E
Mach 66 29 50N 67 20 E
Machado = Jiparana → 126 8 3 S 62 52W
Machagai 124 26 56 S 60 2W
Machakos 90 1 30 S 37 15 E
Machakos □ 90 1 30 S 37 15 E
Machala 126 3 20 S 79 57W
Machanga 93 20 59 S 35 0 E
Machattie, L. 97 24 50 S 139 48 E
Machava 93 25 54 S 32 28 E
Machece 91 19 15 S 35 32 E
Machecoul 18 47 0N 1 49W
Macheng 77 31 12N 115 2 E
Machevna 59 61 20N 172 20 E
Machezo 31 39 21N 4 20W
Machias 107 44 40N 67 28W
Machichaco, Cabo 32 43 28N 2 47W
Machichi → 109 57 3N 92 6W
Machilipatnam 70 16 12N 81 8 E
Machine, La 19 46 54N 3 27 E
Machiques 126 10 4N 72 34W
Machupicchu 126 13 8 S 72 30W
Machynlleth 13 52 36N 3 51W
** Macias Nguema Biyoga 85 3 30N 8 40 E
Maciejowice 28 51 36N 21 26 E
McIlwraith Ra. 97 13 50 S 143 20 E
Măcin 46 45 16N 28 8 E
Macina 84 14 50N 5 0W
McIntosh 116 45 57N 101 20W
McIntosh L. 109 55 45N 105 0W
Macintyre → 97 28 37 S 150 47 E
Macizo Galaico 30 42 30N 7 30W
Mackay, Austral. 97 21 8 S 149 11 E
Mackay, U.S.A. 118 43 58N 113 37W
Mackay → 108 57 10N 111 38W
Mackay, L. 96 22 30 S 129 0 E
McKees Rock 112 40 27N 80 3W
McKeesport 114 40 21N 79 50W
Mackenzie 108 55 20N 123 05W
McKenzie 115 36 10N 88 31W
† Mackenzie □ 104 61 30N 115 0W
Mackenzie →, Austral. 97 23 38 S 149 46 E
Mackenzie →, Can. 104 69 10N 134 20W
McKenzie → 118 44 2N 123 6W
Mackenzie City = Linden 126 6 0N 58 10W
Mackenzie Highway 108 58 0N 117 15W
Mackenzie Mts. 104 64 0N 130 0W
Mackinaw City 114 45 47N 84 44W
McKinlay 98 21 16 S 141 18 E
McKinlay → 98 20 50 S 141 28 E
McKinley, Mt. 104 63 2N 151 0W
McKinley Sea 4 84 0N 10 0W
McKinney 117 33 10N 96 40W
Mackinnon Road 90 3 40 S 39 1 E
McKittrick 119 35 18N 119 39W
Macksville 99 30 40 S 152 56 E
McLaughlin 116 45 50N 100 50W
Maclean 97 29 26 S 153 16 E
McLean 117 35 15N 100 35W
McLeansboro 116 38 5N 88 30W
Maclear 93 31 2 S 28 23 E
Macleay → 97 30 56 S 153 0 E
McLennan 108 55 42N 116 50W
MacLeod, B. 109 62 53N 110 0W
McLeod L. 96 24 9 S 113 47 E
MacLeod Lake 108 54 58N 123 0W
M'Clintock Chan. 104 72 0N 102 0W
McLoughlin, Mt. 118 42 10N 122 19W
McLure 108 51 2N 120 13W

* *Renamed Andulo*
** *Renamed Bioko*
† *Now part of Fort Smith and Inuvik □*

McMechen	**112**	39 57N	80 44W
McMillan L.	**117**	32 40N	104 20W
McMinnville, Oreg., U.S.A.	**118**	45 16N	123 11W
McMinnville, Tenn., U.S.A.	**115**	35 43N	85 45W
McMorran	**109**	51 19N	108 42W
McMurdo Sd.	**5**	77 0S	170 0E
McMurray = Fort McMurray	**108**	56 45N	111 27W
McNary	**119**	34 4N	109 53W
McNaughton L.	**108**	52 0N	118 10W
Macodoene	**93**	23 32S	35 5E
Macomb	**116**	40 25N	90 40W
Macomer	**40**	40 16N	8 48E
Mâcon	**21**	46 19N	4 50E
Macon, Ga., U.S.A.	**115**	32 50N	83 37W
Macon, Miss., U.S.A.	**115**	33 7N	88 31W
Macon, Mo., U.S.A.	**116**	39 40N	92 26W
Macondo	**89**	12 37S	23 46E
Macossa	**91**	17 55S	33 56E
Macoun L.	**109**	56 32N	103 40W
Macovane	**93**	21 30S	35 0E
McPherson	**116**	38 25N	97 40W
Macpherson Ra.	**99**	28 15S	153 15E
Macquarie →	**97**	30 5S	147 30E
Macquarie Harbour	**97**	42 15S	145 23E
Macquarie Is.	**94**	54 36S	158 55E
Macquarie, L.	**100**	33 4S	151 36E
MacRobertson Coast	**5**	68 30S	63 0E
Macroom	**15**	51 54N	8 57W
Macubela	**91**	16 53S	37 49E
Macugnaga	**38**	45 57N	7 58E
Macuiza	**91**	18 7S	34 29E
Macuse	**91**	17 45S	37 10E
Macuspana	**120**	17 46N	92 36W
Macusse	**92**	17 48S	20 23E
Mácuzari, Presa	**120**	27 10N	109 10W
McVille	**116**	47 46N	98 11W
Madā 'in Salih	**86**	26 51N	37 58E
Madagali	**85**	10 56N	13 33E
Madagascar ■	**93**	20 0S	47 0E
Madā'in Sālih	**64**	26 46N	37 57E
Madama	**83**	22 0N	13 40E
Madame I.	**107**	45 30N	60 58W
Madan	**43**	41 30N	24 57E
Madanapalle	**70**	13 33N	78 28E
Madang	**94**	5 12S	145 49E
Madaoua	**85**	14 5N	6 27E
Madara	**85**	11 45N	10 35E
Madaripur	**69**	23 19N	90 15E
Madauk	**67**	17 56N	96 52E
Madawaska	**112**	45 30N	77 55W
Madawaska →	**106**	45 27N	76 21W
Madaya	**67**	22 12N	96 10E
Madbar	**87**	6 17N	30 45E
Maddalena	**40**	41 15N	9 23E
Maddalena, La	**40**	41 13N	9 25E
Maddaloni	**41**	41 4N	14 23E
Madden Dam	**120**	9 13N	79 37W
Madden Lake	**120**	9 20N	79 37W
Madeira	**80**	32 50N	17 0W
Madeira →	**126**	3 22S	58 45W
Madeleine, Is. de la	**107**	47 30N	61 40W
Madera	**119**	37 0N	120 1W
Madha	**70**	18 0N	75 30E
Madhubani	**69**	26 21N	86 7E
Madhya Pradesh □	**68**	21 50N	81 0E
Madill	**117**	34 5N	96 49W
Madimba	**88**	5 0S	15 0E
Madīnat ash Sha'b	**63**	12 50N	45 0E
Madingou	**88**	4 10S	13 33E
Madirovalo	**93**	16 26S	46 32E
Madison, Fla., U.S.A.	**115**	30 29N	83 39W
Madison, Ind., U.S.A.	**114**	38 42N	85 20W
Madison, Nebr., U.S.A.	**116**	41 53N	97 25W
Madison, Ohio, U.S.A.	**112**	41 45N	81 4W
Madison, S.D., U.S.A.	**116**	44 0N	97 8W
Madison, Wis., U.S.A.	**116**	43 5N	89 25W
Madison →	**118**	45 56N	111 30W
Madison Junc.	**118**	44 42N	110 56W
Madisonville, Ky., U.S.A.	**114**	37 20N	87 30W
Madisonville, Tex., U.S.A.	**117**	30 57N	95 55W
Madista	**92**	21 15S	25 6E
Madiun	**73**	7 38S	111 32E
Madley	**13**	52 3N	2 51W
Madol	**87**	9 3N	27 45E
Madon →	**19**	48 36N	6 6E
Madona	**54**	56 53N	26 5E
Madonie, Le	**40**	37 50N	13 50E
Madras, India	**70**	13 8N	80 19E
Madras, U.S.A.	**118**	44 40N	121 10W
Madras = Tamil Nadu □	**70**	11 0N	77 0E
Madre de Dios →	**126**	10 59S	66 8W
Madre de Dios, I.	**128**	50 20S	75 10W
Madre del Sur, Sierra	**120**	17 30N	100 0W
Madre, Laguna, Mexico	**120**	25 0N	97 30W
Madre, Laguna, U.S.A.	**117**	25 0N	97 40W
Madre Occidental, Sierra	**120**	27 0N	107 0W
Madre Oriental, Sierra	**120**	25 0N	100 0W
Madre, Sierra, Mexico	**120**	16 0N	93 0W
Madre, Sierra, Phil.	**73**	17 0N	122 0E
Madri	**68**	24 16N	73 32E
Madrid	**30**	40 25N	3 45W
Madrid □	**30**	40 30N	3 45W
Madridejos	**31**	39 28N	3 33W
Madrigal de las Altas Torres	**30**	41 5N	5 0W
Madrona, Sierra	**31**	38 27N	4 16W
Madroñera	**31**	39 26N	5 42W
Madu	**87**	14 37N	26 4E
Madura, Selat	**73**	7 30S	113 20E
Madurai	**70**	9 55N	78 10E
Madurantakam	**70**	12 30N	79 50E
Madzhalis	**57**	42 9N	47 47E
Mae Hong Son	**71**	19 16N	98 1E
Mae Sot	**71**	16 43N	98 34E
Maebashi	**74**	36 24N	139 4E
Maella	**32**	41 8N	0 7E
Măeruş	**46**	45 53N	25 31E
Maesteg	**13**	51 36N	3 40W
Maestra, Sierra	**121**	20 15N	77 0W
Maestrazgo, Mts. del	**32**	40 30N	0 25W
Maevatanana	**93**	16 56N	46 49E
Ma'fan	**83**	25 56N	14 29E
Mafeking, Can.	**109**	52 40N	101 10W
* Mafeking, S. Afr.	**92**	25 50S	25 38E
Maféré	**84**	5 30N	3 2W
Mafeteng	**92**	29 51S	27 15E
Maffra	**99**	37 53S	146 58E
Mafia	**90**	7 45S	39 50E
Mafra, Brazil	**125**	26 10S	50 0W
Mafra, Port.	**31**	38 55N	9 20W
Mafungabusi Plateau	**91**	18 30S	29 8E
Magadan	**59**	59 38N	150 50E
Magadi	**90**	1 54S	36 19E
Magadi, L.	**90**	1 54S	36 19E
Magaliesburg	**93**	26 1S	27 32E
Magallanes, Estrecho de	**128**	52 30S	75 0W
Magangué	**126**	9 14N	74 45W
Magaria	**85**	13 4N	9 5E
Magburaka	**84**	8 47N	12 0W
Magdalena, Argent.	**124**	35 5S	57 30W
Magdalena, Boliv.	**126**	13 13S	63 57W
Magdalena, Malay.	**72**	4 25N	117 55E
Magdalena, Mexico	**120**	30 50N	112 0W
Magdalena, U.S.A.	**119**	34 10N	107 20W
Magdalena →, Colomb.	**126**	11 6N	74 51W
Magdalena →, Mexico	**120**	30 40N	112 25W
Magdalena, B.	**120**	24 30N	112 10W
Magdalena, I.	**120**	24 40N	112 15W
Magdalena, Llano de la	**120**	25 0N	111 30W
Magdeburg	**24**	52 8N	11 36E
Magdeburg □	**24**	52 20N	11 30E
Magdi'el	**62**	32 10N	34 54E
Magdub	**87**	13 42N	25 5E
Magee	**117**	31 53N	89 45W
Magee, I.	**15**	54 48N	5 44W
Magelang	**73**	7 29S	110 13E
Magellan's Str. = Magallanes, Est. de	**128**	52 30S	75 0W
Magenta	**38**	45 28N	8 53E
Maggia →	**25**	46 18N	8 36E
Maggiorasca, Mte.	**38**	44 33N	9 29E
Maggiore, L.	**38**	46 0N	8 35E
Maghama	**84**	15 32N	12 57W
Maghār	**62**	32 54N	35 24E
Magherafelt	**15**	54 44N	6 37W
Maghnia	**82**	34 50N	1 43W
Magione	**39**	43 10N	12 12E
Maglaj	**42**	44 33N	18 7E
Magliano in Toscana	**39**	42 36N	11 18E
Máglie	**41**	40 8N	18 17E
Magnac-Laval	**20**	46 13N	1 11E
Magnetic Pole, 1976 (North)	**4**	76 12N	100 12W
Magnetic Pole, 1976 (South)	**5**	68 48S	139 30E
Magnisía □	**44**	39 15N	22 45E
Magnitogorsk	**52**	53 27N	59 4E
Magnolia, Ark., U.S.A.	**117**	33 18N	93 12W
Magnolia, Miss., U.S.A.	**117**	31 8N	90 28W
Magnor	**47**	59 56N	12 15E
Magny-en-Vexin	**19**	49 9N	1 47E
Magog	**107**	45 18N	72 9W
Magoro	**90**	1 45N	34 12E
Magosa = Famagusta	**64**	35 8N	33 55E
Magoye	**91**	16 1S	27 30E
Magpie L.	**107**	51 0N	64 41W
Magrath	**108**	49 25N	112 50W
Magro →	**33**	39 11N	0 25W
Magrur, Wadi →	**87**	16 5N	26 30E
Magu □	**90**	2 31S	33 28E
Maguarinho, C.	**127**	0 15S	48 30W
Maguse L.	**109**	61 40N	95 10W
Maguse Pt.	**109**	61 20N	93 50W
Magwe	**67**	20 10N	95 0E
Mahābād	**64**	36 50N	45 45E
Mahabaleshwar	**70**	17 58N	73 43E
Mahabharat Lekh	**69**	28 30N	82 0E
Mahabo	**93**	20 23S	44 40E
Mahad	**70**	18 6N	73 29E
Mahadeo Hills	**68**	22 20N	78 30E
Mahadeopur	**70**	18 48N	80 0E
Mahagi	**90**	2 20N	31 0E
Mahajamba →	**93**	15 33S	47 8E
Mahajamba, Helodranon' i	**93**	15 24S	47 5E
Mahajan	**68**	28 48N	73 56E
Mahajanga □	**93**	17 0S	47 0E
Mahajilo →	**93**	19 42S	45 22E
Mahakam →	**72**	0 35S	117 17E
Mahalapye	**92**	23 1S	26 51E
Maḩallāt	**65**	33 55N	50 30E
Mahanadi →	**69**	20 20N	86 25E
Mahanoro	**93**	19 54S	48 48E
Mahanoy City	**113**	40 48N	76 10W
Maharashtra □	**70**	20 30N	75 30E
Maharès	**83**	34 32N	10 29E
Mahari Mts.	**90**	6 20S	30 0E
Mahasolo	**93**	19 7S	46 22E
Mahaweli → Ganga	**70**	8 30N	81 15E
Mahboobabad	**70**	17 42N	80 2E
Mahbubnagar	**70**	16 45N	77 59E
Mahdia	**83**	35 28N	11 0E
Mahé	**70**	11 42N	75 34E
Mahendra Giri	**70**	8 20N	77 30E
Mahenge	**91**	8 45S	36 41E
Maheno	**101**	45 10S	170 50E
Mahia Pen.	**101**	39 9S	177 55E
Mahirija	**82**	34 0N	3 16W
Mahmiya	**87**	17 12N	33 43E
Mahmud Kot	**68**	30 16N	71 0E
Mahmudia	**46**	45 5N	29 5E
Mahnomen	**116**	47 22N	95 57W
Mahoba	**69**	25 15N	79 55E
Mahón	**32**	39 53N	4 16E
Mahone Bay	**107**	44 39N	64 20W
Mahuta	**85**	11 32N	4 58E
Mai-Ndombe, L.	**88**	2 0S	18 20E
Maîche	**19**	47 16N	6 48E
Maicurú →	**127**	2 14S	54 17W
Máida	**41**	38 51N	16 21E
Maidenhead	**13**	51 31N	0 42W
Maidi	**87**	16 20N	42 45E
Maidstone, Can.	**109**	53 5N	109 20W
Maidstone, U.K.	**13**	51 16N	0 31E
Maiduguri	**85**	12 0N	13 20E
Maignelay	**19**	49 32N	2 30E
Maigudo	**87**	7 30N	37 8E
Maijdi	**69**	22 48N	91 10E

* Renamed Mafikeng

Maikala Ra.	**69**	22 0N	81 0E
Mailly-le-Camp	**19**	48 41N	4 12E
Mailsi	**68**	29 48N	72 15E
Main →, Ger.	**25**	50 0N	8 18E
Main →, U.K.	**15**	54 49N	6 20W
Main Centre	**109**	50 35N	107 21W
Mainburg	**25**	48 37N	11 49E
Maine	**18**	48 0N	0 0E
Maine □	**107**	45 20N	69 0W
Maine →	**15**	52 10N	9 40W
Maine-et-Loire □	**18**	47 31N	0 30W
Maïne-Soroa	**85**	13 13N	12 2E
Maingkwan	**67**	26 15N	96 37E
Mainit, L.	**73**	9 31N	125 30E
Mainland, Orkney, U.K.	**14**	59 0N	3 10W
Mainland, Shetland, U.K.	**14**	60 15N	1 22W
Mainpuri	**68**	27 18N	79 4E
Maintenon	**19**	48 35N	1 35E
Maintirano	**93**	18 3S	44 1E
Mainz	**25**	50 0N	8 17E
Maipú	**124**	36 52S	57 50W
Maiquetía	**126**	10 36N	66 57W
Maira →	**38**	44 49N	7 38E
Mairabari	**67**	26 30N	92 22E
Maisi, Pta. de	**121**	20 10N	74 10W
Maisse	**19**	48 24N	2 21E
Maitland, N.S.W., Austral.	**97**	32 33S	151 36E
Maitland, S. Australia, Austral.	**99**	34 23S	137 40E
Maitland →	**112**	43 45N	81 33W
Maiyema	**85**	12 5N	4 25E
Maizuru	**74**	35 25N	135 22E
Majalengka	**73**	6 55S	108 14E
Majd el Kurūm	**62**	32 56N	35 15E
Majene	**73**	3 38S	118 57E
Majevica Planina	**42**	44 45N	18 50E
Maji	**87**	6 12N	35 30E
Major	**109**	51 52N	109 37W
Majorca, I. = Mallorca	**32**	39 30N	3 0E
Maka	**84**	13 40N	14 10W
Makak	**85**	3 36N	11 0E
Makale	**73**	3 6S	119 51E
Makamba	**90**	4 8S	29 49E
Makari	**88**	12 35N	14 28E
Makarikari = Makgadikgadi Salt Pans	**92**	20 40S	25 45E
Makarovo	**59**	57 40N	107 45E
Makarska	**42**	43 20N	17 2E
Makaryev	**55**	57 52N	43 50E
Makasar = Ujung Pandang	**73**	5 10S	119 20E
Makasar, Selat	**73**	1 0S	118 20E
Makat	**58**	47 39N	53 19E
Makedhonía □	**44**	40 39N	22 0E
Makedonija □	**42**	41 53N	21 40E
Makena	**110**	20 39N	156 27W
Makeni	**84**	8 55N	12 5W
Makeyevka	**56**	48 0N	38 0E
Makgadikgadi Salt Pans	**92**	20 40S	25 45E
Makhachkala	**57**	43 0N	47 30E
Makhambet, U.S.S.R.	**57**	47 43N	51 40E
Makhambet, U.S.S.R.	**57**	47 40N	51 35E
Makharadze	**57**	41 55N	42 2E
Makian	**73**	0 20N	127 20E
** Makin	**94**	3 30N	174 0E
Makindu	**90**	2 18S	37 50E
Makinsk	**58**	52 37N	70 26E
Makkah	**86**	21 30N	39 54E
Makkovik	**107**	55 10N	59 10W
† Maklakovo	**59**	58 16N	92 29E
Makó	**27**	46 14N	20 33E
Makokou	**88**	0 40N	12 50E
Makongo	**90**	3 25N	26 17E
Makoro	**90**	3 10N	29 59E
Makoua	**88**	0 5S	15 50E
Maków Mazowiecki	**28**	52 52N	21 6E
Maków Podhal	**27**	49 43N	19 45E
Makrá	**45**	36 15N	25 54E
Makran	**65**	26 13N	61 30E
Makran Coast Range	**66**	25 40N	64 0E
Makrana	**68**	27 2N	74 46E
Mákri	**44**	40 52N	25 40E
Maksimkin Yar	**58**	58 42N	86 50E
Maktar	**83**	35 48N	9 12E
Mākū	**64**	39 15N	44 31E
Makumbi	**88**	5 50S	20 43E
Makunda	**92**	22 30S	20 7E
Makurazaki	**74**	31 15N	130 20E
Makurdi	**85**	7 43N	8 35E
Makwassie	**92**	27 17S	26 0E
Mal B.	**15**	52 50N	9 30W
Mal i Gjalicës së Lumës	**44**	42 2N	20 25E
Mal i Gribës	**44**	40 17N	19 45E
Mal i Nemërçkës	**44**	40 15N	20 15E
Mal i Tomorit	**44**	40 42N	20 11E
Mala Kapela	**39**	44 45N	15 30E
Mala, Pta.	**121**	7 28N	80 2W
Malabang	**73**	7 36N	124 3E
Malabar Coast	**70**	11 0N	75 0E
Malacca, Str. of	**71**	3 0N	101 0E
Malacky	**27**	48 27N	17 0E
Malad City	**118**	42 10N	112 20E
Málaga	**31**	36 43N	4 23W
Malaga	**117**	32 12N	104 2W
Málaga □	**31**	36 38N	4 58W
Malagarasi	**90**	5 5S	30 50E
Malagarasi →	**90**	5 12S	29 47E
Malagón	**31**	39 11N	3 52W
Malagón →	**31**	37 35N	7 29W
Malaimbandy	**93**	20 20S	45 36E
Malakâl	**87**	9 33N	31 40E
Malakand	**66**	34 40N	71 55E
Malakoff	**117**	32 10N	95 55W
Malamyzh	**59**	50 0N	136 50E
Malang	**73**	7 59S	112 45E
Malanje	**88**	9 36S	16 17E
Mälaren	**48**	59 30N	17 10E
Malargüe	**124**	35 32S	69 30W
Malartic	**106**	48 9N	78 9W
Malatya	**64**	38 25N	38 20E
Malawi ■	**91**	13 0S	34 0E
Malawi, L.	**91**	12 30S	34 30E
Malay Pen.	**71**	7 25N	100 0E
Malaya □	**71**	4 0N	102 0E

* Renamed Peninsular Malaysia
† Renamed Lesosibirsk
** Renamed Butaritari

Malaya Belozërka	**56**	47 12N	34 56E
Malaya Vishera	**54**	58 55N	32 25E
Malaya Viska	**56**	48 39N	31 36E
Malaybalay	**73**	8 5N	125 7E
Malāyer	**64**	34 19N	48 51E
Malaysia ■	**72**	5 0N	110 0E
Malazgirt	**64**	39 10N	42 33E
Malbaie, La	**107**	47 40N	70 10W
Malbon	**98**	21 5S	140 17E
Malbork	**28**	54 3N	19 1E
Malcésine	**38**	45 46N	10 48E
Malchin	**24**	53 43N	12 44E
Malchow	**24**	53 29N	12 25E
Malcolm	**96**	28 51S	121 25E
Malczyce	**28**	51 14N	16 29E
Maldegem	**16**	51 14N	3 26E
Malden, Mass., U.S.A.	**113**	42 26N	71 5W
Malden, Mo., U.S.A.	**117**	36 35N	90 0W
Malden I.	**95**	4 3S	155 1W
Maldives ■	**60**	7 0N	73 0E
Maldonado	**125**	35 0S	55 0W
Maldonado, Punta	**120**	16 19N	98 35W
Malé	**38**	46 20N	10 55E
Malé Karpaty	**27**	48 30N	17 20E
Maléa, Akra	**45**	36 28N	23 7E
Malegaon	**68**	20 30N	74 38E
Malei	**91**	17 12S	36 58E
Malela	**90**	4 22S	26 8E
Målerås	**49**	56 54N	15 34E
Malerkotla	**68**	30 32N	75 58E
Máles	**45**	35 6N	25 35E
Malesherbes	**19**	48 15N	2 24E
Maleshevska Planina	**42**	41 38N	23 7E
Malestroit	**18**	47 49N	2 25W
Malfa	**41**	38 35N	14 50E
Malgobek	**57**	43 30N	44 34E
Malgomaj	**50**	64 40N	16 30E
Malgrat	**32**	41 39N	2 46E
Malha	**81**	15 8N	25 10E
Malheur →	**118**	44 3N	116 59W
Malheur L.	**118**	43 19N	118 42W
Mali	**84**	12 10N	12 20W
Mali ■	**85**	15 0N	2 0W
Mali →	**67**	25 40N	97 40E
Mali Kanal	**42**	45 36N	19 24E
Mali Kyun	**71**	13 0N	98 20E
Malih →	**62**	32 20N	35 34E
Malik	**73**	0 39S	123 16E
Malili	**73**	2 42S	121 6E
Malimba, Mts.	**90**	7 30S	29 30E
Malin	**54**	50 46N	29 3E
Malin Hd.	**15**	55 18N	7 24W
Malinau	**72**	3 35N	116 40E
Malindi	**90**	3 12S	40 5E
Maling	**73**	1 0N	121 0E
Malingping	**73**	6 45S	106 2E
Malinyi	**91**	8 56S	36 0E
Maliqi	**44**	40 45N	20 48E
Malita	**73**	6 19N	125 39E
Maljenik	**42**	43 59N	21 55E
Malkapur, Maharashtra, India	**68**	20 53N	73 58E
Malkapur, Maharashtra, India	**70**	16 57N	73 58E
Małkinia Górna	**28**	52 42N	22 5E
Malko Tŭrnovo	**43**	41 59N	27 31E
Mallacoota	**100**	37 40S	149 40E
Mallacoota Inlet	**97**	37 34S	149 40E
Mallaig	**14**	57 0N	5 50W
Mallawan	**69**	27 4N	80 12E
Mallawi	**86**	27 44N	30 44E
Mallemort	**21**	43 44N	5 11E
Málles Venosta	**38**	46 42N	10 32E
Mállia	**45**	35 17N	25 27E
Mallorca	**32**	39 30N	3 0E
Mallorytown	**113**	44 29N	75 53W
Mallow	**15**	52 8N	8 40W
Malmbäck	**49**	57 34N	14 28E
Malmberget	**50**	67 11N	20 40E
Malmédy	**16**	50 25N	6 2E
Malmesbury	**92**	33 28S	18 41E
Malmö	**49**	55 36N	12 59E
Malmöhus län □	**49**	55 45N	13 30E
Malmslätt	**49**	58 27N	15 33E
Malmyzh	**55**	56 35N	50 41E
Malnaş	**46**	46 2N	25 49E
Malo Konare	**43**	42 12N	24 24E
Maloarkhangelsk	**55**	52 28N	36 30E
Malolos	**73**	14 50N	120 49E
Malombe L.	**91**	14 40S	35 15E
Malomir	**43**	42 16N	26 30E
Malone	**114**	44 50N	74 19W
Malorad	**43**	43 28N	23 41E
Malorita	**54**	51 50N	24 3E
Maloyaroslovets	**55**	55 2N	36 20E
Malozemelskaya Tundra	**52**	67 0N	50 0E
Malpartida	**31**	39 26N	6 30W
Malpelo	**126**	4 3N	81 35W
Malpica	**30**	43 19N	8 50W
Malprabha →	**70**	16 20N	76 5E
Malta, Idaho, U.S.A.	**118**	42 15N	113 30W
Malta, Mont., U.S.A.	**118**	48 20N	107 55W
Malta ■	**36**	35 50N	14 30E
Malta Channel	**40**	36 40N	14 0E
Malton, Can.	**112**	43 42N	79 38W
Malton, U.K.	**12**	54 9N	0 48W
Maluku	**73**	1 0S	127 0E
Maluku □	**73**	3 0S	128 0E
Maluku, Kepulauan	**73**	3 0S	128 0E
Malumfashi	**85**	11 48N	7 39E
Malung	**48**	60 42N	13 44E
Malvalli	**70**	12 28N	77 8E
Malvan	**70**	16 2N	73 30E
Malvern, U.K.	**13**	52 7N	2 19W
Malvern, U.S.A.	**117**	34 22N	92 50W
Malvern Hills	**13**	52 0N	2 19W
Malvérnia	**93**	22 6S	31 42E
Malvik	**47**	63 25N	10 40E
Malvinas, Is. = Falkland Is.	**128**	51 30S	59 0W
Malya	**90**	3 5S	33 38E
Malyy Lyakhovskiy, Ostrov	**59**	74 7N	140 36E
Mama	**59**	58 18N	112 54E
Mamadysh	**55**	55 44N	51 23E
Mamahatun	**64**	39 50N	40 23E

Mamaia Market Harborough

Mamaia 46 44 18N 28 37 E
Mamanguape 127 6 50 S 35 4W
Mamasa 73 2 55 S 119 20 E
Mambasa 90 1 22N 29 3 E
Mamberamo → 73 2 0 S 137 50 E
Mambilima 91 10 31 S 28 45 E
Mambirima 91 11 25 S 27 33 E
Mambo 90 4 52 S 38 22 E
Mambrui 90 3 5 S 40 5 E
Mamburao 73 13 13N 120 39 E
Mameigwess L. 106 52 35N 87 50W
Mamers 18 48 21N 0 22 E
Mamfe 85 5 50N 9 15 E
Mámmola 41 38 23N 16 13 E
Mammoth 119 32 46N 110 43W
Mamoré → 126 10 23 S 65 53W
Mamou 84 10 15N 12 0W
Mampatá 84 11 54N 14 53W
Mampawah 72 0 30N 109 5 E
Mampong 85 7 6N 1 26W
Mamry, Jezioro 28 54 5N 21 50 E
Mamuju 73 2 41 S 118 50 E
Man 84 7 30N 7 40W
Man → 70 17 31N 75 32 E
Man, I. of 12 54 15N 4 30W
Man Na 67 23 27N 97 19 E
Mana 127 5 45N 53 55W
Måna → 47 59 55N 8 50 E
Manaar, Gulf of 70 8 30N 79 0 E
Manacapuru 126 3 16 S 60 37W
Manacor 32 39 34N 3 13 E
Manado 73 1 29N 124 51 E
Managua 121 12 6N 86 20W
Managua, L. 121 12 20N 86 30W
Manakara 93 22 8 S 48 1 E
Manam I. 98 4 5 S 145 0 E
Manamãh, Al 65 26 11N 50 35 E
Manambao → 93 17 35 S 44 0 E
Manambato 93 13 43 S 49 7 E
Manambolo → 93 19 18 S 44 22 E
Manambolosy 93 16 2 S 49 40 E
Mananara 93 16 10 S 49 46 E
Mananara → 93 23 21 S 47 42 E
Mananjary 93 21 13 S 48 20 E
Manantenina 93 24 17 S 47 19 E
Manaos = Manaus 126 3 0 S 60 0W
Manapouri 101 45 34 S 167 39 E
Manapouri, L. 101 45 32 S 167 32 E
Manar → 70 18 50N 77 20 E
Manas 75 44 17N 85 56 E
Manasir 65 24 30N 51 10 E
Manaslu, Mt. 69 28 33N 84 33 E
Manasquan 113 40 7N 74 3W
Manassa 119 37 12N 105 58W
Manaung 67 18 45N 93 40 E
Manaus 126 3 0 S 60 0W
Manawan L. 109 55 24N 103 14W
Manay 73 7 17N 126 33 E
Mancelona 114 44 54N 85 5W
Mancha, La 33 39 10N 2 54W
Mancha Real 31 37 48N 3 39W
Manche ☐ 18 49 10N 1 20W
Manchegorsk 52 67 40N 32 40 E
Manchester, U.K. 12 53 30N 2 15W
Manchester, Conn., U.S.A. 114 41 47N 72 30W
Manchester, Ga., U.S.A. 115 32 53N 84 32W
Manchester, Iowa, U.S.A. 116 42 28N 91 27W
Manchester, Ky., U.S.A. 114 37 9N 83 45W
Manchester, N.H., U.S.A. 114 42 58N 71 29W
Manchester, N.Y., U.S.A. 112 42 56N 77 16W
Manchester, Vt., U.S.A. 113 43 10N 73 5W
Manchester L. 109 61 28N 107 29W
Manciano 39 42 35N 11 30 E
Mancifa 87 6 53N 41 50 E
Mand → 65 28 20N 52 30 E
Manda, Chunya, Tanz. 90 6 51 S 32 29 E
Manda, Ludewe, Tanz. 91 10 30 S 34 40 E
Mandaguari 125 23 32 S 51 42W
Mandal 47 58 2N 7 25 E
Mandalay 67 22 0N 96 4 E
Mandale = Mandalay 67 22 0N 96 4 E
Mandalī 64 33 43N 45 28 E
Mandalya Körfezi 45 37 15N 27 20 E
Mandan 116 46 50N 101 0W
Mandapeta 70 16 47N 81 56 E
Mandar, Teluk 73 3 35 S 119 15 E
Mandas 40 39 40N 9 8 E
Mandasaur 68 24 3N 75 8 E
Mandasor = Mandasaur 68 24 3N 75 8 E
Mandawai (Katingan) → 72 3 30 S 113 0 E
Mandelieu-la-Napoule 21 43 34N 6 57 E
Mandera 90 3 55N 41 53 E
Mandera ☐ 90 3 30N 41 0 E
Mandi 68 31 39N 76 58 E
Mandioli 73 0 40 S 127 20 E
Mandla 69 22 39N 80 30 E
Mandø 49 55 18N 8 33 E
Mandoto 93 19 34 S 46 17 E
Mandoúdhion 45 38 48N 23 29 E
Mandráki 45 36 36N 27 11 E
Mandrare → 93 25 10 S 46 30 E
Mandritsara 93 15 50 S 48 49 E
Mandúria 41 40 25N 17 38 E
Mandvi 68 22 51N 69 22 E
Mandya 70 12 30N 77 0 E
Mandzai 68 30 55N 67 6 E
Mané 85 12 59N 1 21W
Manengouba, Mts. 85 5 0N 9 50 E
Maner → 70 18 30N 79 40 E
Maneroo 98 23 22 S 143 53 E
Maneroo Cr. → 98 23 21 S 143 53 E
Manfalût 86 27 20N 30 52 E
Manfred 99 33 19 S 143 45 E
Manfredónia 41 41 40N 15 55 E
Manfredónia, G. di 41 41 30N 16 10 E
Manga, Niger 85 15 0N 14 0 E
Manga, Upp. Vol. 85 11 40N 1 4W
Mangaia 101 21 55 S 157 55W
Mangalagiri 70 16 26N 80 36 E
Mangalia 46 43 50N 28 35 E
Mangalore 70 12 55N 74 47 E
Manganeses 30 41 45N 5 43W
Mangaon 70 18 15N 73 20 E
Manger 47 60 38N 5 3 E
Manggar 72 2 50 S 108 10 E
Manggawitu 73 4 8 S 133 32 E
Mangkalihat, Tanjung 73 1 2N 118 59 E
Manglaur 68 29 44N 77 49 E
Mangnai 75 37 52N 91 43 E
Mango 85 10 20N 0 30 E
Mangoky → 93 21 29 S 43 41 E
Mangole 73 1 50 S 125 55 E
Mangombe 90 1 20 S 26 48 E
Mangonui 101 35 1 S 173 32 E
Mangualde 30 40 38N 7 48W
Mangueigne 81 10 30N 21 15 E
Mangueira, Lagoa da 125 33 0 S 52 50W
Manguéni, Hamada 83 22 35N 12 40 E
Mangum 117 34 50N 99 30W
Mangyshlak P-ov. 57 44 30N 52 30 E
Mangyshlakskiy Zaliv 57 44 40N 50 50 E
Manhattan, Kans., U.S.A. 116 39 10N 96 40W
Manhattan, Nev., U.S.A. 119 38 31N 117 3W
Manhiça 93 25 23 S 32 49 E
Manhuaçu 127 20 15 S 42 2W
Mania → 93 19 42 S 45 22 E
Maniago 39 46 11N 12 40 E
Manica e Sofala ☐ 93 19 10 S 33 45 E
Manicaland ☐ 91 19 0 S 32 30 E
Manicoré 126 5 48 S 61 16W
Manicouagan → 107 49 30N 68 30W
Manicouagan L. 107 51 25N 68 15W
Manīfah 64 27 44N 49 0 E
Manigotagan 109 51 6N 96 18W
Manigotagan L. 109 50 52N 95 37W
Manihiki 95 10 24 S 161 1W
Manika, Plat. de la 91 10 0 S 25 5 E
Manila, Phil. 73 14 40N 121 3 E
Manila, U.S.A. 118 41 0N 109 44W
Manila B. 73 14 0N 120 0 E
Manilla 99 30 45 S 150 43 E
Manimpé 84 14 11N 5 28W
Manipur ☐ 67 25 0N 94 0 E
Manipur → 67 23 45N 94 20 E
Manisa 64 38 38N 27 30 E
Manistee 114 44 15N 86 20W
Manistee → 114 44 15N 86 21W
Manistique 114 45 59N 86 18W
Manito L. 109 52 43N 109 43W
Manitoba ☐ 109 55 30N 97 0W
Manitoba, L. 109 51 0N 98 45W
Manitou 109 49 15N 98 32W
Manitou I. 106 47 22N 87 30W
Manitou Is. 114 45 8N 86 0W
Manitou L., Ont., Can. 109 49 15N 93 0W
Manitou L., Qué., Can. 107 50 55N 65 17W
Manitou Springs 116 38 52N 104 55W
Manitoulin I. 106 45 40N 82 30W
Manitowaning 106 45 46N 81 49W
Manitowoc 114 44 8N 87 40W
Manizales 126 5 5N 75 32W
Manja 93 21 26 S 44 20 E
Manjakandriana 93 18 55 S 47 47 E
Manjeri 70 11 7N 76 11 E
Manjhand 68 25 50N 68 10 E
Manjil 64 36 46N 49 30 E
Manjimup 96 34 15 S 116 6 E
Manjra → 70 18 49N 77 52 E
Mankato, Kans., U.S.A. 116 39 49N 98 11W
Mankato, Minn., U.S.A. 116 44 8N 93 59W
Mankayana 93 26 38 S 31 6 E
Mankono 84 8 1N 6 10W
Mankota 109 49 25N 107 5W
Manlleu 32 42 2N 2 17 E
Manly 99 33 48 S 151 17 E
Manmad 70 20 18N 74 28 E
Manna 72 4 25 S 102 55 E
Mannahill 99 32 25 S 140 0 E
Mannar 70 9 1N 79 54 E
Mannar, G. of 70 8 30N 79 0 E
Mannar I. 70 9 5N 79 45 E
Mannargudi 70 10 45N 79 51 E
Mannheim 25 49 28N 8 29 E
Manning, Can. 108 56 53N 117 39W
Manning, U.S.A. 115 33 40N 80 9W
Manning → 100 31 52 S 152 43 E
Manning Prov. Park 108 49 5N 120 45W
Mannington 114 39 35N 80 25W
Mannu → 40 39 15N 9 32 E
Mannu, C. 40 40 2N 8 24 E
Mannum 99 34 50 S 139 20 E
Mano 84 8 3N 12 2W
Manokwari 73 0 54 S 134 0 E
Manolás 45 38 4N 21 21 E
Manombo 93 22 57 S 43 28 E
Manono 90 7 15 S 27 25 E
Manosque 21 43 49N 5 47 E
Manouane L. 107 50 45N 70 45W
Manresa 32 41 48N 1 50 E
Mans, Le 18 48 0N 0 10 E
Mansa, Gujarat, India 68 23 27N 72 45 E
Mansa, Punjab, India 68 30 0N 75 27 E
Mansa, Zambia 91 11 13 S 28 55 E
Mansel I. 105 62 0N 80 0W
Mansfield, Austral. 100 37 4 S 146 6 E
Mansfield, U.K. 12 53 8N 1 12W
Mansfield, La., U.S.A. 117 32 2N 93 40W
Mansfield, Mass., U.S.A. 113 42 2N 71 12W
Mansfield, Ohio, U.S.A. 114 40 45N 82 30W
Mansfield, Pa., U.S.A. 112 41 48N 77 4W
Mansfield, Wash., U.S.A. 118 47 51N 119 44W
Mansilla de las Mulas 30 42 30N 5 25W
Mansle 20 45 52N 0 9 E
Mansoa 84 12 0N 15 20W
Manson Creek 108 55 37N 124 32W
Mansoura 83 36 1N 4 31 E
Manta 126 1 0 S 80 40W
Mantalingajan, Mt. 72 8 55N 117 45 E
Mantare 90 2 42 S 33 13 E
Manteca 119 37 50N 121 12W
Manteo 115 35 55N 75 41W
Mantes-la-Jolie 19 49 0N 1 41 E
Manthani 70 18 40N 79 35 E
Manthelan 18 47 9N 0 47 E
Manti 118 39 23N 111 32W
Mantiqueira, Serra da 125 22 0 S 44 0W
Manton 114 44 23N 85 25W
Mantorp 49 58 21N 15 20 E
Mántova 38 45 20N 10 42 E
Mänttä 50 62 0N 24 40 E
Mantua = Mántova 38 45 20N 10 42 E
Manturovo 55 58 30N 44 30 E
Manu 126 12 10 S 70 51W
Manua Is. 101 14 13 S 169 35W
Manuel Alves → 127 11 19 S 48 28W
Manui 73 3 35 S 123 5 E
Manukan 73 8 14N 123 3 E
Manus I. 98 2 0 S 147 0 E
Manvi 70 15 57N 76 59 E
Manville 116 42 48N 104 36W
Manwath 70 19 19N 76 32 E
Many 117 31 36N 93 28W
Manyane 92 23 21 S 21 42 E
Manyara, L. 90 3 40 S 35 50 E
Manych → 57 47 15N 40 0 E
Manych-Gudilo, Oz. 57 46 24N 42 38 E
Manyonga → 90 4 10 S 34 15 E
Manyoni 90 5 45 S 34 55 E
Manyoni ☐ 90 6 30 S 34 30 E
Manzai 68 32 12N 70 15 E
Manzala, Bahra el 86 31 10N 31 56 E
Manzanares 33 39 0N 3 22W
Manzaneda, Cabeza de 30 42 12N 7 15W
Manzanillo, Cuba 121 20 20N 77 31W
Manzanillo, Mexico 120 19 0N 104 20W
Manzanillo, Pta. 121 9 30N 79 40W
Manzano Mts. 119 34 30N 106 45W
Manzhouli 75 49 35N 117 25 E
Manzini 93 26 30 S 31 25 E
Mao 81 14 4N 15 19 E
Maoke, Pegunungan 73 3 40 S 137 30 E
Maoming 75 21 50N 110 54 E
Mapam Yumco 75 30 45N 81 28 E
Mapia, Kepulauan 73 0 50N 134 20 E
Mapimí 120 25 50N 103 50W
Mapimí, Bolsón de 120 27 30N 104 15W
Mapinga 90 6 40 S 39 12 E
Mapinhane 93 22 20 S 35 0 E
Maple Creek 109 49 55N 109 29W
Mapleton 118 44 4N 123 58W
Maplewood 116 38 33N 90 18W
Maprik 98 3 44 S 143 3 E
Mapuca 70 15 36N 73 46 E
Mapuera → 126 1 5 S 57 2W
Maputo 93 25 58 S 32 32 E
Maputo, B. de 93 25 50 S 32 45 E
Maqnā 64 28 25N 34 50 E
Maquela do Zombo 88 6 0 S 15 15 E
Maquinchao 128 41 15 S 68 50W
Maquoketa 116 42 4N 90 40W
Mâr → 47 59 59N 8 46 E
Mar Chiquita, L. 124 30 40 S 62 50W
Mar del Plata 124 38 0 S 57 30W
Mar Menor, L. 33 37 40N 0 45W
Mar, Serra do 125 25 30 S 49 0W
Mara 90 1 30 S 34 32 E
Mara ☐ 90 1 45 S 34 20 E
Maraã 126 1 52 S 65 25W
Marabá 127 5 20 S 49 5W
Maracá, I. de 127 2 10N 50 30W
Maracaibo 126 10 40N 71 37W
Maracaibo, Lago de 126 9 40N 71 30W
Maracaju 125 21 38 S 55 9W
Maracay 126 10 15N 67 28W
Marādah 83 29 15N 19 15 E
Maradi 85 13 29N 8 10 E
Maradun 85 12 35N 6 18 E
Marāgheh 64 37 30N 46 12 E
Marāh 64 25 0N 45 35 E
Marajó, Ilha de 127 1 0 S 49 30W
Maralal 90 1 0N 36 38 E
Maralinga 96 30 13 S 131 32 E
Marama 99 35 10 S 140 10 E
Marampa 84 8 45N 12 28W
Maramureş ☐ 46 47 45N 24 0 E
Marana 119 32 30N 111 9W
Maranchón 32 41 6N 2 15W
Marand 64 38 30N 45 45 E
Marandellas 91 18 5 S 31 42 E
Maranguape 127 3 55 S 38 50W
Maranhão = São Luis 127 2 39 S 44 15W
Maranhão ☐ 127 5 0 S 46 0W
Marano, L. di 39 45 42N 13 13 E
Maranoa → 97 27 50 S 148 37 E
Marañón → 126 4 30 S 73 35W
Maraş 64 37 37N 36 53 E
Mărăşeşti 46 45 52N 27 14 E
Maratea 41 39 59N 15 43 E
Marateca 31 38 34N 8 40W
Marathókambos 45 37 43N 26 42 E
Marathon, Austral. 98 20 51 S 143 32 E
Marathon, Can. 106 48 44N 86 23W
Marathón 45 38 11N 23 58 E
Marathon, N.Y., U.S.A. 113 42 25N 76 3W
Marathon, Tex., U.S.A. 117 30 15N 103 15W
Maratua 73 2 10N 118 35 E
Marbella 31 36 30N 4 57W
Marble Bar 96 21 9 S 119 44 E
Marble Falls 117 30 30N 98 15W
Marblehead 113 42 29N 70 51W
Marburg 24 50 49N 8 36 E
Marby 48 63 7N 14 18 E
Marcal → 27 47 41N 17 32 E
Marcali 27 46 35N 17 25 E
Marcaria 38 45 7N 10 34 E
March 13 52 33N 0 5 E
Marchand = Rommani 82 33 20N 6 40W
Marché 20 46 0N 1 20 E
Marche ☐ 39 43 22N 13 10 E
Marche-en-Famenne 16 50 14N 5 19 E
Marchena 31 37 18N 5 23W
Marches = Marche 39 43 22N 13 10 E
Marciana Marina 38 42 44N 10 12 E
Marcianise 41 41 3N 14 16 E
Marcigny 21 46 17N 4 2 E
Marcillac-Vallon 20 44 29N 2 27 E
Marcillat 20 46 12N 2 38 E
Marck 19 50 57N 1 57 E
Marckolsheim 19 48 10N 7 30 E
Marcos Juárez 124 32 42 S 62 5W
Marcus 94 24 0N 153 45 E
Marcus Necker Ridge 94 20 0N 175 0 E
Marcy Mt. 113 44 7N 73 55W
Mardin 64 37 20N 40 43 E
Maree L. 14 57 40N 5 30W
Mareeba 97 16 59 S 145 28 E
Marek 73 4 41 S 120 24 E
Marek = Stanke Dimitrov 42 42 17N 23 9 E
Maremma 38 42 45N 11 15 E
Maréna 84 14 0N 7 20W
Marenberg 39 46 38N 15 13 E
Marengo 116 41 42N 92 5W
Marennes 20 45 49N 1 7W
Marenyi 90 4 22 S 39 8 E
Marerano 93 21 23 S 44 52 E
Maréttimo 40 37 58N 12 5 E
Mareuil-sur-Lay 20 46 32N 1 14W
Marfa 117 30 15N 104 0W
Marganets 56 47 40N 34 40 E
Margao 70 15 12N 73 58 E
Margaret Bay 108 51 20N 126 35W
Margaret L. 108 58 56N 115 25W
Margarita 120 9 20N 79 55W
Margarita, Isla de 126 11 0N 64 0W
Margaritíon 44 39 22N 20 26 E
Margate, S. Afr. 93 30 50 S 30 20 E
Margate, U.K. 13 51 23N 1 24 E
Margeride, Mts. de la 20 44 43N 3 38 E
Margherita di Savola 41 41 25N 16 5 E
Marghita 46 47 22N 22 22 E
Margonin 28 52 58N 17 5 E
Marguerite 108 52 30N 122 25W
Marhoum 82 34 27N 0 11W
Mari, A.S.S.R. ☐ 55 56 30N 48 0 E
María Elena 124 22 18 S 69 40W
María Grande 124 31 45 S 59 55W
Maria I. 96 14 52 S 135 45 E
Maria van Diemen, C. 101 34 29 S 172 40 E
Mariager 49 56 40N 10 0 E
Mariager Fjord 49 56 42N 10 19 E
Mariakani 90 3 50 S 39 27 E
Marian L. 108 63 0N 116 15W
Mariana Is. 94 17 0N 145 0 E
Mariana Trench 94 13 0N 145 0 E
Marianao 121 23 8N 82 24W
Marianna, Ark., U.S.A. 117 34 48N 90 48W
Marianna, Fla., U.S.A. 115 30 45N 85 15W
Mariannelund 49 57 37N 15 35 E
Mariánské Lázně 26 49 48N 12 41 E
Marias → 118 47 56N 110 30W
Mariato, Punta 121 7 12N 80 52W
Mariazell 26 47 47N 15 19 E
Ma'rib 63 15 25N 45 30 E
Maribo 49 54 48N 11 30 E
Maribor 39 46 36N 15 40 E
Marico → 92 23 35 S 26 57 E
Maricopa, Ariz., U.S.A. 119 33 5N 112 2W
Maricopa, Calif., U.S.A. 119 35 7N 119 27W
Marîdî 87 4 55N 29 25 E
Marîdî, Wadi → 87 6 15N 29 21 E
Marie-Galante 121 15 56N 61 16W
Mariecourt 105 61 30N 72 0W
Mariefred 48 59 15N 17 12 E
Mariehamn 51 60 5N 19 55 E
Marienberg, Ger. 24 50 40N 13 10 E
Marienberg, Neth. 16 52 30N 6 35 E
Marienbourg 16 50 6N 4 31 E
Mariental 92 24 36 S 18 0 E
Marienville 112 41 27N 79 8W
Mariestad 49 58 43N 13 50 E
Marietta, Ga., U.S.A. 115 34 0N 84 30W
Marietta, Ohio, U.S.A. 114 39 27N 81 27W
Marieville 113 45 26N 73 10W
Marignane 21 43 25N 5 13 E
Mariinsk 58 56 10N 87 20 E
Mariinskiy Posad 55 56 10N 47 45 E
Marília 125 22 13 S 50 0W
Marín 30 42 23N 8 42W
Marina di Cirò 41 39 22N 17 8 E
Mariña, La 30 43 30N 7 40W
Marina Plains 98 14 37 S 143 57 E
Marinduque 73 13 25N 122 0 E
Marine City 114 42 45N 82 29W
Marinel, Le 91 10 25 S 25 17 E
Marineo 40 37 57N 13 23 E
Marinette, Ariz., U.S.A. 119 33 41N 112 16W
Marinette, Wis., U.S.A. 114 45 4N 87 40W
Maringá 125 23 26 S 52 2W
Marinha Grande 31 39 45N 8 56W
Marion, Ala., U.S.A. 115 32 33N 87 20W
Marion, Ill., U.S.A. 117 37 45N 88 55W
Marion, Ind., U.S.A. 114 40 35N 85 40W
Marion, Iowa, U.S.A. 116 42 2N 91 36W
Marion, Kans., U.S.A. 116 38 25N 97 2W
Marion, Mich., U.S.A. 114 44 7N 85 8W
Marion, N.C., U.S.A. 115 35 42N 82 0W
Marion, Ohio, U.S.A. 114 40 38N 83 8W
Marion, S.C., U.S.A. 115 34 11N 79 22W
Marion, Va., U.S.A. 115 36 51N 81 29W
Marion, L. 115 33 30N 80 15W
Marion Reef 97 19 10 S 152 17 E
Mariposa 119 37 31N 119 59W
Mariscal Estigarribia 124 22 3 S 60 40W
Maritime Alps = Alpes Maritimes 38 44 10N 7 10 E
Maritsa 43 42 1N 25 50 E
Maritsá 45 36 22N 28 10 E
Maritsa → 43 42 15N 24 0 E
Mariyampole = Kapsukas 54 54 33N 23 19 E
Marka 86 18 14N 41 19 E
Markapur 70 15 44N 79 19 E
Markaryd 49 56 28N 13 35 E
Markdale 112 44 19N 80 39W
Marked Tree 117 35 35N 90 24W
Markelsdorfer Huk 24 54 33N 11 0 E
Marken 16 52 26N 5 12 E
Market Drayton 12 52 55N 2 30W
Market Harborough 13 52 29N 0 55W

Markham Mbulu

Markham 112 43 52N 79 16W
Markham → 98 6 41 S 147 2 E
Markham I. 4 84 0N 0 45W
Markham L. 109 62 30N 102 35W
Markham Mt. 5 83 0 S 164 0 E
Marki 28 52 20N 21 2 E
Markoupoulon 45 37 53N 23 57 E
Markovac 42 44 14N 21 7 E
Markovo 59 64 40N 169 40 E
Markoye 85 14 39N 0 2 E
Marks 55 51 45N 46 50 E
Marksville 117 31 10N 92 2W
Markt Schwaben 25 48 14N 11 49 E
Marktredwitz 25 50 1N 12 2 E
Marlboro 113 42 19N 71 33W
Marlborough 98 22 46 S 149 52 E
Marlborough □ 101 41 45 S 173 33 E
Marlborough Downs 13 51 25N 1 55W
Marle 19 49 43N 3 47 E
Marlin 117 31 25N 96 50W
Marlow, Ger. 24 54 8N 12 34 E
Marlow, U.S.A. 117 34 40N 97 58W
Marmagao 70 15 25N 73 56 E
Marmande 20 44 30N 0 10 E
Marmara 56 40 35N 27 38 E
Marmara Denizi 64 40 45N 28 15 E
Marmara, Sea of = Marmara Denizi 64 40 45N 28 15 E
Marmaris 64 36 50N 28 14 E
Marmarth 116 46 21N 103 52W
Marmion L. 106 48 55N 91 20W
Marmolada, Mte. 39 46 25N 11 55 E
Marmolejo 31 38 3N 4 13W
Marmora 106 44 28N 77 41W
Marnay 19 47 20N 5 48 E
Marne 24 53 57N 9 1 E
Marne □ 19 49 0N 4 10 E
Marne → 19 8 23N 18 36 E
Marnoo 100 36 40 S 142 54 E
Marnueli 57 41 30N 44 48 E
Maroala 93 15 23 S 47 59 E
Maroantsetra 93 15 26 S 49 44 E
Maromandia 93 14 13 S 48 5 E
Maroni → 127 4 0N 52 0W
Marónia 44 40 53N 25 24 E
Maroochydore 99 26 29 S 153 5 E
Maroona 99 37 27 S 142 54 E
Maros → 27 46 15N 20 13 E
Marosakoa 93 15 26 S 46 38 E
Marostica 39 45 44N 11 40 E
Maroua 85 10 40N 14 20 E
Marovoay 93 16 6 S 46 39 E
Marquard 92 28 40 S 27 28 E
Marqueira 31 38 41N 9 9W
Marquesas Is. 95 9 30 S 140 0W
Marquette 114 46 30N 87 21W
Marquise 19 50 50N 1 40 E
Marra, Gebel 87 7 20N 27 35 E
Marradi 39 44 5N 11 37 E
Marrakech 82 31 9N 8 0W
Marrawah 99 40 55 S 144 42 E
Marree 97 29 39 S 138 1 E
Marrimane 93 22 58 S 33 34 E
Marronne → 20 45 4N 1 56 E
Marroquí, Punta 31 36 0N 5 37W
Marrowie Creek 99 33 23 S 145 40 E
Marrubane 91 18 0 S 37 0 E
Marrupa 91 13 8 S 37 30 E
Mars, Le 116 43 0N 96 0W
Marsa Brega 83 30 24N 19 37 E
Marsá Susah 81 32 52N 21 59 E
Marsabit 90 2 18N 38 0 E
Marsabit □ 90 2 45N 37 45 E
Marsala 40 37 48N 12 25 E
Marsaxlokk (Medport) 36 35 47N 14 32 E
Marsciano 39 42 54N 12 20 E
Marsden 99 33 47 S 147 32 E
Marseillan 20 43 23N 3 31 E
Marseille 21 43 18N 5 23 E
Marseilles = Marseille 21 43 18N 5 23 E
Marsh I. 117 29 35N 91 50W
Marsh L. 116 45 5N 96 0W
Marshall, Liberia 84 6 8N 10 22W
Marshall, Ark., U.S.A. 117 35 58N 92 40W
Marshall, Mich., U.S.A. 114 42 17N 84 59W
Marshall, Minn., U.S.A. 116 44 25N 95 45W
Marshall, Mo., U.S.A. 116 39 8N 93 15W
Marshall, Tex., U.S.A. 117 32 29N 94 20W
Marshall Is. 94 9 0N 171 0 E
Marshalltown 116 42 5N 92 56W
Marshfield, Mo., U.S.A. 117 37 20N 92 58W
Marshfield, Wis., U.S.A. 116 44 42N 90 10W
Mársico Nuovo 41 40 26N 15 43 E
Märsta 48 59 37N 17 52 E
Marstal 49 54 51N 10 30 E
Marstrand 49 57 53N 11 35 E
Mart 117 31 34N 96 51W
Marta → 39 42 14N 11 42 E
Martaban 67 16 30N 97 35 E
Martaban, G. of 67 16 5N 96 30 E
Martagne 18 46 59N 0 57W
Martano 41 40 14N 18 18 E
Martapura, Kalimantan, Indon. 72 3 22 S 114 47 E
Martapura, Sumatera, Indon. 72 4 19 S 104 22 E
Marte 85 12 23N 13 46 E
Martel 20 44 57N 1 37 E
Martelange 16 49 49N 5 43 E
Martés, Sierra 33 39 20N 1 0W
Marthaguy Creek → 99 30 16 S 147 35 E
Martha's Vineyard 114 41 25N 70 35W
Martigné-Ferchaud 18 47 50N 1 20W
Martigny 25 46 6N 7 3 E
Martigues 21 43 24N 5 4 E
Martil 82 35 36N 5 15W
Martin, Czech. 27 49 6N 18 48 E
Martin, S.D., U.S.A. 116 43 11N 101 45W
Martin, Tenn., U.S.A. 117 36 23N 88 51W
Martín → 32 41 18N 0 19W
Martin, L. 115 32 45N 85 50W
Martina Franca 41 40 42N 17 20 E
Martinborough 101 41 14 S 175 29 E
Martinique 121 14 40N 61 0W
Martinique Passage 121 15 15N 61 0W
Martinon 45 38 35N 23 15 E
Martinópolis 125 22 11 S 51 12W
Martins Ferry 113 40 5N 80 46W
Martinsberg 26 48 22N 15 9 E
Martinsburg, Pa., U.S.A. 112 40 18N 78 21W
Martinsburg, W. Va., U.S.A. 114 39 30N 77 57W
Martinsville, Ind., U.S.A. 114 39 29N 86 23W
Martinsville, Va., U.S.A. 115 36 41N 79 52W
Marton 101 40 4 S 175 23 E
Martorell 32 41 28N 1 56 E
Martos 31 37 44N 3 58W
Martuni 57 40 9N 45 10 E
Maru 85 12 22N 6 22 E
Marudi 72 4 10N 114 19 E
Ma'ruf 65 31 30N 67 6 E
Marugame 74 34 15N 133 40 E
Marúggio 41 40 20N 17 33 E
Marulan 99 34 43 S 150 3 E
Marunga 92 17 28 S 20 2 E
Marungu, Mts. 90 7 30 S 30 0 E
Mårvatn 47 60 8N 8 14 E
Marvejols 20 44 33N 3 19 E
Marwar 68 25 43N 73 45 E
Mary 58 37 40N 61 50 E
Mary Frances L. 109 63 19N 106 13W
Mary Kathleen 97 20 44 S 139 48 E
Maryborough, Queens., Austral. 97 25 31 S 152 37 E
Maryborough, Vic., Austral. 97 37 0 S 143 44 E
Maryfield 109 49 50N 101 35W
Maryland □ 114 39 10N 76 40W
Maryland Jc. 91 17 45 S 30 31 E
Maryport 12 54 43N 3 30W
Mary's Harbour 107 52 18N 55 51W
Marystown 107 47 10N 55 10W
Marysvale 119 38 25N 112 17W
Marysville, Can. 108 49 35N 116 0W
Marysville, Calif., U.S.A. 118 39 14N 121 40W
Marysville, Kans., U.S.A. 116 39 50N 96 49W
Marysville, Mich., U.S.A. 112 42 55N 82 29W
Marysville, Ohio, U.S.A. 114 40 15N 83 20W
Maryvale 99 28 4 S 152 12 E
Maryville 115 35 50N 84 0W
Marzūq 83 25 53N 13 57 E
Masada = Mesada 62 31 20N 35 19 E
Masahunga 90 2 6 S 33 18 E
Masai Steppe 90 4 30 S 36 30 E
Masaka 90 0 21 S 31 45 E
Masalembo, Kepulauan 72 5 35 S 114 30 E
Masalima, Kepulauan 72 5 4 S 117 5 E
Masamba 73 2 30 S 120 15 E
Masan 76 35 11N 128 32 E
Masanasa 33 39 25N 0 25W
Masandam, Ras 65 26 30N 56 30 E
Masasi 91 10 45 S 38 52 E
Masasi □ 91 10 45 S 38 50 E
Masaya 121 12 0N 86 7W
Masba 85 10 35N 13 1 E
Masbate 73 12 21N 123 36 E
Mascara 82 35 26N 0 6 E
Mascota 120 20 30N 104 50W
Masela 73 8 9 S 129 51 E
Maseru 92 29 18 S 27 30 E
Mashaba 91 20 2 S 30 29 E
Mashābih 64 25 35N 36 30 E
Mashan 77 23 40N 108 11 E
Mashhad 65 36 20N 59 35 E
Mashi 85 13 0N 7 54 E
Mashike 74 43 31N 141 30 E
Mashkel, Hamun-i- 66 28 30N 63 0 E
Mashki Chah 66 29 5N 62 30 E
Mashtaga 57 40 35N 50 0 E
Masi 50 69 26N 23 40 E
Masi Manimba 88 4 40 S 17 54 E
Masindi 90 1 40N 31 43 E
Masindi Port 90 1 43N 32 2 E
Masisea 126 8 35 S 74 22W
Masisi 90 1 23 S 28 49 E
Masjed Soleyman 64 31 55N 49 18 E
Mask, L. 15 53 36N 9 24W
Maski 70 15 56N 76 46 E
Maslen Nos 43 42 18N 27 48 E
Maslinica 39 43 24N 16 13 E
Masnou 32 41 28N 2 20 E
Masoala, Tanjon' i 93 15 59 S 50 13 E
Masoarivo 93 19 3 S 44 19 E
Masohi 73 3 2 S 128 15 E
Masomeloka 93 20 17 S 48 37 E
Mason, S.D., U.S.A. 116 45 12N 103 27W
Mason, Tex., U.S.A. 117 30 45N 99 15W
Mason City, Iowa, U.S.A. 116 43 9N 93 12W
Mason City, Wash., U.S.A. 118 48 0N 119 0W
Masqat 65 23 37N 58 36 E
Massa 38 44 2N 10 7 E
Massa Maríttima 38 43 3N 10 52 E
Massa, O. → 82 30 2N 9 40W
Massachusetts □ 114 42 25N 72 0W
Massachusetts B. 113 42 30N 70 0W
Massada 62 33 41N 35 36 E
Massafra 41 40 35N 17 8 E
Massaguet 81 12 28N 15 26 E
Massakory 81 13 0N 15 49 E
Massangena 93 21 34 S 33 0 E
Massarosa 38 43 53N 10 17 E
Massat 20 42 53N 1 21 E
Massawa = Mitsiwa 87 15 35N 39 25 E
Massena 114 44 52N 74 55W
Massénya 81 11 21N 16 9 E
Masset 108 54 2N 132 10W
Massiac 20 45 15N 3 11 E
Massif Central 20 45 30N 2 21 E
Massillon 114 40 47N 81 30W
Massinga 93 23 46 S 32 4 E
Masson 113 45 32N 75 25W
Masson I. 5 66 10 S 93 20 E
Mastaba 86 20 52N 39 30 E
Mastanli = Momchilgrad 43 41 33N 25 23 E
Masterton 101 40 56 S 175 39 E
Mástikho, Ákra 45 38 10N 26 2 E
Mastuj 69 36 20N 72 36 E
Mastung 66 29 50N 66 56 E
Mastura 86 23 7N 38 52 E
Masuda 74 34 40N 131 51 E
Maswa □ 90 3 30 S 34 0 E
Matabeleland North □ 91 19 0 S 28 0 E
Matabeleland South □ 91 21 0 S 29 0 E
Mataboor 73 1 41 S 138 3 E
Matachel → 31 38 50N 6 17W
Matachewan 106 47 56N 80 39W
Matad 75 47 11N 115 27 E
Matadi 88 5 52 S 13 31 E
Matagalpa 121 13 0N 85 58W
Matagami 106 49 45N 77 34W
Matagami, L. 106 49 50N 77 40W
Matagorda 117 28 43N 96 0W
Matagorda B. 117 28 30N 96 15W
Matagorda I. 117 28 10N 96 40W
Matak, P. 72 3 18N 106 16 E
Matakana 99 32 59 S 145 54 E
Matale 70 7 30N 80 37 E
Matam 84 15 34N 13 17W
Matameye 85 13 26N 8 28 E
Matamoros, Coahuila, Mexico 120 25 33N 103 15W
Matamoros, Puebla, Mexico 120 18 2N 98 17W
Matamoros, Tamaulipas, Mexico 120 25 50N 97 30W
Ma'ṭan as Sarra 81 21 45N 22 0 E
Matandu → 91 8 45 S 34 19 E
Matane 107 48 50N 67 33W
Matankari 85 13 46N 4 1 E
Matanuska 104 61 39N 149 19W
Matanzas 121 23 0N 81 40W
Matapan, C. = Taínaron, Akra 45 36 22N 22 27 E
Matapédia 107 48 0N 66 59W
Matara 70 5 58N 80 30 E
Mataram 72 8 41 S 116 10 E
Matarani 126 77 0 S 72 10W
Mataranka 96 14 55 S 133 4 E
Mataró 32 41 32N 2 29 E
Matarraña → 32 41 14N 0 22 E
Mataruška Banja 42 43 40N 20 45 E
Matatiele 93 30 20 S 28 49 E
Mataura 101 46 11 S 168 51 E
Matehuala 120 23 40N 100 40W
Mateke Hills 91 21 48 S 31 0 E
Matélica 39 43 15N 13 0 E
Matera 41 40 40N 16 37 E
Mátészalka 27 47 58N 22 20 E
Matetsi 91 18 12 S 26 0 E
Mateur 83 37 0N 9 40 E
Matfors 48 62 21N 17 2 E
Matha 20 45 52N 0 20W
Matheson Island 109 51 45N 96 56W
Mathis 117 28 4N 97 48W
Mathura 68 27 30N 77 40 E
Mati 73 6 55N 126 15 E
Mati → 44 41 40N 20 0 E
Matías Romero 120 16 53N 95 2W
Matibane 91 14 49 S 40 45 E
Matima 92 20 15 S 24 26 E
Matlock 12 53 8N 1 32W
Matmata 83 33 37N 9 59 E
Matna 87 13 49N 35 10 E
Mato Grosso □ 127 14 0 S 55 0W
Mato Grosso, Planalto do 127 15 0 S 59 57W
Matochkin Shar 58 73 10N 56 40 E
Matopo Hills 91 20 36 S 28 20 E
Matopos 91 20 20 S 28 29 E
Matosinhos 30 41 11N 8 42W
Matour 21 46 19N 4 29 E
Matrah 65 23 37N 58 30 E
Matrûh 86 31 19N 27 9 E
Matsena 85 13 5N 10 5 E
Matsesta 57 43 34N 39 51 E
Matsue 74 35 25N 133 10 E
Matsumoto 74 36 15N 138 0 E
Matsuyama 74 33 45N 132 45 E
Mattagami → 106 50 43N 81 29W
Mattancheri 70 9 50N 76 15 E
Mattawa 106 46 20N 78 45W
Mattawamkeag 107 45 30N 68 21W
Matterhorn 25 45 58N 7 39 E
Mattersburg 27 47 44N 16 24 E
Matthew Town 121 20 57N 73 40W
Matthew's Ridge 126 7 37N 60 10W
Mattice 106 49 40N 83 20W
Mattituck 113 40 58N 72 32W
Mattmar 48 63 18N 13 45 E
Matua 72 2 58 S 110 46 E
Matuba 93 24 28 S 32 49 E
Matucana 126 11 55 S 76 25W
Matun 66 33 22N 69 58 E
Maturín 126 9 45N 63 11W
Matveyev Kurgan 57 47 35N 38 47 E
Mau-é-ele 93 24 18 S 34 2 E
Mau Escarpment 90 0 40 S 36 0 E
Mau Ranipur 68 25 16N 79 8 E
Maubeuge 19 50 17N 3 57 E
Maubourguet 20 43 29N 0 1 E
Maude 99 34 29 S 144 18 E
Maudheim 5 71 5 S 11 0W
Maudin Sun 67 16 0N 94 30 E
Maués 126 3 20 S 57 45W
Maui 110 20 45N 156 20 E
Mauke 101 20 09 S 157 20W
Maule □ 124 36 5 S 72 30W
Mauléon-Licharre 20 43 14N 0 54W
Maumee 114 41 35N 83 40W
Maumee → 114 41 42N 83 28W
Maumere 73 8 38 S 122 13 E
Maun 92 20 0 S 23 26 E
Mauna Kea 110 19 50N 155 28W
Mauna Loa 110 21 8N 157 10W
Maunath Bhanjan 69 25 56N 83 33 E
Maungmagan Kyunzu 71 14 0N 97 48 E
Maupin 118 45 12N 121 9W
Maure-de-Bretagne 18 47 53N 2 0W
Maurepas L. 117 30 18N 90 35W
Maures 21 43 15N 6 15 E
Mauriac 20 45 13N 2 19 E
Maurice L. 96 29 30 S 131 0 E
Mauritania ■ 80 20 50N 10 0W
Mauritius ■ 3 20 0 S 57 0 E
Mauron 18 48 9N 2 18W
Maurs 20 44 43N 2 12 E
Mauston 116 43 48N 90 5W
Mauterndorf 26 47 9N 13 40 E
Mauvezin 20 43 44N 0 53 E
Mauzé-sur-le-Mignon 20 46 12N 0 41W
Mavelikara 70 9 14N 76 32 E
Mavinga 89 15 50 S 20 21 E
Mavli 68 24 45N 73 55 E
Mavqi'im 62 31 38N 34 32 E
Mavrova 44 40 26N 19 32 E
Mavuradonha Mts. 91 16 30 S 31 30 E
Mawa 90 2 45N 26 40 E
Mawana 68 29 6N 77 58 E
Mawand 68 29 33N 68 38 E
Mawk Mai 67 20 14N 97 37 E
Mawson Base 5 67 30 S 62 53 E
Max 116 47 50N 101 20W
Maxcanú 120 20 40N 92 0W
Maxhamish L. 108 59 50N 123 17W
Maxixe 93 23 54 S 35 17 E
Maxville 113 45 17N 74 51W
Maxwelton 98 20 43 S 142 41 E
May Downs 98 22 38 S 148 55 E
May Glacier Tongue 5 66 08 S 130 35 E
May Pen 121 17 58N 77 15W
Maya 32 43 12N 1 29W
Maya → 59 54 31N 134 41 E
Maya Mts. 120 16 30N 89 0W
Mayaguana 121 22 30N 72 44W
Mayagüez 121 18 12N 67 9W
Mayahi 85 13 58N 7 40 E
Mayals 32 41 22N 0 30 E
Mayarí 121 20 40N 75 41W
Mayavaram = Mayuram 70 11 3N 79 42 E
Maybell 118 40 30N 108 4W
Maychew 87 12 50N 39 31 E
Maydena 99 42 45 S 146 30 E
Maydos 44 40 13N 26 20 E
Mayen 25 50 18N 7 10 E
Mayenne 18 48 20N 0 38W
Mayenne □ 18 48 10N 0 40W
Mayenne → 18 47 30N 0 32W
Mayer 119 34 28N 112 17W
Mayerthorpe 108 53 57N 115 8W
Mayfield 115 36 45N 88 40W
Mayhill 119 32 58N 105 30W
Maykop 57 44 35N 40 25 E
Maymyo 71 22 2N 96 28 E
Maynooth 15 53 22N 6 38W
Mayo 104 63 38N 135 57W
Mayo □ 15 53 47N 9 7W
Mayo → 120 26 45N 109 47W
Mayo L. 104 63 45N 135 0W
Mayon, Mt. 73 13 15N 123 42 E
Mayor I. 101 37 16 S 176 17 E
Mayorga 30 42 10N 5 16W
Mayskiy 57 43 47N 44 2 E
Mayson L. 109 57 55N 107 10W
Maysville 114 38 39N 83 46W
Maythalūn 62 32 21N 35 16 E
Mayu 73 1 30N 126 30 E
Mayuram 70 11 3N 79 42 E
Mayville, N.D., U.S.A. 116 47 30N 97 23W
Mayville, N.Y., U.S.A. 112 42 14N 79 31W
Mayya 59 61 44N 130 18 E
Mazabuka 91 15 52 S 27 44 E
Mazagán = El Jadida 82 33 11N 8 17W
Mazagão 127 0 7 S 51 16W
Mazamet 20 43 30N 2 20 E
Mazán 126 3 30 S 73 0W
Mazan Deran □ 65 36 30N 52 0 E
Mazar-e Sharīf 65 36 41N 67 0 E
Mazar, O. → 82 31 50N 1 36 E
Mazara del Vallo 40 37 40N 12 34 E
Mazarredo 128 47 10 S 66 50W
Mazarrón 33 37 38N 1 19W
Mazarrón, Golfo de 33 37 27N 1 19W
Mazaruni → 126 6 25N 58 35W
Mazatenango 120 14 35N 91 30W
Mazatlán 120 23 10N 106 30W
Mažeikiai 54 56 20N 22 20 E
Māzhān 65 32 30N 59 0 E
Mazīnān 65 36 19N 56 56 E
Mazoe, Mozam. 91 16 42 S 33 7 E
Mazoe, Zimb. 91 17 28 S 30 58 E
Mazrûb 87 14 0N 29 20 E
Mazu Dao 77 26 10N 119 55 E
Mazurian Lakes = Mazurski, Pojezierze 28 53 50N 21 0 E
Mazurski, Pojezierze 28 53 50N 21 0 E
Mazzarino 41 37 19N 14 12 E
Mbaba 84 14 59N 16 44W
Mbabane 93 26 18 S 31 6 E
Mbagne 84 16 6N 14 47W
M'bahiakro 84 7 33N 4 19W
Mbaïki 88 3 53N 18 1 E
Mbala 91 8 46 S 31 24 E
Mbale 90 1 8N 34 12 E
Mbalmayo 88 3 33N 11 33 E
Mbamba Bay 91 11 13 S 34 49 E
Mbandaka 88 0 1N 18 18 E
Mbanga 85 4 30N 9 33 E
Mbanza Congo 88 6 18 S 14 16 E
Mbanza Ngungu 88 5 12 S 14 53 E
Mbarara 90 0 35 S 30 40 E
Mbatto 84 6 28N 4 22W
Mbenkuru → 91 9 25 S 39 50 E
Mberubu 85 6 10N 7 38 E
Mbesuma 91 10 0 S 32 2 E
Mbeya 91 8 54 S 33 29 E
Mbeya □ 90 8 15 S 33 30 E
Mbinga 91 10 50 S 35 0 E
Mbinga □ 91 10 50 S 35 0 E
Mbini = Rio Muni □ 88 1 30N 10 0 E
Mboki 87 5 19N 25 58 E
Mboro 84 15 9N 16 54W
Mboune 84 14 42N 13 34W
Mbour 84 14 22N 16 54W
Mbout 84 16 1N 12 38W
Mbozi □ 91 9 0 S 32 50 E
Mbuji-Mayi 90 6 9 S 23 40 E
Mbulu 90 3 45 S 35 30 E
Mbulu □ 90 3 52 S 35 33 E

Mburucuyá

Miarinarivo

Mburucuyá **124** 28 1 S 58 14W
Mcherrah **82** 27 0N 4 30W
Mchinja **91** 9 44 S 39 45 E
Mchinji **91** 13 47 S 32 58 E
Mdennah **82** 24 37N 6 0W
Mdina **36** 35 51N 14 25 E
Mead, L. **119** 36 1N 114 44W
Meade **117** 37 18N 100 25W
Meadow Lake **109** 54 10N 108 26W
Meadow Lake Prov. Park **109** 54 27N 109 0W
Meadow Valley Wash → **119** 36 39N 114 35W
Meadville **114** 41 39N 80 9W
Meaford **106** 44 36N 80 35W
Mealhada **30** 40 22N 8 27W
Mealy Mts. **107** 53 10N 58 0W
Meander River **108** 59 2N 117 42W
Meares, C. **118** 45 37N 124 0W
Mearim → **127** 3 4 S 44 35W
Meath □ **15** 53 32N 6 40W
Meath Park **109** 53 27N 105 22W
Meaulne **20** 46 36N 2 36 E
Meaux **19** 48 58N 2 50 E
Mecanhelas **91** 15 12 S 35 54 E
Mecca **119** 33 37N 116 3W
Mecca = Makkah **86** 21 30N 39 54 E
Mechanicsburg **112** 40 12N 77 0W
Mechanicville **113** 42 54N 73 41W
Mechara **87** 8 36N 40 20 E
Mechelen **16** 51 2N 4 29 E
Mecheria **82** 33 35N 0 18W
Mechernich **24** 50 35N 6 39 E
Mechetinskaya **57** 46 45N 40 32 E
Mechra Benâbbou **82** 32 39N 7 48W
Mecidiye **44** 40 38N 26 32 E
Mecitözü **56** 40 32N 35 17 E
Meconta **91** 14 59 S 39 50 E
Meda **30** 40 57N 7 18W
Meda → **96** 17 20 S 123 50 E
Medak **70** 18 1N 78 15 E
Medan **72** 3 40N 98 38 E
Medanosa, Pta. **128** 48 8 S 66 0W
Medawachchiya **70** 8 30N 80 30 E
Medéa **82** 36 12N 2 50 E
Mededa **42** 43 44N 19 15 E
Medellín **126** 6 15N 75 35W
Medemblik **16** 52 46N 5 8 E
Médenine **83** 33 21N 10 30 E
Mederdra **84** 17 0N 15 38W
Medford, Oreg., U.S.A. **118** 42 20N 122 52W
Medford, Wis., U.S.A. **116** 45 9N 90 21W
Medgidia **46** 44 15N 28 19 E
Medi **87** 5 4N 30 42 E
Media Agua **124** 31 58 S 68 25W
Media Luna **124** 34 45 S 66 44W
Mediaş **46** 46 9N 24 22 E
Medical Lake **118** 47 35N 117 42W
Medicina **39** 44 29N 11 38 E
Medicine Bow **118** 41 56N 106 11W
Medicine Bow Pk. **118** 41 21N 106 19W
Medicine Bow Ra. **118** 41 10N 106 25W
Medicine Hat **109** 50 0N 110 45W
Medicine Lake **116** 48 30N 104 30W
Medicine Lodge **117** 37 20N 98 37W
Medina, N.D., U.S.A. **116** 46 57N 99 20W
Medina, N.Y., U.S.A. **114** 43 15N 78 27W
Medina, Ohio, U.S.A. **114** 41 9N 81 50W
Medina = Al Madīnah **64** 24 35N 39 35 E
Medina → **117** 29 10N 98 20W
Medina de Ríoseco **30** 41 53N 5 3W
Medina del Campo **30** 41 18N 4 55W
Medina L. **117** 29 35N 98 58W
Medina-Sidonia **31** 36 28N 5 57W
Medinaceli **32** 41 12N 2 30W
Mediterranean Sea **34** 35 0N 15 0 E
Medjerda, O. → **83** 37 7N 10 13 E
Medley **109** 54 25N 110 16W
Médoc **20** 45 10N 0 56W
Medstead **109** 53 19N 108 5W
Medulin **39** 44 49N 13 55 E
Medveda **42** 42 50N 21 32 E
Medveditsa →, R.S.F.S.R., U.S.S.R. **55** 49 35N 42 41 E
Medveditsa →, R.S.F.S.R., U.S.S.R. **55** 57 5N 37 30 E
Medvedok **55** 57 20N 50 1 E
Medvezhi, Ostrava **59** 71 0N 161 0 E
Medvezhyegorsk **52** 63 0N 34 25 E
Medway → **13** 51 28N 0 45 E
Medyn **55** 54 58N 35 52 E
Medzev **27** 48 43N 20 55 E
Medzilaborce **27** 49 17N 21 52 E
Meekatharra **96** 26 32 S 118 29 E
Meeker **118** 40 1N 107 58W
Meerane **24** 50 51N 12 30 E
Meersburg **25** 47 42N 9 16 E
Meerut **68** 29 1N 77 42 E
Meeteetse **118** 44 10N 108 56W
Mega **87** 3 57N 38 19 E
Megálo Khorío **45** 36 27N 27 24 E
Megálo Petalí **45** 38 0N 24 15 E
Megalópolis **45** 37 25N 22 7 E
Meganísi **45** 38 39N 20 48 E
Mégara **45** 37 58N 23 22 E
Megarine **83** 33 14N 6 2 E
Megdhova → **45** 39 10N 21 45 E
Mégève **21** 45 51N 6 37 E
Meghezez, Mt. **87** 9 18N 39 26 E
Meghna → **69** 22 50N 90 50 E
Megiddo **62** 32 36N 35 11 E
Mégiscane, L. **106** 48 35N 75 55W
Megiste **35** 36 8N 29 34 E
Mehadia **46** 44 56N 22 23 E
Mehaïguene, O. → **82** 32 15N 2 59 E
Meharry, Mt. **96** 22 59 S 118 35 E
Mehedinţi □ **46** 44 40N 22 45 E
Meheisa **86** 19 38N 32 57 E
Mehndawal **69** 26 58N 83 5 E
Mehsana **68** 23 39N 72 26 E
Mehun-sur-Yèvre **19** 47 10N 2 13 E
Mei Jiang → **77** 24 25N 116 35 E
Mei Xian **75** 24 16N 116 6 E
Meiganga **88** 6 30N 14 25 E
Meiktila **67** 20 53N 95 54 E
Meiningen **24** 50 32N 10 25 E
Me'ir Shefeya **62** 32 35N 34 58 E
Meira, Sierra de **30** 43 15N 7 15W
Meiringen **25** 46 43N 8 12 E
Meissen **24** 51 10N 13 29 E
Meissner **24** 51 13N 9 51 E
Meitan **77** 27 45N 107 29 E
Méjean, Causse **20** 44 15N 3 30 E
Mejillones **124** 23 10 S 70 30W
Mékambo **88** 1 2N 13 50 E
Mekdela **87** 11 24N 39 10 E
Mekele **87** 13 33N 39 30 E
Meklong = Samut Songkhram **71** 13 24N 100 1 E
Meknès **82** 33 57N 5 33W
Meko **85** 7 27N 2 52 E
Mekong → **71** 9 30N 106 15 E
Mekongga **73** 3 39 S 121 15 E
Melagiri Hills **70** 12 20N 77 30 E
Melah, Sebkhet el **82** 29 20N 1 30W
Melaka **71** 2 15N 102 15 E
Melaka □ **71** 2 20N 102 15 E
Melalap **72** 5 10N 116 5 E
Mélambes **45** 35 8N 24 40 E
Melanesia **94** 4 0 S 155 0 E
Melapalaiyam **70** 8 39N 77 44 E
Melbourne, Austral. **97** 37 50 S 145 0 E
Melbourne, U.S.A. **115** 28 4N 80 35W
Melchor Múzquiz **120** 27 50N 101 30W
Melchor Ocampo (San Pedro Ocampo) **120** 24 52N 101 40W
Méldola **39** 44 7N 12 3 E
Meldorf **24** 54 5N 9 5 E
Mêle-sur-Sarthe, Le **18** 48 31N 0 22 E
Melegnano **38** 45 21N 9 20 E
Melenci **42** 45 32N 20 20 E
Melenki **55** 55 20N 41 37 E
Mélèzes → **105** 57 30N 71 0W
Melfi, Chad **81** 11 0N 17 59 E
Melfi, Italy **41** 41 0N 15 33 E
Melfort, Can. **109** 52 50N 104 37W
Melfort, Zimb. **91** 18 0 S 31 25 E
Melgaço **30** 42 7N 8 15W
Melgar de Fernamental **30** 42 27N 4 17W
Melhus **47** 63 17N 10 18 E
Meligalá **45** 37 15N 21 59 E
Melilla **82** 35 21N 2 57W
Melilot **62** 31 22N 34 37 E
Melipilla **124** 33 42 S 71 15W
Mélissa Óros **45** 37 32N 26 4 E
Melita **109** 49 15N 101 0W
Mélito di Porto Salvo **41** 37 55N 15 47 E
Melitopol **56** 46 50N 35 22 E
Melk **26** 48 13N 15 20 E
Mellan-Fryken **48** 59 45N 13 10 E
Mellansel **50** 63 25N 18 17 E
Melle, France **20** 46 14N 0 10W
Melle, Ger. **24** 52 12N 8 20 E
Mellégue, O. → **83** 36 32N 8 51 E
Mellen **116** 46 19N 90 36W
Mellerud **49** 58 41N 12 28 E
Mellette **116** 45 11N 98 29W
Mellid **30** 42 55N 8 1W
Mellish Reef **97** 17 25 S 155 50 E
Mellit **87** 14 7N 25 34 E
Mellrichstadt **25** 50 26N 10 19 E
Melnik **43** 41 30N 23 25 E
Mělník **26** 50 22N 14 23 E
Melo **125** 32 20 S 54 10W
Melolo **73** 9 53 S 120 40 E
Melovoye **57** 49 25N 40 5 E
Melrhir, Chott **83** 34 25N 6 24 E
Melrose, Austral. **99** 32 42 S 146 57 E
Melrose, U.K. **14** 53 35N 2 44W
Melrose, U.S.A. **117** 34 27N 103 33W
Melstone **118** 46 36N 107 50W
Melsungen **24** 51 8N 9 34 E
Melton Mowbray **12** 52 46N 0 52W
Melun **19** 48 32N 2 39 E
Melur **70** 10 2N 78 23 E
Melut **87** 10 30N 32 13 E
Melville **109** 50 55N 102 50W
Melville B. **97** 12 0 S 136 45 E
Melville, C. **97** 14 11 S 144 30 E
Melville I., Austral. **96** 11 30 S 131 0 E
Melville I., Can. **4** 75 30N 112 0W
Melville, L. **107** 53 30N 60 0W
Melville Pen. **105** 68 0N 84 0W
Melvin → **108** 59 11N 117 31W
Mélykút **27** 46 11N 19 25 E
Memaliaj **44** 40 25N 19 58 E
Memba **91** 14 11 S 40 30 E
Memboro **73** 9 30 S 119 30 E
Membrilla **33** 38 59N 3 21W
Memel **93** 27 38 S 29 36 E
Memel = Klaipeda **54** 55 43N 21 10 E
Memmingen **25** 47 59N 10 12 E
Memphis, Tenn., U.S.A. **117** 35 7N 90 0W
Memphis, Tex., U.S.A. **117** 34 45N 100 30W
Mena **117** 34 40N 94 15W
Mena → **87** 5 40N 40 50 E
Menai Strait **12** 53 14N 4 10W
Ménaka **85** 15 59N 2 18 E
Menan = Chao Phraya → **71** 13 32N 100 36 E
Menarandra → **93** 25 17 S 44 30 E
Menard **117** 30 57N 99 48W
Menasha **114** 44 13N 88 27W
Menate **72** 0 12 S 113 3 E
Mendawai → **72** 3 17 S 113 21 E
Mende **20** 44 31N 3 30 E
Mendebo Mts. **87** 7 0N 39 22 E
Menderes → **64** 37 25N 28 45 E
Mendi, Ethiopia **87** 9 47N 35 4 E
Mendi, P.N.G. **98** 6 11 S 143 39 E
Mendip Hills **13** 51 17N 2 40W
Mendocino **118** 39 26N 123 50W
Mendocino Seascarp **95** 41 0N 140 0W
Mendota, Calif., U.S.A. **119** 36 46N 120 24W
Mendota, Ill., U.S.A. **116** 41 35N 89 5W
Mendoza **124** 32 50 S 68 52W
Mendoza □ **124** 33 0 S 69 0W
Mene Grande **126** 9 49N 70 56W
Menemen **64** 38 34N 27 3 E
Menen **16** 50 47N 3 7 E
Menfi **40** 37 36N 12 57 E
Mengcheng **77** 33 18N 116 31 E
Mengeš **39** 46 24N 14 35 E
Menggala **72** 4 30 S 105 15 E
Mengíbar **31** 37 58N 3 48W
Mengoub **82** 29 49N 5 26W
Mengshan **77** 24 14N 110 55 E
Mengzi **75** 23 20N 103 22 E
Menihek L. **107** 54 0N 67 0W
Menin = Menen **16** 50 47N 3 7 E
Menindee **97** 32 20 S 142 25 E
Menindee, L. **99** 32 20 S 142 25 E
Meningie **99** 35 35 S 139 0 E
Menominee **114** 45 9N 87 39W
Menominee → **114** 45 5N 87 36W
Menomonie **116** 44 50N 91 54W
Menongue **89** 14 48 S 17 52 E
Menorca **32** 40 0N 4 0 E
Mentawai, Kepulauan **72** 2 0 S 99 0 E
Menton **21** 43 50N 7 29 E
Mentor **112** 41 40N 81 21W
Menzel-Bourguiba **83** 39 9N 9 49 E
Menzel Chaker **83** 35 0N 10 26 E
Menzel-Temime **83** 36 46N 11 0 E
Menzelinsk **52** 55 53N 53 1 E
Menzies **96** 29 40 S 120 58 E
Me'ona (Tarshiha) **62** 33 1N 35 15 E
Mepaco **91** 15 57 S 30 48 E
Meppel **16** 52 42N 6 12 E
Meppen **24** 52 41N 7 20 E
Mequinenza **32** 41 22N 0 17 E
Mer Rouge **117** 32 47N 91 48W
Merabéllou, Kólpos **45** 35 10N 25 50 E
Merak **73** 5 56 S 106 0 E
Meran = Merano **39** 46 40N 11 10 E
Merano **39** 46 40N 11 10 E
Merate **38** 45 42N 9 23 E
Merauke **73** 8 29 S 140 24 E
Merbabu **73** 7 30 S 110 40 E
Merbein **99** 34 10 S 142 2 E
Merca **63** 1 48N 44 50 E
Mercadal **32** 39 59N 4 5 E
Mercara **70** 12 30N 75 45 E
Mercato Saraceno **39** 43 57N 12 11 E
Merced **119** 37 18N 120 30W
Mercedes, Buenos Aires, Argent. **124** 34 40 S 59 30W
Mercedes, Corrientes, Argent. **124** 29 10 S 58 5W
Mercedes, San Luis, Argent. **124** 33 40 S 65 21W
Mercedes, Uruguay **124** 33 12 S 58 0W
Merceditas **124** 28 20 S 70 35W
Mercer, N.Z. **101** 37 16 S 175 5 E
Mercer, U.S.A. **112** 41 14N 80 13W
Mercy C. **105** 65 0N 63 30W
Merdrignac **18** 48 11N 2 27W
Meredith C. **128** 52 15 S 60 40W
Meredith, L. **117** 35 30N 101 35W
Merei **46** 45 7N 26 43 E
Méréville **19** 48 20N 2 5 E
Mergenevsky **57** 49 59N 51 15 E
Mergui Arch. = Myeik Kyunzu **71** 11 30N 97 30 E
Mérida, Mexico **120** 20 9N 89 40W
Mérida, Spain **31** 38 55N 6 25W
Mérida, Venez. **126** 8 24N 71 8W
Meriden **114** 41 33N 72 47W
Meridian, Idaho, U.S.A. **118** 43 41N 116 25W
Meridian, Miss., U.S.A. **115** 32 20N 88 42W
Meridian, Tex., U.S.A. **117** 31 55N 97 37W
Mering **25** 48 15N 11 0 E
Meringur **100** 34 20 S 141 19 E
Meriruma **127** 1 15N 54 50W
Merkel **117** 32 30N 100 0W
Merksem **16** 51 16N 4 25 E
Merlebach **19** 49 5N 6 52 E
Merlerault, Le **18** 48 41N 0 16 E
Mern **49** 55 3N 12 3 E
Merowe **86** 18 29N 31 46 E
Merredin **96** 31 28 S 118 18 E
Merrick **14** 55 8N 4 30W
Merrickville **113** 44 55N 75 50W
Merrill, Oregon, U.S.A. **118** 42 2N 121 37W
Merrill, Wis., U.S.A. **116** 45 11N 89 41W
Merriman **116** 42 55N 101 42W
Merritt **108** 50 10N 120 45W
Merriwa **99** 32 6 S 150 22 E
Merriwagga **99** 33 47 S 145 43 E
Merry I. **106** 55 29N 77 31W
Merrygoen **99** 31 51 S 149 12 E
Merryville **117** 30 47N 93 31W
Mersa Fatma **87** 14 57N 40 17 E
Mersch **16** 49 44N 6 7 E
Merseburg **24** 51 20N 12 0 E
Mersey → **12** 53 20N 2 56W
Merseyside □ **12** 53 25N 2 55W
Mersin **64** 36 51N 34 36 E
Mersing **71** 2 25N 103 50 E
Merta **68** 26 39N 74 4 E
Merthyr Tydfil **13** 51 45N 3 23W
Mértola **31** 37 40N 7 40 E
Mertzon **117** 31 17N 100 48W
Méru **19** 49 13N 2 8 E
Meru, Kenya **90** 0 3N 37 40 E
Meru, Tanz. **90** 3 15 S 36 46 E
Meru □ **90** 0 3N 37 46 E
Merville **19** 50 38N 2 38 E
Méry-sur-Seine **19** 48 31N 3 54 E
Merzifon **56** 40 53N 35 32 E
Merzig **25** 49 26N 6 37 E
Merzouga, Erg Tin **83** 24 0N 11 4 E
Mesa **119** 33 20N 111 56W
Mesa, La, Calif., U.S.A. **119** 32 48N 117 5W
Mesa, La, N. Mex., U.S.A. **119** 32 6N 106 48W
Mesach Mellet **83** 24 30N 11 30 E
Mesada **62** 31 20N 35 19 E
Mesagne **41** 40 34N 17 48 E
Mesaras, Kólpos **45** 35 6N 24 47 E
Meschede **24** 51 20N 8 17 E
Mesfinto **87** 13 20N 37 22 E
Mesgouez, L. **106** 51 20N 75 0W
Meshchovsk **54** 54 22N 35 17 E
Meshed = Mashhad **65** 36 20N 59 35 E
Meshoppen **113** 41 36N 76 3W
Meshra er Req **81** 8 25N 29 18 E
Mesick **114** 44 24N 85 42W
Mesilinka → **108** 56 6N 124 30W
Mesilla **119** 32 20N 106 50W
Meslay-du-Maine **18** 47 58N 0 33W
Mesocco **25** 46 23N 9 12 E
Mesolóngion **43** 38 21N 21 28 E
Mesopotamia = Al Jazirah **64** 33 30N 44 0 E
Mesoraca **41** 39 5N 16 47 E
Mésou Volímais **45** 37 53N 20 35 E
Mess Cr. → **108** 57 55N 131 14W
Messac **18** 47 49N 1 50W
Messad **82** 34 8N 3 30 E
Messalo → **91** 12 25 S 39 15 E
Méssaména **85** 3 48N 12 49 E
Messeix **20** 45 37N 2 33 E
Messeue **45** 37 12N 21 58 E
Messina, Italy **41** 38 10N 15 32 E
Messina, S. Afr. **93** 22 20 S 30 0 E
Messina, Str. di **41** 38 5N 15 35 E
Messíni **45** 37 4N 22 1 E
Messínia □ **45** 37 10N 22 0 E
Messiniakós, Kólpos **45** 36 45N 22 5 E
Messkirch **25** 47 59N 9 7 E
Mesta → **43** 41 30N 24 0 E
Mestà, Ákra **45** 38 16N 25 53 E
Mestanza **31** 38 35N 4 4W
Město Teplá **26** 49 59N 12 52 E
Mestre **39** 45 30N 12 13 E
Městys Zelezná Ruda **26** 49 8N 13 15 E
Meta → **126** 6 12N 67 28W
Metairie **117** 29 59N 90 9W
Metalici, Munţii **42** 46 15N 22 50 E
Metaline Falls **118** 48 52N 117 22W
Metán **124** 25 30 S 65 0W
Metauro → **39** 43 50N 13 3 E
Metema **87** 12 56N 36 13 E
Metengobalame **91** 14 49 S 34 30 E
Méthana **45** 37 35N 23 23 E
Methóni **45** 36 49N 21 42 E
Methven **101** 43 38 S 171 40 E
Methy L. **109** 56 28N 109 30W
Metkovets **43** 43 37N 23 10 E
Metković **42** 43 6N 17 39 E
Metlakatla **108** 55 10N 131 33W
Metlaoui **83** 34 24N 8 24 E
Metlika **39** 45 40N 15 20 E
Metropolis **117** 37 10N 88 47W
Métsovon **44** 39 48N 21 12 E
Mettuppalaiyam **70** 11 18N 76 59 E
Mettur **70** 11 48N 77 47 E
Mettur Dam **70** 11 45N 77 45 E
Metulla **62** 33 17N 35 34 E
Metz **19** 49 8N 6 10 E
Meulaboh **72** 4 11N 96 3 E
Meulan **19** 49 0N 1 52 E
Meung-sur-Loire **19** 47 50N 1 40 E
Meureudu **72** 5 19N 96 10 E
Meurthe → **19** 48 47N 6 9 E
Meurthe-et-Moselle □ **19** 48 52N 6 0 E
Meuse □ **19** 49 8N 5 25 E
Meuse → **16** 50 45N 5 41 E
Meuselwitz **24** 51 3N 12 18 E
Mexborough **12** 53 29N 1 18W
Mexia **117** 31 38N 96 32W
Mexiana, I. **127** 0 0 49 30W
Mexicali **120** 32 40N 115 30W
México **120** 19 20N 99 10W
Mexico, Me., U.S.A. **113** 44 35N 70 30W
Mexico, Mo., U.S.A. **116** 39 10N 91 55W
Mexico ■ **120** 20 0N 100 0W
México □ **120** 19 20N 99 10W
Mexico, G. of **120** 25 0N 90 0W
Meyenburg **24** 53 19N 12 15 E
Meymac **20** 45 32N 2 10 E
Meymaneh **65** 35 53N 64 38 E
Meyrargues **21** 43 38N 5 32 E
Meyrueis **20** 44 12N 3 27 E
Meyssac **20** 45 3N 1 40 E
Mezdra **43** 43 12N 23 42 E
Mèze **20** 43 27N 3 36 E
Mezen **52** 65 50N 44 20 E
Mézenc **21** 44 55N 4 11 E
Mezeş, Munţii **46** 47 5N 23 5 E
Mezha → **54** 55 50N 31 45 E
Mézidon **18** 49 5N 0 1W
Mézilhac **21** 44 49N 4 21 E
Mézin **20** 44 4N 0 16 E
Mezöberény **27** 46 49N 21 3 E
Mezöfalva **27** 46 55N 18 49 E
Mezöhegyes **27** 46 19N 20 49 E
Mezökövácsháza **27** 46 25N 20 57 E
Mezökövesd **27** 47 49N 20 35 E
Mézos **20** 44 5N 1 10W
Mezötúr **27** 47 0N 20 41 E
Mezquital **120** 23 29N 104 23W
Mezzolombardo **38** 46 13N 11 5 E
Mgeta **91** 8 22 S 36 6 E
Mglin **54** 53 2N 32 50 E
Mhlaba Hills **91** 18 30 S 30 30 E
Mhow **68** 22 33N 75 50 E
Miahuatlán **120** 16 21N 96 36W
Miajadas **31** 39 9N 5 54W
Mialar **68** 26 15N 70 20 E
Miallo **98** 16 28 S 145 22 E
Miami, Ariz., U.S.A. **119** 33 25N 110 54W
Miami, Fla., U.S.A. **115** 25 45N 80 15W
Miami, Tex., U.S.A. **117** 35 44N 100 38W
Miami → **114** 39 20N 84 40W
Miami Beach **115** 25 49N 80 6W
Miamisburg **114** 39 40N 84 11W
Mian Xian **77** 33 10N 106 32 E
Mianchi **77** 34 48N 111 48 E
Mīāndow āb **64** 37 0N 46 5 E
Miandrivazo **93** 19 31 S 45 29 E
Mīāneh **64** 37 30N 47 40 E
Mianwali **68** 32 38N 71 28 E
Mianyang, Hubei, China **77** 30 25N 113 25 E
Mianyang, Sichuan, China **77** 31 22N 104 47 E
Miaoli **75** 24 37N 120 49 E
Miarinarivo **93** 18 57 S 46 55 E

Miass Mobutu Sese Seko, L.

Miass **52** 54 59N 60 6 E
Miasteczko Kraj **28** 53 7N 17 1 E
Miastko **28** 54 0N 16 58 E
Micăsasa **46** 46 7N 24 7 E
Michalovce **27** 48 47N 21 58 E
Michelstadt **25** 49 40N 9 0 E
Michigan □ **111** 44 40N 85 40W
Michigan City **114** 41 42N 86 56W
Michigan, L. **114** 44 0N 87 0W
Michipicoten **106** 47 55N 84 55W
Michipicoten I. **106** 47 40N 85 40W
Michoacan □ **120** 19 0N 102 0W
Michurin **43** 42 9N 27 51 E
Michurinsk **55** 52 58N 40 27 E
Miclere **98** 22 34 S 147 32 E
Mico, Pta. **121** 12 0N 83 30W
Micronesia **94** 11 0N 160 0 E
Mid Glamorgan □ **13** 51 40N 3 25W
Mid-Indian Ridge **94** 40 0 S 75 0 E
Mid-Oceanic Ridge **94** 42 0 S 90 0 E
Midai, P. **72** 3 0N 107 47 E
Midale **109** 49 25N 103 20W
Midas **118** 41 14N 116 48W
Middagsfjället **48** 63 27N 12 19 E
Middelburg, Neth. **16** 51 30N 3 36 E
Middelburg, C. Prov., S. Afr. **92** 31 30 S 25 0 E
Middelburg, Trans., S. Afr. **93** 25 49 S 29 28 E
Middelfart **49** 55 30N 9 43 E
Middle Alkali L. **118** 41 30N 120 3W
Middle Andaman I. **71** 12 30N 92 30 E
Middle Loup → **116** 41 17N 98 23W
Middleboro **113** 41 56N 70 52W
Middleburg, N.Y., U.S.A. **113** 42 36N 74 19W
Middleburg, Pa., U.S.A. **112** 40 46N 77 5W
Middlebury **113** 44 0N 73 9W
Middleport **114** 39 0N 82 5W
Middlesboro **115** 36 36N 83 43W
Middlesbrough **12** 54 35N 1 14W
Middlesex **113** 40 36N 74 30W
Middleton **107** 44 57N 65 4W
Middleton Cr. → **98** 22 35 S 141 51 E
Middleton P.O. **98** 22 22 S 141 32 E
Middletown, Conn., U.S.A. **114** 41 37N 72 40W
Middletown, N.Y., U.S.A. **114** 41 28N 74 28W
Middletown, Ohio, U.S.A. **114** 39 29N 84 25W
Middletown, Pa., U.S.A. **113** 40 12N 76 44W
Midelt **82** 32 46N 4 44W
Midi, Canal du **20** 43 45N 1 21 E
Midi d'Ossau **32** 42 50N 0 25W
Midland, Austral. **96** 31 54 S 115 59 E
Midland, Can. **106** 44 45N 79 50W
Midland, Mich., U.S.A. **114** 43 37N 84 17W
Midland, Pa., U.S.A. **112** 40 39N 80 27W
Midland, Tex., U.S.A. **117** 32 0N 102 3W
Midlands □ **91** 19 40 S 29 0 E
Midleton **15** 51 52N 8 12W
Midlothian **117** 32 30N 97 0W
Midnapore **69** 22 25N 87 21 E
Midongy Atsimo **93** 23 35 S 47 1 E
Midongy, Tangorombohitr' i **93** 23 30 S 47 0 E
Midour → **20** 43 54N 0 30W
Midouze → **20** 43 48N 0 51W
Midvale **118** 40 39N 111 58W
Midway Is. **94** 28 13N 177 22W
Midwest **118** 43 27N 106 19W
Midyat **64** 37 25N 41 23 E
Midzur **42** 43 24N 22 40 E
Mie □ **74** 34 30N 136 10 E
Miechów **28** 50 21N 20 5 E
Miedwie, Jezioro **28** 53 17N 14 54 E
Międzybód **28** 51 25N 17 34 E
Międzychód **28** 52 35N 15 53 E
Międzylesie **28** 50 8N 16 40 E
Międzyrzec Podlaski **28** 51 58N 22 45 E
Międzyrzecz **28** 52 26N 15 35 E
Międzyzdroje **28** 53 56N 14 26 E
Miejska **28** 51 39N 16 58 E
Miélan **20** 43 27N 0 19 E
Mielec **28** 50 15N 21 25 E
Mienga **92** 17 12 S 19 48 E
Miercurea Ciuc **46** 46 21N 25 48 E
Mieres **30** 43 18N 5 48W
Mieroszów **28** 50 40N 16 11 E
Mieso **87** 9 15N 40 43 E
Mieszkowice **28** 52 47N 14 30 E
Migdāl **62** 32 51N 35 30 E
Migdal Afeq **62** 32 5N 34 58 E
Migennes **19** 47 58N 3 31 E
Migliarino **39** 44 45N 11 56 E
Miguel Alemán, Presa **120** 18 15N 96 40W
Miguel Alves **127** 4 11 S 42 55W
Mihara **74** 34 24N 133 5 E
Mijares → **32** 39 55N 0 1W
Mijas **31** 36 36N 4 40W
Mikese **90** 6 48 S 37 55 E
Mikha-Tskhakaya **57** 42 15N 42 7 E
Mikhailovka **56** 47 36N 35 16 E
Mikhaylov **55** 54 14N 39 0 E
Mikhaylovgrad **43** 43 27N 23 16 E
Mikhaylovka, Azerbaijan, U.S.S.R. **57** 41 31N 48 52 E
Mikhaylovka, R.S.F.S.R., U.S.S.R. **55** 50 3N 43 5 E
Mikhnevo **55** 55 4N 37 59 E
Mikínai **45** 37 43N 22 46 E
Mikindani **91** 10 15 S 40 2 E
Mikkeli **51** 61 43N 27 15 E
Mikkeli □ **50** 62 0N 28 0 E
Mikkwa → **108** 58 25N 114 46W
Mikniya **87** 17 0N 33 45 E
Mikołajki **28** 53 49N 21 37 E
Mikołów **27** 50 10N 18 50 E
Míkonos **45** 37 30N 25 25 E
Mikrí Préspa, Límni **44** 40 47N 21 3 E
Mikrón Dhérion **44** 41 19N 26 6 E
Mikstat **28** 51 32N 17 59 E
Mikulov **27** 48 48N 16 39 E
Mikumi **90** 7 26 S 37 0 E
Mikun **52** 62 20N 50 0 E
Mikura-Jima **74** 33 52N 139 36 E
Milaca **116** 45 45N 93 40W
Milagro **126** 2 11 S 79 36W
Milan, Mo., U.S.A. **116** 40 10N 93 5W
Milan, Tenn., U.S.A. **115** 35 55N 88 45W
Milan = Milano **38** 45 28N 9 10 E
Milange **91** 16 3 S 35 45 E
Milano **38** 45 28N 9 10 E
Milâs **64** 37 20N 27 50 E
Milazzo **41** 38 13N 15 13 E
Milbank **116** 45 17N 96 38W
Milden **109** 51 29N 107 32W
Mildmay **112** 44 3N 81 7W
Mildura **97** 34 13 S 142 9 E
Miléai **44** 39 20N 23 9 E
Miles, Austral. **97** 26 40 S 150 9 E
Miles, U.S.A. **117** 31 39N 100 11W
Miles City **116** 46 24N 105 50W
Milestone **109** 49 59N 104 31W
Mileto **41** 38 37N 16 3 E
Miletto, Mte. **41** 41 26N 14 23 E
Miletus **45** 37 20N 27 33 E
Milevsko **26** 49 27N 14 21 E
Milford, Conn., U.S.A. **113** 41 13N 73 4W
Milford, Del., U.S.A. **114** 38 52N 75 27W
Milford, Mass., U.S.A. **113** 42 8N 71 30W
Milford, Pa., U.S.A. **113** 41 20N 74 47W
Milford, Utah, U.S.A. **119** 38 20N 113 0W
Milford Haven **13** 51 43N 5 2W
Milford Haven, B. **13** 51 40N 5 10W
Milford Sd. **101** 44 41 S 167 47 E
Milḩ, Baḩr al **64** 32 40N 43 35 E
Milḩ, Ras al **81** 31 54N 25 6 E
Miliana, Aïn Salah, Alg. **82** 27 20N 2 32 E
Miliana, Médéa, Alg. **82** 36 20N 2 15 E
Milicz **28** 51 31N 17 19 E
Militello in Val di Catánia **41** 37 16N 14 46 E
Milk → **118** 48 5N 106 15W
Milk River **108** 49 10N 112 5W
Milk, Wadi el → **86** 17 55N 30 20 E
Mill City **118** 44 45N 122 28W
Mill I. **5** 66 0 S 101 30 E
Millau **20** 44 8N 3 4 E
Millbridge **112** 44 41N 77 36W
Millbrook **112** 44 10N 78 29W
Mille **115** 33 7N 83 15W
Mille Lacs, L. **116** 46 10N 93 30W
Mille Lacs, L. des **106** 48 45N 90 35W
Millen **115** 32 50N 81 57W
Miller **116** 44 35N 98 59W
Millerovo **57** 48 57N 40 28 E
Millersburg, Ohio, U.S.A. **112** 40 32N 81 52W
Millersburg, Pa., U.S.A. **112** 40 32N 76 58W
Millerton **113** 41 57N 73 32W
Millevaches, Plateau de **20** 45 45N 2 0 E
Millicent **97** 37 34 S 140 21 E
Millinocket **107** 45 45N 68 45W
Millmerran **99** 27 53 S 151 16 E
Mills L. **108** 61 30N 118 20W
Millsboro **112** 40 0N 80 0W
Milltown Malbay **15** 52 51N 9 25W
Millville **114** 39 22N 75 0W
Millwood Res. **117** 33 45N 94 0W
Milly **19** 48 24N 2 28 E
Milna **39** 43 20N 16 28 E
Milne Inlet **105** 72 30N 80 0W
Milnor **116** 46 19N 97 29W
Milo **108** 50 34N 112 53W
Mílos **45** 36 44N 24 25 E
Miloševo **42** 45 42N 20 20 E
Miłosław **28** 52 12N 17 32 E
Milparinka P.O. **99** 29 46 S 141 57 E
Miltenberg **25** 49 41N 9 13 E
Milton, Can. **112** 43 33N 79 53W
Milton, N.Z. **101** 46 7 S 169 59 E
Milton, U.K. **14** 57 18N 4 32W
Milton, Fla., U.S.A. **115** 30 38N 87 0W
Milton, Pa., U.S.A. **114** 41 0N 76 53W
Milton-Freewater **118** 45 57N 118 24W
Milton Keynes **13** 52 3N 0 42W
Miltou **81** 10 14N 17 26 E
Milverton **112** 43 34N 80 55W
Milwaukee **114** 43 9N 87 58W
Milwaukie **118** 45 27N 122 39W
Mim **84** 6 57N 2 33W
Mimizan **20** 44 12N 1 13W
Mimon **26** 50 38N 14 43 E
Min Jiang →, Fujian, China **75** 26 0N 119 35 E
Min Jiang →, Sichuan, China **75** 28 45N 104 40 E
Min Xian **77** 34 25N 104 0 E
Mina **119** 38 21N 118 9W
Mina Pirquitas **124** 22 40 S 66 30W
Mīnā Su'ud **64** 28 45N 48 28 E
Mīnā'al Aḩmadī **64** 29 5N 48 10 E
Mīnāb **65** 27 10N 57 1 E
Minago → **109** 54 33N 98 59W
Minaki **109** 49 59N 94 40W
Minamata **74** 32 10N 130 30 E
Minas **125** 34 20 S 55 10W
Minas Basin **107** 45 20N 64 12W
Minas de Rio Tinto **31** 37 42N 6 35W
Minas de San Quintín **31** 38 49N 4 23W
Minas Gerais □ **127** 18 50 S 46 0W
Minas, Sierra de las **120** 15 9N 89 31W
Minatitlán **120** 17 58N 94 35W
Minbu **67** 20 10N 94 52 E
Mincio → **38** 45 4N 10 59 E
Mindanao **73** 8 0N 125 0 E
* Mindanao Sea **73** 9 0N 124 0 E
Mindanao Trench **73** 8 0N 128 0 E
Mindel → **25** 48 31N 10 23 E
Mindelheim **25** 48 4N 10 30 E
Minden, Can. **112** 44 55N 78 43W
Minden, Ger. **24** 52 18N 8 45 E
Minden, U.S.A. **117** 32 40N 93 20W
Mindiptana **73** 5 55 S 140 22 E
Mindona, L. **100** 33 6 S 142 6 E
Mindoro **73** 13 0N 121 0 E
Mindoro Strait **73** 12 30N 120 30 E
Mindouli **88** 4 12 S 14 28 E
Minehead **13** 51 12N 3 29W
Mineola **117** 32 40N 95 30W
Mineral Wells **117** 32 50N 98 5W
Mineralnyye Vody **57** 44 2N 43 8 E

* *Renamed Bohol Sea*

Minersville, Pa., U.S.A. **113** 40 11N 76 17W
Minersville, Utah, U.S.A. **119** 38 14N 112 58W
Minerva **112** 40 43N 81 8W
Minervino Murge **41** 41 6N 16 4 E
Minetto **113** 43 24N 76 28W
Mingan **107** 50 20N 64 0W
Mingechaur **57** 40 45N 47 0 E
Mingechaurskoye Vdkhr. **57** 40 56N 47 20 E
Mingela **98** 19 52 S 146 38 E
Mingera Cr. → **98** 20 38 S 138 10 E
Minggang **77** 32 24N 114 3 E
Mingin **67** 22 50N 94 30 E
Minglanilla **32** 39 34N 1 38W
Mingorria **30** 40 45N 4 40W
Mingxi **77** 26 18N 117 12 E
Minićevo **42** 43 42N 22 18 E
Minidoka **118** 42 47N 113 34W
Minigwal L. **96** 29 31 S 123 14 E
Minipi, L. **107** 52 25N 60 45W
Mink L. **108** 61 54N 117 40W
Minna **85** 9 37N 6 30 E
Minneapolis, Kans., U.S.A. **116** 39 11N 97 40W
Minneapolis, Minn., U.S.A. **116** 44 58N 93 20W
Minnedosa **109** 50 14N 99 50W
Minnesota □ **116** 46 40N 94 0W
Minnesund **47** 60 23N 11 14 E
Minnitaki L. **106** 49 57N 92 10W
Miño → **30** 41 52N 8 40W
Minoa **45** 35 6N 25 45 E
Minorca = Menorca **32** 40 0N 4 0 E
Minore **99** 32 14 S 148 27 E
Minot **116** 48 10N 101 15W
Minqing **77** 26 15N 118 50 E
Minquiers, Les **18** 48 58N 2 8W
Minsen **24** 53 43N 7 58 E
Minsk **54** 53 52N 27 30 E
Mińsk Mazowiecki **28** 52 10N 21 33 E
Mintaka Pass **69** 37 0N 74 58 E
Minto **104** 64 55N 149 20W
Minton **109** 49 10N 104 35W
Minturn **118** 39 35N 106 25W
Minturno **40** 41 15N 13 43 E
Minûf **86** 30 26N 30 52 E
Minusinsk **59** 53 50N 91 20 E
Minutang **67** 28 15N 96 30 E
Minvoul **88** 2 9N 12 8 E
Minya el Qamh **86** 30 31N 31 21 E
Mionica **42** 44 14N 20 6 E
Mir **85** 14 5N 11 59 E
Mir-Bashir **57** 40 20N 46 58 E
Mira, Italy **39** 45 26N 12 9 E
Mira, Port. **30** 40 26N 8 44W
Mira → **31** 37 43N 8 47W
Mirabella Eclano **41** 41 3N 14 59 E
Miraflores Locks **120** 8 59N 79 36W
Miraj **70** 16 50N 74 45 E
Miram **98** 21 15 S 148 55 E
Miramar, Argent. **124** 38 15 S 57 50W
Miramar, Mozam. **93** 23 50 S 35 35 E
Miramas **21** 43 33N 4 59 E
Mirambeau **20** 45 23N 0 35W
Miramichi B. **107** 47 15N 65 0W
Miramont-de-Guyenne **20** 44 37N 0 21 E
Miranda **127** 20 10 S 56 15W
Miranda de Ebro **32** 42 41N 2 57W
Miranda do Corvo **30** 40 6N 8 20W
Miranda do Douro **30** 41 30N 6 16W
Mirande **20** 43 31N 0 25 E
Mirandela **30** 41 32N 7 10W
Mirando City **117** 27 28N 98 59W
Mirandola **38** 44 53N 11 2 E
Mirandópolis **125** 21 9 S 51 6W
Mirango **91** 13 32 S 34 58 E
Mirano **39** 45 29N 12 6 E
Mirassol **125** 20 46 S 49 28W
Mirbāţ **63** 17 0N 54 45 E
Mirear **86** 23 15N 35 41 E
Mirebeau, Côte-d'or, France **19** 47 25N 5 20 E
Mirebeau, Vienne, France **18** 46 49N 0 10 E
Mirecourt **19** 48 20N 6 10 E
Mirgorod **54** 49 58N 33 37 E
Miri **72** 4 18N 114 0 E
Miriam Vale **98** 24 20 S 151 33 E
Mirim, Lagoa **125** 32 45 S 52 50W
Mirnyy, Antarct. **5** 66 33 S 93 1 E
Mirnyy, U.S.S.R. **59** 62 33N 113 53 E
Miroč **42** 44 32N 22 16 E
Mirond L. **109** 55 6N 102 47W
Mirosławiec **28** 53 20N 16 5 E
Mirpur Bibiwari **68** 28 33N 67 44 E
Mirpur Khas **68** 25 30N 69 0 E
Mirpur Sakro **68** 24 33N 67 41 E
Mirria **85** 13 43N 9 7 E
Mirror **108** 52 30N 113 7W
Mîrşani **46** 44 1N 23 59 E
Mirsk **28** 50 58N 15 23 E
Miryang **76** 35 31N 128 44 E
Mirzaani **57** 41 24N 46 5 E
Mirzapur-cum-Vindhyachal **69** 25 10N 82 34 E
Miscou I. **107** 47 57N 64 31W
Mish'āb, Ra'as al **64** 28 15N 48 43 E
Mishan **75** 45 37N 131 48 E
Mishawaka **114** 41 40N 86 8W
Mishbih, Gebel **86** 22 38N 34 44 E
Mishima **74** 35 10N 138 52 E
Mishmar Ayyalon **62** 31 52N 34 57 E
Mishmar Ha' Emeq **62** 32 37N 35 7 E
Mishmar Ha Negev **62** 31 22N 34 48 E
Mishmar Ha Yarden **62** 33 0N 35 36 E
Misilmeri **40** 38 2N 13 25 E
Misima I. **98** 10 40 S 152 45 E
Misiones □, Argent. **125** 27 0 S 55 0W
Misiones □, Parag. **124** 27 0 S 56 0W
Miskīn **65** 23 44N 56 52 E
Miskitos, Cayos **121** 14 26N 82 50W
Miskolc **27** 48 7N 20 50 E
Misoke **90** 0 42 S 28 2 E
Misool **73** 1 52 S 130 10 E
Misrātah **83** 32 24N 15 3 E
Misrātah □ **83** 29 0N 16 0 E
Misriç **64** 37 55N 41 40 E
Missanabie **106** 48 20N 84 6W
Missinaibi → **106** 50 43N 81 29W
Missinaibi L. **106** 48 23N 83 40W
Mission, S.D., U.S.A. **116** 43 21N 100 36W
Mission, Tex., U.S.A. **117** 26 15N 98 20W
Mission City **108** 49 10N 122 15W
Missisa L. **106** 52 20N 85 7W
Mississagi → **106** 46 15N 83 9W
Mississippi → **117** 29 0N 89 15W
Mississippi, Delta of the **117** 29 15N 90 30W
Mississippi L. **113** 45 5N 76 10W
Mississippi □ **117** 33 25N 89 0W
Missoula **118** 46 52N 114 0W
Missouri □ **116** 38 25N 92 30W
Missouri → **116** 38 50N 90 8W
Missouri Valley **116** 41 33N 95 53W
Mistake B. **109** 62 8N 93 0W
Mistassini → **107** 48 42N 72 20W
Mistassini L. **106** 51 0N 73 30W
Mistastin L. **107** 55 57N 63 20W
Mistatim **109** 52 52N 103 22W
Mistelbach **27** 48 34N 16 34 E
Misterbianco **41** 37 32N 15 0 E
Mistretta **41** 37 56N 14 20 E
Misty L. **109** 58 53N 101 40W
Mît Ghamr **86** 30 42N 31 12 E
Mitatib **87** 15 59N 36 12 E
Mitchell, Austral. **97** 26 29 S 147 58 E
Mitchell, Can. **112** 43 28N 81 12W
Mitchell, Ind., U.S.A. **114** 38 42N 86 25W
Mitchell, Nebr., U.S.A. **116** 41 58N 103 45W
Mitchell, Oreg., U.S.A. **118** 44 31N 120 8W
Mitchell, S.D., U.S.A. **116** 43 40N 98 0W
Mitchell → **97** 15 12 S 141 35 E
Mitchell, Mt. **115** 35 40N 82 20W
Mitchelstown **15** 52 16N 8 18W
Mitha Tiwana **68** 32 13N 72 6 E
Míthimna **44** 39 20N 26 12 E
Mitiaro, I. **101** 19 49 S 157 43W
Mitilíni **45** 39 6N 26 35 E
Mitilinoí **45** 37 42N 26 56 E
Mitla **120** 16 55N 96 24W
Mito **74** 36 20N 140 30 E
Mitsinjo **93** 16 1 S 45 52 E
Mitsiwa **87** 15 35N 39 25 E
Mitsiwa Channel **87** 15 30N 40 0 E
Mitta Mitta → **100** 36 14 S 147 10 E
Mittagong **99** 34 28 S 150 29 E
Mittelland Kanal **24** 52 23N 7 45 E
Mittenwalde **24** 52 16N 13 33 E
Mitterteich **25** 49 57N 12 15 E
Mittweida **24** 50 59N 13 0 E
Mitú **126** 1 8N 70 3W
Mitumba **90** 7 8 S 31 2 E
Mitumba, Chaîne des **90** 6 0 S 29 0 E
Mitwaba **91** 8 2 S 27 17 E
Mityana **90** 0 23N 32 2 E
Mitzic **88** 0 45N 11 40 E
Mixteco → **120** 18 11N 98 30W
Miyagi □ **74** 38 15N 140 45 E
Miyâh, W. el → **86** 25 0N 33 23 E
Miyake-Jima **74** 34 0N 139 30 E
Miyako **74** 39 40N 141 59 E
Miyakonojō **74** 31 40N 131 5 E
Miyazaki **74** 31 56N 131 30 E
Miyazaki □ **74** 32 30N 131 30 E
Miyazu **74** 35 35N 135 10 E
Miyet, Bahr el **64** 31 30N 35 30 E
Miyun **76** 40 28N 116 50 E
Mizal **64** 23 59N 45 11 E
Mizamis = Ozamiz **73** 8 15N 123 50 E
Mizdah **83** 31 30N 13 0 E
Mizen Hd., Cork, Ireland **15** 51 27N 9 50W
Mizen Hd., Wicklow, Ireland **15** 52 52N 6 4W
Mizhi **76** 37 47N 110 12 E
Mizil **46** 44 59N 26 29 E
Mizoram □ **67** 23 30N 92 40 E
Mizpe Ramon **62** 30 34N 34 49 E
Mjöbäck **49** 57 28N 12 53 E
Mjölby **49** 58 20N 15 10 E
Mjømna **47** 60 55N 4 55 E
Mjörn **49** 57 55N 12 25 E
Mjøsa **47** 60 48N 11 0 E
Mkata **90** 5 45 S 38 20 E
Mkokotoni **90** 5 55 S 39 15 E
Mkomazi **90** 4 40 S 38 7 E
Mkulwe **91** 8 37 S 32 20 E
Mkumbi, Ras **90** 7 38 S 39 55 E
Mkushi **91** 14 25 S 29 15 E
Mkushi River **91** 13 32 S 29 45 E
Mkuze → **93** 27 45 S 32 30 E
Mladá Boleslav **26** 50 27N 14 53 E
Mladenovac **42** 44 28N 20 44 E
Mlala Hills **90** 6 50 S 31 40 E
Mlange **91** 16 2 S 35 33 E
Mlava → **42** 44 45N 21 13 E
Mława **28** 53 9N 20 25 E
Mlinište **39** 44 15N 16 50 E
Mljet **42** 42 43N 17 30 E
Mljetski Kanal **42** 42 48N 17 35 E
Młynąry **28** 54 12N 19 46 E
Młynary **28** 54 12N 19 43 E
Mme **85** 6 18N 10 14 E
Mo **47** 59 28N 7 50 E
Mo i Rana **50** 66 15N 14 7 E
Moa **73** 8 0 S 128 0 E
Moa → **84** 6 59N 11 36 E
Moab **119** 38 40N 109 35W
Moabi **88** 2 24 S 10 59 E
Moala **101** 18 36 S 179 53 E
Moalie Park **99** 29 42 S 143 3 E
Moaña **30** 42 18N 8 43W
Moapa **119** 36 45N 114 37W
Moba **90** 7 0 S 29 48 E
Mobaye **88** 4 25N 21 5 E
Mobayi **88** 4 15N 21 8 E
Moberley **116** 39 25N 92 25W
Moberly → **108** 56 12N 120 55W
Mobile **115** 30 41N 88 3W
Mobile B. **115** 30 30N 88 0W
Mobile, Pt. **115** 30 15N 88 0W
Mobridge **116** 45 31N 100 28W
Mobutu Sese Seko, L. **90** 1 30N 31 0 E

Mocabe Kasari Moosup

Mocabe Kasari	**91**	9 58 S	26 12 E
Moçambique	**91**	15 3 S	40 42 E
Moçambique □	**91**	14 45 S	38 30 E
* Moçâmedes	**89**	15 7 S	12 11 E
* Moçâmedes □	**92**	16 35 S	12 30 E
Mochudi	**92**	24 27 S	26 7 E
Mocimboa da Praia	**91**	11 25 S	40 20 E
Mociu	**46**	46 46N	24 3 E
Möckeln	**49**	56 40N	14 15 E
Moclips	**118**	47 14N	124 10W
Mocoa	**126**	1 7N	76 35W
Mococa	**125**	21 28 S	47 0W
Mocorito	**120**	25 30N	107 53W
Moctezuma	**120**	29 50N	109 0W
Moctezuma →	**120**	21 59N	98 34W
Mocuba	**91**	16 54 S	36 57 E
Modalen	**47**	60 49N	5 48 E
Modane	**21**	45 12N	6 40 E
Modasa	**68**	23 30N	73 21 E
Modder →	**92**	29 2 S	24 37 E
Modderrivier	**92**	29 2 S	24 38 E
Módena	**38**	44 39N	10 55 E
Modena	**119**	37 55N	113 56W
Modesto	**119**	37 43N	121 0W
Módica	**41**	36 52N	14 45 E
Modigliana	**39**	44 9N	11 48 E
Modlin	**28**	52 24N	20 41 E
Mödling	**27**	48 5N	16 17 E
Modo	**87**	5 31N	30 33 E
Modra	**27**	48 19N	17 20 E
Modriča	**42**	44 57N	18 17 E
Moe	**97**	38 12 S	146 19 E
Moebase	**91**	17 3 S	38 41 E
Moei →	**71**	17 25N	98 10 E
Moëlan-sur-Mer	**18**	47 49N	3 38W
Moengo	**127**	5 45N	54 20W
Moffat	**14**	55 20N	3 27W
Moga	**68**	30 48N	75 8 E
Mogadishu = Muqdisho	**63**	2 2N	45 25 E
Mogador = Essaouira	**82**	31 32N	9 48W
Mogadouro	**30**	41 22N	6 47W
Mogami →	**74**	38 45N	140 0 E
Mogaung	**67**	25 20N	97 0 E
Møgeltønder	**49**	54 57N	8 48 E
Mogente	**33**	38 52N	0 45W
Mogho	**87**	4 54N	40 16 E
Mogi das Cruzes	**125**	23 31 S	46 11W
Mogi-Guaçu →	**125**	20 53 S	48 10W
Mogi-Mirim	**125**	22 29 S	47 0W
Mogielnica	**28**	51 42N	20 41 E
Mogilev	**54**	53 55N	30 18 E
Mogilev-Podolskiy	**56**	48 20N	27 40 E
Mogilno	**28**	52 39N	17 55 E
Mogincual	**91**	15 35 S	40 25 E
Mogliano Véneto	**39**	45 33N	12 15 E
Mogocha	**59**	53 40N	119 50 E
Mogoi	**73**	1 55 S	133 10 E
Mogok	**67**	23 0N	96 40 E
Mogollon	**119**	33 25N	108 48W
Mogollon Mesa	**119**	35 0N	111 0W
Moguer	**31**	37 15N	6 52W
Mohács	**27**	45 58N	18 41 E
Mohall	**116**	48 46N	101 30W
Moḩammadābād	**65**	37 52N	59 5 E
Mohammadia	**82**	35 33N	0 3 E
Mohammedia	**82**	33 44N	7 21W
Mohawk	**119**	32 45N	113 50W
Mohawk →	**113**	42 47N	73 42W
Mohe	**76**	53 28N	122 17 E
Moheda	**49**	57 1N	14 35 E
Möhne →	**24**	51 29N	7 57 E
Moholm	**49**	58 37N	14 5 E
Mohon	**19**	49 45N	4 44 E
Mohoro	**90**	8 6 S	39 8 E
Moia	**87**	5 3N	28 2 E
Moidart, L.	**14**	56 47N	5 40W
Moinabad	**70**	17 44N	77 16 E
Moineşti	**46**	46 28N	26 31 E
Mointy	**58**	47 10N	73 18 E
Moirans	**21**	45 20N	5 33 E
Moirans-en-Montagne	**21**	46 26N	5 43 E
Moíres	**45**	35 4N	24 56 E
Moisakula	**54**	58 3N	25 12 E
Moisie	**107**	50 12N	66 1W
Moisie →	**107**	50 14N	66 5W
Moissac	**20**	44 7N	1 5 E
Moïssala	**81**	8 21N	17 46 E
Moita	**31**	38 38N	8 58W
Mojácar	**33**	37 6N	1 55W
Mojados	**30**	41 26N	4 40W
Mojave	**119**	35 8N	118 8W
Mojave Desert	**119**	35 0N	116 30W
Mojo, Boliv.	**124**	21 48 S	65 33W
Mojo, Ethiopia	**87**	8 35N	39 5 E
Mojo, Indon.	**72**	8 10 S	117 40 E
Mojokerto	**73**	7 29 S	112 25 E
Mokai	**101**	38 32 S	175 56 E
Mokambo	**91**	12 25 S	28 20 E
Mokameh	**69**	25 24N	85 55 E
Mokhós	**45**	35 16N	25 27 E
Mokhotlong	**93**	29 22 S	29 2 E
Moknine	**83**	35 35N	10 58 E
Mokokchung	**67**	26 15N	94 30 E
Mokra Gora	**42**	42 50N	20 30 E
Mokronog	**39**	45 57N	15 9 E
Moksha →	**55**	54 45N	41 53 E
Mokshan	**55**	53 25N	44 35 E
Mol	**16**	51 11N	5 5 E
Mola, C. de la	**32**	39 40N	4 20 E
Mola di Bari	**41**	41 3N	17 5 E
Moláoi	**45**	36 49N	22 56 E
Molat	**39**	44 15N	14 50 E
Molchanovo	**58**	57 40N	83 50 E
Mold	**12**	53 10N	3 10W
Moldava nad Bodvou	**27**	48 38N	21 0 E
Moldavia = Moldova	**46**	46 30N	27 0 E
Moldavian S.S.R. □	**56**	47 0N	28 0 E
Molde	**47**	62 45N	7 9 E
Moldova	**46**	46 30N	27 0 E
Moldova Nouă	**42**	44 45N	21 41 E
Moldoveanu	**43**	45 36N	24 45 E
Molepolole	**92**	24 28 S	25 28 E
Molfetta	**41**	41 12N	16 35 E
Molina de Aragón	**32**	40 46N	1 52W
Moline	**116**	41 30N	90 30W
Molinella	**39**	44 38N	11 40 E
Molinos	**124**	25 28 S	66 15W
Moliro	**90**	8 12 S	30 30 E
Molise □	**39**	41 45N	14 30 E
Moliterno	**41**	40 14N	15 50 E
Mollahat	**69**	22 56N	89 48 E
Mölle	**49**	56 17N	12 31 E
Molledo	**30**	43 8N	4 6W
Mollendo	**126**	17 0 S	72 0W
Mollerusa	**32**	41 37N	0 54 E
Mollina	**31**	37 8N	4 38W
Mölln	**24**	53 37N	10 41 E
Mölltorp	**49**	58 30N	14 26 E
Mölndal	**49**	57 40N	12 3 E
Molochansk	**56**	47 15N	35 35 E
Molochnaya →	**56**	47 0N	35 30 E
Molodechno	**54**	54 20N	26 50 E
Molokai	**110**	21 8N	157 0W
Moloma →	**55**	58 20N	48 15 E
Molong	**99**	33 5 S	148 54 E
Molopo →	**92**	28 30 S	20 13 E
Mólos	**45**	38 47N	22 37 E
Moloundou	**88**	2 8N	15 15 E
Molsheim	**19**	48 33N	7 29 E
Molson L.	**109**	54 22N	96 40W
Molteno	**92**	31 22 S	26 22 E
Molu	**73**	6 45 S	131 40 E
Molucca Sea	**73**	4 0 S	124 0 E
Moluccas = Maluku	**73**	1 0 S	127 0 E
Molusi	**92**	20 21 S	24 29 E
Moma, Mozam.	**91**	16 47 S	39 4 E
Moma, Zaîre	**90**	1 35 S	23 52 E
Momanga	**92**	18 7 S	21 41 E
Mombasa	**90**	4 2 S	39 43 E
Mombuey	**30**	42 3N	6 20W
Momchilgrad	**43**	41 33N	25 23 E
Momi	**90**	1 42 S	27 0 E
Mompós	**126**	9 14N	74 26W
Møn	**49**	54 57N	12 15 E
Mon →	**67**	20 25N	94 30 E
Mona, Canal de la	**121**	18 30N	67 45W
Mona, I.	**121**	18 5N	67 54W
Mona, Pta.	**121**	9 37N	82 36W
Mona, Punta	**31**	36 43N	3 45W
Monach Is.	**14**	57 32N	7 40W
Monaco ■	**21**	43 46N	7 23 E
Monadhliath Mts.	**14**	57 10N	4 4W
Monaghan	**15**	54 15N	6 58W
Monaghan □	**15**	54 10N	7 0W
Monahans	**117**	31 35N	102 50W
Monapo	**91**	14 56 S	40 19 E
Monarch Mt.	**108**	51 55N	125 57W
Monastier-sur-Gazeille, Le	**20**	44 57N	3 59 E
Monastir	**83**	35 50N	10 49 E
Monastyriska	**54**	49 8N	25 14 E
Moncada	**32**	39 30N	0 24W
Moncalieri	**38**	45 0N	7 40 E
Moncalvo	**38**	45 3N	8 15 E
Moncão	**30**	42 4N	8 27W
Moncarapacho	**31**	37 5N	7 46W
Moncayo, Sierra del	**32**	41 48N	1 50W
Mönchengladbach	**24**	51 12N	6 23 E
Monchique	**31**	37 19N	8 38W
Monclova	**120**	26 50N	101 30W
Moncontour	**18**	48 22N	2 38W
Moncoutant	**18**	46 43N	0 35W
Moncton	**107**	46 7N	64 51W
Mondego →	**30**	40 9N	8 52W
Mondego, Cabo	**30**	40 11N	8 54W
Mondeodo	**73**	3 34 S	122 9 E
Mondolfo	**39**	43 45N	13 8 E
Mondoñedo	**30**	43 25N	7 23W
Mondoví	**38**	44 23N	7 49 E
Mondovi	**116**	44 37N	91 40W
Mondragon	**21**	44 13N	4 44 E
Mondragone	**40**	41 8N	13 52 E
Monduli □	**90**	3 0 S	36 0 E
Monemvasía	**45**	36 41N	23 3 E
Monessen	**114**	40 9N	79 50W
Monesterio	**31**	38 6N	6 15W
Monestier-de-Clermont	**21**	44 55N	5 38 E
Monêtier-les-Bains, Le	**21**	44 58N	6 30 E
Monett	**117**	36 55N	93 56W
Monfalcone	**39**	45 49N	13 32 E
Monflanquin	**20**	44 32N	0 47 E
Monforte	**31**	39 6N	7 25W
Monforte de Lemos	**30**	42 31N	7 33W
Mong Cai	**71**	21 27N	107 54 E
Mong Hsu	**67**	21 54N	98 30 E
Mong Kung	**67**	21 35N	97 35 E
Mong Lang	**71**	21 29N	97 52 E
Mong Nai	**67**	20 32N	97 46 E
Mong Pawk	**67**	22 4N	99 16 E
Mong Ton	**67**	20 17N	98 45 E
Mong Wa	**67**	21 26N	100 27 E
Mong Yai	**67**	22 21N	98 3 E
Mongalla	**87**	5 8N	31 42 E
Mongers, L.	**96**	29 25 S	117 5 E
Monghyr	**69**	25 23N	86 30 E
Mongla	**69**	22 8N	89 35 E
Mongo	**81**	12 14N	18 43 E
Mongolia ■	**75**	47 0N	103 0 E
Mongonu	**85**	12 40N	13 32 E
Mongororo	**81**	12 3N	22 26 E
Mongu	**89**	15 16 S	23 12 E
Môngua	**92**	16 43 S	15 20 E
Monistrol	**20**	45 57N	3 38 E
Monistrol-St-Loire	**21**	45 17N	4 11 E
Monkey Bay	**91**	14 7 S	35 1 E
Mońki	**28**	53 23N	22 48 E
Monkira	**98**	24 46 S	140 30 E
Monkoto	**88**	1 38 S	20 35 E
Monmouth, U.K.	**13**	51 48N	2 43W
Monmouth, U.S.A.	**116**	40 50N	90 40W
Mono, L.	**119**	38 0N	119 9W
Monongahela	**112**	40 12N	79 56W
Monópoli	**41**	40 57N	17 18 E
Monor	**27**	47 21N	19 27 E
Monóvar	**33**	38 28N	0 53W
Monqoumba	**88**	3 33N	18 40 E
Monreal del Campo	**32**	40 47N	1 20W
Monreale	**40**	38 6N	13 16 E
Monroe, Ga., U.S.A.	**115**	33 47N	83 43W
Monroe, La., U.S.A.	**117**	32 32N	92 4W
Monroe, Mich., U.S.A.	**114**	41 55N	83 26W
Monroe, N.C., U.S.A.	**115**	35 2N	80 37W
Monroe, N.Y., U.S.A.	**113**	41 19N	74 11W
Monroe, Utah, U.S.A.	**119**	38 45N	112 5W
Monroe, Wis., U.S.A.	**116**	42 38N	89 40W
Monroe City	**116**	39 40N	91 40W
Monroeville	**115**	31 33N	87 15W
Monrovia, Liberia	**84**	6 18N	10 47W
Monrovia, U.S.A.	**119**	34 7N	118 1W
Mons	**16**	50 27N	3 58 E
Monsaraz	**31**	38 28N	7 22W
Monse	**73**	4 0 S	123 10 E
Monségur	**20**	44 38N	0 4 E
Monsélice	**39**	45 16N	11 46 E
Mont-de-Marsan	**20**	43 54N	0 31W
Mont d'Or, Tunnel	**19**	46 45N	6 18 E
Mont-Dore, Le	**20**	45 35N	2 50 E
Mont-Joli	**107**	48 37N	68 10W
Mont Laurier	**106**	46 35N	75 30W
Mont-sous-Vaudrey	**19**	46 58N	5 36 E
Mont-St-Michel, Le	**18**	48 40N	1 30W
Mont Tremblant Prov. Park	**106**	46 30N	74 30W
Montabaur	**24**	50 26N	7 49 E
Montagnac	**20**	43 29N	3 28 E
Montagnana	**39**	45 13N	11 29 E
Montagu	**92**	33 45 S	20 8 E
Montagu I.	**5**	58 25 S	26 20W
Montague, Can.	**107**	46 10N	62 39W
Montague, Calif., U.S.A.	**118**	41 47N	122 30W
Montague, Mass., U.S.A.	**113**	42 31N	72 33W
Montague, I.	**120**	31 40N	114 56W
Montague I.	**104**	60 0N	147 0W
Montague Sd.	**96**	14 28 S	125 20 E
Montaigu	**18**	46 59N	1 18W
Montalbán	**32**	40 50N	0 45W
Montalbano di Elicona	**41**	38 1N	15 0 E
Montalbano Iónico	**41**	40 17N	16 33 E
Montalbo	**32**	39 53N	2 42W
Montalcino	**39**	43 4N	11 30 E
Montalegre	**30**	41 49N	7 47W
Montalto di Castro	**39**	42 20N	11 36 E
Montalto Uffugo	**41**	39 25N	16 9 E
Montamarta	**30**	41 39N	5 49W
Montaña	**126**	6 0 S	73 0W
Montana □	**110**	47 0N	110 0W
Montánchez	**31**	39 15N	6 8W
Montargis	**19**	48 0N	2 43 E
Montauban	**20**	44 0N	1 21 E
Montauk	**114**	41 3N	71 57W
Montauk Pt.	**113**	41 4N	71 52W
Montbard	**19**	47 38N	4 20 E
Montbéliard	**19**	47 31N	6 48 E
Montblanch	**32**	41 23N	1 4 E
Montbrison	**21**	45 36N	4 3 E
Montcalm, Pic de	**20**	42 40N	1 25 E
Montceau-les-Mines	**19**	46 40N	4 23 E
Montchanin	**38**	46 47N	4 30 E
Montclair	**113**	40 53N	74 13W
Montcornet	**19**	49 40N	4 0 E
Montcuq	**20**	44 21N	1 13 E
Montdidier	**19**	49 38N	2 35 E
Monte Alegre	**127**	2 0 S	54 0W
Monte Azul	**127**	15 9 S	42 53W
Monte Bello Is.	**96**	20 30 S	115 45 E
Monte-Carlo	**21**	43 46N	7 23 E
Monte Caseros	**124**	30 10 S	57 50W
Monte Comán	**124**	34 40 S	67 53W
Monte Lindo →	**124**	23 56 S	57 12W
Monte Quemado	**124**	25 53 S	62 41W
Monte Redondo	**30**	39 53N	8 50W
Monte San Giovanni	**40**	41 39N	13 33 E
Monte San Savino	**39**	43 20N	11 42 E
Monte Sant' Ángelo	**41**	41 42N	15 59 E
Monte Santu, C. di	**40**	40 5N	9 42 E
Monte Vista	**119**	37 40N	106 8W
Monteagudo	**125**	27 14 S	54 8W
Montealegre	**33**	38 48N	1 17W
Montebello	**106**	45 40N	74 55W
Montebelluna	**39**	45 47N	12 3 E
Montebourg	**18**	49 30N	1 20W
Montecastrilli	**39**	42 40N	12 30 E
Montecatini Terme	**38**	43 55N	10 48 E
Montecristi	**126**	1 0 S	80 40W
Montecristo	**38**	42 20N	10 20 E
Montefalco	**39**	42 53N	12 38 E
Montefiascone	**39**	42 31N	12 2 E
Montefrío	**31**	37 20N	4 0W
Montego Bay	**121**	18 30N	78 0W
Montegranaro	**39**	43 13N	13 38 E
Montehanin	**19**	46 46N	4 44 E
Montejicar	**33**	37 33N	3 30W
Montélimar	**21**	44 33N	4 45 E
Montella	**41**	40 50N	15 0 E
Montellano	**31**	36 59N	5 36W
Montello	**116**	43 49N	89 21W
Montelupo Fiorentino	**38**	43 44N	11 2 E
Montemor-o-Novo	**31**	38 40N	8 12W
Montemor-o-Velho	**30**	40 11N	8 40W
Montemorelos	**120**	25 11N	99 42W
Montendre	**20**	45 16N	0 26W
Montenegro	**125**	29 39 S	51 29W
Montenegro = Crna Gora □	**42**	42 40N	19 20 E
Montenero di Bisaccia	**39**	42 0N	14 47 E
Montepuez	**91**	13 8 S	38 59 E
Montepuez →	**91**	12 32 S	40 27 E
Montepulciano	**39**	43 5N	11 46 E
Montereale	**39**	42 31N	13 13 E
Montereau	**19**	48 22N	2 57 E
Monterey	**119**	36 35N	121 57W
Montería	**126**	8 46N	75 53W
Monteros	**124**	27 11 S	65 30W
Monterotondo	**39**	42 3N	12 36 E
Monterrey	**120**	25 40N	100 30W
Montes Claros	**127**	16 30 S	43 50W
Montesano	**118**	47 0N	123 39W
Montesárchio	**41**	41 5N	14 37 E
Montescaglioso	**41**	40 34N	16 40 E
Montesilvano	**39**	42 30N	14 8 E
Montevarchi	**39**	43 30N	11 32 E
Montevideo	**125**	34 50 S	56 11W
Montezuma	**116**	41 32N	92 35W
Montfaucon, Haute-Loire, France	**21**	45 11N	4 20 E
Montfaucon, Meuse, France	**19**	49 16N	5 8 E
Montfort-l'Amaury	**19**	48 47N	1 49 E
Montfort-sur-Meu	**18**	48 8N	1 58W
Montgenèvre	**21**	44 56N	6 42 E
Montgomery, U.K.	**13**	52 34N	3 9W
Montgomery, Ala., U.S.A.	**115**	32 20N	86 20W
Montgomery, W. Va., U.S.A.	**114**	38 9N	81 21W
Montgomery = Sahiwal	**68**	30 45N	73 8 E
Montguyon	**20**	45 12N	0 12W
Monthey	**25**	46 15N	6 56 E
Monticelli d'Ongina	**38**	45 3N	9 56 E
Monticello, Ark., U.S.A.	**117**	33 40N	91 48W
Monticello, Fla., U.S.A.	**115**	30 35N	83 50W
Monticello, Ind., U.S.A.	**114**	40 40N	86 45W
Monticello, Iowa, U.S.A.	**116**	42 18N	91 12W
Monticello, Ky., U.S.A.	**115**	36 52N	84 50W
Monticello, Minn., U.S.A.	**116**	45 17N	93 52W
Monticello, Miss., U.S.A.	**117**	31 35N	90 8W
Monticello, N.Y., U.S.A.	**113**	41 37N	74 42W
Monticello, Utah, U.S.A.	**119**	37 55N	109 27W
Montichiari	**38**	45 28N	10 29 E
Montier	**19**	48 30N	4 45 E
Montignac	**20**	45 4N	1 10 E
Montigny-les-Metz	**19**	49 7N	6 10 E
Montigny-sur-Aube	**19**	47 57N	4 45 E
Montijo	**31**	38 52N	6 39W
Montijo, Presa de	**31**	38 55N	6 26W
Montilla	**31**	37 36N	4 40W
Montivideo	**116**	44 55N	95 40W
Montlhéry	**19**	48 39N	2 15 E
Montluçon	**20**	46 22N	2 36 E
Montmagny	**107**	46 58N	70 34W
Montmarault	**20**	46 19N	2 57 E
Montmartre	**109**	50 14N	103 27W
Montmédy	**19**	49 30N	5 20 E
Montmélian	**21**	45 30N	6 4 E
Montmirail	**19**	48 51N	3 30 E
Montmoreau-St-Cybard	**20**	45 23N	0 8 E
Montmorency	**107**	46 53N	71 11W
Montmorillon	**20**	46 26N	0 50 E
Montmort	**19**	48 55N	3 49 E
Monto	**97**	24 52 S	151 6 E
Montoire	**18**	47 45N	0 52 E
Montório al Vomano	**39**	42 35N	13 38 E
Montoro	**31**	38 1N	4 27W
Montour Falls	**112**	42 20N	76 51W
Montpelier, Idaho, U.S.A.	**118**	42 15N	111 20W
Montpelier, Ohio, U.S.A.	**114**	41 34N	84 40W
Montpelier, Vt., U.S.A.	**114**	44 15N	72 38W
Montpellier	**20**	43 37N	3 52 E
Montpezat-de-Quercy	**20**	44 15N	1 30 E
Montpon	**20**	45 2N	0 11 E
Montréal, Can.	**106**	45 31N	73 34W
Montréal, France	**20**	43 13N	2 8 E
Montreal L.	**109**	54 20N	105 45W
Montreal Lake	**109**	54 3N	105 46W
Montredon-Labessonniè	**20**	43 45N	2 18 E
Montréjeau	**20**	43 6N	0 35 E
Montrésor	**18**	47 10N	1 10 E
Montreuil	**19**	50 27N	1 45 E
Montreuil-Bellay	**18**	47 8N	0 9W
Montreux	**25**	46 26N	6 55 E
Montrevault	**18**	47 17N	1 2W
Montrevel-en-Bresse	**21**	46 21N	5 8 E
Montrichard	**18**	47 20N	1 10 E
Montrose, U.K.	**14**	56 43N	2 28W
Montrose, Col., U.S.A.	**119**	38 30N	107 52W
Montrose, Pa., U.S.A.	**113**	41 50N	75 55W
Monts, Pte des	**107**	49 20N	67 12W
Monts-sur-Guesnes	**18**	46 55N	0 13 E
Montsalvy	**20**	44 41N	2 30 E
Montsant, Sierra de	**32**	41 17N	1 0 E
Montsauche	**19**	47 13N	4 0 E
Montsech, Sierra del	**32**	42 0N	0 45 E
Montseny	**32**	41 55N	2 25W
Montserrat, Spain	**32**	41 36N	1 49 E
Montserrat, W. Indies	**121**	16 40N	62 10W
Montuenga	**30**	41 3N	4 38W
Montuiri	**32**	39 34N	2 59 E
Monveda	**88**	2 52N	21 30 E
Monywa	**67**	22 7N	95 11 E
Monza	**38**	45 35N	9 15 E
Monze	**91**	16 17 S	27 29 E
Monze, C.	**66**	24 47N	66 37 E
Monzón	**32**	41 52N	0 10 E
Moolawatana	**99**	29 55 S	139 45 E
Moonah →	**98**	22 3 S	138 33 E
Moonbeam	**106**	49 20N	82 10W
Moonie	**99**	27 46 S	150 20 E
Moonie →	**97**	29 19 S	148 43 E
Moonta	**99**	34 6 S	137 32 E
Mooraberree	**99**	25 13 S	140 54 E
Moorcroft	**116**	44 17N	104 58W
Moore, L.	**96**	29 50 S	117 35 E
Moorefield	**114**	39 5N	78 59W
Moores Res.	**113**	44 45N	71 50W
Mooresville	**115**	35 36N	80 45W
Moorfoot Hills	**14**	55 44N	3 8W
Moorhead	**116**	46 51N	96 44W
Mooroopna	**99**	36 25 S	145 22 E
Moorreesburg	**92**	33 6 S	18 38 E
Moosburg	**25**	48 28N	11 57 E
Moose →	**106**	51 20N	80 25W
Moose Factory	**106**	51 16N	80 32W
Moose I.	**109**	51 42N	97 10W
Moose Jaw	**109**	50 24N	105 30W
Moose Jaw Cr. →	**109**	50 34N	105 18W
Moose Lake, Can.	**109**	53 43N	100 20W
Moose Lake, U.S.A.	**116**	46 27N	92 48W
Moose Mountain Cr. →	**109**	49 13N	102 12W
Moose Mountain Prov. Park	**109**	49 48N	102 25W
Moose River	**106**	50 48N	81 17W
Moosehead L.	**107**	45 34N	69 40W
Moosomin	**109**	50 9N	101 40W
Moosonee	**106**	51 17N	80 39W
Moosup	**113**	41 44N	71 52W

** Renamed Namibe*

Mopipi Mullsjö

Mopipi	**92**	21 6S	24 55E
Mopoi	**90**	5 6N	26 54E
Mopti	**84**	14 30N	4 0W
Moqatta	**87**	14 38N	35 50E
Moquegua	**126**	17 15S	70 46W
Mór	**27**	47 25N	18 12E
Móra	**31**	38 55N	8 10W
Mora, Sweden	**48**	61 2N	14 38E
Mora, Minn., U.S.A.	**116**	45 52N	93 19W
Mora, N. Mex., U.S.A.	**119**	35 58N	105 21W
Mora de Ebro	**32**	41 6N	0 38E
Mora de Rubielos	**32**	40 15N	0 45W
Mora la Nueva	**32**	41 7N	0 39E
Morača →	**42**	42 20N	19 9E
Moradabad	**68**	28 50N	78 50E
Morafenobe	**93**	17 50S	44 53E
Morąg	**28**	53 55N	19 56E
Moral de Calatrava	**33**	38 51N	3 33W
Moraleja	**30**	40 6N	6 43W
Moran, Kans., U.S.A.	**117**	37 53N	94 35W
Moran, Wyo., U.S.A.	**118**	43 53N	110 37W
Morano Cálabro	**41**	39 51N	16 8E
Morant Cays	**121**	17 22N	76 0W
Morant Pt.	**121**	17 55N	76 12W
Morar L.	**14**	56 57N	5 40W
Moratalla	**33**	38 14N	1 49W
Moratuwa	**70**	6 45N	79 55E
Morava →	**27**	48 10N	16 59E
Moravia	**116**	40 50N	92 50W
Moravian Hts. = Ceskemoravská V.	**26**	49 30N	15 40E
Moravica →	**42**	43 52N	20 8E
Moravice →	**27**	49 50N	17 43E
Moravița	**42**	45 17N	21 14E
Moravská Třebová	**27**	49 45N	16 40E
Moravské Budějovice	**26**	49 4N	15 49E
Morawhanna	**126**	8 30N	59 40W
Moray Firth	**14**	57 50N	3 30W
Morbach	**25**	49 48N	7 7E
Morbegno	**38**	46 8N	9 34E
Morbihan □	**18**	47 55N	2 50W
Morcenx	**20**	44 0N	0 55W
Mordelles	**18**	48 5N	1 52W
Morden	**109**	49 15N	98 10W
Mordialloc	**100**	38 1S	145 6E
Mordovian A.S.S.R. □	**55**	54 20N	44 30E
Mordovo	**55**	52 6N	40 50E
Mordy	**28**	52 13N	22 31E
Møre og Romsdal fylke □	**47**	62 30N	8 0E
Morea	**9**	37 45N	22 10E
Moreau →	**116**	45 15N	100 43W
Morecambe	**12**	54 5N	2 52W
Morecambe B.	**12**	54 7N	3 0W
Moree	**97**	29 28S	149 54E
Morehead	**114**	38 12N	83 22W
Morehead City	**115**	34 46N	76 44W
Morelia	**120**	19 40N	101 11W
Morella, Austral.	**98**	23 0S	143 52E
Morella, Spain	**32**	40 35N	0 5W
Morelos □	**120**	18 40N	99 10W
Morena, Sierra	**31**	38 20N	4 0W
Morenci	**119**	33 7N	109 20W
Moreni	**46**	44 59N	25 36E
Moresby I.	**108**	52 30N	131 40W
Morestel	**21**	45 40N	5 28E
Moret	**19**	48 22N	2 58E
Moreton	**98**	12 22S	142 30E
Moreton B.	**97**	27 10S	153 10E
Moreton I.	**97**	27 10S	153 25E
Moreuil	**19**	49 46N	2 30E
Morez	**21**	46 31N	6 2E
Morgan, Austral.	**99**	34 0S	139 35E
Morgan, U.S.A.	**118**	41 3N	111 44W
Morgan City	**117**	29 40N	91 15W
Morganfield	**114**	37 40N	87 55W
Morganton	**115**	35 46N	81 48W
Morgantown	**114**	39 39N	79 58W
Morganville	**99**	25 10S	151 50E
Morgat	**18**	48 15N	4 32W
Morgenzon	**93**	26 45S	29 36E
Morges	**25**	46 31N	6 29E
Morhange	**19**	48 55N	6 38E
Mori	**38**	45 51N	10 59E
Moriarty	**119**	35 3N	106 2W
Morice L.	**108**	53 50N	127 40W
Moriki	**85**	12 52N	6 30E
Morinville	**108**	53 49N	113 41W
Morioka	**74**	39 45N	141 8E
Morkalla	**99**	34 23S	141 10E
Morlaàs	**20**	43 21N	0 18W
Morlaix	**18**	48 36N	3 52W
Mormanno	**41**	39 53N	15 59E
Mormant	**19**	48 37N	2 52E
Mornington	**99**	38 15S	145 5E
Mornington I.	**97**	16 30S	139 30E
Mornington, I.	**128**	49 50S	75 30W
Mórnos →	**45**	38 30N	22 0E
Moro	**87**	10 50N	30 9E
Moro G.	**73**	6 30N	123 0E
Morobe	**98**	7 49S	147 38E
Morocco ■	**82**	32 0N	5 50W
Morococha	**126**	11 40S	76 5W
Morogoro	**90**	6 50S	37 40E
Morogoro □	**90**	8 0S	37 0E
Moroleón	**120**	20 8N	101 32W
Morombe	**93**	21 45S	43 22E
Moron	**124**	34 39S	58 37W
Morón	**121**	22 8N	78 39W
Mörön →	**75**	47 14N	110 37E
Morón de Almazán	**32**	41 29N	2 27W
Morón de la Frontera	**31**	37 6N	5 28W
Morondava	**93**	20 17S	44 17E
Morondo	**84**	8 57N	6 47W
Moronou	**84**	6 16N	4 59W
Morotai	**73**	2 10N	128 30E
Moroto	**90**	2 28N	34 42E
Moroto Summit	**90**	2 30N	34 43E
Morozov (Bratan)	**43**	42 30N	25 10E
Morozovsk	**57**	48 25N	41 50E
Morpeth	**12**	55 11N	1 41W
Morphou	**64**	35 12N	32 59E
Morrilton	**117**	35 10N	92 45W
Morrinhos	**127**	17 45S	49 10W
Morrinsville	**101**	37 40S	175 32E
Morris, Can.	**109**	49 25N	97 22W
Morris, Ill., U.S.A.	**114**	41 20N	88 20W
Morris, Minn., U.S.A.	**116**	45 33N	95 56W
Morrisburg	**106**	44 55N	75 7W
Morrison	**116**	41 47N	90 0W
Morristown, Ariz., U.S.A.	**119**	33 54N	112 35W
Morristown, N.J., U.S.A.	**113**	40 48N	74 30W
Morristown, S.D., U.S.A.	**116**	45 57N	101 44W
Morristown, Tenn., U.S.A.	**115**	36 18N	83 20W
Morro Bay	**119**	35 27N	120 54W
Morro, Pta.	**124**	27 6S	71 0W
Morrosquillo, Golfo de	**121**	9 35N	75 40W
Mörrum	**49**	56 12N	14 45E
Mors	**49**	56 50N	8 45E
Morshansk	**55**	53 28N	41 50E
Mörsil	**48**	63 19N	13 40E
Mortagne	**20**	45 28N	0 49W
Mortagne →	**19**	48 33N	6 27E
Mortagne-au-Perche	**18**	48 31N	0 33E
Mortain	**18**	48 40N	0 57W
Mortara	**38**	45 15N	8 43E
Morteau	**19**	47 3N	6 35E
Morteros	**124**	30 50S	62 0W
Mortes, R. das →	**127**	11 45S	50 44W
Mortlake	**99**	38 5S	142 50E
Morton, Tex., U.S.A.	**117**	33 39N	102 49W
Morton, Wash., U.S.A.	**118**	46 33N	122 17W
Morundah	**99**	34 57S	146 19E
Moruya	**99**	35 58S	150 3E
Morvan, Mts. du	**19**	47 5N	4 0E
Morven	**99**	26 22S	147 5E
Morvern	**14**	56 38N	5 44W
Morvi	**68**	22 50N	70 42E
Morwell	**97**	38 10S	146 22E
Moryn	**28**	52 51N	14 22E
Morzhovets, Ostrov	**52**	66 44N	42 35E
Mosalsk	**54**	54 30N	34 55E
Mosbach	**25**	49 21N	9 9E
Moščenice	**39**	45 17N	14 16E
Mosciano Sant' Ángelo	**39**	42 42N	13 52E
Moscos Is.	**72**	14 0N	97 30E
Moscow	**118**	46 45N	116 59W
Moscow = Moskva	**55**	55 45N	37 35E
Mosel →	**16**	50 22N	7 36E
Moselle = Mosel →	**16**	50 22N	7 36E
Moselle □	**19**	48 59N	6 33E
Moses Lake	**118**	47 16N	119 17W
Mosgiel	**101**	45 53S	170 21E
Moshi	**90**	3 22S	37 18E
Moshi □	**90**	3 22S	37 18E
Moshupa	**92**	24 46S	25 29E
Mośina	**28**	52 15N	16 50E
Mosjøen	**50**	65 51N	13 12E
Moskenesøya	**50**	67 58N	13 0E
Moskenstraumen	**50**	67 47N	12 45E
Moskva	**55**	55 45N	37 35E
Moskva →	**55**	55 5N	38 51E
Moslavačka Gora	**39**	45 40N	16 37E
Mosomane (Artesia)	**92**	24 2S	26 19E
Mosonmagyaróvár	**27**	47 52N	17 18E
Mošorin	**42**	45 19N	20 4E
Mospino	**56**	47 52N	38 0E
Mosquera	**126**	2 35N	78 24W
Mosquero	**117**	35 48N	103 57W
Mosqueruela	**32**	40 21N	0 27W
Mosquitos, Golfo de los	**121**	9 15N	81 10W
Moss	**47**	59 27N	10 40E
Moss Vale	**99**	34 32S	150 25E
Mossaka	**88**	1 15S	16 45E
Mossbank	**109**	49 56N	105 56W
Mossburn	**101**	45 41S	168 15E
Mosselbaai	**92**	34 11S	22 8E
Mossendjo	**88**	2 55S	12 42E
Mossgiel	**99**	33 15S	144 5E
Mossman	**97**	16 21S	145 15E
Mossoró	**127**	5 10S	37 15W
Møsstrand	**47**	59 51N	8 4E
Mossuril	**91**	14 58S	40 42E
Mossy →	**109**	54 5N	102 58W
Most	**26**	50 31N	13 38E
Mostaganem	**82**	35 54N	0 5E
Mostar	**42**	43 22N	17 50E
Mostardas	**125**	31 2S	50 51W
Mostefa, Rass	**83**	36 55N	11 3E
Mosterøy	**47**	59 5N	5 37E
Mostiska	**54**	49 48N	23 4E
Mosty	**54**	53 27N	24 38E
Mosul = Al Mawșil	**64**	36 20N	43 5E
Mosvatn	**47**	59 52N	8 5E
Mota del Cuervo	**32**	39 30N	2 52W
Mota del Marqués	**30**	41 38N	5 11W
Motagua →	**120**	15 44N	88 14W
Motala	**49**	58 32N	15 1E
Mothe-Achard, La	**18**	46 37N	1 40W
Motherwell	**14**	55 48N	4 0W
Motihari	**69**	26 30N	84 55E
Motilla del Palancar	**32**	39 34N	1 55W
Motnik	**39**	46 14N	14 54E
Motovun	**39**	45 20N	13 50E
Motozintla de Mendoza	**120**	15 21N	92 14W
Motril	**33**	36 31N	3 37W
Motru →	**46**	44 44N	22 59E
Mott	**116**	46 25N	102 29W
Motte-Chalançon, La	**21**	44 30N	5 21E
Motte, La	**21**	44 20N	6 3E
Móttola	**41**	40 38N	17 0E
Motueka	**101**	41 7S	173 1E
Motul	**120**	21 0N	89 20W
Mouanda	**88**	1 28S	13 7E
Mouchalagane →	**107**	50 56N	68 41W
Moucontant	**18**	46 43N	0 36W
Moúdhros	**44**	39 50N	25 18E
Moudjeria	**84**	17 50N	12 28W
Moudon	**25**	46 40N	6 49E
Mouila	**88**	1 50S	11 0E
Moulamein	**99**	35 3S	144 1E
Moule	**121**	16 20N	61 22W
Moulins	**20**	46 35N	3 19E
Moulmein	**67**	16 30N	97 40E
Moulouya, O. →	**82**	35 5N	2 25W
Moulton	**117**	29 35N	97 8W
Moultrie	**115**	31 11N	83 47W
Moultrie, L.	**115**	33 25N	80 10W
Mound City, Mo., U.S.A.	**116**	40 2N	95 25W
Mound City, S.D., U.S.A.	**116**	45 46N	100 3W
Moúnda, Akra	**45**	38 5N	20 45E
Moundou	**81**	8 40N	16 10E
Moundsville	**114**	39 53N	80 43W
Mount Airy	**115**	36 31N	80 37W
Mount Albert	**112**	44 8N	79 19W
Mount Angel	**118**	45 4N	122 46W
Mount Barker, S.A., Austral.	**99**	35 5S	138 52E
Mount Barker, W.A., Austral.	**96**	34 38S	117 40E
Mount Carmel, Ill., U.S.A.	**114**	38 20N	87 48W
Mount Carmel, Pa., U.S.A.	**114**	40 46N	76 25W
Mount Clemens	**106**	42 35N	82 50W
Mount Coolon	**98**	21 25S	147 25E
Mount Darwin	**91**	16 45S	31 33E
Mount Desert I.	**107**	44 15N	68 25W
Mount Dora	**115**	28 49N	81 32W
Mount Douglas	**98**	21 35S	146 50E
Mount Edgecumbe	**108**	57 8N	135 22W
Mount Enid	**96**	21 42S	116 26E
Mount Forest	**106**	43 59N	80 43W
Mount Gambier	**97**	37 50S	140 46E
Mount Garnet	**98**	17 37S	145 6E
Mount Hope	**114**	37 52N	81 9W
Mount Horeb	**116**	43 0N	89 42W
Mount Howitt	**99**	26 31S	142 16E
Mount Isa	**97**	20 42S	139 26E
Mount Larcom	**98**	23 48S	150 59E
Mount Lofty Ra.	**97**	34 35S	139 5E
Mount McKinley Nat. Park	**104**	64 0N	150 0W
Mount Magnet	**96**	28 2S	117 47E
Mount Margaret	**99**	26 54S	143 21E
Mount Maunganui	**101**	37 40S	176 14E
Mount Morgan	**97**	23 40S	150 25E
Mount Morris	**114**	42 43N	77 50W
Mount Mulligan	**98**	16 45S	144 47E
Mount Nicholas	**96**	22 54S	120 27E
Mount Oxide Mine	**98**	19 30S	139 29E
Mount Pearl	**107**	47 31N	52 47W
Mount Perry	**99**	25 13S	151 42E
Mount Pleasant, Iowa, U.S.A.	**116**	41 0N	91 35W
Mount Pleasant, Mich., U.S.A.	**114**	43 35N	84 47W
Mount Pleasant, Pa., U.S.A.	**112**	40 9N	79 31W
Mount Pleasant, S.C., U.S.A.	**115**	32 45N	79 48W
Mount Pleasant, Tenn., U.S.A.	**115**	35 31N	87 11W
Mount Pleasant, Tex., U.S.A.	**117**	33 5N	95 0W
Mount Pleasant, Ut., U.S.A.	**118**	39 40N	111 29W
Mount Pocono	**113**	41 8N	75 21W
Mount Rainier Nat. Park.	**118**	46 50N	121 43W
Mount Revelstoke Nat. Park	**108**	51 5N	118 30W
Mount Robson	**108**	52 56N	119 15W
Mount Robson Prov. Park	**108**	53 0N	119 0W
Mount Shasta	**118**	41 20N	122 18W
Mount Sterling, Ill., U.S.A.	**116**	40 0N	90 40W
Mount Sterling, Ky., U.S.A.	**114**	38 0N	84 0W
Mount Surprise	**98**	18 10S	144 17E
Mount Union	**112**	40 22N	77 51W
Mount Vernon, Ind., U.S.A.	**116**	38 17N	88 57W
Mount Vernon, N.Y., U.S.A.	**114**	40 57N	73 49W
Mount Vernon, Ohio, U.S.A.	**114**	40 20N	82 30W
Mount Vernon, Wash., U.S.A.	**108**	48 25N	122 20W
Mount Whaleback	**96**	23 18S	119 44E
Mountain City, Nev., U.S.A.	**118**	41 54N	116 0W
Mountain City, Tenn., U.S.A.	**115**	36 30N	81 50W
Mountain Grove	**117**	37 5N	92 20W
Mountain Home, Ark., U.S.A.	**117**	36 20N	92 25W
Mountain Home, Idaho, U.S.A.	**118**	43 11N	115 45W
Mountain Iron	**116**	47 30N	92 37W
Mountain Park.	**108**	52 50N	117 15W
Mountain View, Ark., U.S.A.	**117**	35 52N	92 10W
Mountain View, Calif., U.S.A.	**119**	37 26N	122 5W
Mountainair	**119**	34 35N	106 15W
Mountmellick	**15**	53 7N	7 20W
Moura, Austral.	**98**	24 35S	149 58E
Moura, Brazil	**126**	1 32S	61 38W
Moura, Port.	**31**	38 7N	7 30W
Mourão	**31**	38 22N	7 22W
Mourdi Depression	**81**	18 10N	23 0E
Mourdiah	**84**	14 35N	7 25W
Moure, La	**116**	46 27N	98 17W
Mourenx	**20**	43 23N	0 36W
Mouri	**85**	5 6N	1 14W
Mourilyan	**98**	17 35S	146 3E
Mourmelon-le-Grand	**19**	49 8N	4 22E
Mourne →	**15**	54 45N	7 39W
Mourne Mts.	**15**	54 10N	6 0W
Mouscron	**16**	50 45N	3 12E
Moussoro	**81**	13 41N	16 35E
Mouthe	**19**	46 44N	6 12E
Moutier	**25**	47 16N	7 21E
Moûtiers	**21**	45 29N	6 31E
Moutong	**73**	0 28N	121 13E
Mouy	**19**	49 18N	2 20E
Mouzáki	**44**	39 25N	21 37E
Moville	**15**	55 11N	7 3W
Moy →	**15**	54 5N	8 50W
Moyale, Ethiopia	**87**	3 34N	39 4E
Moyale, Kenya	**90**	3 30N	39 0E
Moyamba	**84**	8 4N	12 30W
Moyen Atlas	**80**	32 0N	5 0W
Moyle □	**15**	55 10N	6 15W
Moyobamba	**126**	6 0S	77 0W
Moyyero →	**59**	68 44N	103 42E
Mozambique = Moçambique	**91**	15 3S	40 42E
Mozambique ■	**91**	19 0S	35 0E
Mozambique Chan.	**93**	20 0S	39 0E
Mozdok	**57**	43 45N	44 48E
Mozhaysk	**55**	55 30N	36 2E
Mozhga	**55**	56 26N	52 15E
Mozirje	**39**	46 22N	14 58E
Mozyr	**54**	52 0N	29 15E
Mpanda	**90**	6 23S	31 1E
Mpanda □	**90**	6 23S	31 40E
Mpésoba	**84**	12 31N	5 39W
Mpika	**91**	11 51S	31 25E
Mpulungu	**91**	8 51S	31 5E
Mpwapwa	**90**	6 23S	36 30E
Mpwapwa □	**90**	6 30S	36 20E
Mrągowo	**28**	53 52N	21 18E
Mramor	**42**	43 20N	21 45E
Mrimina	**82**	29 50N	7 9W
Mrkonjić Grad	**42**	44 26N	17 4E
Mrkopalj	**39**	45 21N	14 52E
Mrocza	**28**	53 16N	17 35E
Msab, Oued en →	**83**	32 25N	5 20E
Msaken	**83**	35 49N	10 33E
Msambansovu	**91**	15 50S	30 3E
M'sila	**83**	35 46N	4 30E
Msta →	**54**	58 25N	31 20E
Mstislavl	**54**	54 0N	31 50E
Mszana Dolna	**27**	49 41N	20 5E
Mszczonów	**28**	51 58N	20 33E
Mtama	**91**	10 17S	39 21E
Mtilikwe →	**91**	21 9S	31 30E
Mtsensk	**55**	53 25N	36 30E
Mtskheta	**57**	41 52N	44 45E
Mtwara-Mikindani	**91**	10 20S	40 20E
Mu Us Shamo	**76**	39 0N	109 0E
Muaná	**127**	1 25S	49 15W
Muang Chiang Rai	**71**	19 52N	99 50E
Muang Lamphun	**71**	18 40N	99 2E
Muang Phichit	**71**	16 29N	100 21E
Muar	**71**	2 3N	102 34E
Muar →	**71**	2 15N	102 48E
Muarabungo	**72**	1 28S	102 52E
Muaradjuloi	**72**	0 12S	114 3E
Muaraenim	**72**	3 40S	103 50E
Muarakaman	**72**	0 2S	116 45E
Muaratebo	**72**	1 30S	102 26E
Muaratembesi	**72**	1 42S	103 8E
Muaratewe	**72**	0 58S	114 52E
Mubarakpur	**69**	26 6N	83 18E
Mubende	**90**	0 33N	31 22E
Mubi	**85**	10 18N	13 16E
Mücheln	**24**	51 18N	11 49E
Muchinga Mts.	**91**	11 30S	31 30E
Muchkapskiy	**55**	51 52N	42 28E
Muck	**14**	56 50N	6 15W
Muckadilla	**99**	26 35S	148 23E
Mucuri	**127**	18 0S	39 36W
Mucusso	**92**	18 1S	21 25E
Mudanjiang	**76**	44 38N	129 30E
Mudanya	**56**	40 25N	28 50E
Muddy →	**119**	38 0N	110 22W
Mudgee	**97**	32 32S	149 31E
Mudjatik →	**109**	56 1N	107 36W
Muecate	**91**	14 55S	39 40E
Muêda	**91**	11 36S	39 28E
Muela, La	**32**	41 36N	1 7W
Muerto, Mar	**120**	16 10N	94 10W
Muertos, Punta de los	**33**	36 57N	1 54W
Mufindi □	**91**	8 30S	35 20E
Mufulira	**91**	12 32S	28 15E
Mufumbiro Range	**90**	1 25S	29 30E
Mugardos	**30**	43 27N	8 15W
Muge	**31**	39 3N	8 40W
Muge →	**31**	39 8N	8 44W
Múggia	**39**	45 36N	13 47E
Mugia	**30**	43 3N	9 10W
Mugila, Mts.	**90**	7 0S	28 50E
Muğla	**64**	37 15N	28 22E
Müglizh	**43**	42 37N	25 32E
Mugshin	**63**	19 35N	54 40E
Mugu	**69**	29 45N	82 30E
Muhammad Qol	**86**	20 53N	37 9E
Muhammad Râs	**86**	27 42N	34 13E
Muhammadabad	**69**	26 4N	83 25E
Muharraqa = Sa'ad	**62**	31 28N	34 33E
Muhesi →	**90**	7 0S	35 20E
Muheza □	**90**	5 0S	39 0E
Mühldorf	**25**	48 14N	12 33E
Mühlhausen	**24**	51 12N	10 29E
Mühlig Hofmann fjella	**5**	72 30S	5 0E
Muhutwe	**90**	1 35S	31 45E
Mui Bai Bung	**71**	8 35N	104 42E
Mui Ron	**71**	18 7N	106 27E
Muikamachi	**74**	37 15N	138 50E
Muine Bheag	**15**	52 42N	6 57W
Muiños	**30**	41 58N	7 59W
Mukachevo	**54**	48 27N	22 45E
Mukah	**72**	2 55N	112 5E
Mukawwa, Geziret	**86**	23 55N	35 53E
Mukden = Shenyang	**76**	41 48N	123 27E
Mukhtolovo	**55**	55 29N	43 15E
Mukishi	**91**	8 30S	24 44E
Mukomuko	**72**	2 30S	101 10E
Mukomwenze	**90**	6 49S	27 15E
Muktsar	**68**	30 30N	74 30E
Mukur	**66**	32 50N	67 42E
Mukutawa →	**109**	53 10N	97 24W
Mukwela	**91**	17 0S	26 40E
Mula	**33**	38 3N	1 33W
Mula →	**70**	18 34N	74 21E
Mulange	**90**	3 40S	27 10E
* Mulatas, Arch. de las	**121**	9 50N	78 31W
Mulchén	**124**	37 45S	72 20W
Mulde →	**24**	51 10N	12 48E
Mule Creek	**116**	43 19N	104 8W
Muleba	**90**	1 50S	31 37E
Muleba □	**90**	2 0S	31 30E
Muleshoe	**117**	34 17N	102 42W
Mulgrave	**107**	45 38N	61 31W
Mulgrave I.	**98**	10 5S	142 10E
Mulhacén	**33**	37 4N	3 20W
Mülheim	**24**	51 26N	6 53E
Mulhouse	**19**	47 40N	7 20E
Muling He →	**76**	45 53N	133 30E
Mull	**14**	56 27N	6 0W
Mullaittvu	**70**	9 15N	80 49E
Mullen	**116**	42 5N	101 0W
Mullengudgery	**99**	31 43S	147 23E
Mullens	**114**	37 34N	81 22W
Muller, Pegunungan	**72**	0 30N	113 30E
Mullet Pen.	**15**	54 10N	10 2W
Mullewa	**96**	28 29S	115 30E
Müllheim	**25**	47 48N	7 37E
Mulligan →	**98**	26 40S	139 0E
Mullin	**117**	31 33N	98 38W
Mullingar	**15**	53 31N	7 20W
Mullins	**115**	34 12N	79 15W
Mullsjö	**49**	57 56N	13 55E

** Renamed San Blas, Arch. de*

Mullumbimby Nanjeko

Mullumbimby 99 28 30S 153 30 E
Mulobezi 91 16 45S 25 7 E
Mulshi L. 70 18 30N 73 48 E
Multai 68 21 50N 78 21 E
Multan 68 30 15N 71 36 E
* Multan □ 68 30 29N 72 29 E
Multrå 48 63 10N 17 24 E
Mulumbe, Mts. 91 8 40S 27 30 E
Mulungushi Dam 91 14 48S 28 48 E
Mulvane 117 37 30N 97 15W
Mulwad 86 18 45N 30 39 E
Mulwala 100 35 59S 146 0 E
Mumra 57 45 45N 47 41 E
Mun → 71 15 17N 103 0 E
Muna 73 5 0S 122 30 E
Munamagi 54 57 43N 27 4 E
Münchberg 25 50 11N 11 48 E
Muncheberg 24 52 30N 14 9 E
München 25 48 8N 11 33 E
Munchen-Gladbach = Mönchengladbach 24 51 12N 6 23 E
Muncho Lake 108 59 0N 125 50W
Muncie 114 40 10N 85 20W
Mundakayam 70 9 30N 76 50 E
Mundala, Puncak 73 4 30S 141 0 E
Mundare 108 53 35N 112 20W
Munday 117 33 26N 99 39W
Münden 24 51 25N 9 42 E
Mundo → 33 38 30N 2 15W
Mundo Novo 127 11 50S 40 29W
Mundra 68 22 54N 69 48 E
Munera 33 39 2N 2 29W
Muneru → 70 16 45N 80 3 E
Mungallala 99 26 28S 147 34 E
Mungallala Cr. → 99 28 53S 147 5 E
Mungana 98 17 8S 144 27 E
Mungaoli 68 24 24N 78 7 E
Mungari 91 17 12S 33 30 E
Mungbere 90 2 36N 28 28 E
Mungindi 97 28 58S 149 1 E
Munhango 89 12 10S 18 38 E
Munich = München 25 48 8N 11 33 E
Munising 114 46 25N 86 39W
Munjiye 86 18 47N 41 20 E
Munka-Ljungby 49 56 16N 12 58 E
Munkedal 49 58 28N 11 40 E
Munkfors 48 59 50N 13 30 E
Munku-Sardyk 59 51 45N 100 20 E
Münnerstadt 25 50 15N 10 11 E
Muñoz Gamero, Pen. 128 52 30S 73 5 E
Munroe L. 109 59 13N 98 35W
Munster, France 19 48 2N 7 8 E
Munster, Ger. 24 52 59N 10 5 E
Münster 24 51 58N 7 37 E
Munster □ 15 52 20N 8 40W
Muntele Mare 46 46 30N 23 12 E
Muntok 72 2 5S 105 10 E
Munyak 58 43 30N 59 15 E
Munyama 91 16 5S 28 31 E
Muon Pak Beng 71 19 51N 101 4 E
Muonio 50 67 57N 23 40 E
Mupa 89 16 5S 15 50 E
Muping 76 37 22N 121 36 E
Muqaddam, Wadi → 86 18 4N 31 30 E
Muqdisho 63 2 2N 45 25 E
Mur → 26 46 18N 16 53 E
Mur-de-Bretagne 18 48 12N 3 0W
Mura → 39 46 18N 16 53 E
Murallón, Cuerro 128 49 48S 73 30W
Muranda 90 1 52S 29 20 E
Murang'a 90 0 45S 37 9 E
Murashi 55 59 30N 49 0 E
Murat 20 45 7N 2 53 E
Murau 26 47 6N 14 10 E
Muravera 40 39 25N 9 35 E
Murça 30 41 24N 7 28W
Murchison → 96 27 45S 114 0 E
Murchison Falls = Kabarega Falls 90 2 15N 31 38 E
Murchison Ra. 96 20 0S 134 10 E
Murchison Rapids 91 15 55S 34 35 E
Murcia 33 38 20N 1 10W
Murcia □ 33 37 50N 1 30W
Murdo 116 43 56N 100 43W
Murdoch Pt. 98 14 37S 144 55 E
Mure, La 21 44 55N 5 48 E
Mureş □ 46 46 45N 24 40 E
Mureş (Mureşul) → 46 46 15N 20 13 E
Muret 20 43 30N 1 20 E
Murfatlar 46 44 10N 28 26 E
Murfreesboro 115 35 50N 86 21W
Murg → 25 48 55N 8 10 E
Murgab 58 38 10N 74 2 E
Murgeni 46 46 12N 28 1 E
Murgon 97 26 15S 151 54 E
Muriaé 125 21 8S 42 23W
Murias de Paredes 30 42 52N 6 11W
Muriel Mine 91 17 14S 30 40 E
Müritz see 24 53 25N 12 40 E
Murka 90 3 27S 38 0 E
Murmansk 52 68 57N 33 10 E
Murnau 25 47 40N 11 11 E
Muro, France 21 42 34N 8 54 E
Muro, Spain 32 39 44N 3 3 E
Muro, C. de 21 41 44N 8 37 E
Muro Lucano 41 40 45N 15 30 E
Murom 55 55 35N 42 3 E
Muroran 74 42 25N 141 0 E
Muros 30 42 45N 9 5W
Muros y de Noya, Ría de 30 42 45N 9 0W
Muroto-Misaki 74 33 15N 134 10 E
Murowana Goślina 28 52 35N 17 0 E
Murphy 118 43 11N 116 33W
Murphysboro 117 37 50N 89 20W
Murrat 86 18 51N 29 33 E
Murray, Ky., U.S.A. 115 36 40N 88 20W
Murray, Utah, U.S.A. 118 40 41N 111 58W
Murray →, Austral. 97 35 20S 139 22 E
Murray →, Can. 108 56 11N 120 45W
Murray Bridge 97 35 6S 139 14 E
Murray Harbour 107 46 0N 62 28W
Murray, L., P.N.G. 98 7 0S 141 35 E

* *Now part of Punjab* □

Murray, L., U.S.A. 115 34 8N 81 30W
Murray Seascarp 95 30 0N 135 0W
Murraysburg 92 31 58S 23 47 E
Murrayville 100 35 16S 141 11 E
Murree 66 33 56N 73 28 E
Murrumbidgee → 97 34 43S 143 12 E
Murrumburrah 99 34 32S 148 22 E
Murrurundi 99 31 42S 150 51 E
Mursala 72 1 41N 98 28 E
Murshid 86 21 40N 31 10 E
Murshidabad 69 24 11N 88 19 E
Murska Sobota 39 46 39N 16 12 E
Murtazapur 68 20 40N 77 25 E
Murtle L. 108 52 8N 119 38W
Murtoa 99 36 35S 142 28 E
Murtosa 30 40 44N 8 40W
Murungu 90 4 12S 31 10 E
Murwara 69 23 46N 80 28 E
Murwillumbah 97 28 18S 153 27 E
Muryo 73 6 36S 110 53 E
Mürz → 26 47 30N 15 25 E
Mürzzuschlag 26 47 36N 15 41 E
Muş 64 38 45N 41 30 E
Musa Khel Bazar 68 30 59N 69 52 E
Mūsá Qal'eh 65 32 20N 64 50 E
Musairik, Wadi → 86 19 30N 43 10 E
Musala 43 42 13N 23 37 E
Musan, Kor., N. 76 42 12N 129 12 E
Musan, Kor., N. 76 42 12N 129 12 E
Musangu 91 10 28S 23 55 E
Musasa 90 3 25S 31 30 E
Musay'īd 65 25 0N 51 33 E
Muscat = Masqat 65 23 37N 58 36 E
Muscat & Oman = Oman ■ 63 23 0N 58 0 E
Muscatine 116 41 25N 91 5W
Musel 30 43 34N 5 42W
Musgrave Ras. 96 26 0S 132 0 E
Mushie 88 2 56S 16 55 E
Mushin 85 6 32N 3 21 E
Musi →, India 70 16 41N 79 40 E
Musi →, Indon. 72 2 20S 104 56 E
Muskeg → 108 60 20N 123 20W
Muskegon 114 43 15N 86 17W
Muskegon → 114 43 25N 86 0W
Muskegon Hts. 114 43 12N 86 17W
Muskogee 117 35 50N 95 25W
Muskwa → 108 58 47N 122 48W
Musmar 86 18 13N 35 40 E
Musofu 91 13 30S 29 0 E
Musoma 90 1 30S 33 48 E
Musoma □ 90 1 50S 34 30 E
Musquaro, L. 107 50 38N 61 5W
Musquodoboit Harbour 107 44 50N 63 9W
Musselburgh 14 55 57N 3 3W
Musselshell → 118 47 21N 107 58W
Mussidan 20 45 2N 0 22 E
Mussomeli 40 37 35N 13 43 E
Mussooree 68 30 27N 78 6 E
Mussuco 92 17 2S 19 3 E
Mustang 69 29 10N 83 55 E
Musters, L. 128 45 20S 69 25W
Muswellbrook 97 32 16S 150 56 E
Muszyna 27 49 22N 20 55 E
Mût 86 25 28N 28 58 E
Mut 64 36 40N 33 28 E
Mutanda, Mozam. 93 21 0S 33 34 E
Mutanda, Zambia 91 12 24S 26 13 E
Mutaray 59 60 56N 101 0 E
Muting 73 7 23S 140 20 E
Mutshatsha 91 10 35S 24 20 E
Muttaburra 97 22 38S 144 29 E
Mutuáli 91 14 55S 37 0 E
Muvatupusha 70 9 53N 76 35 E
Muxima 88 9 33S 13 58 E
Muy, Le 21 43 28N 6 34 E
Muya 59 56 27N 115 50 E
Muyinga 90 3 14S 30 33 E
Muzaffarabad 69 34 25N 73 30 E
Muzaffargarh 68 30 5N 71 14 E
Muzaffarnagar 68 29 26N 77 40 E
Muzaffarpur 69 26 7N 85 23 E
Muzhi 58 65 25N 64 40 E
Muzillac 18 47 35N 2 30W
Muzon C. 108 54 40N 132 40W
Muztag 75 36 20N 87 28 E
Mvôlô 87 6 2N 29 53 E
Mwadui 90 3 26S 33 32 E
Mwambo 91 10 30S 40 22 E
Mwandi 91 17 30S 24 51 E
Mwanza, Tanz. 90 2 30S 32 58 E
Mwanza, Zaïre 90 7 55S 26 43 E
Mwanza, Zambia 91 16 58S 24 28 E
Mwanza □ 90 2 0S 33 0 E
Mwaya 91 9 32S 33 55 E
Mweelrea 15 53 37N 9 48W
Mweka 88 4 50S 21 34 E
Mwenga 90 3 1S 28 28 E
Mweru, L. 91 9 0S 28 40 E
Mweza Range 91 21 0S 30 0 E
Mwilambwe 90 8 7S 25 0 E
Mwimbi 91 8 38S 31 39 E
Mwinilunga 91 11 43S 24 25 E
My Tho 71 10 29N 106 23 E
Mya, O. → 83 30 46N 4 54 E
Myall → 100 32 30S 152 15 E
Myanaung 67 18 18N 95 22 E
Myaungmya 67 16 30N 94 40 E
Mycenae = Mikínai 45 37 43N 22 46 E
Myeik Kyunzu 71 11 30N 97 30 E
Myerstown 113 40 22N 76 18W
Myitkyina 67 25 24N 97 26 E
Myjava 27 48 41N 17 37 E
Mymensingh 69 24 45N 90 24 E
Myndus 45 37 3N 27 14 E
Mynydd ddu 13 51 45N 3 45W
Myrdal 47 60 43N 7 10 E
Mýrdalsjökull 50 63 40N 19 6W
Myrtle Beach 115 33 43N 78 50W
Myrtle Creek 118 43 0N 123 9W
Myrtle Point 118 43 0N 124 4W
Myrtleford 100 36 34S 146 44 E
Mysen 47 59 33N 11 20 E
Myslenice 27 49 51N 19 57 E
Myślibórz 28 52 55N 14 50 E
Mysłowice 27 50 15N 19 12 E
Mysore 70 12 17N 76 41 E
Mysore □ = Karnataka 70 13 15N 77 0 E
Mystic 113 41 21N 71 58W
Mystishchi 55 55 50N 37 50 E
Myszków 28 50 45N 19 22 E
Myszyniec 28 53 23N 21 21 E
Myton 118 40 10N 110 2W
Mývatn 50 65 36N 17 0W
Mze → 26 49 46N 13 24 E
Mzimba 91 11 55S 33 39 E
Mzimvubu → 93 31 38S 29 33 E
Mzuzu 91 11 30S 33 55 E

N

N' Dioum 84 16 31N 14 39W
Naab → 25 49 1N 12 2 E
Na'am 87 9 42N 28 27 E
Na'an 62 31 53N 34 52 E
Naantali 51 60 29N 22 2 E
Naas 15 53 12N 6 40W
Nababiep 92 29 36S 17 46 E
Nabadwip 69 23 34N 88 20 E
Nabas 73 11 47N 122 6 E
Nabburg 25 49 27N 12 11 E
* Nabereznyje Celny 58 55 42N 52 19 E
Nabeul 83 36 30N 10 44 E
Nabha 68 30 26N 76 14 E
Nabire 73 3 15S 135 26 E
Nabisar 68 25 8N 69 40 E
Nabisipi → 107 50 14N 62 13W
Nabiswera 90 1 27N 32 15 E
Nablus = Nābulus 62 32 14N 35 15 E
Naboomspruit 93 24 32S 28 40 E
Nābulus 62 32 14N 35 15 E
Nacala-Velha 91 14 32S 40 34 E
Nacaroa 91 14 22S 39 56 E
Naches 118 46 48N 120 42W
Nachingwea 91 10 23S 38 49 E
Nachingwea □ 91 10 30S 38 30 E
Nachna 68 27 34N 71 41 E
Náchod 27 50 25N 16 8 E
Nacka 48 59 17N 18 12 E
Nackara 99 32 48S 139 12 E
Naco 119 31 24N 109 58W
Nacogdoches 117 31 33N 94 39W
Nacozari 120 30 24N 109 39W
Nadi 86 18 40N 33 41 E
Nadiad 68 22 41N 72 56 E
Nădlac 42 46 10N 20 50 E
Nador 82 35 14N 2 58W
Nadūshan 65 32 2N 53 35 E
Nadvoitsy 52 63 52N 34 14 E
Nadvornaya 56 48 37N 24 30 E
Nadym 58 65 35N 72 42 E
Nadym → 58 66 12N 72 0 E
Nærbø 47 58 40N 5 39 E
Næstved 49 55 13N 11 44 E
Nafada 85 11 8N 11 20 E
Naft-e Shāh 64 34 0N 45 30 E
Nafūd ad Dahy 64 22 0N 45 0 E
Nafūsah, Jabal 83 32 12N 12 30 E
Nag Hammâdi 86 26 2N 32 18 E
Naga 73 13 38N 123 15 E
Naga, Kreb en 82 24 12N 6 0W
Nagagami → 106 49 40N 84 40W
Nagaland □ 67 26 0N 94 30 E
Nagano 74 36 40N 138 10 E
Nagano □ 74 36 15N 138 0 E
Nagaoka 74 37 27N 138 50 E
Nagappattinam 70 10 46N 79 51 E
Nagar Parkar 68 24 28N 70 46 E
Nagari Hills 70 13 3N 79 45 E
Nagarjuna Sagar 70 16 35N 79 17 E
Nagasaki 74 32 47N 129 50 E
Nagasaki □ 74 32 50N 129 40 E
Nagaur 68 27 15N 73 45 E
Nagbhil 70 20 34N 79 55 E
Nagercoil 70 8 12N 77 26 E
Nagina 68 29 30N 78 30 E
Nagīneh 65 34 20N 57 15 E
Nago 77 26 36N 128 0 E
Nagold 25 34 14N 57 2 E
Nagold → 25 48 52N 8 42 E
Nagoorin 98 24 17S 151 15 E
Nagornyy 59 55 58N 124 57 E
Nagorsk 55 59 18N 50 48 E
Nagoya 74 35 10N 136 50 E
Nagpur 68 21 8N 79 10 E
Nagyatád 27 46 14N 17 22 E
Nagyecsed 27 47 53N 22 24 E
Nagykanizsa 27 46 28N 17 0 E
Nagykörös 27 47 5N 19 48 E
Nagyléta 27 47 23N 21 55 E
Naha 77 26 13N 127 42 E
Nahalal 62 32 41N 35 12 E
Nahanni Butte 108 61 2N 123 31W
Nahanni Nat. Park 108 61 15N 125 0W
Nahariyya 62 33 1N 35 5 E
Nahāvand 64 34 10N 48 22 E
Nahe → 25 49 58N 7 57 E
Nahf 62 32 56N 35 18 E
Nahîya, Wadi → 86 28 55N 31 0 E
Nahlin 108 58 55N 131 38W
Nahud 86 18 12N 41 40 E
Naicam 109 52 30N 104 30W
Nā'ifah 63 19 59N 50 46 E
Naila 25 50 19N 11 43 E
Nain 107 56 34N 61 40W
Nā'īn 65 32 54N 53 0 E
Naini Tal 69 29 30N 79 30 E
Naintré 18 46 46N 0 29 E
Naipu 46 44 12N 25 47 E
Naira 73 4 28S 130 0 E
Nairn 14 57 35N 3 54W
Nairobi 90 1 17S 36 48 E
Naivasha 90 0 40S 36 30 E

* *Renamed Brezhnev*

Naivasha L. 90 0 48S 36 20 E
Najac 20 44 14N 1 58 E
Najafābād 65 32 40N 51 15 E
Najd 64 26 30N 42 0 E
Nájera 32 42 26N 2 48W
Najerilla → 32 42 32N 2 48W
Najibabad 68 29 40N 78 20 E
Najin 76 42 12N 130 15 E
Nakalagba 90 2 50N 27 58 E
Nakamura 74 33 0N 133 0 E
Nakfa 87 16 40N 38 32 E
Nakhichevan A.S.S.R. □ 53 39 14N 45 30 E
Nakhl 86 29 55N 33 43 E
Nakhodka 59 42 53N 132 54 E
Nakhon Phanom 71 17 23N 104 43 E
Nakhon Ratchasima (Khorat) 71 14 59N 102 12 E
Nakhon Sawan 71 15 35N 100 10 E
Nakhon Si Thammarat 71 8 29N 100 0 E
Nakina, B.C., Can. 108 59 12N 132 52W
Nakina, Ont., Can. 106 50 10N 86 40W
Nakło nad Noteçią 28 53 9N 17 38 E
Nakodar 68 31 8N 75 31 E
Nakskov 49 54 50N 11 8 E
Näkten 48 62 48N 14 38 E
Naktong → 76 35 7N 128 57 E
Nakuru 90 0 15S 36 4 E
Nakuru □ 90 0 15S 35 5 E
Nakuru, L. 90 0 23S 36 5 E
Nakusp 108 50 20N 117 45W
Nal → 66 25 20N 65 30 E
Nalchik 57 43 30N 43 33 E
Nälden 48 63 21N 14 14 E
Näldsjön 48 63 25N 14 15 E
Nalerigu 85 10 35N 0 25W
Nalgonda 70 17 6N 79 15 E
Nalhati 69 24 17N 87 52 E
Nallamalai Hills 70 15 30N 78 50 E
Nalón → 30 43 32N 6 4W
Nālūt 83 31 54N 11 0 E
Nam Co 75 30 30N 90 45 E
Nam Dinh 71 20 25N 106 5 E
Nam-Phan 72 10 30N 106 0 E
Nam Phong 71 16 42N 102 52 E
Nam Tha 71 20 58N 101 30 E
Nama unde 92 17 18S 15 50 E
Namak, Daryácheh-ye 65 34 30N 52 0 E
Namak, Kavir-e 65 34 30N 57 30 E
Namakkal 70 11 13N 78 13 E
Namaland 92 24 30S 17 0 E
Namangan 58 41 0N 71 40 E
Namapa 91 13 43S 39 50 E
Namaqualand 92 30 0S 18 0 E
Namasagali 90 1 2N 33 0 E
Namatanai 98 3 40S 152 29 E
Namber 73 1 2S 134 49 E
Nambour 97 26 32S 152 58 E
Nambucca Heads 99 30 37S 153 0 E
Namche Bazar 69 27 51N 86 47 E
Namecunda 91 14 54S 37 37 E
Nameh 72 2 34N 116 21 E
Nameponda 91 15 50S 39 50 E
Náměšt' nad Oslavou 27 49 12N 16 10 E
Námestovo 27 49 24N 19 25 E
Nametil 91 15 40S 39 21 E
Namew L. 109 54 14N 101 56W
Namib Desert = Namib Woestyn 92 22 30S 15 0 E
Namib-Woestyn 92 22 30S 15 0 E
Namibia ■ 92 22 0S 18 9 E
Namlea 73 3 18S 127 5 E
Namoi → 99 30 12S 149 30 E
Namous, O. en → 82 31 0N 0 15W
Nampa 118 43 34N 116 34W
Nampula 91 15 6N 39 15 E
Namrole 73 3 46S 126 46 E
Namse Shankou 67 30 0N 82 25 E
Namsen → 50 64 27N 11 42 E
Namsos 50 64 29N 11 30 E
Namtay 59 62 43N 129 37 E
Namtu 67 23 5N 97 28 E
Namtumbo 91 10 30S 36 4 E
Namu 108 51 52N 127 50W
Namucha Shank'ou 69 30 0N 82 28 E
Namur 16 50 27N 4 52 E
Namur □ 16 50 17N 5 0 E
Namutoni 92 18 49S 16 55 E
Namwala 91 15 44S 26 30 E
Namysłów 28 51 6N 17 42 E
Nan 71 18 52N 100 42 E
Nana 46 44 17N 26 34 E
Nanaimo 108 49 10N 124 0W
Nanam 76 41 44N 129 40 E
Nanan 77 24 59N 118 21 E
Nanango 97 26 40S 152 0 E
Nan'ao 77 23 28N 117 5 E
Nanao 74 37 0N 137 0 E
Nanbu 77 31 18N 106 3 E
Nanchang 75 28 42N 115 55 E
Nancheng 77 27 33N 116 35 E
Nanching = Nanjing 75 32 2N 118 47 E
Nanchong 75 30 43N 106 2 E
Nanchuan 77 29 9N 107 6 E
Nancy 19 48 42N 6 12 E
Nanda Devi 69 30 23N 79 59 E
Nandan 77 24 58N 107 29 E
Nander 70 19 10N 77 20 E
Nandewar Ra. 99 30 15S 150 35 E
Nandi 101 17 42S 177 20 E
Nandi □ 90 0 15N 35 0 E
Nandikotkur 70 15 52N 78 18 E
Nandura 68 20 52N 76 25 E
Nandurbar 68 21 20N 74 15 E
Nandyal 70 15 30N 78 30 E
Nanga-Eboko 88 4 41N 12 22 E
Nanga Parbat 69 35 10N 74 35 E
Nangade 91 11 5S 39 36 E
Nangapinoh 72 0 20S 11 44 E
Nangarhár □ 65 34 20N 70 0 E
Nangatayap 72 1 32S 110 34 E
Nangeya Mts. 90 3 30N 33 30 E
Nangis 19 48 33N 3 0 E
Nanjangud 70 12 6N 76 43 E
Nanjeko 91 15 31S 23 30 E

Nanjiang Nevis

Nanjiang **77** 32 28N 106 51 E
Nanjing **75** 32 2N 118 47 E
Nanjirinji **91** 9 41 S 39 5 E
Nankana Sahib **68** 31 27N 73 38 E
Nankang **77** 25 40N 114 45 E
Nanking = Nanjing **75** 32 2N 118 47 E
Nannine **96** 26 51 S 118 18 E
Nanning **75** 22 48N 108 20 E
Nanpara **69** 27 52N 81 33 E
Nanpi **76** 38 2N 116 45 E
Nanping **75** 26 38N 118 10 E
Nanripe **91** 13 52 S 38 52 E
Nansei-Shotō **74** 26 0N 128 0 E
Nansen Sd. **4** 81 0N 91 0W
Nansio **90** 2 3 S 33 4 E
Nant **20** 44 1N 3 18 E
Nantes **18** 47 12N 1 33W
Nanteuil-le-Haudouin **19** 49 9N 2 48 E
Nantiat **20** 46 1N 1 11 E
Nanticoke **114** 41 12N 76 1W
Nanton **108** 50 21N 113 46W
Nantong **77** 32 1N 120 52 E
Nantua **21** 46 10N 5 35 E
Nantucket I. **102** 41 16N 70 3W
Nanuque **127** 17 50 S 40 21W
Nanxiong **77** 25 6N 114 15 E
Nanyang **75** 33 11N 112 30 E
Nanyuan **76** 39 44N 116 22 E
Nanyuki **90** 0 2N 37 4 E
Nanzhang **77** 31 45N 111 50 E
Náo, C. de la **33** 38 44N 0 14 E
Naococane L. **107** 52 50N 70 45W
Naoetsu **74** 37 12N 138 10 E
Naogaon **69** 24 52N 88 52 E
Naoli He ⤳ **76** 47 18N 134 9 E
Náousa **44** 40 42N 22 9 E
Napa **118** 38 18N 122 17W
Napanee **106** 44 15N 77 0W
Napanoch **113** 41 44N 74 22W
Napier **101** 39 30 S 176 56 E
Naples **115** 26 10N 81 45W
Naples = Nápoli **41** 40 50N 14 17 E
Napo ⤳ **126** 3 20 S 72 40W
Napoleon, N. Dak., U.S.A. **116** 46 32N 99 49W
Napoleon, Ohio, U.S.A. **114** 41 24N 84 7W
Nápoli **41** 40 50N 14 17 E
Nápoli, G. di **41** 40 40N 14 10 E
Napopo **90** 4 15N 28 0 E
Nappa Merrie **99** 27 36 S 141 7 E
Naqâda **86** 25 53N 32 42 E
Nara, Japan **74** 34 40N 135 49 E
Nara, Mali **84** 15 10N 7 20W
Nara □ **74** 34 30N 136 0 E
Nara, Canal **68** 24 30N 69 20 E
Nara Visa **117** 35 39N 103 10W
Naracoorte **97** 36 58 S 140 45 E
Naradhan **99** 33 34 S 146 17 E
Narasapur **70** 16 26N 81 40 E
Narasaropet **70** 16 14N 80 4 E
Narathiwat **71** 6 30N 101 48 E
Narayanganj **69** 23 40N 90 33 E
Narayanpet **70** 16 45N 77 30 E
Narbonne **20** 43 11N 3 0 E
Narcea ⤳ **30** 43 33N 6 44W
Nardò **41** 40 10N 18 0 E
Narew **28** 52 55N 23 31 E
Narew ⤳ **28** 52 26N 20 41 E
Nari ⤳ **68** 29 40N 68 0 E
Narindra, Helodranon' i **93** 14 55 S 47 30 E
Narmada ⤳ **68** 21 38N 72 36 E
Narnaul **68** 28 5N 76 11 E
Narni **39** 42 30N 12 30 E
Naro, Ghana **84** 10 22N 2 27W
Naro, Italy **40** 37 18N 13 48 E
Naro Fominsk **55** 55 23N 36 43 E
Narodnaya, G. **52** 65 5N 60 0 E
Narok **90** 1 55 S 33 52 E
Narok □ **90** 1 20 S 36 30 E
Narón **30** 43 32N 8 9W
Narooma **99** 36 14 S 150 4 E
Narowal **68** 32 6N 74 52 E
Narrabri **97** 30 19 S 149 46 E
Narran ⤳ **99** 28 37 S 148 12 E
Narrandera **97** 34 42 S 146 31 E
Narraway ⤳ **108** 55 44N 119 55W
Narrogin **96** 32 58 S 117 14 E
Narromine **97** 32 12 S 148 12 E
Narsampet **70** 17 57N 79 58 E
Narsimhapur **68** 22 54N 79 14 E
Nartkala **57** 43 33N 43 51 E
Narva **54** 59 23N 28 12 E
Narva ⤳ **54** 59 27N 28 2 E
Narvik **50** 68 28N 17 26 E
Narvskoye Vdkhr. **54** 59 18N 28 14 E
Narwana **68** 29 39N 76 6 E
Naryan-Mar **52** 68 0N 53 0 E
Naryilco **99** 28 37 S 141 53 E
Narym **58** 59 0N 81 30 E
Narymskoye **58** 49 10N 84 15 E
Naryn **58** 41 26N 75 58 E
Nasa **50** 66 29N 15 23 E
Nasarawa **85** 8 32N 7 41 E
Năsăud **46** 47 19N 24 29 E
Naseby **101** 45 1 S 170 10 E
Naser, Buheirat en **86** 23 0N 32 30 E
Nashua, Iowa, U.S.A. **116** 42 55N 92 34W
Nashua, Mont., U.S.A. **118** 48 10N 106 25W
Nashua, N.H., U.S.A. **114** 42 50N 71 25W
Nashville, Ark., U.S.A. **117** 33 56N 93 50W
Nashville, Ga., U.S.A. **115** 31 3N 83 15W
Nashville, Tenn., U.S.A. **115** 36 12N 86 46W
Našice **42** 45 32N 18 4 E
Nasielsk **28** 52 35N 20 50 E
Nasik **70** 19 58N 73 50 E
Nasirabad **68** 26 15N 74 45 E
Naskaupi ⤳ **107** 53 47N 60 51W
Naso **41** 38 8N 14 46 E
Nass ⤳ **108** 55 0N 129 40W
Nassau, Bahamas **121** 25 0N 77 20W
Nassau, U.S.A. **113** 42 30N 73 34W
Nassau, Bahía **128** 55 20 S 68 0W
Nasser City = Kôm Ombo **86** 24 25N 32 52 E
Nasser, L. = Naser, Buheiret en **86** 23 0N 32 30 E
Nassian **84** 8 28N 3 28W
Nässjö **49** 57 39N 14 42 E
Nastopoka Is. **106** 57 0N 77 0W
Näsum **49** 56 10N 14 29 E
Näsviken **48** 61 46N 16 52 E
Nat Kyizin **71** 14 57N 97 59 E
Nata **92** 20 12 S 26 12 E
Natagaima **126** 3 37N 75 6W
Natal, Brazil **127** 5 47 S 35 13W
Natal, Can. **108** 49 43N 114 51W
Natal, Indon. **72** 0 35N 99 7 E
Natal □ **93** 28 30 S 30 30 E
Natalinci **42** 44 15N 20 49 E
Naţanz **65** 33 30N 51 55 E
Natashquan **107** 50 14N 61 46W
Natashquan ⤳ **107** 50 7N 61 50W
Natchez **117** 31 35N 91 25W
Natchitoches **117** 31 47N 93 4W
Nathalia **99** 36 1 S 145 13 E
Nathdwara **68** 24 55N 73 50 E
Natick **113** 42 16N 71 19W
Natih **65** 22 25N 56 30 E
Natimuk **99** 36 42 S 142 0 E
Nation ⤳ **108** 55 30N 123 32W
National City **119** 32 39N 117 7W
Natitingou **85** 10 20N 1 26 E
Natividad, I. **120** 27 50N 115 10W
Natoma **116** 39 14N 99 0W
Natron, L. **90** 2 20 S 36 0 E
Natrona **112** 40 39N 79 43W
Natrûn, W. el. ⤳ **86** 30 25N 30 13 E
Natuna Besar, Kepulauan **72** 4 0N 108 15 E
Natuna Selatan, Kepulauan **72** 2 45N 109 0 E
Natural Bridge **113** 44 5N 75 30W
Naturaliste, C. **96** 33 32 S 115 0 E
Naturaliste C. **99** 40 50 S 148 15 E
Naturaliste Channel **96** 25 20 S 113 0 E
Naubinway **106** 46 7N 85 27W
Naucelle **20** 44 13N 2 20 E
Nauders **26** 46 54N 10 30 E
Nauen **24** 52 36N 12 52 E
Naugatuck **113** 41 28N 73 4W
Naujoji Vilnia **54** 54 48N 25 27 E
Naumburg **24** 51 10N 11 48 E
Nauru **94** 1 0 S 166 0 E
Nauru Is. **94** 0 32 S 166 55 E
Nauta **126** 4 31 S 73 35W
Nautla **120** 20 20N 96 50W
Nava del Rey **30** 41 22N 5 6W
Navacerrada, Puerto de **30** 40 47N 4 0W
Navahermosa **31** 39 41N 4 28W
Navajo Res. **119** 36 55N 107 30W
Navalcarnero **30** 40 17N 4 5W
Navalmoral de la Mata **30** 39 52N 5 33W
Navalvillar de Pela **31** 39 9N 5 24W
Navan = An Uaimh **15** 53 39N 6 40W
Navare **20** 43 20N 1 20W
Navarino, I. **128** 55 0 S 67 40W
Navarra □ **32** 42 40N 1 40W
Navarre, France **20** 43 15N 1 20W
Navarre, U.S.A. **112** 40 43N 81 31W
Navarrenx **20** 43 20N 0 45W
Navas del Marqués, Las **30** 40 36N 4 20W
Navasota **117** 30 20N 96 5W
Navassa **121** 18 30N 75 0W
Nave **38** 45 35N 10 17 E
Naver ⤳ **14** 58 34N 4 15W
Navia **30** 43 35N 6 42W
Navia ⤳ **30** 43 15N 6 50W
Navia de Suarna **30** 42 58N 6 59W
Navidad **124** 33 57 S 71 50W
Navlya **54** 52 53N 34 30 E
Navoi **58** 40 9N 65 22 E
Navojoa **120** 27 0N 109 30W
Navolok **52** 62 33N 39 57 E
Návpaktos **45** 38 23N 21 50 E
Návplion **45** 37 33N 22 50 E
Navrongo **85** 10 51N 1 3W
Navsari **68** 20 57N 72 59 E
Nawa Kot **68** 28 21N 71 24 E
Nawabganj, Bangla. **69** 24 35N 88 14 E
Nawabganj, India **69** 26 56N 81 14 E
Nawabganj, Bareilly **69** 28 32N 79 40 E
Nawabshah **68** 26 15N 68 25 E
Nawada **69** 24 50N 85 33 E
Nawakot **69** 27 55N 85 10 E
Nawalgarh **68** 27 50N 75 15 E
Nawapara **69** 20 46N 82 33 E
Nawāsīf, Harrat **64** 21 20N 42 10 E
Nawi **86** 18 32N 30 50 E
Náxos **45** 37 8N 25 25 E
Nay **20** 43 10N 0 18W
Nāy Band **65** 27 20N 52 40 E
Nayakhan **59** 61 56N 159 0 E
Nayarit □ **120** 22 0N 105 0W
Nayé **84** 14 28N 12 12W
Nazaré **31** 39 36N 9 4W
Nazas **120** 25 10N 104 6W
Nazas ⤳ **120** 25 35N 103 25W
Naze, The **13** 51 53N 1 19 E
Nazerat **62** 32 42N 35 17 E
Nazir Hat **67** 22 35N 91 49 E
Nazko **108** 53 1N 123 37W
Nazko ⤳ **108** 53 7N 123 34W
Nazret **87** 8 32N 39 22 E
Nchanga **91** 12 30 S 27 49 E
Ncheu **91** 14 50 S 34 47 E
Ndala **90** 4 45 S 33 15 E
Ndalatando **88** 9 12 S 14 48 E
Ndali **85** 9 50N 2 46 E
Ndareda **90** 4 12 S 35 30 E
Ndélé **81** 8 25N 20 36 E
Ndendé **88** 2 22 S 11 23 E
Ndjamena **81** 12 10N 14 59 E
Ndjolé **88** 0 10 S 10 45 E
Ndola **91** 13 0 S 28 34 E
Ndoto Mts. **90** 2 0N 37 0 E
Nduguti **90** 4 18 S 34 41 E
Nea ⤳ **47** 63 15N 11 0 E
Néa Epídhavros **45** 37 40N 23 7 E
Néa Flippiás **44** 39 12N 20 53 E
Néa Kallikrátia **44** 40 21N 23 1 E
Néa Víssi **44** 41 34N 26 33 E
Neagh, Lough **15** 54 35N 6 25W
Neah Bay **118** 48 25N 124 40W
Neamţ □ **46** 47 0N 26 20 E
Neápolis, Kozan, Greece **44** 40 20N 21 24 E
Neápolis, Lakonia, Greece **45** 36 27N 23 8 E
Near Is. **104** 53 0N 172 0 E
Neath **13** 51 39N 3 49W
Nebbou **85** 11 9N 1 51W
Nebine Cr. ⤳ **99** 29 27 S 146 56 E
Nebit Dag **58** 39 30N 54 22 E
Nebolchy, U.S.S.R. **54** 59 12N 32 58 E
Nebolchy, U.S.S.R. **54** 59 8N 33 18 E
Nebraska □ **116** 41 30N 100 0W
Nebraska City **116** 40 40N 95 52W
Nébrodi, Monti **40** 37 55N 14 50 E
Necedah **116** 44 2N 90 7W
Nechako ⤳ **108** 53 30N 122 44W
Neches ⤳ **117** 29 55N 93 52W
Neckar ⤳ **25** 49 31N 8 26 E
Necochea **124** 38 30 S 58 50W
Nedelišće **39** 46 23N 16 22 E
Nédha ⤳ **45** 37 25N 21 45 E
Nedroma **82** 35 1N 1 45W
Nedstrand **47** 59 21N 5 49 E
Needles **119** 34 50N 114 35W
Needles, The **13** 50 39N 1 35W
Ñeembucú □ **124** 27 0 S 58 0W
Neemuch (Nimach) **68** 24 30N 74 56 E
Neenah **114** 44 10N 88 30W
Neepawa **109** 50 15N 99 30W
Nefta **83** 33 53N 7 50 E
Neftah Sidi Boubekeur **82** 35 1N 0 4 E
Neftegorsk **57** 44 25N 39 45 E
Neftyannyye Kamni **53** 40 20N 50 55 E
Negapatam = Nagappattinam **70** 10 46N 79 50 E
Negaunee **114** 46 30N 87 36W
Negba **62** 31 40N 34 41 E
Negele **87** 5 20N 39 36 E
Negeri Sembilan □ **71** 2 50N 102 10 E
Negev = Hanegev **62** 30 50N 35 0 E
Negoiu **46** 45 35N 24 32 E
Negombo **70** 7 12N 79 50 E
Negotin **42** 44 16N 22 37 E
Negotino **42** 41 29N 22 9 E
Negra, La **124** 23 46 S 70 18W
Negra, Peña **30** 42 11N 6 30W
Negra Pt. **73** 18 40N 120 50 E
Negreira **30** 42 54N 8 45W
Negreşti **46** 46 50N 27 30 E
Négrine **83** 34 30N 7 30 E
Negro ⤳, Argent. **128** 41 2 S 62 47W
Negro ⤳, Brazil **126** 3 0 S 60 0W
Negro ⤳, Uruguay **125** 33 24 S 58 22W
Negros **73** 10 0N 123 0 E
Negru Vodă **46** 43 47N 28 21 E
Nehbandān **65** 31 35N 60 5 E
Neheim-Hüsten **24** 51 27N 7 58 E
Nehoiaşu **46** 45 24N 26 20 E
Nei Monggol Zizhiqu □ **76** 42 0N 112 0 E
Neidpath **109** 50 12N 107 20W
Neihart **118** 47 0N 110 44W
Neijiang **75** 29 35N 104 55 E
Neilton **118** 17 24N 123 52W
Neira de Jusá **30** 42 53N 7 14W
Neisse ⤳ **24** 52 4N 14 46 E
Neiva **126** 2 56N 75 18W
Neixiang **77** 33 10N 111 52 E
Nejanilini L. **109** 59 33N 97 48W
Nejo **87** 9 30N 35 28 E
Nekemte **87** 9 4N 36 30 E
Nêkheb **86** 25 10N 32 48 E
Neksø **49** 55 4N 15 8 E
Nelas **30** 40 32N 7 52W
Nelaug **47** 58 39N 8 40 E
Nelia **98** 20 39 S 142 12 E
Nelidovo **54** 56 13N 32 49 E
Neligh **116** 42 11N 98 2W
Nelkan **59** 57 40N 136 4 E
Nellikuppam **70** 11 46N 79 43 E
Nellore **70** 14 27N 79 59 E
Nelma **59** 47 39N 139 0 E
Nelson, Austral. **100** 38 3 S 141 2 E
Nelson, Can. **108** 49 30N 117 20W
Nelson, N.Z. **101** 41 18 S 173 16 E
Nelson, U.K. **12** 53 50N 2 14W
Nelson, Ariz., U.S.A. **119** 35 35N 113 16W
Nelson, Nev., U.S.A. **119** 35 46N 114 48W
Nelson □ **101** 42 11 S 172 15 E
Nelson ⤳ **109** 54 33N 98 2W
Nelson, C., Austral. **99** 38 26 S 141 32 E
Nelson, C., P.N.G. **98** 9 0 S 149 20 E
Nelson, Estrecho **128** 51 30 S 75 0W
Nelson Forks **108** 59 30N 124 0W
Nelson House **109** 55 47N 98 51W
Nelson L. **109** 55 48N 100 7W
Nelspruit **93** 25 29 S 30 59 E
Néma **84** 16 40N 7 15W
Neman (Nemunas) ⤳ **54** 55 25N 21 10 E
Neméa **45** 37 49N 22 40 E
Nemeiben L. **109** 55 20N 105 20W
Nemira **46** 46 17N 26 19 E
Nemours **19** 48 16N 2 40 E
Nemunas = Neman ⤳ **54** 55 25N 21 10 E
Nemuro **74** 43 20N 145 35 E
Nemuro-Kaikyō **74** 43 30N 145 30 E
Nemuy **59** 55 40N 136 9 E
Nen Jiang ⤳ **76** 45 28N 124 30 E
Nenagh **15** 52 52N 8 11W
Nenana **104** 64 30N 149 20W
Nene ⤳ **12** 52 38N 0 13 E
Nenjiang **75** 49 10N 125 10 E
Neno **91** 15 25 S 34 40 E
Nenusa, Kepulauan **73** 4 45N 127 1 E
Neodesha **117** 37 30N 95 37W
Néon Petrítsi **44** 41 16N 23 15 E
Neosho **117** 36 56N 94 28W
Neosho ⤳ **117** 35 59N 95 10W
Nepal ■ **69** 28 0N 84 30 E
Nepalganj **69** 28 5N 81 40 E
Nephi **118** 39 43N 111 52W
Nephin **15** 54 1N 9 21W
Nepomuk **26** 49 29N 13 35 E
Neptune City **113** 40 13N 74 4W
Néra ⤳ **42** 44 48N 21 25 E
Nérac **20** 44 8N 0 21 E
Nerchinsk **59** 52 0N 116 39 E
Nerchinskiy Zavod **59** 51 20N 119 40 E
Nereju **46** 45 43N 26 43 E
Nerekhta **55** 57 26N 40 38 E
Néret L. **107** 54 45N 70 44W
Neretva ⤳ **42** 43 1N 17 27 E
Neretvanski Kanal **42** 43 7N 17 10 E
Neringa **54** 55 30N 21 5 E
Nerja **31** 36 43N 3 55W
Nerl ⤳ **55** 56 11N 40 34 E
Nerokoúrou **45** 35 29N 24 3 E
Nerpio **33** 38 11N 2 16W
Nerva **31** 37 42N 6 30W
Nes **50** 65 53N 17 24W
Nes Ziyyona **62** 31 56N 34 48W
Nesbyen **47** 60 34N 9 35 E
Nesebŭr **43** 42 41N 27 46 E
Nesflaten **47** 59 38N 6 48 E
Neskaupstaður **50** 65 9N 13 42W
Nesland **47** 59 31N 7 59 E
Neslandsvatn **47** 58 57N 9 10 E
Nesle **19** 49 45N 2 53 E
Nesodden **47** 59 48N 10 40 E
Nesque ⤳ **21** 43 59N 4 59 E
Ness, Loch **14** 57 15N 4 30W
Nestórion Óros **44** 40 24N 21 5 E
Néstos ⤳ **44** 41 20N 24 35 E
Nesttun **47** 60 19N 5 21 E
Nesvizh **54** 53 14N 26 38 E
Netanya **62** 32 20N 34 51 E
Nète ⤳ **16** 51 7N 4 14 E
Nether Stowey **13** 51 0N 3 10W
Netherbury **13** 50 46N 2 45W
Netherdale **97** 21 10 S 148 33 E
Netherlands ■ **16** 52 0N 5 30 E
Netherlands Antilles □ **121** 12 30N 68 0W
Netherlands Guiana = Surinam ■ **127** 4 0N 56 0W
Neto ⤳ **41** 39 13N 17 8 E
Netrakona **69** 24 53N 90 47 E
Nettancourt **19** 48 51N 4 57 E
Nettilling L. **105** 66 30N 71 0W
Nettuno **40** 41 29N 12 40 E
Netzahualcoyotl, Presa **120** 17 10N 93 30W
Neu-Isenburg **25** 50 3N 8 42 E
Neu-Ulm **25** 48 23N 10 2 E
Neubrandenburg **24** 53 33N 13 17 E
Neubrandenburg □ **24** 53 30N 13 20 E
Neubukow **24** 54 1N 11 40 E
Neuburg **25** 48 43N 11 11 E
Neuchâtel **25** 47 0N 6 55 E
Neuchâtel □ **25** 47 0N 6 55 E
Neuchâtel, Lac de **25** 46 53N 6 50 E
Neudau **26** 47 11N 16 6 E
Neuenhaus **24** 52 30N 6 55 E
Neuf-Brisach **19** 48 0N 7 30 E
Neufahrn **25** 48 44N 12 11 E
Neufchâteau, Belg. **16** 49 50N 5 25 E
Neufchâteau, France **19** 48 21N 5 40 E
Neufchâtel **19** 49 43N 1 30 E
Neufchâtel-sur-Aisne **19** 49 26N 4 0 E
Neuhaus **24** 53 16N 10 54 E
Neuillé-Pont-Pierre **18** 47 33N 0 33 E
Neuilly-St-Front **19** 49 10N 3 15 E
Neukalen **24** 53 49N 12 48 E
Neumarkt **25** 49 16N 11 28 E
Neumarkt-Sankt Veit **25** 48 22N 12 30 E
Neumünster **24** 54 4N 9 58 E
Neung-sur-Beuvron **19** 47 30N 1 50 E
Neunkirchen, Austria **26** 47 43N 16 4 E
Neunkirchen, Ger. **25** 49 23N 7 12 E
Neuquén **128** 38 55 S 68 0 E
Neuquén □ **124** 38 0 S 69 50W
Neuruppin **24** 52 56N 12 48 E
Neuse ⤳ **115** 35 5N 76 30W
Neusiedl **27** 47 57N 16 50 E
Neusiedler See **27** 47 50N 16 47 E
Neuss **24** 51 12N 6 39 E
Neussargues-Moissac **20** 45 9N 3 1 E
Neustadt, Baden-W., Ger. **25** 47 54N 8 13 E
Neustadt, Bayern, Ger. **25** 50 23N 11 0 E
Neustadt, Bayern, Ger. **25** 49 42N 12 10 E
Neustadt, Bayern, Ger. **25** 48 48N 11 47 E
Neustadt, Bayern, Ger. **25** 49 34N 10 37 E
Neustadt, Gera, Ger. **24** 50 45N 11 43 E
Neustadt, Hessen, Ger. **24** 50 51N 9 9 E
Neustadt, Niedersachsen, Ger. **24** 52 30N 9 30 E
Neustadt, Potsdam, Ger. **24** 52 50N 12 27 E
Neustadt, Rhld-Pfz., Ger. **25** 49 21N 8 10 E
Neustadt, Schleswig-Holstein, Ger. **24** 54 6N 10 49 E
Neustrelitz **24** 53 22N 13 4 E
Neuvic **20** 45 23N 2 16 E
Neuville, Rhône, France **21** 45 52N 4 51 E
Neuville, Vienne, France **18** 46 41N 0 15 E
Neuville-aux-Bois **19** 48 4N 2 3 E
Neuvy-le-Roi **18** 47 36N 0 36 E
Neuvy-St-Sépulchure **20** 46 35N 1 48 E
Neuvy-sur-Barangeon **19** 47 20N 2 15 E
Neuwerk **24** 53 55N 8 30 E
Neuwied **24** 50 26N 7 29 E
Neva ⤳ **52** 59 50N 30 30 E
Nevada **117** 37 51N 94 22W
Nevada □ **118** 39 20N 117 0W
Nevada City **118** 39 20N 121 0W
Nevada de Sta. Marta, Sa. **126** 10 55N 73 50W
Nevada, Sierra, Spain **33** 37 3N 3 15W
Nevada, Sierra, U.S.A. **118** 39 0N 120 30W
Nevado, Cerro **124** 35 30 S 68 32W
Nevanka **59** 56 31N 98 55 E
Nevasa **70** 19 34N 75 0 E
Nevel **54** 56 0N 29 55 E
Nevers **19** 47 0N 3 9 E
Nevertire **99** 31 50 S 147 44 E
Nevesinje **42** 43 14N 18 6 E
Neville **109** 49 58N 107 39W
Nevinnomyssk **57** 44 40N 42 0 E
Nevis **121** 17 0N 62 30W

Nevlunghavn	**47**	55 58N	9 52 E
Nevrokop = Gotse Delchev	**43**	41 33N	23 46 E
Nevşehir	**64**	38 33N	34 40 E
Nevyansk	**52**	57 30N	60 13 E
New Albany, Ind., U.S.A.	**114**	38 20N	85 50W
New Albany, Miss., U.S.A.	**117**	34 30N	89 0W
New Albany, Pa., U.S.A.	**113**	41 35N	76 28W
New Amsterdam	**126**	6 15N	57 36W
New Bedford	**114**	41 40N	70 52W
New Bern	**115**	35 8N	77 3W
New Bethlehem	**112**	41 0N	79 22W
New Bloomfield	**112**	40 24N	77 12W
New Boston	**117**	33 27N	94 21W
New Braunfels	**117**	29 43N	98 9W
New Brighton, N.Z.	**101**	43 29 S	172 43 E
New Brighton, U.S.A.	**112**	40 42N	80 19W
New Britain, P.N.G.	**94**	5 50 S	150 20 E
New Britain, U.S.A.	**114**	41 41N	72 47W
New Brunswick	**114**	40 30N	74 28W
New Brunswick □	**107**	46 50N	66 30W
New Bussa	**85**	9 53N	4 31 E
New Byrd	**5**	80 0 S	120 0W
New Caledonia = Nouvelle-Calédonie	**94**	21 0 S	165 0 E
New Castile = Castilla La Neuva	**31**	39 45N	3 20W
New Castle, Ind., U.S.A.	**114**	39 55N	85 23W
New Castle, Pa., U.S.A.	**114**	41 0N	80 20W
New City	**113**	41 8N	74 0W
New Cristóbal	**120**	9 22N	79 40W
New Cumberland	**112**	40 30N	80 36W
New Delhi	**68**	28 37N	77 13 E
New Denver	**108**	50 0N	117 25W
New England	**116**	46 36N	102 47W
New England Ra.	**97**	30 20 S	151 45 E
New Forest	**13**	50 53N	1 40W
New Glasgow	**107**	45 35N	62 36W
New Guinea	**94**	4 0 S	136 0 E
New Hamburg	**112**	43 23N	80 42W
New Hampshire □	**114**	43 40N	71 40W
New Hampton	**116**	43 2N	92 20W
New Hanover, P.N.G.	**98**	2 30 S	150 10 E
New Hanover, S. Afr.	**93**	29 22 S	30 31 E
New Haven, Conn., U.S.A.	**114**	41 20N	72 54W
New Haven, Mich., U.S.A.	**112**	42 44N	82 46W
New Hazelton	**108**	55 20N	127 30W
* New Hebrides	**94**	15 0 S	168 0 E
New Iberia	**117**	30 2N	91 54W
New Ireland	**94**	3 20 S	151 50 E
New Jersey □	**114**	40 30N	74 10W
New Kensington	**114**	40 36N	79 43W
New Lexington	**114**	39 40N	82 15W
New Liskeard	**106**	47 31N	79 41W
New London, Conn., U.S.A.	**114**	41 23N	72 8W
New London, Minn., U.S.A.	**116**	45 17N	94 55W
New London, Ohio, U.S.A.	**112**	41 4N	82 25W
New London, Wis., U.S.A.	**116**	44 23N	88 43W
New Madrid	**117**	36 40N	89 30W
New Meadows	**118**	45 0N	116 32W
New Mexico □	**110**	34 30N	106 0W
New Milford, Conn., U.S.A.	**113**	41 35N	73 25W
New Milford, Pa., U.S.A.	**113**	41 50N	75 45W
New Norfolk	**97**	42 46 S	147 2 E
New Orleans	**117**	30 0N	90 5W
New Philadelphia	**114**	40 29N	81 25W
New Plymouth, N.Z.	**101**	39 4 S	174 5 E
New Plymouth, U.S.A.	**118**	43 58N	116 49W
New Providence	**121**	25 25N	78 35W
New Radnor	**13**	52 15N	3 10W
New Richmond	**116**	45 6N	92 34W
New Roads	**117**	30 43N	91 30W
New Rochelle	**113**	40 55N	73 46W
New Rockford	**116**	47 44N	99 7W
New Ross	**15**	52 24N	6 58W
New Salem	**116**	46 51N	101 25W
New Siberian Is. = Novosibirskiye Os.	**59**	75 0N	142 0 E
New Smyrna Beach	**115**	29 0N	80 50W
New South Wales □	**97**	33 0 S	146 0 E
New Town	**116**	47 59N	102 30W
New Ulm	**116**	44 15N	94 30W
New Waterford	**107**	46 13N	60 4W
New Westminster	**108**	49 13N	122 55W
New York □	**114**	42 40N	76 0W
New York City	**114**	40 45N	74 0W
New Zealand ■	**94**	40 0 S	176 0 E
Newala	**91**	10 58 S	39 18 E
Newala □	**91**	10 46 S	39 20 E
Newark, Del., U.S.A.	**114**	39 42N	75 45W
Newark, N.J., U.S.A.	**114**	40 41N	74 12W
Newark, N.Y., U.S.A.	**114**	43 2N	77 10W
Newark, Ohio, U.S.A.	**114**	40 5N	82 24W
Newark-on-Trent	**12**	53 6N	0 48W
Newaygo	**114**	43 25N	85 48W
Newberg	**118**	45 22N	123 0W
Newberry, Mich., U.S.A.	**114**	46 20N	85 32W
Newberry, S.C., U.S.A.	**115**	34 17N	81 37W
Newbrook	**108**	54 24N	112 57W
Newburgh	**114**	41 30N	74 1W
Newbury, U.K.	**13**	51 24N	1 19W
Newbury, U.S.A.	**113**	44 7N	72 6W
Newburyport	**114**	42 48N	70 50W
Newcastle, Austral.	**97**	33 0 S	151 46 E
Newcastle, Can.	**107**	47 1N	65 38W
Newcastle, S. Afr.	**93**	27 45 S	29 58 E
Newcastle, U.K.	**15**	54 13N	5 54W
Newcastle, U.S.A.	**116**	43 50N	104 12W
Newcastle Emlyn	**13**	52 2N	4 29W
Newcastle Ra.	**97**	15 45 S	130 15 E
Newcastle-under-Lyme	**12**	53 2N	2 15W
Newcastle-upon-Tyne	**12**	54 59N	1 37W
Newcastle Waters	**96**	17 30 S	133 28 E
Newdegate	**96**	33 6 S	119 0 E
Newe Etan	**62**	32 30N	35 32 E
Newe Sha'anan	**62**	32 47N	34 59 E
Newe Zohar	**62**	31 9N	35 21 E
Newell	**116**	44 48N	103 25W
Newenham, C.	**104**	58 40N	162 15W
Newfoundland	**107**	48 30N	56 0W
Newfoundland □	**107**	53 0N	58 0W
Newhalem	**108**	48 41N	121 16W
Newham	**13**	51 31N	0 2 E
Newhaven	**13**	50 47N	0 4 E
Newkirk	**117**	36 52N	97 3W
Newman, Mt.	**96**	23 20 S	119 34 E
Newmarket, Can.	**112**	44 3N	79 28W
Newmarket, Ireland	**15**	52 13N	9 0W
Newmarket, U.K.	**13**	52 15N	0 23 E
Newmarket, U.S.A.	**113**	43 4N	70 57W
Newnan	**115**	33 22N	84 48W
Newnes	**99**	33 9 S	150 16 E
Newport, Gwent, U.K.	**13**	51 35N	3 0W
Newport, I. of W., U.K.	**13**	50 42N	1 18W
Newport, Salop, U.K.	**13**	52 47N	2 22W
Newport, Ark., U.S.A.	**117**	35 38N	91 15W
Newport, Ky., U.S.A.	**114**	39 5N	84 23W
Newport, N.H., U.S.A.	**114**	43 23N	72 8W
Newport, Oreg., U.S.A.	**118**	44 41N	124 2W
Newport, Pa., U.S.A.	**112**	40 28N	77 8W
Newport, R.I., U.S.A.	**114**	41 13N	71 19W
Newport, Tenn., U.S.A.	**115**	35 59N	83 12W
Newport, Vt., U.S.A.	**114**	44 57N	72 17W
Newport, Wash., U.S.A.	**118**	48 11N	117 2W
Newport Beach	**119**	33 40N	117 58W
Newport News	**114**	37 2N	76 30W
Newquay	**13**	50 24N	5 6W
Newry	**15**	54 10N	6 20W
Newry & Mourne □	**15**	54 10N	6 15W
Newton, Iowa, U.S.A.	**116**	41 40N	93 3W
Newton, Mass., U.S.A.	**114**	42 21N	71 10W
Newton, Miss., U.S.A.	**117**	32 19N	89 10W
Newton, N.C., U.S.A.	**115**	35 42N	81 10W
Newton, N.J., U.S.A.	**114**	41 3N	74 46W
Newton, Texas, U.S.A.	**117**	30 54N	93 42W
Newton Abbot	**13**	50 32N	3 37W
Newton Boyd	**99**	29 45 S	152 16 E
Newton Stewart	**14**	54 57N	4 30W
Newtonmore	**14**	57 4N	4 7W
Newtown	**13**	52 31N	3 19W
Newtownabbey	**15**	54 40N	5 55W
Newtownabbey □	**15**	54 45N	6 0W
Newtownards	**15**	54 37N	5 40W
Newville	**112**	40 10N	77 24W
Nexon	**20**	45 41N	1 11 E
Neya	**55**	58 21N	43 49 E
Neyrīz	**65**	29 15N	54 19 E
Neyshābūr	**65**	36 10N	58 50 E
Neyyattinkara	**70**	8 26N	77 5 E
Nezhin	**54**	51 5N	31 55 E
Nezperce	**118**	46 13N	116 15W
Ngabang	**72**	0 23N	109 55 E
Ngabordamlu, Tanjung	**73**	6 56 S	134 11 E
Ngambé	**85**	5 48N	11 29 E
Ngami Depression	**92**	20 30 S	22 46 E
Ngamo	**91**	19 3 S	27 32 E
Nganglong Kangri	**67**	33 0N	81 0 E
Nganjuk	**73**	7 32 S	111 55 E
Ngaoundéré	**88**	7 15N	13 35 E
Ngapara	**101**	44 57 S	170 46 E
Ngara	**90**	2 29 S	30 40 E
Ngara □	**90**	2 29 S	30 40 E
Ngau	**101**	18 2 S	179 18 E
Ngawi	**73**	7 24 S	111 26 E
Ngha Lo	**71**	21 33N	104 28 E
Ngiva	**92**	16 48 S	15 50 E
Ngoma	**91**	13 8 S	33 45 E
Ngomahura	**91**	20 26 S	30 43 E
Ngomba	**91**	8 20 S	32 53 E
Ngop	**87**	6 17N	30 9 E
Ngoring Hu	**75**	34 55N	97 5 E
Ngorkou	**84**	15 40N	3 41W
Ngorongoro	**90**	3 11 S	35 32 E
Ngozi	**90**	2 54 S	29 50 E
Ngudu	**90**	2 58 S	33 25 E
Nguigmi	**81**	14 20N	13 20 E
Ngunga	**90**	3 37 S	33 37 E
Ngunza	**88**	11 10 S	13 48 E
Nguru	**85**	12 56N	10 29 E
Nguru Mts.	**90**	6 0 S	37 30 E
Nha Trang	**71**	12 16N	109 10 E
Nhacoongo	**93**	24 18 S	35 14 E
Nhangutazi, L.	**93**	24 0 S	34 30 E
Nhill	**99**	36 18 S	141 40 E
Nia-nia	**90**	1 30N	27 40 E
Niafounké	**84**	16 0N	4 5W
Niagara	**114**	45 45N	88 0W
Niagara Falls, Can.	**106**	43 7N	79 5W
Niagara Falls, U.S.A.	**114**	43 5N	79 0W
Niagara-on-the-Lake	**112**	43 15N	79 4W
Niah	**72**	3 58N	113 46 E
Nialia, L.	**100**	33 20 S	141 42 E
Niamey	**85**	13 27N	2 6 E
Nianforando	**84**	9 37N	10 36W
Nianfors	**48**	61 36N	16 46 E
Niangara	**90**	3 42N	27 50 E
Nianzishan	**76**	47 31N	122 53 E
Nias	**72**	1 0N	97 30 E
Niassa □	**91**	13 30 S	36 0 E
Nibbiano	**38**	44 54N	9 20 E
Nibe	**49**	56 59N	9 38 E
Nibong Tebal	**71**	5 10N	100 29 E
Nicaragua ■	**121**	11 40N	85 30W
Nicaragua, Lago de	**121**	12 0N	85 30W
Nicastro	**41**	39 0N	16 18 E
Nice	**21**	43 42N	7 14 E
Niceville	**115**	30 30N	86 30W
Nichinan	**74**	31 38N	131 23 E
Nicholás, Canal	**121**	23 30N	80 5W
Nicholasville	**114**	37 54N	84 31W
Nichols	**113**	42 1N	76 22W
Nicholson	**113**	41 37N	75 47W
Nicobar Is.	**60**	9 0N	93 0 E
Nicola	**108**	50 12N	120 40W
Nicolet	**106**	46 17N	72 35W
Nicolls Town	**121**	25 8N	78 0W
Nicopolis	**45**	39 2N	20 37 E
Nicosia, Cyprus	**64**	35 10N	33 25 E
Nicosia, Italy	**41**	37 45N	14 22 E
Nicótera	**41**	38 33N	15 57 E
Nicoya, G. de	**121**	10 0N	85 0W
Nicoya, Pen. de	**121**	9 45N	85 40W
Nidd →	**12**	54 1N	1 32W
Nidda	**24**	50 24N	9 2 E
Nidda →	**25**	50 6N	8 34 E
Nidzica	**28**	53 25N	20 28 E
Niebüll	**24**	54 47N	8 49 E
Nied →	**19**	49 23N	6 40 E
Niederaula	**24**	50 48N	9 37 E
Niederbronn	**19**	48 57N	7 39 E
Niedere Tauern	**26**	47 20N	14 0 E
Niedermarsberg	**24**	51 28N	8 52 E
Niederösterreich □	**26**	48 25N	15 40 E
Niedersachsen □	**24**	52 45N	9 0 E
Niellé	**84**	10 5N	5 38W
Niemba	**90**	5 58 S	28 24 E
Niemcza	**28**	50 42N	16 47 E
Niemodlin	**28**	50 38N	17 38 E
Niemur	**100**	35 17 S	144 9 E
Nienburg	**24**	52 38N	9 15 E
Niepołomice	**27**	50 3N	20 13 E
Niers →	**24**	51 45N	5 58 E
Niesky	**24**	51 18N	14 48 E
Nieszawa	**28**	52 52N	18 50 E
Nieuw Amsterdam	**127**	5 53N	55 5W
Nieuw Nickerie	**127**	6 0N	56 59W
Nieuwpoort	**16**	51 8N	2 45 E
Nieves	**30**	42 7N	8 26W
Nièvre □	**19**	47 10N	3 40 E
Niğde	**64**	38 0N	34 40 E
Nigel	**93**	26 27 S	28 25 E
Niger ■	**85**	13 30N	10 0 E
Niger □	**85**	10 0N	5 0 E
Niger →	**85**	5 33N	6 33 E
Nigeria ■	**85**	8 30N	8 0 E
Nightcaps	**101**	45 57 S	168 2 E
Nigríta	**44**	40 56N	23 29 E
Nihtaur	**69**	29 20N	78 23 E
Nii-Jima	**74**	34 20N	139 15 E
Niigata	**74**	37 58N	139 0 E
Niigata □	**74**	37 15N	138 45 E
Niihama	**74**	33 55N	133 16 E
Niihau	**110**	21 55N	160 10W
Níjar	**33**	36 53N	2 15W
Nijkerk	**16**	52 13N	5 30 E
Nijmegen	**16**	51 50N	5 52 E
Nijverdal	**16**	52 22N	6 28 E
Nike	**85**	6 26N	7 29 E
Nikel	**50**	69 24N	30 12 E
Nikiniki	**73**	9 49 S	124 30 E
Nikítas	**44**	40 13N	23 34 E
Nikki	**85**	9 58N	3 12 E
Nikkō	**74**	36 45N	139 35 E
Nikolayev	**56**	46 58N	32 0 E
Nikolayevsk	**55**	50 0N	45 35 E
Nikolayevsk-na-Amur	**59**	53 8N	140 44 E
Nikolsk	**55**	59 30N	45 28 E
Nikolskoye	**59**	55 12N	166 0 E
Nikopol, Bulg.	**43**	43 43N	24 54 E
Nikopol, U.S.S.R.	**56**	47 35N	34 25 E
Niksar	**56**	40 31N	37 2 E
Nīkshahr	**65**	26 15N	60 10 E
Nikšić	**42**	42 50N	18 57 E
Nîl el Abyad →	**87**	15 38N	32 31 E
Nîl el Azraq →	**87**	15 38N	32 31 E
Nîl, Nahr en →	**86**	30 10N	31 6 E
Niland	**119**	33 16N	115 30W
Nile = Nîl, Nahr en →	**86**	30 10N	31 6 E
Nile □	**90**	2 0N	31 30 E
Nile Delta	**86**	31 40N	31 0 E
Niles	**114**	41 8N	80 40W
Nilgiri Hills	**70**	11 30N	76 30 E
Nimach = Neemuch	**68**	24 30N	74 56 E
Nimbahera	**68**	24 37N	74 45 E
Nîmes	**21**	43 50N	4 23 E
Nimfaíon, Ákra-	**44**	40 5N	24 20 E
Nimingarra	**96**	20 31 S	119 55 E
Nimmitabel	**99**	36 29 S	149 15 E
Nimneryskiy	**59**	57 50N	125 10 E
Nimrod Glacier	**5**	82 27 S	161 0 E
Nimule	**87**	3 32N	32 3 E
Nin	**39**	44 16N	15 12 E
Nindigully	**99**	28 21 S	148 50 E
Ninemile	**108**	56 0N	130 7W
Ninety Mile Beach, The	**97**	38 15 S	147 24 E
Nineveh = Nīnawá	**64**	36 25N	43 10 E
Ning'an	**76**	44 22N	129 20 E
Ningbo	**75**	29 51N	121 28 E
Ningde	**75**	26 38N	119 23 E
Ningdu	**77**	26 25N	115 59 E
Ningjin	**76**	37 35N	114 57 E
Ningming	**77**	22 8N	107 4 E
Ningpo = Ningbo	**75**	29 51N	121 28 E
Ningqiang	**77**	32 47N	106 15 E
Ningshan	**77**	33 21N	108 21 E
Ningsia Hui A.R. = Ningxia Huizu Zizhiqu □	**76**	38 0N	106 0 E
Ningwu	**76**	39 0N	112 18 E
Ningxia Huizu Zizhiqu □	**76**	38 0N	106 0 E
Ningxiang	**77**	28 15N	112 30 E
Ningyuan	**77**	25 37N	111 57 E
Ninh Binh	**71**	20 15N	105 55 E
Ninove	**16**	50 51N	4 2 E
Nioaque	**125**	21 5 S	55 50W
Niobrara	**116**	42 48N	97 59W
Niobrara →	**116**	42 45N	98 0W
Niono	**84**	14 15N	6 0W
Nioro du Rip	**84**	13 40N	15 50W
Nioro du Sahel	**84**	15 15N	9 30W
Niort	**20**	46 19N	0 29W
Nipani	**70**	16 20N	74 25 E
Nipawin	**109**	53 20N	104 0W
Nipawin Prov. Park	**109**	54 0N	104 37W
Nipigon	**106**	49 0N	88 17W
Nipigon, L.	**106**	49 50N	88 30W
Nipin →	**109**	55 46N	108 35W
Nipishish L.	**107**	54 12N	60 45W
Nipissing L.	**106**	46 20N	80 0W
Nipomo	**119**	35 4N	120 29W
Niquelândia	**127**	14 33 S	48 23W
Nira →	**70**	17 58N	75 8 E
Nirmal	**70**	19 3N	78 20 E
Nirmali	**69**	26 20N	86 35 E
Niš	**42**	43 19N	21 58 E
Nisa	**31**	39 30N	7 41W
Nişāb	**63**	14 25N	46 29 E
Nišava →	**42**	43 20N	21 46 E
Niscemi	**41**	37 8N	14 21 E
Nishinomiya	**74**	34 45N	135 20 E
Nisíros	**45**	36 35N	27 12 E
Niskibi →	**106**	56 29N	88 9W
Nisko	**28**	50 35N	22 7 E
Nisporeny	**46**	47 4N	28 10 E
Nissafors	**49**	57 25N	13 37 E
Nissan →	**49**	56 40N	12 51 E
Nissedal	**47**	59 10N	8 30 E
Nisser	**47**	59 7N	8 28 E
Nissum Fjord	**49**	56 20N	8 11 E
Nisutlin →	**108**	60 14N	132 34W
Niţā'	**64**	27 15N	48 35 E
Nitchequon	**107**	53 10N	70 58W
Niterói	**125**	22 52 S	43 0W
Nith →	**14**	55 20N	3 5W
Nitra	**27**	48 19N	18 4 E
Nitra →	**27**	47 46N	18 10 E
Nittedal	**47**	60 1N	10 57 E
Nittendau	**25**	49 12N	12 16 E
Niuafo'ou	**101**	15 30 S	175 58W
Niue I. (Savage I.)	**95**	19 2 S	169 54W
Niut	**72**	0 55N	110 6 E
Nivelles	**16**	50 35N	4 20 E
Nivernais	**19**	47 0N	3 40 E
Nixon, Nev., U.S.A.	**118**	39 54N	119 22W
Nixon, Tex., U.S.A.	**117**	29 17N	97 45W
Nizam Sagar	**70**	18 10N	77 58 E
Nizamabad	**70**	18 45N	78 7 E
Nizamghat	**67**	28 20N	95 45 E
Nizhne Kolymsk	**59**	68 34N	160 55 E
Nizhne-Vartovskoye	**58**	60 56N	76 38 E
Nizhneangarsk	**59**	55 47N	109 30 E
Nizhnegorskiy	**56**	45 27N	34 38 E
Nizhneudinsk	**59**	54 54N	99 3 E
Nizhneyansk	**59**	71 26N	136 4 E
Nizhniy Lomov	**55**	53 34N	43 38 E
Nizhniy Novgorod = Gorkiy	**55**	56 20N	44 0 E
Nizhniy Tagil	**52**	57 55N	59 57 E
Nizhnyaya Tunguska →	**59**	64 20N	93 0 E
Nizip	**64**	37 5N	37 50 E
Nizké Tatry	**27**	48 55N	20 0 E
Nizza Monferrato	**38**	44 46N	8 22 E
Njakwa	**91**	11 1 S	33 56 E
Njanji	**91**	14 25 S	31 46 E
Njinjo	**91**	8 48 S	38 54 E
Njombe	**91**	9 20 S	34 50 E
Njombe □	**91**	9 20 S	34 49 E
Njombe →	**90**	6 56 S	35 6 E
Nkambe	**85**	6 35N	10 40 E
Nkana	**91**	12 50 S	28 8 E
Nkawkaw	**85**	6 36N	0 49W
Nkhota Kota	**91**	12 56 S	34 15 E
Nkongsamba	**88**	4 55N	9 55 E
Nkwanta	**84**	6 10N	2 10W
Noatak	**104**	67 32N	162 59W
Nobel	**112**	45 25N	80 6W
Nobeoka	**74**	32 36N	131 41 E
Noblejas	**32**	39 58N	3 26W
Noblesville	**114**	40 1N	85 59W
Noce →	**38**	46 9N	11 4 E
Nocera Inferiore	**41**	40 45N	14 37 E
Nocera Terinese	**41**	39 2N	16 9 E
Nocera Umbra	**39**	43 8N	12 47 E
Noci	**41**	40 47N	17 7 E
Nockatunga	**99**	27 42 S	142 42 E
Nocona	**117**	33 48N	97 45W
Nocrich	**46**	45 55N	24 26 E
Noel	**117**	36 36N	94 29W
Nogales, Mexico	**120**	31 20N	110 56W
Nogales, U.S.A.	**119**	31 33N	110 56W
Nogat →	**28**	54 17N	19 17 E
Nōgata	**74**	33 48N	130 44 E
Nogent-en-Bassigny	**19**	48 0N	5 20 E
Nogent-le-Rotrou	**18**	48 20N	0 50 E
Nogent-sur-Seine	**19**	48 30N	3 30 E
Noginsk, Moskva, U.S.S.R.	**55**	55 50N	38 25 E
Noginsk, Sib., U.S.S.R.	**59**	64 30N	90 50 E
Nogoa →	**97**	23 40 S	147 55 E
Nogoyá	**124**	32 24 S	59 48W
Nógrád □	**27**	48 0N	19 30 E
Nogueira de Ramuin	**30**	42 21N	7 43W
Noguera Pallaresa →	**32**	42 15N	1 0 E
Noguera Ribagorzana →	**32**	41 40N	0 43 E
Nohar	**68**	29 11N	74 49 E
Noi →	**71**	14 50N	100 15 E
Noire, Mt.	**18**	48 11N	3 40W
Noirétable	**20**	45 48N	3 46 E
Noirmoutier	**18**	47 0N	2 15W
Noirmoutier, Î. de	**18**	46 58N	2 10W
Nojane	**92**	23 15 S	20 14 E
Nok Kundi	**66**	28 50N	62 45 E
Nokaneng	**92**	19 40 S	22 17 E
Nokhtuysk	**59**	60 0N	117 45 E
Nokomis	**109**	51 35N	105 0W
Nokomis L.	**109**	57 0N	103 0W
Nol	**49**	57 56N	12 5 E
Nola, C. Afr. Rep.	**88**	3 35N	16 4 E
Nola, Italy	**41**	40 54N	14 29 E
Nolay	**19**	46 58N	4 35 E
Noli, C. di	**38**	44 12N	8 26 E
Nolinsk	**55**	57 28N	49 57 E
Noma Omuramba →	**92**	18 52 S	20 53 E
Noman L.	**109**	62 15N	108 55W
Nome	**104**	64 30N	165 24W
Nonacho L.	**109**	61 42N	109 40W
Nonancourt	**18**	48 47N	1 11 E
Nonant-le-Pin	**18**	48 42N	0 12 E
Nonda	**98**	20 40 S	142 28 E
Nong Khae	**71**	14 29N	100 53 E
Nong Khai	**71**	17 50N	102 46 E
Nong'an	**76**	44 25N	125 5 E
Nonoava	**120**	27 28N	106 44W
Nontron	**20**	45 31N	0 40 E
Noonan	**116**	48 51N	102 59W
Noondoo	**99**	28 35 S	148 30 E
Noord Brabant □	**16**	51 40N	5 0 E
Noord Holland □	**16**	52 30N	4 45 E
Noordbeveland	**16**	51 35N	3 50 E
Noordoostpolder	**16**	52 45N	5 45 E
Noordwijk aan Zee	**16**	52 14N	4 26 E
Nootka	**108**	49 38N	126 38W
Nootka I.	**108**	49 32N	126 42W

* *Renamed Vanuatu* ■

Nóqui	**88**	5 55 S	13 30 E
Nora, Ethiopia	**87**	16 6N	40 4 E
Nora, Sweden	**48**	59 32N	15 2 E
Noranda	**106**	48 20N	79 0W
Norberg	**48**	60 4N	15 56 E
Nórcia	**39**	42 50N	13 5 E
Nord □	**19**	50 15N	3 30 E
Nord-Ostee Kanal	**24**	54 15N	9 40 E
Nord-Süd Kanal	**24**	53 0N	10 32 E
Nord-Trøndelag fylke □	**50**	64 20N	12 0 E
Nordagutu	**47**	59 25N	9 20 E
Nordaustlandet	**4**	79 14N	23 0 E
Nordborg	**49**	55 5N	9 50 E
Nordby, Århus, Denmark	**49**	55 58N	10 32 E
Nordby, Ribe, Denmark	**49**	55 27N	8 24 E
Norddal	**47**	62 15N	7 14 E
Norddalsfjord	**47**	61 39N	5 23 E
Norddeich	**24**	53 37N	7 10 E
Nordegg	**108**	52 29N	116 5W
Norden	**24**	53 35N	7 12 E
Nordenham	**24**	53 29N	8 28 E
Norderhov	**47**	60 7N	10 17 E
Norderney	**24**	53 42N	7 15 E
Nordfjord	**47**	61 55N	5 30 E
Nordfriesische Inseln	**24**	54 40N	8 20 E
Nordhausen	**24**	51 29N	10 47 E
Nordhorn	**24**	52 27N	7 4 E
Nordjyllands Amtskommune □	**49**	57 0N	10 0 E
Nordkapp, Norway	**50**	71 10N	25 44 E
Nordkapp, Svalb.	**4**	80 31N	20 0 E
Nordkinn	**9**	71 8N	27 40 E
Nordland fylke □	**50**	65 40N	13 0 E
Nördlingen	**25**	48 50N	10 30 E
Nordrhein-Westfalen □	**24**	51 45N	7 30 E
Nordstrand	**24**	54 27N	8 50 E
Nordvik	**59**	74 2N	111 32 E
Nore	**47**	60 10N	9 0 E
Nore →	**15**	52 40N	7 20W
Norefjell	**47**	60 16N	9 29 E
Norembega	**106**	48 59N	80 43W
Noresund	**47**	60 11N	9 37 E
Norfolk, Nebr., U.S.A.	**116**	42 3N	97 25W
Norfolk, Va., U.S.A.	**114**	36 40N	76 15W
Norfolk □	**12**	52 39N	1 0 E
Norfolk Broads	**12**	52 30N	1 15 E
Norfolk I.	**94**	28 58 S	168 3 E
Norfork Res.	**117**	36 13N	92 15W
Norilsk	**59**	69 20N	88 6 E
Norley	**99**	27 45 S	143 48 E
Norma, Mt.	**98**	20 55 S	140 42 E
Normal	**116**	40 30N	89 0W
Norman	**117**	35 12N	97 30W
Norman →	**97**	17 28 S	140 49 E
Norman Wells	**104**	65 17N	126 51W
Normanby →	**97**	14 23 S	144 10 E
Normanby I.	**98**	10 55 S	151 5 E
Normandie	**18**	48 45N	0 10 E
Normandie, Collines de	**18**	48 55N	0 45W
Normandin	**106**	48 49N	72 31W
Normandy = Normandie	**18**	48 45N	0 10 E
Normanton	**97**	17 40 S	141 10 E
Norquay	**109**	51 53N	102 5W
Norquinco	**128**	41 51 S	70 55W
Norrahammar	**49**	57 43N	14 7 E
Norrbotten □	**50**	66 30N	22 30 E
Norrby	**50**	64 55N	18 15 E
Nørre Åby	**49**	55 27N	9 52 E
Nørre Nebel	**49**	55 47N	8 17 E
Nørresundby	**49**	57 5N	9 52 E
Norris	**118**	45 40N	111 40W
Norristown	**114**	40 9N	75 21W
Norrköping	**49**	58 37N	16 11 E
Norrland □	**50**	66 50N	18 0 E
Norrtälje	**48**	59 46N	18 42 E
Norsholm	**49**	58 31N	15 59 E
Norsk	**59**	52 30N	130 0 E
North Adams	**114**	42 42N	73 6W
North America	**102**	40 0N	100 0W
North Andaman I.	**71**	13 15N	92 40 E
North Atlantic Ocean	**6**	30 0N	50 0W
North Battleford	**109**	52 50N	108 17W
North Bay	**106**	46 20N	79 30W
North Belcher Is.	**106**	56 50N	79 50W
North Bend, Can.	**108**	49 50N	121 27W
North Bend, Oreg., U.S.A.	**118**	43 28N	124 14W
North Bend, Pa., U.S.A.	**112**	41 20N	77 42W
North Berwick, U.K.	**14**	56 4N	2 44W
North Berwick, U.S.A.	**113**	43 18N	70 43W
North Buganda □	**90**	1 0N	32 0 E
North Canadian →	**117**	35 17N	95 31W
North C., Antarct.	**5**	71 0 S	166 0 E
North C., Can.	**107**	47 2N	60 20W
North C., N.Z.	**101**	34 23 S	173 4 E
North Caribou L.	**106**	52 50N	90 40W
North Carolina □	**115**	35 30N	80 0W
North Channel, Br. Is.	**14**	55 0N	5 30W
North Channel, Can.	**106**	46 0N	83 0W
North Chicago	**114**	42 19N	87 50W
North Dakota □	**116**	47 30N	100 0W
North Down □	**15**	54 40N	5 45W
North Downs	**13**	51 17N	0 30 E
North East	**112**	42 17N	79 50W
North East Frontier Agency = Arunachal Pradesh □	**67**	28 0N	95 0 E
North East Providence Chan.	**121**	26 0N	76 0W
North Eastern □	**90**	1 30N	40 0 E
North Esk →	**14**	56 44N	2 25W
North European Plain	**9**	55 0N	20 0 E
North Foreland	**13**	51 22N	1 28 E
North Frisian Is. = Nordfr'sche Inseln	**24**	54 50N	8 20 E
North Henik L.	**109**	61 45N	97 40W
North Horr	**90**	3 20N	37 8 E
North I., Kenya	**90**	4 5N	36 5 E
North I., N.Z.	**101**	38 0 S	175 0 E
North Kingsville	**112**	41 53N	80 42W
North Knife →	**109**	58 53N	94 45W
North Koel →	**69**	24 45N	83 50 E
North Korea ■	**76**	40 0N	127 0 E
North Lakhimpur	**67**	27 14N	94 7 E
North Las Vegas	**119**	36 15N	115 6W
North Loup →	**116**	41 17N	98 23W
North Mashonaland □	**91**	16 30 S	30 0 E
North Minch	**14**	58 5N	5 55W
North Nahanni →	**108**	62 15N	123 20W
North Ossetian A.S.S.R. □	**57**	43 30N	44 30 E
North Palisade	**119**	37 6N	118 32W
North Platte	**116**	41 10N	100 50W
North Platte →	**116**	41 15N	100 45W
North Pt.	**107**	47 5N	64 0W
North Pole	**4**	90 0N	0 0 E
North Portal	**109**	49 0N	102 33W
North Powder	**118**	45 2N	117 59W
North Ronaldsay	**14**	59 20N	2 30W
North Sea	**8**	56 0N	4 0 E
North Sentinel I.	**71**	11 35N	92 15 E
North Sporades = Voríai Sporádhes	**45**	39 15N	23 30 E
North Stradbroke I.	**97**	27 35 S	153 28 E
North Sydney	**107**	46 12N	60 15W
North Thompson →	**108**	50 40N	120 20W
North Tonawanda	**114**	43 5N	78 50W
North Troy	**113**	44 59N	72 24W
North Truchas Pk.	**119**	36 0N	105 30W
North Twin I.	**106**	53 20N	80 0W
North Tyne →	**12**	54 59N	2 7W
North Uist	**14**	57 40N	7 15W
North Vancouver	**108**	49 25N	123 3W
North Vernon	**114**	39 0N	85 35W
North Village	**121**	32 15N	64 45W
North Wabiskaw L.	**108**	56 0N	113 55W
North Walsham	**12**	52 49N	1 22 E
North West Basin	**96**	25 45 S	115 0 E
North West C.	**96**	21 45 S	114 9 E
North West Christmas I. Ridge	**95**	6 30N	165 0W
North West Highlands	**14**	57 35N	5 2W
North West Providence Channel	**121**	26 0N	78 0W
North West River	**107**	53 30N	60 10W
North Western □	**91**	13 30 S	25 30 E
North York Moors	**12**	54 25N	0 50W
North Yorkshire □	**12**	54 15N	1 25W
Northallerton	**12**	54 20N	1 26W
Northam	**96**	31 35 S	116 42 E
Northampton, Austral.	**96**	28 27 S	114 33 E
Northampton, U.K.	**13**	52 14N	0 54W
Northampton, Mass., U.S.A.	**114**	42 22N	72 31W
Northampton, Pa., U.S.A.	**113**	40 38N	75 24W
Northampton □	**13**	52 16N	0 55W
Northampton Downs	**98**	24 35 S	145 48 E
Northbridge	**113**	42 12N	71 40W
Northeim	**24**	51 42N	10 0 E
Northern □, Malawi	**91**	11 0 S	34 0 E
Northern □, Uganda	**90**	3 5N	32 30 E
Northern □, Zambia	**91**	10 30 S	31 0 E
Northern Circars	**70**	17 30N	82 30 E
Northern Group	**101**	10 00 S	160 00W
Northern Indian L.	**109**	57 20N	97 20W
Northern Ireland □	**15**	54 45N	7 0W
Northern Light, L.	**106**	48 15N	90 39W
Northern Province □	**84**	9 15N	11 30W
Northern Territory □	**96**	16 0 S	133 0 E
Northfield	**116**	44 30N	93 10W
Northome	**116**	47 53N	94 15W
Northport, Ala., U.S.A.	**115**	33 15N	87 35W
Northport, Mich., U.S.A.	**114**	45 8N	85 39W
Northport, Wash., U.S.A.	**118**	48 55N	117 48W
Northumberland □	**12**	55 12N	2 0W
Northumberland, C.	**97**	38 5 S	140 40 E
Northumberland Is.	**98**	21 30 S	149 50 E
Northumberland Str.	**107**	46 20N	64 0W
Northwest Territories □	**104**	65 0N	100 0W
Northwich	**12**	53 16N	2 30W
Northwood, Iowa, U.S.A.	**116**	43 27N	93 0W
Northwood, N.D., U.S.A.	**116**	47 44N	97 30W
Norton, U.S.A.	**116**	39 50N	99 53W
Norton, Zimb.	**91**	17 52 S	30 40 E
Norton Sd.	**104**	64 0N	164 0W
Nortorf	**24**	54 14N	9 47 E
Norwalk, Conn., U.S.A.	**114**	41 9N	73 25W
Norwalk, Ohio, U.S.A.	**114**	41 13N	82 38W
Norway	**114**	45 46N	87 57W
Norway House	**109**	53 59N	97 50W
Norwegian Dependency	**5**	66 0 S	15 0 E
Norwegian Sea	**6**	66 0N	1 0 E
Norwich, Can.	**112**	42 59N	80 36W
Norwich, U.K.	**12**	52 38N	1 17 E
Norwich, Conn., U.S.A.	**113**	41 33N	72 5W
Norwich, N.Y., U.S.A.	**114**	42 32N	75 30W
Norwood, Can.	**112**	44 23N	77 59W
Norwood, U.S.A.	**113**	42 10N	71 10W
Nosok	**58**	70 10N	82 20 E
Nosovka	**54**	50 50N	31 37 E
Noşratābād	**65**	29 55N	60 0 E
Noss Hd.	**14**	58 29N	3 4W
Nossebro	**49**	58 12N	12 43 E
Nossob →	**92**	26 55 S	20 37 E
Nosy Boraha	**93**	16 50 S	49 55 E
Nosy Varika	**93**	20 35 S	48 32 E
Noteć →	**28**	52 44N	15 26 E
Notigi Dam	**109**	56 40N	99 10W
Notikewin →	**108**	57 2N	117 38W
Notios Evvoïkos Kólpos	**45**	38 20N	24 0 E
Noto	**41**	36 52N	15 4 E
Noto, G. di	**41**	36 50N	15 10 E
Noto-Hanto	**74**	37 0N	137 0 E
Notodden	**47**	59 35N	9 17 E
Notre-Dame	**107**	46 18N	64 46W
Notre Dame B.	**107**	49 45N	55 30W
Notre Dame de Koartac	**105**	60 55N	69 40W
Notsé	**85**	7 0N	1 17 E
Nottaway →	**106**	51 22N	78 55W
Nøtterøy	**47**	59 14N	10 24 E
Nottingham	**12**	52 57N	1 10W
Nottingham □	**12**	53 10N	1 0W
Nottoway →	**114**	36 33N	76 55W
Notwani →	**92**	23 35 S	26 58 E
Nouâdhibou	**80**	20 54N	17 0W
Nouâdhibou, Ras	**80**	20 50N	17 0W
Nouakchott	**84**	18 9N	15 58W
Noumea	**94**	22 17 S	166 30 E
Noupoort	**92**	31 10 S	24 57 E
Nouveau Comptoir (Paint Hills)	**106**	53 0N	78 49W
Nouvelle Calédonie	**94**	21 0 S	165 0 E
Nouzonville	**19**	49 48N	4 44 E
Nová Baňa	**27**	48 28N	18 39 E
Nová Bystřice	**26**	49 2N	15 8 E
† Nova Chaves	**88**	10 31 S	21 15 E
Nova Cruz	**127**	6 28 S	35 25W
Nova Esperança	**125**	23 8 S	52 24W
Nova Friburgo	**125**	22 16 S	42 30W
Nova Gaia	**88**	10 10 S	17 35 E
Nova Gradiška	**42**	45 17N	17 28 E
Nova Iguaçu	**125**	22 45 S	43 28W
Nova Iorque	**127**	7 0 S	44 5W
Nova Lamego	**84**	12 19N	14 11W
Nova Lima	**125**	19 59 S	43 51W
Nova Lisboa = Huambo	**89**	12 42 S	15 44 E
Nova Lusitânia	**91**	19 50 S	34 34 E
Nova Mambone	**93**	21 0 S	35 3 E
Nova Mesto	**39**	45 47N	15 12 E
Nova Paka	**26**	50 29N	15 30 E
Nova Scotia □	**107**	45 10N	63 0W
Nova Sofala	**93**	20 7 S	34 42 E
Nova Varoš	**42**	43 29N	19 48 E
Nova Venécia	**127**	18 45 S	40 24W
Nova Zagora	**43**	42 32N	25 59 E
Novaci, Romania	**46**	45 10N	23 42 E
Novaci, Yugo.	**42**	41 5N	21 29 E
Noval Iorque	**127**	6 48 S	44 0W
Novaleksandrovskaya	**57**	45 29N	41 17 E
Novannenskiy	**55**	50 32N	42 39 E
Novara	**38**	45 27N	8 36 E
Novaya Kakhovka	**56**	46 42N	33 27 E
Novaya Ladoga	**52**	60 7N	32 16 E
Novaya Lyalya	**58**	59 10N	60 35 E
Novaya Sibir, O.	**59**	75 10N	150 0 E
Novaya Zemlya	**58**	75 0N	56 0 E
Nové Město	**27**	48 45N	17 50 E
Nové Zámky	**27**	48 0N	18 8 E
Novelda	**33**	38 24N	0 45W
Novellara	**38**	44 50N	10 43 E
Noventa Vicentina	**39**	45 18N	11 30 E
Novgorod	**54**	58 30N	31 25 E
Novgorod-Severskiy	**54**	52 2N	33 10 E
Novi Bečej	**42**	45 36N	20 10 E
Novi Grad	**39**	45 19N	13 33 E
Novi Kneževa	**42**	46 4N	20 8 E
* Novi Krichim	**43**	42 8N	24 31 E
Novi Lígure	**38**	44 45N	8 47 E
Novi Pazar, Bulg.	**43**	43 25N	27 15 E
Novi Pazar, Yugo.	**42**	43 12N	20 28 E
Novi Sad	**42**	45 18N	19 52 E
Novi Vinodolski	**39**	45 10N	14 48 E
Novigrad	**39**	44 10N	15 32 E
Nôvo Hamburgo	**125**	29 37 S	51 7W
Novo-Zavidovskiy	**55**	56 32N	36 29 E
Novoakrainka	**56**	48 25N	31 30 E
Novoaltaysk	**58**	53 30N	84 0 E
Novoazovsk	**56**	47 15N	38 4 E
Novobelitsa	**54**	52 27N	31 2 E
Novobogatinskoye	**57**	47 20N	51 11 E
Novocherkassk	**57**	47 27N	40 5 E
Novodevichye	**55**	53 37N	48 50 E
Novograd-Volynskiy	**54**	50 34N	27 35 E
Novogrudok	**54**	53 40N	25 50 E
Novokayakent	**57**	42 30N	47 52 E
Novokazalinsk	**58**	45 48N	62 6 E
Novokhopersk	**55**	51 5N	41 39 E
Novokuybyshevsk	**55**	53 7N	49 58 E
Novokuznetsk	**58**	53 45N	87 10 E
Novomirgorod	**56**	48 45N	31 33 E
Novomoskovsk, R.S.F.S.R., U.S.S.R.	**55**	54 5N	38 15 E
Novomoskovsk, Ukraine, U.S.S.R.	**56**	48 33N	35 17 E
Novopolotsk	**54**	55 32N	28 37 E
Novorossiysk	**56**	44 43N	37 46 E
Novorybnoye	**59**	72 50N	105 50 E
Novorzhev	**54**	57 3N	29 25 E
Novoselitsa	**56**	48 14N	26 15 E
Novoshakhtinsk	**57**	47 46N	39 58 E
Novosibirsk	**58**	55 0N	83 5 E
Novosibirskiye Ostrava	**59**	75 0N	142 0 E
Novosil	**55**	52 58N	36 58 E
Novosokolniki	**54**	56 33N	30 5 E
Novotroitsk	**52**	51 10N	58 15 E
Novotulskiy	**55**	54 10N	37 43 E
Novouzensk	**55**	50 32N	48 17 E
Novovolynsk	**54**	50 45N	24 4 E
Novovyatsk	**55**	58 29N	49 44 E
Novozybkov	**54**	52 30N	32 0 E
Novska	**42**	45 19N	17 0 E
Novvy Port	**58**	67 40N	72 30 E
Novy Bug	**56**	47 34N	32 29 E
Nový Bydzov	**26**	50 14N	15 29 E
Novy Dwór Mazowiecki	**28**	52 26N	20 44 E
Nový Jičín	**27**	49 30N	18 0 E
Novyy Afon	**57**	43 7N	40 50 E
Novyy Oskol	**55**	50 44N	37 55 E
Now Shahr	**65**	36 40N	51 30 E
Nowa Deba	**28**	50 26N	21 41 E
Nowa Huta	**27**	50 5N	20 30 E
Nowa Ruda	**28**	50 35N	16 30 E
Nowa Skalmierzyce	**28**	51 43N	18 0 E
Nowa Sól	**28**	51 48N	15 44 E
Nowe	**28**	53 41N	18 44 E
Nowe Miasteczko	**28**	51 42N	15 42 E
Nowe Miasto	**28**	51 38N	20 34 E
Nowe Miasto Lubawskie	**28**	53 27N	19 33 E
Nowe Warpno	**28**	53 42N	14 18 E
Nowgong	**67**	26 20N	92 50 E
Nowingi	**100**	34 33 S	142 15 E
Nowogard	**28**	53 41N	15 10 E
Nowogród	**28**	53 14N	21 53 E
Nowra	**97**	34 53 S	150 35 E
Nowy Dwór, Białystok, Poland	**28**	53 40N	23 30 E
Nowy Dwór, Gdansk, Poland	**28**	54 13N	19 7 E
Nowy Korczyn	**28**	50 19N	20 48 E
Nowy Sącz	**27**	49 40N	20 41 E
Nowy Sącz □	**27**	49 30N	20 30 E
Nowy Staw	**28**	54 13N	19 2 E
Nowy Tomyśl	**28**	52 19N	16 10 E
Noxen	**113**	41 25N	76 4W
Noxon	**118**	48 0N	115 43W
Noya	**30**	42 48N	8 53W
Noyant	**18**	47 30N	0 6 E
Noyers	**19**	47 40N	4 0 E
Noyes I.	**108**	55 30N	133 40W
Noyon	**19**	49 34N	3 0 E
Nozay	**18**	47 34N	1 38W
Nsa, O. en →	**83**	32 28N	5 24 E
Nsanje	**91**	16 55 S	35 12 E
Nsawam	**85**	5 50N	0 24W
Nsomba	**91**	10 45 S	29 51 E
Nsukka	**85**	6 51N	7 29 E
Nuanetsi →	**91**	22 40 S	31 50 E
Nuba Mts. = Nubah, Jibalan	**87**	12 0N	31 0 E
Nubah, Jibalan	**87**	12 0N	31 0 E
Nûbîya, Es Sahrâ En	**86**	21 30N	33 30 E
Ñuble □	**124**	37 0 S	72 0W
Nuboai	**73**	2 10 S	136 30 E
Nueces →	**117**	27 50N	97 30W
Nueima →	**62**	31 54N	35 25 E
Nueltin L.	**109**	60 30N	99 30W
Nueva Gerona	**121**	21 53N	82 49W
Nueva Imperial	**128**	38 45 S	72 58W
Nueva Palmira	**124**	33 52 S	58 20W
Nueva Rosita	**120**	28 0N	101 11W
Nueva San Salvador	**120**	13 40N	89 18W
Nuéve de Julio	**124**	35 30 S	61 0W
Nuevitas	**121**	21 30N	77 20W
Nuevo, Golfo	**128**	43 0 S	64 30W
Nuevo Laredo	**120**	27 30N	99 30W
Nuevo León □	**120**	25 0N	100 0W
Nugget Pt.	**101**	46 27 S	169 50 E
Nugrus, Gebel	**86**	24 47N	34 35 E
Nuhaka	**101**	39 3 S	177 45 E
Nuits	**19**	47 44N	4 12 E
Nuits-St-Georges	**19**	47 10N	4 56 E
Nukheila (Merga)	**86**	19 1N	26 21 E
Nuku'alofa	**101**	21 10 S	174 0W
Nukus	**58**	42 20N	59 7 E
Nulato	**104**	64 40N	158 10W
Nules	**32**	39 51N	0 9W
Nullagine	**96**	21 53 S	120 6 E
Nullarbor Plain	**96**	30 45 S	129 0 E
Numalla, L.	**99**	28 43 S	144 20 E
Numan	**85**	9 29N	12 3 E
Numata	**74**	36 45N	139 4 E
Numatinna →	**87**	7 38N	27 20 E
Numazu	**74**	35 7N	138 51 E
Numfoor	**73**	1 0 S	134 50 E
Numurkah	**99**	36 5 S	145 26 E
Nunaksaluk I.	**107**	55 49N	60 20W
Nuneaton	**13**	52 32N	1 29W
Nungo	**91**	13 23 S	37 43 E
Nungwe	**90**	2 48 S	32 2 E
Nunivak	**104**	60 0N	166 0W
Nunkun	**69**	33 57N	76 2 E
Nunspeet	**16**	52 21N	5 45 E
Nuomin He →	**76**	46 45N	126 55 E
Nuoro	**40**	40 20N	9 20 E
Nuqayy, Jabal	**83**	23 11N	19 30 E
Nure →	**38**	45 3N	9 49 E
Nuremburg = Nürnberg	**25**	49 26N	11 5 E
Nuriootpa	**99**	34 27 S	139 0 E
Nurlat	**55**	54 29N	50 45 E
Nürnberg	**25**	49 26N	11 5 E
Nurran, L. = Terewah, L.	**99**	29 52 S	147 35 E
Nurri	**40**	39 43N	9 13 E
Nurzec →	**28**	52 37N	22 25 E
Nusa Barung	**73**	8 22 S	113 20 E
Nusa Kambangan	**73**	7 47 S	109 0 E
Nusa Tenggara Barat □	**72**	8 50 S	117 30 E
Nusa Tenggara Timur □	**73**	9 30 S	122 0 E
Nushki	**66**	29 35N	66 0 E
Nutak	**105**	57 28N	61 59W
Nuwakot	**69**	28 10N	83 55 E
Nuwara Eliya	**70**	6 58N	80 48 E
Nuweiba'	**86**	28 58N	34 40 E
Nuweveldberge	**92**	32 10 S	21 45 E
Nuyts Arch.	**96**	32 35 S	133 20 E
Nuyts, Pt.	**96**	35 4 S	116 38 E
Nuzvid	**70**	16 47N	80 53 E
Nxau-Nxau	**92**	18 57 S	21 4 E
Nyaake (Webo)	**84**	4 52N	7 37W
Nyabing	**96**	33 30 S	118 7 E
Nyack	**113**	41 5N	73 57W
Nyadal	**48**	62 48N	17 59 E
Nyah West	**100**	35 16 S	143 21 E
Nyahanga	**90**	2 20 S	33 37 E
Nyahua	**90**	5 25 S	33 23 E
Nyahururu	**90**	0 2N	36 27 E
Nyainqentanglha Shan	**75**	30 0N	90 0 E
Nyakanazi	**90**	3 2 S	31 10 E
Nyakrom	**85**	5 40N	0 50W
Nyâlâ	**87**	12 2N	24 58 E
Nyamandhlovu	**91**	19 55 S	28 16 E
Nyambiti	**90**	2 48 S	33 27 E
Nyamwaga	**90**	1 27 S	34 33 E
Nyandekwa	**90**	3 57 S	32 32 E
Nyanding →,	**87**	8 40N	32 41 E
Nyandoma	**52**	61 40N	40 12 E
Nyangana	**92**	18 0 S	20 40 E
Nyanguge	**90**	2 30 S	33 12 E
Nyankpala	**85**	9 21N	0 58W
Nyanza, Burundi	**90**	4 21 S	29 36 E
Nyanza, Rwanda	**90**	2 20 S	29 42 E
Nyanza □	**90**	0 10 S	34 15 E
Nyarling →	**108**	60 41N	113 23W
Nyasa, L. = Malawi, L.	**91**	12 0 S	34 30 E
Nyazepetrovsk	**52**	56 3N	59 36 E
Nyazwidzi →	**91**	20 0 S	31 17 E
Nyborg	**49**	55 18N	10 47 E
Nybro	**49**	56 44N	15 55 E
Nyda	**58**	66 40N	72 58 E
Nyeri	**90**	0 23 S	36 56 E
Nyerol	**87**	8 41N	32 1 E
Nyhem	**48**	62 54N	15 37 E
Nyiel	**87**	6 9N	31 13 E
Nyinahin	**84**	6 43N	2 3W
Nyirbátor	**27**	47 49N	22 9 E
Nyíregyháza	**27**	47 58N	21 47 E
Nykarleby	**50**	63 22N	22 31 E
Nykøbing, Sjælland, Denmark	**49**	55 55N	11 40 E
Nykøbing, Storstrøm, Denmark	**49**	54 56N	11 52 E
Nykøbing, Viborg, Denmark	**49**	56 48N	8 51 E
Nyköping	**49**	58 45N	17 0 E

* *Renamed Stamboliyski*

† *Renamed Muconda*

Nykroppa Onehunga

Nykroppa 48 59 37N 14 18 E
Nykvarn 48 59 11N 17 25 E
Nyland 48 63 1N 17 45 E
Nylstroom 93 24 42 S 28 22 E
Nymagee 99 32 7 S 146 20 E
Nymburk 26 50 10N 15 1 E
Nynäshamn 48 58 54N 17 57 E
Nyngan 99 31 30 S 147 8 E
Nyon 25 46 23N 6 14 E
Nyong → 85 3 17N 9 54 E
Nyons 21 44 22N 5 10 E
Nyord 49 55 4N 12 13 E
Nyou 85 12 42N 2 1W
Nysa 28 50 30N 17 22 E
Nysa →, Poland/Poland 28 52 4N 14 46 E
Nysa →, Poland 28 50 49N 17 40 E
Nyssa 118 43 56N 117 2W
Nysted 49 54 40N 11 44 E
Nyunzu 90 5 57 S 27 58 E
Nyurba 59 63 17N 118 28 E
Nzega 90 4 10 S 33 12 E
Nzega □ 90 4 10 S 33 10 E
N'Zérékoré 84 7 49N 8 48W
Nzeto 88 7 10 S 12 52 E
Nzilo, Chutes de 91 10 18 S 25 27 E
Nzubuka 90 4 45 S 32 50 E

O

Oacoma 116 43 50N 99 26W
Oahe 116 44 33N 100 29W
Oahe Dam 116 44 28N 100 25W
Oahe Res. 116 45 30N 100 25W
Oahu 110 21 30N 158 0W
Oak Creek 118 40 15N 106 59W
Oak Harb. 118 48 20N 122 38W
Oak Hill 114 38 0N 81 7W
Oak Park 114 41 55N 87 45W
Oak Ridge 115 36 1N 84 12W
Oakbank 99 33 4 S 140 33 E
Oakdale, Calif., U.S.A. 119 46 14N 98 4W
Oakdale, La., U.S.A. 117 30 50N 92 38W
Oakengates 12 52 42N 2 29W
Oakes 116 46 14N 98 4W
Oakesdale 118 47 11N 117 15W
Oakey 99 27 25 S 151 43 E
Oakham 12 52 40N 0 43W
Oakland, Calif., U.S.A. 119 37 50N 122 18W
Oakland, Oreg., U.S.A. 118 43 23N 123 18W
Oakland City 114 38 20N 87 20W
Oakleigh 100 37 54 S 145 6 E
Oakley, Id., U.S.A. 118 42 14N 113 55W
Oakley, Kans., U.S.A. 116 39 8N 100 51W
Oakridge 118 43 47N 122 31W
Oakwood 117 31 35N 94 45W
Oamaru 101 45 5 S 170 59 E
Oates Coast 5 69 0 S 160 0 E
Oatman 119 35 1N 114 19W
Oaxaca 120 17 2N 96 40W
Oaxaca □ 120 17 0N 97 0W
Ob → 58 66 45N 69 30 E
Oba 106 49 4N 84 7W
Obala 85 4 9N 11 32 E
Oban, N.Z. 101 46 55 S 168 10 E
Oban, U.K. 14 56 25N 5 30W
Obbia 63 5 25N 48 30 E
Obed 108 53 30N 117 10W
Obera 125 27 21 S 55 2W
Oberammergau 25 47 35N 11 3 E
Oberdrauburg 26 46 44N 12 58 E
Oberengadin 25 46 35N 9 55 E
Oberhausen 24 51 28N 6 50 E
Oberkirch 25 48 31N 8 5 E
Oberlin, Kans., U.S.A. 116 39 52N 100 31W
Oberlin, La., U.S.A. 117 30 42N 92 42W
Oberlin, Ohio, U.S.A. 112 41 15N 82 10W
Obernai 19 48 28N 7 30 E
Oberndorf 25 48 17N 8 35 E
Oberon 99 33 45 S 149 52 E
Oberösterreich □ 26 48 10N 14 0 E
Oberpfälzer Wald 25 49 30N 12 25 E
Oberstdorf 25 47 25N 10 16 E
Obi, Kepulauan 73 1 23 S 127 45 E
Obiaruku 85 5 51N 6 9 E
Óbidos, Brazil 127 1 50 S 55 30W
Óbidos, Port. 31 39 19N 9 10W
Obihiro 74 42 56N 143 12 E
Obilatu 73 1 25 S 127 20 E
Obilnoye 57 47 32N 44 30 E
Obing 25 48 0N 12 25 E
Obisfelde 24 52 27N 10 57 E
Objat 20 45 16N 1 24 E
Obluchye 59 49 1N 131 4 E
Obninsk 55 55 8N 36 37 E
Obo, C. Afr. Rep. 90 5 20N 26 32 E
Obo, Ethiopia 87 3 46N 38 52 E
Oboa, Mt. 90 1 45N 34 45 E
Obock 87 12 0N 43 20 E
Oborniki 28 52 39N 16 50 E
Oborniki Śląskie 28 51 17N 16 53 E
Oboyan 55 51 13N 36 37 E
Obrenovac 42 44 40N 20 11 E
Obrovac 39 44 11N 15 41 E
Observatory Inlet 108 55 10N 129 54W
Obshchi Syrt 9 52 0N 53 0 E
Obskaya Guba 58 69 0N 73 0 E
Obuasi 85 6 17N 1 40W
Obubra 85 6 8N 8 20 E
Obzor 43 42 50N 27 52 E
Ocala 115 29 11N 82 5W
Ocampo 120 28 9N 108 24W
Ocaña 32 39 55N 3 30W
Oconomowoc 116 43 7N 88 30W
Ocate 117 36 12N 104 59W
Occidental, Cordillera 126 5 0N 76 0W
Ocean City 114 39 18N 74 34W
Ocean, I. = Banaba 94 0 52 S 169 35 E
Ocean Park 118 46 30N 124 2W
Oceanlake 118 45 0N 124 0W
Oceanport 113 40 20N 74 3W
Oceanside 119 33 13N 117 26W
Ochagavia 32 42 55N 1 5W
Ochamchire 57 42 46N 41 32 E
Ochil Hills 14 56 14N 3 40W
Ochre River 109 51 4N 99 47W
Ochsenfurt 25 49 38N 10 3 E
Ochsenhausen 25 48 4N 9 57 E
Ocilla 115 31 35N 83 12W
Ockelbo 48 60 54N 16 45 E
Ocmulgee → 115 31 58N 82 32W
Ocna Mureş 46 46 23N 23 55 E
Ocna Sibiului 46 45 52N 24 2 E
Ocnele Mari 46 45 8N 24 18 E
Oconee → 115 31 58N 82 32W
Oconto 114 44 52N 87 53W
Oconto Falls 114 44 52N 88 10W
Ocotal 121 13 41N 86 31W
Ocotlán 120 20 21N 102 42W
Ocreza → 31 39 32N 7 50W
Ócsa 27 47 17N 19 15 E
Octave 119 34 10N 112 43W
Octeville 18 49 38N 1 40W
Ocumare del Tuy 126 10 7N 66 46W
Ocussi 73 9 20 S 124 23 E
Oda 85 5 50N 0 51W
Oda, Jebel 86 20 21N 36 39 E
Ódáðahraun 50 65 5N 17 0W
Ödåkra 49 56 7N 12 45 E
Odawara 74 35 20N 139 6 E
Odda 47 60 3N 6 35 E
Odder 49 55 58N 10 10 E
Oddur 63 4 11N 43 52 E
Ödeborg 49 58 32N 11 58 E
Odei → 109 56 6N 96 54W
Odemira 31 37 35N 8 40W
Ödemiş 64 38 15N 28 0 E
Odendaalsrus 92 27 48 S 26 45 E
Odense 49 55 22N 10 23 E
Odenwald 25 49 40N 9 0 E
Oder → 24 53 33N 14 38 E
Oderzo 39 45 47N 12 29 E
Odessa, Can. 113 44 17N 76 43W
Odessa, Tex., U.S.A. 117 31 51N 102 23W
Odessa, Wash., U.S.A. 118 47 19N 118 35W
Odessa, U.S.S.R. 56 46 30N 30 45 E
Odiakwe 92 20 12 S 25 17 E
Odiel → 31 37 10N 6 55W
Odienné 84 9 30N 7 34W
Odobeşti 46 45 43N 27 4 E
Odolanów 28 51 34N 17 40 E
O'Donnell 117 33 0N 101 48W
Odorheiul Secuiesc 46 46 21N 25 21 E
Odoyevo 55 53 56N 36 42 E
Odra →, Poland 28 53 33N 14 38 E
Odra →, Spain 30 42 14N 4 17W
Odžaci 42 45 30N 19 17 E
Odžak 42 45 3N 18 18 E
Oeiras, Brazil 127 7 0 S 42 8W
Oeiras, Port. 31 38 41N 9 18W
Oelrichs 116 43 11N 103 14W
Oelsnitz 24 50 24N 12 11 E
Oelwein 116 42 41N 91 55W
Ofanto → 41 41 22N 16 13 E
Offa 85 8 13N 4 42 E
Offaly □ 15 53 15N 7 30W
Offenbach 25 50 6N 8 46 E
Offenburg 25 48 29N 7 56 E
Offerdal 48 63 28N 14 0 E
Offida 39 42 56N 13 40 E
Offranville 18 49 52N 1 0 E
Ofidhousa 45 36 33N 26 8 E
Ofotfjorden 50 68 27N 16 40 E
Oga-Hantō 74 39 58N 139 47 E
Ogahalla 106 50 6N 85 51W
Ōgaki 74 35 21N 136 37 E
Ogallala 116 41 12N 101 40W
Ogbomosho 85 8 1N 4 11 E
Ogden, Iowa, U.S.A. 116 42 3N 94 0W
Ogden, Utah, U.S.A. 118 41 13N 112 1W
Ogdensburg 114 44 40N 75 27W
Ogeechee → 115 31 51N 81 6W
Oglio → 38 45 2N 10 39 E
Ogmore 98 22 37 S 149 35 E
Ogna 47 58 31N 5 48 E
Ognon → 19 47 16N 5 28 E
Ogoja 85 6 38N 8 39 E
Ogoki → 106 51 38N 85 57W
Ogoki L. 106 50 50N 87 10W
Ogoki Res. 106 50 45N 88 15W
Ogooué → 88 1 0 S 10 0 E
Ogosta → 43 43 48N 23 55 E
Ogowe = Ogooué → 88 1 0 S 10 0 E
Ograźden 42 41 30N 22 50 E
Ogrein 86 17 55N 34 50 E
Ogulin 39 45 16N 15 16 E
Ogun □ 85 7 0N 3 0 E
Oguta 85 5 44N 6 44 E
Ogwashi-Uku 85 6 15N 6 30 E
Ogwe 85 5 0N 7 14 E
Ohai 101 44 55 S 168 0 E
Ohakune 101 39 24 S 175 24 E
Ohau, L. 101 44 15 S 169 53 E
Ohey 16 50 26N 5 8 E
O'Higgins □ 124 34 15 S 70 45W
Ohio □ 114 40 20N 14 10 E
Ohio → 114 38 0N 86 0W
Ohre →, Czech. 26 50 30N 14 10 E
Ohre →, Ger. 24 52 18N 11 47 E
Ohrid 42 41 8N 20 52 E
Ohridsko, Jezero 42 41 8N 20 52 E
Ohrigstad 93 24 19 S 30 36 E
Öhringen 25 49 11N 9 31 E
Oil City 114 41 26N 79 40W
Oinousa 45 38 33N 26 14 E
Oise □ 19 49 28N 2 30 E
Oise → 19 49 0N 2 4 E
Ōita 74 33 14N 131 36 E
Ōita □ 74 33 15N 131 30 E
Oiticica 127 5 3 S 41 5W
Ojai 119 34 28N 119 16W
Ojinaga 120 29 34N 104 25W
Ojos del Salado, Cerro 124 27 0 S 68 40W
Oka → 55 56 20N 43 59 E
Okaba 73 8 6 S 139 42 E
Okahandja 92 22 0 S 16 59 E
Okahukura 94 38 48 S 175 14 E
Okanagan L. 108 50 0N 119 30W
Okandja 88 0 35 S 13 45 E
Okanogan 118 48 6N 119 43W
Okanogan → 118 48 6N 119 43W
Okány 27 46 52N 21 21 E
Okaputa 92 20 5 S 17 0 E
Okara 68 30 50N 73 31 E
Okarito 101 43 15 S 170 9 E
Okavango Swamps 92 18 45 S 22 45 E
Okaya 74 36 0N 138 10 E
Okayama 74 34 40N 133 54 E
Okayama □ 74 35 0N 133 50 E
Okazaki 74 34 57N 137 10 E
Oke-Iho 85 8 1N 3 18 E
Okeechobee 115 27 16N 80 46W
Okeechobee L. 115 27 0N 80 50W
Okefenokee Swamp 115 30 50N 82 15W
Okehampton 13 50 44N 4 1W
Okene 85 7 32N 6 11 E
Oker → 24 52 30N 10 22 E
Okha 59 53 40N 143 0 E
Ókhi Óros 45 38 5N 24 25 E
Okhotsk 59 59 20N 143 10 E
Okhotsk, Sea of 59 55 0N 145 0 E
Okhotskiy Perevoz 59 61 52N 135 35 E
Okhotsko Kolymskoye 59 63 0N 157 0 E
Oki-Shotō 74 36 5N 133 15 E
Okiep 92 29 39 S 17 53 E
Okigwi 85 5 52N 7 20 E
Okija 85 5 54N 6 55 E
Okinawa □ 77 26 40N 128 0 E
Okitipupa 85 6 31N 4 50 E
Oklahoma □ 117 35 20N 97 30W
Oklahoma City 117 35 25N 97 30W
Okmulgee 117 35 38N 96 0W
Oknitsa 56 48 25N 27 30 E
Okolo 90 2 37N 31 8 E
Okolona 117 34 0N 88 45W
Okondeka 92 21 38 S 15 37 E
Okonek 28 53 32N 16 51 E
Okrika 85 4 40N 7 10 E
Oktabrsk 58 49 28N 57 25 E
Oktyabrsk 55 53 11N 48 40 E
Oktyabrskiy, Byelorussia, U.S.S.R. 54 52 38N 28 53 E
Oktyabrskiy, R.S.F.S.R., U.S.S.R. 52 54 28N 53 28 E
Oktyabrskoy Revolyutsii, Os. 59 79 30N 97 0 E
Oktyabrskoye 58 62 28N 66 3 E
Oktyabrskoye = Zhovtnevoye 56 47 54N 32 2 E
Okulovka 54 58 25N 33 19 E
Okuru 101 43 55 S 168 55 E
Okushiri-Tō 74 42 15N 139 30 E
Okuta 85 9 14N 3 12 E
Okwa → 92 22 30 S 23 0 E
Ola 117 35 2N 93 10W
Ólafsfjörður 50 66 4N 18 39W
Ólafsvík 50 64 53N 23 43W
Olancha 119 36 15N 118 1W
Olanchito 121 15 30N 86 30W
Öland 49 56 45N 16 38 E
Olargues 20 43 34N 2 53 E
Olary 99 32 18 S 140 19 E
Olascoaga 124 35 15 S 60 39W
Olathe 116 38 50N 94 50W
Olavarría 124 36 55 S 60 20W
Oława 28 50 57N 17 20 E
Ólbia 40 40 55N 9 30 E
Ólbia, G. di 40 40 55N 9 35 E
Old Bahama Chan. = Bahama, Canal Viejo de 121 22 10N 77 30W
Old Castile = Castilla la Vieja □ 30 41 55N 4 0W
Old Castle 15 53 46N 7 10W
Old Cork 98 22 57 S 141 52 E
Old Crow 104 67 30N 140 5 E
Old Dongola 86 18 11N 30 44 E
Old Forge, N.Y., U.S.A. 113 43 43N 74 58W
Old Forge, Pa., U.S.A. 113 41 20N 75 46W
Old Fort → 109 58 36N 110 24W
Old Shinyanga 90 3 33 S 33 27 E
Old Speckle, Mt. 113 44 35N 70 57W
Old Town 107 45 0N 68 41W
Old Wives L. 109 50 5N 106 0W
Oldbury 13 51 38N 2 30W
Oldeani 90 3 22 S 35 35 E
Oldenburg, Niedersachsen, Ger. 24 53 10N 8 10 E
Oldenburg, Schleswig-Holstein, Ger. 24 54 16N 10 53 E
Oldenzaal 16 52 19N 6 53 E
Oldham 12 53 33N 2 8W
Oldman → 108 49 57N 111 42W
Olds 108 51 50N 114 10W
Olean 114 42 8N 78 25W
Olecko 28 54 2N 22 31 E
Oléggio 38 45 36N 8 38 E
Oleiros 30 39 56N 7 56W
Olekma → 59 60 22N 120 42 E
Olekminsk 59 60 25N 120 30 E
Olenegorsk 52 68 9N 33 18 E
Olenek 59 68 28N 112 18 E
Olenek → 59 73 0N 120 10 E
Olenino 54 56 15N 33 30 E
Oléron, Île d' 20 45 55N 1 15W
Oleśnica 28 51 13N 17 22 E
Olesno 28 50 51N 18 26 E
Olevsk 54 51 12N 27 39 E
Olga 59 43 50N 135 14 E
Olga, L. 106 49 47N 77 15W
Olga, Mt. 96 25 20 S 130 50 E
Olgastretet 4 78 35N 25 0 E
Ølgod 49 55 49N 8 36 E
Olhão 31 37 3N 7 48W
Olib 39 44 23N 14 44 E
Olib, I. 39 44 23N 14 44 E
Oliena 40 40 18N 9 22 E
Oliete 32 41 1N 0 41W
Olifants → 93 24 5 S 31 20 E
Olifantshoek 92 27 57 S 22 42 E
Ólimbos 45 35 44N 27 11 E
Ólimbos, Óros 44 40 6N 22 23 E
Olímpia 125 20 44 S 48 54W
Olimpo □ 124 20 30 S 58 45W
Olite 32 42 29N 1 40W
Oliva, Argent. 124 32 0 S 63 38W
Oliva, Spain 33 38 58N 0 9W
Oliva de la Frontera 31 38 17N 6 54W
Oliva, Punta del 30 43 37N 5 28W
Olivares 32 39 46N 2 20W
Oliveira 127 20 39 S 44 50W
Oliveira de Azemeis 30 40 49N 8 29W
Olivença 91 11 47 S 35 13 E
Olivenza 31 38 41N 7 9W
Oliver 108 49 13N 119 37W
Oliver L. 109 56 56N 103 22W
Olkhovka 57 49 48N 44 32 E
Olkusz 28 50 18N 19 33 E
Ollagüe 124 21 15 S 68 10W
Olmedo 30 41 20N 4 43W
Olney, Ill., U.S.A. 114 38 40N 88 0W
Olney, Tex., U.S.A. 117 33 25N 98 45W
Olofström 49 56 17N 14 32 E
Oloma 85 3 29N 11 19 E
Olomane → 107 50 14N 60 37W
Olomouc 27 49 38N 17 12 E
Olonets 52 61 10N 33 0 E
Olongapo 73 14 50N 120 18 E
Oloron, Gave d' 20 43 33N 1 5W
Oloron-Ste-Marie 20 43 11N 0 38W
Olot 32 42 11N 2 30 E
Olovo 42 44 8N 18 35 E
Olovyannaya 59 50 58N 115 35 E
Oloy → 59 66 29N 159 29 E
Olpe 24 51 2N 7 50 E
Olshanka 56 48 16N 30 58 E
Olshany 56 50 3N 35 53 E
Olsztyn 28 53 48N 20 29 E
Olsztyn □ 28 54 0N 21 0 E
Olsztynek 28 53 34N 20 19 E
Olt □ 46 44 20N 24 30 E
Olt → 46 43 50N 24 40 E
Olten 25 47 21N 7 53 E
Olteniţa 46 44 7N 26 42 E
Olton 117 34 16N 102 7W
Oltu 64 40 35N 41 58 E
Olvega 32 41 47N 2 0W
Olvera 31 36 55N 5 18W
Olympia, Greece 45 37 39N 21 39 E
Olympia, U.S.A. 118 47 0N 122 58W
Olympic Mts. 118 47 50N 123 45W
Olympic Nat. Park 118 47 48N 123 30W
Olympus, Mt. 118 47 52N 123 40W
Olympus, Mt. = Ólimbos, Óros 44 40 6N 22 23 E
Olyphant 113 41 27N 75 36W
Om → 58 54 59N 73 22 E
Om Hajer 87 14 20N 36 41 E
Ōmachi 74 36 30N 137 50 E
Omagh 15 54 36N 7 20W
Omagh □ 15 54 35N 7 15W
Omaha 116 41 15N 96 0W
Omak 118 48 24N 119 31W
Oman ■ 63 23 0N 58 0 E
Oman, G. of 65 24 30N 58 30 E
Omaruru 92 21 26 S 16 0 E
Omaruru → 92 22 7 S 14 15 E
Omate 126 16 45 S 71 0W
Ombai, Selat 73 8 30 S 124 50 E
Ombo 47 59 18N 6 0 E
Omboué 88 1 35 S 9 15 E
Ombrone → 38 42 39N 11 0 E
Omchi 83 21 22N 17 53 E
Omdurmân 87 15 40N 32 28 E
Omegna 38 45 52N 8 23 E
Omeonga 90 3 40 S 24 22 E
Ometepe, Isla de 121 11 32N 85 35W
Ometepec 120 16 39N 98 23W
Omez 62 32 22N 35 0 E
Omineca → 108 56 3N 124 16W
Omiš 39 43 28N 16 40 E
Omišalj 39 45 13N 14 32 E
Omitara 92 22 16 S 18 2 E
Ōmiya 74 35 54N 139 38 E
Omme Å → 49 55 56N 8 32 E
Ommen 16 52 31N 6 26 E
Omo → 81 6 25N 36 10 E
Omolon → 59 68 42N 158 36 E
Omsk 58 55 0N 73 12 E
Omsukchan 59 62 32N 155 48 E
Omul, Vf. 46 45 27N 25 29 E
Omulew → 28 53 5N 21 33 E
Ōmura 74 32 56N 130 0 E
Omurtag 43 43 8N 26 26 E
Ōmuta 74 33 0N 130 26 E
Omutninsk 55 58 45N 52 4 E
Oña 32 42 43N 3 25W
Onaga 116 39 32N 96 12W
Onalaska 116 43 53N 91 14W
Onamia 116 46 4N 93 38W
Onancock 114 37 42N 75 49W
Onang 73 3 2 S 118 49 E
Onaping L. 106 47 3N 81 30W
Onarheim 47 59 57N 5 35 E
Oñate 32 43 3N 2 25W
Onavas 120 28 28N 109 30W
Onawa 116 42 2N 96 2W
Onaway 114 45 21N 84 11W
Oncesti 46 43 56N 25 52 E
Oncócua 92 16 30 S 13 25 E
Onda 32 39 55N 0 17W
Ondangua 92 17 57 S 16 4 E
Ondárroa 32 43 19N 2 25W
Ondava → 27 48 27N 21 48 E
Ondo 85 7 4N 4 47 E
Ondo □ 85 7 0N 5 0 E
Öndörhaan 75 47 19N 110 39 E
Öndverðarnes 50 64 52N 24 0W
Onega 52 64 0N 38 10 E
Onega → 52 63 58N 37 55 E
Onega, G. of = Onezhskaya G. 52 64 30N 37 0 E
Onega, L. = Onezhskoye Oz. 52 62 0N 35 30 E
Onehunga 101 36 55 S 174 48 E

Oneida Ouesso

Oneida	**114**	43 5N	75 40W
Oneida L.	**114**	43 12N	76 0W
O'Neill	**116**	42 30N	98 38W
Onekotan, Ostrov	**59**	49 25N	154 45 E
Onema	**90**	4 35 S	24 30 E
Oneonta, Ala., U.S.A.	**115**	33 58N	86 29W
Oneonta, N.Y., U.S.A.	**114**	42 26N	75 5W
Onezhskaya Guba	**52**	64 30N	37 0 E
Onezhskoye Ozero	**52**	62 0N	35 30 E
Ongarue	**101**	38 42 S	175 19 E
Ongniud Qi	**76**	43 0N	118 38 E
Ongoka	**90**	1 20 S	26 0 E
Ongole	**70**	15 33N	80 2 E
Onguren	**59**	53 38N	107 36 E
Oni	**57**	42 33N	43 26 E
Onida	**116**	44 42N	100 5W
Onilahy →	**93**	23 34 S	43 45 E
Onitsha	**85**	6 6N	6 42 E
Onoda	**74**	34 2N	131 25 E
Ons, Islas d'	**30**	42 23N	8 55W
Onsala	**49**	57 26N	12 0 E
Onslow	**96**	21 40 S	115 12 E
Onslow B.	**115**	34 20N	77 20W
Onstwedde	**16**	53 2N	7 4 E
Ontake-San	**74**	35 53N	137 29 E
Ontaneda	**30**	43 12N	3 57W
Ontario, Calif., U.S.A.	**119**	34 2N	117 40W
Ontario, Oreg., U.S.A.	**118**	44 1N	117 1W
Ontario □	**106**	52 0N	88 10W
Ontario, L.	**106**	43 40N	78 0W
Onteniente	**33**	38 50N	0 35W
Ontonagon	**116**	46 52N	89 19W
Ontur	**33**	38 38N	1 29W
Oodnadatta	**96**	27 33 S	135 30 E
Ooldea	**96**	30 27 S	131 50 E
Oona River	**108**	53 57N	130 16W
Oorindi	**98**	20 40 S	141 1 E
Oost-Vlaanderen □	**16**	51 5N	3 50 E
Oostende	**16**	51 15N	2 50 E
Oosterhout	**16**	51 39N	4 47 E
Oosterschelde	**16**	51 33N	4 0 E
Ootacamund	**70**	11 30N	76 44 E
Ootsa L.	**108**	53 50N	126 2W
Ootsi	**92**	25 2 S	25 45 E
Opaka	**43**	43 28N	26 10 E
Opala, U.S.S.R.	**59**	51 58N	156 30 E
Opala, Zaïre	**88**	0 40 S	24 20 E
Opalenica	**28**	52 18N	16 24 E
Opan	**43**	42 13N	25 41 E
Opanake	**70**	6 35N	80 40 E
Opasatika	**106**	49 30N	82 50W
Opasquia	**109**	53 16N	93 34W
Opatija	**39**	45 21N	14 17 E
Opatów	**28**	50 50N	21 27 E
Opava	**27**	49 57N	17 58 E
Opelousas	**117**	30 35N	92 7W
Opémisca L.	**106**	50 0N	75 0W
Opheim	**118**	48 52N	106 30W
Ophir	**104**	63 10N	156 40W
Ophthalmia Ra.	**96**	23 15 S	119 30 E
Opi	**85**	6 36N	7 28 E
Opinaca →	**106**	52 15N	78 2W
Opinaca L.	**106**	52 39N	76 20W
Opiskotish, L.	**107**	53 10N	67 50W
Opobo	**85**	4 35N	7 34 E
Opochka	**54**	56 42N	28 45 E
Opoczno	**28**	51 22N	20 18 E
Opole	**28**	50 42N	17 58 E
Opole □	**28**	50 40N	17 56 E
Oporto = Porto	**30**	41 8N	8 40W
Opotiki	**101**	38 1 S	177 19 E
Opp	**115**	31 19N	86 13W
Oppegård	**47**	59 48N	10 48 E
Oppenheim	**25**	49 50N	8 22 E
Óppido Mamertina	**41**	38 16N	15 59 E
Oppland fylke □	**47**	61 15N	9 40 E
Oppstad	**47**	60 17N	11 40 E
Oprtalj	**39**	45 23N	13 50 E
Opua	**101**	35 19 S	174 9 E
Opunake	**101**	39 26 S	173 52 E
Opuzen	**42**	43 1N	17 34 E
Or Yehuda	**62**	32 2N	34 50 E
Ora, Israel	**62**	30 55N	35 1 E
Ora, Italy	**39**	46 20N	11 19 E
Oracle	**119**	32 36N	110 46W
Oradea	**46**	47 2N	21 58 E
Öræfajökull	**50**	64 2N	16 39W
Orahovac	**42**	42 24N	20 40 E
Orahovica	**42**	45 35N	17 52 E
Orai	**69**	25 58N	79 30 E
Oraison	**21**	43 55N	5 55 E
Oran, Alg.	**82**	35 45N	0 39W
Oran, Argent.	**124**	23 10 S	64 20W
Orange, Austral.	**97**	33 15 S	149 7 E
Orange, France	**21**	44 8N	4 47 E
Orange, Mass., U.S.A.	**113**	42 35N	72 15W
Orange, Tex., U.S.A.	**117**	30 10N	93 50W
Orange, Va., U.S.A.	**114**	38 17N	78 5W
Orange, C.	**127**	4 20N	51 30W
Orange Free State = Oranje Vrystaat □	**92**	28 30 S	27 0 E
Orange Grove	**117**	27 57N	97 57W
Orange Walk	**120**	18 6N	88 33W
Orangeburg	**115**	33 35N	80 53W
Orangeville	**106**	43 55N	80 5W
Oranienburg	**24**	52 45N	13 15 E
Oranje →	**92**	28 41 S	16 28 E
Oranje Vrystaat □	**92**	28 30 S	27 0 E
Oranjemund	**92**	28 38 S	16 29 E
Or'Aquiva	**62**	32 30N	34 54 E
Oras	**73**	12 9N	125 28 E
Orašje	**42**	45 1N	18 42 E
Orăştie	**46**	45 50N	23 10 E
Oraşul Stalin = Braşov	**46**	45 38N	25 35 E
Orava →	**27**	49 24N	19 20 E
Oravita	**42**	45 2N	21 43 E
Orb →	**20**	43 17N	3 17 E
Orba →	**38**	44 53N	8 37 E
Ørbæk	**49**	55 17N	10 39 E
Orbe	**25**	46 43N	6 32 E
Orbec	**18**	49 1N	0 23 E
Orbetello	**39**	42 26N	11 11 E
Órbigo →	**30**	42 5N	5 42W
Orbost	**97**	37 40 S	148 29 E
Örbyhus	**48**	60 15N	17 43 E
Orce	**33**	37 44N	2 28W
Orce →	**33**	37 44N	2 28W
Orchies	**19**	50 28N	3 14 E
Orchila, Isla	**126**	11 48N	66 10W
Orco →	**38**	45 10N	7 52 E
Ord →	**96**	15 33 S	138 15 E
Ord, Mt.	**96**	17 20 S	125 34 E
Ordenes	**30**	43 5N	8 29W
Orderville	**119**	37 18N	112 43W
Ordos = Mu Us Shamo	**76**	39 0N	109 0 E
Ordu	**64**	40 55N	37 53 E
Orduña, Álava, Spain	**32**	42 58N	2 58 E
Orduña, Granada, Spain	**33**	37 20N	3 30W
Ordway	**116**	38 15N	103 42W
Ordzhonikidze, R.S.F.S.R., U.S.S.R.	**57**	43 0N	44 43 E
Ordzhonikidze, Ukraine S.S.R., U.S.S.R.	**56**	47 39N	34 3 E
Ore, Sweden	**48**	61 8N	15 10 E
Ore, Zaïre	**90**	3 17N	29 30 E
Ore Mts. = Erzgebirge	**24**	50 25N	13 0 E
Orebić	**42**	43 0N	17 11 E
Örebro	**48**	59 20N	15 18 E
Örebro län □	**48**	59 27N	15 0 E
Oregon	**116**	42 1N	89 20W
Oregon □	**118**	44 0N	121 0W
Oregon City	**118**	45 21N	122 35W
Öregrund	**48**	60 21N	18 30 E
Öregrundsgrepen	**48**	60 25N	18 15 E
Orekhov	**56**	47 30N	35 48 E
Orekhovo-Zuyevo	**55**	55 50N	38 55 E
Orel	**55**	52 57N	36 3 E
Orel →	**56**	48 30N	34 54 E
Orellana, Canal de	**31**	39 2N	6 0W
Orellana la Vieja	**31**	39 1N	5 32W
Orellana, Pantano de	**31**	39 5N	5 10W
Orem	**118**	40 20N	111 45W
Oren	**45**	37 3N	27 57 E
Orenburg	**52**	51 45N	55 6 E
Orense	**30**	42 19N	7 55W
Orense □	**30**	42 15N	7 51W
Orepuki	**101**	46 19 S	167 46 E
Orestiás	**44**	41 30N	26 33 E
Øresund	**49**	55 45N	12 45 E
Orford Ness	**13**	52 6N	1 31 E
Orgañà	**32**	42 13N	1 20 E
Orgaz	**31**	39 39N	3 53W
Orgeyev	**56**	47 24N	28 50 E
Orgon	**21**	43 47N	5 3 E
Orgūn	**65**	32 55N	69 12 E
Orhon Gol →	**75**	49 30N	106 0 E
Ória	**41**	40 30N	17 38 E
Orient	**99**	28 7 S	142 50 E
Oriental, Cordillera	**126**	6 0N	73 0W
Oriente	**124**	38 44 S	60 37W
Origny-Ste-Benoîte	**19**	49 50N	3 30 E
Orihuela	**33**	38 7N	0 55W
Orihuela del Tremedal	**32**	40 33N	1 39W
Oriku	**44**	40 20N	19 30 E
Orinoco →	**126**	9 15N	61 30W
Orissa □	**69**	20 0N	84 0 E
Oristano	**40**	39 54N	8 35 E
Oristano, Golfo di	**40**	39 50N	8 22 E
Orizaba	**120**	18 50N	97 10W
Orizare	**43**	42 44N	27 39 E
Ørje	**47**	59 29N	11 39 E
Orjen	**42**	42 35N	18 34 E
Orjiva	**33**	36 53N	3 24W
Orkanger	**47**	63 18N	9 52 E
Orkelljunga	**49**	56 17N	13 17 E
Örkény	**27**	47 9N	19 26 E
Orkla →	**47**	63 18N	9 51 E
Orkney	**92**	26 58 S	26 40 E
Orkney □	**14**	59 0N	3 0W
Orkney Is.	**14**	59 0N	3 0W
Orla	**28**	52 42N	23 20 E
Orland	**118**	39 46N	122 12W
Orlando	**115**	28 30N	81 25W
Orlando, C. d'	**41**	38 10N	14 43 E
Orléanais	**19**	48 0N	2 0 E
Orléans	**19**	47 54N	1 52 E
Orleans	**113**	44 49N	72 10W
Orléans, Î. d'	**107**	46 54N	70 58W
Orlice →	**26**	50 5N	16 10 E
Orlické Hory	**27**	50 15N	16 30 E
Orlik	**59**	52 30N	99 55 E
Orlov	**27**	49 17N	20 51 E
Orlov Gay	**55**	50 56N	48 19 E
Orlovat	**42**	45 14N	20 33 E
Ormara	**66**	25 16N	64 33 E
Ormea	**38**	44 9N	7 54 E
Ormília	**44**	40 16N	23 39 E
Ormoc	**73**	11 0N	124 37 E
Ormond, N.Z.	**101**	38 33 S	177 56 E
Ormond, U.S.A.	**115**	29 13N	81 5W
Ormož	**39**	46 25N	16 10 E
Ormstown	**113**	45 8N	74 0W
Ornans	**19**	47 7N	6 10 E
Orne □	**18**	48 40N	0 5 E
Orne →	**18**	49 18N	0 15W
Orneta	**28**	54 8N	20 9 E
Ørnhøj	**49**	56 13N	8 34 E
Ornö	**48**	59 4N	18 24 E
Örnsköldsvik	**48**	63 17N	18 40 E
Oro →	**120**	25 35N	105 2W
Orocué	**126**	4 48N	71 20W
Orodo	**85**	5 34N	7 4 E
Orogrande	**119**	32 20N	106 4W
Orol	**30**	43 34N	7 39W
Oromocto	**107**	45 54N	66 29W
Oron	**85**	4 48N	8 14 E
Orono	**112**	43 59N	78 37W
Oropesa	**30**	39 57N	5 10W
Oroqen Zizhiqi	**76**	50 34N	123 43 E
Oroquieta	**73**	8 32N	123 44 E
Orós	**127**	6 15 S	38 55W
Orosei, G. di	**40**	40 15N	9 40 E
Orosháza	**27**	46 32N	20 42 E
Orotukan	**59**	62 16N	151 42 E
Oroville, Calif., U.S.A.	**118**	39 31N	121 30W
Oroville, Wash., U.S.A.	**118**	48 58N	119 30W
Orrefors	**49**	56 50N	15 45 E
Orroroo	**99**	32 43 S	138 38 E
Orrville	**112**	40 50N	81 46W
Orsa	**48**	61 7N	14 37 E
Orsara di Púglia	**41**	41 17N	15 16 E
Orsasjön	**48**	61 7N	14 37 E
Orsha	**54**	54 30N	30 25 E
Orsk	**52**	51 12N	58 34 E
Ørslev	**49**	55 3N	11 56 E
Orsogna	**39**	42 13N	14 17 E
Orşova	**46**	44 41N	22 25 E
Ørsted	**49**	56 30N	10 20 E
Orta, L. d'	**38**	45 48N	8 21 E
Orta Nova	**41**	41 20N	15 40 E
Orte	**39**	42 28N	12 23 E
Ortegal, C.	**30**	43 43N	7 52W
Orthez	**20**	43 29N	0 48W
Ortigueira	**30**	43 40N	7 50W
Ortles	**38**	46 31N	10 33 E
Ortón →	**126**	10 50 S	67 0W
Ortona	**39**	42 21N	14 24 E
Orune	**40**	40 25N	9 20 E
Oruro	**126**	18 0 S	67 9W
Orust	**49**	58 10N	11 40 E
Orūzgān □	**65**	33 30N	66 0 E
Orvault	**18**	47 17N	1 38W
Orvieto	**39**	42 43N	12 8 E
Orwell	**112**	41 32N	80 52W
Orwell →	**13**	52 2N	1 12 E
Oryakhovo	**43**	43 40N	23 57 E
Orzinuovi	**38**	45 24N	9 55 E
Orzyc →	**28**	52 46N	21 14 E
Orzysz	**28**	53 50N	21 58 E
Os	**47**	60 9N	5 30 E
Osa	**52**	57 17N	55 26 E
Osa →	**28**	53 33N	18 46 E
Osa, Pen. de	**121**	8 0N	84 0W
Osage, Iowa, U.S.A.	**116**	43 15N	92 50W
Osage, Wyo., U.S.A.	**116**	43 59N	104 25W
Osage →	**116**	38 35N	91 57W
Osage City	**116**	38 43N	95 51W
Ōsaka	**74**	34 40N	135 30 E
Osaka □	**74**	34 30N	135 30 E
Osawatomie	**116**	38 30N	94 55W
Osborne	**116**	39 30N	98 45W
Osby	**49**	56 23N	13 59 E
Osceola, Ark., U.S.A.	**117**	35 40N	90 0W
Osceola, Iowa, U.S.A.	**116**	41 0N	93 20W
Oschatz	**24**	51 17N	13 8 E
Oschersleben	**24**	52 2N	11 13 E
Óschiri	**40**	40 43N	9 7 E
Oscoda	**114**	44 26N	83 20W
Oscoda-Au-Sable	**112**	44 26N	83 20W
Osečina	**42**	44 23N	19 34 E
Ösel = Saaremaa	**54**	58 30N	22 30W
Osëry	**55**	54 52N	38 28 E
Osh	**58**	40 37N	72 49 E
Oshawa	**106**	43 50N	78 50W
ŌShima	**74**	34 44N	139 24 E
Oshkosh, Nebr., U.S.A.	**116**	41 27N	102 20W
Oshkosh, Wis., U.S.A.	**116**	44 3N	88 35W
Oshmyany	**54**	54 26N	25 52 E
Oshogbo	**85**	7 48N	4 37 E
Oshwe	**88**	3 25 S	19 28 E
Osica de Jos	**46**	44 14N	24 20 E
Osieczna	**28**	51 55N	16 40 E
Osijek	**42**	45 34N	18 41 E
Ósilo	**40**	40 45N	8 41 E
Osimo	**39**	43 28N	13 30 E
Osintorf	**54**	54 40N	30 39 E
Osipenko = Berdyansk	**56**	46 45N	36 50 E
Osipovichi	**54**	53 19N	28 33 E
Oskaloosa	**116**	41 18N	92 40W
Oskarshamn	**49**	57 15N	16 27 E
Oskélanéo	**106**	48 5N	75 15W
Oskol →	**55**	49 6N	37 25 E
Oslo	**47**	59 55N	10 45 E
Oslob	**73**	9 31N	123 26 E
Oslofjorden	**47**	59 20N	10 35 E
Osmanabad	**70**	18 5N	76 10 E
Osmancık	**56**	40 45N	34 47 E
Osmaniye	**64**	37 5N	36 10 E
Ösmo	**48**	58 58N	17 55 E
Osnabrück	**24**	52 16N	8 2 E
Ośno Lubuskie	**28**	52 28N	14 51 E
Osobláha	**27**	50 17N	17 44 E
Osogovska Planina	**42**	42 10N	22 30 E
Osor	**38**	44 42N	14 24 E
Osorio	**125**	29 53 S	50 17W
Osorno, Chile	**128**	40 25 S	73 0W
Osorno, Spain	**30**	42 24N	4 22W
Osoyoos	**108**	49 0N	119 30W
Ospika →	**108**	56 20N	124 0W
Osprey Reef	**97**	13 52 S	146 36 E
Oss	**16**	51 46N	5 32 E
Ossa de Montiel	**33**	38 58N	2 45W
Ossa, Mt.	**97**	41 52 S	146 3 E
Óssa, Oros	**44**	39 47N	22 42 E
Ossabaw I.	**115**	31 45N	81 8W
Osse →	**20**	44 7N	0 17 E
Ossining	**114**	41 9N	73 50W
Ossipee	**113**	43 41N	71 9W
Ossokmanuan L.	**107**	53 25N	65 0W
Ossora	**59**	59 20N	163 13 E
Ostashkov	**54**	57 4N	33 2 E
Oste →	**24**	53 30N	9 12 E
Ostend = Oostende	**16**	51 15N	2 50 E
Oster	**54**	50 57N	30 53 E
Osterburg	**24**	52 47N	11 44 E
Osterburken	**25**	49 26N	9 25 E
Österbybruk	**48**	60 13N	17 55 E
Österbymo	**49**	57 49N	15 15 E
Östergötlands län □	**49**	58 35N	15 45 E
Osterholz-Scharmbeck	**24**	53 14N	8 48 E
Østerild	**49**	57 2N	8 51 E
Österkorsberga	**49**	57 18N	15 6 E
Osterøya	**47**	60 32N	5 30 E
Östersund	**48**	63 10N	14 38 E
Østfold fylke □	**47**	59 25N	11 25 E
Ostfreisland	**24**	53 20N	7 30 E
Ostfriesische Inseln	**24**	53 45N	7 15 E
Óstia, Lido di (Lido di Roma)	**40**	41 43N	12 17 E
Ostiglía	**39**	45 4N	11 9 E
Ostra	**39**	43 40N	13 5 E
Ostrava	**27**	49 51N	18 18 E
Ostróda	**28**	53 42N	19 58 E
Ostrog	**54**	50 20N	26 30 E
Ostrogozhsk	**55**	50 55N	39 7 E
Ostrogróg Sźamotuły	**28**	52 37N	16 33 E
Ostrołeka	**28**	53 4N	21 32 E
Ostrołeka □	**28**	53 0N	21 30 E
Ostrov, Bulg.	**43**	43 40N	24 9 E
Ostrov, Romania	**46**	44 6N	27 24 E
Ostrov, U.S.S.R.	**54**	57 25N	28 20 E
Ostrów Lubelski	**28**	51 29N	22 51 E
Ostrów Mazowiecka	**28**	52 50N	21 51 E
Ostrów Wielkopolski	**28**	51 36N	17 44 E
Ostrowiec-Świętokrzyski	**28**	50 55N	21 22 E
Ostrozac	**42**	43 43N	17 49 E
Ostrzeszów	**28**	51 25N	17 52 E
Ostseebad-Külungsborn	**24**	54 10N	11 40 E
Ostuni	**41**	40 44N	17 34 E
Osum →	**43**	43 40N	24 50 E
Osumi →	**44**	40 40N	20 10 E
Ōsumi-Kaikyō	**74**	30 55N	131 0 E
Osuna	**31**	37 14N	5 8W
Oswego	**114**	43 29N	76 30W
Oswestry	**12**	52 52N	3 3W
Oświecim	**27**	50 2N	19 11 E
Otago □	**101**	44 44 S	169 10 E
Otago Harb.	**101**	45 47 S	170 42 E
Ōtake	**74**	34 12N	132 13 E
Otaki	**101**	40 45 S	175 10 E
Otaru	**74**	43 10N	141 0 E
Otava →	**26**	49 26N	14 12 E
Otavalo	**126**	0 13N	78 20W
Otavi	**92**	19 40 S	17 24 E
Otchinjau	**92**	16 30 S	13 56 E
Otelec	**42**	45 36N	20 50 E
Otero de Rey	**30**	43 6N	7 36W
Othello	**118**	46 53N	119 8W
Othonoí	**44**	39 52N	19 22 E
Óthris, Óros	**45**	39 4N	22 42 E
Otira Gorge	**101**	42 53 S	171 33 E
Otis	**116**	40 12N	102 58W
Otjiwarongo	**92**	20 30 S	16 33 E
Otmuchów	**28**	50 28N	17 10 E
Otočac	**39**	44 53N	15 12 E
Otorohanga	**101**	38 12 S	175 14 E
Otoskwin →	**106**	52 13N	88 6W
Otosquen	**109**	53 17N	102 1W
Otra →	**47**	58 8N	8 1 E
Otranto	**41**	40 9N	18 28 E
Otranto, C. d'	**41**	40 7N	18 30 E
Otranto, Str. of	**41**	40 15N	18 40 E
Ōtsu	**74**	35 0N	135 50 E
Otta	**47**	61 46N	9 32 E
Otta →	**47**	61 46N	9 31 E
Ottapalam	**70**	10 46N	76 23 E
Ottawa, Can.	**106**	45 27N	75 42W
Ottawa, Ill., U.S.A.	**116**	41 20N	88 55W
Ottawa, Kans., U.S.A.	**116**	38 40N	95 6W
Ottawa = Outaouais →	**106**	45 27N	74 8W
Ottawa Is.	**105**	59 35N	80 10W
Ottélé	**85**	3 38N	11 19 E
Ottenby	**49**	56 15N	16 24 E
Otter L.	**109**	55 35N	104 39W
Otter Rapids, Ont., Can.	**106**	50 11N	81 39W
Otter Rapids, Sask., Can.	**109**	55 38N	104 44W
Otterberg	**25**	49 30N	7 46 E
Otterndorf	**24**	53 47N	8 52 E
Ottersheim	**26**	48 21N	14 12 E
Otterup	**49**	55 30N	10 22 E
Otterville	**112**	42 55N	80 36W
Otto Beit Bridge	**91**	15 59 S	28 56 E
Ottosdal	**92**	26 46 S	25 59 E
Ottoshoop	**92**	25 45 S	25 58 E
Ottsjö	**48**	63 13N	13 2 E
Ottumwa	**116**	41 0N	92 25W
Otu	**85**	8 14N	3 22 E
Otukpa (Al Owuho)	**85**	7 9N	7 41 E
Oturkpo	**85**	7 16N	8 8 E
Otway, Bahía	**128**	53 30 S	74 0W
Otway, C.	**97**	38 52 S	143 30 E
Otwock	**28**	52 5N	21 20 E
Ötz	**26**	47 13N	10 53 E
Ötz →	**26**	47 14N	10 50 E
Ötztaler Alpen	**26**	46 45N	11 0 E
Ou →	**71**	20 4N	102 13 E
Ou-Sammyaku	**74**	39 20N	140 35 E
Ouachita →	**117**	31 38N	91 49W
Ouachita, L.	**117**	34 40N	93 25W
Ouachita Mts.	**117**	34 50N	94 30W
Ouadâne	**80**	20 50N	11 40W
Ouadda	**81**	8 15N	22 20 E
Ouagadougou	**85**	12 25N	1 30W
Ouahigouya	**84**	13 31N	2 25W
Ouahila	**82**	27 50N	5 0W
Ouahran = Oran	**82**	35 49N	0 39W
Oualâta	**84**	17 20N	6 55W
Ouallene	**82**	24 41N	1 11 E
Ouanda Djallé	**81**	8 55N	22 53 E
Ouango	**88**	4 19N	22 30 E
Ouargla	**83**	31 59N	5 16 E
Ouarkziz, Djebel	**82**	28 50N	8 0W
Ouarzazate	**82**	30 55N	6 50W
Ouatagouna	**85**	15 11N	0 43 E
Oubangi →	**88**	1 0N	17 50 E
Oubarakai, O. →	**83**	27 20N	9 0 E
Ouche →	**19**	47 6N	5 16 E
Ouddorp	**16**	51 50N	3 57 E
Oude Rijn →	**16**	52 12N	4 24 E
Oudenaarde	**16**	50 50N	3 37 E
Oudon	**18**	47 22N	1 19W
Oudon →	**18**	47 38N	1 18 E
Oudtshoorn	**92**	33 35 S	22 14 E
Oued Zem	**82**	32 52N	6 34W
Ouellé	**84**	7 26N	4 1W
Ouenza	**83**	35 57N	8 4 E
Ouessa	**84**	11 4N	2 47W
Ouessant, Île d'	**18**	48 28N	5 6W
Ouesso	**88**	1 37N	16 5 E

Ouest, Pte. — Papua New Guinea

Ouest, Pte. 107 49 52N 64 40W
Ouezzane 82 34 51N 5 35W
Ouidah 85 6 25N 2 0 E
Ouistreham 18 49 17N 0 18W
Oujda 82 34 41N 1 55W
Oujeft 80 20 2N 13 0W
Ould Yenjé 84 15 38N 12 16W
Ouled Djellal 83 34 28N 5 2 E
Ouled Naïl, Mts. des 82 34 30N 3 30 E
Oulmès 82 33 17N 6 0W
Oulu 50 65 1N 25 29 E
Oulu □ 50 65 10N 27 20 E
Oulujärvi 50 64 25N 27 15 E
Oulujoki ⤳ 50 65 1N 25 30 E
Oulx 38 45 2N 6 49 E
Oum Chalouba 81 15 48N 20 46 E
Oum-el-Bouaghi 83 35 55N 7 6 E
Oum el Ksi 82 29 4N 6 59W
Oum-er-Rbia, O. ⤳ 82 33 19N 8 21W
Oumé 84 6 21N 5 27W
Ounane, Dj. 83 25 4N 7 19 E
Ounguati 92 21 54 S 15 46 E
Ounianga-Kébir 81 19 4N 20 29 E
Ounianga Sérir 81 18 54N 19 51 E
Our ⤳ 16 49 55N 6 5 E
Ouray 119 38 3N 107 40W
Ourcq ⤳ 19 49 1N 3 1 E
Oureg, Oued el ⤳ 82 32 34N 2 10 E
Ouricuri 127 7 53 S 40 5W
Ourinhos 125 23 0 S 49 54W
Ourique 31 37 38N 8 16W
Ouro Fino 125 22 16 S 46 25W
Ouro Prêto 125 20 20 S 43 30W
Ouro Sogui 84 15 36N 13 19W
Oursi 85 14 41N 0 27W
Ourthe ⤳ 16 50 29N 5 35 E
Ouse 99 42 38 S 146 42 E
Ouse ⤳, Sussex, U.K. 13 50 43N 0 3 E
Ouse ⤳, Yorks., U.K. 12 54 3N 0 7 E
Oust 20 42 52N 1 13 E
Oust ⤳ 18 47 35N 2 6W
Outaouais ⤳ 106 45 27N 74 8W
Outardes ⤳ 107 49 24N 69 30W
Outat Oulad el Haj 82 33 22N 3 42W
Outer Hebrides 14 57 30N 7 40W
Outer I. 107 51 10N 58 35W
Outes 30 42 52N 8 55W
Outjo 92 20 5 S 16 7 E
Outlook, Can. 109 51 30N 107 0W
Outlook, U.S.A. 116 48 53N 104 46W
Outreau 19 50 40N 1 36 E
Ouvèze ⤳ 21 43 59N 4 51 E
Ouyen 97 35 1 S 142 22 E
Ouzouer-le-Marché 18 47 54N 1 32 E
Ovada 38 44 39N 8 40 E
Ovalau 101 17 40 S 178 48 E
Ovalle 124 30 33 S 71 18W
Ovar 30 40 51N 8 40W
Ovens ⤳ 100 36 2 S 146 12 E
Over Flakkee 16 51 45N 4 5 E
Overijssel □ 16 52 25N 6 35 E
Overpelt 16 51 12N 5 20 E
Overton 119 36 32N 114 31W
Övertorneå 50 66 23N 23 38 E
Overum 49 58 0N 16 20 E
Ovid 116 41 0N 102 17W
Ovidiopol 56 46 15N 30 30 E
Oviedo 30 43 25N 5 50W
Oviedo □ 30 43 20N 6 0W
Oviken 48 63 0N 14 23 E
Oviksfjällen 48 63 0N 13 49 E
Ovoro 85 5 26N 7 16 E
Övre Sirdal 47 58 48N 6 43 E
Ovruch 54 51 25N 28 45 E
Owaka 101 46 27 S 169 40 E
Owambo 92 17 20 S 16 30 E
Owase 74 34 7N 136 12 E
Owatonna 116 44 3N 93 10W
Owbeh 65 34 28N 63 10 E
Owego 114 42 6N 76 17W
Owen Falls 90 0 30N 33 5 E
Owen Sound 106 44 35N 80 55W
Owen Stanley Range 98 8 30 S 147 0 E
Owendo 88 0 17N 9 30 E
Owens L. 119 36 20N 118 0W
Owensboro 114 37 40N 87 5W
Owensville 116 38 20N 91 30W
Owerri 85 5 29N 7 0 E
Owl ⤳ 109 57 51N 92 44W
Owo 85 7 10N 5 39 E
Owosso 114 43 0N 84 10W
Owyhee 118 42 0N 116 3W
Owyhee ⤳ 118 43 46N 117 2W
Owyhee Res. 118 43 40N 117 16W
Ox Mts. 15 54 6N 9 0W
Oxberg 48 61 7N 14 11 E
Oxelösund 49 58 43N 17 15 E
Oxford, N.Z. 101 43 18 S 172 11 E
Oxford, U.K. 13 51 45N 1 15W
Oxford, Miss., U.S.A. 117 34 22N 89 30W
Oxford, N.C., U.S.A. 115 36 19N 78 36W
Oxford, Ohio, U.S.A. 114 39 30N 84 40W
Oxford □ 13 51 45N 1 15W
Oxford L. 109 54 51N 95 37W
Oxía 45 38 16N 21 5 E
Oxílithos 45 38 35N 24 7 E
Oxley 99 34 11 S 144 6 E
Oxnard 119 34 10N 119 14W
Oya 72 2 55N 111 55 E
Oyem 88 1 34N 11 31 E
Oyen 109 51 22N 110 28W
Öyeren 47 59 50N 11 15 E
Oykel ⤳ 14 57 55N 4 26W
Oymyakon 59 63 25N 142 44 E
Oyo 85 7 46N 3 56 E
Oyo □ 85 8 0N 3 30 E
Oyonnax 21 46 16N 5 40 E
Oyster B. 113 40 52N 73 32W
Øystese 47 60 22N 6 9 E
Ozamis (Mizamis) 73 8 15N 123 50 E
Ozark, Ala., U.S.A. 115 31 29N 85 39W
Ozark, Ark., U.S.A. 117 35 30N 93 50W
Ozark, Mo., U.S.A. 117 37 0N 93 15W
Ozark Plateau 117 37 20N 91 40W
Ozarks, L. of 116 38 10N 92 40W
Ózd 27 48 14N 20 15 E
Ozieri 40 40 35N 9 0 E
Ozimek 28 50 41N 18 11 E
Ozona 117 30 43N 101 11W
Ozorków 28 51 57N 19 16 E
Ozren 42 43 55N 18 29 E
Ozuluama 120 21 40N 97 50W
Ozun 46 45 47N 25 50 E

P

Pa 84 11 33N 3 19W
Pa-an 67 16 51N 97 40 E
Pa Sak ⤳ 71 15 30N 101 0 E
Paar ⤳ 25 48 13N 10 59 E
Paarl 92 33 45 S 18 56 E
Paatsi ⤳ 50 68 55N 29 0 E
Paauilo 110 20 3N 155 22W
Pab Hills 66 26 30N 66 45 E
Pabianice 28 51 40N 19 20 E
Pabna 69 24 1N 89 18 E
Pabo 90 3 1N 32 10 E
Pacaja ⤳ 127 1 56 S 50 50W
Pacaraima, Sierra 126 4 0N 62 30W
Pacasmayo 126 7 20 S 79 35W
Pacaudière, La 20 46 11N 3 52 E
Paceco 40 37 59N 12 32 E
Pachhar 68 24 40N 77 42 E
Pachino 41 36 43N 15 4 E
Pachora 68 20 38N 75 29 E
Pachuca 120 20 10N 98 40W
Pacific 108 54 48N 128 28W
Pacific-Antarctic Basin 95 46 0 S 95 0W
Pacific-Antarctic Ridge 95 43 0 S 115 0W
Pacific Grove 119 36 38N 121 58W
Pacific Ocean 94 10 0N 140 0W
Pacitan 73 8 12 S 111 7 E
Pacofi 108 53 0N 132 30W
Pacov 26 49 27N 15 0 E
Pacsa 27 46 44N 17 2 E
Paczków 28 50 28N 17 0 E
Padaido, Kepulauan 73 1 5 S 138 0 E
Padalarang 73 7 50 S 107 30 E
Padang 72 1 0 S 100 20 E
Padangpanjang 72 0 40 S 100 20 E
Padangsidempuan 72 1 30N 99 15 E
Padborg 49 54 49N 9 21 E
Paddockwood 109 53 30N 105 30W
Paderborn 24 51 42N 8 44 E
Padeşul 46 45 40N 22 22 E
Padina 46 44 50N 27 8 E
Padloping Island 105 67 0N 62 50W
Padmanabhapuram 70 8 16N 77 17 E
Pádova 39 45 24N 11 52 E
Padra 68 22 15N 73 7 E
Padrauna 69 26 54N 83 59 E
Padre I. 117 27 0N 97 20W
Padrón 30 42 41N 8 39W
Padstow 12 50 33N 4 57W
Padua = Pádova 39 45 24N 11 52 E
Paducah, Ky., U.S.A. 114 37 0N 88 40W
Paducah, Tex., U.S.A. 117 34 3N 100 16W
Padul 31 37 1N 3 38W
Padula 41 40 20N 15 40 E
Padwa 70 18 27N 82 47 E
Paeroa 101 37 23 S 175 41 E
Paesana 38 44 40N 7 18 E
Pag 39 44 30N 14 50 E
Paga 85 11 1N 1 8W
Pagadian 73 7 55N 123 30 E
Pagai Selatan 72 3 0 S 100 15W
Pagai Utara 72 2 35 S 100 0 E
Pagalu = Annobón 79 1 25 S 5 36 E
Pagastikós Kólpos 44 39 15N 23 0 E
Pagatan 72 3 33 S 115 59 E
Page, Ariz., U.S.A. 119 36 57N 111 27W
Page, N.D., U.S.A. 116 47 11N 97 37W
Paglieta 39 42 10N 14 30 E
Pagny-sur-Moselle 19 48 59N 6 2 E
Pago Pago 101 14 16 S 170 43W
Pagosa Springs 119 37 16N 107 4W
Pagwa River 106 50 2N 85 14W
Pahala 110 19 12N 155 25W
Pahang □ 71 3 40N 102 20 E
Pahang ⤳ 71 3 30N 103 9 E
Pahiatua 101 40 27 S 175 50 E
Pahokee 115 26 50N 80 40W
Pahrump 119 36 15N 116 0W
Paia 110 20 54N 156 22W
Paide 54 58 57N 25 31 E
Paignton 13 50 26N 3 33W
Päijänne, L. 51 61 30N 25 30 E
Pailin 71 12 46N 102 36 E
Paimbœuf 18 47 17N 2 0W
Paimpol 18 48 48N 3 4W
Painan 72 1 21 S 100 34 E
Painesville 114 41 42N 81 18W
Paint I. 109 55 28N 97 57W
Paint Rock 117 31 30N 99 56W
Painted Desert 119 36 0N 111 30W
Paintsville 114 37 50N 82 50W
Paisley, Can. 112 44 18N 81 16W
Paisley, U.K. 14 55 51N 4 27W
Paisley, U.S.A. 118 42 43N 120 40W
Paita 126 5 11 S 81 9W
Paiva ⤳ 30 41 4N 8 16W
Pajares 30 43 1N 5 46W
Pajares, Puerto de 30 43 0N 5 46W
Pajeczno 28 51 10N 19 0 E
Pak Lay 71 18 15N 101 27 E
Pakala 70 13 29N 79 8 E
Pakanbaru 72 0 30N 101 15 E
Pakaraima Mts. 126 6 0N 60 0W
Pakistan ■ 66 30 0N 70 0 E
Pakistan, East = Bangladesh ■ 67 24 0N 90 0 E
Pakokku 67 21 20N 95 0 E
Pakosc 28 52 48N 18 6 E
Pakpattan 68 30 25N 73 27 E
Pakrac 42 45 27N 17 12 E
Paks 27 46 38N 18 55 E
Pakse 71 15 5N 105 52 E
Paktīā □ 65 33 0N 69 15 E
Pakwach 90 2 28N 31 27 E
Pala, Chad 81 9 25N 15 5 E
Pala, Zaïre 90 6 45 S 29 30 E
Palabek 90 3 22N 32 33 E
Palacios 117 28 44N 96 12W
Palafrugell 32 41 55N 3 10 E
Palagiano 41 40 35N 17 0 E
Palagonía 41 37 20N 14 43 E
Palagruža 39 42 24N 16 15 E
Palaiokastron 45 35 12N 26 18 E
Palaiokhóra 45 35 16N 23 39 E
Pálairos 45 38 45N 20 51 E
Palais, Le 18 47 20N 3 10W
Palakol 70 16 31N 81 46 E
Palam 70 19 0N 77 0 E
Palamás 44 39 26N 22 4 E
Palamós 32 41 50N 3 10 E
Palampur 68 32 10N 76 30 E
Palana, Austral. 99 39 45 S 147 55 E
Palana, U.S.S.R. 59 59 10N 159 59 E
Palanan 73 17 8N 122 29 E
Palanan Pt. 73 17 17N 122 30 E
Palangkaraya 72 2 16 S 113 56 E
Palanpur 68 24 10N 72 25 E
Palapye 92 22 30 S 27 7 E
Palar ⤳ 70 12 27N 80 13 E
Palatka, U.S.A. 115 29 40N 81 40W
Palatka, U.S.S.R. 59 60 6N 150 54 E
* Palau Is. 94 7 30N 134 30 E
Palauig 73 15 26N 119 54 E
Palauk 71 13 10N 98 40 E
Palavas 20 43 32N 3 56 E
Palawan 72 9 30N 118 30 E
Palayancottai 70 8 45N 77 45 E
Palazzo San Gervásio 41 40 53N 15 58 E
Palazzolo Acreide 41 37 4N 14 54 E
Paldiski 54 59 23N 24 9 E
Pale 42 43 50N 18 38 E
Paleleh 73 1 10N 121 50 E
Palembang 72 3 0 S 104 50 E
Palencia 30 42 1N 4 34W
Palencia □ 30 42 31N 4 33W
Palermo, Italy 40 38 8N 13 20 E
Palermo, U.S.A. 118 39 30N 121 37W
Palestine, Asia 62 32 0N 35 0 E
Palestine, U.S.A. 117 31 42N 95 35W
Palestrina 40 41 50N 12 52 E
Paletwa 67 21 10N 92 50 E
Palghat 70 10 46N 76 42 E
Pali 68 25 50N 73 20 E
Palinuro, C. 41 40 1N 15 14 E
Palisade 116 40 21N 101 10W
Palitana 68 21 32N 71 49 E
Palizada 120 18 18N 92 8W
Palizzi 41 37 58N 15 59 E
Palk Bay 70 9 30N 79 15 E
Palk Strait 70 10 0N 79 45 E
Palkonda 70 18 36N 83 48 E
Palkonda Ra. 70 13 50N 79 20 E
Pallanza = Verbánia 38 45 50N 8 55 E
Pallasovka 55 50 4N 47 0 E
Palleru ⤳ 70 16 45N 80 2 E
Pallisa 90 1 12N 33 43 E
Pallu 68 28 59N 74 14 E
Palm Beach 115 26 46N 80 0W
Palm Is. 97 18 40 S 146 35 E
Palm Springs 119 33 51N 116 35W
Palma, Canary Is. 8 28 40N 17 50W
Palma, Mozam. 91 10 46 S 40 29 E
Palma ⤳ 127 12 33 S 47 52W
Palma, B. de 33 39 30N 2 39 E
Palma de Mallorca 32 39 35N 2 39 E
Palma del Río 31 37 43N 5 17W
Palma di Montechiaro 40 37 12N 13 46 E
Palma, La, Canary Is. 80 28 40N 17 50W
Palma, La, Panama 121 8 15N 78 0W
Palma, La, Spain 31 37 21N 6 38W
Palma Soriano 121 20 15N 76 0W
Palmahim 62 31 56N 34 44 E
Palmanova 39 45 54N 13 18 E
Palmares 127 8 41 S 35 28W
Palmarola 40 40 57N 12 50 E
Palmas 125 26 29 S 52 0W
Palmas, C. 84 4 27N 7 46W
Pálmas, G. di 40 39 0N 8 30 E
Palmdale 119 34 36N 118 7W
Palmeira dos Índios 127 9 25 S 36 37W
Palmeirinhas, Pta. das 88 9 2 S 12 57 E
Palmela 31 38 32N 8 57W
Palmer, Alaska, U.S.A. 104 61 35N 149 10W
Palmer, Mass., U.S.A. 113 42 9N 72 21W
Palmer ⤳, N. Terr., Austral. 96 24 46 S 133 25 E
Palmer ⤳, Queens., Austral. 98 15 34 S 142 26 E
Palmer Arch 5 64 15 S 65 0W
Palmer Lake 116 39 10N 104 52W
Palmer Land 5 73 0 S 60 0W
Palmerston 112 43 50N 80 51W
Palmerston, C. 97 21 32 S 149 29 E
Palmerston North 101 40 21 S 175 39 E
Palmerton 113 40 47N 75 36W
Palmetto 115 27 33N 82 33W
Palmi 41 38 21N 15 51 E
Palmira, Argent. 124 32 59 S 68 34W
Palmira, Colomb. 126 3 32N 76 16W
Palms 112 43 37N 82 47W
Palmyra, Mo., U.S.A. 116 39 45N 91 30W
Palmyra, N.Y., U.S.A. 112 42 5N 77 18W
Palmyra = Tudmur 64 34 30N 37 17 E
Palmyra Is. 95 5 52N 162 6W
Palni 70 10 30N 77 30 E
Palni Hills 70 10 14N 77 33 E
Palo Alto 119 37 25N 122 8W
Palo del Colle 41 41 4N 16 43 E
Paloma, La 124 30 35 S 71 0W
Palombara Sabina 39 42 4N 12 45 E
Palopo 73 3 0 S 120 16 E
Palos, Cabo de 33 37 38N 0 40W
Palouse 118 46 59N 117 5W
Palparara 98 24 47 S 141 28 E
Pålsboda 49 59 3N 15 22 E
Palu, Indon. 73 1 0 S 119 52 E
Palu, Turkey 64 38 45N 40 0 E
Paluan 73 13 26N 120 29 E
Palwal 68 28 8N 77 19 E
Pama 85 11 19N 0 44 E
Pamamaroo, L. 100 32 17 S 142 28 E
Pamanukan 73 6 16 S 107 49 E
Pamban I. 70 9 15N 79 20 E
Pamekasan 73 7 10 S 113 29 E
Pameungpeuk 73 7 38 S 107 44 E
Pamiers 20 43 7N 1 39 E
Pamir 58 37 40N 73 0 E
Pamlico ⤳ 115 35 25N 76 30W
Pamlico Sd. 115 35 20N 76 0W
Pampa 117 35 35N 100 58W
Pampa de las Salinas 124 32 1 S 66 58W
Pampa, La □ 124 36 50 S 66 0W
Pampanua 73 4 16 S 120 8 E
Pamparato 38 44 16N 7 54 E
Pampas, Argent. 124 35 0 S 63 0W
Pampas, Peru 126 12 20 S 74 50W
Pamplona, Colomb. 126 7 23N 72 39W
Pamplona, Spain 32 42 48N 1 38W
Pampoenpoort 92 31 3 S 22 40 E
Pana 116 39 25N 89 10W
Panaca 119 37 51N 114 23W
Panagyurishte 43 42 30N 24 15 E
Panaitan 73 6 35 S 105 10 E
Panaji (Panjim) 70 15 25N 73 50 E
Panamá 121 9 0N 79 25W
Panama ■ 121 8 48N 79 55W
Panama Canal 121 9 10N 79 37W
Panama City 115 30 10N 85 41W
Panamá, Golfo de 121 8 4N 79 20W
Panamint Mts. 119 36 30N 117 20W
Panão 126 9 55 S 75 55W
Panarea 41 38 38N 15 3 E
Panaro ⤳ 38 44 55N 11 25 E
Panarukan 73 7 40 S 113 52 E
Panay 73 11 10N 122 30 E
Panay, G. 73 11 0N 122 30 E
Pancake Ra. 119 38 30N 116 0W
Pančevo 42 44 52N 20 41 E
Panciu 46 45 54N 27 8 E
Panco 73 8 42 S 118 40 E
Pancorbo, Paso 32 42 32N 3 5W
Pandan 73 11 45N 122 10 E
Pandeglang 73 6 25 S 106 0 E
Pandharpur 70 17 41N 75 20 E
Pandhurna 68 21 36N 78 35 E
Pandilla 32 41 32N 3 43W
Pando 125 34 44 S 56 0W
Pando, L. = Hope L. 99 28 24 S 139 18 E
Panevezys 54 55 42N 24 25 E
Panfilov 58 44 10N 80 0 E
Panfilovo 55 50 25N 42 46 E
Pang-Long 67 23 11N 98 45 E
Pang-Yang 67 22 7N 98 48 E
Panga 90 1 52N 26 18 E
Pangaíon Óros 44 40 50N 24 0 E
Pangalanes, Canal des 93 22 48 S 47 50 E
Pangani 90 5 25 S 38 58 E
Pangani □ 90 5 25 S 39 0 E
Pangani ⤳ 90 5 26 S 38 58 E
Pangfou = Bengbu 77 32 56N 117 20 E
Pangil 90 3 10 S 26 35 E
Pangkah, Tanjung 73 6 51 S 112 33 E
Pangkalanberandan 72 4 1N 98 20 E
Pangkalanbuun 72 2 41 S 111 37 E
Pangkalansusu 72 4 2N 98 13 E
Pangkoh 72 3 5 S 114 8 E
Pangnirtung 105 66 8N 65 54W
Pangrango 73 6 46 S 107 1 E
Panguitch 119 37 52N 112 30W
Pangutaran Group 73 6 18N 120 34 E
Panhandle 117 35 23N 101 23W
Pani Mines 68 22 29N 73 50 E
Pania-Mutombo 90 5 11 S 23 51 E
Panipat 68 29 25N 77 2 E
Panjal Range 68 32 30N 76 50 E
Panjgur 66 27 0N 64 5 E
Panjim = Panaji 70 15 25N 73 50 E
Panjinad Barrage 65 29 22N 71 15 E
Pankajene 73 4 46 S 119 34 E
Pankalpinang 72 2 0 S 106 0 E
Pankshin 85 9 16N 9 25 E
Panna 69 24 40N 80 15 E
Panna Hills 69 24 40N 81 15 E
Pannuru 70 16 5N 80 34 E
Panorama 125 21 21 S 51 51W
Panruti 70 11 46N 79 35 E
Panshan 76 41 3N 122 2 E
Panshi 76 42 58N 126 5 E
Pantano 119 32 0N 110 32W
Pantar 73 8 28 S 124 10 E
Pantelleria 40 36 52N 12 0 E
Pantón 30 42 31N 7 37W
Pánuco 120 22 0N 98 15W
Panyam 85 9 27N 9 8 E
Panyu 77 22 51N 113 20 E
Páola 41 39 21N 16 2 E
Paola 116 38 36N 94 50W
Paonia 119 38 56N 107 37W
Paoting = Baoding 76 38 50N 115 28 E
Paot'ou = Baotou 76 40 32N 110 2 E
Paoua 88 7 9N 16 20 E
Papá 27 47 22N 17 30 E
Papagayo ⤳ 120 16 36N 99 43W
Papagayo, Golfo de 121 10 30N 85 50W
Papagni ⤳ 70 15 35N 77 45 E
Papakura 101 37 4 S 174 59 E
Papantla 120 20 30N 97 30W
Papar 72 5 45N 116 0 E
Pápas, Ákra 45 38 13N 21 20 E
Papenburg 24 53 7N 7 25 E
Papigochic ⤳ 120 29 9N 109 40W
Paposo 124 25 0 S 70 30W
Papua, Gulf of 98 9 0 S 144 50 E
Papua New Guinea ■ 94 8 0 S 145 0 E

* Renamed Belau

Papuča	**39**	44 22N	15 30 E
Papudo	**124**	32 29S	71 27W
Papuk	**42**	45 30N	17 30 E
Papun	**67**	18 0N	97 30 E
Pará = Belém	**127**	1 20S	48 30W
Pará □	**127**	3 20S	52 0W
Parábita	**41**	40 3N	18 8 E
Paraburdoo	**96**	23 14S	117 32 E
Paracatu	**127**	17 10S	46 50W
Parachilna	**99**	31 10S	138 21 E
Parachinar	**66**	33 55N	70 5 E
Paraćin	**42**	43 54N	21 27 E
Paradas	**31**	37 18N	5 29W
Paradela	**30**	42 44N	7 37W
Paradip	**69**	20 15N	86 35 E
Paradise	**118**	47 27N	114 17W
Paradise →	**107**	53 27N	57 19W
Paradise Valley	**118**	41 30N	117 28W
Parado	**73**	8 42S	118 30 E
Paradyz	**28**	51 19N	20 2 E
Paragould	**117**	36 5N	90 30W
Paragua →	**126**	6 55N	62 55W
Paragua, La	**126**	6 50N	63 20W
Paraguaçu →	**127**	12 45S	38 54W
Paraguaçu Paulista	**125**	22 22S	50 35W
Paraguaná, Pen. de	**126**	12 0N	70 0W
Paraguarí	**124**	25 36S	57 0W
Paraguarí □	**124**	26 0S	57 10W
Paraguay ■	**124**	23 0S	57 0W
Paraguay →	**124**	27 18S	58 38W
Paraíba = João Pessoa	**127**	7 10S	35 0W
Paraíba □	**127**	7 0S	36 0W
Paraíba do Sul →	**125**	21 37S	41 3W
Parainen	**51**	60 18N	22 18 E
Parakhino Paddubye	**54**	58 26N	33 10 E
Parakou	**85**	9 25N	2 40 E
Parálion-Astrous	**45**	37 25N	22 45 E
Paramagudi	**70**	9 31N	78 39 E
Paramaribo	**127**	5 50N	55 10W
Paramithiá	**44**	39 30N	20 35 E
Paramushir, Ostrov	**59**	50 24N	156 0 E
Paran →	**62**	30 20N	35 10 E
Paraná	**124**	31 45S	60 30W
Paranã	**127**	12 30S	47 48W
Paraná □	**125**	24 30S	51 0W
Paraná →	**124**	33 43S	59 15W
Paranaguá	**125**	25 30S	48 30W
Paranaíba →	**127**	20 6S	51 4W
Paranapanema →	**125**	22 40S	53 9W
Paranapiacaba, Serra do	**125**	24 31S	48 35W
Paranavaí	**125**	23 4S	52 56W
Parang, Jolo, Phil.	**73**	5 55N	120 54 E
Parang, Mindanao, Phil.	**73**	7 23N	124 16 E
Parapóla	**45**	36 55N	23 27 E
Paraspóri, Ákra	**45**	35 55N	27 15 E
Paratinga	**127**	12 40S	43 10W
Paratoo	**99**	32 42S	139 40 E
Parattah	**99**	42 22S	147 23 E
Paray-le-Monial	**21**	46 27N	4 7 E
Parbati →	**68**	25 50N	76 30 E
Parbhani	**68**	19 8N	76 52 E
Parchim	**24**	53 25N	11 50 E
Parczew	**28**	51 40N	22 52 E
Pardes Hanna	**62**	32 28N	34 57 E
Pardilla	**30**	41 33N	3 43W
Pardo →, Bahia, Brazil	**127**	15 40S	39 0W
Pardo →, Mato Grosso, Brazil	**125**	21 46S	52 9W
Pardo →, São Paulo, Brazil	**127**	20 10S	48 38W
Pardubice	**26**	50 3N	15 45 E
Pare	**73**	7 43S	112 12 E
Pare □	**90**	4 10S	38 0 E
Pare Mts.	**90**	4 0S	37 45 E
Parecis, Serra dos	**126**	13 0S	60 0W
Paredes de Nava	**30**	42 9N	4 42W
Paren	**59**	62 30N	163 15 E
Parent	**106**	47 55N	74 35W
Parent, Lac.	**106**	48 31N	77 1W
Parentis-en-Born	**20**	44 21N	1 4W
Parepare	**73**	4 0S	119 40 E
Parfino	**54**	57 59N	31 34 E
Parfuri	**93**	22 28S	31 17 E
Parguba	**52**	62 20N	34 27 E
Parham	**113**	44 39N	76 43W
Pariaguán	**126**	8 51N	64 34W
Pariaman	**72**	0 47S	100 11 E
Paricutín, Cerro	**120**	19 28N	102 15W
Parigi, Java, Indon.	**73**	7 42S	108 29 E
Parigi, Sulawesi, Indon.	**73**	0 50S	120 5 E
Parika	**126**	6 50N	58 20W
Parima, Serra	**126**	2 30N	64 0W
Parinari	**126**	4 35S	74 25W
Parincea	**46**	46 27N	27 9 E
Parîng	**46**	45 20N	23 37 E
Parintins	**127**	2 40S	56 50W
Pariparit Kyun	**67**	14 55S	93 45 E
Paris, Can.	**106**	43 12N	80 25W
Paris, France	**19**	48 50N	2 20 E
Paris, Idaho, U.S.A.	**118**	42 13N	111 30W
Paris, Ky., U.S.A.	**114**	38 12N	84 12W
Paris, Tenn., U.S.A.	**115**	36 20N	88 20W
Paris, Tex., U.S.A.	**117**	33 40N	95 30W
Paris, Ville de □	**19**	48 50N	2 20 E
Parish	**113**	43 24N	76 9W
Pariti	**73**	10 15S	123 45 E
Park City	**118**	40 42N	111 35W
Park Falls	**116**	45 58N	90 27W
Park Range	**118**	40 0N	106 30W
Park Rapids	**116**	46 56N	95 0W
Park River	**116**	48 25N	97 43W
Park Rynie	**93**	30 25S	30 45 E
Park View	**119**	36 45N	106 37W
Parker, Ariz., U.S.A.	**119**	34 8N	114 16W
Parker, S.D., U.S.A.	**116**	43 25N	97 7W
Parker Dam	**119**	34 13N	114 5W
Parkersburg	**114**	39 18N	81 31W
Parkerview	**109**	51 21N	103 18W
Parkes, A.C.T., Austral.	**97**	35 18S	149 8 E
Parkes, N.S.W., Austral.	**97**	33 9S	148 11 E
Parkside	**109**	53 10N	106 33W
Parkston	**116**	43 25N	98 0W
Parksville	**108**	49 20N	124 21W
Parlakimedi	**70**	18 45N	84 5 E
Parma, Italy	**38**	44 50N	10 20 E
Parma, Idaho, U.S.A.	**118**	43 49N	116 59W
Parma, Ohio, U.S.A.	**112**	41 25N	81 42W
Parma →	**38**	44 56N	10 26 E
Parnaguá	**127**	10 10S	44 38W
Parnaíba, Piauí, Brazil	**127**	2 54S	41 47W
Parnaíba, São Paulo, Brazil	**127**	19 34S	51 14W
Parnaíba →	**127**	3 0S	41 50W
Parnassós	**45**	38 35N	22 30 E
Párnis	**45**	38 14N	23 45 E
Párnon Óros	**45**	37 15N	22 45 E
Pärnu	**54**	58 28N	24 33 E
Parola	**68**	20 47N	75 7 E
Paroo →	**97**	31 28S	143 32 E
Paroo Chan.	**97**	30 50S	143 35 E
Páros, Greece	**45**	37 5N	25 9 E
Páros, Greece	**45**	37 5N	25 12 E
Parowan	**119**	37 54N	112 56W
Parpaillon	**21**	44 30N	6 40 E
Parral	**124**	36 10S	71 52W
Parramatta	**99**	33 48S	151 1 E
Parras	**120**	25 30N	102 20W
Parrett →	**13**	51 7N	2 58W
Parris I.	**115**	32 20N	80 30W
Parrsboro	**107**	45 30N	64 25W
Parry Is.	**4**	77 0N	110 0W
Parry Sound	**106**	45 20N	80 0W
Parsberg	**25**	49 10N	11 43 E
Parseta →	**28**	54 11N	15 34 E
Parshall	**116**	47 56N	102 11W
Parsnip →	**108**	55 10N	123 2W
Parsons	**117**	37 20N	95 17W
Partabpur	**70**	20 0N	80 42 E
Partanna	**40**	37 43N	12 51 E
Partapgarh	**68**	24 2N	74 40 E
Parthenay	**18**	46 38N	0 16W
Partinico	**40**	38 3N	13 6 E
Partur	**70**	19 40N	76 14 E
Paru →	**127**	1 33S	52 38W
Parur	**70**	10 13N	76 14 E
Paruro	**126**	13 45S	71 50W
Parvān □	**65**	35 0N	69 0 E
Parvatipuram	**70**	18 50N	83 25 E
Parys	**92**	26 52S	27 29 E
Pas-de-Calais □	**19**	50 30N	2 30 E
Pasadena, Calif., U.S.A.	**119**	34 5N	118 9W
Pasadena, Tex., U.S.A.	**117**	29 45N	95 14W
Pasaje	**126**	3 23S	79 50W
Pasaje →	**124**	25 39S	63 56W
Pascagoula	**117**	30 21N	88 30W
Pascagoula →	**117**	30 21N	88 35W
Paşcani	**46**	47 14N	26 45 E
Pasco	**118**	46 10N	119 0W
Pasco, Cerro de	**126**	10 45S	76 10W
Pasewalk	**24**	53 30N	14 0 E
Pasfield L.	**109**	58 24N	105 20W
Pasha →	**54**	60 29N	32 55 E
Pashmakli = Smolyan	**43**	41 36N	24 38 E
Pasing	**25**	48 9N	11 27 E
Pasir Mas	**71**	6 2N	102 8 E
Pasir Puteh	**71**	5 50N	102 24 E
Pasirian	**73**	8 13S	113 8 E
Pasłeka →	**28**	54 26N	19 46 E
Pasley, C.	**96**	33 52S	123 35 E
Pašman	**39**	43 58N	15 20 E
Pasni	**66**	25 15N	63 27 E
Paso de Indios	**128**	43 55S	69 0W
Paso de los Libres	**124**	29 44S	57 10W
Paso de los Toros	**124**	32 45S	56 30W
Paso Robles	**119**	35 40N	120 45W
Paspébiac	**107**	48 3N	65 17W
Pasrur	**68**	32 16N	74 43 E
Passage West	**15**	51 52N	8 20W
Passaic	**113**	40 50N	74 8W
Passau	**25**	48 34N	13 27 E
Passero, C.	**41**	36 42N	15 8 E
Passo Fundo	**125**	28 10S	52 20W
Passos	**127**	20 45S	46 37W
Passow	**24**	53 13N	14 10 E
Passy	**21**	45 55N	6 41 E
Pastaza →	**126**	4 50S	76 52W
Pastęk	**28**	54 3N	19 41 E
Pasto	**126**	1 13N	77 17W
Pastrana	**32**	40 27N	2 53W
Pasuruan	**73**	7 40S	112 44 E
Pasym	**28**	53 48N	20 49 E
Pásztó	**27**	47 52N	19 43 E
Patagonia, Argent.	**128**	45 0S	69 0W
Patagonia, U.S.A.	**119**	31 35N	110 45W
Patan, Gujarat, India	**70**	17 22N	73 57 E
Patan, Maharashtra, India	**68**	23 54N	72 14 E
Patani	**73**	0 20N	128 50 E
Pataudi	**68**	28 18N	76 48 E
Patay	**19**	48 2N	1 40 E
Patchewollock	**99**	35 22S	142 12 E
Patchogue	**114**	40 46N	73 1W
Patea	**101**	39 45S	174 30 E
Pategi	**85**	8 50N	5 45 E
Patensie	**92**	33 46S	24 49 E
Paternò	**41**	37 34N	14 53 E
Paternoster, Kepulauan	**72**	7 5S	118 15 E
Pateros	**118**	48 4N	119 58W
Paterson, Austral.	**100**	32 37S	151 39 E
Paterson, U.S.A.	**114**	40 55N	74 10W
Pathankot	**68**	32 18N	75 45 E
Pathfinder Res.	**118**	42 30N	107 0W
Pati	**73**	6 45S	111 3 E
Patiala	**68**	30 23N	76 26 E
Patine Kouka	**84**	12 45N	13 45W
Patkai Bum	**67**	27 0N	95 30 E
Pátmos	**45**	37 21N	26 36 E
Patna	**69**	25 35N	85 12 E
Patonga	**90**	2 45N	33 15 E
Patos de Minas	**127**	18 35S	46 32W
Patos, Lag. dos	**125**	31 20S	51 0 E
Patosi	**44**	40 42N	19 38 E
Patquía	**124**	25 30N	102 11W
Pátrai	**45**	38 14N	21 47 E
Pátraikós, Kólpos	**45**	38 17N	21 30 E
Patrocínio	**127**	18 57S	47 0W
Patta	**90**	2 10S	41 0 E
Pattada	**40**	40 35N	9 7 E
Pattanapuram	**70**	9 6N	76 50 E
Pattani	**71**	6 48N	101 15 E
Patten	**107**	45 59N	68 28W
Patterson, Calif., U.S.A.	**119**	37 30N	121 9W
Patterson, La., U.S.A.	**117**	29 44N	91 20W
Patti, India	**68**	31 17N	74 54 E
Patti, Italy	**41**	38 8N	14 57 E
Pattoki	**68**	31 5N	73 52 E
Patton	**112**	40 38N	78 40W
Pattukkottai	**70**	10 25N	79 20 E
Patuakhali	**69**	22 20N	90 25 E
Patuca →	**121**	15 50N	84 18W
Patuca, Punta	**121**	15 49N	84 14W
Pátzcuaro	**120**	19 30N	101 40W
Pau	**20**	43 19N	0 25W
Pau, Gave de	**20**	43 33N	1 12W
Pauillac	**20**	45 11N	0 46W
Pauini →	**126**	1 42S	62 50W
Pauk	**67**	21 27N	94 30 E
Paul I.	**107**	56 30N	61 20W
Paulhan	**20**	43 33N	3 28 E
Paulis = Isiro	**90**	2 47N	27 37 E
Paulistana	**127**	8 9S	41 9W
Paullina	**116**	42 55N	95 40W
Paulo Afonso	**127**	9 21S	38 15W
Paulpietersburg	**93**	27 23S	30 50 E
Pauls Valley	**117**	34 40N	97 17W
Pauni	**69**	20 48N	79 40 E
Pavelets	**55**	53 49N	39 14 E
Pavia	**38**	45 10N	9 10 E
Pavlikeni	**43**	43 14N	25 20 E
Pavlodar	**58**	52 33N	77 0 E
Pavlograd	**56**	48 30N	35 52 E
Pavlovo, Gorkiy, U.S.S.R.	**55**	55 58N	43 5 E
Pavlovo, Yakut A.S.S.R., U.S.S.R.	**59**	63 5N	115 25 E
Pavlovsk	**55**	50 26N	40 5 E
Pavlovskaya	**57**	46 17N	39 47 E
Pavlovskiy-Posad	**55**	55 47N	38 42 E
Pavullo nel Frignano	**38**	44 20N	10 50 E
Pawhuska	**117**	36 40N	96 25W
Pawling	**113**	41 35N	73 37W
Pawnee	**117**	36 24N	96 50W
Pawnee City	**116**	40 8N	96 10W
Pawtucket	**114**	41 51N	71 22W
Paximádhia	**45**	35 0N	24 35 E
Paxoí	**44**	39 14N	20 12 E
Paxton, Ill., U.S.A.	**114**	40 25N	88 7W
Paxton, Nebr., U.S.A.	**116**	41 12N	101 27W
Paya Bakri	**71**	2 3N	102 44 E
Payakumbah	**72**	0 20S	100 35 E
Payerne	**25**	46 49N	6 56 E
Payette	**118**	44 0N	117 0W
Paymogo	**31**	37 44N	7 21W
Payne L.	**105**	59 30N	74 30W
Paynesville, Liberia	**84**	6 20N	10 45W
Paynesville, U.S.A.	**116**	45 21N	94 44W
Pays Basque	**20**	43 15N	1 0W
Paysandú	**124**	32 19S	58 8W
Payson, Ariz., U.S.A.	**119**	34 17N	111 15W
Payson, Utah, U.S.A.	**118**	40 8N	111 41W
Paz →	**120**	13 44N	90 10W
Paz, Bahía de la	**120**	24 15N	110 25W
Paz, La, Entre Ríos, Argent.	**124**	30 50S	59 45W
Paz, La, San Luis, Argent.	**124**	33 30S	67 20W
Paz, La, Boliv.	**126**	16 20S	68 10W
Paz, La, Hond.	**120**	14 20N	87 47W
Paz, La, Mexico	**120**	24 10N	110 20W
Pazar	**64**	41 10N	40 50 E
Pazardzhik	**43**	42 12N	24 20 E
Pazin	**39**	45 14N	13 56 E
Pčinja →	**42**	41 50N	21 45 E
Pe Ell	**118**	46 30N	123 18W
Peabody	**113**	42 31N	70 56W
Peace →	**108**	59 0N	111 25W
Peace Point	**108**	59 7N	112 27W
Peace River	**108**	56 15N	117 18W
Peach Springs	**119**	35 36N	113 30W
Peak Downs	**98**	22 14S	148 0 E
Peak Hill	**99**	32 47S	148 11 E
Peak Range	**97**	22 50S	148 20 E
Peak, The	**12**	53 24N	1 53W
Peake	**99**	35 25S	140 0 E
Peale Mt.	**119**	38 25N	109 12W
Pearce	**119**	31 57N	109 56W
Pearl →	**117**	30 23N	89 45W
Pearl Banks	**70**	8 45N	79 45 E
Pearl City	**110**	21 24N	158 0W
Pearsall	**117**	28 55N	99 8W
Pearse I.	**108**	54 52N	130 14W
Peary Land	**4**	82 40N	33 0W
Pease →	**117**	34 12N	99 7W
Pebane	**91**	17 10S	38 8 E
Pebas	**126**	3 10S	71 46W
Peč	**42**	42 40N	20 17 E
Péccioli	**38**	43 32N	10 43 E
Pechea	**46**	45 36N	27 49 E
Pechenezhin	**56**	48 30N	24 48 E
Pechenga	**52**	69 30N	31 25 E
Pechnezhskoye Vdkhr.	**55**	50 0N	37 10 E
Pechora →	**52**	68 13N	54 15 E
Pechorskaya Guba	**52**	68 40N	54 0 E
Pechory	**54**	57 48N	27 40 E
Pecica	**42**	46 10N	21 3 E
Pečka	**42**	44 18N	19 33 E
Pécora, C.	**40**	39 28N	8 23 E
Pecos	**117**	31 25N	103 35W
Pecos →	**117**	29 42N	102 30W
Pécs	**27**	46 5N	18 15 E
Peddapalli	**70**	18 40N	79 24 E
Peddapuram	**70**	17 6N	82 5 E
Pedra Azul	**127**	16 2S	41 17W
Pedreiras	**127**	4 32S	44 40W
Pedrera, La	**126**	1 18S	69 43W
Pedro Afonso	**127**	9 0S	48 10W
Pedro Cays	**121**	17 5N	77 48W
Pedro de Valdivia	**124**	22 55S	69 38W
Pedro Juan Caballero	**125**	22 30S	55 40W
Pedro Miguel Locks	**120**	9 1N	79 36W
Pedro Muñoz	**33**	39 25N	2 56W
Pedrógão Grande	**30**	39 55N	8 9W
Peduyim	**62**	31 20N	34 37 E
Peebinga	**99**	34 52S	140 57 E
Peebles	**14**	55 40N	3 12W
Peekskill	**114**	41 18N	73 57W
Peel	**12**	54 14N	4 40W
Peel →, Austral.	**99**	30 50S	150 29 E
Peel →, Can.	**104**	67 0N	135 0W
Peene →	**24**	54 9N	13 46 E
Peera Peera Poolanna L.	**99**	26 30S	138 0 E
Peers	**108**	53 40N	116 0W
Pegasus Bay	**101**	43 20S	173 10 E
Peggau	**26**	47 12N	15 21 E
Pegnitz	**25**	49 45N	11 33 E
Pegnitz →	**25**	49 29N	10 59 E
Pego	**33**	38 51N	0 8W
Pegu Yoma	**67**	19 0N	96 0 E
Pehčevo	**42**	41 41N	22 55 E
Pehuajó	**124**	35 45S	62 0W
Peine, Chile	**124**	23 45S	68 8W
Peine, Ger.	**24**	52 19N	10 12 E
Peip'ing = Beijing	**76**	39 55N	116 20 E
Peiss	**25**	47 58N	11 47 E
Peissenberg	**25**	47 48N	11 4 E
Peitz	**24**	51 50N	14 23 E
Peixe	**127**	12 0S	48 40W
Pek →	**42**	44 45N	21 29 E
Pekalongan	**73**	6 53S	109 40 E
Pekan	**71**	3 30N	103 25 E
Pekin	**116**	40 35N	89 40W
Peking = Beijing	**76**	39 55N	116 20 E
Pelabuhan Ratu, Teluk	**73**	7 5S	106 30 E
Pelabuhanratu	**73**	7 0S	106 32 E
Pélagos	**44**	39 17N	24 4 E
Pelaihari	**72**	3 55S	114 45 E
Pelat, Mont	**21**	44 16N	6 42 E
Pełczyce	**28**	53 3N	15 16 E
Peleaga	**46**	45 22N	22 55 E
Pelee I.	**106**	41 47N	82 40W
Pelée, Mt.	**121**	14 48N	61 0W
Pelee, Pt.	**106**	41 54N	82 31W
Pelekech, mt.	**90**	3 52N	35 8 E
Peleng	**73**	1 20S	123 30 E
Pelham	**115**	31 5N	84 6W
Pelhřimov	**26**	49 24N	15 12 E
Pelican L.	**109**	52 28N	100 20W
Pelican Narrows	**109**	55 10N	102 56W
Pelican Portage	**108**	55 51N	112 35W
Pelican Rapids	**109**	52 45N	100 42W
Peljesac	**42**	42 55N	17 25 E
Pelkosenniemi	**50**	67 6N	27 28 E
Pella, Greece	**44**	40 46N	22 23 E
Pella, U.S.A.	**116**	41 30N	93 0W
Pélla □	**44**	40 52N	22 0 E
Péllaro	**41**	38 1N	15 40 E
Pellworm	**24**	54 30N	8 40 E
Pelly →	**104**	62 47N	137 19W
Pelly Bay	**105**	68 38N	89 50W
Pelly L.	**104**	66 0N	102 0W
Peloponnes = Pelóponnisos □	**45**	37 10N	22 0 E
Pelopónnisos □	**45**	37 10N	22 0 E
Peloritani, Monti	**41**	38 2N	15 25 E
Peloro, C.	**41**	38 15N	15 40 E
Pelorus Sound	**101**	40 59S	173 59 E
Pelotas	**125**	31 42S	52 23W
Pelòvo	**43**	43 26N	24 17 E
Pelvoux, Massif de	**21**	44 52N	6 20 E
Pemalang	**73**	6 53S	109 23 E
Pematang	**72**	0 12S	102 4 E
Pematangsiantar	**72**	2 57N	99 5 E
Pemba, Mozam.	**91**	12 58S	40 30 E
Pemba, Tanz.	**90**	5 0S	39 45 E
Pemba, Zambia	**91**	16 30S	27 28 E
Pemba Channel	**90**	5 0S	39 37 E
Pemberton, Austral.	**96**	34 30S	116 0 E
Pemberton, Can.	**108**	50 25N	122 50W
Pembina	**109**	48 58N	97 15W
Pembina →	**109**	49 0N	98 12W
Pembine	**114**	45 38N	87 59W
Pembino	**116**	48 58N	97 15W
Pembroke, Can.	**106**	45 50N	77 7W
Pembroke, U.K.	**13**	51 41N	4 57W
Pembroke, U.S.A.	**115**	32 5N	81 32W
Pen-y-Ghent	**12**	54 10N	2 15W
Peña de Francia, Sierra de	**30**	40 32N	6 10W
Peña, Sierra de la	**32**	42 32N	0 45W
Penafiel	**30**	41 12N	8 17W
Peñafiel	**30**	41 35N	4 7W
Peñaflor	**31**	37 43N	5 21W
Peñalara, Pico	**30**	40 51N	3 57W
Penamacôr	**30**	40 10N	7 10W
Penang = Pinang	**71**	5 25N	100 15 E
Penápolis	**125**	21 30S	50 0W
Peñaranda de Bracamonte	**30**	40 53N	5 13W
Peñarroya-Pueblonuevo	**31**	38 19N	5 16W
Peñas, C. de	**30**	43 42N	5 52W
Peñas de San Pedro	**33**	38 44N	2 0W
Penas, G. de	**128**	47 0S	75 0W
Peñausende	**30**	41 17N	5 52W
Pench'i = Benxi	**76**	41 20N	123 48 E
Pend Oreille →	**118**	49 4N	117 37W
Pend Oreille, L.	**118**	48 0N	116 30W
Pendálofon	**44**	40 14N	21 12 E
Pendelikón	**45**	38 10N	23 53 E
Pendembu	**84**	9 7N	12 14W
Pendleton	**118**	45 35N	118 50W
Penedo	**127**	10 15S	36 36W
Penetanguishene	**106**	44 50N	79 55W
Pengalengan	**73**	7 9S	107 30 E
Penge, Kasai Oriental, Congo	**90**	5 30S	24 33 E
Penge, Kivu, Congo	**90**	4 27S	28 25 E
Penglai	**76**	37 48N	120 42 E
Pengshui	**77**	29 17N	108 12 E
Penguin	**99**	41 8S	146 6 E
Penhalonga	**91**	18 52S	32 40 E
Peniche	**31**	39 19N	9 22W
Penicuik	**14**	55 50N	3 14W
Penida	**72**	8 45S	115 30 E
Peñíscola	**32**	40 22N	0 24 E
Penmarch	**18**	47 49N	4 21W
Penmarch, Pte. de	**18**	47 48N	4 22W
Pennabilli	**39**	43 50N	12 17 E
Pennant	**109**	50 32N	108 14W
Penne	**39**	42 28N	13 56 E

Pennel Glacier Piorini, L.

Pennel Glacier **5** 69 20 S 157 27 E
Penner → **70** 14 35N 80 10 E
Pennine, Alpi **38** 46 4N 7 30 E
Pennines **12** 54 50N 2 20W
Pennino, Mte. **39** 43 6N 12 54 E
Pennsylvania □ **114** 40 50N 78 0W
Penny **108** 53 51N 121 20W
Pennyan **114** 42 39N 77 7W
Peno **54** 57 2N 32 49 E
Penola **97** 37 25 S 140 21 E
Penong **96** 31 59 S 133 5 E
Penonomé **121** 8 31N 80 21W
Penrhyn Is. **95** 9 0 S 158 30W
Penrith, Austral. **97** 33 43 S 150 38 E
Penrith, U.K. **12** 54 40N 2 45W
Pensacola **115** 30 30N 87 10W
Pensacola Mts. **5** 84 0 S 40 0W
Pense **109** 50 25N 104 59W
Penshurst **99** 37 49 S 142 20 E
Penticton **108** 49 30N 119 38W
Pentland **97** 20 32 S 145 25 E
Pentland Firth **14** 58 43N 3 10W
Pentland Hills **14** 55 48N 3 25W
Penukonda **70** 14 5N 77 38 E
Penylan L. **109** 61 50N 106 20W
Penza **55** 53 15N 45 5 E
Penzance **13** 50 7N 5 32W
Penzberg **25** 47 46N 11 23 E
Penzhino **59** 63 30N 167 55 E
Penzhinskaya Guba **59** 61 30N 163 0 E
Penzlin **24** 53 32N 13 6 E
Peoria, Ariz., U.S.A. **119** 33 40N 112 15W
Peoria, Ill., U.S.A. **116** 40 40N 89 40W
Pepperwood **118** 40 23N 124 0W
Peqini **44** 41 4N 19 44 E
Pera Hd. **98** 12 55 S 141 37 E
Perabumilih **72** 3 27 S 104 15 E
Perak → **71** 5 10N 101 4 E
Perakhóra **45** 38 2N 22 56 E
Perales de Alfambra **32** 40 38N 1 0W
Perales del Puerto **30** 40 10N 6 40W
Peralta **32** 42 21N 1 49W
Pérama **45** 35 20N 24 40 E
Perast **42** 42 31N 18 47 E
Percé **107** 48 31N 64 13W
Perche **18** 48 31N 1 1 E
Perche, Collines du **18** 48 30N 0 40 E
Percy **18** 48 55N 1 11W
Percy Is. **98** 21 39 S 150 16 E
Pereira **126** 4 49N 75 43W
Perekerten **99** 34 55 S 143 40 E
Perekop **56** 46 10N 33 42 E
Pereslavi-Zalesskiy **55** 56 45N 38 50 E
Pereyaslav Khmelnitskiy **54** 50 3N 31 28 E
Pérez, I. **120** 22 24N 89 42W
Perg **26** 48 15N 14 38 E
Pergamino **124** 33 52 S 60 30W
Pérgine Valsugano **39** 46 4N 11 15 E
Pérgola **39** 43 35N 12 50 E
Perham **116** 46 36N 95 36W
Perhentian, Kepulauan **71** 5 54N 102 42 E
Periam **42** 46 2N 20 59 E
Péribonca → **107** 48 45N 72 5W
Péribonca, L. **107** 50 1N 71 10W
Perico **124** 24 20 S 65 5W
Pericos **120** 25 3N 107 42W
Périers **18** 49 11N 1 25W
Périgord **20** 45 0N 0 40 E
Périgueux **20** 45 10N 0 42 E
Perijá, Sierra de **126** 9 30N 73 3W
Peristéra **45** 39 15N 23 58 E
Periyakulam **70** 10 5N 77 30 E
Periyar → **70** 10 15N 76 10 E
Periyar, L. **70** 9 25N 77 10 E
Perkam, Tg. **73** 1 35 S 137 50 E
Perković **39** 43 41N 16 10 E
Perlas, Arch. de las **121** 8 41N 79 7W
Perlas, Punta de **121** 12 30N 83 30W
Perleberg **24** 53 5N 11 50 E
Perlevka **55** 51 48N 38 57 E
Perlez **42** 45 11N 20 22 E
Perlis □ **71** 6 30N 100 15 E
Perm (Molotov) **52** 58 0N 57 10 E
Përmeti **44** 40 15N 20 21 E
Pernambuco = Recife **127** 8 0 S 35 0W
Pernambuco □ **127** 8 0 S 37 0W
Pernik **42** 42 35N 23 2 E
Péronne **19** 49 55N 2 57 E
Perosa Argentina **38** 44 57N 7 11 E
Perow **108** 54 35N 126 10W
Perpendicular Pt. **99** 31 37 S 152 52 E
Perpignan **20** 42 42N 2 53 E
Perros-Guirec **18** 48 49N 3 28W
Perry, Fla., U.S.A. **115** 30 9N 83 40W
Perry, Ga., U.S.A. **115** 32 25N 83 41W
Perry, Iowa, U.S.A. **116** 41 48N 94 5W
Perry, Maine, U.S.A. **115** 44 59N 67 20W
Perry, Okla., U.S.A. **117** 36 20N 97 20W
Perryton **117** 36 28N 100 48W
Perryville **117** 37 42N 89 50W
Persberg **48** 59 47N 14 15 E
Persepolis **65** 29 55N 52 50 E
Persia = Iran ■ **65** 35 0N 50 0 E
Persian Gulf **65** 27 0N 50 0 E
Perstorp **49** 56 10N 13 25 E
Perth, Austral. **96** 31 57 S 115 52 E
Perth, Can. **106** 44 55N 76 15W
Perth, U.K. **14** 56 24N 3 27W
Perth Amboy **114** 40 31N 74 16W
Perthus, Le **20** 42 30N 2 53 E
Pertuis **21** 43 42N 5 30 E
Peru, Ill., U.S.A. **116** 41 18N 89 12W
Peru, Ind., U.S.A. **114** 40 42N 86 0W
Peru ■ **126** 8 0 S 75 0W
Peru-Chile Trench **95** 20 0 S 72 0W
Perúgia **39** 43 6N 12 24 E
Perušić **39** 44 40N 15 22 E
Pervomaysk, R.S.F.S.R., U.S.S.R. **55** 54 56N 43 58 E
Pervomaysk, Ukraine S.S.R., U.S.S.R. **56** 48 10N 30 46 E
Pervouralsk **52** 56 55N 60 0 E
Pésaro **39** 43 55N 12 53 E
Pescara **39** 42 28N 14 13 E
Pescara → **39** 42 28N 14 13 E
Peschanokopskoye **57** 46 14N 41 4 E
Péscia **38** 43 54N 10 40 E
Pescina **39** 42 0N 13 39 E
Peshawar **66** 34 2N 71 37 E
* Peshawar □ **66** 33 30N 71 20 E
Peshkopia **44** 41 41N 20 25 E
Peshtera **43** 42 2N 24 18 E
Peshtigo **114** 45 4N 87 46W
Peski **55** 51 14N 42 29 E
Peskovka **55** 59 23N 52 20 E
Pêso da Régua **30** 41 10N 7 47W
Pesqueira **127** 8 20 S 36 42W
Pesqueria → **120** 25 54N 99 11W
Pessac **20** 44 48N 0 37W
Pest □ **27** 47 29N 19 5 E
Pestovo **54** 58 33N 35 42 E
Pestravka **55** 52 28N 49 57 E
Péta **45** 39 10N 21 2 E
Petah Tiqwa **62** 32 6N 34 53 E
Petalidhion **45** 36 57N 21 55 E
Petaling Jaya **71** 3 4N 101 42 E
Petaluma **118** 38 13N 122 39W
Petange **16** 49 33N 5 55 E
Petatlán **120** 17 31N 101 16W
Petauke **91** 14 14 S 31 20 E
Petawawa **106** 45 54N 77 17W
Petén Itzá, Lago **120** 16 58N 89 50W
Peter 1st, I. **5** 69 0 S 91 0W
Peter Pond L. **109** 55 55N 108 44W
Peterbell **106** 48 36N 83 21W
Peterborough, Austral. **97** 32 58 S 138 51 E
Peterborough, Can. **112** 44 20N 78 20W
Peterborough, U.K. **13** 52 35N 0 14W
Peterborough, U.S.A. **113** 42 55N 71 59W
Peterhead **14** 57 30N 1 49W
Petersburg, Alas., U.S.A. **108** 56 50N 133 0W
Petersburg, Ind., U.S.A. **114** 38 30N 87 15W
Petersburg, Va., U.S.A. **114** 37 17N 77 26W
Petersburg, W. Va., U.S.A. **114** 38 59N 79 10W
Petford **98** 17 20 S 144 58 E
Petília Policastro **41** 39 7N 16 48 E
Petit Bois I. **115** 30 16N 88 25W
Petit-Cap **107** 48 3N 64 30W
Petit Goâve **121** 18 27N 72 51W
Petit-Quevilly, Le **18** 49 26N 1 0 E
Petit Saint Bernard, Col du **38** 45 40N 6 52 E
Petitcodiac **107** 45 57N 65 11W
Petite Baleine → **106** 55 50N 77 0W
Petite Saguenay **107** 48 15N 70 4W
Petitsikapau, L. **107** 54 37N 66 25W
Petlad **68** 22 30N 72 45 E
Peto **120** 20 10N 88 53W
Petone **101** 41 13 S 174 53 E
Petoskey **106** 45 22N 84 57W
Petra, Jordan **62** 30 20N 35 22 E
Petra, Spain **32** 39 37N 3 6 E
Petra, Ostrova **4** 76 15N 118 30 E
Petralia **41** 37 49N 14 4 E
Petrel **33** 38 30N 0 46W
Petrich **43** 41 24N 23 13 E
Petrijanec **39** 46 23N 16 17 E
Petrikov **54** 52 11N 28 29 E
Petrila **46** 45 29N 23 29 E
Petrinja **39** 45 28N 16 18 E
Petrolândia **127** 9 5 S 38 20W
Petrolia **106** 42 54N 82 9W
Petrolina **127** 9 24 S 40 30W
Petromagoúla **45** 38 31N 23 0 E
Petropavlovsk **58** 54 53N 69 13 E
Petropavlovsk-Kamchatskiy **59** 53 3N 158 43 E
Petrópolis **125** 22 33 S 43 9W
Petroşeni **46** 45 28N 23 20 E
Petroskey **114** 45 22N 84 57W
Petrova Gora **39** 45 15N 15 45 E
Petrovac, Crna Gora, Yugo. **42** 42 13N 18 57 E
Petrovac, Srbija, Yugo. **42** 44 22N 21 26 E
Petrovaradin **42** 45 16N 19 55 E
Petrovsk **55** 52 22N 45 19 E
Petrovsk-Zabaykalskiy **59** 51 20N 108 55 E
Petrovskoye = Svetlograd **57** 45 25N 42 58 E
Petrozavodsk **52** 61 41N 34 20 E
Petrus Steyn **93** 27 38 S 28 8 E
Petrusburg **92** 29 4 S 25 26 E
Petukhovka **54** 53 42N 30 54 E
Peumo **124** 34 21 S 71 12W
Peureulak **72** 4 48N 97 45 E
Pevek **59** 69 41N 171 19 E
Peveragno **38** 44 20N 7 37 E
Peyrehorade **20** 43 34N 1 7W
Peyruis **21** 44 1N 5 56 E
Pézenas **20** 43 28N 3 24 E
Pezinok **27** 48 17N 17 17 E
Pfaffenhofen **25** 48 31N 11 31 E
Pfarrkirchen **25** 48 25N 12 57 E
Pfeffenhausen **25** 48 40N 11 58 E
Pforzheim **25** 48 53N 8 43 E
Pfullendorf **25** 47 55N 9 15 E
Pfungstadt **25** 49 47N 8 36 E
Phala **92** 23 45 S 26 50 E
Phalodi **68** 27 12N 72 24 E
Phalsbourg **19** 48 46N 7 15 E
Phan Rang **71** 11 34N 109 0 E
Phan Thiet **71** 11 1N 108 9 E
Phanae **45** 38 8N 25 87 E
Phangan, Ko **71** 9 45N 100 0 E
Phangnga **71** 8 28N 98 30 E
Phanh Bho Ho Chi Minh **71** 10 58N 106 40 E
Pharenda **69** 27 5N 83 17 E
Phatthalung **71** 7 39N 100 6 E
Phelps, N.Y., U.S.A. **112** 42 57N 77 5W
Phelps, Wis., U.S.A. **116** 46 2N 89 2W
Phelps L. **109** 59 15N 103 15W
Phenix City **115** 32 30N 85 0W
Phetchabun **71** 16 25N 101 8 E
Phetchabun, Thiu Khao **71** 16 0N 101 20 E
Phetchaburi **71** 13 1N 99 55 E
Phichai **71** 17 22N 100 10 E
Philadelphia, Miss., U.S.A. **117** 32 47N 89 5W
Philadelphia, N.Y., U.S.A. **113** 44 9N 75 40W
Philadelphia, Pa., U.S.A. **114** 40 0N 75 10W
Philip **116** 44 4N 101 42W
Philippeville **16** 50 12N 4 33 E
Philippi **44** 41 1N 24 16 E
Philippi L. **98** 24 20 S 138 55 E
Philippines ■ **73** 12 0N 123 0 E
Philippolis **92** 30 15 S 25 16 E
Philippopolis = Plovdiv **43** 42 8N 24 44 E
Philipsburg, Mont., U.S.A. **118** 46 20N 113 21W
Philipsburg, Pa., U.S.A. **112** 40 53N 78 10W
Philipstown **92** 30 28 S 24 30 E
Phillip **97** 38 30 S 145 12 E
Phillips, Texas, U.S.A. **117** 35 48N 101 17W
Phillips, Wis., U.S.A. **116** 45 41N 90 22W
Phillipsburg, Kans., U.S.A. **116** 39 48N 99 20W
Phillipsburg, Pa., U.S.A. **113** 40 43N 75 12W
Phillott **99** 27 53 S 145 50 E
Philmont **113** 42 14N 73 37W
Philomath **118** 44 28N 123 21W
Phitsanulok **71** 16 50N 100 12 E
Phnom Dangrek **71** 14 20N 104 0 E
Phnom Penh **71** 11 33N 104 55 E
Phnom Thbeng **71** 13 50N 104 56 E
Phoenix, Ariz., U.S.A. **119** 33 30N 112 10W
Phoenix, N.Y., U.S.A. **113** 43 13N 76 18W
Phoenix Is. **94** 3 30 S 172 0W
Phoenixville **113** 40 12N 75 29W
Phong Saly **71** 21 42N 102 9 E
Phra Chedi Sam Ong **71** 15 16N 98 23 E
Phra Nakhon Si Ayutthaya **71** 14 25N 100 30 E
Phrae **71** 18 7N 100 9 E
Phrao **71** 19 23N 99 15 E
Phu Doan **71** 21 40N 105 10 E
Phu Loi **71** 20 14N 103 14 E
Phu Ly **71** 20 35N 105 50 E
Phu Qui **71** 19 20N 105 20 E
Phuket **71** 7 52N 98 22 E
Phulera (Phalera) **68** 26 52N 75 16 E
† Phuoc Le **71** 10 30N 107 10 E
Piacenza **38** 45 2N 9 42 E
Piádena **38** 45 8N 10 22 E
Pialba **97** 25 20 S 152 45 E
Pian Cr. → **99** 30 2 S 148 12 E
Piana **21** 42 15N 8 34 E
Pianella **39** 42 24N 14 5 E
Pianoro **39** 44 20N 11 20 E
Pianosa, Puglia, Italy **39** 42 12N 15 44 E
Pianosa, Toscana, Italy **38** 42 36N 10 4 E
Piapot **109** 49 59N 109 8W
Piare → **39** 45 32N 12 44 E
Pias **31** 38 1N 7 29W
Piaseczno **28** 52 5N 21 2 E
Piaski **28** 51 8N 22 52 E
Piastów **28** 52 12N 20 48 E
Piatra **46** 43 51N 25 9 E
Piatra Neamţ **46** 46 56N 26 21 E
Piatra Olt **46** 44 22N 24 16 E
Piauí □ **127** 7 0 S 43 0W
Piave → **39** 45 32N 12 44 E
Piazza Armerina **41** 37 21N 14 20 E
Pibor → **87** 7 35N 33 0 E
Pibor Post **87** 6 47N 33 3 E
Pica **126** 20 35 S 69 25W
Picardie **19** 50 0N 2 15 E
Picardie, Plaine de **19** 50 0N 2 0 E
Picardy = Picardie **19** 50 0N 2 15 E
Picayune **117** 30 31N 89 40W
Picerno **41** 40 40N 15 37 E
Pichilemu **124** 34 22 S 72 0W
Pickerel L. **106** 48 40N 91 25W
Pickle Lake **106** 51 30N 90 12W
Pico **8** 38 28N 28 18W
Pico Truncado **128** 46 40 S 68 0W
Picos Ancares, Sierra de **30** 42 51N 6 52W
Picquigny **19** 49 56N 2 10 E
Picton, Austral. **99** 34 12 S 150 34 E
Picton, Can. **106** 44 1N 77 9W
Picton, N.Z. **101** 41 18 S 174 3 E
Pictou **107** 45 41N 62 42W
Picture Butte **108** 49 55N 112 45W
Picún Leufú **128** 39 30 S 69 5W
Pidurutalagala **70** 7 10N 80 50 E
Piedad, La **120** 20 20N 102 1W
Piedicavallo **38** 45 41N 7 57 E
Piedmont **115** 33 55N 85 39W
Piedmont = Piemonte **38** 45 0N 7 30 E
Piedmont Plat. **115** 34 0N 81 30W
Piedmonte d'Alife **41** 41 22N 14 22 E
Piedra → **32** 41 18N 1 47W
Piedrabuena **31** 39 0N 4 10W
Piedrahita **30** 40 28N 5 23W
Piedras Blancas Pt. **119** 35 45N 121 18W
Piedras Negras **120** 28 35N 100 35W
Piedras, R. de las → **126** 12 30 S 69 15W
Piemonte □ **38** 45 0N 7 30 E
Piensk **28** 51 16N 15 2 E
Pierce **118** 46 29N 115 53W
Piercefield **113** 44 13N 74 35W
Pieria □ **44** 40 13N 22 25 E
Pierre, France **19** 46 54N 5 13 E
Pierre, U.S.A. **116** 44 23N 100 20W
Pierre Benite, Barrage **21** 45 42N 4 49 E
Pierrefeu **21** 43 8N 6 9 E
Pierrefonds **19** 49 20N 3 0 E
Pierrefontaine **19** 47 14N 6 32 E
Pierrefort **20** 44 55N 2 50 E
Pierrelatte **21** 44 23N 4 43 E
Piešťany **27** 48 38N 17 55 E
Piesting → **27** 48 6N 16 40 E
Pieszyce **28** 50 43N 16 33 E
Piet Retief **93** 27 1 S 30 50 E
Pietarsaari **50** 63 40N 22 43 E
Pietermaritzburg **93** 29 35 S 30 25 E
Pietersburg **93** 23 54 S 29 25 E
Pietraperzia **41** 37 26N 14 8 E
Pietrasanta **38** 43 57N 10 12 E
Pietrosu **46** 47 12N 25 8 E
Pietrosul **46** 47 35N 24 43 E
Pieve di Cadore **39** 46 25N 12 22 E
Pieve di Teco **38** 44 3N 7 54 E
Pievepélago **38** 44 12N 10 35 E
Pigádhia **45** 35 30N 27 12 E
Pigadhítsa **44** 39 59N 21 23 E
Pigeon **114** 43 50N 83 17W
Pigeon I. **70** 14 2N 74 20 E
Piggott **117** 36 20N 90 10W
Pigna **38** 43 57N 7 40 E
Pigüe **124** 37 36 S 62 25W
Pihani **69** 27 36N 80 15 E
Pikalevo **54** 59 37N 34 0 E
Pikes Peak **116** 38 50N 105 10W
Piketberg **92** 32 55 S 18 40 E
Pikeville **114** 37 30N 82 30W
Pikwitonei **109** 55 35N 97 9W
Piła **28** 53 10N 16 48 E
Pila **33** 38 16N 1 11W
Piła □ **28** 53 0N 17 0 E
Pilaia **44** 40 32N 22 59 E
Pilani **68** 28 22N 75 33 E
Pilar, Brazil **127** 9 36 S 35 56W
Pilar, Parag. **124** 26 50 S 58 20W
Pilas **73** 6 39N 121 37 E
Pilawa **28** 51 57N 21 32 E
Pilbara **96** 21 15 S 118 16 E
Pilcomayo → **124** 25 21 S 57 42W
Pili **45** 36 50N 27 15 E
Pilibhit **69** 28 40N 79 50 E
Pilica → **28** 51 52N 21 17 E
Pilion **44** 39 27N 23 7 E
Pilis **27** 47 17N 19 35 E
Pilisvörösvár **27** 47 38N 18 56 E
Pilkhawa **68** 28 43N 77 42 E
Pilos **45** 36 55N 21 42 E
Pilot Mound **109** 49 15N 98 54W
Pilot Point **117** 33 26N 97 0W
Pilot Rock **118** 45 30N 118 50W
Pilsen = Plzen **26** 49 45N 13 22 E
Pilštanj **39** 46 8N 15 39 E
Pilzno **27** 50 0N 21 16 E
Pima **119** 32 54N 109 50W
Pimba **97** 31 18 S 136 46 E
Pimenta Bueno **126** 11 35 S 61 10W
Pimentel **126** 6 45 S 79 55W
Pina **32** 41 29N 0 33W
Pinang **71** 5 25N 100 15 E
Pinar del Río **121** 22 26N 83 40W
Pinaroo **97** 35 17 S 140 53 E
Pincehely **27** 46 41N 18 27 E
Pincher Creek **108** 49 30N 113 57W
Pinchi L. **108** 54 38N 124 30W
Pinckneyville **116** 38 5N 89 20W
Pîncota **42** 46 20N 21 45 E
Pińczów **28** 50 32N 20 32 E
Pind Dadan Khan **68** 32 36N 73 7 E
Pindiga **85** 9 58N 10 53 E
Pindos Óros **44** 40 0N 21 0 E
Pindus Mts. = Pindos Óros **44** 40 0N 21 0 E
Pine **119** 34 27N 111 30W
Pine → **109** 58 50N 105 38W
Pine Bluff **117** 34 10N 92 0W
Pine, C. **107** 46 37N 53 32W
Pine City **116** 45 46N 93 0W
Pine Creek **96** 13 50 S 132 10 E
Pine Falls **109** 50 34N 96 11W
Pine, La **118** 43 40N 121 30W
Pine Pass **108** 55 25N 122 42W
Pine Point **108** 60 50N 114 28W
Pine Ridge **116** 43 0N 102 35W
Pine River, Can. **109** 51 45N 100 30W
Pine River, U.S.A. **116** 46 43N 94 24W
Pinedale **119** 34 23N 110 16W
Pinega → **52** 64 8N 46 54 E
Pinehill **98** 23 38 S 146 57 E
Pinerolo **38** 44 47N 7 21 E
Pineto **39** 42 36N 14 4 E
Pinetop **119** 34 10N 109 57W
Pinetown **93** 29 48 S 30 54 E
Pinetree **118** 43 42N 105 52W
Pineville, Ky., U.S.A. **115** 36 42N 83 42W
Pineville, La., U.S.A. **117** 31 22N 92 30W
Piney **19** 48 22N 4 21 E
Ping → **71** 15 42N 100 9 E
Pingding **76** 37 47N 113 38 E
Pingdingshan **77** 33 43N 113 27 E
Pingdong **75** 22 39N 120 30 E
Pingdu **76** 36 42N 119 59 E
Pingguo **77** 23 19N 107 36 E
Pinghe **77** 24 17N 117 21 E
Pingjiang **77** 28 45N 113 36 E
Pingle **77** 24 40N 110 40 E
Pingliang **76** 35 35N 106 31 E
Pingluo **76** 38 52N 106 30 E
Pingnan **77** 23 33N 110 22 E
Pingtan Dao **77** 25 29N 119 47 E
Pingwu **75** 32 25N 104 30 E
Pingxiang, Guangxi Zhuangzu, China **75** 22 6N 106 46 E
Pingxiang, Jiangxi, China **77** 27 43N 113 48 E
Pingyao **76** 37 12N 112 10 E
Pinhal **125** 22 10 S 46 46W
Pinhel **30** 40 50N 7 1W
Pini **72** 0 10N 98 40 E
Piniós →, Ilia, Greece **45** 37 48N 21 20 E
Piniós →, Trikkala, Greece **44** 39 55N 22 10 E
Pinjarra **96** 32 37 S 115 52 E
Pink → **109** 56 50N 103 50W
Pinkafeld **27** 47 22N 16 9 E
Pinneberg **24** 53 39N 9 48 E
Pinos **120** 22 20N 101 40W
Pinos, I. de **121** 21 40N 82 40W
Pinos Pt. **119** 36 38N 121 57W
Pinos Puente **31** 37 15N 3 45W
Pinrang **73** 3 46 S 119 41 E
Pinsk **54** 52 10N 26 1 E
Pintados **126** 20 35 S 69 40W
Pinyang **77** 27 42N 120 31 E
Pinyug **52** 60 5N 48 0 E
Pinzolo **38** 46 9N 10 45 E
Pioche **119** 38 0N 114 35W
Piombino **38** 42 54N 10 30 E
Piombino, Canale di **38** 42 50N 10 25 E
Pioner, Os. **59** 79 50N 92 0 E
Pionki **28** 51 29N 21 28 E
Piorini, L. **126** 3 15 S 62 35W

* *Now part of North West Frontier* □

† *Renamed Ba Ria*

Piotrków Trybunalski 28 51 23N 19 43 E
Piotrków Trybunalski □ 28 51 30N 19 45 E
Piove di Sacco 39 45 18N 12 1 E
Pip 65 26 45N 60 10 E
Pipar 68 26 25N 73 31 E
Pipariya 68 22 45N 78 23 E
Pipéri 44 39 20N 24 19 E
Pipestone 116 44 0N 96 20W
Pipestone → 106 52 53N 89 23W
Pipestone Cr. → 109 49 42N 100 45W
Pipmuacan, Rés. 107 49 45N 70 30W
Pipriac 18 47 49N 1 58W
Piqua 114 40 10N 84 10W
Piquiri → 125 24 3 S 54 14W
Piracicaba 125 22 45 S 47 40W
Piracuruca 127 3 50 S 41 50W
Piræus = Piraiévs 45 37 57N 23 42 E
Piraiévs 45 37 57N 23 42 E
Piraiévs □ 45 37 0N 23 30 E
Piráino 41 38 10N 14 52 E
Pirajuí 125 21 59 S 49 29W
Piran (Pirano) 39 45 31N 13 33 E
Pirané 124 25 42 S 59 6W
Pirapora 127 17 20 S 44 56W
Pirdop 43 42 40N 24 10 E
Pirganj 69 25 51N 88 24 E
Pirgos, Ilía, Greece 45 37 40N 21 27 E
Pirgos, Messinia, Greece 45 36 50N 22 16 E
Pirgovo 43 43 44N 25 43 E
Piriac-sur-Mer 18 47 22N 2 33W
Piribebuy 124 25 26 S 57 2W
Pirin Planina 43 41 40N 23 30 E
Pirineos 32 42 40N 1 0 E
Piripiri 127 4 15 S 41 46W
Pirmasens 25 49 12N 7 30 E
Pirna 24 50 57N 13 57 E
Pirojpur 69 22 35N 90 1 E
Pirot 42 43 9N 22 39 E
Pirtleville 119 31 25N 109 35W
Piru 73 3 4 S 128 12 E
Piryatin 54 50 15N 32 25 E
Piryí 45 38 13N 25 59 E
Pisa 38 43 43N 10 23 E
Pisa → 28 53 14N 21 52 E
Pisagua 126 19 40 S 70 15W
Pisarovina 39 45 35N 15 50 E
Pisciotta 41 40 7N 15 12 E
Pisco 126 13 50 S 76 12W
Piscu 46 45 30N 27 43 E
Písek 26 49 19N 14 10 E
Pishan 75 37 30N 78 33 E
Pising 73 5 8 S 121 53 E
Pissos 20 44 19N 0 49W
Pisticci 41 40 24N 16 33 E
Pistóia 38 43 57N 10 53 E
Pistol B. 109 62 25N 92 37W
Pisuerga → 30 41 33N 4 52W
Pisz 28 53 38N 21 49 E
Pitarpunga, L. 99 34 24 S 143 30 E
Pitcairn I. 95 25 5 S 130 5W
Pite älv → 50 65 20N 21 25 E
Piteå 50 65 20N 21 25 E
Piterka 55 50 41N 47 29 E
Piteşti 46 44 52N 24 54 E
Pithapuram 70 17 10N 82 15 E
Píthion 44 41 24N 26 40 E
Pithiviers 19 48 10N 2 13 E
Pitigliano 39 42 38N 11 40 E
Pitlochry 14 56 43N 3 43W
Pitt I. 108 53 30N 129 50W
Pittsburg, Calif., U.S.A. 118 38 1N 121 50W
Pittsburg, Kans., U.S.A. 117 37 21N 94 43W
Pittsburg, Tex., U.S.A. 117 32 59N 94 58W
Pittsburgh 114 40 25N 79 55W
Pittsfield, Ill., U.S.A. 116 39 35N 90 46W
Pittsfield, Mass., U.S.A. 114 42 28N 73 17W
Pittsfield, N.H., U.S.A. 113 43 17N 71 18W
Pittston 114 41 19N 75 50W
Pittsworth 99 27 41 S 151 37 E
Pituri → 98 22 35 S 138 30 E
Piura 126 5 15 S 80 38W
Piva → 42 43 20N 18 50 E
Piwniczna 27 49 27N 20 42 E
Piyai 44 39 17N 21 25 E
Pizzo 41 38 44N 16 10 E
Placentia 107 47 20N 54 0W
Placentia B. 107 47 0N 54 40W
Placerville 118 38 47N 120 51W
Placetas 121 22 15N 79 44W
Plačkovica 42 41 45N 22 30 E
Plain Dealing 117 32 56N 93 41W
Plainfield 114 40 37N 74 28W
Plains, Kans., U.S.A. 117 37 20N 100 35W
Plains, Mont., U.S.A. 118 47 27N 114 57W
Plains, Tex., U.S.A. 117 33 11N 102 50W
Plainview, Nebr., U.S.A. 116 42 25N 97 48W
Plainview, Tex., U.S.A. 117 34 10N 101 40W
Plainville 116 39 18N 99 19W
Plainwell 114 42 28N 85 40W
Plaisance 20 43 36N 0 3 E
Pláka 44 40 0N 25 24 E
Plakenska Planina 42 41 14N 21 2 E
Plakhino 58 67 45N 86 5 E
Planá 26 49 50N 12 44 E
Plancoët 18 48 32N 2 13W
Plandište 42 45 16N 21 10 E
Planina, Slovenija, Yugo. 39 46 10N 15 20 E
Planina, Slovenija, Yugo. 39 45 47N 14 19 E
Plankinton 116 43 45N 98 27W
Plano 117 33 0N 96 45W
Plant City 115 28 0N 82 8W
Plant, La 116 45 11N 100 40W
Plaquemine 117 30 20N 91 15W
Plasencia 30 40 3N 6 8W
Plaški 39 45 4N 15 22 E
Plassen 48 61 9N 12 30 E
Plaster Rock 107 46 53N 67 22W
Plata, La 124 35 0 S 57 55W
Plata, Río de la 124 34 45 S 57 30W
Platani → 40 37 23N 13 16 E
Plateau 5 79 55 S 40 0 E
Plateau □ 85 8 0N 8 30 E
Plateau du Coteau du Missouri 116 47 9N 101 5W
Platí, Ákra- 44 40 27N 24 0 E
Plato 126 9 47N 74 47W
Platte 116 43 28N 98 50W
Platte → 116 39 16N 94 50W
Platteville 116 40 18N 104 47W
Plattling 25 48 46N 12 53 E
Plattsburg 114 44 41N 73 30W
Plattsmouth 116 41 0N 95 50W
Plau 24 53 27N 12 16 E
Plauen 24 50 29N 12 9 E
Plav 42 42 38N 19 57 E
Plavinas 54 56 35N 25 46 E
Plavnica 42 42 20N 19 13 E
Plavsk 55 53 40N 37 18 E
Playgreen L. 109 54 0N 98 15W
Pleasant Bay 107 46 51N 60 48W
Pleasant Hill 116 38 48N 94 14W
Pleasanton 117 29 0N 98 30W
Pleasantville 114 39 25N 74 30W
Pléaux 20 45 8N 2 13 E
Pleiku (Gia Lai) 71 13 57N 108 0 E
Plélan-le-Grand 18 48 0N 2 7W
Plémet 18 48 11N 2 36W
Pléneuf-Val-André 18 48 35N 2 32W
Plenita 46 44 14N 23 10 E
Plenty, Bay of 101 37 45 S 177 0 E
Plentywood 116 48 45N 104 35W
Plesetsk 52 62 40N 40 10 E
Plessisville 107 46 14N 71 47W
Plestin-les-Grèves 18 48 40N 3 39W
Pleszew 28 51 53N 17 47 E
Pleternica 42 45 17N 17 48 E
Pletipi L. 107 51 44N 70 6W
Pleven 43 43 26N 24 37 E
Plevlja 42 43 21N 19 21 E
Ploče 42 43 4N 17 26 E
Płock 28 52 32N 19 40 E
Płock □ 28 52 30N 19 45 E
Plöcken Passo 39 46 37N 12 57 E
Ploëmeur 18 47 44N 3 26W
Ploërmel 18 47 55N 2 26W
Ploieşti 46 44 57N 26 5 E
Plomárion 45 38 58N 26 24 E
Plomb du Cantal 20 45 2N 2 48 E
Plombières 19 47 59N 6 27 E
Plomin 39 45 8N 14 10 E
Plön 24 54 8N 10 22 E
Plöner See 24 45 10N 10 22 E
Plonge, Lac La 109 55 8N 107 20W
Płońsk 28 52 37N 20 21 E
Płoty 28 53 48N 15 18 E
Plouaret 18 48 37N 3 28W
Plouay 18 47 55N 3 21W
Ploučnice → 26 50 46N 14 13 E
Ploudalmézeau 18 48 34N 4 41W
Plougasnou 18 48 42N 3 49W
Plouha 18 48 41N 2 57W
Plouhinec 18 48 0N 4 29W
Plovdiv 43 42 8N 24 44 E
Plum I. 113 41 10N 72 12W
Plummer 118 47 21N 116 59W
Plumtree 91 20 27 S 27 55 E
Plunge 54 55 53N 21 59 E
Pluvigner 18 47 46N 3 1W
Plymouth, U.K. 13 50 23N 4 9W
Plymouth, Ind., U.S.A. 114 41 20N 86 19W
Plymouth, Mass., U.S.A. 113 41 58N 70 40W
Plymouth, N.C., U.S.A. 115 35 54N 76 46W
Plymouth, N.H., U.S.A. 113 43 44N 71 41W
Plymouth, Pa., U.S.A. 113 41 17N 76 0W
Plymouth, Wis., U.S.A. 114 43 42N 87 58W
Plymouth Sd. 13 50 20N 4 10W
Plynlimon = Pumlumon Fawr 13 52 29N 3 47W
Plyussa 54 58 40N 29 20 E
Plyussa → 54 58 40N 29 0 E
Plzen 26 49 45N 13 22 E
Pniewy 28 52 31N 16 16 E
Pô 85 11 14N 1 5W
Po → 38 44 57N 12 4 E
Po, Foci del 39 44 55N 12 30 E
Po Hai = Bo Hai 76 39 0N 120 0 E
Pobé 85 7 0N 2 56 E
Pobeda 59 65 12N 146 12 E
Pobedino 59 49 51N 142 49 E
Pobedy Pik 58 40 45N 79 58 E
Pobiedziska 28 52 29N 17 11 E
Pobla de Lillet, La 32 42 16N 1 59 E
Pobla de Segur 32 42 15N 0 58 E
Pobladura de Valle 30 42 6N 5 44W
Pocahontas, Arkansas, U.S.A. 117 36 18N 91 0W
Pocahontas, Iowa, U.S.A. 116 42 41N 94 42W
Pocatello 118 42 50N 112 25W
Počátky 26 49 15N 15 14 E
Pochep 54 52 58N 33 29 E
Pochinki 55 54 41N 44 59 E
Pochinok 54 54 28N 32 29 E
Pöchlarn 26 48 12N 15 12 E
Pochontas 108 53 10N 117 51W
Pochutla 120 15 50N 96 31W
Pocomoke City 114 38 4N 75 32W
Poços de Caldas 125 21 50 S 46 33W
Poddebice 28 51 54N 18 58 E
Poděbrady 26 50 9N 15 8 E
Podensac 20 44 40N 0 22W
Podgorač 42 45 27N 18 13 E
Podgorica = Titograd 42 42 30N 19 19 E
Podkamennaya Tunguska → 59 61 50N 90 13 E
Podlapac 39 44 37N 15 47 E
Podmokly 26 50 48N 14 10 E
Podoleni 46 46 46N 26 39 E
Podolínec 27 49 16N 20 31 E
Podolsk 55 55 25N 37 30 E
Podor 84 16 40N 15 2W
Podporozhy 52 60 55N 34 2 E
Podravska Slatina 42 45 42N 17 45 E
Podu Turcului 46 46 11N 27 25 E
Podujevo 42 42 54N 21 10 E
Poel 24 54 0N 11 25 E
Pofadder 92 29 10 S 19 22 E
Pogamasing 106 46 55N 81 50W
Poggiardo 41 40 3N 18 21 E
Poggibonsi 39 43 27N 11 8 E
Pogoanele 46 44 55N 27 0 E
Pogorzcla 28 51 50N 17 12 E
Pogradeci 44 40 57N 20 37 E
Poh 73 0 46 S 122 51 E
Pohang 76 36 1N 129 23 E
Pohorelá 27 48 50N 20 2 E
Pohořelice 27 48 59N 16 31 E
Pohorje 39 46 30N 15 20 E
Poiana Mare 46 43 57N 23 5 E
Poiana Ruscăi, Munţii 46 45 45N 22 25 E
Poinsett, C. 5 65 42 S 113 18 E
Point Edward 106 43 0N 82 30W
Point Pedro 70 9 50N 80 15 E
Point Pleasant, U.S.A. 113 40 5N 74 4W
Point Pleasant, W. Va., U.S.A. 114 38 50N 82 7W
Pointe-à-la Hache 117 29 35N 89 55W
Pointe-à-Pitre 121 16 10N 61 30W
Pointe Noire 88 4 48 S 11 53 E
Poirino 38 44 55N 7 50 E
Poissy 19 48 55N 2 0 E
Poitiers 18 46 35N 0 20 E
Poitou, Plaines et Seuil du 20 46 30N 0 1W
Poix 19 49 47N 2 0 E
Poix-Terron 19 49 38N 4 38 E
Pojoaque 119 35 55N 106 0W
Pokataroo 99 29 30 S 148 36 E
Poko, Sudan 87 5 41N 31 55 E
Poko, Zaïre 90 3 7N 26 52 E
Pokrov 55 55 55N 39 7 E
Pokrovsk 59 61 29N 126 12 E
Pol 30 43 9N 7 20W
Pola de Allande 30 43 16N 6 37W
Pola de Gordón, La 30 42 51N 5 41W
Pola de Lena 30 43 10N 5 49W
Pola de Siero 30 43 24N 5 39W
Pola de Somiedo 30 43 5N 6 15W
Polacca 119 35 52N 110 25W
Polan 65 25 30N 61 10 E
Poland ■ 28 52 0N 20 0 E
Polanów 28 54 7N 16 41 E
Polar Sub-Glacial Basin 5 85 0 S 110 0 E
Polcura 124 37 17 S 71 43W
Połczyn Zdrój 28 53 47N 16 5 E
Polden Hills 13 51 7N 2 50W
Polessk 54 54 50N 21 8 E
Polevskoy 52 56 26N 60 11 E
Polewali, Sulawesi, Indon. 73 4 8 S 119 43 E
Polewali, Sulawesi, Indon. 73 3 21 S 119 23 E
Polgar 27 47 54N 21 6 E
Poli 88 8 34N 13 15 E
Poliaigos 45 36 45N 24 38 E
Policastro, Golfo di 41 39 55N 15 35 E
Police 28 53 33N 14 33 E
Polička 27 49 43N 16 15 E
Polignano a Mare 41 41 0N 17 12 E
Poligny 19 46 50N 5 42 E
Polikhnitas 45 39 4N 26 10 E
Polillo Is. 73 14 56N 122 0 E
Polístena 41 38 25N 16 4 E
Políyiros 44 40 23N 23 25 E
Polk 112 41 22N 79 57W
Polkowice 28 51 29N 16 3 E
Polla 41 40 31N 15 27 E
Pollachi 70 10 35N 77 0 E
Pollensa 32 39 54N 3 1 E
Pollensa, B. de 32 39 53N 3 8 E
Póllica 41 40 13N 15 3 E
Pollino, Mte. 41 39 54N 16 13 E
Pollock 116 45 58N 100 18W
Polna 54 58 31N 28 0 E
Polnovat 58 63 50N 65 54 E
Polo 116 42 0N 89 38W
Pologi 56 47 29N 36 15 E
Polonnoye 54 50 6N 27 30 E
Polotsk 54 55 30N 28 50 E
Polski Trŭmbesh 43 43 20N 25 38 E
Polsko Kosovo 43 43 23N 25 38 E
Polson 118 47 45N 114 12W
Poltava 56 49 35N 34 35 E
Polunochnoye 52 60 52N 60 25 E
Polur 70 12 32N 79 11 E
Polyanovgrad 43 42 39N 26 59 E
Polyarny 52 69 8N 33 20 E
Polynesia 95 10 0 S 162 0W
Pomarance 38 43 18N 10 51 E
Pomarico 41 40 31N 16 33 E
Pombal, Brazil 127 6 45 S 37 50W
Pombal, Port. 30 39 55N 8 40W
Pómbia 45 35 0N 24 51 E
Pomeroy, Ohio, U.S.A. 114 39 0N 82 0W
Pomeroy, Wash., U.S.A. 118 46 30N 117 33W
Pomona 119 34 2N 117 49W
Pomorie 43 42 32N 27 41 E
Pomoshnaya 56 48 13N 31 36 E
Pompano Beach 115 26 12N 80 6W
Pompei 41 40 45N 14 30 E
Pompey 19 48 50N 6 2 E
Pompeys Pillar 118 46 0N 108 0W
Ponape 94 6 55N 158 10 E
Ponask, L. 106 54 0N 92 41W
Ponass L. 109 52 16N 103 58W
Ponca 116 42 38N 96 41W
Ponca City 117 36 40N 97 5W
Ponce 121 18 1N 66 37W
Ponchatoula 117 30 27N 90 25W
Poncheville, L. 106 50 10N 76 55W
Poncin 21 46 6N 5 25 E
Pond Inlet 105 72 40N 77 0W
Pondicherry 70 11 59N 79 50 E
Pondoland 93 31 10 S 29 30 E
Ponds, I. of 107 53 27N 55 52W
Ponferrada 30 42 32N 6 35W
Pongo, Wadi → 87 8 42N 27 40 E
Poniatowa 28 51 11N 22 3 E
Poniec 28 51 48N 16 50 E
Ponikva 39 46 16N 15 26 E
Ponnaiyar → 70 11 50N 79 45 E
Ponnani 70 10 45N 75 59 E
Ponneri 70 13 20N 80 15 E
Ponnyadaung 67 22 0N 94 10 E
Ponoi 52 67 0N 41 0 E
Ponoi → 52 66 59N 41 17 E
Ponoka 108 52 42N 113 40W
Ponorogo 73 7 52 S 111 29 E
Pons, France 20 45 35N 0 34W
Pons, Spain 32 41 55N 1 12 E
Ponsul → 31 39 40N 7 31W
Pont-à-Mousson 19 48 54N 6 1 E
Pont-Audemer 18 49 21N 0 30 E
Pont-Aven 18 47 51N 3 47W
Pont Canavese 38 45 24N 7 33 E
Pont-de-Roide 19 47 23N 6 45 E
Pont-de-Salars 20 44 18N 2 44 E
Pont-de-Vaux 19 46 26N 4 56 E
Pont-de-Veyle 21 46 17N 4 53 E
Pont-l'Abbé 18 47 52N 4 15W
Pont-l'Évêque 18 49 18N 0 11 E
Pont-St-Esprit 21 44 16N 4 40 E
Pont-sur-Yonne 19 48 18N 3 10 E
Ponta Grossa 125 25 7 S 50 10W
Ponta Pora 125 22 20 S 55 35W
Pontacq 20 43 11N 0 8W
Pontailler 19 47 18N 5 24 E
Pontarlier 19 46 54N 6 20 E
Pontassieve 39 43 47N 11 25 E
Pontaubault 18 48 40N 1 20W
Pontaumur 20 45 52N 2 40 E
Pontcharra 21 45 26N 6 1 E
Pontchartrain, L. 117 30 12N 90 0W
Pontchâteau 18 47 25N 2 5W
Ponte da Barca 30 41 48N 8 25W
Ponte de Sor 31 39 17N 7 57W
Ponte dell 'Olio 38 44 52N 9 39 E
Ponte di Legno 38 46 15N 10 30 E
Ponte do Lima 30 41 46N 8 35W
Ponte do Pungué 91 19 30 S 34 33 E
Ponte Leccia 21 42 28N 9 13 E
Ponte Macassar 73 9 30 S 123 58 E
Ponte nell' Alpi 39 46 10N 12 18 E
Ponte Nova 125 20 25 S 42 54W
Ponte San Martino 38 45 36N 7 47 E
Ponte San Pietro 38 45 42N 9 35 E
Pontebba 39 46 30N 13 17 E
Pontecorvo 40 41 28N 13 40 E
Pontedera 38 43 40N 10 37 E
Pontefract 12 53 42N 1 19W
Ponteix 109 49 46N 107 29W
Pontelandolfo 41 41 17N 14 41 E
Pontevedra 30 42 26N 8 40W
Pontevedra □ 30 42 25N 8 39W
Pontevedra, R. de → 30 42 22N 8 45W
Pontevico 38 45 16N 10 6 E
Pontiac, Ill., U.S.A. 116 40 50N 88 40W
Pontiac, Mich., U.S.A. 114 42 40N 83 20W
Pontian Kechil 71 1 29N 103 23 E
Pontianak 72 0 3 S 109 15 E
Pontine Is. = Ponziane, Isole 40 40 55N 13 0 E
Pontine Mts. = Karadeniz D. 64 41 30N 35 0 E
Pontinia 40 41 25N 13 2 E
Pontivy 18 48 5N 3 0W
Pontoise 19 49 3N 2 5 E
Ponton → 108 58 27N 116 11W
Pontorson 18 48 34N 1 30W
Pontrémoli 38 44 22N 9 52 E
Pontrieux 18 48 42N 3 10W
Ponts-de-Cé, Les 18 47 25N 0 30W
Pontypool, Can. 112 44 6N 78 38W
Pontypool, U.K. 13 51 42N 3 1W
Pontypridd 13 51 36N 3 21W
Ponza 40 40 55N 12 57 E
Ponziane, Isole 40 40 55N 13 0 E
Poole 13 50 42N 1 58W
Pooley I. 108 52 45N 128 15W
Poona = Pune 70 18 29N 73 57 E
Poonamallee 70 13 3N 80 10 E
Pooncarie 99 33 22 S 142 31 E
Poopelloe, L. 99 31 40 S 144 0 E
Poopó, Lago de 126 18 30 S 67 35W
Popayán 126 2 27N 76 36W
Poperinge 16 50 51N 2 42 E
Popigay 59 72 1N 110 39 E
Popilta, L. 99 33 10 S 141 42 E
Popina 43 44 7N 26 57 E
Popio, L. 99 33 10 S 141 52 E
Poplar 116 48 3N 105 9W
Poplar →, Man., Can. 109 53 0N 97 19W
Poplar →, N.W.T., Can. 108 61 22N 121 52W
Poplar Bluff 117 36 45N 90 22W
Poplarville 117 30 55N 89 30W
Popocatepetl 120 19 10N 98 40W
Popokabaka 88 5 41 S 16 40 E
Pópoli 39 42 12N 13 50 E
Popondetta 98 8 48 S 148 17 E
Popovača 39 45 30N 16 41 E
Popovo 43 43 21N 26 18 E
Poprád 27 49 3N 20 18 E
Poprád → 27 49 38N 20 42 E
Porbandar 68 21 44N 69 43 E
Porcher I. 108 53 50N 130 30W
Porcuna 31 37 52N 4 11W
Porcupine →, Can. 109 59 11N 104 46W
Porcupine →, U.S.A. 104 66 35N 145 15W
Pordenone 39 45 58N 12 40 E
Pordim 43 43 23N 24 51 E
Poreč 39 45 14N 13 36 E
Poretskoye 55 55 9N 46 21 E
Pori 51 61 29N 21 48 E
Porí 45 35 58N 23 13 E
Porjus 50 66 57N 19 50 E
Porkhov 54 57 45N 29 38 E
Porkkala 51 59 59N 24 26 E
Porlamar 126 10 57N 63 51W
Porlezza 38 46 2N 9 8 E
Porma → 30 42 49N 5 28W
Pornic 18 47 7N 2 5W
Poronaysk 59 49 13N 143 0 E
Póros 45 37 30N 23 30 E
Poroshiri-Dake 74 42 41N 142 52 E
Poroszló 27 47 39N 20 40 E
Poroto Mts. 91 9 0 S 33 30 E
Porquerolles, Îles de 21 43 0N 6 13 E
Porrentruy 25 47 25N 7 6 E
Porreras 32 39 31N 3 2 E

Pripyat Quillabamba

Pripyat → **54** 51 20N 30 9 E
Prislop, Pasul **46** 47 37N 25 15 E
Pristen **55** 51 15N 36 44 E
Priština **42** 42 40N 21 13 E
Pritchard **115** 30 47N 88 5W
Pritzwalk **24** 53 10N 12 11 E
Privas **21** 44 45N 4 37 E
Priverno **40** 41 29N 13 10 E
Privolzhsk **55** 57 23N 41 16 E
Privolzhskaya Vozvyshennost **55** 51 0N 46 0 E
Privolzhskiy **55** 51 25N 46 3 E
Privolzhye **55** 52 52N 48 33 E
Priyutnoye **57** 46 12N 43 40 E
Prizren **42** 42 13N 20 45 E
Prizzi **40** 37 44N 13 24 E
Prnjavor **42** 44 52N 17 43 E
Probolinggo **73** 7 46 S 113 13 E
Prochowice **28** 51 17N 16 20 E
Procida **40** 40 46N 14 0 E
Proddatur **70** 14 45N 78 30 E
Proença-a-Nova **31** 39 45N 7 54W
Progreso **120** 21 20N 89 40W
Prokhladnyy **57** 43 50N 44 2 E
Prokletije **44** 42 30N 19 45 E
Prokopyevsk **58** 54 0N 86 45 E
Prokuplje **42** 43 16N 21 36 E
Proletarskaya **57** 46 42N 41 50 E
Prome = Pyè **67** 18 45N 95 30 E
Prophet → **108** 58 48N 122 40W
Propriá **127** 10 13 S 36 51W
Propriano **21** 41 41N 8 52 E
Proserpine **97** 20 21 S 148 36 E
Prosna **28** 51 1N 18 30 E
Prosser **118** 46 11N 119 52W
Prostějov **27** 49 30N 17 9 E
Prostki **28** 53 42N 22 25 E
Proston **99** 26 8 S 151 32 E
Proszowice **27** 50 13N 20 16 E
Protection **117** 37 16N 99 30W
Próti **45** 37 5N 21 32 E
Provadiya **43** 43 12N 27 30 E
Provence **21** 43 40N 5 46 E
Providence, Ky., U.S.A. **114** 37 25N 87 46W
Providence, R.I., U.S.A. **114** 41 50N 71 28W
Providence Bay **106** 45 41N 82 15W
Providence Mts. **119** 35 0N 115 30W
Providencia, I. de **121** 13 25N 81 26W
Provideniya **59** 64 23N 173 18W
Provins **19** 48 33N 3 15 E
Provo **118** 40 16N 111 37W
Provost **109** 52 25N 110 20W
Prozor **42** 43 50N 17 34 E
Prud'homme **109** 52 20N 105 54W
Prudnik **28** 50 20N 17 38 E
Prüm **25** 50 14N 6 22 E
Pruszcz Gd. **28** 54 17N 18 40 E
Pruszków **28** 52 9N 20 49 E
Prut → **46** 46 3N 28 10 E
Pruzhany **54** 52 33N 24 28 E
Prvič **39** 44 55N 14 47 E
Prydz B. **5** 69 0 S 74 0 E
Pryor **117** 36 17N 95 20W
Przasnysz **28** 53 2N 20 45 E
Przedbórz **28** 51 6N 19 53 E
Przedecz **28** 52 20N 18 53 E
Przemyśl **27** 49 50N 22 45 E
Przeworsk **27** 50 6N 22 32 E
Przewóz **28** 51 28N 14 57 E
Przhevalsk **58** 42 30N 78 20 E
Przysuchla **28** 51 22N 20 38 E
Psakhná **45** 38 34N 23 35 E
Psará **45** 38 37N 25 38 E
Psathoúra **44** 39 30N 24 12 E
Psel → **56** 49 5N 33 20 E
Pserimos **45** 36 56N 27 12 E
Pskov **54** 57 50N 28 25 E
Psunj **42** 45 25N 17 19 E
Pszczyna **27** 49 59N 18 58 E
Pteleón **45** 39 3N 22 57 E
Ptich → **54** 52 9N 28 52 E
Ptolemais **44** 40 30N 21 43 E
Ptuj **39** 46 28N 15 50 E
Ptujska Gora **39** 46 23N 15 47 E
Puán **124** 37 30 S 62 45W
Pucallpa **126** 8 25 S 74 30W
Pucheng **77** 27 59N 118 31 E
Puchezh **46** 45 12N 25 17 E
Pučišće **39** 43 22N 16 43 E
Puck **28** 54 45N 18 23 E
Pucka, Zatoka **28** 54 30N 18 40 E
Pudozh **52** 61 48N 36 32 E
Pudukkottai **70** 10 28N 78 47 E
Puebla **120** 19 0N 98 10W
Puebla □ **120** 18 30N 98 0W
Puebla de Alcocer **31** 38 59N 5 14W
Puebla de Cazalla, La **31** 37 10N 5 20W
Puebla de Don Fadrique **33** 37 58N 2 25W
Puebla de Don Rodrigo **31** 39 5N 4 37W
Puebla de Guzmán **31** 37 37N 7 15W
Puebla de los Infantes, La **31** 37 47N 5 24W
Puebla de Montalbán, La **30** 39 52N 4 22W
Puebla de Sanabria **30** 42 4N 6 38W
Puebla de Trives **30** 42 20N 7 10W
Puebla del Caramiñal **30** 42 37N 8 56W
Puebla, La **32** 39 46N 3 1 E
Pueblo **116** 38 20N 104 40W
Pueblo Bonito **119** 36 4N 107 57W
Pueblo Hundido **124** 26 20 S 70 5W
Puelches **124** 38 5 S 65 51W
Puelén **124** 37 32 S 67 38W
Puente Alto **124** 33 32 S 70 35W
Puente del Arzobispo **30** 39 48N 5 10W
Puente-Genil **31** 37 22N 4 47W
Puente la Reina **32** 42 40N 1 49W
Puenteareas **30** 42 10N 8 28W
Puentedeume **30** 43 24N 8 10W
Puentes de Garcia Rodriguez **30** 43 27N 7 50W
Puerco → **119** 34 22N 107 50W
Puerta, La **33** 38 22N 2 45W
Puerto Aisén **128** 45 27 S 73 0W
Puerto Armuelles **121** 8 20N 82 51W
Puerto Ayacucho **126** 5 40N 67 35W
Puerto Barrios **120** 15 40N 88 32W
Puerto Bermejo **124** 26 55 S 58 34W
Puerto Bermúdez **126** 10 20 S 75 0W
Puerto Bolívar **126** 3 19 S 79 55W
Puerto Cabello **126** 10 28N 68 1W
Puerto Cabezas **121** 14 0N 83 30W
Puerto Capaz = Jebba **82** 35 11N 4 43W
Puerto Carreño **126** 6 12N 67 22W
Puerto Castilla **121** 16 0N 86 0W
Puerto Chicama **126** 7 45 S 79 20W
Puerto Coig **128** 50 54 S 69 15W
Puerto Cortes **121** 8 55N 84 0W
Puerto Cortés **120** 15 51N 88 0W
Puerto Cumarebo **126** 11 29N 69 30W
Puerto de Santa María **31** 36 36N 6 13W
Puerto del Rosario **80** 28 30N 13 52W
Puerto Deseado **128** 47 55 S 66 0W
Puerto Heath **126** 12 34 S 68 39W
Puerto Juárez **120** 21 11N 86 49W
Puerto La Cruz **126** 10 13N 64 38W
Puerto Leguízamo **126** 0 12 S 74 46W
Puerto Libertad **120** 29 55N 112 41W
Puerto Lobos **128** 42 0 S 65 3W
Puerto Lumbreras **33** 37 34N 1 48W
Puerto Madryn **128** 42 48 S 65 4W
Puerto Maldonado **126** 12 30 S 69 10W
Puerto Mazarrón **33** 37 34N 1 15W
Puerto Montt **128** 41 28 S 73 0W
Puerto Morelos **120** 20 49N 86 52W
Puerto Natales **128** 51 45 S 72 15W
Puerto Padre **121** 21 13N 76 35W
Puerto Páez **126** 6 13N 67 28W
Puerto Peñasco **120** 31 20N 113 33W
Puerto Pinasco **124** 22 36 S 57 50W
Puerto Pirámides **128** 42 35 S 64 20W
Puerto Plata **121** 19 48N 70 45W
Puerto Princesa **73** 9 46N 118 45 E
Puerto Quellón **128** 43 7 S 73 37W
Puerto Quepos **121** 9 29N 84 6W
Puerto Real **31** 36 33N 6 12W
Puerto Rico ■ **121** 18 15N 66 45W
Puerto Sastre **124** 22 2 S 57 55W
Puerto Suárez **126** 18 58 S 57 52W
Puerto Vallarta **120** 20 36N 105 15W
Puerto Wilches **126** 7 21N 73 54W
Puertollano **31** 38 43N 4 7W
Puertomarin **30** 42 48N 7 36W
Pueyrredón, L. **128** 47 20 S 72 0W
Pugachev **55** 52 0N 48 49 E
Puge **90** 4 45 S 33 11 E
Puget Sd. **118** 47 15N 122 30W
Puget-Théniers **21** 43 58N 6 53 E
Púglia □ **41** 41 0N 16 30 E
Pugu **90** 6 55 S 39 4 E
Pui **46** 45 30N 23 4 E
Puieşti **46** 46 25N 27 33 E
Puig Mayor, Mte. **32** 39 48N 2 47 E
Puigcerdá **32** 42 24N 1 50 E
Puigmal **32** 42 23N 2 7 E
Puisaye, Collines de **19** 47 34N 3 18 E
Puiseaux **19** 48 11N 2 30 E
Puka **44** 42 2N 19 53 E
Pukaki L. **101** 44 4 S 170 1 E
Pukatawagan **109** 55 45N 101 20W
Pukekohe **101** 37 12 S 174 55 E
Pukou **77** 32 7N 118 38 E
Pula **40** 39 0N 9 0 E
Pula (Pola) **39** 44 54N 13 57 E
Pulaski, N.Y., U.S.A. **114** 43 32N 76 9W
Pulaski, Tenn., U.S.A. **115** 35 10N 87 0W
Pulaski, Va., U.S.A. **114** 37 4N 80 49W
Pulawy **28** 51 23N 21 59 E
Pulgaon **68** 20 44N 78 21 E
Pulicat, L. **70** 13 40N 80 15 E
Puliyangudi **70** 9 11N 77 24 E
Pullman **118** 46 49N 117 10W
Pulog, Mt. **73** 16 40N 120 50 E
Puloraja **72** 4 55N 95 24 E
Pułtusk **28** 52 43N 21 6 E
Pumlumon Fawr **13** 52 29N 3 47W
Puna **126** 19 45 S 65 28W
Puná, I. **126** 2 55 S 80 5W
Punakha **69** 27 42N 89 52 E
Punalur **70** 9 0N 76 56 E
Punasar **68** 27 6N 73 6 E
Punata **126** 17 32 S 65 50W
Punch **69** 33 48N 74 4 E
Pune **70** 18 29N 73 57 E
Pungue, Ponte de **91** 19 0 S 34 0 E
Puning **77** 23 20N 116 12 E
Punjab □ **68** 31 0N 76 0 E
Puno **126** 15 55 S 70 3W
Punta Alta **128** 38 53 S 62 4W
Punta Arenas **128** 53 10 S 71 0W
Punta de Díaz **124** 28 0 S 70 45W
Punta Gorda, Belize **120** 16 10N 88 45W
Punta Gorda, U.S.A. **115** 26 55N 82 0W
Puntarenas **121** 10 0N 84 50W
Punto Fijo **126** 11 50N 70 13W
Punxsutawney **114** 40 56N 79 0W
Puqi **77** 29 40N 113 50 E
Puquio **126** 14 45 S 74 10W
Pur → **58** 67 31N 77 55 E
Purace, Vol. **126** 2 21N 76 23W
Puračić **42** 44 33N 18 28 E
Purari → **98** 7 49 S 145 0 E
Purbeck, Isle of **13** 50 40N 2 5W
Purcell **117** 35 0N 97 25W
Purchena Tetica **33** 37 21N 2 21W
Puri **69** 19 50N 85 58 E
Purli **68** 18 50N 76 35 E
Purmerend **16** 52 30N 4 58 E
Purna → **70** 19 6N 77 2 E
Purnea **69** 25 45N 87 31 E
Pursat **71** 12 34N 103 50 E
Purukcahu **72** 0 35 S 114 35 E
Purulia **69** 23 17N 86 24 E
Purus → **126** 3 42 S 61 28W
Pŭrvomay **43** 42 8N 25 17 E
Purwakarta **73** 6 35 S 107 29 E
Purwodadi, Jawa, Indon. **73** 7 51 S 110 0 E
Purwodadi, Jawa, Indon. **73** 7 7 S 110 55 E
Purwokerto **73** 7 25 S 109 14 E
Purworedjo **73** 7 43 S 110 2 E
Pus → **70** 19 55N 77 55 E
Pusad **70** 19 56N 77 36 E
Pusan **76** 35 5N 129 0 E
Pushchino **59** 54 10N 158 0 E
Pushkin **54** 59 45N 30 25 E
Pushkino, R.S.F.S.R., U.S.S.R. **55** 51 16N 47 0 E
Pushkino, R.S.F.S.R., U.S.S.R. **55** 56 2N 37 49 E
Püspökladány **27** 47 19N 21 6 E
Pustoshka **54** 56 20N 29 30 E
Puszczykowo **28** 52 18N 16 49 E
Putahow L. **109** 59 54N 100 40W
Putao **67** 27 28N 97 30 E
Putaruru **101** 38 2 S 175 50 E
Putbus **24** 54 19N 13 29 E
Puţeni **46** 45 49N 27 42 E
Puthein Myit → **67** 15 56N 94 18 E
Putian **77** 25 23N 119 0 E
Putignano **41** 40 50N 17 5 E
Puting, Tanjung **72** 3 31 S 111 46 E
Putlitz **24** 53 15N 12 3 E
Putna **46** 47 50N 25 33 E
Putna → **46** 45 42N 27 26 E
Putnam **113** 41 55N 71 55W
Putnok **27** 48 18N 20 26 E
Putorana, Gory **59** 69 0N 95 0 E
Puttalam Lagoon **70** 8 15N 79 45 E
Putten **16** 52 16N 5 36 E
Puttgarden **24** 54 28N 11 15 E
Puttur **70** 12 46N 75 12 E
Putumayo → **126** 3 7 S 67 58W
Putussibau **72** 0 50N 112 56 E
Puy-de-Dôme **20** 45 46N 2 57 E
Puy-de-Dôme □ **20** 45 47N 3 0 E
Puy-de-Sancy **20** 45 32N 2 48 E
Puy-Guillaume **20** 45 57N 3 29 E
Puy, Le **20** 45 3N 3 52 E
Puy l'Évêque **20** 44 31N 1 9 E
Puyallup **118** 47 10N 122 22W
Puyang **76** 35 40N 115 1 E
Puylaurens **20** 43 35N 2 0 E
Puyôo **20** 43 33N 0 56W
Pwani □ **90** 7 0 S 39 0 E
Pweto **91** 8 25 S 28 51 E
Pwllheli **12** 52 54N 4 26W
Pya-ozero **52** 66 5N 30 58 E
Pyana → **55** 55 30N 46 0 E
Pyapon **67** 16 20N 95 40 E
Pyasina → **59** 73 30N 87 0 E
Pyatigorsk **57** 44 2N 43 6 E
Pyatikhatki **56** 48 28N 33 38 E
Pydna **44** 40 20N 22 34 E
Pyinmana **67** 19 45N 96 12 E
Pyŏngyang **76** 39 0N 125 30 E
Pyote **117** 31 34N 103 5W
Pyramid L. **118** 40 0N 119 30W
Pyramids **86** 29 58N 31 9 E
Pyrénées **20** 42 45N 0 18 E
Pyrenees = Pyrénées **20** 42 45N 0 18 E
Pyrénées-Atlantiques □ **20** 43 15N 1 0W
Pyrénées-Orientales □ **20** 42 35N 2 26 E
Pyrzyce **28** 53 10N 14 55 E
Pyshchug **55** 58 57N 45 47 E
Pytalovo **54** 57 5N 27 55 E
Pyttegga **47** 62 13N 7 42 E
Pyu **67** 18 30N 96 28 E
Pyzdry **28** 52 11N 17 42 E

Q

Qabalān **62** 32 8N 35 17 E
Qabātiyah **62** 32 25N 35 16 E
Qaidam Pendi **75** 37 0N 95 0 E
Qa'iya **64** 24 33N 43 15 E
Qal' at Shajwa **86** 25 2N 38 57 E
Qala-i-Jadid (Spin Baldak) **68** 31 1N 66 25 E
Qalāt **65** 32 15N 66 58 E
Qal'at al Akhḍar **64** 28 0N 37 10 E
Qal'at al Mu'azzam **64** 27 45N 37 31 E
Qal'at Saura **86** 26 10N 38 40 E
Qal'eh-ye Now **65** 35 0N 63 5 E
Qalqīlya **62** 32 12N 34 58 E
Qalyûb **86** 30 12N 31 11 E
Qam **62** 32 36N 35 43 E
Qamar, Ghubbat al **63** 16 20N 52 30 E
Qamruddin Karez **68** 31 45N 68 20 E
Qāna **62** 33 12N 35 17 E
Qâra **86** 29 38N 26 30 E
Qarachuk **64** 37 0N 42 2 E
Qārah **64** 29 55N 40 3 E
Qardud **87** 10 20N 29 56 E
Qarqan **75** 38 5N 85 20 E
Qarqan He → **75** 39 30N 88 30 E
Qarrasa **87** 14 38N 32 5 E
Qasim **64** 26 0N 43 0 E
Qāsim **62** 32 59N 36 2 E
Qaşr Bū Hadi **83** 31 1N 16 45 E
Qaşr-e Qand **65** 26 15N 60 45 E
Qasr Farâfra **86** 27 0N 28 1 E
Qatar ■ **65** 25 30N 51 15 E
Qattâra **86** 30 12N 27 3 E
Qattâra Depression = Qattâra, Munkhafed el **86** 29 30N 27 30 E
Qattâra, Munkhafed el **86** 29 30N 27 30 E
Qāyen **65** 33 40N 59 10 E
Qazvin **64** 36 15N 50 0 E
Qena **86** 26 10N 32 43 E
Qena, Wadi → **86** 26 12N 32 44 E
Qeshm **65** 26 55N 56 10 E
Qezi'ot **62** 30 52N 34 26 E
Qian Xian **77** 34 31N 108 15 E
Qianshan **77** 30 37N 116 35 E
Qianxi **77** 27 3N 106 3 E
Qianyang **77** 27 18N 110 10 E
Qijiang **77** 28 57N 106 35 E
Qila Safed **66** 29 0N 61 30 E
Qila Saifulla **68** 30 45N 68 17 E
Qilian Shan **75** 38 30N 96 0 E
Qin Ling = Qinling Shandi **77** 33 50N 108 10 E
Qin'an **77** 34 48N 105 40 E
Qingdao **76** 36 5N 120 20 E
Qinghai □ **75** 36 0N 98 0 E
Qinghai Hu **75** 36 40N 100 10 E
Qingjiang, Jiangsu, China **77** 33 30N 119 2 E
Qingjiang, Jiangxi, China **77** 28 4N 115 29 E
Qingliu **77** 26 11N 116 48 E
Qingshuihe **76** 39 55N 111 35 E
Qingyang **76** 36 2N 107 55 E
Qingyuan **77** 23 40N 112 59 E
Qinhuangdao **76** 39 56N 119 30 E
Qinling Shandi **77** 33 50N 108 10 E
Qinyang **77** 35 7N 112 57 E
Qinyuan **76** 36 29N 112 20 E
Qinzhou **75** 21 58N 108 38 E
Qiongshan **77** 19 51N 110 26 E
Qiongzhou Haixia **77** 20 10N 110 15 E
Qiqihar **75** 47 26N 124 0 E
Qiryat 'Anavim **62** 31 49N 35 7 E
Qiryat Ata **62** 32 47N 35 6 E
Qiryat Bialik **62** 32 50N 35 5 E
Qiryat Gat **62** 31 32N 34 46 E
Qiryat Hayyim **62** 32 49N 35 4 E
Qiryat Mal'akhi **62** 31 44N 34 44 E
Qiryat Shemona **62** 33 13N 35 35 E
Qiryat Yam **62** 32 51N 35 4 E
Qishan **77** 22 52N 120 25 E
Qishon → **62** 32 49N 35 2 E
Qishrān **86** 20 14N 40 2 E
Qitai **75** 44 2N 89 35 E
Qiyahe **76** 53 0N 120 35 E
Qiyang **77** 26 35N 111 50 E
Qizan **87** 16 57N 42 34 E
Qizān **63** 17 0N 42 20 E
Qom **65** 34 40N 51 0 E
Qomolangma Feng (Mt. Everest) **75** 28 0N 86 45 E
Qondūz **65** 36 50N 68 50 E
Qondūz □ **65** 36 50N 68 50 E
Qu Jiang → **77** 30 1N 106 24 E
Qu Xian, Sichuan, China **77** 30 48N 106 58 E
Qu Xian, Zhejiang, China **75** 28 57N 118 54 E
Quackenbrück **24** 52 40N 7 59 E
Quakertown **113** 40 27N 75 20W
Quambatook **99** 35 49 S 143 34 E
Quambone **99** 30 57 S 147 53 E
Quan Long = Ca Mau **71** 9 7N 105 8 E
Quanan **117** 34 20N 99 45W
Quandialla **99** 34 1 S 147 47 E
Quang Ngai **71** 15 13N 108 58 E
Quang Yen **71** 20 56N 106 52 E
Quantock Hills **13** 51 8N 3 10W
Quanzhou, Fujian, China **75** 24 55N 118 34 E
Quanzhou, Guangxi Zhuangzu, China **77** 25 57N 111 5 E
Quaraí **124** 30 15 S 56 20W
Quarré-les-Tombes **19** 47 21N 4 0 E
Quartu Sant' Elena **40** 39 15N 9 10 E
Quartzsite **119** 33 44N 114 16W
Quatsino **108** 50 30N 127 40W
Quatsino Sd. **108** 50 25N 127 58W
Qubab = Mishmar Ayyalon **62** 31 52N 34 57 E
Qūchān **65** 37 10N 58 27 E
† Que Que **91** 18 58 S 29 48 E
Queanbeyan **97** 35 17 S 149 14 E
Québec **107** 46 52N 71 13W
Québec □ **107** 50 0N 70 0W
Quedlinburg **24** 51 47N 11 9 E
Queen Alexandra Ra. **5** 85 0 S 170 0 E
Queen Charlotte **108** 53 15N 132 2W
Queen Charlotte Is. **108** 53 20N 132 10W
Queen Charlotte Str. **108** 51 0N 128 0W
Queen Elizabeth Is. **102** 76 0N 95 0W
Queen Elizabeth Nat. Park **90** 0 0 S 30 0 E
Queen Mary Coast **5** 70 0 S 95 0 E
Queen Maud G. **104** 68 15N 102 30W
Queen Maud Ra. **5** 86 0 S 160 0W
Queens Chan. **96** 15 0 S 129 30 E
Queenscliff **97** 38 16 S 144 39 E
Queensland □ **97** 22 0 S 142 0 E
Queenstown, Austral. **97** 42 4 S 145 35 E
Queenstown, N.Z. **101** 45 1 S 168 40 E
Queenstown, S. Afr. **92** 31 52 S 26 52 E
Queguay Grande → **124** 32 9 S 58 9W
Queimadas **127** 11 0 S 39 38W
Quela **88** 9 10 S 16 56 E
Quelimane **91** 17 53 S 36 58 E
Quelpart = Cheju Do **77** 33 29N 126 34 E
Quemado, N. Mex., U.S.A. **119** 34 17N 108 28W
Quemado, Tex., U.S.A. **117** 28 58N 100 35W
Quemú-Quemú **124** 36 3 S 63 36W
Quequén **124** 38 30 S 58 30W
Querétaro **120** 20 40N 100 23W
Querétaro □ **120** 20 30N 100 0W
Querfurt **24** 51 22N 11 33 E
Querqueville **18** 49 40N 1 42W
Quesada **33** 37 51N 3 4W
Queshan **77** 32 55N 114 2 E
Quesnel **108** 53 0N 122 30W
Quesnel → **108** 52 58N 122 29W
Quesnel L. **108** 52 30N 121 20W
Quesnoy, Le **19** 50 15N 3 38 E
Questa **119** 36 45N 105 35W
Questembert **18** 47 40N 2 28W
Quetico Prov. Park **106** 48 30N 91 45W
Quetta **66** 30 15N 66 55 E
* Quetta □ **66** 30 15N 66 55 E
Quezaltenango **120** 14 50N 91 30W
Quezon City **73** 14 38N 121 0 E
Qui Nhon **71** 13 40N 109 13 E
Quiaca, La **124** 22 5 S 65 35W
Quibaxe **88** 8 24 S 14 27 E
Quibdo **126** 5 42N 76 40W
Quiberon **18** 47 29N 3 9W
Quick **108** 54 36N 126 54W
Quickborn **24** 53 42N 9 52 E
Quiet L. **108** 61 5N 133 5W
Quiindy **124** 25 58 S 57 14W
Quilán, C. **128** 43 15 S 74 30W
Quilengues **89** 14 12 S 14 12 E
Quilimarí **124** 32 5 S 71 30W
Quilino **124** 30 14 S 64 29W
Quillabamba **126** 12 50 S 72 50W

* *Now part of Baluchistan* □

† *Renamed Kwekwe*

Quillagua Red Rock, L.

Quillagua **124** 21 40 S 69 40W
Quillaicillo **124** 31 17 S 71 40W
Quillan **20** 42 53N 2 10 E
Quillebeuf **18** 49 28N 0 30 E
Quillota **124** 32 54 S 71 16W
Quilmes **124** 34 43 S 58 15W
Quilon **70** 8 50N 76 38 E
Quilpie **97** 26 35 S 144 11 E
Quilpué **124** 33 5 S 71 33W
Quilua **91** 16 17 S 39 54 E
Quimilí **124** 27 40 S 62 30W
Quimper **18** 48 0N 4 9W
Quimperlé **18** 47 53N 3 33W
Quincy, Calif., U.S.A. **118** 39 56N 121 0W
Quincy, Fla., U.S.A. **115** 30 34N 84 34W
Quincy, Ill., U.S.A. **116** 39 55N 91 20W
Quincy, Mass., U.S.A. **114** 42 14N 71 0W
Quincy, Wash., U.S.A. **118** 47 22N 119 56W
Quines **124** 32 13 S 65 48W
Quinga **91** 15 49 S 40 15 E
Quingey **19** 47 7N 5 52 E
Quintana de la Serena **31** 38 45N 5 40W
Quintana Roo □ **120** 19 0N 88 0W
Quintanar de la Orden **32** 39 36N 3 5W
Quintanar de la Sierra **32** 41 57N 2 55W
Quintanar del Rey **33** 39 21N 1 56W
Quintero **124** 32 45 S 71 30W
Quintin **18** 48 26N 2 56W
Quinto **32** 41 25N 0 32W
Quinyambie **99** 30 15 S 141 0 E
Quípar → **33** 38 15N 1 40W
Quirihue **124** 36 15 S 72 35W
Quirindi **99** 31 28 S 150 40 E
Quiroga **30** 42 28N 7 18W
Quissac **21** 43 55N 4 0 E
Quissanga **91** 12 24 S 40 28 E
Quitilipi **124** 26 50 S 60 13W
Quitman, Ga., U.S.A. **115** 30 49N 83 35W
Quitman, Miss., U.S.A. **115** 32 2N 88 42W
Quitman, Tex., U.S.A. **117** 32 48N 95 25W
Quito **126** 0 15 S 78 35W
Quixadá **127** 4 55 S 39 0W
Quixaxe **91** 15 17 S 40 4 E
Qul'ân, Jazâ'ir **86** 24 22N 35 31 E
Qumrān **62** 31 43N 35 27 E
Quneitra **62** 33 7N 35 48 E
Quoin Pt. **92** 34 46 S 19 37 E
Quondong **99** 33 6 S 140 18 E
Quorn **97** 32 25 S 138 0 E
Qurein **87** 13 30N 34 50 E
Qûs **86** 25 55N 32 50 E
Quseir **86** 26 7N 34 16 E
Qusrah **62** 32 5N 35 20 E
Quthing **93** 30 25 S 27 36 E
Qytet Stalin (Kuçove) **44** 40 47N 19 57 E

R

Råå **49** 56 0N 12 45 E
Raab **26** 48 21N 13 39 E
Raahe **50** 64 40N 24 28 E
Ra'ananna **62** 32 12N 34 52 E
Raasay **14** 57 25N 6 4W
Raasay, Sd. of **14** 57 30N 6 8W
Rab **39** 44 45N 14 45 E
Raba **73** 8 36 S 118 55 E
Rába → **27** 47 38N 17 38 E
Raba → **27** 50 8N 20 30 E
Rabaçal → **30** 41 30N 7 12W
Rabah **85** 13 5N 5 30 E
Rabai **90** 3 50 S 39 31 E
Rabastens, Hautes-Pyrénées, France **20** 43 25N 0 10 E
Rabastens, Tarn, France **20** 43 50N 1 43 E
Rabat, Malta **36** 35 53N 14 25 E
Rabat, Moroc. **82** 34 2N 6 48W
Rabaul **94** 4 24 S 152 18 E
Rabbit → **108** 59 41N 127 12W
Rabbit Lake **109** 53 8N 107 46W
Rabbitskin → **108** 61 47N 120 42W
Rābigh **64** 22 50N 39 5 E
Rabka **27** 49 37N 19 59 E
Rača **42** 44 14N 21 0 E
Rácale **41** 39 57N 18 6 E
Racalmuto **40** 37 25N 13 41 E
Răcăşdia **42** 44 59N 21 36 E
Racconigi **38** 44 47N 7 41 E
Race, C. **107** 46 40N 53 5W
Rach Gia **71** 10 5N 105 5 E
Raciąż **28** 52 46N 20 10 E
Racibórz **27** 50 7N 18 18 E
Racine **114** 42 41N 87 51W
Radama, Nosy **93** 14 0 S 47 47 E
Radama, Saikanosy **93** 14 16 S 47 53 E
Radan **42** 42 59N 21 29 E
Rădăuţi **46** 47 50N 25 59 E
Radbuza → **26** 49 35N 13 5 E
Räde **47** 59 21N 10 53 E
Radeburg **24** 51 6N 13 55 E
Radeče **39** 46 5N 15 14 E
Radekhov **54** 50 25N 24 32 E
Radew → **28** 54 2N 15 52 E
Radford **114** 37 8N 80 32W
Radhanpur **68** 23 50N 71 38 E
Radhwa, Jabal **64** 24 34N 38 18 E
Radiska → **42** 41 38N 20 37 E
Radisson **109** 52 30N 107 20W
Radium Hill **97** 32 30 S 140 42 E
Radium Hot Springs **108** 50 35N 116 2W
Radja, Kepulauan **73** 0 30 S 130 00 E
Radków **28** 50 30N 16 24 E
Radlin **27** 50 3N 18 29 E
Radna **42** 46 7N 21 41 E
Radnevo **43** 42 17N 25 58 E
Radnice **26** 49 51N 13 35 E
Radnor Forest **13** 52 17N 3 10W
Radolfzell **25** 47 44N 8 58 E
Radom **28** 51 23N 21 12 E
Radom □ **28** 51 30N 21 0 E
Radomir **42** 42 37N 23 4 E
Radomka → **28** 51 31N 21 11 E
Radomsko **28** 51 5N 19 28 E
Radomyshl **54** 50 30N 29 12 E
Radomysl Wielki **27** 50 14N 21 15 E
Radoszyce **28** 51 4N 20 15 E
Radoviš **42** 41 38N 22 28 E
Radovljica **39** 46 22N 14 12 E
Radstadt **26** 47 24N 13 28 E
Radstock **13** 51 17N 2 25W
Răducăneni **46** 46 58N 27 54 E
Raduša **42** 42 7N 21 15 E
Radviliškis **54** 55 49N 23 33 E
Radville **109** 49 30N 104 15W
Radymno **27** 49 59N 22 52 E
Radzanów **28** 52 56N 20 8 E
Radziejów **28** 52 40N 18 30 E
Radzymin **28** 52 25N 21 11 E
Radzyń Chełmiński **28** 53 23N 18 55 E
Radzyń Podlaski **28** 51 47N 22 37 E
Rae **108** 62 50N 116 3W
Rae Bareli **69** 26 18N 81 20 E
Rae Isthmus **105** 66 40N 87 30W
Raeren **16** 50 41N 6 7 E
Raeside, L. **96** 29 20 S 122 0 E
Raetihi **101** 39 25 S 175 17 E
Rafaela **124** 31 10 S 61 30W
Rafah **86** 31 18N 34 14 E
Rafai **90** 4 59N 23 58 E
Raffadali **40** 37 23N 13 29 E
Rafḩā **64** 29 35N 43 35 E
Rafsanjān **65** 30 30N 56 5 E
Ragag **87** 10 59N 24 40 E
Raglan, Austral. **98** 23 42 S 150 49 E
Raglan, N.Z. **101** 37 55 S 174 55 E
Ragunda **48** 63 6N 16 23 E
Ragusa **41** 36 56N 14 42 E
Raha **73** 4 55 S 123 0 E
Rahad al Bardī **81** 11 20N 23 40 E
Rahad, Nahr ed → **87** 14 28N 33 31 E
Rahden **24** 52 26N 8 36 E
Raheita **87** 12 46N 43 4 E
Rahimyar Khan **68** 28 30N 70 25 E
Raichur **70** 16 10N 77 20 E
Raiganj **69** 25 37N 88 10 E
Raigarh, Madhya Pradesh, India **69** 21 56N 83 25 E
Raigarh, Orissa, India **70** 19 51N 82 6 E
Raiis **64** 23 33N 38 43 E
Raijua **73** 10 37 S 121 36 E
Railton **99** 41 25 S 146 28 E
Rainbow Lake **108** 58 30N 119 23W
Rainier **118** 46 4N 123 0W
Rainier, Mt. **118** 46 50N 121 50W
Rainy L. **109** 48 42N 93 10W
Rainy River **109** 48 43N 94 29W
Raipur **69** 21 17N 81 45 E
Raja, Kepulauan **73** 0 30 S 129 40 E
Raja, Ujung **72** 3 40N 96 25 E
Rajahmundry **70** 17 1N 81 48 E
Rajang → **72** 2 30N 112 0 E
Rajapalaiyam **70** 9 25N 77 35 E
Rajasthan □ **68** 26 45N 73 30 E
Rajasthan Canal **68** 28 0N 72 0 E
Rajbari **69** 23 47N 89 41 E
Rajgarh, Mad. P., India **68** 24 2N 76 45 E
Rajgarh, Raj., India **68** 28 40N 75 25 E
Rajgród **28** 53 42N 22 42 E
Rajhenburg **39** 46 1N 15 29 E
Rajkot **68** 22 15N 70 56 E
Rajmahal Hills **69** 24 30N 87 30 E
Rajnandgaon **69** 21 5N 81 5 E
Rajojooseppi **50** 68 25N 28 30 E
Rajpipla **68** 21 50N 73 30 E
Rajpura **68** 30 25N 76 32 E
Rajshahi **69** 24 22N 88 39 E
Rajshahi □ **69** 25 0N 89 0 E
Rakaia **101** 43 45 S 172 1 E
Rakaia → **101** 43 36 S 172 15 E
Rakan, Ra's **65** 26 10N 51 20 E
Rakaposhi **69** 36 10N 74 25 E
Rakha **86** 18 25N 41 30 E
Rakhni **68** 30 4N 69 56 E
Rakitovo **43** 41 59N 24 5 E
Rakkestad **47** 59 25N 11 21 E
Rakoniewice **28** 52 10N 16 16 E
Rakops **92** 21 1 S 24 28 E
Rákospalota **27** 47 30N 19 5 E
Rakov **54** 53 58N 26 59 E
Rakovica **39** 44 59N 15 38 E
Rakovník **26** 50 6N 13 42 E
Rakovski **43** 42 21N 24 57 E
Rakvere **54** 59 30N 26 25 E
Raleigh **115** 35 47N 78 39W
Raleigh B. **115** 34 50N 76 15W
Ralja **42** 44 33N 20 34 E
Ralls **117** 33 40N 101 20W
Ram → **108** 62 1N 123 41W
Rām Allāh **62** 31 55N 35 10 E
Rama **62** 32 56N 35 21 E
Ramacca **41** 37 24N 14 40 E
Ramachandrapuram **70** 16 50N 82 4 E
Ramales de la Victoria **32** 43 15N 3 28W
Ramanathapuram **70** 9 25N 78 55 E
Ramanetaka, B. de **93** 14 13 S 47 52 E
Ramas C. **70** 15 5N 73 55 E
Ramat Gan **62** 32 4N 34 48 E
Ramat HaSharon **62** 32 7N 34 50 E
Ramatlhabama **92** 25 37 S 25 33 E
Rambervillers **19** 48 20N 6 38 E
Rambipuji **73** 8 12 S 113 37 E
Rambla, La **31** 37 37N 4 45W
Rambouillet **19** 48 40N 1 48 E
Ramdurg **70** 15 58N 75 22 E
Rame Hd. **99** 37 47 S 149 30 E
Ramea **107** 47 28N 57 4W
Ramechhap **69** 27 25N 86 10 E
Ramelau **73** 8 55 S 126 22 E
Ramenskoye **55** 55 32N 38 15 E
Ramgarh, Bihar, India **69** 23 40N 85 35 E
Ramgarh, Rajasthan, India **68** 27 16N 75 14 E
Ramgarh, Rajasthan, India **68** 27 30N 70 36 E
Rāmhormoz **64** 31 15N 49 35 E
Ramla **62** 31 55N 34 52 E
Ramlat Zalţan **83** 28 30N 19 30 E
Ramlu **87** 13 32N 41 40 E
Ramme **49** 56 30N 8 11 E
Rammūn **62** 31 55N 35 17 E
Ramnad = Ramanathapuram **70** 9 25N 78 55 E
Ramnäs **48** 59 46N 16 12 E
Ramon **55** 51 55N 39 21 E
Ramon, Har **62** 30 30N 34 38 E
Ramona **119** 33 1N 116 56W
Ramore **106** 48 30N 80 25W
Ramos → **120** 25 35N 105 3W
Ramoutsa **92** 24 50 S 25 52 E
Rampart **104** 65 0N 150 15W
Rampur, H.P., India **68** 31 26N 77 43 E
Rampur, Mad. P., India **68** 23 25N 73 53 E
Rampur, Orissa, India **69** 21 48N 83 58 E
Rampur, U.P., India **68** 28 50N 79 5 E
Rampura **68** 24 30N 75 27 E
Rampurhat **69** 24 10N 87 50 E
Ramree Kyun **67** 19 0N 94 0 E
Ramsey, Can. **106** 47 25N 82 20W
Ramsey, U.K. **12** 54 20N 4 21W
Ramsgate **13** 51 20N 1 25 E
Ramsjö **48** 62 11N 15 37 E
Ramtek **69** 21 20N 79 15 E
Ramu → **98** 4 0 S 144 41 E
Ramvik **48** 62 49N 17 51 E
Ranaghat **69** 23 15N 88 35 E
Ranahu **68** 25 55N 69 45 E
Ranau **72** 6 2N 116 40 E
Rancagua **124** 34 10 S 70 50W
Rance → **18** 48 34N 1 59W
Rance, Barrage de la **18** 48 30N 2 3W
Rancheria → **108** 60 13N 129 7W
Ranchester **118** 44 57N 107 12W
Ranchi **69** 23 19N 85 27 E
Rancu **46** 44 32N 24 15 E
Rand **100** 35 33 S 146 32 E
Randan **20** 46 2N 3 21 E
Randazzo **41** 37 53N 14 56 E
Randers **49** 56 29N 10 1 E
Randers Fjord **49** 56 37N 10 20 E
Randfontein **93** 26 8 S 27 45 E
Randolph, Mass., U.S.A. **113** 42 10N 71 3W
Randolph, N.Y., U.S.A. **112** 42 10N 78 59W
Randolph, Utah, U.S.A. **118** 41 43N 111 10W
Randolph, Vt., U.S.A. **113** 43 55N 72 39W
Randsburg **119** 35 22N 117 44W
Randsfjorden **47** 60 15N 10 25 E
Råne älv → **50** 65 50N 22 20 E
Rangaunu B. **101** 34 51 S 173 15 E
Rångedala **49** 57 47N 13 9 E
Rangeley **114** 44 58N 70 33W
Rangely **118** 40 3N 108 53W
Ranger **117** 32 30N 98 42W
Rangia **67** 26 28N 91 38 E
Rangiora **101** 43 19 S 172 36 E
Rangitaiki → **101** 37 54 S 176 49 E
Rangitata → **101** 43 45 S 171 15 E
Rangkasbitung **73** 6 22 S 106 16 E
Rangon → **67** 16 28N 96 40 E
Rangoon **67** 16 45N 96 20 E
Ranibennur **70** 14 35N 75 30 E
Raniganj **69** 23 40N 87 5 E
Ranipet **70** 12 56N 79 23 E
Rankin **117** 31 16N 101 56W
Rankin Inlet **104** 62 30N 93 0W
Rankins Springs **99** 33 49 S 146 14 E
Rannoch, L. **14** 56 41N 4 20W
Rannoch Moor **14** 56 38N 4 48W
Ranobe, Helodranon' i **93** 23 3 S 43 33 E
Ranohira **93** 22 29 S 45 24 E
Ranomafana, Tamatave, Madag. **93** 18 57 S 48 50 E
Ranomafana, Tuléar, Madag. **93** 24 34 S 47 0 E
Ranong **71** 9 56N 98 40 E
Ransiki **73** 1 30 S 134 10 E
Rantau **72** 2 56 S 115 9 E
Rantauprapat **72** 2 15N 99 50 E
Rantemario **73** 3 15 S 119 57 E
Rantīs **62** 32 4N 35 3 E
Rantoul **114** 40 18N 88 10W
Ranum **49** 56 54N 9 14 E
Ranwanlenau **92** 19 37 S 22 49 E
Raohe **76** 46 47N 134 0 E
Raon l'Étape **19** 48 24N 6 50 E
Raoui, Erg er **82** 29 0N 2 0W
Rapa Iti **95** 27 35 S 144 20W
Rapallo **38** 44 21N 9 12 E
Rapang **73** 3 45 S 119 55 E
Rāpch **65** 25 40N 59 15 E
Rapid → **108** 59 15N 129 5W
Rapid City **116** 44 0N 103 0W
Rapid River **114** 45 55N 87 0W
Rapides des Joachims **106** 46 13N 77 43W
Rapla **54** 59 1N 24 52 E
Rarotonga **95** 21 30 S 160 0W
Ra's al Khaymah **65** 25 50N 56 5 E
Ra's al-Unuf **83** 30 25N 18 15 E
Ras Bânâs **81** 23 57N 35 59 E
Ras Dashen **87** 13 8N 38 26 E
Ras el Ma **82** 34 26N 0 50W
Ras Mallap **86** 29 18N 32 50 E
Ra's Tannūrah **64** 26 40N 50 10 E
Râs Timirist **84** 19 21N 16 30W
Rasa, Punta **128** 40 50 S 62 15W
Raseiniai **54** 55 25N 23 5 E
Rashad **87** 11 55N 31 0 E
Rashîd **86** 31 21N 30 22 E
Rashîd, Masabb **86** 31 22N 30 17 E
Rasht **64** 37 20N 49 40 E
Rasipuram **70** 11 30N 78 15 E
Raška **42** 43 19N 20 39 E
Rason, L. **96** 28 45 S 124 25 E
Raşova **46** 44 15N 27 55 E
Rasovo **43** 43 42N 23 17 E
Rasra **69** 25 50N 83 50 E
Rass el Oued **83** 35 57N 5 2 E
Rasskazovo **55** 52 35N 41 50 E
Rastatt **25** 48 50N 8 12 E
Rastu **46** 43 53N 23 16 E
Raszków **28** 51 43N 17 40 E
Rat Buri **71** 13 30N 99 54 E
Rat Is. **104** 51 50N 178 15 E
Rat River **108** 61 7N 112 36W
Ratangarh **68** 28 5N 74 35 E
Rath **69** 25 36N 79 37 E
Rath Luirc (Charleville) **15** 52 21N 8 40W
Rathdrum, Ireland **15** 52 57N 6 13W
Rathdrum, U.S.A. **118** 47 50N 116 58W
Rathenow **24** 52 38N 12 23 E
Rathkeale **15** 52 32N 8 57W
Rathlin I. **15** 55 18N 6 14W
Rathlin O'Birne I. **15** 54 40N 8 50W
Ratibor = Racibórz **27** 50 7N 18 18 E
Rätikon **26** 47 0N 9 55 E
Ratlam **68** 23 20N 75 0 E
Ratnagiri **70** 16 57N 73 18 E
Ratnapura **70** 6 40N 80 20 E
Raton **117** 37 0N 104 30W
Ratten **26** 47 28N 15 44 E
Rattray Hd. **14** 57 38N 1 50W
Rättvik **48** 60 52N 15 7 E
Ratz, Mt. **108** 57 23N 132 12W
Ratzeburg **24** 53 41N 10 46 E
Raub **71** 3 47N 101 52 E
Rauch **124** 36 45 S 59 5W
Raufarhöfn **50** 66 27N 15 57W
Raufoss **47** 60 44N 10 37 E
Raukumara Ra. **101** 38 5 S 177 55 E
Rauland **47** 59 43N 8 0 E
Rauma **51** 61 10N 21 30 E
Rauma → **47** 62 34N 7 43 E
Raundal **47** 60 40N 6 37 E
Raung **73** 8 8 S 114 4 E
Raurkela **69** 22 14N 84 50 E
Rava Russkaya **54** 50 15N 23 42 E
Ravanusa **40** 37 16N 13 58 E
Rāvar **65** 31 20N 56 51 E
Ravena **113** 42 28N 73 49W
Ravenna, Italy **39** 44 28N 12 15 E
Ravenna, Nebr., U.S.A. **116** 41 3N 98 58W
Ravenna, Ohio, U.S.A. **112** 41 11N 81 15W
Ravensburg **25** 47 48N 9 38 E
Ravenshoe **97** 17 37 S 145 29 E
Ravensthorpe **96** 33 35 S 120 2 E
Ravenswood, Austral. **98** 20 6 S 146 54 E
Ravenswood, U.S.A. **114** 38 58N 81 47W
Ravi → **68** 30 35N 71 49 E
Ravna Gora **39** 45 24N 14 50 E
Ravna Reka **42** 43 59N 21 35 E
Rawa Mazowiecka **28** 51 46N 20 12 E
Rawalpindi **66** 33 38N 73 8 E
Rawāndūz **64** 36 40N 44 30 E
Rawang **71** 3 20N 101 35 E
Rawdon **106** 46 3N 73 40W
Rawene **101** 35 25 S 173 32 E
Rawicz **28** 51 36N 16 52 E
Rawka → **28** 52 9N 20 8 E
Rawlinna **96** 30 58 S 125 28 E
Rawlins **118** 41 50N 107 20W
Rawlinson Range **96** 24 40 S 128 30 E
Rawson **128** 43 15 S 65 0W
Ray **116** 48 21N 103 6W
Ray, C. **107** 47 33N 59 15W
Rayachoti **70** 14 4N 78 50 E
Rayadrug **70** 14 40N 76 50 E
Rayagada **70** 19 15N 83 20 E
Raychikhinsk **59** 49 46N 129 25 E
Raymond, Can. **108** 49 30N 112 35W
Raymond, U.S.A. **118** 46 45N 123 48W
Raymondville **117** 26 30N 97 50W
Raymore **109** 51 25N 104 31W
Rayne **117** 30 16N 92 16W
Rayong **71** 12 40N 101 20 E
Rayville **117** 32 30N 91 45W
Raz, Pte. du **18** 48 2N 4 47W
Ražana **42** 44 6N 19 55 E
Ražanj **42** 43 40N 21 31 E
Razdelna **43** 43 13N 27 41 E
Razdel'naya **56** 46 50N 30 2 E
Razdolnoye **56** 45 46N 33 29 E
Razelm, Lacul **46** 44 50N 29 0 E
Razgrad **43** 43 33N 26 34 E
Razlog **43** 41 53N 23 28 E
Razmak **68** 32 45N 69 50 E
Razole **70** 16 36N 81 48 E
Ré, Île de **20** 46 12N 1 30W
Reading, U.K. **13** 51 27N 0 57W
Reading, U.S.A. **114** 40 20N 75 53W
Realicó **124** 35 0 S 64 15W
Réalmont **20** 43 48N 2 10 E
Ream **71** 10 34N 103 39 E
Rebais **19** 48 50N 3 10 E
Rebi **73** 6 23 S 134 7 E
Rebiana **81** 24 12N 22 10 E
Rebun-Tō **74** 45 23N 141 2 E
Recanati **39** 43 24N 13 32 E
Recaş **42** 45 46N 21 30 E
Recherche, Arch. of the **96** 34 15 S 122 50 E
Rechitsa **54** 52 13N 30 15 E
Recife **127** 8 0 S 35 0W
Recklinghausen **24** 51 36N 7 10 E
Reconquista **124** 29 10 S 59 45W
Recreo **124** 29 25 S 65 10W
Recz **28** 53 16N 15 31 E
Red →, Can. **109** 50 24N 96 48W
Red →, Minn., U.S.A. **116** 48 10N 97 0W
Red →, Tex., U.S.A. **117** 31 0N 91 40W
Red Bank **113** 40 21N 74 4W
Red Bay **107** 51 44N 56 25W
Red Bluff **118** 40 11N 122 11W
Red Bluff L. **117** 31 59N 103 58W
Red Cloud **116** 40 8N 98 33W
Red Deer **108** 52 20N 113 50W
Red Deer →, Alta., Can. **109** 50 58N 110 0W
Red Deer →, Man., Can. **109** 52 53N 101 1W
Red Deer L. **109** 52 55N 101 20W
Red Indian L. **107** 48 35N 57 0W
Red Lake **109** 51 3N 93 49W
Red Lake Falls **116** 47 54N 96 15W
Red Lodge **118** 45 10N 109 10W
Red Oak **116** 41 0N 95 10W
Red Rock **106** 48 55N 88 15W
Red Rock, L. **116** 41 30N 93 15W

Red Sea Röbel

Red Sea 63 25 0N 36 0 E
Red Sucker L 109 54 9N 93 40W
Red Tower Pass = Turnu Rosu P. 46 45 33N 24 17 E
Red Wing 116 44 32N 92 35W
Reda 28 54 40N 18 19 E
Redbridge 13 51 35N 0 7 E
Redcar 12 54 37N 1 4W
Redcliff 109 50 10N 110 50W
Redcliffe 99 27 12 S 153 0 E
Reddersburg 92 29 41 S 26 10 E
Redding 118 40 30N 122 25W
Redditch 13 52 18N 1 57W
Redfield 116 45 0N 98 30W
Redknife → 108 61 14N 119 22W
Redlands 119 34 0N 117 11W
Redmond 118 44 19N 121 11W
Redon 18 47 40N 2 6W
Redonda 121 16 58N 62 19W
Redondela 30 42 15N 8 38W
Redondo 31 38 39N 7 37W
Redondo Beach 119 33 52N 118 26W
Redrock Pt. 108 62 11N 115 2W
Redruth 13 50 14N 5 14W
Redvers 109 49 35N 101 40W
Redwater 108 53 55N 113 6W
Redwood 113 44 18N 75 48W
Redwood City 119 37 30N 122 15W
Redwood Falls 116 44 30N 95 2W
Ree, L. 15 53 35N 8 0W
Reed City 114 43 52N 85 30W
Reed, L 109 54 38N 100 30W
Reeder 116 46 7N 102 52W
Reedley 119 36 36N 119 27W
Reedsburg 116 43 34N 90 5W
Reedsport 118 43 45N 124 4W
Reefton 101 42 6 S 171 51 E
Reftele 49 57 11N 13 35 E
Refugio 117 28 18N 97 17W
Rega → 28 54 10N 15 18 E
Regalbuto 41 37 40N 14 38 E
Regavim 62 32 32N 35 2 E
Regen 25 48 58N 13 9 E
Regen → 25 49 2N 12 6 E
Regensburg 25 49 1N 12 7 E
Réggio di Calábria 41 38 7N 15 38 E
Réggio nell' Emilia 38 44 42N 10 38 E
Regina 109 50 27N 104 35W
Registro 125 24 29 S 47 49W
Reguengos de Monsaraz 31 38 25N 7 32W
Rehar → 69 23 55N 82 40 E
Rehoboth 92 23 15 S 17 4 E
Rehovot 62 31 54N 34 48 E
Rei-Bouba 81 8 40N 14 15 E
Reichenbach 24 50 36N 12 19 E
Reid River 98 19 40 S 146 48 E
Reidsville 115 36 21N 79 40W
Reigate 13 51 14N 0 11W
Reillo 32 39 54N 1 53W
Reims 19 49 15N 4 0 E
Reina 62 32 43N 35 18 E
Reina Adelaida, Arch. 128 52 20 S 74 0W
Reinbeck 116 42 18N 92 0W
Reindeer → 109 55 36N 103 11W
Reindeer I. 109 52 30N 98 0W
Reindeer L. 109 57 15N 102 15W
Reine, La 32 48 50N 79 30W
Reinga, C. 101 34 25 S 172 43 E
Reinosa 30 43 2N 4 15W
Reinosa, Paso 30 42 56N 4 10W
Reitz 93 27 48 S 28 29 E
Reivilo 92 27 36 S 24 8 E
Rejmyra 49 58 50N 15 55 E
Rejowiec Fabryczny 28 51 5N 23 17 E
Reka → 39 45 40N 14 0 E
Rekinniki 59 60 51N 163 40 E
Rekovac 42 43 51N 21 3 E
Reliance 109 63 0N 109 20W
Remad, Oued → 82 33 28N 1 20W
Rémalard 18 48 26N 0 47 E
Remanso 127 9 41 S 42 4W
Remarkable, Mt. 99 32 48 S 138 10 E
Rembang 73 6 42 S 111 21 E
Remchi 82 35 2N 1 26W
Remeshk 65 26 55N 58 50 E
Remetea 46 46 45N 25 29 E
Remich 16 49 32N 6 22 E
Remiremont 19 48 0N 6 36 E
Remo 87 6 48N 41 20 E
Remontnoye 57 46 34N 43 37 E
Remoulins 21 43 55N 4 35 E
Remscheid 24 51 11N 7 12 E
Rena 47 61 8N 11 20 E
Rena → 47 61 8N 11 23 E
Rende 41 39 19N 16 11 E
Rendina 45 39 4N 21 58 E
Rendsburg 24 54 18N 9 41 E
Rene 59 66 2N 179 25W
Renfrew, Can. 106 45 30N 76 40W
Renfrew, U.K. 14 55 52N 4 24W
Rengat 72 0 30 S 102 45 E
Rengo 124 34 24 S 70 50W
Renhuai 77 27 48N 106 24 E
Reni 56 45 28N 28 15 E
Renigunta 70 13 38N 79 30 E
Renk 81 11 50N 32 50 E
Renkum 16 51 58N 5 43 E
Renmark 97 34 11 S 140 43 E
Rennell Sd. 108 53 23N 132 35W
Renner Springs T.O. 96 18 20 S 133 47 E
Rennes 18 48 7N 1 41W
Rennes, Bassin de 18 48 12N 1 33W
Rennesøy 47 59 6N 5 43 E
Reno 118 39 30N 119 50W
Reno → 39 44 37N 12 17 E
Renovo 114 41 20N 77 47W
Rensselaer, Ind., U.S.A. 114 40 57N 87 10W
Rensselaer, N.Y., U.S.A. 113 42 38N 73 41W
Renteria 32 43 19N 1 54W
Renton 118 47 30N 122 9W
Réo 84 12 28N 2 35W
Réole, La 20 44 35N 0 1W
Reotipur 69 25 33N 83 45 E
Repalle 70 16 2N 80 45 E
Répcelak 27 47 24N 17 1 E
Republic, Mich., U.S.A. 114 46 25N 87 59W
Republic, Wash., U.S.A. 118 48 38N 118 42W
Republican → 116 39 3N 96 48W
Republican City 116 40 9N 99 20W
Repulse B., Antarct. 5 64 30 S 99 30 E
Repulse B., Austral. 97 20 31 S 148 45 E
Repulse Bay 105 66 30N 86 30W
Requena, Peru 126 5 5 S 73 52W
Requena, Spain 33 39 30N 1 4W
Resele 48 63 20N 17 5 E
Resen 42 41 5N 21 0 E
Reserve, Can. 109 52 28N 102 39W
Reserve, U.S.A. 119 33 50N 108 54W
Resht = Rasht 64 37 20N 49 40 E
Resistencia 124 27 30 S 59 0W
Reşiţa 42 45 18N 21 53 E
Resko 28 53 47N 15 25 E
Resolution I., Can. 105 61 30N 65 0W
Resolution I., N.Z. 101 45 40 S 166 40 E
Ressano Garcia 93 25 25 S 32 0 E
Reston 109 49 33N 101 6W
Reszel 28 54 4N 21 10 E
Retalhuleu 120 14 33N 91 46W
Reteag 46 47 10N 24 0 E
Retenue, Lac de 91 11 0 S 27 0 E
Rethel 19 49 30N 4 20 E
Rethem 24 52 47N 9 25 E
Réthímnon 45 35 18N 24 30 E
Réthímnon □ 45 35 23N 24 28 E
Rétiers 18 47 55N 1 25W
Retortillo 30 40 48N 6 21W
Rétság 27 47 58N 19 10 E
Réunion 3 22 0 S 56 0 E
Reus 32 41 10N 1 5 E
Reuss → 25 47 16N 8 24 E
Reuterstadt Stavenhagen 24 53 41N 12 54 E
Reutlingen 25 48 28N 9 13 E
Reutte 26 47 29N 10 42 E
Reval = Tallinn 54 59 29N 24 58 E
Revda 52 56 48N 59 57 E
Revel 20 43 28N 2 0 E
Revelganj 69 25 50N 84 40 E
Revelstoke 108 51 0N 118 10W
Reventazón 126 6 10 S 81 0W
Revigny 19 48 50N 5 0 E
Revilla Gigedo, Is. 95 18 40N 112 0W
Revillagigedo I. 108 55 50N 131 20W
Revin 19 49 55N 4 39 E
Revuè → 91 19 50 S 34 0 E
Rewa 69 24 33N 81 25 E
Rewari 68 28 15N 76 40 E
Rexburg 118 43 55N 111 50W
Rey Malabo 88 3 45N 8 50 E
Rey, Rio del → 85 4 30N 8 48 E
Reykjahlið 50 65 40N 16 55W
Reykjanes 50 63 48N 22 40W
Reykjavík 50 64 10N 21 57 E
Reynolds 109 49 40N 95 55W
Reynolds Ra. 96 22 30 S 133 0 E
Reynoldsville 112 41 5N 78 58W
Reynosa 120 26 5N 98 18W
Rezā'īyeh 64 37 40N 45 0 E
Rezā'īyeh, Daryācheh-ye 64 37 50N 45 30 E
Rezekne 54 56 30N 27 17 E
Rezovo 43 42 0N 28 0 E
Rgotina 42 44 1N 22 17 E
Rhamnus 45 38 12N 24 3 E
Rharis, O. → 83 26 0N 5 4 E
Rhayader 13 52 19N 3 30W
Rheden 16 52 0N 6 3 E
Rhein 109 51 25N 102 15W
Rhein → 24 51 52N 6 20 E
Rhein-Main-Donau-Kanal 25 49 1N 11 27 E
Rheinbach 24 50 38N 6 54 E
Rheine 24 52 17N 7 25 E
Rheinland-Pfalz □ 25 50 0N 7 0 E
Rheinsberg 24 53 6N 12 52 E
Rheriss, Oued → 82 30 50N 4 34W
Rheydt 24 51 10N 6 24 E
Rhin → Rhein → 24 51 52N 6 20 E
Rhinau 19 48 19N 7 43 E
Rhine = Rhein → 24 51 52N 6 20 E
Rhinelander 116 45 38N 89 29W
Rhino Camp 90 3 0N 31 22 E
Rhir, Cap 82 30 38N 9 54W
Rho 38 45 31N 9 2 E
Rhode Island □ 114 41 38N 71 37W
Rhodes = Ródhos 45 36 15N 28 10 E
Rhodes' Tomb 91 20 30 S 28 30 E
Rhodesia = Zimbabwe ■ 91 20 0 S 30 0 E
Rhodope Mts. = Rhodopi Planina 43 41 40N 24 20 E
Rhodopi Planina 43 41 40N 24 20 E
Rhondda 13 51 39N 3 30W
Rhône □ 21 45 54N 4 35 E
Rhône → 21 43 28N 4 42 E
Rhum 14 57 0N 6 20W
Rhumney 13 51 32N 3 7W
Rhyl 12 53 19N 3 29W
Ri-Aba 85 3 28N 8 40 E
Riachão 127 7 20 S 46 37W
Riaño 30 42 59N 5 0W
Rians 21 43 37N 5 44 E
Riansares → 32 39 32N 3 18W
Riasi 69 33 10N 74 50 E
Riau □ 72 0 0 102 35 E
Riau, Kepulauan 72 0 30N 104 20 E
Riaza 32 41 18N 3 30W
Riaza → 32 41 42N 3 55W
Riba de Saelices 32 40 55N 2 17W
Ribadavia 30 42 17N 8 8W
Ribadeo 30 43 35N 7 5W
Ribadesella 30 43 30N 5 7W
Ribas 32 42 19N 2 15 E
Ribble → 12 54 13N 2 20W
Ribe 49 55 19N 8 44 E
Ribeauvillé 19 48 10N 7 20 E
Ribécourt 19 49 30N 2 55 E
Ribeira 30 42 36N 8 58W
Ribeirão Prêto 125 21 10 S 47 50W
Ribemont 19 49 47N 3 27 E
Ribera 40 37 30N 13 13 E
Ribérac 20 45 15N 0 20 E
Riberalta 126 11 0 S 66 0W
Ribnica 39 45 45N 14 45 E
Ribnitz-Damgarten 24 54 14N 12 24 E
Ričany 26 50 0N 14 40 E
Riccarton 101 43 32 S 172 37 E
Riccia 41 41 30N 14 50 E
Riccione 39 44 0N 12 39 E
Rice L. 112 44 12N 78 10W
Rice Lake 116 45 30N 91 42W
Riceys, Les 19 47 59N 4 22 E
Rich 82 32 16N 4 30W
Rich Hill 117 38 5N 94 22W
Richards Bay 93 28 48 S 32 6 E
Richards L. 109 59 10N 107 10W
Richardson → 109 58 25N 111 14W
Richardton 116 46 56N 102 22W
Richelieu 18 47 0N 0 20 E
Richey 116 47 42N 105 5W
Richfield, Idaho, U.S.A. 118 43 2N 114 5W
Richfield, Utah, U.S.A. 119 38 50N 112 0W
Richford 113 45 0N 72 40W
Richibucto 107 46 42N 64 54W
Richland, Ga., U.S.A. 115 32 7N 84 40W
Richland, Oreg., U.S.A. 118 44 49N 117 9W
Richland, Wash., U.S.A. 118 46 15N 119 15W
Richland Center 116 43 21N 90 22W
Richlands 114 37 7N 81 49W
Richmond, N.S.W., Austral. 100 33 35 S 150 42 E
Richmond, Queens., Austral. 97 20 43 S 143 8 E
Richmond, N.Z. 101 41 20 S 173 12 E
Richmond, S. Afr. 93 29 51 S 30 18 E
Richmond, N. Yorks., U.K. 12 54 24N 1 43W
Richmond, Surrey, U.K. 13 51 28N 0 18W
Richmond, Calif., U.S.A. 118 37 58N 122 21W
Richmond, Ind., U.S.A. 114 39 50N 84 50W
Richmond, Ky., U.S.A. 114 37 40N 84 20W
Richmond, Mich., U.S.A. 112 42 47N 82 45W
Richmond, Mo., U.S.A. 116 39 15N 93 58W
Richmond, Tex., U.S.A. 117 29 32N 95 42W
Richmond, Utah, U.S.A. 118 41 55N 111 48W
Richmond, Va., U.S.A. 114 37 33N 77 27W
Richmond, Ra. 99 29 0 S 152 45 E
Richton 115 31 23N 88 58W
Richwood 114 38 17N 80 32W
Ricla 32 41 31N 1 24W
Riddarhyttan 48 59 49N 15 33 E
Ridgedale 109 53 0N 104 10W
Ridgeland 115 32 30N 80 58W
Ridgelands 98 23 16 S 150 17 E
Ridgetown 106 42 26N 81 52W
Ridgewood 113 40 59N 74 7W
Ridgway 114 41 25N 78 43W
Riding Mt. Nat. Park 109 50 50N 100 0W
Ried 26 48 14N 13 30 E
Riedlingen 25 48 9N 9 28 E
Rienza → 39 46 49N 11 47 E
Riesa 24 51 19N 13 19 E
Riesi 41 37 16N 14 4 E
Rieti 39 42 23N 12 50 E
Rieupeyroux 20 44 19N 2 12 E
Riez 21 43 49N 6 6 E
Rifle 118 39 40N 107 50W
Rifstangi 50 66 32N 16 12W
Rift Valley □ 90 0 20N 36 0 E
Rig Rig 81 14 13N 14 25 E
Riga 54 56 53N 24 8 E
Riga, G. of = Rīgas Jūras Līcis 54 57 40N 23 45 E
Rīgas Jūras Līcis 54 57 40N 23 45 E
Rigaud 113 45 29N 74 18W
Rigby 118 43 41N 111 58W
Rīgestān □ 65 30 15N 65 0 E
Riggins 118 45 29N 116 26W
Rignac 20 44 25N 2 16 E
Rigolet 107 54 10N 58 23W
Riihimäki 51 60 45N 24 48 E
Riiser-Larsen-halvøya 5 68 0 S 35 0 E
Rijau 85 11 8N 5 17 E
Rijeka 39 45 20N 14 21 E
Rijeka Crnojevica 42 42 24N 19 1 E
Rijn → 16 52 12N 4 21 E
Rijssen 16 52 19N 6 30 E
Rijswijk 16 52 4N 4 22 E
Rike 87 10 50N 39 53 E
Rila 43 42 7N 23 7 E
Rila Planina 42 42 10N 23 0 E
Riley 118 43 35N 119 33W
Rilly 19 49 11N 4 3 E
Rima → 85 13 4N 5 10 E
Rimah, Wadi ar → 64 26 5N 41 30 E
Rimavská Sobota 27 48 22N 20 2 E
Rimbey 108 52 35N 114 15W
Rimbo 48 59 44N 18 21 E
Rimforsa 49 58 6N 15 43 E
Rimi 85 12 58N 7 43 E
Rimini 39 44 3N 12 33 E
Rîmna → 46 45 36N 27 3 E
Rîmnicu Sărat 46 45 26N 27 3 E
Rîmnicu Vîlcea 46 45 9N 24 21 E
Rimouski 107 48 27N 68 30W
Rinca 73 8 45 S 119 35 E
Rinconada 124 22 26 S 66 10W
Rineanna 15 52 42N 8 57W
Ringarum 49 58 21N 16 26 E
Ringe 49 55 13N 10 28 E
Ringgim 85 12 13N 9 10 E
Ringkøbing 49 56 5N 8 15 E
Ringling 118 46 16N 110 56W
Ringsaker 47 60 54N 10 45 E
Ringsjön 49 55 55N 13 30 E
Ringsted 49 55 25N 11 46 E
Ringvassøy 50 69 56N 19 15 E
Rinía 45 37 23N 25 13 E
Rinjani 72 8 24 S 116 28 E
Rinteln 24 52 11N 9 3 E
Rio Branco 126 9 58 S 67 49W
Río Branco 125 32 40 S 53 40W
Rio Brilhante 125 21 48 S 54 33W
Rio Claro, Brazil 125 22 19 S 47 35W
Rio Claro, Trin. 121 10 20N 61 25W
Río Colorado 128 39 0 S 64 0W
Río Cuarto 124 33 10 S 64 25W
Rio das Pedras 93 23 8 S 35 28 E
Rio de Janeiro 125 23 0 S 43 12W
Rio de Janeiro □ 125 22 50 S 43 0W
Rio do Sul 125 27 13 S 49 37W
Río Gallegos 128 51 35 S 69 15W
Río Grande 128 53 50 S 67 45W
Rio Grande 125 32 0 S 52 20W
Rio Grande → 117 25 57N 97 9W
Rio Grande City 117 26 23N 98 49W
Río Grande del Norte → 110 26 0N 97 0W
Rio Grande do Norte □ 127 5 40 S 36 0W
Rio Grande do Sul □ 125 30 0 S 53 0W
Rio Largo 127 9 28 S 35 50W
Rio Maior 31 39 19N 8 57W
Rio Marina 38 42 48N 10 25 E
Río Mulatos 126 19 40 S 66 50W
Río Muni □ 88 1 30N 10 0 E
Rio Negro 125 26 0 S 50 0W
Rio Pardo 125 30 0 S 52 30W
Río, Punta del 33 36 49N 2 24W
Río Segundo 124 31 40 S 63 59W
Río Tercero 124 32 15 S 64 8W
Rio Tinto 30 41 11N 8 34W
Rio Verde 127 17 50 S 51 0W
Río Verde 120 21 56N 99 59W
Rio Vista 118 38 11N 121 44W
Ríobamba 126 1 50 S 78 45W
Ríohacha 126 11 33N 72 55W
Rioja, La, Argent. 124 29 20 S 67 0W
Rioja, La, Spain 32 42 20N 2 20W
Rioja, La □ 124 29 30 S 67 0W
Riom 20 45 54N 3 7 E
Riom-ès-Montagnes 20 45 17N 2 39 E
Rion-des-Landes 20 43 55N 0 56W
Rionero in Vúlture 41 40 55N 15 40 E
Rioni → 57 42 5N 41 50 E
Rios 30 41 58N 7 16W
Riosucio 126 5 30N 75 40W
Riosucio 126 7 27N 77 7W
Riou L. 109 59 7N 106 25W
Rioz 19 47 25N 6 04 E
Riparia, Dora → 38 45 7N 7 24 E
Ripatransone 39 43 0N 13 45 E
Ripley, Can. 112 44 4N 81 35W
Ripley, N.Y., U.S.A. 112 42 16N 79 44W
Ripley, Tenn., U.S.A. 117 35 43N 89 34W
Ripoll 32 42 15N 2 13 E
Ripon, U.K. 12 54 8N 1 31W
Ripon, U.S.A. 114 43 51N 88 50W
Riposto 41 37 44N 15 12 E
Risan 42 42 32N 18 42 E
Riscle 20 43 39N 0 5W
Rishiri-Tō, Japan 74 45 11N 141 15 E
Rishiri-Tō, Japan 74 45 11N 141 15 E
Rishon le Ziyyon 62 31 58N 34 48 E
Rishpon 62 32 12N 34 49 E
Risle → 18 49 26N 0 23 E
Rîsnov 46 45 35N 25 27 E
Rison 117 33 57N 92 11W
Risør 47 58 43N 9 13 E
Ritchies Archipelago 71 12 5N 94 0 E
Riti 85 7 57N 9 41 E
Rittman 112 40 57N 81 48W
Ritzville 118 47 10N 118 21W
Riva Bella 18 49 17N 0 18W
Riva del Garda 38 45 53N 10 50 E
Rivadavia, Buenos Aires, Argent. 124 35 29 S 62 59W
Rivadavia, Mendoza, Argent. 124 33 13 S 68 30W
Rivadavia, Salta, Argent. 124 24 5 S 62 54W
Rivadavia, Chile 124 29 57 S 70 35W
Rivarolo Canavese 38 45 20N 7 42 E
Rivas 121 11 30N 85 50W
Rive-de-Gier 21 45 32N 4 37 E
River Cess 84 5 30N 9 32W
Rivera 125 31 0 S 55 50W
Riverdsale 92 34 7 S 21 15 E
Riverhead 114 40 53N 72 40W
Riverhurst 109 50 55N 106 50W
Riverina 97 35 30 S 145 20 E
Rivers 109 50 2N 100 14W
Rivers □ 85 5 0N 6 30 E
Rivers Inl. 108 51 40N 127 20W
Rivers, L. of the 109 49 49N 105 44W
Riverside, Calif., U.S.A. 119 34 0N 117 22W
Riverside, Wyo., U.S.A. 118 41 12N 106 57W
Riversleigh 98 19 5 S 138 40 E
Riverton, Austral. 99 34 10 S 138 46 E
Riverton, Can. 109 51 1N 97 0W
Riverton, N.Z. 101 46 21 S 168 0 E
Riverton, U.S.A. 118 43 1N 108 27W
Rives 21 45 21N 5 31 E
Rivesaltes 20 42 47N 2 50 E
Riviera 38 44 0N 8 30 E
Riviera di Levante 36 44 23N 9 15 E
Riviera di Ponente 36 43 50N 7 58 E
Rivière-à-Pierre 107 46 59N 72 11W
Rivière-au-Renard 107 48 59N 64 23W
Rivière-du-Loup 107 47 50N 69 30W
Rivière-Pentecôte 107 49 57N 67 1W
Rivoli 38 45 3N 7 31 E
Rivoli B. 99 37 32 S 140 3 E
Riyadh = Ar Riyāḍ 64 24 41N 46 42 E
Rize 64 41 0N 40 30 E
Rizhao 77 35 25N 119 30 E
Rizzuto, C. 41 38 54N 17 5 E
Rjukan 47 59 54N 8 33 E
Rjuven 47 59 9N 7 8 E
Roa, Norway 47 60 17N 10 37 E
Roa, Spain 30 41 41N 3 56W
Roag, L. 14 58 10N 6 55W
Roanne 21 46 3N 4 4 E
Roanoke, Ala., U.S.A. 115 33 9N 85 23W
Roanoke, Va., U.S.A. 114 37 19N 79 55W
Roanoke → 115 35 56N 76 43W
Roanoke I. 115 35 55N 75 40W
Roanoke Rapids 115 36 28N 77 42W
Roatán 121 16 18N 86 35W
Robbins I. 99 40 42 S 145 0 E
Robe → 15 53 38N 9 10W
Robe, Mt. 100 31 40 S 141 20 E
Röbel 24 53 24N 12 37 E

Robert Lee Rujen

Robert Lee	117	31 55N	100 26W
Roberts	118	43 44N	112 8W
Robertsganj	69	24 44N	83 4 E
Robertson	92	33 46 S	19 50 E
Robertson I.	5	65 15 S	59 30W
Robertsport	84	6 45N	11 26W
Robertstown	99	33 58 S	139 5 E
Roberval	107	48 32N	72 15W
Robeson Ch.	4	82 0N	61 30W
Robinson Crusoe I.	95	33 38 S	78 52W
Robinson Ranges	96	25 40 S	119 0 E
Robinvale	99	34 40 S	142 45 E
Robla, La	30	42 50N	5 41W
Roblin	109	51 14N	101 21W
Roboré	126	18 10 S	59 45W
Robson, Mt.	108	53 10N	119 10W
Robstown	117	27 47N	97 40W
Roc, Pointe du	18	48 50N	1 37W
Roca, C. da	31	38 40N	9 31W
Rocas, I.	127	4 0 S	34 1W
Rocca d'Aspidé	41	40 27N	15 10 E
Rocca San Casciano	39	44 3N	11 45 E
Roccalbegna	39	42 47N	11 30 E
Roccastrada	39	43 0N	11 10 E
Roccella Iónica	41	38 20N	16 24 E
Rocha	125	34 30 S	54 25W
Rochdale	12	53 36N	2 10W
Roche-Bernard, La	18	47 31N	2 19W
Roche-Canillac, La	20	45 12N	1 57 E
Roche, La	21	46 4N	6 19 E
Roche-sur-Yon, La	18	46 40N	1 25W
Rochechouart	20	45 50N	0 49 E
Rochefort, Belg.	16	50 9N	5 12 E
Rochefort, France	20	45 56N	0 57W
Rochefort-en-Terre	18	47 42N	2 22W
Rochefoucauld, La	20	45 44N	0 24 E
Rochelle	116	41 55N	89 5W
Rochelle, La	20	46 10N	1 9W
Rocher River	108	61 23N	112 44W
Rocheservière	18	46 57N	1 30W
Rochester, Austral.	100	36 22 S	144 41 E
Rochester, Can.	108	54 22N	113 27W
Rochester, U.K.	13	51 22N	0 30 E
Rochester, Ind., U.S.A.	114	41 5N	86 15W
Rochester, Minn., U.S.A.	116	44 1N	92 28W
Rochester, N.H., U.S.A.	114	43 19N	70 57W
Rochester, N.Y., U.S.A.	114	43 10N	77 40W
Rochester, Pa., U.S.A.	112	40 41N	80 17W
Rociana	31	37 19N	6 35W
Rociu	46	44 43N	25 2 E
Rock →	108	60 7N	127 7W
Rock Hill	115	34 55N	81 2W
Rock Island	116	41 30N	90 35W
Rock Port	116	40 26N	95 30W
Rock Rapids	116	43 25N	96 10W
Rock River	118	41 49N	106 0W
Rock Sound	121	24 54N	76 12W
Rock Sprs., Ariz., U.S.A.	119	34 2N	112 11W
Rock Sprs., Mont., U.S.A.	118	46 55N	106 11W
Rock Sprs., Tex., U.S.A.	117	30 2N	100 11W
Rock Sprs., Wyo., U.S.A.	118	41 40N	109 10W
Rock Valley	116	43 10N	96 17W
Rockall	8	57 37N	13 42W
Rockdale	117	30 40N	97 0W
Rockefeller Plat.	5	80 0 S	140 0W
Rockford	116	42 20N	89 0W
Rockglen	109	49 11N	105 57W
Rockhampton	97	23 22 S	150 32 E
Rockingham B.	98	18 5 S	146 10 E
Rockingham Forest	13	52 28N	0 42W
Rocklake	116	48 50N	99 13W
Rockland, Can.	113	45 33N	75 17W
Rockland, Idaho, U.S.A.	118	42 37N	112 57W
Rockland, Me., U.S.A.	107	44 6N	69 6W
Rockland, Mich., U.S.A.	116	46 40N	89 10W
Rocklands Reservoir	100	37 15 S	142 5 E
Rockmart	115	34 1N	85 2W
Rockport	117	28 2N	97 3W
Rockville, Conn., U.S.A.	113	41 51N	72 27W
Rockville, Md., U.S.A.	114	39 7N	77 10W
Rockwall	117	32 55N	96 30W
Rockwell City	116	42 20N	94 35W
Rockwood	115	35 52N	84 40W
Rocky Ford	116	38 7N	103 45W
Rocky Lane	108	58 31N	116 22W
Rocky Mount	115	35 55N	77 48W
Rocky Mountain House	108	52 22N	114 55W
Rocky Mts.	108	55 0N	121 0W
Rocky Pt.	96	33 30 S	123 57 E
Rocky River	112	41 30N	81 40W
Rockyford	108	51 14N	113 10W
Rocroi	19	49 55N	4 30 E
Rod	66	28 10N	63 5 E
Roda, La, Albacete, Spain	33	39 13N	2 15W
Roda, La, Sevilla, Spain	31	37 12N	4 46W
Rødberg	47	60 17N	8 56 E
Rødby	49	54 41N	11 23 E
Rødbyhavn	49	54 39N	11 22 E
Roddickton	107	50 51N	56 8W
Rødding	49	55 23N	9 3 E
Rødekro	49	55 4N	9 20 E
Rødenes	47	59 35N	11 34 E
Rodenkirchen	24	53 24N	8 26 E
Roderick I.	108	52 38N	128 22W
Rodez	20	44 21N	2 33 E
Rodholívas	44	40 55N	24 0 E
Rodhópi □	44	41 5N	25 30 E
Ródhos	45	36 15N	28 10 E
Rodi Garganico	41	41 55N	15 53 E
Rodna	46	47 25N	24 50 E
Rodnei, Munţii	46	47 35N	24 35 E
Rodney	112	42 34N	81 41W
Rodney, C.	101	36 17 S	174 50 E
Rodniki	55	57 7N	41 47 E
Rodriguez	3	19 45 S	63 20 E
Rodstock, C.	96	33 12 S	134 20 E
Roe →	15	55 10N	6 59W
Roebling	113	40 7N	74 45W
Roebourne	96	20 44 S	117 9 E
Roebuck B.	96	18 5 S	122 20 E
Roermond	16	51 12N	6 0 E
Roes Welcome Sd.	105	65 0N	87 0W
Roeselare	16	50 57N	3 7 E
Rogachev	54	53 8N	30 5 E
Rogaçica	42	44 4N	19 40 E
Rogagua, L.	126	13 43 S	66 50W
Rogaland fylke □	47	59 12N	6 20 E
Rogaška Slatina	39	46 15N	15 42 E
Rogatec	39	46 15N	15 46 E
Rogatica	42	43 47N	19 0 E
Rogatin	54	49 24N	24 36 E
Rogers	117	36 20N	94 5W
Rogers City	114	45 25N	83 49W
Rogerson	118	42 10N	114 40W
Rogersville	115	36 27N	83 1W
Roggan	106	54 25N	79 32W
Roggeveldberge	92	32 10 S	20 10 E
Roggiano Gravina	41	39 37N	16 9 E
Rogliano, France	21	42 57N	9 30 E
Rogliano, Italy	41	39 11N	16 20 E
Rogoaguado, L.	126	13 0 S	65 30W
Rogowo	28	52 43N	17 38 E
Rogozno	28	52 45N	16 59 E
Rogue →	118	42 30N	124 0W
Rohan	18	48 4N	2 45W
Rohrbach	19	49 3N	7 15 E
Rohri	68	27 45N	68 51 E
Rohri Canal	68	26 15N	68 27 E
Rohtak	68	28 55N	76 43 E
Roi Et	71	16 4N	103 40 E
Roisel	19	49 58N	3 6 E
Rojas	124	34 10 S	60 45W
Rojo, C.	120	21 33N	97 20W
Rokan →	72	2 0N	100 50 E
Rokeby	98	13 39 S	142 40 E
Rokiskis	54	55 55N	25 35 E
Rokitno	54	50 57N	35 56 E
Rokycany	26	49 43N	13 35 E
Rolândia	125	23 18 S	51 23W
Røldal	47	59 47N	6 50 E
Rolette	116	48 42N	99 50W
Rolla, Kansas, U.S.A.	117	37 10N	101 40W
Rolla, Mo., U.S.A.	117	37 56N	91 42W
Rolla, N. Dak., U.S.A.	116	48 50N	99 36W
Rollag	47	60 2N	9 18 E
Rolleston	98	24 28 S	148 35 E
Rollingstone	98	19 2 S	146 24 E
Rom	87	9 54N	32 16 E
Roma, Austral.	97	26 32 S	148 49 E
Roma, Italy	40	41 54N	12 30 E
Roman, Bulg.	43	43 8N	23 54 E
Roman, Romania	46	46 57N	26 55 E
Roman, U.S.S.R.	59	66 4N	112 14 E
Roman-Kosh, Gora	56	44 37N	34 15 E
Romana, La	121	18 27N	68 57W
Romanche →	21	45 5N	5 43 E
Romang	73	7 30 S	127 20 E
Români	86	30 59N	32 38 E
Romania ■	46	46 0N	25 0 E
Romanija Planina	42	43 50N	18 45 E
Romano, Cayo	121	22 0N	77 30W
Romano di Lombardia	38	45 32N	9 45 E
Romanovka = Bessarabka	56	46 21N	28 58 E
Romans	21	45 3N	5 3 E
Romanshorn	25	47 33N	9 22 E
Romblon	73	12 33N	122 17 E
Rombo □	90	3 10 S	37 30 E
Rome, Ga., U.S.A.	115	34 20N	85 0W
Rome, N.Y., U.S.A.	114	43 14N	75 29W
Rome = Roma	40	41 54N	12 30 E
Romeleåsen	49	55 34N	13 33 E
Romenay	21	46 30N	5 1 E
Romerike	47	60 7N	11 10 E
Romilly	19	48 31N	3 44 E
Romîni	46	44 59N	24 11 E
Rommani	82	33 31N	6 40W
Romney	114	39 21N	78 45W
Romney Marsh	13	51 0N	1 0 E
Romny	54	50 48N	33 28 E
Rømø	49	55 10N	8 30 E
Romodan	54	50 0N	33 15 E
Romodanovo	55	54 26N	45 23 E
Romont	25	46 42N	6 54 E
Romorantin-Lanthenay	19	47 21N	1 45 E
Romsdalen	47	62 25N	8 0 E
Rona	14	57 33N	6 0W
Ronan	118	47 30N	114 6W
Roncador, Cayos	121	13 32N	80 4W
Roncador, Serra do	127	12 30 S	52 30W
Roncesvalles, Paso	32	43 1N	1 19W
Ronceverte	114	37 45N	80 28W
Ronciglione	39	42 18N	12 12 E
Ronco →	39	44 24N	12 12 E
Ronda	31	36 46N	5 12W
Ronda, Serranía de	31	36 44N	5 3W
Rondane	47	61 57N	9 50 E
Rondônia □	126	11 0 S	63 0W
Rondonópolis	127	16 28 S	54 38W
Rong, Koh	71	10 45N	103 15 E
Rong Xian	77	29 23N	104 22 E
Rong'an	77	25 14N	109 22 E
Ronge, L. la	109	55 6N	105 17W
Ronge, La	109	55 5N	105 20W
Rongshui	77	25 5N	109 12 E
Ronne Land	5	83 0 S	70 0W
Ronneby	49	56 12N	15 17 E
Ronse	16	50 45N	3 35 E
Roof Butte	119	36 29N	109 5W
Roorkee	68	29 52N	77 59 E
Roosendaal	16	51 32N	4 29 E
Roosevelt, Minn., U.S.A.	116	48 51N	95 2W
Roosevelt, Utah, U.S.A.	118	40 19N	110 1W
Roosevelt I.	5	79 30 S	162 0W
Roosevelt, Mt.	108	58 26N	125 20W
Roosevelt Res.	119	33 46N	111 0W
Ropczyce	27	50 4N	21 38 E
Roper →	96	14 43 S	135 27 E
Ropesville	117	33 25N	102 10W
Roque Pérez	124	35 25 S	59 24W
Roquebrou, La	20	44 58N	2 12 E
Roquefort	20	44 2N	0 20W
Roquefort-sur-Soulzon	20	43 58N	2 59 E
Roquemaure	21	44 3N	4 48 E
Roquetas	32	40 50N	0 30 E
Roquevaire	21	43 20N	5 36 E
Roraima □	126	2 0N	61 30W
Roraima, Mt.	126	5 10N	60 40W
Rorketon	109	51 24N	99 35W
Røros	47	62 35N	11 23 E
Rorschach	25	47 28N	9 30 E
Rosa	91	9 33 S	31 15 E
Rosa, C.	83	37 0N	8 16 E
Rosa, Monte	25	45 57N	7 53 E
Rosal	30	41 57N	8 51W
Rosal de la Frontera	31	37 59N	7 13W
Rosalia	118	47 14N	117 25W
Rosans	21	44 24N	5 29 E
Rosario	124	33 0 S	60 40W
Rosário	127	3 0 S	44 15W
Rosario, Baja Calif. N., Mexico	120	30 0N	115 50W
Rosario, Durango, Mexico	120	26 30N	105 35W
Rosario, Sinaloa, Mexico	120	23 0N	105 52W
Rosario, Parag.	124	24 30 S	57 35W
Rosario de la Frontera	124	25 50 S	65 0W
Rosario de Lerma	124	24 59 S	65 35W
Rosario del Tala	124	32 20 S	59 10W
Rosário do Sul	125	30 15 S	54 55W
Rosarno	41	38 29N	15 59 E
Rosas	32	42 19N	3 10 E
Roscoe	116	45 27N	99 20W
Roscoff	18	48 44N	4 0W
Roscommon, Ireland	15	53 38N	8 11W
Roscommon, U.S.A.	114	44 27N	84 35W
Roscommon □	15	53 40N	8 15W
Roscrea	15	52 58N	7 50W
Rose Blanche	107	47 38N	58 45W
Rose Harbour	108	52 15N	131 10W
Rose Pt.	108	54 11N	131 39W
Rose Valley	109	52 19N	103 49W
Roseau, Domin.	121	15 20N	61 24W
Roseau, U.S.A.	116	48 51N	95 46W
Rosebery	99	41 46 S	145 33 E
Rosebud, Austral.	100	38 21 S	144 54 E
Rosebud, U.S.A.	117	31 5N	97 0W
Roseburg	118	43 10N	123 20W
Rosedale, Austral.	98	24 38 S	151 53 E
Rosedale, U.S.A.	117	33 51N	91 0W
Rosemary	108	50 46N	112 5W
Rosenberg	117	29 30N	95 48W
Rosendaël	19	51 3N	2 24 E
Rosenheim	25	47 51N	12 9 E
Roseto degli Abruzzi	39	42 40N	14 2 E
Rosetown	109	51 35N	107 59W
Rosetta = Rashîd	86	31 21N	30 22 E
Roseville	118	38 46N	121 17W
Rosewood	99	27 38 S	152 36 E
Rosh Haniqra, Kefar	62	33 5N	35 5 E
Rosh Pinna	62	32 58N	35 32 E
Rosières	19	49 49N	2 43 E
Rosignano Marittimo	38	43 23N	10 28 E
Rosignol	126	6 15N	57 30W
Roşiori de Vede	46	44 9N	25 0 E
Rositsa	43	43 57N	27 57 E
Rositsa →	43	43 10N	25 30 E
Roskilde	49	55 38N	12 3 E
Roskilde Amtskommune □	49	55 35N	12 5 E
Roskilde Fjord	49	55 50N	12 2 E
Roslavl	54	53 57N	32 55 E
Roslyn	99	34 29 S	149 37 E
Rosmaninhal	31	39 44N	7 5W
Røsnæs	49	55 44N	10 55 E
Rosolini	41	36 49N	14 58 E
Rosporden	18	47 57N	3 50W
Ross, Austral.	99	42 2 S	147 30 E
Ross, N.Z.	101	42 53 S	170 49 E
Ross Dependency □	5	70 0 S	170 5W
Ross I.	5	77 30 S	168 0 E
Ross Ice Shelf	5	80 0 S	180 0W
Ross L.	118	48 50N	121 5W
Ross on Wye	13	51 55N	2 34W
Ross Sea	5	74 0 S	178 0 E
Rossan Pt.	15	54 42N	8 47W
Rossano Cálabro	41	39 36N	16 39 E
Rossburn	109	50 40N	100 49W
Rosseau	112	45 16N	79 39W
Rossignol, L., N.S., Can.	107	44 12N	65 10W
Rossignol, L., Qué., Can.	106	52 43N	73 40W
Rossland	108	49 6N	117 50W
Rosslare	15	52 17N	6 23W
Rosslau	24	51 52N	12 15 E
Rosso	84	16 40N	15 45W
Rossosh	57	50 15N	39 28 E
Rossport	106	48 50N	87 30W
Røssvatnet	50	65 45N	14 5 E
Rossville	98	15 48 S	145 15 E
Rosthern	109	52 40N	106 20W
Rostock	24	54 4N	12 9 E
Rostock □	24	54 10N	12 30 E
Rostov, Don, U.S.S.R.	57	47 15N	39 45 E
Rostov, Moskva, U.S.S.R.	55	57 14N	39 25 E
Rostrenen	18	48 14N	3 21W
Roswell	117	33 26N	104 32W
Rosyth	14	56 2N	3 26W
Rota	31	36 37N	6 20W
Rotälven →	48	61 15N	14 3 E
Rotan	117	32 52N	100 30W
Rotenburg	24	53 6N	9 24 E
Roth	25	49 15N	11 6 E
Rothaargebirge	22	51 0N	8 20 E
Rothenburg ob der Tauber	25	49 21N	10 11 E
Rother →	13	50 59N	0 40 E
Rotherham	12	53 26N	1 21W
Rothes	14	57 31N	3 12W
Rothesay, Can.	107	45 23N	66 0W
Rothesay, U.K.	14	55 50N	5 3W
Roti	73	10 50 S	123 0 E
Roto	97	33 0 S	145 30 E
Rotondella	41	40 10N	16 30 E
Rotoroa, L.	101	41 55 S	172 39 E
Rotorua	101	38 9 S	176 16 E
Rotorua, L.	101	38 5 S	176 18 E
Rott →	25	48 26N	13 26 E
Rottenburg	25	48 28N	8 56 E
Rottenmann	26	47 31N	14 22 E
Rotterdam	16	51 55N	4 30 E
Rottumeroog	16	53 33N	6 34 E
Rottweil	25	48 9N	8 38 E
Rotuma	94	12 25 S	177 5 E
Roubaix	19	50 40N	3 10 E
Roudnice	26	50 25N	14 15 E
Rouen	18	49 27N	1 4 E
Rouillac	20	45 47N	0 4W
Rouleau	109	50 10N	104 56W
Round Mt.	97	30 26 S	152 16 E
Round Mountain	118	38 46N	117 3W
Roundup	118	46 25N	108 35W
Rousay	14	59 10N	3 2W
Rouses Point	113	44 58N	73 22W
Rousse, L'Île	21	42 37N	8 57 E
Roussillon, Isère, France	21	45 24N	4 49 E
Roussillon, Pyrénées-Or., France	20	42 30N	2 35 E
Rouxville	92	30 25 S	26 50 E
Rouyn	106	48 20N	79 0W
Rovaniemi	50	66 29N	25 41 E
Rovato	38	45 34N	10 0 E
Rovenki	57	48 5N	39 21 E
Rovereto	38	45 53N	11 3 E
Rovigo	39	45 4N	11 48 E
Rovinari	46	44 56N	23 10 E
Rovinj	39	45 5N	13 40 E
Rovno	54	50 40N	26 10 E
Rovnoye	55	50 52N	46 3 E
Rovuma →	91	10 29 S	40 28 E
Rowena	99	29 48 S	148 55 E
Rowley Shoals	96	17 30 S	119 0 E
Roxa	84	11 15N	15 45W
Roxas	73	11 36N	122 49 E
Roxboro	115	36 24N	78 59W
Roxborough Downs	98	22 30 S	138 45 E
Roxburgh	101	45 33 S	169 19 E
Roxen	49	58 30N	15 40 E
Roy, Mont., U.S.A.	118	47 17N	109 0W
Roy, N. Mex., U.S.A.	117	35 57N	104 8W
Roy, Le	117	38 8N	95 35W
Roya, Peña	32	40 25N	0 40W
Royal Oak	114	42 30N	83 5W
Royan	20	45 37N	1 2W
Roye	19	49 42N	2 48 E
Røyken	47	59 45N	10 23 E
Rožaj	42	42 50N	20 15 E
Rózan	28	52 52N	21 25 E
Rozay	19	48 40N	2 56 E
Rozhishche	54	50 54N	25 15 E
Rozier, Le	20	44 13N	3 12 E
Rôžnava	27	48 37N	20 35 E
Rozogi	28	53 48N	21 9 E
Rozoy-sur-Serre	19	49 40N	4 8 E
Rozwadów	28	50 37N	22 2 E
Rrësheni	44	41 47N	19 49 E
Rrogozhino	44	41 2N	19 50 E
Rtanj	42	43 45N	21 50 E
Rtishchevo	55	55 16N	43 50 E
Rúa	30	42 24N	7 6W
Ruacaná	92	17 20 S	14 12 E
Ruahine Ra.	101	39 55 S	176 2 E
Ruapehu	101	39 17 S	175 35 E
Ruapuke I.	101	46 46 S	168 31 E
Ruaus, Wadi →	83	30 26N	15 24 E
Rubeho Mts.	90	6 50 S	36 25 E
Rubezhnoye	56	49 6N	38 25 E
Rubh a' Mhail	14	55 55N	6 10W
Rubha Hunish	14	57 42N	6 20W
Rubicone →	39	44 8N	12 28 E
Rubino	84	6 4N	4 18W
Rubio	126	7 43N	72 22W
Rubtsovsk	58	51 30N	81 10 E
Ruby	104	64 40N	155 35W
Ruby L.	118	40 10N	115 28W
Ruby Mts.	118	40 30N	115 30W
Rubyvale	98	23 25 S	147 45 E
Rucava	54	56 9N	21 12 E
Ruciane-Nida	28	53 40N	21 32 E
Rud	47	60 1N	10 1 E
Ruda	49	57 6N	16 7 E
Ruda Śląska	28	50 16N	18 50 E
Ruden	24	54 13N	13 47 E
Rüdersdorf	24	52 28N	13 48 E
Rudewa	91	10 7 S	34 40 E
Rudkøbing	49	54 56N	10 41 E
Rudna	28	51 30N	16 17 E
Rudnichnyy	52	59 38N	52 26 E
Rudnik, Bulg.	43	42 36N	27 30 E
Rudnik, Poland	28	50 26N	22 15 E
Rudnik, Yugo.	42	44 8N	20 30 E
Rudnik, Yugo.	43	44 7N	20 35 E
Rudnogorsk	59	57 15N	103 42 E
Rudnya	54	54 55N	31 7 E
Rudnyy	58	52 57N	63 7 E
Rudo	42	43 41N	19 23 E
Rudolf, Ostrov	58	81 45N	58 30 E
Rudolstadt	24	50 44N	11 20 E
Rudozem	43	41 29N	24 51 E
Rudyard	114	46 14N	84 35W
Rue	19	50 15N	1 40 E
Ruelle	20	45 41N	0 14 E
Rufa'a	87	14 44N	33 22 E
Ruffec-Charente	20	46 2N	0 12 E
Rufiji □	90	8 0 S	38 30 E
Rufiji →	90	7 50 S	39 15 E
Rufino	124	34 20 S	62 50W
Rufisque	84	14 40N	17 15W
Rufunsa	91	15 4 S	29 34 E
Rugao	77	32 23N	120 31 E
Rugby, U.K.	13	52 23N	1 16W
Rugby, U.S.A.	116	48 21N	100 0W
Rügen	24	54 22N	13 25 E
Rugles	18	48 50N	0 40 E
Ruhama	62	31 31N	34 43 E
Ruhengeri	90	1 30 S	29 36 E
Ruhla	24	50 53N	10 21 E
Ruhland	24	51 27N	13 52 E
Ruhr →	24	51 25N	6 44 E
Ruhuhu →	91	10 31 S	34 34 E
Rui'an	77	27 47N	120 40 E
Ruidosa	117	29 59N	104 39W
Ruidoso	119	33 19N	105 39W
Ruj	42	42 52N	22 42 E
Rujen	42	42 9N	22 30 E

Ruk St-Junien

Ruk	**68**	27 50N	68 42 E
Rukwa □	**90**	7 0S	31 30 E
Rukwa L.	**90**	8 0S	32 20 E
Rum Cay	**121**	23 40N	74 58W
Rum Jungle	**96**	13 0S	130 59 E
Ruma	**42**	45 0N	19 50 E
Rumāḩ	**64**	25 29N	47 10 E
Rumania = Romania ■	**46**	46 0N	25 0 E
Rumbêk	**87**	6 54N	29 37 E
Rumburk	**26**	50 57N	14 32 E
Rumford	**114**	44 30N	70 30W
Rumia	**28**	54 37N	18 25 E
Rumilly	**21**	45 53N	5 56 E
Rumoi	**74**	43 56N	141 39W
Rumonge	**90**	3 59S	29 26 E
Rumsey	**108**	51 51N	112 48W
Rumula	**98**	16 35S	145 20 E
Rumuruti	**90**	0 17N	36 32 E
Runan	**77**	33 0N	114 30 E
Runanga	**101**	42 25S	171 15 E
Runaway, C.	**101**	37 32S	178 2 E
Runcorn	**12**	53 20N	2 44W
Rungwa	**90**	6 55S	33 32 E
Rungwa →	**90**	7 36S	31 50 E
Rungwe	**91**	9 11S	33 32 E
Rungwe □	**91**	9 25S	33 32 E
Runka	**85**	12 28N	7 20 E
Runn	**48**	60 30N	15 40 E
Ruoqiang	**75**	38 55N	88 10 E
Rupa	**67**	27 15N	92 21 E
Rupar	**68**	31 2N	76 38 E
Rupat	**72**	1 45N	101 40 E
Rupea	**46**	46 2N	25 13 E
Rupert →	**106**	51 29N	78 45W
Rupert House = Fort Rupert	**106**	51 30N	78 40W
Rupsa	**69**	21 44N	89 30 E
Rur →	**24**	51 20N	6 0 E
Rurrenabaque	**126**	14 30S	67 32W
Rus →	**33**	39 30N	2 30W
Rusambo	**91**	16 30S	32 4 E
Rusape	**91**	18 35S	32 8 E
Ruschuk = Ruse	**43**	43 48N	25 59 E
Ruse	**43**	43 48N	25 59 E
Ruşeţu	**46**	44 57N	27 14 E
Rushden	**13**	52 17N	0 37W
Rushford	**116**	43 48N	91 46W
Rushville, Ill., U.S.A.	**116**	40 6N	90 35W
Rushville, Ind., U.S.A.	**114**	39 38N	85 22W
Rushville, Nebr., U.S.A.	**116**	42 43N	102 28W
Rushworth	**100**	36 32S	145 1 E
Rusken	**49**	57 15N	14 20 E
Russas	**127**	4 55S	37 50W
Russell, Can.	**109**	50 50N	101 20W
Russell, N.Z.	**101**	35 16S	174 10 E
Russell, U.S.A.	**116**	38 56N	98 55W
Russell L., Man., Can.	**109**	56 15N	101 30W
Russell L., N.W.T., Can.	**108**	63 5N	115 44W
Russellkonda	**69**	19 57N	84 42 E
Russellville, Ala., U.S.A.	**115**	34 30N	87 44W
Russellville, Ark., U.S.A.	**117**	35 15N	93 8W
Russellville, Ky., U.S.A.	**115**	36 50N	86 50W
Russi	**39**	44 21N	12 1 E
Russian S.F.S.R. □	**59**	62 0N	105 0 E
Russkaya Polyana	**58**	53 47N	73 53 E
Russkoye Ustie	**4**	71 0N	149 0 E
Rust	**27**	47 49N	16 42 E
Rustavi	**57**	41 30N	45 0 E
Rustenburg	**92**	25 41S	27 14 E
Ruston	**117**	32 30N	92 58W
Rutana	**90**	3 55S	30 0 E
Rute	**31**	37 19N	4 23W
Ruteng	**73**	8 35S	120 30 E
Ruth, Mich., U.S.A.	**112**	43 42N	82 45W
Ruth, Nev., U.S.A.	**118**	39 15N	115 1W
Rutherglen, Austral.	**100**	36 5S	146 29 E
Rutherglen, U.K.	**14**	55 50N	4 11W
Rutigliano	**41**	41 1N	17 0 E
Rutland I.	**71**	11 25N	92 40 E
Rutland Plains	**98**	15 38S	141 43 E
Rutledge →	**109**	61 4N	112 0W
Rutledge L.	**109**	61 33N	110 47W
Rutshuru	**90**	1 13S	29 25 E
Ruurlo	**16**	52 5N	6 24 E
Ruvo di Púglia	**41**	41 7N	16 27 E
Ruvu	**90**	6 49S	38 43 E
Ruvu →	**90**	6 23S	38 52 E
Ruvuma □	**91**	10 20S	36 0 E
Ruwenzori	**90**	0 30N	29 55 E
Ruyigi	**90**	3 29S	30 15 E
Ruzayevka	**55**	54 4N	45 0 E
Růzhevo Konare	**43**	42 23N	24 46 E
Ružomberok	**27**	49 3N	19 17 E
Rwanda ■	**90**	2 0S	30 0 E
Ry	**49**	56 5N	9 45 E
Ryakhovo	**43**	44 0N	26 18 E
Ryan, L.	**14**	55 0N	5 2W
Ryazan	**55**	54 40N	39 40 E
Ryazhsk	**55**	53 45N	40 3 E
Rybache	**58**	46 40N	81 20 E
Rybachiy Poluostrov	**52**	69 43N	32 0 E
*Rybinsk	**55**	58 5N	38 50 E
Rybinskoye Vdkhr.	**55**	58 30N	38 25 E
Rybnik	**27**	50 6N	18 32 E
Rybnitsa	**56**	47 45N	29 0 E
Rybnoye	**55**	54 45N	39 30 E
Rychwał	**28**	52 4N	18 10 E
Ryd	**49**	56 27N	14 42 E
Ryde	**13**	50 44N	1 9W
Rydöbruk	**49**	56 58N	13 7 E
Rydsnäs	**49**	57 47N	15 9 E
Rydułtowy	**27**	50 4N	18 23 E
Rydzyna	**28**	51 47N	16 39 E
Rye	**13**	50 57N	0 46 E
Rye →	**12**	54 12N	0 53W
Rye Patch Res.	**118**	40 38N	118 20W
Ryegate	**118**	46 21N	109 15W
Ryki	**28**	51 38N	21 56 E
Rylsk	**54**	51 36N	34 43 E
Rylstone	**99**	32 46S	149 58 E
Rymanów	**27**	49 35N	21 51 E
Ryn	**28**	53 57N	21 34 E
Rypin	**28**	53 3N	19 25 E
Ryūkyū Is. = Nansei-Shotō	**74**	26 0N	128 0 E
Rzepin	**28**	52 20N	14 49 E
Rzeszów	**27**	50 5N	21 58 E
Rzeszów □	**27**	50 0N	22 0 E
Rzhev	**54**	56 20N	34 20 E
S			
Sa Dec	**71**	10 20N	105 46 E
Sa'ad (Muharraqa)	**62**	31 28N	34 33 E
Sa'ādatābād	**65**	30 10N	53 5 E
Saale →	**24**	51 57N	11 56 E
Saaler Bodden	**24**	54 20N	12 25 E
Saalfeld	**24**	50 39N	11 21 E
Saalfelden	**26**	47 25N	12 51 E
Saane →	**25**	46 23N	7 18 E
Saar (Sarre) →	**19**	49 42N	6 34 E
Saarbrücken	**25**	49 15N	6 58 E
Saarburg	**25**	49 36N	6 32 E
Saaremaa	**54**	58 30N	22 30 E
Saariselkä	**50**	68 16N	28 15 E
Saarland □	**25**	49 15N	7 0 E
Saarlouis	**25**	49 19N	6 45 E
Saba	**121**	17 42N	63 26W
Šabac	**42**	44 48N	19 42 E
Sabadell	**32**	41 28N	2 7 E
Sabagalet	**72**	1 36S	98 40 E
Sabah □	**72**	6 0N	117 0 E
Sábana de la Mar	**121**	19 7N	69 24W
Sábanalarga	**126**	10 38N	74 55W
Sabang	**72**	5 50N	95 15 E
Sabará	**127**	19 55S	43 46W
Sabarania	**73**	2 5S	138 18 E
Sabari →	**70**	17 35N	81 16 E
Sabasţiyah	**62**	32 17N	35 12 E
Sabattis	**113**	44 6N	74 40W
Sabáudia	**40**	41 17N	13 2 E
Sabhah	**83**	27 9N	14 29 E
Sabhah □	**83**	26 0N	14 0 E
Sabie	**93**	25 10S	30 48 E
Sabinal, Mexico	**120**	30 58N	107 25W
Sabinal, U.S.A.	**117**	29 20N	99 27W
Sabinal, Punta del	**33**	36 43N	2 44W
Sabinas	**120**	27 50N	101 10W
Sabinas Hidalgo	**120**	26 33N	100 10W
Sabine	**117**	29 42N	93 54W
Sabine →	**117**	30 0N	93 35W
Sabine L.	**117**	29 50N	93 50W
Sabinov	**27**	49 6N	21 5 E
Sabirabad	**57**	40 5N	48 30 E
Sabkhat Tāwurghā'	**83**	31 48N	15 30 E
Sablayan	**73**	12 50N	120 50 E
Sable, C., Can.	**107**	43 29N	65 38W
Sable, C., U.S.A.	**121**	25 13N	81 0W
Sable I.	**107**	44 0N	60 0W
Sablé-sur-Sarthe	**18**	47 50N	0 20W
Sables-d'Olonne, Les	**20**	46 30N	1 45W
Sabolev	**59**	54 20N	155 30 E
Sabor →	**30**	41 10N	7 7W
Sabou	**84**	12 1N	2 15W
Sabrātah	**83**	32 47N	12 29 E
Sabria	**83**	33 22N	8 45 E
Sabrina Coast	**5**	68 0S	120 0 E
Sabugal	**30**	40 20N	7 5W
Sabzevār	**65**	36 15N	57 40 E
Sabzvārān	**65**	28 45N	57 50 E
Sac City	**116**	42 26N	95 0W
Sacedón	**32**	40 29N	2 41W
Sachigo →	**106**	55 6N	88 58W
Sachigo, L.	**106**	53 50N	92 12W
Sachkhere	**57**	42 25N	43 28 E
Sacile	**39**	45 58N	12 30 E
Sackets Harbor	**113**	43 56N	76 7W
Säckingen	**25**	47 34N	7 56 E
Saco, Me., U.S.A.	**115**	43 30N	70 27W
Saco, Mont., U.S.A.	**118**	48 28N	107 19W
Sacramento	**118**	38 33N	121 30 E
Sacramento →	**118**	38 3N	121 56W
Sacramento Mts.	**119**	32 30N	105 30W
Sacratif, Cabo	**33**	36 42N	3 28W
Săcueni	**46**	47 20N	22 5 E
Sada	**30**	43 22N	8 15W
Sádaba	**32**	42 19N	1 12W
Sadani	**90**	5 58S	38 35 E
Sadao	**71**	6 38N	100 26 E
Sadasivpet	**70**	17 38N	77 59 E
Sadd el Aali	**86**	23 54N	32 54 E
Sade	**85**	11 22N	10 45 E
Sadimi	**91**	9 25S	23 32 E
Sado	**74**	38 0N	138 25 E
Sado →	**31**	38 29N	8 55W
Sado, Shima	**74**	38 15N	138 30 E
Sadon, Burma	**67**	25 28N	98 0 E
Sadon, U.S.S.R.	**57**	42 52N	43 58 E
Sæby	**49**	57 21N	10 30 E
Saegerstown	**112**	41 42N	80 10W
Saelices	**32**	39 55N	2 49W
Safaga	**86**	26 42N	34 0 E
Safaha	**86**	26 25N	39 0 E
Šafárikovo	**27**	48 25N	20 20 E
Säffle	**48**	59 8N	12 55 E
Safford	**119**	32 50N	109 43W
Saffron Walden	**13**	52 2N	0 15 E
Safi	**82**	32 18N	9 20W
Safīd Kūh	**65**	34 45N	63 0 E
Safonovo	**54**	55 4N	33 16 E
Safranbolu	**56**	41 15N	32 41 E
Sag Harbor	**113**	40 59N	72 17W
Saga	**73**	2 40S	132 55 E
Saga □	**74**	33 15N	130 20 E
Sagala	**84**	14 9N	6 38W
Sagara	**70**	14 14N	75 6 E
Sagara, L.	**90**	5 20S	31 0 E
Saghīr, Zab al	**64**	35 10N	43 20 E
Sagil	**75**	50 15N	91 15 E
Saginaw	**114**	43 26N	83 55W
Saginaw B.	**106**	43 50N	83 40W
Sagleipie	**84**	7 0N	8 52W
Saglouc (Sugluk)	**105**	62 10N	74 40W
Sagone	**21**	42 7N	8 42 E
Sagone, G. de	**21**	42 4N	8 40 E
Sagra, La >	**33**	37 57N	2 35W
Sagres	**31**	37 0N	8 58W
Sagua la Grande	**121**	22 50N	80 10W
Saguache	**119**	38 10N	106 10W
Saguenay →	**107**	48 22N	71 0W
Sagunto	**32**	39 42N	0 18W
Sahaba	**86**	18 57N	30 25 E
Sahagún	**30**	42 18N	5 2W
Saham	**62**	32 42N	35 46 E
Saḩam al Jawlān	**62**	32 45N	35 55 E
Sahand, Kūh-e	**64**	37 44N	46 27 E
Sahara	**82**	23 0N	5 0 E
Saharanpur	**68**	29 58N	77 33 E
Saharien Atlas	**82**	33 30N	1 0 E
Sahasinaka	**93**	21 49S	47 49 E
Sahaswan	**68**	28 5N	78 45 E
Sahel, Canal du	**84**	14 20N	6 0W
Sahibganj	**69**	25 12N	87 40 E
Sahiwal	**68**	30 45N	73 8 E
Sahtaneh →	**108**	59 2N	122 28W
Sahuaripa	**120**	29 0N	109 13W
Sahuarita	**119**	31 58N	110 59W
Sahuayo	**120**	20 4N	102 43W
Sahy	**27**	48 4N	18 55 E
Saibai I.	**98**	9 25S	142 40 E
Sa'id Bundas	**81**	8 24N	24 48 E
Saïda	**82**	34 50N	0 11 E
Saīdābād	**65**	29 30N	55 45 E
Saïdia	**82**	35 5N	2 14W
Saidu	**69**	34 43N	72 24 E
Saignes	**20**	45 20N	2 31 E
Saigon = Thanh Bho Ho Chi Minh	**71**	10 46N	106 40 E
Saih-al-Malih	**65**	23 37N	58 31 E
Saijō	**74**	33 55N	133 11 E
Saikhoa Ghat	**67**	27 50N	95 40 E
Saiki	**74**	32 58N	131 51 E
Saillans	**21**	44 42N	5 12 E
Sailolof	**73**	1 7S	130 46 E
St. Abb's Head	**14**	55 55N	2 10W
St. Aegyd	**26**	47 52N	15 33 E
St-Affrique	**20**	43 57N	2 53 E
St-Agrève	**21**	45 0N	4 23 E
St-Aignan	**18**	47 16N	1 22 E
St. Alban's	**107**	47 51N	55 50W
St. Albans, U.K.	**13**	51 44N	0 19W
St. Albans, Vt., U.S.A.	**114**	44 49N	73 7W
St. Albans, W. Va., U.S.A.	**114**	38 21N	81 50W
St. Alban's Head	**13**	50 34N	2 3W
St. Albert	**108**	53 37N	113 32W
St-Amand	**19**	50 25N	3 26 E
St-Amand-en-Puisaye	**19**	47 32N	3 5 E
St-Amand-Mont-Rond	**20**	46 43N	2 30 E
St-Amarin	**19**	47 54N	7 2 E
St-Amour	**21**	46 26N	5 21 E
St-André-de-Cubzac	**20**	44 59N	0 26W
St-André-de-l'Eure	**18**	48 54N	1 16 E
St-André-les-Alpes	**21**	43 58N	6 30 E
St. André, Tanjona	**93**	16 11S	44 27 E
St. Andrew's	**107**	47 45N	59 15W
St. Andrews	**14**	56 20N	2 48W
St-Anicet	**113**	45 8N	74 22W
St. Ann B.	**107**	46 22N	60 25W
St. Anne	**18**	49 43N	2 11W
St. Anthony, Can.	**107**	51 22N	55 35W
St. Anthony, U.S.A.	**118**	44 0N	111 40W
St-Antonin-Noble-Val	**20**	44 10N	1 45 E
St. Arnaud	**99**	36 40S	143 16 E
St. Arthur	**107**	47 33N	67 46W
St. Asaph	**12**	53 15N	3 27W
St-Astier	**20**	45 8N	0 31 E
St-Aubin-du-Cormier	**18**	48 15N	1 26W
St. Augustin	**93**	23 33S	43 46 E
St-Augustin-Saguenay	**107**	51 13N	58 38W
St. Augustine	**115**	29 52N	81 20W
St. Austell	**13**	50 20N	4 48W
St-Avold	**19**	49 6N	6 43 E
St.-Barthélemy, I.	**121**	17 50N	62 50W
St. Bee's Hd.	**12**	54 30N	3 38 E
St-Benoît-du-Sault	**20**	46 26N	1 25 E
St. Bernard, Col du Grand	**25**	45 53N	7 11 E
St. Boniface	**109**	49 53N	97 5W
St-Bonnet	**21**	44 40N	6 5 E
St-Brévin-les-Pins	**18**	47 14N	2 10W
St-Brice-en-Coglès	**18**	48 25N	1 22W
St. Bride's	**107**	46 56N	54 10W
St. Bride's B.	**13**	51 48N	5 15W
St-Brieuc	**18**	48 30N	2 46W
St-Calais	**18**	47 55N	0 45 E
St-Cast	**18**	48 37N	2 18W
St. Catharines	**106**	43 10N	79 15W
St. Catherines I.	**115**	31 35N	81 10W
St. Catherine's Pt.	**13**	50 34N	1 18W
St-Céré	**20**	44 51N	1 54 E
St.-Cergue	**25**	46 27N	6 10 E
St-Cernin	**20**	45 5N	2 25 E
St-Chamond	**21**	45 28N	4 31 E
St. Charles, Ill., U.S.A.	**114**	41 55N	88 21W
St. Charles, Mo., U.S.A.	**116**	38 46N	90 30W
St-Chély-d'Apcher	**20**	44 48N	3 17 E
St-Chinian	**20**	43 25N	2 56 E
St. Christopher (St. Kitts)	**121**	17 20N	62 40W
St-Ciers-sur-Gironde	**20**	45 17N	0 37W
St. Clair, Mich, U.S.A.	**112**	42 47N	82 27W
St. Clair, Pa., U.S.A.	**113**	40 42N	76 12W
St. Clair, L.	**106**	42 30N	82 45W
St. Clairsville	**112**	40 5N	80 53W
St-Claud	**20**	45 54N	0 28 E
St. Claude	**109**	49 40N	98 20W
St-Claude	**21**	46 22N	5 52 E
St-Cloud	**18**	48 51N	2 12 E
St. Cloud, Fla., U.S.A.	**115**	28 15N	81 15W
St. Cloud, Minn., U.S.A.	**116**	45 30N	94 11W
St-Coeur de Marie	**107**	48 39N	71 43W
St. Croix	**121**	17 45N	64 45W
St. Croix →	**116**	44 45N	92 50W
St. Croix Falls	**116**	45 18N	92 22W
St-Cyprien	**20**	42 37N	3 0 E
St-Cyr	**21**	43 11N	5 43 E
St. David's, Can.	**107**	48 12N	58 52W
St. David's, U.K.	**13**	51 54N	5 16W
St. David's Head	**13**	51 55N	5 16W
St-Denis	**19**	48 56N	2 22 E
St-Denis-d'Orques	**18**	48 2N	0 17W
St-Dié	**19**	48 17N	6 56 E
St-Dizier	**19**	48 40N	5 0 E
St-Egrève	**21**	45 14N	5 41 E
St. Elias, Mt.	**104**	60 14N	140 50W
St Elias Mts.	**108**	60 33N	139 28W
St-Éloy-les-Mines	**20**	46 10N	2 51 E
St-Émilion	**20**	44 53N	0 9W
St-Étienne	**21**	45 27N	4 22 E
St-Étienne-de-Tinée	**21**	44 16N	6 56 E
St. Eugène	**113**	45 30N	74 28W
St. Eustatius	**121**	17 20N	63 0W
St-Félicien	**106**	48 40N	72 25W
St-Florent	**21**	42 41N	9 18 E
St-Florent-sur-Cher	**19**	46 59N	2 15 E
St-Florentin	**19**	48 0N	3 45 E
St-Flour	**20**	45 2N	3 6 E
St-Fons	**21**	45 42N	4 52 E
St. Francis	**116**	39 48N	101 47W
St. Francis →	**117**	34 38N	90 36W
St. Francis, C.	**92**	34 14S	24 49 E
St. Francis, L.	**113**	45 10N	74 22W
St. Francisville	**117**	30 48N	91 22W
St-Fulgent	**18**	46 50N	1 10W
St-Gabriel-de-Brandon	**106**	46 17N	73 24W
St-Gaudens	**20**	43 6N	0 44 E
St-Gengoux-le-National	**21**	46 37N	4 40 E
St-Geniez-d'Olt	**20**	44 27N	2 58 E
St. George, Austral.	**97**	28 1S	148 30 E
St. George, Berm.	**121**	32 24N	64 42W
St. George, Can.	**107**	45 11N	66 50W
St. George, S.C., U.S.A.	**115**	33 13N	80 37W
St. George, Utah, U.S.A.	**119**	37 10N	113 35W
St. George, C., Can.	**107**	48 30N	59 16W
St. George, C., U.S.A.	**115**	29 36N	85 2W
St-Georges	**16**	50 37N	5 20 E
St. George's	**107**	48 26N	58 31W
St. Georges	**106**	46 42N	72 35W
St-Georges	**107**	46 8N	70 40W
St. Georges	**127**	4 0N	52 0W
St. George's	**121**	12 5N	61 43W
St. George's B.	**107**	48 24N	58 53W
Saint George's Channel	**98**	4 10S	152 20 E
St. George's Channel	**11**	52 0N	6 0W
St-Georges-de-Didonne	**20**	45 36N	1 0W
St. Georges Head	**100**	35 12S	150 42 E
St-Germain	**19**	48 53N	2 5 E
St-Germain-Lembron	**20**	45 27N	3 14 E
St-Germain-de-Calberte	**20**	44 13N	3 48 E
St-Germain-des-Fossés	**20**	46 12N	3 26 E
St-Germain-du-Plain	**19**	46 42N	4 58 E
St-Germain-Laval	**21**	45 50N	4 1 E
St-Gers	**18**	48 18N	0 37W
St-Gervais, Haute Savoie, France	**21**	45 53N	6 42 E
St-Gervais, Puy de Dôme, France	**20**	46 4N	2 50 E
St-Gildas, Pte. de	**18**	47 8N	2 14W
St-Gilles-Croix-de-Vie	**18**	46 41N	1 55W
St-Gilles-du-Gard	**21**	43 40N	4 26 E
St-Girons	**20**	42 59N	1 8 E
St. Goar	**25**	50 12N	7 43 E
St-Gualtier	**18**	46 39N	1 26 E
St-Guénolé	**18**	47 49N	4 23W
St. Helena, Atl. Oc.	**7**	15 55S	5 44W
St. Helena, U.S.A.	**118**	38 29N	122 30W
St. Helenabaai	**92**	32 40S	18 10 E
St. Helens, U.K.	**12**	53 28N	2 44W
St. Helens, U.S.A.	**118**	45 55N	122 50W
St. Helier	**18**	49 11N	2 6W
St-Hilaire	**18**	48 35N	1 7W
St-Hippolyte	**19**	47 20N	6 50 E
St-Hippolyte-du-Fort	**20**	43 58N	3 52 E
St-Honoré	**19**	46 54N	3 50 E
St-Hubert	**16**	50 2N	5 23 E
St-Hyacinthe	**106**	45 40N	72 58W
St. Ignace	**114**	45 53N	84 43W
St. Ignace I.	**106**	48 45N	88 0W
St. Ignatius	**118**	47 19N	114 8W
St-Imier	**25**	47 9N	6 58 E
St. Ives, Cambs., U.K.	**13**	52 20N	0 5W
St. Ives, Cornwall, U.K.	**13**	50 13N	5 29W
St-James	**18**	48 31N	1 20W
St. James	**116**	43 57N	94 40W
St. Jean	**106**	45 20N	73 20W
St-Jean	**21**	45 30N	5 10 E
St-Jean →	**107**	50 17N	64 20W
St. Jean Baptiste	**109**	49 15N	97 20W
St-Jean-d'Angély	**20**	45 57N	0 31W
St-Jean-de-Maurienne	**21**	45 16N	6 21 E
St-Jean-de-Luz	**20**	43 23N	1 39W
St-Jean-de-Monts	**18**	46 47N	2 4W
St-Jean-du-Gard	**20**	44 7N	3 52 E
St-Jean-en-Royans	**21**	45 1N	5 18 E
St-Jean, L.	**107**	48 40N	72 0W
St-Jean-Port-Joli	**107**	47 15N	70 13W
St-Jérôme, Qué., Can.	**106**	45 47N	74 0W
St-Jérôme, Qué., Can.	**107**	48 26N	71 53W
St. John, Can.	**107**	45 20N	66 8W
St. John, Kans., U.S.A.	**117**	37 59N	98 45W
St. John, N.D., U.S.A.	**116**	48 58N	99 40W
St. John →	**107**	45 15N	66 4W
St. John, C.	**107**	50 0N	55 32W
St. John's, Antigua	**121**	17 6N	61 51W
St. John's, Can.	**107**	47 35N	52 40W
St. Johns, Ariz., U.S.A.	**119**	34 31N	109 26W
St. Johns, Mich., U.S.A.	**114**	43 0N	84 31W
St. John's →	**115**	30 20N	81 30W
St. Johnsbury	**114**	44 25N	72 1W
St. Johnsville	**113**	43 0N	74 43W
St. Joseph, La., U.S.A.	**117**	31 55N	91 15W
St. Joseph, Mich., U.S.A.	**114**	42 5N	86 30W
St. Joseph, Mo., U.S.A.	**116**	39 46N	94 50W
St. Joseph →	**114**	42 7N	86 30W
St. Joseph, I.	**106**	46 12N	83 58W
St. Joseph, L.	**106**	51 10N	90 35W
St-Jovite	**106**	46 8N	74 38W
St-Juéry	**20**	43 55N	2 12 E
St-Julien	**21**	46 8N	6 5 E
St-Julien-Chapteuil	**21**	45 2N	4 4 E
St-Julien-du-Sault	**19**	48 1N	3 17 E
St-Junien	**20**	45 53N	0 55 E

*Renamed Andropov

St-Just-en-Chaussée San Constanzo

St-Just-en-Chaussée 19 49 30N 2 25 E
St-Just-en-Chevalet 20 45 55N 3 50 E
St-Justin 20 43 59N 0 14W
St. Kilda, N.Z. 101 45 53 S 170 31 E
St. Kilda, U.K. 8 57 9N 8 34W
St. Kitts-Nevis ■ 121 17 20N 62 40W
St. Laurent 109 50 25N 97 58W
St-Laurent 127 5 29N 54 3W
St-Laurent-du-Pont 21 45 23N 5 45 E
St-Laurent-en-Grandvaux 21 46 35N 5 58 E
St. Lawrence 107 46 54N 55 23W
St. Lawrence → 107 49 30N 66 0W
St. Lawrence, Gulf of 107 48 25N 62 0W
St. Lawrence I. 104 63 0N 170 0W
St. Leonard 107 47 12N 67 58W
St-Léonard-de-Noblat 20 45 49N 1 29 E
St. Lewis → 107 52 26N 56 11W
St-Lô 18 49 7N 1 5W
St-Louis 84 16 8N 16 27W
St. Louis, Mich., U.S.A. 114 43 27N 84 38W
St. Louis, Mo., U.S.A. 116 38 40N 90 12W
St. Louis → 116 47 15N 92 45W
St-Loup-sur-Semouse 19 47 53N 6 16 E
St. Lucia ■ 121 14 0N 60 50W
St. Lucia, C. 93 28 32 S 32 29 E
St. Lucia Channel 121 14 15N 61 0W
St. Lucia, Lake 93 28 5 S 32 30 E
St. Lunaire-Griquet 107 51 31N 55 28W
St. Maarten 121 18 0N 63 5W
St-Maixent-l'École 20 46 24N 0 12W
St-Malo 18 48 39N 2 1W
St-Malo, G. de 18 48 50N 2 30W
St-Mandrier 21 43 4N 5 56 E
St-Marc 121 19 10N 72 41W
St-Marcellin 21 45 9N 5 20 E
St-Marcouf, Îs. 18 49 30N 1 10W
St. Maries 118 47 17N 116 34W
St-Martin, Charente-M., France 20 46 12N 1 22W
St-Martin, Pas-de-Calais, France 19 50 42N 1 38 E
St-Martin, I. 121 18 0N 63 0W
St. Martin L. 109 51 40N 98 30W
St-Martin-Vésubie 21 44 4N 7 15 E
St. Martins 107 45 22N 65 34W
St. Martinsville 117 30 10N 91 50W
St-Martory 20 43 9N 0 56 E
St. Mary B. 107 46 50N 53 50W
St. Mary Is. 70 13 20N 74 35 E
St. Mary Pk. 97 31 32 S 138 34 E
St. Marys, Austral. 97 41 35 S 148 11 E
St. Marys, Can. 112 43 20N 81 10W
St. Mary's, U.K. 13 49 55N 6 17W
St. Mary's, U.S.A. 114 40 33N 84 20W
St. Marys 114 41 27N 78 33W
St. Marys Bay 107 44 25N 66 10W
St. Mary's, C. 107 46 50N 54 12W
St. Mathews I. = Zadetkyi Kyun 71 10 0N 98 25 E
St-Mathieu, Pte. de 18 48 20N 4 45W
St-Maur-des-Fossés 19 48 48N 2 30 E
St-Maurice → 106 46 21N 72 31W
St-Médard-de-Guizières 20 45 1N 0 4W
St-Méen-le-Grand 18 48 11N 2 12W
St. Michaels 119 35 38N 109 5W
St. Michael's Mt. 13 50 7N 5 30W
St-Michel 21 45 15N 6 29 E
St-Mihiel 19 48 54N 5 30 E
St-Nazaire 18 47 17N 2 12W
St. Neots 13 52 14N 0 16W
St-Nicolas-de-Port 19 48 38N 6 18 E
St-Omer 19 50 45N 2 15 E
St. Ouen 19 48 50N 2 20 E
St-Ouen 19 50 2N 2 7 E
St-Pacome 107 47 24N 69 58W
St-Palais 20 45 40N 1 8W
St-Pamphile 107 46 58N 69 48W
St-Pardoux-la-Rivière 20 45 29N 0 45 E
St. Pascal 107 47 32N 69 48W
St. Paul, Can. 108 54 0N 111 17W
St. Paul, Ind. Oc. 3 30 40 S 77 34 E
St. Paul, Minn., U.S.A. 116 44 54N 93 5W
St. Paul, Nebr., U.S.A. 116 41 15N 98 30W
St-Paul-de-Fenouillet 20 42 50N 2 28 E
St. Paul, I. 107 47 12N 60 9W
St-Péray 21 44 57N 4 50 E
St-Père-en-Retz 18 47 11N 2 2W
St. Peter 116 44 21N 93 57W
St. Peter Port 18 49 27N 2 31W
St. Peters, N.S., Can. 107 45 40N 60 53W
St. Peters, P.E.I., Can. 107 46 25N 62 35W
St. Petersburg 115 27 45N 82 40W
St-Philbert-de-Grand-Lieu 18 47 2N 1 39W
St Pierre 107 46 46N 56 12W
St-Pierre-d'Oléron 20 45 57N 1 19W
St-Pierre-Église 18 49 40N 1 24W
St-Pierre-en-Port 18 49 48N 0 30 E
St-Pierre et Miquelon □ 107 46 55N 56 10W
St-Pierre, L. 106 46 12N 72 52W
St-Pierre-le-Moûtier 19 46 47N 3 7 E
St.-Pierre-sur-Dives 18 49 2N 0 1W
St.-Pol 19 50 21N 2 20 E
St-Pol-de-Léon 18 48 41N 4 0W
St-Pol-sur-Mer 19 51 1N 2 20 E
St-Pons 20 43 30N 2 45 E
St-Pourçain-sur-Sioule 20 46 18N 3 18 E
St-Quay-Portrieux 18 48 39N 2 51W
St-Quentin 19 49 50N 3 16 E
St-Rambert-d'Albon 21 45 17N 4 49 E
St-Raphaël 21 43 25N 6 46 E
St. Regis, Mont., U.S.A. 118 47 20N 115 3W
St. Regis, N.Y., U.S.A. 113 44 39N 74 34W
St-Rémy-de-Provence 21 43 48N 4 50 E
St-Renan 18 48 26N 4 37W
St-Saëns 18 49 41N 1 16 E
St-Sauveur-en-Puisaye 19 47 37N 3 12 E
St-Sauveur-le-Vicomte 18 49 23N 1 32W
St-Savin 20 46 34N 0 50 E
St-Savinien 20 45 53N 0 42W
St. Sebastien, Tanjon' i 93 12 26 S 48 44 E
St-Seine-l'Abbaye 19 47 26N 4 47 E
St-Sernin 20 43 54N 2 35 E
St-Servan-sur-Mer 18 48 38N 2 0W
St-Sever 20 43 46N 0 34W
St-Sever-Calvados 18 48 50N 1 3W
St-Siméon 107 47 51N 69 54W
St. Stephen 107 45 16N 67 17W
St-Sulpice-Laurière 20 46 3N 1 29 E
St-Sulpice-la-Pointe 20 43 46N 1 41 E
St-Thégonnec 18 48 31N 3 57W
St. Thomas, Can. 106 42 45N 81 10W
St. Thomas, W. Indies 121 18 21N 64 55W
St-Tite 106 46 45N 72 34W
St-Tropez 21 43 17N 6 38 E
St. Troud = Sint Truiden 16 50 48N 5 10 E
St-Vaast-la-Hougue 18 49 35N 1 17W
St-Valéry 19 50 10N 1 38 E
St-Valéry-en-Caux 18 49 52N 0 43 E
St-Vallier 21 45 11N 4 50 E
St-Vallier-de-Thiey 21 43 42N 6 51 E
St-Varent 18 46 53N 0 13W
St. Vincent 6 18 0N 26 1W
St. Vincent ■ 121 13 10N 61 10W
St-Vincent-de-Tyrosse 20 43 39N 1 18W
St. Vincent, G. 97 35 0 S 138 0 E
St. Vincent Passage 121 13 30N 61 0W
St. Vincent, Tanjona 93 21 58 S 43 20 E
St-Vith 16 50 17N 6 9 E
St-Yrieux-la-Perche 20 45 31N 1 12 E
Ste-Adresse 18 49 31N 0 5 E
Ste-Agathe-des-Monts 106 46 3N 74 17W
Ste Anne de Beaupré 107 47 2N 70 58W
Ste-Anne-des-Monts 107 49 8N 66 30W
Ste-Énimie 20 44 22N 3 26 E
Ste-Foy-la-Grande 20 44 50N 0 13 E
Ste. Genevieve 116 37 59N 90 2W
Ste-Hermine 20 46 32N 1 4W
Ste-Livrade-sur-Lot 20 44 24N 0 36 E
Ste-Marguerite → 107 50 9N 66 36W
Ste Marie 121 14 48N 61 1W
Ste-Marie-aux-Mines 19 48 10N 7 12 E
Ste-Marie de la Madeleine 107 46 26N 71 0W
Ste-Maure-de-Touraine 18 47 7N 0 37 E
Ste-Maxime 21 43 19N 6 39 E
Ste-Menehould 19 49 5N 4 54 E
Ste-Mère-Église 18 49 24N 1 19W
Ste-Rose 121 16 20N 61 45W
Ste.-Rose du lac 109 51 4N 99 30W
Saintes 20 45 45N 0 37W
Saintes, Île des 121 15 50N 61 35W
Saintes-Maries-de-la-Mer 21 43 26N 4 26 E
Saintonge 20 45 40N 0 50W
Sairang 67 23 50N 92 45 E
Sairecábur, Cerro 124 22 43 S 67 54W
Saitama □ 74 36 25N 139 30 E
Sajama 126 18 7 S 69 0W
Sajan 42 45 50N 20 20 E
Sajószentpéter 27 48 12N 20 44 E
Sakai 74 34 30N 135 30 E
Sakākah 64 30 0N 40 8 E
Sakami, L. 106 53 15N 77 0W
Sâkâne, 'Erg i-n 82 20 30N 1 30W
Sakania 91 12 43 S 28 30 E
Sakarya → 56 41 7N 30 39 E
Sakata 74 38 55N 139 50 E
Sakeny → 93 20 0 S 45 25 E
Sakété 85 6 40N 2 45 E
Sakhalin, Ostrov 59 51 0N 143 0 E
Sakhi Gopal 69 19 58N 85 50 E
Sakhnīn 62 32 52N 35 12 E
Saki 56 45 9N 33 34 E
Sakiai 54 54 59N 23 0 E
Sakołow Małopolski 28 50 10N 22 9 E
Sakon Nakhon 71 17 10N 104 9 E
Sakrand 68 26 10N 68 15 E
Sakri 68 21 2N 74 20 E
Sakskøbing 49 54 49N 11 39 E
Sal → 57 47 31N 40 45 E
Sal'a 27 48 10N 17 50 E
Sala 48 59 58N 16 35 E
Sala Consilina 41 40 23N 15 35 E
Sala-y-Gómez 95 26 28 S 105 28W
Salaberry-de-Valleyfield 106 45 15N 74 8W
Saladas 124 28 15 S 58 40W
Saladillo 124 35 40 S 59 55W
Salado →, Buenos Aires, Argent. 124 35 44 S 57 22W
Salado →, La Pampa, Argent. 128 37 30 S 67 0W
Salado →, Santa Fe, Argent. 124 31 40 S 60 41W
Salado →, Mexico 120 26 52N 99 19W
Salaga 85 8 31N 0 31W
Sălaj □ 46 47 15N 23 0 E
Salala, Liberia 84 6 42N 10 7W
Salala, Sudan 86 21 17N 36 16 E
Salālah 63 16 56N 53 59 E
Salamanca, Chile 124 31 46 S 70 59W
Salamanca, Spain 30 40 58N 5 39W
Salamanca, U.S.A. 114 42 10N 78 42W
Salamanca □ 30 40 57N 5 40W
Salamis 45 37 56N 23 30 E
Salar de Atacama 124 23 30 S 68 25W
Salar de Uyuni 126 20 30 S 67 45W
Sălard 46 47 12N 22 3 E
Salas 30 43 25N 6 15W
Salas de los Infantes 32 42 2N 3 17W
Salatiga 73 7 19 S 110 30 E
Salavat 52 53 21N 55 55 E
Salaverry 126 8 15 S 79 0W
Salawati 73 1 7 S 130 52 E
Salayar 73 6 7 S 120 30 E
Salazar → 32 42 40N 1 0W
Salbris 19 47 25N 2 3 E
Salcia 46 43 56N 24 55 E
Salcombe 13 50 14N 3 47W
Saldaña 30 42 32N 4 48W
Saldanha 92 33 0 S 17 58 E
Saldanhabaai 92 33 6 S 18 0 E
Saldus 54 56 38N 22 30 E
Sale 97 38 6 S 147 6 E
Salé 82 34 3N 6 48W
Sale 12 53 26N 2 19W
Salebabu 73 3 55N 126 40 E
Salekhard 58 66 30N 66 35 E
Salem, India 70 11 40N 78 11 E
Salem, Ind., U.S.A. 114 38 38N 86 6W
Salem, Mass., U.S.A. 114 42 29N 70 53W
Salem, Mo., U.S.A. 117 37 40N 91 30W
Salem, N.J., U.S.A. 114 39 34N 75 29W
Salem, Ohio, U.S.A. 114 40 52N 80 50W
Salem, Oreg., U.S.A. 118 45 0N 123 0W
Salem, S.D., U.S.A. 116 43 44N 97 23W
Salem, Va., U.S.A. 114 37 19N 80 8W
Salemi 40 37 49N 12 47 E
Salernes 21 43 34N 6 15 E
Salerno 41 40 40N 14 44 E
Salerno, G. di 41 40 35N 14 45 E
Salfīt 62 32 5N 35 11 E
Salford 12 53 30N 2 17W
Salgir → 56 45 38N 35 1 E
Salgótarján 27 48 5N 19 47 E
Salies-de-Béarn 20 43 28N 0 56W
Salina, Italy 41 38 35N 14 50 E
Salina, U.S.A. 116 38 50N 97 40W
Salina Cruz 120 16 10N 95 10W
Salinas, Brazil 127 16 10 S 42 10W
Salinas, Chile 124 23 31 S 69 29W
Salinas, Ecuador 126 2 10 S 80 58W
Salinas, U.S.A. 119 36 40N 121 41W
Salinas →, Mexico 120 16 28N 90 31W
Salinas →, U.S.A. 119 36 45N 121 48W
Salinas Ambargasta 124 29 0 S 65 0W
Salinas, B. de 121 11 4N 85 45W
Salinas, C. de 33 39 16N 3 4 E
Salinas (de Hidalgo) 120 22 30N 101 40W
Salinas Grandes 124 30 0 S 65 0W
Salinas, Pampa de las 124 31 58 S 66 42W
Saline →, Ark., U.S.A. 117 33 10N 92 8W
Saline →, Kans., U.S.A. 116 38 51N 97 30W
Salinópolis 127 0 40 S 47 20W
Salins 19 46 57N 5 53 E
Salins-les-Bains 19 46 58N 5 52 E
Salir 31 37 14N 8 2W
Salisbury, Austral. 99 34 46 S 138 40 E
Salisbury, U.K. 13 51 4N 1 48W
Salisbury, Md., U.S.A. 114 38 20N 75 38W
Salisbury, N.C., U.S.A. 115 35 20N 80 29W
• Salisbury, Zimb. 91 17 43 S 31 2 E
Salisbury Plain 13 51 13N 1 50W
Săliște 46 45 45N 23 56 E
Salka 85 10 20N 4 58 E
Salle, La 116 41 20N 89 6W
Sallent 32 41 49N 1 54 E
Salles-Curan 20 44 11N 2 48 E
Salling 49 56 40N 8 55 E
Sallisaw 117 35 26N 94 45W
Sallom Junction 86 19 17N 37 6 E
Salmerón 32 40 33N 2 29W
Salmo 108 49 10N 117 20W
Salmon 118 45 12N 113 56W
Salmon →, Can. 108 54 3N 122 40W
Salmon →, U.S.A. 118 45 51N 116 46W
Salmon Arm 108 50 40N 119 15W
Salmon Falls 118 42 48N 114 59W
Salmon Res. 107 48 05N 56 00W
Salmon River Mts. 118 45 0N 114 30W
Salo 51 60 22N 23 10 E
Salò 38 45 37N 10 32 E
Salobreña 31 36 44N 3 35W
Salome 119 33 51N 113 37W
Salon-de-Provence 21 43 39N 5 6 E
Salonica = Thessaloníki 44 40 38N 22 58 E
Salonta 46 46 49N 21 42 E
Salop = Shropshire □ 13 52 36N 2 45W
Salor → 31 39 39N 7 3W
Salou, Cabo 32 41 3N 1 10 E
Salsacate 124 31 20 S 65 5W
Salses 20 42 50N 2 55 E
Salsette I. 70 19 5N 72 50 E
Salsk 57 46 28N 41 30 E
Salso → 41 37 6N 13 55 E
Salsomaggiore 38 44 48N 9 59 E
Salt →, Can. 108 60 0N 112 25W
Salt →, U.S.A. 119 33 23N 112 18W
Salt Creek 99 36 8 S 139 38 E
Salt Fork → 117 36 37N 97 7W
Salt Lake City 118 40 45N 111 58W
Salt Range 68 32 30N 72 25 E
Salta 124 24 57 S 65 25W
Salta □ 124 24 48 S 65 30W
Saltcoats 14 55 38N 4 47W
Saltee Is. 15 52 7N 6 37W
Saltfjorden 50 67 15N 14 10 E
Saltholm 49 55 38N 12 43 E
Salthólmavík 50 65 24N 21 57W
Saltillo 120 25 30N 100 57W
Salto, Argent. 124 34 20 S 60 15W
Salto, Uruguay 124 31 27 S 57 50W
Salton Sea 119 33 20N 115 50W
Saltpond 85 5 15N 1 3W
Saltsjöbaden 49 59 15N 18 20 E
Saltspring 108 48 54N 123 37W
Saltville 114 36 53N 81 46W
Saluda → 115 34 0N 81 4W
Salûm 86 31 31N 25 7 E
Salûm, Khâlig el 86 31 30N 25 9 E
Salur 70 18 27N 83 18 E
Saluzzo 38 44 39N 7 29 E
Salvador, Brazil 127 13 0 S 38 30W
Salvador, Can. 109 52 10N 109 32W
Salvador, L. 117 29 46N 90 16W
Salvaterra de Magos 31 39 1N 8 47W
Sálvora, Isla 30 42 30N 8 58W
Salwa 65 24 45N 50 55 E
Salween → 67 16 31N 97 37 E
Salyany 53 39 10N 48 50 E
Salyersville 114 37 45N 83 4W
Salza → 26 47 40N 14 43 E
Salzach → 26 48 12N 12 56 E
Salzburg 26 47 48N 13 2 E
Salzburg □ 26 47 15N 13 0 E
Salzgitter 24 52 13N 10 22 E
Salzwedel 24 52 50N 11 11 E
Sam Neua 71 20 29N 104 0 E
Sam Ngao 71 17 18N 99 0 E
Sam Rayburn Res. 117 31 15N 94 20W
Sama 58 60 12N 60 22 E
Sama de Langreo 30 43 18N 5 40W
Samagaltai 59 50 36N 95 3 E
Samales Group 73 6 0N 122 0 E
Samalkot 70 17 3N 82 13 E
Samâlût 86 28 20N 30 42 E
Samana 68 30 10N 76 13 E
Samanga 91 8 20 S 39 13 E
Samangán □ 65 36 15N 68 3 E
Samangwa 90 4 23 S 24 10 E
Samar 73 12 0N 125 0 E
Samarai 98 10 39 S 150 41 E
Samaria = Shōmrōn 62 32 15N 35 13 E
Samarinda 72 0 30 S 117 9 E
Samarkand 58 39 40N 66 55 E
Sāmarrā" 64 34 16N 43 55 E
Samastipur 69 25 50N 85 50 E
Samatan 20 43 29N 0 55 E
Samba 90 4 38 S 26 22 E
Sambalpur 69 21 28N 84 4 E
Sambar, Tanjung 72 2 59 S 110 19 E
Sambas 72 1 20N 109 20 E
Sambava 93 14 16 S 50 10 E
Sambawizi 91 18 24 S 26 13 E
Sambhal 68 28 35N 78 37 E
Sambhar 68 26 52N 75 6 E
Sambiase 41 38 58N 16 16 E
Sambonifacio 38 45 24N 11 16 E
Sambor, Camb. 71 12 46N 106 0 E
Sambor, U.S.S.R. 54 49 30N 23 10 E
Sambre → 16 50 27N 4 52 E
Sambuca di Sicilia 40 37 39N 13 6 E
Samburu □ 90 1 10N 37 0 E
Samchŏk 76 37 30N 129 10 E
Same 90 4 2 S 37 38 E
Samer 19 50 38N 1 44 E
Samfya 91 11 22 S 29 31 E
Sámi 45 38 15N 20 39 E
Samna 86 25 12N 37 17 E
Samnū 83 27 15N 14 55 E
Samo Alto 124 30 22 S 71 0W
Samobor 39 45 47N 15 44 E
Samoëns 21 46 5N 6 45 E
Samokov 43 42 18N 23 35 E
Samoorombón, Bahía 124 36 5 S 57 20W
Samorogouan 84 11 21N 4 57W
Sámos 45 37 45N 26 50 E
Samos 30 42 44N 7 20W
Samoš 42 45 13N 20 49 E
Samotharáki 44 39 48N 19 31 E
Samothráki 44 40 28N 25 28 E
Samoylovka 55 51 12N 43 43 E
Sampa 84 8 0N 2 36W
Sampacho 124 33 20 S 64 50W
Sampang 73 7 11 S 113 13 E
Samper de Calanda 32 41 11N 0 28W
Sampit 72 2 34 S 113 0 E
Sampit, Teluk 72 3 5 S 113 3 E
Samra 64 25 35N 41 0 E
Samsø 49 55 50N 10 35 E
Samsø Bælt 49 55 45N 10 45 E
Samsun 64 41 15N 36 22 E
Samsun Daği 45 37 45N 27 10 E
Samtredia 57 42 7N 42 24 E
Samui, Ko 71 9 30N 100 0 E
Samur → 57 41 53N 48 32 E
Samusole 91 10 2 S 24 0 E
Samut Prakan 71 13 32N 100 40 E
Samut Sakhon 71 13 31N 100 13 E
Samut Songkhram (Mekong) 71 13 24N 100 1 E
Samwari 68 28 30N 66 46 E
San 84 13 15N 4 57W
San → 27 50 45N 21 51 E
San Adrián, C. de 30 43 21N 8 50W
San Agustin, C. 73 6 20N 126 13 E
San Agustín de Valle Fértil 124 30 35 S 67 30W
San Ambrosio 95 26 28 S 79 53W
San Andreas 118 38 0N 120 39W
San Andrés, I. de 121 12 42N 81 46W
San Andres Mts. 119 33 0N 106 45W
San Andrés Tuxtla 120 18 30N 95 20W
San Angelo 117 31 30N 100 30W
San Antonio, Chile 124 33 40 S 71 40W
San Antonio, N. Mex., U.S.A. 119 33 58N 106 57W
San Antonio, Tex., U.S.A. 117 29 30N 98 30W
San Antonio → 117 28 30N 96 50W
San Antonio Abad 33 38 59N 1 19 E
San Antonio, C., Argent. 124 36 15 S 56 40W
San Antonio, C., Cuba 121 21 50N 84 57W
San Antonio, C. de 33 38 48N 0 12 E
San Antonio de los Baños 121 22 54N 82 31W
San Antonio de los Cobres 124 24 10 S 66 17W
San Antonio Oeste 128 40 40 S 65 0W
San Augustine 117 31 30N 94 7W
San Bartolomeo in Galdo 41 41 23N 15 2 E
San Benedetto 38 45 2N 10 57 E
San Benedetto del Tronto 39 42 57N 13 52 E
San Benito 117 26 5N 97 39W
San Bernardino 119 34 7N 117 18W
San Bernardino Str. 73 13 0N 125 0 E
San Bernardo 124 33 40 S 70 50W
San Bernardo, I. de 126 9 45N 75 50W
San Blas 120 26 4N 108 46W
San Blas, C. 115 29 40N 85 12W
San Borja 126 14 50 S 66 52W
San Buenaventura 120 27 5N 101 32W
San Carlos, Argent. 124 33 50 S 69 0W
San Carlos, Chile 124 36 10 S 72 0W
San Carlos, Mexico 120 29 0N 100 54W
San Carlos, Nic. 121 11 12N 84 50W
San Carlos, Phil. 73 10 29N 123 25 E
San Carlos, Uruguay 125 34 46 S 54 58W
San Carlos, U.S.A. 119 33 24N 110 27W
San Carlos, Amazonas, Venez. 126 1 55N 67 4W
San Carlos, Cojedes, Venez. 126 9 40N 68 36W
San Carlos = Butuku-Luba 85 3 29N 8 33 E
San Carlos de Bariloche 128 41 10 S 71 25W
San Carlos de la Rápita 32 40 37N 0 35 E
San Carlos del Zulia 126 9 1N 71 55W
San Carlos L. 119 33 15N 110 25W
San Cataldo 40 37 30N 13 58 E
San Celoni 32 41 42N 2 30 E
San Clemente, Chile 124 35 30 S 71 29W
San Clemente, Spain 33 39 24N 2 25W
San Clemente, U.S.A. 119 33 29N 117 36W
San Clemente I. 119 32 53N 118 30W
San Constanzo 39 43 46N 13 5 E

• Renamed Harare

San Cristóbal Santéramo in Colle

San Cristóbal, Argent.	**124**	30 20 S	61 10W
San Cristóbal, Dom. Rep.	**121**	18 25N	70 6W
San Cristóbal, Venez.	**126**	16 50N	92 40W
San Cristóbal de las Casas	**120**	16 50N	92 33W
San Damiano d'Asti	**38**	44 51N	8 4 E
San Daniele del Friuli	**39**	46 10N	13 0 E
San Demétrio Corone	**41**	39 34N	16 22 E
San Diego, Calif., U.S.A.	**119**	32 43N	117 10W
San Diego, Tex., U.S.A.	**117**	27 47N	98 15W
San Diego, C.	**128**	54 40 S	65 10W
San Donà di Piave	**39**	45 38N	12 34 E
San Elpídio a Mare	**39**	43 16N	13 41 E
San Estanislao	**124**	24 39 S	56 26W
San Esteban de Gormaz	**32**	41 34N	3 13W
San Felice sul Panaro	**38**	44 51N	11 9 E
San Felipe, Chile	**124**	32 43 S	70 42W
San Felipe, Mexico	**120**	31 0N	114 52W
San Felipe, Venez.	**126**	10 20N	68 44W
San Felíu de Guíxols	**32**	41 45N	3 1 E
San Felíu de Llobregat	**32**	41 23N	2 2 E
San Félix	**95**	26 23 S	80 0W
San Fernando, Chile	**124**	34 30 S	71 0W
San Fernando, Mexico	**120**	30 0N	115 10W
San Fernando, Luzon, Phil.	**73**	16 40N	120 23 E
San Fernando, Luzon, Phil.	**73**	15 5N	120 37 E
San Fernando, Spain	**31**	36 28N	6 17W
San Fernando, Trin.	**121**	10 20N	61 30W
San Fernando, U.S.A.	**119**	34 15N	118 29W
San Fernando →	**120**	24 55N	98 10W
San Fernando de Apure	**126**	7 54N	67 15W
San Fernando de Atabapo	**126**	4 3N	67 42W
San Fernando di Púglia	**41**	41 18N	16 5 E
San Francisco, Argent.	**124**	31 30 S	62 5W
San Francisco, U.S.A.	**119**	37 47N	122 30W
San Francisco →	**119**	32 59N	109 22W
San Francisco de Macorîs	**121**	19 19N	70 15W
San Francisco del Monte de Oro	**124**	32 36 S	66 8W
San Francisco del Oro	**120**	26 52N	105 50W
San Francisco Javier	**33**	38 42N	1 26 E
San Francisco, Paso de	**124**	27 0 S	68 0W
San Fratello	**41**	38 1N	14 33 E
San Gavino Monreale	**40**	39 33N	8 47 E
San Gil	**126**	6 33N	73 8W
San Gimignano	**38**	43 28N	11 3 E
San Giórgio di Nogaro	**39**	45 50N	13 13 E
San Giórgio Iónico	**41**	40 27N	17 23 E
San Giovanni Bianco	**38**	45 52N	9 40 E
San Giovanni in Fiore	**41**	39 16N	16 42 E
San Giovanni in Persieceto	**39**	44 39N	11 12 E
San Giovanni Rotondo	**41**	41 41N	15 42 E
San Giovanni Valdarno	**39**	43 32N	11 30 E
San Giuliano Terme	**38**	43 45N	10 26 E
San Gottardo, Paso del	**25**	46 33N	8 33 E
San Grcángelo	**40**	40 14N	16 14 E
San Gregorio	**125**	32 37 S	55 40W
San Guiseppe Iato	**40**	37 57N	13 11 E
San Ignacio, Boliv.	**126**	16 20 S	60 55W
San Ignacio, Parag.	**124**	26 52 S	57 3W
San Ignacio, Laguna	**120**	26 50N	113 11W
San Ildefonso, C.	**73**	16 0N	122 1 E
San Isidro	**124**	34 29 S	58 31W
San Javier, Misiones, Argent.	**125**	27 55 S	55 5W
San Javier, Santa Fe, Argent.	**124**	30 40 S	59 55W
San Javier, Boliv.	**126**	16 18 S	62 30W
San Javier, Chile	**124**	35 40 S	71 45W
San Javier, Spain	**33**	37 49N	0 50W
San Joaquin →	**119**	37 4N	121 51W
San Jorge	**124**	31 54 S	61 50W
San Jorge, Bahía de	**120**	31 20N	113 20W
San Jorge, Golfo	**128**	46 0 S	66 0W
San Jorge, G. de	**32**	40 50N	0 55W
San José, Boliv.	**126**	17 53 S	60 50W
San José, C. Rica	**121**	10 0N	84 2W
San José, Guat.	**120**	14 0N	90 50W
San José, Mexico	**120**	25 0N	110 50W
San Jose, Luzon, Phil.	**73**	15 45N	120 55 E
San Jose, Mindoro, Phil.	**73**	12 27N	121 4 E
San Jose, Panay, Phil.	**73**	10 50N	122 5 E
San José	**33**	38 55N	1 18 E
San Jose, Calif., U.S.A.	**119**	37 20N	121 53W
San Jose, N. Mex., U.S.A.	**119**	35 26N	105 30W
San Jose →	**119**	34 58N	106 7W
San José de Feliciano	**124**	30 26 S	58 46W
San José de Jáchal	**124**	30 15 S	68 46W
San José de Mayo	**124**	34 27 S	56 40W
San José de Ocune	**126**	4 15N	70 20W
San José del Cabo	**120**	23 0N	109 40W
San José del Guaviare	**126**	2 35N	72 38W
San Juan, Argent.	**124**	31 30 S	68 30W
San Juan, Dom. Rep.	**121**	18 45N	72 45W
San Juan, Mexico	**120**	21 20N	102 50W
San Juan, Phil.	**73**	8 25N	126 20 E
San Juan, Pto. Rico	**121**	18 28N	66 8W
San Juan □	**124**	31 9 S	69 0W
San Juan →, Argent.	**124**	32 20 S	67 25W
San Juan →, Nic.	**121**	10 56N	83 42W
San Juan →, U.S.A.	**119**	37 20N	110 20W
San Juan Bautista, Parag.	**124**	26 37 S	57 6W
San Juan Bautista, Spain	**33**	39 5N	1 31 E
San Juan, C.	**88**	1 5N	9 20 E
San Juan Capistrano	**119**	33 29N	117 40W
San Juan de los Morros	**126**	9 55N	67 21W
San Juan del Norte, B. de	**121**	11 0N	83 40W
San Juan del Puerto	**31**	37 20N	6 50W
San Juan del Río	**120**	20 25N	100 0W
San Juan del Sur	**121**	11 20N	85 51W
San Juan Mts.	**119**	38 30N	108 30W
San Julián	**128**	49 15 S	67 45W
San Just, Sierra de	**32**	40 45N	0 49W
San Justo	**124**	30 47 S	60 30W
San Lázaro, C.	**120**	24 50N	112 18W
San Lázaro, Sa. de	**120**	23 25N	110 0W
San Leandro	**119**	37 40N	122 6W
San Leonardo	**32**	41 51N	3 5W
San Lorenzo, Argent.	**124**	32 45 S	60 45W
San Lorenzo, Ecuador	**126**	1 15N	78 50W
San Lorenzo, Parag.	**124**	25 20 S	57 32W
San Lorenzo →	**120**	24 15N	107 24W
San Lorenzo de la Parrilla	**32**	39 51N	2 22W
San Lorenzo de Morunys	**32**	42 8N	1 35 E
San Lorenzo, I., Mexico	**120**	28 35N	112 50W
San Lorenzo, I., Peru	**126**	12 7 S	77 15W
San Lorenzo, Mt.	**128**	47 40 S	72 20W
San Lucas, Boliv.	**126**	20 5 S	65 7W
San Lucas, Mexico	**120**	27 10N	112 14W
San Lucas, C. de	**120**	22 50N	110 0W
San Lúcido	**41**	39 18N	16 3 E
San Luis, Argent.	**124**	33 20 S	66 20W
San Luis, U.S.A.	**119**	37 3N	105 26W
San Luis □	**124**	34 0 S	66 0W
San Luis de la Paz	**120**	21 19N	100 32W
San Luis, I.	**120**	29 58N	114 26W
San Luis Obispo	**119**	35 21N	120 38W
San Luis Potosí	**120**	22 9N	100 59W
San Luis Potosí □	**120**	22 10N	101 0W
San Luis Río Colorado	**120**	32 29N	114 58W
San Luis, Sierra de	**124**	32 30 S	66 10W
San Marco Argentano	**41**	39 34N	16 8 E
San Marco dei Cavoti	**41**	41 20N	14 50 E
San Marco in Lámis	**41**	41 43N	15 38 E
San Marcos, Guat.	**120**	14 59N	91 52W
San Marcos, Mexico	**120**	27 13N	112 6W
San Marcos, U.S.A.	**117**	29 53N	98 0W
San Marino	**39**	43 56N	12 25 E
San Marino ■	**39**	43 56N	12 25 E
San Martín	**124**	33 5 S	68 28W
San Martín de Valdeiglesias	**30**	40 21N	4 24W
San Martín, L.	**128**	48 50 S	72 50W
San Martino de Calvi	**38**	45 57N	9 41 E
San Mateo, Spain	**32**	40 28N	0 10 E
San Mateo, U.S.A.	**119**	37 32N	122 19W
San Matías	**126**	16 25 S	58 20W
San Matías, Golfo	**128**	41 30 S	64 0W
San Matias, G. of	**122**	41 30 S	64 0W
San Miguel, El Sal.	**120**	13 30N	88 12W
San Miguel, Spain	**33**	39 3N	1 26 E
San Miguel, U.S.A.	**119**	35 45N	120 42W
San Miguel →	**126**	13 52 S	63 56W
San Miguel de Salinas	**33**	37 59N	0 47W
San Miguel de Tucumán	**124**	26 50 S	65 20W
San Miguel del Monte	**124**	35 23 S	58 50W
San Miniato	**38**	43 40N	10 50 E
San Narciso	**73**	15 2N	120 3 E
San Nicolás de los Arroyas	**124**	33 25 S	60 10W
San Nicolas I.	**119**	33 16N	119 30W
San Pablo	**124**	21 43 S	66 38W
San Paolo di Civitate	**41**	41 44N	15 16 E
San Pedro, Buenos Aires, Argent.	**125**	26 30 S	54 10W
San Pedro, Jujuy, Argent.	**124**	24 12 S	64 55W
San-Pédro	**84**	4 50N	6 33W
San Pedro □	**124**	24 0 S	57 0W
San Pedro →, Chihuahua, Mexico	**120**	28 20N	106 10W
San Pedro →, Nayarit, Mexico	**120**	21 45N	105 30W
San Pedro →, U.S.A.	**119**	33 0N	110 50W
San Pedro de Atacama	**124**	22 55 S	68 15W
San Pedro de Jujuy	**124**	24 12 S	64 55W
San Pedro de las Colonias	**120**	25 50N	102 59W
San Pedro de Lloc	**126**	7 15 S	79 28W
San Pedro de Macorís	**121**	18 30N	69 18W
San Pedro del Paraná	**124**	26 43 S	56 13W
San Pedro del Pinatar	**33**	37 50N	0 50W
San Pedro Mártir, Sierra	**120**	31 0N	115 30W
San Pedro Mixtepec	**120**	16 2N	97 7W
San Pedro Ocampo = Melchor Ocampo	**120**	24 52N	101 40W
San Pedro, Pta.	**124**	25 30 S	70 38W
San Pedro, Sierra de	**31**	39 18N	6 40W
San Pedro Sula	**120**	15 30N	88 0W
San Pedro,Pta.	**124**	25 30 S	70 38W
San Pietro, I.	**40**	39 9N	8 17 E
San Pietro Vernótico	**41**	40 28N	18 0 E
San Quintin	**73**	16 1N	120 56 E
San Rafael, Argent.	**124**	34 40 S	68 21W
San Rafael, Calif., U.S.A.	**118**	37 59N	122 32W
San Rafael, N. Mex., U.S.A.	**119**	35 6N	107 58W
San Ramón de la Nueva Orán	**124**	23 10 S	64 20W
San Remo	**38**	43 48N	7 47 E
San Roque, Argent.	**124**	28 25 S	58 45W
San Roque, Spain	**31**	36 17N	5 21W
San Rosendo	**124**	37 16 S	72 43W
San Saba	**117**	31 12N	98 45W
San Salvador	**120**	13 40N	89 10W
San Salvador de Jujuy	**124**	24 10 S	64 48W
San Salvador I.	**121**	24 0N	74 32W
San Sebastián, Argent.	**128**	53 10 S	68 30W
San Sebastián, Spain	**32**	43 17N	1 58W
San Serverino Marche	**39**	43 13N	13 10 E
San Simon	**119**	32 14N	109 16W
San Stéfano di Cadore	**39**	46 34N	12 33 E
San Valentin, Mte.	**128**	46 30 S	73 30W
San Vicente de Alcántara	**31**	39 22N	7 8W
San Vicente de la Barquera	**30**	43 23N	4 29W
San Vincenzo	**38**	43 6N	10 29 E
San Vito	**40**	39 26N	9 32 E
San Vito al Tagliamento	**39**	45 55N	12 50 E
San Vito, C.	**40**	38 11N	12 41 E
San Vito Chietino	**39**	42 19N	14 27 E
San Vito dei Normanni	**41**	40 40N	17 40 E
San Ygnacio	**117**	27 6N	99 24W
Sana'	**63**	15 27N	44 12 E
Sana →	**39**	45 3N	16 23 E
Sanaba	**84**	12 25N	3 47W
Sanabria, La	**30**	42 0N	6 30W
Sanâfir	**86**	27 55N	34 37 E
Sanaga →	**88**	3 35N	9 38 E
Sanak I.	**104**	53 30N	162 30W
Sanana	**73**	2 5 S	125 59 E
Sanand	**68**	22 59N	72 25 E
Sanandaj	**64**	35 18N	47 1 E
Sanandita	**124**	21 40 S	63 45W
Sanary	**21**	43 7N	5 48 E
Sanawad	**68**	22 11N	76 5 E
Sancergues	**19**	47 10N	2 54 E
Sancerre	**19**	47 20N	2 50 E
Sancerrois, Coll. du	**19**	47 20N	2 40 E
Sancha He →	**77**	26 48N	106 7 E
Sanchor	**68**	24 45N	71 55 E
Sanco, Pt.	**73**	8 15N	126 24 E
Sancoins	**19**	46 47N	2 55 E
Sancti-Spíritus	**121**	21 52N	79 33W
Sand →	**93**	22 25 S	30 5 E
Sand Springs	**117**	36 12N	96 5W
Sandah	**86**	20 35N	39 32 E
Sandakan	**72**	5 53N	118 4 E
Sandan	**71**	12 46N	106 0 E
Sandanski	**43**	41 35N	23 16 E
Sandaré	**84**	14 40N	10 15W
Sanday	**14**	59 15N	2 30W
Sande, Möre og Romsdal, Norway	**47**	62 15N	5 27 E
Sande, Sogn og Fjordane, Norway	**47**	61 20N	5 47 E
Sandefjord	**47**	59 10N	10 15 E
Sandeid	**47**	59 33N	5 52 E
Sanders	**119**	35 12N	109 25W
Sanderson	**117**	30 5N	102 30W
Sandfly L.	**109**	55 43N	106 6W
Sandgate	**99**	27 18 S	153 3 E
Sandía	**126**	14 10 S	69 30W
Sandıklı	**64**	38 30N	30 20 E
Sandnes	**47**	58 50N	5 45 E
Sandness	**14**	60 18N	1 38W
Sandoa	**88**	9 41 S	23 0 E
Sandomierz	**28**	50 40N	21 43 E
Sandover →	**97**	21 43 S	136 32 E
Sandoway	**67**	18 20N	94 30 E
Sandpoint	**118**	48 20N	116 34W
Sandringham	**12**	52 50N	0 30 E
Sandslån	**48**	63 2N	17 49 E
Sandspit	**108**	53 14N	131 49W
Sandstone	**96**	27 59 S	119 16 E
Sandusky, Mich., U.S.A.	**106**	43 26N	82 50W
Sandusky, Ohio, U.S.A.	**114**	41 25N	82 40W
Sandvig	**49**	55 18N	14 48 E
Sandviken	**48**	60 38N	16 46 E
Sandwich B., Can.	**107**	53 40N	57 15W
Sandwich B., S. Afr.	**92**	23 25 S	14 20 E
Sandwich, C.	**98**	18 14 S	146 18 E
Sandwich Group	**5**	57 0 S	27 0W
Sandwip Chan.	**67**	22 35N	91 35 E
Sandy C., Queens., Austral.	**97**	24 42 S	153 15 E
Sandy C., Tas., Austral.	**97**	41 25 S	144 45 E
Sandy Cr. →	**118**	41 15N	109 47W
Sandy L.	**106**	53 2N	93 0W
Sandy Lake	**106**	53 0N	93 15W
Sandy Narrows	**109**	55 5N	103 4W
Sanford, Fla., U.S.A.	**115**	28 45N	81 20W
Sanford, Me., U.S.A.	**113**	43 28N	70 47W
Sanford, N.C., U.S.A.	**115**	35 30N	79 10W
Sanford →	**96**	27 22 S	115 53 E
Sanford Mt.	**104**	62 30N	143 0W
Sanga	**91**	12 22 S	35 21 E
Sanga →	**88**	1 5 S	17 0 E
Sanga-Tolon	**59**	61 50N	149 40 E
Sangamner	**70**	19 37N	74 15 E
Sangar	**59**	64 2N	127 31 E
Sangasanga	**72**	0 36 S	117 13 E
Sange	**90**	6 58 S	28 21 E
Sangeang	**73**	8 12 S	119 6 E
Sanger	**119**	36 41N	119 35W
Sangerhausen	**24**	51 28N	11 18 E
Sanggan He →	**76**	38 12N	117 15 E
Sanggau	**72**	0 5N	110 30 E
Sangihe, Kepulauan	**73**	3 0N	126 0 E
Sangihe, P.	**73**	3 45N	125 30 E
Sangkapura	**72**	5 52 S	112 40 E
Sangli	**70**	16 55N	74 33 E
Sangmélina	**88**	2 57N	12 1 E
Sangonera →	**33**	37 59N	1 4W
Sangre de Cristo Mts.	**117**	37 0N	105 0W
Sangro →	**39**	42 14N	14 32 E
Sangudo	**108**	53 50N	114 54W
Sangüesa	**32**	42 37N	1 17W
Sanguinaires, Îs.	**21**	41 51N	8 36 E
Sangzhi	**77**	29 25N	110 12 E
Sanhala	**84**	10 3N	6 51W
Sanish	**116**	48 0N	102 30W
Sanje	**90**	0 49 S	31 30 E
Sanjiang	**77**	25 48N	109 37 E
Sankaranayinarkovil	**70**	9 10N	77 35 E
Sankeshwar	**70**	16 23N	74 32 E
Sankt Andra	**26**	46 46N	14 50 E
Sankt Blasien	**25**	47 47N	8 7 E
Sankt Gallen	**25**	47 26N	9 22 E
Sankt Gallen □	**25**	47 25N	9 22 E
Sankt Gotthard P. = San Gottardo, Paso del	**25**	46 33N	8 33 E
Sankt Ingbert	**25**	49 16N	7 6 E
Sankt Johann, Salzburg, Austria	**26**	47 22N	13 12 E
Sankt Johann, Tirol, Austria	**26**	47 30N	12 25 E
Sankt Moritz	**25**	46 30N	9 50 E
Sankt Olof	**49**	55 37N	14 8 E
Sankt Pölten	**26**	48 12N	15 38 E
Sankt Valentin	**26**	48 11N	14 33 E
Sankt Veit	**26**	46 54N	14 22 E
Sankt Wendel	**25**	49 27N	7 9 E
Sankt Wolfgang	**26**	47 43N	13 27 E
Sankuru →	**88**	4 17 S	20 25 E
Sanlúcar de Barrameda	**31**	36 46N	6 21W
Sanlúcar la Mayor	**31**	37 26N	6 18W
Sanluri	**40**	39 35N	8 55 E
Sanmenxia	**77**	34 47N	111 12 E
Sannaspos	**92**	29 6 S	26 34 E
Sannicandro Gargánico	**41**	41 50N	15 34 E
Sannidal	**47**	58 55N	9 15 E
Sannieshof	**92**	26 30 S	25 47 E
Sanok	**27**	49 35N	22 10 E
Sanquhar	**14**	55 21N	3 56W
Sansanding Dam	**84**	13 48N	6 0W
Sansepolcro	**39**	43 34N	12 8 E
Sanshui	**75**	23 10N	112 56 E
Sanski Most	**39**	44 46N	16 40 E
Sant' Ágata de Goti	**41**	41 6N	14 30 E
Sant' Ágata di Militello	**41**	38 2N	14 8 E
Santa Ana, Boliv.	**126**	13 50 S	65 40W
Santa Ana, Ecuador	**126**	1 16 S	80 20W
Santa Ana, El Sal.	**120**	14 0N	89 31W
Santa Ana, Mexico	**120**	30 31N	111 8W
Santa Ana, U.S.A.	**119**	33 48N	117 55W
Sant' Ángelo Lodigiano	**38**	45 14N	9 25 E
Sant' Antíoco	**40**	39 2N	8 30 E
Sant' Arcángelo di Romagna	**39**	44 4N	12 26 E
Santa Bárbara, Mexico	**120**	26 48N	105 50W
Santa Bárbara, Spain	**32**	40 42N	0 29 E
Santa Barbara	**119**	34 25N	119 40W
Santa Bárbara, Mt.	**33**	37 23N	2 50W
Santa Catalina	**120**	25 40N	110 50W
Santa Catalina, G. of	**119**	33 0N	118 0W
Santa Catalina I.	**119**	33 20N	118 30W
Santa Catarina □	**125**	27 25 S	48 30W
Santa Catarina, I. de	**125**	27 30 S	48 40W
Santa Caterina Villarmosa	**41**	37 37N	14 1 E
Santa Cecília	**125**	26 56 S	50 18W
Santa Clara, Cuba	**121**	22 20N	80 0W
Santa Clara, Calif., U.S.A.	**119**	37 21N	122 0W
Santa Clara, Utah, U.S.A.	**119**	37 10N	113 38W
Santa Clara de Olimar	**125**	32 50 S	54 54W
Santa Clara Pk.	**119**	35 58N	106 45W
Santa Clotilde	**126**	2 33 S	73 45W
Santa Coloma de Farnés	**32**	41 50N	2 39 E
Santa Coloma de Gramanet	**32**	41 27N	2 13 E
Santa Comba	**30**	43 2N	8 49W
Santa Croce Camerina	**41**	36 50N	14 30 E
Santa Croce di Magliano	**41**	41 43N	14 59 E
Santa Cruz, Argent.	**128**	50 0 S	68 32W
Santa Cruz, Boliv.	**126**	17 43 S	63 10W
Santa Cruz, Chile	**124**	34 38 S	71 27W
Santa Cruz, C. Rica	**121**	10 15N	85 35W
Santa Cruz, Phil.	**73**	14 20N	121 24 E
Santa Cruz, Calif., U.S.A.	**119**	36 55N	122 1W
Santa Cruz, N. Mexico, U.S.A.	**119**	35 59N	106 1W
Santa Cruz □	**126**	17 43 S	63 10W
Santa Cruz →	**128**	50 10 S	68 20W
Santa Cruz de Mudela	**33**	38 39N	3 28W
Sta. Cruz de Tenerife	**80**	28 28N	16 15W
Santa Cruz del Retamar	**30**	40 8N	4 14W
Santa Cruz del Sur	**121**	20 44N	78 0W
Santa Cruz do Rio Pardo	**125**	22 54 S	49 37W
Santa Cruz do Sul	**125**	29 42 S	52 25W
Santa Cruz I.	**119**	34 0N	119 45W
Santa Cruz, Is.	**94**	10 30 S	166 0 E
Santa Domingo, Cay	**121**	21 25N	75 15W
Santa Elena, Argent.	**124**	30 58 S	59 47W
Santa Elena, Ecuador	**126**	2 16 S	80 52W
Santa Elena, C.	**121**	10 54N	85 56W
Sant' Eufémia, Golfo di	**41**	38 50N	16 10 E
Santa Eulalia	**33**	38 59N	1 32 E
Santa Fe, Argent.	**124**	31 35 S	60 41W
Santa Fe, Spain	**31**	37 11N	3 43W
Santa Fe, U.S.A.	**119**	35 40N	106 0W
Santa Fé □	**124**	31 50 S	60 55W
Santa Filomena	**127**	9 6 S	45 50W
Santa Genoveva	**120**	23 18N	109 52W
Santa Inés	**31**	38 32N	5 37W
Santa Inés, I.	**128**	54 0 S	73 0W
Santa Isabel, Argent.	**124**	36 10 S	66 54W
Santa Isabel, Brazil	**127**	11 45 S	51 30W
Santa Isabel = Rey Malabo	**85**	3 45N	8 50 E
Santa Isabel, Pico	**85**	3 36N	8 49 E
Santa Lucía, Corrientes, Argent.	**124**	28 58 S	59 5W
Santa Lucía, San Juan, Argent.	**124**	31 30 S	68 30W
Santa Lucía, Spain	**33**	37 35N	0 58W
Santa Lucia	**124**	34 27 S	56 24W
Santa Lucia Range	**119**	36 0N	121 20W
Santa Margarita, Argent.	**124**	38 28 S	61 35W
Santa Margarita, Mexico	**120**	24 30N	111 50W
Santa Margherita	**38**	44 20N	9 11 E
Santa María	**124**	26 40 S	66 0W
Santa Maria, Brazil	**125**	29 40 S	53 48W
Santa Maria, Spain	**32**	39 38N	2 47 E
Santa Maria, U.S.A.	**119**	34 58N	120 29W
Santa Maria, Zambia	**91**	11 5 S	29 58 E
Santa María →	**120**	31 0N	107 14W
Santa María, Bahía de	**120**	25 10N	108 40W
Santa Maria, Cabo de	**31**	36 58N	7 53W
Santa Maria Capua Vetere	**41**	41 3N	14 15 E
Santa Maria da Vitória	**127**	13 24 S	44 12W
Santa María del Oro	**120**	25 58N	105 20W
Santa Maria di Leuca, C.	**41**	39 48N	18 20 E
Santa María la Real de Nieva	**30**	41 4N	4 24W
Santa Marta, Colomb.	**126**	11 15N	74 13W
Santa Marta, Spain	**31**	38 37N	6 39W
Santa Marta Grande, C.	**125**	28 43 S	48 50W
Santa Marta, Ría de	**30**	43 44N	7 45W
Santa Marta, Sierra Nevada de	**126**	10 55N	73 50W
Santa Maura = Levkás	**45**	38 40N	20 43 E
Santa Monica	**119**	34 0N	118 30W
Santa Olalla, Huelva, Spain	**31**	37 54N	6 14W
Santa Olalla, Toledo, Spain	**30**	40 2N	4 25W
Sant' Onofrio	**41**	38 42N	16 10 E
Santa Paula	**119**	34 20N	119 2W
Santa Pola	**33**	38 13N	0 35W
Santa Rita	**119**	32 50N	108 0W
Santa Rosa, La Pampa, Argent.	**124**	36 40 S	64 17W
Santa Rosa, San Luis, Argent.	**124**	32 21 S	65 10W
Santa Rosa, Boliv.	**126**	10 36 S	67 20W
Santa Rosa, Brazil	**125**	27 52 S	54 29W
Santa Rosa, Calif., U.S.A.	**118**	38 26N	122 43W
Santa Rosa, N. Mexico, U.S.A.	**117**	34 58N	104 40W
Santa Rosa de Copán	**120**	14 47N	88 46W
Santa Rosa de Río Primero	**124**	31 8 S	63 20W
Santa Rosa I., Calif., U.S.A.	**119**	34 0N	120 6W
Santa Rosa I., Fla., U.S.A.	**115**	30 23N	87 0W
Santa Rosa Mts.	**118**	41 45N	117 30W
Santa Rosalía	**120**	27 20N	112 20W
Santa Sofia	**39**	43 57N	11 55 E
Santa Sylvina	**124**	27 50 S	61 10W
Santa Tecla = Nueva San Salvador	**120**	13 40N	89 25W
Santa Teresa	**124**	33 25 S	60 47W
Santa Teresa di Riva	**41**	37 58N	15 21 E
Santa Teresa Gallura	**40**	41 14N	9 12 E
Santa Vitória do Palmar	**125**	33 32 S	53 25W
Santadi	**40**	39 5N	8 42 E
Santai	**75**	31 5N	104 58 E
Santana, Coxilha de	**125**	30 50 S	55 35W
Santana do Livramento	**125**	30 55 S	55 30W
Santanayi	**33**	39 20N	3 5 E
Santander	**30**	43 27N	3 51W
Santander □	**30**	43 25N	4 0W
Santander Jiménez	**120**	24 11N	98 29W
Santaquin	**118**	40 0N	111 51W
Santarém, Brazil	**127**	2 25 S	54 42W
Santarém, Port.	**31**	39 12N	8 42W
Santarém □	**31**	39 10N	8 40W
Santaren Channel	**121**	24 0N	79 30W
Santéramo in Colle	**41**	40 48N	16 45 E

Santerno Scunthorpe

Santerno → 39 44 10N 11 38 E
Santhia 38 45 20N 8 10 E
Santiago, Brazil 125 29 11 S 54 52W
Santiago, Chile 124 33 24 S 70 40W
Santiago, Panama 121 8 0N 81 0W
Santiago □ 124 33 30 S 70 50W
Santiago de Compostela 30 42 52N 8 37W
Santiago de Cuba 121 20 0N 75 49W
Santiago de los Cabelleros 121 19 30N 70 40W
Santiago del Estero 124 27 50 S 64 15W
Santiago del Estero □ 124 27 40 S 63 15W
Santiago do Cacém 31 38 1N 8 42W
Santiago Ixcuintla 120 21 50N 105 11W
Santiago Papasquiaro 120 25 0N 105 20W
Santiago, Punta de 85 3 12N 8 40 E
Santiaguillo, L. de 120 24 50N 104 50W
Santillana del Mar 30 43 24N 4 6W
Santipur 69 23 17N 88 25 E
Santisteban del Puerto 33 38 17N 3 15W
Santo Amaro 127 12 30 S 38 43W
Santo Anastácio 125 21 58 S 51 39W
Santo André 125 23 39 S 46 29W
Santo Ângelo 125 28 15 S 54 15W
Santo Antonio 127 15 50 S 56 0W
Santo Corazón 126 18 0 S 58 45W
Santo Domingo, Dom. Rep. 121 18 30N 64 54W
Santo Domingo, Baja Calif. N., Mexico 120 30 43N 116 2W
Santo Domingo, Baja Calif. S., Mexico 120 25 32N 112 2W
Santo Domingo, Nic. 121 12 14N 84 59W
Santo Domingo de la Calzada 32 42 26N 2 57W
Santo Stéfano di Camastro 41 38 1N 14 22 E
Santo Stino di Livenza 39 45 45N 12 40 E
Santo Tirso 30 41 21N 8 28W
Santo Tomás 126 14 26 S 72 8W
Santo Tomé 125 28 40 S 56 5W
Santo Tomé de Guayana 126 8 22N 62 40W
Santoña 30 43 29N 3 27W
Santos 125 24 0 S 46 20W
Santos Dumont 125 22 55 S 43 10W
Santos, Sierra de los 31 38 7N 5 12W
Şanūr 62 32 22N 35 15 E
Sanvignes-les-Mines 19 46 40N 4 18 E
Sanyuan 77 34 35N 108 58 E
Sanza Pombo 88 7 18 S 15 56 E
São Anastácio 125 22 0 S 51 40W
São Bartolomeu de Messines 31 37 15N 8 17W
São Borja 125 28 39 S 56 0W
São Bras d'Alportel 31 37 8N 7 37W
São Carlos 125 22 0 S 47 50W
São Cristóvão 127 11 1 S 37 15W
São Domingos 127 13 25 S 46 19W
São Francisco 127 16 0 S 44 50W
São Francisco → 127 10 30 S 36 24W
São Francisco do Sul 125 26 15 S 48 36W
São Gabriel 125 30 20 S 54 20W
São Gonçalo 125 22 48 S 43 5W
Sao Hill 91 8 20 S 35 12 E
São João da Boa Vista 125 22 0 S 46 52W
São João da Pesqueira 30 41 8N 7 24W
São João del Rei 125 21 8 S 44 15W
São João do Araguaia 127 5 23 S 48 46W
São João do Piauí 127 8 21 S 42 15W
São José do Rio Prêto 125 20 50 S 49 20W
São José dos Campos 125 23 7 S 45 52W
São Leopoldo 125 29 50 S 51 10W
São Lourenço 125 22 7 S 45 3W
São Lourenço → 127 17 53 S 57 27W
São Luís Gonzaga 125 28 25 S 55 0W
São Luís (Maranhão) 127 2 39 S 44 15W
São Marcos → 127 18 15 S 47 37W
São Marcos, B. de 127 2 0 S 44 0W
São Martinho 30 40 18N 8 8W
São Mateus 127 18 44 S 39 50W
São Miguel 8 37 33N 25 27W
São Paulo 125 23 32 S 46 37W
São Paulo □ 125 22 0 S 49 0W
Sao Paulo, I. 6 0 50N 31 40W
São Pedro do Sul 30 40 46N 8 4W
São Roque, C. de 127 5 30 S 35 16W
São Sebastião do Paraíso 125 20 54 S 46 59W
São Sebastião, I. de 125 23 50 S 45 18W
São Teotónio 31 37 30N 8 42W
São Tomé 79 0 10N 6 39 E
São Tomé, C. de 125 22 0 S 40 59W
São Vicente 125 23 57 S 46 23W
São Vicente, Cabo de 31 37 0N 9 0W
Saona, I. 121 18 10N 68 40W
Saône → 19 45 44N 4 50 E
Saône-et-Loire □ 19 46 25N 4 50 E
Saonek 73 0 22 S 130 55 E
Saoura, O. → 82 29 0N 0 55W
Sápai 44 41 2N 25 43 E
Saparua 73 3 33 S 128 40 E
Sapele 85 5 50N 5 40 E
Sapelo I. 115 31 28N 81 15W
Sapiéntza 45 36 45N 21 43 E
Sapone 85 12 3N 1 35W
Saposoa 126 6 55 S 76 45W
Sapozhok 55 53 59N 40 41 E
Sapphire Mts. 118 46 20N 113 45W
Sapporo 74 43 0N 141 21 E
Sapri 41 40 5N 15 37 E
Sapudi 73 7 2 S 114 17 E
Sapulpa 117 36 0N 96 0W
Saqqez 64 36 15N 46 20 E
Sar-e Pol 65 36 10N 66 0 E
Sar Planina 42 42 10N 21 0 E
Sara 84 11 40N 3 53W
Sarāb 64 38 0N 47 30 E
Saragossa = Zaragoza 32 41 39N 0 53W
Saraguro 126 3 35 S 79 16W
Saraipalli 69 21 20N 82 59 E
Sarajevo 42 43 52N 18 26 E
Saralu 46 44 43N 28 10 E
Saran 86 19 35N 40 30 E
Saran, G. 72 0 30 S 111 25 E
Saranac Lake 114 44 20N 74 10W
Saranda, Alb. 44 39 52N 19 55 E
Saranda, Tanz. 90 5 45 S 34 59 E
Sarandí del Yi 125 33 18 S 55 38W
Sarandí Grande 124 33 44 S 56 20W
Sarangani B. 73 6 0N 125 13 E
Sarangani Is. 73 5 25N 125 25 E
Sarangarh 69 21 30N 83 5 E
Saransk 55 54 10N 45 10 E
Sarapul 52 56 28N 53 48 E
Sarasota 115 27 20N 82 30W
Saratoga 118 41 30N 106 48W
Saratoga Springs 114 43 5N 73 47W
Saratov 55 51 30N 46 2 E
Saravane 71 15 43N 106 25 E
Sarawak □ 72 2 0N 113 0 E
Saraya 84 12 50N 11 45W
Sarbāz 65 26 38N 61 19 E
Sarbīsheh 65 32 30N 59 40 E
Sârbogård 27 46 50N 18 40 E
Sarca → 38 45 52N 10 52 E
Sardalas 83 25 50N 10 34 E
Sardarshahr 68 28 30N 74 29 E
Sardegna 40 39 57N 9 0 E
Sardhana 68 29 9N 77 39 E
Sardinia = Sardegna 40 39 57N 9 0 E
Šarengrad 42 45 14N 19 16 E
Saréyamou 84 16 7N 3 10W
Sargasso Sea 6 27 0N 72 0W
Sargent 116 41 42N 99 24W
Sargodha 68 32 10N 72 40 E
* Sargodha □ 68 31 50N 72 0 E
Sarh 81 9 5N 18 23 E
Sarhro, Djebel 82 31 6N 5 0W
Sārī 65 36 30N 53 4 E
Sária 45 35 54N 27 17 E
Sarida → 62 32 4N 34 45 E
Sarikamiş 64 40 22N 42 35 E
Sarikei 72 2 8N 111 30 E
Sarina 97 21 22 S 149 13 E
Sariñena 32 41 47N 0 10W
Sarīr Tibasti 83 22 50N 18 30 E
Sarita 117 27 14N 97 49W
Sariyer 43 41 10N 29 3 E
Sark 18 49 25N 2 20W
Sarkad 27 46 47N 21 23 E
Sarlat-la-Canéda 20 44 54N 1 13 E
Sarles 116 48 58N 99 0W
Sărmaşu 46 46 45N 24 13 E
Sarmi 73 1 49 S 138 44 E
Sarmiento 128 45 35 S 69 5W
Särna 48 61 41N 13 8 E
Sarnano 39 43 2N 13 17 E
Sarnen 25 46 53N 8 13 E
Sarnia 106 42 58N 82 23W
Sarno 41 40 48N 14 35 E
Sarnowa 28 51 39N 16 53 E
Sarny 54 51 17N 26 40 E
Särö 49 57 31N 11 57 E
Sarolangun 72 2 19 S 102 42 E
Saronikós Kólpos 45 37 45N 23 45 E
Saronno 38 45 38N 9 2 E
Saros Körfezi 44 40 30N 26 15 E
Sárospatak 27 48 18N 21 33 E
Sarosul Românesc 42 45 34N 21 43 E
Sarova 55 54 55N 43 19 E
Sarpsborg 47 59 16N 11 12 E
Sarracín 32 42 15N 3 45W
Sarralbe 19 48 55N 7 1 E
Sarre = Saar → 19 49 7N 7 4 E
Sarre, La 106 48 45N 79 15W
Sarre-Union 19 48 55N 7 4 E
Sarrebourg 19 48 43N 7 3 E
Sarreguemines 19 49 1N 7 4 E
Sarriá 30 42 49N 7 29W
Sarrión 32 40 9N 0 49W
Sarro 84 13 40N 5 15W
Sarstedt 24 52 13N 9 50 E
Sartène 21 41 38N 8 58 E
Sarthe □ 18 47 58N 0 10 E
Sarthe → 18 47 33N 0 31W
Sartilly 18 48 45N 1 28W
Sartynya 58 63 22N 63 11 E
Sarum 86 21 11N 39 10 E
Sarūr 65 23 17N 58 4 E
Sárvár 27 47 15N 16 56 E
Sarvestān 65 29 20N 53 10 E
Särvfjället 48 62 42N 13 30 E
Sárviz → 27 46 24N 18 41 E
Sary-Tash 58 39 44N 73 15 E
Sarych, Mys. 56 44 25N 33 45 E
Saryshagan 58 46 12N 73 38 E
Sarzana 38 44 5N 9 59 E
Sarzeau 18 47 31N 2 48W
Sasa 62 33 2N 35 23 E
Sasabeneh 63 7 59N 44 43 E
Sasaram 69 24 57N 84 5 E
Sasca Montană 42 44 50N 21 45 E
Sasebo 74 33 10N 129 43 E
Saser Mt. 69 34 50N 77 50 E
Saskatchewan □ 109 54 40N 106 0W
Saskatchewan → 109 53 37N 100 40W
Saskatoon 109 52 10N 106 38W
Saskylakh 59 71 55N 114 1 E
Sasnovka 55 56 20N 51 4 E
Sasolburg 93 26 46 S 27 49 E
Sasovo 55 54 25N 41 55 E
Sassandra 84 5 0N 6 8W
Sassandra → 84 4 58N 6 5W
Sássari 40 40 44N 8 33 E
Sassnitz 24 54 29N 13 39 E
Sasso Marconi 39 44 22N 11 12 E
Sassocorvaro 39 43 47N 12 30 E
Sassoferrato 39 43 26N 12 51 E
Sassuolo 38 44 31N 10 47 E
Sástago 32 41 19N 0 21W
Sastown 84 4 45N 8 27W
Sasumua Dam 90 0 45 S 36 40 E
Sasyk, Ozero 46 45 45N 30 0 E
Sata-Misaki 74 30 59N 130 40 E
Satadougou 84 12 25N 11 25W
Satanta 117 37 30N 101 0W
Satara 70 17 44N 73 58 E
Satilla → 115 30 59N 81 28W
Satka 52 55 3N 59 1 E
Satkhira 69 22 43N 89 8 E
Satmala Hills 70 20 15N 74 40 E
Satna 69 24 35N 80 50 E
Sator 39 44 11N 16 37 E
Sátoraljaújhely 27 48 25N 21 41 E
Satpura Ra. 68 21 25N 76 10 E
Satrup 24 54 39N 9 38 E
Sattenapalle 70 16 25N 80 6 E
Satu Mare 46 47 46N 22 55 E
Satui 72 3 50 S 115 27 E
Satumare □ 46 47 45N 23 0 E
Satun 71 6 43N 100 2 E
Saturnina → 126 12 15 S 58 10W
Sauce 124 30 5 S 58 46W
Saucillo 120 28 1N 105 17W
Sauda 47 59 40N 6 20 E
Sauðarkrókur 50 65 45N 19 40W
Saudi Arabia ■ 64 26 0N 44 0 E
Sauerland 24 51 0N 8 0 E
Saugeen → 112 44 30N 81 22W
Saugerties 114 42 4N 73 58W
Saugues 20 44 58N 3 32 E
Sauherad 47 59 25N 9 15 E
Saujon 20 45 41N 0 55W
Sauk Center 116 45 42N 94 56W
Sauk Rapids 116 45 35N 94 10W
Saulgau 25 48 4N 9 32 E
Saulieu 19 47 17N 4 14 E
Sault 21 44 6N 5 24 E
Sault Ste. Marie, Can. 106 46 30N 84 20W
Sault Ste. Marie, U.S.A. 114 46 27N 84 22W
Saumlaki 73 7 55 S 131 20 E
Saumur 18 47 15N 0 5W
Saunders C. 101 45 53 S 170 45 E
Saunders I. 5 57 48 S 26 28W
Saurbær, Borgarfjarðarsýsla, Iceland 50 64 24N 21 35W
Saurbær, Eyjafjarðarsýsla, Iceland 50 65 27N 18 13W
Sauri 85 11 42N 6 44 E
Saurimo 88 9 40 S 20 12 E
Sauveterre 20 43 25N 0 57W
Sauzé-Vaussais 20 46 8N 0 8 E
Sava 39 40 28N 17 32 E
Sava → 39 44 50N 20 26 E
Savage 116 47 27N 104 20W
Savai'i 101 13 28 S 172 24W
Savalou 85 7 57N 1 58 E
Savane 91 19 37 S 35 8 E
Savanna 116 42 5N 90 10W
Savanna la Mar 121 18 10N 78 10W
Savannah, Ga., U.S.A. 115 32 4N 81 4W
Savannah, Mo., U.S.A. 116 39 55N 94 46W
Savannah, Tenn., U.S.A. 115 35 12N 88 18W
Savannah → 115 32 2N 80 53W
Savannakhet 71 16 30N 104 49 E
Savant L. 106 50 16N 90 44W
Savant Lake 106 50 14N 90 40W
Savantvadi 70 15 55N 73 54 E
Savanur 70 14 59N 75 21 E
Savda 68 21 9N 75 56 E
Savé 85 8 2N 2 29 E
Save → 20 43 47N 1 17 E
Sāveh 64 35 2N 50 20 E
Savelugu 85 9 38N 0 54W
Savenay 18 47 20N 1 55W
Saverdun 20 43 14N 1 34 E
Saverne 19 48 39N 7 20 E
Savigliano 38 44 39N 7 40 E
Savigny-sur-Braye 18 47 53N 0 49 E
Saviñao 30 42 35N 7 38W
Savio → 39 44 19N 12 20 E
Šavnik 42 42 59N 19 10 E
Savoie □ 21 45 26N 6 35 E
Savona 38 44 19N 8 29 E
Savonlinna 52 61 52N 28 53 E
Sävsjö 49 57 20N 14 40 E
Sävsjøström 49 57 1N 15 25 E
Sawahlunto 72 0 40 S 100 52 E
Sawai 73 3 0 S 129 5 E
Sawai Madhopur 68 26 0N 76 25 E
Sawara 74 35 55N 140 30 E
Sawatch Mts. 119 38 30N 106 30W
Sawdā, Jabal as 83 28 51N 15 12 E
Sawel, Mt. 15 54 48N 7 5W
Sawfajjin, W. 83 31 46N 14 30 E
Sawknah 81 29 4N 15 47 E
Sawmills 91 19 30 S 28 2 E
Sawu 73 10 35 S 121 50 E
Sawu Sea 73 9 30 S 121 50 E
Sawyerville 113 45 20N 71 34W
Saxby → 98 18 25 S 140 53 E
Saxony, Lower = Niedersachsen □ 24 52 45N 9 0 E
Saxton 112 40 12N 78 18W
Say 85 13 8N 2 22 E
Saya 85 9 30N 3 18 E
Sayabec 107 48 35N 67 41W
Sayán 126 11 8 S 77 12W
Sayan, Vostochnyy 59 54 0N 96 0 E
Sayan, Zapadnyy 59 52 30N 94 0 E
Sayasan 57 42 56N 46 15 E
Saydā 64 33 35N 35 25 E
Şayghān 65 35 10N 67 55 E
Sayḥut 63 15 12N 51 10 E
Saynshand 75 44 55N 110 11 E
Sayre, Okla., U.S.A. 117 35 20N 99 40W
Sayre, Pa., U.S.A. 114 42 0N 76 30W
Sayula 120 19 50N 103 40W
Sayville 113 40 45N 73 7W
Sazan 44 40 30N 19 20 E
Sázava → 26 49 53N 14 24 E
Sazin 69 35 35N 73 30 E
Sazlika → 43 41 59N 25 50 E
Sbeïtla 83 35 12N 9 7 E
Scaër 18 48 2N 3 42W
Scafell Pikes 12 54 26N 3 14W
Scalea 41 39 49N 15 47 E
Scalpay 14 57 51N 6 40W
Scandia 108 50 20N 112 0W
Scandiano 38 44 36N 10 40 E
Scandinavia 9 64 0N 12 0 E
Scansano 39 42 40N 11 20 E
Scapa Flow 14 58 52N 3 6W
Scarborough, Trin. 121 11 11N 60 42W
Scarborough, U.K. 12 54 17N 0 24W
Scarpe → 19 50 31N 3 27 E
Ščedro 39 43 6N 16 43 E
Scenic 116 43 49N 102 32W
Schaal See 24 53 40N 10 57 E
Schaffhausen □ 25 47 42N 8 36 E
Schagen 16 52 49N 4 48 E
Schärding 26 48 27N 13 27 E
Scharhörn 24 53 58N 8 24 E
Scharnitz 26 47 23N 11 15 E
Scheessel 24 53 10N 9 33 E
Schefferville 107 54 48N 66 50W
Scheibbs 26 48 1N 15 9 E
Schelde → 16 51 15N 4 16 E
Schenectady 114 42 50N 73 58W
Scherfede 24 51 32N 9 2 E
Schesslitz 25 49 59N 11 2 E
Scheveningen 16 52 6N 4 16 E
Schiedam 16 51 55N 4 25 E
Schiermonnikoog 16 53 30N 6 15 E
Schifferstadt 25 49 22N 8 23 E
Schiltigheim 19 48 35N 7 45 E
Schio 39 45 42N 11 21 E
Schirmeck 19 48 29N 7 12 E
Schladming 26 47 23N 13 41 E
Schlei → 24 54 45N 9 52 E
Schleiden 24 50 32N 6 26 E
Schleiz 24 50 35N 11 49 E
Schleswig 24 54 32N 9 34 E
Schleswig-Holstein □ 24 54 10N 9 40 E
Schlüchtern 25 50 20N 9 32 E
Schmalkalden 24 50 43N 10 28 E
Schmölln 24 50 54N 12 22 E
Schmölln 24 53 15N 14 6 E
Schneeberg, Austria 26 47 47N 15 48 E
Schneeberg, Ger. 24 50 35N 12 39 E
Schofield 116 44 54N 89 39W
Schönberg, Rostock, Ger. 24 53 50N 10 55 E
Schönberg, Schleswig-Holstein, Ger. 24 54 23N 10 20 E
Schönebeck 24 52 2N 11 42 E
Schongau 25 47 49N 10 54 E
Schöningen 24 52 8N 10 57 E
Schortens 24 53 37N 7 51 E
Schouten I. 99 42 20 S 148 20 E
Schouten, Kepulauan 73 1 0 S 136 0 E
Schouwen 16 51 43N 3 45 E
Schramberg 25 48 12N 8 24 E
Schrankogl 26 47 3N 11 7 E
Schreiber 106 48 45N 87 20W
Schrobenhausen 25 48 33N 11 16 E
Schruns 26 47 5N 9 56 E
Schuler 109 50 20N 110 6W
Schumacher 106 48 30N 81 16W
Schurz 118 38 57N 118 48W
Schuyler 116 41 30N 97 3W
Schuylkill Haven 113 40 37N 76 11W
Schwabach 25 49 19N 11 3 E
Schwäbisch Gmünd 25 48 49N 9 48 E
Schwäbisch Hall 25 49 7N 9 45 E
Schwäbische Alb 25 48 30N 9 30 E
Schwabmünchen 25 48 11N 10 45 E
Schwandorf 25 49 20N 12 7 E
Schwarmstedt 24 52 41N 9 37 E
Schwarzach → 26 46 56N 12 35 E
Schwärze 24 52 50N 13 49 E
Schwarzenberg 24 50 31N 12 49 E
Schwarzwald 25 48 0N 8 0 E
Schwaz 26 47 20N 11 44 E
Schwedt 24 53 4N 14 18 E
Schweinfurt 25 50 3N 10 12 E
Schweizer Reneke 92 27 11 S 25 18 E
Schwerin 24 53 37N 11 22 E
Schwerin □ 24 53 35N 11 20 E
Schweriner See 24 53 45N 11 26 E
Schwetzingen 25 49 22N 8 35 E
Schwyz 25 47 2N 8 39 E
Schwyz □ 25 47 2N 8 39 E
Sciacca 40 37 30N 13 3 E
Scicli 41 36 48N 14 41 E
Scie, La 107 49 57N 55 36W
Scilla 41 38 18N 15 44 E
Scilly, Isles of 13 49 55N 6 15W
Ščinawa 28 51 25N 16 26 E
Scione 44 39 57N 23 36 E
Scioto → 114 38 44N 83 0W
Scobey 116 48 47N 105 30W
Scone, Austral. 99 32 5 S 150 52 E
Scone, U.K. 14 56 25N 3 26W
Scordia 41 37 19N 14 50 E
Scoresbysund 4 70 20N 23 0W
Scorno, Punta dello 40 41 7N 8 23 E
Scotia, Calif., U.S.A. 118 40 36N 124 4W
Scotia, N.Y., U.S.A. 113 42 50N 73 58W
Scotia Sea 5 56 5 S 56 0W
Scotland 116 43 10N 97 45W
Scotland □ 13 57 0N 4 0W
Scotland Neck 115 36 6N 77 32W
Scott 5 77 0 S 165 0 E
Scott, C. 5 71 30 S 168 0 E
Scott City 116 38 30N 100 52W
Scott Glacier 5 66 15 S 100 5 E
Scott I. 5 67 0 S 179 0 E
Scott Inlet 105 71 0N 71 0W
Scott Is. 108 50 48N 128 40W
Scott L. 109 59 55N 106 18W
Scott Reef 96 14 0 S 121 50 E
Scottburgh 93 30 15 S 30 47 E
Scottdale 112 40 8N 79 35W
Scottsbluff 116 41 55N 103 35W
Scottsboro 115 34 40N 86 0W
Scottsburg 114 38 40N 85 46W
Scottsdale 97 41 9 S 147 31 E
Scottsville, Ky., U.S.A. 115 36 48N 86 10W
Scottsville, N.Y., U.S.A. 112 43 2N 77 47W
Scottville, Austral. 98 20 33 S 147 49 E
Scottville, U.S.A. 114 43 57N 86 18W
Scranton 114 41 22N 75 41W
Scugog, L. 112 44 10N 78 55W
Scunthorpe 12 53 35N 0 38W

* *Now part of Punjab □*

Scusciuban Shāhrūd

Scusciuban 63 10 18N 50 12 E
Sea Breeze 112 43 12N 77 32W
Seaford, Austral. 100 38 10 S 145 11 E
Seaford, U.S.A. 114 38 37N 75 36W
Seaforth 106 43 35N 81 25W
Seagraves 117 32 56N 102 30W
Seal → 109 58 50N 97 30W
Seal Cove 107 49 57N 56 22W
Seal L. 107 54 20N 61 30W
Sealy 117 29 46N 96 9W
Searchlight 119 35 31N 114 55W
Searcy 117 35 15N 91 45W
Searles L. 119 35 47N 117 17W
Seaside 118 45 59N 123 55W
Seaspray 99 38 25 S 147 15 E
Seattle 118 47 41N 122 15W
Seaview Ra. 97 18 40 S 145 45 E
Sebastián Vizcaíno, Bahía 120 28 0N 114 30W
Sebastopol 118 38 24N 122 49W
Sebastopol = Sevastopol 56 44 35N 33 30 E
Sebderat 87 15 26N 36 42 E
Sebdou 82 34 38N 1 19W
Sebeş 46 45 58N 23 34 E
Sebeşului, Munţii 46 45 36N 23 40 E
Sebewaing 114 43 45N 83 27W
Sebezh 54 56 14N 28 22 E
Sébi 84 15 50N 4 12W
Şebinkarahisar 56 40 22N 38 28 E
Sebiş 46 46 23N 22 13 E
Sebkhet Te-n-Dghâmcha 84 18 30N 15 55W
Sebkra Azzel Mati 82 26 10N 0 43 E
Sebkra Mekerghene 82 26 21N 1 30 E
Sebnitz 24 50 58N 14 17 E
Sebou, Oued → 82 34 16N 6 40W
Sebring, Fla., U.S.A. 115 27 30N 81 26W
Sebring, Ohio, U.S.A. 112 40 55N 81 2W
Sebringville 112 43 24N 81 4W
Sebta = Ceuta 82 35 52N 5 19W
Sebuku 72 3 30 S 116 25 E
Sebuku, Teluk 72 4 0N 118 10 E
Sečanj 42 45 25N 20 47 E
Secchia → 38 44 4N 11 0 E
Sechelt 108 49 25N 123 42W
Sechura, Desierto de 126 6 0 S 80 30W
Seclin 19 50 33N 3 2 E
Secondigny 18 46 37N 0 26W
Sečovce 27 48 42N 21 40 E
Secretary I. 101 45 15 S 166 56 E
Secunderabad 70 17 28N 78 30 E
Sedalia 116 38 40N 93 18W
Sedan, Austral. 99 34 34 S 139 19 E
Sedan, France 19 49 43N 4 57 E
Sedan, U.S.A. 117 37 10N 96 11W
Sedano 32 42 43N 3 49W
Seddon 101 41 40 S 174 7 E
Seddonville 101 41 33 S 172 1 E
Sede Ya'aqov 62 32 43N 35 7 E
Sedgewick 108 52 48N 111 41W
Sedhiou 84 12 44N 15 30W
Sedičany 26 49 40N 14 25 E
Sedico 39 46 8N 12 6 E
Sedienie 43 42 16N 24 33 E
Sedley 109 50 10N 104 0W
Sedom 62 31 5N 35 20 E
Sedova, Pik 58 73 29N 54 58 E
Sedrata 83 36 7N 7 31 E
Sedro Woolley 118 48 30N 122 15W
Seduva 54 55 45N 23 45 E
Sedziszów Małapolski 27 50 5N 21 45 E
Seebad Ahlbeck 24 53 56N 14 10 E
Seefeld 26 47 19N 11 13 E
Seehausen 24 52 52N 11 43 E
Seeheim 92 26 50 S 17 45 E
Seekoe → 92 30 18 S 25 1 E
Seelaw 24 52 32N 14 22 E
Se'elim, Nahal 62 31 21N 35 24 E
Sées 18 48 38N 0 10 E
Seesen 24 51 53N 10 10 E
Sefadu 84 8 35N 10 58W
Séfeto 84 14 8N 9 49W
Sefrou 82 33 52N 4 52W
Sefwi Bekwai 84 6 10N 2 25W
Seg-ozero 54 63 0N 33 10 E
Segamat 71 2 30N 102 50 E
Segarcea 46 44 6N 23 43 E
Segbwema 84 8 0N 11 0W
Seget 73 1 24 S 130 58 E
Segezha 52 63 44N 34 19 E
Segqueur, O. → 82 32 4N 2 4 E
Segid 87 16 55N 42 0 E
Segonzac 20 45 36N 0 14W
Segorbe 32 39 50N 0 30W
Ségou 84 13 30N 6 16W
Segovia 30 40 57N 4 10W
Segovia = Coco → 121 15 0N 83 8W
Segovia □ 30 40 55N 4 10W
Segré 18 47 40N 0 52W
Segre → 32 41 40N 0 43 E
Séguéla 84 7 55N 6 40W
Seguin 117 29 34N 97 58W
Segundo 117 37 12N 104 50W
Segundo → 124 30 53 S 62 44W
Segura → 33 38 6N 0 54W
Segura, Sierra de 33 38 5N 2 45W
Sehore 68 23 10N 77 5 E
Sehwan 68 26 28N 67 53 E
Şeica Mare 46 46 1N 24 7 E
Seiland 50 70 25N 23 15 E
Seiling 117 36 10N 98 56W
Seille →, Moselle, France 19 49 7N 6 11 E
Seille →, Saône-et-Loire, France 21 46 31N 4 57 E
Sein, Î. de 18 48 2N 4 52W
Seinäjoki → 50 62 40N 22 45 E
Seine → 18 49 26N 0 26 E
Seine, B. de la 18 49 40N 0 40W
Seine-et-Marne □ 19 48 45N 3 0 E
Seine-Maritime □ 18 49 40N 1 0 E
Seine-Saint-Denis □ 19 48 58N 2 24 E
Seini 46 47 44N 23 21 E
Seistan 65 30 50N 61 0 E
Seistan-Balūchestān □ 65 27 0N 62 0 E
Sejerø 49 55 54N 11 9 E
Sejerø Bugt 49 55 53N 11 15 E
Sejny 28 54 6N 23 21 E
Seka 87 8 10N 36 52 E
Sekayu 72 2 51 S 103 51 E
Seke 90 3 20 S 33 31 E
Sekenke 90 4 18 S 34 11 E
Sekiu 118 48 16N 124 18W
Sekken Veøy 47 62 45N 7 30 E
Sekondi-Takoradi 84 4 58N 1 45W
Sekuma 92 24 36 S 23 50 E
Selah 118 46 44N 120 30W
Selama 71 5 12N 100 42 E
Selangor □ 71 3 20N 101 30 E
Selárgius 40 39 14N 9 14 E
Selaru 73 8 9 S 131 0 E
Selb 25 50 9N 12 9 E
Selby, U.K. 12 53 47N 1 5W
Selby, U.S.A. 116 45 34N 100 2W
Selca 39 43 20N 16 50 E
Selden 116 39 33N 100 39W
Seldovia 104 59 30N 151 45W
Sele → 41 40 27N 14 58 E
Selemdzha → 59 51 42N 128 53 E
Selenge → 75 49 25N 103 59 E
Selenica 44 40 33N 19 39 E
Selenter See 24 54 19N 10 26 E
Sélestat 19 48 16N 7 26 E
Seletan, Tg. 72 4 10 S 114 40 E
Seletin 46 47 50N 25 12 E
Selevac 42 44 28N 20 52 E
Selfridge 116 46 3N 100 57W
Sélibabi 84 15 10N 12 15W
Seliger, Oz. 54 57 15N 33 0 E
Seligman 119 35 17N 112 56W
Şelim 57 40 30N 42 46 E
Selîma, El Wâhât el 86 21 22N 29 19 E
Selinda Spillway 92 18 35 S 23 10 E
Selinoús 45 37 35N 21 37 E
Selizharovo 54 56 51N 33 27 E
Selje 47 62 3N 5 22 E
Seljord 47 59 30N 8 40 E
Selkirk, Can. 109 50 10N 96 55W
Selkirk, U.K. 14 55 33N 2 50W
Selkirk I. 109 53 20N 99 6W
Selkirk Mts. 108 51 15N 117 40W
Selles-sur-Cher 19 47 16N 1 33 E
Sellières 19 46 50N 5 32 E
Sells 119 31 57N 111 57W
Sellye 27 45 52N 17 51 E
Selma, Ala., U.S.A. 115 32 30N 87 0W
Selma, Calif., U.S.A. 119 36 39N 119 39W
Selma, N.C., U.S.A. 115 35 32N 78 15W
Selmer 115 35 9N 88 36W
Selo 44 41 10N 25 53 E
Selongey 19 47 36N 5 10 E
Selowandoma Falls 91 21 15 S 31 50 E
Selpele 73 0 1 S 130 5 E
Selsey Bill 13 50 44N 0 47W
Seltz 19 48 48N 8 4 E
Selu 73 7 32 S 130 55 E
Selukwe 91 19 40 S 30 0 E
Sélune → 18 48 38N 1 22W
Selva, Argent. 124 29 50 S 62 0W
Selva, Italy 39 46 33N 11 46 E
Selva, Spain 32 41 13N 1 8 E
Selva, La 32 42 0N 2 45 E
Selvas 126 6 30 S 67 0W
Selwyn L. 109 60 0N 104 30W
Selwyn P.O. 97 21 32 S 140 30 E
Selwyn Ra. 97 21 10 S 140 0 E
Seman → 44 40 45N 19 50 E
Semara 82 26 48N 11 41W
Semarang 73 7 0 S 110 26 E
Semau 73 10 13 S 123 22 E
Sembabule 90 0 4 S 31 25 E
Sémé 84 15 4N 13 41W
Semeih 87 12 43N 30 53 E
Semenov 55 56 43N 44 30 E
Semenovka, Ukraine S.S.R., U.S.S.R. 54 52 8N 32 36 E
Semenovka, Ukraine S.S.R., U.S.S.R. 56 49 37N 33 10 E
Semeru 73 8 4 S 112 55 E
Semiluki 55 51 41N 39 2 E
Seminoe Res. 118 42 0N 107 0W
Seminole, Okla., U.S.A. 117 35 15N 96 45W
Seminole, Tex., U.S.A. 117 32 41N 102 38W
Semiozernoye 58 52 22N 64 8 E
Semipalatinsk 58 50 30N 80 10 E
Semirara Is. 73 12 0N 121 20 E
Semisopochnoi 104 52 0N 179 40W
Semitau 72 0 29N 111 57 E
Semiyarskoye 58 50 55N 78 23 E
Semmering Pass 26 47 41N 15 45 E
Semnān 65 35 55N 53 25 E
Semnān □ 65 36 0N 54 0 E
Semois → 16 49 53N 4 44 E
Semporna 73 4 30N 118 33 E
Semuda 72 2 51 S 112 58 E
Semur-en-Auxois 19 47 30N 4 20 E
Sen → 71 13 45N 105 12 E
Sena 91 17 25 S 35 0 E
Sena Madureira 126 9 5 S 68 45W
Senador Pompeu 127 5 40 S 39 20W
Senai 71 1 38N 103 38 E
Senaja 72 6 45N 117 3 E
Senanga 92 16 2 S 23 14 E
Senatobia 117 34 38N 89 57W
Sendafa 87 9 11N 39 3 E
Sendai, Kagoshima, Japan 74 31 50N 130 20 E
Sendai, Miyagi, Japan 74 38 15N 140 53 E
Sendamangalam 70 11 17N 78 17 E
Sendeling's Drift 92 28 12 S 16 52 E
Sendenhorst 24 51 50N 7 49 E
Sendurjana 68 21 32N 78 17 E
Senec 27 48 12N 17 23 E
Seneca, Oreg., U.S.A. 118 44 10N 119 2W
Seneca, S.C., U.S.A. 115 34 43N 82 59W
Seneca Falls 114 42 55N 76 50W
Seneca L. 114 42 40N 76 58W
Senegal ■ 84 14 30N 14 30W
Senegal → 84 15 48N 16 32W
Senekal 93 28 30 S 27 36 E
Senftenberg 24 51 30N 14 1 E
Senga Hill 91 9 19 S 31 11 E
Senge Khambab (Indus) → 68 28 40N 70 10 E
Sengerema □ 90 2 10 S 32 20 E
Sengiley 55 53 58N 48 46 E
Sengkang 73 4 8 S 120 1 E
Sengua → 91 17 7 S 28 5 E
Senhor-do-Bonfim 127 10 30 S 40 10W
Senica 27 48 41N 17 25 E
Senigállia 39 43 42N 13 12 E
Senio → 39 44 35N 12 15 E
Senise 40 40 6N 16 15 E
Senj 39 45 0N 14 58 E
Senja 50 69 25N 17 30 E
Senlis 19 49 13N 2 35 E
Senmonorom 71 12 27N 107 12 E
Sennâr 87 13 30N 33 35 E
Senneterre 106 48 25N 77 15W
Senniquelle 84 7 19N 8 38W
Senno 54 54 45N 29 43 E
Sennori 40 40 49N 8 36 E
Senonches 18 48 34N 1 2 E
Senorbì 40 39 33N 9 8 E
Senožeče 39 45 43N 14 3 E
Sens 19 48 11N 3 15 E
Senta 42 45 55N 20 3 E
Sentein 20 42 53N 0 58 E
Sentery 90 5 17 S 25 42 E
Sentinel 119 32 45N 113 13W
Sentolo 73 7 55 S 110 13 E
Senya Beraku 85 5 28N 0 31W
Seo de Urgel 32 42 22N 1 23 E
Seohara 68 29 15N 78 33 E
Seoni 69 22 5N 79 30 E
Seoriuarayan 69 21 45N 82 34 E
Seoul = Sŏul 76 37 31N 127 6 E
Separation Point 107 53 37N 57 25W
Sepik → 98 3 49 S 144 30 E
Sępólno Krajeńskie 28 53 26N 17 30 E
Sepone 71 16 45N 106 13 E
Sepopa 92 18 49 S 22 12 E
Sepopol 28 54 16N 21 2 E
Sept-Îles 107 50 13N 66 22W
Septemvri 43 42 13N 24 6 E
Septimus 98 21 13 S 148 47 E
Sepúlveda 30 41 18N 3 45W
Sequeros 30 40 31N 6 2W
Sequim 118 48 3N 123 9W
Sequoia Nat. Park 119 36 30N 118 30W
Serafimovich 57 49 36N 42 43 E
Seraing 16 50 35N 5 32 E
Seram 73 3 10 S 129 0 E
Seram Sea 73 2 30 S 128 30 E
Serampore 69 22 44N 88 21 E
Serang 73 6 8 S 106 10 E
Serasan 72 2 29N 109 4 E
Seravezza 38 43 59N 10 13 E
Serbia = Srbija 42 43 30N 21 0 E
Sercaia 46 45 49N 25 9 E
Serdo 87 11 56N 41 14 E
Serdobsk 55 52 28N 44 10 E
Seredka 54 58 12N 28 10 E
Seregno 38 45 40N 9 12 E
Seremban 71 2 43N 101 53 E
Serena, La, Chile 124 29 55 S 71 10W
Serena, La, Spain 31 38 45N 5 40W
Serengeti □ 90 2 0 S 34 30 E
Serengeti Plain 90 2 40 S 35 0 E
Sereth = Siret → 46 47 58N 26 5 E
Sergach 55 55 30N 45 30 E
Serge → 32 41 54N 0 50 E
Sergino 58 62 30N 65 38 E
Sergipe □ 127 10 30 S 37 30W
Seria 72 4 37N 114 23 E
Serian 72 1 10N 110 31 E
Seriate 38 45 42N 9 43 E
Seribu, Kepulauan 72 5 36 S 106 33 E
Sérifontaine 19 49 20N 1 45 E
Sérifos 45 37 9N 24 30 E
Sérignan 20 43 17N 3 17 E
Sermaize-les-Bains 19 48 47N 4 54 E
Sermata 73 8 15 S 128 50 E
Sérmide 39 45 0N 11 17 E
Sernovodsk 55 53 54N 51 16 E
Serny Zavod 58 39 59N 58 50 E
Serock 28 52 31N 21 4 E
Serón 33 37 20N 2 29W
Serós 32 41 27N 0 24 E
Serov 58 59 29N 60 35 E
Serowe 92 22 25 S 26 43 E
Serpa 31 37 57N 7 38 E
Serpeddi, Punta 40 39 19N 9 18 E
Serpentara 40 39 8N 9 38 E
Serpis → 33 38 59N 0 9W
Serpukhov 55 54 55N 37 28 E
Serra San Bruno 41 38 31N 16 23 E
Serracapriola 41 41 47N 15 12 E
Serradilla 30 39 50N 6 9W
Sérrai 44 41 5N 23 31 E
Sérrai □ 44 41 5N 23 37 E
Serramanna 40 39 26N 8 56 E
Serrat, C. 83 37 14N 9 10 E
Serre-Poncon, Barrage de 21 44 22N 6 20 E
Serres 21 44 26N 5 43 E
Serrezuela 124 30 40 S 65 20W
Serrinha 127 11 39 S 39 0W
Sersale 41 39 1N 16 44 E
Sertã 30 39 48N 8 6W
Sertânia 127 8 5 S 37 20W
Sertanópolis 125 23 4 S 51 2W
Serua 73 6 18 S 130 1 E
Serui 73 1 53 S 136 10 E
Serule 92 21 57 S 27 20 E
Sérvia 44 40 9N 21 58 E
Sese Is. 90 0 20 S 32 20 E
Sesepe 73 1 30 S 127 59 E
Sesfontein 92 19 7 S 13 39 E
Sesheke 92 17 29 S 24 13 E
Sesia → 38 45 5N 8 37 E
Sesimbra 31 38 28N 9 6W
Sessa Aurunca 40 41 14N 13 55 E
Sestao 32 43 18N 3 0W
Sesto S. Giovanni 38 45 32N 9 14 E
Sestos 44 40 16N 26 23 E
Sestri Levante 38 44 17N 9 22 E
Sestrières 38 44 58N 6 56 E
Sestrunj 39 44 10N 15 0 E
Sestu 40 39 18N 9 6 E
Sète 20 43 25N 3 42 E
Sete Lagôas 127 19 27 S 44 16W
Sétif 83 36 9N 5 26 E
Setonaikai 74 34 20N 133 30 E
Settat 82 33 0N 7 40W
Setté-Cama 88 2 32 S 9 45 E
Séttimo Tor 38 45 9N 7 46 E
Setting L. 109 55 0N 98 38W
Settle 12 54 5N 2 18W
Settlement Pt. 115 26 40N 79 0W
Setto Calende 38 45 44N 8 37 E
Setúbal 31 38 30N 8 58W
Setúbal □ 31 38 25N 8 35W
Setúbal, B. de 31 38 40N 8 56W
Seugne → 20 45 42N 0 32W
Seul, Lac-Rés. 106 50 25N 92 30W
Seulimeum 72 5 27N 95 15 E
Sevan 57 40 33N 44 56 E
Sevan, Ozero 57 40 30N 45 20 E
Sevastopol 56 44 35N 33 30 E
Seven Sisters 108 54 56N 128 10W
Sever → 31 39 40N 7 32W
Sévérac-le-Château 20 44 20N 3 5 E
Severn →, Can. 106 56 2N 87 36W
Severn →, U.K. 13 51 35N 2 38W
Severn L. 106 53 54N 90 48W
Severnaya Zemlya 59 79 0N 100 0 E
Severnyye Uvaly 52 58 0N 48 0 E
Severo-Kurilsk 59 50 40N 156 8 E
Severo-Yeniseyskiy 59 60 22N 93 1 E
Severočeský □ 26 50 30N 14 0 E
Severodinsk 52 64 27N 39 58 E
Severodonetsk 57 48 58N 38 30 E
Severomoravský □ 27 49 38N 17 40 E
Severomorsk 52 69 5N 33 27 E
Severouralsk 52 60 9N 59 57 E
Sevier 119 38 39N 112 11W
Sevier → 119 39 10N 113 6W
Sevier L. 118 39 0N 113 20W
Sevilla 31 37 23N 6 0W
Sevilla □ 31 37 25N 5 30W
Seville = Sevilla 31 37 23N 6 0W
Sevlievo 43 43 2N 25 3 E
Sevnica 39 46 2N 15 19 E
Sèvre-Nantaise → 18 47 12N 1 33W
Sèvre Niortaise → 20 46 18N 1 8W
Sevsk 54 52 10N 34 30 E
Seward, Alaska, U.S.A. 104 60 6N 149 26W
Seward, Nebr., U.S.A. 116 40 55N 97 6W
Seward Pen. 104 65 0N 164 0W
Sewell 124 34 10 S 70 23W
Sewer 73 5 53 S 134 40 E
Sewickley 112 40 33N 80 12W
Sexsmith 108 55 21N 118 47W
Seychelles ■ 3 5 0 S 56 0 E
Seyðisfjörður 50 65 16N 14 0W
Seym → 54 51 27N 32 34 E
Seymchan 59 62 54N 152 30 E
Seymour, Austral. 99 37 0 S 145 10 E
Seymour, Conn., U.S.A. 113 41 23N 73 5W
Seymour, Ind., U.S.A. 114 39 0N 85 50W
Seymour, Tex., U.S.A. 117 33 35N 99 18W
Seymour, Wis., U.S.A. 114 44 30N 88 20W
Seyne 21 44 21N 6 22 E
Seyne-sur-Mer, La 21 43 7N 5 52 E
Seyssel 21 45 57N 5 50 E
Sežana 39 45 43N 13 41 E
Sézanne 19 48 40N 3 40 E
Sezze 40 41 30N 13 3 E
Sfax 83 34 49N 10 48 E
Sfintu Gheorghe 46 45 52N 25 48 E
Sha Xian 77 26 23N 117 45 E
Shaanxi □ 77 35 0N 109 0 E
Shaba 90 8 0 S 25 0 E
† Shabani 91 20 17 S 30 2 E
Shabla 43 43 31N 28 32 E
Shabunda 90 2 40 S 27 16 E
Shache 75 38 20N 77 10 E
Shackleton 5 78 30 S 36 1W
Shackleton Ice Shelf 5 66 0 S 100 0 E
Shackleton Inlet 5 83 0 S 160 0 E
Shaddad 86 21 25N 40 2 E
Shadrinsk 58 56 5N 63 32 E
Shaffa 85 10 30N 12 6 E
Shafter, Calif., U.S.A. 119 35 32N 119 14W
Shafter, Tex., U.S.A. 117 29 49N 104 18W
Shaftesbury 13 51 0N 2 12W
Shagamu 85 6 51N 3 39 E
Shah Bunder 68 24 13N 67 56 E
* Shah Faisalabad 68 31 30N 73 5 E
Shahabad, Andhra Pradesh, India 70 17 10N 76 54 E
Shahabad, Punjab, India 68 30 10N 76 55 E
Shahabad, Raj., India 68 25 15N 77 11 E
Shahabad, Ut. P., India 69 27 36N 79 56 E
Shāhābād, Kermanshāhān, Iran 64 34 10N 46 30 E
Shāhābād, Khorāsān, Iran 65 37 40N 56 50 E
Shahada 68 21 33N 74 30 E
Shahadpur 68 25 55N 68 35 E
Shahapur 70 15 50N 74 34 E
Shahdād 65 30 30N 57 40 E
Shahdadkot 68 27 50N 67 55 E
Shahganj 69 26 3N 82 44 E
Shahḥāt 81 32 48N 21 54 E
Shāhī 65 36 30N 52 55 E
Shahjahanpur 69 27 54N 79 57 E
Shahpur, Mad. P., India 68 22 12N 77 58 E
Shahpur, Mysore, India 70 16 40N 76 48 E
Shahpūr 64 38 12N 44 45 E
Shahpur 68 28 46N 68 27 E
Shahpura 69 23 10N 80 45 E
Shahr Kord 65 32 15N 50 55 E
Shahrezā 65 32 0N 51 55 E
Shahrig 68 30 15N 67 40 E
Shāhrūd 65 36 30N 55 0 E

* Renamed Faisalabad

† Renamed Zvishavane

Shahsād, Namakzār-e Siliguri

Shahsād, Namakzār-e	**65**	30 20N	58 20 E
Shahsavār	**65**	36 45N	51 12 E
Shaibara	**86**	25 26N	36 47 E
Shaikhabad	**66**	34 2N	68 45 E
Shajapur	**68**	23 27N	76 21 E
Shakargarh	**68**	32 17N	75 10 E
Shakawe	**92**	18 28 S	21 49 E
Shaker Heights	**112**	41 29N	81 36W
Shakhty	**57**	47 40N	40 16 E
Shakhunya	**55**	57 40N	46 46 E
Shaki	**85**	8 41N	3 21 E
Shakopee	**116**	44 45N	93 30W
Shala, L.	**87**	7 30N	38 30 E
Shallow Lake	**112**	44 36N	81 5W
Sham, J. ash	**65**	23 10N	57 5 E
Shamâl Dârfûr □	**87**	15 0N	25 0 E
Shamâl Kordofân □	**87**	15 0N	30 0 E
Shamattawa	**109**	55 51N	92 5W
Shamattawa →	**106**	55 1N	85 23W
Shambe	**87**	7 8N	30 46 E
Shambu	**87**	9 32N	37 3 E
Shamgong Dzong	**69**	27 13N	90 35 E
Shamīl	**65**	27 30N	56 55 E
Shamkhor	**57**	40 50N	46 0 E
Shamli	**68**	29 32N	77 18 E
Shammar, Jabal	**64**	27 40N	41 0 E
Shamo, L.	**87**	5 45N	37 30 E
Shamokin	**114**	40 47N	76 33W
Shamrock	**117**	35 15N	100 15W
Shan □	**67**	21 30N	98 30 E
Shanan →	**87**	8 0N	40 20 E
Shanchengzhen	**76**	42 20N	125 20 E
Shandong □	**76**	36 0N	118 0 E
Shang Xian	**77**	33 50N	109 58 E
Shangalowe	**91**	10 50 S	26 30 E
Shangani	**91**	19 41 S	29 20 E
Shangani →	**91**	18 41 S	27 10 E
Shangbancheng	**76**	40 50N	118 1 E
Shangcheng	**77**	31 47N	115 26 E
Shangchuan Dao	**77**	21 40N	112 50 E
Shangdu	**76**	41 30N	113 30 E
Shanggao	**77**	28 17N	114 55 E
Shanghai	**75**	31 15N	121 26 E
Shangqiu	**77**	34 26N	115 36 E
Shangrao	**75**	28 25N	117 59 E
Shangshui	**77**	33 42N	114 35 E
Shangsi	**77**	22 8N	107 58 E
Shangyou	**77**	25 48N	114 32 E
Shangzhi	**76**	45 22N	127 56 E
Shani	**85**	10 14N	12 2 E
Shaniko	**118**	45 0N	120 50W
Shannon, Greenl.	**4**	75 10N	18 30W
Shannon, N.Z.	**101**	40 33 S	175 25 E
Shannon →	**15**	52 35N	9 30W
Shansi = Shanxi □	**76**	37 0N	112 0 E
Shantar, Ostrov Bolshoy	**59**	55 9N	137 40 E
Shantou	**75**	23 18N	116 40 E
Shantung = Shandong □	**76**	36 0N	118 0 E
Shanxi □	**76**	37 0N	112 0 E
Shanyang	**77**	33 31N	109 55 E
Shaoguan	**75**	24 48N	113 35 E
Shaowu	**75**	27 22N	117 28 E
Shaoxing	**75**	30 0N	120 35 E
Shaoyang	**75**	27 14N	111 25 E
Shapinsay	**14**	59 2N	2 50W
Shaqrā', Si. Arab.	**64**	25 15N	45 16 E
Shaqrā', Yemen, S.	**63**	13 22N	45 44 E
Sharafa (Ogr)	**87**	11 59N	27 7 E
Sharavati →	**70**	14 20N	74 25 E
Sharbot Lake	**113**	44 46N	76 41W
Shark B.	**96**	25 55 S	113 32 E
Sharm el Sheikh	**86**	27 53N	34 15 E
Sharon, Mass., U.S.A.	**113**	42 5N	71 11W
Sharon, Pa., U.S.A.	**114**	41 18N	80 30W
Sharon, Plain of = Hasharon	**62**	32 12N	34 49 E
Sharon Springs	**116**	38 54N	101 45W
Sharp Pt.	**98**	10 58 S	142 43 E
Sharpe L.	**109**	54 5N	93 40W
Sharpsville	**112**	41 16N	80 28W
Shary	**64**	27 14N	43 29 E
Sharya	**55**	58 22N	45 20 E
Shasha	**87**	6 29N	35 59 E
Shashemene	**87**	7 13N	38 33 E
Shashi	**75**	30 25N	112 14 E
Shashi →	**91**	21 14 S	29 20 E
Shasta, Mt.	**118**	41 30N	122 12W
Shasta Res.	**118**	40 50N	122 15W
Shatsk	**55**	54 0N	41 45 E
Shattuck	**117**	36 17N	99 55W
Shatura	**55**	55 34N	39 31 E
Shaumyani	**57**	41 22N	41 45 E
Shaunavon	**109**	49 35N	108 25W
Shaw →	**96**	20 21 S	119 17 E
Shaw I.	**98**	20 30 S	149 2 E
Shawan	**75**	44 34N	85 50 E
Shawanaga	**112**	45 31N	80 17W
Shawano	**114**	44 45N	88 38W
Shawinigan	**106**	46 35N	72 50W
Shawnee	**117**	35 15N	97 0W
Shayib el Banat, Bebel	**86**	26 59N	33 29 E
Shchekino	**55**	54 1N	37 34 E
Shcherbakov = Rybinsk	**55**	58 5N	38 50 E
Shchigri	**55**	51 55N	36 58 E
Shchors	**54**	51 48N	31 56 E
Shchuchiosk	**58**	52 56N	70 12 E
She Xian	**77**	29 50N	118 25 E
Shebekino	**55**	50 28N	36 54 E
Shebele, Wabi →	**87**	2 0N	44 0 E
Sheboygan	**114**	43 46N	87 45W
Shechem	**62**	32 13N	35 21 E
Shediac	**107**	46 14N	64 32W
Sheelin, Lough	**15**	53 48N	7 20W
Sheep Haven	**15**	55 12N	7 55W
Sheerness	**13**	51 26N	0 47 E
Sheet Harbour	**107**	44 56N	62 31W
Shefar'am	**62**	32 48N	35 10 E
Sheffield, U.K.	**12**	53 23N	1 28W
Sheffield, Ala., U.S.A.	**115**	34 45N	87 42W
Sheffield, Mass., U.S.A.	**113**	42 6N	73 23W
Sheffield, Pa., U.S.A.	**112**	41 42N	79 3W
Sheffield, Tex., U.S.A.	**117**	30 42N	101 49W
Shegaon	**68**	20 48N	76 47 E
Sheho	**109**	51 35N	103 13W
Shehojele	**87**	10 40N	35 9 E
Sheikhpura	**69**	25 9N	85 53 E
Shek Hasan	**87**	12 5N	35 58 E
Shekhupura	**68**	31 42N	73 58 E
Sheki	**57**	41 10N	47 5 E
Sheksna →	**55**	59 0N	38 30 E
Shelburne, N.S., Can.	**107**	43 47N	65 20W
Shelburne, Ont., Can.	**106**	44 4N	80 15W
Shelburne, U.S.A.	**113**	44 23N	73 15W
Shelburne B.	**97**	11 50 S	142 50 E
Shelburne Falls	**113**	42 36N	72 45W
Shelby, Mich., U.S.A.	**114**	43 34N	86 27W
Shelby, Mont., U.S.A.	**118**	48 30N	111 52W
Shelby, N.C., U.S.A.	**115**	35 18N	81 34W
Shelby, Ohio, U.S.A.	**112**	40 52N	82 40W
Shelbyville, Ill., U.S.A.	**116**	39 25N	88 45W
Shelbyville, Ind., U.S.A.	**114**	39 30N	85 42W
Shelbyville, Tenn., U.S.A.	**115**	35 30N	86 25W
Sheldon	**116**	43 6N	95 40W
Sheldrake	**107**	50 20N	64 51W
Shelikhova, Zaliv	**59**	59 30N	157 0 E
Shell Creek Ra.	**118**	39 15N	114 30W
Shell Lake	**109**	53 19N	107 2W
Shellbrook	**109**	53 13N	106 24W
Shellharbour	**97**	34 31 S	150 51 E
Shelling Rocks	**15**	51 45N	10 35W
Shelon →	**54**	58 10N	30 30 E
Shelton, Conn., U.S.A.	**113**	41 18N	73 7W
Shelton, Wash., U.S.A.	**118**	47 15N	123 6W
Shemakha	**57**	40 38N	48 37 E
Shenandoah, Iowa, U.S.A.	**116**	40 50N	95 25W
Shenandoah, Pa., U.S.A.	**114**	40 49N	76 13W
Shenandoah, Va., U.S.A.	**114**	38 30N	78 38W
Shenandoah →	**114**	39 19N	77 44W
Shenchi	**76**	39 8N	112 10 E
Shencottah	**70**	8 59N	77 18 E
Shendam	**85**	8 49N	9 30 E
Shendî	**87**	16 46N	33 22 E
Shendurni	**70**	20 39N	75 36 E
Sheng Xian	**77**	29 35N	120 50 E
Shëngjergji	**44**	41 17N	20 10 E
Shëngjini	**44**	41 50N	19 35 E
Shenmëria	**44**	42 7N	20 13 E
Shenmu	**76**	38 50N	110 29 E
Shenqiucheng	**77**	33 24N	115 2 E
Shensi = Shaanxi □	**77**	35 0N	109 0 E
Shenyang	**76**	41 48N	123 27 E
Shepetovka	**54**	50 10N	27 10 E
Shephelah = Hashefela	**62**	31 30N	34 43 E
Shepparton	**97**	36 23 S	145 26 E
Sheqi	**77**	33 12N	112 57 E
Sherada	**87**	7 18N	36 30 E
Sherborne	**13**	50 56N	2 31W
Sherbro I.	**84**	7 30N	12 40W
Sherbrooke	**107**	45 28N	71 57W
Sherda	**83**	20 7N	16 46 E
Shereik	**86**	18 44N	33 47 E
Sheridan, Ark., U.S.A.	**117**	34 20N	92 25W
Sheridan, Col., U.S.A.	**116**	39 44N	105 3W
Sheridan, Wyo., U.S.A.	**118**	44 50N	107 0W
Sherkot	**68**	29 22N	78 35 E
Sherman	**117**	33 40N	96 35W
Sherpur	**69**	25 0N	90 0 E
Sherridon	**109**	55 8N	101 5W
Sherwood, N.D., U.S.A.	**116**	48 59N	101 36W
Sherwood, Tex., U.S.A.	**117**	31 18N	100 45W
Sherwood Forest	**12**	53 5N	1 5W
Sheslay	**108**	58 17N	131 52W
Sheslay →	**108**	58 48N	132 5W
Shethanei L.	**109**	58 48N	97 50W
Shetland □	**14**	60 30N	1 30W
Shetland Is.	**14**	60 30N	1 30W
Shevaroy Hills	**70**	11 58N	78 12 E
Shewa □	**87**	9 33N	38 10 E
Shewa Gimira	**87**	7 4N	35 51 E
Sheyenne	**116**	47 52N	99 8W
Sheyenne →	**116**	47 5N	96 50W
Shibām	**63**	16 0N	48 36 E
Shibîn El Kôm	**86**	30 31N	30 55 E
Shibîn el Qanâtir	**86**	30 19N	31 19 E
Shibogama L.	**106**	53 35N	88 15W
Shibushi	**74**	31 25N	131 8 E
Shidao	**76**	36 50N	122 25 E
Shiel, L.	**14**	56 48N	5 32W
Shiga □	**74**	35 20N	136 0 E
Shigaib	**81**	15 5N	23 35 E
Shiguaigou	**76**	40 52N	110 15 E
Shihchiachuangi = Shijiazhuang	**76**	38 2N	114 28 E
Shijaku	**44**	41 21N	19 33 E
Shijiazhuang	**76**	38 2N	114 28 E
Shikarpur, India	**68**	28 17N	78 7 E
Shikarpur, Pak.	**68**	27 57N	68 39 E
Shikoku	**74**	33 30N	133 30 E
Shikoku □	**74**	33 30N	133 30 E
Shikoku-Sanchi	**74**	33 30N	133 30 E
Shilabo	**63**	6 22N	44 32 E
Shilka	**59**	52 0N	115 55 E
Shilka →	**59**	53 20N	121 26 E
Shillelagh	**15**	52 46N	6 32W
Shillong	**67**	25 35N	91 53 E
Shilo	**62**	32 4N	35 18 E
Shilong	**75**	23 5N	113 52 E
Shilovo	**55**	54 25N	40 57 E
Shimabara	**74**	32 48N	130 20 E
Shimada	**74**	34 49N	138 10 E
Shimane □	**74**	35 0N	132 30 E
Shimanovsk	**59**	52 15N	127 30 E
Shimizu	**74**	35 0N	138 30 E
Shimodate	**74**	36 20N	139 55 E
Shimoga	**70**	13 57N	75 32 E
Shimoni	**90**	4 38 S	39 20 E
Shimonoseki	**74**	33 58N	131 0 E
Shimpuru Rapids	**92**	17 45 S	19 55 E
Shimsha →	**70**	13 15N	77 10 E
Shimsk	**54**	58 15N	30 50 E
Shin, L.	**14**	58 7N	4 30W
Shin-Tone →	**74**	35 44N	140 51 E
Shinano →	**74**	36 50N	138 30 E
Shīndand	**65**	33 12N	62 8 E
Shingleton	**106**	46 25N	86 33W
Shingū	**74**	33 40N	135 55 E
Shinkafe	**85**	13 8N	6 29 E
Shinyanga	**90**	3 45 S	33 27 E
Shinyanga □	**90**	3 50 S	34 0 E
Shio-no-Misaki	**74**	33 25N	135 45 E
Ship I.	**117**	30 16N	88 55W
Shipehenski Prokhod	**43**	42 45N	25 15 E
Shippegan	**107**	47 45N	64 45W
Shippensburg	**114**	40 4N	77 32W
Shiprock	**119**	36 51N	108 45W
Shiqian	**77**	27 32N	108 13 E
Shiqma, N. →	**62**	31 37N	34 30 E
Shiquan	**77**	33 5N	108 15 E
Shīr Kūh	**65**	31 39N	54 3 E
Shīrāz	**65**	29 42N	52 30 E
Shirbin	**86**	31 11N	31 32 E
Shire →	**91**	17 42 S	35 19 E
Shiretoko-Misaki	**74**	44 21N	145 20 E
Shiringushi	**55**	53 51N	42 46 E
Shiriya-Zaki	**74**	41 25N	141 30 E
Shirol	**70**	16 47N	74 41 E
Shirpur	**68**	21 21N	74 57 E
Shīrvān	**65**	37 30N	57 50 E
Shishmanova	**43**	42 58N	23 12 E
Shisur	**63**	17 30N	54 0 E
Shitai	**77**	30 12N	117 25 E
Shivali (Sirkali)	**70**	11 15N	79 41 E
Shivpuri	**68**	25 26N	77 42 E
Shivta	**62**	30 53N	34 40 E
Shiwei	**76**	51 19N	119 55 E
Shixing	**77**	24 46N	114 5 E
Shiyata	**86**	29 25N	25 7 E
Shizuishan	**76**	39 15N	106 50 E
Shizuoka	**74**	35 0N	138 24 E
Shizuoka □	**74**	35 15N	138 40 E
Shklov	**54**	54 16N	30 15 E
Shkoder = Shkodra	**44**	42 6N	19 1 E
Shkodra	**44**	42 6N	19 20 E
Shkodra □	**44**	42 25N	19 20 E
Shkumbini →	**44**	41 5N	19 50 E
Shmidt, O.	**59**	81 0N	91 0 E
Shoal Lake	**109**	50 30N	100 35W
Shoalhaven →	**100**	34 54 S	150 42 E
Shoeburyness	**13**	51 31N	0 49 E
Sholapur	**70**	17 43N	75 56 E
Shologontsy	**59**	66 13N	114 0 E
Shomera	**62**	33 4N	35 17 E
Shōmrōn	**62**	32 15N	35 13 E
Shongopovi	**119**	35 49N	110 37W
Shoranur	**70**	10 46N	76 19 E
Shorapur	**70**	16 31N	76 48 E
Shoshone	**118**	43 0N	114 27W
Shoshone L.	**118**	44 30N	110 40W
Shoshone Mts.	**118**	39 30N	117 30W
Shoshong	**92**	22 56 S	26 31 E
Shoshoni	**118**	43 13N	108 5W
Shostka	**54**	51 57N	33 32 E
Shouyang	**76**	37 54N	113 8 E
Show Low	**119**	34 16N	110 0W
Shpola	**56**	49 1N	31 30 E
Shreveport	**117**	32 30N	93 50W
Shrewsbury	**12**	52 42N	2 45W
Shrivardhan	**70**	18 4N	73 3 E
Shropshire □	**13**	52 36N	2 45W
Shuangcheng	**76**	45 20N	126 15 E
Shuangliao	**76**	43 29N	123 30 E
Shuangyashan	**75**	46 28N	131 5 E
Shucheng	**77**	31 28N	116 57 E
Shu'eib, Wadi	**62**	31 54N	35 38 E
Shuguri Falls	**91**	8 33 S	37 22 E
Shujalpur	**68**	23 18N	76 46 E
Shulan	**76**	44 28N	127 0 E
Shule	**75**	39 25N	76 3 E
Shumagin Is.	**104**	55 0N	159 0W
Shumerlya	**55**	55 30N	46 25 E
Shumikha	**58**	55 10N	63 15 E
Shunchang	**77**	26 54N	117 48 E
Shunde	**77**	22 42N	113 14 E
Shungay	**57**	48 30N	46 45 E
Shungnak	**104**	66 55N	157 10W
Shuo Xian	**76**	39 20N	112 33 E
Shūr →	**65**	28 30N	55 0 E
Shurma	**55**	56 58N	50 21 E
Shūsf	**65**	31 50N	60 5 E
Shūshtar	**64**	32 0N	48 50 E
Shuswap L.	**108**	50 55N	119 3W
Shuwaykah	**62**	32 20N	35 1 E
Shuya	**55**	56 50N	41 28 E
Shwebo	**67**	22 30N	95 45 E
Shwegu	**67**	24 15N	96 26 E
Shweli →	**67**	23 45N	96 45 E
Shyok	**69**	34 15N	78 12 E
Shyok →	**69**	35 13N	75 53 E
Si Kiang = Xi Jiang →	**75**	22 5N	113 20 E
Si Racha	**71**	13 10N	100 48 E
Siah	**64**	22 0N	47 0 E
Siahan Range	**66**	27 30N	64 40 E
Siaksrinderapura	**72**	0 51N	102 0 E
Sialkot	**68**	32 32N	74 30 E
Siam = Thailand ■	**71**	16 0N	102 0 E
Siam, G. of	**71**	11 30N	101 0 E
Sian = Xi'an	**77**	34 15N	109 0 E
Siantan, P.	**72**	3 10N	106 15 E
Sīāreh	**65**	28 5N	60 14 E
Siargao	**73**	9 52N	126 3 E
Siasi	**73**	5 34N	120 50 E
Siátista	**44**	40 15N	21 33 E
Siau	**73**	2 50N	125 25 E
Siauliai	**54**	55 56N	23 15 E
Siaya □	**90**	0 0N	34 20 E
Siazan	**57**	41 3N	49 10 E
Sibâi, Gebel el	**86**	25 45N	34 10 E
Sibari	**41**	39 47N	16 27 E
Sibay	**52**	52 42N	58 39 E
Sibaya, L.	**93**	27 20 S	32 45 E
Šibenik	**39**	43 48N	15 54 E
Siberia	**60**	60 0N	100 0 E
Siberut	**72**	1 30 S	99 0 E
Sibi	**68**	29 30N	67 54 E
Sibil	**73**	4 59 S	140 35 E
Sibiti	**88**	3 38 S	13 19 E
Sibiu	**46**	45 45N	24 9 E
Sibiu □	**46**	45 50N	24 15 E
Sibley, Iowa, U.S.A.	**116**	43 21N	95 43W
Sibley, La., U.S.A.	**117**	32 34N	93 16W
Sibolga	**72**	1 42N	98 45 E
Sibsagar	**67**	27 0N	94 36 E
Sibu	**72**	2 18N	111 49 E
Sibuco	**73**	7 20N	122 10 E
Sibuguey B.	**73**	7 50N	122 45 E
Sibutu	**73**	4 45N	119 30 E
Sibutu Passage	**73**	4 50N	120 0 E
Sibuyan	**73**	12 25N	122 40 E
Sibuyan Sea	**73**	12 30N	122 20 E
Sicamous	**108**	50 49N	119 0W
Siccus →	**99**	31 42 S	139 25 E
Sichuan □	**75**	31 0N	104 0 E
Sicilia	**41**	37 30N	14 30 E
Sicilia, Canale di	**40**	37 25N	12 30 E
Sicilian Channel = Sicilia, Canale di	**40**	37 25N	12 30 E
Sicily = Sicilia	**41**	37 30N	14 30 E
Sicuani	**126**	14 21 S	71 10W
Siculiana	**40**	37 20N	13 23 E
Šid	**42**	45 8N	19 14 E
Sidamo □	**87**	5 0N	37 50 E
Sidaouet	**85**	18 34N	8 3 E
Siddipet	**70**	18 0N	78 51 E
Sidéradougou	**84**	10 42N	4 12W
Siderno Marina	**41**	38 16N	16 17 E
Sidheros, Ákra	**45**	35 19N	26 19 E
Sidhirókastron	**44**	41 13N	23 24 E
Sidhpur	**68**	23 56N	72 25 E
Sîdi Abd el Rahmân	**86**	30 55N	29 44 E
Sîdi Barrâni	**86**	31 38N	25 58 E
Sidi-bel-Abbès	**82**	35 13N	0 39W
Sidi Bennour	**82**	32 40N	8 25W
Sidi Haneish	**86**	31 10N	27 35 E
Sidi Kacem	**82**	34 11N	5 49W
Sidi Moussa, O. →	**82**	26 58N	3 54 E
Sidi Omar	**86**	31 24N	24 57 E
Sidi Slimane	**82**	34 16N	5 56W
Sidi Smaïl	**82**	32 50N	8 31W
Sidlaw Hills	**14**	56 32N	3 10W
Sidley, Mt.	**5**	77 2 S	126 2W
Sidmouth	**13**	50 40N	3 13W
Sidmouth, C.	**98**	13 25 S	143 36 E
Sidney, Can.	**108**	48 39N	123 24W
Sidney, Mont., U.S.A.	**116**	47 42N	104 7W
Sidney, N.Y., U.S.A.	**114**	42 18N	75 20W
Sidney, Ohio, U.S.A.	**114**	40 18N	84 6W
Sidoarjo	**73**	7 30 S	112 46 E
Sidra, G. of = Khalīj Surt	**35**	31 40N	18 30 E
Siedlce	**28**	52 10N	22 20 E
Siedlce □	**28**	52 0N	22 0 E
Sieg →	**24**	50 46N	7 7 E
Siegburg	**24**	50 48N	7 12 E
Siegen	**24**	50 52N	8 2 E
Siem Reap	**71**	13 20N	103 52 E
Siena	**39**	43 20N	11 20 E
Sieniawa	**27**	50 11N	22 38 E
Sieradź	**28**	51 37N	18 41 E
Sieraków	**28**	52 39N	16 2 E
Sierck-les-Bains	**19**	49 26N	6 20 E
Sierpc	**28**	52 55N	19 43 E
Sierra Blanca, N. Mex., U.S.A.	**119**	33 20N	105 54W
Sierra Blanca, Tex., U.S.A.	**119**	31 11N	105 17W
Sierra City	**118**	39 34N	120 42W
Sierra Colorada	**128**	40 35 S	67 50W
Sierra de Yeguas	**31**	37 7N	4 52W
Sierra Gorda	**124**	22 50 S	69 15W
Sierra Leone ■	**84**	9 0N	12 0W
Sierra Mojada	**120**	27 19N	103 42W
Sierre	**25**	46 17N	7 31 E
Sif Fatima	**83**	31 6N	8 41 E
Sífnos	**45**	37 0N	24 45 E
Sifton	**109**	51 21N	100 8W
Sifton Pass	**108**	57 52N	126 15W
Sig	**82**	35 32N	0 12W
Sigdal	**47**	60 4N	9 38 E
Sigean	**20**	43 2N	2 58 E
Sighetul Marmatiei	**46**	47 57N	23 52 E
Sighişoara	**46**	46 12N	24 50 E
Sigli	**72**	5 25N	96 0 E
Siglufjörður	**50**	66 12N	18 55W
Sigma	**73**	11 29N	122 40 E
Sigmaringen	**25**	48 5N	9 13 E
Signakhi	**57**	41 40N	45 57 E
Signy I.	**5**	60 45 S	45 56W
Signy-l'Abbaye	**19**	49 40N	4 25 E
Sigsig	**126**	3 0 S	78 50W
Sigtuna	**48**	59 36N	17 44 E
Sigüenza	**32**	41 3N	2 40W
Siguiri	**84**	11 31N	9 10W
Sigulda	**54**	57 10N	24 55 E
Sigurd	**119**	38 49N	112 0W
Sihanoukville = Kompong Som	**71**	10 40N	103 30 E
Sihui	**77**	23 20N	112 40 E
Si'īr	**62**	31 35N	35 9 E
Siirt	**64**	37 57N	41 55 E
Sijarira Ra.	**91**	17 36 S	27 45 E
Sikar	**68**	27 33N	75 10 E
Sikasso	**84**	11 18N	5 35W
Sikeston	**117**	36 52N	89 35W
Sikhote Alin, Khrebet	**59**	46 0N	136 0 E
Sikiá.	**44**	40 2N	23 56 E
Síkinos	**45**	36 40N	25 8 E
Sikkani Chief →	**108**	57 47N	122 15W
Sikkim □	**69**	27 50N	88 30 E
Siklós	**27**	45 50N	18 19 E
Sil →	**30**	42 27N	7 43W
Sila, La	**41**	39 15N	16 35 E
Silandro	**38**	46 38N	10 48 E
Sīlat aẓ Ẓahr	**62**	32 19N	35 11 E
Silba	**39**	44 24N	14 41 E
Silchar	**67**	24 49N	92 48 E
Silcox	**109**	57 12N	94 10W
Siler City	**115**	35 44N	79 30W
Sileru →	**70**	17 49N	81 24 E
Silesia = Slask	**22**	51 0N	16 30 E
Silet	**82**	22 44N	4 37 E
Silgarhi Doti	**69**	29 15N	81 0 E
Silghat	**67**	26 35N	93 0 E
Silifke	**64**	36 22N	33 58 E
Siliguri	**69**	26 45N	88 25 E

Siling Co Sobótka

Siling Co 75 31 50N 89 20 E
Siliqua 40 39 20N 8 49 E
Silistra 43 44 6N 27 19 E
Siljan, L. 48 60 55N 14 45 E
Silkeborg 49 56 10N 9 32 E
Sillajhuay, Cordillera 126 19 46S 68 40W
Sillé-le-Guillaume 18 48 10N 0 8W
Siloam Springs 117 36 15N 94 31W
Silogui 72 1 10S 9 0 E
Silsbee 117 30 20N 94 8W
Silute 54 55 21N 21 33 E
Silva Porto = Bié 89 12 22S 16 55 E
Silver City, Panama 120 9 19N 79 53W
Silver City, N. Mex., U.S.A. 119 32 50N 108 18W
Silver City, Nev., U.S.A. 118 39 15N 119 48W
Silver Cr. → 118 43 16N 119 13W
Silver Creek 114 42 33N 79 9W
Silver Lake 118 43 9N 121 4W
Silverton, Austral. 100 31 52S 141 10 E
Silverton, Colo., U.S.A. 119 37 51N 107 45W
Silverton, Tex., U.S.A. 117 34 30N 101 16W
Silves 31 37 11N 8 26W
Silvi 39 42 32N 14 5 E
Silvies → 118 43 22N 118 48W
Silvretta Gruppe 25 46 50N 10 6 E
Silwa Bahari 86 24 45N 32 55 E
Silwād 62 31 59N 35 15 E
Silz 26 47 16N 10 56 E
Sim, C. 82 31 26N 9 51W
Simanggang 72 1 15N 111 32 E
Simard, L. 106 47 40N 78 40W
Simărtin 46 46 19N 25 58 E
Simba 90 2 10S 37 36 E
Simbach 25 48 16N 13 3 E
Simbo 90 4 51S 29 41 E
Simcoe 106 42 50N 80 20W
Simcoe, L. 106 44 25N 79 20W
Simenga 59 62 42N 108 25 E
Simeto → 41 37 25N 15 10 E
Simeulue 72 2 45N 95 45 E
Simferopol 56 44 55N 34 3 E
Simi 45 36 35N 27 50 E
Simikot 69 30 0N 81 50 E
Simitli 42 41 52N 23 7 E
Simla 68 31 2N 77 9 E
Şimleu-Silvaniei 46 47 17N 22 50 E
Simmern 25 49 59N 7 32 E
Simmie 109 49 56N 108 6W
Simojärvi 50 66 5N 27 3 E
Simojoki → 50 65 35N 25 1 E
Simonette → 108 55 9N 118 15W
Simonstown 92 34 14S 18 26 E
Simontornya 27 46 45N 18 33 E
Simpang, Indon. 72 1 16S 104 5 E
Simpang, Malay. 71 4 50N 100 40 E
Simplon Pass 25 46 15N 8 0 E
Simplon Tunnel 25 46 15N 8 7 E
Simpson Des. 97 25 0S 137 0 E
Simrishamn 49 55 33N 14 22 E
Simunjan 72 1 25N 110 45 E
Simushir, Ostrov 59 46 50N 152 30 E
Sina → 70 17 30N 75 55 E
Sinabang 72 2 30N 96 24 E
Sinadogo 63 5 50N 47 0 E
Sinai = Es Sînâ' 86 29 0N 34 0 E
Sinai, Mt. = Mûsa, G. 86 28 32N 33 59 E
Sinaia 46 45 21N 25 38 E
Sinaloa 120 25 50N 108 20W
Sinaloa □ 120 25 0N 107 30W
Sinalunga 39 43 12N 11 43 E
Sinan 77 27 56N 108 13 E
Sînandrei 46 45 52N 21 13 E
Sināwan 83 31 0N 10 37 E
Sincelejo 126 9 18N 75 24W
Sinclair 118 41 47N 107 10W
Sinclair Mills 108 54 5N 121 40W
Sincorá, Serra do 127 13 30S 41 0W
Sind 68 26 0N 68 30 E
Sind Sagar Doab 68 32 0N 71 30 E
Sindal 49 57 28N 10 10 E
Sindangan 73 8 10N 123 5 E
Sindangbarang 73 7 27S 107 1 E
Sinde 91 17 28S 25 51 E
Sinegorski 57 48 0N 40 52 E
Sinelnikovo 56 48 25N 35 30 E
Sines 31 37 56N 8 51W
Sines, Cabo de 31 37 58N 8 53W
Sineu 32 39 38N 3 1 E
Sinfra 84 6 35N 5 56W
Singa 87 13 10N 33 57 E
Singanallur 70 11 2N 77 1 E
Singaparna 73 7 23S 108 4 E
Singapore ■ 71 1 17N 103 51 E
Singapore, Straits of 71 1 15N 104 0 E
Singaraja 72 8 6S 115 10 E
Singen 25 47 45N 8 50 E
Singida 90 4 49S 34 48 E
Singida □ 90 6 0S 34 30 E
Singitikós Kólpos 44 40 6N 24 0 E
Singkaling Hkamti 67 26 0N 95 39 E
Singkawang 72 1 0N 108 57 E
Singkep 72 0 30S 104 20 E
Singleton 97 32 33S 151 0 E
Singleton, Mt. 96 29 27S 117 15 E
Singö 48 60 12N 18 45 E
Singoli 68 25 0N 75 22 E
Siniátsikon, Óros 44 40 25N 21 35 E
Siniscóla 40 40 35N 9 40 E
Sinj 39 43 42N 16 39 E
Sinjai 73 5 7S 120 20 E
Sinjajevina, Planina 42 42 57N 19 22 E
Sinjār 64 36 19N 41 52 E
Sinjil 62 32 3N 35 15 E
Sinkat 86 18 55N 36 49 E
Sinkiang Uighur = Xinjiang Uygur □ 75 42 0N 86 0 E
Sinnai 40 39 18N 9 13 E
Sinnar 70 19 48N 74 0 E
Sinni → 41 40 9N 16 42 E
Sînnicolau Maré 42 46 5N 20 39 E
Sinnuris 86 29 26N 30 31 E
Sinoe, L. 46 44 35N 28 50 E
Sinoia 91 17 20S 30 8 E
Sinop 64 42 1N 35 11 E
Sinskoye 59 61 8N 126 48 E
Sint Maarten 121 18 0N 63 5W
Sint Niklaas 16 51 10N 4 9 E
Sint Truiden 16 50 48N 5 10 E
Sîntana 46 46 20N 21 30 E
Sintang 72 0 5N 111 35 E
Sinton 117 28 1N 97 30W
Sintra 31 38 47N 9 25W
Sinŭiju 76 40 5N 124 24 E
Sinyukha → 56 48 3N 30 51 E
Siocon 73 7 40N 122 10 E
Siófok 27 16 39S 23 36 E
Sioma 92 16 25S 23 28 E
Sion 25 46 14N 7 20 E
Sioux City 116 42 32N 96 25W
Sioux Falls 116 43 35N 96 40W
Sioux Lookout 106 50 10N 91 50W
Šipan 42 42 45N 17 52 E
Siping 76 43 8N 124 21 E
Sipiwesk L. 109 55 5N 97 35W
Sipora 72 2 18S 99 40 E
Siquia → 121 12 10N 84 20W
Siquijor 73 9 12N 123 35 E
Sir Edward Pellew Group 97 15 40S 137 10 E
Sira 70 13 41N 76 49 E
Siracusa 41 37 4N 15 17 E
Sirajganj 69 24 25N 89 47 E
Sirakoro 84 12 41N 9 14W
Sirasso 84 9 16N 6 6W
Siret 46 47 55N 26 5 E
Siret → 46 47 58N 26 5 E
Şiria 42 46 16N 21 38 E
Sirino, Monte 41 40 7N 15 50 E
Sirkali (Shivali) 70 11 15N 79 41 E
Sirna. 45 36 22N 26 42 E
Sirohi 68 24 52N 72 53 E
Široki Brijeg 42 43 21N 17 36 E
Sironj 68 24 5N 77 39 E
Siros 45 37 28N 24 57 E
Sirsa 68 29 33N 75 4 E
Sirsi 70 14 40N 74 49 E
Siruela 31 38 58N 5 3W
Sisak 39 45 30N 16 21 E
Sisaket 71 15 8N 104 23 E
Sisante 33 39 25N 2 12W
Sisargas, Islas 30 43 21N 8 50W
Sishen 92 27 47S 22 59 E
Sishui 77 34 48N 113 15 E
Sisipuk L. 109 55 45N 101 50W
Sisophon 71 13 38N 102 59 E
Sisseton 116 45 43N 97 3W
Sissonne 19 49 34N 3 51 E
Sistema Central 30 40 40N 5 55W
Sistema Iberico 32 41 0N 2 10W
Sisteron 21 44 12N 5 57 E
Sisters 118 44 21N 121 32W
Sitamarhi 69 26 37N 85 30 E
Sitapur 69 27 38N 80 45 E
Siteki 93 26 32S 31 58 E
Sitges 32 41 17N 1 47 E
Sithoniá 44 40 0N 23 45 E
Sitía 45 35 13N 26 6 E
Sitka 104 57 9N 135 20W
Sitoti 92 23 15S 23 40 E
Sitra 86 28 40N 26 53 E
Sittang → 67 17 10N 96 58 E
Sittang Myit → 67 17 20N 96 45 E
Sittard 16 51 0N 5 52 E
Sittensen 24 53 17N 9 32 E
Sittona 87 14 25N 37 23 E
Situbondo 73 7 45S 114 0 E
Sivaganga 70 9 50N 78 28 E
Sivagiri 70 9 16N 77 26 E
Sivakasi 70 9 24N 77 47 E
Sivana 68 28 37N 78 6 E
Sīvand 65 30 5N 52 55 E
Sivas 64 39 43N 36 58 E
Siverek 64 37 50N 39 19 E
Sivomaskinskiy 52 66 40N 62 35 E
Sivrihisar 64 39 30N 31 35 E
Sîwa 86 29 11N 25 31 E
Sîwa, El Wâhât es 86 29 10N 25 30 E
Siwalik Range 69 28 0N 83 0 E
Siwan 69 26 13N 84 21 E
Siyâl, Jazâ'ir 86 22 49N 36 12 E
Sizewell 13 52 13N 1 38 E
Sjælland 49 55 30N 11 30 E
Sjællands Odde 49 56 0N 11 15 E
Själevad 48 63 18N 18 36 E
Sjarinska Banja 42 42 45N 21 38 E
Sjenica 42 43 16N 20 0 E
Sjoa 47 61 41N 9 33 E
Sjöbo 49 55 37N 13 45 E
Sjösa 49 58 47N 17 4 E
Skadarsko Jezero 42 42 10N 19 20 E
Skadovsk 56 46 17N 32 52 E
Skagafjörður 50 65 54N 19 35W
Skagastølstindane 47 61 28N 7 52 E
Skagen 49 57 43N 10 35 E
Skagern 48 59 0N 14 20 E
Skagerrak 49 57 30N 9 0 E
Skagway 104 59 23N 135 20W
Skaidi 50 70 26N 24 30 E
Skala Podolskaya 56 48 50N 26 15 E
Skalat 54 49 23N 25 55 E
Skalbmierz 28 50 20N 20 25 E
Skalica 27 48 50N 17 15 E
Skalni Dol = Kamenyak 43 43 24N 26 57 E
Skals 49 56 34N 9 24 E
Skanderborg 49 56 2N 9 55 E
Skånevik 47 59 43N 5 53 E
Skänninge 49 58 24N 15 5 E
Skanör 49 55 24N 12 50 E
Skantzoúra 45 39 5N 24 6 E
Skara 49 58 25N 13 30 E
Skaraborgs län □ 49 58 20N 13 30 E
Skardu 69 35 20N 75 44 E
Skarrild 49 55 58N 8 53 E
Skarszewy 28 54 4N 18 25 E
Skaryszew 28 51 19N 21 15 E
Skarzysko Kamienna 28 51 7N 20 52 E
Skattungbyn 48 61 10N 14 56 E
Skebokvarn 48 59 7N 16 45 E
Skeena → 108 54 9N 130 5W
Skeena Mts. 108 56 40N 128 30W
Skegness 12 53 9N 0 20 E
Skeldon 126 5 55N 57 20W
Skellefte älv → 50 64 45N 21 10 E
Skellefteå 50 64 45N 20 58 E
Skelleftehamn 50 64 47N 20 59 E
Skender Vakuf 42 44 29N 17 22 E
Skene 49 57 30N 12 37 E
Skerries, The 12 53 27N 4 40W
Skhíza 45 36 41N 21 40 E
Skhoinoúsa 45 36 53N 25 31 E
Skhwaner, Pegunungan 72 1 0S 112 30 E
Ski 47 59 43N 10 52 E
Skiathos 45 39 12N 23 30 E
Skibbereen 15 51 33N 9 16W
Skiddaw 12 54 39N 3 9W
Skien 47 59 12N 9 35 E
Skierniewice 28 51 58N 20 10 E
Skierniewice □ 28 52 0N 20 10 E
Skikda 83 36 50N 6 58 E
Skillingaryd 49 57 27N 14 5 E
Skillinge 49 55 30N 14 16 E
Skillingmark 48 59 48N 12 1 E
Skinári, Ákra 45 37 56N 20 40 E
Skipton, Austral. 99 37 39S 143 40 E
Skipton, U.K. 12 53 57N 2 1W
Skiropoúla 45 38 50N 24 21 E
Skiros 45 38 55N 24 34 E
Skivarp 49 55 26N 13 34 E
Skive 49 56 33N 9 2 E
Skjåk 47 61 52N 8 22 E
Skjálfandafljót → 50 65 59N 17 25W
Skjálfandi 50 66 5N 17 30W
Skjeberg 47 59 12N 11 12 E
Skjern 49 55 57N 8 30 E
Skoczów 27 49 49N 18 45 E
Skodje 47 62 30N 6 43 E
Škofja Loka 39 46 9N 14 19 E
Skoghall 48 59 20N 13 30 E
Skoki 28 52 40N 17 11 E
Skole 54 49 3N 23 30 E
Skópelos 45 39 9N 23 47 E
Skopin 55 53 55N 39 32 E
Skopje 42 42 1N 21 32 E
Skórcz 28 53 47N 18 30 E
Skottfoss 47 59 12N 9 30 E
Skovorodino 59 54 0N 125 0 E
Skowhegan 107 44 49N 69 40W
Skownan 109 51 58N 99 35W
Skradin 39 43 52N 15 53 E
Skreanäs 49 56 52N 12 35 E
Skrwa → 28 52 35N 19 32 E
Skull 15 51 32N 9 40W
Skultorp 49 58 24N 13 51 E
Skunk → 116 40 42N 91 7W
Skuodas 54 56 21N 21 45 E
Skurup 49 55 28N 13 30 E
Skutskär 49 60 37N 17 25 E
Skvira 56 49 44N 29 40 E
Skwierzyna 28 52 33N 15 30 E
Skye 14 57 15N 6 10W
Skykomish 118 47 43N 121 16W
Skyros = Skíros 45 38 52N 24 37 E
Slagelse 49 55 23N 11 19 E
Slamet, G. 72 7 16S 109 8 E
Slaney → 15 52 52N 6 45W
Slangerup 49 55 50N 12 11 E
Slănic 46 45 14N 25 58 E
Slankamen 42 45 8N 20 15 E
Slano 42 42 48N 17 53 E
Slantsy 54 59 7N 28 5 E
Slany 26 50 13N 14 6 E
Slask 22 51 0N 16 30 E
Slate Is. 106 48 40N 87 0W
Slatina 46 44 28N 24 22 E
Slaton 117 33 27N 101 38W
Slave → 108 61 18N 113 39W
Slave Coast 85 6 0N 2 30 E
Slave Lake 108 55 17N 114 43W
Slave Pt. 108 61 11N 115 56W
Slavgorod 58 53 1N 78 37 E
Slavinja 42 43 9N 22 50 E
Slavkov (Austerlitz) 27 49 10N 16 52 E
Slavnoye 54 54 24N 29 15 E
Slavonska Požega 42 45 20N 17 40 E
Slavonski Brod 42 45 11N 18 0 E
Slavuta 54 50 15N 27 2 E
Slavyansk 56 48 55N 37 36 E
Slavyansk-na-Kubani 56 45 15N 38 11 E
Sława 28 51 52N 16 2 E
Sławno 28 54 20N 16 41 E
Sławoborze 28 53 55N 15 42 E
Sleaford 12 53 0N 0 22W
Sleat, Sd. of 14 57 5N 5 47W
Sleeper Is. 105 58 30N 81 0W
Sleepy Eye 116 44 15N 94 45W
Sleman 73 7 40S 110 20 E
Slemon L. 108 63 13N 116 4W
Ślesin 28 52 22N 18 14 E
Slidell 117 30 20N 89 48W
Sliedrecht 16 51 50N 4 45 E
Slieve Aughty 15 53 4N 8 30W
Slieve Bloom 15 53 4N 7 40W
Slieve Donard 15 54 10N 5 57W
Slieve Gullion 15 54 8N 6 26W
Slieve Mish 15 52 12N 9 50W
Slievenamon 15 52 25N 7 37W
Sligo 15 54 17N 8 28W
Sligo □ 15 54 10N 8 35W
Sligo B. 15 54 20N 8 40W
Slite 51 57 42N 18 48 E
Sliven 43 42 42N 26 19 E
Slivnitsa 42 42 50N 23 0 E
Sljeme 39 45 57N 15 58 E
Sloansville 113 42 45N 74 22W
Slobodskoy 52 58 40N 50 6 E
Slobozia, Ialomiţa, Romania 46 44 34N 27 23 E
Slobozia, Valahia, Romania 46 44 30N 25 14 E
Slocan 108 49 48N 117 28W
Slochteren 16 53 12N 6 48 E
Slöinge 49 56 51N 12 42 E
Słomniki 28 50 16N 20 4 E
Slonim 54 53 4N 25 19 E
Slough 13 51 30N 0 35W
Slovakia = Slovensko 27 48 30N 19 0 E
Slovakian Ore Mts. = Slovenské Rudohorie 27 48 45N 20 0 E
Slovenia = Slovenija 39 45 58N 14 30 E
Slovenija □ 39 45 58N 14 30 E
Slovenj Gradec 39 46 31N 15 5 E
Slovenska Bistrica 39 46 24N 15 35 E
Slovenská Socialisticka Republika □ 27 48 30N 10 0 E
Slovenské Rudohorie 27 48 45N 20 0 E
Slovensko □ 27 48 30N 19 0 E
Słubice 28 52 22N 14 35 E
Sluch → 54 51 37N 26 38 E
Sluis 16 51 18N 3 23 E
Slunchev Bryag 43 42 40N 27 41 E
Slunj 39 45 6N 15 33 E
Słupca 28 52 15N 17 52 E
Słupia → 28 54 35N 16 51 E
Słupsk 28 54 30N 17 3 E
Słupsk □ 28 54 15N 17 30 E
Slurry 92 25 49S 25 42 E
Slutsk 54 53 2N 27 31 E
Slyne Hd. 15 53 25N 10 10W
Slyudyanka 59 51 40N 103 40 E
Smålandsfarvandet 49 55 10N 11 20 E
Smalandsstenar 49 57 9N 13 24 E
Smalltree L. 109 61 0N 105 0W
Smallwood Reservoir 107 54 20N 63 10W
Smarje 39 46 15N 15 34 E
Smart Syndicate Dam 92 30 45S 23 10 E
Smeaton 109 53 30N 104 49W
Smederevo 42 44 40N 20 57 E
Smederevska Palanka 42 44 22N 20 58 E
Smela 56 49 15N 31 58 E
Smethport 112 41 50N 78 28W
Smidovich 59 48 36N 133 49 E
Smigiel 28 52 1N 16 32 E
Smiley 109 51 38N 109 29W
Smilyan 43 41 29N 24 46 E
Smith 108 55 10N 114 0W
Smith → 108 59 34N 126 30W
Smith Arm 104 66 15N 123 0W
Smith Center 116 39 50N 98 50W
Smith Sund 4 78 30N 74 0W
Smithburne → 98 17 3S 140 57 E
Smithers 108 54 45N 127 10W
Smithfield, Madag. 93 30 9S 26 30 E
Smithfield, N.C., U.S.A. 115 35 31N 78 16W
Smithfield, Utah, U.S.A. 118 41 50N 111 50W
Smiths Falls 106 44 55N 76 0W
Smithton 99 40 53S 145 6 E
Smithtown 99 30 58S 152 48 E
Smithville, Can. 112 43 6N 79 33W
Smithville, U.S.A. 117 30 2N 97 12W
Smoky → 108 56 10N 117 21W
Smoky Falls 106 50 4N 82 10W
Smoky Hill → 116 39 3N 96 48W
Smoky Lake 108 54 10N 112 30W
Smøla 47 63 23N 8 3 E
Smolensk 54 54 45N 32 0 E
Smolikas, Óros 44 40 9N 20 58 E
Smolník 27 48 43N 20 44 E
Smolyan 43 41 36N 24 38 E
Smooth Rock Falls 106 49 17N 81 37W
Smoothstone L. 109 54 40N 106 50W
Smorgon 54 54 20N 26 24 E
Smulţi 46 45 57N 27 44 E
Smyadovo 43 43 2N 27 1 E
Smyrna = İzmir 64 38 25N 27 8 E
Snaefell 12 54 18N 4 26W
Snaefellsjökull 50 64 45N 23 46W
Snake → 118 46 12N 119 2W
Snake I. 99 38 47S 146 33 E
Snake L. 109 55 32N 106 35W
Snake Ra. 118 39 0N 114 30W
Snake River 118 44 10N 110 42W
Snake River Plain 118 43 13N 113 0W
Snarum 47 60 1N 9 54 E
Snedsted 49 56 55N 8 32 E
Sneek 16 53 2N 5 40 E
Snejbjerg 49 56 8N 8 54 E
Snezhnoye 57 48 0N 38 58 E
Sněžka 26 50 41N 15 50 E
Snežnik 39 45 36N 14 35 E
Sniadowo 28 53 2N 22 0 E
Sniardwy, Jezioro 28 53 48N 21 50 E
Snigirevka 56 47 2N 32 49 E
Snina 27 49 0N 22 9 E
Snizort, L. 14 57 33N 6 28W
Snøhetta 47 62 19N 9 16 E
Snohomish 118 47 53N 122 6W
Snonuten 47 59 31N 6 50 E
Snow Hill 114 38 10N 75 21W
Snow Lake 109 54 52N 100 3W
Snowbird L. 109 60 45N 103 0W
Snowdon 12 53 4N 4 8W
Snowdrift 109 62 24N 110 44W
Snowdrift → 109 62 24N 110 44W
Snowflake 119 34 30N 110 4W
Snowshoe Pk. 118 48 13N 115 41W
Snowtown 99 33 46S 138 14 E
Snowville 118 41 59N 112 47W
Snowy → 97 37 46S 148 30 E
Snowy Mts. 99 36 30S 148 20 E
Snyatyn 56 48 30N 25 50 E
Snyder, Okla., U.S.A. 117 34 40N 99 0W
Snyder, Tex., U.S.A. 117 32 45N 100 57W
Soahanina 93 18 42S 44 13 E
Soalala 93 16 6S 45 20 E
Soanierana-Ivongo 93 16 55S 49 35 E
Soap Lake 118 47 23N 119 31W
Sobat, Nahr → 87 9 22N 31 33 E
Soběslav 26 49 16N 14 45 E
Sobhapur 68 22 47N 78 17 E
Sobinka 55 56 0N 40 0 E
Sobótka 28 50 54N 16 44 E

Sobrado Spragge

Sobrado 30 43 2N 8 2W
Sobral 127 3 50S 40 20W
Sobreira Formosa 31 39 46N 7 51W
Soča → 39 46 20N 13 40 E
Sochaczew 28 52 15N 20 13 E
Soch'e = Shache 75 38 20N 77 10 E
Sochi 57 43 35N 39 40 E
Société, Is. de la 95 17 0S 151 0W
Society Is. = Société, Is. de la 95 17 0S 151 0W
Socompa, Portezuelo de 124 24 27S 68 18W
Socorro, Colomb. 126 6 29N 73 16W
Socorro, U.S.A. 119 34 4N 106 54W
Socotra 63 12 30N 54 0 E
Socúellmos 33 39 16N 2 47W
Soda L. 119 35 7N 116 2W
Soda Plains 69 35 30N 79 0 E
Soda Springs 118 42 40N 111 40W
Söderfors 48 60 23N 17 25 E
Söderhamn 48 61 18N 17 10 E
Söderköping 48 58 31N 16 20 E
Södermanlands län □ 48 59 10N 16 30 E
Södertälje 48 59 12N 17 39 E
Sodiri 81 14 27N 29 0 E
Sodo 87 7 0N 37 41 E
Södra Vi 49 57 45N 15 45 E
Sodražica 39 45 45N 14 39 E
Sodus 112 43 13N 77 5W
Soekmekaar 93 23 30S 29 55 E
Soest, Ger. 24 51 34N 8 7 E
Soest, Neth. 16 52 9N 5 19 E
Sofádhes 44 39 20N 22 4 E
Sofara 84 13 59N 4 9W
Sofia = Sofiya 43 42 45N 23 20 E
Sofia → 93 15 27S 47 23 E
Sofievka 56 48 6N 33 55 E
Sofiiski 59 52 15N 133 59 E
Sofikón 45 37 47N 23 3 E
Sofiya 43 42 45N 23 20 E
Sogad 73 10 30N 125 0 E
Sogakofe 85 6 2N 0 39 E
Sogamoso 126 5 43N 72 56W
Sögel 24 52 50N 7 32 E
Sogn og Fjordane fylke □ 47 61 40N 6 0 E
Sognefjorden 47 61 10N 5 50 E
Sohâg 86 26 33N 31 43 E
Soignies 16 50 35N 4 5 E
Soira, Mt. 87 14 45N 39 30 E
Soissons 19 49 25N 3 19 E
Sōja 74 34 40N 133 45 E
Sojat 68 25 55N 73 45 E
Sok → 55 53 24N 50 8 E
Sokal 54 50 31N 24 15 E
Söke 45 37 48N 27 28 E
Sokelo 91 9 55S 24 36 E
Sokhós 44 40 48N 23 22 E
Sokki, Oued In → 82 29 30N 3 42 E
Sokna 47 60 16N 9 50 E
Soknedal 47 62 57N 10 13 E
Soko Banja 42 43 40N 21 51 E
Sokodé 85 9 0N 1 11 E
Sokol 55 59 30N 40 5 E
Sokolac 42 43 56N 18 48 E
Sokółka 28 53 25N 23 30 E
Sokolo 84 14 53N 6 8W
Sokolov 26 50 12N 12 40 E
Sokołów Małpolski 27 50 12N 22 7 E
Sokołów Podlaski 28 52 25N 22 15 E
Sokoły 28 52 59N 22 42 E
Sokoto 85 13 2N 5 16 E
Sokoto □ 85 12 30N 5 0 E
Sokoto → 85 11 20N 4 10 E
Sol Iletsk 52 51 10N 55 0 E
Sola 47 58 53N 5 36 E
Sola → 27 50 4N 19 15 E
Solai 90 0 2N 36 12 E
Solana, La 33 38 59N 3 14W
Solano 73 16 31N 121 15 E
Solares 30 43 23N 3 43W
Solberga 49 57 45N 14 43 E
Solca 46 47 40N 25 50 E
Solec Kujawski 28 53 5N 18 14 E
Soledad, U.S.A. 119 36 27N 121 16W
Soledad, Venez. 126 8 10N 63 34W
Solent, The 13 50 45N 1 25W
Solenzara 21 41 53N 9 23 E
Solesmes 19 50 10N 3 30 E
Solfonn 47 60 2N 6 57 E
Soligalich 55 59 5N 42 10 E
Soligorsk 54 52 51N 27 27 E
Solikamsk 58 59 38N 56 50 E
Solila 93 21 25S 46 37 E
Solimões → = Amazonas → 126 2 15S 66 30W
Solingen 24 51 10N 7 4 E
Sollebrunn 49 58 8N 12 32 E
Sollefteå 48 63 12N 17 20 E
Sollentuna 48 59 26N 17 56 E
Sóller 32 39 46N 2 43 E
Solling 24 51 44N 9 36 E
Solna 48 59 22N 18 1 E
Solnechnogorsk 55 56 10N 36 57 E
Sologne 19 47 40N 2 0 E
Solok 72 0 45S 100 40 E
Sololá 120 14 49N 91 10 E
Solomon Is. ■ 94 6 0S 155 0 E
Solomon, N. Fork → 116 39 29N 98 26W
Solomon Sea 98 7 0S 150 0 E
Solomon, S. Fork → 116 39 25N 99 12W
Solomon's Pools = Birak Sulaymān 62 31 42N 35 7 E
Solon 75 46 32N 121 10 E
Solon Springs 116 46 19N 91 47W
Solor 73 8 27S 123 0 E
Solotcha 55 54 48N 39 53 E
Solothurn 25 47 13N 7 32 E
Solothurn □ 25 47 18N 7 40 E
Solsona 32 42 0N 1 31 E
Solt 27 46 45N 19 1 E
Solta 39 43 24N 16 15 E
Solṭānābād 65 36 29N 58 5 E
Solṭāniyeh 64 36 20N 48 55 E
Soltau 24 52 59N 9 50 E
Soltsy 54 58 10N 30 30 E
Solund 47 61 5N 4 50 E
Solunska Glava 42 41 44N 21 31 E
Solvay 114 43 5N 76 17W
Sölvesborg 49 56 5N 14 35 E
Solvychegodsk 52 61 21N 46 56 E
Solway Firth 12 54 45N 3 38W
Solwezi 91 12 11S 26 21 E
Somali Rep. ■ 63 7 0N 47 0 E
Sombe Dzong 69 27 13N 89 8 E
Sombernon 19 47 20N 4 40 E
Sombor 42 45 46N 19 9 E
Sombra 112 42 43N 82 29W
Sombrerete 120 23 40N 103 40W
Sombrero 121 18 37N 63 30W
Somers 118 48 4N 114 18W
Somerset, Berm. 121 32 16N 64 55W
Somerset, Can. 109 49 25N 98 39W
Somerset, Colo., U.S.A. 119 38 55N 107 30W
Somerset, Ky., U.S.A. 114 37 5N 84 40W
Somerset, Mass., U.S.A. 113 41 45N 71 10W
Somerset, Pa., U.S.A. 112 40 1N 79 4W
Somerset □ 13 51 9N 3 0W
Somerset East 92 32 42S 25 35 E
Somerset I. 104 73 30N 93 0W
Somerset West 92 34 8S 18 50 E
Somersworth 113 43 15N 70 51W
Somerton 119 32 35N 114 47W
Somerville 113 40 34N 74 36W
Someș → 46 47 15N 23 45 E
Someșul Mare → 46 47 18N 24 30 E
Somma Lombardo 38 45 41N 8 42 E
Somma Vesuviana 41 40 52N 14 23 E
Sommariva 99 26 24S 146 36 E
Sommatino 40 37 20N 14 0 E
Somme □ 19 50 0N 2 20 E
Somme, B. de la 18 50 14N 1 33 E
Sommen 49 58 12N 15 0 E
Sommen, L. 49 58 0N 15 15 E
Sommepy-Tahure 19 49 15N 4 31 E
Sömmerda 24 51 10N 11 8 E
Sommesous 19 48 44N 4 12 E
Sommières 21 43 47N 4 6 E
Somogy □ 27 46 19N 17 30 E
Somogyszob 27 46 18N 17 20 E
Sompolno 28 52 26N 18 30 E
Somport, Paso 32 42 48N 0 31W
Somport, Puerto de 32 42 48N 0 31W
Son, Norway 47 59 32N 10 42 E
Son, Spain 30 42 43N 8 58W
Son La 71 21 20N 103 50 E
Sonamukhi 69 23 18N 87 27 E
Soncino 38 45 24N 9 52 E
Sondags → 92 33 44S 25 51 E
Sóndalo 38 46 20N 10 20 E
Sønder Omme 49 55 50N 8 54 E
Sønder Ternby 49 57 31N 9 58 E
Sønderborg 49 54 55N 9 49 E
Sonderjyllands Amtskommune □ 49 55 10N 9 10 E
Sondershausen 24 51 22N 10 50 E
Sóndrio 38 46 10N 9 53 E
Sone 91 17 23S 34 55 E
Sonepat 68 29 0N 77 5 E
Sonepur 69 20 55N 83 50 E
Song Cau 71 13 27N 109 18 E
Song Xian 77 34 12N 112 8 E
Songea 91 10 40S 35 40 E
Songea □ 91 10 30S 36 0 E
Songeons 19 49 32N 1 50 E
Songhua Hu 76 43 35N 126 50 E
Songhua Jiang → 75 47 45N 132 30 E
Songjiang 77 31 1N 121 12 E
Songkhla 71 7 13N 100 37 E
Songling 76 48 2N 121 9 E
Songpan 75 32 40N 103 30 E
Songtao 77 28 11N 109 10 E
Songwe 90 3 20S 26 16 E
Songwe → 91 9 44S 33 58 E
Songzi 77 30 12N 111 45 E
Sonkovo 55 57 50N 37 5 E
Sonmiani 66 25 25N 66 40 E
Sonnino 40 41 25N 13 13 E
Sono → 127 9 58S 48 11W
Sonora, Calif., U.S.A. 119 37 59N 120 27W
Sonora, Texas, U.S.A. 117 30 33N 100 37W
Sonora □ 120 29 0N 111 0W
Sonora → 120 28 50N 111 33W
Sonora P. 118 38 17N 119 35W
Sonsomate 120 13 43N 89 44W
Sonthofen 25 47 31N 10 16 E
Soo Junction 114 46 20N 85 14W
Soochow = Suzhou 75 31 19N 120 38 E
Sopi 73 2 34N 128 28 E
Sopo, Nahr → 87 8 40N 26 30 E
Sopot, Poland 28 54 27N 18 31 E
Sopot, Yugo. 42 44 29N 20 30 E
Sopotnica 42 41 23N 21 13 E
Sopron 27 47 45N 16 32 E
Sop's Arm 107 49 46N 56 56W
Sør-Rondane 5 72 0S 25 0 E
Sør-Trøndelag fylke □ 47 63 0N 10 0 E
Sora 40 41 45N 13 36 E
Sorada 70 19 45N 84 26 E
Sorah 68 27 13N 68 56 E
Söråker 48 62 30N 17 32 E
Sorano 39 42 40N 11 42 E
Sorata 126 15 50S 68 40W
Sorbas 33 37 6N 2 7W
Sorel 106 46 0N 73 10W
Sorento 99 38 22S 144 47 E
Soreq, N. → 62 31 57N 34 43 E
Soresina 38 45 17N 9 51 E
Sorgono 40 40 01N 9 06 E
Sorgues 21 44 1N 4 53 E
Soria 32 41 43N 2 32W
Soria □ 32 41 46N 2 28W
Soriano 124 33 24S 58 19W
Soriano nel Cimino 39 42 25N 12 14 E
Sorkh, Kuh-e 65 35 40N 58 30 E
Sorø 49 55 26N 11 32 E
Soro 84 10 9N 9 48W
Sorocaba 125 23 31S 47 27W
Sorochinsk 52 52 26N 53 10 E
Soroki 56 48 8N 28 12 E
Soroksár 27 47 24N 19 9 E
Soron 68 27 55N 78 45 E
Sorong 73 0 55S 131 15 E
Soroti 90 1 43N 33 35 E
Sørøya 50 70 40N 22 30 E
Sørøyane 47 62 25N 5 32 E
Sørøysundet 50 70 25N 23 0 E
Sorraia → 31 38 55N 8 53W
Sorrento 41 40 38N 14 23 E
Sorris Sorris 92 21 0S 14 46 E
Sorsele 50 65 31N 17 30 E
Sorso 40 40 50N 8 34 E
Sorsogon 73 13 0N 124 0 E
Sortavala 52 61 42N 30 41 E
Sortino 41 37 9N 15 1 E
Sorvizhi 55 57 52N 48 32 E
Sos 32 42 30N 1 13W
Soscumica, L. 106 50 15N 77 27W
Sosna → 55 52 42N 38 55 E
Sosnogorsk 52 63 37N 53 51 E
Sosnovka, R.S.F.S.R., U.S.S.R. 55 53 13N 41 24 E
Sosnovka, R.S.F.S.R., U.S.S.R. 59 54 9N 109 35 E
Sosnowiec 28 50 20N 19 10 E
Sospel 21 43 52N 7 27 E
Šoštanj 39 46 23N 15 4 E
Sosva 52 59 10N 61 50 E
Soto la Marina → 120 23 40N 97 40W
Soto y Amío 30 42 46N 5 53W
Sotteville-lès-Rouen 18 49 24N 1 5 E
Sotuta 120 20 29N 89 43W
Souanké 88 2 10N 14 3 E
Soúdhas, Kólpos 45 35 25N 24 10 E
Souflíon 44 41 12N 26 18 E
Souillac 20 44 53N 1 29 E
Souk-Ahras 83 36 23N 7 57 E
Souk el Arba du Rharb 82 34 43N 5 59W
Sŏul 76 37 31N 126 58 E
Soulac-sur-Mer 20 45 30N 1 7W
Soultz 19 48 57N 7 52 E
Soúnion, Ákra 45 37 37N 24 1 E
Sour el Ghozlane 83 36 10N 3 45 E
Sources, Mt. aux 93 28 45S 28 50 E
Sourdeval 18 48 43N 0 55W
Soure, Brazil 127 0 35S 48 30W
Soure, Port. 30 40 4N 8 38W
Souris, Man., Can. 109 49 40N 100 20W
Souris, P.E.I., Can. 107 46 21N 62 15W
Souris → 109 49 40N 99 34W
Soúrpi 45 39 6N 22 54 E
Sousa 127 6 45S 38 10W
Sousel, Brazil 127 2 38S 52 29W
Sousel, Port. 31 38 57N 7 40W
Souss, O. → 82 30 27N 9 31W
Sousse 83 35 50N 10 38 E
Soustons 20 43 45N 1 19W
Souterraine, La 20 46 15N 1 30 E
South Africa, Rep. of, ■ 89 32 0S 17 0 E
South America 122 10 0S 60 0W
South Atlantic Ocean 7 20 0S 10 0W
South Aulatsivik I. 107 56 45N 61 30W
South Australia □ 96 32 0S 139 0 E
South Baldy, Mt. 119 34 6N 107 27W
South Bend, Ind., U.S.A. 114 41 38N 86 20W
South Bend, Wash., U.S.A. 118 46 44N 123 52W
South Boston 115 36 42N 78 58W
South Branch 107 47 55N 59 2W
South Brook 107 49 26N 56 5W
South Buganda □ 90 0 15S 31 30 E
South Carolina □ 115 33 45N 81 0W
South Charleston 114 38 20N 81 40W
South China Sea 71 10 0N 113 0 E
South Dakota □ 116 45 0N 100 0W
South Downs 13 50 53N 0 10W
South East C. 97 43 40S 146 50 E
South-East Indian Rise 94 43 0S 80 0 E
South Esk → 14 56 44N 3 3W
South Foreland 13 51 7N 1 23 E
South Fork → 118 47 54N 113 15W
South Gamboa 120 9 4N 79 40W
South Georgia 5 54 30S 37 0W
South Glamorgan □ 13 51 30N 3 20W
South Grafton 99 29 41S 152 57 E
South Haven 114 42 22N 86 20W
South Henik, L. 109 61 30N 97 30W
South Honshu Ridge 94 23 0N 143 0 E
South Horr 90 2 12N 36 56 E
South I., Kenya 90 2 35N 36 35 E
South I., N.Z. 101 44 0S 170 0 E
South Invercargill 101 46 26S 168 23 E
South Knife → 109 58 55N 94 37W
South Korea ■ 76 36 0N 128 0 E
South Loup → 116 41 4N 98 40W
South Mashonaland □ 91 18 0S 31 30 E
South Milwaukee 114 42 50N 87 52W
South Molton 13 51 1N 3 50W
South Nahanni → 108 61 3N 123 21W
South Negril Pt. 121 18 14N 78 30W
South Orkney Is. 5 63 0S 45 0W
South Pass 118 42 20N 108 58W
South Passage 96 26 07S 113 09 E
South Pines 115 35 10N 79 25W
South Pittsburg 115 35 1N 85 42W
South Platte → 116 41 7N 100 42W
South Pole 5 90 0S 0 0 E
South Porcupine 106 48 30N 81 12W
South River, Can. 106 45 52N 79 23W
South River, U.S.A. 113 40 27N 74 23W
South Ronaldsay 14 58 46N 2 58W
South Sandwich Is. 7 57 0S 27 0W
South Saskatchewan → 109 53 15N 105 5W
South Seal → 109 58 48N 98 8W
South Sentinel I. 71 11 1N 92 16 E
South Shetland Is. 5 62 0S 59 0W
South Shields 12 54 59N 1 26W
South Sioux City 116 42 30N 96 24W
South Taranaki Bight 101 39 40S 174 5 E
South Thompson → 108 50 40N 120 20W
South Twin I. 106 53 7N 79 52W
South Tyne → 12 54 46N 2 25W
South Uist 14 57 20N 7 15W
South West Africa = Namibia ■ 92 22 0S 18 9 E
South West C. 99 43 34S 146 3 E
South Yemen ■ 63 15 0N 48 0 E
South Yorkshire □ 12 53 30N 1 20W
Southampton, Can. 106 44 30N 81 25W
Southampton, U.K. 13 50 54N 1 23W
Southampton, U.S.A. 114 40 54N 72 22W
Southampton I. 105 64 30N 84 0W
Southbridge, N.Z. 101 43 48S 172 16 E
Southbridge, U.S.A. 113 42 4N 72 2W
Southeast Pacific Basin 95 16 30S 92 0W
Southend 109 56 19N 103 22W
Southend-on-Sea 13 51 32N 0 42 E
Southern □, Malawi 91 15 0S 35 0 E
Southern □, S. Leone 84 8 0N 12 30W
Southern □, Zambia 91 16 20S 26 20 E
Southern Alps 101 43 41S 170 11 E
Southern Cross 96 31 12S 119 15 E
Southern Indian L. 109 57 10N 98 30W
Southern Ocean 5 62 0S 60 0 E
Southern Uplands 14 55 30N 3 3W
Southington 113 41 37N 72 53W
Southold 113 41 4N 72 26W
Southport, Austral. 97 27 58S 153 25 E
Southport, U.K. 12 53 38N 3 1W
Southport, U.S.A. 115 33 55N 78 0W
Southwestern Pacific Basin 94 42 0S 170 0W
Southwold 13 52 19N 1 41 E
Soutpansberge 93 23 0S 29 30 E
Souvigny 20 46 33N 3 10 E
Sovata 46 46 35N 25 3 E
Sovetsk, Lithuania, U.S.S.R. 54 55 6N 21 50 E
Sovetsk, R.S.F.S.R., U.S.S.R. 55 57 38N 48 53 E
Sovetskaya 57 49 1N 42 7 E
Sovetskaya Gavan 59 48 50N 140 0 E
Sovicille 39 43 16N 11 12 E
Sovra 42 42 44N 17 34 E
Sōya-Misaki 74 45 30N 142 0 E
Soyo 88 6 13S 12 20 E
Sozh → 54 51 57N 30 48 E
Sozopol 43 42 23N 27 42 E
Spa 16 50 29N 5 53 E
Spain ■ 29 40 0N 5 0W
Spalding, Austral. 99 33 30S 138 37 E
Spalding, U.K. 12 52 47N 0 9W
Spalding, U.S.A. 116 41 45N 98 27W
Spangereid 47 58 3N 7 9 E
Spangler 112 40 39N 78 48W
Spaniard's Bay 107 47 38N 53 20W
Spanish 106 46 12N 82 20W
Spanish Fork 118 40 10N 111 37W
Spanish Town 121 18 0N 76 57W
Sparks 118 39 30N 119 45W
Sparta, Ga., U.S.A. 115 33 18N 82 59W
Sparta, Wis., U.S.A. 116 43 55N 90 47W
Sparta = Spárti 45 37 5N 22 25 E
Spartanburg 115 35 0N 82 0W
Spartansburg 112 41 48N 79 43W
Spartel, C. 82 35 47N 5 56W
Spárti 45 37 5N 22 25 E
Spartivento, C., Calabria, Italy 41 37 56N 16 4 E
Spartivento, C., Sard., Italy 40 38 52N 8 50 E
Spas-Demensk 54 54 20N 34 0 E
Spas-Klepiki 55 55 10N 40 10 E
Spassk-Dalniy 59 44 40N 132 48 E
Spassk-Ryazanskiy 55 54 24N 40 25 E
Spátha, Akra 45 35 42N 23 43 E
Spatsizi → 108 57 42N 128 7W
Spearfish 116 44 32N 103 52W
Spearman 117 36 15N 101 10W
Speers 109 52 43N 107 34W
Speightstown 121 13 15N 59 39W
Speke Gulf 90 2 20S 32 50 E
Spenard 104 61 11N 149 50W
Spence Bay 104 69 32N 93 32W
Spencer, Idaho, U.S.A. 118 44 18N 112 8W
Spencer, Iowa, U.S.A. 116 43 5N 95 19W
Spencer, N.Y., U.S.A. 113 42 14N 76 30W
Spencer, Nebr., U.S.A. 116 42 52N 98 43W
Spencer, W. Va., U.S.A. 114 38 47N 81 24W
Spencer B. 92 25 30S 14 47 E
Spencer, C. 97 35 20S 136 53 E
Spencer G. 97 34 0S 137 20 E
Spencerville 113 44 51N 75 33W
Spences Bridge 108 50 25N 121 20W
Spenser Mts. 101 42 15S 172 45 E
Sperkhiós → 45 38 57N 22 3 E
Sperrin Mts. 15 54 50N 7 0W
Spessart 25 50 10N 9 20 E
Spétsai 45 37 15N 23 10 E
Spey → 14 57 26N 3 25W
Speyer 25 49 19N 8 26 E
Speyer → 25 49 19N 8 27 E
Spézia, La 38 44 8N 9 50 E
Spezzano Albanese 41 39 41N 16 19 E
Spiekeroog 24 53 45N 7 42 E
Spielfeld 39 46 43N 15 38 E
Spiez 25 46 40N 7 40 E
Spíli 45 35 13N 24 31 E
Spilimbergo 39 46 7N 12 53 E
Spinazzola 41 40 58N 16 5 E
Spind 47 58 6N 6 53 E
Spineni 46 44 43N 24 37 E
Spirit Lake 118 47 56N 116 56W
Spirit River 108 55 45N 118 50W
Spiritwood 109 53 24N 107 33W
Spišská Nová Ves 27 48 58N 20 34 E
Spišské Podhradie 27 49 0N 20 48 E
Spital 26 47 42N 14 18 E
Spithead 13 50 43N 1 5W
Spittal 26 46 48N 13 31 E
Spitzbergen = Svalbard 4 78 0N 17 0 E
Split 39 43 31N 16 26 E
Split L. 109 56 8N 96 15W
Splitski Kanal 39 43 31N 16 20 E
Splügenpass 25 46 30N 9 20 E
Spofford 117 29 10N 100 27W
Spokane 118 47 45N 117 25W
Spoleto 39 42 46N 12 47 E
Spooner 116 45 49N 91 51W
Sporádhes 45 39 0N 24 30 E
Sporyy Navolok, Mys 58 75 50N 68 40 E
Spragge 106 46 15N 82 40W

Sprague Suceava

Sprague 118 47 18N 117 59W
Sprague River 118 42 28N 121 31W
Spratly, I. 72 8 20N 112 0 E
Spray 118 44 50N 119 46W
Spree → 24 52 32N 13 13 E
Spring City 118 39 31N 111 28W
Spring Mts. 119 36 20N 115 43W
Spring Valley, Minn., U.S.A. 116 43 40N 92 23W
Spring Valley, N.Y., U.S.A. 113 41 7N 74 4W
Springbok 92 29 42 S 17 54 E
Springburn 101 43 40 S 171 32 E
Springdale, Can. 107 49 30N 56 6W
Springdale, Ark., U.S.A. 117 36 10N 94 5W
Springdale, Wash., U.S.A. 118 48 1N 117 50W
Springe 24 52 12N 9 35 E
Springer 117 36 22N 104 36W
Springerville 119 34 10N 109 16W
Springfield, Can. 112 42 50N 80 56W
Springfield, N.Z. 101 43 19 S 171 56 E
Springfield, Colo., U.S.A. 117 37 26N 102 40W
Springfield, Ill., U.S.A. 116 39 48N 89 40W
Springfield, Mass., U.S.A. 114 42 8N 72 37W
Springfield, Mo., U.S.A. 117 37 15N 93 20W
Springfield, Ohio, U.S.A. 114 39 58N 83 48W
Springfield, Oreg., U.S.A. 118 44 2N 123 0W
Springfield, Tenn., U.S.A. 115 36 35N 86 55W
Springfield, Vt., U.S.A. 113 43 20N 72 30W
Springfontein 92 30 15 S 25 40 E
Springhill 107 45 40N 64 4W
Springhouse 108 51 56N 122 7W
Springhurst 99 36 10 S 146 31 E
Springs 93 26 13 S 28 25 E
Springsure 97 24 8 S 148 6 E
Springvale, Austral. 98 23 33 S 140 42 E
Springvale, U.S.A. 113 43 28N 70 48W
Springville, N.Y., U.S.A. 114 42 31N 78 41W
Springville, Utah, U.S.A. 118 40 14N 111 35W
Springwater 109 51 58N 108 23W
Spruce-Creek 112 40 36N 78 9W
Spur 117 33 28N 100 50W
Spurn Hd. 12 53 34N 0 8 E
Spuž 42 42 32N 19 10 E
Spuzzum 108 49 37N 121 23W
Squam L. 113 43 45N 71 32W
Squamish 108 49 45N 123 10W
Square Islands 107 52 47N 55 47W
Squillace, Golfo di 41 38 43N 16 35 E
Squinzano 41 40 27N 18 1 E
Sragen 73 7 28 S 110 59 E
Srbac 42 45 7N 17 30 E
Srbija □ 42 43 30N 21 0 E
Srbobran 42 45 32N 19 48 E
Sre Umbell 71 11 8N 103 46 E
Srebrnica 42 44 10N 19 18 E
Sredinnyy Khrebet 59 57 0N 160 0 E
Središče 39 46 24N 16 17 E
Sredna Gora 43 42 40N 24 20 E
Sredne Tambovskoye 59 50 55N 137 45 E
Srednekolymsk 59 67 27N 153 40 E
Srednevilyuysk 59 63 50N 123 5 E
Sredni Rodopi 43 41 40N 24 45 E
Śrem 28 52 6N 17 2 E
Sremska Mitrovica 42 44 59N 19 33 E
Sremski Karlovci 42 45 12N 19 56 E
Sretensk 59 52 10N 117 40 E
Sri Lanka ■ 70 7 30N 80 50 E
Sriharikota, I. 70 13 40N 80 20 E
Srikakulam 70 18 14N 83 58 E
Srinagar 66 34 5N 74 50 E
Sripur 69 24 14N 90 30 E
Srirangam 70 10 54N 78 42 E
Srirangapatnam 70 12 26N 76 43 E
Srivilliputtur 70 9 31N 77 40 E
Środa Śląska 28 51 10N 16 36 E
Środa Wielkopolski 28 52 15N 17 19 E
Srokowo 28 54 13N 21 31 E
Srpska Crnja 42 45 38N 20 44 E
Srpska Itabej 42 45 35N 20 44 E
Staaten → 98 16 24 S 141 17 E
Staberhuk 24 54 23N 11 18 E
Stade 24 53 35N 9 31 E
Staðarhólskirkja 50 65 23N 21 58W
Städjan 48 61 56N 12 52 E
Stadlandet 47 62 10N 5 10 E
Stadskanaal 16 53 4N 6 55 E
Stadthagen 24 52 20N 9 14 E
Stadtlohn 24 52 0N 6 52 E
Stadtroda 24 50 51N 11 44 E
Stafafell 50 64 25N 14 52W
Staffa 14 56 26N 6 21W
Stafford, U.K. 12 52 49N 2 9W
Stafford, U.S.A. 117 38 0N 98 35W
Stafford □ 12 52 53N 2 10W
Stafford Springs 113 41 58N 72 20W
Stagnone 40 37 50N 12 28 E
Staines 13 51 26N 0 30W
Stainz 26 46 53N 15 17 E
Stalač 42 43 43N 21 28 E
Stalingrad = Volgograd 57 48 40N 44 25 E
Staliniri = Tskhinvali 57 42 14N 44 1 E
Stalino = Donetsk 56 48 0N 37 45 E
Stalinogorsk = Novomoskovsk 55 54 5N 38 15 E
Stalowa Wola 28 50 34N 22 3 E
Stalybridge 12 53 29N 2 4W
Stamford, Austral. 98 21 15 S 143 46 E
Stamford, U.K. 13 52 39N 0 29W
Stamford, Conn., U.S.A. 114 41 5N 73 30W
Stamford, Tex., U.S.A. 117 32 58N 99 50W
Stamps 117 33 22N 93 30W
Stanberry 116 40 12N 94 32W
Standerton 93 26 55 S 29 7 E
Standish 114 43 58N 83 57W
Stanford 118 47 11N 110 10W
Stange 47 60 43N 11 5 E
Stanger 93 29 27 S 31 14 E
Stanišić 42 45 56N 19 10 E
Stanislav = Ivano-Frankovsk 54 49 0N 24 40 E
Stanisławów 28 52 18N 21 33 E
Stanke Dimitrov 42 42 17N 23 9 E
Stanley, Austral. 99 40 46 S 145 19 E
Stanley, N.B., Can. 107 46 20N 66 44W
Stanley, Sask., Can. 109 55 24N 104 22W
Stanley, Falk. Is. 128 51 40 S 59 51W
Stanley, Idaho, U.S.A. 118 44 10N 114 59W
Stanley, N.D., U.S.A. 116 48 20N 102 23W
Stanley, N.Y., U.S.A. 112 42 48N 77 6W
Stanley, Wis., U.S.A. 116 44 57N 91 0W
Stanley Res. 70 11 50N 77 40 E
Stann Creek 120 17 0N 88 13W
Stanovoy Khrebet 59 55 0N 130 0 E
Stanthorpe 97 28 36 S 151 59 E
Stanton 117 32 8N 101 45W
Staples 116 46 21N 94 48W
Stapleton 116 41 30N 100 31W
Staporków 28 51 9N 20 31 E
Star City 109 52 50N 104 20W
Stara-minskaya 57 46 33N 39 0 E
Stara Moravica 42 45 50N 19 30 E
Stara Pazova 42 45 0N 20 10 E
Stara Planina 43 43 15N 23 0 E
Stara Zagora 43 42 26N 25 39 E
Starachowice 28 51 3N 21 2 E
Starashcherbinovskaya 57 46 40N 38 53 E
Staraya Russa 54 57 58N 31 23 E
Starbuck I. 95 5 37 S 155 55W
Stargard 24 53 29N 13 19 E
Stargard Szczeciński 28 53 20N 15 0 E
Stari Bar 42 42 7N 19 13 E
Stari Trg 39 45 29N 15 7 E
Staritsa 54 56 33N 35 0 E
Starke 115 30 0N 82 10W
Starkville, Colo., U.S.A. 117 37 10N 104 31W
Starkville, Miss., U.S.A. 115 33 26N 88 48W
Starnberg 25 48 0N 11 20 E
Starnberger See 25 47 55N 11 20 E
Starobelsk 57 49 16N 39 0 E
Starodub 54 52 30N 32 50 E
Starogard 28 53 59N 18 30 E
Starokonstantinov 56 49 48N 27 10 E
Starosielce 28 53 8N 23 5 E
Start Pt. 13 50 13N 3 38W
Stary Sącz 27 49 33N 20 35 E
Staryy Biryuzyak 57 44 46N 46 50 E
Staryy Chartoriysk 54 51 15N 25 54 E
Staryy Kheydzhan 59 60 0N 144 50 E
Staryy Krym 56 45 3N 35 8 E
Staryy Oskol 55 51 19N 37 55 E
Stassfurt 24 51 51N 11 34 E
Staszów 28 50 33N 21 10 E
State College 114 40 47N 77 49W
Staten I. 113 40 35N 74 10W
Staten, I. = Los Estados, I. de 128 54 40 S 64 30W
Statesboro 115 32 26N 81 46W
Statesville 115 35 48N 80 51W
Staunton, Ill., U.S.A. 116 39 0N 89 49W
Staunton, Va., U.S.A. 114 38 7N 79 4W
Stavanger 47 58 57N 5 40 E
Stavelot 16 50 23N 5 55 E
Staveren 16 52 53N 5 22 E
Stavern 47 59 0N 10 1 E
Stavre 48 62 51N 15 19 E
Stavropol 57 45 5N 42 0 E
Stavroúpolis 44 41 12N 24 45 E
Stawell 97 37 5 S 142 47 E
Stawell → 98 20 20 S 142 55 E
Stawiski 28 53 22N 22 9 E
Stawiszyn 28 51 56N 18 4 E
Stayner 112 44 25N 80 5W
Steamboat Springs 118 40 30N 106 50W
Stębark 28 53 30N 20 10 E
Stebleva 44 41 18N 20 33 E
Steele 116 46 56N 99 52W
Steelton 114 40 17N 76 50W
Steelville 117 37 57N 91 21W
Steen River 108 59 40N 117 12W
Steenvoorde 19 50 48N 2 33 E
Steenwijk 16 52 47N 6 7 E
Steep Pt. 96 26 08 S 113 8 E
Steep Rock 109 51 30N 98 48W
Ştefăneşti 46 47 44N 27 15 E
Stefanie L. = Chew Bahir 87 4 40N 36 50 E
Stefansson Bay 5 67 20 S 59 8 E
Stege 49 55 0N 12 18 E
Steiermark □ 26 47 26N 15 0 E
Steigerwald 25 49 45N 10 30 E
Steinbach 109 49 32N 96 40W
Steinfort 16 49 39N 5 55 E
Steinheim 24 51 50N 9 6 E
Steinhuder Meer 24 52 48N 9 20 E
Steinkjer 50 63 59N 11 31 E
Stellaland 92 26 45 S 24 50 E
Stellarton 107 45 32N 62 30W
Stellenbosch 92 33 58 S 18 50 E
Stemshaug 47 63 19N 8 44 E
Stendal 24 52 36N 11 50 E
Stensele 50 65 3N 17 8 E
Stenstorp 49 58 17N 13 45 E
Stepanakert 53 39 40N 46 25 E
Stephan 116 48 30N 96 53W
Stephens Creek 99 31 50 S 141 30 E
Stephens I. 108 54 10N 130 45W
Stephenville, Can. 107 48 31N 58 35W
Stephenville, U.S.A. 117 32 12N 98 12W
Stepnica 28 53 38N 14 36 E
Stepnoi = Elista 57 46 16N 44 14 E
Stepnyak 58 52 50N 70 50 E
Steppe 60 50 0N 50 0 E
Stereá Ellas □ 45 38 50N 22 0 E
Sterkstroom 92 31 32 S 26 32 E
Sterling, Colo., U.S.A. 116 40 40N 103 15W
Sterling, Ill., U.S.A. 116 41 45N 89 45W
Sterling, Kans., U.S.A. 116 38 17N 98 13W
Sterling City 117 31 50N 100 59W
Sterling Run 112 41 25N 78 12W
Sterlitamak 52 53 40N 56 0 E
Sternberg 24 53 42N 11 48 E
Šternberk 27 49 45N 17 15 E
Stettin = Szczecin 28 53 27N 14 27 E
Stettiner Haff 24 53 50N 14 25 E
Stettler 108 52 19N 112 40W
Steubenville 114 40 21N 80 39W
Stevens Port 116 44 32N 89 34W
Stevenson L. 109 53 55N 96 0W
Stevns Klint 49 55 17N 12 28 E
Stewart, B.C., Can. 108 55 56N 129 57W
Stewart, N.W.T., Can. 104 63 19N 139 26W
Stewart, I. 128 54 50 S 71 15W
Stewart I. 101 46 58 S 167 54 E
Stewiacke 107 45 9N 63 22W
Steynsburg 92 31 15 S 25 49 E
Steyr 26 48 3N 14 25 E
Steyr → 26 48 17N 14 15 E
Steytlerville 92 33 17 S 24 19 E
Stia 39 43 48N 11 41 E
Stigler 117 35 19N 95 6W
Stigliano 41 40 24N 16 13 E
Stigsnæs 49 55 13N 11 18 E
Stigtomta 49 58 47N 16 48 E
Stikine → 104 56 40N 132 30W
Stilfontein 92 26 50 S 26 50 E
Stilis 45 38 55N 22 47 E
Stillwater, Minn., U.S.A. 116 45 3N 92 47W
Stillwater, N.Y., U.S.A. 113 42 55N 73 41W
Stillwater, Okla., U.S.A. 117 36 5N 97 3W
Stillwater Mts. 118 39 45N 118 6W
Stilwell 117 35 52N 94 36W
Štimfalías, L. 45 37 51N 22 27 E
Štip 42 41 42N 22 10 E
Stíra 45 38 9N 24 14 E
Stiring-Wendel 19 49 12N 6 57 E
Stirling, Austral. 98 17 12 S 141 35 E
Stirling, Can. 108 49 30N 112 30W
Stirling, U.K. 14 56 7N 3 57W
Stirling Ra. 96 34 23 S 118 0 E
Stittsville 113 45 15N 75 55W
Stockach 25 47 51N 9 01 E
Stockaryd 49 57 19N 14 36 E
Stockerau 27 48 24N 16 12 E
Stockett 118 47 23N 111 7W
Stockholm 48 59 20N 18 3 E
Stockholms län □ 48 59 30N 18 20 E
Stockinbingal 100 34 30 S 147 53 E
Stockport 12 53 25N 2 11W
Stockton, Austral. 100 32 50 S 151 47 E
Stockton, Calif., U.S.A. 119 38 0N 121 20W
Stockton, Kans., U.S.A. 116 39 30N 99 20W
Stockton, Mo., U.S.A. 117 37 40N 93 48W
Stockton-on-Tees 12 54 34N 1 20W
Stockvik 48 62 17N 17 23 E
Stoczek Łukowski 28 51 58N 22 0 E
Stöde 48 62 28N 16 35 E
Stogovo 42 41 31N 20 38 E
Stoke-on-Trent 12 53 1N 2 11W
Stokes Bay 106 45 0N 81 28W
Stokes Pt. 99 40 10 S 143 56 E
Stokkseyri 50 63 50N 21 2W
Stokksnes 50 64 14N 14 58W
Stolac 42 43 8N 17 59 E
Stolberg 24 50 48N 6 13 E
Stolbovaya, R.S.F.S.R., U.S.S.R. 55 55 10N 37 32 E
Stolbovaya, R.S.F.S.R., U.S.S.R. 59 64 50N 153 50 E
Stolbovoy, Ostrov 59 56 44N 163 14 E
Stolbtsy 54 53 30N 26 43 E
Stolin 54 51 53N 26 50 E
Stolnici 46 44 31N 24 48 E
Ston 42 42 51N 17 43 E
Stonehaven 14 56 58N 2 11W
Stonehenge 98 24 22 S 143 17 E
Stonewall 109 50 10N 97 19W
Stonington I. 5 68 11 S 67 0W
Stony L., Man., Can. 109 58 51N 98 40W
Stony L., Ont., Can. 112 44 30N 78 0W
Stony Rapids 109 59 16N 105 50W
Stony Tunguska = Tunguska, Nizhnyaya → 59 65 48N 88 4 E
Stopnica 28 50 27N 20 57 E
Stora Gla 48 59 30N 12 30 E
Stora Karlsö 49 57 17N 17 59 E
Stora Lulevatten 50 67 10N 19 30 E
Stora Sjöfallet 50 67 29N 18 40 E
Storavan 50 65 45N 18 10 E
Stordal 47 63 28N 10 56 E
Store Bælt 49 55 20N 11 0 E
Store Creek 99 32 54 S 149 6 E
Store Heddinge 49 55 18N 12 23 E
Støren 47 63 3N 10 18 E
Storfjorden 47 62 25N 6 30 E
Storm B. 97 43 10 S 147 30 E
Storm Lake 116 42 35N 95 11W
Stormberg 92 31 16 S 26 17 E
Stormsrivier 92 33 59 S 23 52 E
Stornoway 14 58 12N 6 23W
Storozhinets 56 48 14N 25 45 E
Storsjö 48 62 49N 13 5 E
Storsjöen, Hedmark, Norway 47 60 20N 11 40 E
Storsjöen, Hedmark, Norway 47 61 30N 11 14 E
Storsjön, Gävleborg, Sweden 48 60 35N 16 45 E
Storsjön, Jämtland, Sweden 48 62 50N 13 8 E
Storstrøms Amt. □ 49 54 50N 11 45 E
Storuman 50 65 5N 17 10 E
Storuman,sjö 50 65 13N 16 50 E
Storvik 48 60 35N 16 33 E
Stoughton 109 49 40N 103 0W
Stour →, Dorset, U.K. 13 50 48N 2 7W
Stour →, Here. & Worcs., U.K. 13 52 25N 2 13W
Stour →, Suffolk, U.K. 13 51 55N 1 5 E
Stour (Gt. Stour) → 13 51 15N 1 20 E
Stourbridge 13 52 28N 2 8W
Stout, L. 109 52 0N 94 40W
Stowmarket 13 52 11N 1 0 E
Strabane 15 54 50N 7 28W
Strabane □ 15 54 45N 7 25W
Stracin 42 42 13N 22 2 E
Stradella 38 45 4N 9 20 E
Strahan 97 42 9 S 145 20 E
Strakonice 26 49 15N 13 53 E
Straldzha 43 42 35N 26 40 E
Stralsund 24 54 17N 13 5 E
Strand, Norway 47 61 17N 11 17 E
Strand, S. Afr. 92 34 9 S 18 48 E
Stranda 47 62 19N 6 58 E
Strandebarm 47 60 17N 6 0 E
Strandvik 47 60 9N 5 41 E
Strangford, L. 15 54 30N 5 37W
Strängnäs 48 59 23N 17 2 E
Stranraer 14 54 54N 5 0W
Strasbourg, Can. 109 51 4N 104 55W
Strasbourg, France 19 48 35N 7 42 E
Strasburg, Ger. 24 53 30N 13 44 E
Strasburg, U.S.A. 116 46 12N 100 9W
Stratford, Austral. 100 37 59 S 147 7 E
Stratford, Can. 106 43 23N 81 0W
Stratford, N.Z. 101 39 20 S 174 19 E
Stratford, Calif., U.S.A. 119 36 10N 119 49W
Stratford, Conn., U.S.A. 113 41 13N 73 8W
Stratford, Tex., U.S.A. 117 36 20N 102 3W
Stratford-on-Avon 13 52 12N 1 42W
Strath Spey 14 57 15N 3 40W
Strathalbyn 99 35 13 S 138 53 E
Strathclyde □ 14 56 0N 4 50W
Strathcona Prov. Park 108 49 38N 125 40W
Strathmore, Austral. 98 17 50 S 142 35 E
Strathmore, Can. 108 51 5N 113 18W
Strathmore, U.K. 14 56 40N 3 4W
Strathnaver 108 53 20N 122 33W
Strathpeffer 14 57 35N 4 32W
Strathroy 106 42 58N 81 38W
Strathy Pt. 14 58 35N 4 0W
Stratton, U.K. 12 51 41N 1 45W
Stratton, U.S.A. 116 39 20N 102 36W
Straubing 25 48 53N 12 35 E
Straumnes 50 66 26N 23 8W
Strausberg 24 52 40N 13 52 E
Strawberry Res. 118 40 10N 111 7W
Strawn 117 32 36N 98 30W
Strážnice 27 48 54N 17 19 E
Streaky Bay 96 32 48 S 134 13 E
Streator 116 41 9N 88 52W
Středočeský □ 26 49 55N 14 30 E
Středoslovenský □ 27 48 30N 19 15 E
Streeter 116 46 39N 99 21W
Streetsville 112 43 35N 79 42W
Strehaia 46 44 37N 23 10 E
Strelcha 43 42 25N 24 19 E
Strelka 59 58 5N 93 3 E
Strésa 38 45 52N 8 28 E
Strezhevoy 58 60 42N 77 34 E
Stříbro 26 49 44N 13 0 E
Strickland → 98 7 35 S 141 36 E
Strimón → 44 40 46N 23 51 E
Strimonikós Kólpos 44 40 33N 24 0 E
Strofádhes 45 37 15N 21 0 E
Strombacka 48 61 58N 16 44 E
Strómboli 41 38 48N 15 12 E
Stromeferry 14 57 20N 5 33W
Stromness 14 58 58N 3 18W
Ströms vattudal 50 64 15N 14 55 E
Strömsnäsbruk 49 56 35N 13 45 E
Strömstad 48 58 55N 11 15 E
Strömsund 50 63 51N 15 33 E
Stróngoli 41 39 16N 17 2 E
Stronsay 14 59 8N 2 38W
Stronsburg 116 41 7N 97 36W
Stropkov 27 49 13N 21 39 E
Stroud 13 51 44N 2 12W
Stroud Road 99 32 18 S 151 57 E
Stroudsberg 113 40 59N 75 15W
Struer 49 56 30N 8 35 E
Struga 42 41 13N 20 44 E
Strugi Krasnyye 54 58 21N 29 1 E
Strumica 42 41 28N 22 41 E
Strumica → 42 41 20N 22 22 E
Struthers, Can. 106 48 41N 85 51W
Struthers, U.S.A. 114 41 6N 80 38W
Stryama 43 42 16N 24 54 E
Stryi 54 49 16N 23 48 E
Stryker 108 48 40N 114 44W
Stryków 28 51 55N 19 33 E
Strzegom 28 50 58N 16 20 E
Strzelce Krajeńskie 28 52 52N 15 33 E
Strzelce Opolskie 28 50 31N 18 18 E
Strzelecki Cr. → 97 29 37 S 139 59 E
Strzelin 28 50 46N 17 2 E
Strzelno 28 52 35N 18 9 E
Strzybnica 28 50 28N 18 48 E
Strzyzów 27 49 52N 21 47 E
Stuart, Fla., U.S.A. 115 27 11N 80 12W
Stuart, Nebr., U.S.A. 116 42 39N 99 8W
Stuart → 108 54 0N 123 35W
Stuart L. 108 54 30N 124 30W
Stuart Range 96 29 10 S 134 56 E
Stuart Town 100 32 44 S 149 4 E
Stubbekøbing 49 54 53N 12 9 E
Stuben 26 47 10N 10 8 E
Studen Kladenets, Yazovir 43 41 37N 25 30 E
Stugun 48 63 10N 15 40 E
Stühlingen 25 47 44N 8 26 E
Stull, L. 109 54 24N 92 34W
Stung Treng 71 13 31N 105 58 E
Stupart → 109 56 0N 93 25W
Stupino 55 54 57N 38 2 E
Sturgeon B. 109 52 0N 97 50W
Sturgeon Bay 114 44 52N 87 20W
Sturgeon Falls 106 46 25N 79 57W
Sturgeon L., Alta., Can. 108 55 6N 117 32W
Sturgeon L., Ont., Can. 106 50 0N 90 45W
Sturgeon L., Ont., Can. 112 44 28N 78 43W
Sturgis, Mich., U.S.A. 114 41 50N 85 25W
Sturgis, S.D., U.S.A. 116 44 25N 103 30W
Sturkö 49 56 5N 15 42 E
Štúrovo 27 47 48N 18 41 E
Sturt Cr. → 96 20 8 S 127 24 E
Stutterheim 92 32 33 S 27 28 E
Stuttgart, Ger. 25 48 46N 9 10 E
Stuttgart, U.S.A. 117 34 30N 91 33W
Stuyvesant 113 42 23N 73 45W
Stykkishólmur 50 65 2N 22 40W
Styr → 54 52 7N 26 35 E
Styria = Steiermark □ 26 47 26N 15 0 E
Su Xian 77 33 41N 116 59 E
Suakin 86 19 8N 37 20 E
Suaqui 120 29 12N 109 41W
Subang 73 6 34 S 107 45 E
Subi 72 2 58N 108 50 E
Subiaco 39 41 56N 13 5 E
Subotica 42 46 6N 19 49 E
Success 109 50 28N 108 6W
Suceava 46 47 38N 26 16 E

Suceava
Tabatinga, Serra da

Suceava □ **46** 47 37N 25 40 E
Suceava ⤳ **46** 47 38N 26 16 E
Sucha-Beskidzka **27** 49 44N 19 35 E
Suchan **28** 53 18N 15 18 E
Suchedniów **28** 51 3N 20 49 E
Suchitoto **120** 13 56N 89 0W
Suchou = Suzhou **75** 31 18N 120 36 E
Süchow = Xuzhou **77** 34 18N 117 10 E
Suchowola **28** 53 33N 23 3 E
Suck ⤳ **15** 53 17N 8 18W
Suckling, Mt. **98** 9 49 S 148 53 E
Sucre **126** 19 0 S 65 15W
Sućuraj **39** 43 10N 17 8 E
Sud-Ouest, Pte. du **107** 49 23N 63 36W
Sud, Pte. **107** 49 3N 62 14W
Suda ⤳ **55** 59 0N 37 40 E
Sudair **64** 26 0N 45 0 E
Sudak **56** 44 51N 34 57 E
Sudan **117** 34 4N 102 32W
Sudan ■ **81** 15 0N 30 0 E
Suday **55** 59 0N 43 0 E
Sudbury **106** 46 30N 81 0W
Sûdd **87** 8 20N 30 0 E
Süderbrarup **24** 54 38N 9 47 E
Süderlügum **24** 54 50N 8 55 E
Süderoog-Sand **24** 54 27N 8 30 E
Sudetan Mts. = Sudety **27** 50 20N 16 45 E
Sudety **27** 50 20N 16 45 E
Sudi **91** 10 11 S 39 57 E
Sudirman, Pegunungan **73** 4 30 S 137 0 E
Sudiţi **46** 44 35N 27 38 E
Sudogda **55** 55 55N 40 50 E
Sudr **86** 29 40N 32 42 E
Sudzha **54** 51 14N 35 17 E
Sueca **33** 39 12N 0 21W
Suedala **49** 55 30N 13 15 E
Sueur, Le **116** 44 25N 93 52W
Suez = El Suweis **86** 28 40N 33 0 E
Suez Canal = Suweis, Qanâl es **86** 31 0N 33 20 E
Sūf **62** 32 19N 35 49 E
Şufaynah **64** 23 6N 40 33 E
Suffield **109** 50 12N 111 10W
Suffolk **114** 36 47N 76 33W
Suffolk □ **13** 52 16N 1 0 E
Sufuk **65** 23 50N 51 50 E
Şugag **46** 45 47N 23 37 E
Sugar City **116** 38 18N 103 38W
Sugluk = Sagloue **105** 62 30N 74 15W
Suhaia, L. **46** 43 45N 25 15 E
Suhār **65** 24 20N 56 40 E
Suhbaatar **75** 50 17N 106 10 E
Suhl **24** 50 35N 10 40 E
Suhl □ **24** 50 37N 10 43 E
Sui Xian, Henan, China **77** 34 25N 115 2 E
Sui Xian, Henan, China **77** 31 42N 113 24 E
Suichang **77** 28 29N 119 15 E
Suichuan **77** 26 20N 114 32 E
Suide **76** 37 30N 110 12 E
Suifenhe **76** 44 25N 131 10 E
Suihua **75** 46 32N 126 55 E
Suining, Hunan, China **77** 26 35N 110 10 E
Suining, Sichuan, China **77** 30 26N 105 35 E
Suiping **77** 33 10N 113 59 E
Suippes **19** 49 8N 4 30 E
Suir ⤳ **15** 52 15N 7 10W
Suixi **77** 21 19N 110 18 E
Suizhong **76** 40 21N 120 20 E
Sujangarh **68** 27 42N 74 31 E
Sujica **42** 43 52N 17 11 E
Sukabumi **73** 6 56 S 106 50 E
Sukadana, Kalimantan, Indon. **72** 1 10 S 110 0 E
Sukadana, Sumatera, Indon. **72** 5 5 S 105 33 E
Sukaradja **72** 2 28 S 110 25 E
Sukarnapura = Jayapura **73** 2 37 S 140 38 E
Sukhindol **43** 43 11N 25 10 E
Sukhinichi **54** 54 8N 35 10 E
Sukhona ⤳ **52** 60 30N 45 0 E
Sukhumi **57** 43 0N 41 0 E
Sukkur **68** 27 42N 68 54 E
Sukkur Barrage **68** 27 40N 68 50 E
Sukma **70** 18 24N 81 45 E
Sukovo **42** 43 4N 22 37 E
Sukunka ⤳ **108** 55 45N 121 15W
Sula ⤳ **54** 49 40N 32 41 E
Sula, Kepulauan **73** 1 45 S 125 0 E
Sulaiman Range **68** 30 30N 69 50 E
Sulak ⤳ **57** 43 20N 47 34 E
Sulam Tsor **62** 33 4N 35 6 E
Sulawesi □ **73** 2 0 S 120 0 E
Sulechów **28** 52 5N 15 40 E
Sulęcin **28** 52 26N 15 10 E
Sulejów **28** 51 26N 19 53 E
Sulejówek **28** 52 13N 21 17 E
Sulima **84** 6 58N 11 32W
Sulina **46** 45 10N 29 40 E
Sulingen **24** 52 41N 8 47 E
Suliţa **46** 47 39N 26 59 E
Sulitälma **50** 67 17N 17 28 E
Sulitjelma **50** 67 9N 16 3 E
Sułkowice **27** 49 50N 19 49 E
Sullana **126** 4 52 S 80 39W
Sullivan, Ill., U.S.A. **116** 39 40N 88 40W
Sullivan, Ind., U.S.A. **114** 39 5N 87 26W
Sullivan, Mo., U.S.A. **116** 38 10N 91 10W
Sullivan Bay **108** 50 55N 126 50W
Sully-sur-Loire **19** 47 45N 2 20 E
Sulmierzyce **28** 51 37N 17 32 E
Sulmona **39** 42 3N 13 55 E
Sulphur, La., U.S.A. **117** 30 13N 93 22W
Sulphur, Okla., U.S.A. **117** 34 35N 97 0W
Sulphur Pt. **108** 60 56N 114 48W
Sulphur Springs **117** 33 5N 95 36W
Sulphur Springs, Cr. ⤳ **117** 32 12N 101 36W
Sultan **106** 47 36N 82 47W
Sultanpur **69** 26 18N 82 4 E
Sultsa **52** 63 27N 46 2 E
Sulu Arch. **73** 6 0N 121 0 E
Sulu Sea **73** 8 0N 120 0 E
Sululta **87** 9 10N 38 43 E
Suluq **83** 31 44N 20 14 E
Sulzbach **25** 49 18N 7 4 E
Sulzbach-Rosenberg **25** 49 30N 11 46 E
Sumalata **73** 1 0N 122 31 E
Sumampa **124** 29 25 S 63 29W
Sumatera □ **72** 0 40N 100 20 E
Sumatera Barat □ **72** 1 0 S 100 0 E
Sumatera Selatan □ **72** 3 30 S 104 0 E
Sumatera Utara □ **72** 2 0N 99 0 E
Sumatra **118** 46 38N 107 31W
Sumatra = Sumatera □ **72** 0 40N 100 20 E
Sumba **73** 9 45 S 119 35 E
Sumba, Selat **73** 9 0 S 118 40 E
Sumbawa **72** 8 26 S 117 30 E
Sumbawa Besar **72** 8 30 S 117 26 E
Sumbawanga □ **90** 8 0 S 31 30 E
Sumbing **73** 7 19 S 110 3 E
Sumburgh Hd. **14** 59 52N 1 17W
Sumedang **73** 6 49 S 107 56 E
Sümeg **27** 46 59N 17 20 E
Sumenep **73** 7 3 S 113 51 E
Sumgait **57** 40 34N 49 38 E
Summer L. **118** 42 50N 120 50W
Summerland **108** 49 32N 119 41W
Summerside **107** 46 24N 63 47W
Summerville, Ga., U.S.A. **115** 34 30N 85 20W
Summerville, S.C., U.S.A. **115** 33 2N 80 11W
Summit Lake **108** 54 20N 122 40W
Summit Pk. **119** 37 20N 106 48W
Sumner **116** 42 49N 92 7W
Sumperk **27** 49 59N 17 0 E
Sumter **115** 33 55N 80 22W
Sumy **54** 50 57N 34 50 E
Sunart, L. **14** 56 42N 5 43W
Sunburst **118** 48 56N 111 59W
Sunbury, Austral. **99** 37 35 S 144 44 E
Sunbury, U.S.A. **114** 40 50N 76 46W
Sunchales **124** 30 58 S 61 35W
Suncho Corral **124** 27 55 S 63 27W
Sunchon **77** 34 52N 127 31 E
Suncook **113** 43 8N 71 27W
Sunda Is. **94** 5 0 S 105 0 E
Sunda Kecil, Kepulauan **72** 7 30 S 117 0 E
Sunda, Selat **72** 6 20 S 105 30 E
Sundance **116** 44 27N 104 27W
Sundarbans, The **69** 22 0N 89 0 E
Sundargarh **69** 22 4N 84 5 E
Sundays = Sondags ⤳ **92** 33 44 S 25 51 E
Sundbyberg **48** 59 22N 17 58 E
Sunderland, Can. **112** 44 16N 79 4W
Sunderland, U.K. **12** 54 54N 1 22W
Sunderland, U.S.A. **113** 42 27N 72 36W
Sundre **108** 51 49N 114 38W
Sundridge **106** 45 45N 79 25W
Sunds **49** 56 13N 9 1 E
Sundsjö **48** 62 59N 15 9 E
Sundsvall **48** 62 23N 17 17 E
Sungaigerong **72** 2 59 S 104 52 E
Sungailiat **72** 1 51 S 106 8 E
Sungaipakning **72** 1 19N 102 0 E
Sungaipenuh **72** 2 1 S 101 20 E
Sungaitiram **72** 0 45 S 117 8 E
Sungari = Songhua Jiang ⤳ **76** 47 45N 132 30 E
Sungei Patani **71** 5 38N 100 29 E
Sungei Siput **71** 4 51N 101 6 E
Sungguminasa **73** 5 17 S 119 30 E
Sunghua Chiang = Songhua Jiang ⤳ **76** 47 45N 132 30 E
Sungikai **87** 12 20N 29 51 E
Sungtao Hu **77** 19 20N 109 35 E
Sungurlu **56** 40 12N 34 21 E
Sunja **39** 45 21N 16 35 E
Sunndalsøra **47** 62 40N 8 33 E
Sunne **48** 59 52N 13 5 E
Sunnfjord **47** 61 25N 5 18 E
Sunnyside, Utah, U.S.A. **118** 39 34N 110 24W
Sunnyside, Wash., U.S.A. **118** 46 24N 120 2W
Sunray **117** 36 1N 101 47W
Sunshine **100** 37 48 S 144 52 E
Suntar **59** 62 15N 117 30 E
Sunyani **84** 7 21N 2 22W
Suoyarvi **52** 62 12N 32 23 E
Supai **119** 36 14N 112 44W
Supaul **69** 26 10N 86 40 E
Superior, Ariz., U.S.A. **119** 33 19N 111 9W
Superior, Mont., U.S.A. **118** 47 15N 114 57W
Superior, Nebr., U.S.A. **116** 40 3N 98 2W
Superior, Wis., U.S.A. **116** 46 45N 92 5W
Superior, L. **111** 47 40N 87 0W
Supetar **39** 43 25N 16 32 E
Suphan Buri **71** 14 14N 100 10 E
Suphan Daği **64** 38 54N 42 48 E
Supraśl **28** 53 13N 23 19 E
Suq al Jum'ah **83** 32 58N 13 12 E
Sūq ash Shūyukh **64** 30 53N 46 28 E
Suqian **77** 33 54N 118 8 E
Sūr, Leb. **62** 33 19N 35 16 E
Sūr, Oman **65** 22 34N 59 32 E
Sur, Pt. **119** 36 18N 121 54W
Sura ⤳ **55** 56 6N 46 0 E
Surabaja = Surabaya **73** 7 17 S 112 45 E
Surabaya **73** 7 17 S 112 45 E
Surahammar **48** 59 43N 16 13 E
Suraia **46** 45 40N 27 25 E
Surakarta **73** 7 35 S 110 48 E
Surakhany **57** 40 25N 50 1 E
Surandai **70** 8 58N 77 26 E
Šurany **27** 48 6N 18 10 E
Surat, Austral. **99** 27 10 S 149 6 E
Surat, India **68** 21 12N 72 55 E
Surat Thani **71** 9 6N 99 20 E
Suratgarh **68** 29 18N 73 55 E
Suraz **28** 52 57N 22 57 E
Surazh, Byelorussia, U.S.S.R. **54** 55 25N 30 44 E
Surazh, R.S.F.S.R., U.S.S.R. **54** 53 5N 32 27 E
Surduc **46** 47 15N 23 25 E
Surduc Pasul **46** 45 21N 23 23 E
Surdulica **42** 42 41N 22 11 E
Sûre ⤳ **16** 49 44N 6 31 E
Surendranagar **68** 22 45N 71 40 E
Surgères **20** 46 7N 0 47W
Surgut **58** 61 14N 73 20 E
Suri **69** 23 50N 87 34 E
Surianu **46** 45 33N 23 31 E
Suriapet **70** 17 10N 79 40 E
Şūrīf **62** 31 40N 35 4 E
Surigao **73** 9 47N 125 29 E
Surin **71** 14 50N 103 34 E
Surinam ■ **127** 4 0N 56 0W
Suriname ⤳ **127** 5 50N 55 15W
Surmene **57** 41 0N 40 1 E
Surovikino **57** 48 32N 42 55 E
Surprise L. **108** 59 40N 133 15W
Surrey □ **13** 51 16N 0 30W
Sursee **25** 47 11N 8 6 E
Sursk **55** 53 3N 45 40 E
Surt **83** 31 11N 16 39 E
Surt, Al Hammadah al **83** 30 0N 17 50 E
Surt, Khalīj **83** 31 40N 18 30 E
Surtsey **50** 63 20N 20 30W
Suruga-Wan **74** 34 45N 138 30 E
Susa **38** 45 8N 7 3 E
Suså ⤳ **49** 55 20N 11 42 E
Sušac **39** 42 46N 16 30 E
Susak **39** 44 30N 14 18 E
Sūsangerd **64** 31 35N 48 6 E
Susanino **59** 52 50N 140 14 E
Susanville **118** 40 28N 120 40W
Sušice **26** 49 17N 13 30 E
Susquehanna ⤳ **114** 39 33N 76 5W
Susquehanna Depot **113** 41 55N 75 36W
Susques **124** 23 35 S 66 25W
Sussex, Can. **107** 45 45N 65 37W
Sussex, U.S.A. **113** 41 12N 74 38W
Sussex, E. □ **13** 51 0N 0 20 E
Sussex, W. □ **13** 51 0N 0 30W
Sustut ⤳ **108** 56 20N 127 30W
Susuman **59** 62 47N 148 10 E
Susunu **73** 3 20 S 133 25 E
Susz **28** 53 44N 19 20 E
Şuţeşti **46** 45 13N 27 27 E
Sutherland, S. Afr. **92** 32 33 S 20 40 E
Sutherland, U.S.A. **116** 41 12N 101 11W
Sutherland Falls **101** 44 48 S 167 46 E
Sutherland Pt. **97** 28 15 S 153 35 E
Sutherlin **118** 43 28N 123 16W
Sutivan **39** 43 23N 16 30 E
Sutlej ⤳ **68** 29 23N 71 3 E
Sutton, Can. **113** 45 6N 72 37W
Sutton, U.S.A. **116** 40 40N 97 50W
Sutton ⤳ **106** 55 15N 83 45W
Sutton-in-Ashfield **12** 53 7N 1 20W
Suttor ⤳ **98** 21 36 S 147 2 E
Suva **94** 18 6 S 178 30 E
Suva Gora **42** 41 45N 21 3 E
Suva Planina **42** 43 10N 22 5 E
Suva Reka **42** 42 21N 20 50 E
Suvo Rudïste **42** 43 17N 20 49 E
Suvorov **55** 54 7N 36 30 E
Suvorov Is. = Suwarrow Is. **95** 13 15 S 163 30W
Suvorovo **43** 43 20N 27 35 E
Suwałki **28** 54 8N 22 59 E
Suwałki □ **28** 54 0N 22 30 E
Suwannee ⤳ **115** 29 18N 83 9W
Suwanose Jima **74** 29 26N 129 30 E
Suwarrow Is. **95** 15 0 S 163 0W
Suweis, Khalîg el **86** 28 40N 33 0 E
Suweis, Qanâl es **86** 31 0N 32 20 E
Suwŏn **76** 37 17N 127 1 E
Suzdal **55** 56 29N 40 26 E
Suze, La **18** 47 54N 0 2 E
Suzhou **75** 31 19N 120 38 E
Suzu-Misaki **74** 37 31N 137 21 E
Suzuka **74** 34 55N 136 36 E
Suzzara **38** 45 0N 10 45 E
Svalbard **4** 78 0N 17 0 E
Svalbarð **50** 66 12N 15 43W
Svalöv **49** 55 57N 13 8 E
Svanvik **50** 69 25N 30 3 E
Svappavaara **50** 67 40N 21 03 E
Svarstad **47** 59 27N 9 56 E
Svartisen **50** 66 40N 13 50 E
Svartvik **48** 62 19N 17 24 E
Svatovo **56** 49 35N 38 11 E
Svay Rieng **71** 11 9N 105 45 E
Sveio **47** 59 33N 5 23 E
Svendborg **49** 55 4N 10 35 E
Svene **47** 59 45N 9 31 E
Svenljunga **49** 57 29N 13 5 E
Svenstrup **49** 56 58N 9 50 E
Sverdlovsk, R.S.F.S.R., U.S.S.R. **52** 56 50N 60 30 E
Sverdlovsk, Ukraine S.S.R., U.S.S.R. **57** 48 5N 39 37 E
Sverdrup Is. **4** 79 0N 97 0W
Svetac **39** 43 3N 15 43 E
Sveti Ivan Zelina **39** 45 57N 16 16 E
Sveti Jurij **39** 46 14N 15 24 E
Sveti Lenart **39** 46 36N 15 48 E
Sveti Nikola, Prokhad **42** 43 27N 22 6 E
Sveti Nikole **42** 41 51N 21 56 E
Sveti Rok **39** 40 1N 9 6 E
Sveti Trojica **39** 46 37N 15 50 E
Svetlogorsk **54** 52 38N 29 46 E
Svetlograd **57** 45 25N 42 58 E
Svetlovodsk **54** 49 2N 33 13 E
Svetozarevo **42** 44 5N 21 15 E
Svidník **27** 49 20N 21 37 E
Svilaja Pl. **39** 43 49N 16 31 E
Svilajnac **42** 44 15N 21 11 E
Svilengrad **43** 41 49N 26 12 E
Svir ⤳ **52** 60 30N 32 48 E
Svishtov **43** 43 36N 25 23 E
Svisloch **54** 53 3N 24 2 E
Svitava ⤳ **27** 49 30N 16 37 E
Svitavy **27** 49 47N 16 28 E
Svobodnyy **59** 51 20N 128 0 E
Svoge **43** 42 59N 23 23 E
Svolvær **50** 68 15N 14 34 E
Svratka ⤳ **27** 49 11N 16 38 E
Svrljig **42** 43 25N 22 6 E
Swabian Alps = Schäbischer Alb **25** 48 30N 9 30 E
Swain Reefs **97** 21 45 S 152 20 E
Swainsboro **115** 32 38N 82 22W
Swakopmund **92** 22 37 S 14 30 E
Swale ⤳ **12** 54 5N 1 20W
Swan ⤳ **96** 32 3 S 115 45 E
Swan Hill **97** 35 20 S 143 33 E
Swan Hills **108** 54 42N 115 24W
Swan Islands **121** 17 22N 83 57W
Swan L. **109** 52 30N 100 40W
Swan River **109** 52 10N 101 16W
Swanage **13** 50 36N 1 59W
Swansea, Austral. **99** 33 3 S 151 35 E
Swansea, U.K. **13** 51 37N 3 57W
Swartberge **92** 33 20 S 22 0 E
Swartruggens **92** 25 39 S 26 42 E
Swarzędz **28** 52 25N 17 4 E
Swastika **106** 48 7N 80 6W
Swatow = Shantou **76** 23 18N 116 40 E
Swaziland ■ **93** 26 30 S 31 30 E
Sweden ■ **50** 67 0N 15 0 E
Swedru **85** 5 32N 0 41W
Sweet Home **118** 44 26N 122 25W
Sweetwater **117** 32 30N 100 28W
Sweetwater ⤳ **118** 42 31N 107 2W
Swellendam **92** 34 1 S 20 26 E
Swider ⤳ **28** 52 6N 21 14 E
Świdnica **28** 50 50N 16 30 E
Świdnik **28** 51 13N 22 39 E
Świdwin **28** 53 47N 15 49 E
Świebodzice **28** 50 51N 16 20 E
Świebodzin **28** 52 15N 15 31 E
Świecie **28** 53 25N 18 30 E
Świętokrzyskie, Góry **28** 51 0N 20 30 E
Swift Current **109** 50 20N 107 45W
Swiftcurrent ⤳ **109** 50 38N 107 44W
Swilly, L. **15** 55 12N 7 35W
Swindle, I. **108** 52 30N 128 35W
Swindon **13** 51 33N 1 47W
Swinemünde = Świnoujście **28** 53 54N 14 16 E
Świnoujście **28** 53 54N 14 16 E
Switzerland ■ **25** 46 30N 8 0 E
Swords **15** 53 27N 6 15W
Syasstroy **54** 60 5N 32 15 E
Sychevka **54** 55 59N 34 16 E
Syców **28** 51 19N 17 40 E
Sydney, Austral. **97** 33 53 S 151 10 E
Sydney, Can. **107** 46 7N 60 7W
Sydney, U.S.A. **116** 41 12N 103 0W
Sydney Mines **107** 46 18N 60 15W
Sydprøven **4** 60 30N 45 35W
Sydra G. of = Surt, Khalīj **35** 31 40N 18 30 E
Syke **24** 52 55N 8 50 E
Syktyvkar **52** 61 45N 50 40 E
Sylacauga **115** 33 10N 86 15W
Sylarna **50** 63 2N 12 13 E
Sylhet **67** 24 54N 91 52 E
Sylt **24** 54 50N 8 20 E
Sylvan Lake **108** 52 20N 114 03W
Sylvania **115** 32 45N 81 37W
Sylvester **115** 31 31N 83 50W
Sym **58** 60 20N 88 18 E
Syracuse, Kans., U.S.A. **117** 38 0N 101 46W
Syracuse, N.Y., U.S.A. **114** 43 4N 76 11W
Syrdarya ⤳ **58** 46 3N 61 0 E
Syria ■ **64** 35 0N 38 0 E
Syriam **69** 16 44N 96 19 E
Syrian Desert **60** 31 0N 40 0 E
Syul'dzhyukyor **59** 63 14N 113 32 E
Syutkya **43** 41 50N 24 16 E
Syzran **55** 53 12N 48 30 E
Szabolcs-Szatmár □ **27** 48 2N 21 45 E
Szamocin **28** 53 2N 17 7 E
Szamos ⤳ **27** 48 7N 22 20 E
Szaraz ⤳ **27** 46 28N 20 44 E
Szarvas **27** 46 50N 20 38 E
Szazhalombatta **27** 47 20N 18 58 E
Szczawnica **27** 49 26N 20 30 E
Szczebrzeszyn **28** 50 42N 22 59 E
Szczecin **28** 53 27N 14 27 E
Szczecin □ **28** 53 25N 14 32 E
Szczecinek **28** 53 43N 16 41 E
Szczekocimy **28** 50 38N 19 48 E
Szczucin **28** 50 18N 21 4 E
Szczuczyn **28** 53 36N 22 19 E
Szczytno **28** 53 33N 21 0 E
Szechwan = Sichuan □ **75** 31 0N 104 0 E
Szécsény **27** 48 7N 19 30 E
Szeged **27** 46 16N 20 10 E
Szeghalom **27** 47 1N 21 10 E
Székesfehérvár **27** 47 15N 18 25 E
Szekszárd **27** 46 22N 18 42 E
Szendrö **27** 48 24N 20 41 E
Szentendre **27** 47 39N 19 4 E
Szentes **27** 46 39N 20 21 E
Szentgotthárd **27** 46 58N 16 19 E
Szentlörinc **27** 46 3N 18 1 E
Szerencs **27** 48 10N 21 12 E
Szigetvár **27** 46 3N 17 46 E
Szikszó **27** 48 12N 20 56 E
Szkwa ⤳ **28** 53 11N 21 43 E
Szlichtyngowa **28** 51 42N 16 15 E
Szob **27** 47 48N 18 53 E
Szolnok **27** 47 10N 20 15 E
Szolnok □ **27** 47 15N 20 30 E
Szombathely **27** 47 14N 16 38 E
Szprotawa **28** 51 33N 15 35 E
Sztum **28** 53 55N 19 1 E
Sztutowo **28** 54 20N 19 15 E
Szubin **28** 53 1N 17 45 E
Szydłowiec **28** 51 15N 20 51 E
Szypliszki **28** 54 17N 23 2 E

T

Tabacal **124** 23 15 S 64 15W
Tabaco **73** 13 22N 123 44 E
Tabagné **84** 7 59N 3 4W
Ţābah **64** 26 55N 42 38 E
Tabar Is. **98** 2 50 S 152 0 E
Tabarca, Isla de **33** 38 17N 0 30W
Tabarka **83** 36 56N 8 46 E
Ţabas, Khorāsān, Iran **65** 33 35N 56 55 E
Ţabas, Khorāsān, Iran **65** 32 48N 60 12 E
Tabasará, Serranía de **121** 8 35N 81 40W
Tabasco □ **120** 17 45N 93 30W
Tabatinga, Serra da **127** 10 30 S 44 0W

Tabelbala, Kahal de
Tarp

Tabelbala, Kahal de 82 28 47N 2 0W
Tabelkaza 80 29 50N 0 55 E
Taber 108 49 47N 112 8W
Tabernas 33 37 4N 2 26W
Tabernes de Valldigna 33 39 5N 0 13W
Tablas 73 12 25N 122 2 E
Table B. 107 53 40N 56 25W
Table Mt. 92 34 0S 18 22 E
Table Top, Mt. 98 23 24S 147 11 E
Tábor 26 49 25N 14 39 E
Tabor 62 32 42N 35 24 E
Tabora 90 5 2S 32 50 E
Tabora □ 90 5 0S 33 0 E
Tabou 84 4 30N 7 20W
Tabrīz 64 38 7N 46 20 E
Tabuenca 32 41 42N 1 33W
Tabūk 64 28 23N 36 36 E
Tacheng 75 46 40N 82 58 E
Tach'ing Shan = Daqing Shan 76 40 40N 111 0 E
Tachov 26 49 47N 12 39 E
Tácina → 41 38 57N 16 55 E
Tacloban 73 11 15N 124 58 E
Tacna 126 18 0S 70 20W
Tacoma 118 47 15N 122 30W
Tacuarembó 125 31 45S 56 0W
Tademaït, Plateau du 82 28 30N 2 30 E
Tadent, O. → 83 22 25N 6 40 E
Tadjerdjeri, O. → 83 26 0N 8 0W
Tadjerouna 82 33 31N 2 3 E
Tadjettaret, O. → 83 21 20N 7 22 E
Tadjmout, Atlas, Alg. 82 33 52N 2 30 E
Tadjmout, Sahara, Alg. 82 25 37N 3 48 E
Tadjoura 87 11 50N 42 55 E
Tadjoura, Golfe de 87 11 50N 43 0 E
Tadmor 101 41 27S 172 45 E
Tadoule, L. 109 58 36N 98 20W
Tadoussac 107 48 11N 69 42W
Tadzhik S.S.R. □ 58 35 30N 70 0 E
Taegu 76 35 50N 128 37 E
Taejŏn 76 36 20N 127 28 E
Tafalla 32 42 30N 1 41W
Tafar 87 6 52N 28 15 E
Ţafas 62 32 44N 36 5 E
Tafassasset, O. → 83 22 0N 9 57 E
Tafelbaai 92 33 35S 18 25 E
Tafelney, C. 82 31 3N 9 51W
Tafermaar 73 6 47S 134 10 E
Taffermit 82 29 37N 9 15W
Tafí Viejo 124 26 43S 65 17W
Tafiré 84 9 4N 5 4W
Tafnidilt 82 28 47N 10 58W
Tafraoute 82 29 50N 8 58W
Taft, Phil. 73 11 57N 125 30 E
Taft, Calif., U.S.A. 119 35 9N 119 28W
Taft, Tex., U.S.A. 117 27 58N 97 23W
Taga Dzong 69 27 5N 89 55 E
Taganrog 57 47 12N 38 50 E
Taganrogskiy Zaliv 56 47 0N 38 30 E
Tagânt 84 18 20N 11 0W
Tagbilaran 73 9 39N 123 51 E
Tággia 38 43 52N 7 50 E
Taghrīfat 83 29 5N 17 26 E
Taghzout 82 33 30N 4 49W
Tagish 108 60 19N 134 16W
Tagish L. 104 60 10N 134 20W
Tagliacozzo 39 42 4N 13 13 E
Tagliamento → 39 45 38N 13 5 E
Táglio di Po 39 45 0N 12 12 E
Tagomago, I. de 33 39 2N 1 39 E
Taguatinga 127 12 16S 42 26W
Tagula I. 98 11 30S 153 30 E
Tagum (Hijo) 73 7 33N 125 53 E
Tagus = Tajo → 29 39 44N 5 50W
Tahakopa 101 46 30S 169 23 E
Tahala 82 34 0N 4 28W
Tahan, Gunong 71 4 34N 102 17 E
Tahat 83 23 18N 5 33 E
Tāherī 65 27 43N 52 20 E
Tahiti 95 17 37S 149 27W
Tahoe City 118 39 12N 120 9W
Tahoe, L. 118 39 0N 120 9W
Tahoua 85 14 57N 5 16 E
Tahta 86 26 44N 31 32 E
Tahulandang 73 2 27N 125 23 E
Tahuna 73 3 38N 125 30 E
Taï 84 5 55N 7 30W
Tai Hu 75 31 5N 120 10 E
Tai Shan 76 36 25N 117 20 E
Tai'an 76 36 12N 117 8 E
Taibei 75 25 4N 121 29 E
Taibus Qi 76 41 54N 115 22 E
T'aichung = Taizhong 75 24 10N 120 38 E
Taidong 75 22 43N 121 9 E
Taieri → 101 46 3S 170 12 E
Taiga Madema 83 23 46N 15 25 E
Taigu 76 37 28N 112 30 E
Taihang Shan 76 36 0N 113 30 E
Taihape 101 39 41S 175 48 E
Taihe 77 26 47N 114 52 E
Taihu 77 30 22N 116 20 E
Taijiang 77 26 39N 108 21 E
Taikang, Heilongjiang, China 76 46 50N 124 25 E
Taikang, Henan, China 77 34 5N 114 50 E
Taikkyi 69 17 20N 96 0 E
Tailai 76 46 23N 123 24 E
Tailem Bend 99 35 12S 139 29 E
Tailfingen 25 48 15N 9 1 E
Taimyr = Taymyr 59 75 0N 100 0 E
Taimyr, Oz. 59 74 20N 102 0 E
Tain 14 57 49N 4 4W
Tainan 77 23 17N 120 18 E
Taínaron, Ákra 45 36 22N 22 27 E
Taining 77 26 54N 117 9 E
T'aipei = Taibei 75 25 4N 121 29 E
Taiping 71 4 51N 100 44 E
Taishan 77 22 14N 112 41 E
Taishun 77 27 30N 119 42 E
Taita □ 90 4 0S 38 30 E
Taita Hills 90 3 25S 38 15 E
Taitao, Pen. de 128 46 30S 75 0W
Taivalkoski 50 65 33N 28 12 E
Taiwan ■ 75 24 0N 121 0 E
Taïyetos Óros 45 37 0N 22 23 E
Taiyib → 62 31 55N 35 17 E
Taiyiba 62 32 36N 35 27 E
Taiyuan 76 37 52N 112 33 E
Taizhong 77 24 12N 120 35 E
Taizhou 77 32 28N 119 55 E
Ta'izz 63 13 35N 44 2 E
Tajarḥī 83 24 21N 14 28 E
Tajo → 31 38 40N 9 24W
Tajumulco, Volcán de 120 15 2N 91 50W
Tājūrā 83 32 51N 13 21 E
Tak 71 16 52N 99 8 E
Takada 74 37 7N 138 15 E
Takaka 101 40 51S 172 50 E
Takamatsu 74 34 20N 134 5 E
Takanabe 74 32 8N 131 30 E
Takaoka 74 36 47N 137 0 E
Takapuna 101 36 47S 174 47 E
Takasaki 74 36 20N 139 0 E
Takatsuki 74 34 51N 135 37 E
Takaungu 90 3 38S 39 52 E
Takayama 74 36 18N 137 11 E
Takefu 74 35 50N 136 10 E
Takengeun 72 4 45N 96 50 E
Takeo 71 10 59N 104 47 E
Tåkern 49 58 22N 14 45 E
Tākestān 64 36 0N 49 40 E
Takhar □ 65 36 40N 70 0 E
Takla L. 108 55 15N 125 45W
Takla Landing 108 55 30N 125 50W
Takla Makan 60 39 0N 83 0 E
Takla Makan = Taklimakan Shamo 75 38 0N 83 0 E
Taklimakan Shamo 75 38 0N 83 0 E
Taku → 108 58 30N 133 50W
Takua Pa 71 7 18N 9 59 E
Takum 85 7 18N 9 36 E
Tala 125 34 21S 55 46W
Talagante 124 33 40S 70 50W
Talaïnt 82 29 41N 9 40W
Talak 85 18 0N 5 0 E
Talamanca, Cordillera de 121 9 20N 83 20W
Talara 126 4 38S 81 18 E
Talas 58 42 30N 72 13 E
Talasea 98 5 20S 150 2 E
Talata Mafara 85 12 38N 6 4 E
Talaud, Kepulauan 73 4 30N 127 10 E
Talavera de la Reina 30 39 55N 4 46W
Talayan 73 6 52N 124 24 E
Talbert, Sillon de 18 48 53N 3 5W
Talbot, C. 96 13 48S 126 43 E
Talbragar → 99 32 12S 148 37 E
Talca 124 35 28S 71 40W
Talca □ 124 35 20S 71 46W
Talcahuano 124 36 40S 73 10W
Talcher 69 21 0N 85 18 E
Talcho 85 14 44N 3 28 E
Taldy Kurgan 58 45 10N 78 45 E
Ţalesh, Kūhhā-ye 64 39 0N 48 30 E
Talfit 62 32 5N 35 17 E
Talguharai 86 18 19N 35 56 E
Tali Post 87 5 55N 30 44 E
Taliabu 73 1 45S 125 0 E
Talibon 73 10 9N 124 20 E
Talihina 117 34 45N 95 1W
Talikoti 70 16 29N 76 17 E
Taling Sung 71 15 5N 99 11 E
Taliwang 72 8 50S 116 55 E
Talkeetna 104 62 20N 150 9W
Tall 62 33 0N 35 6 E
Tall 'Afar 64 36 22N 42 27 E
Tall 'Asūr 62 31 59N 35 17 E
Talla 86 28 5N 30 43 E
Talladega 115 33 28N 86 2W
Tallahassee 115 30 25N 84 15W
Tallangatta 99 36 15S 147 19 E
Tallarook 99 37 5S 145 6 E
Tällberg 48 60 51N 15 2 E
Tallering Pk. 96 28 6S 115 37 E
Tallinn 54 59 22N 24 48 E
Tallulah 117 32 25N 91 12W
Ţallūzā 62 32 17N 35 18 E
Tălmaciu 46 45 38N 24 19 E
Talmest 82 31 48N 9 21W
Talmont 20 46 27N 1 37W
Talnoye 56 48 50N 30 44 E
Taloda 68 21 34N 74 11 E
Talodi 87 10 35N 30 22 E
Talovaya 55 51 6N 40 45 E
Talsi 54 57 10N 22 30 E
Talsinnt 82 32 33N 3 27W
Taltal 124 25 23S 70 33W
Taltson → 108 61 24N 112 46W
Taltson L. 109 61 30N 110 15W
Talwood 99 28 29S 149 29 E
Talyawalka Cr. → 99 32 28S 142 22 E
Tama 116 41 56N 92 37W
Tamale 85 9 22N 0 50W
Taman 56 45 14N 36 41 E
Tamanar 82 31 1N 9 46W
Tamano 74 34 29N 133 59 E
Tamanrasset 83 22 50N 5 30 E
Tamanrasset, O. → 82 22 0N 2 0 E
Tamaqua 113 40 46N 75 58W
Tamar → 13 50 33N 4 15W
Tamarite de Litera 32 41 52N 0 25 E
Tamási 27 46 40N 18 18 E
Tamaské 85 14 49N 5 43 E
Tamaulipas □ 120 24 0N 99 0W
Tamaulipas, Sierra de 120 23 30N 98 20W
Tamazula 120 24 55N 106 58W
Tamba-Dabatou 84 11 50N 10 40W
Tambacounda 84 13 45N 13 40W
Tambelan, Kepulauan 72 1 0N 107 30 E
Tambo 98 24 54S 146 14 E
Tambo de Mora 126 13 30S 76 8W
Tambohorano 93 17 30S 43 58 E
Tambora 72 8 12S 118 5 E
Tambov 55 52 45N 41 28 E
Tambre → 30 42 49N 8 53W
Tambuku 73 7 8S 113 40 E
Tamburâ 87 5 40N 27 25 E
Tâmchekket 84 17 25N 10 40W
Tamega → 30 41 5N 8 21W
Tamelelt 82 31 50N 7 32W
Tamenglong 67 25 0N 93 35 E
Tamerza 83 34 23N 7 58 E
Tamgak, Mts. 80 19 12N 8 35 E
Tamiahua, Laguna de 120 21 30N 97 30W
Tamil Nadu □ 70 11 0N 77 0 E
Tamluk 69 22 18N 87 58 E
Tammerfors = Tampere 51 61 30N 23 50 E
Tammisaari 51 60 0N 23 26 E
Ţammūn 62 32 18N 35 23 E
Tämnaren 48 60 10N 17 25 E
Tamo Abu, Pegunungan 72 3 10N 115 0 E
Tampa 115 27 57N 82 38W
Tampa B. 115 27 40N 82 40W
Tampere 51 61 30N 23 50 E
Tampico 120 22 20N 97 50W
Tampin 71 2 28N 102 13 E
Tamri 82 30 49N 9 50W
Tamrida = Hadibu 63 12 35N 54 2 E
Tamsagbulag 75 47 14N 117 21 E
Tamsalu 54 59 11N 26 8 E
Tamsweg 26 47 7N 13 49 E
Tamu 67 24 13N 94 12 E
Tamuja → 31 39 38N 6 29W
Tamworth, Austral. 97 31 7S 150 58 E
Tamworth, U.K. 13 52 38N 1 41W
Tan-tan 82 28 29N 11 1W
Tana 50 70 26N 28 14 E
Tana →, Kenya 90 2 32S 40 31 E
Tana →, Norway 50 70 30N 28 23 E
Tana, L. 87 13 5N 37 30 E
Tana River 90 2 0S 39 30 E
Tanafjorden 50 70 45N 28 25 E
Tanagro → 41 40 35N 15 25 E
Tanahbala 72 0 30S 98 30 E
Tanahgrogot 72 1 55S 116 15 E
Tanahjampea 73 7 10S 120 35 E
Tanahmasa 72 0 12S 98 39 E
Tanahmerah 73 6 5S 140 16 E
Tanakura 74 37 10N 140 20 E
Tanami Des. 96 18 50S 132 0 E
Tanana 104 65 10N 152 15W
Tanana → 104 65 9N 151 55W
Tananarive = Antananarivo 93 18 55S 47 35 E
Tanannt 82 31 54N 6 56W
Tánaro → 38 45 1N 8 47 E
Tanaunella 40 40 42N 9 45 E
Tancarville 18 49 29N 0 28 E
Tanchŏn 76 40 27N 128 54 E
Tanda, U.P., India 68 28 57N 78 56 E
Tanda, U.P., India 69 26 33N 82 35 E
Tanda, Ivory C. 84 7 48N 3 10W
Tandag 73 9 4N 126 9 E
Tandaia 91 9 25S 34 15 E
Tăndărei 46 44 39N 27 40 E
Tandaué 92 16 58S 18 5 E
Tandil 124 37 15S 59 6W
Tandil, Sa. del 124 37 30S 59 0W
Tandlianwala 68 31 3N 73 9 E
Tando Adam 68 25 45N 68 40 E
Tandou L. 99 32 40S 142 5 E
Tandsbyn 48 63 0N 14 45 E
Tandur 70 19 11N 79 30 E
Tane-ga-Shima 74 30 30N 131 0 E
Taneatua 101 38 4S 177 1 E
Tanen Tong Dan 67 16 30N 98 30 E
Tanew → 28 50 29N 22 16 E
Tanezrouft 82 23 9N 0 11 E
Tanga 88 5 5S 39 2 E
Tanga □ 90 5 20S 38 0 E
Tanga Is. 98 3 20S 153 15 E
Tangail 69 24 15N 89 55 E
Tanganyika, L. 90 6 40S 30 0 E
Tanger 82 35 50N 5 49W
Tangerang 73 6 12S 106 39 E
Tangerhütte 24 52 26N 11 50 E
Tangermünde 24 52 32N 11 57 E
Tanggu 76 39 2N 117 40 E
Tanggula Shan 75 32 40N 92 10 E
Tanghe 77 32 47N 112 50 E
Tangier = Tanger 82 35 50N 5 49W
Tangkak 71 2 18N 102 34 E
Tangorin P.O. 98 21 47S 144 12 E
Tangshan 76 39 38N 118 10 E
Tanguiéta 85 10 35N 1 21 E
Tanimbar, Kepulauan 73 7 30S 131 30 E
Taninges 21 46 7N 6 36 E
Tanjay 73 9 30N 123 5 E
Tanjore = Thanjavur 70 10 48N 79 12 E
Tanjung 72 2 10S 115 25 E
Tanjungbalai 72 2 55N 99 44 E
Tanjungbatu 72 2 23N 118 3 E
Tanjungkarang 72 5 20S 105 10 E
Tanjungpandan 72 2 43S 107 38 E
Tanjungpinang 72 1 5N 104 30 E
Tanjungpriok 73 6 8S 106 55 E
Tanjungredeb 72 2 9N 117 29 E
Tanjungselor 72 2 55N 117 25 E
Tank 68 32 14N 70 25 E
Tänndalen 48 62 33N 12 18 E
Tannis Bugt 49 57 40N 10 15 E
Tannu-Ola 59 51 0N 94 0 E
Tano → 84 5 7N 2 56W
Tanout 85 14 50N 8 55 E
Tanta 86 30 45N 30 57 E
Tantoyuca 120 21 21N 98 10W
Tantung = Dandong 76 40 10N 124 20 E
Tantūra = Dor 62 32 37N 34 55 E
Tanuku 70 16 45N 81 44 E
Tanumshede 49 58 42N 11 20 E
Tanunda 99 34 30S 139 0 E
Tanur 70 11 1N 75 52 E
Tanus 20 44 8N 2 19 E
Tanzania ■ 90 6 40S 34 0 E
Tanzilla → 108 58 8N 130 43W
Tao'an 76 45 22N 122 40 E
Taormina 41 37 52N 15 16 E
Taos 119 36 28N 105 35W
Taoudenni 82 22 40N 3 55W
Taoudrart, Adrar 82 24 25N 2 24 E
Taounate 82 34 25N 4 41W
Taourirt, Alg. 82 26 37N 0 20 E
Taourirt, Moroc. 82 34 25N 2 53W
Taouz 82 30 53N 4 0W
Taoyuan, China 77 28 55N 111 16 E
Taoyuan, Taiwan 77 25 0N 121 13 E
Tapa 54 59 15N 25 50 E
Tapa Shan = Daba Shan 75 31 50N 109 20 E
Tapachula 120 14 54N 92 17W
Tapah 71 4 12N 101 15 E
Tapajós → 127 2 24S 54 41W
Tapaktuan 72 3 15N 97 10 E
Tapanui 101 45 56S 169 18 E
Tapauá → 126 5 40S 64 21W
Tapeta 84 6 29N 8 52W
Tapia 30 43 34N 6 56W
Tápiószele 27 47 25N 19 55 E
Tapirapecó, Serra 126 1 10N 65 0W
Tapolca 27 46 53N 17 29 E
Tappahannock 114 37 56N 76 50W
Tapti → 68 21 8N 72 41 E
Tapuaenuku, Mt. 101 42 0S 173 39 E
Tapul Group 73 5 35N 120 50 E
Taquara 125 29 36S 50 46W
Taquari → 126 19 15S 57 17W
Tar Island 108 57 3N 111 40W
Tara, Austral. 99 27 17S 150 31 E
Tara, Can. 112 44 28N 81 9W
Tara, U.S.S.R. 58 56 55N 74 24 E
Tara, Zambia 91 16 58S 26 45 E
Tara →, U.S.S.R. 58 56 42N 74 36 E
Tara →, Yugo. 42 43 21N 18 51 E
Tarabagatay, Khrebet 58 48 0N 83 0 E
Tarābulus, Leb. 64 34 31N 35 50 E
Tarābulus, Libya 83 32 49N 13 7 E
Tarahouahout 83 22 41N 5 59 E
Tarakan 72 3 20N 117 35 E
Tarakit, Mt. 90 2 2N 35 10 E
Taralga 99 34 26S 149 52 E
Taranagar 68 28 43N 74 50 E
Taranaki □ 101 39 5S 174 51 E
Tarancón 32 40 1N 3 1W
Taranga 68 23 56N 72 43 E
Taranga Hill 68 24 0N 72 40 E
Táranto 41 40 30N 17 11 E
Táranto, G. di 41 40 0N 17 15 E
Tarapacá 126 2 56S 69 46W
Tarapacá □ 124 20 45S 69 30W
Tarare 21 45 54N 4 26 E
Tararua Range 101 40 45S 175 25 E
Tarascon, Ariège, France 20 42 50N 1 37 E
Tarascon, Bouches-du-Rhône, France 21 43 48N 4 39 E
Tarashcha 56 49 30N 30 31 E
Tarat 80 25 55N 9 3 E
Tarat, Bj. 83 26 13N 9 18 E
Tarauacá 126 8 6S 70 48W
Tarauacá → 126 6 42S 69 48W
Taravo → 21 41 42N 8 49 E
Tarawera 101 39 2S 176 36 E
Tarawera L. 101 38 13S 176 27 E
Tarazona 32 41 55N 1 43W
Tarazona de la Mancha 33 39 16N 1 55W
Tarbat Ness 14 57 52N 3 48W
Tarbert, Strathclyde, U.K. 14 55 55N 5 25W
Tarbert, W. Isles, U.K. 14 57 54N 6 49W
Tarbes 20 43 15N 0 3 E
Tarboro 115 35 55N 77 30W
Tarbrax 98 21 7S 142 26 E
Tarbū 83 26 0N 15 5 E
Tarcento 39 46 12N 13 12 E
Tarcoola 96 30 44S 134 36 E
Tarcoon 99 30 15S 146 43 E
Tardets-Sorholus 20 43 8N 0 52W
Tardoire → 20 45 52N 0 14 E
Taree 97 31 50S 152 30 E
Tarentaise 21 45 30N 6 35 E
Tarf, Ras 82 35 40N 5 11W
Tarf Shaqq al Abd 86 26 50N 36 6 E
Tarfa, Wadi el → 86 28 25N 30 50 E
Tarfaya 80 27 55N 12 55W
Targon 20 44 44N 0 16W
Targuist 82 34 59N 4 14W
Tărhăus 46 46 40N 26 8 E
Tărhăus, Munţii 46 46 39N 26 7 E
Tarhbalt 82 30 39N 5 20W
Tarhit 82 30 58N 2 0W
Tarhūnah 83 32 27N 13 36 E
Tarib, Wadi → 86 18 30N 43 23 E
Tarifa 31 36 1N 5 36W
Tarija 124 21 30S 64 40W
Tarija □ 124 21 30S 63 30W
Tariku → 73 2 55S 138 26 E
Tarim He → 75 39 30N 88 30 E
Tarim Pendi 75 40 0N 84 0 E
Tarime □ 90 1 15S 34 0 E
Taritatu → 73 2 54S 138 27 E
Tarka → 92 32 10S 26 0 E
Tarkastad 92 32 0S 26 16 E
Tarkhankut, Mys 56 45 25N 32 30 E
Tarko Sale 58 64 55N 77 50 E
Tarkwa 84 5 20N 2 0W
Tarlac 73 15 29N 120 35 E
Tarm 49 55 56N 8 31 E
Tarma 126 11 25S 75 45W
Tarn □ 20 43 49N 2 8 E
Tarn → 20 44 5N 1 6 E
Tarn-et-Garonne □ 20 44 8N 1 20 E
Tarna → 27 47 31N 19 59 E
Tårnby 49 55 37N 12 36 E
Tarnica 27 49 4N 22 44 E
Tarnobrzeg 28 50 35N 21 41 E
Tarnobrzeg □ 28 50 40N 22 0 E
Tarnogród 28 50 22N 22 45 E
Tarnów 27 50 3N 21 0 E
Tarnów □ 27 50 0N 21 0 E
Tarnowskie Góry 28 50 27N 18 54 E
Táro → 38 45 0N 10 15 E
Tarong 99 26 47S 151 51 E
Taroom 97 25 36S 149 48 E
Taroudannt 82 30 30N 8 52W
Tarp 24 54 40N 9 25 E

Tarpon Springs　　Thaon

Tarpon Springs	**115**	28 8N	82 42W
Tarquínia	**39**	42 15N	11 45 E
Tarqūmiyah	**62**	31 35N	35 1 E
Tarragona	**32**	41 5N	1 17 E
Tarragona □	**32**	41 . 0N	1 0 E
Tarrasa	**32**	41 34N	2 1 E
Tárrega	**32**	41 39N	1 9 E
Tarrytown	**113**	41 5N	73 52W
Tarshiha = Me'ona	**62**	33 1N	35 15 E
Tarso Emissi	**83**	21 27N	18 36 E
Tarso Ourari	**83**	21 27N	17 27 E
Tarsus	**64**	36 58N	34 55 E
Tartagal	**124**	22 30 S	63 50W
Tartas	**20**	43 50N	0 49W
Tartna Point	**99**	32 54 S	142 24 E
Tartu	**54**	58 20N	26 44 E
Tarţūs	**64**	34 55N	35 55 E
Tarussa	**55**	54 44N	37 10 E
Tarutao, Ko	**71**	6 33N	99 40 E
Tarutung	**72**	2 0N	98 54 E
Tarvisio	**39**	46 31N	13 35 E
Tarz Ulli	**83**	25 32N	10 8 E
Tasāwah	**83**	26 0N	13 30 E
Taschereau	**106**	48 40N	78 40W
Taseko →	**108**	52 4N	123 9W
Tasgaon	**70**	17 2N	74 39 E
Tash-Kumyr	**58**	41 40N	72 10 E
Ta'shan	**87**	16 31N	42 33 E
Tashauz	**58**	41 49N	59 58 E
Tashi Chho Dzong = Thimphu	**69**	27 31N	89 45 E
Tashkent	**58**	41 20N	69 10 E
Tashtagol	**58**	52 47N	87 53 E
Tasikmalaya	**73**	7 18 S	108 12 E
Tåsjön	**50**	64 15N	16 0 E
Taskan	**59**	62 59N	150 20 E
Taskopru	**56**	41 30N	34 15 E
Tasman B.	**101**	40 59 S	173 25 E
Tasman Mts.	**101**	41 3 S	172 25 E
Tasman Pen.	**97**	43 10 S	148 0 E
Tasman Sea	**94**	36 0 S	160 0 E
Tasmania □	**97**	42 0 S	146 30 E
Tăşnad	**46**	47 30N	22 33 E
Tassil Tin-Rerhoh	**82**	20 5N	3 55 E
Tassili n-Ajjer	**83**	25 47N	8 1 E
Tassili-Oua-n-Ahaggar	**83**	20 41N	5 30 E
Tasu Sd.	**108**	52 47N	132 2W
Tata, Hung.	**27**	47 37N	18 19 E
Tata, Moroc.	**82**	29 46N	7 56W
Tatabánya	**27**	47 32N	18 25 E
Tatahouine	**83**	32 57N	10 29 E
Tatar A.S.S.R. □	**52**	55 30N	51 30 E
Tatarbunary	**56**	45 50N	29 39 E
Tatarsk	**58**	55 14N	76 0 E
* Tatarskiy Proliv	**59**	54 0N	141 0 E
Tateyama	**74**	35 0N	139 50 E
Tathlina L.	**108**	60 33N	117 39W
Tathra	**99**	36 44 S	149 59 E
Tatinnai L.	**109**	60 55N	97 40W
Tatnam, C.	**109**	57 16N	91 0W
Tatra = Tatry	**27**	49 20N	20 0 E
Tatry	**27**	49 20N	20 0 E
Tatta	**68**	24 42N	67 55 E
Tatuī	**125**	23 25 S	47 53W
Tatum	**117**	33 16N	103 16W
Tat'ung = Datong	**76**	40 6N	113 12 E
Tatura	**100**	36 29 S	145 16 E
Tatvan	**64**	38 31N	42 15 E
Taubaté	**125**	23 0 S	45 36W
Tauberbischofsheim	**25**	49 37N	9 40 E
Taucha	**24**	51 22N	12 31 E
Tauern	**26**	47 15N	12 40 E
Tauern-tunnel	**26**	47 0N	13 12 E
Taufikia	**87**	9 24N	31 37 E
Taumarunui	**101**	38 53 S	175 15 E
Taumaturgo	**126**	8 54 S	72 51W
Taung	**92**	27 33 S	24 47 E
Taungdwingyi	**67**	20 1N	95 40 E
Taunggyi	**67**	20 50N	97 0 E
Taungup	**67**	18 51N	94 14 E
Taungup Pass	**67**	18 40N	94 45 E
Taunsa Barrage	**68**	30 42N	70 50 E
Taunton, U.K.	**13**	51 1N	3 7W
Taunton, U.S.A.	**114**	41 54N	71 6W
Taunus	**25**	50 15N	8 20 E
Taupo	**101**	38 41 S	176 7 E
Taupo, L.	**101**	38 46 S	175 55 E
Taurage	**54**	55 14N	22 16 E
Tauranga	**101**	37 42 S	176 11 E
Tauranga Harb.	**101**	37 30 S	176 5 E
Taurianova	**41**	38 22N	16 1 E
Taurus Mts. = Toros Dağlari	**64**	37 0N	35 0 E
Tauste	**32**	41 58N	1 18W
Tauz	**57**	41 0N	45 40 E
Tavda	**58**	58 7N	65 8 E
Tavda →	**58**	59 20N	63 28 E
Taverny	**19**	49 2N	2 13 E
Taveta	**90**	3 23 S	37 37 E
Taveuni	**101**	16 51 S	179 58W
Tavignano →	**21**	42 7N	9 33 E
Tavira	**31**	37 8N	7 40W
Tavistock, Can.	**112**	43 19N	80 50W
Tavistock, U.K.	**13**	50 33N	4 9W
Tavolara	**40**	40 55N	9 40 E
Távora →	**30**	41 8N	7 35W
Tavoy	**71**	14 2N	98 12 E
Taw →	**13**	17 37 S	177 55 E
Tawas City	**114**	44 16N	83 31W
Tawau	**72**	4 20N	117 55 E
Tawitawi	**73**	5 10N	120 0 E
Tāwurgha'	**83**	32 1N	15 2 E
Tay →	**14**	56 37N	3 38W
Tay, Firth of	**14**	56 25N	3 8W
Tay, L.	**14**	56 30N	4 10W
Tay Ninh	**71**	11 20N	106 5 E
Tayabamba	**126**	8 15 S	77 16W
Taylakovy	**58**	59 13N	74 0 E
Taylor, Can.	**108**	56 13N	120 40W
Taylor, Ariz., U.S.A.	**119**	34 28N	110 5W
Taylor, Nebr., U.S.A.	**116**	41 46N	99 23W
Taylor, Pa., U.S.A.	**113**	41 23N	75 43W
Taylor, Tex., U.S.A.	**117**	30 30N	97 30W
Taylor Mt.	**119**	35 16N	107 36W
Taylorville	**116**	39 32N	89 20W
Taymā'	**64**	27 35N	38 45 E
Taymyr, P-ov.	**59**	75 0N	100 0 E
Tayport	**14**	56 27N	2 52W
Ţayr Zibnā	**62**	33 14N	35 23 E
Tayshet	**59**	55 58N	98 1 E
Tayside □	**14**	56 25N	3 30W
Taytay	**73**	10 45N	119 30 E
Taz →	**58**	67 32N	78 40 E
Taza	**82**	34 16N	4 6W
Tazenakht	**82**	30 35N	7 12W
Tazin →	**109**	60 26N	110 45W
Tazin L.	**109**	59 44N	108 42W
Tazoult	**83**	35 29N	6 11 E
Tazovskiy	**58**	67 30N	78 44 E
Tbilisi (Tiflis)	**57**	41 43N	44 50 E
Tchad (Chad) ■	**81**	12 30N	17 15 E
Tchad, L.	**81**	13 30N	14 30 E
Tch'ang-k'ing = Changqing	**75**	29 35N	106 35 E
Tchaourou	**85**	8 58N	2 40 E
Tch'eng-tou = Chengdu	**75**	30 38N	104 2 E
Tchentlo L.	**108**	55 15N	125 0W
Tchibanga	**88**	2 45 S	11 0 E
Tchin Tabaraden	**85**	15 58N	5 56 E
Tczew	**28**	54 8N	18 50 E
Te Anau, L.	**101**	45 15 S	167 45 E
Te Aroha	**101**	37 32 S	175 44 E
Te Awamutu	**101**	38 1 S	175 20 E
Te Kuiti	**101**	38 20 S	175 11 E
Te Puke	**101**	37 46 S	176 22 E
Te Waewae B.	**101**	46 13 S	167 33 E
Teaca	**46**	46 55N	24 30 E
Teague	**117**	31 40N	96 20W
Teano	**41**	41 15N	14 1 E
Teapa	**120**	18 35N	92 56W
Teba	**31**	36 59N	4 55W
Tebakang	**72**	1 6N	110 30 E
Teberda	**57**	43 30N	41 46 E
Tébessa	**83**	35 22N	8 8 E
Tebicuary →	**124**	26 36 S	58 16W
Tebingtinggi, Bengkulu, Indon.	**72**	3 38 S	103 9 E
Tebingtinggi, Sumatera Utara, Indon.	**72**	3 20N	99 9 E
Tébourba	**83**	36 49N	9 51 E
Téboursouk	**83**	36 29N	9 10 E
Tebulos	**57**	42 36N	45 17 E
Tech →	**20**	42 36N	3 3 E
Techiman	**84**	7 35N	1 58W
Techirghiol	**46**	44 4N	28 32 E
Tecuala	**120**	22 23N	105 27W
Tecuci	**46**	45 51N	27 27 E
Tecumseh	**114**	42 1N	83 59W
Tedzhen	**58**	37 23N	60 31 E
Tees →	**12**	54 36N	1 25W
Teesside	**12**	54 37N	1 13W
Teeswater	**112**	43 59N	81 17W
Tefé	**126**	3 25 S	64 50W
Tegal	**73**	6 52 S	109 8 E
Tegelen	**16**	51 20N	6 9 E
Tegernsee	**25**	47 43N	11 46 E
Teggiano	**41**	40 24N	15 32 E
Teghra	**69**	25 30N	85 34 E
Tegid, L.	**12**	52 53N	3 38W
Tegina	**85**	10 5N	6 11 E
Tegucigalpa	**121**	14 5N	87 14W
Tehachapi	**119**	35 11N	118 29W
Tehachapi Mts.	**119**	35 0N	118 40W
Tehamiyam	**86**	18 20N	36 32 E
Tehilla	**86**	17 42N	36 6 E
Téhini	**84**	9 39N	3 40W
Tehrān	**65**	35 44N	51 30 E
Tehrān □	**65**	35 0N	49 30 E
Tehuacán	**120**	18 30N	97 30W
Tehuantepec	**120**	16 21N	95 13W
Tehuantepec, Golfo de	**120**	15 50N	95 0W
Tehuantepec, Istmo de	**120**	17 0N	94 30W
Teich, Le	**20**	44 38N	0 59W
Teifi →	**13**	52 4N	4 14W
Teign →	**13**	50 41N	3 42W
Teignmouth	**13**	50 33N	3 30W
Teil, Le	**21**	44 33N	4 40 E
Teilleul, Le	**18**	48 32N	0 53W
Teiuş	**46**	46 12N	23 40 E
Teixeira Pinto	**84**	12 3N	16 0W
Tejo →	**31**	38 40N	9 24W
Tekamah	**116**	41 48N	96 22W
Tekapo, L.	**101**	43 53 S	170 33 E
Tekax	**120**	20 11N	89 18W
Tekeli	**58**	44 50N	79 0 E
Tekeze →	**87**	14 20N	35 50 E
Tekija	**42**	44 42N	22 26 E
Tekirdağ	**64**	40 58N	27 30 E
Tekkali	**70**	18 37N	84 15 E
Tekoa	**118**	47 19N	117 4W
Tekouiât, O. →	**82**	22 25N	2 35 E
Tel Adashim	**62**	32 30N	35 17 E
Tel Aviv-Yafo	**62**	32 4N	34 48 E
Tel Lakhish	**62**	31 34N	34 51 E
Tel Megiddo	**62**	32 35N	35 11 E
Tel Mond	**62**	32 15N	34 56 E
Tela	**120**	15 40N	87 28W
Télagh	**82**	34 51N	0 32W
Telanaipura = Jambi	**72**	1 38 S	103 37 E
Telavi	**57**	42 0N	45 30 E
Telciu	**46**	47 25N	24 24 E
Telegraph Cr.	**108**	58 0N	131 10W
Telekhany	**54**	52 30N	25 46 E
Telemark fylke □	**47**	59 25N	8 30 E
Telén	**124**	36 15 S	65 31W
Teleneshty	**46**	47 35N	28 24 E
Teleño	**30**	42 23N	6 22W
Teleorman □	**46**	44 0N	25 0 E
Teleorman →	**46**	44 15N	25 20 E
Teles Pires →	**126**	7 21 S	58 3W
Telescope Peak	**119**	36 6N	117 7W
Teletaye	**85**	16 31N	1 30 E
Telford	**12**	52 42N	2 31W
Telfs	**26**	47 19N	11 4 E
Telgte	**24**	51 59N	7 46 E
Télimélé	**84**	10 54N	13 2W
Telkwa	**108**	54 41N	127 5W
Tell City	**114**	38 0N	86 44W
Tellicherry	**70**	11 45N	75 30 E
Telluride	**119**	37 58N	107 48W
Telok Anson	**71**	4 3N	101 0 E
Telom →	**71**	4 20N	101 46 E
Telpos Iz	**52**	63 35N	57 30 E
Telsen	**128**	42 30 S	66 50W
Telšiai	**54**	55 59N	22 14 E
Teltow	**24**	52 24N	13 15 E
Telukbetung	**72**	5 29 S	105 17 E
Telukbutun	**72**	4 13N	108 12 E
Telukdalem	**72**	0 33N	97 50 E
Tema	**85**	5 41N	0 0 E
Temanggung	**73**	7 18 S	110 10 E
Temax	**120**	21 10N	88 50W
Tembe	**90**	0 16 S	28 14 E
Tembeling →	**71**	4 20N	102 23 E
Tembleque	**32**	39 41N	3 30W
Tembuland	**93**	31 35 S	28 0 E
Teme →	**13**	52 23N	2 15W
Temecula	**119**	33 26N	117 6W
Temerloh	**71**	3 27N	102 25 E
Temir	**58**	49 21N	57 3 E
Temirtau, Kazakh, U.S.S.R.	**58**	50 5N	72 56 E
Temirtau, R.S.F.S.R., U.S.S.R.	**58**	53 10N	87 30 E
Témiscaming	**106**	46 44N	79 5W
Temma	**99**	41 12 S	144 48 E
Temnikov	**55**	54 40N	43 11 E
Temo →	**40**	40 20N	8 30 E
Temora	**99**	34 30 S	147 30 E
Temosachic	**120**	28 58N	107 50W
Tempe	**119**	33 26N	111 59W
Tempino	**72**	1 42 S	103 30 E
Témpio Pausania	**40**	40 53N	9 6 E
Temple	**117**	31 5N	97 22W
Temple B.	**97**	12 15 S	143 3 E
Templemore	**15**	52 48N	7 50W
Templeton →	**98**	21 0 S	138 40 E
Templin	**24**	53 8N	13 31 E
Temryuk	**56**	45 15N	37 24 E
Temska →	**42**	43 17N	22 33 E
Temuco	**128**	38 45 S	72 40W
Temuka	**101**	44 14 S	171 17 E
Tenabo	**120**	20 2N	90 12W
Tenaha	**117**	31 57N	94 25W
Tenali	**70**	16 15N	80 35 E
Tenancingo	**120**	19 0N	99 33W
Tenango	**120**	19 7N	99 33W
Tenasserim	**71**	12 6N	99 3 E
Tenasserim □	**71**	14 0N	98 30 E
Tenay	**21**	45 55N	5 30 E
Tenby	**13**	51 40N	4 42W
Tendaho	**87**	11 48N	40 54 E
Tende	**21**	44 5N	7 35 E
Tende, Col de	**21**	44 9N	7 32 E
Tendelti	**87**	13 1N	31 55 E
Tendjedi, Adrar	**83**	23 41N	7 32 E
Tendrara	**82**	33 3N	1 58W
Teneida	**86**	25 30N	29 19 E
Ténéré	**85**	19 0N	10 30 E
Tenerife	**80**	28 15N	16 35W
Ténès	**82**	36 31N	1 14 E
Teng →	**71**	20 30N	98 10 E
Teng Xian, Guangxi Zhuangzu, China	**77**	23 21N	110 56 E
Teng Xian, Shandong, China	**77**	35 5N	117 10 E
Tengah □	**73**	2 0 S	122 0 E
Tengah Kepulauan	**72**	7 5 S	118 15 E
Tengchong	**75**	25 0N	98 28 E
Tenggara □	**73**	3 0 S	122 0 E
Tenggarong	**72**	0 24 S	116 58 E
Tengiz, Ozero	**58**	50 30N	69 0 E
Tenille	**115**	32 58N	82 50W
Tenkasi	**70**	8 55N	77 20 E
Tenke, Congo	**91**	11 22 S	26 40 E
Tenke, Zaïre	**91**	10 32 S	26 7 E
Tenkodogo	**85**	11 54N	0 19W
Tenna →	**39**	43 12N	13 47 E
Tennant Creek	**96**	19 30 S	134 15 E
Tennessee □	**111**	36 0N	86 30W
Tennessee →	**114**	34 30N	86 20W
Tennsift, Oued →	**82**	32 3N	9 28W
Tenom	**72**	5 4N	115 57 E
Tenosique	**120**	17 30N	91 24W
Tenryū-Gawa →	**74**	35 39N	137 48 E
Tent L.	**109**	62 25N	107 54W
Tenterfield	**97**	29 0 S	152 0 E
Teófilo Otoni	**127**	17 50 S	41 30W
Teotihuacán	**120**	19 44N	98 50W
Tepa	**73**	7 52 S	129 31 E
Tepalcatepec →	**120**	18 35N	101 59W
Tepelena	**44**	40 17N	20 2 E
Tepic	**120**	21 30N	104 54W
Teplice	**26**	50 40N	13 48 E
Tepoca, C.	**120**	30 20N	112 25W
Tequila	**120**	20 54N	103 47W
Ter →	**32**	42 0N	3 12 E
Ter Apel	**16**	52 53N	7 5 E
Téra	**85**	14 0N	0 45 E
Tera →	**30**	41 54N	5 44W
Téramo	**39**	42 40N	13 40 E
Terang	**99**	38 15 S	142 55 E
Terazit, Massif de	**83**	20 2N	8 30 E
Terceira	**8**	38 43N	27 13W
Tercero →	**124**	32 58 S	61 47W
Terdal	**70**	16 33N	75 3 E
Terebovlya	**54**	49 18N	25 44 E
Teregova	**46**	45 10N	22 16 E
Terek →, U.S.S.R.	**56**	43 55N	47 30 E
Terek →, U.S.S.R.	**57**	44 0N	47 30 E
Terembone Cr. →	**99**	30 25 S	148 50 E
Terengganu □	**71**	4 55N	103 0 E
Tereshka →	**55**	51 48N	46 26 E
Teresina	**127**	5 9 S	42 45W
Terespol	**28**	52 5N	23 37 E
Terewah L.	**99**	29 52 S	147 35 E
Terges →	**31**	37 49N	7 41W
Tergnier	**19**	49 40N	3 17 E
Terhazza	**82**	23 38N	5 22W
Terlizzi	**41**	41 8N	16 32 E
Terme	**56**	41 11N	37 0 E
Termez	**58**	37 15N	67 15 E
Términi Imerese	**40**	37 58N	13 42 E
Términos, Laguna de	**120**	18 35N	91 30W
Térmoli	**39**	42 0N	15 0 E
Ternate	**73**	0 45N	127 25 E
Terneuzen	**16**	51 20N	3 50 E
Terney	**59**	45 3N	136 37 E
Terni	**39**	42 34N	12 38 E
Ternitz	**26**	47 43N	16 2 E
Ternopol	**54**	49 30N	25 40 E
Terra Nova B.	**5**	74 50 S	164 40 E
Terrace	**108**	54 30N	128 35W
Terrace Bay	**106**	48 47N	87 5W
Terracina	**40**	41 17N	13 12 E
Terralba	**40**	39 42N	8 38 E
Terranuova Bracciolini	**39**	43 31N	11 35 E
Terrasini Favarotta	**40**	38 10N	13 4 E
Terrasson	**20**	45 7N	1 19 E
Terre Haute	**114**	39 28N	87 24W
Terrebonne B.	**117**	29 15N	90 28W
Terrecht	**82**	20 10N	0 10W
Terrell	**117**	32 44N	96 19W
Terrenceville	**107**	47 40N	54 44W
Terrick Terrick	**98**	24 44 S	145 5 E
Terry	**116**	46 47N	105 20W
Terschelling	**16**	53 25N	5 20 E
Terter →	**57**	40 35N	47 22 E
Teruel	**32**	40 22N	1 8W
Teruel □	**32**	40 48N	1 0W
Tervel	**43**	43 45N	27 28 E
Tervola	**50**	66 6N	24 49 E
Teryaweyna L.	**99**	32 18 S	143 22 E
Tešanj	**42**	44 38N	17 59 E
Teseney	**87**	15 5N	36 42 E
Tesha →	**55**	55 38N	42 9 E
Teshio-Gawa →	**74**	44 53N	141 45 E
Tešica	**42**	43 27N	21 45 E
Tesiyn Gol →	**75**	50 40N	93 20 E
Teslić	**42**	44 37N	17 54 E
Teslin	**104**	60 10N	132 43W
Teslin →	**108**	61 34N	134 35W
Teslin L.	**108**	60 15N	132 57W
Tessalit	**85**	20 12N	1 0 E
Tessaoua	**85**	13 47N	7 56 E
Tessin	**24**	54 2N	12 28 E
Tessit	**85**	15 13N	0 18 E
Test →	**13**	51 7N	1 30W
Testa del Gargano	**41**	41 50N	16 10 E
Teste, La	**20**	44 37N	1 8W
Tét	**27**	47 30N	17 33 E
Têt →	**20**	42 44N	3 2 E
Tetachuck L.	**108**	53 18N	125 55W
Tetas, Pta.	**124**	23 31 S	70 38W
Tete	**91**	16 13 S	33 33 E
Tete □	**91**	15 15 S	32 40 E
Teterev →	**54**	51 1N	30 5 E
Teterow	**24**	53 45N	12 34 E
Teteven	**43**	42 58N	24 17 E
Tethul →	**108**	60 35N	112 12W
Tetiyev	**56**	49 22N	29 38 E
Teton →	**118**	47 58N	111 0W
Tétouan	**82**	35 35N	5 21W
Tetovo	**42**	42 1N	21 2 E
Tetuán = Tétouan	**82**	35 30N	5 25W
Tetyushi	**55**	54 55N	48 49 E
Teuco →	**124**	25 35 S	60 11W
Teulada	**40**	38 59N	8 47 E
Teulon	**109**	50 23N	97 16W
Teun	**73**	6 59 S	129 8 E
Teutoburger Wald	**22**	52 5N	8 20 E
Tevere →	**39**	41 44N	12 14 E
Teverya	**62**	32 47N	35 32 E
Teviot →	**14**	55 21N	2 51W
Tewantin	**99**	26 27 S	153 3 E
Tewkesbury	**13**	51 59N	2 8W
Texada I.	**108**	49 40N	124 25W
Texarkana, Ark., U.S.A.	**117**	33 25N	94 0W
Texarkana, Tex., U.S.A.	**117**	33 25N	94 3W
Texas	**99**	28 49 S	151 9 E
Texas □	**117**	31 40N	98 30W
Texas City	**117**	29 20N	94 55W
Texel	**16**	53 5N	4 50 E
Texhoma	**117**	36 32N	101 47W
Texline	**117**	36 26N	103 0W
Texoma L.	**117**	34 0N	96 38W
Teykovo	**55**	56 55N	40 30 E
Teyvareh	**65**	33 30N	64 24 E
Teza →	**55**	56 32N	41 53 E
Teziutlán	**120**	19 50N	97 22W
Tezpur	**67**	26 40N	92 45 E
Tezzeron L.	**108**	54 43N	124 30W
Tha-anne →	**109**	60 31N	94 37W
Tha Nun	**71**	8 12N	98 17 E
Thaba Putsoa	**93**	29 45 S	28 0 E
Thabana Ntlenyana	**93**	29 30 S	29 16 E
Thabazimbi	**93**	24 40 S	27 21 E
Thabor, Mt.	**21**	45 7N	6 34 E
Thai Nguyen	**71**	21 35N	105 55 E
Thailand (Siam) ■	**71**	16 0N	102 0 E
Thakhek	**71**	17 25N	104 45 E
Thal	**66**	33 28N	70 33 E
Thal Desert	**68**	31 10N	71 30 E
Thala	**83**	35 35N	8 40 E
Thala La	**67**	28 25N	97 23 E
Thallon	**99**	28 39 S	148 49 E
Thalwil	**25**	47 17N	8 35 E
Thame →	**13**	51 35N	1 8W
Thames	**101**	37 7 S	175 34 E
Thames →, Can.	**106**	42 20N	82 25W
Thames →, U.K.	**13**	51 30N	0 35 E
Thames →, U.S.A.	**113**	41 18N	72 9W
Thamesford	**112**	43 4N	81 0W
Thamesville	**112**	42 33N	81 59W
Thāmit, W.	**83**	30 51N	16 14 E
Thana	**70**	19 12N	72 59 E
Thanesar	**68**	30 1N	76 52 E
Thanet, I. of	**13**	51 21N	1 20 E
Thang Binh	**71**	15 50N	108 20 E
Thangool	**98**	24 38 S	150 42 E
Thanh Hoa	**71**	19 48N	105 46 E
Thanjavur (Tanjore)	**70**	10 48N	79 12 E
Thanlwin Myit →	**67**	20 0N	98 0 E
Thann	**19**	47 48N	7 5 E
Thaon	**19**	48 15N	6 25 E

* *Renamed Sakhalinskiy Zaliv*

Thar Tocina

Thar (Great Indian) Desert **68** 28 0N 72 0 E
Tharad **68** 24 30N 71 44 E
Thargomindah **97** 27 58 S 143 46 E
Tharrawaddy **67** 17 38N 95 48 E
Thasopoúla **44** 40 49N 24 45 E
Thásos, Greece **44** 40 50N 24 42 E
Thásos, Greece **44** 40 40N 24 40 E
Thatcher, Ariz., U.S.A. **119** 32 54N 109 46W
Thatcher, Colo., U.S.A. **117** 37 38N 104 6W
Thaton **67** 16 55N 97 22 E
Thau, Étang de **20** 43 23N 3 36 E
Thaungdut **67** 24 30N 94 40 E
Thayer **117** 36 34N 91 34W
Thayetmyo **67** 19 20N 95 10 E
Thazi **67** 21 0N 96 5 E
The Bight **121** 24 19N 75 24W
The Dalles **118** 45 40N 121 11W
The English Company's Is. **97** 11 50 S 136 32 E
The Flatts **121** 32 16N 64 45W
The Frome → **99** 29 8 S 137 54 E
The Granites **96** 20 35 S 130 21 E
The Grenadines, Is. **121** 12 40N 61 20W
The Hague = s'-Gravenhage **16** 52 7N 4 14 E
The Hamilton → **96** 26 40 S 135 19 E
The Johnston Lakes **96** 32 25 S 120 30 E
The Macumba → **97** 27 52 S 137 12 E
The Pas **109** 53 45N 101 15W
The Range **91** 19 2 S 31 2 E
The Rock **99** 35 15 S 147 2 E
The Salt Lake **99** 30 6 S 142 8 E
The Warburton → **99** 28 4 S 137 28 E
Thebes **86** 25 40N 32 35 E
Thebes = Thívai **45** 38 19N 23 19 E
Thedford, Can. **112** 43 9N 81 51W
Thedford, U.S.A. **116** 41 59N 100 31W
Theebine **99** 25 57 S 152 34 E
Theil, Le **18** 48 16N 0 42 E
Thekulthili L. **109** 61 3N 110 0W
Thelon → **109** 62 35N 104 3W
Thénezay **18** 46 44N 0 2W
Thenia **83** 36 44N 3 33 E
Thenon **20** 45 9N 1 4 E
Theodore **97** 24 55 S 150 3 E
Thérain → **19** 49 15N 2 27 E
Theresa **113** 44 13N 75 50W
Thermaïkos Kólpos **44** 40 15N 22 45 E
Thermopolis **118** 43 35N 108 10W
Thermopylae P. **45** 38 48N 22 35 E
Thesprotía □ **44** 39 27N 20 22 E
Thessalía □ **44** 39 30N 22 0 E
Thessalon **106** 46 20N 83 30W
Thessaloníki **44** 40 38N 22 58 E
Thessaloníki □ **44** 40 45N 23 0 E
Thessaly = Thessalía **44** 39 30N 22 0 E
Thetford **13** 52 25N 0 44 E
Thetford Mines **107** 46 8N 71 18W
Theunissen **92** 28 26 S 26 43 E
Thiámis → **44** 39 15N 20 6 E
Thiberville **18** 49 8N 0 27 E
Thibodaux **117** 29 48N 90 49W
Thicket Portage **109** 55 19N 97 42W
Thief River Falls **116** 48 15N 96 48W
Thiel Mts. **5** 85 15 S 91 0W
Thiene **39** 45 42N 11 29 E
Thiérache **19** 49 51N 3 45 E
Thiers **20** 45 52N 3 33 E
Thies **84** 14 50N 16 51W
Thiet **87** 7 37N 28 49 E
Thika **90** 1 1 S 37 5 E
Thikombia **101** 15 44 S 179 55W
Thille-Boubacar **84** 16 31N 15 5W
Thillot, Le **19** 47 53N 6 46 E
Thimphu (Tashi Chho Dzong) **69** 27 31N 89 45 E
Þingvallavatn **50** 64 11N 21 9W
Thionville **19** 49 20N 6 10 E
Thíra **45** 36 23N 25 27 E
Thirasía **45** 36 26N 25 21 E
Thirsk **12** 54 15N 1 20W
Thistle I. **96** 35 0 S 136 8 E
Thívai **45** 38 19N 23 19 E
Thiviers **20** 45 25N 0 54 E
Thizy **21** 46 2N 4 18 E
Þjórsá → **50** 63 47N 20 48W
Thlewiaza →, Man., Can. **109** 59 43N 100 5W
Thlewiaza →, N.W.T., Can. **109** 60 29N 94 40W
Thoa → **109** 60 31N 109 47W
Thoissey **21** 46 12N 4 48 E
Thomas, Okla., U.S.A. **117** 35 48N 98 48W
Thomas, W. Va., U.S.A. **114** 39 10N 79 30W
Thomas, L. **99** 26 4 S 137 58 E
Thomaston **115** 32 54N 84 20W
Thomasville, Ala., U.S,A. **115** 31 55N 87 42W
Thomasville, Ga., U.S.A. **115** 30 50N 84 0W
Thomasville, N.C., U.S.A. **115** 35 55N 80 4W
Thompson **109** 55 45N 97 52W
Thompson →, Can. **108** 50 15N 121 24W
Thompson →, U.S.A. **116** 39 46N 93 37W
Thompson Falls **118** 47 37N 115 20W
Thompson Landing **109** 62 56N 110 40W
Thompson Pk. **118** 41 0N 123 3W
Thompsons **119** 39 0N 109 50W
Thompsonville **113** 42 0N 72 37W
Thomson → **97** 25 11 S 142 53 E
Thomson's Falls = Nyahururu **90** 0 2N 36 27 E
Thon Buri **71** 13 43N 100 29 E
Thônes **21** 45 54N 6 18 E
Thonon-les-Bains **21** 46 22N 6 29 E
Thorez **57** 48 4N 38 34 E
Þórisvatn **50** 64 20N 18 55W
Þorlákshöfn **50** 63 51N 21 22W
Thornaby on Tees **12** 54 36N 1 19W
Thornbury **112** 44 34N 80 26W
Thorne Glacier **5** 87 30 S 150 0W
Thorold **112** 43 7N 79 12W
Þórshöfn **50** 66 12N 15 20W
Thouarcé **18** 47 17N 0 30W
Thouars **18** 46 58N 0 15W
Thrace = Thráki □ **44** 41 10N 25 30 E
Thráki □ **44** 41 9N 25 30 E
Thrakikón Pélagos **44** 40 30N 25 0 E
Three Forks **118** 45 55N 111 32W
Three Hills **108** 51 43N 113 15W
Three Hummock I. **99** 40 25 S 144 55 E
Three Lakes **116** 45 48N 89 10W
Three Points, C. **84** 4 42N 2 6W
Three Rivers **117** 28 30N 98 10W
Three Sisters, Mt. **118** 44 10N 121 46W
Throssell Ra. **96** 22 3 S 121 43 E
Thrun Pass **26** 47 20N 12 25 E
Thubun Lakes **109** 61 30N 112 0W
Thuddungra **100** 34 8 S 148 8 E
Thueyts **21** 44 41N 4 9 E
Thuin **16** 50 20N 4 17 E
Thuir **20** 42 38N 2 45 E
Thule, Antarct. **5** 59 27 S 27 19W
Thule, Greenl. **4** 77 40N 69 0W
Thun **25** 46 45N 7 38 E
Thunder B. **114** 45 0N 83 20W
Thunder Bay **106** 48 20N 89 15W
Thunersee **25** 46 43N 7 39 E
Thung Song **71** 8 10N 99 40 E
Thunkar **69** 27 55N 91 0 E
Thur → **25** 47 32N 9 10 E
Thurgau □ **25** 47 34N 9 10 E
Thüringer Wald **24** 50 35N 11 0 E
Thurles **15** 52 40N 7 53W
Thurloo Downs **99** 29 15 S 143 30 E
Thurn P. **25** 47 20N 12 25 E
Thursday I. **97** 10 30 S 142 3 E
Thurso, Can. **106** 45 36N 75 15W
Thurso, U.K. **14** 58 34N 3 31W
Thurston I. **5** 72 0 S 100 0W
Thury-Harcourt **18** 49 0N 0 30W
Thutade L. **108** 57 0N 126 55W
Thyborøn **49** 56 42N 8 12 E
Thylungra **99** 26 4 S 143 28 E
Thyolo **91** 16 7 S 35 5 E
Thysville = Mbanza Ngungu **88** 5 12 S 14 53 E
Ti-n-Barraouene, O. → **85** 18 40N 4 5 E
Ti-n-Medjerdam, O. → **82** 25 45N 1 30 E
Ti-n-Tarabine, O. → **83** 21 0N 7 25 E
Ti-n-Zaouaténe **82** 20 0N 2 55 E
Tia **99** 31 10 S 150 34 E
Tian Shan **75** 43 0N 84 0 E
Tiandu **77** 18 18N 109 36 E
Tian'e **77** 25 1N 107 9 E
Tianhe **77** 24 48N 108 40 E
Tianjin **76** 39 8N 117 10 E
Tiankoura **84** 10 47N 3 17W
Tianshui **77** 34 32N 105 40 E
Tianyang **77** 23 42N 106 53 E
Tianzhen **76** 40 24N 114 5 E
Tiaret **82** 35 20N 1 21 E
Tiassalé **84** 5 58N 4 57W
Tibagi **125** 24 30 S 50 24W
Tibagi → **125** 22 47 S 51 1W
Tibati **85** 6 22N 12 30 E
Tiber = Tevere → **39** 41 44N 12 14 E
Tiber Res. **118** 48 20N 111 15W
Tiberias, L. = Kinneret, Yam **62** 32 45N 35 35 E
Tibesti **83** 21 0N 17 30 E
Tibet = Xizang □ **75** 32 0N 88 0 E
Tibiri **85** 13 34N 7 4 E
Ţibleş **46** 47 32N 24 15 E
Tibnīn **62** 33 12N 35 24 E
Tibooburra **97** 29 26 S 142 1 E
Tibro **49** 58 28N 14 10 E
Tiburón **120** 29 0N 112 30W
Tîchît **84** 18 21N 9 29W
Ticho **87** 7 50N 39 32 E
Ticino □ **25** 46 20N 8 45 E
Ticino → **38** 45 9N 9 14 E
Ticonderoga **114** 43 50N 73 28W
Ticul **120** 20 20N 89 31W
Tidaholm **49** 58 12N 13 55 E
Tiddim **67** 23 28N 93 45 E
Tideridjaouine, Adrar **82** 23 0N 2 15 E
Tidikelt **82** 26 58N 1 30 E
Tidjikja **84** 18 29N 11 35W
Tidore **73** 0 40N 127 25 E
Tiébissou **84** 7 9N 5 10W
Tiéboro **83** 21 20N 17 7 E
Tiel, Neth. **16** 51 53N 5 26 E
Tiel, Senegal **84** 14 55N 15 5W
Tieling **76** 42 20N 123 55 E
Tielt **16** 51 0N 3 20 E
Tien Shan = Tian Shan **65** 42 0N 80 0 E
Tien-tsin = Tianjin **75** 39 8N 117 10 E
T'ienching = Tianjin **76** 39 8N 117 10 E
Tienen **16** 50 48N 4 57 E
Tiénigbé **84** 8 11N 5 43W
Tientsin = Tianjin **76** 39 8N 117 10 E
Tierp **48** 60 20N 17 30 E
Tierra Amarilla, Chile **124** 27 28 S 70 18W
Tierra Amarilla, U.S.A. **119** 36 42N 106 33W
Tierra de Barros **31** 38 40N 6 30W
Tierra de Campos **30** 42 10N 4 50W
Tierra del Fuego, I. Gr. de **128** 54 0 S 69 0W
Tiétar → **30** 39 50N 6 1W
Tieté → **125** 20 40 S 51 35W
Tifarit **82** 26 9N 10 33W
Tiffin **114** 41 8N 83 10W
Tiflèt **82** 33 54N 6 20W
Tiflis = Tbilisi **57** 41 43N 44 50 E
Tifrah **62** 31 19N 34 42 E
Tifton **115** 31 28N 83 32W
Tifu **73** 3 39 S 126 24 E
Tigil **59** 57 49N 158 40 E
Tignish **107** 46 58N 64 2W
Tigre □ **87** 13 35N 39 15 E
Tigre → **126** 4 30 S 74 10W
Tigris = Dijlah, Nahr → **64** 31 0N 47 25 E
Tiguentourine **83** 27 52N 9 8 E
Tigveni **46** 45 10N 24 31 E
Tigyaing **67** 23 45N 96 10 E
Tigzerte, O. → **82** 28 10N 9 37W
Tîh, Gebel el **86** 29 32N 33 26 E
Tihama **64** 22 0N 39 0 E
Tihodaine, Dunes de **83** 25 15N 7 15 E
Tijesno **39** 43 48N 15 39 E
Tijī **83** 32 0N 11 18 E
Tijuana **120** 32 30N 117 10W
Tikal **120** 17 13N 89 24W
Tikamgarh **68** 24 44N 78 50 E
Tikhoretsk **57** 45 56N 40 5 E
Tikhvin **54** 59 35N 33 30 E
Tikkadouine, Adrar **82** 24 28N 1 30 E
Tiko **85** 4 4N 9 20 E
Tikrīt **64** 34 35N 43 37 E
Tiksi **59** 71 40N 128 45 E
Tilamuta **73** 0 32N 122 23 E
Tilburg **16** 51 31N 5 6 E
Tilbury, Can. **106** 42 17N 82 23W
Tilbury, U.K. **13** 51 27N 0 24 E
Tilcara **124** 23 36 S 65 23W
Tilden, Nebr., U.S.A. **116** 42 3N 97 45W
Tilden, Tex., U.S.A. **117** 28 28N 98 33W
Tilemses **85** 15 37N 4 44 E
Tilemsi, Vallée du **85** 17 42N 0 15 E
Tilhar **69** 28 0N 79 45 E
Tilia, O. → **82** 27 32N 0 55 E
Tilichiki **59** 60 27N 166 5 E
Tiligul → **56** 47 4N 30 57 E
Tililane **82** 27 49N 0 6W
Tílissos **45** 35 2N 25 0 E
Till → **12** 55 35N 2 3W
Tillabéri **85** 14 28N 1 28 E
Tillamook **118** 45 29N 123 55W
Tillberga **48** 59 52N 16 39 E
Tillia **85** 16 8N 4 47 E
Tillsonburg **106** 42 53N 80 44W
Tílos **45** 36 27N 27 27 E
Tilpa **99** 30 57 S 144 24 E
Tilrhemt **82** 33 9N 3 22 E
Tilsit = Sovetsk **54** 55 6N 21 50 E
Tilt → **14** 56 50N 3 50W
Tilton **113** 43 25N 71 36W
Timagami L. **106** 47 0N 80 10W
Timanskiy Kryazh **52** 65 58N 50 5 E
Timaru **101** 44 23 S 171 14 E
Timashevsk **57** 45 35N 39 0 E
Timau, Italy **39** 46 35N 13 0 E
Timau, Kenya **90** 0 4N 37 15 E
Timbákion **45** 35 4N 24 45 E
Timbedgha **84** 16 17N 8 16W
Timber Lake **116** 45 29N 101 6W
Timboon **99** 38 30 S 142 58 E
Timbuktu = Tombouctou **84** 16 50N 3 0W
Timdjaouine **82** 21 37N 4 30 E
Timellouline **83** 29 22N 8 55 E
Timétrine Montagnes **85** 19 25N 1 0W
Timfi Óros **44** 39 59N 20 45 E
Timfristós, Óros **45** 38 57N 21 50 E
Timhadit **82** 33 15N 5 4W
Tîmia **85** 18 4N 8 40 E
Timimoun **82** 29 14N 0 16 E
Timimoun, Sebkha de **82** 28 50N 0 46 E
Timiş □ **42** 45 40N 21 30 E
Timiş → **46** 45 30N 21 0 E
Timişoara **42** 45 43N 21 15 E
Timmins **106** 48 28N 81 25W
Timok → **42** 44 10N 22 40 E
Timon **127** 5 8 S 42 52W
Timor **73** 9 0 S 125 0 E
Timor □ **73** 9 0 S 125 0 E
Timor Sea **97** 10 0 S 127 0 E
Tin Alkoum **83** 24 42N 10 17 E
Tin Gornai **85** 16 38N 0 38W
Tin Gornaï → **85** 20 30N 4 35 E
Tîna, Khalîg el **86** 31 20N 32 42 E
Tinaca Pt. **73** 5 30N 125 25 E
Tinafak, O. → **83** 27 10N 7 0 E
Tinca **46** 46 46N 21 58 E
Tinchebray **18** 48 47N 0 45W
Tindivanam **70** 12 15N 79 41 E
Tindouf **82** 27 42N 8 10W
Tinee → **21** 43 55N 7 11 E
Tineo **30** 43 21N 6 27W
Tinerhir **82** 31 29N 5 31W
Tinfouchi **82** 28 52N 5 49W
Tinglev **49** 54 57N 9 13 E
Tingo Maria **126** 9 10 S 75 54W
Tingsryd **49** 56 31N 15 0 E
Tinjoub **82** 29 45N 5 40W
Tinnoset **47** 59 55N 9 3 E
Tinnsjø **47** 59 55N 8 54 E
Tinogasta **124** 28 5 S 67 32W
Tínos **45** 37 33N 25 8 E
Tiñoso, C. **33** 37 32N 1 6W
Tintina **124** 27 2 S 62 45W
Tintinara **99** 35 48 S 140 2 E
Tinto → **31** 37 12N 6 55W
Tioga **112** 41 54N 77 9W
Tioman, Pulau **71** 2 50N 104 10 E
Tione di Trento **38** 46 3N 10 44 E
Tionesta **112** 41 29N 79 28W
Tior **87** 6 26N 31 11 E
Tioulilin **82** 27 1N 0 2W
Tipongpani **67** 27 20N 95 55 E
Tipperary **15** 52 28N 8 10W
Tipperary □ **15** 52 37N 7 55W
Tipton, U.K. **13** 52 32N 2 4W
Tipton, Calif., U.S.A. **119** 36 3N 119 19W
Tipton, Ind., U.S.A. **114** 40 17N 86 0W
Tipton, Iowa, U.S.A. **116** 41 45N 91 12W
Tiptonville **117** 36 22N 89 30W
Tiptur **70** 13 15N 76 26 E
Tirahart, O. **82** 23 45N 3 10 E
Tīrān **65** 32 45N 51 8 E
Tirân **86** 27 56N 34 45 E
Tirana **44** 41 18N 19 49 E
Tirana-Durrësi □ **44** 41 35N 20 0 E
Tirano **38** 46 13N 10 11 E
Tiraspol **56** 46 55N 29 35 E
Tirat Karmel **62** 32 46N 34 58 E
Tirat Yehuda **62** 32 1N 34 56 E
Tirat Zevi **62** 32 26N 35 31 E
Tiratimine **82** 25 56N 3 37 E
Tirdout **85** 16 7N 1 5W
Tire **64** 38 5N 27 50 E
Tirebolu **64** 40 58N 38 45 E
Tiree **14** 56 31N 6 55W
Tîrgovişte **46** 44 55N 25 27 E
Tîrgu Frumos **46** 47 12N 27 2 E
Tîrgu-Jiu **46** 45 5N 23 19 E
Tîrgu Mureş **46** 46 31N 24 38 E
Tîrgu Neamţ **46** 47 12N 26 25 E
Tîrgu Ocna **46** 46 16N 26 39 E
Tîrgu Secuiesc **46** 46 0N 26 10 E
Tirich Mir **66** 36 15N 71 55 E
Tiriola **41** 38 57N 16 32 E
Tirna → **70** 18 4N 76 57 E
Tîrnava Mare → **46** 46 15N 24 30 E
Tîrnava Mică → **46** 46 17N 24 30 E
Tîrnăveni **46** 46 19N 24 13 E
Tírnavos **44** 39 45N 22 18 E
Tîrnova **46** 45 23N 22 1 E
Tirodi **69** 21 40N 79 44 E
Tirol □ **26** 47 3N 10 43 E
Tirschenreuth **25** 49 51N 12 20 E
Tirso → **40** 39 52N 8 33 E
Tirso, L. del **40** 40 8N 8 56 E
Tiruchchirappalli **70** 10 45N 78 45 E
Tiruchendur **70** 8 30N 78 11 E
Tiruchengodu **70** 11 23N 77 56 E
Tirumangalam **70** 9 49N 77 58 E
Tirunelveli (Tinnevelly) **70** 8 45N 77 45 E
Tirupati **70** 13 39N 79 25 E
Tiruppattur **70** 12 30N 78 30 E
Tiruppur **70** 11 5N 77 22 E
Tiruturaipundi **70** 10 32N 79 41 E
Tiruvadaimarudur **70** 11 2N 79 27 E
Tiruvallar **70** 13 9N 79 57 E
Tiruvannamalai **70** 12 15N 79 5 E
Tiruvarur **70** 10 46N 79 38 E
Tiruvatipuram **70** 12 39N 79 33 E
Tiruvottiyur **70** 13 10N 80 22 E
Tisa → **42** 45 15N 20 17 E
Tisdale **109** 52 50N 104 0W
Tishomingo **117** 34 14N 96 38W
Tisjön **48** 60 56N 13 0 E
Tisnaren **48** 58 58N 15 56 E
Tišnov **27** 49 21N 16 25 E
Tisovec **27** 48 41N 19 56 E
Tissemsilt **82** 35 35N 1 50 E
Tissint **82** 29 57N 7 16W
Tissø **49** 55 35N 11 18 E
Tista → **69** 25 23N 89 43 E
Tisza → **27** 46 8N 20 2 E
Tiszaföldvár **27** 47 0N 20 14 E
Tiszafüred **27** 47 38N 20 50 E
Tiszalök **27** 48 0N 21 10 E
Tiszavasvári **27** 47 58N 21 18 E
Tit, Ahaggar, Alg. **83** 23 0N 5 10 E
Tit, Tademait, Alg. **82** 27 0N 1 29 E
Tit-Ary **59** 71 55N 127 2 E
Titaguas **32** 39 53N 1 6W
Titel **42** 45 10N 20 18 E
Titicaca, L. **126** 15 30 S 69 30W
Titilagarh **70** 20 15N 83 11 E
Titiwa **85** 12 14N 12 53 E
Titograd **42** 42 30N 19 19 E
Titov Veles **42** 41 46N 21 47 E
Titova Korenica **39** 44 45N 15 41 E
Titovo Užice **42** 43 55N 19 50 E
Titule **90** 3 15N 25 31 E
Titusville, Fla., U.S.A. **115** 28 37N 80 49W
Titusville, Pa., U.S.A. **114** 41 35N 79 39W
Tivaouane **84** 14 56N 16 45W
Tivat **42** 42 28N 18 43 E
Tiveden **49** 58 50N 14 30 E
Tiverton **13** 50 54N 3 30W
Tívoli **39** 41 58N 12 45 E
Tiwī **65** 22 45N 59 12 E
Tiyo **87** 14 41N 40 15 E
Tizga **82** 32 1N 5 9W
Ti'zi N'Isli **82** 32 28N 5 47W
Tizi-Ouzou **83** 36 42N 4 3 E
Tizimín **120** 21 0N 88 1W
Tiznit **82** 29 48N 9 45W
Tjeggelvas **50** 66 37N 17 45 E
Tjirebon = Cirebon **73** 6 45 S 108 32 E
Tjöme **47** 59 8N 10 26 E
Tjörn **49** 58 0N 11 35 E
Tkibuli **57** 42 26N 43 0 E
Tkvarcheli **57** 42 47N 41 42 E
Tlahualilo **120** 26 20N 103 30W
Tlaxcala **120** 19 20N 98 14W
Tlaxcala □ **120** 19 30N 98 20W
Tlaxiaco **120** 17 18N 97 40W
Tlell **108** 53 34N 131 56W
Tlemcen **82** 34 52N 1 21W
Tleta Sidi Bouguedra **82** 32 16N 9 59W
Tlumach, U.S.S.R. **54** 48 46N 25 0 E
Tlumach, U.S.S.R. **56** 48 51N 25 0 E
Tłuszcz **28** 52 25N 21 25 E
Tlyarata **57** 42 9N 46 26 E
Tmassah **83** 26 19N 15 51 E
Tnine d'Anglou **82** 29 50N 9 50W
Toad → **108** 59 25N 124 57W
Toala **73** 1 30 S 121 40 E
Toamasina **93** 18 10 S 49 25 E
Toamasina □ **93** 18 0 S 49 0 E
Toay **124** 36 43 S 64 38W
Toba **74** 34 30N 136 51 E
Toba, Danau **72** 2 40N 98 50 E
Toba Kakar **68** 31 30N 69 0 E
Toba Tek Singh **68** 30 55N 72 25 E
Tobago **121** 11 10N 60 30W
Tobarra **33** 38 37N 1 44W
Tobelo **73** 1 45N 127 56 E
Tobermorey **98** 22 12 S 137 51 E
Tobermory, Can. **106** 45 12N 81 40W
Tobermory, U.K. **14** 56 37N 6 4W
Tobin L. **109** 53 35N 103 30W
Toboali **72** 3 0 S 106 25 E
Tobol **58** 52 40N 62 39 E
Toboli **73** 0 38 S 120 5 E
Tobolsk **58** 58 15N 68 10 E
Tobruk = Tubruq **81** 32 7N 23 55 E
Tobyhanna **113** 41 10N 75 25W
Tocantinópolis **127** 6 20 S 47 25W
Tocantins → **127** 1 45 S 49 10W
Toccoa **115** 34 32N 83 17W
Toce → **38** 45 56N 8 29 E
Tochigi **74** 36 25N 139 45 E
Tochigi □ **74** 36 45N 139 45 E
Tocina **31** 37 37N 5 44W

Tocopilla Treuenbrietzen

Tocopilla 124 22 5S 70 10W
Tocumwal 99 35 51S 145 31E
Tocuyo → 126 11 3N 68 23W
Todeli 73 1 38S 124 34E
Todenyang 90 4 35N 35 56E
Todi 39 42 47N 12 24E
Todos os Santos, Baía de 127 12 48S 38 38W
Todos Santos 120 23 27N 110 13W
Todtnau 25 47 50N 7 56E
Toecé 85 11 50N 1 16W
Tofield 108 53 25N 112 40W
Tofino 108 49 11N 125 55W
Töfsingdalens nationalpark 48 62 15N 12 44E
Toftlund 49 55 11N 9 2E
Tofua 101 19 45S 175 05W
Togba 84 17 26N 10 12W
Togian, Kepulauan 73 0 20S 121 50E
Togliatti 55 53 32N 49 24E
Togo ■ 85 6 15N 1 35E
Togtoh 76 40 15N 111 10E
Toinya 87 6 17N 29 46E
Tojo 73 1 20S 121 15E
Tokaj 27 48 8N 21 27E
Tōkamachi 74 37 8N 138 43E
Tokanui 101 46 34S 168 56E
Tokar 81 18 27N 37 56E
Tokara Kaikyō 74 30 0N 130 0E
Tokarahi 101 44 56S 170 39E
Tokat 64 40 22N 36 35E
Tokelau Is. ■ 94 9 0S 171 45W
Tokmak 58 42 49N 75 15E
Toko Ra. 98 23 5S 138 20E
Tokong 71 5 27N 100 23E
Tokushima 74 34 4N 134 34E
Tokushima □ 74 34 15N 134 0E
Tokuyama 74 34 3N 131 50E
Tōkyō 74 35 45N 139 45E
Tōkyō □ 74 35 40N 139 30E
Tolbukhin 43 43 37N 27 49E
Toledo, Spain 30 39 50N 4 2W
Toledo, Ohio, U.S.A. 114 41 37N 83 33W
Toledo, Oreg., U.S.A. 118 44 40N 123 59W
Toledo, Wash., U.S.A. 118 46 29N 122 51W
Toledo, Montes de 31 39 33N 4 20W
Tolentino 39 43 12N 13 17E
Tolga, Alg. 83 34 40N 5 22E
Tolga, Norway 47 62 26N 11 1E
Toliara 93 23 21S 43 40E
Toliara □ 93 21 0S 45 0E
Tolima, Vol. 126 4 40N 75 19W
Tolitoli 73 1 5N 120 50E
Tolkmicko 28 54 19N 19 31E
Tollarp 49 55 55N 13 58E
Tolleson 119 33 29N 112 10W
Tolmachevo 54 58 56N 29 51E
Tolmezzo 39 46 23N 13 0E
Tolmin 39 46 11N 13 45E
Tolna 27 46 25N 18 48E
Tolna □ 27 46 30N 18 30E
Tolo 88 2 55S 18 34E
Tolo, Teluk 73 2 20S 122 10E
Tolochin 54 54 25N 29 42E
Tolosa 32 43 8N 2 5W
Tolox 31 36 41N 4 54W
Toluca 120 19 20N 99 40W
Tom Burke 93 23 5S 28 4E
Tom Price 96 22 40S 117 48E
Tomah 116 43 59N 90 30W
Tomahawk 116 45 28N 89 40W
Tomar 31 39 36N 8 25W
Tómaros Óros 44 39 29N 20 48E
Tomaszów Mazowiecki 28 51 30N 19 57E
Tombé 87 5 53N 31 40E
Tombigbee → 115 31 4N 87 58W
Tombouctou 84 16 50N 3 0W
Tombstone 119 31 40N 110 4W
Tomé 124 36 36S 72 57W
Tomelilla 49 55 33N 13 58E
Tomelloso 33 39 10N 3 2W
Tomingley 99 32 6S 148 16E
Tomini 73 0 30N 120 30E
Tomini, Teluk 73 0 10S 122 0E
Tominian 84 13 17N 4 35W
Tomiño 30 41 59N 8 46W
Tommot 59 59 4N 126 20E
Tomnavoulin 14 57 19N 3 18W
Toms River 113 39 59N 74 12W
Tomsk 58 56 30N 85 5E
Tomtabacken 49 57 30N 14 30E
Tonalá 120 16 8N 93 41W
Tonale, Passo del 38 46 15N 10 34E
Tonalea 119 36 17N 110 58W
Tonantins 126 2 45S 67 45W
Tonasket 118 48 45N 119 30W
Tonawanda 114 43 0N 78 54W
Tonbridge 13 51 12N 0 18E
Tondano 73 1 35N 124 54E
Tondela 30 40 31N 8 5W
Tønder 49 54 58N 8 50E
Tondi 70 9 45N 79 4E
Tondi Kiwindi 85 14 28N 2 02E
Tondibi 85 16 39N 0 14W
Tong Xian 76 39 55N 116 35E
Tonga ■ 101 19 50S 174 30W
Tonga Trench 94 18 0S 175 0W
Tongaat 93 29 33S 31 9E
Tongaland 93 27 0S 32 0E
Tongareva 95 9 0S 158 0W
Tongatapu 101 21 10S 174 0W
Tongcheng 77 31 4N 116 56E
Tongchuan 77 35 6N 109 3E
Tongdao 77 26 10N 109 42E
Tongeren 16 50 47N 5 28E
Tongguan 77 34 40N 110 25E
Tonghua 76 41 42N 125 58E
Tongio 99 37 14S 147 44E
Tongjiang, Heilongjiang, China 75 47 40N 132 27E
Tongjiang, Sichuan, China 77 31 58N 107 11E
Tongking = Tonkin, G. of 71 20 0N 108 0E
Tongliao 76 43 38N 122 18E
Tongling 77 30 55N 117 48E
Tonglu 77 29 45N 119 37E
Tongnan 77 30 9N 105 50E
Tongobory 93 23 32S 44 20E
Tongoy 124 30 16S 71 31W
Tongren 75 27 43N 109 11E
Tongres = Tongeren 16 50 47N 5 28E
Tongue 14 58 29N 4 25W
Tongue → 116 46 24N 105 52W
Tongyu 76 44 45N 123 4E
Tongzi 77 28 9N 106 49E
Tonj 87 7 20N 28 44E
Tonk 68 26 6N 75 54E
Tonkawa 117 36 44N 97 22W
Tonkin = Bac-Phan 71 22 0N 105 0E
Tonlé Sap 71 13 0N 104 0E
Tonnay-Charente 20 45 56N 0 55W
Tonneins 20 44 23N 0 19E
Tonnerre 19 47 51N 3 59E
Tönning 24 54 18N 8 57E
Tonopah 119 38 4N 117 12W
Tønsberg 47 59 19N 10 25E
Tonstad 47 58 40N 6 45E
Tonto Basin 119 33 56N 111 27W
Tooele 118 40 30N 112 20W
Toompine 99 27 15S 144 19E
Toonpan 98 19 28S 146 48E
Toora 99 38 39S 146 23E
Toora-Khem 59 52 28N 96 17E
Toowoomba 97 27 32S 151 56E
Top-ozero 52 65 35N 32 0E
Topalu 46 44 31N 28 3E
Topeka 116 39 3N 95 40W
Topki 58 55 20N 85 35E
Topl'a → 27 48 45N 21 45E
Topley 108 54 49N 126 18W
Toplica → 42 43 15N 21 49E
Toplița 46 46 55N 25 20E
Topocalma, Pta. 124 34 10S 72 2W
Topock 119 34 46N 114 29W
Topola 42 44 17N 20 41E
Topolčani 42 41 14N 21 56E
Topoľčany 27 48 35N 18 12E
Topoli 57 47 59N 51 38E
Topolnitsa → 43 42 11N 24 18E
Topolobampo 120 25 40N 109 4W
Topolovgrad 43 42 5N 26 20E
Topolvätu Mare 42 45 46N 21 41E
Toppenish 118 46 27N 120 16W
Topusko 39 45 18N 15 59E
Tor Bay 96 35 5S 117 50E
Torá 32 41 49N 1 25E
Tora Kit 87 11 2N 32 36E
Toraka Vestale 93 16 20S 43 58E
Torata 126 17 23S 70 1W
Torbat-e Ḩeydārīyeh 65 35 15N 59 12E
Torbat-e Jām 65 35 16N 60 35E
Torbay, Can. 107 47 40N 52 42W
Torbay, U.K. 13 50 26N 3 31W
Tørdal 47 59 10N 8 45E
Tordesillas 30 41 30N 5 0W
Tordoya 30 43 6N 8 36W
Töreboda 49 58 41N 14 7E
Torey 59 50 33N 104 50E
Torfajökull 50 63 54N 19 0W
Torgau 24 51 32N 13 0E
Torgelow 24 53 40N 13 59E
Torhout 16 51 5N 3 7E
Tori 87 7 53N 33 35E
Torigni-sur-Vire 18 49 3N 0 58W
Torija 32 40 44N 3 2W
Torin 120 27 33N 110 15W
Toriñana, C. 30 43 3N 9 17W
Torino 38 45 4N 7 40E
Torit 87 4 27N 32 31E
Torkovichi 54 58 51N 30 21E
Tormac 42 45 30N 21 30E
Tormentine 107 46 6N 63 46W
Tormes → 30 41 18N 6 29W
Tornado Mt. 108 49 55N 114 40W
Torne älv → 50 65 50N 24 12E
Torneträsk 50 68 24N 19 15E
Tornio 50 65 50N 24 12E
Tornionjoki → 50 65 50N 24 12E
Tornquist 124 38 8S 62 15W
Toro 30 41 35N 5 24W
Torö 49 58 48N 17 50E
Toro, Cerro del 124 29 10S 69 50W
Toro, Pta. 120 9 22N 79 57W
Törökszentmiklós 27 47 11N 20 27E
Toroníios Kólpos 44 40 5N 23 30E
Toronto, Austral. 99 33 0S 151 30E
Toronto, Can. 106 43 39N 79 20W
Toronto, U.S.A. 114 40 27N 80 36W
Toronto, L. 120 27 40N 105 30W
Toropets 54 56 30N 31 40E
Tororo 90 0 45N 34 12E
Toros Dağlari 64 37 0N 35 0E
Torpshammar 48 62 29N 16 20E
Torquay, Can. 109 49 9N 103 30W
Torquay, U.K. 13 50 27N 3 31W
Torquemada 30 42 2N 4 19W
Torralba de Calatrava 31 39 1N 3 44W
Torrão 31 38 16N 8 11W
Torre Annunziata 41 40 45N 14 26E
Tôrre de Moncorvo 30 41 12N 7 8W
Torre del Greco 41 40 47N 14 22E
Torre del Mar 31 36 44N 4 6W
Torre-Pacheco 33 37 44N 0 57W
Torre Pellice 38 44 49N 7 13E
Torreblanca 32 40 14N 0 12E
Torrecampo 31 38 29N 4 41W
Torrecilla en Cameros 32 42 15N 2 38W
Torredembarra 32 41 9N 1 24E
Torredonjimeno 31 37 46N 3 57W
Torrejoncillo 30 39 54N 6 28W
Torrelaguna 32 40 50N 3 38W
Torrelavega 30 43 20N 4 5W
Torremaggiore 41 41 42N 15 17E
Torremolinos 31 36 38N 4 30W
Torrens Cr. → 98 22 23S 145 9E
Torrens Creek 98 20 48S 145 3E
Torrens, L. 97 31 0S 137 50E
Torrente 33 39 27N 0 28W
Torrenueva 33 38 38N 3 22W
Torréon 120 25 33N 103 25W
Torreperogil 33 38 2N 3 17W
Torres 120 28 46N 110 47W
Torres Novas 31 39 27N 8 33W
Torres Strait 97 9 50S 142 20E
Torres Vedras 31 39 5N 9 15W
Torrevieja 33 37 59N 0 42W
Torrey 119 38 18N 111 25W
Torridge → 13 50 51N 4 10W
Torridon, L. 14 57 35N 5 50W
Torrijos 30 39 59N 4 18W
Torrington, Conn., U.S.A. 114 41 50N 73 9W
Torrington, Wyo., U.S.A. 116 42 5N 104 8W
Torroella de Montgri 32 42 2N 3 8E
Torrox 31 36 46N 3 57W
Torsås 49 56 24N 16 0E
Torsby 48 60 7N 13 0E
Torsö 49 58 48N 13 45E
Tortola 121 18 19N 65 0W
Tórtoles de Esgueva 30 41 49N 4 2W
Tortona 38 44 53N 8 54E
Tortoreto 39 42 50N 13 55E
Tortorici 41 38 2N 14 48E
Tortosa 32 40 49N 0 31E
Tortosa, C. 32 40 41N 0 52E
Tortosendo 30 40 15N 7 31W
Tortue, Î. de la 121 20 5N 72 57W
Tortuga, La 126 11 0N 65 22W
Ţorūd 65 35 25N 55 5E
Toruń 28 53 0N 18 39E
Toruń □ 28 53 20N 19 0E
Torup, Denmark 49 57 5N 9 5E
Torup, Sweden 49 56 57N 13 5E
Tory I. 15 55 17N 8 12W
Torysa → 27 48 39N 21 21E
Torzhok 54 57 5N 34 55E
Tosa-Wan 74 33 15N 133 30E
Toscana 38 43 30N 11 5E
Toscano, Arcipelago 38 42 30N 10 30E
Tosno 54 59 38N 30 46E
Tossa 32 41 43N 2 56E
Tostado 124 29 15S 61 50W
Tostedt 24 53 17N 9 42E
Tosya 64 41 1N 34 2E
Toszek 28 50 27N 18 32E
Totak 47 59 40N 7 45E
Totana 33 37 45N 1 30W
Toten 47 60 37N 10 53E
Toteng 92 20 22S 22 58E
Tôtes 18 49 41N 1 3E
Tótkomlós 27 46 24N 20 45E
Totma 55 60 0N 42 40E
Totnes 13 50 26N 3 41W
Totonicapán 120 14 58N 91 12W
Totten Glacier 5 66 45S 116 10E
Tottenham, Austral. 99 32 14S 147 21E
Tottenham, Can. 112 44 1N 79 49W
Tottori 74 35 30N 134 15E
Tottori □ 74 35 30N 134 12E
Touat 82 27 27N 0 30E
Touba 84 8 22N 7 40W
Toubkal, Djebel 82 31 0N 8 0W
Toucy 19 47 44N 3 15E
Tougan 84 13 11N 2 58W
Touggourt 83 33 10N 6 0E
Tougué 84 11 25N 11 50W
Toukmatine 83 24 49N 7 11E
Toul 19 48 40N 5 53E
Toulepleu 84 6 32N 8 24W
Toulon 21 43 10N 5 55E
Toulouse 20 43 37N 1 27E
Toummo 83 22 45N 14 8E
Toummo Dhoba 83 22 30N 14 31E
Toumodi 84 6 32N 5 4W
Tounassine, Hamada 82 28 48N 5 0W
Toungoo 67 19 0N 96 30E
Touques → 18 49 22N 0 8E
Touquet-Paris-Plage, Le 19 50 30N 1 36E
Tour-du-Pin, La 21 45 33N 5 27E
Touraine 18 47 20N 0 30E
Tourcoing 19 50 42N 3 10E
Tournai 16 50 35N 3 25E
Tournan-en-Brie 19 48 44N 2 46E
Tournay 20 43 13N 0 13E
Tournon 21 45 4N 4 50E
Tournon-St-Martin 18 46 45N 0 58E
Tournus 21 46 35N 4 54E
Tours 18 47 22N 0 40E
Touside, Pic 83 21 1N 16 29E
Touwsrivier 92 33 20S 20 0E
Tovarkovskiy 55 53 40N 38 14E
Tovdal 47 58 47N 8 10E
Tovdalselva → 47 58 15N 8 5E
Towamba 99 37 6S 149 43E
Towanda 114 41 46N 76 30W
Towang 67 27 37N 91 50E
Tower 116 47 49N 92 17W
Towerhill Cr. → 98 22 28S 144 35E
Towner 116 48 25N 100 26W
Townsend 118 46 25N 111 32W
Townshend, C. 97 22 18S 150 30E
Townshend I. 97 22 10S 150 31E
Townsville 97 19 15S 146 45E
Towson 114 39 26N 76 34W
Towyn 13 52 36N 4 5W
Toyah 117 31 20N 103 48W
Toyahvale 117 30 58N 103 45W
Toyama 74 36 40N 137 15E
Toyama □ 74 36 45N 137 30E
Toyama-Wan 74 37 0N 137 30E
Toyohashi 74 34 45N 137 25E
Toyokawa 74 34 48N 137 27E
Toyonaka 74 34 50N 135 28E
Toyooka 74 35 35N 134 48E
Toyota 74 35 3N 137 7E
Tozeur 83 33 56N 8 8E
Trabancos → 30 41 36N 5 15W
Traben Trarbach 25 49 57N 7 7E
Trabzon 64 41 0N 39 45E
Tracadie 107 47 30N 64 55W
Tracy, Calif., U.S.A. 119 37 46N 121 27W
Tracy, Minn., U.S.A. 116 44 12N 95 38W
Tradate 38 45 43N 8 54E
Trafalgar 100 38 14S 146 12E
Trafalgar, C. 31 36 10N 6 2W
Trăghân 83 26 0N 14 30E
Traian 46 45 2N 28 15E
Trail 108 49 5N 117 40W
Trainor L. 108 60 24N 120 17W
Tralee 15 52 16N 9 42W
Tralee B. 15 52 17N 9 55W
Tramore 15 52 10N 7 10W
Tran Ninh, Cao Nguyen 71 19 30N 103 10E
Tranås 49 58 3N 14 59E
Trancas 124 26 11S 65 20W
Tranche, La 20 46 20N 1 26W
Tranche-sur-Mer, La 18 46 20N 1 27W
Trancoso 30 40 49N 7 21W
Tranebjerg 49 55 51N 10 36E
Tranemo 49 57 30N 13 20E
Trang 71 7 33N 99 38E
Trangahy 93 19 7S 44 31E
Trangan 73 6 40S 134 20E
Trangie 99 32 4S 148 0E
Trångsviken 48 63 19N 14 0E
Trani 41 41 17N 16 24E
Tranoroa 93 24 42S 45 4E
Tranquebar 70 11 1N 79 54E
Tranqueras 125 31 13S 55 45W
Trans Nzoia □ 90 1 0N 35 0E
Transcona 109 49 55N 97 0W
Transilvania 46 46 19N 25 0E
Transkei □ 93 32 15S 28 15E
Transtrand 48 61 6N 13 20E
Transvaal □ 92 25 0S 29 0E
Transylvania = Transilvania 46 46 19N 25 0E
Transylvanian Alps 46 45 30N 25 0E
Trápani 40 38 1N 12 30E
Trapper Peak 118 45 56N 114 29W
Traralgon 97 38 12S 146 34E
Traryd 49 56 35N 13 45E
Trarza □ 84 17 30N 15 0W
Trasacco 39 41 58N 13 30E
Trăscău, Munţii 46 46 14N 23 14E
Trasimeno, L. 39 43 10N 12 5E
Trat 71 12 14N 102 33E
Traun 26 48 14N 14 15E
Traunsee 26 47 55N 13 50E
Traunstein 25 47 52N 12 40E
Tråvad 49 58 15N 13 5E
Traveller's L. 99 33 20S 142 0E
Travemünde 24 53 58N 10 52E
Travers, Mt. 101 42 1S 172 45E
Traverse City 114 44 45N 85 39W
Traverse Is. 5 57 0S 28 0W
Travnik 42 44 17N 17 39E
Trazo 30 43 0N 8 30W
Trbovlje 39 46 12N 15 5E
Trébbia → 38 45 4N 9 41E
Trebel → 24 53 55N 13 1E
Třebíč 26 49 14N 15 55E
Trebinje 42 42 44N 18 22E
Trebisacce 41 39 52N 16 32E
Trebišnica → 42 42 47N 18 8E
Trebišov 27 48 38N 21 41E
Trebižat → 42 43 15N 17 30E
Trebnje 39 45 54N 15 1E
Třeboň 26 48 59N 14 48E
Trebujena 31 36 52N 6 11W
Trecate 38 45 26N 8 42E
Tredegar 13 51 47N 3 16W
Tregaron 13 52 14N 3 56W
Trégastel-Plage 18 48 49N 3 31W
Tregnago 39 45 31N 11 10E
Tréguier 18 48 47N 3 16W
Trégune 18 47 51N 3 51W
Treherne 109 49 38N 98 42W
Tréia 39 43 20N 13 20E
Treignac 20 45 32N 1 48E
Treinta y Tres 125 33 16S 54 17W
Treis 25 50 9N 7 19E
Treklyano 42 42 33N 22 36E
Trekveld 92 30 35S 19 45E
Trelde Næs 49 55 38N 9 53E
Trelew 128 43 10S 65 20W
Trelissac 20 45 11N 0 47E
Trelleborg 49 55 20N 13 10E
Trélon 19 50 5N 4 6E
Tremblade, La 20 45 46N 1 8W
Tremiti 39 42 8N 15 30E
Tremonton 118 41 45N 112 10W
Tremp 32 42 10N 0 52E
Trenary 114 46 12N 86 59W
Trenche → 106 47 46N 72 53W
Trenčín 27 48 52N 18 4E
Trenggalek 73 8 5S 111 38E
Trenque Lauquen 124 36 5S 62 45W
Trent → 12 53 33N 0 44W
Trentino-Alto Adige □ 38 46 30N 11 0E
Trento 38 46 5N 11 8E
Trenton, Can. 106 44 10N 77 34W
Trenton, Mo., U.S.A. 116 40 5N 93 37W
Trenton, N.J., U.S.A. 114 40 15N 74 41W
Trenton, Nebr., U.S.A. 116 40 14N 101 4W
Trenton, Tenn., U.S.A. 117 35 58N 88 57W
Trepassey 107 46 43N 53 25W
Tréport, Le 18 50 3N 1 20E
Trepuzzi 41 40 26N 18 4E
Tres Arroyos 124 38 26S 60 20W
Três Corações 125 21 44S 45 15W
Três Lagoas 127 20 50S 51 43W
Tres Marías 120 21 25N 106 28W
Tres Montes, C. 128 46 50S 75 30W
Três Pontas 125 21 23S 45 29W
Tres Puentes 124 27 50S 70 15W
Tres Puntas, C. 128 47 0S 66 0W
Três Rios 125 22 6S 43 15W
Treska → 42 42 0N 21 20E
Treskavika Planina 42 43 40N 18 20E
Trespaderne 32 42 47N 3 24W
Trets 21 43 27N 5 41E
Treuchtlingen 25 48 58N 10 55E
Treuenbrietzen 24 52 6N 12 51E

Trevíglio	**38**	45 31N	9 35 E
Trevínca, Peña	**30**	42 15N	6 46W
Treviso	**39**	45 40N	12 15 E
Trévoux	**21**	45 57N	4 47 E
Treysa	**24**	50 55N	9 12 E
Trgovište	**42**	42 20N	22 10 E
Triabunna	**99**	42 30 S	147 55 E
Triánda	**45**	36 25N	28 10 E
Triaucourt-en-Argonne	**19**	48 59N	5 2 E
Tribsees	**24**	54 4N	12 46 E
Tribulation, C.	**97**	16 5 S	145 29 E
Tribune	**116**	38 30N	101 45W
Tricárico	**41**	40 37N	16 9 E
Tricase	**41**	39 56N	18 20 E
Trichinopoly = Tiruchchirappalli	**70**	10 45N	78 45 E
Trichur	**70**	10 30N	76 18 E
Trida	**99**	33 1 S	145 1 E
Trier	**25**	49 45N	6 37 E
Trieste	**39**	45 39N	13 45 E
Trieste, G. di	**39**	45 37N	13 40 E
Trieux →	**18**	48 50N	3 3W
Triggiano	**41**	41 4N	16 58 E
Triglav	**39**	46 21N	13 50 E
Trigno →	**39**	42 4N	14 48 E
Trigueros	**31**	37 24N	6 50W
Tríkeri	**45**	39 6N	23 5 E
Trikhonis, Límni	**45**	38 34N	21 30 E
Tríkkala	**44**	39 34N	21 47 E
Tríkkala □	**44**	39 41N	21 30 E
Trikora, Puncak	**73**	4 15 S	138 45 E
Trilj	**39**	43 38N	16 42 E
Trillo	**32**	40 42N	2 35W
Trim	**15**	53 34N	6 48W
Trincomalee	**70**	8 38N	81 15 E
Trindade, I.	**7**	20 20 S	29 50W
Trinidad, Boliv.	**126**	14 46 S	64 50W
Trinidad, Colomb.	**126**	5 25N	71 40W
Trinidad, Cuba	**121**	21 48N	80 0W
Trinidad, Uruguay	**124**	33 30 S	56 50W
Trinidad, U.S.A.	**117**	37 15N	104 30W
Trinidad, W. Indies	**121**	10 30N	61 15W
Trinidad & Tobago ■	**121**	10 30N	61 20W
Trinidad →	**120**	17 49N	95 9W
Trinidad, I.	**128**	39 10 S	62 0W
Trinitápoli	**41**	41 22N	16 5 E
Trinity, Can.	**107**	48 59N	53 55W
Trinity, U.S.A.	**117**	30 59N	95 25W
Trinity →, Calif., U.S.A.	**118**	41 11N	123 42W
Trinity →, Tex., U.S.A.	**117**	30 30N	95 0W
Trinity B., Austral.	**97**	16 30 S	146 0 E
Trinity B., Can.	**107**	48 20N	53 10W
Trinity Mts.	**118**	40 20N	118 50W
Trinkitat	**81**	18 45N	37 51 E
Trino	**38**	45 10N	8 18 E
Trion	**115**	34 35N	85 18W
Trionto C.	**41**	39 38N	16 47 E
Triora	**38**	44 0N	7 46 E
Tripoli = Tarābulus, Leb.	**64**	34 31N	35 50 E
Tripoli = Tarābulus, Libya	**83**	32 58N	13 12 E
Trípolis	**45**	37 31N	22 25 E
Tripp	**116**	43 16N	97 58W
Tripura □	**67**	24 0N	92 0 E
Trischen	**24**	54 3N	8 32 E
Tristan da Cunha	**7**	37 6 S	12 20W
Trivandrum	**70**	8 41N	77 0 E
Trivento	**41**	41 48N	14 31 E
Trnava	**27**	48 23N	17 35 E
Trobriand Is.	**98**	8 30 S	151 0 E
Trochu	**108**	51 50N	113 13W
Trodely I.	**106**	52 15N	79 26W
Troezen	**45**	37 25N	23 15 E
Trogir	**39**	43 32N	16 15 E
Troglav	**39**	43 56N	16 36 E
Trøgstad	**47**	59 37N	11 16 E
Tróia	**41**	41 22N	15 19 E
Troilus, L.	**106**	50 50N	74 35W
Troina	**41**	37 47N	14 34 E
Trois Fourches, Cap des	**82**	35 26N	2 58W
Trois-Pistoles	**107**	48 5N	69 10W
Trois-Riviéres	**106**	46 25N	72 34W
Troitsk	**58**	54 10N	61 35 E
Troitsko Pechorsk	**52**	62 40N	56 10 E
Trölladyngja	**50**	64 54N	17 16W
Trollhättan	**49**	58 17N	12 20 E
Trollheimen	**47**	62 46N	9 1 E
Troms fylke □	**50**	68 56N	19 0 E
Tromsø	**50**	69 40N	18 56 E
Tronador	**128**	41 10 S	71 50W
Trondheim	**47**	63 36N	10 25 E
Trondheimsfjorden	**47**	63 35N	10 30 E
Trönninge	**49**	56 37N	12 51 E
Trönö	**48**	61 22N	16 54 E
Tronto →	**39**	42 54N	13 55 E
Troon	**14**	55 33N	4 40W
Tropea	**41**	38 40N	15 53 E
Tropic	**119**	37 36N	112 4W
Tropoja	**44**	42 23N	20 10 E
Trossachs, The	**14**	56 14N	4 24W
Trostan	**15**	55 4N	6 10W
Trostberg	**25**	48 2N	12 33 E
Trostyanets	**54**	50 33N	34 59 E
Trotternish	**14**	57 32N	6 15W
Troup	**117**	32 10N	95 3W
Trout →	**108**	61 19N	119 51W
Trout L., N.W.T., Can.	**108**	60 40N	121 40W
Trout L., Ont., Can.	**109**	51 20N	93 15W
Trout Lake	**106**	46 10N	85 2W
Trout River	**107**	49 29N	58 8W
Trouville	**18**	49 21N	0 5 E
Trowbridge	**13**	51 18N	2 12W
Troy, Turkey	**44**	39 57N	26 12 E
Troy, Turkey	**64**	39 55N	26 20 E
Troy, Ala., U.S.A.	**115**	31 50N	85 58W
Troy, Idaho, U.S.A.	**118**	46 44N	116 46W
Troy, Kans., U.S.A.	**116**	39 47N	95 2W
Troy, Mo., U.S.A.	**116**	38 56N	90 59W
Troy, Montana, U.S.A.	**118**	48 30N	115 58W
Troy, N.Y., U.S.A.	**114**	42 45N	73 39W
Troy, Ohio, U.S.A.	**114**	40 0N	84 10W
Troyan	**43**	42 57N	24 43 E
Troyes	**19**	48 19N	4 3 E
Trpanj	**42**	43 1N	17 15 E
Trstena	**27**	49 21N	19 37 E
Trstenik	**42**	43 36N	21 0 E
Trubchevsk	**54**	52 33N	33 47 E
Trucial States = United Arab Emirates ■	**65**	24 0N	54 30 E
Truckee	**118**	39 20N	120 11W
Trujillo, Hond.	**121**	16 0N	86 0W
Trujillo, Peru	**126**	8 6 S	79 0W
Trujillo, Spain	**31**	39 28N	5 55W
Trujillo, U.S.A.	**117**	35 34N	104 44W
Trujillo, Venez.	**126**	9 22N	70 38W
Truk	**94**	7 25N	151 46 E
Trumann	**117**	35 42N	90 32W
Trumbull, Mt.	**119**	36 25N	113 8W
Trŭn	**42**	42 51N	22 38 E
Trun	**18**	48 50N	0 2 E
Trundle	**99**	32 53 S	147 35 E
Trung-Phan	**72**	16 0N	108 0 E
Truro, Can.	**107**	45 21N	63 14W
Truro, U.K.	**13**	50 17N	5 2W
Trustrup	**49**	56 20N	10 46 E
Truth or Consequences	**119**	33 9N	107 16W
Trutnov	**26**	50 37N	15 54 E
Truyère →	**20**	44 38N	2 34 E
Tryavna	**43**	42 54N	25 25 E
Tryon	**115**	35 15N	82 16W
Tryonyille	**112**	41 42N	79 48W
Trzcianka	**28**	53 3N	16 25 E
Trzciel	**28**	52 23N	15 50 E
Trzcińsko Zdrój	**28**	52 58N	14 35 E
Trzebiatów	**28**	54 3N	15 18 E
Trzebiez	**28**	53 38N	14 31 E
Trzebinia-Siersza	**27**	50 11N	19 18 E
Trzebnica	**28**	51 20N	17 1 E
Trzemeszno	**28**	52 33N	17 48 E
Tržič	**39**	46 22N	14 18 E
Tsageri	**57**	42 39N	42 46 E
Tsamandás	**44**	39 46N	20 21 E
Tsaratanana	**93**	16 47 S	47 39 E
Tsaratanana, Mt. de	**93**	14 0 S	49 0 E
Tsarevo = Michurin	**43**	42 9N	27 51 E
Tsarichanka	**56**	48 55N	34 30 E
Tsaritsáni	**44**	39 53N	22 14 E
Tsau	**92**	20 8 S	22 22 E
Tsebrikovo	**56**	47 9N	30 10 E
Tselinograd	**58**	51 10N	71 30 E
Tsetserleg	**75**	47 36N	101 32 E
Tshabong	**92**	26 2 S	22 29 E
Tshane	**92**	24 5 S	21 54 E
Tshela	**88**	4 57 S	13 4 E
Tshesebe	**93**	21 51 S	27 32 E
Tshibeke	**90**	2 40 S	28 35 E
Tshibinda	**90**	2 23 S	28 43 E
Tshikapa	**88**	6 28 S	20 48 E
Tshilenge	**90**	6 17 S	23 48 E
Tshinsenda	**91**	12 20 S	28 0 E
Tshofa	**90**	5 13 S	25 16 E
Tshwane	**92**	22 24 S	22 1 E
Tsigara	**92**	20 22 S	25 54 E
Tsihombe	**93**	25 18 S	45 29 E
Tsimlyansk	**57**	47 40N	42 6 E
Tsimlyanskoye Vdkhr.	**57**	48 0N	43 0 E
Tsinan = Jinan	**76**	36 38N	117 1 E
Tsineng	**92**	27 05 S	23 05 E
Tsínga	**44**	41 23N	24 44 E
Tsinghai = Qinghai □	**75**	36 0N	98 0 E
Tsingtao = Qingdao	**76**	36 5N	120 20 E
Tsinjomitondraka	**93**	15 40 S	47 8 E
Tsiroanomandidy	**93**	18 46 S	46 2 E
Tsivilsk	**55**	55 50N	47 25 E
Tsivory	**93**	24 4 S	46 5 E
Tskhinali	**53**	42 22N	43 52 E
Tskhinvali	**57**	42 14N	44 1 E
Tsna →	**55**	54 55N	41 58 E
Tsodilo Hill	**92**	18 49 S	21 43 E
Tsu	**74**	34 45N	136 25 E
Tsu L.	**108**	60 40N	111 52W
Tsuchiura	**74**	36 5N	140 15 E
Tsugaru-Kaikyō	**74**	41 35N	141 0 E
Tsumeb	**92**	19 9 S	17 44 E
Tsumis	**92**	23 39 S	17 29 E
Tsuruga	**74**	35 45N	136 2 E
Tsushima	**74**	34 20N	129 20 E
Tsvetkovo	**56**	49 8N	31 33 E
Tua →	**30**	41 13N	7 26W
Tual	**73**	5 38 S	132 44 E
Tuam	**15**	53 30N	8 50W
Tuamotu Arch.	**95**	17 0 S	144 0W
Tuamotu Ridge	**95**	20 0 S	138 0W
Tuao	**73**	17 55N	122 22 E
Tuapse	**57**	44 5N	39 10 E
Tuatapere	**101**	46 8 S	167 41 E
Tuba City	**119**	36 8N	111 18W
Tubac	**119**	31 37N	111 20W
Tuban	**73**	6 54 S	112 3 E
Tubarão	**125**	28 30 S	49 0W
Tūbās	**62**	32 20N	35 22 E
Tubau	**72**	3 10N	113 40 E
Tübingen	**25**	48 31N	9 4 E
Tubja, W. →	**86**	25 27N	38 45 E
Ţubruq	**81**	32 7N	23 55 E
Tubuai Is.	**95**	25 0 S	150 0W
Tucacas	**126**	10 48N	68 19W
Tuchodi →	**108**	58 17N	123 42W
Tuchola	**28**	53 33N	17 52 E
Tuchów	**27**	49 54N	21 1 E
Tucker's Town	**121**	32 17N	64 43W
Tucson	**119**	32 14N	110 59W
Tucumán □	**124**	26 48 S	66 2W
Tucumcari	**117**	35 12N	103 45W
Tucupita	**126**	9 2N	62 3W
Tucuruí	**127**	3 42 S	49 44W
Tuczno	**28**	53 13N	16 10 E
Tudela	**32**	42 4N	1 39W
Tudela de Duero	**30**	41 37N	4 39W
Tudmur	**64**	34 36N	38 15 E
Tudor, Lac	**107**	55 50N	65 25W
Tudora	**46**	47 31N	26 45 E
Tuella →	**30**	41 30N	7 12W
Tufi	**98**	9 8 S	149 19 E
Tuguegarao	**73**	17 35N	121 42 E
Tugur	**59**	53 44N	136 45 E
Tukangbesi, Kepulauan	**73**	6 0 S	124 0 E
Tukarak I.	**106**	56 15N	78 45W
Tûkh	**86**	30 21N	31 12 E
Tukobo	**84**	5 1N	2 47W
Tūkrah	**83**	32 30N	20 37 E
Tuktoyaktuk	**104**	69 27N	133 2W
Tukums	**54**	57 2N	23 10 E
Tukuyu	**91**	9 17 S	33 35 E
Tula, Hidalgo, Mexico	**120**	20 0N	99 20W
Tula, Tamaulipas, Mexico	**120**	23 0N	99 40W
Tula, Nigeria	**85**	9 51N	11 27 E
Tula, U.S.S.R.	**55**	54 13N	37 38 E
Tulak	**65**	33 55N	63 40 E
Tulancingo	**120**	20 5N	99 22W
Tulare	**119**	36 15N	119 26W
Tulare Lake	**119**	36 0N	119 53W
Tularosa	**119**	33 4N	106 1W
Tulbagh	**92**	33 16 S	19 6 E
Tulcán	**126**	0 48N	77 43W
Tulcea	**46**	45 13N	28 46 E
Tulcea □	**46**	45 0N	29 0 E
Tulchin	**56**	48 41N	28 49 E
Tulemalu L.	**109**	62 58N	99 25W
Tulgheş	**46**	46 58N	25 45 E
Tuli, Indon.	**73**	1 24 S	122 26 E
Tuli, Zimb.	**91**	21 58 S	29 13 E
Ţūlkarm	**62**	32 19N	35 2 E
Tulla	**117**	34 35N	101 44W
Tullahoma	**115**	35 23N	86 12W
Tullamore, Austral.	**99**	32 39 S	147 36 E
Tullamore, Ireland	**15**	53 17N	7 30W
Tulle	**20**	45 16N	1 46 E
Tullibigeal	**99**	33 25 S	146 44 E
Tullins	**21**	45 18N	5 29 E
Tulln	**26**	48 20N	16 4 E
Tullow	**15**	52 48N	6 45W
Tullus	**87**	11 7N	24 31 E
Tully	**98**	17 56 S	145 55 E
Ţulmaythah	**81**	32 40N	20 55 E
Tulmur	**98**	22 40 S	142 20 E
Tulnici	**46**	45 51N	26 38 E
Tulovo	**43**	42 33N	25 32 E
Tulsa	**117**	36 10N	96 0W
Tulsequah	**108**	58 39N	133 35W
Tulu Milki	**87**	9 55N	38 20 E
Tulu Welel	**87**	8 56N	34 47 E
Tulua	**126**	4 6N	76 11W
Tulun	**59**	54 32N	100 35 E
Tulungagung	**72**	8 5 S	111 54 E
Tum	**73**	3 36 S	130 21 E
Tuma	**55**	55 10N	40 30 E
Tuma →	**121**	13 6N	84 35W
Tumaco	**126**	1 50N	78 45W
Tumatumari	**126**	5 20N	58 55W
Tumba	**48**	59 12N	17 48 E
Tumba, L.	**88**	0 50 S	18 0 E
Tumbarumba	**99**	35 44 S	148 0 E
Tumbaya	**124**	23 50 S	65 26W
Túmbes	**126**	3 37 S	80 27W
Tumbwe	**91**	11 25 S	27 15 E
Tumen	**76**	43 0N	129 50 E
Tumen Jiang →	**76**	42 20N	130 35 E
Tumeremo	**126**	7 18N	61 30W
Tumkur	**70**	13 18N	77 6 E
Tummel, L.	**14**	56 43N	3 55W
Tump	**66**	26 7N	62 16 E
Tumpat	**71**	6 11N	102 10 E
Tumsar	**69**	21 26N	79 45 E
Tumu	**84**	10 56N	1 56W
Tumucumaque, Serra	**127**	2 0N	55 0W
Tumut	**97**	35 16 S	148 13 E
Tumwater	**118**	47 0N	122 58W
Tunas de Zaza	**121**	21 39N	79 34W
Tunbridge Wells	**13**	51 7N	0 16 E
Tuncurry	**99**	32 17 S	152 29 E
Tunduru	**91**	11 8 S	37 25 E
Tunduru □	**91**	11 5 S	37 22 E
Tundzha →	**43**	41 40N	26 35 E
Tune	**47**	59 16N	11 2 E
Tunga →	**70**	15 0N	75 50 E
Tunga Pass	**67**	29 0N	94 14 E
Tungabhadra →	**70**	15 57N	78 15 E
Tungabhadra Dam	**70**	15 0N	75 50 E
Tungaru	**81**	10 9N	30 52 E
Tungla	**121**	13 24N	84 21W
Tungnafellsjökull	**50**	64 45N	17 55W
Tungsten, Can.	**108**	61 57N	128 16W
Tungsten, U.S.A.	**118**	40 50N	118 10W
Tunguska, Nizhnyaya →	**59**	65 48N	88 4 E
Tunguska, Podkamennaya →	**59**	61 36N	90 18 E
Tuni	**70**	17 22N	82 36 E
Tunica	**117**	34 43N	90 23W
Tunis	**83**	36 50N	10 11 E
Tunis, Golfe de	**83**	37 0N	10 30 E
Tunisia ■	**83**	33 30N	9 10 E
Tunja	**126**	5 33N	73 25W
Tunkhannock	**113**	41 32N	75 46W
Tunliu	**76**	36 13N	112 52 E
Tunnsjøen	**50**	64 45N	13 25 E
Tunungayualok I.	**107**	56 0N	61 0W
Tunuyán	**124**	33 35 S	69 0W
Tunuyán →	**124**	33 33 S	67 30W
Tunxi	**75**	29 42N	118 25 E
Tuolumne	**119**	37 59N	120 16W
Tuoy-Khaya	**59**	62 32N	111 25 E
Tupã	**125**	21 57 S	50 28W
Tupelo	**115**	34 15N	88 42W
Tupik, U.S.S.R.	**54**	55 42N	33 22 E
Tupik, U.S.S.R.	**59**	54 26N	119 57 E
Tupinambaranas	**126**	3 0 S	58 0W
Tupiza	**124**	21 30 S	65 40W
Tupižnica	**42**	43 43N	22 10 E
Tupper	**108**	55 32N	120 1W
Tupper L.	**114**	44 18N	74 30W
Tupungato, Cerro	**124**	33 15 S	69 50W
Tuquan	**76**	45 18N	121 38 E
Tuque, La	**106**	47 30N	72 50W
Túquerres	**126**	1 5N	77 37W
Tura, India	**69**	25 30N	90 16 E
Tura, U.S.S.R.	**59**	64 20N	100 17 E
Turaba, Wadi →	**86**	21 15N	41 32 E
Turabah	**64**	28 20N	43 15 E
Turaiyur	**70**	11 9N	78 38 E
Tūrān	**65**	35 39N	56 42 E
Turan	**59**	51 55N	95 0 E
Turayf	**64**	31 41N	38 39 E
Turbacz	**27**	49 30N	20 8 E
Turbe	**42**	44 15N	17 35 E
Turda	**46**	46 34N	23 47 E
Turégano	**30**	41 9N	4 1W
Turek	**28**	52 3N	18 30 E
Turfan = Turpan	**75**	43 58N	89 10 E
Turfan Depression = Turpan Hami	**75**	42 40N	89 25 E
Tŭrgovishte	**43**	43 17N	26 38 E
Turgutlu	**64**	38 30N	27 48 E
Turhal	**56**	40 24N	36 5 E
Turia →	**33**	39 27N	0 19W
Turiaçu	**127**	1 40 S	45 19W
Turiaçu →	**127**	1 36 S	45 19W
Turiec →	**27**	49 07N	18 55 E
Turin	**108**	49 47N	112 24W
Turin = Torino	**38**	45 3N	7 40 E
Turka	**54**	49 10N	23 2 E
Turkana □	**90**	3 0N	35 30 E
Turkana, L.	**90**	3 30N	36 5 E
Turkestan	**58**	43 17N	68 16 E
Túrkeve	**27**	47 6N	20 44 E
Turkey ■	**64**	39 0N	36 0 E
Turki	**55**	52 0N	43 15 E
Turkmen S.S.R. □	**58**	39 0N	59 0 E
Turks Is.	**121**	21 20N	71 20W
Turks Island Passage	**121**	21 30N	71 30W
Turku	**51**	60 30N	22 19 E
Turkwe →	**90**	3 6N	36 6 E
Turlock	**119**	37 30N	120 55W
Turnagain →	**108**	59 12N	127 35W
Turnagain, C.	**101**	40 28 S	176 38 E
Turneffe Is.	**120**	17 20N	87 50W
Turner	**118**	48 52N	108 25W
Turner Valley	**108**	50 40N	114 17W
Turners Falls	**113**	42 36N	72 34W
Turnhout	**16**	51 19N	4 57 E
Türnitz	**26**	47 55N	15 29 E
Turnor L.	**109**	56 35N	108 35W
Turnov	**26**	50 34N	15 10 E
Tŭrnovo	**43**	43 5N	25 41 E
Turnovo	**43**	43 5N	25 41 E
Turnu Măgurele	**46**	43 46N	24 56 E
Turnu Rosu Pasul	**46**	45 33N	24 17 E
Turnu-Severin	**46**	44 39N	22 41 E
Turobin	**28**	50 50N	22 44 E
Turon	**117**	37 48N	98 27W
Turpan	**75**	43 58N	89 10 E
Turpan Hami	**75**	42 40N	89 25 E
Turrës, Kalaja e	**44**	41 10N	19 28 E
Turriff	**14**	57 32N	2 28W
Tursha	**55**	56 55N	47 36 E
Tursi	**41**	40 15N	16 27 E
Turtle Hd. I.	**98**	10 56 S	142 37 E
Turtle L., Can.	**109**	53 36N	108 38W
Turtle L., U.S.A.	**116**	45 22N	92 10W
Turtle Lake	**116**	47 30N	100 55W
Turtleford	**109**	53 23N	108 57W
Turukhansk	**59**	65 21N	88 5 E
Turun ja Porin lääni □	**51**	60 27N	22 15 E
Turzovka	**27**	49 25N	18 35 E
Tuscaloosa	**115**	33 13N	87 31W
Tuscánia	**39**	42 25N	11 53 E
Tuscany = Toscana	**38**	43 28N	11 15 E
Tuscola, Ill., U.S.A.	**114**	39 48N	88 15W
Tuscola, Tex., U.S.A.	**117**	32 15N	99 48W
Tuscumbia	**115**	34 42N	87 42W
Tuskar Rock	**15**	52 12N	6 10W
Tuskegee	**115**	32 24N	85 39W
Tustna	**47**	63 10N	8 5 E
Tuszyn	**28**	51 36N	19 33 E
Tutayev	**55**	57 53N	39 32 E
Tuticorin	**70**	8 50N	78 12 E
Tutin	**42**	43 0N	20 20 E
Tutóia	**127**	2 45 S	42 20W
Tutong	**72**	4 47N	114 40 E
Tutova →	**46**	46 20N	27 30 E
Tutrakan	**43**	44 2N	26 40 E
Tutshi L.	**108**	59 56N	134 30W
Tuttle	**116**	47 9N	100 00W
Tuttlingen	**25**	47 59N	8 50 E
Tutuala	**73**	8 25 S	127 15 E
Tutuila	**101**	14 19 S	170 50W
Tuva A.S.S.R. □	**59**	51 30N	95 0 E
Tuvalu ■	**94**	8 0 S	178 0 E
Tuxpan	**120**	20 58N	97 23W
Tuxtla Gutiérrez	**120**	16 50N	93 10W
Tuy	**30**	42 3N	8 39W
Tuy Hoa	**71**	13 5N	109 10 E
Tuya L.	**108**	59 7N	130 35W
Tuyen Hoa	**71**	17 50N	106 10 E
Tuz Gölü	**64**	38 45N	33 30 E
Ţūz Khurmātū	**64**	34 56N	44 38 E
Tuzla	**42**	44 34N	18 41 E
Tuzlov →	**57**	47 28N	39 45 E
Tvååker	**49**	57 4N	12 25 E
Tvedestrand	**47**	58 38N	8 58 E
Tvŭrditsa	**43**	42 42N	25 53 E
Twardogóra	**28**	51 23N	17 28 E
Tweed	**112**	44 29N	77 19W
Tweed →	**14**	55 42N	2 10W
Tweedsmuir Prov. Park	**108**	53 0N	126 20W
Twentynine Palms	**119**	34 10N	116 4W
Twillingate	**107**	49 42N	54 45W
Twin Bridges	**118**	45 33N	112 23W
Twin Falls	**118**	42 30N	114 30W
Twin Valley	**116**	47 18N	96 15W
Twisp	**118**	48 21N	120 5W
Twistringen	**24**	52 48N	8 38 E
Two Harbors	**116**	47 1N	91 40W
Two Hills	**108**	53 43N	111 52W
Two Rivers	**114**	44 10N	87 31W
Twofold B.	**97**	37 8 S	149 59 E
Tychy	**27**	50 9N	18 59 E
Tyczyn	**27**	49 58N	22 2 E
Tydal	**47**	63 4N	11 34 E
Tykocin	**28**	53 13N	22 46 E
Tyldal	**47**	62 8N	10 48 E

Tyler Uvira

Tyler, Minn., U.S.A. 116 44 18N 96 8W
Tyler, Tex., U.S.A. 117 32 18N 95 18W
Týn nad Vltavou 26 49 13N 14 26 E
Tynda 59 55 10N 124 43 E
Tyne & Wear □ 12 54 55N 1 35W
Tyne → 12 54 58N 1 28W
Tynemouth 12 55 1N 1 27W
Tynset 47 62 17N 10 47 E
Tyre = Sūr 62 33 12N 35 11 E
Tyrifjorden 47 60 2N 10 8 E
Tyringe 49 56 9N 13 35 E
Tyristrand 47 60 5N 10 5 E
Tyrnyauz 57 43 21N 42 45 E
Tyrol = Tirol 26 47 3N 10 43 E
Tyrone 112 40 39N 78 10W
Tyrrell → 100 35 26 S 142 51 E
Tyrrell Arm 109 62 27N 97 30W
Tyrrell, L. 99 35 20 S 142 50 E
Tyrrell L. 109 63 7N 105 27W
Tyrrhenian Sea 34 40 0N 12 30 E
Tysfjorden 50 68 7N 16 25 E
Tysnes 47 60 1N 5 30 E
Tysnesøy 47 60 0N 5 35 E
Tyssedal 47 60 7N 6 35 E
Tystberga 49 58 51N 17 15 E
Tyub Karagan, M. 57 44 40N 50 19 E
Tyuleniy 57 44 28N 47 30 E
Tyulgan 52 52 22N 56 12 E
Tyumen 58 57 11N 65 29 E
Tywi → 13 51 48N 4 20W
Tzaneen 93 23 47 S 30 9 E
Tzermiadhes Neápolis 46 35 11N 25 29 E
Tzoumérka, Óros 44 39 30N 21 26 E
Tzukong = Zigong 75 29 15N 104 48 E

U

Uad Erni, O. → 82 26 45N 10 47W
Uanda 98 21 37 S 144 55 E
Uarsciek 63 2 28N 45 55 E
Uasin □ 90 0 30N 35 20 E
Uato-Udo 73 9 7 S 125 36 E
Uatumã → 126 2 26 S 57 37W
Uaupés 126 0 8 S 67 5W
Ub 42 44 28N 20 6 E
Ubá 125 21 8 S 43 0W
Ubaitaba 127 14 18 S 39 20W
Ubangi = Oubangi → 88 1 0N 17 50 E
Ubauro 68 28 15N 69 45 E
Ubaye → 21 44 28N 6 18 E
Ube 74 33 56N 131 15 E
Ubeda 33 38 3N 3 23W
Uberaba 127 19 50 S 47 55W
Uberlândia 127 19 0 S 48 20W
Überlingen 25 47 46N 9 10 E
Ubiaja 85 6 41N 6 22 E
Ubombo 93 27 31 S 32 4 E
Ubon Ratchathani 71 15 15N 104 50 E
Ubondo 90 0 55 S 25 42 E
Ubort → 54 52 6N 28 30 E
Ubrique 31 36 41N 5 27W
Ubundu 90 0 22 S 25 30 E
Ucayali → 126 4 30 S 73 30W
Uchi Lake 109 51 5N 92 35W
Uchiura-Wan 74 42 25N 140 40 E
Uchte 24 52 29N 8 52 E
Uchur → 59 58 48N 130 35 E
Ucluelet 108 48 57N 125 32W
Ucuriş 46 46 41N 21 58 E
Uda → 59 54 42N 135 14 E
Udaipur 68 24 36N 73 44 E
Udaipur Garhi 69 27 0N 86 35 E
Udamalpet 70 10 35N 77 15 E
Udbina 39 44 31N 15 47 E
Uddeholm 48 60 1N 13 38 E
Uddevalla 49 58 21N 11 55 E
Uddjaur 50 65 25N 21 15 E
Udgir 70 18 25N 77 5 E
Udi 85 6 23N 7 21 E
Udine 39 46 5N 13 10 E
Udipi 70 13 25N 74 42 E
Udmurt A.S.S.R. □ 52 57 30N 52 30 E
Udon Thani 71 17 29N 102 46 E
Udvoy Balkan 43 42 50N 26 50 E
Udzungwa Range 91 9 30 S 35 10 E
Ueckermünde 24 53 45N 14 1 E
Ueda 74 36 24N 138 16 E
Uedineniya, Os. 4 78 0N 85 0 E
Uelen 59 66 10N 170 0W
Uelzen 24 53 0N 10 33 E
Uere → 88 3 45N 24 45 E
Ufa 52 54 45N 55 55 E
Ufa → 52 54 40N 56 0 E
Uffenheim 25 49 32N 10 15 E
Ugalla → 90 5 8 S 30 42 E
Uganda ■ 90 2 0N 32 0 E
Ugento 41 39 55N 18 10 E
Ugep 85 5 53N 8 2 E
Ugie 93 31 10 S 28 13 E
Ugijar 33 36 58N 3 7W
Ugine 21 45 45N 6 25 E
Ugla 86 25 40N 37 42 E
Uglegorsk 59 49 5N 142 2 E
Uglich 55 57 33N 38 20 E
Ugljane 39 43 35N 16 46 E
Ugolyak 59 64 33N 120 30 E
Ugra → 54 54 30N 36 7 E
Ugürchin 43 43 6N 24 26 E
Uh → 27 48 7N 21 25 E
Uherske Hradiště 27 49 4N 17 30 E
Uhersky Brod 27 49 1N 17 40 E
Uhlava → 26 49 45N 13 24 E
Uhrichsville 114 40 23N 81 22W
Uige 88 7 30 S 14 40 E
Uiju 76 40 15N 124 35 E
Uinta Mts. 118 40 45N 110 30W
Uitenhage 92 33 40 S 25 28 E
Uithuizen 16 53 24N 6 41 E
Újfehértó 27 47 49N 21 41 E
Ujhani 68 28 0N 79 6 E
Ujjain 68 23 9N 75 43 E
Újpest 27 47 32N 19 6 E
Újszász 27 47 19N 20 7 E
Ujung Pandang 73 5 10 S 119 20 E
Uka 59 57 50N 162 0 E
Ukara I. 90 1 50 S 33 0 E
Ukerewe □ 90 2 0 S 32 30 E
Ukerewe I. 90 2 0 S 33 0 E
Ukholovo 55 53 47N 40 30 E
Ukhrul 67 25 10N 94 25 E
Ukhta 52 63 55N 54 0 E
Ukiah 118 39 10N 123 9W
Ukmerge 54 55 15N 24 45 E
Ukrainian S.S.R. □ 56 49 0N 32 0 E
Ukwi 92 23 29 S 20 30 E
Ulaanbaatar 75 47 54N 106 52 E
Ulaangom 75 50 0N 92 10 E
Ulamba 91 9 3 S 23 38 E
Ulan Bator = Ulaanbaatar 75 47 54N 106 52 E
Ulan Ude 59 51 45N 107 40 E
Ulanga □ 91 8 40 S 36 50 E
Ulanów 28 50 30N 22 16 E
Ulaya, Morogoro, Tanz. 90 7 3 S 36 55 E
Ulaya, Tabora, Tanz. 90 4 25 S 33 30 E
Ulcinj 42 41 58N 19 10 E
Ulco 92 28 21 S 24 15 E
Ulefoss 47 59 17N 9 16 E
Ulëza 44 41 46N 19 57 E
Ulfborg 49 56 16N 8 20 E
Ulhasnagar 70 19 15N 73 10 E
Uljma 42 45 2N 21 10 E
Ulla → 30 42 39N 8 44W
Ulladulla 99 35 21 S 150 29 E
Ullånger 48 62 58N 18 10 E
Ullapool 14 57 54N 5 10W
Ullared 49 57 8N 12 42 E
Ulldecona 32 40 36N 0 20 E
Ullswater 12 54 35N 2 52W
Ullung-do 76 37 30N 130 30 E
Ulm 25 48 23N 10 0 E
Ulmarra 99 29 37 S 153 4 E
Ulmeni 46 45 4N 26 40 E
Ulricehamn 49 57 46N 13 26 E
Ulsberg 47 62 45N 9 59 E
Ulsteinvik 47 62 21N 5 53 E
Ulster □ 15 54 35N 6 30W
Ulstrem 43 42 1N 26 27 E
Ulubaria 69 22 31N 88 4 E
Uluguru Mts. 90 7 15 S 37 40 E
Ulungur He 75 47 1N 87 24 E
Ulutau 58 48 39N 67 1 E
Ulverston 12 54 13N 3 7W
Ulverstone 97 41 11 S 146 11 E
Ulvik 47 60 35N 6 54 E
Ulya 59 59 10N 142 0 E
Ulyanovsk 55 54 20N 48 25 E
Ulyasutay (Javhlant) 75 47 56N 97 28 E
Ulysses 117 37 39N 101 25W
Umag 39 45 26N 13 31 E
Umala 126 17 25 S 68 5W
Uman 56 48 40N 30 12 E
Umarkhed 70 19 37N 77 46 E
Umatilla 118 45 58N 119 17W
Umba 52 66 50N 34 20 E
Umbertide 39 43 18N 12 20 E
Umboi I. 98 5 40 S 148 0 E
Umbrella Mts. 101 45 35 S 169 5 E
Umbria □ 39 42 53N 12 30 E
Ume älv → 50 63 45N 20 20 E
Umeå 50 63 45N 20 20 E
Umera 73 0 12 S 129 37 E
Umfuli → 91 17 30 S 29 23 E
Umgusa 91 19 29 S 27 52 E
Umka 42 44 40N 20 19 E
Umkomaas 93 30 13 S 30 48 E
Umm al Arānib 83 26 10N 14 43 E
Umm al Qaywayn 65 25 30N 55 35 E
Umm Arda 87 15 17N 32 31 E
Umm az Zamul 65 22 42N 55 18 E
Umm Bel 87 13 35N 28 0 E
Umm Dubban 87 15 23N 32 52 E
Umm el Fahm 62 32 31N 35 9 E
Umm Koweika 87 13 10N 32 16 E
Umm Lajj 64 25 0N 37 23 E
Umm Merwa 86 18 4N 32 30 E
Umm Qays 62 32 40N 35 41 E
Umm Rumah 86 25 50N 36 30 E
Umm Ruwaba 87 12 50N 31 20 E
Umm Sidr 87 14 29N 25 10 E
Ummanz 24 54 29N 13 9 E
Umnak 104 53 20N 168 20W
Umniati → 91 16 49 S 28 45 E
Umpang 71 16 3N 98 54 E
Umpqua → 118 43 42N 124 3W
Umrer 68 20 51N 79 18 E
Umreth 68 22 41N 73 4 E
Umshandige Dam 91 20 10 S 30 40 E
* Umtali 91 18 58 S 32 38 E
Umtata 93 31 36 S 28 49 E
Umuahia 85 5 33N 7 29 E
Umvukwe Ra. 91 16 45 S 30 45 E
Umvukwes 91 17 0 S 30 57 E
Umvuma 91 19 16 S 30 30 E
Umzimvubu 93 31 38 S 29 33 E
Umzingwane → 91 22 12 S 29 56 E
Umzinto 93 30 15 S 30 45 E
Una 68 20 46N 71 8 E
Una → 39 45 16N 16 55 E
Unac → 39 44 30N 16 9 E
Unadilla 113 42 20N 75 17W
Unalaska 104 53 40N 166 40W
Uncastillo 32 42 21N 1 8W
Uncia 126 18 25 S 66 40W
Uncompahgre Pk. 119 38 5N 107 32W
Unden 49 58 45N 14 25 E
Underbool 99 35 10 S 141 51 E
Undersaker 48 63 19N 13 21 E
Undersvik 48 61 36N 16 20 E
Undredal 47 60 57N 7 6 E
Unecha 54 52 50N 32 37 E
Ungarie 99 33 38 S 146 56 E

* *Renamed Mutare*

Ungava B. 105 59 30N 67 30W
Ungeny 56 47 11N 27 51 E
Unggi 76 42 16N 130 28 E
Ungwatiri 87 16 52N 36 10 E
Uni 55 56 44N 51 47 E
União da Vitória 125 26 13 S 51 5W
Uniejów 28 51 59N 18 46 E
Unije 39 44 40N 14 15 E
Unimak 104 55 0N 164 0W
Unimak Pass. 104 53 30N 165 15W
Union, Miss, U.S.A. 117 32 34N 89 14W
Union, Mo., U.S.A. 116 38 25N 91 0W
Union, S.C., U.S.A. 115 34 43N 81 39W
Union City, N.J., U.S.A. 113 40 47N 74 5W
Union City, Ohio, U.S.A. 114 40 11N 84 49W
Union City, Pa., U.S.A. 114 41 53N 79 50W
Union City, Tenn., U.S.A. 117 36 25N 89 0W
Union Gap 118 46 38N 120 29W
Unión, La, Chile 128 40 10 S 73 0W
Unión, La, El Sal. 120 13 20N 87 50W
Unión, La, Spain 33 37 38N 0 53W
Union, Mt. 119 34 34N 112 21W
Union of Soviet Socialist Republics ■ 59 60 0N 100 0 E
Union Springs 115 32 9N 85 44W
Uniondale 92 33 39 S 23 7 E
Uniontown 114 39 54N 79 45W
Unionville 116 40 29N 93 1W
Unirea 46 44 15N 27 35 E
United Arab Emirates ■ 65 23 50N 54 0 E
United Kingdom ■ 11 55 0N 3 0W
United States of America ■ 111 37 0N 96 0W
United States Trust Terr. of the Pacific Is. 94 10 0N 160 0 E
Unity 109 52 30N 109 5W
Universales, Mtes. 32 40 18N 1 33W
Unjha 68 23 46N 72 24 E
Unnao 69 26 35N 80 30 E
Uno, Ilha 84 11 15N 16 13W
Unst 14 60 50N 0 55W
Unstrut → 24 51 10N 11 48 E
Unuk → 108 56 5N 131 3W
Ünye 56 41 5N 37 15 E
Unzha 55 58 0N 44 0 E
Unzha → 55 57 30N 43 40 E
Upa → 27 50 35N 16 15 E
Upata 126 8 1N 62 24W
Upemba, L. 91 8 30 S 26 20 E
Upernavik 4 72 49N 56 20W
Upington 92 28 25 S 21 15 E
Upleta 68 21 46N 70 16 E
Upolu 101 13 58 S 172 0W
Upper Alkali Lake 118 41 47N 120 8W
Upper Arrow L. 108 50 30N 117 50W
Upper Austria = Oberösterreich 26 48 10N 14 0 E
Upper Foster L. 109 56 47N 105 20W
Upper Hutt 101 41 8 S 175 5 E
Upper Klamath L. 118 42 16N 121 55W
Upper L. Erne 15 54 14N 7 22W
Upper Lake 118 39 10N 122 55W
Upper Musquodoboit 107 45 10N 62 58W
Upper Red L. 116 48 0N 95 0W
Upper Sandusky 114 40 50N 83 17W
Upper Taimyr → 59 74 15N 99 48 E
*Upper Volta ■ 84 12 0N 1 0W
Upphärad 49 58 9N 12 19 E
Uppsala 48 59 53N 17 38 E
Uppsala län □ 48 60 0N 17 30 E
Upstart, C. 98 19 41 S 147 45 E
Upton 116 44 8N 104 35W
Ur 64 30 55N 46 25 E
Uracara 126 2 20 S 57 50W
Urach 25 48 29N 9 25 E
Urad Qianqi 76 40 40N 108 30 E
Ural → 58 47 0N 51 48 E
Ural, Mt. 99 33 21 S 146 12 E
Ural Mts. = Uralskie Gory 52 60 0N 59 0 E
Uralla 99 30 37 S 151 29 E
Uralsk 52 51 20N 51 20 E
Uralskie Gory 52 60 0N 59 0 E
Urambo 90 5 4 S 32 0 E
Urambo □ 90 5 0 S 32 0 E
Urana 100 35 15 S 146 21 E
Urandangie 97 21 32 S 138 14 E
Uranium City 109 59 34N 108 37W
Uravakonda 70 14 57N 77 12 E
Urawa 74 35 50N 139 40 E
Uray 58 60 5N 65 15 E
Urbana, Ill., U.S.A. 114 40 7N 88 12W
Urbana, Ohio, U.S.A. 114 40 9N 83 44W
Urbana, La 126 7 8N 66 56W
Urbánia 39 43 40N 12 31 E
Urbel → 32 42 21N 3 40W
Urbino 39 43 43N 12 38 E
Urbión, Picos de 32 42 1N 2 52W
Urcos 126 13 40 S 71 38W
Urda, Spain 31 39 25N 3 43W
Urda, U.S.S.R. 57 48 52N 47 23 E
Urdinarrain 124 32 37 S 58 52W
Urdos 20 42 51N 0 35W
Urdzhar 58 47 5N 81 38 E
Ure → 12 54 20N 1 25W
Uren 55 57 35N 45 55 E
Urengoy 58 65 58N 28 25 E
Ures 120 29 30N 110 30W
Urfa 64 37 12N 38 50 E
Urfahr 26 48 19N 14 17 E
Urgench 58 41 40N 60 41 E
Uri □ 25 46 43N 8 35 E
Uribia 126 11 43N 72 16W
Urim 62 31 18N 34 32 E
Uriondo 124 21 41 S 64 41W
Urique → 120 26 29N 107 58W
Urk 16 52 39N 5 36 E
Urla 64 38 20N 26 47 E
Urlati 46 44 59N 26 15 E
Urmia = Rezā'īyeh 64 37 40N 45 0 E
Urmia, L. = Rezā'īyeh, Daryācheh-ye 64 37 30N 45 30 E
Uroševac 42 42 23N 21 10 E
Urshult 49 56 31N 14 50 E
Ursus 28 52 12N 20 53 E

**Renamed Burkina Faso*

Uruana 127 15 30 S 49 41W
Uruapan 120 19 30N 102 0W
Urubamba 126 13 20 S 72 10W
Urubamba → 126 10 43 S 73 48W
Uruçuí 127 7 20 S 44 28W
Uruguai → 125 26 0 S 53 30W
Uruguaiana 124 29 50 S 57 0W
Uruguay ■ 124 32 30 S 56 30W
Uruguay → 124 34 12 S 58 18W
Urumchi = Ürümqi 75 43 45N 87 45 E
Ürümqi 75 43 45N 87 45 E
Urup → 57 46 0N 41 10 E
Urup, Os. 59 46 0N 151 0 E
Uryung-Khaya 59 72 48N 113 23 E
Uryupinsk 55 50 45N 41 58 E
Urzhum 55 57 10N 49 56 E
Urziceni 46 44 40N 26 42 E
Usa → 52 65 67N 56 55 E
Uşak 64 38 43N 29 28 E
Usakos 92 22 0 S 15 31 E
Ušće 42 43 30N 20 39 E
Usedom 24 53 50N 13 55 E
Usfan 86 21 58N 39 27 E
Ush-Tobe 58 45 16N 78 0 E
Ushakova, O. 4 82 0N 80 0 E
Ushant = Ouessant, Île d' 18 48 25N 5 5W
Ushashi 90 1 59 S 33 57 E
Ushat 87 7 59N 29 28 E
Ushuaia 128 54 50 S 68 23W
Ushumun 59 52 47N 126 32 E
Usk → 13 51 37N 2 56W
Uskedal 47 59 56N 5 53 E
Üsküdar 64 41 0N 29 5 E
Uslar 24 51 39N 9 39 E
Usman 55 52 5N 39 48 E
Usoke 90 5 7 S 32 19 E
Usolye Sibirskoye 59 52 48N 103 40 E
Usoro 85 5 33N 6 11 E
Uspallata, P. de 124 32 37 S 69 22W
Uspenskiy 58 48 41N 72 43 E
Ussel 20 45 32N 2 18 E
Ussuriysk 59 43 48N 131 59 E
Ust-Aldan = Batamay 59 63 30N 129 15 E
Ust Amginskoye = Khandyga 59 62 42N 135 0 E
Ust-Bolsheretsk 59 52 50N 156 15 E
Ust Buzulukskaya 55 50 8N 42 11 E
Ust chaun 59 68 47N 170 30 E
Ust-Donetskiy 57 47 35N 40 55 E
Ust'-Ilga 59 55 5N 104 55 E
Ust Ilimpeya = Yukti 59 63 20N 105 0 E
Ust-Ilimsk 59 58 3N 102 39 E
Ust Ishim 58 57 45N 71 10 E
Ust-Kamchatsk 59 56 10N 162 28 E
Ust-Kamenogorsk 58 50 0N 82 36 E
Ust-Karenga 59 54 25N 116 30 E
Ust Khayryuzova 59 57 15N 156 45 E
Ust-Kut 59 56 50N 105 42 E
Ust Kuyga 59 70 1N 135 43 E
Ust-Labinsk 57 45 15N 39 41 E
Ust Luga 54 59 35N 28 20 E
Ust Maya 59 60 30N 134 28 E
Ust-Mil 59 59 40N 133 11 E
Ust-Nera 59 64 35N 143 15 E
Ust-Nyukzha 59 56 34N 121 37 E
Ust Olenek 59 73 0N 119 48 E
Ust-Omchug 59 61 9N 149 38 E
Ust Port 58 69 40N 84 26 E
Ust Tsilma 52 65 25N 52 0 E
Ust-Tungir 59 55 25N 120 36 E
Ust Urt = Ustyurt, Plato 58 44 0N 55 0 E
Ust Usa 52 66 0N 56 30 E
Ust Vorkuta 58 67 24N 64 0 E
Ustaoset 47 60 30N 8 2 E
Ustaritz 20 43 24N 1 27W
Uste 55 59 35N 39 40 E
Ústí nad Labem 26 50 41N 14 3 E
Ústí nad Orlicí 27 49 58N 16 24 E
Ustica 40 38 42N 13 10 E
Ustka 28 54 35N 16 55 E
Ustroń 27 49 43N 18 48 E
Ustrzyki Dolne 27 49 27N 22 40 E
Ustye 59 57 46N 94 37 E
Ustyurt, Plato 58 44 0N 55 0 E
Ustyuzhna 55 58 50N 36 32 E
Usu 75 44 27N 84 40 E
Usuki 74 33 8N 131 49 E
Usulután 120 13 25N 88 28W
Usumacinta → 120 17 0N 91 0W
Usure 90 4 40 S 34 22 E
Uta 73 4 33 S 136 0 E
Utah □ 118 39 30N 111 30W
Utah, L. 118 40 10N 111 58W
Ute Cr. 117 35 21N 103 45W
Utena 54 55 27N 25 40 E
Ütersen 24 53 40N 9 40 E
Utete 90 8 0 S 38 45 E
Uthai Thani 71 15 22N 100 3 E
Utiariti 126 13 0 S 58 10W
Utica, N.Y., U.S.A. 114 43 5N 75 18W
Utica, Ohio, U.S.A. 112 40 13N 82 26W
Utiel 32 39 37N 1 11W
Utik L. 109 55 15N 96 0W
Utikuma L. 108 55 50N 115 30W
Utrecht, Neth. 16 52 5N 5 8 E
Utrecht, S. Afr. 93 27 38 S 30 20 E
Utrecht □ 16 52 6N 5 7 E
Utrera 31 37 12N 5 48W
Utsjoki 50 69 51N 26 59 E
Utsunomiya 74 36 30N 139 50 E
Uttar Pradesh □ 69 27 0N 80 0 E
Uttaradit 71 17 36N 100 5 E
Uttoxeter 12 52 53N 1 50W
Ütze 24 52 28N 10 11 E
Uusikaarlepyy 50 63 32N 22 31 E
Uusikaupunki 51 60 47N 21 25 E
Uva 52 56 59N 52 13 E
Uvac → 42 43 35N 19 40 E
Uvalde 117 29 15N 99 48W
Uvarovo 55 51 59N 42 14 E
Uvat 58 59 5N 68 50 E
Uvinza 90 5 5 S 30 24 E
Uvira 90 3 22 S 29 3 E

Uvs Nuur Verdigre

Uvs Nuur **75** 50 20N 92 30 E
Uwajima **74** 33 10N 132 35 E
Uweinat, Jebel **86** 21 54N 24 58 E
Uxbridge **112** 44 6N 79 7W
Uxin Qi **76** 38 50N 109 5 E
Uxmal **120** 20 22N 89 46W
Uyandi **59** 69 19N 141 0 E
Uyo **85** 5 1N 7 53 E
Uyuni **126** 20 28 S 66 47W
Uzbek S.S.R. □ **58** 41 30N 65 0 E
Uzen **53** 43 27N 53 10 E
Uzen, Bol. → **55** 50 0N 49 30 E
Uzen, Mal. → **55** 50 0N 48 30 E
Uzerche **20** 45 25N 1 34 E
Uzès **21** 44 1N 4 26 E
Uzh → **54** 51 15N 30 12 E
Uzhgorod **54** 48 36N 22 18 E
Uzlovaya **55** 54 0N 38 5 E
Uzunköprü **43** 41 16N 26 43 E

V

Vaal → **92** 29 4 S 23 38 E
Vaaldam **93** 27 0 S 28 14 E
Vaalwater **93** 24 15 S 28 8 E
Vaasa **50** 63 6N 21 38 E
Vaasan lääni □ **50** 63 2N 22 50 E
Vabre **20** 43 42N 2 24 E
Vác **27** 47 49N 19 10 E
Vacaria **125** 28 31 S 50 52W
Vacaville **118** 38 21N 122 0W
Vaccarès, Étang de **21** 43 32N 4 34 E
Vach → **58** 60 45N 76 45 E
Vache, Î.-à- **121** 18 2N 73 35W
Väddö **48** 59 55N 18 50 E
Vadnagar **68** 23 47N 72 40 E
Vado Lígure **38** 44 16N 8 26 E
Vadodara **68** 22 20N 73 10 E
Vadsø **50** 70 3N 29 50 E
Vadstena **49** 58 28N 14 54 E
Vaduz **25** 47 8N 9 31 E
Værøy **50** 67 40N 12 40 E
Vagney **19** 48 1N 6 43 E
Vagnhärad **48** 58 57N 17 33 E
Vagos **30** 40 33N 8 42W
Váh → **27** 47 55N 18 0 E
Vahsel B. **5** 75 0 S 35 0W
Vaigach **58** 70 10N 59 0 E
Vaigai → **70** 9 15N 79 10 E
Vaiges **18** 48 2N 0 30W
Vaihingen **25** 48 55N 8 58 E
Vaijapur **70** 19 58N 74 45 E
Vaikam **70** 9 45N 76 25 E
Vailly Aisne **19** 49 25N 3 30 E
Vaippar → **70** 9 0N 78 25 E
Vaison **21** 44 14N 5 4 E
Vajpur **68** 21 24N 73 17 E
Vakarel **43** 42 35N 23 40 E
Vaksdal **47** 60 29N 5 45 E
Vál **27** 47 22N 18 40 E
Val-d'Ajol, Le **19** 47 55N 6 30 E
Val-de-Marne □ **19** 48 45N 2 28 E
Val-d'Oise □ **19** 49 5N 2 10 E
Val d'Or **106** 48 7N 77 47W
Val Marie **109** 49 15N 107 45W
Valadares **30** 41 5N 8 38W
Valahia **46** 44 35N 25 0 E
Valais □ **25** 46 12N 7 45 E
Valandovo **42** 41 19N 22 34 E
Valašské Meziříčí **27** 49 29N 17 59 E
Valáxa **45** 38 50N 24 29 E
Vălcani **42** 46 0N 20 26 E
Valcheta **128** 40 40 S 66 8W
Valdagno **39** 45 38N 11 18 E
Valdahon, Le **19** 47 8N 6 20 E
Valday **54** 57 58N 33 9 E
Valdayskaya Vozvyshennost **54** 57 0N 33 30 E
Valdeazogues → **31** 38 45N 4 55W
Valdemarsvik **49** 58 14N 16 40 E
Valdepeñas, Ciudad Real, Spain **31** 38 43N 3 25W
Valdepeñas, Jaén, Spain **31** 37 33N 3 47W
Valderaduey → **30** 41 31N 5 42W
Valderrobres **32** 40 53N 0 9 E
Valdés, Pen. **128** 42 30 S 63 45W
Valdez **104** 61 14N 76 17W
Valdivia **128** 39 50 S 73 14W
Valdobbiádene **39** 45 53N 12 0 E
Valdosta **115** 30 50N 83 20W
Valdoviño **30** 43 36N 8 8W
Valdres **47** 60 55N 9 28 E
Vale, U.S.A. **118** 44 0N 117 15W
Vale, U.S.S.R. **57** 41 30N 42 58 E
Valea lui Mihai **46** 47 32N 22 11 E
Valença, Brazil **127** 13 20 S 39 5W
Valença, Port. **30** 42 1N 8 34W
Valença do Piauí **127** 6 20 S 41 45W
Valençay **19** 47 9N 1 34 E
Valence **21** 44 57N 4 54 E
Valence-d'Agen **20** 44 8N 0 54 E
Valencia, Spain **33** 39 27N 0 23W
Valencia, Venez. **126** 10 11N 68 0W
Valencia □ **33** 39 20N 0 40W
Valencia, Albufera de **33** 39 20N 0 27W
Valencia de Alcántara **31** 39 25N 7 14W
Valencia de Don Juan **30** 42 17N 5 31W
Valencia del Ventoso **31** 38 15N 6 29W
Valencia, G. de **33** 39 30N 0 20 E
Valenciennes **19** 50 20N 3 34 E
Văleni **46** 44 15N 24 45 E
Valensole **21** 43 50N 5 59 E
Valentia Hr. **15** 51 56N 10 17W
Valentia I. **15** 51 54N 10 22W
Valentim, Sa. do **127** 6 0 S 43 30W
Valentine, Nebr., U.S.A. **116** 42 50N 100 35W
Valentine, Tex., U.S.A. **117** 30 36N 104 28W
Valenza **38** 45 2N 8 39 E
Våler **47** 60 41N 11 50 E
Valera **126** 9 19N 70 37W
Valga **54** 57 44N 26 0 E
Valguarnera Caropepe **41** 37 30N 14 22 E
Valier **118** 48 25N 112 9W
Valinco, G. de **21** 41 40N 8 52 E
Valjevo **42** 44 18N 19 53 E
Valkenswaard **16** 51 21N 5 29 E
Vall de Uxó **32** 39 49N 0 15W
Valla **48** 59 2N 16 20 E
Valladolid, Mexico **120** 20 40N 88 11W
Valladolid, Spain **30** 41 38N 4 43W
Valladolid □ **30** 41 38N 4 43W
Vallata **41** 41 3N 15 16 E
Valldemosa **32** 39 43N 2 37 E
Valle **47** 59 13N 7 33 E
Valle d'Aosta □ **38** 45 45N 7 22 E
Valle de Arán **32** 42 50N 0 55 E
Valle de Cabuérniga **30** 43 14N 4 18W
Valle de la Pascua **126** 9 13N 66 0W
Valle de Santiago **120** 20 25N 101 15W
Valle Fértil, Sierra del **124** 30 20 S 68 0W
Valle Hermoso **120** 25 35N 97 40W
Vallecas **30** 40 23N 3 41W
Vallejo **118** 38 12N 122 15W
Vallenar **124** 28 30 S 70 50W
Valleraugue **20** 44 6N 3 39 E
Vallet **18** 47 10N 1 15W
Valletta **36** 35 54N 14 30 E
Valley City **116** 46 57N 98 0W
Valley Falls **118** 42 33N 120 16W
Valleyview **108** 55 5N 117 17W
Valli di Comácchio **39** 44 40N 12 15 E
Vallimanca, Arroyo **124** 35 40 S 59 10W
Vallo della Lucánia **41** 40 14N 15 16 E
Vallon **21** 44 25N 4 23 E
Vallorbe **25** 46 42N 6 20 E
Valls **32** 41 18N 1 15 E
Vallsta **48** 61 31N 16 22 E
Valmaseda **32** 43 11N 3 12W
Valmiera **54** 57 37N 25 29 E
Valmont **18** 49 45N 0 30 E
Valmontone **40** 41 48N 12 55 E
Valmy **19** 49 5N 4 45 E
Valnera, Mte. **32** 43 9N 3 40W
Valognes **18** 49 30N 1 28W
Valona = Vlóra **44** 40 32N 19 28 E
Valongo **30** 41 8N 8 30W
Valpaços **30** 41 36N 7 17W
Valparaiso, Chile **124** 33 2 S 71 40W
Valparaiso, Mexico **120** 22 50N 103 32W
Valparaiso **114** 41 27N 87 2W
Valparaiso □ **124** 33 2 S 71 40W
Valpovo **42** 45 39N 18 25 E
Valréas **21** 44 24N 5 0 E
Vals **25** 46 39N 9 11 E
Vals → **92** 27 23 S 26 30 E
Vals-les-Bains **21** 44 42N 4 24 E
Vals, Tanjung **73** 8 26 S 137 25 E
Valsbaai **92** 34 15 S 18 40 E
Valskog **48** 59 27N 15 57 E
Válta **44** 40 3N 23 25 E
Valtellina **38** 46 9N 9 55 E
Valuyki **55** 50 10N 38 5 E
Valverde del Camino **31** 37 35N 6 47W
Valverde del Fresno **30** 40 15N 6 51W
Vama **46** 47 34N 25 42 E
Vámos **45** 35 24N 24 13 E
Vamsadhara → **70** 18 21N 84 8 E
Van **64** 38 30N 43 20 E
Van Alstyne **117** 33 25N 96 36W
Van Bruyssel **107** 47 56N 72 9W
Van Buren, Can. **107** 47 10N 67 55W
Van Buren, Ark., U.S.A. **117** 35 28N 94 18W
Van Buren, Me., U.S.A. **115** 47 10N 68 1W
Van Buren, Mo., U.S.A. **117** 37 0N 91 0W
Van der Kloof Dam **92** 30 04 S 24 40 E
Van Diemen, C. **97** 16 30 S 139 46 E
Van Diemen G. **96** 11 45 S 132 0 E
Van Gölü **64** 38 30N 43 0 E
Van Horn **117** 31 3N 104 55W
Van Reenen P. **93** 28 22 S 29 27 E
Van Rees, Pegunungan **73** 2 35 S 138 15 E
Van Tassell **116** 42 40N 104 3W
Van Tivu **70** 8 51N 78 15 E
Van Wert **114** 40 52N 84 31W
Vanavara **59** 60 22N 102 16 E
Vancouver, Can. **108** 49 15N 123 10W
Vancouver, U.S.A. **118** 45 44N 122 41W
Vancouver I. **108** 49 50N 126 0W
Vandalia, Ill., U.S.A. **116** 38 57N 89 4W
Vandalia, Mo., U.S.A. **116** 39 18N 91 30W
Vandeloos Bay **70** 8 0N 81 45 E
Vanderbijlpark **93** 26 42 S 27 54 E
Vandergrift **114** 40 36N 79 33W
Vanderhoof **108** 54 0N 124 0W
Vanderlin I. **97** 15 44 S 137 2 E
Vandyke **98** 24 10 S 147 51 E
Vänern **49** 58 47N 13 30 E
Vänersborg **49** 58 26N 12 19 E
Vang Vieng **71** 18 58N 102 32 E
Vanga **90** 4 35 S 39 12 E
Vangaindrano **93** 23 21 S 47 36 E
Vanguard **109** 49 55N 107 20W
Vanier **106** 45 27N 75 40W
Vanimo **98** 2 42 S 141 21 E
Vanivilasa Sagara **70** 13 45N 76 30 E
Vaniyambadi **70** 12 46N 78 44 E
Vankarem **59** 67 51N 175 50 E
Vankleek Hill **106** 45 32N 74 40W
Vanna **50** 70 6N 19 50 E
Vännäs **50** 63 58N 19 48 E
Vannes **18** 47 40N 2 47W
Vanoise, Massif de la **21** 45 25N 6 40 E
Vanrhynsdorp **92** 31 36 S 18 44 E
Vanrook **98** 16 57 S 141 57 E
Vans, Les **21** 44 25N 4 7 E
Vansbro **48** 60 32N 14 15 E
Vanse **47** 58 6N 6 41 E
Vansittart B. **96** 14 3 S 126 17 E
Vanthli **68** 21 28N 70 25 E
Vanua Levu **101** 16 33 S 179 15 E
Vanua Mbalavu **101** 17 40 S 178 57W
Vanwyksvlei **92** 30 18 S 21 49 E
Vanylven **47** 62 5N 5 33 E
Vapnyarka **56** 48 32N 28 45 E
Var □ **21** 43 27N 6 18 E
Var → **21** 43 39N 7 12 E
Vara **49** 58 16N 12 55 E
Varada → **70** 15 0N 75 40 E
Varades **18** 47 25N 1 1W
Varaita → **38** 44 49N 7 36 E
Varaldsøy **47** 60 6N 5 59 E
Varallo **38** 45 50N 8 13 E
Varanasi (Benares) **69** 25 22N 83 0 E
Varangerfjorden **50** 70 3N 29 25 E
Varaždin **39** 46 20N 16 20 E
Varazze **38** 44 21N 8 36 E
Varberg **49** 57 6N 12 20 E
Vardar → **42** 40 35N 22 50 E
Varde **49** 55 38N 8 29 E
Varde Å **49** 55 35N 8 19 E
Varel **24** 53 23N 8 9 E
Varena **54** 54 12N 24 30 E
Varennes-sur-Allier **20** 46 19N 3 24 E
Vareš **42** 44 12N 18 23 E
Varese **38** 45 49N 8 50 E
Varese Lígure **38** 44 22N 9 33 E
Vårgårda **49** 58 2N 12 49 E
Varginha **125** 21 33 S 45 25W
Vargön **49** 58 22N 12 20 E
Varhaug **47** 58 37N 5 41 E
Variadero **117** 35 43N 104 17W
Varillas **124** 24 0 S 70 10W
Väring **49** 58 30N 14 0 E
Värmeln **48** 59 35N 12 54 E
Värmlands län □ **48** 60 0N 13 20 E
Varna **43** 43 13N 27 56 E
Varna → **70** 16 48N 74 32 E
Värnamo **49** 57 10N 14 3 E
Varnsdorf **26** 50 55N 14 35 E
Värö **49** 57 16N 12 11 E
Vars **113** 45 21N 75 21W
Varteig **47** 59 23N 11 12 E
Varvarin **42** 43 43N 21 20 E
Varzaneh **65** 32 25N 52 40 E
Varzi **38** 44 50N 9 12 E
Varzo **38** 46 12N 8 15 E
Varzy **19** 47 22N 3 20 E
Vas □ **27** 47 10N 16 55 E
Vasa **50** 63 6N 21 38 E
Vasa Barris → **127** 11 10 S 37 10W
Vásárosnamény **27** 48 9N 22 19 E
Vascão → **31** 37 31N 7 31W
Vaşcău **46** 46 28N 22 30 E
Vascongadas **32** 42 50N 2 45W
Väse **48** 59 23N 13 52 E
Vasht = Khāsh **65** 28 14N 61 14 E
Vasilevichi **54** 52 15N 29 50 E
Vasilikón **45** 38 25N 23 40 E
Vasilkov **54** 50 7N 30 15 E
Vaslui **46** 46 38N 27 42 E
Vaslui □ **46** 46 30N 27 45 E
Väsman **48** 60 9N 15 5 E
Vassar, Can. **109** 49 10N 95 55W
Vassar, U.S.A. **114** 43 23N 83 33W
Västerås **49** 59 37N 16 38 E
Västerbottens län □ **50** 64 58N 18 0 E
Västernorrlands län □ **48** 63 30N 17 30 E
Västervik **49** 57 43N 16 43 E
Västmanlands län □ **48** 59 45N 16 20 E
Vasto **39** 42 8N 14 40 E
Vasvár **27** 47 3N 16 47 E
Vatan **19** 47 4N 1 50 E
Vathí, Ithákí, Greece **45** 38 18N 20 40 E
Vathí, Sámos, Greece **45** 37 46N 27 1 E
Váthia **45** 36 29N 22 29 E
Vatican City ■ **39** 41 54N 12 27 E
Vaticano, C. **40** 38 40N 15 48 E
Vatin **42** 45 12N 21 20 E
Vatnajökull **50** 64 30N 16 48W
Vatnås **47** 59 58N 9 37 E
Vatne **47** 62 33N 6 38 E
Vatneyri **50** 65 35N 24 0W
Vatoa **101** 19 50 S 178 13W
Vatoloha, Mt. **93** 17 52 S 47 48 E
Vatomandry **93** 19 20 S 48 59 E
Vatra-Dornei **46** 47 22N 25 22 E
Vättern **49** 58 25N 14 30 E
Vaucluse □ **21** 44 3N 5 10 E
Vaucouleurs **19** 48 37N 5 40 E
Vaud □ **25** 46 35N 6 30 E
Vaughan **119** 34 37N 105 12W
Vaughn **118** 47 37N 111 36W
Vaupés → **126** 0 2N 67 16W
Vauvert **21** 43 42N 4 17 E
Vauxhall **108** 50 5N 112 9W
Vava'u **101** 18 36 S 174 0W
Vavincourt **19** 48 49N 5 12 E
Vavoua **84** 7 23N 6 29W
Vaxholm **48** 59 25N 18 20 E
Växjö **49** 56 52N 14 50 E
Vaygach, Ostrov **58** 70 0N 60 0 E
Vazovgrad **43** 42 39N 24 45 E
Vechta **24** 52 47N 8 18 E
Vechte → **16** 52 34N 6 6 E
Vecilla, La **30** 42 51N 5 27W
Vecsés **27** 47 26N 19 19 E
Vedaraniam **70** 10 25N 79 50 E
Veddige **49** 57 17N 12 20 E
Vedea → **46** 44 0N 25 20 E
Vedia **124** 34 30 S 61 31W
Vedra, I. del **33** 38 52N 1 12 E
Veendam **16** 53 5N 6 52 E
Veenendaal **16** 52 2N 5 34 E
Vefsna → **50** 65 48N 13 10 E
Vega, Norway **50** 65 40N 11 55 E
Vega, U.S.A. **117** 35 18N 102 26W
Vega, La **121** 19 20N 70 30W
Vegadeo **30** 43 27N 7 4W
Vegafjorden **50** 65 37N 12 0 E
Vegesack **24** 53 10N 8 38 E
Veggli **47** 60 3N 9 9 E
Veghel **16** 51 37N 5 32 E
Vegorritis, Límni **44** 40 45N 21 45 E
Vegreville **108** 53 30N 112 5W
Vegusdal **47** 58 32N 8 10 E
Veii **39** 42 0N 12 24 E
Vejen **49** 55 30N 9 9 E
Vejer de la Frontera **31** 36 15N 5 59W
Vejle **49** 55 43N 9 30 E
Vejle Fjord **49** 55 40N 9 50 E
Vela Luka **39** 42 59N 16 44 E
Velanai I. **70** 9 45N 79 45 E
Velarde **119** 36 11N 106 1W
Velasco **117** 29 0N 95 20W
Velasco, Sierra de. **124** 29 20 S 67 10W
Velay, Mts. du **20** 45 0N 3 40 E
Velddrif **92** 32 42 S 18 11 E
Velebit Planina **39** 44 50N 15 20 E
Velebitski Kanal **39** 44 45N 14 55 E
Veleka → **43** 42 4N 27 58 E
Velenje **39** 46 23N 15 8 E
Velestínon **44** 39 23N 22 43 E
Veleta, La **31** 37 1N 3 22W
Vélez **126** 6 1N 73 41W
Velež **42** 43 19N 18 2 E
Vélez Blanco **33** 37 41N 2 5W
Vélez Málaga **31** 36 48N 4 5W
Vélez Rubio **33** 37 41N 2 5W
Velhas → **127** 17 13 S 44 49W
Velika **42** 45 27N 17 40 E
Velika Gorica **39** 45 44N 16 5 E
Velika Gradište **42** 44 46N 21 29 E
Velika Kapela **39** 45 10N 15 5 E
Velika Kladuša **39** 45 11N 15 48 E
Velika Morava → **42** 44 43N 21 3 E
Velika Plana **42** 44 20N 21 1 E
Velikaya → **54** 57 48N 28 20 E
Velikaya Lepetikha **56** 47 2N 33 58 E
Veliké Kapušany **27** 48 34N 22 5 E
Velike Lašče **39** 45 49N 14 45 E
Veliki Backa Kanal **42** 45 45N 19 15 E
Veliki Jastrebac **42** 43 25N 21 30 E
Veliki Popović **42** 44 8N 21 18 E
Veliki Ustyug **52** 60 47N 46 20 E
Velikiye Luki **54** 56 25N 30 32 E
Velikonda Range **70** 14 45N 79 10 E
Velikoye, Oz. **55** 55 15N 40 10 E
Velingrad **43** 42 4N 23 58 E
Velino, Mte. **39** 42 10N 13 20 E
Velizh **54** 55 36N 31 11 E
Velké Karlovice **27** 49 20N 18 17 E
Velke Meziřici **26** 49 21N 16 1 E
Vel'ký ostrov Žitný **27** 48 5N 17 20 E
Vellar → **70** 11 30N 79 36 E
Velletri **40** 41 43N 12 43 E
Vellinge **49** 55 29N 13 0 E
Vellore **70** 12 57N 79 10 E
Velsen-Noord **16** 52 27N 4 40 E
Velsk **52** 61 10N 42 5 E
Velten **24** 52 40N 13 11 E
Velva **116** 48 6N 100 56W
Velvendós **44** 40 15N 22 6 E
Vembanad Lake **70** 9 36N 76 15 E
Veme **47** 60 14N 10 7 E
Ven **49** 55 55N 12 45 E
Vena **49** 57 31N 16 0 E
Venado **120** 22 56N 101 10W
Venado Tuerto **124** 33 50 S 62 0W
Venafro **41** 41 28N 14 3 E
Venarey-les-Laumes **19** 47 32N 4 26 E
Venaria **38** 45 6N 7 39 E
Venčane **42** 44 24N 20 28 E
Vence **21** 43 43N 7 6 E
Vendas Novas **31** 38 39N 8 27W
Vendée □ **18** 46 50N 1 35W
Vendée → **18** 46 20N 1 10W
Vendée, Collines de **18** 46 35N 0 45W
Vendeuvre-sur-Barse **19** 48 14N 4 28 E
Vendôme **18** 47 47N 1 3 E
Vendrell **32** 41 10N 1 30 E
Vendsyssel **49** 57 22N 10 0 E
Véneta, Laguna **39** 45 23N 12 25 E
Véneto □ **39** 45 40N 12 0 E
Venev **55** 54 22N 38 17 E
Venézia **39** 45 27N 12 20 E
Venézia, Golfo di **39** 45 20N 13 0 E
Venezuela ■ **126** 8 0N 65 0W
Venezuela, Golfo de **126** 11 30N 71 0W
Vengurla **70** 15 53N 73 45 E
Vengurla Rocks **70** 15 55N 73 22 E
Venice = Venézia **39** 45 27N 12 20 E
Vénissieux **21** 45 43N 4 53 E
Venkatagiri **70** 14 0N 79 35 E
Venkatapuram **70** 18 20N 80 30 E
Venlo **16** 51 22N 6 11 E
Vennesla **47** 58 15N 8 0 E
Venraij **16** 51 31N 6 0 E
Venta de Cardeña **31** 38 16N 4 20W
Venta de San Rafael **30** 40 42N 4 12W
Ventana, Punta de la **120** 24 4N 109 48W
Ventana, Sa. de la **124** 38 0 S 62 30W
Ventersburg **92** 28 7 S 27 9 E
Ventimíglia **38** 43 50N 7 39 E
Ventnor **13** 50 35N 1 12W
Ventotene **40** 40 48N 13 25 E
Ventoux **21** 44 10N 5 17 E
Ventspils **54** 57 25N 21 32 E
Ventuari → **126** 3 58N 67 2W
Ventura **119** 34 16N 119 18W
Vera, Argent. **124** 29 30 S 60 20W
Vera, Spain **33** 37 15N 1 51W
Veracruz **120** 19 10N 96 10W
Veracruz □ **120** 19 0N 96 15W
Veraval **68** 20 53N 70 27 E
Verbánia **38** 45 56N 8 43 E
Verbicaro **41** 39 46N 15 54 E
Vercelli **38** 45 19N 8 25 E
Verchovchevo **56** 48 32N 34 10 E
Verdalsøra **50** 63 48N 11 30 E
Verde →, Argent. **128** 41 56 S 65 5W
Verde →, Chihuahua, Mexico **120** 26 29N 107 58W
Verde →, Oaxaca, Mexico **120** 15 59N 97 50W
Verde →, Veracruz, Mexico **120** 21 10N 102 50W
Verde →, Parag. **124** 23 9 S 57 37W
Verde, Cay **121** 23 0N 75 5W
Verden **24** 52 58N 9 18 E
Verdhikoúsa **44** 39 47N 21 59 E
Verdigre **116** 42 38N 98 0W

Verdon Visoko

Verdon → 21 43 43N 5 46 E
Verdon-sur-Mer, Le 20 45 33N 1 4W
Verdun 19 49 12N 5 24 E
Verdun-sur-le Doubs 19 46 54N 5 0 E
Vereeniging 93 26 38 S 27 57 E
Vérendrye, Parc Prov. de la 106 47 20N 76 40W
Verga, C. 84 10 30N 14 10W
Vergara 32 43 9N 2 28W
Vergato 38 44 18N 11 8 E
Vergemont 98 23 33 S 143 1 E
Vergemont Cr. → 98 24 16 S 143 16 E
Vergennes 113 44 9N 73 15W
Vergt 20 45 2N 0 43 E
Verín 30 41 57N 7 27W
Veriña 30 43 32N 5 43W
Verkhnedvinsk 54 55 45N 27 58 E
Verkhnevilyuysk 59 63 27N 120 18 E
Verkhneye Kalinino 59 59 54N 108 8 E
Verkhniy Baskunchak 57 48 14N 46 44 E
Verkhovye 55 52 55N 37 15 E
Verkhoyansk 59 67 35N 133 25 E
Verkhoyanskiy Khrebet 59 66 0N 129 0 E
Verlo 109 50 19N 108 35W
Verma 47 62 21N 8 3 E
Vermenton 19 47 40N 3 42 E
Vermilion 109 53 20N 110 50W
Vermilion →, Alta., Can. 109 53 22N 110 51W
Vermilion →, Qué., Can. 106 47 38N 72 56W
Vermilion, B. 117 29 45N 91 55W
Vermilion Bay 109 49 51N 93 34W
Vermilion Chutes 108 58 22N 114 51W
Vermilion L. 116 47 53N 92 25W
Vermillion 116 42 50N 96 56W
Vermont □ 114 43 40N 72 50W
Vernal 118 40 28N 109 35W
Verner 106 46 25N 80 8W
Verneuil-sur-Avre 18 48 45N 0 55 E
Vernon, Can. 108 50 20N 119 15W
Vernon, France 18 49 5N 1 30 E
Vernon, U.S.A. 117 34 10N 99 20W
Vero Beach 115 27 39N 80 23W
Véroia 44 40 34N 22 12 E
Verolanuova 38 45 20N 10 5 E
Véroli 40 41 43N 13 24 E
Verona 38 45 27N 11 0 E
Veropol 59 65 15N 168 40 E
Versailles 19 48 48N 2 8 E
Vert, C. 84 14 45N 17 30W
Vertou 18 47 10N 1 28W
Vertus 19 48 54N 4 0 E
Verulam 93 29 38 S 31 2 E
Verviers 16 50 37N 5 52 E
Vervins 19 49 50N 3 53 E
Verwood 109 49 30N 105 40W
Verzej 39 46 34N 16 13 E
Veselí nad Lužnicí 26 49 12N 14 43 E
Veseliye 43 42 18N 27 38 E
Veselovskoye Vdkhr. 57 47 0N 41 0 E
Veshenskaya 57 49 35N 41 44 E
Vesle → 19 49 23N 3 38 E
Vesoul 19 47 40N 6 11 E
Vessigebro 49 56 58N 12 40 E
Vest-Agder fylke □ 47 58 30N 7 15 E
Vestby 47 59 37N 10 45 E
Vestfjorden 50 67 55N 14 0 E
Vestfold-fylke □ 47 59 15N 10 0 E
Vestmannaeyjar 50 63 27N 20 15W
Vestmarka 47 59 56N 11 59 E
Vestnes 47 62 39N 7 5 E
Vestone 38 45 43N 10 25 E
Vestsjællands Amtskommune □ 49 55 30N 11 20 E
Vestspitsbergen 4 78 40N 17 0 E
Vestvågøy 50 68 18N 13 50 E
Vesuvio 41 40 50N 14 22 E
Vesuvius, Mt. = Vesuvio 41 40 50N 14 22 E
Vesyegonsk 55 58 40N 37 16 E
Veszprém 27 47 8N 17 57 E
Veszprém □ 27 47 5N 17 55 E
Vésztő 27 46 55N 21 16 E
Vetapalem 70 15 47N 80 18 E
Vetlanda 49 57 24N 15 3 E
Vetluga 55 57 53N 45 45 E
Vetluzhskiy 55 57 17N 45 12 E
Vetovo 43 43 42N 26 16 E
Vetralia 39 42 20N 12 2 E
Vetren 43 42 15N 24 3 E
Vettore, Monte 39 42 49N 13 16 E
Veurne 16 51 5N 2 40 E
Vevey 25 46 28N 6 51 E
Vévi 44 40 47N 21 38 E
Veynes 21 44 32N 5 49 E
Veys 64 31 30N 49 0 E
Vézelise 19 48 30N 6 5 E
Vézère → 20 44 53N 0 53 E
Vezhen 43 42 50N 24 20 E
Viacha 126 16 39 S 68 18W
Viadana 38 44 55N 10 30 E
Viana, Brazil 127 3 13 S 45 0W
Viana, Spain 32 42 31N 2 22W
Viana del Bollo 30 42 11N 7 6W
Viana do Alentejo 31 38 17N 7 59W
Viana do Castelo 30 41 42N 8 50W
Vianna do Castelo □ 30 41 50N 8 30W
Vianópolis 127 16 40 S 48 35W
Viar → 31 37 36N 5 50W
Viaréggio 38 43 52N 10 13 E
Viaur → 20 44 8N 1 58 E
Vibank 109 50 20N 103 56W
Vibo Valéntia 41 38 40N 16 5 E
Viborg 49 56 27N 9 23 E
Vibraye 18 48 3N 0 44 E
Vic-en-Bigorre 20 43 24N 0 3 E
Vic-Fézensac 20 43 47N 0 19 E
Vic-sur-Cère 20 44 59N 2 38 E
Vic-sur-Seille 19 48 45N 6 33 E
Vicenza 39 45 32N 11 31 E
Vich 32 41 58N 2 19 E
Vichuga 55 57 12N 41 55 E
Vichy 20 46 9N 3 26 E
Vicksburg, Mich., U.S.A. 114 42 10N 85 30W
Vicksburg, Miss., U.S.A. 117 32 22N 90 56W
Vico del Gargaro 41 41 54N 15 57 E
Vico, L. di 39 42 20N 12 10 E
Viçosa 127 9 28 S 36 14W
Victor, Colo., U.S.A. 116 38 43N 105 7W
Victor, N.Y., U.S.A. 112 42 58N 77 24W
Victor Harbour 97 35 30 S 138 37 E
Victoria, Argent. 124 32 40 S 60 10W
Victoria, Camer. 88 4 1N 9 10 E
Victoria, Can. 108 48 30N 123 25W
Victoria, Chile 128 38 13 S 72 20W
* Victoria, Guin. 84 10 50N 14 32W
Victoria, H. K. 75 22 16N 114 15 E
Victoria, Malay. 72 5 20N 115 14 E
Victoria, Kans., U.S.A. 116 38 52N 99 8W
Victoria, Tex., U.S.A. 117 28 50N 97 0W
Victoria □, Austral. 97 37 0 S 144 0 E
Victoria □, Zimb. 91 21 0 S 31 30 E
Victoria → 96 15 10 S 129 40 E
Victoria Beach 109 50 40N 96 35W
Victoria de las Tunas 121 20 58N 76 59W
Victoria Falls 91 17 58 S 25 52 E
Victoria, Grand L. 106 47 31N 77 30W
Victoria Harbour 106 44 45N 79 45W
Victoria I. 104 71 0N 111 0W
Victoria, L. 90 1 0 S 33 0 E
Victoria Ld. 5 75 0 S 160 0 E
Victoria, Mt. 98 8 55 S 147 32 E
Victoria Nile → 90 2 14N 31 26 E
Victoria Res. 107 48 20N 57 27W
Victoria River Downs 96 16 25 S 131 0 E
Victoria Taungdeik 67 21 15N 93 55 E
Victoria West 92 31 25 S 23 4 E
Victoriaville 107 46 4N 71 56W
Victorica 124 36 20 S 65 30W
Victorville 119 34 32N 117 18W
Vicuña 124 30 0 S 70 50W
Vicuña Mackenna 124 33 53 S 64 25W
Vidalia 115 32 13N 82 25W
Vidauban 21 43 25N 6 27 E
Vidigueira 31 38 12N 7 48W
Vidin 42 43 59N 22 50 E
Vidio, Cabo 30 43 35N 6 14W
Vidisha (Bhilsa) 68 23 28N 77 53 E
Vidöstern 49 57 5N 14 0 E
Vidra 46 45 56N 26 55 E
Viduša 42 42 55N 18 21 E
Vidzy 54 55 23N 26 37 E
Viechtach 25 49 5N 12 53 E
Viedma 128 40 50 S 63 0W
Viedma, L. 128 49 30 S 72 30W
Vieira 30 41 38N 8 8W
Viella 32 42 43N 0 44 E
Vien Pou Kha 71 20 45N 101 5 E
Vienenburg 24 51 57N 10 35 E
Vienna 117 37 29N 88 54W
Vienna = Wien 27 48 12N 16 22 E
Vienne 21 45 31N 4 53 E
Vienne □ 20 46 30N 0 42 E
Vienne → 18 47 13N 0 5 E
Vientiane 71 17 58N 102 36 E
Vientos, Paso de los 121 20 0N 74 0W
Viersen 24 51 15N 6 23 E
Vierwaldstättersee 25 47 0N 8 30 E
Vierzon 19 47 13N 2 5 E
Vieste 40 41 52N 16 14 E
Vietnam ■ 71 19 0N 106 0 E
Vieux-Boucau-les-Bains 20 43 48N 1 23W
Vif 21 45 5N 5 41 E
Vigan 73 17 35N 120 28 E
Vigan, Le 20 44 0N 3 36 E
Vigévano 38 45 18N 8 50 E
Vigia 127 0 50 S 48 5W
Vignacourt 19 50 1N 2 15 E
Vignemale, Pic du 20 42 47N 0 10W
Vigneulles 19 48 59N 5 40 E
Vignola 38 44 29N 11 0 E
Vigo 30 42 12N 8 41W
Vigo, Ría de 30 42 15N 8 45W
Vihiers 18 47 10N 0 30W
Vijayadurg 70 16 30N 73 25 E
Vijayawada (Bezwada) 70 16 31N 80 39 E
Vikedal 47 59 30N 5 55 E
Viken 49 58 39N 14 20 E
Vikersund 47 59 58N 10 2 E
Viking 108 53 7N 111 50W
Vikna 50 64 55N 10 58 E
Vikramasingapuram 70 8 40N 76 47 E
Viksjö 48 62 45N 17 26 E
Vikulovo 58 56 50N 70 40 E
Vila Aiferes Chamusca 93 24 27 S 33 0 E
Vila Caldas Xavier 91 14 28 S 33 0 E
Vila Coutinho 91 14 37 S 34 19 E
Vila da Maganja 91 17 18 S 37 30 E
Vila de João Belo = Xai-Xai 93 25 6 S 33 31 E
Vila de Junqueiro 91 15 25 S 36 58 E
Vila de Manica 91 18 58 S 32 59 E
Vila de Rei 31 39 41N 8 9W
Vila do Bispo 31 37 5N 8 53W
Vila do Chibuto 93 24 40 S 33 33 E
Vila do Conde 30 41 21N 8 45W
Vila Fontes 91 17 51 S 35 24 E
Vila Franca de Xira 31 38 57N 8 59W
Vila Gamito 91 14 12 S 33 0 E
Vila Gomes da Costa 93 24 20 S 33 37 E
Vila Luisa 93 25 45 S 32 35 E
Vila Machado 91 19 15 S 34 14 E
Vila Mouzinho 91 14 48 S 34 25 E
Vila Nova de Foscôa 30 41 5N 7 9W
Vila Nova de Ourém 31 39 40N 8 35W
Vila Novo de Gaia 30 41 4N 8 40W
Vila Paiva de Andrada 91 18 44 S 34 2 E
Vila Pouca de Aguiar 30 41 30N 7 38W
Vila Real 30 41 17N 7 48W
Vila Real de Santo António 31 37 10N 7 28W
Vila Vasco da Gama 91 14 54 S 32 14 E
Vila Velha 125 20 20 S 40 17W
Vila Veríssimo Sarmento 88 8 7 S 20 38 E
Vila Viçosa 31 38 45N 7 27W
Vilaboa 30 42 21N 8 39W
Vilaine → 18 47 30N 2 27W
Vilanculos 93 22 1 S 35 17 E
Vilar Formosa 30 40 38N 6 45W
Vilareal □ 30 41 36N 7 35W
Vilaseca-Salou 32 41 7N 1 9 E
Vilcea □ 46 45 0N 24 10 E
Vileyka 54 54 30N 26 53 E
Vilhelmina 50 64 35N 16 39 E
Vilhena 126 12 40 S 60 5W
Viliga 59 61 36N 156 56 E
Viliya → 54 55 54N 23 53 E
Viljandi 54 58 28N 25 30 E
Vilkovo 56 45 28N 29 32 E
Villa Abecia 124 21 0 S 68 18W
Villa Ahumada 120 30 38N 106 30W
Villa Ana 124 28 28 S 59 40W
Villa Ángela 124 27 34 S 60 45W
Villa Bella 126 10 25 S 65 22W
Villa Bens = Tarfaya 80 27 55N 12 55W
Villa Cañás 124 34 0 S 61 35W
Villa Cisneros = Dakhla 80 23 50N 15 53W
Villa Colón 124 31 38 S 68 20W
Villa Constitución 124 33 15 S 60 20W
Villa de María 124 29 55 S 63 43W
Villa Dolores 124 31 58 S 65 15W
Villa Guillermina 124 28 15 S 59 29W
Villa Hayes 124 25 0 S 57 20W
Villa Iris 124 38 12 S 63 12W
Villa María 124 32 20 S 63 10W
Villa Mazán 124 28 40 S 66 30W
Villa Minozzo 38 44 21N 10 30 E
Villa Montes 124 21 10 S 63 30W
Villa Ocampo 124 28 30 S 59 20W
Villa Ojo de Agua 124 29 30 S 63 44W
Villa San Giovanni 41 38 13N 15 38 E
Villa San José 124 32 12 S 58 15W
Villa San Martín 124 28 15 S 64 9W
Villa Santina 39 46 25N 12 55 E
Villablino 30 42 57N 6 19W
Villacañas 32 39 38N 3 20W
Villacarlos 32 39 53N 4 17 E
Villacarriedo 32 43 14N 3 48W
Villacarrillo 33 38 7N 3 3W
Villacastín 30 40 46N 4 25W
Villach 26 46 37N 13 51 E
Villaciado 40 39 27N 8 45 E
Villada 30 42 15N 4 59W
Villadiego 30 42 31N 4 1W
Villadóssola 38 46 4N 8 16 E
Villafeliche 32 41 10N 1 30W
Villafranca 32 42 17N 1 46W
Villafranca de los Barros 31 38 35N 6 18W
Villafranca de los Caballeros 33 39 26N 3 21W
Villafranca del Bierzo 30 42 38N 6 50W
Villafranca del Cid 32 40 26N 0 16W
Villafranca del Panadés 32 41 21N 1 40 E
Villafranca di Verona 38 45 20N 10 51 E
Villagarcía de Arosa 30 42 34N 8 46W
Villagrán 120 24 29N 99 29W
Villaguay 124 32 0 S 59 0W
Villaharta 31 38 9N 4 54W
Villahermosa, Mexico 120 18 0N 92 50W
Villahermosa, Spain 33 38 46N 2 52W
Villaines-la-Juhel 18 48 21N 0 20W
Villajoyosa 33 38 30N 0 12W
Villalba 30 43 26N 7 40W
Villalba de Guardo 30 42 42N 4 49W
Villalcampo, Pantano de 30 41 31N 6 0W
Villalón de Campos 30 42 5N 5 4W
Villalpando 30 41 51N 5 25W
Villaluenga 30 40 2N 3 54W
Villamanán 30 42 19N 5 35W
Villamartín 31 36 52N 5 38W
Villamayor 32 39 50N 2 59W
Villamblard 20 45 2N 0 32 E
Villanova Monteleone 40 40 30N 8 28 E
Villanueva 119 35 16N 105 23W
Villanueva de Castellón 33 39 5N 0 31W
Villanueva de Córdoba 31 38 20N 4 38W
Villanueva de la Fuente 33 38 42N 2 42W
Villanueva de la Serena 31 38 59N 5 50W
Villanueva de la Sierra 30 40 12N 6 24W
Villanueva de los Castillejos 31 37 30N 7 15W
Villanueva del Arzobispo 33 38 10N 3 0W
Villanueva del Duque 31 38 20N 5 0W
Villanueva del Fresno 31 38 23N 7 10W
Villanueva y Geltrú 32 41 13N 1 40 E
Villaodrid 30 43 20N 7 11W
Villaputzu 40 39 28N 9 33 E
Villar del Arzobispo 32 39 44N 0 50W
Villar del Rey 31 39 7N 6 50W
Villarcayo 32 42 56N 3 34W
Villard-Bonnet 21 45 14N 5 53 E
Villard-de-Lans 21 45 3N 5 33 E
Villarino de los Aires 30 41 18N 6 23W
Villarosa 41 37 36N 14 9 E
Villarramiel 30 42 2N 4 55W
Villarreal 32 39 55N 0 3W
Villarrica, Chile 128 39 15 S 72 15W
Villarrica, Parag. 124 25 40 S 56 30W
Villarrobledo 33 39 18N 2 36W
Villarroya de la Sierra 32 41 27N 1 46W
Villarrubia de los Ojos 33 39 14N 3 36W
Villars 21 46 0N 5 2 E
Villarta de San Juan 33 39 15N 3 25W
Villasayas 32 41 24N 2 39W
Villaseca de los Gamitos 30 41 2N 6 7W
Villastar 32 40 17N 1 9W
Villatobas 32 39 54N 3 20W
Villavicencio, Argent. 124 32 28 S 69 0W
Villavicencio, Colomb. 126 4 9N 73 37W
Villaviciosa 30 43 32N 5 27W
Villazón 124 22 0 S 65 35W
Ville-Marie 106 47 20N 79 30W
Ville Platte 117 30 45N 92 17W
Villedieu 18 48 50N 1 12W
Villefort 20 44 28N 3 56 E
Villefranche 19 47 19N 1 46 E
Villefranche-de-Lauragais 20 43 25N 1 44 E
Villefranche-de-Rouergue 20 44 21N 2 2 E
Villefranche-du-Périgord 20 44 38N 1 5 E
Villefranche-sur-Saône 21 45 59N 4 43 E
Villel 32 40 14N 1 12W
Villemaur 19 48 14N 3 40 E
Villemur-sur-Tarn 20 43 51N 1 31 E
Villena 33 38 39N 0 52W
Villenauxe 19 48 36N 3 30 E
Villenave 20 44 46N 0 33W
Villeneuve, France 19 48 42N 2 25 E
Villeneuve, Italy 38 45 40N 7 10 E
Villeneuve-l'Archevêque 19 48 14N 3 32 E
Villeneuve-lès-Avignon 21 43 57N 4 49 E
Villeneuve-sur-Allier 20 46 40N 3 13 E
Villeneuve-sur-Lot 20 44 24N 0 42 E
Villeréal 20 44 38N 0 45 E
Villers-Bocage 18 49 3N 0 40W
Villers-Bretonneux 19 49 50N 2 30 E
Villers-Cotterêts 19 49 15N 3 4 E
Villers-Outreaux 19 50 2N 3 18 E
Villers-sur-Mer 18 49 21N 0 2W
Villersexel 19 47 33N 6 26 E
Villerupt 19 49 28N 5 55 E
Villerville 18 49 26N 0 5 E
Villiers 93 27 2 S 28 36 E
Villingen 25 48 4N 8 28 E
Villingen-Schwenningen 25 48 3N 8 29 E
Villisca 116 40 55N 94 59W
Villupuram 70 11 59N 79 31 E
Vilna 108 54 7N 111 55W
Vilnius 54 54 38N 25 19 E
Vils 26 47 33N 10 37 E
Vils → 25 48 38N 13 11 E
Vilsbiburg 25 48 27N 12 23 E
Vilshofen 25 48 38N 13 11 E
Vilskutskogo, Proliv 59 78 0N 103 0 E
Vilusi 42 42 44N 18 34 E
Vilvoorde 16 50 56N 4 26 E
Vilyuy → 59 64 24N 126 26 E
Vilyuysk 59 63 40N 121 35 E
Vimercate 38 45 38N 9 25 E
Vimiosa 30 41 35N 6 31W
Vimmerby 49 57 40N 15 55 E
Vimoutiers 18 48 57N 0 10 E
Vimperk 26 49 3N 13 46 E
Viña del Mar 124 33 0 S 71 30W
Vinaroz 32 40 30N 0 27 E
Vincennes 114 38 42N 87 29W
Vinchina 124 28 45 S 68 15W
Vindel älven → 50 63 55N 19 50 E
Vindeln 50 64 12N 19 43 E
Vinderup 49 56 29N 8 45 E
Vindhya Ra. 68 22 50N 77 0 E
Vineland 114 39 30N 75 0W
Vinga 42 46 0N 21 14 E
Vingnes 47 61 7N 10 26 E
Vinh 71 18 45N 105 38 E
Vinhais 30 41 50N 7 0W
Vinica, Hrvatska, Yugo. 39 46 20N 16 9 E
Vinica, Slovenija, Yugo. 39 45 28N 15 16 E
Vinita 117 36 40N 95 12W
Vinkovci 42 45 19N 18 48 E
Vinnitsa 56 49 15N 28 30 E
Vinson Massif 5 78 35 S 85 25W
Vinstra 47 61 37N 9 44 E
Vinton, Iowa, U.S.A. 116 42 8N 92 1W
Vinton, La., U.S.A. 117 30 13N 93 35W
Vinţu de Jos 46 46 0N 23 30 E
Viöl 24 54 32N 9 12 E
Vipava 39 45 51N 13 58 E
Vipiteno 39 46 55N 11 25 E
Viqueque 73 8 52 S 126 23 E
Vir 39 44 17N 15 3 E
Virac 73 13 30N 124 20 E
Virago Sd. 108 54 0N 132 30W
Virajpet 70 12 10N 75 50 E
Viramgam 68 23 5N 72 0 E
Viranşehir 64 37 13N 39 45 E
Virarajendrapet = Virajpet 70 12 10N 75 50 E
Viravanallur 70 8 40N 77 30 E
Virden 109 49 50N 100 56W
Vire 18 48 50N 0 53W
Vire → 18 49 20N 1 7W
Vírgenes, C. 128 52 19 S 68 21W
Virgin →, Can. 109 57 2N 108 17W
Virgin →, U.S.A. 119 36 50N 114 10W
Virgin Gorda 121 18 30N 64 26W
Virgin Is. 121 18 40N 64 30W
Virginia, S. Afr. 92 28 8 S 26 55 E
Virginia, U.S.A. 116 47 30N 92 32W
Virginia □ 114 37 45N 78 0W
Virginia Beach 114 36 54N 75 58W
Virginia City, Mont., U.S.A. 118 45 18N 111 58W
Virginia City, Nev., U.S.A. 118 39 19N 119 39W
Virginia Falls 108 61 38N 125 42W
Virginiatown 106 48 9N 79 36W
Virieu-le-Grand 21 45 51N 5 39 E
Virje 42 46 4N 16 59 E
Viroqua 116 43 33N 90 57W
Virovitica 42 45 51N 17 21 E
Virpazar 42 42 14N 19 6 E
Virserum 49 57 20N 15 35 E
Virton 16 49 35N 5 32 E
Virtsu 54 58 32N 23 33 E
Virudunagar 70 9 30N 78 0 E
Vis 39 43 0N 16 10 E
Vis Kanal 39 43 4N 16 5 E
Visalia 119 36 25N 119 18W
Visayan Sea 73 11 30N 123 30 E
Visby 49 57 37N 18 18 E
Viscount Melville Sd. 4 74 10N 108 0W
Visé 16 50 44N 5 41 E
Višegrad 42 43 47N 19 17 E
Viseu, Brazil 127 1 10 S 46 5W
Viseu, Port. 30 40 40N 7 55W
Viseu □ 30 40 40N 7 55W
Vişeu de Sus 46 47 45N 24 25 E
Vishakhapatnam 70 17 45N 83 20 E
Vishnupur 69 23 8N 87 20 E
Visikoi I. 5 56 43 S 27 15W
Visingsö 49 58 2N 14 20 E
Viskafors 49 57 37N 12 50 E
Vislanda 49 56 46N 14 30 E
Vislinskil Zaliv (Zalew Wislany) 28 54 20N 19 50 E
Visnagar 68 23 45N 72 32 E
Višnja Gora 39 45 58N 14 45 E
Viso del Marqués 33 38 32N 3 34W
Viso, Mte. 38 44 38N 7 5 E
Visoko 42 43 58N 18 10 E

* Renamed Limbe

Visp Wangdu

Visp 25 46 17N 7 52 E
Visselhövede 24 52 59N 9 36 E
Vistonikos, Ormos 44 41 0N 25 7 E
Vistula = Wisła → 28 54 22N 18 55 E
Vit → 43 43 30N 24 30 E
Vitanje 39 46 25N 15 18 E
Vitebsk 54 55 10N 30 15 E
Viterbo 39 42 25N 12 8 E
Viti Levu 101 17 30 S 177 30 E
Vitiaz Str. 98 5 40 S 147 10 E
Vitigudino 30 41 1N 6 26W
Vitim 59 59 28N 112 35 E
Vitim → 59 59 26N 112 34 E
Vitína 45 37 40N 22 10 E
Vitina 42 43 17N 17 29 E
Vitória 127 20 20 S 40 22W
Vitoria 32 42 50N 2 41W
Vitória da Conquista 127 14 51 S 40 51W
Vitória de São Antão 127 8 10 S 35 20W
Vitré 18 48 8N 1 12W
Vitry-le-François 19 48 43N 4 33 E
Vitsi, Óros 44 40 40N 21 25 E
Vitteaux 19 47 24N 4 30 E
Vittel 19 48 12N 5 57 E
Vittória 41 36 58N 14 30 E
Vittório Véneto 39 45 59N 12 18 E
Vitu Is. 98 4 50 S 149 25 E
Viver 32 39 55N 0 36W
Vivero 30 43 39N 7 38W
Viviers 21 44 30N 4 40 E
Vivonne 20 46 25N 0 15 E
Vizcaíno, Desierto de 120 27 40N 113 50W
Vizcaíno, Sierra 120 27 30N 114 0W
Vizcaya □ 32 43 15N 2 45W
Vizianagaram 70 18 6N 83 30 E
Vizille 21 45 5N 5 46 E
Viziňada 39 45 20N 13 46 E
Viziru 46 45 0N 27 43 E
Vizovice 27 49 12N 17 56 E
Vizzini 41 37 9N 14 43 E
Vjosa → 44 40 37N 19 42 E
Vlaardingen 16 51 55N 4 21 E
Vlădeasa 46 46 47N 22 50 E
Vladicin Han 42 42 42N 22 1 E
Vladimir 55 56 15N 40 30 E
Vladimir Volynskiy 54 50 50N 24 18 E
Vladimirci 42 44 36N 19 45 E
Vladimirovac 42 45 1N 20 53 E
Vladimirovka, R.S.F.S.R., U.S.S.R. 57 48 27N 46 10 E
Vladimirovka, R.S.F.S.R., U.S.S.R. 57 44 45N 44 41 E
Vladimirovo 43 43 32N 23 22 E
Vladislavovka 56 45 15N 35 15 E
Vladivostok 59 43 10N 131 53 E
Vlasenica 42 44 11N 18 59 E
Vlašić 42 44 19N 17 37 E
Vlašim 26 49 40N 14 53 E
Vlasinsko Jezero 42 42 44N 22 22 E
Vlasotinci 42 42 59N 22 7 E
Vlieland 16 53 16N 4 55 E
Vlissingen 16 51 26N 3 34 E
Vlóra 44 40 32N 19 28 E
Vlóra □ 44 40 12N 20 0 E
Vlorës, Gjiri i 44 40 29N 19 27 E
Vltava → 26 50 21N 14 30 E
Vobarno 38 45 38N 10 30 E
Voćin 42 45 37N 17 33 E
Vöcklabruck 26 48 1N 13 39 E
Vodice 39 43 47N 15 47 E
Vodňany 26 49 9N 14 11 E
Vodnjan 39 44 59N 13 52 E
Vogelkop = Doberai, Jazirah 73 1 25 S 133 0 E
Vogelsberg 24 50 37N 9 15 E
Voghera 38 44 59N 9 1 E
Vohibinany 93 18 49 S 49 4 E
Vohimarina 93 13 25 S 50 0 E
Vohimena, Tanjon' i 93 25 36 S 45 8 E
Vohipeno 93 22 22 S 47 51 E
Voi 90 3 25 S 38 32 E
Void 19 48 40N 5 36 E
Voineşti, Iaşi, Romania 46 47 5N 27 27 E
Voineşti, Prahova, Romania 46 45 5N 25 14 E
Voiotía □ 45 38 20N 23 0 E
Voiron 21 45 22N 5 35 E
Voisey B. 107 56 15N 61 50W
Voitsberg 26 47 3N 15 9 E
Voíviïs Límni 44 39 30N 22 45 E
Vojens 49 55 16N 9 18 E
Vojmsjön 50 64 55N 16 40 E
Vojnik 38 46 18N 15 19 E
Vojnió 39 45 19N 15 43 E
Vojvodina, Auton. Pokrajina □ 42 45 20N 20 0 E
Vokhma 55 59 0N 46 45 E
Vokhma → 55 56 20N 46 20 E
Vokhtoga 55 58 46N 41 8 E
Volary 26 48 54N 13 52 E
Volborg 116 45 50N 105 44W
Volcano Is. 94 25 0N 141 0 E
Volchansk 55 50 17N 36 58 E
Volchayevka 59 48 40N 134 30 E
Volchya → 56 48 0N 37 0 E
Volda 47 62 9N 6 5 E
Volga 55 57 58N 38 16 E
Volga → 57 48 30N 46 0 E
Volga Hts. = Privolzhskaya V. S. 53 51 0N 46 0 E
Volgodonsk 57 47 33N 42 5 E
Volgograd 57 48 40N 44 25 E
Volgogradskoye Vdkhr. 55 50 0N 45 20 E
Volgorechensk 55 57 28N 41 14 E
Volissós 45 38 29N 25 54 E
Volkach 25 49 52N 10 14 E
Völkermarkt 26 46 39N 14 39 E
Volkhov 54 59 55N 32 15 E
Volkhov → 54 60 8N 32 20 E
Völklingen 25 49 15N 6 50 E
Volkovysk 54 53 9N 24 30 E
Volksrust 93 27 24 S 29 53 E
Vollenhove 16 52 40N 5 58 E
Vol'n'ansk 56 47 55N 35 29 E
Volnovakha 56 47 35N 37 30 E
Volochanka 59 71 0N 94 28 E
Volodarsk 55 56 12N 43 15 E
Vologda 55 59 10N 40 0 E
Volokolamsk 55 56 5N 35 57 E
Volokonovka 55 50 33N 37 52 E
Vólos 44 39 24N 22 59 E
Volosovo 54 59 27N 29 32 E
Volozhin 54 54 3N 26 30 E
Volsk 55 52 5N 47 22 E
Volta → 85 5 46N 0 41 E
Volta, L. 85 7 30N 0 15 E
Volta Redonda 125 22 31 S 44 5W
Volterra 38 43 24N 10 50 E
Voltri 38 44 25N 8 43 E
Volturara Áppula 41 41 30N 15 2 E
Volturno → 41 41 1N 13 55 E
Volubilis 82 34 2N 5 33W
Volujak 42 43 53N 17 47 E
Vólvi, L. 44 40 40N 23 34 E
Volzhsk 55 55 57N 48 23 E
Volzhskiy 57 48 56N 44 46 E
Vondrozo 93 22 49 S 47 20 E
Voorburg 16 52 5N 4 24 E
Vopnafjörður 50 65 45N 14 40W
Vorarlberg □ 26 47 20N 10 0 E
Vóras Óros 44 40 57N 21 45 E
Vorbasse 49 55 39N 9 6 E
Vorderrhein → 25 46 49N 9 25 E
Vordingborg 49 55 0N 11 54 E
Voreppe 21 45 18N 5 39 E
Voríai Sporádhes 45 39 15N 23 30 E
Vórios Evvoïkos Kólpos 45 38 45N 23 15 E
Vorkuta 52 67 48N 64 20 E
Vorma → 47 60 9N 11 27 E
Vorona → 55 51 22N 42 3 E
Voronezh, R.S.F.S.R., U.S.S.R. 55 51 40N 39 10 E
Voronezh, Ukraine, U.S.S.R. 54 51 47N 33 28 E
Voronezh → 55 51 56N 37 17 E
Vorontsovo-Aleksandrovskoye = Zelenokumsk 57 44 30N 44 1 E
Voroshilovgrad 57 48 38N 39 15 E
Vorovskoye 59 54 30N 155 50 E
Vorskla → 56 48 50N 34 10 E
Võru 54 57 48N 26 54 E
Vorupør 49 56 58N 8 22 E
Vosges 19 48 20N 7 10 E
Vosges □ 19 48 12N 6 20 E
Voskopoja 44 40 40N 20 33 E
Voskresensk 55 55 19N 38 43 E
Voskresenskoye 55 56 51N 45 30 E
Voss 47 60 38N 6 26 E
Vostochnyy Sayan 59 54 0N 96 0 E
Vostok I. 95 10 5 S 152 23W
Votice 26 49 38N 14 39 E
Votkinsk 52 57 0N 53 55 E
Votkinskoye Vdkhr. 52 57 30N 55 0 E
Vouga → 30 40 41N 8 40W
Vouillé 18 46 38N 0 10 E
Voulte-sur-Rhône, La 21 44 48N 4 46 E
Vouvray 18 47 25N 0 48 E
Voúxa, Ákra 45 35 37N 23 32 E
Vouzela 30 40 43N 8 7W
Vouziers 19 49 22N 4 40 E
Voves 19 48 15N 1 38 E
Voxna 48 61 20N 15 40 E
Vozhe Oz. 52 60 45N 39 0 E
Vozhgaly 55 58 9N 50 11 E
Voznesenka 59 56 40N 95 3 E
Voznesensk 56 47 35N 31 21 E
Voznesenye 52 61 0N 35 45 E
Vráble 27 48 15N 18 16 E
Vraćevšnica 42 44 2N 20 34 E
Vrådal 47 59 20N 8 25 E
Vraka 44 42 8N 19 28 E
Vrakhnéïka 45 38 10N 21 40 E
Vrancea □ 46 45 50N 26 45 E
Vrancei, Munţii 46 46 0N 26 30 E
Vrangelya, Ostrov 59 71 0N 180 0 E
Vranica 42 43 55N 17 50 E
Vranje 42 42 34N 21 54 E
Vranjska Banja 42 42 34N 22 1 E
Vranov 27 48 53N 21 40 E
Vransko 39 46 17N 14 58 E
Vratsa 43 43 13N 23 30 E
Vrbas 42 45 40N 19 40 E
Vrbas → 42 45 8N 17 29 E
Vrbnik 39 45 4N 14 40 E
Vrbovec 39 45 53N 16 28 E
Vrbovsko 39 45 24N 15 5 E
Vrchlabí 26 50 38N 15 37 E
Vrede 93 27 24 S 29 6 E
Vredefort 92 27 0 S 26 22 E
Vredenburg 92 32 51 S 18 0 E
Vredendal 92 31 41 S 18 35 E
Vrena 49 58 54N 16 41 E
Vrgorac 42 43 12N 17 20 E
Vrhnika 39 45 58N 14 15 E
Vriddhachalam 70 11 30N 79 20 E
Vridi 84 5 15N 4 3W
Vrindaban 68 27 37N 77 40 E
Vrnograč 39 45 10N 15 57 E
Vrondádhes 45 38 25N 26 7 E
Vrpolje 42 45 13N 18 24 E
Vršac 42 45 8N 21 18 E
Vrsacki Kanal 42 45 15N 21 0 E
Vryburg 92 26 55 S 24 45 E
Vryheid 93 27 45 S 30 47 E
Vsetin 27 49 20N 18 0 E
Vucha → 43 42 10N 24 26 E
Vučitrn 42 42 49N 20 59 E
Vught 16 51 38N 5 20 E
Vukovar 42 45 21N 18 59 E
Vulcan, Can. 108 50 25N 113 15W
Vulcan, Romania 46 45 23N 23 17 E
Vulcan, U.S.A. 114 45 46N 87 51W
Vulcano 41 38 25N 14 58 E
Vŭlchedruma 43 43 42N 23 27 E
Vulci 39 42 23N 11 37 E
Vulkaneshty 56 45 35N 28 30 E
Vunduzi → 91 18 56 S 34 1 E
Vung Tau 71 10 21N 107 4 E
Vŭrbitsa 43 42 59N 26 40 E
Vurshets 43 43 15N 23 23 E
Vutcani 46 46 26N 27 59 E
Vuyyuru 70 16 28N 80 50 E
Vyara 68 21 8N 73 28 E
Vyasniki 55 56 10N 42 10 E
Vyatka → 52 56 30N 51 0 E
Vyatskiye Polyany 52 56 5N 51 0 E
Vyazemskiy 59 47 32N 134 45 E
Vyazma 54 55 10N 34 15 E
Vyborg 52 60 43N 28 47 E
Vychegda → 52 61 18N 46 36 E
Vychodné Beskydy 27 49 30N 22 0 E
Východočeský □ 26 50 20N 15 45 E
Východoslovenský □ 27 48 50N 21 0 E
Vyg-ozero 52 63 30N 34 0 E
Vyksa 55 55 19N 42 11 E
Vypin 70 10 10N 76 15 E
Vyrnwy, L. 12 52 48N 3 30W
Vyshniy Volochek 54 57 30N 34 30 E
Vyškov 27 49 17N 17 0 E
Vysoké Mýto 27 49 58N 10 10 E
Vysokovsk 55 56 22N 36 30 E
Vysotsk 54 51 43N 26 32 E
Vyšší Brod 26 48 37N 14 19 E
Vytegra 52 61 0N 36 27 E

W

W.A.C. Bennett Dam 108 56 2N 122 6W
Wa 84 10 7N 2 25W
Waal → 16 51 59N 4 30 E
Wabakimi L. 106 50 38N 89 45W
Wabana 107 47 40N 53 0W
Wabasca 108 55 57N 113 56W
Wabash 114 40 48N 85 46W
Wabash → 114 37 46N 88 2W
Wabeno 114 45 25N 88 40W
Wabi → 87 7 45N 40 50 E
Wabigoon L. 109 49 44N 92 44W
Wabowden 109 54 55N 98 38W
Wąbrzeźno 28 53 16N 18 57 E
Wabuk Pt. 106 55 20N 85 5W
Wabush 107 52 55N 66 52W
Wabuska 118 39 9N 119 13W
Wächtersbach 25 50 16N 9 18 E
Waco 117 31 33N 97 5W
Waconichi, L. 106 50 8N 74 0W
Wad Ban Naqa 87 16 32N 33 9 E
Wad Banda 87 13 10N 27 56 E
Wad el Haddad 87 13 50N 33 30 E
Wad en Nau 87 14 10N 33 34 E
Wad Hamid 87 16 30N 32 45 E
Wâd Medanî 87 14 28N 33 30 E
Waddān 83 29 9N 16 10 E
Waddān, Jabal 83 29 0N 16 15 E
Waddeneilanden 16 53 25N 5 10 E
Waddenzee 16 53 6N 5 10 E
Waddington 113 44 51N 75 12W
Waddington, Mt. 108 51 23N 125 15W
Waddy Pt. 99 24 58 S 153 21 E
Wadena, Can. 109 51 57N 103 47W
Wadena, U.S.A. 116 46 25N 95 8W
Wädenswil 25 47 14N 8 40 E
Wadesboro 115 35 2N 80 2W
Wadhams 108 51 30N 127 30W
Wādī ash Shāţi' 83 27 30N 15 0 E
Wādī Banī Walīd 83 31 49N 14 0 E
Wadi Gemâl 86 24 35N 35 10 E
Wadi Halfa 86 21 53N 31 19 E
Wadi Masila 63 16 30N 49 0 E
Wadi Şabāḩ 64 23 50N 48 30 E
Wadlew 28 51 31N 19 23 E
Wadowice 27 49 52N 19 30 E
Wadsworth 118 39 38N 119 22W
Wafrah 64 28 33N 47 56 E
Wageningen 16 51 58N 5 40 E
Wager B. 105 65 26N 88 40W
Wager Bay 105 65 56N 90 49W
Wagga Wagga 97 35 7 S 147 24 E
Waghete 73 4 10 S 135 50 E
Wagin 96 33 17 S 117 25 E
Wagon Mound 117 36 1N 104 44W
Wagoner 117 36 0N 95 20W
Wagrowiec 28 52 48N 17 11 E
Wahai 73 2 48 S 129 35 E
Wahiawa 110 21 30N 158 2W
Wahoo 116 41 15N 96 35W
Wahpeton 116 46 20N 96 35W
Wai 70 17 56N 73 57 E
Waiau → 101 42 47 S 173 22 E
Waiawe Ganga → 70 6 15N 81 0 E
Waibeem 73 0 30 S 132 59 E
Waiblingen 25 48 49N 9 20 E
Waidhofen, Niederösterreich, Austria 26 48 49N 15 17 E
Waidhofen, Niederösterreich, Austria 26 47 57N 14 46 E
Waigeo 73 0 20 S 130 40 E
Waihi 101 37 23 S 175 52 E
Waihou → 101 37 15 S 175 40 E
Waika 90 2 22 S 25 42 E
Waikabubak 73 9 45 S 119 25 E
Waikaremoana 101 38 42 S 177 12 E
Waikari 101 42 58 S 172 41 E
Waikato → 101 37 23 S 174 43 E
Waikerie 99 34 9 S 140 0 E
Waikokopu 101 39 3 S 177 52 E
Waikouaiti 101 45 36 S 170 41 E
Waimate 101 44 45 S 171 3 E
Wainganga → 69 18 50N 79 55 E
Waingapu 73 9 35 S 120 11 E
Wainwright, Can. 109 52 50N 110 50W
Wainwright, U.S.A. 104 70 39N 160 1W
Waiouru 101 39 28 S 175 41 E
Waipara 101 43 3 S 172 46 E
Waipawa 101 39 56 S 176 38 E
Waipiro 101 38 2 S 178 22 E
Waipu 101 35 59 S 174 29 E
Waipukurau 101 40 1 S 176 33 E
Wairakei 101 38 37 S 176 6 E
Wairarapa, L. 101 41 14 S 175 15 E
Wairoa 101 39 3 S 177 25 E
Waitaki → 101 44 56 S 171 7 E
Waitara 101 38 59 S 174 15 E
Waitsburg 118 46 15N 118 0W
Waiuku 101 37 15 S 174 45 E
Wajima 74 37 30N 137 0 E
Wajir 90 1 42N 40 5 E
Wajir □ 90 1 42N 40 20 E
Wakasa-Wan 74 35 40N 135 30 E
Wakatipu, L. 101 45 5 S 168 33 E
Wakaw 109 52 39N 105 44W
Wakayama 74 34 15N 135 15 E
Wakayama-ken □ 74 33 50N 135 30 E
Wake Forest 115 35 58N 78 30W
Wake I. 94 19 18N 166 36 E
Wakefield, N.Z. 101 41 24 S 173 5 E
Wakefield, U.K. 12 53 41N 1 31W
Wakefield, Mass., U.S.A. 113 42 30N 71 3W
Wakefield, Mich., U.S.A. 116 46 28N 89 53W
Wakema 67 16 30N 95 11 E
Wakkanai 74 45 28N 141 35 E
Wakkerstroom 93 27 24 S 30 10 E
Wakool 99 35 28 S 144 23 E
Wakool → 99 35 5 S 143 33 E
Wakre 73 0 19 S 131 5 E
Wakuach L. 107 55 34N 67 32W
Walamba 91 13 30 S 28 42 E
Wałbrzych 28 50 45N 16 18 E
Walbury Hill 13 51 22N 1 28W
Walcha 99 30 55 S 151 31 E
Walcheren 16 51 30N 3 35 E
Walcott 118 41 50N 106 55W
Wałcz 28 53 17N 16 27 E
Wald 25 47 17N 8 56 E
Waldbröl 24 50 52N 7 36 E
Waldeck 24 51 12N 9 4 E
Walden, Colo., U.S.A. 118 40 47N 106 20W
Walden, N.Y., U.S.A. 113 41 32N 74 13W
Waldport 118 44 30N 124 2W
Waldron, Can. 109 50 53N 102 35W
Waldron, U.S.A. 117 34 52N 94 4W
Waldshut 25 47 37N 8 12 E
Walembele 84 10 30N 1 58W
Wales □ 11 52 30N 3 30W
Walewale 85 10 21N 0 50W
Walgett 97 30 0 S 148 5 E
Walgreen Coast 5 75 15 S 105 0W
Walhalla, Austral. 99 37 56 S 146 29 E
Walhalla, U.S.A. 109 48 55N 97 55W
Walker 116 47 4N 94 35W
Walker L., Man., Can. 109 54 42N 95 57W
Walker L., Qué., Can. 107 50 20N 67 11W
Walker L., U.S.A. 118 38 56N 118 46W
Walkerston 98 21 11 S 149 8 E
Walkerton 112 44 10N 81 10W
Wall 116 44 0N 102 14W
Walla Walla 118 46 3N 118 25W
Wallabadah 98 17 57 S 142 15 E
Wallace, Idaho, U.S.A. 118 47 30N 116 0W
Wallace, N.C., U.S.A. 115 34 44N 77 59W
Wallace, Nebr., U.S.A. 116 40 51N 101 12W
Wallaceburg 106 42 34N 82 23W
Wallachia = Valahia 46 44 35N 25 0 E
Wallal 99 26 32 S 146 7 E
Wallaroo 97 33 56 S 137 39 E
Wallasey 12 53 26N 3 2W
Walldürn 25 49 34N 9 23 E
Wallerawang 99 33 25 S 150 4 E
Wallingford, U.K. 12 51 40N 1 15W
Wallingford, U.S.A. 113 41 27N 72 50W
Wallis Arch. 94 13 18 S 176 10W
Wallowa 118 45 40N 117 35W
Wallowa, Mts. 118 45 20N 117 30W
Wallsend, Austral. 99 32 55 S 151 40 E
Wallsend, U.K. 12 54 59N 1 30W
Wallula 118 46 3N 118 59W
Wallumbilla 99 26 33 S 149 9 E
Walmer 92 33 57 S 25 35 E
Walmsley, L. 109 63 25N 108 36W
Walney, Isle of 12 54 5N 3 15W
Walnut Ridge 117 36 7N 90 58W
Walsall 13 52 36N 1 59W
Walsenburg 117 37 42N 104 45W
Walsh 117 37 28N 102 15W
Walsh → 98 16 31 S 143 42 E
Walsh P.O. 98 16 40 S 144 0 E
Walsrode 24 52 51N 9 37 E
Waltair 70 17 44N 83 23 E
Walterboro 115 32 53N 80 40W
Walters 117 34 25N 98 20W
Waltershausen 24 50 53N 10 33 E
Waltham 113 42 22N 71 12W
Waltham Sta. 106 45 57N 76 57W
Waltman 118 43 8N 107 15W
Walton 113 42 12N 75 9W
Walvisbaai 92 23 0S 14 28 E
Wamba, Kenya 90 0 58N 37 19 E
Wamba, Zaïre 90 2 10N 27 57 E
Wamego 116 39 14N 96 22W
Wamena 73 4 4 S 138 57 E
Wampsville 113 43 4N 75 42W
Wamsasi 73 3 27 S 126 7 E
Wana 68 32 20N 69 32 E
Wanaaring 99 29 38 S 144 9 E
Wanaka L. 101 44 33 S 169 7 E
Wan'an 77 26 26N 114 49 E
Wanapiri 73 4 30 S 135 59 E
Wanapitei L. 106 46 45N 80 40W
Wanbi 99 34 46 S 140 17 E
Wanda Shan 76 46 0N 132 0 E
Wanderer 91 19 36 S 30 1 E
Wandiwash 70 12 30N 79 30 E
Wandoan 97 26 5 S 149 55 E
Wang Kai (Ghâbat el Arab) 87 9 3N 29 23 E
Wang Saphung 71 17 18N 101 46 E
Wanga 90 2 58N 29 12 E
Wangal 73 6 8 S 134 9 E
Wanganella 99 35 6 S 144 49 E
Wanganui 101 39 56 S 175 3 E
Wangaratta 97 36 21 S 146 19 E
Wangdu 76 38 40N 115 7 E

Wangerooge Wetzlar

Wangerooge 24 53 47N 7 52 E
Wangi 90 1 58 S 40 58 E
Wangiwangi 73 5 22 S 123 37 E
Wangjiang 77 30 10N 116 42 E
Wangqing 76 43 12N 129 42 E
Wankaner 68 22 35N 71 0 E
* Wankie 91 18 18 S 26 30 E
* Wankie Nat. Park 92 19 0 S 26 30 E
Wanless 109 54 11N 101 21W
Wanning 77 18 48N 110 22 E
Wannon → 100 37 38 S 141 25 E
Wanquan 76 40 50N 114 40 E
Wanxian 75 30 42N 108 20 E
Wanyuan 77 32 4N 108 3 E
Wanzai 77 28 7N 114 30 E
Wapakoneta 114 40 35N 84 10W
Wapato 118 46 30N 120 25W
Wapawekka L. 109 54 55N 104 40W
Wappingers Falls 113 41 35N 73 56W
Wapsipinicon → 116 41 44N 90 19W
Waranga Res. 100 36 32 S 145 5 E
Warangal 70 17 58N 79 35 E
Waratah 99 41 30 S 145 30 E
Waratah B. 99 38 54 S 146 5 E
Warburg 24 51 29N 9 10 E
Warburton 99 37 47 S 145 42 E
Warburton → 97 28 4 S 137 28 E
Ward 101 41 49 S 174 11 E
Ward → 99 26 28 S 146 6 E
Ward Cove 108 55 25N 132 43W
Ward Hunt, C. 98 8 2 S 148 10 E
Wardak □ 65 34 0N 68 0 E
Warden 93 27 50 S 29 0 E
Wardha 68 20 45N 78 39 E
Wardlow 108 50 56N 111 31W
Ware, Can. 108 57 26N 125 41W
Ware, U.S.A. 113 42 16N 72 15W
Wareham 113 41 45N 70 44W
Waren 24 53 30N 12 41 E
Warendorf 24 51 57N 8 0 E
Warialda 97 29 29 S 150 33 E
Wariap 73 1 30 S 134 5 E
Warka 28 51 47N 21 12 E
Warkopi 73 1 12 S 134 9 E
Warley 13 52 30N 2 0W
Warm Springs, Mont., U.S.A. 118 46 11N 112 48W
Warm Springs, Nev., U.S.A. 119 38 16N 116 32W
Warman 109 52 19N 106 30W
Warmbad, Namibia 92 28 25 S 18 42 E
Warmbad, S. Afr. 93 24 51 S 28 19 E
Warmeriville 19 49 20N 4 13 E
Warnambool Downs 98 22 48 S 142 52 E
Warnemünde 24 54 9N 12 5 E
Warner 108 49 17N 112 12W
Warner Range, Mts. 118 41 30 S 120 20W
Warner Robins 115 32 41N 83 36W
Warnow → 24 54 6N 12 9 E
Warora 70 20 14N 79 1 E
Warracknabeal 100 36 9 S 142 26 E
Warragul 99 38 10 S 145 58 E
Warrego → 97 30 24 S 145 21 E
Warrego Ra. 97 24 58 S 146 0 E
Warren, Austral. 99 31 42 S 147 51 E
Warren, Ark., U.S.A. 117 33 35N 92 3W
Warren, Minn., U.S.A. 116 48 12N 96 46W
Warren, Ohio, U.S.A. 114 41 18N 80 52W
Warren, Pa., U.S.A. 114 41 52N 79 10W
Warrenpoint 15 54 7N 6 15W
Warrensburg 116 38 45N 93 45W
Warrenton, S. Afr. 92 28 9 S 24 47 E
Warrenton, U.S.A. 118 46 11N 123 59W
Warrenville 99 25 48 S 147 22 E
Warri 85 5 30N 5 41 E
Warrina 96 28 12 S 135 50 E
Warrington, U.K. 12 53 25N 2 38W
Warrington, U.S.A. 115 30 22N 87 16W
Warrnambool 97 38 25 S 142 30 E
Warroad 116 48 54N 95 19W
Warsa 73 0 47 S 135 55 E
Warsaw, Ind., U.S.A. 114 41 14N 85 50W
Warsaw, N.Y., U.S.A. 112 42 46N 78 10W
Warsaw, Ohio, U.S.A. 112 40 20N 82 0W
Warsaw = Warszawa 28 52 13N 21 0 E
Warstein 24 51 26N 8 20 E
Warszawa 28 52 13N 21 0 E
Warszawa □ 28 52 30N 21 0 E
Warta 28 51 43N 18 38 E
Warta → 28 52 35N 14 39 E
Waru 73 3 30 S 130 36 E
Warud 68 21 30N 78 16 E
Warwick, Austral. 97 28 10 S 152 1 E
Warwick, U.K. 13 52 17N 1 36W
Warwick, U.S.A. 114 41 43N 71 25W
Warwick □ 13 52 20N 1 30W
Wasa 108 49 45N 115 50W
Wasaga Beach 112 44 31N 80 1W
Wasatch, Ra. 118 40 30N 111 15W
Wasbank 93 28 15 S 30 9 E
Wasco, Calif., U.S.A. 119 35 37N 119 16W
Wasco, Oreg., U.S.A. 118 45 36N 120 46W
Waseca 116 44 3N 93 31W
Wasekamio L. 109 56 45N 108 45W
Wash, The 12 52 58N 0 20 E
Washago 112 44 45N 79 20W
Washburn, N.D., U.S.A. 116 47 17N 101 0W
Washburn, Wis., U.S.A. 116 46 38N 90 55W
Washington, D.C., U.S.A. 114 38 52N 77 0W
Washington, Ga., U.S.A. 115 33 45N 82 45W
Washington, Ind., U.S.A. 114 38 40N 87 8W
Washington, Iowa, U.S.A. 116 41 20N 91 45W
Washington, Mo, U.S.A. 116 38 35N 91 1W
Washington, N.C., U.S.A. 115 35 35N 77 1W
Washington, N.J., U.S.A. 113 40 45N 74 59W
Washington, Pa., U.S.A. 114 40 10N 80 20W
Washington, Utah, U.S.A. 119 37 10N 113 30W
Washington □ 118 47 45N 120 30W
† Washington I., Pac. Oc. 95 4 43N 160 25W
Washington I., U.S.A. 114 45 24N 86 54W
Washington Mt. 114 44 15N 71 18W
Wasian 73 1 47 S 133 19 E
Wasilków 28 53 12N 23 13 E
Wasior 73 2 43 S 134 30 E
Waskaiowaka, L. 109 56 33N 96 23W
Waskesiu Lake 109 53 55N 106 5W
Wasm 86 18 2N 41 32 E
Wassenaar 16 52 8N 4 24 E
Wasserburg 25 48 4N 12 15 E
Wasserkuppe 24 50 30N 9 56 E
Wassy 19 48 30N 4 58 E
Waswanipi 106 49 40N 76 29W
Waswanipi, L. 106 49 35N 76 40W
Watangpon 73 4 29 S 120 25 E
Water Park Pt. 98 22 56 S 150 47 E
Water Valley 117 34 9N 89 38W
Waterberg, Namibia 92 20 30 S 17 18 E
Waterberg, S. Afr. 93 24 14 S 28 0 E
Waterbury, Conn., U.S.A. 114 41 32N 73 0W
Waterbury, Vt., U.S.A. 113 44 22N 72 44W
Waterbury L. 109 58 10N 104 22W
Waterdown 112 43 20N 79 53W
Waterford, Can. 112 42 56N 80 17W
Waterford, Ireland 15 52 16N 7 8W
Waterford □ 15 52 10N 7 40W
Waterford Harb. 15 52 10N 6 58W
Waterhen L., Man., Can. 109 52 10N 99 40W
Waterhen L., Sask., Can. 109 54 28N 108 25W
Waterloo, Belg. 16 50 43N 4 25 E
Waterloo, Ont., Can. 106 43 30N 80 32W
Waterloo, Qué., Can. 113 45 22N 72 32W
Waterloo, S. Leone 84 8 26N 13 8W
Waterloo, Ill., U.S.A. 116 38 22N 90 6W
Waterloo, Iowa, U.S.A. 116 42 27N 92 20W
Waterloo, N.Y., U.S.A. 112 42 54N 76 53W
Watersmeet 116 46 15N 89 12W
Waterton Lakes Nat. Park 108 49 5N 114 15W
Watertown, Conn., U.S.A. 113 41 36N 73 7W
Watertown, N.Y., U.S.A. 114 43 58N 75 57W
Watertown, S.D., U.S.A. 116 44 57N 97 5W
Watertown, Wis., U.S.A. 116 43 15N 88 45W
Waterval-Boven 93 25 40 S 30 18 E
Waterville, Can. 113 45 16N 71 54W
Waterville, Me., U.S.A. 107 44 35N 69 40W
Waterville, N.Y., U.S.A. 113 42 56N 75 23W
Waterville, Pa., U.S.A. 112 41 19N 77 21W
Waterville, Wash., U.S.A. 118 47 38N 120 1W
Watervliet 114 42 46N 73 43W
Wates 73 7 53 S 110 6 E
Watford, Can. 112 42 57N 81 53W
Watford, U.K. 13 51 38N 0 23W
Watford City 116 47 50N 103 23W
Wathaman → 109 57 16N 102 59W
Watkins Glen 114 42 25N 76 55W
Watling I. = San Salvador 121 24 0N 74 40W
Watonga 117 35 51N 98 24W
Watrous, Can. 109 51 40N 105 25W
Watrous, U.S.A. 117 35 50N 104 55W
Watsa 90 3 4N 29 30 E
Watseka 114 40 45N 87 45W
Watson 109 52 10N 104 30W
Watson Lake 104 60 6N 128 49W
Watsonville 119 36 55N 121 49W
Wattwil 25 47 18N 9 6 E
Watuata = Batuata 73 6 12 S 122 42 E
Watubela, Kepulauan 73 4 28 S 131 35 E
Wau 98 7 21 S 146 47 E
Waubamik 112 45 27N 80 1W
Waubay 116 45 22N 97 17W
Waubra 99 37 21 S 143 39 E
Wauchope 99 31 28 S 152 45 E
Wauchula 115 27 35N 81 50W
Waugh 109 49 40N 95 11W
Waukegan 114 42 22N 87 54W
Waukesha 114 43 0N 88 15W
Waukon 116 43 14N 91 33W
Wauneta 116 40 27N 101 25W
Waupaca 116 44 22N 89 8W
Waupun 116 43 38N 88 44W
Waurika 117 34 12N 98 0W
Wausau 116 44 57N 89 40W
Wautoma 116 44 3N 89 20W
Wauwatosa 114 43 6N 87 59W
Wave Hill 96 17 32 S 131 0 E
Waveney → 13 52 24N 1 20 E
Waverley 101 39 46 S 174 37 E
Waverly, Iowa, U.S.A. 116 42 40N 92 30W
Waverly, N.Y., U.S.A. 114 42 0N 76 33W
Wavre 16 50 43N 4 38 E
Wâw 87 7 45N 28 1 E
Waw al Kabir 81 25 20N 17 20 E
Wâw al Kabîr 83 25 20N 16 43 E
Wâw an Nâmûs 83 24 55N 17 46 E
Wawa, Can. 106 47 59N 84 47W
Wawa, Nigeria 85 9 54N 4 27 E
Wawa, Sudan 86 20 30N 30 22 E
Wawanesa 109 49 36N 99 40W
Wawoi → 98 7 48 S 143 16 E
Waxahachie 117 32 22N 96 53W
Waxweiler 25 50 6N 6 22 E
Wayabula Rau 73 2 29N 128 17 E
Wayatinah 99 42 19 S 146 27 E
Waycross 115 31 12N 82 25W
Wayi 87 5 8N 30 10 E
Wayne, Nebr., U.S.A. 116 42 16N 97 0W
Wayne, W. Va., U.S.A. 114 38 15N 82 27W
Waynesboro, Ga., U.S.A. 115 33 6N 82 1W
Waynesboro, Miss., U.S.A. 115 31 40N 88 39W
Waynesboro, Pa., U.S.A. 114 39 46N 77 32W
Waynesboro, Va., U.S.A. 114 38 4N 78 57W
Waynesburg 114 39 54N 80 12W
Waynesville 115 35 31N 83 0W
Waynoka 117 36 38N 98 53W
Wâzin 83 31 58N 10 40 E
Wazirabad 68 32 30N 74 8 E
Wda → 28 53 25N 18 29 E
We 72 5 51N 95 18 E
Weald, The 13 51 7N 0 9 E
Wear → 12 54 55N 1 22W
Weatherford, Okla., U.S.A. 117 35 30N 98 45W
Weatherford, Tex., U.S.A. 117 32 45N 97 48W
Weaverville 118 40 44N 122 56W
Webb City 117 37 9N 94 30W
Webster, Mass., U.S.A. 113 42 4N 71 54W
Webster, N.Y., U.S.A. 112 43 11N 77 27W
Webster, S.D., U.S.A. 116 45 24N 97 33W
Webster, Wis., U.S.A. 116 45 53N 92 25W
Webster City 116 42 30N 93 50W
Webster Green 116 38 38N 90 20W
Webster Springs 114 38 30N 80 25W
Weda 73 0 21N 127 50 E
Weda, Teluk 73 0 30N 127 50 E
Weddell I. 128 51 50 S 61 0W
Weddell Sea 5 72 30 S 40 0W
Wedderburn 99 36 26 S 143 33 E
Wedge I. 96 30 50 S 115 11 E
Wedgeport 107 43 44N 65 59W
Wedza 91 18 40 S 31 33 E
Wee Waa 99 30 11 S 149 26 E
Weed 118 41 29N 122 22W
Weedsport 113 43 3N 76 35W
Weedville 112 41 17N 78 28W
Weemelah 99 29 2 S 149 15 E
Weenen 93 28 48 S 30 7 E
Weener 24 53 10N 7 23 E
Weert 16 51 15N 5 43 E
Wegierska-Gorka 27 49 36N 19 7 E
Wegliniec 28 51 18N 15 10 E
Węgorzewo 28 54 13N 21 43 E
Węgrów 28 52 24N 22 0 E
Wei He →, Hebei, China 76 36 10N 115 45 E
Wei He →, Shaanxi, China 77 34 38N 110 15 E
Weida 24 50 47N 12 3 E
Weiden 25 49 40N 12 10 E
Weifang 76 36 44N 119 7 E
Weihai 76 37 30N 122 6 E
Weilburg 24 50 28N 8 17 E
Weilheim 25 47 50N 11 9 E
Weimar 24 51 0N 11 20 E
Weinan 77 34 31N 109 29 E
Weingarten 25 47 49N 9 39 E
Weinheim 25 49 33N 8 40 E
Weipa 97 12 40 S 141 50 E
Weir →, Austral. 99 28 20 S 149 50 E
Weir →, Can. 109 56 54N 93 21W
Weir River 109 56 49N 94 6W
Weirton 112 40 23N 80 35W
Weiser 118 44 10N 117 0W
Weishan 77 34 47N 117 5 E
Weissenburg 25 49 2N 10 58 E
Weissenfels 24 51 11N 12 0 E
Weisswasser 24 51 30N 14 36 E
Wéitra 26 48 41N 14 54 E
Weiyuan 76 35 7N 104 10 E
Weiz 26 47 13N 15 39 E
Weizhou Dao 77 21 0N 109 5 E
Wejherowo 28 54 35N 18 12 E
Wekusko 109 54 30N 99 45W
Wekusko L. 109 54 40N 99 50W
Welby 109 50 33N 101 29W
Welch 114 37 29N 81 36W
Weldya 87 11 50N 39 34 E
Welega □ 87 9 25N 34 20 E
Welkite 87 8 15N 37 42 E
Welkom 92 28 0 S 26 50 E
Welland 106 43 0N 79 15W
Welland → 12 52 43N 0 10W
Wellesley Is. 97 16 42 S 139 30 E
Wellin 16 50 5N 5 6 E
Wellingborough 13 52 18N 0 41W
Wellington, Austral. 97 32 35 S 148 59 E
Wellington, Can. 106 43 57N 77 20W
Wellington, N.Z. 101 41 19 S 174 46 E
Wellington, S. Afr. 92 33 38 S 18 57 E
Wellington, U.K. 13 50 58N 3 13W
Wellington, Col., U.S.A. 116 40 43N 105 0W
Wellington, Kans., U.S.A. 117 37 15N 97 25W
Wellington, Nev., U.S.A. 118 38 47N 119 28W
Wellington, Ohio, U.S.A. 112 41 9N 82 12W
Wellington, Tex., U.S.A. 117 34 55N 100 13W
Wellington □ 101 40 8 S 175 36 E
Wellington, I. 128 49 30 S 75 0W
Wellington, L. 99 38 6 S 147 20 E
Wellington (Telford) 12 52 42N 2 31W
Wells, Norfolk, U.K. 12 52 57N 0 51 E
Wells, Somerset, U.K. 13 51 12N 2 39W
Wells, Me., U.S.A. 113 43 18N 70 35W
Wells, Minn., U.S.A. 116 43 44N 93 45W
Wells, Nev., U.S.A. 118 41 8N 115 0W
Wells Gray Prov. Park 108 52 30N 120 15W
Wells L. 96 26 44 S 123 15 E
Wells River 113 44 9N 72 4W
Wellsboro 114 41 45N 77 20W
Wellsburg 112 40 15N 80 36W
Wellsville, Mo., U.S.A. 116 39 4N 91 30W
Wellsville, N.Y., U.S.A. 114 42 9N 77 53W
Wellsville, Ohio, U.S.A. 114 40 36N 80 40W
Wellsville, Utah, U.S.A. 118 41 35N 111 59W
Wellton 119 32 39N 114 6W
Welmel, Wabi → 87 5 38N 40 47 E
Wełna → 28 52 46N 17 32 E
Welo □ 87 11 50N 39 48 E
Wels 26 48 9N 14 1 E
Welshpool 13 52 40N 3 9W
Welwyn 109 50 20N 101 30W
Wem 12 52 52N 2 45W
Wembere → 90 4 10 S 34 15 E
Wen Xian 77 32 43N 104 36 E
Wenatchee 118 47 30N 120 17W
Wenchang 77 19 38N 110 42 E
Wenchi 84 7 46N 2 8W
Wenchow = Wenzhou 75 28 0N 120 38 E
Wendell 118 42 50N 114 42W
Wendeng 76 37 15N 122 5 E
Wendesi 73 2 30 S 134 17 E
Wendo 87 6 40N 38 27 E
Wendover 118 40 49N 114 1W
Wengcheng 77 24 22N 113 50 E
Wenlock 98 13 6 S 142 58 E
Wenlock → 97 12 2 S 141 55 E
Wensu 75 41 15N 80 10 E
Wentworth 97 34 2 S 141 54 E
Wenut 73 3 11 S 133 19 E
Wenxi 77 35 20N 111 10 E
Wenzhou 75 28 0N 120 38 E
Weott 118 40 19N 123 56W
Wepener 92 29 42 S 27 3 E
Werda 92 25 24 S 23 15 E
Werdau 24 50 45N 12 20 E
Werder, Ethiopia 63 6 58N 45 1 E
Werder, Ger. 24 52 23N 12 56 E
Werdohl 24 51 15N 7 47 E
Wereilu 87 10 40N 39 28 E
Weri 73 3 10 S 132 38 E
Werne 24 51 38N 7 38 E
Werneck 25 49 59N 10 6 E
Wernigerode 24 51 49N 10 45 E
Werra → 24 51 26N 9 39 E
Werribee 99 37 54 S 144 40 E
Werrimull 99 34 25 S 141 38 E
Werris Creek 99 31 18 S 150 38 E
Wersar 73 1 30 S 131 55 E
Wertach → 25 48 24N 10 53 E
Wertheim 25 49 44N 9 32 E
Wertingen 25 48 33N 10 41 E
Wesel 24 51 39N 6 34 E
Weser → 24 53 33N 8 30 E
Wesiri 73 7 30 S 126 30 E
Wesleyville, Can. 107 49 8N 53 36W
Wesleyville, U.S.A. 112 42 9N 80 1W
Wessel Is. 97 11 10 S 136 45 E
Wesselburen 24 54 11N 8 53 E
Wessington 116 44 30N 98 40W
Wessington Springs 116 44 10N 98 35W
West 117 31 50N 97 5W
West B. 117 29 5N 89 27W
West Bend 114 43 25N 88 10W
West Bengal □ 69 23 0N 88 0 E
West Branch 114 44 16N 84 13W
West Bromwich 13 52 32N 2 1W
West Chazy 113 44 49N 73 28W
West Chester 114 39 58N 75 36W
West Columbia 117 29 10N 95 38W
West Des Moines 116 41 30N 93 45W
West Falkland 128 51 40 S 60 0W
West Frankfurt 116 37 56N 89 0W
West Germany ■ 24 52 0N 9 0 E
West Glamorgan □ 13 51 40N 3 55W
West Hartford 113 41 45N 72 45W
West Haven 113 41 18N 72 57W
West Helena 117 34 30N 90 40W
West Ice Shelf 5 67 0 S 85 0 E
West Indies 121 15 0N 70 0W
West Looe 13 50 21N 4 29W
West Lorne 112 42 36N 81 36W
West Lunga → 91 13 6 S 24 39 E
West Magpie → 107 51 2N 64 42W
West Memphis 117 35 5N 90 11W
West Midlands □ 13 52 30N 1 55W
West Monroe 117 32 32N 92 7W
West Moors 12 50 49N 1 50W
West Newton 112 40 14N 79 46W
West Nicholson 91 21 2 S 29 20 E
West Palm Beach 115 26 44N 80 3W
West Pittston 113 41 19N 75 49W
West Plains 117 36 45N 91 50W
West Point, Ga., U.S.A. 115 32 54N 85 10W
West Point, Miss., U.S.A. 115 33 36N 88 38W
West Point, Nebr., U.S.A. 116 41 50N 96 43W
West Point, Va., U.S.A. 114 37 35N 76 47W
West Pokot □ 90 1 30N 35 15 E
West Road → 108 53 18N 122 53W
West Rutland 114 43 38N 73 0W
West Schelde → = Westerschelde 16 51 25N 3 25 E
West Siberian Plain 60 62 0N 75 0 E
West Sussex □ 13 50 55N 0 30W
West-Terschelling 16 53 22N 5 13 E
West Virginia □ 114 39 0N 81 0W
West-Vlaanderen □ 16 51 0N 3 0 E
West Wyalong 100 33 56 S 147 10 E
West Yellowstone 118 44 47N 111 4W
West Yorkshire □ 12 53 45N 1 40W
Westbrook, Maine, U.S.A. 115 43 40N 70 22W
Westbrook, Tex., U.S.A. 117 32 25N 101 0W
Westbury 99 41 30 S 146 51 E
Westby 116 48 52N 104 3W
Westerland 24 54 51N 8 20 E
Western □, Kenya 90 0 30N 34 30 E
Western □, Uganda 90 1 45N 31 30 E
Western □, Zambia 91 15 15 S 24 30 E
Western Australia □ 96 25 0 S 118 0 E
Western Ghats 70 14 0N 75 0 E
Western Isles □ 14 57 30N 7 10W
Western Samoa ■ 101 14 0 S 172 0W
Westernport 114 39 30N 79 5W
Westerschelde → 16 51 25N 3 25 E
Westerstede 24 53 15N 7 55 E
Westerwald 24 50 39N 8 0 E
Westfield, Mass., U.S.A. 113 42 9N 72 49W
Westfield, N.Y., U.S.A. 112 42 20N 79 38W
Westfield, Pa., U.S.A. 112 41 54N 77 32W
Westhope 116 48 55N 101 0W
Westland □ 101 43 33 S 169 59 E
Westland Bight 101 42 55 S 170 5 E
Westlock 108 54 9N 113 55W
Westmeath □ 15 53 30N 7 30W
Westminster 114 39 34N 77 1W
Westmorland 119 33 2N 115 42W
Weston, Malay. 72 5 10N 115 35 E
Weston, Oreg., U.S.A. 118 45 50N 118 30W
Weston, W. Va., U.S.A. 114 39 3N 80 29W
Weston I. 106 52 33N 79 36W
Weston-super-Mare 13 51 20N 2 59W
Westport, Can. 113 44 40N 76 25W
Westport, Ireland 15 53 44N 9 31W
Westport, N.Z. 101 41 46 S 171 37 E
Westport, U.S.A. 118 46 48N 124 4W
Westray, Can. 109 53 36N 101 24W
Westray, U.K. 14 59 18N 3 0W
Westree 106 47 26N 81 34W
Westview 108 49 50N 124 31W
Westville, Ill., U.S.A. 114 40 3N 87 36W
Westville, Okla., U.S.A. 117 36 0N 94 33W
Westwood 118 40 26N 121 0W
Wetar 73 7 30 S 126 30 E
Wetaskiwin 108 52 55N 113 24W
Wethersfield 113 41 43N 72 40W
Wetteren 16 51 0N 3 53 E
Wetzlar 24 50 33N 8 30 E

* Renamed Hwange

† Renamed Teraina

Wewak Workington

Wewak **98** 3 38 S 143 41 E
Wewaka **117** 35 10N 96 35W
Wexford **15** 52 20N 6 28W
Wexford □ **15** 52 20N 6 25W
Wexford Harb. **15** 52 20N 6 25W
Weyburn **109** 49 40N 103 50W
Weyburn L. **108** 63 0N 117 59W
Weyer **26** 47 51N 14 40 E
Weyib → **87** 7 15N 40 15 E
Weymouth, Can. **107** 44 30N 66 1W
Weymouth, U.K. **13** 50 36N 2 28W
Weymouth, U.S.A. **113** 42 13N 70 53W
Weymouth, C. **97** 12 37 S 143 27 E
Whakatane **101** 37 57 S 177 1 E
Whale → **107** 58 15N 67 40W
Whale Cove **104** 62 11N 92 36W
Whales, B. of **5** 78 0 S 165 0W
Whalsay **14** 60 22N 1 0W
Whangamomona **101** 39 8 S 174 44 E
Whangarei **101** 35 43 S 174 21 E
Whangarei Harbour **101** 35 45 S 174 28 E
Wharfe → **12** 53 55N 1 30W
Wharfedale **12** 54 7N 2 4W
Wharton, N.J., U.S.A. **113** 40 53N 74 36W
Wharton, Pa., U.S.A. **112** 41 31N 78 1W
Wharton, Tex., U.S.A. **117** 29 20N 96 6W
Wheatland **116** 42 4N 104 58W
Wheatley **112** 42 6N 82 27W
Wheaton **116** 45 50N 96 29W
Wheeler, Oreg., U.S.A. **118** 45 50N 123 57W
Wheeler, Tex., U.S.A. **117** 35 29N 100 15W
Wheeler → **109** 57 25N 105 30W
Wheeler Pk., N. Mex., U.S.A. **119** 36 34N 105 25W
Wheeler Pk., Nev., U.S.A. **119** 38 57N 114 15W
Wheeling **114** 40 2N 80 41W
Whernside **12** 54 14N 2 24W
Whidbey I. **108** 48 15N 122 40W
Whidbey Is. **96** 34 30 S 135 3 E
Whiskey Gap **108** 49 0N 113 3W
Whiskey Jack L. **109** 58 23N 101 55W
Whistler **115** 30 50N 88 10W
Whitby, Can. **112** 43 52N 78 56W
Whitby, U.K. **12** 54 29N 0 37W
White →, Ark., U.S.A. **117** 33 53N 91 3W
White →, Colo., U.S.A. **118** 40 8N 109 41W
White →, Ind., U.S.A. **114** 38 25N 87 44W
White →, S.D., U.S.A. **116** 43 45N 99 30W
White B. **107** 50 0N 56 35W
White Bear Res. **107** 48 10N 57 5W
White Bird **118** 45 46N 116 21W
White Butte **116** 46 23N 103 19W
White City **116** 38 50N 96 45W
White Cliffs **99** 30 50 S 143 10 E
White Deer **117** 35 30N 101 8W
White Hall **116** 39 25N 90 27W
White Haven **113** 41 3N 75 47W
White I. **101** 37 30 S 177 13 E
White L., Can. **113** 45 18N 76 31W
White L., U.S.A. **117** 29 45N 92 30W
White Mts., Calif., U.S.A. **119** 37 30N 118 15W
White Mts., N.H., U.S.A. **113** 44 15N 71 15W
White Nile = Nîl el Abyad → **87** 15 38N 32 31 E
White Nile Dam **87** 15 24N 32 30 E
White Otter L. **106** 49 5N 91 55W
White Pass **104** 59 40N 135 3W
White Plains **113** 41 2N 73 44W
White River, Can. **106** 48 35N 85 20W
White River, S. Afr. **93** 25 20 S 31 00 E
White River, U.S.A. **116** 43 34N 100 45W
White River Junc. **113** 43 38N 72 20W
White Russia = Byelorussian S.S.R. □ **54** 53 30N 27 0 E
White Sea = Beloye More **52** 66 30N 38 0 E
White Sulphur Springs, Mont., U.S.A. **118** 46 35N 110 54W
White Sulphur Springs, W. Va., U.S.A. **114** 37 50N 80 16W
White Volta (Volta Blanche) → **85** 9 10N 1 15W
Whitecliffs **101** 43 26 S 171 55 E
Whitecourt **108** 54 10N 115 45W
Whiteface **117** 33 35N 102 40W
Whitefield **113** 44 23N 71 37W
Whitefish **118** 48 25N 114 22W
Whitefish L. **109** 62 41N 106 48W
Whitefish Pt. **114** 46 45N 85 0W
Whitegull, L. **107** 55 27N 64 17W
Whitehall, Mich., U.S.A. **114** 43 21N 86 20W
Whitehall, Mont., U.S.A. **118** 45 52N 112 4W
Whitehall, N.Y., U.S.A. **114** 43 32N 73 28W
Whitehall, Wis., U.S.A. **116** 44 20N 91 19W
Whitehaven **12** 54 33N 3 35W
Whitehorse **104** 60 43N 135 3W
Whitehorse, Vale of **13** 51 37N 1 30W
Whiteman Ra. **98** 5 55 S 150 0 E
Whitemark **99** 40 7 S 148 3 E
Whitemouth **109** 49 57N 95 58W
Whiteplains **84** 6 28N 10 40W
Whitesail, L. **108** 53 35N 127 45W
Whitesboro, N.Y., U.S.A. **113** 43 8N 75 20W
Whitesboro, Tex., U.S.A. **117** 33 40N 96 58W
Whiteshell Prov. Park **109** 50 0N 95 40W
Whitetail **116** 48 54N 105 15W
Whiteville **115** 34 20N 78 40W
Whitewater **114** 42 50N 88 45W
Whitewater Baldy, Mt. **119** 33 20N 108 44W
Whitewater L. **106** 50 50N 89 10W
Whitewood, Austral. **98** 21 28 S 143 30 E
Whitewood, Can. **109** 50 20N 102 20W
Whitfield **99** 36 42 S 146 24 E
Whithorn **14** 54 44N 4 25W
Whitianga **101** 36 47 S 175 41 E
Whitman **113** 42 4N 70 55W
Whitmire **115** 34 33N 81 40W
Whitney **106** 45 31N 78 14W
Whitney, Mt. **119** 36 35N 118 14W
Whitney Pt. **113** 42 19N 75 59W
Whitstable **13** 51 21N 1 2 E
Whitsunday I. **97** 20 15 S 149 4 E
Whittier **104** 60 46N 148 48W
Whittlesea **99** 37 27 S 145 9 E
Whitwell **115** 35 15N 85 30W
Wholdaia L. **109** 60 43N 104 20W
Whyalla **97** 33 2 S 137 30 E
Whyjonta **99** 29 41 S 142 28 E
Wiarton **106** 44 40N 81 10W
Wiawso **84** 6 10N 2 25W
Wiazów **28** 50 50N 17 10 E
Wibaux **116** 47 0N 104 13W
Wichita **117** 37 40N 97 20W
Wichita Falls **117** 33 57N 98 30W
Wick **14** 58 26N 3 5W
Wickenburg **119** 33 58N 112 45W
Wickett **117** 31 37N 102 58W
Wickham, C. **99** 39 35 S 143 57 E
Wickliffe **112** 41 36N 81 29W
Wicklow **15** 53 0N 6 2W
Wicklow □ **15** 52 59N 6 25W
Wicklow Hd. **15** 52 59N 6 3W
Wicklow Mts. **15** 53 0N 6 30W
Widawa **28** 51 27N 18 51 E
Widawka **28** 51 7N 19 36 E
Widnes **12** 53 22N 2 44W
Więcbork **28** 53 21N 17 30 E
Wiedenbrück **24** 51 52N 8 15 E
Wiek **24** 54 37N 13 17 E
Wielbark **28** 53 24N 20 55 E
Wieleń **28** 52 53N 16 9 E
Wieliczka **27** 50 0N 20 5 E
Wieluń **28** 51 15N 18 34 E
Wien **27** 48 12N 16 22 E
Wiener Neustadt **27** 47 49N 16 16 E
Wieprz →, Koszalin, Poland **28** 54 26N 16 35 E
Wieprz →, Lublin, Poland **28** 51 34N 21 49 E
Wierden **16** 52 22N 6 35 E
Wieruszów **28** 51 19N 18 9 E
Wiesbaden **25** 50 7N 8 17 E
Wiesental **25** 49 15N 8 30 E
Wigan **12** 53 33N 2 38W
Wiggins, Colo., U.S.A. **116** 40 16N 104 3W
Wiggins, Miss., U.S.A. **117** 30 53N 89 9W
Wight, I. of **13** 50 40N 1 20W
Wigry, Jezioro **28** 54 2N 23 8 E
Wigtown **14** 54 52N 4 27W
Wigtown B. **14** 54 46N 4 15W
Wil **25** 47 28N 9 3 E
Wilamowice **27** 49 55N 19 9 E
Wilber **116** 40 34N 96 59W
Wilberforce **112** 45 2N 78 13W
Wilberforce, C. **97** 11 54 S 136 35 E
Wilburton **117** 34 55N 95 15W
Wilcannia **97** 31 30 S 143 26 E
Wilcox **112** 41 34N 78 43W
Wildbad **25** 48 44N 8 32 E
Wildeshausen **24** 52 54N 8 25 E
Wildon **26** 46 52N 15 31 E
Wildrose **116** 48 36N 103 11W
Wildspitze **26** 46 53N 10 53 E
Wildwood **114** 38 59N 74 46W
Wilga → **28** 51 52N 21 18 E
Wilhelm II Coast **5** 68 0 S 90 0 E
Wilhelm Mt. **98** 5 50 S 145 1 E
Wilhelm-Pieck-Stadt Guben **24** 51 59N 14 48 E
Wilhelmsburg, Austria **26** 48 6N 15 36 E
Wilhelmsburg, Ger. **24** 53 28N 10 1 E
Wilhelmshaven **24** 53 30N 8 9 E
Wilhelmstal **92** 21 58 S 16 21 E
Wilkes Barre **114** 41 15N 75 52W
Wilkes Land **5** 69 0 S 120 0 E
Wilkes Sub-Glacial Basin **5** 75 0 S 130 0 E
Wilkesboro **115** 36 10N 81 9W
Wilkie **109** 52 27N 108 42W
Wilkinsburg **112** 40 26N 79 50W
Willamina **118** 45 9N 123 32W
Willandra Billabong Creek → **99** 33 22 S 145 52 E
Willapa, B. **118** 46 44N 124 0W
Willard, N. Mex., U.S.A. **119** 34 35N 106 1W
Willard, Utah, U.S.A. **118** 41 28N 112 1W
Willcox **119** 32 13N 109 53W
Willemstad **121** 12 5N 69 0W
William → **109** 59 8N 109 19W
Williams **119** 35 16N 112 11W
Williams Lake **108** 52 10N 122 10W
Williamsburg, Ky., U.S.A. **115** 36 45N 84 10W
Williamsburg, Pa., U.S.A. **112** 40 27N 78 14W
Williamsburg, Va., U.S.A. **114** 37 17N 76 44W
Williamson, N.Y., U.S.A. **112** 43 14N 77 15W
Williamson, W. Va., U.S.A. **114** 37 46N 82 17W
Williamsport **114** 41 18N 77 1W
Williamston **115** 35 50N 77 5W
Williamstown, Austral. **99** 37 51 S 144 52 E
Williamstown, Mass., U.S.A. **113** 42 41N 73 12W
Williamstown, N.Y., U.S.A. **113** 43 25N 75 54W
Williamsville **117** 37 0N 90 33W
Willimantic **113** 41 45N 72 12W
Williston, S. Afr. **92** 31 20 S 20 53 E
Williston, Fla., U.S.A. **115** 29 25N 82 28W
Williston, N.D., U.S.A. **116** 48 10N 103 35W
Williston L. **108** 56 0N 124 0W
Willits **118** 39 28N 123 17W
Willmar **116** 45 5N 95 0W
Willoughby **112** 41 38N 81 26W
Willow Bunch **109** 49 20N 105 35W
Willow L. **108** 62 10N 119 8W
Willow Lake **116** 44 40N 97 40W
Willow River **108** 54 6N 122 28W
Willow Springs **117** 37 0N 92 0W
Willowlake → **108** 62 42N 123 8W
Willowmore **92** 33 15 S 23 30 E
Willows, Austral. **98** 23 39 S 147 25 E
Willows, U.S.A. **118** 39 30N 122 10W
Wills Cr. → **98** 22 43 S 140 2 E
Wills Pt. **117** 32 42N 95 57W
Willunga **99** 35 15 S 138 30 E
Wilmette **114** 42 6N 87 44W
Wilmington, Austral. **99** 32 39 S 138 7 E
Wilmington, Del., U.S.A. **114** 39 45N 75 32W
Wilmington, Ill., U.S.A. **114** 41 19N 88 10W
Wilmington, N.C., U.S.A. **115** 34 14N 77 54W
Wilmington, Ohio, U.S.A. **114** 39 27N 83 50W
Wilpena Cr. → **99** 31 25 S 139 29 E
Wilsall **118** 45 59N 110 40W
Wilson **115** 35 44N 77 54W
Wilson → **99** 27 38 S 141 24 E
Wilson, Mt. **119** 37 55N 108 3W
Wilson's Promontory **97** 38 55 S 146 25 E
Wilster **24** 53 55N 9 23 E
Wilton, U.K. **13** 51 5N 1 52W
Wilton, U.S.A. **116** 47 12N 100 47W
Wiltshire □ **13** 51 20N 2 0W
Wiltz **16** 49 57N 5 55 E
Wiluna **96** 26 36 S 120 14 E
Wimereux **19** 50 45N 1 37 E
Wimmera **97** 36 30 S 142 0 E
Wimmera → **99** 36 8 S 141 56 E
Winam G. **90** 0 20 S 34 15 E
Winburg **92** 28 30 S 27 2 E
Winchendon **113** 42 40N 72 3W
Winchester, U.K. **13** 51 4N 1 19W
Winchester, Conn., U.S.A. **113** 41 53N 73 9W
Winchester, Idaho, U.S.A. **118** 46 11N 116 32W
Winchester, Ind., U.S.A. **114** 40 10N 84 56W
Winchester, Ky., U.S.A. **114** 38 0N 84 8W
Winchester, Mass., U.S.A. **113** 42 28N 71 10W
Winchester, N.H., U.S.A. **113** 42 47N 72 22W
Winchester, Tenn., U.S.A. **115** 35 11N 86 8W
Winchester, Va., U.S.A. **114** 39 14N 78 8W
Wind → **118** 43 8N 108 12W
Wind River Range **118** 43 0N 109 30W
Windber **114** 40 14N 78 50W
Windermere, L. **12** 54 20N 2 57W
Windfall **108** 54 12N 116 13W
Windflower L. **108** 62 52N 118 30W
Windhoek **92** 22 35 S 17 4 E
Windischgarsten **26** 47 42N 14 21 E
Windom **116** 43 48N 95 3W
Windorah **97** 25 24 S 142 36 E
Window Rock **119** 35 47N 109 4W
Windrush → **13** 51 48N 1 35W
Windsor, Austral. **99** 33 37 S 150 50 E
Windsor, N.S., Can. **107** 44 59N 64 5W
Windsor, Newf., Can. **107** 48 57N 55 40W
Windsor, Ont., Can. **106** 42 18N 83 0W
Windsor, U.K. **13** 51 28N 0 36W
Windsor, Col., U.S.A. **116** 40 33N 104 45W
Windsor, Conn., U.S.A. **113** 41 50N 72 40W
Windsor, Mo., U.S.A. **116** 38 32N 93 31W
Windsor, N.Y., U.S.A. **113** 42 5N 75 37W
Windsor, Vt., U.S.A. **114** 43 30N 72 25W
Windsorton **92** 28 16 S 24 44 E
Windward Is., Atl. Oc. **121** 13 0N 63 0W
Windward Is., Pac. Oc. **95** 18 0 S 149 0W
Windward Passage = Vientos, Paso de los **121** 20 0N 74 0W
Windy L. **109** 60 20N 100 2W
Winefred L. **109** 55 30N 110 30W
Winejok **87** 9 1N 27 30 E
Winfield **117** 37 15N 97 0W
Wingen **99** 31 54 S 150 54 E
Wingham, Austral. **99** 31 48 S 152 22 E
Wingham, Can. **106** 43 55N 81 20W
Winifred **118** 47 30N 109 28W
Winisk **106** 55 20N 85 15W
Winisk → **106** 55 17N 85 5W
Winisk L. **106** 52 55N 87 22W
Wink **117** 31 49N 103 9W
Winkler **109** 49 10N 97 56W
Winklern **26** 46 52N 12 52 E
Winlock **118** 46 29N 122 56W
Winneba **85** 5 25N 0 36W
Winnebago **116** 43 43N 94 8W
Winnebago L. **114** 44 0N 88 20W
Winnemucca **118** 41 0N 117 45W
Winnemucca, L. **118** 40 25N 119 21W
Winner **116** 43 23N 99 52W
Winnetka **114** 42 8N 87 46W
Winnett **118** 47 2N 108 21W
Winnfield **117** 31 57N 92 38W
Winnibigoshish L. **116** 47 25N 94 12W
Winnipeg **109** 49 54N 97 9W
Winnipeg → **109** 50 38N 96 19W
Winnipeg Beach **109** 50 30N 96 58W
Winnipeg, L. **109** 52 0N 97 0W
Winnipegosis **109** 51 39N 99 55W
Winnipegosis L. **109** 52 30N 100 0W
Winnipesaukee, L. **113** 43 38N 71 21W
Winnsboro, La., U.S.A. **117** 32 10N 91 41W
Winnsboro, S.C., U.S.A. **115** 34 23N 81 5W
Winnsboro, Tex., U.S.A. **117** 32 56N 95 15W
Winokapau, L. **107** 53 15N 62 50W
Winona, Miss., U.S.A. **117** 33 30N 89 42W
Winona, Wis., U.S.A. **116** 44 2N 91 39W
Winooski **114** 44 31N 73 11W
Winschoten **16** 53 9N 7 3 E
Winsen **24** 53 21N 10 11 E
Winslow **119** 35 2N 110 41W
Winsted **113** 41 55N 73 5W
Winston-Salem **115** 36 7N 80 15W
Winter Garden **115** 28 33N 81 35W
Winter Haven **115** 28 0N 81 42W
Winter Park **115** 28 34N 81 19W
Winterberg **24** 51 12N 8 30 E
Winters **117** 31 58N 99 58W
Winterset **116** 41 18N 94 0W
Wintersville **112** 40 22N 80 38W
Winterswijk **16** 51 58N 6 43 E
Winterthur **25** 47 30N 8 44 E
Winthrop, Minn., U.S.A. **116** 44 31N 94 25W
Winthrop, Wash., U.S.A. **118** 48 27N 120 6W
Winton, Austral. **97** 22 24 S 143 3 E
Winton, N.Z. **101** 46 8 S 168 20 E
Winton, N.C., U.S.A. **115** 36 25N 76 58W
Winton, Pa., U.S.A. **113** 41 27N 75 33W
Wintzenheim **19** 48 4N 7 17 E
Wipper → **24** 51 17N 11 10 E
Wirral **12** 53 25N 3 0W
Wisbech **12** 52 39N 0 10 E
Wisconsin □ **116** 44 30N 90 0W
Wisconsin → **116** 43 0N 91 15W
Wisconsin Dells **116** 43 38N 89 45W
Wisconsin Rapids **116** 44 25N 89 50W
Wisdom **118** 45 37N 113 27W
Wishaw **14** 55 46N 3 55W
Wishek **116** 46 20N 99 35W
Wisła **27** 49 38N 18 53 E
Wisła → **28** 54 22N 18 55 E
Wisłok → **27** 50 13N 22 32 E
Wisłoka → **27** 50 27N 21 23 E
Wismar **24** 53 53N 11 23 E
Wisner **116** 42 0N 96 46W
Wissant **19** 50 52N 1 40 E
Wissembourg **19** 49 2N 7 57 E
Wistoka → **27** 49 50N 21 28 E
Wisznice **28** 51 48N 23 13 E
Witbank **93** 25 51 S 29 14 E
Witdraai **92** 26 58 S 20 48 E
Witham → **12** 53 3N 0 8W
Withernsea **12** 53 43N 0 2 E
Witkowo **28** 52 26N 17 45 E
Witney **13** 51 47N 1 29W
Witnossob → **92** 26 55 S 20 37 E
Wittdün **24** 54 38N 8 23 E
Witten **24** 51 26N 7 19 E
Wittenberg **24** 51 51N 12 39 E
Wittenberge **24** 53 0N 11 44 E
Wittenburg **24** 53 30N 11 4 E
Wittenoom **96** 22 15 S 118 20 E
Wittingen **24** 52 43N 10 43 E
Wittlich **25** 50 0N 6 54 E
Wittmund **24** 53 39N 7 45 E
Wittow **24** 54 37N 13 21 E
Wittstock **24** 53 10N 12 30 E
Witzenhausen **24** 51 20N 9 50 E
Wkra → **28** 52 27N 20 44 E
Władysławowo **28** 54 48N 18 25 E
Wlen **28** 51 0N 15 39 E
Wlingi **73** 8 5 S 112 25 E
Włocławek □ **28** 52 50N 19 10 E
Włocławek **28** 52 40N 19 3 E
Włodawa **28** 51 33N 23 31 E
Włoszczowa **28** 50 50N 19 55 E
Woburn **113** 42 31N 71 7W
Wodonga **99** 36 5 S 146 50 E
Wodzisław Śląski **27** 50 1N 18 26 E
Woerth **19** 48 57N 7 45 E
Woëvre, Plaine de la **19** 49 15N 5 45 E
Wokam **73** 5 45 S 134 28 E
Woking **108** 55 35N 118 50W
Wolbrom **28** 50 24N 19 45 E
Wołczyn **28** 51 1N 18 3 E
Woldegk **24** 53 27N 13 35 E
Wolf → **108** 60 17N 132 33W
Wolf Creek **118** 47 1N 112 2W
Wolf L. **108** 60 24N 131 40W
Wolf Point **116** 48 6N 105 40W
Wolfe I. **106** 44 7N 76 20W
Wolfenbüttel **24** 52 10N 10 33 E
Wolfenden **108** 52 0N 119 25W
Wolfsberg **26** 46 50N 14 52 E
Wolfsburg **24** 52 27N 10 49 E
Wolgast **24** 54 3N 13 46 E
Wolhusen **25** 47 4N 8 4 E
Wolin, Poland **28** 53 50N 14 37 E
Wolin, Poland **28** 54 0N 14 40 E
Wollaston, Islas **128** 55 40 S 67 30W
Wollaston L. **109** 58 7N 103 10W
Wollaston Pen. **104** 69 30N 115 0W
Wollondilly → **100** 34 12 S 150 18 E
Wollongong **97** 34 25 S 150 54 E
Wolmaransstad **92** 27 12 S 26 13 E
Wolmirstedt **24** 52 15N 11 35 E
Wołomin **28** 52 19N 21 15 E
Wołów **28** 51 20N 16 38 E
Wolseley, Austral. **99** 36 23 S 140 54 E
Wolseley, Can. **109** 50 25N 103 15W
Wolseley, S. Afr. **92** 33 26 S 19 7 E
Wolstenholme Fjord **4** 76 0N 70 0W
Wolsztyn **28** 52 8N 16 5 E
Wolvega **16** 52 52N 6 0 E
Wolverhampton **13** 52 35N 2 6W
Wondai **97** 26 20 S 151 49 E
Wonder Gorge **91** 14 40 S 29 0 E
Wongalarroo L. **99** 31 32 S 144 0 E
Wŏnju **76** 37 22N 127 58 E
Wonosari **73** 7 58 S 110 36 E
Wŏnsan **76** 39 11N 127 27 E
Wonthaggi **97** 38 37 S 145 37 E
Woocalla **99** 31 42 S 137 12 E
Wood Buffalo Nat. Park **108** 59 0N 113 41W
Wood L. **109** 55 17N 103 17W
Wood Lake **116** 42 38N 100 14W
Woodbridge **112** 43 47N 79 36W
Woodburn **99** 29 6 S 153 23 E
Woodend **99** 37 20 S 144 33 E
Woodland **118** 38 40N 121 50W
Woodlark I. **98** 9 10 S 152 50 E
Woodpecker **108** 53 30N 122 40W
Woodridge **109** 49 20N 96 9W
Woodroffe, Mt. **96** 26 20 S 131 45 E
Woodruff, Ariz., U.S.A. **119** 34 51N 110 1W
Woodruff, Utah, U.S.A. **118** 41 30N 111 4W
Woods, L., Austral. **96** 17 50 S 133 30 E
Woods, L., Can. **107** 54 30N 65 13W
Woods, L. of the **109** 49 15N 94 45W
Woodside **100** 38 31 S 146 52 E
Woodstock, Austral. **98** 19 35 S 146 50 E
Woodstock, N.B., Can. **107** 46 11N 67 37W
Woodstock, Ont., Can. **106** 43 10N 80 45W
Woodstock, U.K. **13** 51 51N 1 20W
Woodstock, Ill., U.S.A. **116** 42 17N 88 30W
Woodstock, Vt., U.S.A. **113** 43 37N 72 31W
Woodsville **114** 44 10N 72 0W
Woodville, N.Z. **101** 40 20 S 175 53 E
Woodville, U.S.A. **117** 30 45N 94 25W
Woodward **117** 36 24N 99 28W
Woolamai, C. **99** 38 30 S 145 23 E
Woombye **99** 26 40 S 152 55 E
Woomera **97** 31 30 S 137 10 E
Woonona **100** 34 21 S 150 54 E
Woonsocket **114** 42 0N 71 30W
Woonsockett **116** 44 5N 98 15W
Wooramel → **96** 25 47 S 114 10 E
Wooster **114** 40 48N 81 55W
Worcester, S. Afr. **92** 33 39 S 19 27 E
Worcester, U.K. **13** 52 12N 2 12W
Worcester, Mass., U.S.A. **114** 42 14N 71 49W
Worcester, N.Y., U.S.A. **113** 42 35N 74 45W
Wörgl **26** 47 29N 12 3 E
Workington **12** 54 39N 3 34W

Worksop Yining

Worksop 12 53 19N 1 9W
Workum 16 52 59N 5 26 E
Worland 118 44 0N 107 59W
Wormhoudt 19 50 52N 2 28 E
Worms 25 49 37N 8 21 E
Wörth 25 49 1N 12 24 E
Wortham 117 31 48N 96 27W
Wörther See 26 46 37N 14 10 E
Worthing 13 50 49N 0 21W
Worthington 116 43 35N 95 36W
Wosi 73 0 15 S 128 0 E
Wou-han = Wuhan 75 30 31N 114 18 E
Wour 83 21 14N 16 0 E
Wowoni 73 4 5 S 123 5 E
Wozniki 28 50 35N 19 4 E
Wrangell 104 56 30N 132 25W
Wrangell, I. 108 56 20N 132 10W
Wrangell Mts. 104 61 40N 143 30W
Wrath, C. 14 58 38N 5 0W
Wray 116 40 8N 102 18W
Wrekin, The 12 52 41N 2 35W
Wrens 115 33 13N 82 23W
Wrexham 12 53 5N 3 0W
Wriezen 24 52 43N 14 9 E
Wright, Can. 108 51 52N 121 40W
Wright, Phil. 73 11 42N 125 2 E
Wrightson, Mt. 119 31 43N 110 56W
Wrigley 104 63 16N 123 37W
Wrocław 28 51 5N 17 5 E
Wrocław □ 28 51 0N 17 0 E
Wronki 28 52 41N 16 21 E
Września 28 52 21N 17 36 E
Wschowa 28 51 48N 16 20 E
Wu Jiang → 75 29 40N 107 20 E
Wuchang 76 44 55N 127 5 E
Wuchuan 77 28 25N 108 3 E
Wuding He → 76 37 2N 110 23 E
Wugang 77 26 44N 110 35 E
Wugong Shan 77 27 30N 114 0 E
Wuhan 75 30 31N 114 18 E
Wuhsi = Wuxi 75 31 33N 120 18 E
Wuhu 75 31 22N 118 21 E
Wukari 85 7 51N 9 42 E
Wulehe 85 8 39N 0 0
Wuliaru 73 7 27 S 131 0 E
Wulumuchi = Ürümqi 75 43 45N 87 45 E
Wum 85 6 24N 10 2 E
Wuning 77 29 17N 115 5 E
Wunnummin L. 106 52 55N 89 10W
Wunsiedel 25 50 2N 12 0 E
Wunstorf 24 52 26N 9 29 E
Wuntho 67 23 55N 95 45 E
Wuping 77 25 5N 116 5 E
Wuppertal, Ger. 24 51 15N 7 8 E
Wuppertal, S. Afr. 92 32 13 S 19 12 E
Wuqing 76 39 23N 117 4 E
Wurung 98 19 13 S 140 38 E
Würzburg 25 49 46N 9 55 E
Wurzen 24 51 21N 12 45 E
Wushan 77 31 7N 109 54 E
Wustrow 24 54 4N 11 33 E
Wutach → 25 47 37N 8 15 E
Wutongqiao 75 29 22N 103 50 E
Wuwei, Anhui, China 77 31 18N 117 54 E
Wuwei, Gansu, China 75 37 57N 102 34 E
Wuxi, Jiangsu, China 75 31 33N 120 18 E
Wuxi, Sichuan, China 77 31 23N 109 35 E
Wuxing 77 30 51N 120 8 E
Wuyi, Hebei, China 76 37 46N 115 56 E
Wuyi, Zhejiang, China 77 28 52N 119 50 E
Wuyi Shan 75 27 0N 117 0 E
Wuying 76 47 53N 129 56 E
Wuyo 85 10 23N 11 50 E
Wuyuan 76 41 2N 108 20 E
Wuzhai 76 38 54N 111 48 E
Wuzhi Shan 75 18 45N 109 45 E
Wuzhong 76 38 2N 106 12 E
Wuzhou 75 23 30N 111 18 E
Wyaaba Cr. → 98 16 27 S 141 35 E
Wyalusing 113 41 40N 76 16W
Wyandotte 114 42 14N 83 13W
Wyandra 97 27 12 S 145 56 E
Wyangala Res. 100 33 54 S 149 0 E
Wyara, L. 99 28 42 S 144 14 E
Wycheproof 99 36 0 S 143 17 E
Wye → 13 51 36N 2 40W
Wyk 24 54 41N 8 33 E
Wymondham 13 52 45N 0 42W
Wymore 116 40 10N 96 40W
Wynberg 92 34 2 S 18 28 E
Wyndham, Austral. 96 15 33 S 128 3 E
Wyndham, N.Z. 101 46 20 S 168 51 E
Wyndmere 116 46 23N 97 7W
Wynne 117 35 15N 90 50W
Wynnum 99 27 27 S 153 9 E
Wynyard 109 51 45N 104 10W
Wyoming □ 110 42 48N 109 0W
Wyong 99 33 14 S 151 24 E
Wyrzysk 28 53 10N 17 17 E
Wysoka 28 53 13N 17 2 E
Wysokie 28 50 55N 22 40 E
Wysokie Mazowieckie 28 52 55N 22 30 E
Wyszków 28 52 36N 21 25 E
Wyszogród 28 52 23N 20 9 E
Wytheville 114 37 0N 81 3W

X

Xai-Xai 93 25 6 S 33 31 E
Xainza 75 30 58N 88 35 E
Xangongo 92 16 45 S 15 0 E
Xanten 24 51 40N 6 27 E
Xánthi 44 41 10N 24 58 E
Xánthi □ 44 41 10N 24 58 E
Xapuri 126 10 35 S 68 35W
Xau, L. 92 21 15 S 24 44 E
Xavantina 125 21 15 S 52 48W
Xenia 114 39 42N 83 57W
Xi Jiang → 75 22 5N 113 20 E
Xi Xian 76 36 41N 110 58 E
Xiachengzi 76 44 40N 130 18 E
Xiachuan Dao 77 21 40N 112 40 E
Xiaguan 75 25 32N 100 16 E
Xiajiang 77 27 30N 115 10 E
Xiamen 75 24 25N 118 4 E
Xi'an 77 34 15N 109 0 E
Xianfeng 77 29 40N 109 8 E
Xiang Jiang → 75 28 55N 112 50 E
Xiangfan 75 32 2N 112 8 E
Xiangning 76 35 58N 110 50 E
Xiangtan 75 27 51N 112 54 E
Xiangxiang 77 27 43N 112 28 E
Xiangyang 75 32 1N 112 8 E
Xiangyin 77 28 38N 112 54 E
Xiangzhou 77 23 58N 109 40 E
Xianju 77 28 51N 120 44 E
Xianyang 77 34 20N 108 40 E
Xiao Hinggan Ling 75 49 0N 127 0 E
Xiaogan 77 30 52N 113 55 E
Xiapu 75 26 54N 119 59 E
Xichang 75 27 51N 102 19 E
Xichuan 77 33 0N 111 30 E
Xieng Khouang 71 19 17N 103 25 E
Xifeng 77 27 7N 106 42 E
Xigazê 75 29 5N 88 45 E
Xihe 77 34 2N 105 20 E
Xiliao He → 76 43 32N 123 35 E
Xilin 77 24 30N 105 6 E
Xilókastron 45 38 4N 22 43 E
Xin Xian 76 38 22N 112 46 E
Xinavane 93 25 2 S 32 47 E
Xinbin 76 41 40N 125 2 E
Xincheng 77 24 5N 108 39 E
Xinfeng 77 25 27N 114 58 E
Xing'an 75 25 38N 110 40 E
Xingan 77 27 46N 115 20 E
Xingcheng 76 40 40N 120 45 E
Xingguo 77 26 21N 115 21 E
Xinghua 77 32 58N 119 48 E
Xinghua Wan 77 25 15N 119 20 E
Xingning 77 24 3N 115 42 E
Xingren 75 25 24N 105 11 E
Xingshan 77 31 15N 110 45 E
Xingtai 76 37 3N 114 32 E
Xingu → 127 1 30 S 51 53W
Xingyang 77 34 45N 112 52 E
Xinhua 77 27 42N 111 13 E
Xiniás, L. 45 39 2N 22 12 E
Xining 75 36 34N 101 40 E
Xinjiang 76 35 34N 111 11 E
Xinjiang Uygur Zizhiqu □ 75 42 0N 86 0 E
Xinjin 76 39 25N 121 58 E
Xinle 76 38 25N 114 40 E
Xinmin 76 41 59N 122 50 E
Xinning 77 26 28N 110 50 E
Xinxiang 77 35 18N 113 50 E
Xinyang 75 32 6N 114 3 E
Xinzheng 77 34 20N 113 45 E
Xinzhou 77 19 43N 109 17 E
Xinzhu 75 24 49N 120 57 E
Xiongyuecheng 76 40 12N 122 5 E
Xiping 77 33 22N 114 0 E
Xique-Xique 127 10 50 S 42 40W
Xiuyan 76 40 18N 123 11 E
Xixabangma Feng 67 28 20N 85 40 E
Xixiang 77 33 0N 107 44 E
Xizang □ 75 32 0N 88 0 E
Xuancheng 77 30 56N 118 43 E
Xuan'en 77 30 0N 109 30 E
Xuanhan 77 31 18N 107 38 E
Xuanhua 76 40 40N 115 2 E
Xuchang 77 34 2N 113 48 E
Xuguit Qi 76 49 17N 120 44 E
Xunke 76 49 35N 128 27 E
Xupu 77 27 53N 110 32 E
Xuwen 77 20 20N 110 10 E
Xuyong 77 28 10N 105 22 E
Xuzhou 77 34 18N 117 10 E

Y

Ya 'Bad 62 32 27N 35 10 E
Yaamba 98 23 8 S 150 22 E
Ya'an 75 29 58N 103 5 E
Yaapeet 99 35 45 S 142 3 E
Yabassi 85 4 30N 9 57 E
Yabelo 87 4 50N 38 8 E
Yablanitsa 43 43 2N 24 5 E
Yablonovy Khrebet 59 53 0N 114 0 E
Yabrīn 64 23 17N 48 58 E
Yacheng 77 18 22N 109 6 E
Yacuiba 124 22 0 S 63 43W
Yadgir 70 16 45N 77 5 E
Yadkin → 115 35 23N 80 3W
Yadrin 55 55 57N 46 12 E
Yagaba 85 10 14N 1 20W
Yagodnoye 59 62 33N 149 40 E
Yagoua 88 10 20N 15 13 E
Yagur 62 32 45N 35 4 E
Yahila 90 0 13N 24 28 E
Yahk 108 49 6N 116 10W
Yahuma 88 1 0N 23 10 E
Yajua 85 11 27N 12 49 E
Yakima 118 46 42N 120 30W
Yakima → 118 47 0N 120 30W
Yako 84 12 59N 2 15W
Yakoruda 43 42 1N 23 39 E
Yakut A.S.S.R. □ 59 62 0N 130 0 E
Yakutat 104 59 29N 139 44W
Yakutsk 59 62 5N 129 50 E
Yala 71 6 33N 101 18 E
Yalabusha → 117 33 30N 90 12W
Yalboroo 98 20 50 S 148 40 E
Yale 112 43 9N 82 47W
Yalgoo 96 28 16 S 116 39 E
Yalinga 88 6 33N 23 10 E
Yalkubul, Punta 120 21 32N 88 37W
Yalleroi 98 24 3 S 145 42 E
Yallourn 97 38 10 S 146 18 E
Yalong Jiang → 75 26 40N 101 55 E
Yalpukh, Oz. 46 45 30N 28 41 E
Yalta 56 44 30N 34 10 E
Yalu Chiang → 76 41 30N 126 30 E
Yalu He → 76 46 56N 123 30 E
Yalu Jiang → 76 40 0N 124 22 E
Yalutorovsk 58 56 41N 66 12 E
Yam Kinneret 62 32 45N 35 35 E
Yamagata 74 38 15N 140 15 E
Yamagata □ 74 38 30N 140 0 E
Yamaguchi 74 34 10N 131 32 E
Yamaguchi □ 74 34 20N 131 40 E
Yamal, Poluostrov 58 71 0N 70 0 E
Yamama 64 24 5N 47 30 E
Yamanashi □ 74 35 40N 138 40 E
Yamantau 52 54 20N 57 40 E
Yamantau, Gora 52 54 15N 58 6 E
Yamba 99 29 26 S 153 23 E
Yâmbiô 87 4 35N 28 16 E
Yambol 43 42 30N 26 36 E
Yamdena 73 7 45 S 131 20 E
Yamil 85 12 53N 8 4 E
Yamma-Yamma, L. 97 26 16 S 141 20 E
Yampa → 118 40 37N 108 59W
Yampi Sd. 96 16 8 S 123 38 E
Yampol 56 48 15N 28 15 E
Yamrat 85 10 11N 9 55 E
Yamrukchal 43 42 44N 24 52 E
Yamuna (Jumna) → 68 25 30N 81 53 E
Yamzho Yumco 75 28 48N 90 35 E
Yan 85 10 5N 12 11 E
Yan → 70 9 0N 81 10 E
Yana → 59 71 30N 136 0 E
Yanac 99 36 8 S 141 25 E
Yanai 74 33 58N 132 7 E
Yanam 70 16 47N 82 15 E
Yan'an 76 36 35N 109 26 E
Yanaul 52 56 25N 55 0 E
Yanbu 'al Baḥr 64 24 0N 38 5 E
Yancannia 99 30 12 S 142 35 E
Yanchang 76 36 43N 110 1 E
Yancheng, Henan, China 77 33 35N 114 0 E
Yancheng, Jiangsu, China 77 33 23N 120 8 E
Yanchi 76 37 48N 107 20 E
Yanchuan 76 36 51N 110 10 E
Yanco 100 34 38 S 146 27 E
Yandaran 98 24 43 S 152 6 E
Yanfolila 84 11 11N 8 9W
Yangambi 90 0 47N 24 20 E
Yangch'ü = Taiyuan 76 37 52N 112 33 E
Yangchun 75 22 11N 111 48 E
Yanggao 76 40 21N 113 55 E
Yangi-Yer 58 40 17N 68 48 E
Yangjiang 75 21 50N 110 59 E
Yangquan 76 37 58N 113 31 E
Yangshan 77 24 30N 112 40 E
Yangshuo 77 24 48N 110 29 E
Yangtze Kiang = Chang Jiang → 75 31 20N 121 52 E
Yangxin 77 29 50N 115 12 E
Yangzhou 77 32 21N 119 26 E
Yanhee Res. 71 17 30N 98 45 E
Yanji 76 42 59N 129 30 E
Yankton 116 42 55N 97 25W
Yanna 99 26 58 S 146 0 E
Yanonge 90 0 35N 24 38 E
Yanqi 75 42 5N 86 35 E
Yanqing 76 40 30N 115 58 E
Yanshan 77 28 15N 117 41 E
Yantabulla 99 29 21 S 145 0 E
Yantai 76 37 34N 121 22 E
Yanting 77 31 11N 105 24 E
Yantra → 43 43 40N 25 37 E
Yanzhou 76 35 35N 116 49 E
Yao 81 12 56N 17 33 E
Yaoundé 88 3 50N 11 35 E
Yap 94 9 31N 138 6 E
Yapen 73 1 50 S 136 0 E
Yapen, Selat 73 1 20 S 136 10 E
Yappar → 98 18 22 S 141 16 E
Yaqui → 120 27 37N 110 39W
Yar 55 58 14N 52 5 E
Yar-Sale 58 66 50N 70 50 E
Yaraka 97 24 53 S 144 3 E
Yarangüme 64 37 35N 29 8 E
Yaransk 55 57 22N 47 49 E
Yaratishky 54 54 3N 26 0 E
Yare → 13 52 36N 1 28 E
Yarensk 52 61 10N 49 8 E
Yarfa 86 24 40N 38 35 E
Yari → 126 0 20 S 72 20W
Yarkand = Shache 75 38 20N 77 10 E
Yarker 113 44 23N 76 46W
Yarkhun → 69 36 17N 72 30 E
Yarmouth 107 43 50N 66 7W
Yarmuk → 62 32 38N 35 34 E
Yarmûk → 62 32 42N 35 40 E
Yaroslavl 55 57 35N 39 55 E
Yarra → 100 37 50 S 144 53 E
Yarram 99 38 29 S 146 9 E
Yarraman 99 26 50 S 152 0 E
Yarranvale 99 26 50 S 145 20 E
Yarras 99 31 25 S 152 20 E
Yarrawonga 100 36 0 S 146 0 E
Yartsevo, R.S.F.S.R., U.S.S.R. 54 55 6N 32 43 E
Yartsevo, R.S.F.S.R., U.S.S.R. 59 60 20N 90 0 E
Yasawa Group 101 17 00 S 177 23 E
Yaselda → 54 52 7N 26 28 E
Yashi 85 12 23N 7 54 E
Yasinovataya 56 48 7N 37 57 E
Yasinski, L. 106 53 16N 77 35W
Yasothon 71 15 50N 104 10 E
Yass 97 34 49 S 148 54 E
Yas'ur 62 32 54N 35 10 E
Yatağn 45 37 20N 28 10 E
Yates Center 117 37 53N 95 45W
Yathkyed L. 109 62 40N 98 0W
Yatsushiro 74 32 30N 130 40 E
Yatta Plateau 90 2 0 S 38 0 E
Yaṭṭah 62 31 27N 35 6 E
Yauyos 126 12 19 S 75 50W
Yaval 68 21 10N 75 42 E
Yavari → 126 4 21 S 70 2W
Yavne 62 31 52N 34 45 E
Yavorov 54 49 55N 23 20 E
Yawatahama 74 33 27N 132 24 E
Yawri B. 84 8 22N 13 0W
Yazd (Yezd) 65 31 55N 54 27 E
Yazdān 65 33 30N 60 50 E
Yazoo → 117 32 35N 90 50W
Yazoo City 117 32 48N 90 28W
Ybbs 26 48 12N 15 4 E
Ye Xian 76 37 8N 119 57 E
Yebbi-Souma 83 21 7N 17 54 E
Yebyu 67 14 15N 98 13 E
Yecla 33 38 35N 1 5W
Yedintsy 56 48 9N 27 18 E
Yefremov 55 53 8N 38 3 E
Yegorlyk → 57 46 33N 41 40 E
Yegorlykskaya 57 46 35N 40 35 E
Yegoryevsk 55 55 27N 38 55 E
Yegros 124 26 20 S 56 25W
Yehuda, Midbar 62 31 35N 35 15 E
Yei 87 4 9N 30 40 E
Yei, Nahr → 87 6 15N 30 13 E
Yelabuga 52 55 45N 52 4 E
Yelan 55 50 55N 43 43 E
Yelan-Kolenovski 55 51 16N 41 4 E
Yelandur 70 12 6N 77 0 E
Yelanskoye 59 61 25N 128 0 E
Yelarbon 99 28 33 S 150 38 E
Yelatma 55 55 0N 41 45 E
Yelets 55 52 40N 38 30 E
Yélimané 84 15 9N 10 34W
Yell 14 60 35N 1 5W
Yell Sd. 14 60 33N 1 15W
Yellamanchilli (Elamanchili) 70 17 33N 82 50 E
Yellow Mt. 100 32 31 S 146 52 E
Yellow Sea 76 35 0N 123 0 E
Yellowhead P. 108 52 53N 118 25W
Yellowknife 108 62 27N 114 29W
Yellowknife → 104 62 31N 114 19W
Yellowstone → 116 47 58N 103 59W
Yellowstone L. 118 44 30N 110 20W
Yellowstone National Park 118 44 35N 110 0W
Yellowtail Res. 118 45 6N 108 8W
Yelnya 54 54 35N 33 15 E
Yelsk 54 51 50N 29 10 E
Yelvertoft 98 20 13 S 138 45 E
Yelwa 85 10 49N 4 41 E
Yemen ■ 63 15 0N 44 0 E
Yenakiyevo 56 48 15N 38 15 E
Yenangyaung 67 20 30N 95 0 E
Yenda 99 34 13 S 146 14 E
Yendéré 84 10 12N 4 59W
Yendi 85 9 29N 0 1W
Yenisaía 44 41 1N 24 57 E
Yenisey → 58 71 50N 82 40 E
Yeniseysk 59 58 27N 92 13 E
Yeniseyskiy Zaliv 58 72 20N 81 0 E
Yenne 21 45 43N 5 44 E
Yenotayevka 57 47 15N 47 0 E
Yenyuka 59 57 57N 121 15 E
Yeo, L. 96 28 0 S 124 30 E
Yeola 70 20 0N 74 30 E
Yeotmal 70 20 20N 78 15 E
Yeovil 13 50 57N 2 38W
Yepes 32 39 55N 3 39W
Yeppoon 97 23 5 S 150 47 E
Yeráki 45 37 0N 22 42 E
Yerbent 58 39 30N 58 50 E
Yerbogachen 59 61 16N 108 0 E
Yerevan 57 40 10N 44 31 E
Yerla → 70 16 50N 74 30 E
Yermak 58 52 2N 76 55 E
Yermakovo 59 52 25N 126 20 E
Yermo 119 34 58N 116 50W
Yerofey Pavlovich 59 54 0N 122 0 E
Yershov 55 51 22N 48 16 E
Yerushalayim 62 31 47N 35 10 E
Yerville 18 49 40N 0 53 E
Yes Tor 13 50 41N 3 59W
Yesnogorsk 55 54 32N 37 38 E
Yeso 117 34 29N 104 37W
Yessentuki 57 44 0N 42 53 E
Yessey 59 68 29N 102 10 E
Yeste 33 38 22N 2 19W
Yeu, I. d' 18 46 42N 2 20W
Yevlakh 57 40 39N 47 7 E
Yevpatoriya 56 45 15N 33 20 E
Yevstratovskiy 55 50 11N 39 45 E
Yeya → 57 46 40N 38 40 E
Yeysk 56 46 40N 38 12 E
Yhati 124 25 45 S 56 35W
Yhú 125 25 0 S 56 0W
Yi → 124 33 7 S 57 8W
Yi Xian 76 41 30N 121 22 E
Yiali 45 36 41N 27 11 E
Yi'allaq, G. 86 30 21N 33 31 E
Yiáltra 45 38 51N 22 59 E
Yianisádhes 45 35 20N 26 10 E
Yiannitsa 44 40 46N 22 24 E
Yibin 75 28 45N 104 32 E
Yichang 75 30 40N 111 20 E
Yicheng 76 35 42N 111 40 E
Yichuan 76 36 2N 110 10 E
Yichun, Heilongjiang, China 75 47 44N 128 52 E
Yichun, Jiangxi, China 77 27 48N 114 22 E
Yidhá 44 40 35N 22 53 E
Yidu 76 36 43N 118 28 E
Yihuang 77 27 30N 116 12 E
Yijun 76 35 28N 109 8 E
Yilan, China 76 46 19N 129 34 E
Yilan, Taiwan 75 24 51N 121 44 E
Yilehuli Shan 76 51 20N 124 20 E
Yimianpo 76 45 7N 128 2 E
Yinchuan 76 38 30N 106 15 E
Ying He → 77 32 30N 116 30 E
Ying Xian 76 39 32N 113 10 E
Yingcheng 77 30 56N 113 35 E
Yingde 77 24 10N 113 25 E
Yingkou 76 40 37N 122 18 E
Yingshan 77 30 41N 115 32 E
Yingshang 77 32 38N 116 12 E
Yingtan 75 28 12N 117 0 E
Yining 75 43 58N 81 10 E

Yinjiang Zikhron Ya'Aqov

Yinjiang 77 28 1N 108 21 E
Yinkanie 99 34 22 S 140 17 E
Yinnietharra 96 24 39 S 116 12 E
Yioúra, Greece 44 39 23N 24 10 E
Yioúra, Greece 45 37 32N 24 40 E
Yipinglang 75 25 10N 101 52 E
Yirga Alem 87 6 48N 38 22 E
Yirshi 76 47 18N 119 49 E
Yishan 75 24 28N 108 38 E
Yíthion 45 36 46N 22 34 E
Yitong 76 43 13N 125 20 E
Yitulihe 76 50 38N 121 34 E
Yixing 77 31 21N 119 48 E
Yiyang, Henan, China 77 34 27N 112 10 E
Yiyang, Hunan, China 75 28 35N 112 18 E
Yizhang 77 25 27N 112 57 E
Yizre'el 62 32 34N 35 19 E
Ylitornio 50 66 19N 23 39 E
Ylivieska 50 64 4N 24 28 E
Yngaren 49 58 50N 16 35 E
Ynykchanskiy 59 60 15N 137 35 E
Yoakum 117 29 20N 97 20W
Yog Pt. 73 14 6N 124 12 E
Yogan 85 6 23N 1 30 E
Yogyakarta 73 7 49 S 110 22 E
Yoho Nat. Park 108 51 25N 116 30W
Yojoa, L. de 120 14 53N 88 0W
Yokadouma 88 3 26N 15 6 E
Yokkaichi 74 35 0N 136 38 E
Yoko 85 5 32N 12 20 E
Yokohama 74 35 27N 139 28 E
Yokosuka 74 35 20N 139 40 E
Yola 85 9 10N 12 29 E
Yolaina, Cordillera de 121 11 30N 84 0W
Yonago 74 35 25N 133 19 E
Yong Peng 71 2 0N 103 3 E
Yong'an 77 25 59N 117 25 E
Yongchun 77 25 16N 118 20 E
Yongding 77 24 43N 116 45 E
Yongfeng 77 27 20N 115 22 E
Yongfu 77 24 59N 109 59 E
Yonghe 76 36 46N 110 38 E
Yongji 77 34 52N 110 28 E
Yongshun 77 29 2N 109 51 E
Yongxin 77 26 58N 114 15 E
Yongxing 77 26 9N 113 8 E
Yongxiu 77 29 2N 115 42 E
Yonibana 84 8 30N 12 19W
Yonkers 114 40 57N 73 51W
Yonne □ 19 47 50N 3 40 E
Yonne → 19 48 23N 2 58 E
Yoqne'am 62 32 40N 35 6 E
York, Austral. 96 31 52 S 116 47 E
York, U.K. 12 53 58N 1 7W
York, Ala., U.S.A. 115 32 30N 88 18W
York, Nebr., U.S.A. 116 40 55N 97 35W
York, Pa., U.S.A. 114 39 57N 76 43W
York, C. 97 10 42 S 142 31 E
York, Kap 4 75 55N 66 25W
York Sd. 96 14 50 S 125 5 E
Yorke Pen. 97 34 50 S 137 40 E
Yorkshire Wolds 12 54 0N 0 30W
Yorkton 109 51 11N 102 28W
Yorktown 117 29 0N 97 29W
Yosemite National Park 119 38 0N 119 30W
Yoshkar Ola 55 56 38N 47 55 E
Yŏsu 77 34 47N 127 45 E
Yotvata 62 29 55N 35 2 E
You Jiang → 75 23 22N 110 3 E
Youbou 108 48 53N 124 13W
Youghal 15 51 58N 7 51W
Youghal B. 15 51 55N 7 50W
Youkounkoun 84 12 35N 13 11W
Young, Austral. 97 34 19 S 148 18 E
Young, Can. 109 51 47N 105 45W
Young, Uruguay 124 32 44 S 57 36W
Young, U.S.A. 119 34 9N 110 56W
Younghusband Pen. 99 36 0 S 139 25 E
Youngstown, Can. 109 51 35N 111 10W
Youngstown, N.Y., U.S.A. 112 43 16N 79 2W
Youngstown, Ohio, U.S.A. 114 41 7N 80 41W
Youngsville 112 41 51N 79 21W
Youssoufia 82 32 16N 8 31W
Youyang 77 28 47N 108 42 E
Youyu 76 40 10N 112 20 E
Yozgat 64 39 51N 34 47 E
Ypané → 124 23 29 S 57 19W
Yport 18 49 45N 0 15 E
Ypres = Ieper 16 50 51N 2 53 E
Ypsilanti 114 42 18N 83 40W
Yreka 118 41 44N 122 40W
Ysleta 119 31 45N 106 24W
Yssingeaux 21 45 9N 4 8 E
Ystad 49 55 26N 13 50 E
Ythan → 14 57 26N 2 12W
Ytterhogdal 48 62 12N 14 56 E
Ytyk-Kel 59 62 30N 133 45 E
Yu Shan 75 23 30N 120 58 E
Yu Xian, Hebei, China 76 39 50N 114 35 E
Yu Xian, Henan, China 77 34 10N 113 28 E
Yuan Jiang → 75 28 55N 111 50 E
Yuanling 75 28 29N 110 22 E
Yuanyang 75 23 10N 102 43 E
Yuba City 118 39 12N 121 37W
Yucatán □ 120 21 30N 86 30W
Yucatán, Canal de 121 22 0N 86 30W
Yucca 119 34 56N 114 6W
Yucheng 76 36 55N 116 32 E
Yuci 76 37 42N 112 46 E
Yudino, R.S.F.S.R., U.S.S.R. 55 55 51N 48 55 E
Yudino, R.S.F.S.R., U.S.S.R. 58 55 10N 67 55 E
Yudu 77 25 59N 115 30 E
Yueqing 77 28 9N 120 59 E
Yueyang 77 29 21N 113 5 E
Yugan 77 28 43N 116 37 E
Yugoslavia ■ 37 44 0N 20 0 E
Yuhuan 77 28 9N 121 12 E
Yujiang 77 28 10N 116 43 E
Yukhnov 54 54 44N 35 15 E
Yukon Territory □ 104 63 0N 135 0W
Yukti 59 63 26N 105 42 E
Yule → 96 20 41 S 118 17 E
Yuli 85 9 44N 10 12 E
Yülin 77 18 10N 109 31 E
Yulin, Guangxi Zhuangzu, China 77 22 40N 110 8 E
Yulin, Shaanxi, China 76 38 20N 109 30 E
Yuma, Ariz., U.S.A. 119 32 45N 114 37W
Yuma, Colo., U.S.A. 116 40 10N 102 43W
Yuma, B. de 121 18 20N 68 35W
Yumbe 90 3 28N 31 15 E
Yumbi 90 1 12 S 26 15 E
Yumen 75 39 50N 97 30 E
Yun Xian 75 32 50N 110 46 E
Yungas 126 17 0 S 66 0W
Yungay 124 37 10 S 72 5W
Yunhe 77 28 8N 119 33 E
Yunlin 77 23 42N 120 30 E
Yunnan □ 75 25 0N 102 0 E
Yunquera de Henares 32 40 47N 3 11W
Yunta 99 32 34 S 139 36 E
Yunxiao 77 23 59N 117 18 E
Yur 59 59 52N 137 41 E
Yurgao 58 55 42N 84 51 E
Yuribei 58 71 8N 76 58 E
Yurimaguas 126 5 55 S 76 7W
Yurya 55 59 1N 49 13 E
Yuryev-Polskiy 55 56 30N 39 40 E
Yuryevets 55 57 25N 43 2 E
Yuscarán 121 13 58N 86 45W
Yushu, Jilin, China 76 44 43N 126 38 E
Yushu, Qinghai, China 75 33 5N 96 55 E
Yuyao 77 30 3N 121 10 E
Yuzha 55 56 34N 42 1 E
Yuzhno-Sakhalinsk 59 46 58N 142 45 E
Yvelines □ 19 48 40N 1 45 E
Yverdon 25 46 47N 6 39 E
Yvetot 18 49 37N 0 44 E

Z

Zaandam 16 52 26N 4 49 E
Zab, Monts du 83 34 55N 5 0 E
Žabalj 42 45 21N 20 5 E
Žabari 42 44 22N 21 15 E
Zabarjad 86 23 40N 36 12 E
Zabaykalskiy 59 49 40N 117 25 E
Zabid 63 14 0N 43 10 E
Ząbkowice Śląskie 28 50 35N 16 50 E
Žabljak 42 43 18N 19 7 E
Zabłudów 28 53 0N 23 19 E
Žabno 27 50 9N 20 53 E
Zābol 65 31 0N 61 32 E
Zābolī 65 27 10N 61 35 E
Zabré 85 11 12N 0 36W
Zabrze 28 50 18N 18 50 E
Zabul □ 65 32 0N 67 0 E
Zacapa 120 14 59N 89 31W
Zacatecas 120 22 49N 102 34W
Zacatecas □ 120 23 30N 103 0W
Zacatecoluca 120 13 29N 88 51W
Zacoalco 120 20 14N 103 33W
Zadar 39 44 8N 15 14 E
Zadawa 85 11 33N 10 19 E
Zadetkyi Kyun 72 10 0N 98 25 E
Zadonsk 55 52 25N 38 56 E
Zafora 45 36 5N 26 24 E
Zafra 31 38 26N 6 30W
Zafriya 62 31 59N 34 51 E
Żagań 28 51 39N 15 22 E
Zagazig 86 30 40N 31 30 E
Zaghouan 83 36 23N 10 10 E
Zaglivérion 44 40 36N 23 15 E
Zaglou 82 27 17N 0 3W
Zagnanado 85 7 18N 2 28 E
Zagorá 44 39 27N 23 6 E
Zagora 82 30 22N 5 51W
Zagórów 28 52 10N 17 54 E
Zagorsk 55 56 20N 38 10 E
Zagórz 27 49 30N 22 14 E
Zagreb 39 45 50N 16 0 E
Zāgros, Kudhā-ye 65 33 45N 47 0 E
Žagubica 42 44 15N 21 47 E
Zaguinaso 84 10 1N 6 14W
Zagyva → 27 47 5N 20 4 E
Zāhedān 65 29 30N 60 50 E
Zahirabad 70 17 43N 77 37 E
Zahlah 64 33 52N 35 50 E
Zahna 24 51 54N 12 47 E
Zahrez Chergui 82 35 0N 3 30 E
Zahrez Rharbi 82 34 50N 2 55 E
Zaïr 82 29 47N 5 51W
Zaïre → 88 6 4 S 12 24 E
Zaïre, Rep. of ■ 88 3 0 S 23 0 E
Zaječar 42 43 53N 22 18 E
Zakamensk 59 50 23N 103 17 E
Zakataly 57 41 38N 46 35 E
Zakavkazye 57 42 0N 44 0 E
Zākhū 64 37 10N 42 50 E
Zákinthos 45 37 47N 20 54 E
Zaklików 28 50 46N 22 7 E
Zakopane 27 49 18N 19 57 E
Zakroczym 28 52 26N 20 38 E
Zala □ 27 46 42N 16 50 E
Zala → 27 46 43N 17 16 E
Zalaegerszeg 27 46 53N 16 47 E
Zalakomár 27 46 33N 17 10 E
Zalalövö 27 46 51N 16 35 E
Zalamea de la Serena 31 38 40N 5 38W
Zalamea la Real 31 37 41N 6 38W
Zalău 46 47 12N 23 3 E
Zalazna 55 58 39N 52 31 E
Žalec 39 46 16N 15 10 E
Zaleshchiki 56 48 45N 25 45 E
Zalewo 28 53 50N 19 41 E
Zalingei 81 12 51N 23 29 E
Zaltan, Jabal 83 28 46N 19 45 E
Zambeke 90 2 8N 25 17 E
Zambeze → 91 18 55 S 36 4 E
Zambezi 89 13 30 S 23 15 E
Zambezi = Zambeze → 91 18 55 S 36 4 E
Zambezia □ 91 16 15 S 37 30 E
Zambia ■ 89 15 0 S 28 0 E
Zamboanga 73 6 59N 122 3 E
Zambrów 28 52 59N 22 14 E
Zametchino 55 53 30N 42 30 E
Zamora, Mexico 120 20 0N 102 21W
Zamora, Spain 30 41 30N 5 45W
Zamora □ 30 41 30N 5 46W
Zamość 28 50 43N 23 15 E
Zamość □ 28 50 40N 23 10 E
Zamzam, W. 83 31 0N 14 30 E
Zan 85 9 26N 0 17W
Zanaga 88 2 48 S 13 48 E
Záncara → 33 39 18N 3 18W
Zandvoort 16 52 22N 4 32 E
Zanesville 114 39 56N 82 2W
Zangue → 91 17 50 S 35 21 E
Zanjan 64 36 40N 48 35 E
Zannone 40 40 58N 13 2 E
Zante = Zákinthos 45 37 47N 20 54 E
Zanthus 96 31 2 S 123 34 E
Zanzibar 90 6 12 S 39 12 E
Zanzūr 83 32 55N 13 1 E
Zaouiet El-Kala = Bordj Omar Driss 83 28 4N 6 40 E
Zaouiet Reggane 82 26 32N 0 3 E
Zapadna Morava → 42 43 38N 21 30 E
Zapadnaya Dvina 54 56 15N 32 3 E
Zapadnaya Dvina → 54 57 4N 24 3 E
Západné Beskydy 27 49 30N 19 0 E
Zapadni Rodopi 43 41 50N 24 0 E
Zapadočeský □ 26 49 35N 13 0 E
Západoslovenský □ 27 48 30N 17 30 E
Zapala 128 39 0 S 70 5W
Zapaleri, Cerro 124 22 49 S 67 11W
Zapata 117 26 56N 99 17W
Zapatón → 31 39 0N 6 49W
Zapodnyy Sayan 59 52 30N 94 0 E
Zapolyarnyy 52 69 26N 30 51 E
Zaporozhye 56 47 50N 35 10 E
Zapponeta 41 41 27N 15 57 E
Zara 64 39 58N 37 43 E
Zaragoza, Coahuila, Mexico 120 28 30N 101 0W
Zaragoza, Nuevo León, Mexico 120 24 0N 99 46W
Zaragoza, Spain 32 41 39N 0 53W
Zaragoza □ 32 41 35N 1 0W
Zarand 65 30 46N 56 34 E
Zărandului, Munţii 46 46 14N 22 7 E
Zaranj 65 30 55N 61 55 E
Zarasai 54 55 40N 26 20 E
Zarate 124 34 7 S 59 0W
Zaraysk 55 54 48N 38 53 E
Zarembo I. 108 56 20N 132 50W
Zaria 85 11 0N 7 40 E
Zarisberge 92 24 30 S 16 15 E
Zárkon 44 39 38N 22 6 E
Żarów 28 50 56N 16 29 E
Zarqā' → 62 32 10N 35 37 E
Zaruma 126 3 40 S 79 38W
Żary 28 51 37N 15 10 E
Zarza de Alange 31 38 49N 6 13W
Zarza de Granadilla 30 40 14N 6 3W
Zarza, La 31 37 42N 6 51W
Zarzaïtine 83 28 15N 9 34 E
Zarzis 83 33 31N 11 2 E
Zas 30 43 4N 8 53W
Zashiversk 59 67 25N 142 40 E
Zaskar Mountains 69 33 15N 77 30 E
Zastron 92 30 18 S 27 7 E
Žatec 26 50 20N 13 32 E
Zator 27 49 59N 19 28 E
Zavala 42 42 50N 17 59 E
Zavarāh 65 33 29N 52 28 E
Zavetnoye 57 47 13N 43 50 E
Zavidoviči 42 44 27N 18 13 E
Zavitinsk 59 50 10N 129 20 E
Zavodoski 5 56 0 S 27 45W
Zavolzhsk 55 57 30N 42 10 E
Zavolzhye 55 56 37N 43 26 E
Zawadzkie 28 50 37N 18 28 E
Zawichost 28 50 48N 21 51 E
Zawidów 28 51 1N 15 1 E
Zawiercie 28 50 30N 19 24 E
Zāwiyat al Bayḍā 81 32 30N 21 40 E
Zawyet Shammâs 86 31 30N 26 37 E
Zâwyet Um el Rakham 86 31 18N 27 1 E
Zâwyet Ungeîla 86 31 23N 26 42 E
Zāyandeh → 65 32 35N 52 0 E
Zayarsk 59 56 12N 102 55 E
Zaysan 58 47 28N 84 52 E
Zaysan, Oz. 58 48 0N 83 0 E
Zaytā 62 32 23N 35 2 E
Zāzamt, W. 83 30 29N 14 30 E
Zazir, O. → 83 22 0N 5 40 E
Zázrivá 27 49 16N 19 7 E
Zbarazh 54 49 43N 25 44 E
Zbąszyń 28 52 14N 15 56 E
Zbąszynek 28 52 16N 15 51 E
Zblewo 28 53 56N 18 19 E
Zdolbunov 54 50 30N 26 15 E
Ždrelo 42 44 16N 21 28 E
Zduńska Wola 28 51 37N 18 59 E
Zduny 28 51 39N 17 21 E
Zeballos 108 49 59N 126 50W
Zebediela 93 24 20 S 29 17 E
Zeebrugge 16 51 19N 3 12 E
Zeehan 97 41 52 S 145 25 E
Zeeland □ 16 51 30N 3 50 E
Ze'elim 62 31 13N 34 32 E
Zeerust 92 25 31 S 26 4 E
Zefat 62 32 58N 35 29 E
Zegdou 82 29 51N 4 45W
Zege 87 11 43N 37 18 E
Zégoua 84 10 32N 5 35W
Zehdenick 24 52 59N 13 20 E
Zeila 63 11 21N 43 30 E
Zeist 16 52 5N 5 15 E
Zeitz 24 51 3N 12 9 E
Żelechów 28 51 49N 21 54 E
Zelengora 42 43 22N 18 30 E
Zelenika 42 42 27N 18 37 E
Zelenodolsk 55 55 55N 48 30 E
Zelenogradsk 54 54 53N 20 29 E
Zelenokumsk 57 44 24N 43 53 E
Zelënyy 57 48 6N 50 45 E
Zeleznik 42 44 43N 20 23 E
Zell, Baden, Ger. 25 47 42N 7 50 E
Zell, Rhld-Pfz., Ger. 25 50 2N 7 11 E
Zell am See 26 47 19N 12 47 E
Zella Mehlis 24 50 40N 10 41 E
Zelów 28 51 28N 19 14 E
Zelzate 16 51 13N 3 47 E
Zembra, I. 83 37 5N 10 56 E
Zémio 90 5 2N 25 5 E
Zemlya Frantsa Iosifa 4 81 0N 55 0 E
Zemmora 82 35 44N 0 51 E
Zemoul, O. → 82 29 15N 7 0W
Zemun 42 44 51N 20 25 E
Zengbe 85 5 46N 13 4 E
Zenica 42 44 10N 17 57 E
Zenina 82 34 30N 2 37 E
Žepče 42 44 28N 18 2 E
Zeraf, Bahr ez → 87 9 42N 30 52 E
Zerbst 24 51 59N 12 8 E
Zerhamra 82 29 58N 2 30W
Żerków 28 52 4N 17 32 E
Zermatt 25 46 2N 7 46 E
Zernez 25 46 42N 10 7 E
Zernograd 57 46 52N 40 19 E
Zerqani 44 41 30N 20 20 E
Zestafoni 57 42 6N 43 0 E
Zetel 24 53 25N 7 57 E
Zeulenroda 24 50 39N 12 0 E
Zeven 24 53 17N 9 19 E
Zévio 38 45 23N 11 10 E
Zeya 59 53 48N 127 14 E
Zeya → 59 53 13N 127 35 E
Zêzere → 31 39 28N 8 20W
Zgierz 28 51 50N 19 27 E
Zgorzelec 28 51 10N 15 0 E
Zhabinka 54 52 13N 24 2 E
Zhailma 58 51 37N 61 33 E
Zhangguangcai Ling 76 45 0N 129 0 E
Zhanghua 75 24 6N 120 29 E
Zhangjiakou 76 40 48N 114 55 E
Zhangping 77 25 17N 117 23 E
Zhangpu 77 24 8N 117 35 E
Zhangwu 76 42 43N 123 52 E
Zhangye 75 38 50N 100 23 E
Zhangzhou 75 24 30N 117 35 E
Zhanhua 76 37 40N 118 8 E
Zhanjiang 75 21 15N 110 20 E
Zhanyi 75 25 38N 103 48 E
Zhanyu 76 44 30N 122 30 E
Zhao Xian 76 37 43N 114 45 E
Zhao'an 77 23 41N 117 10 E
Zhaoping 77 24 11N 110 48 E
Zhaoqing 77 23 0N 112 20 E
Zhaotong 75 27 20N 103 44 E
Zhaoyuan 76 37 20N 120 23 E
Zharkovskiy 54 55 56N 32 19 E
Zhashkov 56 49 15N 30 5 E
Zhdanov 56 47 5N 37 31 E
Zhecheng 77 34 7N 115 20 E
Zhejiang □ 75 29 0N 120 0 E
Zheleznodorozhny 52 62 35N 50 55 E
Zheleznogorsk 54 52 22N 35 23 E
Zheleznogorsk-Ilimskiy 59 56 34N 104 8 E
Zheltyye Vody 56 48 21N 33 31 E
Zhen'an 77 33 27N 109 9 E
Zhenfeng 77 25 22N 105 40 E
Zheng'an 77 28 32N 107 27 E
Zhengding 76 38 8N 114 32 E
Zhenghe 77 27 20N 118 50 E
Zhengyang 77 32 37N 114 22 E
Zhengyangguan 77 32 30N 116 29 E
Zhengzhou 77 34 45N 113 34 E
Zhenjiang 75 32 11N 119 26 E
Zhenlai 76 45 50N 123 5 E
Zhenning 77 26 4N 105 45 E
Zhenyuan, Gansu, China 76 35 35N 107 30 E
Zhenyuan, Guizhou, China 75 27 4N 108 21 E
Zherdevka 55 51 56N 41 29 E
Zhigansk 59 66 48N 123 27 E
Zhigulevsk 55 53 28N 49 30 E
Zhijiang 75 27 27N 109 42 E
Zhirnovsk 55 50 57N 44 49 E
Zhitomir 54 50 20N 28 40 E
Zhizdra 54 53 45N 34 40 E
Zhlobin 54 52 55N 30 0 E
Zhmerinka 56 49 2N 28 2 E
Zhodino 54 54 5N 28 17 E
Zhokhova, Ostrov 59 76 4N 152 40 E
Zhong Xian 77 30 21N 108 1 E
Zhongdian 75 27 48N 99 42 E
Zhongshan 77 22 26N 113 20 E
Zhongwei 76 37 30N 105 12 E
Zhongxiang 77 31 12N 112 34 E
Zhoushan Dao 77 28 5N 122 10 E
Zhouzhi 77 34 10N 108 12 E
Zhovtnevoye 56 46 54N 32 3 E
Zhuanghe 76 39 40N 123 0 E
Zhucheng 76 36 0N 119 27 E
Zhugqu 76 33 40N 104 30 E
Zhuji 77 29 40N 120 10 E
Zhukovka 54 53 35N 33 50 E
Zhumadian 75 32 59N 114 2 E
Zhuo Xian 76 39 28N 115 58 E
Zhupanovo 59 53 40N 159 52 E
Zhushan 77 32 15N 110 13 E
Zhuxi 77 32 25N 109 40 E
Zhuzhou 75 27 49N 113 12 E
Ziarat 68 30 25N 67 49 E
Zibo 76 36 47N 118 3 E
Zidarovo 43 42 20N 27 24 E
Ziębice 28 50 37N 17 2 E
Zielona Góra 28 51 57N 15 31 E
Zielona Góra □ 28 51 57N 15 30 E
Zierikzee 16 51 40N 3 55 E
Ziesar 24 52 16N 12 19 E
Zifta 86 30 43N 31 14 E
Zigey 81 14 43N 15 50 E
Zigong 75 29 15N 104 48 E
Zigui 75 31 0N 110 40 E
Ziguinchor 84 12 35N 16 20W
Zikhron Ya'Aqov 62 32 34N 34 56 E

Zile	64 40 15N 35 52 E	Ziz, Oued →	82 31 40N 4 15W	Zorra Island	120 9 18N 79 52W
Žilina	27 49 12N 18 42 E	Zizhong	77 29 48N 104 47 E	Zorritos	126 3 43 S 80 40W
Zillah	83 28 30N 17 33 E	Zlarin	39 43 42N 15 49 E	Zory	27 50 3N 18 44 E
Zillertaler Alpen	26 47 6N 11 45 E	Zlatar, Hrvatska, Yugo.	39 46 5N 16 3 E	Zorzor	84 7 46N 9 28W
Zima	59 54 0N 102 5 E	Zlatar, Srbija, Yugo.	42 43 25N 19 47 E	Zossen	24 52 13N 13 28 E
Zimane, Adrar in	82 22 10N 4 30 E	Zlataritsa	43 43 2N 25 55 E	Zou Xiang	77 35 30N 116 58 E
Zimapán	120 20 54N 99 20W	Zlatibor	42 43 45N 19 43 E	Zouar	83 20 30N 16 32 E
Zimba	91 17 20 S 26 11 E	Zlatitsa	43 42 41N 24 7 E	Zouérate	80 22 44N 12 21W
Zimbabwe	91 20 16 S 30 54 E	Zlatna	46 46 8N 23 11 E	Zousfana, O. →	82 31 28N 2 17W
Zimbabwe ■	91 20 0S 30 0 E	Zlatograd	43 41 22N 25 7 E	Zoutkamp	16 53 20N 6 18 E
Zimnicea	46 43 40N 25 22 E	Zlatoust	52 55 10N 59 40 E	Zrenjanin	42 45 22N 20 23 E
Zimovniki	57 47 10N 42 25 E	Zletovo	42 41 59N 22 17 E	Zuarungu	85 10 49N 0 46W
Zinder	85 13 48N 9 0 E	Žlitan	83 32 32N 14 35 E	Zuba	85 9 11N 7 12 E
Zinga	91 9 16 S 38 49 E	Złocieniec	28 53 30N 16 1 E	Zubair, Jazāir	87 15 0N 42 10 E
Zingst	24 54 24N 12 45 E	Złoczew	28 51 24N 18 35 E	Zubia	31 37 8N 3 33W
Ziniaré	85 12 35N 1 18W	Zlot	42 44 1N 22 0 E	Zubtsov	54 56 10N 34 34 E
Zinjibār	63 13 5N 45 23 E	Złotoryja	28 51 8N 15 55 E	Zuénoula	84 7 34N 6 3W
Zinkgruvan	49 58 50N 15 6 E	Złotów	28 53 22N 17 2 E	Zuera	32 41 51N 0 49W
Zinnowitz	24 54 5N 13 54 E	Złoty Stok	28 50 27N 16 53 E	Zuetina	83 30 58N 20 7 E
Zion Nat. Park	119 37 25N 112 50W	Zmeinogorsk	58 51 10N 82 13 E	Zufar	63 17 40N 54 0 E
Zipaquirá	126 5 0N 74 0W	Żmigród	28 51 28N 16 53 E	Zug	25 47 10N 8 31 E
Zippori	62 32 45N 35 16 E	Zmiyev	56 49 39N 36 27 E	Zugdidi	57 42 30N 41 55 E
Zirc	27 47 17N 17 42 E	Znamenka	56 48 45N 32 30 E	Zugersee	25 47 7N 8 35 E
Žiri	39 46 5N 14 5 E	Znamensk	54 54 37N 21 17 E	Zugspitze	25 47 25N 10 59 E
Žirje	39 43 39N 15 42 E	Žnin	28 52 51N 17 44 E	Zuid-Holland □	16 52 0N 4 35 E
Zirko	65 25 0N 53 40 E	Znojmo	26 48 50N 16 2 E	Zuidhorn	16 53 15N 6 23 E
Zirl	26 47 17N 11 14 E	Zoar	92 33 30 S 21 26 E	Zújar	33 37 34N 2 50W
Zisterdorf	27 48 33N 16 45 E	Zobia	90 3 0N 25 59 E	Zújar →	31 39 1N 5 47W
Zitácuaro	120 19 28N 100 21W	Zogno	38 45 49N 9 41 E	Zújar, Pantano del	31 38 55N 5 35W
Zitava →	27 48 14N 18 21 E	Zolochev	54 49 45N 24 51 E	Zula	87 15 17N 39 40 E
Žitište	42 45 30N 20 32 E	Zolotonosha	56 49 39N 32 5 E	Zulpich	24 50 41N 6 38 E
Zitsa	44 39 47N 20 40 E	Zomba	91 15 22 S 35 19 E	Zululand	93 43 19N 2 15 E
Zittau	24 50 54N 14 47 E	Zongo	88 4 20N 18 35 E	Zumaya	32 43 19N 2 15W
Zitundo	93 26 48 S 32 47 E	Zonguldak	56 41 28N 31 50 E	Zumbo	91 15 35 S 30 26 E
Živinice	42 44 27N 18 36 E	Zorgo	85 12 15N 0 35W	Zummo	85 9 51N 12 59 E
Ziway, L.	87 8 0N 38 50 E	Zorita	31 39 17N 5 39W	Zungeru	85 9 48N 6 8 E
Zixi	77 27 45N 117 4 E	Zorleni	46 46 14N 27 44 E	Zunhua	76 40 18N 117 58 E
Ziyang	77 32 32N 108 31 E	Zornitsa	43 42 23N 26 58 E	Zuni	119 35 7N 108 57W

Zunyi	75 27 42N 106 53 E
Županja	42 45 4N 18 43 E
Zuqar	87 14 0N 42 40 E
Žur	42 42 13N 20 34 E
Zürich	25 47 22N 8 32 E
Zürich □	25 47 26N 8 40 E
Zürichsee	25 47 18N 8 40 E
Zuromin	28 53 4N 19 51 E
Zuru	85 11 20N 5 11 E
Žut	39 43 52N 15 17 E
Zutphen	16 52 9N 6 12 E
Zuwārah	83 32 58N 12 1 E
Zuyevka	55 58 25N 51 10 E
Žužemberk	39 45 52N 14 56 E
Zvenigorodka	56 49 4N 30 56 E
Zverinogolovskoye	58 54 23N 64 40 E
Zvezdets	43 42 6N 27 26 E
Zvolen	27 48 33N 19 10 E
Zvonce	42 42 57N 22 34 E
Zvornik	42 44 26N 19 7 E
Zwedru (Tchien)	84 5 59N 8 15W
Zweibrücken	25 49 15N 7 20 E
Zwenkau	24 51 13N 12 19 E
Zwettl	26 48 35N 15 9 E
Zwickau	24 50 43N 12 30 E
Zwiesel	25 49 1N 13 14 E
Zwischenahn	24 53 12N 8 1 E
Zwoleń	28 51 21N 21 36 E
Zwolle, Neth.	16 52 31N 6 6 E
Zwolle, U.S.A.	117 31 38N 93 38W
Żychlin	28 52 15N 19 37 E
Zymoetz →	108 54 33N 128 31W
Żyrardów	28 52 3N 20 28 E
Zyrya	57 40 20N 50 15 E
Zyryanka	59 65 45N 150 51 E
Zyryanovsk	58 49 43N 84 20 E
Żywiec	27 49 42N 19 10 E

Recent Place Name Changes

The following place name changes have recently occurred.
The new names are on the maps but the former names are in the index.

India

Former name	New name
Ambarnath	Amarnath
Arrah	Ara
Aruppukottai	Aruppukkottai
Barrackpur	Barakpur
Berhampore	Baharampur
Bokharo Steel City	Bokaro
Budge Budge	Baj Baj
Burdwam	Barddhaman
Chapra	Chhapra
Cooch Behar	Koch Bihar
Dohad	Dahod
Dhulia	Dhule
English Bazar	Ingraj Bazar
Farrukhabad-cum-Fatehgarh	Fategarh
Ferozepore	Firozpur
Gadag-Batgeri	Gadag
Gudiyatam	Gudiyattam
Hardwar	Haridwar
Hooghly-Chinsura	Chunchura
Howrah	Haora
Hubli-Dharwar	Dharwad
Kadayanallur	Kadaiyanallur
Manaar, Gulf of	Mannar, Gulf of
Maunath Bhanjan	Mau
Mehsana	Mahesana
Midnapore	Medinipur
Monghyr	Munger
Morvi	Morbi
Nabadwip	Navadwip
Nander	Nanded
Palayancottai	Palayankottai
Purnea	Purnia
Rajnandgaon	Raj Nandgaon
Santipur	Shantipur
Serampore	Shrirampur
Siliguri	Shiliguri
Sonepat	Sonipat
South Suburban	Behala

Iran

Former name	New name
Bandar-e Pahlavi	Bandar-e Anzalī
Bandar-e Shāh	Bandar-e Torkeman
Bandar-e Shahpur	Bandar-e Khomeynī
Dezh Shāhpūr	Marīvan
Gach Sārān	Gachsārān
Herowābād	Khalkhāl
Kermānshāh	Bakhtāran
Naft-e Shāh	Naftshahr
Reza'īyeh	Orūmīyeh
Reza'īyeh, Daryācheh-ye	Orūmīyeh, Daryācheh-ye
Shāhābād	Āshkhāneh
Shāhābād	Eslāmābād-e Gharb
Shāhī	Qā 'emshahr
Shahrezā	Qomsheh
Shāhrud	Emāmrūd
Shahsavār	Tonekābon
Solţāniyeh	Sa'īdīyeh

Mozambique

Former name	New name
Augusto Cardosa	Metangula
Entre Rios	Malema
Malvérnia	Chicualacuala
Miranda	Macalogue
Olivença	Lupilichi
Vila Alferes Chamusca	Guijá
Vila Caldas Xavier	Muende
Vila Coutinho	Ulonguè
Vila Fontes	Caia
Vila de Junqueiro	Gurué
Vila Luísa	Marracuene
Vila Paiva de Andrada	Gorongoza

Zimbabwe

Former name	New name
Balla Balla	Mbalabala
Belingwe	Mberengwa
Chipinga	Chipinge
Dett	Dete
Enkeldoorn	Chivhu
Essexvale	Esigodini
Fort Victoria	Masvingo
Gwelo	Gweru
Hartley	Chegutu
Gatooma	Kadoma
Inyazura	Nyazura
Marandellas	Marondera
Mashaba	Mashava
Melsetter	Chimanimani
Mrewa	Murewa
Mtoko	Mutoko
Nuanetsi	Mwenezi
Que Que	Kwekwe
Salisbury	Harare
Selukwe	Shurugwi
Shabani	Zvishavane
Sinoia	Chinhoyi
Somabula	Somabhula
Tjolotjo	Tsholotsho
Umvuma	Mvuma
Umtali	Mutare
Wankie	Hwange